ANNUAL REVIEW OF PSYCHOLOGY

ANNUAL REVIEW OF PSYCHOLOGY

VOLUME 43, 1992

MARK R. ROSENZWEIG, *Editor*

University of California, Berkeley

LYMAN W. PORTER, *Editor*

University of California, Irvine

ANNUAL REVIEWS INC.   4139 EL CAMINO WAY   P.O. BOX 10139   PALO ALTO, CALIFORNIA 94303-0897

ANNUAL REVIEWS INC.
Palo Alto, California, USA

International Standard Serial Number: 0066–4308
International Standard Book Number: 0–8243–0243-5
Library of Congress Catalog Card Number: 50-13143

Annual Review and publication titles are registered trademarks of Annual Reviews Inc.

⊗ The paper used in this publication meets the minimum requirements of American National Standard for Information Sciences—Permanence of Paper for Printed
Library Materials, ANSI Z39.48-1984.

Annual Reviews Inc. and the Editors of its publications assume no responsibility for the statements expressed by the contributors to this *Review*.

Typesetting by Kachina Typesetting Inc., Tempe, Arizona; John Olson, President;
Janis Hoffman, Typesetting Coordinator; and by the Annual Reviews Inc. Editorial Staff

PRINTED AND BOUND IN THE UNITED STATES OF AMERICA

PREFACE

In the continuing progress of psychological science, certain events serve as markers. One such event is the XXV International Congress of Psychology in Brussels, July 19–24, 1992. (The first International Congress of Psychology took place in Paris in 1889.) To mark this occasion, as with other major international congresses of psychology, this volume of the *Annual Review of Psychology* provides an informative article on psychology in the host country, Belgium.

A few years after the first International Congress, the American Psychological Association was founded (1892); it celebrates its centenary at its convention in Washington this year. In connection with that centenary, the Smithsonian Institution is playing host during the summer of 1992 to a major Traveling Exhibition of Psychology that illustrates many of the themes of research treated in our review chapters.

Decisions about chapter coverage and invitations to prospective authors are the responsibilty of the Members of the Editorial Committee, which meets once a year, usually in the spring. Members are named to the Editorial Committee for a five-year term. Two members completed terms of service with the 1991 meeting: Albert Bandura and Frances Degen Horowitz. We are grateful to both of them for putting their extensive knowledge of psychology and psychologists at the service of the *ARP*. Auke Tellegen was persuaded to extend his term of service for an additional year so that there would not be too great a turnover of experienced members in a single year.

Readers who belong to certain scientific/professional societies can purchase the *Annual Review of Psychology* and other Annual Review volumes at reduced prices. The following societies, for example, currently participate in such an arrangement with Annual Reviews Inc.: American Psychological Society, Australian Psychological Society, Canadian Psychological Association, European Neuroscience Association, German Society for Psychology, Interamerican Society of Psychology, International Council of Psychologists, Nederlands Instituut van Psychologen, and the Society for Research in Child Development. To receive the society discount, members must place their orders through their society.

The Editors are always happy to hear from readers who wish to comment on coverage of the *Annual Reviews of Psychology* and to suggest topics to be included in future volumes.

Mark R. Rosenzweig
Lyman W. Porter
Coeditors

Annual Review of Psychology
Volume 43 (1992)

CONTENTS

CHAPTERS OF INTEREST FROM OTHER *ANNUAL REVIEWS*

From the *Annual Review of Anthropology,* Volume 20 (1991)

Human Behavioral Ecology, Lee Cronk

From the *Annual Review of Public Health,* Volume 13 (1992)

Depression: Current Understanding and Changing Trends, Myrna M. Weissman, Gerald L. Klerman

The Impact of Patient Education and Counseling on Blood Pressure Control, Douglas A. Mains, Ramon Velez, Mary Ann Richardson

Acute Confusional States in Older Adults and the Role of Polypharmacy, William E. Hale, Ronald B. Stewart

Cognitive Impairment: Dementia and Alzheimer's Disease, Eric Larson, Walter A. Kukull, Robert L. Katzman

From *The Annual Review of Sociology,* Volume 17 (1991)

The Design and Administration of Mail Surveys, Don A. Dillman

Ethnic Minorities and Mental Health, William A. Vega and Rubén G. Rumbaut

Sport and Society, James H. Frey and D. Stanley Eitzen

The Evolution of New Organizational Forms, Elaine Romanelli

Networks of Corporate Power: A Comparative Assessment, John Scott

Work Experiences and Family Interaction Processes: The Long Reach of the Job?, Elizabeth G. Menaghan

Policy Domains: Organization, Culture, and Policy Outcomes, Paul Burstein

From the *Annual Review of Neuroscience,* Volume 14 (1991)

Evolution in Nervous Systems, E. A. Arbas, I. A. Meinertzhagen, and S. R. Shaw

Modulation of Neural Networks for Behavior, Ronald M. Harris-Warrick and Eve Marder

Mechanisms of Fast and Slow Axonal Transport, Richard B. Vallee and George S. Bloom

Plasticity of Sensory and Motor Maps in Adult Mammals, Jon H. Kaas

The Neural Basis of Behavior: A Neuroethological View, Walter Heiligenberg

Molecular Approaches to Hereditary Diseases of the Nervous System: Huntington's Disease as a Paradigm, N. S. Wexler, E. A. Rose, and D. E. Housman

For the convenience of readers, a detachable order form/envelope is bound into the back of this volume.

Harold H Kelley

Annu. Rev. Psychol. 1992. 43:1–23

COMMON-SENSE PSYCHOLOGY AND SCIENTIFIC PSYCHOLOGY

Harold H. Kelley

Department of Psychology, University of California, Los Angeles, California 90024

KEY WORDS: common concepts, common beliefs, implicit theories, obviousness

CONTENTS

For some years I have been concerned about the issues that arise from the interplay between common-sense psychology (CS-ψ) and scientific psychology (S-ψ). The invitation to write this chapter provides a welcome occasion to examine this interplay. The relevant writings are found under such rubrics as "common sense," "naive psychology," "ethnopsychology," "indigenous psychologies," and "implicit theories." The issues seem to be of particular interest to social psychologists, and I have drawn on excellent essays by Farr (1981), Fletcher (1984), Furnham (1983), and Wegner & Vallacher (1981). Our area's interest in these matters has been greatly stimulated by the fruitfulness of Heider's (1958) analyses of naive psychology. Our interest also reflects the obvious fact that the interplay between CS-ψ and S-ψ involves social processes—the processes by which the common culture affects scien-

1

0066-4308/92/0201-0001$02.00

tists' thought and activities, and the reverse processes, by which the products of science modify the common culture. These observations notwithstanding, I would emphasize that the problems arising from the interplay are not unique to social psychology. As my examples will suggest, they occur in all psychological research areas that deal with molar behavior and that rely on common language.

SOME GENERAL ISSUES

What is Common-Sense Psychology?

Presumably we all know what S-ψ encompasses, but the scope of CS-ψ requires some explanation. Examples will be useful. The first is John Houston's study of "lay knowledge of the principles of psychology" (Houston 1983, 1985). He constructed 21 multiple-choice questions about various memory and learning phenomena. The items were stated in everyday language, dealt with both human and animal learning, and referred to such phenomena as extinction, subjective organization, partial reinforcement, and secondary reinforcement. For example, the item on levels of processing read as follows:

> What should be the best way to think about words if you want to remember them?
> a. to think about what they sound like (e.g. think about where the accent falls, or whether the word has an "r" sound in it).
> b. to think about what the word looks like (e.g. think about how many syllables the word has, or whether it has any curved letters in it).
> c. to think about the meaning of the word (e.g. can it fit into your hand, or how pleasant is it).
> d. all of these ways of thinking about words will lead to equal recall.

Houston first gave this "test" to 50 introductory psychology students before they had been formally exposed to the pertinent principles. On 15 of the 21 items, more students answered correctly than would be expected by chance. To reduce the likelihood that this result was attributable to general test-taking skills or to information gained in other college courses, Houston gave the questionnaire to a heterogeneous sample of 50 people found in a city park on a Sunday afternoon. They answered 16 of the items more accurately than expected by chance. (In both samples, the "levels of processing" item, above, was among those answered correctly more often than expected by chance.) Some caution must be exercised in interpreting "chance" levels for multiple-choice questions, but Houston's results make a strong case for his conclusion that "a great many of psychology's basic principles are self-evident. One gets the uneasy feeling that we have often been dealing with the obvious and did not know it" (1983:207).

A second example comes from questionnaires that Jorge Manzi and I have given to the members of young heterosexual couples. We asked each member separately to rate their own and their partner's degree of involvement in the relationship. We then asked them to make similar ratings of each one's worrying that the other would leave the relationship, the likelihood that each would leave, and the amount of "say" each has in their relationship. In a parallel identical section of the questionnaire, we told them how two hypothetical people like themselves had rated their respective degrees of involvement (sometimes, high; sometimes, low, etc), and asked them to rate, for each member of that hypothetical pair, degree of worry, likelihood of leaving, and amount of "say." It will be apparent that the purpose of the first set of questions is to obtain their "reports" about their own relationships and that of the second set to obtain their "beliefs" about how such relationships work. (These are the beliefs shared among the respondents in the sample, inasmuch as the correlations between relative involvement and the other variables are calculated over the sample.) Without going into detail, it may be reported that over a number of different samples, the results from the report and the belief data yield essentially the same picture: The more involved partner is both reported and believed to be the one who is less likely to leave the relationship, more likely to worry about the partner's leaving, more likely to take steps to enhance the other's involvement, and less likely to have much say about the relationship's affairs. In other words, these people have beliefs or expectations about relationships that are consistent with what, by their reports, actually happens in relationships. Like Houston's data, these results suggest that the "principles" we derive from the study of interpersonal relationships—in this case, principles about the consequences of unequal dependence—are already part of common knowledge.

[The particular structure of the two-part questionnaire employed by Manzi and myself leads one to wonder whether the report data may not simply reflect the respondents' beliefs, or, conversely, whether the belief data may not reflect their experience in their own relationships—i.e. their reports. We examined these questions in a number of ways (as by varying order of presentation) and could find little evidence of influence in either direction. Taking advantage of the fact that we have two independent reports about each relationship (provided by its two members), we were able to find clear evidence that the reports do reflect a "reality" of each relationship, as defined consensually by the pair. These results bear on an issue discussed much later in this review, as to whether behavioral ratings reflect actual covariations in behavior or simply the semantic or logical relations implicit in everyday language.]

These two lines of work illustrate ways of studying CS-ψ, and they illustrate what is meant here by the term. From two research areas, we have examples of what Heider (1958) calls "naive psychology": ". . . the ordinary person has a great and profound understanding of himself and other people which . . .[is]. . . unformulated or only vaguely conceived.. . . "it is expressed in our everyday language and experience. . .[and] will be referred to as common-sense or naive psychology. . ." (pp. 2, 4). In a similar vein, Smedslund (1978:10) defines common-sense psychology as "the network of concepts pertaining to psychological phenomena, imbedded in ordinary language."

Here I consider CS-ψ to include common people's ideas about their own and other persons' behavior and about the antecedents and consequences of that behavior. These ideas are expressed in the labels and terms that we, as common folk, use to describe people and in the familiar sayings and stories that we tell each other about individuals, kinds of people, and people in general. In short, and as both Heider and Smedslund emphasize, CS-ψ is embedded in and carried by our everyday language.

The foregoing specifies the particular "contents" of common thought that constitute CS-ψ. Several authors (Fletcher 1984; Wegner & Vallacher 1977) have also included the "how," or the processes of common thought in the CS-ψ domain. I am uncomfortable with this inclusion because CS-ψ then becomes equivalent to all of cognitive psychology. For example, like O'Hare & Duck (1981), I consider attribution theory to be "a psychology *about* common sense," not common sense itself. Of course, there are everyday beliefs about how people make attributions, and S-ψ may study such common-sense meta-attribution theories. It may also be true, as Gergen (1973) and O'Hare & Duck (1981) have suggested, that S-ψ theory about how attributions are made has been subtly influenced by the uncritical incorporation of certain causal concepts from common thought. For example, my ANOVA model of attribution (1967) makes sense only if "persons" and "situations" are viewed as independent causal factors, and that independence has been repeatedly challenged.

The Interplay between CS-ψ and S-ψ

It sometimes serves our purposes explicitly to study "common sense," as illustrated above by Houston's and Kelley & Manzi's work. However, much more frequent and important are the occasions when CS-ψ enters into our S-ψ work implicitly. We all are members of the common culture and users of the common language long before we become scientific psychologists. Insofar as we address our scientific efforts to the behavioral phenomena encompassed by common terms and beliefs, they inevitably influence the concepts and theories we develop for our scientific purposes. CS-ψ affects our work when we communicate verbally with our subjects/respondents, when we interact with one another, and, of course, in our private verbally mediated thoughts.

The above statement emphasizes the effects of CS-ψ upon our S-ψ activities. This chapter focuses on those effects. It is also obvious that, over time, the ideas and information developed within the S-ψ realm are likely to influence the terms and beliefs in the CS-ψ realm. To supplement this chapter the interested reader may wish to refer to the rich literature on these effects. I merely mention a few here. (*a*) In their writings on "social representation," Serge Moscovici and his colleagues (e.g. Moscovici 1961; Herzlich 1973) make detailed analyses of how such things as psychoanalytic concepts and medical knowledge have become incorporated into the common domain. (*b*) In a strong critique, Wallach & Wallach (1983) describe the dangers that S-ψ serves to legitimize ego-centrism and selfish behavior in the common culture. (*c*) In a commentary on social psychology's role, Gergen (1973) emphasizes its probable quantitative impact on common thought and expresses a concern that common people's acquisition of scientific knowledge will "alter the character of causal relations in social interaction" (p. 310). Schlenker (1974) takes strong issue with Gergen on these points. (*d*) Krech & Crutchfield (1948) observed that although "many people are impatient with psychology because it does not know enough" (p. 6), perhaps just as many are afraid that it knows or will know too much. This thought is echoed by Kazak & Reppucci (1980) in relation to the study of love: "There seems to be a strong fear that by studying love we will somehow destroy its 'spontaneity and magical powers'" (p. 213).

The brief comments above may whet the reader's appetite for essays on the influence of S-ψ upon CS-ψ. Here I turn my attention exclusively to effects of the opposite kind.

The Extent and Validity of CS-ψ

In all that follows, questions about the extent and validity of CS-ψ will be in the background, if not at the focus, of my discussion: With respect to what kinds of phenomena may we expect CS-ψ to be most extensive and valid?

Of course, the validity of CS-ψ is largely irrelevant to the question of whether CS-ψ affects human behavior. Whether CS-ψ squares with empirical findings or not, we may assume that the way people conceptualize and explain behavior affects their behavior. However, validity is clearly an important issue when we find that S-ψ explicitly relies on CS-ψ or is subtly influenced by it.

To gain some sense of when CS-ψ is likely to be extensive and valid, it is useful to speculate about its origins. Like other human intellectual achievements, CS-ψ is created and transmitted by language-using adults. They have occasions to observe and learn about, at first and second hand, how people behave and the conditions under which variations in behavior occur. They think and converse about these matters, develop and use labels for behavior and persons, and create stories and aphorisms about important regularities and deviations.

These CS-ψ-generating intellectual and interactional activities occur under a wide variety of conditions. I would suggest that the most important ways those conditions vary are with respect to *level, familiarity,* and *personal involvement.* My hypothesis is that CS-ψ is most likely to be both extensive and valid when it refers to events that exist at a middle level (rather than at a macro- or microlevel), that are familiar (rather than alien), and of which people are observers (rather than involved participants).

Space does not permit a thorough justification of my hypothesis, but the factor of level requires some explanation. Most of subjective daily life is carried on at what I am here calling a middle level, or [following Vollmer (1984); see below] *mesolevel.* This is the level of molar individual behavior (the level of planned, goal-directed activity), immediate and direct consequences, time-spans of minutes to days, and face-to-face interaction of small numbers of people. This level is the focus of attention in everyday life, and it provides information that permits conscious and deliberate processing. This also happens to be the level to which most social, motivational, and personality psychologists direct their attention. In contrast, *macrolevel* phenomena involve many people and long time spans (e.g. life-span developmental trends, institutional and historical changes, economic and political trends). *Microlevel* events include what might be described as "molecular" behavior—i.e. events that occur rapidly (in seconds or milliseconds), in small scales of magnitude and mass (e.g. small contractions of the facial muscles or shifts in eye fixation), and often invisibly (e.g. muscle innervations, gland secretions). [See Koffka (1935) for the distinction between molar and molecular behavior.]

Thus one claim of my hypothesis is that people are not very good at drawing valid macrolevel generalizations—i.e. generalizations about events that occur over broad time spans and/or in large populations. Social psychology has repeatedly demonstrated that common beliefs about groups of people—ethnic, national, gender stereotypes—are exaggerated at best, and wholly inaccurate at worst. Such beliefs illustrate errors in the "common wisdom" that occur at the macrolevel with respect to unfamiliar phenomena. Social psychology emphasizes that these beliefs are more strongly fed by outgroup prejudice and ingroup consensus than by factual information.

My hypothesis also asserts that common beliefs are often wrong at the microlevel. A behavioral example is provided by Kaye (1977), who observed that a mother nursing her infant tends to jiggle the child when it pauses during the process. Mothers believe, reasonably enough, that this stimulates the child to return immediately to the nursing. Kaye's micro-analysis of the interaction process revealed that this belief is in error. Jiggling the infant actually delays its return to nursing. The erroneous belief here illustrates the inability of mothers to process information with the precision that Kaye's observers, one looking at the mother and the other at the infant, were able to attain. It may also indicate that the psychology of the tiny infant is in some sense "alien" to the mother.

When I described to Greg Schmidt my hunch about the role of mesolevel conditions in the development of CS-ψ, he pointed out that a similar idea has been proposed in evolutionary epistemology. Vollmer (1984) summarizes the point this way:

> The world to which our cognitive apparatus was adapted during evolution is but a *section* of the real world. . . . Every organism has its own cognitive niche or ambient, and so does man. Man's cognitive niche we shall call '*mesocosm.*' Our mesocosm is that section of the real world we cope with in perceiving and acting, sensually and motorially. . . . Mesocosm is, crudely speaking, a world of medium dimensions..." (p. 87). ". . . our sense organs, perceptual powers, structures of experience, ordinary language, and elementary inferential habits, are well adapted to this mesocosm and are *adequate* for mesocosmic needs. The same is true for our forms of intuition. Our powers of visualization are adapted to and fit everyday needs" (p. 88, emphases in original).

The behavioral categories assumed by CS-ψ are thus well adapted (through evolutionary, cultural, and developmental processes) to the mesocosm constituted by molar behavior and interaction. It is at the mesolevel that S-ψ will encounter an extensive supply of useful (i.e. somewhat valid) categories and theories. It is at the macrolevels of institutional and collective behavior and the microlevels of fine-grain behavior that S-ψ is least likely to find useful CS-ψ concepts and most likely to disconfirm CS-ψ beliefs.

The Effects of CS-ψ on S-ψ

In discussing these effects, it is convenient to refer to certain components of the two realms that are parallel or analogous. The *scientific concepts* of S-ψ parallel the *common terms* of everyday language; concomitantly, running parallel to *common beliefs* within the folk or popular culture are *scientific propositions* about how the phenomena related to certain concepts covary or are causally linked.

In the following sections, I first consider two parallel phenomena: (*a*) How common terms affect scientific concepts and (*b*) how common beliefs affect scientific propositions. Finally, I consider a more complex case, illustrating (*c*) how common terms may affect scientific propositions. Most of my examples come from social and interpersonal psychology. However, I emphasize again that the relevant phenomena are not unique to social psychology. They appear in all the fields of psychology that deal with molar behavior and use information available for encoding into everyday language by common people.

SOME SPECIFIC ISSUES

How Common Terms May Affect Scientific Concepts

Like any psychologist who has begun work in a new area, I have encountered the problem of terminology. How shall I denote the concepts particular to my work? The problem always sends me scurrying to the dictionary in search of common language that might work, but it also often makes me toy with the idea of inventing a new term (see below). Occasionally I later find that a term chosen earlier was not the best one: It has unintended implications, it is difficult to explain to readers, etc, but I am now stuck with it. We encounter similar problems as readers of technical terms that other psychologists have adopted. They do not have the proper connotations for us. We have to remind ourselves and our students that they are "not quite right." We can think of a better term and wish the earlier writer had used it instead.

The question of common terms also arises when we operationalize a concept. In research that relies on verbal reports, the fact that our scientific concept has been drawn directly from the common vocabulary tempts us to use it in our questions. For example, how might we assess the "commitment" to each other of two partners in a close relationship? An obvious way is to ask them. Sharing the term with them ("commitment" occurs in the ordinary speech of our typical respondent), we simply ask, "How committed to this relationship are you?" Our respondents rarely ask what "comitted" means, probably because they assume that we expect them to know the term.

During development, use, and operationalization of S-ψ concepts, common language is both a help and a hinderance. On the plus side, it suggests the categories into which our phenomena might usefully be sorted, it provides convenient terms for thinking about those categories, and it enables us to tap into the store of information our respondents may have about the phenomena. On the negative side, common terms may not sort things out in the most precise ways, may tempt us lazily to skip over preliminary conceptual analysis (i.e. to turn that job over to our respondents), and may encourage us to rely too greatly on verbal reports (thereby possibly delaying development of methods that could replace them).

These competing considerations leave most of us ambivalent about using common terms. Although uncomfortable with reliance on them, few of us are willing entirely to turn our backs on them. For example, in measuring "investment" in a relationship, Rusbult (1980a,b) asks questions about specific things "put into" the relationship (time, money, shared possessions, mutual friends), but she also uses the target concept itself (". . . what is the size of your investment in this relationship?"). The latter is sometimes used as a marker variable, to determine whether the concrete measures are all tapping the desired common concept. In a similar manner, Berscheid et al (1989) used their concrete measures of relationship "closeness" (detailed reports of time spent with the partner, number of activities done alone with the partner in past week, and degree to which respondent had been influenced by the partner in various decisions), but also a "subjective" measure that required the respondents directly to estimate the closeness of their relationship. This study is of special interest here because the investigators have a theory about the limitations of the common-sense concept of closeness. Their idea is that the common concept includes a strong component of "positive feeling," which was not a part of the phenomenon conceptualized as "closeness" by the investigators. Berscheid et al were not surprised to find that the subjective measure was only marginally related to the aggregate of the concrete measures. Thus, even though people's extensive knowledge about their own relationships makes it reasonable to ask them to judge their "closeness," from the perspective of Bersheid et al this question is inappropriate because the lay conception of the term is askew from what theory indicates to be correct.

In operationalizing a concept, psychologists typically try to develop a set of measures or questionnaire items, working from the common term and trying to express or exemplify it in a variety of ways. A common procedure is to obtain ideas from prior research, one's colleagues, and lay persons themselves. For example, in developing scales to measure "love" vs "liking," Rubin (1970) scanned writings on love and research on interpersonal attraction. He then asked panels of students and colleagues to sort the items into love and liking categories.

This reasonable procedure sometimes has the unnoticed and unwanted result that the set of indicators comes to include variables measuring the antecedents and/or consequences of the focal variable. For example, Rubin's (1970) liking scale includes not only such direct items as "_____ is one of the most likable people I know," but also items about "_____'s intelligence and similarity to self" (which other investigators might wish to examine as antecedents of liking) and about "voting for _____ in a class or group election" (which other investigators might consider to be a consequence of liking).

This inclusion of antecedents and consequences reveals how the network of associations that exists around a common concept includes not only semantic synonyms but also an implicit theory about the causal network in which lay persons assume the referent phenomenon to exist. I develop this point further below. Here, we may note that an omnibus instrument intended to measure a focal concept may (a) pick up what other investigators, pursuing particular causal hypotheses, may wish to exclude; (b) have items in common with scales measuring different concepts; and (c) lose validity through the effects of irrelevant causal factors on certain component measures. (For example, in a measure of interpersonal attraction, items concerning the amount of time one person spends with another—a presumed consequence of attraction—may reflect opportunities rather than positivity of attitudes.)

Another locus of ambivalence in the process of selecting S-ψ concepts is at the point of deciding whether to adopt a common term or develop a special "scientific" one. New terms are often necessary, precisely to enable us to escape from the grip of common terms that have inappropriate connotations. On the other hand, the invention and use of special terms opens S-ψ to the charge that it proliferates "scientistic jargon." This charge implies that the terms are unnecessary because they could readily be replaced by more common ones and that the new terms are motivated by a desire to create the mere trappings of "science." For these various reasons, throughout our S-ψ work we often experience a tension between using common terms that are moderately appropriate for the job and inventing more precise scientific ones. Of course, one hopes that uncritical use of common terms or the phoniness of pseudo-scientific concepts will be exposed through scientific interaction. A more formal approach to some of these problems is provided by prototype analysis.

PROTOTYPE ANALYSIS: A SYSTEMATIC PROCEDURE FOR MOVING FROM COMMON TERMS TO SCIENTIFIC CONCEPTS   This method is based on Eleanor Rosch's (1978) research on category systems. Her theory is that category systems have both a horizontal and vertical dimension. For example, the category defined by the concept "love" includes (horizontally) a number of different examples—different manifestations of love. Those instances are differentiated as to how well they represent the category, ranging from instances that are prototypic of the category (e.g. caring) to other instances that are less so (e.g. protectiveness). The concept also exists (vertically) within a hierarchy comprised of a higher-order concept (e.g. attraction) that includes it along with other concepts (e.g. not only love, but also liking and respect) and of lower-order concepts included within it (specific kinds of love, such as romantic love or filial love).

Assessment of the horizontal dimension is illustrated by Buss & Craik's study of the category of "dominance" (1980). In creating items for a personality scale, they asked an initial sample of ordinary people (undergraduate students) to think of the most dominant people they knew and to describe the behaviors that illustrate their dominance. A reduced version of the resulting long list of examples was then given to a second sample, who rated how good an example of "dominance" each item is. By this procedure, the items considered most characteristic of the category were identified. These prototypic items included the following:

He forbade her to leave the room.
She demanded that he run an errand.

He assigned roles and got the game going.
On the auto trip, she decided which direction to take when they got lost.

Prototype analysis of category content is a formalization of methods researchers have long used for assembling test items. It provides a more
systematic understanding of a concept than do the earlier methods. This
procedure has been used with a number of different concepts and for a variety
of purposes. In general, the goal is to extract from CS-ψ the essence of
everyday terms that lend themselves to S-ψ uses. For example, in his study of
the concepts of intelligence, creativity, and wisdom, Sternberg (1981, 1985)
points out that the prototype analysis reveals in detail what people mean
when, in judging each other, they use these terms. He also describes how the
analysis may provide a basis for broadening the scientific concept. He found,
for example, that common people place more emphasis on "the practical and
worldly side" of intelligence than do typical tests of the construct.

Fehr (1988) compared the prototypic features of love and commitment in
order to evaluate several current S-ψ views about their interrelation. Thus,
Fehr used the common categories to evaluate competing scientific views.
Other researchers might not be comfortable with this implied dependency of
scientific categories upon common categories, and might wish to have their
theoretical ideas play a stronger role in setting up the S-ψ categories. For
example, certain S-ψ theories of commitment view it as having two components, internal constraints (e.g. loyalty, living up to your word) and
external constraints (e.g. social arrangements that keep one "trapped" within a
relationship). Fehr's data show that the latter are rather peripheral to the
common category, with "feeling trapped" having low ratings on prototypicality. Do these S-ψ theories require a different term or might the common-sense
category benefit from some theory-based reshaping?

Prototype analysis is useful for introducing CS-ψ terms into S-ψ discourse,
but my impression is that the theory and procedures have not yet been fully
exploited for this purpose. Explorations of the horizontal dimension have
outpaced work on the vertical dimension.

An example of work on the vertical dimension (in this case, identifying the
subcategories within a broad category) is provided by my own study of
"dominance." When I examined the results of the Buss & Craik (1980)
prototype analysis of "dominance," it struck me that the instances rated as
most prototypic (see above) included two distinct types of phenomena that, on
theoretical grounds, I would want to differentiate: Some of the prototypical
items (e.g. the two listed first above) imply a promise-threat scenario and
others (the two listed last) an initiative-taking scenario. [These two scenarios
are based in two contrasting patterns of interdependence which, according to
the Thibaut & Kelley (1959) theory, are basic in interpersonal relations.]

I tested my impression by having students evaluate the items Buss & Craik had found to have the highest prototypicality ratings for dominance. This time the subjects were to judge whether each item most closely conformed to a schematic threat-promise scenario ("Person used threat or promise, implicitly or explicitly, to induce other to do something the person wanted") or to a schematic initiative scenario ("Person acted first, pre-empted, took initiative, and expected other to follow—to coordinate with, accommodate to person"). Of the items tested (which had previously been judged most prototypic of dominance), some were now judged to illustrate the threat-promise scenario and others the initiative scenario. Perhaps more important is the fact that when the schematic scenarios and a sample of Buss & Craik's items were rated on prototypicality for "dominance," the schematic items received ratings as high as the best of those derived from everyday examples of the concept. Thus it may be important to dissect common categories, rather than taking them as they come. This is what is involved in analyzing the vertical dimension of a category system. Such dissection can be aided by viewing common conceptual categories through the lenses of S-ψ theory. For example, theory can be used to construct conceptually prototypic examples which, like my schematic scenarios, can then be used to assess and compare the common-sense categories.

I am expressing here some uneasiness about undue dependence on common thought for clues about how S-ψ should slice up its phenomena. There must surely be an important role for S-ψ analysis that enables our conceptual work to come partially under the guidance of logical and theoretical considerations and to avoid total dependence on common terms. It would be unfortunate if the elegance of such procedures as prototype and hierarchical analysis led us to focus our attention on empirical analysis of common terms to the exclusion of theoretical analysis.

How Common Beliefs May Affect Scientific Propositions

In their formulation of theoretical propositions, social and personality psychologists are influenced, implicitly or explicitly, by their own everyday experiences and by ideas that are part of the common culture. The terms in their hypotheses are based partly on common usage (as discussed above), and the postulated relationships among variables are influenced by informally observed and socially labeled covariations. The linkage between the CS-ψ and S-ψ domains revealed by the latter process raises many issues. I consider two below.

THE QUESTION OF "OBVIOUSNESS"   "Psychology, it seems, is a science which specializes not in discovery but in re-discovery." Joynson's crisp observation (1974:34) provides the theme for this discussion. To the degree S-ψ draws its propositions from the mesolevel of everyday experience, common people will regard it as revealing facts they already know. (It may be noted that the pejorative label "obvious" reflects people's "social representations" of science—the belief that science is an enterprise that specializes in revealing the unknown.) And in any case, whatever the source of S-ψ hypotheses, the vast extent of common knowledge at the mesolevel makes it probable that many scientific facts adduced at that level will be recognized by common people. One consequence of this recognition is that doubts are raised about the value of the S-ψ enterprise: It reveals no new information, only what people already know.

In social psychology we have a term for what is already known about human behavior—namely, "bubba psychology." "Bubba" (sometimes spelled "bubbe") is Yiddish for "grandmother." One's grandmother can recall a rich store of folk sayings and stories. When her grandson describes the findings from his recent doctoral dissertation, she readily assimilates them to some idea or theme from her experience, and may sarcastically inquire, "So what else is new?" Some social psychologists try to avoid doing "bubba psychology." They'd generally like to surprise their grandmothers.

Of the many things to be said on this matter, I merely raise several interrelated points.

What is "obvious" is not obvious   One wonders whether a person who labels a proposition "obvious" could have explicated the hypothesis in advance. And might not that same person have found the counter-proposition "obvious" as well? In describing how social scientists other than psychologists are sensitive to the charge that they never discover anything new, Farr (1981) writes:

> Stouffer, for example, found that when he reported his survey findings concerning the opinions of American soldiers during World War II, military commanders typically responded by claiming that they already knew the information which he was reporting. On one significant occasion in his oral presentation he reversed all of his actual findings and met with the same response. Lazarsfield . . . played a similar ruse on the readers in one of his articles. . . . The lesson which one can draw from these two relatively minor incidents concerns the versatility of the human listener in being able to 'make sense' both of actual data and of the opposite of these data" (p. 306).

Several phenomena are involved here. More is obvious in hindsight than in foresight (Fischhoff 1975). And as we will see below, common sense encompasses beliefs on both sides of many issues. We may also note that what is "obvious" undoubtedly changes over time (Brickman 1980), as people acquire new understandings of the principles of human behavior.

Common-sense beliefs are self-contradictory   This fact accounts in part for the ease with which the charge of "obviousness" is leveled at generalizations about molar behavior. Common understanding encompasses numerous contradictory principles. One common textbook strategy for immunizing student readers against uncritically rendering judgments of "obviousness" is to present a list of common aphorisms that are contradictory, for example, "birds of a feather flock together" versus "opposites attract," "you can't teach an old dog new tricks" versus "never too old to learn," and "look before you leap" versus "he who hesitates is lost."

The fact that mesolevel CS-ψ is replete with contradictory ideas should probably be examined in the light of comments in S-ψ to the effect that "All reasonable hypotheses are likely to be valid" (Gergen 1978:521), or, as McGuire expressed it in his seventh koan, "The opposite of a great truth is also true" (McGuire 1973:455). Both CS-ψ and S-ψ often identify relationships among variables that hold only under a restricted set of circumstances; the total circumstantial domain includes locations at which the opposite relationships hold.

The consequences of concern about "obviousness"   To avoid the "obvious" one can seek out combinations of circumstances at the mesolevel that produce counterintuitive effects. In its reaction to the charge that it was "bubba psychology," in the early 1960s social psychology developed a strong theme—one might say an ethos—of "demonstrating the non-obvious." This was most notable in research on cognitive dissonance theory—in the demonstrations, for example, that under certain circumstances, small incentives produce greater effects than large ones.

Social psychology's focus on the "non-obvious" has had many consequences: It has (*a*) generated excitement in the field, (*b*) identified unusual combinations of conditions that produce out-of-the-ordinary relationships between variables, (*c*) produced debates and counter-research on the plausibility of alternative, more "obvious" interpretations of findings, and (*d*) caused the development of various implicit strategies for lending the appearance of non-obviousness to research (e.g. by imputing false or oversimple beliefs to "common sense" in order to provide a straw man that the research can then demolish, or by creating gaps between the conceptualization of the work (cast in non-obvious terms) and its operationalization (rather obvious when stripped of ts technical jargon). Finally, one might argue that the ethos of "non-obviousr ess" has played an important role in the reductionistic shift in social psychology—the shift from studying group, interpersonal, and molar behavioral phenomena at the mesolevel to studying molecular behavior and cognitive and emotional mediating processes. In a sense, the quest for a result that will surprise Bubba has produced work at the microlevel about which she is poorly informed and by which she is easily impressed. This shift occasionally worries me. I fear that widespread reductionism runs the risk of our losing sight of the structure of the molar processes for which mediational analyses are needed; that is, I worry that the molar phenomena will no longer "set the agenda" for the mediational work. However, the agenda is probably sustained implicitly both by the prevalence of knowledge about molar phenomena, and by possession of this knowledge by even those scientists most inclined to reductionism.

How to make science interesting   In a marvelous paper to which Dan Wegner referred me, Murray Davis (1971) argues that a theorist is considered great not because the theory is true but because it is interesting. "All *interesting* theories . . . constitute an attack on the taken-for-granted world of their audience" (p. 311, emphasis Davis's). If a theory does not challenge their existing assumptions and practices, the audience will reject its value even while affirming its truth. The general form of an interesting proposition, according to Davis, is that it states (or implies) what *seems* to be true of a particular phenomenon and then specifies what *is* true. For example, Festinger's central proposition in cognitive dissonance theory might be paraphrased as "What seems to be important in behavior is the pre-decision process; what is in fact important is the post-decision process." From Davis's perspective, the genius of great theorists lies in their ability to recognize the "assumption-ground" of their audience and to place their propositions in a refutative position relative to that ground.

Davis's analysis provides a fascinating view of the problems of developing and presenting our propositions in ways that will interest our colleagues, students, and lay audiences. The analysis suggests both how to make our work truly more interesting (e.g. through sensitivity to the assumptions of our audiences) and how to make it *appear* more interesting (e.g. crudely illustrated by certain common writing gambits: "It has long been thought . . ... But that is false . . ... We have seen instead that. . .").

The importance of studying the "obvious"   When all is said and done, there are good—even (by Davis's criteria) interesting—reasons for studying propositions that seem "obvious." The contradictions found among common beliefs suggest that common sense is more attuned to the main effects of variables than to their interactions. This implies that an important task for S-ψ research is to reconcile the contradictions by identifying the conditions under which the relation corresponding to a particular belief occurs and the contrasting conditions under which its opposite appears. The relevant "interesting proposition" prototype, from Davis's analysis, is "What seems to be disorganized is, in reality, organized." The scientist also often identifies background factors which, overlooked in the contrasts that common observers make, can be shown by broader comparisons to be important (Cheng & Novick 1990). The relevant Davis prototype is "What seem to be assorted heterogeneous phenomena are, in reality, manifestations of a single element." The classic example is provided by Newton's "interesting" insights into the motions of apples and planets. The detection of organization underlying apparent disorganization and of singularity underlying apparent heterogeneity should be viewed as special cases of S-ψ's broader functions of systematizing and quantifying common sense. The systematization consists of developing general theory that reveals the framework within which the piecemeal ideas of common sense are located. This was clearly Heider's goal in his analysis of naive psychology. I should also emphasize the gains that science makes by quantitative measurement of variables and by description of the relations among them in quantitative terms. The level of detailed observation and assembly of information necessary for developing integrative frameworks and precise quantitative formulations is what sets the S-ψ enterprise apart from everyday experience and enables S-ψ to begin with but then rise above CS-ψ.

RELIANCE ON BELIEFS AS DATA ABOUT REALITY   To the degree common beliefs reflect accurately observed and encoded experience, whether in each individual's direct experience or in the culture's collective experience, S-ψ can rely on those beliefs as information about reality. This possibility holds forth many possible benefits, including economy of research, information about private and otherwise unobservable events, and information about dangerous and disturbing events that it may be unethical to create or observe.

Several different data sources are implied here, ranging from (*a*) people's *reports* of what they and/or their associates do or have done in certain situations; (*b*) people's *predictions* of what they or acquaintances would do in certain situations, which may be common or "hypothetical" ones; and (*c*) people's *beliefs* about what certain kinds of persons do or would do in certain situations. The latter source involves procedures variously referred to as "hypothetical situations," "vignettes," "scenarios," or "simulations." In general, as we move from source *a* to *c* in the above list, our method shifts from reliance on memory-based reports of experienced events to reliance on beliefs about "what people do," this last being the belief component of CS-ψ.

As suggested by an analogous but unresolved controversy in social psychology about the relative merits of laboratory experiments and role-playing procedures, we are not yet in a position to render confident judgments about the relative merits of these various procedures. However, it may be helpful to consider an example of the use of scenarios to gain access to thoughts and feelings that mediate behavior. The example is provided by Weiner's (1980) scenario-based research on helping behavior. The procedure used situational descriptions based on the naturalistic experiment of Piliavin et al (1969). Subjects were asked to imagine themselves in a subway car, seeing a person, who was apparently either ill or drunk, stagger and fall. They were then asked to rate the causes of the falling, what they would feel toward the victim, and whether they would be likely to go to the victim's aid. In other cases, the scenario procedure enabled Weiner to ask subjects to assume that they are experiencing certain feelings or thoughts about causality, and then to predict their degree of helping. The procedure yields results confirming Weiner's hypothesis that helping is mediated in part by a particular chain of attribution and emotion—one in which the victim is seen as not responsible for the problem and is regarded with pity. (Weiner does *not* assume that helping in such situations is solely mediated by attributions or "reasons".)

One is hard put to propose alternative, practicable ways to investigate such important mediational hypotheses. Yet one wonders about the relevance of the scenario-derived metacognitively mediated beliefs to the processes occurring in the course of the "real" situation. In response to such doubts, Weiner points out that the scenario simulation produces patterns of anticipated behavior (helping or not) that correspond to those actually observed by Piliavin et al.

As a basis for thinking about this problem, I return to my earlier hypothesis, that common beliefs are most likely to be veridical when they concern the mesolevel of behavioral phenomena, the familiar, and those events of which the person has principally been an uninterested observer. Helping a victim is a molar event and one with which we typically have had some first-hand and considerable second-hand experience (e.g. in what our elders have told us about when people should and do provide help). Beliefs about that behavior and its occurrence under various conditions should thus be fairly veridical. My doubts would be directed more at beliefs about the mediating processes, those being at the microlevel (fast moving, transient, not easily accessible). We might consider the possibility that in situations of the sort constructed by Piliavin et al, helping may typically be controlled by mediating processes that entail rules of thumb, learned habits, unconditioned reflexes, and such. These fast-acting mediators, well adapted to the exigencies of unanticipated and quickly developing situations, may well reflect the more "reasonable" (i.e. mediated by "reason") considerations picked up in the beliefs that the helping scenarios tap. Thus the scenario procedures may give the same "behavioral" results as the experiment, and the scenarios may also suggest the adaptive underpinnings of the actual mediational processes. However, those processes may involve shortcuts, response habits, etc that carry out the adaptive logic but do not directly involve it.

How Common Terms May Affect Scientific Propositions

S-ψ's postulates about relations among variables may be influenced by explicit common beliefs about the causes and consequences of behavior. However, the propositions we develop may also be affected by relationships *implicit* in everyday terms. The network of meaning in which common terms are embedded always includes subtle ideas about what goes with what and what causes what. Figuratively speaking, common psychological terms "reach out" in various directions, carrying with them other, associated terms and often an implicit theory about a causal sequence in which the referent phenomena occur. Their very usage induces people to think of patterns of associated meaning and of simple models of causality.

Two types of critiques leveled at the products of S-ψ stem from the phenomena just described. Both types assert that certain relationships that S-ψ takes as facts about behavior have their true source in common terms and their implications. The critiques claim that (*a*) patterns of semantic similarity have been taken to represent patterns of real behavior, and (*b*) the causal relationships implied in common concepts have formed the basis for "laws of behavior" that are in fact unfalsifiable.

PATTERNS OF SEMANTIC SIMILARITY   This criticism was initiated by D'Andrade (1965) and vigorously advanced by Shweder (1975, 1977), both anthropologists. An example of their research is provided by Shweder (1975). Common people (students naive about the relevant S-ψ theory) are asked to judge the conceptual similarity between pairs of items from a personality or behavioral rating scale. Shweder then shows that the matrix of average similarity judgments (the *Conceptual Similarity Matrix*) corresponds rather closely to the matrix of inter-item correlations obtained when the scale items are used to obtain ratings of behavior (the *Rated Behavior Matrix*).

From some ten analyses of this sort, Shweder and D'Andrade conclude that the rating-based data on which S-ψ often relies reflect semantic similarity rather than behavioral covariation: ". . .the factors described in ratings are the property of trait terms as linguistic elements without being the property of the persons described by those terms" (Shweder 1975:457). CS-ψ judgments of "what *is like* what" are responsible for inferences made in S-ψ about "what *goes with* what."

This critique was the center of a heated controversy in the 1970s, and the technical issues are too complicated to present here. Perhaps the final round of the debate was staged in papers by Block et al (1979) and Shweder & D'Andrade (1979). It now seems clear that (*a*) the critique does not cut the ground out from under individual-difference research, with its broad set of measurement and validation strategies, but (*b*) it undoubtedly has something important to say about the factors that contribute to the *memory-based* ratings (including self-ratings) commonly used in personality and social psychology.

The participants in this controversy have recognized that it raises but leaves unanswered the question of where the CS-ψ conceptual system comes from. This question takes us into a running philosophical debate in which "realist" vs "constructionist" positions are counterposed. The latter position is expressed by Shweder (1977): "What is disputed is that the *categories* . . . into which people sort themselves and others can be induced from experience. Cultural *constructs* are not empirical generalizations" (p. 938, emphases in original). The realist position is expressed, though more moderately, by Block et al (1979): "Our own view is that although cultural constructs need not be evolved from living in the world, they very often are.. . ...[I]ndividually evolved and yet consensual structurings of interpersonal experience provide the basis, we suggest, for many learned cultural constructs" (p. 1071). It must be emphasized that the realist-constructionist issue is independent of the critique summarized above. Common sense categories may, in general, reflect the structure of an underlying reality; but any particular data set (e.g. a set of behavioral ratings) may be only poorly anchored in the corresponding "behavioral reality." Such an individual data set may instead be largely influenced by the common-sense category system.

CAUSAL IMPLICATIONS OF CONCEPTS   The issue here is closely related to the preceding one except that the focus is on the causal sequences implied by particular terms. Psychologists have studied the causal theories implicit in common terms. Examples include Au's (1986) research on the causes and consequences of events described by interpersonal verbs, and Shaver et al (1987) have noted the similar implications of common terms for emotions.

From an implicit recognition of the causal networks associated with common terms, both Smedslund (1978) and Ossorio (1981a,b) have written critiques of S-ψ. In essence, both argue (and I'll use Smedslund's statement of the position) that theories in psychology are often merely "explications of conceptual relationships imbedded in ordinary language (common sense). This conceptual network is *anterior* to both observation and theorizing. [In an] analogy between the tasks of pre-Euclidean geometry and contemporary psychology . . .[both] tasks are seen as involving explication of our implicit concepts of respectively space and people. One consequence of [this] view is that much psychological research is pointless since it attempts to verify logically necessary statements by empirical methods" (Smedslund 1978:1, emphasis in original).

Ossorio (1981a) illustrates his critique by examining the S-ψ formula "Frustration leads to aggression," which he reformulates as, "Provocation by O elicits a correspondingly hostile response by P." This, he asserts, "represents neither an empirical discovery nor a stipulative definition. Instead, it is a partial formulation of our familiar four-thousand-year-old concept of anger" (p. 49). In this, Ossorio implicitly recognizes the causal network implied by the term "anger," shown by Shaver et al's (1987) prototype analysis to include provocation and hostile responses as antecedents and consequences, respectively. Ossorio's point is that a S-ψ proposition such as that above is a "non-empirical formula." "What is not empirical is the content of the formula and the logical interconnections among the elements of the formula..." (p. 52). Empirical research on such formulations is appropriate only to establish "their range of effective applicability."

Smedslund's critique can be illustrated by his translation of Bandura's (1977) self-efficacy theory into a set of common-sense theorems (Smedslund 1978). For example, Bandura's proposition that "The strength of people's convictions in their own effectiveness is likely to affect whether they will even try to cope with given situations" Smedslund restates, in part, in these terms: "If P wants to do something and believes with complete certainty that he can do it, then P will try to do it." This theorem, Smedslund notes, is "logically necessary" by virtue of the implication, built into the word "trying," that P both wants to do something and believes he can. The causal implications of the concept "trying" link it back to the two antecedents of "wanting" and "belief in ability." To describe trying as a consequence of wanting and belief is simply to provide what all users of the English language would regard as "an acceptable explanation." The proof of the theorem is found in the fact that the alternative assertion, that trying reflects a person's not believing and/or not wanting, would not be considered an acceptable explanation.

Smedslund's rendering of S-ψ theories involves stripping the common terms of the technical jargon in which they have been clothed, and then showing that the (simpler, more naked) propositions follow from the implications of those common terms. Like Ossorio, Smedslund assigns only a limited role to empirical research in relation to the "logically necessary theorems." It may provide reminders of the complexities of human behavior, yield assessment of practical procedures implied by the theorems, and determine whether the theorems apply to a particular set of real circumstances.

These critiques of S-ψ theories are essentially sophisticated ways of labeling them "obvious." As a consequence, Bandura's (1978) brief reply to Smedslund's critique is, in essence, a summary of the most weighty responses to the charge of "obviousness," implied in my earlier discussion.

Smedslund notes the strong similarity between the simple terms he finds useful and those identified by Heider (1958) in his "naive analysis of action." For example, Smedslund's argument, outlined above, is essentially a reprise of Heider's schematization of the relations among "intention," "can," and "trying." However, there are some sharp contrasts. Heider explicitly recognized that the implicational links are generated by the causal connotations of CS-ψ terms, describing these terms as "fundamental concept[s] . . . linked with causation." Furthermore, Heider viewed himself as contributing to the development of S-ψ theory where Smedslund is, in some sense, debunking it. Heider's analysis was framed to provide a foundation for theories such as

Bandura's, and in fact, it has provided the starting point for Weiner's (1986) attributional theory of motivation and emotion. Weiner's work shows how it is possible for S-ψ to refine and organize the common-sense notions, by explicitly and systematically analyzing the categories and dimensions of causality they imply. This suggests that CS-ψ can become a foundation for S-ψ theory. The creative work here lies in analyzing CS-ψ and revealing its underlying framework. Once any such theory is completed, we should hardly be surprised that, taken separately and viewed from the CS-ψ perspective, most of the specific S-ψ propositions will appear to be truisms.

An overview of the common thrust of Heider's, Ossorio's, and Smedslund's work is provided by Shotter & Burton (1983). They see this work as "concerned with constructing formulations within which to describe the structure of social behavior systematically." They designate the work as "descriptive formulation research, to emphasize that the main activity involved is a back and forth productive process working between explicit formulations and the implicit social knowledge such formulations are meant to specify and describe" (p. 272). This locates the effort squarely in a symmetrical interplay between CS-ψ and S-ψ. As to the value of the work, Shotter & Burton advance the provocative (and in my view, dubious) qualification that, being characterized by an ineradicable vagueness, CS-ψ is "a source of indefinitely many formulations. . . ." Thus the formulations of the three theorists discussed above are to be regarded "as exemplary and not as in any way definitive" (p. 278.) They write that Heider "is not *clarifying concepts* as he says, but is *constructing idealizations,* [because] . . . formulation involves the further specification of what is initially and intrinsically vague" (p. 279; emphasis in the original).

CONCLUSION

In thinking about the overall influence of CS-ψ on S-ψ, I come to the same ambivalent conclusions as have many authors who have preceded me: It is impossible for us to avoid the effects of CS-ψ, but easy for us to be unaware of them. These effects provide us with both opportunities and risks. As Fletcher (1984) writes, "common sense is a valuable but inherently dangerous resource available to psychologists" (p. 203).

It is easy to overlook the risks entailed in the many CS-ψ-to-S-ψ linkages. However, to do so introduces ambiguity and confusion into our work. We must be more explicitly aware of the effects and more analytic in thinking about them. This chapter describes many instances of such awareness and various empirical and conceptual approaches to analyzing the linkages.

I have become convinced that despite the large literature bearing on the issues described in this chapter, they deserve more widespread attention than they presently receive. For example, although I am uncertain about where it would fit into their curriculum, I would think that graduate students should be sensitized to how CS-ψ intrudes into the early, fundamental stages of research—the stages at which we define our concepts and formulate our hypotheses.

The inevitable effects of CS-ψ on S-ψ are neither all good nor all bad. Proposals that we break entirely free from CS-ψ are misguided. Discarding our CS-ψ "baggage" would require us needlessly to separate ourselves from the vast sources of knowledge gained in the course of human history. And in any case, such suggestions are unrealistic: The thoughts, writings, and conversations of human researchers are heavily saturated with common language. Common-sense psychology constitutes both a bondage and a heritage for scientific psychology. Like all that we inherit, we have little or no choice in the matter. And like other inheritances, at the same time that it constrains and creates problems for us, it provides a useful and potentially rich foundation for development and growth.

ACKNOWLEDGMENTS

I am deeply grateful to John Houston and Bernard Weiner for their thoughtful reactions to a first draft of this manuscript.

Literature Cited

Au, T. K.-F. 1986. A verb is worth a thousand words: the causes and consequences of interpersonal events implicit in language. *J. Mem. Lang.* 25:104–22

Bandura, A. 1977. Self-efficacy: toward a theory of behavioral change. *Psychol. Rev.* 84:191–215

Bandura, A. 1978. On distinguishing between logical and empirical verification. A comment on Smedslund. *Scand. J. Psychol.* 19:97–9

Berscheid, E., Snyder, M., Omoto, A. L. 1989. The relationship closeness inventory: assessing the closeness of interpersonal relationships. *J. Pers. Soc. Psychol.* 57:792–807

Block, J., Weiss, D. S., Thorne, A. 1979. How relevant is a semantic similarity interpretation of personality ratings? *J. Pers. Soc. Psychol.* 37:1055–74

Brickman, P. 1980. A social psychology of human concerns. In *The Development of Social Psychology,* ed. R. Gilmour, S. Duck, pp. 5–25. London: Academic

Buss, D. M., Craik, K. H. 1980. The frequency concept of disposition: dominance and prototypically dominant acts. *J. Pers.* 48:379–92

Cheng, P. W., Novick, L. R. 1990. A probabilistic contrast model of causal induction. *J. Pers. Soc. Psychol.* 58:545–67

D'Andrade, R. G. 1965. Trait psychology and componential analysis. *Am. Anthro.* 67:215–28

Davis, M. S. 1971. That's interesting! Towards a phenomenology of sociology and a sociology of phenomenology. *Philos. Soc. Sci.* 1:309–44

Farr, R. M. 1981. On the nature of human nature and the science of behaviour. See Heelas & Lock 1981, pp. 303–17

Fehr, B. 1988. Prototype analysis of the concepts of love and commitment. *J. Pers. Soc. Psychol.* 55:557–79

Fischhoff, B. 1975. Hindsight $\neq$ foresight: the effect of outcome knowledge on judgment under uncertainty. *J. Exp. Psychol.: Hum. Percep. Perform.* 1:288–99

Fletcher, G. J. O. 1984. Psychology and common sense. *Am. Psychol.* 39:203–13

Furnham, A. 1983. Social psychology as common sense. *Bull. Br. Psychol. Soc.* 36:105–9

Gergen, K. J. 1973. Social psychology as history. *J. Pers. Soc. Psychol.* 26:309–20

Gergen, K. J. 1978. Experimentation in social psychology: a reappraisal. *Eur. J. Soc. Psychol.* 8:507–27

Heelas, P., Lock, A., eds. 1981. *Indigenous Psychologies: The Anthropology of the Self.* London: Academic

Heider, F. 1958. *The Psychology of Interpersonal Relations.* New York: John Wiley & Sons

Herzlich, C. 1973. *Health and Illness: A Social Psychological Analysis.* London: Academic

Houston, J. P. 1983. Psychology: a closed system of self-evident information? *Psychol. Rep.* 52:203–8

Houston, J. P. 1985. Untutored lay knowledge of the principles of psychology: Do we know anything they don't? *Psychol. Rep.* 57:567–70

Joynson, R. B. 1974. *Psychology and Common Sense.* London: Routledge & Kegan Paul

Kaye, K. 1977. Toward the origin of dialogue. In *Studies in mother-infant interaction,* ed. H. R. Schaffer, pp. 89–117. New York: Academic

Kazak, A. E., Reppucci, N. D. 1980. Romantic love as a social institution. In *On Love and Loving: Psychological Perspectives on the Nature and Experience of Romantic Love,* ed. K. S. Pope and Associates, pp. 209–27. San Francisco: Jossey-Bass

Kelley, H. H. 1967. Attribution theory in social psychology. In *Nebraska Symposium on Motivation,* ed. D. Levine, pp. 192–38. Lincoln: Univ. Nebraska Press

Koffka, K. 1935. *Principles of Gestalt Psychology.* New York: Harcourt, Brace

Krech, D., Crutchfield, R. S. 1948. *Theories and Problems of Social Psychology.* New York: McGraw-Hill

McGuire, W. J. 1973. The Ying and Yang of progress in social psychology: seven koan. *J. Pers. Soc. Psychol.* 26:446–56

Moscovici, S. 1961. *La psychanalyse, son image et son public. Etude sur la représentation sociale de la psychanalyse.* Paris: Presses Universitaires de France

O'Hare, D., Duck, S. 1981. Implicit psychology and ordinary explanation. See Heelas & Lock 1981, pp. 285–302

Ossorio, P. B. 1981a. Explanation, falsifiability, and rule-following. *Adv. Descrip. Psychol.* 1:37–55

Ossorio, P. B. 1981b. Outline of descriptive psychology for personality theory and clinical applications. *Adv. Descrip. Psychol.* 1:57–81

Piliavin, I. M., Rodin, J., Piliavin, J. A. 1969. Good Samaritanism: an underground phenomenon? *J. Pers. Soc. Psychol.* 13:289–99

Rosch, E. 1978. Principles of categorization. In *Cognition and Categorization,* ed. E. Rosch, B. B. Lloyd, pp. 27–48. Hillsdale, NJ: Erlbaum

Rubin, Z. 1970. Measurement of romantic love. *J. Pers. Soc. Psychol.* 16:265–73

Rusbult, C. E. 1980a. Commitment and satisfaction in romantic associations: a test of the investment model. *J. Exp. Soc. Psychol.* 16:172–86

Rusbult, C. E. 1980b. Satisfaction and commitment in friendships. *Rep. Res. Soc. Psychol.* 11:96–105

Schlenker, B. R. 1974. Social psychology and science. *J. Pers. Soc. Psychol.* 29:1–15

Shaver, P., Schwartz, J., Kirson, D., O'Connor, C. 1987. *J. Pers. Soc. Psychol.* 52:1061-86

Shotter, J., Burton, M. 1983. Common sense accounts of human action: the descriptive formulations of Heider, Smedslund, and Ossorio. *Rev. Pers. Soc. Psychol.* 4:272–96

Shweder, R. A. 1975. How relevant is an individual difference theory of personality? *J. Pers.* 43:455–84

Shweder, R. A. 1977. Illusory correlation and the MMPI controversy. *J. Couns. Clin. Psychol.* 45:917–24

Shweder, R. A., D'Andrade, R. G. 1979. Accurate reflection or semantic distortion? A reply to Block, Weiss, and Thorne. *J. Pers. Soc. Psychol.* 37:1075–84

Smedslund, J. 1978. Bandura's theory of self-efficacy: a set of common sense theorems. *Scand. J. Psychol.* 19:1–14

Sternberg, R. J. 1981. People's conceptions of intelligence. *J. Pers. Soc. Psychol.* 41:37–55

Sternberg, R. J. 1985. Implicit theories of intelligence, creativity, and wisdom. *J. Pers. Soc. Psychol.* 49:607–27

Thibaut, J. W., Kelley, H. H. 1959. *The Social Psychology of Groups.* New York: John Wiley & Sons

Vollmer, G. 1984. Mesocosm and objective knowledge. In *Concepts and Approaches to Evolutionary Epistemology: Towards an Evolutionary Theory of Knowledge,* ed. F. M. Wuketits, pp. 69–121. Dordrecht: D. Reidel

Wallach, M. A., Wallach, L. 1983. *Psychology's Sanction for Selfishness: The Error of Egoism in Theory and Therapy.* San Francisco: W. H. Freeman

Wegner, D. M., Vallacher, R. R. 1977. *Implicit Psychology.* New York: Oxford Univ. Press

Wegner, D. M., Vallacher, R. R. 1981. Common-sense psychology. In *Social Cognition: Perspectives on Everyday Understanding,* ed. J. P. Forgas, pp. 224–46. London: Academic

Weiner, B. 1980. A cognitive (attribution)-emotion-action model of motivated behavior: an analysis of judgments of helpgiving. *J. Pers. Soc. Psychol.* 39:186-200

Weiner, B. 1986. *An Attributional Theory of Motivation and Emotion.* New York: Springer-Verlag

Annu. Rev. Psychol. 1992. 43:25–53

SIMILARITY SCALING AND COGNITIVE PROCESS MODELS

Robert M. Nosofsky

Department of Psychology, Indiana University, Bloomington, Indiana 47405

KEY WORDS: multidimensional scaling, multidimensional signal detection theory, categorization, generalization, psychological distance

Contents

INTRODUCTION

A well-known virtue of similarity-scaling techniques such as multi-dimensional scaling, Thurstonian modeling, and clustering is that they reveal hidden structure underlying psychological data. By applying these techniques, complex matrixes of similarity data such as similarity ratings, identification confusions, and same-different errors can be efficiently described, summarized, and displayed, and a deeper insight into the underlying basis of the similarity data can be derived.

25

0066-4308/92/0201-0025$02.00

Beyond describing and summarizing data, however, scaling techniques can be viewed as psychological models for the mental representation of interobject similarity. In this chapter I review the role of similarity-scaling techniques as components in formal psychological models of perceptual and cognitive processes.

Cognitive models are often conceptualized as representation-process pairs (e.g. Anderson 1976). Objects that are perceived or remembered receive some internal representation. Various cognitive processes are then assumed to act upon that representation. The particular processes that operate are task dependent—they will vary depending on whether subjects are asked to discriminate among objects; identify, categorize or recognize them; supply similarity ratings; make preference judgments, and so forth. Thus, to understand performance in tasks involving similarity data we must specify not only an underlying similarity representation, but also the cognitive processes that act on that representation.

The beauty of deriving a similarity-scaling representation by modeling performance in a given task is that the derived representation can then be used to predict performance in independent tasks involving the same objects and stimulus conditions (e.g. Cliff 1973; Henley 1969; Hutchinson & Lockhead 1977; Monahan & Lockhead 1977). For each task, one needs to specify the cognitive processes that are operating, but key aspects of the underlying similarity representation may be invariant. Thus, similarity-scaling techniques allow one to characterize how performance across independent tasks is related. I believe that the characterization of such invariant relations should be one of the central goals of psychological science.

I also argue that any evaluation of how well a scaling representation accounts for similarity data must occur within the framework of formal process models. Mispredictions involving a proposed scaling representation may reflect inadequacies in the scaling model, but they may also indicate a failure to specify adequately the cognitive processes that operate on the representation.

I organize this chapter into two main parts. Part 1 focuses on models incorporating deterministic multidimensional scaling (MDS) approaches, Part 2 on probabilistic MDS approaches. I distinguish between the two as follows: In deterministic MDS, each object is represented as a single point in the spatial representation, whereas in probabilistic MDS, each object is represented as a probabilistic distribution of points. (Note that by this definition, many deterministic MDS models can still have probabilistic components. For example, although each object is represented as a fixed point, the distance-judgment process itself may be noisy.) Because of space limitations I review only spatial models, although the role of discrete-feature and network approaches as components in cognitive process models is of equal importance.

The last review article on scaling was that of Gescheider (1988), who also emphasized linkages between scaling methods and perceptual and cognitive processes. However, Gescheider's (1988) review was concerned with classic psychophysical tasks involving unidimensional scaling, such as magnitude estimation, whereas the present review focuses on multidimensional cognitive processes involving similarity data. I do not attempt to match the broad and comprehensive reviews on multidimensional scaling provided in the chapters by Carroll & Arabie (1980) and Young (1984a), but rather focus on the intersection between similarity scaling and cognitive-process models. Ashby's (1992) edited volume, *Multidimensional Models of Perception and Cognition*, covers more extensively many of the MDS-based models discussed here.

DETERMINISTIC MULTIDIMENSIONAL SCALING APPROACHES

Universal Laws of Generalization and Similarity

A major recent contribution in the use of MDS techniques for understanding cognitive processes was Shepard's (1987) "Toward a universal law of generalization for psychological science." As argued by Shepard, an organism's generalization from one situation to another must surely stand among the most fundamental psychological processes. The process of generalization is often studied within the context of identification learning paradigms. In these paradigms, subjects learn to associate a unique response with each member of a set of stimuli. Generalization or similarity is measured in terms of the probability of interstimulus-confusion errors. A well-known quantitative measure of generalization or similarity between stimuli i and j is given by $g_{ij} = [(p_{ij} \cdot p_{ji})/(p_{ii} \cdot p_{jj})]^{1/2}$, where p_{ij} is the probability that stimulus i is identified as stimulus j. An intuitive justification for this measure is provided by Shepard (1958a). The major theoretical justification is that this quantity gives an estimate of the similarity parameters in the classic similarity choice model (SCM) for predicting identification confusions (Luce 1963; Shepard 1957). I discuss the SCM extensively in the following section.

The similarity measures obtained in generalization experiments can be used as input to nonmetric multidimensional scaling algorithms, and an MDS solution for the stimuli can be derived. The generalization measures g_{ij} can then be plotted against the corresponding distances d_{ij} between points in the derived solution to discover the form of the gradient relating generalization to distance in the psychological space. Shepard (1987) presents 12 different plots of these derived generalization gradients, the generalization measures having been obtained in experiments involving both human and animal subjects, and both visual and auditory stimuli. As summarized by Shepard (1987:1319), "in every case, the decrease of generalization with psychological distance is monotonic, generally concave upward, and more or less approximates a simple exponential decay function. . . ."

It is critical to realize that in discovering this exponential law relating generalization to psychological distance, Shepard (1987) operates at an entirely psychological level of analysis. Distances between objects are derived by using MDS techniques that rely on only the generalization measures themselves. "Psychophysics" is not involved, in the sense that no physical measurements are ever taken on the stimuli. Indeed, Shepard (1987:1318) argues that the invariant law of generalization was "attainable only by formulating that law with respect to the appropriate abstract psychological space."

When more than one dimension is required to describe the similarity structure of a set of stimuli, the generalization data also provide information about the metric structure of the psychological space. Noting the extensive literature on this subject, Shepard (1987) suggests that for stimuli composed of relatively unanalyzable, "integral" dimensions, such as colors varying in lightness and saturation, the distance structure of psychological space is well approximated by the Euclidean metric; whereas for stimuli composed of highly analyzable, "separable" dimensions, such as forms varying in size and orientation, the distance structure is generally best approximated by the "city-block" metric (see Garner 1974 and Shepard 1991 for reviews).

Given these observed regularities in the form of the generalization gradient and the metric structure of psychological space, Shepard then proposes a cognitive process model to account for the laws. Assume that an experience with an object has had some significant consequence for an organism. The organism must decide which new objects are enough like the old one that they are likely to have the same consequence. A class of objects with the same consequence corresponds to a region in the organism's psychological space that Shepard terms a *consequential region*.

In finding a given object to be consequential, the organism learns that there is some consequential region that overlaps the point in psychological space corresponding to that object. Probability of generalization to a new object would be determined by estimating the conditional probability that the consequential region also overlaps the point corresponding to the second object. To determine this conditional probability precisely, one needs information concerning the probability that the consequential regions in an organism's psychological space are of given shapes, sizes, and locations, and then needs to integrate over the hypothesized forms of the consequential regions. Nevertheless, given remarkably weak assumptions, many justified by evolutionary considerations, Shepard (1987) demonstrates that the conditional probability of overlap is always well approximated by an exponential decay function of the distance between the objects in the psychological space. He concludes, "Evidently, the form of [the generalization gradient] is a relatively robust consequence of the probabilistic geometry of consequential regions" (Shepard 1987:1320). Finally, Shepard's (1987) cognitive process model also provides an account of why the Euclidean and city-block metrics closely approximate the distance structure for integral-dimension and separable-dimension stimuli, respectively.

CHALLENGES   The proposed universal law of generalization has not gone unchallenged. Work reported by Nosofsky (1985a,b; 1986, 1989) raised questions about the universality of the exponential-decay generalization gradient, although these questions have now been largely resolved (Ennis 1988; Ennis et al 1988; Nosofsky 1988b; Shepard 1986, 1987, 1988). Using essentially the same theoretical approach as described by Shepard (1987), Nosofsky found evidence that in some identification-confusion experiments, the plot of similarity against psychological distance was Gaussian in form rather than exponential (see also Ashby & Lee 1991). The main difference between the experiments conducted by Nosofsky (1985b, 1989) and those discussed by Shepard (1987) is that Nosofsky's studies involved protracted identification training involving asymptotic performance with highly confusable stimuli, whereas the studies considered by Shepard involved identification learning of fairly discriminable stimuli. Shepard (1986:60) suggested that the Gaussian similarity functions observed by Nosofsky (1985a,b) reflected limitations on discrimination performance resulting from "irreducible noise in the perceptual/memory system," and not the cognitive form of similarity intrinsic to the process of generalization.

The difference in the situations considered by Shepard (1987) and Nosofsky (1985a,b) can be viewed theoretically in the following way. Because of noise in the perceptual/memory system, presentation of an object does not result in the same internal representation on every trial. Rather, over trials, presentation of an object gives rise to a probabilistic distribution of points in the observer's psychological space (see the second part of this chapter). Nevertheless, in Shepard's situations, the distance between the means of the object representations is so great, relative to the variability of these representations, that each object can be represented as essentially a single point in the psychological space. By contrast, in Nosofsky's situations, overlap among the alternative object distributions is substantial, so each object should really be represented as a distribution of points rather than as a single point. As will be seen in the section on probabilistic MDS, Ennis and his colleagues have demonstrated that such a model reconciles Shepard's proposed universal law of generalization with the findings reported by Nosofsky.

RELATED WORK   Alternative process models to account for the form of the generalization gradient have also been proposed. Staddon & Reid (1990) proposed a simple neural network model in which activation received by individual units tends, over time, to spread to neighboring units in the network. When a given stimulus is presented for a moderate number of iterations, the activation gradient that it produces is approximately exponential in form. But when the stimulus is withdrawn, the diffusion process eventually produces a gradient that is Gaussian in form. Shepard (1990) notes that this neural network model is formally identical to his earlier proposed trace-diffusion model of stimulus generalization (Shepard 1958a). He argues that a limitation of both diffusion models is that they fail to predict that with continued training, subjects can eventually learn to discriminate perfectly between objects that are members of contrasting consequential regions. Shepard & Kannappan (1991) present a multi-layered, neural-network embodiment of the 1987 cognitive theory of generalization, which successfully predicts the form of the generalization gradient under different conditions of discrimination training. Finally, Gluck (1991) suggests that the configural-cue adaptive network model proposed by Gluck & Bower (1988) produces, in discrete-dimension domains, a generalization gradient that approximates the exponential.

In work related to Shepard's, Blough (1988) observed highly regular results relating reaction time in visual search tasks to distances in multidimensional psychological space. Pigeons were trained to peck at a unique target embedded in a field of identical distractors, and visual search reaction time (RT) was measured. The targets and distractors were drawn from fixed stimulus sets, such as squares varying in size, and rectangles varying in height and width. In most experiments, all possible pairs of forms from each set served as targets and distractors across trials, yielding a complete matrix of mean RTs, one for each pair of forms. MDS solutions were derived for the forms by using these matrixes of mean RTs as input. Blough then plotted the mean RT for each pair of forms against their distance (D) in the derived scaling solution, and found that for all stimulus sets, the RT gradients were well fitted by the function $RT - k = c \cdot \exp(- b \cdot D)$, where k, c, and b are estimated parameters. Thus, just as occurs for generalization, there is the suggestion of lawful relations between visual search speed and psychological distance (see also Shepard et al 1975, for reports of lawful relations between discrimination RT and psychological distance).

Identification, Categorization, and Recognition

The MDS-based models of generalization and identification learning discussed by Shepard (1987) have been extended to account for categorization and recognition performance. Whereas in identification each stimulus is to be assigned a unique response, in categorization stimuli are to be classified into groups. Recognition refers to a memory experiment in which subjects judge whether items are "old" or "new."

IDENTIFICATION   One of the classic models for predicting identification performance is the *similarity choice model* (SCM) proposed by Shepard (1957) and Luce (1963), whose formal properties have been further investigated by researchers such as Smith (1980, 1982), Townsend (1971; Townsend & Landon 1982), Nosofsky (1985b, 1990), and Takane & Shibayama (1985). According to the model, the probability that stimulus i is identified as stimulus j is given by

$$P(R_j|S_i) = b_j \, \eta_{ij} \, / \, \Sigma b_k \, \eta_{ik}, \qquad\qquad 1.$$

where η_{ij} $(0 \leq \eta_{ij}, \eta_{ij} = \eta_{ji})$ denotes the similarity between stimuli i and j, and b_j $(0 \leq b_j \leq 1, \Sigma b_j = 1)$ is often interpreted as the bias for making response j. Although descriptive in nature, a variety of process interpretations for the SCM have been proposed (e.g. Marley 1992; Nosofsky 1990; Smith 1980; Townsend & Landon 1983).

The SCM usually provides excellent descriptions of the detailed quantitative structure of identification-confusion matrixes. However, assuming n stimuli, fitting the model requires estimation of $n(n - 1)/2$ freely varying similarity parameters (one similarity parameter for each pair of unique stimuli), and $n - 1$ freely varying bias parameters. Furthermore, simply fitting the full version of the model provides little insight into the psychological processes and similarity structure that underlie identification performance.

A vast reduction in the number of free parameters and a deeper understanding of identification processes can be achieved by testing and comparing restricted versions of the SCM in which theories of similarity are used to constrain the η_{ij} parameters. One classic approach, initiated in Shepard's (1957, 1958b) original formulation of the model, is to derive an MDS solution for the set of stimuli, and assume that the η_{ij} parameters are functionally related to distances in the derived scaling solution. Systematic comparisons among different versions of this MDS-choice model can provide insights into the underlying dimensions of the stimuli, the metric structure of the psychological space, the extent to which values on different dimensions are perceived independently of one another, and so forth.

As one example, Nosofsky (1985b) collected confusion data in which two subjects identified stimuli varying along two continuous dimensions (size and angle). There were four orthogonally varying values per dimension, yielding a 16-member stimulus set (and, therefore, a 256-cell identification-confusion matrix). Nosofsky (1985b) found that by representing each stimulus as a point in a two-dimensional psychological space, computing similarities between stimuli on the basis of their distance in the space, and substituting these similarities into the SCM response rule (Equation 1), excellent predictions of the identification-confusion data could be achieved. Indeed, the fits of this

MDS-choice model were not significantly worse than those of the full SCM for either subject, suggesting that the MDS solution provided a precise quantitative account of the similarity structure inherent in each subject's data. Moreover, for one of the subjects, a constrained MDS-choice model with only six freely varying MDS coordinate parameters accounted for the data essentially as well as the full SCM with 120 freely varying similarity parameters. In this constrained model, all stimuli with a given physical value of angle were assumed to have the same psychological value on the angle dimension, and likewise for the size dimension. The excellent fits of this constrained MDS-choice model provided evidence that the subject perceived the size and angle dimensions in a separable manner. Other illustrative applications of the MDS-choice model are provided by Shepard (1958b), Getty et al (1979), Nosofsky (1985a, 1987, 1989), Takane & Shibayama (1985), and Heiser (1988).

CATEGORIZATION   A classic issue in cognitive psychology is whether the principles of stimulus generalization and similarity that underlie identification performance also underlie categorization performance. Indeed, perhaps the most straightforward view of categorization, formalized in what are known today as *exemplar models* (e.g. Estes 1986; Hintzman 1986; Medin & Schaffer 1978; Nosofsky 1986), is that classification of an object is determined by how similar it is to the individual members of alternative categories.

Seminal investigations of this idea were conducted by Shepard et al (1961) and Shepard & Chang (1963). These researchers measured similarities among the individual objects in a set in terms of the probability of pairwise confusions in identification learning paradigms. The measured similarities were then used to quantitatively predict the difficulty of learning different category structures. Intuitively, if an exemplar-based generalization view is correct, it should be easier to learn structures in which within-category similarities among objects are large, and between-category similarities are small. In a situation involving relatively unanalyzable, integral-dimension stimuli, Shepard & Chang (1963) found that the difficulty of learning different category structures could indeed be predicted well on the basis of pairwise confusions in identification learning tasks. But in a situation involving highly analyzable, separable-dimension stimuli there were systematic failures of the exemplar-based generalization hypothesis. Shepard et al (1961) attributed these failures to the intervention of a selective-attention process, in which subjects focused attention on those dimensions of the stimuli that were relevant to solving a given categorization problem. Such a selective-attention process should be particularly efficient for separable-dimension stimuli.

Nosofsky (1984, 1986) formalized these early ideas involving exemplar-based generalization and selective attention within an integrated model. This model, which is a generalization of the *context model* of categorization proposed by Medin & Schaffer (1978), builds directly on the multidimensional scaling–SCM framework discussed in the previous section. According to the generalized context model (GCM), the evidence favoring Category J given presentation of stimulus i is found by summing the (weighted) similarity of stimulus i to all exemplars of Category J, and then multiplying by the response bias for Category J. This evidence is then divided by the sum of evidences for all categories to predict the conditional probability with which stimulus i is classified in Category J:

$$P(R_J \mid S_i) = (b_J \sum_{j \epsilon C_J} M_j \; \eta_{ij}) \; / \; (\sum_K b_K \sum_{k \epsilon C_K} M_k \; \eta_{ik}), \qquad 2.$$

where η_{ij} denotes the similarity between exemplars i and j; b_J denotes the Category J response bias; and M_j denotes the strength with which exemplar j is stored in memory.

The relation between the decision rules in the GCM (Equation 2) and the SCM (Equation 1) is readily apparent. However, because of the selective-attention processes discussed by Shepard et al (1961), Shepard (1964), Tversky (1977), Garner (1974), Medin & Schaffer (1978), and others, the η_{ij} similarity parameters in Equations 1 and 2 may be not invariant across the identification and categorization paradigms.

Nosofsky (1984, 1986) adopted the Individual Differences Scaling approach to multidimensional scaling (Carroll & Wish 1974) as a theory for explaining attention-based changes in similarities. The distance between exemplars i and j (d_{ij}) in a multidimensional psychological space is given by

$$d_{ij} = [\sum_m w_m \mid x_{im} - x_{jm} \mid ^r]^{1/r}, \qquad 3.$$

where x_{im} is the psychological value of exemplar i on dimension m; the value of r defines the distance metric (e.g. $r = 1$, city-block; $r = 2$, Euclidean); and w_m ($0 \leq w_m$, $\Sigma w_m = 1$) is the "attention-weight" given to dimension m. Large values of w_m serve to "stretch" the psychological space along dimension m, and small values of w_m serve to "shrink" the space along that dimension. The distance d_{ij} is converted to a similarity measure by using the function

$$\eta_{ij} = \exp(-c \cdot d_{ij}^p), \qquad 4.$$

where c is a general sensitivity parameter; and the value of p defines the similarity gradient (e.g. $p = 1$, exponential; $p = 2$, Gaussian).

The general approach to predicting and relating identification and categorization in terms of this multidimensional scaling framework is as follows. First, by fitting the MDS-choice model (Equations 1, 3, and 4) to a set of identification-confusion data, a maximum-likelihood MDS solution is derived for a set of stimuli. This MDS solution can then be used in conjunction with the GCM (Equations 2, 3, and 4) to predict performance in any given categorization paradigm involving the same set of stimuli. Because the MDS solution will have been derived from the identification-confusion data, a minimum of parameters remain to be estimated for predicting categorization. The critical parameters tend to be the weights (w_m) in the distance function (Equation 3), which describe the role of the selective attention process in modifying similarities across identification and categorization.

Nosofsky (e.g. 1984, 1986, 1987, 1989, 1991c) has demonstrated numerous successful quantitative applications of the GCM, in situations involving both integral and separable-dimension stimuli. These demonstrations are important because they illustrate that the fundamental processes of identification and categorization can be understood within a unified theoretical framework, and that precise quantitative predictions of performance in each paradigm can be achieved within this framework. Furthermore, the predictions of categorization are achieved with a minimum of parameter estimation. Finally, the estimated attention-weight parameters vary in psychologically meaningful ways. In particular, Nosofsky (e.g. 1984, 1986, 1991c) has provided evidence that subjects often distribute attention over psychological dimensions so as to nearly optimize their categorization performance—i.e. maximize their average percentage of correct categorization choices. A variety of mechanistic models have recently been proposed for how the attention weights in the GCM may be learned trial by trial (e.g. Hurwitz 1990; Kruschke 1990).

The role of MDS in developing these theoretical relations is critical. Note that it is not "similarity" that is invariant across identification and categorization; rather, the MDS solution for the stimuli is invariant. Because of the selective-attention processes assumed to operate on the scaling representation, similarities among exemplars are systematically modified.

The MDS-based exemplar model accounts successfully for the effects of a number of fundamental variables on categorization performance. As one example, Nosofsky (1988c, 1991c) established experimental learning conditions in which the frequency of individual exemplars was manipulated. In the GCM, increasing the frequency of an exemplar is assumed to increase its "strength" in memory. Exemplar memory-strength is modeled by the M_j parameters in Equation 2. Because memory strength combines multiplicatively with interexemplar similarity, the GCM predicts an interactive effect of frequency and similarity on categorization performance. The interactive effect is observed: Classification accuracy and confidence increase for exemplars that are presented with high frequency, and for items that are similar to the high-frequency exemplars. Little effect of frequency occurs for items that are dissimilar to the high-frequency exemplars. It is as if the high-frequency exemplar acts as a "magnet" in the psychological space, drawing nearby objects toward it.

Alternative models of categorization can also be formulated within an MDS framework. According to prototype models, classification is determined by the similarity of an item to the central tendency of the distributions of category exemplars in the multidimensionally scaled psychological space (e.g. Nosofsky 1987, 1991c; Reed 1972; Shin 1990). Prototype models tend not to fare as well as exemplar models, however, in their quantitative predictions of classification performance (see Nosofsky 1992, for a review).

The fuzzy logical model of perception (FLMP) of Massaro, Oden, and their colleagues (e.g. Massaro 1987; Massaro & Friedman 1990; Oden & Massaro 1978) can also be construed as an MDS-based prototype model, although here the prototype of a category is defined more generally as an "ideal point" in the psychological space rather than as the central tendency. In a typical experimental paradigm for testing the FLMP, the stimuli vary along M orthogonal continuous dimensions, and the subject is required to classify each object into one of K categories. According to the model, the probability that stimulus i is classified in Category J is given by

$$P(R_J \mid S_i) = \eta_{iPJ} / \Sigma \; \eta_{iPK}, \qquad\qquad 5.$$

where η_{iPJ} denotes the similarity (or "fuzzy logical degree of match") of stimulus i to the prototype of Category J. This similarity is given by the multiplicative rule

$$\eta_{iPJ} = \Pi \; s(i_m, J_m), \qquad\qquad 6.$$

where $s(i_m, J_m)$ denotes the similarity of stimulus i to Prototype J on dimension m. This interdimensional multiplicative rule for computing similarities between exemplars was also proposed by Medin & Schaffer (1978) in their original formulation of the context model, although they restricted attention to binary-valued dimensions.

The FLMP has accounted impressively for numerous phenomena involving forms of information integration in diverse domains (Massaro 1987). In most previous applications of the model, however, all the individual $s(i_m, J_M)$ values were treated essentially as free parameters. As noted by Nosofsky (1984, 1986), the multiplicative similarity rule (Equation 6) has a natural MDS interpretation that would allow for a much more parsimonious application of the FLMP. In particular, an interdimensional multiplicative rule arises whenever $p = r$ in Equations 3 and 4. For example, when distance in psychological space is described by a city-block metric ($r = 1$), and similarity is an exponential decay function of psychological distance ($p = 1$), then we would have

$$\eta_{iPJ} = \exp\left[-c\left(\Sigma\, w_m\,\middle|\, x_{im}\text{-}x_{Jm}\,\middle|\right)\right]$$
$$= \Pi\, \exp\left(-c \cdot w_m\,\middle|\, x_{im}\text{-}x_{Jm}\,\middle|\right), \qquad\qquad 7.$$

which is Equation 6 with $s(i_m, J_m) = \exp(-\,c \cdot w_m\,|\,x_{im}\text{-}x_{Jm}\,|)$. Thus, by deriving in independent tasks similarity-scaling solutions for the objects under study, the FLMP could be applied to predict categorization with a minimum of parameter estimation.

Recently, Anderson (1990) proposed a rational model of categorization. According to the rational model, exemplars are grouped into clusters during the category learning process. The probability that an exemplar joins a cluster is determined jointly by the current size of each cluster, the similarity of the exemplar to the cluster's central tendency, and the value of a "coupling" parameter, which is a free parameter in the model. There are also mechanisms in the model for determining the probability that membership in each cluster signals a given category label. Roughly, the probability that stimulus i is classified in Category J is found by summing the similarity of i to each cluster's central tendency, weighted by the category-label J probability associated with the cluster. Similarity to the central tendency of each cluster is computed by using a multiplicative-similarity rule that is isomorphic to the one assumed in the context model and the FLMP. With the addition of some technical assumptions, Nosofsky (1991a) proved that in domains involving binary-valued dimensions, the rational model generalizes both the context model and the FLMP. Intuitively, when the value of the coupling parameter is zero, each exemplar forms its own cluster, and the rational model becomes the context model. By contrast, when the value of the coupling parameter is unity, the clusters that are formed correspond to prototypes for each of the experimentally defined categories, and the rational model is essentially the FLMP. For intermediate values of the coupling parameter, the rational model functions as a multiple-prototype model. A natural direction of future research will involve the use of MDS techniques in conjunction with the rational model, as I have described previously for the context model and the FLMP.

RECOGNITION   The MDS-based exemplar model (the GCM) has also been used to model old-new recognition memory performance (Nosofsky 1988a, 1991c; Nosofsky et al 1989). Following previous investigators (e.g. Gillund & Shiffrin 1984; Hintzman 1986), Nosofsky made the central assumption that recognition judgments are based on the overall summed similarity of an item to all exemplars stored in memory. This summed similarity gives a measure of overall "familiarity," with higher familiarity values leading to higher recognition probabilities. Specifically, the familiarity for item i (F_i) is given by

$$F_i = \Sigma \Sigma M_k \, \eta_{ik}, \qquad\qquad 8.$$

where the M_k and η_{ik} parameters are defined as before (see Equation 2), and the sum is over all exemplars stored in memory. Nosofsky (1991c) demonstrated that by deriving MDS solutions for sets of objects, and using these MDS solutions in conjunction with the model (Equations 3, 4, and 8), fine-grained differences in old-new recognition judgments could be predicted on the basis of fine-grained differences in similarities among items.

Note that categorization and recognition are presumed to involve different decision rules. According to the exemplar model, categorization decisions involve a relative-similarity rule (Equation 2), whereas recognition decisions involve an absolute-similarity rule (Equation 8). Thus, the exemplar model can predict markedly different patterns of performance across the two tasks, as are often observed. However, a unified account of categorization and recognition is provided by the model in the sense that both judgments are assumed to be based on the similarity of an item to the exemplars in a multidimensionally scaled psychological space.

Same-Different Judgments and Reaction Time

Takane & Sergent (1983) and Sergent & Takane (1987) proposed and tested a scaling-based process model for jointly characterizing accuracy and reaction time data in "same-different" judgment tasks. The model has three main components. The representation component specifies the function used to compute distances among objects in a psychological space. Takane & Sergent assume that error is introduced into these distance judgments. The error component of their model specifies the nature of the error perturbations operating on the distances. The distribution of error perturbations is assumed to be log-normal in form, with variance that increases as the true distance increases. [This assumption is the same as the one used by Ramsay (1977) in his maximum-likelihood method for scaling similarity judgments.] Finally, the response component of their model relates observed reaction times and same-different judgments to the error-perturbed distances. If the judged distance exceeds a threshold then a "different" response is made, else a "same" response is made. Based on the log-normal assumption for the distribution of errors, the log of the distribution of "different" reaction times for each stimulus pair is assumed to be normal in form, with a mean that decreases linearly with the difference between the (log) distance and (log) threshold. Thus, "different" RTs get faster as stimuli become more dissimilar. By contrast, the distribution of "same" RTs is assumed to have a mean that increases with the difference between (log) distance and (log) threshold, reflecting Podgorny & Garner's (1979) finding that "same" RT increases as stimuli become more dissimilar.

Using maximum-likelihood methods, Sergent & Takane (1987) fitted the model to same-different data obtained for a variety of stimulus sets. One of the central purposes of their study was to gain "information about similarity structure of stimulus sets as they actually emerge under conditions of speeded judgment process" (Sergent & Takane 1987:312). The argument is that similarity structure and the nature of dimensional interactions may be functions not only of stimulus characteristics, but also of perceptual processes. Similarity relations among objects may differ depending on whether the objects are processed under speeded or unspeeded conditions. Indeed, Sergent & Takane (1987) found that under their process-limited conditions, the best-fitting distance metric for a set of separable-dimension stimuli (circles varying in size, and in the orientation of a radial line) was Euclidean rather than city-block, in contrast to the usual finding obtained under process-unlimited conditions (for similar evidence, see Nosofsky 1985b).

Cognitive Processes and the Metric Axioms

In their well-known and elegant work, Tversky and his colleagues have called into question the psychological validity of the fundamental metric axioms underlying traditional MDS approaches (e.g. Gati & Tversky 1982; Tversky 1977; Tversky & Gati 1982). Using an extensive array of similarity data, including direct judgments and recognition confusions, Tversky's demonstrations suggest, for example, that similarities can be asymmetric, that stimuli can have differing degrees of self-similarity, and that similarity data often entail violations of the triangle inequality. As an alternative to spatial MDS models, Tversky (1977) proposed a set-theoretic model of similarity based on feature matching, which has been extremely influential and widely used, and which can account for the patterns of similarity data noted above.

I believe that some of the force of Tversky's demonstrations is diminished, however, when MDS representations are viewed as components of cognitive process models. As I have argued previously, observed behavior reflects only indirectly the underlying similarity representation. Process models that incorporate symmetric-similarity representations can predict asymmetric patterns of proximity data. A straightforward example involves identification-confusion data, which are often highly asymmetric (e.g. the probability of identifying object i as object j may be far greater than the probability of identifying object j as object i). Despite these asymmetries, the symmetric-similarity SCM usually accounts accurately for the structure of identification-confusion matrixes. It accounts for the asymmetries by virtue of the bias parameters in the model (Luce 1963; Shepard 1957), as well as the nature of the decision rule itself (e.g. see Getty et al 1979).

A very general reason why similarity data are often asymmetric may be that in addition to the role of pairwise similarities, properties of individual objects play a fundamental role in cognitive processes. For example, suppose that in a categorization experiment a particular exemplar is presented with high frequency. According to the GCM, the exemplar receives a strong memory representation, and the strength with which that individual item is stored in memory plays a fundamental role in subsequent classification. According to the model, a strong item is activated by a weak item far more than the weak item is activated by the strong, leading to asymmetries in classification behavior.

Holman (1979) presented a series of hierarchically organized models for describing asymmetric proximity data. These models incorporate a symmetric-similarity function together with individual item bias functions. "Bias" is defined very generally as a property associated with an individual object. According to one of the stronger models he presents, the proximity of i to j [p(i,j)] is given by

$$p(i,j) = F[s(i,j) + r(i) + c(j)], \qquad\qquad 9.$$

where $s(i,j)$ is the symmetric similarity between i and j, $r(i)$ is the "row" bias for item i (the "subject" of the object pair), $c(j)$ is the "column" bias for item j (the "referent" of the object pair), and F is an increasing function. In general, we have $p(i,j) > p(j,i)$ whenever $r(i) + c(j) > r(j) + c(i)$. Various models that have successfully accounted for asymmetric proximities are special cases of this "additive similarity and bias model," including the additive version of Tversky's (1977) feature-contrast model, Krumhansl's (1978) distance-density model, and the SCM for predicting identification confusions. Carroll's (1976) hybrid model, which combines spatial and hierarchical components, is a symmetric special case of Equation 9. Nosofsky (1991b) reviews a wide variety of phenomena involving asymmetric proximities that appear to be readily interpretable in terms of symmetric similarities together with individual item biases, as described by Holman's (1979) model. [It should be noted in this section, however, that in tests of Krumhansl's (1978) model, Corter (1987) conducted a series of experimental manipulations involving stimulus density, but failed to observe effects of this variable on similarity judgments.]

Self-proximities are also bound to be influenced by properties of the individual objects. For example, in a same-different judgment task, it should take more time to respond "same" for a complex object than for a simple one. In their modeling of same-different judgments, Takane & Sergent (1983) discuss a representation based on Equation 9 in which the bias terms are assumed to reflect stimulus complexity.

Another diagnostic used to question the psychological validity of MDS models is nearest-neighbor analysis of proximity data (Tversky & Hutchinson 1986). Low-dimensional spatial solutions are unable to account for patterns of proximity data in which a single item is the nearest neighbor (most proximal) to many other items in the set. Such data arise frequently in semantic domains that include a single focal element such as the superordinate of a category. However, as noted by Tversky & Hutchinson (1986), by augmenting the spatial representation with individual item-bias components to model the hierarchical structure of the set, one can readily account for such patterns of proximity data. One interpretation is that above and beyond "similarity," properties of individual objects play a fundamental role in cognitive processes.

According to the triangle inequality, for any three points a, b, and c, the psychological distance from a to c must be less than or equal to the sum of the distances from a to b and b to c. Although the triangle inequality cannot be tested directly on the basis of ordinal data, in a clever experimental design Tversky & Gati (1982) were able to infer systematic violations of the triangle inequality. These violations occurred in situations involving highly separable–dimension stimuli, in which objects a and b coincided on one dimension, and b and c coincided on a second dimension. Tversky & Gati provided corroborating evidence of these qualitative violations in a series of MDS analyses that showed that a value of $r < 1$ in the Minkowski power model (Equation 3) yielded a best fit to the similarity data. A process-interpretation for $r < 1$ is that, in making their similarity judgments, subjects systematically give greater attention weight to those dimensions along which stimuli are more similar (Tversky & Gati 1982:150). This process interpretation is consistent with Sjoberg & Thorslund's (1979) suggestion that, in making similarity judgments, subjects carry out an active search for the ways stimuli are similar.

Summary

In the first part of this chapter I discussed MDS-based models for predicting a variety of performances, including generalization, identification, categorization, recognition, same-different accuracy and reaction time, and similarity judgment. The MDS-based similarity representation is a fundamental component of these models. In the case of categorization, for example, it is important to specify whether the representation consists of a prototype, multiple prototypes, individual exemplars, and so forth. Furthermore, to apply the models, the representational objects must be located as points in the psychological scaling solution. But a complete account of performance in each task also requires specification of the cognitive processes that operate on the similarity representation. Some of the critical processes that were discussed were the nature of the decision rule, the role of selective attention in modifying the structure of the psychological space, and the influence of individual item properties such as memory strength. Testing the process models and deriving the scaling representations are mutually dependent, and one cannot proceed without the other.

Even after specifying the processing mechanisms, however, a potential shortcoming of all the models just reviewed is that they involve deterministic scaling representations, in which each object is represented as a single point in the psychological space. More general cognitive-process models make use of probabilistic scaling representations, which I review in the second part of this chapter.

PROBABILISTIC MULTIDIMENSIONAL SCALING APPROACHES

Probabilistic MDS models represent individual objects as probabilistic distributions of points in a multidimensional space, an extension of Thurstone's (1927a) classic framework for scaling unidimensional psychological magnitudes. As in deterministic models, presentation of an object is assumed to give rise to some internal representation. Because of noise in the system, however, the same internal representation is not yielded on every trial. Rather, across trials, presentation of an object gives rise to a probabilistic distribution of internal representations. Conceptually, such probabilistic representations are necessary in situations in which there is a good deal of noise in the perceptual processing system. Also, probabilistic models are needed for situations in which there is uncertainty in subjects' memory for the previously presented objects, as might occur because of diffusion of memory traces over time.

Each of the deterministic MDS models discussed in Part 1 of this chapter can be generalized by allowing the single-point representations of the objects to become probabilistic in nature. In addition, once one allows probabilistic representations, a variety of new process models suggest themselves. In the following, I focus primarily on these new models.

Probabilistic Scaling of Distance Judgments

Zinnes & MacKay (1983) developed maximum-likelihood procedures to obtain estimates of the parameters in the Hefner (1958) model. In this model, each object is represented as an n-dimensional random-vector, where the values on each dimension have been drawn at random from independent normal distributions of equal variance. Thus, each object is characterized on each dimension by a location parameter (the mean of the distribution) and a variability parameter. Although a given stimulus is assumed to have the same variance on each dimension, the variance associated with different stimuli can be unequal. When the model is applied at the level of individual subjects, one interpretation of the variance parameter is that it represents the subject's level of unfamiliarity with, or uncertainty about, the nature of the stimulus.

Because each stimulus has the same variance on each of its dimensions, the Hefner (1958) model is isotropic, in the sense that there are no dominant directions in the space. MacKay (1989) generalized the model to allow each stimulus to have different variances on each of its dimensions, yielding an anisotropic model. In addition, he allowed the coordinates of each stimulus to be correlated. Techniques for obtaining maximum-likelihood estimates of the parameters were proposed and tested.

It is assumed in these models that in judging the distance between objects i and j, a point from each of the object distributions is randomly and independently sampled, and the Euclidean distance between the points is computed. This momentary distance, d_{ij}, is a random variable, and is conceptually distinct from the distance between the means of the object distributions (D_{ij}), which Zinnes & MacKay (1983) term the "true" distance. The expected value of d_{ij}, $E(d_{ij})$, also differs from the true distance D_{ij}. Indeed, even if D_{ij} is zero, $E(d_{ij})$ will become indefinitely large as the variance of the object distributions approaches infinity.

Thus, in the Hefner model, the expected distance between objects is not related to the "true" distance in a simple, monotonic way. This property of nonmonotonicity can lead to highly pathological solutions if a deterministic MDS algorithm is used to analyze data generated from a probabilistic MDS process. As one example, Zinnes & MacKay (1983) constructed a configuration in which the objects were positioned along an inner and an outer hexagon, the variances of the points forming the inner hexagon being larger than those forming the outer hexagon. Simulated distance judgments were then used as input to a nonmetric (deterministic) scaling program and to the maximum-likelihood (ML) procedure developed by Zinnes & MacKay. The ML procedure accurately recovered the true configuration, but the deterministic model actually interchanged the positions of the inner and outer hexagons. The reason is that the expected value of the interpoint distances strongly reflected the large variances of the inner hexagon stimuli, so the deterministic program incorrectly "perceived" the inner hexagon to be large.

In general, by fitting alternative restricted versions of the general anisotropic model to sets of distance judgments, and systematically comparing the fits, one can statistically test hypotheses concerning the dimensionality of the space, the values of the coordinates, whether the space is isotropic or anisotropic, and whether individual stimuli have common variance-covariance structures.

General Recognition Theory

The general recognition theory (GRT) of Ashby, Townsend, and their associates (e.g. Ashby & Perrin 1988; Ashby & Townsend 1986; Kadlec & Townsend 1992) is a multidimensional generalization of signal detection theory (Green & Swets 1966) and of Thurstone's (1927b) law of categorical judgment. Besides assuming probabilistic internal representations, the critical assumption in this theory is that the observer establishes *decision boundaries* to partition the psychological space into response regions. Any internal representation or "perceptual effect" falling in Region A would lead to an A response. Most applications of the GRT have assumed that the perceptual effects are distributed as multivariate normal random variables, an assumption that I make in the following discussion.

FUNDAMENTAL CONSTRUCTS   Ashby & Townsend (1986) discuss a variety of fundamental constructs and their interrelations within the framework of the GRT. For simplicity, imagine a complete identification experiment in which there are two physically manipulated dimensions, A and B, with r levels on dimension A and q levels on dimension B that are factorially combined. Assume further that the psychological dimensions along which the objects are represented correspond to the physically manipulated dimensions. Thus, over trials, each stimulus gives rise to a bivariate normal distribution. On each trial the subject is required to identify the level on each dimension of the presented stimulus (or provide an informationally equivalent response).

Perceptual independence for a pair of dimensions in a particular stimulus holds if the perceptual effects of the two dimensions are statistically independent, which, for the bivariate normal distribution, occurs if there is zero correlation between the perceptual effects on each dimension. Note that perceptual independence is a property of an individual stimulus.

Perceptual separability holds if, across stimuli, the perceptual effects of a given level of one dimension do not depend on the level of the other dimension. Consider, for example, the set of stimuli A_iB_j constructed from dimension A at level i and dimension B at level j. Dimension A would be perceptually separable from dimension B if, for each i, the perceptual effects of A_i do not depend on the level of B. In the case of the normal distribution, this property holds if, for each i, the stimuli A_iB_1, A_iB_2, ..., A_iB_q have the same mean and variance on dimension A. Note that dimension A can be perceptually separable from dimension B without the converse relation holding. Also, whereas perceptual independence is a property pertaining to an individual stimulus, perceptual separability is a property pertaining to a set of stimuli.

Decisional separability on dimension A holds if a subject's decision about the level of dimension A does not depend on the value of the perceptual effect associated with dimension B. This property holds if the subject's decision boundaries are perpendicular to the Dimension A coordinate axis (or, equivalently, parallel to the Dimension B axis). As is the case for perceptual separability, note that decisional separability can hold on Dimension A without holding on Dimension B, and vice versa.

Perceptual independence, perceptual separability, and decisional separability are all logically independent from one another. However, Ashby & Townsend (1986) and Kadlec & Townsend (1992) prove a number of fundamental theorems that allow the constructs to be interrelated by means of observable response probabilities in an identification experiment. For example, in an identification experiment with two levels on each of the two dimensions, *sampling independence* in stimulus A_iB_j holds if the probability of A2 and B2 both being reported given presentation of stimulus A_iB_j is equal to the product of the individual probabilities of A_2 being reported and B_2 being reported (given stimulus A_iB_j). Ashby & Townsend (1986) prove that if decisional separability holds on both dimensions, then sampling independence is equivalent to perceptual independence. This simple example is intended to give only a flavor of the rich web of interrelated concepts that the GRT provides for investigating the structure of subjects' internal representations of multidimensional stimuli. Other methods for investigating the properties of perceptual independence, perceptual separability, and decisional separability are discussed and illustrated by Ashby (1988) and Wickens & Olzak (1989).

MODELS OF CLASSIFICATION   The GRT provides a powerful and flexible language for expressing numerous different models of stimulus classification. These models differ in terms of the types of decision boundaries that the subject uses for partitioning the multidimensional space into response regions.

Ashby & Gott (1988) distinguish between independent-decisions boundaries and several types of information-integration boundaries (cf Shaw 1982). Imagine, for example, that there are two categories, A and B, composed of objects varying on two dimensions. Both categories of objects are distributed as bivariate normal random variables, with members of Category A tending to have low values on both of dimensions 1 and 2, and members of Category B having high values on both dimensions. According to an independent-decisions model, the subject would establish a separate criterion on each dimension for partitioning low versus high values. Given presentation of a stimulus, separate decisions would be made about its value on each dimension, and these decisions would then be combined in making a response. "Low-low" decisions would result in a Category A response and high-high decisions would result in a Category B response. Low-high and high-low decisions provide ambiguous information, so the subject would be forced to guess. In terms of the GRT, this decision strategy corresponds to establishing two orthogonal boundaries that are parallel to the coordinate axes (i.e. decisional separability holds on both dimensions). Percepts falling in the lower-left quadrant would be classified in Category A, whereas percepts falling in the upper-right quadrant would be classified in Category B. Percepts falling in the remaining two quadrants provide ambiguous information and the subject must guess.

By contrast, according to information-integration models, subjects are able to combine information from both dimensions into an integrated percept, and a single decision is then made with regard to that integrated information. Ashby & Gott (1988) discuss a variety of information-integration models in terms of the types of decision boundaries they entail. A *minimum distance boundary* is a linear boundary that bisects and is perpendicular to the segment that connects the central tendencies (prototypes) of Categories A and B. Minimum distance bounds arise when classification decisions are based on distance to the prototype: If the percept is closer to the prototype of Category A, then respond A; else respond B. *General linear boundaries* generalize minimum distance bounds by allowing the slope and y-intercept of the linear boundary to be free parameters. These boundaries can be interpreted in terms of a (biased) prototype model in which differential weight is given to each dimension in calculating distance. *Optimal boundaries* (that maximize probability of correct classification) are those in which the subject computes the overall likelihood of the percept coming from Category distribution A or B, and responds with the category with greater likelihood. There are close formal relations between these optimal likelihood–based boundaries and the decision boundaries that are predicted by certain types of exemplar storage models (Estes 1986; Nosofsky 1990).

Ashby & Gott (1988) and Ashby & Maddox (1990, 1992) have conducted a number of experimental studies to investigate the types of decision boundaries that subjects adopt. Using a procedure known as the general recognition randomization technique, which involves the systematic addition of multivariate external noise to the prototypes of each category, they have obtained convincing evidence that in their paradigm: 1. subjects adopt information-integration strategies rather than independent-decisions strategies (Ashby & Gott 1988), even if the underlying perceptual dimensions are highly separable in nature (Ashby & Maddox 1990); 2. if given sufficient motivation and training, subjects can adopt decision boundaries that are highly nonlinear, and sometimes close to optimal (Ashby & Maddox 1992); and 3. rather than using probabilistic decision rules, subjects use decision rules that are deterministic in nature (or close to it). The latter finding means that each percept in the psychological space has an associated category response probability that is essentially 0 or 1, in contrast to the predictions of models that postulate competing response tendencies such as Nosofsky's (1986) GCM. Finally, in recent work, Ashby & Lee (1991) demonstrated successful applications in which versions of the GRT performed as well or better than the SCM and GCM at predicting identification and categorization data. These applications were in standard designs that did not involve the introduction of external noise.

SIMILARITY   Ashby & Perrin (1988) proposed to model similarity judgments in terms of the GRT by assuming that the judged similarity of A to B is related to the proportion of the A distribution that overlaps the B response region. A virtue of the model is that it contains the general Euclidean scaling model (Young 1984b) as a special case. For example, in the GRT, differential weighting of dimensions corresponds to differential variances of the distributions of perceptual effects, and oblique dimensions correspond to dependencies (correlations) in the distributions of perceptual effects. Unlike the general Euclidean scaling model, however, the GRT similarity model is not constrained by the metric axioms. Ashby & Perrin (1988) demonstrated support for the model by conducting an experiment in which distance between the prototypes of distributions A and B was held constant, but overlap between the A and B distributions was varied across conditions. Overall similarity judgments were observed to increase as the proportion of overlap increased.

In my view, this application of the GRT seems reasonable as a model of the similarity between categories, or as a model of similarity between objects with substantial variability. But in numerous experimental situations, one judges the similarity between pairs of individual objects with essentially no psychological variability. The applicability of the GRT similarity model in these situations seems more limited. Another interesting challenge for the model would be to explain the exponential gradient of similarity discussed by Shepard (1987), as well as why the metric of psychological space depends systematically on the types of dimensions that compose the stimuli.

COMPARING THE GCM AND THE GRT   Because the GCM and the GRT are two MDS-based models that have been applied rigorously in recent years to relate similarity, identification, and categorization data, it is of some interest to compare and contrast them. First, in the GCM, each object is represented as a single point in psychological space, whereas the GRT represents each object as a probabilistic distribution of points. In situations involving substantial perceptual or memorial variability, the single-point assumption of the GCM clearly needs to be modified. Second, the GCM assumes a probabilistic decision rule, whereas the GRT incorporates a deterministic decision rule. Ashby & Gott (1988) provided convincing evidence of the use of deterministic decision rules in experiments involving the recognition randomization technique, but the generalizability of these results to more standard designs is open to question. It may well be that the use of probabilistic versus deterministic decision rules depends on the experimental situation.

The most fundamental difference between the GCM and the GRT concerns the presumed nature of the category representation. In the GCM it is assumed that people classify items on the basis of their summed similarity to the exemplars of alternative categories. By contrast, in the GRT, it is assumed that people form "decision boundaries" to partition the multidimensional space into response regions. The GRT should be viewed as providing a general and powerful language for expressing alternative models of classification. To use the GRT to predict classification probabilities, one needs to specify the types of decision boundaries that the subject uses to partition the multidimensional space. In recent work, Ashby & Maddox (1992) propose that subjects adopt quadratic bounds, which is the form that likelihood-ratio bounds take when the category distributions are normal in form. They have also discussed (mainly as foils) independent-decisions bounds, minimum distance bounds, general linear bounds, and bilinear bounds. My view is that each different type of boundary that is assumed constitutes an alternative model of classification. An infinite variety of such models is available within the general framework provided by the GRT. Indeed, one could formulate an exemplar-similarity model in its framework by assuming an exemplar-similarity boundary: The decision rule is to classify a percept into Category A if its summed similarity to the Category A exemplars exceeds its summed similarity to the Category B exemplars, else classify it in Category B. Thus, with modifications in some of the technical differences noted above, the exemplar-based GCM can be expressed within the language of the GRT.

Multivariate Discrimination Methods

Ennis, Mullen, and their colleagues (e.g. Ennis 1988, 1992; Ennis & Mullen 1986; Ennis et al 1988; Mullen & Ennis 1987 have developed a number of multivariate models for discrimination and grouping methods, such as the duo-trio method and the triangular method. They have also extended these models to account for same-different judgments and identification performance. Among other things, Ennis (1988; Ennis et al 1988) showed how these models could be used to reconcile Nosofsky's (1985a,b) observations of a Gaussian similarity gradient with Shepard's (1987) proposed universal law of generalization.

I illustrate the nature of the discrimination modelling by reviewing Ennis & Mullen's (1986) multivariate Euclidean model for the triangular method. In the triangular method, the subject is instructed to select out of three stimuli (two sampled from one stimulus distribution and one from another) the stimulus that is perceptually different from the other two. In the Ennis &

Mullen (1986) model, each stimulus distribution is assumed to be multivariate normal in form. The stimuli sampled from each distribution are assumed to be mutually independently distributed. The decision rule is to group together the two stimuli that are the shortest Euclidean distance apart. A correct response occurs if these shortest-distance stimuli were the ones that were sampled from the same distribution.

Ennis & Mullen (1986) developed a mathematical formulation of the triangular-method model for the bivariate case, and used Monte Carlo simulations to evaluate the more general multivariate model. Of most general conceptual importance regarding their findings was that discrimination performance is not a function solely of the distance between the means of the stimulus distributions, but depends critically on such characteristics of the distributions as their dimensionality, correlation structure, relative orientation, and variances.

In an extension of these methods to account for same-different judgments, similarity, and identification, Ennis (1988, 1992; Ennis et al 1988) combined assumptions about the stochastic, multivariate representation of the stimulus objects with the kinds of distance-based similarity judgments assumed in the models of Shepard (1957, 1987) and Nosofsky (1986). Assume that a pair of stimuli has been presented and the subject must judge whether they are the "same" or "different." As described previously, it is assumed that each stimulus gives rise to a momentary psychological representation (i.e. a point) in the perceptual space. The distance (d) between these points is computed by using the Minkowski power model, and the similarity between the objects is then given by $g(d) = \exp(-d^\alpha)$, where $\alpha > 0$ (cf Nosofsky 1986; Shepard 1957, 1987). In one version of the same-different model, Ennis et al (1988) take g(d) to be the (unbiased) probability that the subject judges the pair of stimuli to be the "same" on the given trial.

To predict the probability that a pair of stimuli is judged "same" during the course of the experiment, one would compute the expected value of g(d), E[g(d)]. (Note that because the stimulus representations are stochastic, the distance between stimuli is a random variable in the model.) Ennis et al (1988) provide expressions for E[g(d)] in the case in which the stimuli are distributed as multivariate normal random variables. They also illustrate that the parameters of the stimulus distributions can be accurately recovered by fitting the model to generated matrixes of same-different judgments. Thus, the model provides a viable approach to obtaining probabilistic MDS solutions for sets of multidimensional stimuli.

In further analyses, Ennis et al (1988) investigated the effect of the multivariate stochastic portion of the model on the presumed form of the similarity gradient. In particular, suppose that one modeled a set of similarity data by using a deterministic MDS model, but that the similarity data had actually been generated by the probabilistic MDS process discussed above. Ennis et al (1988) provided evidence that the gradient relating similarity to distance between points in the space could look Gaussian in form, even if the true similarity judgment function was exponential. (Intuitively, the Gaussian-distributed dispersions associated with each stimulus can swamp the exponential similarity function that operates within trials.) Thus, Nosofsky's (1985b) observation of a Gaussian similarity gradient (which was obtained within a deterministic MDS framework) can be reconciled with Shepard's (1987) proposed exponential law. Conceptually, Shepard's (1987) law concerns a cognitive similarity-judgment process that operates at the level of individual trials, but when the stimuli are highly confusable, one needs to also model the variability that is associated with the stimulus representations across trials.

FUTURE DIRECTIONS

The recent influx of probabilistic scaling approaches to the study of similarity and classification is a welcome development. In addition to the increased power and generality that is afforded by probabilistic scaling models, the fundamental assumption that objects give rise to probabilistic representations in perception and memory seems conceptually well motivated. With this increased power and flexibility, however, it becomes even more important to search for invariances across tasks when fitting these models to similarity data. Thus, the probabilistic scaling representation that is derived by fitting a model to a matrix of same-different data should be useful for predicting how subjects will identify, classify, and recognize the same set of objects.

What lies in the near future regarding the intersection between similarity scaling and cognitive process models? One direction likely to be pursued will involve the use of similarity scaling to constrain connectionist/distributed models of perception and cognition. The recent explosion of studies that demonstrate the potential power of connectionist models is slowly giving way to efforts to test these models rigorously on their psychological validity and predictive, quantitative accuracy. An impediment to developing rigorous tests is that there is often no associated theory of stimulus representation in these models. A particular form of input representation might be assumed a priori, or the investigators might search for an input representation that "works" (in the sense that when used with the model, it delivers the desired behavior).

The process-model approach to scaling that I advocate in this chapter could easily be incorporated in the connectionist-modeling domain. For example, suppose that one wanted to test the quantitative predictions of a given connectionist model of category learning. As a first step, one could fit the model to a set of identification learning data. This step would involve searching for the input representation of the stimuli that maximized the likelihood of the data with respect to the model—the portion of the modeling in which a scaling representation is derived. Then, using the same basic connectionist architecture and scaling representation, one could use the model to predict category learning in situations involving the same set of objects. With an invariant scaling representation, we gain greater confidence that a successful connectionist model captures psychological processes in a meaningful way.

ACKNOWLEDGMENTS

Preparation of this chapter was supported by NSF Grant BNS 87-19938 to Indiana University. My thanks to Greg Ashby, Roger Shepard, and Jim Townsend for their comments on an earlier version.

Literature Cited

Anderson, J. R. 1976. *Language, Memory, and Thought.* Hillsdale, NJ: Erlbaum

Anderson, J. R. 1990. *The Adaptive Character of Thought.* Hillsdale, NJ: Erlbaum

Ashby, F. G. 1988. Estimating the parameters of multidimensional signal detection theory from simultaneous ratings on separate stimulus components. *Percept. Psychophys.* 44:195–204

Ashby, F. G., ed. 1992. *Multidimensional Models of Perception and Cognition.* Hillsdale, NJ: Erlbaum

Ashby, F. G., Gott, R. E. 1988. Decision rules in the perception and categorization of multidimensional stimuli. *J. Exp. Psychol.: Learn. Mem. Cognit.* 14:33–53

Ashby, F. G., Lee, W. W. 1991. Predicting similarity and categorization from identification. *J. Exp. Psychol.: General.* 120:150–72

Ashby, F. G., Maddox, W. T. 1990. Integrating information from separable psychological dimensions. *J. Exp. Psychol.: Hum. Percept. Perform.* 16:598–612

Ashby, F. G., Maddox, W. T. 1992. Complex decision rules in categorization: contrasting novice and experienced performance. *J. Exp. Psychol.: Hum. Percept. Perform.* In press

Ashby, F. G., Perrin, N. A. 1988. Toward a unified theory of similarity and recognition. *Psychol. Rev.* 95:124–50

Ashby, F. G.,Townsend, J. T. 1986. Varieties of perceptual independence. *Psychol. Rev.* 93:154–79

Blough, D. S. 1988. Quantitative relations between visual search speed and target-distractor similarity. *Percept. Psychophys.* 43:57–71

Carroll, J. D. 1976. Spatial, non-spatial, and hybrid models for scaling. *Psychometrika* 41:439–63

Carroll, J. D., Arabie, P. 1980. Multidimensional scaling. *Annu. Rev. Psychol.* 31:607–49

Carroll, J. D., Wish, M. 1974. Models and methods for three-way multidimensional scaling. In *Contemporary Developments in Mathematical Psychology,* ed. D. H. Krantz, R. C. Atkinson, R. D. Luce, P. Suppes, pp. 57–105. San Francisco: W. H. Freeman

Cliff, N. 1973. Scaling. *Annu. Rev. Psychol.* 21:473–506

Corter, J. E. 1987. Similarity, confusability, and the density hypothesis. *J. Exp. Psychol.: General* 116:238–49.

Ennis, D. M. 1988. Confusable and discriminable stimuli: comment on Nosofsky 1986 and Shepard 1986. *J. Exp. Psychol.: General* 117:408–11

Ennis, D. M. 1992. Modelling similarity and identification when there are momentary fluctuations in psychological magnitudes. See Ashby 1992. In press

Ennis, D. M., Mullen, K. 1986. A multivariate model for discrimination methods. *J. Math. Psychol.* 30:206–19

Ennis, D. M., Palen, J., Mullen, K. 1988. A multidimensional stochastic theory of similarity. *J. Math. Psychol.* 32:449–65

Estes, W. K. 1986. Array models for category learning. *Cognit. Psychol.* 18:500–49

Garner, W. R. 1974. *The Processing of Information and Structure.* New York: Wiley

Gati, I., Tversky, A. 1982. Representations of qualitative and quantitative dimensions. *J.*

Exp. Psychol.: Hum. Percept. Perform. 8:325–40

Gescheider, G. A. 1988. Psychophysical scaling. *Annu. Rev. Psychol.* 39:169–200

Getty, D. J., Swets, J. B., Swets, J. A., Green, D. M. 1979. On the prediction of confusion matrices from similarity judgments. *Percept. Psychophys.* 26:1–19

Gillund, G., Shiffrin, R. M. 1984. A retrieval model for both recognition and recall. *Psychol. Rev.* 91:1–67

Gluck, M. A. 1991. Stimulus generalization and representation in adaptive network models of category learning. *Psychol. Sci.* 2:50–55

Gluck, M. A., Bower, G. H. 1988. Evaluating an adaptive network model of human learning. *J. Mem. Lang.* 27:166–95

Green, D. M., Swets, J. A. 1966. *Signal Detection Theory and Psychophysics.* New York: Wiley

Hefner, R. A. 1958. *Extensions of the law of comparative judgment to discriminable and multidimensional stimuli.* PhD thesis. Univ. Michigan

Heiser, W. J. 1988. Selecting a stimulus set with prescribed structure from empirical confusion frequencies. *Brit. J. Math. Stat. Psychol.* 41:37–51

Henley, N. M. 1969. A psychological study of the semantics of animal terms. *J. Verb. Learn. Verb. Behav.* 8:176–84

Hintzman, D. L. 1986. "Schema abstraction" in a multiple-trace memory model. *Psychol. Rev.* 93:411–28

Holman, E. W. 1979. Monotonic models for asymmetric proximities. *J. Math. Psychol.* 20:1–15

Hurwitz, J. B. 1990. *A hidden-pattern unit network model of category learning.* PhD thesis. Harvard Univ.

Hutchinson, J. W., Lockhead, G. R. 1977. Similarity as distance: a structural principle for semantic memory. *J. Exp. Psychol.: Hum. Learn. Mem.* 3:660–78

Kadlec, H., Townsend, J. T. 1992. Implications of marginal and conditional detection parameters for the separabilities and independence of perceptual dimensions. *J. Math. Psychol.* In press

Krumhansl, C. L. 1978. Concerning the applicability of geometric models to similarity data: the interrelationship between similarity and spatial density. *Psychol. Rev.* 85:445–63

Kruschke, J. K. 1990. *A connectionist model of category learning.* PhD thesis. Univ. Calif. Berkeley

Luce, R. D. 1963. Detection and recognition. In *Handbook of Mathematical Psychology,* ed. R. D. Luce, R. R. Bush, E. Galanter, 1:103–90. New York: Wiley

MacKay, D. B. 1989. Probabilistic multi-dimensional scaling: an anisotropic model for distance judgments. *J. Math. Psychol.* 33:187–205

Marley, A. A. J. 1992. Developing and characterizing multidimensional Thurstone and Luce models for identification and preference. See Ashby 1992, In press

Massaro, D. W. 1987. *Speech Perception by Ear and Eye: A Paradigm for Psychological Inquiry.* Hillsdale, NJ: Erlbaum

Massaro, D. W., Friedman, D. 1990. Models of integration given multiple sources of information. *Psychol. Rev.* 97:225–52

Medin, D. L., Schaffer, M. M. 1978. Context theory of classification learning. *Psychol. Rev.* 85:207–38

Monahan, J. S., Lockhead, G. R. 1977. Identification of integral stimuli. *J. Exp. Psychol.: General* 106:94–110

Mullen, K., Ennis, D. M. 1987. Mathematical formulation of multivariate Euclidean models for discrimination methods. *Psychometrika* 52:235–49

Nosofsky, R. M. 1984. Choice, similarity, and the context theory of classification. *J. Exp. Psychol.: Learn. Mem. Cognit.* 10:104–14

Nosofsky, R. M. 1985a. Luce's choice model and Thurstone's categorical judgment model compared: Kornbrot's data revisited. *Percept. Psychophys.* 37:89–91

Nosofsky, R. M. 1985b. Overall similarity and the identification of separable-dimension stimuli: a choice model analysis. *Percept. Psychophys.* 38:415–32

Nosofsky, R. M. 1986. Attention, similarity, and the identification-categorization relationship. *J. Exp. Psychol.: General* 115:39–57

Nosofsky, R. M. 1987. Attention and learning processes in the identification and categorization of integral stimuli. *J. Exp. Psychol.: Learn. Mem. Cognit.* 13:87–109

Nosofsky, R. M. 1988a. Exemplar-based accounts of relations between classification, recognition, and typicality. *J. Exp. Psychol.: Learn. Mem. Cognit.* 14:700–8

Nosofsky, R. M. 1988b. On exemplar-based exemplar representations: reply to Ennis (1988). *J. Exp. Psychol.: General* 117:412–14

Nosofsky, R. M. 1988c. Similarity, frequency, and category representations. *J. Exp. Psychol.: Learn. Mem. Cognit.* 14:54–65

Nosofsky, R. M. 1989. Further tests of an exemplar-similarity approach to relating identification and categorization. *Percept. Psychophys.* 45:279–90

Nosofsky, R. M. 1990. Relations between exemplar-similarity and likelihood models of classification. *J. Math. Psychol.* 34:393–418

Nosofsky, R. M. 1991a. Relation between the

rational model and the context model of classification. *Cognit. Sci. Rep.* 39, Indiana Univ.

Nosofsky, R. M. 1991b. Stimulus bias, asymmetric similarity, and classification. *Cognit. Psychol.* 23:94–140

Nosofsky, R. M. 1991c. Tests of an exemplar model for relating perceptual classification and recognition memory. *J. Exp. Psychol.: Hum. Percept. Perform.* 17:3–27

Nosofsky, R. M. 1992. Exemplars, prototypes, and similarity rules. In *Essays in Honor of William K. Estes,* Vol. 1, ed. A. Healy, S. Kosslyn, R. Shiffrin. Hillsdale, NJ: Erlbaum. In press

Nosofsky, R. M., Clark, S. E., Shin, H. J. 1989. Rules and exemplars in categorization, identification, and recognition. *J. Exp. Psychol.: Learn. Mem. Cognit.* 15:282–304

Oden, G. C., Massaro, D. W. 1978. Integration of featural information in speech perception. *Psychol. Rev.* 85:172–91

Podgorny, P., Garner, W. R. 1979. Reaction time as a measure of inter- and intraobject visual similarity: letters of the alphabet. *Percept. Psychophys.* 26:37–52

Ramsay, J. O. 1977. Maximum-likelihood estimation in multidimensional scaling. *Psychometrika* 42:241–66

Reed, S. K. 1972. Pattern recognition and categorization. *Cognit. Psychol.* 3:382–407

Sergent, J., Takane, Y. 1987. Structures in two-choice reaction- time data. *J. Exp. Psych.: Hum. Percept. Perform.* 13:300–15

Shaw, M. L. 1982. Attending to multiple sources of information: I. The integration of information in decision making. *Cognit. Psychol.* 14:353–409

Shepard, R. N. 1957. Stimulus and response generalization: a stochastic model relating generalization to distance in psychological space. *Psychometrika* 22:325–45

Shepard, R. N. 1958a. Stimulus and response generalization: deduction of the generalization gradient from a trace model. *Psychol. Rev.* 65:242–56

Shepard, R. N. 1958b. Stimulus and response generalization: tests of a model relating generalization to distance in psychological space. *J. Exp. Psychol.* 55:509–23

Shepard, R. N. 1964. Attention and the metric structure of the stimulus space. *J. Math. Psychol.* 1:54–87

Shepard, R. N. 1986. Discrimination and generalization in identification and classification: comment on Nosofsky. *J. Exp. Psychol.: General* 115:58–61

Shepard, R. N. 1987. Toward a universal law of generalization for psychological science. *Science* 237:1317–23

Shepard, R. N. 1988. Time and distance in

generalization and discrimination: reply to Ennis (1988). *J. Exp. Psychol.: General* 117:415–16

Shepard, R. N. 1990. Neural nets for generalization and classification: comment on Staddon and Reid (1990). *Psychol. Rev.* 97:579–80

Shepard, R. N. 1991. Integrality versus separability of stimulus dimensions: evolution of the distinction and a proposed theoretical basis. In *Perception of Structure,* ed. J. Pomerantz, G. Lockhead. Washington, DC: APA. In press

Shepard, R. N., Chang, J. J. 1963. Stimulus generalization in the learning of classifications. *J. Exp. Psychol.* 65:94–102

Shepard, R. N., Hovland, C. I., Jenkins, H. M. 1961. Learning and memorization of classifications. *Psychol. Monogr.* 75:1–41

Shepard, R. N., Kannappan, S. 1991. Connectionist implementation of a theory of generalization. In *Advances in Neural Information Processing Systems,* ed. R. Lippmann, J. Moody, D. Touretzky, Vol. 3. San Mateo, CA: Morgan Kaufman. In press

Shepard, R. N., Kilpatric, D. W., Cunningham, J. P. 1975. The internal representation of numbers. *Cognit. Psychol.* 7:82- 138

Shin, H. J. 1990. *Similarity-scaling studies of "dot patterns" classification and recognition.* PhD thesis. Indiana Univ.

Sjoberg, L., Thorslund, C. 1979. A classificatory theory of similarity. *Psychol. Res.* 40:223–47

Smith, J. E. K. 1980. Models of identification. In *Attention and performance,* ed. R. Nickerson, 8:129–58. Hillsdale, NJ: Erlbaum

Smith, J. E. K. 1982. Recognition models evaluated: a commentary on Keren and Baggen. *Percept. Psychophys.* 31:183–89

Staddon, J. E. R., Reid, A. K. 1990. On the dynamics of generalization. *Psychol. Rev.* 97:576–78

Takane, Y., Sergent, J. 1983. Multidimensional models for reaction times and same-different judgments. *Psychometrika* 48:393–423

Takane, Y., Shibayama, T. 1985. Comparison of models for stimulus recognition data. In *Proceedings of the Multidimensional Data Analysis Workshop.* Leiden: DSWO Press

Thurstone, L. L. 1927a. A law of comparative judgment. *Psychol. Rev.* 34:273–86

Thurstone, L. L. 1927b. Psychophysical analysis. *Am. J. Psychol.* 38:368–89

Townsend, J. T. 1971. Theoretical analysis of an alphabetic confusion matrix. *Percept. Psychophys.* 9:40–50

Townsend, J. T., Landon, D. E. 1982. An experimental and theoretical investigation of the constant-ratio rule and other models of visual letter confusion. *J. Math. Psychol.* 25:119–62

Townsend, J. T., Landon, D. E. 1983. Mathematical models of recognition and confusion in psychology. *Math. Soc. Sci.* 4:25–71

Tversky, A. 1977. Features of similarity. *Psychol. Rev.* 84:327–52

Tversky, A., Gati, I. 1982. Similarity, separability, and the triangle inequality. *Psychol. Rev.* 89:123–54

Tversky, A., Hutchinson, J. W. 1986. Nearest neighbor analysis of psychological spaces. *Psychol. Rev.* 93:3–22

Wickens, T. D., Olzak, L. A. 1989. The statistical analysis of concurrent detection ratings. *Percept. Psychophys.* 45:514–28

Young, F. W. 1984a. Scaling. *Annu. Rev. Psychol.* 35:55–81

Young, F. W. 1984b. The general Euclidean model. In *Three-Mode Models for Data Analysis,* ed. H. Law, C. Snyder, R. McDonald, J. Hattie. New York: Praeger

Zinnes, J. L., MacKay, D. B. 1983. Probabilistic multidimensional scaling: complete and incomplete data. *Psychometrika.* 48:27–48

Annu. Rev. Psychol. 1992. 43:55–85

HUMAN EMOTIONS: FUNCTION AND DYSFUNCTION

Keith Oatley

Center for Applied Cognitive Science, Ontario Institute for Studies in Education, Toronto M5S 1V6, Canada

Jennifer M Jenkins

Institute of Child Study, University of Toronto, Toronto M5R 2X2, Canada

KEY WORDS: emotional development, continuity, stress, psychopathology, consciousness

CONTENTS

0066-4308/92/0201-0055$02.00

INTRODUCTION

In the second half of the 19th century research on emotions began in earnest, particularly with the work of Darwin (1872) and James (1890). Until recently the currents of this research were fitful and uneven. Now the mainstream of publications has swelled far beyond any possibility of a six-years' comprehensive review: Even a review of the limited area of facial expression of emotion (Fridlund et al 1987) contained more than 450 references. Nevertheless the swelling volume of material allows us to discern with more confidence some principal themes.

Scope of This Article

Our main focus is on publications from 1985, when Leventhal & Tomarken (1986) finished their scan of the literature for the most recent coverage of this subject in the *Annual Review of Psychology,* through 1990.

We concentrate on two main issues. (*a*) One of those issues concerns the functions of emotions—their roles in action and interaction. Thinking about functions also gives a perspective on the dysfunctional. (*b*) The other issue involves interrelating research on emotions from various disciplines. Of all topics, it seems to us, understanding of emotions needs a multidisciplinary approach. Therefore we have ranged more widely than usual for the psychology of emotions. This has exacted a cost in terms of depth and detail, but we have considered principal themes within different subdisciplines of psychology, as well as between psychology and some neighboring disciplines with substantial literatures on emotions, including psychiatry (Lane & Schwartz 1987), philosophy (De Sousa 1987), anthropology (Levy & Wellenkamp 1989), history (Stearns 1989), sociology (Kemper 1990), psychophysiology (Wagner & Manstead 1989), psychobiology (Panksepp 1989), and even artificial intelligence (Pfeiffer 1988).

The Legacy of Darwin and James

During the period of this review the influences of Darwin (1872) and James (1890) were still very much present. Darwin's evolutionary theory is the basis for many theories of emotions today (e.g. Plutchik 1991). Darwin's 1872 book laid foundations for work on facial expression (discussed below). Darwin also introduced the idea of continuities of emotional reactions both among species and during individual development (e.g. Lamb et al 1985). Not all of Darwin's legacy is so positive: His study of 1872 gives the sense that expressions of emotions in adult humans are not quite proper. They derive from beasts and infants. His book resonated strongly with a Western distrust of emotions, placing them in a corner of the museum along with the fossils of dinosaurs, exotic but obsolete. As Hinde (1985) has argued, moreover, Darwin's term "emotional expression" may be misleading. It implies something within—an emotion—which is expressed. Thus expressions become indexes of inner states. This idea links to James's (1890) proposal that emotions are "feelings" of inner states. An unintentional side effect of this idea of emotions as "inner" entities [a questionable metaphor (Solomon 1984)] is the notion that they may need to be contained lest they spill out. Such a metaphor may reinforce the notion prevalent today that unwanted emotions can be ventilated and hence disposed of under controlled conditions (Stearns 1989). For alternatives to such ideas see the next section.

Within the Jamesian tradition stress is laid on the individual's experience of emotions as they occur, a perspective of renewed importance (Ellis 1991), and also on psycho-physiological relations (Cacioppo & Tassinary 1990). In this tradition, too, regulation of emotions (Izard 1990) and management of one's own and others' emotions (Hochschild 1989; Saarni 1991) could later become issues for research. James's idea also lends itself to analyses of emotions as valenced (i.e. pleasant or unpleasant, positive or negative) (Ortony et al 1988; Lang et al 1990), as implying approach or avoidance (Hammond 1990), and as reinforcements (Rolls 1990). This effect is seen in an experiment of Lewis et al (1990) on infants aged 2–8 months: Those whose arm movements were reinforced by appearance of a color slide and a snatch of song made more joyful facial expressions during learning phases, and more angry expressions during an extinction phase, than control subjects for whom audiovisual stimuli were not contingent on their actions.

James's theory continues to inspire research. Thus, Zajonc et al (1989) proposed that facial actions in emotional expressions regulate blood supply to the brain, and hence warm or cool it. These changes detected by the brain then influence subjective feeling. As a warning against any assumption that all emotions are due to changes in blood supply caused by making faces, Zajonc et al say: "We would not expect someone who has just learned that he has cancer to turn his grief to joy by the mere contraction of the zygomatic muscle" (p. 412). Matsuomoto (1987) found in a meta-analysis that the effects of facial muscle actions on mood are small, and perhaps overestimated. The difficulty here, as elsewhere in psychology, is in distinguishing effects that are important from those that are merely significant. Some facial inductions of emotion, however, can be substantial. Schiff & Lamon (1989) induced emotions, which were sometimes strong, by having subjects contract muscles on one side of their faces. Now that induction of moods by imagination, memory, self talk, music etc has become common in ex-

-quality

perimentation, Schiff & Lamon's procedure may become important because this induction seems to occur without conscious mediation. The effects of unilateral contractions, moreover, are among a growing number of indications that processing of emotions takes place differently in the two cerebral hemispheres (Davidson 1991).

While James's theory emphasizes phenomenology, in some ways it may trivialize emotions (Solomon 1984; Gordon 1987). James thought folk theories wrong in their assumption that an external event causes an emotion and the emotion causes an action. In the correct sequence, he claimed, an emotion is the feeling of the reaction to the event. A corollary is that emotions have no effect on action as such but comprise the color and warmth of experience.

Neo-Jamesians have sought to rescue James's theory from some of its embarrassments. Notably Schachter & Singer (1962) proposed that emotion was perception of a generalized arousal plus an attributional label. The idea still inspires interesting research, though in smaller amounts than formerly. In one series of studies Mandler (1990) argues that emotions are typically based on arousal caused by discrepancy between expectation and eventuality, and on evaluating what produced the discrepancy. This analysis has been applied to enjoying music (Gaver & Mandler 1987) and to playing a computer adventure game (MacDowell & Mandler 1989). In the latter study events that were unexpected caused the largest increases in arousal as measured by heart rate. Berscheid (e.g. 1988), moreover, argues that though the problem is not simple, arousal of sexual excitement may be the major cause of erotic love.

The neo-Jamesian tradition is also represented in studies of attribution (e.g. Wiener 1986). Some emotions depend on attributional labels indicating their cause. For instance pride depends on attributing success to the self. Wiener & Graham (1989) also suggest that emotions function as a "bridge between the past and the future" (p. 401). In their studies they showed how attributionally based emotions influence future plans. For instance, subjects judging vignettes believe that people experience gratitude when they perceive that someone has voluntarily taken helpful action, and helpful action is believed to elicit reciprocal favors.

The current mainstream of research has swung away from James's idea that we are afraid because we perceive internal effects of running away. It now supports the folk theoretical idea that we run away because we are afraid. And research continues that tends to refute James's position. For instance Bermond et al (1991) used improved methodology on an old problem. Hohmann (1966) had reported that people experienced less intense emotions after spinal injuries that diminished inner sensations. Bermond et al interviewed spinally injured subjects, asking each to recall an incident of fear before injury and one after it, elicited by circumstances that were as similar as possible on the two occasions. Data were also collected for incidents of anger. There was no evidence of lowered subjective intensity of fear or anger following the injury. Indeed for these two emotions, remembered subjective intensities of the emotions were significantly greater following injury, although as expected on pure anatomical grounds lowered intensity of physiological disturbance was reported (see also Lowe & Carroll 1985; Chwalisz et al 1988).

As Campos et al (1989) have pointed out, Darwin and to an even greater extent James taught psychologists to see emotions as end points—individual states extending no further than the body. As end points, of course, emotions can be pleasant or unpleasant reinforcers. But many cognitive and developmental psychologists now investigate other contributions of emotions to controlling action, and try also to discover how they extend beyond the body to affect social interaction.

Recent Answers to James's Question: What Is an Emotion?

Recent answers to James's (1884) question "What is an emotion?" thus tend to emphasize specificity and function. Emotions are now often thought of as communications. As Oatley & Johnson-Laird (1987) put it, emotions are communications to oneself and others. Buck (1991) regards emotions as readouts, some of which are communicative. As Lang (1988) has demonstrated, there are often substantial differences between a person's conscious awareness and behavioral or physiological indications of emotions. Hence communications of emotion, which are picked up from behavioral signs, need not be consciously recognized by the person emitting these signs.

As communications to oneself, emotions signal the occurrence of events relevant to important goals. Perhaps primarily emotions are changes of action readiness (Frijda 1986), and they set goal priorities. Emotions also function to insert and maintain in consciousness information about the events that caused them and about the possible consequences of these events (Oatley 1992). As communications to others, emotions can have destinations: At 10 months, infant smiles are made more frequently to someone present, than when infants are alone (Jones et al 1991). Emotional signals indicate intentions and changes of intention. They affect other peoples' actions, tending to set pairs or groups of people into particular modes of interaction (see below).

According to recent treatments, an emotion is a mental state (Ortony et al 1988) or a process (Frijda 1986); it is usually elicited by an external event. By analogy with motor movements, emotions are phasic: They have a defined onset, perhaps rising to one or more peaks of intensity, and a decline (Frijda et al 1991). At any moment an emotion has an intensity that can be measured behaviorally (e.g. from facial expressions), physiologically (e.g. from autonomic variables such as heart rate or skin conductance), or by self-report (Plutchik & Kellerman 1989). What is not always so clear is how well different measures correlete with each other in specific instances. Researchers on facial expressions or physiological changes tend to see emotions as lasting between a few seconds and a few minutes, while those whose research is on verbal reports see them lasting from a few minutes to a few hours. All are agreed, however, that moods can last for many hours. They are like muscle tone, and they may lack subjectively apparent beginnings or ends. Cognition theorists agree, we believe, in distinguishing the functions of emotions from the functions of mood. Emotions function to rearrange the priorities of goals. If, as Frijda (1986) argues, emotions are types of action readiness, they change the flow of action. Fear, for instance, interrupts the current of action, makes ready for flight or fight, and directs attention to the environment for signs of danger. The role of moods is the converse: They maintain a distinctive readiness that continues despite events that might disturb it: In irritability, for example, we maintain a disposition to react angrily.

Most researchers agree that emotions are usually elicited by evaluating events that concern a person's important needs or goals—concerns as Frijda (1986) calls them. Such evaluations in relation to goals seem to be innate and often unconscious. To two-hour-old babies Rosenstein & Oster (1988) presented fluids that adults find sweet, salty, sour, and bitter. The babies' facial expressions were judged appropriate to pleasure when given the sweet fluids, and to displeasure when given salty and bitter ones. These facial expressions are taken as indexes of positive and negative emotions that are innately organized in relation to goals of obtaining sweet and avoiding bitter substances. Comparable conclusions about goal relevance derive from cross-cultural considerations. For instance, from a review of anthropological research Lutz (1988) concluded that the following are universal goal-based problems of social life: (a) conflicting goals of multiple actors (b), an individual's violation of cultural standards, (c) danger to ego or significant others, (d) loss of significant relationship or threat of such loss, and (e) needs to obtain tangible or symbolic resources. Negative emotions are generally thought to occur when such problems arise, and positive emotions when they are resolved.

The conditions that elicit an emotion distinguish it from other emotions (e.g. Ellsworth & Smith 1988). Most cognitive theorists (e.g. Frijda 1986; Oatley & Johnson-Laird 1987; Ortony et al 1988; Fischer et al 1990) agree that achievements tend to cause happiness, losses tend to cause sadness, frustration tends to cause anger, threats or goal conflicts tend to cause fear. In addition, toxic substances cause the specific emotion of disgust (Rozin & Fallon 1987). An emotion typically includes a distinct subjective experience (see e.g. Scherer et al 1986). It has differentiating physiological accompaniments (Levenson et al 1990 and perhaps also a specific neural substrate (Gray 1989). It is also accompanied by compulsive thoughts (Shaver et al 1987). It involves facial and other expressions, as well as distinctive actions. Thus happiness functions to prompt continuation with a current action, sadness prompts cessation, anger prompts aggression, and so forth. Moreover, emotions are labeled socially, and thus may be interpreted, commented upon, suppressed, and moulded (Thoits 1989).

A tenet of most cognitive theorists is that people are often conscious of emotions, and that information about emotion conveyed in ordinary language is meaningful—indeed essential to ordinary discourse. Thus, Stein & Levine (1989) asked three- and six-year-old children and adults to assess small stories in which goals and outcomes of goals were varied. Children and adults made similar inferences about what emotions the protagonist would feel apropos various goal attributes and outcomes in the story. Both groups could say what plans the protagonist would be likely to have next. Children and adults understand emotions in terms of goals and outcomes—i.e. as being followed by plans to maintain, reinstate, relinquish, or change goals. Emotions function conceptually, therefore, in explanations to ourselves or to others of intention and action. In folk theory they are the pivots around which sequences of action turn.

THE ROLE OF EMOTIONS IN DEVELOPMENT

Normal Functions of One's Own and Others' Emotions

ATTACHMENT   The best-established tradition of research on the interpersonal function of emotions has been done in child development. One aspect has been work on infant attachment. Bowlby (1969) described how infants use their mothers as secure bases from which to explore, and how they become distressed at separation. He saw the infant's distress as functional in evolutionary terms—to keep the mother nearby. It is also vital for mothers to be responsive to their infants. Corter & Fleming (1990) discuss psychosocial processes in maternal responsiveness and consider interactions with endocrine mechanisms.

Ainsworth et al (1978) examined infants' responses to brief separations from their caregivers and observed their behavior on reunion in laboratory setting. This procedure has become known as the "strange situation" test. Infants with a "securely attached" style are distressed at separation but can seek and be comforted by the caregiver on her return. "Ambivalently attached" infants want proximity but also show angry resistant behavior on the caregiver's return. "Avoidantly attached" infants avoid interaction with the caregiver on her return. A fourth style of "disoriented/disorganized attachment" was added by Main & Solomon (1986), in which children show disorientation and contradictory reactions to separation.

Attachment styles are thought to reflect the history of caregivers' sensitivity to their child. Mothers of the securely attached react to their babies more sensitively than mothers of the insecurely attached (Grossmann & Grossmann 1990; Smith & Pederson 1988; Isabella et al 1989). Depressed mothers and those who have physically abused their children are more likely than nondisturbed mothers to have insecurely attached infants (Carlson et al 1989; Radke-Yarrow et al 1985).

It should be noted however that the causal sequence in the creation of attachment styles is not clear. Mothers may be reacting to behavior that originates with the infant. There is indeed evidence that differential attachment styles can result from infant factors such as temperament or emotional reactivity (Goldsmith & Alansky 1987). Miyake et al (1985) found that Japanese infants rated as irritable neonates later showed resistant reunion patterns in the strange situation at 12 months. Thompson et al (1988) found that temperament of American infants was associated with distress on separation. This distress in turn affected how the infant behaved towards the mother at reunion. Other researchers have found interactions between child temperament and maternal characteristics in predicting attachment status (Mangeldorf et al 1990; Bohlin et al 1989). Thus both infants and their mothers contribute to the quality of their emotional relationship, and the extent to which they adjust to each other is important in predicting whether children are easily comforted after separation.

The importance of the attachment classification is based on the assumption that it predicts socio-emotional development in older children and adults. Attachment status has been found to predict children's behavior over the medium term. For instance, securely attached children at one year were more sociable and communicative at three (Lutkenhaus et al 1985) and five years (Main et al 1985). Some hypothesize that effects may continue into adulthood: In several studies (Shaver et al 1988; Feeney & Noller; 1990) infant attachment styles, assessed retrospectively, were associated with adult relationships with lovers, implying either that people fall in love with those whose interaction styles are familiar to them or that they mould their partners to their expectations. Other researchers (Crowell & Feldman 1988; Grossmann et al 1988) have found transgenerational links in attachment, such that people who reported an insecure attachment to their own parents in infancy were more likely to have infants with insecure attachments. These studies suffer, however, from the obvious methodological problems of retrospective accounts, and thus results must be viewed cautiously.

Certain inconsistencies have also been observed in studies relating infant attachment status to later childhood behavior: Effects have been found for girls but not boys (La Freniere & Sroufe 1985), in one setting but not another (Oppenheim et al 1988), and sometimes for only a small number of the hypothesized variables in spite of careful and sound methodology (Fagot & Kavanagh 1990; Goldberg et al 1989). Most studies do not exclude the possibility that predictions from attachment style result from a stability in the caregiver-child relationship, such that the observed correlations are actually the product of contemporaneous associations (Lamb et al 1985).

Overall, attachment studies have demonstrated that emotions act as signals between mothers and babies in their accommodation to each other. Certainly some of the extreme effects of nonaccommodation have been demonstrated. However, emotional events other than those of attachment have been found to be just as strongly and consistently linked with children's future adjustment [e.g. parental disharmony, parental criticism of children (Richman et al 1982)]. The concentration of research effort on attachment status has meant that such processes, which are of comparable importance for an understanding of the interpersonal effects of emotions, have been underresearched.

SOCIAL REFERENCING   The idea behind social referencing was that infants are guided in exploration by their mothers' emotional expressions. Sorce et al (1985) found that with a visual cliff adjusted to a height that produced no clear avoidance, 74% of one-year-old infants crossed the cliff if their mother looked happy but none crossed when she posed a fearful expression. The hypothesis was that maternal expressions functioned to disambiguate such situations. This may help account for why infants are so good at discriminating mothers' expressions within the first year: Haviland & Lelwica (1987) showed that ten-week-olds could respond differentially to their mothers' expressing happiness, sadness, and anger.

Since the first discussions of social referencing, research has indicated that the phenomenon is not as strong as one might expect if this is an important mechanism helping children to avoid danger. For instance, Zarbatany & Lamb (1985) found only a trend towards children approaching a toy spider when their mother or a stranger looked happy rather than fearful. Also, instead of approaching the mother more when she looked fearful (as the social referencing hypothesis predicted), children approached her more when she looked happy. Strong age effects have been observed: Negative parental expressions inhibited a child's action more in a 10–12-month age group than when the children were either younger or older (Walden & Ogan 1988). Also troubling for the hypothesis is the observation that in most experiments children are excluded from the sample because they do not "reference" their caretaker in a measurable way (21% were excluded in Sorce et al's 1985 study, and 34% by Zarbatany & Lamb 1985). When Hornik & Gunnar (1988) introduced a pet rabbit to mothers and infants in a semi-naturalistic study,

16% of the children never referenced, and only a third did so on the first introduction of the rabbit. Of those who did reference, looking at the mother was not necessarily followed by a change of behavior.

Despite these setbacks to the hypothesis of social referencing, it is clear that children do actively monitor their mothers' facial expressions. These expressions are likely one among many sources of information prompting approach and avoidance. For other reasons as well, it is probably important for a child to keep an eye on what mother is feeling—reasons that concern issues other than whether or not to explore.

Development of People's Concepts of Emotions

There is a growing literature on children's conceptions of emotion. We indicate here some of the transitions that occur in these conceptions. For a review of the development of emotions up to age 30 months, see Lewis (1990).

At least from age two children use terms denoting emotion, and by age three are making causal statements about emotions in their everyday lives (Bretherton et al 1986; Dunn et al 1987). At first children tend to speak mainly of emotions that are considered basic, using terms like happy, sad, mad, and scared. Later they develop subcategories and more complex concepts (Bretherton et al 1986; Ridgeway et al 1985), with emotional developments influencing intellectual developments, and vice versa (Case et al 1988). Smiley & Huttenlocher (1989) argue that children first acquire emotion categories for their own emotion states, then for observable features of another person's behavior, and finally to describe the inferred mental states of another.

Theorists debate the age at which children begin to represent the mental states of other persons and to understand their emotions (Harris 1989). Infants under two years old react to the emotions of another person and show the beginnings of empathic concern (Dunn 1988; Zahn-Waxler & Radke Yarrow 1991), but the ability to form a concept of emotion emerges later. Brown & Dunn (1991) found that two-year-olds speak mainly about their own desires and feelings in terms of satisfying immediate needs but by three years show interest in other people's feelings, and talk in more mentalistic terms about their own. By the time they're five or six years old, children can represent and analyze the goals of another person, a capability Stein & Trabasso (1989) argue is prerequisite to understanding emotion in others. Another landmark is the ability to recognize the existence of two emotions at once. Harter & Buddin (1987), using Fischer et al's (e.g 1990) developmental theory of emotion, investigated concepts of the simultaneous experience of two emotions in children from four to twelve years old. They found that emotions of different valence directed towards the same target only emerge late in this sequence. Other developments in the early school years involve understanding the distinction between feeling an emotion and hiding it (Harris 1989), and taking personal information into account to evaluate the emotions of others (Gnepp & Chilamkurti 1988). Some emotions, such as guilt and embarrassment, require a mature sense of self before they can emerge (Lewis 1990).

Though there is controversy about how emotion concepts are represented mentally, either as prototypes or in terms of necessary and sufficient conditions (see Russell 1991 and the reply by Clore & Ortony 1991), by adulthood people in most cultures have complex concepts about how emotions are elicited and what their consequences are. It is hard to escape the conclusion that without such concepts we would be unable to make sense of important aspects of our own or of other people's behavior (Gordon 1987).

ADULT EMOTIONS

When and Where Do Emotions Occur?

Adults' concepts of specific emotions are differentiated by features of the eliciting event. Thus Roseman et al (1990) investigated the following categories of appraisal: motive consistent vs inconsistent, rewarding vs punishing, certain vs uncertain, strong vs weak; positive outcome deserved vs negative outcome deserved; and agency attributed to circumstances vs other person vs self. They compared their results with those of other appraisal theorists and found their categories good at discriminating among emotions remembered by subjects. A complementary analysis of emotion incidents in terms of their consequences has been made by Frijda et al (1989), who found that types of action readiness showed associations to 32 emotion words which were as distinctive as were appraisals of eliciting events to these emotion words.

A central tenet of most cognitive emotional theories is that emotions are elicited not merely by events but by events in relation to important goals. Appraisal studies support this hypothesis.

It is something of an embarrassment for emotion researchers that most studies of the causation of emotions in adult humans can be regarded primarily as tapping folk theories about the elicitation of emotion, rather than as observing the causes of emotions directly. Such an interpretation probably applies to Smith's (1989) laudable attempt to measure facial action, autonomic variables, and appraisals when subjects responded with emotionally toned images to specially written scenarios. Ideally, different indexes of emotions must be interrelated in ecologically valid sets of studies, though methodological and conceptual problems remain severe (Cacioppo & Tassinary 1990). In one study on elicitation that cross-validated several measures Stemmler (1989) found that real occurrences of fear, anger, and happiness were discriminable on autonomic variables as well as self-reports, whereas physiological measures obtained while recalling fearful and angry scenes did not allow supposedly fearful and angry states to be discriminated. For behavioral confirmation that specific goal-relevant events cause human emotions we must often rely on studies such as those reviewed in the previous section—e.g. studies showing that an infant's separation from a caregiver does cause distress, and that reunion causes relief for the securely attached and occasions anger in many of the insecurely attached.

Effects of Emotions on Attention and Memory

Several developments in the last decade have prompted interest in the effects of emotions. (For the relevance of these developments to psychopathology, see below.) For example, the hypothesis that high arousal (or more specifically anxiety) narrows attention has been tested more carefully. MacLeod et al (1986) showed that when clinically anxious, but not depressed, subjects looked at words displayed on a screen, they had faster reaction times to a spot of light appearing in the position of a threat word than to one appearing in the position of a neutral word. Apparently their attention was focussed more closely on the threat words. Comparable experimental effects have been observed for other attentional tasks (Mathews et al 1990).

Effects of happy emotions have been studied by Isen, Clark, and others. For example, induction of mild happiness improved creative problem solving (Isen et al 1987). Isen (1990) proposed that happiness can change cognitive organization, making the range of associations broader and processing more flexible. Recently Isen & Baron (1991) have applied their findings on the effects of emotions to understanding organizational behavior, including helpfulness, risk taking, and negotiation. Clark & Williamson (1989) have reviewed the literature on the effects of mood on judgments of self, others, and environmental objects. They conclude that such effects are found more consistently with positive than with negative moods.

Emotions also affect memory. In his review Blaney (1986) distinguished state-dependent memory from mood congruence. The hypothesis of state-dependency is that recall of any material is better if mood at recall is the same as it was at acquisition. The mood-congruence hypothesis, on the other hand, holds that material is better acquired and/or recalled if the material itself has an emotional significance congruent with mood at acquisition and/or recall. Some of the reported state-dependent effects have been difficult to replicate; and Bower, who previously supported the hypothesis, has become sceptical about its generality (Bower 1987). He concludes that state-dependent effects occur but are difficult to capture in the laboratory. He argues that they may be more robust in autobiographical memory because the event being remembered is causally related to the mood being investigated. Blaney argues that many experiments confound state-dependency and mood-congruency: The latter explanation, he holds, has greater empirical support. In addition, it accounts for the finding of easier access to those autobiographical memories that have the same emotional tone as the mood at recall. Another line of evidence concerns the representation of emotions in memory. Conway (1990) has found that emotion concepts, in contrast to other kinds of information, are stored in terms of autobiographical incidents during which particular emotions were experienced. In some people, called repressors, memories of negative emotions are less accessible than for nonrepressors (Hansen & Hansen 1988).

It would make sense if emotions, hypothesized as forms of action readiness, were to affect attention and other aspects of cognitive organization, and also gave access to information about comparable emotional events in the past. As Lazarus (1991) has pointed out, an emotion typically prompts attempts to cope with the event that caused it. Indexing autobiographical examples of coping plans by means of specific emotions would be cognitively efficient, because retrieval of a stored plan together with the effects it had could be better than generating a new plan on each occasion. (However, as we note below, this mechanism may also underlie some types of psychopathology).

Functions and Effects of Emotions in Social Interaction

By far the most extensive body of data in the field of human emotions is that on facial expressions of emotions. Ekman (1989) and Fridlund et al (1987) describe a scheme for coding facial expressions (FACS). Based on contraction of each facial muscle, FACS can describe any facial movement. These investigators have found expressions specific to discrete emotions. Emotions may be considered discrete in the sense that they are produced and recognized pan-culturally, that they are accompanied by specific autonomic nervous system activity (Levenson et al 1990), and/or that they are likely to have had survival value during the course of evolution. Principal alternative coding schemes are those designed by Izard (Phillips & Izard 1988) for maximum discrimination among primary emotions. These schemes have also produced many data on infants and adults, indicating that facial expressions of emotion are specific and recognizable. There is comparable though less extensive evidence that tones of voice signal emotions (Scherer 1986).

Facial and vocal expressions have interpersonal effects that occur independently of any words spoken (McHugo et al 1985; Ohman 1986), although generally the more channels of information available the more accurate is the judgment of emotion (Wallbott & Scherer 1986). And just as it has been argued that we are biologically wired to send certain emotion signals, so there is evidence of a biological predisposition to detect and interpret them: Dimberg (1990) argues from conditioning experiments that humans are biologically prepared to associate perceptions of angry faces, but not of smiling faces, with aversive outcomes.

Communication of emotion can promote certain kinds of action in another person—e.g. helping (Carlson et al 1988). Emotions can also set groups into particular modes of interaction. In a naturalistic study of families with depressed and nondepressed mothers (10 1-hr sessions), Hops et al (1987) found that depressed mothers emitted more dysphoric signals and fewer happy ones than the nondepressed. Depressed mothers' dysphoric mood resulted in a suppression of aggressive affect in other family members, while these members' aggressive affect suppressed the display of her dysphoria. Hops et al suggest that the displays of emotion they studied provided brief respites from the aversiveness of other family members' aggression or dysphoria. Levenson & Gottman (e.g. 1985) studied the anger communicated during arguments between spouses and found that the degree to which one spouse mirrored the physiological state of the other in angry arousal accounted for 60% of the variance on marital dissatisfaction measures.

Both emotional facial patterns and prosodic features of speech that signal emotions (Fernald 1989) function to communicate intentions and needs. Interpersonal emotional communications transform relationships (De Rivera & Grinkis 1986) or change patterns of joint action, while moods tend to maintain such patterns.

DYSFUNCTIONS IN EMOTIONAL LIFE

Normal and Abnormal Emotions

Although the term "emotional disorder" is a common synonym for "psychiatric syndrome," one wishes for more links between the literatures on emotions and on abnormal psychology. There are, of course, problems: Syndromes are defined in psychiatry in terms of the disability they cause rather than in terms of emotional intensity or duration. Reflecting this, a psychiatric state is indicated not on the continuous scales preferred by psychologists but on dichotomous scales—i.e. a person either does or does not receive a given diagnosis (Widiger & Trull 1991). A second problem is that although emotional disturbance may well be a feature of every category of psychiatric diagnosis (Lane & Schwartz 1987), psychiatric syndromes are not themselves emotions or moods, and cannot be extrapolated simply from emotions or moods.

Might not the emotions recognized in psychiatry be normal in eliciting conditions and consequences, although more intense and long lasting than in people who have no psychiatric syndrome? Clinicians, on the whole, assume that diagnosed patients' emotions are abnormal in some way. As to sufferer's estimates, Thoits (1985) has argued that one attribute of those who seek psychiatric help may be that they label their own emotions as abnormal.

In this section we concentrate not on these knotty problems but on the extent to which emotions contribute to causing or sustaining psychopathology. We do not imply that emotions are the most important of such influences—it is clear that psychopathology has many causes, but we point out a growing literature in which the intrapersonal and interpersonal influences of emotions are being recognized in psychiatry.

Continuities of Emotional Response as Seen in Psychiatric Disorders

One of the venerable ideas about psychopathology is that people have traits that start in childhood and persist. These traits are manifested in dispositions and in repeated reactions to certain kinds of event. They also form bases for certain kinds of psychopathology. The question brought by research on emotions is whether such traits and psychopathological vulnerability could be understood in terms of research on emotional reactions.

A basic issue, then, is how stable our fundamental emotional patterns are over short and long periods (Robins & Rutter 1990). Over shorter periods continuities can be quite marked, particularly for negative emotions. Izard et al (1987) examined children's expressions of anger and sadness during inoculations on three occasions between 2 and 7 months of age, and again at 19 months. Aggregate measures of the proportion of time spent expressing anger and sadness before 7 months predicted 19 month-old-expressions of anger (r = 0.53) and sadness (r = 0.56). Malatesta et al (1989) also reported a significant continuity of negative expression from 7 to 22 months. Personality measures generally are heavily weighted with issues concerning emotions. Costa & McCrea (1988) found stability in adults of about 0.7 or more on individual traits in neuroticism, extraversion, and openness domains over six years as derived from spouse reports. In other studies they discuss, stability of personality has been recorded for even longer periods.

Temperament is postulated as a biological patterning of behavioral tendencies, involving emotionality as a component (Bates 1989). Its neurological signs are being investigated (e.g. Davidson 1991). Chess & Thomas (1990) followed 133 middle-class children into early adulthood. Some had "difficult temperament," characterized by irregularity, withdrawal, slow adaptability to change, high intensity, and generally negative mood. Others had "easy temperament," characterized by the opposite traits, including generally positive mood. Chess & Thomas measured adult temperament by questionnaire and interview and found significant correlations from year to year in childhood on specific items such as adaptability. Though there were few correlations from childhood to adulthood on specific items, a composite score on an easy-vs-difficult constellation indicated that from Year 3 and Year 4 of childhood to adulthood there were significant correlations (r = 0.31 and 0.37), but from Year 5 to adulthood the correlation was not significant (r = 0.15). According to these studies there was some long-term continuity of temperament, but it was relatively small. Higher correlations have been found for the easy/difficult dimension of temperament in the early years—e.g. Lee & Bates (1985) found a correlation between measures at 6 and 24 months on difficult temperament of r = 0.57.

As part of a program of research over many years, Caspi et al (1990) note that consistency in personality is affected by changes in emotional demands during the course of life. They gave clinical interviews to mothers of 8–10-year-old children, from which ratings were made on five-point scales of the children's temper tantrums and anger: Severe reactions included kicking and screaming. Similar ratings were made for shyness: Severe ratings were for panic in social situations. Personality assessments were then made of the subjects when they reached ages 30 and 40. Most striking was the association in males between earlier ratings and life course: By midlife, ill-tempered boys of the middle-class were indistinguishable from even-tempered counterparts of lower socioeconomic status on occupational level, and 53% of them were downwardly mobile, compared to 28% of their even-tempered middle-class peers. Ill temper was associated with leaving school earlier, and this afforded fewer possibilities in work. Men who were ill tempered as children made poorer marriages, with significantly more divorces. Shy boys had different life-course patterns, although again with continuities between childhood and adulthood: They were significantly older when they married, when they first became fathers, and when they entered a stable career, even controlling for class, educational level, and military service.

We now turn to continuities in psychopathology (Zeitlin 1990)—not because disorders are synonymous with emotions but because particular emotions are evident in particular disorders. For instance, both childhood conduct disorder and its adult equivalent, antisocial personality disorder, involve aggression, destructive acts, disobedience, delinquency, etc. The syndromes involve anger rather than other emotions. Similarly, affective disorders such as depression or anxiety states are more characteristic of sadness or fear, respectively. These continuities are discussed to indicate how patterns of response, which involve emotions, may be established. We do not argue that continuities can be explained in terms of continuity of emotions without taking into account factors such as genetics, social stressors, and cognitive factors.

Conduct disorder has high childhood-adult continuity: About 50% of boys with conduct disorder show personality disorder as adults (Robins 1978). Robins (1986) found that the strongest predictor of later antisocial problems was the extent of conduct disorder in childhood. People are likely to exhibit the same kind of disorder (i.e. affective or conduct disorder as two broad categories) in adulthood as in childhood. Quinton et al (1990) followed-up children with psychiatric disorder in childhood who had a parent who was a psychiatric patient. Of the boys with conduct disorder as children and a disorder of some kind as adults, the adult disorder was antisocial personality disorder. For girls with conduct disorder in childhood, however, the disorder in adulthood was affective. For both sexes affective problems in childhood only led to affective problems in adulthood. Continuity was mediated by continuing parental discord in the home. Although the sample size in this study was small, the continuity of affective disturbance in both boys and girls, and the discontinuity for antisocial disturbance only in girls, are striking. Robins (1986) also reported that conduct-disordered girls who continue to show disorder show a mixture of affective and antisocial symptoms in adulthood. Harrington et al (1990) carried out a follow-up study of two groups of sex- and age-matched adults—one depressed as children and one with a childhood psychiatric disorder but not depression. Those who had been depressed as children were much more likely than the others to have episodes of depression as adults. Taken together these studies demonstrate a high level of continuity from childhood to adulthood in the type of psychiatric disorder expressed.

Intergenerational continuities in emotional behavior have also been described (see also the section above on attachment). Angry or harsh parenting has been found to be more common in parents who have themselves been harshly parented (Egeland et al 1988; Quinton & Rutter 1988; Simons et al 1991). The mechanism for such an effect is as yet obscure. However, effects of parental maltreatment on children are pervasive. Socio-emotional, cognitive, and representational aspects of development are affected (Cicchetti 1990). For instance Dodge et al (1990), examining the effect of parental maltreatment in a representative sample of four-year-olds, found that by comparison to nonabused children, abused children show deviant patterns of processing social information and behave more aggressively towards their peers. Abnormal patterns in abused children's reactions to other peoples' emotions are evident early. Main & George (1985) and Klimes-Dougan & Kistner (1990) have shown that toddlers and preschool children who have been physically abused are likely to respond to other children's distress with aggression.

Bowlby's (e.g. 1988) concept of internal working models has been used to explain continuities in emotional responses, including intergenerational continuities (Egeland et al 1988). These models are dynamic representations of attachment figures, and of the self in interaction with them, built up through successive interactions with caregivers (Bretherton 1990). Stern (1985) has developed the concept of "representations of interactions that have become generalized" (RIGs). He postulates mechanisms by means of which individuals organize their emotional experience and interactions with others, and suggests ways that early emotional interactions might affect long-term behavior.

Repetitive patterns of emotional response, whether caused by endogenous or situational processes, can become dysfunctional. For instance, people can maintain a predominantly angry or predominantly fearful pattern of responding. If extreme, such patterns can handicap or at least restrict people (cf Main et al 1985) in comparison with those who respond to situations in an easier or more flexible way. While it is adaptive for emotions to prompt patterns of action, if responses such as frustration or fear are overgeneralized to most social situations they can form the basis of personality traits or dispositions and become maladaptive.

Stress and Its Emotional Effects

Modern work on stress is often traced back to the 1930s. Much of it has been concerned with undifferentiated responses and corresponds to a line of emotion research, represented by Mandler (1990), in which emotion is based on generalized autonomic arousal. Life-event checklists cumulate scores from a heterogeneous set of events on the hypothesis that all change is stressful and stresses are additive. Stress gauged in this fashion is mildly correlated with illnesses such as coronary heart disease (Rahe 1988).

Is each emotion correlated with a specific kind of pathology? Let us take one definition of stress—the state that results from suffering a serious loss or threat, or from the experience of a chronic difficulty. Brown & Harris (1978) developed an interview to determine what adverse events and difficulties had occurred in a person's life, and a procedure for making judgments about their severity. In 1978 they were able to go well beyond the evidence of checklists to explain a large majority of nonpsychotic psychiatric breakdowns in randomly chosen community respondents, and these breakdowns almost invariably involved depression, sometimes also accompanied by a clinical anxiety state. Brown & Harris found that 89% of women with onsets of depression (compared with 30% of women who had no onset of depression) had suffered a severe event or difficulty within 38 weeks prior to onset. Severe events and difficulties were found to cause depression only if the subject had a vulnerability factor, such as lack of social support. This work has now been firmly established (Oatley & Bolton 1985) and extended (Brown & Harris 1989). Severe losses and threats, occurring in conjunction with vulnerability factors, can cause the psychiatric syndrome of depression at the case level, with or without an anxiety syndrome. Such states, perhaps if they are particularly severe or long lasting, may give rise to physical illness (Brown & Harris 1989; Cohen & Williamson 1991).

A second kind of stress is internal, and can better be conceptualized in terms of personality traits than of events. Such traits, of course, can be understood as emotional rigidities in interactions with others, as discussed above. There is growing evidence that some such personality traits are associated with physical disease (Friedman & Booth-Kewley 1987), though much of the association may be with illness behavior (Cohen & Williamson 1991). Repeated elicitations of anxiety or frustration may bring about illness. The correlation between the Type-A personality and coronary heart disease is an hypothesis of this kind. Recently it has been argued that the aspect of this personality type that correlates with coronary heart disease is hostility/anger/ aggression (Booth-Kewley & Friedman 1987; Spielberger et al 1988). A current difficulty with this particular linkage between emotion and illness, however, is that, as Booth-Kewley & Friedman show, depression and anxiety also predict coronary heart disease. The etiology of heart disease is not well understood.

In future research it should not be assumed that stress causes generalized arousal, or is identical to arousal. Studies are needed of how differentiated events, in the context of people's lives and aspirations, ordinarily cause specific emotions. Other research should examine predispositions to certain kinds of emotional response. In some circumstances events or predispositions may contribute to psychiatric syndromes that include emotions, and perhaps also to some kinds of physical disease.

Emotions Eliciting or Sustaining Psychopathology

The emotions and moods of one person can affect psychopathology in others.

CHILDREN EXPOSED TO DEPRESSION   In a number of studies children of depressed mothers have been found to be at increased risk of affective disorders (see Downey & Coyne 1990 for review). Depressed women display negative affect to their children more frequently than nondepressed women (Cohn et al 1990; Hops et al 1987). Depressed mothers are slower to respond to their infant's vocalizations (Bettes 1988). They show fewer affectionate contact behaviors, are less active, imitate less, and play fewer games (Field et al 1988; Fleming et al 1988). Depressed mothers may be less well synchronized with their infants than are nondepressed mothers (Field et al 1988), although this is not found in all studies (Cohn et al 1990). Field et al found that infants of depressed mothers had lower rates of activity and vocalization, increased rates of fussiness, and more negative affect. These depressed behaviors of infants carry over into interactions with strangers.

Such studies help to elucidate how negative affect is communicated to young babies and how it can influence behavior in the short term. They do not, however, employ designs allowing psychopathology in children of depressed parents to be explained. Sad affect is just one component of clinical depression. Children experiencing parents' depression are typically exposed to several kinds of negative affect that may contribute to their psychopathology. For instance, parental marital disharmony is much more common in people with psychiatric disorders and is itself related to psychopathology. In a longitudinal study of children of psychiatric patients, most of whom had affective disorders, Quinton & Rutter (1985) found that children had increased rates of psychopathology only when parental disturbance was coupled with marital discord. Genetic influences also play a part in increasing risk, but their extent has not yet been determined (Plomin & Rende 1991).

EXPOSING CHILDREN TO ANGER   Cummings (1987) has shown that exposure to adult anger increases children's aggression toward peers. Children were exposed to two adult strangers in an acted argument. During the argument children would freeze, make distressed facial expressions, and seek their mothers. The children more frequently hit, kicked, and pushed each other after the argument than after periods when they had not witnessed an argument. The children's aggression was not based on imitation of the adult actors, since the actors did not make physical contact.

This work complements the epidemiological evidence on the effects of parental disharmony on children's behavior. Children in disharmonious homes are at risk of developing emotional and behavioral problems (see Grych & Fincham 1990, for review). In a general population study on the effects of marital disharmony on 9–12-year-old children, Jenkins & Smith (1991) showed how the frequency and severity of overt parental conflict (exposure to high levels of interparental anger) was the most damaging aspect of a poor marriage. It was more strongly associated with children's conduct problems (aggression, disobedience, etc) than with their affective problems (e.g. anxiety, depressed mood, etc). Silent and unexpressed parental tension was not independently associated with children's disturbance, suggesting that some negative affective styles in the home are more detrimental for children's socio-emotional development than others. Most children intervened actively in an attempt to stop parental conflict; the more frequent and severe the conflict, the more the children intervened. Children were found to be skilled at assessing the seriousness of different kinds of conflict and altering their own behavior accordingly (Jenkins et al 1989).

ADULT INTERPERSONAL INFLUENCES   In adults, too, emotions can be important to an understanding of psychopathology. In the 1960s it was observed that the "expressed emotion" of the relatives of schizophrenic patients predicted relapse of symptoms (see Leff & Vaughn 1985). "Expressed emotion" is a measure derived from the number of critical comments made during a semi-structured interview, and from evidence of emotional overinvolvement. In most studies, schizophrenic patients returning home from hospital to families high in expressed emotion were more liable to relapse than those returning to families with low expressed emotion (Goldstein et al 1986). Though several groups have had therapeutic success in helping high-expressed-emotion families to become low-expressed-emotion families, producing the predicted improvement in prognosis for their schizophrenic relatives (Koenigsberg & Handley 1986), the effect is not yet well understood. Expressed emotion and patient's perceptions of criticism by spouses also predict relapse in patients who have been hospitalized with unipolar depressive disorder (Hooley & Teasdale 1989).

INDIVIDUAL COGNITIVE EFFECTS IN ADULTS   A quite different hypothetical mechanism in the maintenance of psychopathology (Williams et al 1988) derives from cognitive biases of the kind discussed in the section above on the effects of emotions. Patients with depressed mood, for example, have a bias towards recalling episodes of loss and failure. Attributing such failures to the self tends to prolong the depression in a vicious cycle (Brewin 1988). As Blaney (1986) has remarked, however, the hypothesis that depression is maintained by memory bias explains too much: It is not clear how discouraging memories could cease coming to mind under the bias of depressed mood, causing yet more discouragement and depression. Recent modifications have sought to repair this defect in the theory (e.g. Parrott & Sabini 1990)

A comparable mechanism has been proposed to account for the maintenance of anxiety states, its effects operating not via memory but via attention to cues of threat. In anxious people, threat cues elicit maladaptive cognitive schemata from which beliefs are generated about the self and the future (Beck & Emery 1985). Such cue-schema couplings may be biologically based (Hamm et al 1990). Such a mechanism might help to explain why some people are generally more fearful than others, despite the absence of serious dangers in their past. Not only people who are generally anxious but also those suffering from posttraumatic stress disorder following war combat show changes in attention (McNally et al 1990), and these changes may help explain the repeated intrusive thoughts and images that are a feature of this disorder.

EMOTIONS AND CONSCIOUSNESS

The Role of Emotions in Narrative Literature

Emotions figure prominently in narrative: In what ways can we analyze them? Narratives are basically accounts of action. If a narrative character encounters vicissitudes, the character is described as experiencing an emotion. Adults and children are good both at generating stories on request to imply occurrence of a specific emotion and at inferring an appropriate emotion when asked to judge these stories (Camras & Allison 1989). Drawing on folk theories, novelists depict emotions either as prompting the next phase of action or as being maintained (as in "... they lived happily ever after"). Computer programs for narrative understanding (Wegman 1985; Dyer 1987) depend on knowledge about what causes emotions and what follows from them. Such programs are attempts to formalize and explore these folk beliefs, and they have been successful in making the kinds of inference that humans make when understanding stories. As Miall (1989) has argued, however, they depend on fixed schemas, whereas when humans read literary texts the emotions they feel help them to form new schemas; new interpretations are produced by each reader, and in each reading.

De Sousa (1987) has described "paradigm scenarios of emotion." According to De Sousa, such scenarios teach us how emotions are elicited and what the appropriate responsive actions are. If emotions and the readiness they prompt are innate, then part of what we learn are names for such kinds of readiness. We also learn elaborations and the implications of such states in our culture. These scenarios are depicted in narrative literature, which thus becomes a vehicle for emotional education. Paradigm scenarios are, in other words, higher-order components of folk theories of emotions. They correspond to scripts as described by Tomkins (1979), and to the slightly different idea of script proposed by Shaver et al (1987), to hierarchical structures (Leventhal & Scherer 1987), to plot units in computational analysis of narrative (Lehnert & Vine 1987), to emotion schemata as described by Lutz (1987), and to response-based images proposed by Lang (1987); they may also correspond to the autobiographical memories of emotion postulated by Conway (1990).

At least since Freud (1905) said that his therapy was based on asking the patient "to give [him] the whole story of his life and illness" (p. 16), therapy of many kinds has included the attempt to let the patient understand his or her life in narrative terms. This involves identifying emotions in the course of action, sometimes re-experiencing emotions from the past, and often reinterpreting them.

Why are emotions and narrative form so important to therapy? There are many possibilities. People may be unclear about their emotions. Greenberg & Safran (1989) propose that fuller conscious experience of emotions enhances ability to function; Scheff (1987) suggests that it improves creativity. Emotions can indicate goals or intentions of which a person may be unaware (Oatley 1992; cf also Dahl 1991). Also, as Luborsky & Crits-Christoph (1990) have proposed, emotion scenarios (called by them Core Conflictual Relationship Themes) can emerge in therapy, and their identification can help to elucidate some of the more mysterious dynamics between persons. In addition, the narrative that emerges in therapy is an equivalent of the psychologist's idea of personality—but one the client can appropriate for himself or herself.

Work that integrates such themes is research on literary texts—relating emotions to actions and other issues that are described. Thus Haviland (1984) has analyzed Virginia Woolf's diaries and letters from childhood to age 30, counting mentions of emotion and instances of the thematic scripts of the kind described by Tomkins (1979). She discovered continuities in some of Woolf's emotional episodes—for instance, close associations between intense joys and intense despairs, as well as a linkage to a theme of affiliation, as she broods on absences of friends, and to the theme of control, including control of her own emotions. Haviland finds evidence of emotional continuity and discontinuity, as discussed above; she establishes bases for the understanding of Woolf's personality—perhaps even of Woolf's eventual suicide; and she examines the structure of the narrative accounts according to which Woolf tried to make sense of her life.

The Functions of Our Consciousness of Emotions

We can approach the role of our consciousness of emotions in several ways. First, people talk frequently about emotions. Emotions are essential concepts in our folk theories of action and interaction. To put it at its simplest, we assume that we can correctly identify emotions in ourselves and others. We use emotion terms widely in almost every kind of discourse, with the exception of the scientific and technical. A priori, then, emotions have functions in most of what is written and spoken. The specific kinds of function have been less well understood, but they include enabling us to explain and plan our own actions, and to rely on the actions of others whose emotional signals reassure us.

Are we humans largely correct, as many emotion researchers believe, in assuming that emotions as ordinarily experienced and talked about have causal roles in actions and interactions? Or is it the case, as Nisbett & Wilson (1977) have argued, that introspective access to any such putative causes of behavior, or even to peripheral changes in emotion (Rimé et al 1990), is so poor that they should usually be ignored? Answering yes to the latter question would amount to agreeing with what James thought in 1890 and to what Churchland thinks in 1989, that folk theories are likely to be plain wrong.

Second, an emotion can induce concentration on the issue that elicited it. In this regard psychologists have emphasized pathological variants of emotion—the obsessive ruminations of depression, the concentration on danger in anxiety states. But it may be the case that the kinds of control of memory and attention that emotions exert in depression and anxiety are also important to cognitive re-structuring in the nontraumatic realm: We vividly recall the attributes of someone we have just fallen in love with, in sadness we tend to reconsider when a plan miscarries, and in anger we may think intently about the implications of an impulse toward revenge.

How do the conceptualizing and interpreting of emotions function within a culture? We can approach the question by noting that among the Chewong studied by Howell (1981) emotions are identified mainly for the purpose of suppressing them. As Stearns (1989) shows, in American culture too we can see such effects: Anger and jealousy have in this century been seen as problematic, and taboos are applied. By conceiving of emotions as certain kinds of states, culture can mould them. This process can go further: Hochschild (1983) has shown how airline stewardesses are trained to maintain a happy mood and produce a pleasant emotional tone in the cabin. Thus in Western culture emotions can become products, which some people in the service industry may create in themselves and in others, thus giving an extra twist to the idea of emotion regulation.

CONCLUSION

Emotions have a biological basis. The most plausible current hypothesis is that they function (a) within individuals in the control of goal priorities, and (b) between people to communicate intentions and set outline structures for interaction. Emotions often become conscious. Each can give preferential access to stored autobiographical information relevant to that state and direct attention. This may be important in planning future actions and interactions.

Emotions are essential elements in folk theories of our selves and others. In much research on emotions a correspondence is assumed between biological bases and folk theoretical categories, though by no means all relevant work investigates such correspondence. Serious consequences can follow from some questionable tenets of folk theory—e.g. that women and men differ widely in emotionality (Shields 1987). For researchers on normal emotions one advantage of following work in psychopathology is that psychiatric research can validate certain folk theoretical categories. Cross-validations have been made from interview identification of emotions to physiological measures (e.g. Sturgeon et al 1981, for expressed emotion in relation to schizophrenia). Moreover, continuities of emotional response from childhood to adulthood are validated by independent ratings from parents' reports of emotions in childhood to self-reports and demographic measures in adulthood (e.g. Caspi et al 1990). Perhaps most compelling are the findings that emotions as described in terms of folk categories can have effects on physical illness as studied in the pathology laboratory.

In general, interrelating research on emotions from several disciplines helps to demonstrate not only that emotions can be studied, but also that they are of considerable importance in psychological function and dysfunction.

ACKNOWLEDGMENTS

We are grateful for a Grant from the Ontario Institute for Studies in Education for help in preparing this review, and to Mary Medved and Maria Guzman for their bibliographic assistance. We thank Bernard Schiff and Phil Shaver for their excellently thoughtful and constructive comments on a draft of this chapter.

Literature Cited

Ainsworth, M. D. S., Blehar, M. C., Waters, E., Wall, S. 1978. *Patterns of Attachment: A Psychological Study of the Strange Situation*. Hillsdale, NJ: Erlbaum

Bates, J. E. 1989. Concepts and measures of temperament. In *Temperament in Childhood*, ed. G. A. Kohnstamm, J. E. Bates, M. K. Rothbart, pp. 3–26. Chichester: Wiley

Beck, A. T., Emery, G. 1985. *Anxiety Disorders and Phobias: A Cognitive Perspective*. New York: Basic Books

Bermond, B., Fasotti, L., Nieuwenhuyse, B., Schuerman, J. 1991. Spinal cord lesions, peripheral feedback and intensities of emotional feelings. *Cognit. Emot.* 5:201–20

Berscheid, E. 1988. Some comments on love's anatomy: or whatever happened to old-fashioned lust? In *The Psychology of Love*, ed. R. J. Sternberg, M. L. Barnes, pp. 359–74. New Haven: Yale Univ. Press

Bettes, B. A. 1988. Maternal depression and motherese: temporal and intonational features. *Child Dev.* 59:1089–96

Blaney, P. H. 1986. Affect and memory: a review. *Psychol. Bull.* 99:229–46

Bohlin, G., Hagekull, B., Germer, M., Andersson, K., Lindberg, L. 1989. Avoidant and resistant reunion behaviors as predicted by maternal interactive behavior and infant temperament. *Infant Behav. Dev.* 12:105–17

Booth-Kewley, S., Friedman, H. S. 1987. Psychological predictors of heart disease: a quantitative review. *Psychol. Bull.* 101: 343–62

Bower, G. H. 1987. Commentary on mood and memory. *Behav. Res. Ther.* 25:443–55

Bowlby, J. 1969. *Attachment and Loss*, Vol. 1, *Attachment*. London: Hogarth Press

Bowlby, J. 1988. *A Secure Base: Parent-Child Attachment and Healthy Human Development*. New York: Basic Books

Bretherton, I. 1990. Open communication and internal working models. *Nebraska Symp. Motiv.* 36:57–113

Bretherton, I., Fritz, J., Zahn-Waxler, C., Ridgeway, D. 1986. Talking about internal states: a functionalist perspective. *Child Dev.* 57:529–48

Brewin, C. R. 1988. *Cognitive Foundations of Clinical Psychology*. Hove: Erlbaum

Brown, G. W., Harris, T. 1978. *The Social Origins of Depression*. London: Tavistock

Brown, G. W., Harris, T. 1989. *Life Events and Illness*. London: Unwin Hyman

Brown, J. R., Dunn, J. 1991. "You can cry mum": the social and developmental implications of talk about internal states. *Br. J. Dev. Psychol.* In press

Buck, R. 1991. Motivation, emotion and cogntion: a developmental-interactionist view. In *International Review of Studies on Emotion*, ed. K. T. Strongman, 1:101–42. Chichester: Wiley

Cacioppo, J. T., Tassinary, L. G. 1990. Inferring psychological significance from physiological signals. *Am. Psychol.* 45:16–28

Campos, J. J., Campos, R. G., Barrett, K. C. 1989. Emergent themes in the study of emotional development and emotion regulation. *Dev. Psychol.* 25:394–402

Camras, L. A., Allison, K. 1989. Children's and adults' beliefs about emotion elicitation. *Motiv. Emot.* 13:53–70

Carlson, M., Charlin, V., Miller, N. 1988. Positive mood and helping behavior: a test of six hypotheses. *J. Pers. Soc. Psychol.* 55:211–29

Carlson, V., Cicchetti, D., Barnett, D., Braunwald, K. 1989. Disorganized/disoriented attachment relationships in maltreated infants. *Dev. Psychol.* 25:525–31

Case, R., Hayward, S., Lewis, M., Hurst, P. 1988. Toward a neo-Piagetian theory of cognitive and emotional development. *Dev. Rev.* 8:1–51

Caspi, A., Elder, G. H., Herbener, E. 1990. Childhood personality and the prediction of life-course patterns. See Robins & Rutter 1990, pp. 13–35

80   OATLEY & JENKINS

Chess, S., Thomas, A. 1990. Continuities and discontinuities in temperament. See Robins & Rutter 1990, pp. 205–20

Churchland, P. 1989. A Neurocomputational Perspective: The Nature of Mind and the Structure of Science. Cambridge, MA: MIT Press

Chwalisz, K., Diener, E., Gallagher, D. 1988. Autonomic arousal feedback and emotional experience: evidence from the spinal cord injured. J. Pers. Soc. Psychol. 54:820–28

Cicchetti, D. 1990. The organization and coherence of socioemotional, cognitive and representational development: illustrations through a developmental psychopathology perspective on down syndrome and child maltreatment. Nebraska Symp. Motiv. 36: 259–366

Clark, M. S., Williamson, G. M. 1989. Moods and social judgement. See Wagner & Manstead 1989, pp. 347–70

Clore, G. L., Ortony, A. 1991. What more is there to emotion concepts than prototypes? J. Pers. Soc. Psychol. 60:48–50

Cohen, S., Williamson, G. M. 1991. Stress and infectious disease in humans. Psychol. Bull. 109:5–24

Cohn, J. F., Campbell, S. B., Matias, R., Hopkins, J. 1990. Face-to-face interactions of postpartum depressed and nondepressed mother-infant pairs at 2 months. Dev. Psychol. 261:15–23

Conway, M. A. 1990. Conceptual representation of emotions: The role of autobiographical memories. In Lines of Thinking: Reflections on the Psychology of Thought. Vol. 2. Skills, Emotion, Creative Processes, Individual Differences and Teaching Thinking, ed. K. J. Gilhooly, M. T. G. Keene, R. H. Logie, G. Erdos, pp. 133–43. Chichester: Wiley

Corter, C. M., Fleming, A. S. 1990. Maternal responsiveness in humans: emotional, cognitive and biological factors. Adv. Stud. Behav. 19:83–136

Costa, P. T., McCrae, R. R. 1988. Personality in adulthood: a six-year longitudinal study of self reports and spouse ratings on the NEO Personality Inventory. J. Pers. Soc. Psychol. 54:853–63

Crowell, J. A., Feldman, S. S. 1988. Mothers' internal models of relationships and children's behavioral and developmental status: a study of mother-child interaction. Child Dev. 59:1273–85

Cummings, E. M. 1987. Coping with background anger in early childhood. Child Dev. 58:976–84

Dahl, H. 1991. The key to understanding change: emotions as appetitive wishes and beliefs about their fulfilment. In Emotion, Psychotherapy and Change, ed. J. D. Saf-

ran, L. S. Greenberg, pp. 130–65. New York: Guilford Press

Darwin, C. 1872. The Expression of the Emotions in Man and the Animals. Reprinted 1965. Chicago, IL: Univ. Chigaco Press

Davidson, R. J. 1991. Anterior cerebral asymmetry and the nature of emotion. Brain Cognit. In press

De Rivera, J., Grinkis, C. 1986. Emotions as social relationships. Motiv. Emot. 10:351–69

De Sousa, R. 1987. The Rationality of Emotions. Cambridge, MA: MIT Press

Dimberg, U. 1990. Facial electromyography and emotional reactions. Psychophysiology 27:481–94

Dodge, K. A., Bates, J. E., Pettit, G. S. 1990. Mechanisms in the cycle of violence. Science 250:1678–83

Downey, G., Coyne, J. C. 1990. Children of depressed parents: an integrative review. Psychol. Bull. 108:50–76

Dunn, J. 1988. The Beginnings of Social Understanding. Cambridge, MA: Harvard Univ. Press

Dunn, J., Bretherton, I., Munn, P. 1987. Conversations about feeling states between mothers and their young children. Dev. Psychol. 23:132–39

Dyer, M. G. 1987. Emotions and their computations: three computer models. Cognit. Emot. 1:323–47

Egeland, B., Jacobvitz, D., Sroufe, L. A. 1988. Breaking the cycle of abuse. Child Dev. 59:1080–88

Ekman, P. 1989. The argument and evidence about universals in facial expressions of emotion. See Wagner & Manstead 1989, pp. 143–64

Ellis, C. 1991. Sociological introspection and emotional experience. Symb. Interact. 14: 23–50

Ellsworth, P. C., Smith, C. A. 1988. From appraisal to emotion: differences among unpleasant feelings. Motiv. Emot. 12:271–302

Fagot, B., Kavanagh, L. 1990. The prediction of antisocial behavior from avoidant attachment classification. Child Dev. 61:864–73

Feeney, J. A., Noller, P. 1990. Attachment style as a predictor of adult romantic relationships. J. Pers. Soc. Psychol. 58:281–91

Fernald, A. 1989. Intonation and communicative intent in mothers' speech to infants: Is the melody the message? Child Dev. 60:1497–510

Field, T., Healy, B., Goldstein, S., Perry, S., Bendel, D., et al. 1988. Infants of depressed mothers show "depressed" behavior even with nondepressed adults. Child Dev. 59:1569–79

Fischer, K. W., Shaver, P. R., Carnochan, P. 1990. How emotions develop and how they organize behavior. Cognit. Emot. 4:81–127

Fleming, A. S., Ruble, D. N., Flett, G. L., Shaul, D. L. 1988. Postpartum adjustment in first-time mothers: relations between mood, maternal attitudes and mother-infant interactions. *Dev. Psychol.* 24:71–81

Freud, S. 1905. Fragment of an analysis of a case of hysteria. In *The Complete Psychological Works of Sigmund Freud,* Standard Edition, ed. & transl. J. Strachey, 7:7–122. London: Hogarth Press

Fridlund, A. J., Ekman, P., Oster, H. 1987. Facial expressions of emotion: a review of the literature. In *Nonverbal Behavior and Communication,* ed. A. W. Siegman, S. Feldstein, pp. 143–224. Hillsdale, NJ: Erlbaum. 2nd ed.

Friedman, H. S., Booth-Kewley, S. 1987. The Disease-Prone Personality: a meta-analytic view of the construct. *Am. Psychol.* 42:539–55

Frijda, N. H. 1986. *The Emotions.* Cambridge: Cambridge Univ. Press

Frijda, N. H., Kuipers, P., ter Schure, E. 1989. Relations among emotion, appraisal, and emotional action readiness. *J. Pers. Soc. Psychol.* 57:212–28

Frijda, N. H., Mesquita, B., Sonnemans, J., van Goozen, S. 1991. The duration of affective phenomena or emotions, sentiments and passions. In *International Review of Research on Emotion,* ed. K. T. Strongman, Vol. 1. Chichester: Wiley

Gaver, W. W., Mandler, G. 1987. Play it again Sam: on liking music. *Cognit. Emot.* 1:259–82

Gnepp, J., Chilamkurti, C. 1988. Children's use of personality attibutions to predict other people's emotional and behavioral reactions. *Child Dev.* 59:743–54

Goldberg, S., Lojkasek, M., Gartner, G., Corter, C. 1989. Maternal responsiveness and social development in preterm infants. In *Maternal Responsiveness: Characteristics and consequences.* New Directions for Child Development, No. 43, ed. M. H. Bornstein, pp. 89–103. San Francisco: Jossey-Bass

Goldsmith, H. H., Alansky, J. A. 1987. Maternal and infant temperamental predictors of attachment: a meta-analytic review. *J. Consult. Clin. Psychol.* 55:805–16

Goldstein, M. J., Hand, I., Hahlweg, K. 1986. *Treatment of Schizophrenia: Family Assessment and Intervention.* Berlin: Springer-Verlag

Gordon, R. M. 1987. *The Structure of Emotions: Investigations in Cognitive Philosophy.* Cambridge: Cambridge Univ. Press

Gray, J. A. 1989. Fundamental systems of emotion in the mammalian brain. In *Coping with Uncertainty: Biological, Behavioral and Developmental Perspectives,* ed. D.

S. Palermo, pp. 173–95. Hillsdale, NJ: Erlbaum

Greenberg, L. S., Safran, J. D. 1989. Emotion in psychotherapy. *Am. Psychol.* 44:19–29

Grossmann, K., Fremmer-Bombik, E., Rudolph, J., Grossmann, K. E. 1988. Maternal attachment representations as related to patterns of infant-mother attachment and maternal care during the first year. In *Relationships within Families,* ed. R. A. Hinde, J. Stevenson-Hinde, pp. 241–60. Oxford: Oxford Univ. Press

Grossmann, K., Grossmann, K. E. 1990. Newborn behavior and later development. In *The Cultural Context of Infancy,* ed. J. K. Nugent, B. M. Lester, T. B. Brazelton, pp. 3–38. New York: Ablex

Grych, J. H., Fincham, F. D. 1990. Marital conflict and children's adjustment: a cognitive-contextual framework. *Psychol. Bull.* 108:267–90

Hamm, A. O., Vaitl, D., Lang, P. J. 1990. Fear conditioning, meaning and belongingness: a selective association analysis. *J. Abnorm. Psychol.* 98:395–406

Hammond, M. 1990. Affective maximization: a new macro-theory in the sociology of emotion. See Kemper 1990, pp. 58–81

Hansen, R. D., Hansen, C. H. 1988. Repression of emotionally tagged memories: the architecture of less complex emotions. *J. Pers. Soc. Psychol.* 55:811–18

Harrington, R., Fudge, H., Rutter, M., Pickles, A., Hill, J. 1990. Adult outcomes of childhood and adolescent depression: 1. Psychiatric status. *Arch. Gen. Psychiat.* 47:465–73

Harris, P. L. 1989. *Children and Emotion: The Development of Psychological Understanding.* Oxford: Blackwell

Harter, S., Buddin, B. J. 1987. Children's understanding of the simultaneity of two emotions: a five-stage developmental acquistion sequence. *Dev. Psychol.* 23:388–99

Haviland, J. M. 1984. Thinking and feeling in Woolf's writing: from childhood to adulthood. In *Emotions, Cognition and Behavior,* ed. C. E. Izard, J. Kagan, R. B. Zajonc, pp. 513–46. Cambridge: Cambridge Univ. Press

Haviland, J., Lelwica, M. 1987. The induced affect response: 10-week old infants' responses to three emotional expressions. *Dev. Psychol.* 23:97–104

Hinde, R. A. 1985. Was the "the expression of emotions" a misleading phrase? *Anim. Behav.* 33:985–92

Hochschild, A. R. 1983. *The Managed Heart: The Commercialization of Human Feeling.* Berkeley: Univ. Calif. Press

Hochschild, A. R. 1989. *The Second Shift:*

82   OATLEY & JENKINS

Working Parents and the Revolution at Home. New York: Viking-Penguin

Hohmann, G. W. 1966. Some effects of spinal cord lesions on experienced emotional feelings. *Psychophysiology* 3:143–56

Hooley, J. M., Teasdale, J. D. 1989. Predictors of relapse in unipolar despressives: expressed emotion, marital distress, and perceived criticism. *J. Abnorm. Psychol.* 98:229–35

Hops, H., Biglan, A., Sherman, L., Arthur, J., Friedman, L., Osteen, V. 1987. Home observations of family interaction of depressed women. *J. Consult. Clin. Psychol.* 55:341–46

Hornik, R., Gunnar, M. R. 1988. A descriptive analysis of infant social referencing. *Child Dev.* 59:626–34

Howell, S. 1981. Rules not words. In *Indiginous Psychologies: The Anthropology of the Self*, ed. P. Heelas, A. Lock, pp. 133–43. London: Academic

Isabella, R. A., Belsky, J., von Eye, A. 1989. Origins of infant-mother attachment: an examination of interactional synchrony during the infant's first year. *Dev. Psychol.* 25:12–21

Isen, A. M. 1990. The influence of positive and negative affect on cognitive organization: some implications for development. In *Psychological and Biological Processes in the Development of Emotion*, ed. N. Stein, B. Leventhal, T. Trabasso, pp. 75–94. Hillsdale, NJ: Erlbaum

Isen, A. M., Baron, R. A. 1991. Positive affect as a factor in organizational behavior. In *Research in Organizational Behavior*, ed. L. L. Cummings, B. L. Staw, 13:1–53. Greenwich, CT: JAI Press

Isen, A. M., Daubman, K. A., Nowicki, G. P. 1987. Positive affect facilitates creative problem solving. *J. Pers. Soc. Psychol.* 52:1122–31

Izard, C. 1990. Facial expressions and the regulation of emotions. *J. Pers. Soc. Psychol.* 58:487–98

Izard, C. E., Hembree, E. A., Huebner, R. R. 1987. Infants' expressions to acute pain: developmental change and stability of individual differences. *Dev. Psychol.* 23:105–13

James, W. 1884. What is an emotion? *Mind* 9:188–205

James, W. 1890. *The Principles of Psychology.* New York: Holt

Jenkins, J. M., Smith, M. A., Graham, P. J. 1989. Coping with parental quarrels. *J. Am. Acad. Child. Adoles. Psychiat.* 28:182–89

Jenkins, J. M., Smith, M. A. 1991. Marital disharmony and children's behavioural problems: aspects of a poor marriage that affect children adversely. *J. Child Psychol. Psychiat.* In press

Jones, S. S., Collins, K., Hong, H.-W. 1991. An audience effect on smile production in 10-month old infants. *Psychol. Sci.* 2:45–49

Kemper, T. D., ed. 1990. *Research Agendas in the Sociology of Emotions.* Albany: SUNY Press

Klimes-Dougan, B., Kistner, J. 1990. Physically abused preschoolers' responses to peers' distress. *Dev. Psychol.* 26:599–602

Koeningsberg, H. W., Handley, R. 1986. Expressed emotion: from predictive index to clinical construct. *Am. J. Psychiat.* 143:1361–73

La Freniere, P. J., Sroufe, L. A. 1985. Profiles of peer competence in the preschool: interrelations between measures, influence of social ecology, and relation to attachment history. *Dev. Psychol.* 21:56–69

Lamb, M. E., Thompson, R. A., Gardner, W., Charnov, E. L., Connell, J. P. 1985. *Infant-Mother Attachment: The Origins and Developmental Significance of Individual Differences in Strange Situation Behavior.* Hillsdale, NJ: Erlbaum

Lane, R. D., Schwartz, G. E. 1987. Levels of emotional awareness: a cognitive developmental theory and its application to psychopathology. *Am. J. Psychiat.* 144:133–43

Lang, P. J. 1988. What are the data of emotion? In *Cognitive Perspectives on Emotion and Motivation*, ed. V. Hamilton, G. H. Bower, N. H. Frijda, pp. 173–91. Kluwer: Dordrecht

Lang, P. J. 1987. Image as action: a reply to Watts and Blackstock. *Cognit. Emot.* 1:407–26

Lang, P. J., Bradley, M. M., Cuthbert, B. N. 1990. Emotion, attention and the startle reflex. *Psychol. Rev.* 97:377–95

Lazarus, R. L. 1991. Cognition and motivation in emotion. *Am. Psychol.* 46:352–67

Lee, C. L., Bates, J. E. 1985. Mother-child interaction at age two years and perceived difficult temperament. *Child Dev.* 56:1314–25

Leff, J., Vaughn, C. E. 1985. *Expressed Emotion in Families.* New York: Guilford Press

Lehnert, W. G., Vine, E. L. 1987. The role of affect in narrative structure. *Cognit. Emot.* 1:299–322

Levenson, R. W., Ekman, P., Friesen, W. 1990. Voluntary facial action generates emotion-specific autonomic nervous system activity. *Psychophysiology* 27:363–85

Levenson, R. W., Gottman, J. M. 1985. Physiological and affective predictors of change in relationship satisfaction. *J. Pers. Soc. Psychol.* 49:85–94

Leventhal, H., Scherer, K. R. 1987. The relationship of emotion to cognition: a functional approach to a semantic controversy. *Cognit. Emot.* 1:3–28

Leventhal, H., Tomarken, A. J. 1986. Emotion: today's problems. *Annu. Rev. Psychol.* 37:365–610

Levy, R. I., Wellenkamp, J. C. 1989. Methodology in the anthopological study of emotion. In *Emotion: Theory, Research and Experience*, ed. R. Plutchik, H. Kellerman, pp. 4:205–32. San Diego: Academic

Lewis, M. 1990. Self-knowledge and social development in early life. In *Handbook of Personality: Theory and Research*, ed. L. A. Pervin, pp. 277–300. New York: Guilford Press

Lewis, M., Alessandri, S. M., Sullivan, M. W. 1990. Violation of expectancy, loss of control and anger expressions in young infants. *Dev. Psychol.* 26:745–51

Lowe, J., Carroll, D. 1985. The effects of spinal injury on the intensity of emotional experience. *Br. J. Clin. Psychol.* 14:135–36

Luborsky, L., Crits-Christoph, P. 1990. *Understanding Transference: The CCRT Method*. New York: Basic Books

Lutkenhaus, P., Grossmann, K. E., Grossmann, K. 1985. Infant-mother attachment at twelve months and style of interaction with a stranger at the age of three years. *Child Dev.* 56:1538–42

Lutz, C. 1987. Goals, events and understanding in Ifaluk emotion theory. In *Cultural Models in Language and Thought*, ed. D. Holland, N. Quinn, pp. 290–312. Cambridge: Cambridge Univ. Press

Lutz, C. 1988. Ethnographic perspectives on the emotion lexicon. See Lang 1988, pp. 399–419

MacDowell, K. A., Mandler, G. 1989. Constructions of emotion: discrepancy, arousal and mood. *Motiv. Emot.* 13:105–24

MacLeod, C., Mathews, A., Tata, P. 1986. Attentional bias in emotional disorders. *J. Abnorm. Psychol.* 95:15–20

Main, M., George, C. 1985. Responses of abused and disadvantaged toddlers to distress in agemates: a study in the day care setting. *Dev. Psychol.* 21:407–12

Main, M., Kaplan, K., Cassidy, J. 1985. Security in infancy, childhood and adulthood: a move to the level of representation. In *Growing Points of Attachment Theory and Research*. Monogr. Soc. Res. Child Dev. 50, Ser. No. 209, pp. 66–104

Main, M., Solomon, J. 1986. Discovery of a disorganized/disoriented attachment pattern. In *Affective Development in Infancy*, ed. T. B. Brazelton , M. W. Yogman, pp. 95–124. Norwood, NJ: Ablex

Malatesta, C. Z., Cullver, C., Tesman, J., Shepard, B. 1989. The development of emotion expression during the first two years of life. In *Growing Points of Attachment Theory and Research*. Monogr. Soc. Res. Child Dev. 50, Ser. No. 219

Mandler, G. 1990. Interruption discrepancy theory: review and extensions. In *On the move: The Psychology of Change and Transition*, ed. S. Fisher, C. L. Cooper, pp. 13–32. Chicester: Wiley

Mangelsdorf, S., Gunnar, M., Kestenbaum, R., Lang, S., Andreas, D. 1990. Infant proneness to distress temperament, maternal personality, and mother-infant attachment: association and goodness of fit. *Child Dev.* 61:820–31

Mathews, A. M., May, J., Mogg, K., Eysenck, M. 1990. Attentional bias in anxiety: selective search of defective filtering. *J. Abnorm. Psychol.* 99:166–73

Matsuomoto, D. 1987. The role of facial response in the experience of emotion: more methodological problems and a meta-analysis. *J. Pers. Soc. Psychol.* 52:769–74

McHugo, G. J., Lanzetta, J. L., Sullivan, D. G., Masters, R. D., Englis, B. D. 1985. Emotional reactions to a political leader's expressive displays. *J. Pers. Soc. Psychol.* 49:1513–29

McNally, R. J., Kaspi, S. P., Riemann, B. C., Zeitlin, S. B. 1990. Selective processing of threat cues in posttraumatic stress disorder. *J. Abnorm. Psychol.* 99:398–402

Miall, D. 1989. Beyond the schema given: comprehension of literary narratives. *Cognit. Emot.* 3:55–78

Miyake, K., Chen, S.-J., Campos, J. J. 1985. Infant temperament, mother's mode of interaction, and attachment in Japan: an interim report. In *Growing Points of Attachment Theory and Research*. Monogr. Soc. Res. Child Dev. 50, Ser. No. 209

Nisbett, R. E., Wilson, T. D. 1977. Telling more than we can know: verbal reports on mental processes. *Psychol. Rev.* 84:231–59

Oatley, K. 1992. *Best Laid Schemes: The Psychology of Emotions*. New York: Cambridge Univ. Press

Oatley, K., Bolton, W. 1985. A social-cognitive theory of depression in reaction to life events. *Psychol. Rev.* 92:372–88

Oatley, K., Johnson-Laird, P. N. 1987. Towards a cognitive theory of emotion. *Cognit. Emot.* 1:29–50

Ohman, A. 1986. Face the beast and fear the face: animal and social fears as prototypes for evolutionary analyses of emotion. *Psychophysiology* 23:123–45

Oppenheim, D., Sagi, A., Lamb, M. E. 1988. Infant-adult attachments on the kibbutz and their relation to socioemotional development 4 years later. *Dev. Psychol.* 24:427–33

Ortony, A., Clore, G. L., Collins, A. 1988. *The Cognitive Structure of Emotions*. New York: Cambridge Univ. Press

Panksepp, J. 1989. The psychobiology of

emotions: the animal side of human feelings. *Exp. Brain Res.* 18:31–55

Parrott, W. G., Sabini, J. 1990. Mood and memory under natural conditions: evidence for mood incongruent recall. *J. Pers. Soc. Psychol.* 59:321–36

Pfeiffer, R. 1988. Artificial Intelligence models of emotion. See Lang 1988, pp. 287–343

Phillips, R. D., Izard, C. 1988. Understanding facial expressions of emotion. In *Handbook of Research on Face Processing*, ed. A. W. Young, H. D. Ellis, pp. 163–69. New York: Elsevier

Plomin, R., Rende, R. 1991. Human behavioral genetics. *Annu. Rev. Psychol.* 42:161–90

Plutchik, R. 1991. Emotions and evolution. In *International Review of Studies on Emotion*, ed. K. T. Strongman, 1:37–58. Chichester: Wiley

Plutchik, R., Kellerman, H. 1989. *Emotion: Theory, Research and Experience*, Vol. 4. San Diego: Academic

Quinton, D., Rutter, M. 1985. Family pathology and child psychiatric disorder: a 4-year prospective study. In *Longitudinal Studies in Child Psychology and Psychiatry*, ed. A. R. Nicol, pp. 91–134. Chichester: Wiley

Quinton, D., Rutter, M. 1988. *Parenting Breakdown: The Making and Breaking of Intergenerational Links*. Aldershot: Avebury

Quinton, D., Rutter, M., Gulliver, L. 1990. Continuities in psychiatric disorders from childhood to adulthood in the children of psychiatric patients. See Robins & Rutter 1990, pp. 259–28

Radke-Yarrow, M., Cummings, E. M., Kuczynski, L., Chapman, M. 1985. Patterns of attachment in two-and three-year-olds in normal families and families with parental depression. *Child Dev.* 56:884–93

Rahe, R. H. 1988. Recent life changes and coronary heart disease: 10 years research. In *Handbook of Life Stress, Cognition and Health*, ed. S. Fisher, J. Reason, pp. 317–33. Chichester: Wiley

Richman, N., Graham, P. J., Stevenson, J. 1982. *Preschool to School*. London: Academic

Ridgeway, D., Waters, E., Kucza, S. A. 1985. Acquisition of emotion-descriptive language: receptive and productive vocabulary norms for ages 18 months to 6 years. *Dev. Psychol.* 21:901–8

Rimé, B., Philipott, P., Cisamolo, D. 1990. Social schemata of peripheral changes in emotion. *J. Pers. Soc. Psychol.* 59:38–49

Robins, L. N. 1978. Sturdy childhood predictors of adult antisocial behavior: replications from longitudinal studies. *Psychol. Med.* 8:611–22

Robins, L. N. 1986. The consequences of conduct disorder in girls. In *Development of Antisocial and Prosocial Behavior*, ed. D. Olweus, J. Block, M. Radke-Yarrow, pp. 385–414. Orlando, FL: Academic

Robins, L. N., Rutter, M. 1990. *Straight and Devious Pathways from Childhood to Adulthood*. Cambridge: Cambridge Univ. Press

Rolls, E. 1990. A theory of emotion and its application to understanding the neural basis of emotion. *Cognit. Emot.* 4:161–90

Roseman, I. J., Spindel, M. S., Jose, P. E. 1990. Appraisals of emotion-eliciting events: testing a theory of discrete emotions. *J. Pers. Soc. Psychol.* 59:899–915

Rosenstein, D., Oster, H. 1988. Differential facial responses to four basic tastes in newborns. *Child Dev.* 59:1555–68

Rozin, P., Fallon, A. E. 1987. A perspective on disgust. *Psychol. Rev.* 94:23–41

Russell, J. A. 1991. In defense of a prototype approach to emotion concepts. *J. Pers. Soc. Psychol.* 60:37–47

Saarni, C. 1991. Children's emotional expressive behaviors as regulators of others' happy and sad emotional states. *New Dir. Child Dev.* In press

Schachter, S., Singer, J. 1962. Cognitive, social and physiological determinants of emotional state. *Psychol. Rev.* 69:379–99

Scheff, T. 1987. Creativity and repetition: a theory of the coarse emotions. In *Advances in Psychoanalytic Sociology*, ed. J. Rabow, G. Platt, M. Goldman, pp. 70–100. Malibor, FL: Kreiger

Scherer, K. R. 1986. Vocal affect expression. A review and a model for future research. *Psychol. Bull.* 99:143–65

Scherer, K. R., Wallbott, H. G., Summerfield, A. B. 1986. *Experiencing Emotion: A Cross-Cultural Study*. Cambridge: Cambridge Univ. Press

Schiff, B. B., Lamon, M. 1989. Inducing emotion by unilateral contraction of facial muscles: a new look at hemispheric specialization and the experience of emotion. *Neuropsychologia* 27:923–25

Shaver, P., Hazan, C., Bradshaw, D. 1988. Love as attachment: the integration of three behavioral systems. See Berscheid 1988, pp. 68–99

Shaver, P., Schwartz, J., Kirson, D., O'Connor, C. 1987. Emotion knowledge: further exploration of a prototype approach. *J. Pers. Soc. Psychol.* 52:1061–86

Shields, S. A. 1987. Women, men, and the dilemma of emotion. In *Review of Personality and Social Psychology: Sex and Gender*, ed. P. Shaver, C. Hendrick, pp. 229–50. Beverly Hills: Sage

Simons, R. L., Whitbeck, L. B., Conger, R., Chyi-In, W. 1991. Intergenerational transmission of harsh parenting. *Dev. Psychol.* 27:159–71

Smiley, P., Huttenlocher, J. 1989. Young children's acquisition of emotion concepts. In *Children's Understanding of Changing Emotional States,* ed. C. Saarni, P. L. Harris, pp. 27–49. New York: Cambridge Univ. Press

Smith, C. A. 1989. Dimensions of appraisal and physiological response in emotion. *J. Pers. Soc. Psychol.* 56:339–53

Smith, P. B., Pederson, D. R. 1988. Maternal sensitivity and patterns of infant-mother attachment. *Child Dev.* 59:1097–1101

Solomon, R. C. 1984. Getting angry: the Jamesian theory of emotion in anthropology. In *Culture Theory: Essays on Mind, Self and Emotion,* ed. R. A. Schweder, R. A. LeVine, pp. 238–54. Cambridge: Cambridge Univ. Press

Sorce, J. F., Emde, R. N., Campos, J. J., Klinnert, M. D. 1985. Maternal emotional signalling: its effect on the visual cliff behavior of 1-year-olds. *Dev. Psychol.* 21:195–200

Spielberger, C. D., Krasner, S. S., Solomon, E. P. 1988. The experience, expression and control of anger. In *Health Psychology: Individual Differences and Stress,* ed. M. P. Janissa, pp. 89–108. New York: Springer Verlag

Stearns, P. 1989. Suppressing unpleasant emotions: the development of a Twentieth-Century American Style. In *Social History and Issues in Human Consciousness,* ed. A. E. Barnes, P. N. Stearns, pp. 230–61. New York: New York Univ. Press

Stein, N. L., Levine, L. J. 1989. The causal organisation of emotional knowledge: a developmental study. *Cognit. Emot.* 3:343–78

Stein, N. L., Trabasso, T. 1989. Children's understanding of changing emotional states. In *Children's Understanding of Changing Emotional States,* ed. C. Saarni, P. L. Harris, pp. 50–77. New York: Cambridge Univ. Press

Stemmler, G. 1989. The autonomic differentiation of emotions revisited: convergent and discriminant validation. *Psychophysiology* 26:617–32

Stern, D. N. 1985. *Interpersonal World of the Infant.* New York: Basic Books

Sturgeon, D., Kuipers, L., Berkowitz, R., Turpin, G., Leff, J. 1981. Psychophysiological responses of schizophrenic patients

to high and low expressed emotion relatives. *Br. J. Psychiat.* 138:40–45

Thoits, P. 1985. Self labelling processes in mental illness: the role of emotional deviance. *Am. J. Sociol.* 91:221–49

Thoits, P. 1989. The sociology of emotions. *Annu. Rev. Sociol.* 15:317–42

Thompson, R. A., Connell, J. P., Bridges, L. J. 1988. Temperament, emotion, and social interactive behavior in the strange situation: a component process analysis of attachment system functioning. *Child Dev.* 59:1102–10

Tomkins, S. S. 1979. Script theory: differential magnification of affect. *Nebraska Symp. Motiv.* 26:201–40

Wagner, H., Manstead, A. 1989. *Handbook of Social Psychophysiology.* Chichester: Wiley

Walden, T. A., Ogan, T. A. 1988. The development of social referencing. *Child Dev.* 59:1230–40

Wallbott, H. G., Scherer, K. R. 1986. Cues and channels in emotion recognition. *J. Pers. Soc. Psychol.* 51:690–99

Wegman, C. 1985. *Psychoanalysis and Cognitive Psychology: A Formulation of Freud's Earliest Theory.* London: Academic

Widiger, T. A., Trull, T. J. 1991. Diagnosis and clinical assessment. *Annu. Rev. Psychol.* 42:109–33

Wiener, B. 1986. *An Attributional Theory of Motivation and Emotion.* New York: Springer

Wiener, B., Graham, S. 1989. Understanding the motivational role of affect: life-span research from an attributional perspective. *Cognit. Emot.* 3:401–19

Williams, J. M. G., Watts, F. N., MacLeod, C., Mathews, A. M. 1988. *Cognitive Psychology and the Emotional Disorders.* Chichester: Wiley

Zahn Waxler, C., Radke-Yarrow, M. 1991. The origins of empathic concern. *Motiv. Emot.* In press

Zajonc, R. B., Murphy, S. T., Inglehart, M. 1989. Feeling and facial efference: implications of the vascular theory of emotion. *Psychol. Rev.* 96:395–416

Zarbatany, L., Lamb, M. E. 1985. Social referencing as a function of information source: mothers versus strangers. *Infant Behav. Dev.* 8:25–33

Zeitlin, H. 1990. Current interests in child-adult psychopathological continuities. *J. Child Psychol. Psychiat.* 31:671–79

Annu. Rev. Psychol. 1992. 43:87–131

BEHAVIORAL DECISION RESEARCH: A CONSTRUCTIVE PROCESSING PERSPECTIVE

John W. Payne and James R. Bettman

Fuqua School of Business, Duke University, Durham, North Carolina 27706

Eric J. Johnson

Wharton School, University of Pennsylvania, Philadelphia, Pennsylvania 19104

KEY WORDS: judgment, choice, uncertainty, preference, values

CONTENTS

INTRODUCTION

Almost 40 years ago, Ward Edwards (1954) provided the first major review for psychologists of research on decision behavior done by economists, statisticians, and philosophers. He argued that work by economists and others on both normative and predictive decision models should be important to psychologists interested in judgment and choice. About the same time, Herbert Simon (1955) argued that if economists were interested in understanding actual decision behavior, then research would need to focus on the perceptual, cognitive, and learning factors that cause human decision behavior to deviate from that predicted by the normative "economic man" model. Simon emphasized that the limited computational capabilities of the decision-maker interact with the complexity of task environments to produce bounded rationality— i.e. decision behavior that reflects information processing bounds. As a consequence, Simon suggested that actual decision behavior might not even approximate the behavior predicted by normative models of decision tasks (Simon 1978).

Nearly four decades later, a clear and separate area of inquiry has emerged, which we refer to as Behavioral Decision Research (BDR). This area is intensely interdisciplinary, employing concepts and models from economics, social and cognitive psychology, statistics, and other fields. It is also nearly unique among subdisciplines in psychology, because it often proceeds by testing the descriptive adequacy of normative theories of judgment and choice; in doing so, it makes substantial use of psychological concepts in general, and cognitive mechanisms in particular.

This chapter reviews behavioral decision research for the period 1983– 1991. We have noticed several trends in the course of our review. First, behavioral decision research concepts and methods are being widely adopted. A substantial amount of research in the area, for example, is conducted by scholars with primary interests in many applied areas, including accounting, environmental studies, finance, law, marketing, and medicine (Ashton et al 1989; Froot & Thaler 1990; Noll & Krier 1990; Schwartz & Griffin 1986; Simonson 1989). In addition, researchers are using behavioral decision concepts to gain insights into such complex, multiperson phenomena as negotiations and the behavior of experimental markets (Carroll et al 1988; Camerer

1992). Second, there is a growing focus on the problem structuring and learning elements of decision behavior, although the amount of such research is still small. Examples include research on alternative generation (Gettys et al 1987; Keller & Ho 1988) and studies of how cues for inference are learned from outcome feedback (Klayman 1988). Third, the richness of methods and problem descriptions used in decision research continues to increase. For example, process-tracing techniques, case methods, computer-game simulations, and even the presentation of data via radar screens are being used (Ford et al 1989; Eisenhardt 1989; Brehmer 1990; Lusk & Hammond 1991). These trends can be found in the thousand-plus articles and chapters that have been written on behavioral decision topics during the past eight years. However, given page constraints, our review is selective rather than exhaustive; we focus on a fourth major trend of much recent behavioral decision research: a theoretical concern with the constructive nature of judgment and choice. See Abelson & Levi 1985, Slovic et al 1988, and Stevenson et al 1990 for reviews of behavioral decision research that cover a longer time span and offer alternative perspectives.

THE CONSTRUCTIVE NATURE OF PREFERENCES AND BELIEFS

An underlying theme of much recent decision research is that preferences for and beliefs about objects or events of any complexity are often constructed—not merely revealed—in the generation of a response to a judgment or choice task (Slovic et al 1990). March (1978) attributes the constructiveness of preferences to the same limits on information processing capacity emphasized by Simon. In his words, "Human beings have unstable, inconsistent, incompletely evoked, and imprecise goals at least in part because human abilities limit preference orderliness" (March 1978:598). March's argument about preference applies to belief judgments as well, and the constructive view is a major organizing theme of this review.

The idea of constructive preferences goes beyond a mere denial that observed preferences result from reference to a master list in memory. The notion of constructive preferences means as well that preferences are not necessarily generated by some consistent and invariant algorithm such as expected value calculation (Tversky et al 1988). It appears that decision-makers have a repertoire of methods for identifying their preferences and developing their beliefs. These multiple methods or strategies result from both experience and training (Fong et al 1986; Kruglanski 1989; Larrick et al 1990).

Descriptive research on decision-making processes has shown that the information and strategies used to construct preferences or beliefs appear to be highly contingent upon and predictable from a variety of task, context, and individual-difference factors. Task factors are general characteristics of a decision problem, such as response mode (judgment or choice, for example), which do not depend upon the particular values of the alternatives. Context factors such as similarity of alternatives, on the other hand, are associated with the particular values of the alternatives. Task and context factors cause different aspects of the problem to be salient and evoke different processes for combining information. Thus, characteristics of the decision problem, such as the response mode or similarity, can evoke different strategies that at least partially determine the preferences and beliefs we observe. Further, the characteristics to which people are sensitive are from a normative perspective often, although certainly not always, irrelevant (Tversky & Kahneman 1986; Tversky et al 1988). Consequently, people sometimes ignore normatively relevant information such as base-rates, and sometimes use base-rate information in an appropriate fashion. Hence an important question in current decision research is the identification of the task conditions that determine when normatively important information like base-rates will and will not be used (Gigerenzer et al 1988; Ginossar & Trope 1987).

Also related to the constructive nature of decision behavior are the multiple and sometimes conflicting meta-goals adopted for the decision episode—e.g. maximize accuracy or justifiability; or minimize effort, regret, or conflict (Einhorn & Hogarth 1981; Tetlock 1985). Finally, how a solution to a decision problem is constructed will also, of course, be a function of individual-difference factors such as processing capacities (Bettman et al 1990) and prior knowledge or expertise (Shanteau 1988). Another important ongoing issue is the extent to which individual differences in values and beliefs are related across task and context changes (MacCrimmon & Wehrung 1990; Schoemaker 1990).

Thus many current issues in behavioral decision research can be related to the notion of the constructive nature of human preferences and beliefs and the contingent use of multiple approaches for solving decision problems. We use this theme in organizing our review. We first consider two central elements of decisions—preferences and beliefs about uncertain events—focusing on the use of multiple strategies in such judgments and the factors that influence which strategies are used. Then we consider decision-making under risk and uncertainty, again focusing on contingent strategy use. This prevalence of evidence for contingent strategy use leads us to consider possible frameworks explaining such contingencies. Finally, we consider how the research and concepts reviewed can be applied to improve assessments of preferences, beliefs, and decisions.

PREFERENCES

Common sense suggests that good decisions are consistent decisions and that small changes in how a question is asked or how options are presented should not change what we prefer. In more formal terms, we would expect our choices and judgments to possess procedural invariance: Normatively equivalent procedures for assessing preferences should result in the same preference order (Tversky et al 1988). Similarly, we would expect descriptive invariance to hold: Different representations of the same choice problem should yield the same preference (Tversky & Kahneman 1986). As discussed below, a great deal of research demonstrates that both procedural and descriptive invariance often fail to hold. In fact, Shafer (1986) has called the failure of decisions to be invariant across procedures and descriptions "the most fundamental result of three decades of empirical investigation" (p. 464) in behavioral decision-making.

Why does invariance fail? A constructive view of decision-making suggests at least three sources of such failures. First, decisions often involve conflicting values, where we must decide how much we value one attribute relative to another. In trying to deal with such conflicts, individuals often adopt different strategies in different situations, potentially leading to variance in preferences. Second, decisions are often complex, containing many attributes or alternatives. Since these problems are simplified by decision-makers in different ways, failures of invariance might be related to task complexity. Finally, although we may know what we get when we choose an option, we may not know how we feel about it. A prestigious Ivy League school may offer a competitive and high-pressure graduate program, but we might be uncertain about how we would like that environment. Hence, invariance may fail because of uncertainty in values, even when we know what we will receive.

Below, we consider the underlying theme of the constructive nature of judgment and choice. We review investigations of how individuals respond to decisions made difficult by conflicting values, decision complexity, and uncertainty in values. In addition, we consider how individuals may restructure problems or construct arguments in assessing their preferences.

Conflicting Values

Conflict among values arises because decisions generally involve a choice among options where no option best meets all of our objectives. Conflict has long been recognized as a major source of decision difficulty (Shepard 1964). The presence of conflict and the fact that a rule for resolving the conflict cannot readily be drawn from memory are also reasons why decision-making, even in the simplest laboratory tasks, is often characterized by tentativeness and the use of relatively weak methods (heuristics). The use of such heuristics is often associated with novice-like problem solving rather than the kind of recognize-and-calculate processes associated with expertise (Chi et al 1988; Langley et al 1987).

In cases where there is clearly a dominating option—i.e. option A is at least as good as option B on all valued attributes and strictly better on one or more attributes—there is no conflict, and the choice of the dominating option is easy. In fact, the idea that the dominant option should be chosen in such a case is the most widely accepted principle of rational decision-making. When the relation of dominance is highly transparent, people indeed choose the dominating option; however, the principle of dominance can be violated if the relation of dominance is masked by the way a decision is presented (Tversky & Kahneman 1986) or by erroneous beliefs such as the fixed-pie assumption in negotiations (Bazerman 1990).

How do people make decisions among multiattribute alternatives when no alternative dominates, and hence conflict exists? People use a variety of evaluation strategies, some of which can be thought of as conflict confronting and others as conflict avoiding (Hogarth 1987). The most common assumption is that such decisions are made by considering the extent to which one is willing to trade off more of one valued attribute (e.g. economy) against less of another valued attribute (e.g. safety). That is, conflict among values is confronted and resolved. A decision model often used to represent the trading-off process is the weighted additive value model, in which a measure of the relative importance (weight) of the attribute is multiplied by the attribute value for the particular alternative and the products are summed over all attributes. The alternative with the highest overall evaluation is chosen.

Exactly how people think of "weights" in such decisions is the subject of investigation. There is some evidence that weights are sometimes interpreted in a local sense: The relative weights reflect the ranges of attribute values across the alternatives in the choice set—i.e. the greater the range, the greater the importance of the attribute (Goldstein 1990). At other times, subjects interpret the weight given to an attribute more globally—e.g. safety might always be viewed as much more important than costs, without much consideration of local ranges of values (Beattie & Baron 1992).

To the extent that people make decisions consistent with an additive model, the key research problems are to measure the weights and values a person assigns to the attributes describing the decision alternatives. Unfortunately, the tradeoffs people exhibit among conflicting attributes are highly contingent on a host of task and context factors. Individuals also use strategies other than weighted adding in many situations, depending upon task and context factors. Many of the heuristics used are noncompensatory, meaning that a good value on one attribute cannot compensate for a bad value on another. Hence, tradeoffs may not be made explicitly in many cases.

PROCEDURAL VARIANCE   One of the most important task variables demonstrating procedural variance in preference assessments is the method by which the decision-maker is asked to respond. Different response modes can lead to differential weighting of attributes and different preference assessments. Research on choice vs matching tasks and on preference reversals documents such response mode effects.

Choice vs Matching   An excellent illustration of the contingent weighing of attributes as a function of response mode is provided by the so-called "prominence effect" investigated by Tversky et al (1988). They show that the predominant attribute (e.g. lives saved in comparison to the cost of a safety program) is given even more weight when preferences are assessed using a choice mode than when preferences are assessed using a matching task.

Let us illustrate the difference between a matching task and a choice task. Imagine that you are asked to consider two programs for dealing with traffic accidents. The programs are both described to you both in terms of yearly dollar costs and in terms of the number of casualties per year each will result in: Program A is expected to lead to 570 casualties and cost \$12 million, while Program B is expected to lead to 500 casualties and cost \$X. In a matching task you are asked to provide an estimate X for the cost for program B— presumably an amount greater than \$12 million—that will make Program B equal in overall value to Program A.

In a choice task, on the other hand, values for the cost and casualties of both programs are given (e.g. you know all the values in the example above, and you know that Program B will cost \$55 million). You are asked to choose the program you prefer. Most people choose B over A in this situation, implying that saving 70 lives is more important than saving \$43 million. In a matching task, on the other hand, people estimate X at less than \$55 million, implying that a cost difference of less than \$43 million is equivalent to the difference in casualties of 70. Hence, the tradeoffs when performing matching tasks differ from those when performing choice tasks.

Tversky et al (1988) suggest that different heuristics or computational schemes are likely to be used in the two kinds of tasks. Of the two, choice is thought to involve more qualitative reasoning, such as that involved in the lexicographic choice strategy (i.e. select the option that is ordinally superior on the most important attribute). Lexicographic reasoning is viewed as both cognitively easier than explicit tradeoffs and easier to justify to oneself and others. A lexicographic strategy for choice also avoids rather than confronts conflict. Matching, on the other hand, requires a more quantitative assessment. In order to perform the matching task, one must consider the size of the intervals for both attributes and the relative weights of the attributes.

More generally, Tversky et al suggest a principle of strategy compatibility between the nature of the required response, ordinal or cardinal, and the types of reasoning employed by a decision-maker. Choice, for example, requires an ordinal response and is hypothesized to evoke arguments (processes) based on the ordering of the attribute values.

Preference reversals   As discussed by Fischer & Hawkins (1989), an idea related to, but distinct from, the concept of strategy compatibility is that of "scale compatibility," which states that the weight of a stimulus attribute is enhanced by its compatibility with the response scale. The idea of scale compatibility has been in the literature for some time and has played a major role in elucidating the classic preference reversal phenomenon (Lichtenstein & Slovic 1971). In the standard preference-reversal paradigm, two bets of comparable expected values are evaluated. One of the bets offers a high probability of winning a small amount of money while the other bet offers a low probability of winning a much larger amount of money. When asked to choose between the two bets, most people prefer the bet with the higher probability of winning. When asked to bid on (assign a cash equivalent to) each bet separately, most people assign a higher value to the low-probability, high-payoff bet. Tversky et al (1990) show that overpricing of the low-probability, high-payoff bet, as suggested by the scale compatibility of payoff amount with the bid response mode, is a major cause of preference reversals (see also Bostic et al 1990). Schkade & Johnson (1989), using a computer-based method for monitoring information-acquisition behavior, also found support for the notion that scale compatibility is a factor underlying preference reversals.

Scale compatibility clearly plays a role in preference reversals; however, other mechanisms may also contribute to preference reversals. For example, Goldstein & Einhorn (1987) assume that the evaluation process is the same for all response modes. They locate the principal source of procedural variance in the expression of the underlying internal evaluation on different response scales.

Hershey & Schoemaker (1985) suggest that preference reversals also may be understood in terms of how individuals reframe decisions with certain response modes. Suppose that a person is given a sure-thing option and a gamble offering the possibility of either a specified greater-amount outcome or a specified lesser-amount outcome, and that the person is asked to set (match) a probability p of obtaining the greater amount in order to make the sure-thing option and the gamble equal in value. Hershey & Schoemaker suggest that the person uses the amount of the sure thing as a reference point, with the two outcomes of the gamble then coded as a gain and as a loss. With other response modes the framing of the problem is assumed to be different (see Bell 1985 for the suggestion that the expected value (EV) of a gamble serves as a natural reference point in a bidding mode). Casey (1991) emphasizes the related idea of an aspiration level in his explanation of a new form of preference reversal. Finally, Johnson & Schkade (1989), using process-tracing methods, show that the more an individual uses a reframing and an anchoring and adjustment strategy, the greater the extent to which value assessments differ across response modes. We have more to say about framing effects and anchoring and adjustment below.

As suggested by the strategy-compatibility hypothesis discussed above, preference reversals may also be due to changes in evaluation processes as a function of response mode (e.g. Johnson et al 1988; Mellers et al 1992; Schkade & Johnson 1989). People may use different strategies to generate each type of response, thus leading to reversals. In a series of experiments pitting strategy compatibility and scale compatibility against one another, Fischer & Hawkins (1989) found strategy compatibility effects to be stronger as explanations of procedural variance.

To summarize, various preference-reversal explanations locate the cause of the phenomenon at either the framing, strategy selection, weighting of information, or expression of preferences stage of decisions. However, as suggested by several authors (e.g. Goldstein & Einhorn 1987), the preference-reversal phenomenon may be so robust because there are multiple underlying causes, each of which may be operative in some situations but not others. In any event, it is now clear that the answer to how much you like a decision option can depend greatly on how you ask the question.

DESCRIPTIVE VARIANCE   Research conducted in the past eight years confirms that the manner in which problems are presented affects preferences, even when the descriptions or presentations are normatively equivalent (Tversky & Kahneman 1986). Two major streams of research that demonstrate descriptive variance are investigations of framing effects and effects of information presentation.

Framing effects   Framing involves the determination of the effective acts, contingencies, and outcomes of a decision. Framing is influenced by how the decision problem is presented and by the norms, habits, and expectations of the decision-maker (Tversky & Kahneman 1986). Tversky & Kahneman (1981) illustrated the impact of presentation on framing by showing that simple wording changes—e.g. from describing outcomes in terms of lives saved to describing them in terms of lives lost—can lead to different preferences. Numerous other researchers have demonstrated such wording effects (Fagley & Miller 1987; Huber et al 1987; Kramer 1989; Levin & Gaeth 1988; Puto 1987). These studies most often distinguish between (*a*) framing that leads one to code outcomes as gains and (*b*) frames that result in outcomes' being coded as losses. It is clear that people treat negative consequences and positive consequences differently. Tversky & Kahneman (1992) have emphasized the importance of this difference in the concept of loss aversion, which states that the impact of a difference on a dimension is greater when that difference is seen as a loss than when it is seen as a gain. We believe that this concept will prove important in understanding decision behavior.

More generally, however, a complete theory of framing has proven difficult to formalize, although progress has been made in identifying important elements of framing. For instance, Thaler (1985; Thaler & Johnson 1990) has suggested that framing may be an active process rather than simply a passive response to the decision problem as given. He examined the hypothesis that people prefer outcomes framed to make the options appear the most pleasant or the least unpleasant. Using the prospect theory value function (Kahneman & Tversky 1979) as a starting point, Thaler (1985) argued that people generally prefer to have gains kept separate (segregated) and to have all negative outcomes integrated (packaged together) into one total.

Thaler & Johnson (1990) term this view *hedonic editing* and asked whether people actively edit options to a more pleasant frame. Their study examined how prior gains and losses (e.g. sunk costs) influence subsequent choices (Arkes & Blumer 1985; Laughhunn & Payne 1984; Staw 1981). Their results suggest a more complex picture of hedonic editing; for example, people apparently prefer to have financial losses separated temporally. They also report a "break-even" effect, in which the impact of a prior loss on risk-taking is influenced by whether the choice of a new gamble will or will not offer the possibility of getting back to some original reference position or break-even point.

Linville & Fischer (1991) also provide evidence that the original hedonic-framing hypothesis does not account for peoples' preferences for temporally separating or combining good and bad news. They find that people prefer to segregate bad news but to combine a positive and negative event on the same day. They suggest that frames are driven by the need to conserve the limited, but renewable, physiological, cognitive, and social resources available to people for dealing with emotional events. Like Thaler, they see framing as at times a proactive process.

The concept of a reference point, target level, or aspiration level that contributes to framing effects, and perhaps to procedural variance, is a venerable one in theories of decision-making (Siegel 1957; Simon 1955).

Simon, for example, suggested that individuals can simplify choice problems by coding an outcome as being one of two types: satisfactory if the outcome is above the aspiration level or unsatisfactory if it is below. Substantial evidence indicates that choice depends on the reference level used in the coding of outcomes (Fischer et al 1986; Payne et al 1984; Tversky & Kahneman 1990). A particularly important form of reference-level effect is the status quo bias (Samuelson & Zeckhauser 1988; Kahneman et al 1990), in which the retention of the status quo option is favored over other options. Recently, Hogarth & Einhorn (1991) have emphasized the role of a reference point in the encoding of evidence for the purpose of updating beliefs.

Framing effects are dramatic examples of descriptive variance. Hence, understanding how frames are selected would be very important. Fischhoff (1983) found it hard to predict when certain frames would be used. However, Puto (1987) was able to relate the selection of reference points to expectations and objectives in an industrial buying context. Given the crucial nature of framing effects in decision behavior, much more research on this topic is needed.

Information presentation effects   Differences in modes of information presentation also affect decision behavior. For example, Stone & Schkade (1991) found that representing attribute values with words led to less compensatory processing than representing the values numerically. Wallsten and his colleagues (Budescu et al 1988; Erev & Cohen 1990; Wallsten 1990) have carried out an important related series of experiments testing differences between numerical and verbal representations of probability information. In general, people prefer to receive information about probabilities of events in numerical form but prefer to express the probabilities of events to others in words (e.g. doubtful, likely).

The format or structure of information presentation also can influence how information is processed. Jarvenpaa (1989, 1990), extending an earlier result by Bettman & Kakkar (1977), found that how information was processed tended to be consistent with how graphic displays were organized—i.e. by alternative or by attribute. MacGregor & Slovic (1986) also show that people will use a less important cue in predictive judgments simply because it is more salient in the display. While the finding that information acquisition proceeds in a fashion consistent with display format is not surprising (see Slovic 1972, for an early statement of this idea), it does have important implications both for aiding decision behavior using relatively simple changes in information presentation and for the design of graphics for computer-based decision support systems.

Another series of experiments has dealt with a third aspect of information presentation, the completeness of information displays (Dube-Rioux & Russo

1988; Hirt & Castellan 1988; Weber et al 1988). Those studies show that the apparent completeness of a display can blind a decision-maker to the possibility that important information is missing from a problem description (a result earlier obtained by Fischhoff et al 1978). Individuals may respond differently to the problem if they do not realize that information is missing.

Finally, Fischer et al (1987) found that when a more fundamental attribute (e.g, health effects) is represented by a proxy attribute (e.g. levels of pollutants in the air) there was a strong bias toward overweighting the proxy attribute (relative to an expectation model of the value of the proxy). Fischer et al suggest that this bias is due to the inference processes people use to construct values when they do not have well-articulated preferences for tradeoffs among attributes.

Complexity of Decisions

Studies showing procedural and descriptive variance in how individuals deal with conflicting values provide clear examples of constructive decision behavior; however, other striking examples exist of multiple strategy use and contingent judgment and choice. Many of these examples concern how people adapt their decision processes to deal with decision complexity. The primary hypothesis underlying most of this research is that the more complex the decision problem, the more people will use simplifying decision heuristics. This hypothesis has been supported by a number of studies conducted during the past eight years. Decision complexity has been manipulated using the number of alternatives, number of attributes, and time pressure, among other factors.

Perhaps the most well-established task-complexity effect is the impact of changes in the number of alternatives available. When faced with two alternatives, people use compensatory decision strategies like the weighted additive model; these involve trading off a better value on one attribute against a poorer value on another. However, when faced with multi-alternative decision tasks, people prefer noncompensatory choice strategies (Biggs et al 1985; Billings & Marcus 1983; Johnson et al 1989; Klayman 1985; Onken et al 1985; Sundstrom 1987).

Varying the amount of attribute information is another way to manipulate decision complexity. A number of studies, though not all, indicate that decision quality can decrease with increases in the number of attributes after a certain level of complexity has been reached (Keller & Staelin 1987; Shields 1983; Sundstrom 1987). These studies of "information overload" effects have been criticized on a variety of methodological grounds (e.g. Meyer & Johnson 1989). Nonetheless, it is clear that people use selective attention to deal with increased task complexity. The crucial question is how people focus on the most important information and avoid getting distracted by irrelevant information. Grether & Wilde (Grether & Wilde 1983; Grether et al 1986) argue that in "real" tasks people are able to ignore the less-relevant information, and hence overload is not a serious issue. On the other hand, Gaeth & Shanteau (1984) found that judgments were adversely influenced by irrelevant factors, although that influence could be reduced with training. Research on the strategies people use for selectively attending to information would be valuable.

People also respond in several ways when faced with decision problems varying in time pressure. These coping mechanisms include the acceleration of processing, selectivity in processing, and shifts in decision strategies. As time constraints are made more severe, the amount of time spent processing an item of information decreases substantially (Ben Zur & Breznitz 1981). Under time stress, processing is focused on the more important and/or more negative information about alternatives (Ben Zur & Breznitz 1981; Svenson & Edland 1987; Wallsten & Barton 1982; Payne et al 1988). There is also evidence that decision strategies may shift as a function of increased time pressure (Zakay 1985; Payne et al 1988). Finally, there may be a hierarchy of responses to time pressure. Payne et al (1988) found that under moderate time pressure subjects accelerated processing and to a lesser extent became more selective in their processing. Under more severe time pressure, people accelerated processing, focused on a subset of information, and changed processing strategies.

Research on decision complexity, therefore, also documents the constructive nature of judgment and choice, since people respond to complex decisions using different strategies depending upon the nature of the task.

Uncertainty in Values

Rational choice involves two kinds of guesses: "guesses about future consequences of current actions and guesses about future preferences for those consequences" (March 1978:40). Decisions are difficult whenever either kind of uncertainty (need to guess) is present. Below, we review research on how people assess the probabilities of uncertain events that link future consequences to actions. In the current section we examine research considering the second kind of uncertainty. How well do people assess uncertainties about their own future preferences, and how do people make choices when their values are ambiguous?

Kahneman & Snell (1990), for instance, have explored how people predict future experiences of enjoyment or discomfort (i.e. future utility values). They conclude that people have difficulty evaluating the utilities of future consequences. People also have trouble estimating the utilities of consequences that will result after a series of repetitive experiences with the same outcome.

Choice among alternatives whose outcomes occur at different points in time is related to prediction of utilities for consequences over time. The standard approach to such choice problems is to assume a discount function that permits an individual to make value comparisons between immediate and delayed consumption. Stevenson (1986) and Benzion et al (1989) provide experimental studies of discounting.

Loewenstein (1988) extends the discounting analysis by including the concept of a reference point used by individuals in the evaluation of immediate and delayed consumption options. For example, Loewenstein argues that delay in consumption of a good assumed to have already been purchased will be framed as a loss, and a high level of compensation for that loss will be demanded. A speed-up in delivery of a consumption item, on the other hand, will not be valued as much: the "speed-up cost" will be lower than the delay premium demanded. Loewenstein shows that different methods of eliciting intertemporal preferences yield different estimates of subjects' relative preferences for immediate and delayed consumption in ways consistent with the concept of a reference-point effect and inconsistent with standard discounting models. While the focus of Loewenstein's paper is on framing and intertemporal preferences, his studies also provide an example of the more general phenomenon of procedural variance in the elicitation of preferences.

Norm Theory also deals with uncertainty in preferences and the context-dependent aspects of judgment. Kahneman & Miller (1986) suggest that the particular subjective value given to an attribute score—e.g. travel time to an apartment from campus—will be constructed ad hoc on the basis of the recall or generation in memory of a comparison class of objects or decision episodes that seem relevant to the task at hand. The value assigned to an attribute score of a particular stimulus will reflect the distribution of scores for that attribute within the set of exemplars of that object evoked in memory. Kahneman & Miller also suggest that the attributes that control judgments may often not be the most central attributes, given that the generated set of exemplars may not be seen as varying much on the most central attributes.

An obvious hypothesis is that the more uncertainty (ambiguity) in one's preferences, the more one's expressed preferences will be subject to procedural and descriptive effects. For example, preferences for events further and further in the future may be more susceptible to framing effects. As another example, Alba & Hutchinson (1987) contend that consumers less familiar or less expert in a product class are more likely than familiar buyers to select information based on non-task related cues, such as display form (see also Hoch & Ha 1986; Levin & Gaeth 1988). Conversely, people who have more experience in making decisions within a particular domain may be less susceptible to effects such as the prominence effect of choice vs matching. A key research issue is whether the major determinant of susceptibility to procedural and display variables is the number of facts, the knowledge possessed about a domain, or the number of tradeoff decisions made within a domain.

Restructuring Decision Problems

Researchers typically assume that a decision-maker takes the decision problem as initially presented and seeks to find the preferred alternative given that structure—what Slovic (1972) refers to as the concreteness principle. However, a decision-maker might restructure the problem. Restructuring might involve transformations of information (e.g. rounding off, standardizing, or performing calculations), rearranging information (e.g. the order of brands or attributes), or simplifying by eliminating information. The restructuring might serve to reduce either the amount of perceived conflict in the decision or the degree of complexity.

The restructuring phenomenon expresses our theme that preferences are often constructed. Montgomery (1983), for example, has proposed that people actively restructure decision problems until one alternative is seen to be dominant, which provides a (relatively) conflict-free way to make the decision. The restructuring may involve such operations as collapsing two or more attributes into a more comprehensive one, emphasizing an attribute, or adding new attributes to the problem representation that will bolster one alternative.

Coupey (1990) suggests that various restructuring activities might also ease the total cognitive effort of solving a given decision problem. She allowed some of her subjects to take notes while solving decision problems and then coded the restructuring operations evident in the notes. Individuals who received information sequentially, or information that was poorly structured, used notes to generate alternative × attribute matrixes. Individuals who restructured were more likely ultimately to utilize alternative-based strategies. Hence, one interpretation of these data is that individuals put effort into restructuring so that later they can use a more accurate heuristic with a reasonable amount of effort.

Other researchers have also stressed restructuring in their accounts of decision behavior (M. Johnson 1984, 1989; Ranyard 1989). Michael Johnson's work deserves special note for its innovative look at the problem of preferences among more noncomparable alternatives. Most decision research has examined choices among options easily defined on a common set of attributes—e.g. alternative brands of television. In contrast, Johnson explored how people choose among items from different product classes (e.g. a new television vs a vacation) that possess different attributes. He identified several processes used by people to deal with such noncomparable choice options, including the generation of more abstract attributes, a form of restructuring. Bettman & Sujan (1987) argue that the criteria individuals construct for such choices are a function of how the problem is framed.

Argument-Based Decisions

A final concept related to the notion of constructive preferences is that choice is based on arguments that are generated in support of one option over another (Shafer 1986; Slovic 1975; Tversky 1988). Simonson (1989), for example, has shown that choice phenomena that are difficult to explain with more traditional models can be explained in terms of a search for reasons (arguments) to prefer one option over another. Specifically, he showed that the size of the asymmetric dominance (attraction) effect, in which the addition of an asymmetrically dominated alternative to a choice set (i.e. dominated by one alternative but not another) increases the probability of choosing the dominating alternative (Huber et al 1982; Ratneshwar et al 1987), was increased by the need to justify one's decisions to others. Further, he showed that the choice of the dominating alternative was felt by subjects to be less likely to be criticized and to provide a better argument.

To summarize, there is ample evidence that preferences are often constructed in response to a judgment or choice task. Next we consider evidence that people use multiple strategies to construct assessments of uncertainty. Following that discussion, we consider choice involving both uncertainty and values in more detail.

BELIEFS ABOUT UNCERTAIN EVENTS

The question of how people judge the probabilities or likelihoods of uncertain events has been a major focus in behavioral decision research for a number of years, and interest continued during the period under review. Efforts to compare intuitive probability judgments to the rules of statistics continue to be a major focus, as detailed below. The fact that such intuitive judgments often deviate from the laws of probability is now widely accepted, although some investigators question both the meaning and the relevance of errors in intuitive judgments (von Winterfeldt & Edwards 1986).

Much of the recent work on how people assess the probability of an event has adopted many of the same concepts used to explain preferential choice. That is, people are seen as having available several ways of assessing beliefs about uncertain events, and individuals use different modes of probabilistic reasoning in a highly contingent fashion. In addition, probability judgment can be thought of as the construction of arguments (Shafer & Tversky 1985). In the following sections, we consider different strategies for probabilistic reasoning and then consider evidence for the contingent use of such strategies.

Strategies for Probabilistic Reasoning

Specific heuristics involved in probabilistic thinking (e.g. availability, representativeness, and anchoring and adjustment) continue to be investigated. The availability heuristic refers to the assessment of the probability of an event based on the ease with which instances of that event come to mind. The representativeness heuristic involves an assessment of the probability of an event by judging the degree to which that event corresponds to an appropriate mental model such as a sample and a population, an instance and a category, or an act and an actor. Anchoring and adjustment is a general judgment process in which an initially generated or given response serves as an anchor and other information is used to adjust that response. It is generally assumed that the adjustment is insufficient.

The availability heuristic has been investigated in relation to judgments of political events (Levi & Pryor 1987), perceptions of the risk of consumer products (Folkes 1988), the generation of hypotheses by accountants (Libby 1985), and judgments about others (Shedler & Manis 1986). More generally, the relationship between memory access and judgment has been examined by Lichtenstein & Srull (1985) and Hastie & Park (1986).

A detailed study of the representativeness heuristic is offered by Bar-Hillel (1984). In an innovative study, Camerer (1987) has shown that representativeness affects prices in experimental markets, although the effect is smaller for subjects with greater experience in that market.

Finally, the anchoring and adjustment heuristic has been investigated in a variety of domains, including accounting (Butler 1986), marketing (Davis et al 1986), the assessment of real estate values (Northcraft & Neale 1987), and as a general process by which belief-updating tasks are performed (Hogarth & Einhorn 1991).

Contingent Usage of Strategies for Assessing Uncertainty

One characteristic of the use of heuristics is the neglect of potentially relevant problem information. As discussed more fully below, the adaptive use of heuristics, even though neglecting some information, can save substantial cognitive effort and still produce good solutions to decision problems. However, in many situations people do make systematic errors in forming probability judgments. As illustrated below, the question is no longer whether biases exist, but under what conditions relevant information will or will not be used to construct a response to a probability judgment task. We examine this issue for usage of base-rate information, the conjunction fallacy, and the effects of expertise on uncertainty judgments.

THE USE/MISUSE OF BASE-RATE INFORMATION   Almost 20 years ago, Kahneman & Tversky (1973) reported a series of studies that involved presenting subjects with a brief personality description of a person and a list of different categories to which the person might belong. The task for the subject was to indicate the category to which the person was most likely to belong. The striking finding was that subjects all but ignored the relative sizes of the different categories—i.e. the base rates; instead, judgments were based almost exclusively on the extent to which the given description matched the various category stereotypes (representativeness). Since then, many researchers have investigated when and how base-rate information is utilized in decision-making (see Bar-Hillel 1990 for an overview of base-rate studies). Base-rate information is often, but by no means always ignored. For example, Medin & Edelson (1988) report that in one series of studies "participants use base-rate information appropriately, ignore base-rate information, or use base-rate information inappropriately (predict that the rare disease is more likely to be present)" (p. 68).

Evidence that base-rate information is sometimes neglected and sometimes used appropriately in assessing the probability of an event has led to the view that probabilistic reasoning involves contingent processing. Two recent examples of contingent-processing approaches to base-rate use are provided by Gigerenzer et al (1988) and Ginossar & Trope (1987). Both studies show that the use of base-rate information is highly sensitive to a variety of task and context variables. For example, Gigerenzer et al found that a change of problem context from guessing the profession of a person to predicting the outcome of a soccer game influenced the use of base-rate information, with the use of base-rates greater in the soccer problem. They argued that "the content of the problem strongly influenced both subjects' performance and their *reported strategies*" (p. 523, emphasis added).

Ginossar & Trope (1987) propose that people have a variety of rules for making probabilistic judgments, including both statistical and nonstatistical inference principles. Which rule is used to solve a particular judgment task is contingent upon the recency and frequency of prior activation of the rules, the relation of the rules to task goals, and their applicability to the givens of the problem. More generally, Ginossar & Trope view strategies for thinking under uncertainty as sequences of production rules whose application depends on the same general cognitive factors that determine production rule application in other task domains (Anderson 1982). They conclude that instead of asking whether people are inherently good or bad statisticians, attention should be directed to understanding the cognitive factors that determine when different inferential rules, statistical or nonstatistical, will be applied. The Ginossar & Trope viewpoint is one we share completely and is consistent with much of the research on preferences reported above.

THE CONJUNCTION FALLACY   The idea that the same person will use a variety of approaches to solving probabilistic reasoning tasks also arises in discussions of the conjunction fallacy. Tversky & Kahneman (1983) distinguish intuitive (holistic) reasoning about the probabilities of events from more extensional (decomposed) reasoning, where events are analyzed into exhaustive lists of possibilities or compound probabilities are evaluated by aggregating elementary ones. A fundamental law of probability derived from extensional logic is the conjunction rule: The probability of a conjunction of events, $P(A \& B)$, cannot exceed the probability of any one of its constituents, $P(A)$ and $P(B)$. Intuitive reasoning, on the other hand, is seen by Tversky & Kahneman as being based on "natural assessments" such as representativeness and availability, which "are often neither deliberate nor conscious" (p. 295). Consistent with the hypothesis that probabilistic reasoning is often intuitive, Tversky & Kahneman demonstrate numerous instances where people state that the probability of $A \& B$ is greater than the probability of B, violating the conjunction rule. Additional evidence of violations of the conjunction rule can be found in several studies (Crandall & Greenfield 1986; Thuring & Jungermann 1990; Wells 1985; Yates & Carlson 1986). Einhorn & Hogarth (1986b) relate causal reasoning to the conjunction fallacy and suggest that there is a link between the need for multiple causes of an event and the conjunction fallacy.

Tversky & Kahneman argue that violations of the conjunction rule are both systematic and sizable; however, they also note that "probability judgments are not always dominated by nonextensional heuristics . . .[and] judgments of probability vary in the degree to which they follow a decompositional or holistic approach" (p. 310). Thus, understanding when the decision-maker will use one approach or another in solving problems under uncertainty is of the same crucial importance as understanding the use of different strategies in the assessment of preferences. A related argument is offered by Beach et al (1986), who propose that a person has a repertoire of strategies for making forecasts that includes both strategies utilizing aleatory reasoning (extensional) and explicit reasoning (unique characteristics). They suggest that the selection of a forecasting strategy will depend on a variety of task factors. Beach et al also make a useful distinction between task factors that determine which strategy will be used and environmental factors that determine the vigor with which a strategy will be applied. They suggest that a variable like the extrinsic benefit of making an accurate forecast will be more likely to determine how rigorously a strategy is applied than to determine which strategy is applied.

EXPERTISE AND UNCERTAINTY JUDGMENTS   The studies of base-rate use, violations of the conjunction rule, and, more generally, intuitive vs statistical reasoning in the solving of uncertainty problems illustrate constructive decision behavior. In discussing such contingent judgments and choices, we have emphasized elements of the task as determinants of behavior; however, it is clear that the processes used to construct a solution to a decision problem may differ as a function of individual differences as well.

One question of current interest is the extent to which the strategies for assessing uncertainties found in studies of novices doing laboratory tasks generalize to the judgments of experts dealing with tasks relevant to their areas of expertise. It is clear that experience does not necessarily improve judgment. Garb (1989), for example, provides a review of the effects of training and experience on the validity of clinical judgment in mental health fields. He concludes that "the results on validity generally fail to support the value of experience in mental health fields. However, the results do provide limited support for the value of training" (p. 391). Garb also argues that experienced judges do seem better at knowing which of their judgments are likely to be correct; that is, their judgments are better calibrated.

Other research demonstrates that expertise is not a panacea for making assessments of uncertain events. Experts, too, use heuristics such as representativeness and show such biases as the misuse of base-rate information. Cox & Summers (1987), for example, found that experienced retail buyers used the same heuristics when making sales forecasts (i.e. representativeness) and displayed biases similar to those found with novice subjects. The extent to which the heuristics and potential biases that have been observed in studies using college students will also be observed in "real-world" settings using experts continues to be a subject of much debate (see, for example Bunn & Wright 1991; Shanteau 1988).

Why might expertise not lead to better assessments in some cases? The prediction of future events often depends on learning from and understanding past events. One factor that may cause people to learn less from experience than they should is the hindsight bias (Fischhoff 1975) or the "I knew it all along" phenomenon. An excellent review of the research on hindsight is offered by Hawkins & Hastie (1990). They conclude that the hindsight phenomenon extends to the judgments of experts in nonlaboratory settings. For other reasons why expertise may not lead to better assessments, see Camerer & Johnson (1991).

Next we examine in more detail an area of research that draws upon and combines findings from studies both of preferences and of judgments about uncertain events, namely how people make decisions under risk and uncertainty.

DECISIONS UNDER RISK AND UNCERTAINTY

The study of how people make decisions that involve tradeoffs between the desirability of consequences and the likelihood of consequences—e.g. choice among gambles—continues to be one of the most active areas of decision research. Not only do responses to gambles provide insight into basic psychological processes of judgment and choice, but understanding decision-making under uncertainty and risk has direct relevance for improving decisions in business and public policy. Increasingly, as might be expected, decisions under risk are seen as being sensitive to the same types of context and task variables described above for preferences among multi-attribute alternatives and for the assessment of uncertainties. In the following sections, we consider research on generalizations of expected-utility models (how values depend upon the specific set of available options and interactions between payoffs and probabilities), on responses to repeated-play gambles, and on ambiguity and risky choice.

Generalizations of Expected-Utility Models

Expected-utility (EU) theory (von Neuman & Morgenstern 1947) has long been the standard model for decisions under risk, although the descriptive validity of the expected-utility model has also long been questioned. An economist, Mark Machina, recently summarized risky-decision research by noting that "choice under uncertainty is a field in flux" (Machina 1987:121). We agree; evidence of violations of the standard EU model has accumulated to the point that numerous theorists have offered alternatives to the standard EU model. The goal has been to model risky decisions in ways that will allow the tradeoffs between probabilities and values to reflect contextual factors. One approach has been to develop generalizations of the expected-utility model. Decision weights that may not be additive over outcomes, for example, are used in place of linear probabilities. Another type of generalization allows the value of an outcome of a gamble to differ depending on the specific gamble of which it is a part (Becker & Sarin 1987). A related idea is that the value placed on the outcome of one gamble depends on the outcome that would have been received if a second gamble had been chosen and the same random event had occurred—i.e. the notion of regret (Bell 1982; Loomes & Sugden 1987). Regret is a good example of a contextual factor that may effect decisions.

Many of the proposed generalizations of EU also reflect a weakening of the view that the disentanglement of belief and value is essential to rational decision-making (Shafer 1986). For example, one can weight the probabilities (decision weights) of outcomes by the rank order of the attractiveness of the outcomes. The lowest-ranked, least-attractive outcomes, for instance, might be given relatively greater weight (Quiggin 1982; Segal 1989). One could also allow decision weights to differ for gain outcomes and loss outcomes (Einhorn & Hogarth 1986a). Weber et al (1992) extend the idea of sign-dependent decision weights to judgments of the riskiness of gambles as well as to attractiveness judgments.

Another generalization of the expected-utility model allows the decision weights assigned to the outcomes to vary as a function of both the rank *and* the sign of the payoffs. Luce (1990; Luce & Fishburn 1991) and Tversky & Kahneman (1990) propose models with this property. In the Luce model, a framing or "plausible accounting" assumption is that gambles that have a mixture of gains and losses are decomposed into two subgambles, one consisting of gain outcomes and null consequences and another consisting of loss outcomes and null consequences. Within the gain and loss subgambles, respectively, the decision weights are rank dependent. The decision weights for the gain and loss consequences are allowed to differ.

Recently, Tversky & Kahneman (1990) have offered a generalization of prospect theory that also allows for different decision weights for gains and losses. The decision weights are also rank dependent based upon the marginal contributions of the events ordered by payoffs. The new theory, called Cumulative Prospect Theory, is extended to cover both probabilistic and uncertain (ambiguous probability) gambles. Cumulative Prospect Theory retains the major features of the original versions of prospect theory. In particular, the prediction of reflection of risk attitudes for gains and losses is preserved; risk aversion and risk seeking are predicted, respectively, for gains and losses of moderate or high probability—e.g. $p > .5$. However, for small probabilities—e.g. $p < .1$—the prediction is for risk seeking for gains and risk aversion for losses. These risk attitude predictions are derived from the principles of (a) diminishing sensitivity for both value functions (from a reference point) and weighting functions (from certainty and impossible events) and (b) loss aversion.

The predictive power of rank- and sign-dependent models is impressive; however, Tversky & Kahneman note that formal models of the valuation of risky options are at best approximate and incomplete, arguing that "choice is a constructive and contingent process. When faced with a complex decision problem, people employ a variety of heuristic procedures in order to simplify the representation and the evaluation of prospects. The heuristics of choice do not readily lend themselves to formal analysis, because their application is contingent on the method of elicitation, the formulation of the problem and the context of choice" (p. 36). While we agree with their assessment that judgment and choice are often constructive and characterized by contingent usage of heuristics, we believe that the contingent use of heuristics is more susceptible to formal analyses than implied above (e.g. see Payne et al 1988).

To what extent do generalizations of EU much beyond those already proposed represent the best direction for theory development in the attempt to understand risky decision behavior (Camerer 1989)? One suggestion, offered by Shafir et al (1989), is to combine the absolute approach of expectation models, in which the attractiveness of a gamble is assumed to be independent of other alternatives, with a comparative approach, in which the attractiveness of a gamble depends on the alternatives to which it is compared. Another suggestion, offered by Lopes (1987; Schneider & Lopes 1986), is to move away from expectation models of decisions to models that more directly reflect the multiple and conflicting goals that people may have in solving risky decision problems. Some suggested goals are maximizing security, maximizing potential gain, and maximizing the probability of coming out ahead . The Lopes concept of multiple goals is similar in spirit to the early idea of characterizing gambles by risk dimensions rather than moments (Slovic & Lichtenstein 1968; also see Aschenbrenner 1984 for a test of dimensional vs moment-based explanations of risky decisions).

Repeated-Play Gambles

Whether people respond differently to gambles involving a single play versus repeated-play gambles may be related to the notion that multiple goals can underlie risky choice. People may pay attention to different goals depending on how often a gamble will be played (Lopes 1981) or whether the decision involves a single individual or a group of comparable individuals (Redelmeir & Tversky 1990). Recent work provides substantial empirical support for the need to distinguish between risky-choice behavior for unique and repeated gambles (Keren & Wagenaar 1987; Joag et al 1990). Wedell & Bockenholt (1990), for example, show that the frequency of preference reversals is less under repeated-play conditions. They offer an interpretation of the effects of multiple plays that emphasizes the concept of an aspiration level in both choice and pricing. An interesting connection exists between the repeated play of gambles and the question of when people will reason statistically. As suggested by Kahneman & Lovallo (1992), framing an apparently unique risky decision as part of a much larger set of risky choices may lead to behavior more in line with a considered tradeoff of beliefs and values.

Ambiguity and Risky Choice

In most discussions of decision-making under risk, it is assumed that the probabilities representing the decision-maker's uncertainties about events are well specified. However, there is often ambiguity concerning the probabilities of events. That is, a decision-maker might tell you that his or her best guess is that the probability of an event is .4, but he or she may also tell you that the estimate is shaky. While the standard theory of subjective expected utility prescribes that an "expected probability" adequately represents the individual's uncertainty about an event, it is clear that people respond differently to decisions under uncertainty as a function of the uncertainty about uncertainties, even when the expectations of the probabilities are the same. Thus, the presence or absence of ambiguity about the probabilities may represent an important context variable affecting risky decisions. As illustrated by the classic Ellsberg paradox (Ellsberg 1961) and subsequent experimental results, individual choices often exhibit an aversion to ambiguity, at least when the probabilities of the events are moderate (e.g. .5) or larger. Frisch & Baron (1988) suggest a number of reasons why it may be reasonable for an individual to show ambiguity aversion. Ambiguity seeking, however, can occur for lower-probability events (Curley & Yates 1989), a result suggested by Ellsberg.

A number of researchers have investigated ambiguity and risky decisions during the period under review (Curley & Yates 1985, 1989; Curley et al 1986; Einhorn & Hogarth 1985; Frisch & Baron 1988; Gardenfors & Sahlin 1983; Hogarth & Einhorn 1990; Hogarth & Kunreuther 1985; Kahn & Sarin 1988). This interest reflects both a theoretical concern with the limits of the standard expected-utility model and a recognition that ambiguity is a prevalent feature of real-world decision problems. Ritov & Baron (1990), for example, suggest that ambiguity lowers the willingness to vaccinate a child against potentially deadly diseases.

Einhorn & Hogarth (1985) offer a model of how people adjust probabilities under ambiguity to reflect what might be imagined. Imagination is likened to a mental simulation process. The adjustment is from an anchor that corresponds to an initial estimate of the probability of an event. The size of the adjustment depends on the amount of ambiguity as well as on the value of the initial probability. Hogarth & Kunreuther (1985, 1989) use the ambiguity model as a basis for understanding when, and at what prices, insurance coverage for different uncertainties will be offered. Hogarth & Einhorn (1990) also propose a model of how people assess decision weights in evaluating risky options which is based upon their model for ambiguous probabilities. The adjustment of decision weights in the Hogarth & Einhorn model is affected by the size as well as the sign of the payoffs, as is the case for several of the generalizations of expected utility noted above.

Curley et al (1986) provide evidence that concern about the evaluation of one's decisions by others is at least a partial explanation for ambiguity avoidance. In the standard Ellsberg task, where there is one urn containing 50 red balls and 50 black balls and another urn containing 100 red and black balls in unknown proportions, the preference for a bet based on the known 50:50 urn is enhanced by the anticipation that the contents of the unknown urn will be shown to others.

Heath & Tversky (1991) have extended the study of ambiguity to domains where the judged probabilities are based on knowledge rather than chance. They argue that the willingness to bet on an uncertain event depends on one's feelings of knowledge or competence in a given context, as well as on the estimated likelihood of that event and the precision of that estimate. In support of their idea, they report that subjects who felt knowledgeable about a domain (e.g. politics) were more likely to prefer a bet based on a judged probability event than on a matched lottery (chance) bet. The chance bet was preferred over a matched judgmental bet in content domains in which one felt less competent. Heath & Tversky conclude that the effect of knowledge or competence far outweighs the contribution of ambiguity or vagueness in understanding how beliefs and preferences interact in determining risky decisions. In other words, factors beyond simple beliefs about the likelihoods of events and values (e.g. feelings of competence) may determine risk-taking behavior.

The research outlined above suggests a variety of methods individuals may use to construct probability assessments or make decisions when confronting ambiguity. How individuals use these methods in a contingent fashion has not been investigated; however, given the prevalence of contingent-strategy usage in the areas reviewed thus far, examining how individuals respond contingently to ambiguity would be a fertile area for future research.

FRAMEWORKS FOR CONTINGENT-DECISION BEHAVIOR

We have now reviewed research on preferences, judgments of beliefs about uncertain events, and risky decision-making. In all cases, we have seen substantial evidence for contingent use of multiple strategies for dealing with such decision tasks. Awareness of the highly contingent nature of decision behavior has led several researchers to propose frameworks within which constructive decision behavior could be understood. Some of these frameworks emphasize the cognitive costs and benefits of the various strategies people might use in constructing preferences and beliefs. In that regard, such frameworks are direct extensions of the bounded-rationality concept. Other frameworks emphasize more perceptual processes of problem representation, formulation, or framing that determine which strategies, values, and beliefs will be used to solve a particular problem.

Cost/Benefit Frameworks

The most frequently used approach to explaining contingent decision behavior assumes that people have available or can generate a repertoire of strategies or heuristics for solving decision problems. The available strategies or abilities may have been acquired through formal training (Larrick et al 1990) or natural experience (Kruglanski 1989), and their availability in any given situation will be a function of the frequency and recency of prior use (Ginossar & Trope 1987). It is also assumed that the strategies have differing expected advantages (benefits) and disadvantages (costs). The selection of a strategy then involves the consideration of the anticipated benefits and costs of each strategy given the specific task environment.

Beach & Mitchell and their colleagues offer one version of a cost/benefit framework (Beach & Mitchell 1978; Beach et al 1986; Waller & Mitchell 1984). Beach & Mitchell identify three broad categories of strategies: 1. "aided-analytic", 2. "unaided-analytic", and 3. "nonanalytic." Task factors assumed to influence strategy selection include complexity, ambiguity of goals (values), significance of outcomes, and accountability. Recently, Beach & Mitchell have argued that their original model is too limited and have proposed a new model called "Image Theory" that stresses the intuitive and automatic aspects of decision-making (Beach 1990; Mitchell & Beach 1990). The emphasis in Image Theory is on noncompensatory tests of the acceptability or compatibility of a single alternative (candidate option) with the decision-maker's values or goals (images). They stress that individuals make judgments about the compatibility of an option with one's image; this is seen as a rapid, smooth process that can be called "intuitive" decision-making. The more analytical processes specified in the original Beach & Mitchell model are assumed to be evoked only if there is more than one acceptable alternative.

A comparison between analytical and intuitive decision-making is also stressed by Hammond and his associates (Hammond et al 1987).They argue that the cognitive processes (modes of thought) available to a decision-maker can be seen as falling on a continuum from intuition (characterized by rapid data processing, low cognitive control, and low awareness of processing) to analysis (characterized by slow data processing, high cognitive control, and high awareness of processing). Hammond et al claim that properties of the decision task, such as whether information is presented pictorially or presented via bar graphs or numbers, lead to one mode of cognition versus another. An important feature of their framework is the distinction they make between the frequency and the size of judgmental errors assumed to result from intuitive and analytical modes of thought. Analysis is viewed as leading to fewer but larger errors than intuition. Hammond et al (1987) provide a good example of a computational error (execution of analysis) in decision-making involving an engineer who wrote down a weight of .8 for a cue instead of the .08 that he intended, thus reducing his judgmental accuracy to little better than chance.

The Beach & Mitchell and the Hammond frameworks deal with contingent decision processing at a fairly general level of analytic vs nonanalytic and analytic vs intuitive modes of thought. Explaining contingent strategy selection at a more detailed information processing level has been the focus of a series of studies by Payne et al (summarized in Payne et al 1990a). They investigate the costs and benefits of solving complex preferential choice problems using specific decision strategies such as satisficing (Simon 1955), lexicographic choice (Tversky 1969), elimination-by-aspects (Tversky 1972), equal weighting (Einhorn & Hogarth 1975), and more normative strategies like additive utility.While Payne et al acknowledge the importance of factors like decision accuracy, avoidance of conflict, and accountability in strategy selection, they focus on the role played in strategy choice by the cognitive effort (mental resources) required to execute a strategy in a specific task environment (Simon 1955; Russo & Dosher 1983). Payne et al note that different decision strategies require different amounts of computational effort and that a measure of such cognitive effort in decision-making can be obtained by decomposing strategies like elimination-by-aspects and weighted adding into sets of elementary information processes (EIPs) (see O. Huber 1989 for similar ideas). Examples of EIPs are reading an alternative's value on an attribute into working memory, comparing two alternatives on an attribute, and adding the values of two attributes in working memory. Bettman et al (1990) show that a weighted EIP model provides good predictions of the response times and subjective effort reports associated with the use of various decision strategies in different task environments.

By combining measures of strategy effort with measures of decision accuracy, Johnson & Payne (1985), Payne et al (1988), and Payne et al (1990b) use simulation to show that adaptive choice of decision heuristics can often provide reasonable effort/accuracy tradeoffs. Their studies of the adaptiveness of actual decision behavior to changes in decision tasks, contexts, and goals show that people often adapt their behavior in ways that seem reasonable given a concern for both decision effort and decision accuracy (Payne et al 1988; Creyer et al 1990). However, Klayman & Ha (1987) argue that people may not always be as adaptive to task demands as they should be. In the case of hypothesis testing, for instance, Klayman & Ha argue that people generally rely on a "positive test strategy" that often works very well, but can lead to systematic errors or inefficiencies. Overgeneralizing the applicability of reasonable heuristics is perhaps a typical failure of adaptivity (Baron 1988). Klayman & Ha (1987), like Tversky & Kahneman (1986), suggest that the use of more optimal strategies may require that the relationships between task variables and strategy performance be highly transparent.

Most current attempts to explain contingent or constructive decision behavior focus on goals and strategies that the decision-maker brings to the task, which are assumed to interact with task structure and context in determining strategy use. However, people can decide how to decide not only at the beginning of a decision episode but also as they learn more about a problem in the course of solving it. That is, people can be opportunistic (data driven) as well as top-down (goal driven) (Hayes-Roth and Hayes-Roth 1979). One argument for a more opportunistic view of strategy use is that people may store procedures for decision-making in terms of simple processing operations such as comparison processes rather than in the form of more complete strategies like elimination-by-aspects (Bettman & Park 1980; Biehal & Chakravarti 1986). It has been suggested that opportunistic or constructive processes will be more likely to be used as decision problems become more complex or stressful (Klein & Yadav 1989). Evidence that people scan alternatives in a more nonsystematic fashion under stress, and therefore may be more data driven, is provided by Keinan (1987). Information display factors may also impact the degree of bottom-up vs top-down processing (Jarvenpaa 1990).

Perceptual Frameworks

As reviewed above, some of the most dramatic demonstrations of the lack of invariance in human decision behavior have come from studies of framing effects (Tversky & Kahneman 1986). Tversky & Kahneman acknowledge that contingent processing in decision-making can sometimes be explained in terms of mental effort; however, they prefer to trace contingent decision behavior to more basic perceptual principles governing the formulation or representation of decision problems. Examples of such principles include the diminishing sensitivity of values and decision weights and the coding of outcomes from a reference point discussed earlier. Tversky & Kahneman stress that "in the persistence of their appeal, framing effects resemble visual illusion more than computational errors" (Tversky & Kahneman 1986:S260).

Another approach to the issue of multiple decision strategy use which blends cost/benefit and perceptual approaches has been offered by Montgomery and his associates (Lindberg et al 1989; Montgomery 1983; Montgomery & Svenson 1983). As noted earlier, Montgomery sees decision-making as series of structuring and restructuring activities. The various compensatory and noncompensatory decision rules like elimination-by-aspects are seen as operators used in the restructuring of the decision problem. Thus, like Tversky & Kahneman, Montgomery emphasizes problem formulation or representation activities in his account of the constructive nature of decision behavior. Montgomery also emphasizes the justifiability of the decision process as a goal of the decision-maker.

A key distinction between the perceptual perspective and that offered by the cost/benefit approach concerns the role of incentives in determining decision behavior. If the only factors influencing decision behavior were a concern with accuracy and a concern for decision effort, then one would expect that violations of rational decision principles could be eliminated by proper incentives. For example, many economists continue to argue that the lack of incentives may cause individuals to perform suboptimally (e.g. Harrison

1989). Further, as was found by Creyer et al (1990), the processes used in decision-making should become more consistent with normative models as incentives are increased. However, errors in preferential choice and probabilistic reasoning persist even in the presence of monetary payoffs (Grether & Plott 1979; Tversky & Kahneman 1983). Even a casual view of decision-making in the real world suggests that reasoning errors sometimes occur in important decisions. Consequently, much recent research has examined the effects of incentives on decision behavior, leading to a view that incentives can both help and hinder decision performance (Ashton 1992; Berg & Dickhaut 1990; Hogarth et al 1991).

As noted by Tversky & Kahneman (1986), incentives do not work by magic. Generally, what incentives do is prolong deliberation or attention to a problem; people generally work harder on more important problems. More effort is generally believed to lead to better performance. However, as reported in Paese & Sniezek (1991), increased effort may lead to increased confidence in judgment without accompanying increases in accuracy. Devoting more effort to using a flawed decision strategy can lead to poorer performance (Arkes et al 1986).

For incentives to change decision strategies and increase performance, several conditions seem necessary. First, one must believe that one's current decision strategy is insufficient in terms of desired accuracy (i.e. if you don't think it's broken, you won't fix it). Failure to adapt may result from overconfidence in assessing the likelihood that a current strategy will lead to a successful outcome. In many decision environments feedback is often not sufficient to sway such assessments (Einhorn 1980). A related factor that may cause people to overestimate the quality of their current judgments is the hindsight bias. A failure to adapt can also result from difficulty in properly assessing the task environment and the relationship between the environment and the strategy. For example, the degree of intercorrelation among cues or attributes affects the accuracy of heuristics, yet correlations are difficult to estimate (Alloy & Tabachnik 1984).

Second, for incentives to lead to a strategy shift, a better strategy must be available. If one doesn't know what else to do, a belief that one is stuck with a flawed strategy may lead to a panic response under high incentives (Janis 1989). There is evidence that better strategies are sometimes unavailable. For example, several effective memory strategies for encoding and retrieval are not possessed by young children (John & Cole 1986). Deficits in strategy knowledge for solving certain classes of problems have recently been examined by Kaplan & Simon (1990). Brehmer (1990) makes the related point that knowledge of suboptimality in the process of solving a complex and dynamic decision problem is not a primary perceptual datum. Instead, "it is an inference based on a normative model of the task, and, if the decision-maker does not have a well-developed model of the task, the possibility of doing better will not be detected" (Brehmer 1990:267). Thus, it is certainly possible that better decision strategies for some situation are not known by most decision-makers. On a more positive note, however, recent work by Nisbett & Fong and their colleagues has shown that the teaching of statistical and decision principles increases the likelihood of using statistical and decision theoretic reasoning processes (Fong et al 1986; Larrick et al 1990).

Third, one must believe that one is capable of executing the new, hopefully more optimal strategy. For complex problems there may be a constraint on which strategies are believed to be feasible. In the words of Simon (1981), "what a person cannot do he will not do, no matter how much he wants to do it" (p. 36). More generally, incentive effects can be seen as one more question concerning the conflicting goals (i.e. accuracy, effort minimization, conflict avoidance, and justifiability) that a decision-maker might have in constructing a solution to a decision problem.

Integrating the Cost/Benefit and Perceptual Frameworks

The perceptual framework clearly complements the cost/benefit framework, because it is difficult to see how simple wording changes alone (e.g. as seen in "lives saved" versus "lives lost" in Tversky & Kahneman 1981) change either cognitive effort or the desire for accuracy. On the other hand, it is not clear how the perceptual framework would handle contingent behavior due to the number of alternatives, for example, yet that phenomenon fits nicely into a cost/benefit framework. There are opportunities to integrate cost/benefit and perceptual frameworks. For example, Tversky & Kahneman (1990) suggest that the framing process is governed by such rules of mental economy (effort saving) as the general tendency to accept the problem as given and the segregation of the decision problem at hand from its broader context. In addition, during the course of constructing a heuristic, decision-makers may cycle between noticing aspects or characteristics of the choice set (e.g. extreme values across alternatives) and deciding how to exploit those aspects. Perceptual frameworks may be most relevant for the noticing process, whereas cost/benefit notions may be more relevant for determining what to do to take advantage of what has been noticed. A third opportunity for integrating the two frameworks would be to consider that individuals' assessments of costs and benefits for any heuristic may be greatly influenced by perceptual concerns such as how information is presented or how the problem is framed.

The concepts of multiple strategies and constructive decision-making also provide a point of integration between decision research and other areas of psychology. For example, Weber et al (1991) suggest that research on memory processes can shed light on the possible decay, distortion, or confusion of intermediate computations in the execution (implementation) of a decision strategy. They also suggest that the idea of parallel processing in memory may require a rethinking of our measures of decision effort. Another area of integration is between the concept of decision strategies and mood or affect (Isen 1987; Mano 1992). Mano, for instance, shows that people employ simpler strategies when under distress.

APPLICATIONS

Behavioral decision research is often motivated by the desire to improve the decision-making process. Several approaches to improving decisions are identifiable in the literature. Some stress changes in the task environment facing the decision-maker. For example, the fact that decision behavior is often descriptively variant (i.e. information presentation matters) suggests that decisions might be improved through rather straightforward, inexpensive changes to the information environments in which individuals make judgments and choices.

Other approaches, such as decision analysis, stress changes in the capacity of the decision-maker for dealing with decision tasks. The concept of information-processing limits on decision behavior, for instance, suggests that tasks might be restructured (decomposed) to make required judgments and choices easier for the decision-maker and hopefully more accurate. Decision analysts also often try to improve directly the capacity of a decision-maker to cope with complex decisions through the provision of decision aids such as computer-based decision support systems and through training in statistical and decision-theoretic reasoning. Of course, combinations of improvements in information provision, decomposition of tasks, decision aids, and training are possible.

The approaches to aiding decision mentioned above can be thought of as methods for improving the match between task and person. An alternative approach is to replace the computations or processing done in the head with an automated decision procedure (a formula or model). Finally, when societal decisions (e.g. whether to improve some aspect of the environment at some cost to the public) affect, or depend upon, the preferences of others, providing decision-makers with better information on the values and beliefs of other people should also improve the decision process (see Lichtenstein et al 1990, for a discussion of some of the dilemmas facing a societal decision-maker).

Changing Information Environments to Aid Decisions.

The great adaptability of human decision behavior makes it possible to improve decisions by improving the information environments in which decisions are made. For example, the processing of current information can be made cognitively easier—without making more information available.

That is, the *processability* of currently available information can be improved (Russo 1977).

In a now classic study, Russo (1977) showed that providing a rank-ordered list of unit-price information at the point of purchase resulted in shifts in purchasing patterns and increased cost savings for consumers. In a recent extension of that study, Russo et al (1986) found that using an organized display to provide nutritional information on proteins, minerals, and vitamins had little impact on consumer behavior; but when the nutritional information concerned negative attributes such as sodium, sugar, and calories, the organized information display had an impact. Russo et al offer a cost/benefit explanation of this difference in results: Most consumers were not concerned about deficiencies in vitamins, but they were concerned about getting too much sodium, sugar, and calories. The importance of improved formats is also borne out in studies of hazard-warning labels on household products (Viscusi et al 1986) and the provision of information on radon in homes (Smith et al 1988).

The processability of information depends on the congruence between (*a*) the format and organization of information and (*b*) the type of processing (judgment) to be done (Bettman et al 1986). There are two basic approaches to congruence. The first, a reactive approach, is to attempt to determine how decision-makers are currently processing information and to make that processing easier. Typical displays of information in *Consumer Reports* illustrate this approach. Consumers would generally like to compare information on several attributes across several alternatives. By providing matrix displays of such information and by using comparative rating scales, *Consumer Reports* makes any comparison process easier. A second and more proactive approach is to determine the types of processing one wishes to encourage and then design formats that facilitate such processing. The Russo unit-price study is an example of this approach if one wanted to encourage comparisons based upon unit price, since the rank-ordered list contained only that information for the various brands. This latter approach may be particularly relevant for public policy decision-makers, although obvious issues arise concerning the degree to which processing should be guided.

Decision Analysis

Decision analysis is a set of methods and procedures designed to help people structure and simplify the task of making complex, confusing, and stressful decisions. Decision analysis depends heavily on human assessments of beliefs and/or preferences as inputs. Increasingly, decision analysis as a field of research and practice is sensitive to the contingent nature of decision behavior. Behavioral research is causing decision theorists to revise both models and procedures (Watson & Buede 1987; von Winterfeldt & Edwards 1986).

Bell (1985), for example, suggests that psychological factors such as the possibility of disappointment or regret might well be included in formal decision analyses. Instead of the alternative-focused thinking that is used in most decision problems, Keeney (1988) suggests that people would be better served by a more value-focused approach, in which one asks whether one could do better in achieving one's values than is suggested by the most readily apparent alternatives. Keller & Ho (1988) offer suggestions for how new alternatives might be constructed.

As noted above, a key feature of decision analysis is the incorporation of human beliefs and preferences into the analysis. The essential idea is to provide a structure by means of which a complex decision problem may be decomposed into a series of cognitively simpler judgments. Research continues on how decomposition of judgments might improve decisions (Henrion et al 1992; MacGregor et al 1988; Ravinder et al 1988); however, the constructive nature of even the simplest tradeoff and belief judgments raises questions regarding the validity of the subjective inputs into decision analyses. Consequently, a variety of new methods have been proposed for eliciting the beliefs and values necessary to operationalize decision models. These new methods are designed to avoid some of the context factors influencing probability and preference assessments. For instance, the most common procedures for assessing von Neumann-Morgenstern utility functions involve the matching of a sure-thing option with a gamble. This procedure is subject to the so-called certainty effect, in which outcomes that occur with certainty are given more weight. McCord & de Neufville (1986) have suggested a utility-assessment method designed to reduce this effect that involves the comparison of one gamble against a second gamble. Another approach commonly suggested for dealing with contingent judgments is sensitivity analysis, in which utility is measured in several ways and any discrepancies are explicitly reconciled by the decision-maker (von Winterfeldt & Edwards 1986). One of the major advantages of the new computer-based packages for decision analysis is the ease with which such sensitivity analysis can be conducted. Finally, Slovic et al (1988) discuss how a deeper understanding of task and context effects could help us deliberately to manage our own preferences more effectively, a proactive approach to contingent decision behavior.

Formulas or Models Versus Heads

The focus of our review so far has been on understanding how a decision-maker combines or processes information mentally. Alternatively, a decision-maker could use a mathematical, statistical, or mechanical procedure to combine the information when asked to make a judgment or choice. The process of combining information in the head is often called clinical judgment. The use of a formula or model to combine information may involve the automation of a human judge's decision rules, or it may reflect empirically established relations between data and the outcomes of interest—i.e. an actuarial approach (Dawes et al 1989). Numerous studies have shown that judgments are generally better if made using a formula (Dawes et al 1989; Kleinmuntz 1990), and organizations do use formulas instead of clinical judgment for some decision problems. The use of statistical judgment in place of clinical is more the exception than the rule, however. Consequently, recent research has emphasized two questions. First, what factors influence the use of an automated decision procedure? Second, how can models and humans complement rather than compete with one another as decision systems?

Dawes et al (1989) suggest several reasons why we still use our heads instead of formulas: lack of familiarity with the evidence showing the benefits of formulas, a belief that the evidence does not apply to case-by-case decisions, and an inflated belief in the accuracy of clinical judgment. Kleinmuntz (1990) offers several other reasons why formulas are not often used, including the error possibilities in the execution of a formula (Hammond et al 1987). Arkes et al (1986) show empirically that a simple decision formula was used less in solving a probabilistic judgment task when incentives for performance existed, when outcome feedback was available, and when people felt themselves to have more domain expertise. Under the conditions of incentives, feedback, and felt expertise, people frequently shift strategies, apparently in the hope that they will be able to beat the odds inherent in the probabilistic nature of the judgment task.

Einhorn (1986) suggests that people generally find it difficult to accept some level of explicit error associated with the use of a decision rule, even though the use of the statistical rule would lead to fewer overall errors in prediction. Einhorn (1986) also suggests that the degree to which one decides to use a statistical formula depends on whether one believes the phenomenon being predicted is inherently random (a formula is more likely) or systematic in nature; and as Einhorn notes, people tend to believe even random events are systematic (see also Gilovich et al 1985; Lopes & Oden 1987). Similarly, Kahneman & Tversky (1982) hypothesize that the laws of probability are more likely to be accepted (and used) when uncertainty is attributed to the external world and a distributional mode of reasoning is adopted. Given the contingent nature of probabilistic reasoning, one might be able to frame problems as being more external and distributional and thus increase the acceptability of formal statistical and decision models.

An old idea that has received much recent emphasis is to combine the use of formulas and judgment in the head. One approach is to use experts to measure the inputs to a model but to combine the subjective inputs mechanically (e.g. Libby & Libby 1989). At a more aggregated level, a judgment from a model and an intuitive judgment might be integrated in several ways. The model might be used as one input to be combined with other information known to the decision-maker (Peterson & Pitz 1986). The model could also be used as a baseline judgment, which should only be modified by the judge in special cases. Finally, the judgment by formula and the judgment in the head might be aggregated using another formula—e.g. 50% human judgment and 50% model (Blattberg & Hoch 1990).

The Measurement of Values   .

The measurement of human values (preferences) has practical significance in a number of different domains. Marketing, for example, has long been concerned with understanding and predicting the preferences of consumers in the hope that such understanding will lead to better managerial decisions (Green & Srinivasan 1990). Sophisticated methods of measuring preferences are also being used to guide decisions in a variety of nontraditional areas, such as medicine, law, and public policy (Keeney et al 1990). For example, the method of contingent valuation (CVM) is being used to assess the value of environmental goods (Cummings et al 1986; Fischhoff & Furby 1988; Mitchell & Carson 1989) both to guide policy decisions about protection of the environment and to establish liability in the case of damages to the environment. A contingent valuation (CV) study typically involves the assessment of tradeoffs by a large sample of respondents. Essentially, CV studies assess preferences by asking a respondent to match an option defined by an environmental good (level of air quality) at a clearly specified level (1) and a wealth level (1) against a second option defined by an environmental good at a specified second (more preferred) level (2) and an alternative (less preferred) wealth level (2). In the typical willingness-to-pay (WTP) task, the respondent is asked to specify an amount by which he/she would be willing to reduce his/her current wealth level—i.e. move down from level 1 to level 2—in order to gain an environmental improvement—a move up from level 1 to level 2. A subject of much practical import is the extent to which the assessed value of a public good (e.g. clean air) is contingent on a host of procedural variables (such as the order in which questions are asked; whether one matches by considering a potential gain or a potential loss in the level of a public good; or whether the event to be assessed—environmental damage—may occur or has already occurred) (Kahneman & Knetsch 1992; Schulze & McClelland 1990).

  The constructive nature of human preferences, particularly in domains where people do not commonly make tradeoff decisions, raises the question of the extent to which any technique such as CV creates values as much as it reveals them. Fischhoff & Furby (1988) offer one response to the labile (constructive) nature of values that emphasizes a careful provision of information to the respondent. Gregory & McDaniels (1987) suggest another approach that involves the explicit construction of values using multi-attribute decision analysis. On the other hand, in the spirit of decision theory, one should also ask whether there is an alternative to the measurement, however flawed, of individual values as input to policy decisions. Using an unstructured intuitive approach to judge the value of some environmental good may be even more biased. Ignoring the value of an environmental good because it is difficult to measure is a questionable response. We hope that increased understanding of the details of procedural and descriptive variance can lead to the development of better value assessment tools.

CONCLUSION

Behavioral decision research has made much progress between 1983 and 1991. We now better understand and appreciate the constructive nature of decision behavior. Behavioral decision research is also being used increasingly to inform a variety of applied areas of study, including health, business, and public policy.

The highly contingent nature of decision behavior both poses problems (costs) and creates opportunities (benefits) for decision researchers. At the theoretical level, the fact that decision processes are not invariant across task environments complicates the search for a small set of underlying principles (models) that can describe behavior. In addition, as noted by Hogarth & Einhorn (1991), the importance and pervasiveness of task and context effects may create a view of decision research as a fragmented and chaotic field. Nonetheless, as researchers ask questions about the conditions under which different types of information and different decision processes are likely to be used, generalizations about decision behavior seem to be emerging. Well established, for example, are the effects of task complexity on decision strategy use, the importance of the gain-vs-loss distinction in both risky and riskless preference, and the prevalence of the anchoring and adjustment process in judgment. In addition, phenomena like loss aversion suggest that general principles of value can be discovered. Thus, the constructivist view does not imply that there is no reflection of underlying beliefs and values in generating a decision.

Also on the theoretical level, the need to predict and explain the constructive aspects of decision behavior should contribute to a greater integration of decision research with other areas of psychology. For example, Norm Theory, which emphasizes context as a factor in making decisions (Kahneman & Miller 1986), clearly depends on cognitive psychology and an understanding of how memory is structured and operates. Similarly, Ginossar & Trope (1987) stress that the strategies used for assessing beliefs will depend on the same cognitive factors that influence use of procedural knowledge in other task domains. Finally, the importance of accountability, justifiability, and argument-based reasoning in decision-making helps reinforce the long-standing connections between decision research and social/organizational psychology.

The constructive and contingent nature of decision behavior has important implications at the level of application as well. We have summarized some of those implications for the design of information environments, the practice of decision analysis, the design of combined judgment/formula decision systems, and the measurement of values. Behavioral decision research continues to reflect a rich interplay between basic and applied disciplines and between descriptive and prescriptive concerns.

ACKNOWLEDGMENTS

Support for this review was provided by the Office of Naval Research and the National Science Foundation. In addition, the support of our respective institutions and the Graduate School of Management, University of California, Irvine is gratefully acknowledged. We also wish to thank Jonathan Baron, Colin Camerer, Gregory Fischer, Robin Hogarth, and Amos Tversky for their comments on an earlier draft of the manuscript.

Literature Cited

Abelson, R. P., Levi, A. 1985. Decision making and decision theory. In *The Handbook of Social Psychology*, Vol. 1, ed. G. Lindzey, E. Aronson. New York: Random House

Alba, J. W., Hutchinson, J. W. 1987. Dimensions of consumer expertise. *J. Consum. Res.* 13:411–54

Alloy, L. B., Tabachnik, N. 1984. Assessment of covariation by humans and animals: the joint influence of prior expectations and current situational information. *Psychol. Rev.* 91:112–49

Anderson, J. R. 1982. Acquisition of cognitive skill. *Psychol. Rev.* 89:369–406

Arkes, H. R., Blumer, C. 1985. The psychology of sunk costs. *Organ. Behav. Hum. Decis. Process.* 35:124–40

Arkes, H. R., Dawes, R. M., Christensen, C. 1986. Factors influencing the use of a decision rule in a probabilistic task. *Organ. Behav. Hum. Decis. Process.* 37:93–110

Aschenbrenner, K. M. 1984. Moment versus dimension-oriented theories of risky choice: a (fairly) general test involving single-peaked preferences. *J. Exp. Psychol.: Learn. Mem. Cogn.* 10:513–35

Ashton, R. H. 1992. Pressure and performance in accounting decision settings: paradoxical effects of incentives, feedback, and justification. *J. Acct. Res.* In press

Ashton, R. H., Kleinmuntz, D. N., Sullivan, J. B., Tomassini, L. A. 1989. Audit decision making. In *Research Opportunities in Auditing: The Second Decade*, ed. A. R. Abdel-Khalik, I. Solomon, pp. 95–132. Sarasota, FL: Am. Account. Assoc., Auditing Sect.

Bar-Hillel, M. 1984. Representativeness and fallacies of probability judgment. *Acta Psychol.* 55:91–107

Bar-Hillel, M. 1990. Back to base-rates. See Hogarth 1990, pp. 200–16

Baron, J. 1988. *Thinking and Deciding*. Cambridge: Cambridge Univ. Press

Bazerman, M. H. 1990. *Judgment in Managerial Decision Making*. New York: John Wiley. 2nd ed.

Beach, L. R. 1990. *Image Theory: Decision Making in Personal and Organizational Contexts*. New York: John Wiley

Beach, L. R., Barnes, V. E., Christensen-Szalanski, J. J. J. 1986. Beyond heuristics and biases: a contingency model of judgmental forecasting. *J. Forecast.* 5:143–57

Beach, L. R., Mitchell, T. R. 1978. A contingency model for the selection of decision strategies. *Acad. Manage. Rev.* 3:439–49

Beach, L. R., Mitchell, T. R. 1987. Image theory: principles, plans, and goals in decision making. *Acta Psychol.* 66:201–20

Beattie, J., Baron, J. 1992. Investigating the effect of stimulus range on attribute weight. *J. Exp. Psychol.: Hum. Percept. Perform.* In press

Becker, J. L., Sarin, R. K. 1987. Lottery dependent utility. *Manage. Sci.* 33:1367–82

Bell, D. E. 1982. Regret in decision making under uncertainty. *Oper. Res.* 30:961–81

Bell, D. E. 1985. Disappointment in decision making under uncertainty. *Oper. Res.* 33:1–27

Benzion, U., Rapoport, A., Yagil, J. 1989. Discount rates inferred from decisions: an experimental study. *Manage. Sci.* 35:270–84

Ben Zur, H., Breznitz, S. J. 1981. The effects of time pressure on risky choice behavior. *Acta Psychol.* 47:89–104

Bettman, J. R., Johnson, E. J., Payne, J. W. 1990. A componential analysis of cognitive effort in choice. *Organ. Behav. Hum. Decis. Process.* 45:111–39

Bettman, J. R., Kakkar, P. 1977. Effects of information presentation format on consumer information acquisition strategies. *J. Consum. Res.* 3:233–40

Bettman, J. R., Park, C. W. 1980. Effects of prior knowledge, experience, and phase of the choice process on consumer decision processes: a protocol analysis. *J. Consum. Res.* 7:234–48

Bettman, J. R., Payne, J. W., Staelin, R. 1986. Cognitive considerations in designing effective labels for presenting risk information. *J. Mark. Pub. Pol.* 5:1–28

Bettman, J. R., Sujan, M. 1987. Effects of framing on evaluation of comparable and noncomparable alternatives by expert and novice consumers. *J. Consum. Res.* 14:141–54

Biehal, G. J., Chakravarti, D. 1986. Consumers' use of memory and external information in choice: macro and micro processing perspectives. *J. Consum. Res.* 12:382–405

Biggs, S. F., Bedard, J. C., Gaber, B. G., Linsmeier, T. J. 1985. The effects of task size and similarity on the decision behavior of bank loan officers. *Manage. Sci.* 31:970–87

Billings, R. S., Marcus, S. A. 1983. Measures of compensatory and noncompensatory models of decision behavior: process tracing versus policy capturing. *Organ. Behav. Hum. Perform.* 31:331–52

Blattberg, R. C., Hoch, S. J. 1990. Database models and managerial intuition: 50% model and 50% manager. *Manage. Sci.* 36:887–99

Bostic, R., Herrnstein, R. J., Luce, R. D. 1990. The effect on the preference-reversal phenomenon of using choice indifferences. *J. Econ. Behav. Organ.* 13:193–212

Brehmer, B. 1990. Strategies in real-time dynamic decision making. See Hogarth 1990, pp. 262–79

Budescu, D. V., Weinberg, S., Wallsten, T. S. 1988. Decisions based on numerically and verbally expressed uncertainties. *J. Exp. Psychol.: Hum. Percept. Perform.* 14:281–94

Bunn, D., Wright, G. 1991. Interaction of judgmental and statistical forecasting methods: issues & analysis. *Manage. Sci.* 37:501–18

Butler, S. A. 1986. Anchoring in the judgmental evaluation of audit samples. *Account. Rev.* 61:101–11

Camerer, C. F. 1987. Do biases in probability judgment matter in markets? Experimental evidence. *Am. Econ. Rev.* 77:981–97

Camerer, C. F. 1989. An experimental test of several generalized utility theories. *J. Risk Uncertain.* 2:61–104

Camerer, C. 1992. The rationality of prices and volume in experimental markets. *Organ. Behav. Hum. Decis. Process.* In press

Camerer, C., Johnson, E. J. 1991. The process-performance paradox in expert judgment: How can experts know so much and predict so badly? In *Toward a General Theory of Expertise: Prospects and Limits,* ed. A. Ericsson, J. Smith, pp. 195–207. Cambridge: Cambridge Univ. Press

Carroll, J. S., Bazerman, M. H., Maury, R. 1988. Negotiator cognition: a descriptive approach to negotiators understanding their opponents. *Organ. Behav. Hum. Decis. Process.* 41:352–70

Casey, J. T. 1991. Reversal of the preference reversal phenomenon. *Organ. Behav. Hum. Decis. Process.* 48:224–51

Chi, M. T. H., Glaser, R., Farr, M. J., eds. 1988. *The Nature of Expertise.* Hillsdale, NJ: Lawrence Erlbaum

Coupey, E. 1990. Decision Restructuring in consumer Choice. PhD thesis. Fuqua School of Business, Duke Univ.

Cox, A. D., Summers, J. D. 1987. Heuristics and biases in the intuitive projection of retail sales. *J. Mark. Res.* 24:290–97

Crandall, C. S., Greenfield, B. 1986. Understanding the conjunction fallacy: a conjunction of effects? *Soc. Cognit.* 4:408–19

Creyer, E. H., Bettman, J. R., Payne, J. W. 1990. The impact of accuracy and effort feedback and goals on adaptive decision behavior. *J. Behav. Decis. Making* 3:1–16

Cummings, R. G., Brookshire, D. S., Schulze, W. D. 1986. *Valuing Environmental Goods: An assessement of the Contingent Valuation Method.* Totawa, NJ: Rowman & Allanheld

Curley, S. P., Yates, J. F. 1985. The center and range of the probability interval as factors affecting ambiguity preferences.

Organ. Behav. Hum. Decis. Process. 36:273–87

Curley, S. P., Yates, J. F. 1989. An empirical evaluation of decriptive models of ambiguity reactions in choice situations. *J. Math. Psychol.* 33:397–427

Curley, S. P., Yates, J. F., Abrams, R. A. 1986. Psychological sources of ambiguity avoidance. *Organ. Behav. Hum. Decis. Process.* 38:230–56

Davis, H. L., Hoch, S. J., Ragsdale, E. K. 1986. An anchoring and adjustment model of spousal predictions. *J. Consum. Res.* 13:25–37

Dawes, R. M., Faust, D., Meehl, P. E. 1989. Clinical versus actuarial judgment. *Science* 243:1668–74

Dube-Rioux, L., Russo, J. E. 1988. An availability bias in professional judgment. *J. Behav. Decis. Making* 1:223–37

Edwards, W. 1954. The theory of decision making. *Psychol. Bull.* 51:380–417

Einhorn, H. J. 1980. Learning from experience and suboptimal rules in decision making. In *Cognitive Processes in Choice and Decision Behavior*, ed. T. S. Wallsten, pp. 1–20. Hillsdale, NJ: Erlbaum

Einhorn, H. J. 1986. Accepting error to make less error. *J. Personal. Assess.* 50:387–95

Einhorn, H. J., Hogarth, R. M. 1975. Unit weighting schemes for decision making. *Organ. Behav. Hum. Perform.* 13:171–92

Einhorn, H. J., Hogarth, R. M. 1981. Behavioral decision theory: processes of judgment and choice. *Annu. Rev. Psychol.* 32:53–88

Einhorn, H. J., Hogarth, R. M. 1985. Ambiguity and uncertainty in probabilistic inference. *Psychol. Rev.* 93:433–61

Einhorn, H. J., Hogarth, R. M. 1986a. Decision making under ambiguity. *J. Bus.* 59: S225–50

Einhorn, H. J., Hogarth, R. M. 1986a. Judging probable cause. *Psychol. Bull.* 99:3–19

Eisenhardt, K. M. 1989. Making fast strategic decisions in high velocity environments. *Acad. Manage. J.* 32:543–76

Ellsberg, D. 1961. Risk, ambiguity, and the Savage axioms. *Q. J. Econ.* 75:643–69

Erev, I., Cohen, B. L. 1990. Verbal versus numerical probabilities: efficiency, biases, and the preference paradox. *Organ. Behav. Hum. Decis. Process.* 45:1–18

Fagley, N. S., Miller, P. M. 1987. The effects of decision framing on choice of risky vs. certain options. *Organ. Behav. Hum. Decis. Process.* 39:264–77

Fischer, G. W., Damodaran, W., Laskey, K. B., Lincoln, D. 1987. Preferences for proxy attributes. *Manage. Sci.* 33:198–214

Fischer, G. W., Hawkins, S. A. 1989. The prominence bias in multiattribute decision making: Scale compatibility, strategy com-

patibility and the contingent strategies hypothesis. Working paper, Carnegie Mellon Univ.

Fischer, G. W., Kamlet, M. S., Fienberg, S. E., Schkade, D. 1986. Risk preferences for gains and losses in multiple objective decision making. *Manage. Sci.* 32:1065–86

Fischhoff, B. 1975. Hindsight ≠ foresight: the effect of outcome knowledge on judgment under uncertainty. *J. Exp. Psychol.: Hum. Percept. Perform.* 1:288–99

Fischhoff, B. 1983. Predicting frames. *J. Exp. Psychol.: Learn. Mem. Cogn.* 9:103–16

Fischhoff, B. Furby, L. 1988. Measuring values: a conceptual framework for interpreting transactions with special reference to contingent valuations of visibility. *J. Risk Uncertain.* 1:147–84

Fischhoff, B., Slovic P., Lichtenstein, S. 1978. Fault trees: sensitivity of estimated failure probabilities to problem representation. *J. Exp. Psychol.: Hum. Percept. Perform.* 1:330–44

Folkes, V. S. 1988. The availability heuristic and perceived risk. *J. Consum. Res.* 15:13–23

Fong, G. T., Krantz, D. H., Nisbett, R. E. 1986. The effects of statistical training on thinking about everyday problems. *Cogn. Psychol.* 18:253–92

Ford, J. K., Schmitt, N., Schechtman, S. L., Hults, B. M., Doherty, M. L. 1989. Process tracing methods: contributions, problems, and neglected research questions. *Organ. Behav. Hum. Decis. Process.* 43:75–117

Froot, K. A., Thaler, R. H. 1990. Anomalies—foreign exchange. *J. Econ. Perspect.* 4:179–92

Frisch, D., Baron, J. 1988. Ambiguity and rationality. *J. Behav. Decis. Making* 1:149–57

Gaeth, G. J., Shanteau, J. 1984. Reducing the influence of irrelevant information on experienced decision makers. *Organ. Behav. Hum. Perform.* 33:263–82

Garb, H. N. 1989. Clinicial judgment, clinical training and professional experience. *Psychol. Bull.* 105:387–96

Gardenfors, P., Sahlin, N. 1983. Decision making with unreliable probabilities. *Brit. J. Math. Stat. Psychol.* 36:240–51

Gettys, C. F., Pliske, R. M., Manning, C., Casey, J. T. 1987. An evaluation of human act generation performance. *Organ. Behav. Hum. Decis. Process.* 39:23–51

Gigerenzer, G., Hell, W., Blank, H. 1988. Presentation and content: the use of base rates as a continuous variable. *J. Exp. Psychol.: Hum. Percept. Perform.* 14:513–25

Gilovich, T., Vallone, R., Tversky, A. 1985. The hot hand in basketball: on the misperception of random sequences. *Cogn. Psychol.* 17:295–314

Ginossar, Z., Trope, Y. 1987. Problem solving in judgment under uncertainty. *J. Pers. Soc. Psychol.* 17:464–74

Goldstein, W. M. 1990. Judgments of relative importance in decision making: global vs. local interpretations of subjective weight. *Organ. Behav. Hum. Decis. Process.* 47: 313–36

Goldstein, W. M., Einhorn, H. J. 1987. Expression theory and the preference reversal phenomena. *Psychol. Rev.* 94:236–54

Green, P. E., Srinivasan, V. 1990. Conjoint analysis in marketing research: new developments and directions. *J. Market.* 54:3–19

Gregory, R., McDaniels, T. 1987. Valuing environmental losses: What promise does the right measure hold? *Policy Sci.* 20:11–26

Grether, D. M., Plott, C. 1979. Economic theory of choice and the preference reversal phenomenon. *Am. Econ. Rev.* 69:623–38

Grether, D. M., Schwartz, A., Wilde, L. L. 1986. The irrelevance of information overload: an analysis of search and disclosure. *S. Calif. Law Rev.* 59:277–303

Grether, D. M., Wilde, L. L. 1983. Consumer choice and information: new experimental evidence. *Inform. Econ. Policy* 1:115–44

Hammond, K. R., Hamm, R. M., Grassia, J., Pearson, T. 1987. Direct comparison of the efficacy of intuitive and analytical cognition in expert judgment. *IEEE Trans. System. Man. Cyber.* 17:753–70

Harrison, G. 1989. Theory and misbehavior of first price auctions. *Am. Econ. Rev.* 79: 749–62

Hastie, R., Park, B. 1986. The relationship between memory and judgment depends on whether the judgment task is memory-based or on-line. *Psychol. Rev.* 93:258–68

Hawkins, S. A., Hastie, R. 1990. Hindsight: biased judgments of past events after the outcomes are known. *Psychol. Bull.* 107: 311–27

Hayes-Roth, B., Hayes-Roth, F. 1979. A cognitive model of planning. *Cogn. Sci.* 3:275–310

Heath, C., Tversky, A. 1991. Preference and belief: ambiguity and competence in choice under uncertainty. *J. Risk Uncertain.* 4:5–28

Henrion, M., Fischer, G. W., Mullin, T. 1992. Divide and conquer? Effects of decomposition on the accuracy and calibration of subjective probability distributions. *Organ. Behav. Hum. Decis. Process.* In press

Hershey, J. C., Schoemaker, P. J. H. 1985. Probability versus certainty equivalence methods in utility measurement: Are they equivalent? *Manage. Sci.* 31:1213–31

Hirt, E. R., Castellan, N. J. 1988. Probability and category redefinition in the fault tree paradigm. *J. Exp. Psychol.: Hum. Percept. Perform.* 14:122–31

Hoch, S. J., Ha, Y. 1986. Consumer learning: advertising and the ambiguity of product experience. *J. Consum. Res.* 13:221–33

Hogarth, R. M. 1987. *Judgement and Choice.* New York: John Wiley. 2nd ed.

Hogarth, R. M., ed. 1990. *Insights in Decision Making: A Tribute to Hillel J. Einhorn.* Chicago: Univ. Chicago Press

Hogarth, R. M., Einhorn, H. J. 1990. Venture theory: a model of decision weights. *Manage. Sci.* 36:780–803

Hogarth, R. M., Einhorn, H. J. 1991. Order effects in belief updating: the belief-adjustment model. *Cogn. Psychol.* 23

Hogarth, R. M., Gibbs, B. J., McKenzie, C. R. M., Marquis, M. A. 1991. Learning from feedback: exactingness and incentives. *J. Exp. Psychol.: Learn. Mem. Cognit.* 17:734–52

Hogarth, R. M., Kunreuther, H. 1985. Ambiguity and insurance decisions. *Am. Econ. Rev.* 75:386–90

Hogarth, R. M., Kunreuther, H. 1989. Risk, ambiguity, and insurance. *J. Risk Uncertain.* 2:5–35

Huber, J., Payne, J. W., Puto, C. P. 1982. Adding asymmetrically dominated alternatives: violations of regularity and the similarity hypothesis. *J. Consum. Res.* 9:90–98

Huber, O. 1989. Information-processing operators in decision making. In *Process and Structure in Human Decision Making*, ed. H. Montgomery, O. Svenson, pp. 3–22. Chichester: Wiley

Huber, V. L., Neale, M. A., Northcraft, G. B. 1987. Decision bias and personnel selection strategies. *Organ. Behav. Hum. Decis. Process.* 40:136–47

Isen, A. 1987. Positive affect, cognitive processes, and social behavior. *Adv. Exp. Soc. Psychol.* 20:203–53

Janis, I. L. 1989. *Crucial Decisions.* New York: Free Press

Jarvenpaa, S. L. 1989. The effect of task demands and graphical format on information processing strategies. *Manage. Sci.* 35:285–303

Jarvenpaa, S. L. 1990. Graphic displays in decision making—the visual salience effect. *J. Behav. Decis. Making* 3:247–62

Joag, S. G., Mowen, J. C., Gentry, J. W. 1990. Risk perception in a simulated industrial purchasing task: the effects of single versus multi-play decisions. *J. Behav. Decis. Making* 3:91–108

John, D. R., Cole, C. A. 1986. Age differences in information processing: understanding deficits in young and elderly consumers. *J. Consum. Res.* 13:297–315

Johnson, E. J., Meyer, R. M., Ghose, S. 1989. When choice models fail: compensatory representations in negatively correlated environments. *J. Mark. Res.* 26:255–70

Johnson, E. J., Payne, J. W. 1985. Effort and accuracy in choice. *Manage. Sci.* 31:394–414

Johnson, E. J., Payne, J. W., Bettman, J. R. 1988. Information displays and preference reversals. *Organ. Behav. Hum. Dec. Process* 42:1–21

Johnson, E. J., Schkade, D. A. 1989. Bias in utility assessments: further evidence and explanations. *Manage. Sci.* 35:406–24

Johnson, M. D. 1984. Consumer choice strategies for comparing noncomparable alternatives. *J. Consum. Res.* 11:741–53

Johnson, M. D. 1989. The differential processing of product category and noncomparable choice alternatives. *J. Consum. Res.* 16:300–9

Kahn, B. E., Sarin, R. K. 1988. Modeling ambiguity in decisions under uncertainty. *J. Consum. Res.* 15:265–72

Kahneman, D., Knetsch, J. 1992. Valuing public goods: the purchase of moral satisfaction. *J. Econ. Environ. Manage.* In press

Kahneman, D., Knetsch, J. L., Thaler, R. H. 1990. Experimental tests of the endowment effect and the Coase theorem. *J. Polit. Econ.* 98:1325–48

Kahneman, D., Lovallo, D. 1992. Timid decisions and bold forecasts: a cognitive perspective on risk taking. In *Fundamental Issues in Strategy,* ed. R. Rumelt, D. Schendel, D. Teece. Cambridge, MA: Harvard Univ. Press

Kahneman, D., Miller, D. T. 1986. Norm theory: comparing reality to its alternatives. *Psychol. Rev.* 93:136–53

Kahneman, D., Snell, J. 1990. Predicting utility. See Hogarth 1990, pp. 295–310

Kahneman, D., Tversky, A. 1973. On the psychology of prediction. *Psychol. Rev.* 80:237–51

Kahneman, D., Tversky, A. 1979. Prospect theory: an analysis of decision making under risk. *Econometrica* 47:263–91

Kahneman, D. Tversky, A 1982. Variants of uncertainty. In *Judgment Under Uncertainty: Heuristics and Biases,* ed. D. Kahneman, P. Slovic, A. Tversky, pp. 509–20. New York: Cambridge Univ. Press

Kaplan, C. A., Simon, H. A. 1990. In search of insight. *Cogn. Psychol.* 22:374–419

Keeney, R. L. 1988. Structuring objectives for problems of public interest. *Oper. Res.* 36:396–405

Keeney, R. L., Von Winterfeldt, D., Eppel, T. 1990. Eliciting public values for complex policy decisions. *Manage. Sci.* 36:1011–30

Keinan, G. 1987. Decision making under stress: scanning of alternatives under controllable and uncontrollable threats. *J. Pers. Soc. Psychol.* 52:639–44

Keller, K. L., Staelin, R. 1987. Effects of quality and quantity of information on decision effectiveness. *J. Consum. Res.* 14:200–13

Keller, L. R., Ho, J. L. 1988. Decision problem structuring: generating options. *IEEE Trans. System. Man. Cyber.* 18:715–28

Keren, G., Wagenaar, W. A. 1987. Violation of utility theory in unique and repeated gambles. *J. Exp. Psychol.: Learn. Mem. Cogn.* 13:387–91

Klayman, J. 1985. Children's decision strategies and their adaptation to task characteristics. *Organ. Behav. Hum. Decis. Process.* 35:179–201

Klayman, J. 1988. Cue discovery in probabilistic environments: uncertainty and experimentation. *J. Exp. Psychol.: Learn. Mem. Cogn.* 14:317–30

Klayman, J., Ha, Y. 1987. Confirmation, disconfirmation, and information in hypothesis testing. *Psychol. Rev.* 94:211–28

Klein, N. M., Yadav, M. S. 1989. Context effects on effort and accuracy in choice: an enquiry into adaptive decision making. *J. Consum. Res.* 15:411–21

Kleinmuntz, B. 1990. Why we still use our heads instead of formulas: toward an integrative approach. *Psychol. Bull.* 107:296–310

Kramer, R. M. 1989. Windows of vulnerability or cognitive illusions? Cognitive processes and the nuclear arms race. *J. Exp. Soc. Psychol.* 25:79–100

Kruglanski, A. W. 1989. The psychology of being "right": the problem of accuracy in social perception and cognition. *Psychol. Bull.* 106:395–409

Langley, P., Simon, H. A., Bradshaw, G. L., Zytkow, J. M. 1987. *Scientific Discovery: Computational Explorations of the Creative Process.* Cambridge, MA: MIT Press

Larrick, R. P., Morgan, J. N., Nisbett, R. E. 1990. Teaching the use of cost-benefit reasoning in everyday life. *Psychol. Sci.* 1:362–70

Laughhunn, D. J., Payne, J. W. 1984. The impact of sunk outcomes on risky choice behavior. *INFOR (Can. J. Oper. Res. Inform. Process.)* 22:151–81

Levi, A. S., Pryor, J. B. 1987. Use of the availability heuristic in probability estimates of future events: the effects of imagining outcomes versus imagining reasons. *Organ. Behav. Hum. Decis. Process.* 40:219–34

Levin, I. P., Gaeth, G. J. 1988. How consumers are affected by the framing of attribute information before and after consuming the product. *J. Consum. Res.* 15:374–78

Libby, R. 1985. Availability and the generation of hypotheses in analytical review. *J. Account. Res.* 23:648–67

Libby, R., Libby, P. A. 1989. Expert measurement and mechanical combination in control reliance decisions. *Account. Rev.* 64:729–47

Lichtenstein, M., Srull, T. K. 1985. Conceptual and methodological issues in examining the relationship between consumer memory and judgment. In *Psychological Processes and Advertising Effects: Theory, Research, and Application*, ed. L. F. Alwitt, A. A. Mitchell, pp. 113–128. Hillsdale, NJ: Lawrence Erlbaum

Lichtenstein, S., Gregory, R., Slovic, P., Wagenaar, W. A. 1990. When lives are in your hands: Dilemmas of the societal decision maker. See Hogarth 1990, pp. 91–106

Lichtenstein, S., Slovic, P. 1971. Reversals of preference between bids and choices in gambling decisions. *J. Exp. Psychol.* 89:46–55

Lindberg, E., Garling, T., Montgomery, H. 1989. Differential predictability of preferences and choices. *J. Behav. Decis. Making* 2:205–19

Linville, P. W., Fischer, G. W. 1991. Preferences for separating or combining events. *J. Pers. Soc. Psychol.* 59:5–21

Loewenstein, G. F. 1988. Frames of mind in intertemporal choice. *Manage. Sci.* 34:200–14

Loomes, G., Sugden, R. 1987. Some implications of a more general form of regret. *J. Econ. Theory* 41:270–87

Lopes, L. L. 1981. Decision making in the short run. *J. Exp. Psychol.: Hum. Learn. Mem.* 7:377–85

Lopes, L. L. 1987. Between hope and fear: the psychology of risk. *Adv. Exper. Soc. Psychol.* 20:255–95

Lopes, L. L., Oden, G. C. 1987. Distinguishing between random and nonrandom events. *J. Exp. Psychol.: Learn. Mem. Cogn.* 13:392–400

Luce, R. D. 1990. Rational versus plausible accounting equivalences in preference judgments. *Psychol. Sci.* 1:225–34

Luce, R. D., Fishburn, P. C. 1991. Rank-and sign-dependent linear utility models for finite first-order gambles. *J. Risk Uncertain.* 1:29–59

Lusk, C. M., Hammond, K. R. 1991. Judgment in a dynamic task: microburst forecasting. *J. Behav. Decis. Making* 4:55–73

MacCrimmon, K. R., Wehrung, D. A. 1990. Characteristics of risk taking executives. *Manage. Sci.* 36:422–35

MacGregor, D., Lichtenstein, S., Slovic, P. 1988. Structuring knowledge retrieval: an analysis of decomposed quantitative judgments. *Organ. Behav. Hum. Decis. Process.* 42:303–23

MacGregor, D., Slovic, P. 1986. Graphical representation of judgmental information. *Hum.-Comput. Interact.* 2:179–200

Machina, M. J. 1987. Decision-making in the presence of risk. *Science* 236:537–43

Mano, H. 1992. Judgments under distress: assessing the role of unpleasantness and arousal in judgment formation. *Organ. Behav. Hum. Decis. Process.* In press

March, J. G. 1978. Bounded rationality, ambiguity, and the engineering of choice. *Bell J. Econ.* 9:587–608

McCord, M. R., DeNeufville, R. 1986. "Lottery equivalents": reduction of the certainty effect problem in utiltity assessment. *Manage. Sci.* 32:56–60

Medin, D. L., Edelson, S. M. 1988. Problem structure and the use of base-rate information from experience. *J. Exp. Psychol.: Gen.* 117:68–85

Mellers, B. A., Ordonez, L. D., Birnbaum, M. H. 1992. A change of process theory for contextual effects and preference reversals in risky decision making. *Organ. Behav. Hum. Decis. Process.* In press

Meyer, R. J., Johnson, E. J. 1989. Information overload and the nonrobustness of linear models: a comment on Keller and Staelin. *J. Consum. Res.* 15:498–503

Mitchell, R. C., Carson, R. T. 1989. *Using Surveys to Value Public Goods: The Contingent Valuation Method.* Washington, DC: Resources for the Future

Mitchell, T. R., Beach L. R. 1990. "... Do I love thee? Let me count..." Toward an understanding of intuitive and automatic decision making. *Organ. Behav. Hum. Decis. Process.* 47:1–20

Montgomery, H. 1983. Decision rules and the search for a dominance structure: towards a process model of decision making. In *Analyzing and Aiding Decision Processes*, ed. P. C. Humphreys, O. Svenson, A. Vari, pp. 343–69. Amsterdam: North Holland

Montgomery, H., Svenson, O. 1983. A think-aloud study of dominance structuring in decision processes. In *Aspiration Levels in Bargaining and Economic Decision Making*, ed. R. Tietz, pp. 366–83. Berlin: Springer-Verlag

Noll, R. G., Krier, J. E. 1990. Some implications of cognitive psychology for risk regulation. *J. Legal Stud.* 19:747–79

Northcraft, G. B., Neale, M. A. 1987. Experts, amateurs, and real estate: an anchoring-and-adjustment perspective on property pricing decisions. *Organ. Behav. Hum. Decis. Process.* 39:84–97

Onken, J., Hastie, R., Revelle, W. 1985. Individual differences in the use of simplification strategies in a complex decision-making task. *J. Exp. Psychol.: Hum. Percept. Perform.* 11:14–27

Paese, P. W., Sniezek, J. A. 1991. Influences on the appropriateness of confidence in judgment: practice, effort, information, and decision-making. *Organ. Behav. Hum. Decis. Process.* 48:100–30

Payne, J. W., Bettman, J. R., Johnson, E. J. 1988. Adaptive strategy selection in decision making. *J. Exp. Psychol.: Learn. Mem. Cogn.* 14:534–52

Payne, J. W., Bettman, J. R., Johnson, E. J. 1990a. The adaptive decision maker: effort and accuracy in choice. See Hogarth 1990, pp. 129–53

Payne, J. W., Johnson, E. J., Bettman, J. R., Coupey, E. 1990b. Understanding contingent choice: a computer simulation approach. *IEEE Trans. System. Man. Cyber.* 20:296–309

Payne, J. W., Laughhunn, D. J., Crum, R. 1984. Multiattribute risky choice behavior: the editing of complex prospects. *Manage. Sci.* 30:1350–61

Peterson, D. K., Pitz, G. F. 1986. Explicit cue weighting in a prediction task. *Organ. Behav. Hum. Decis. Process.* 36:289–304

Puto, C. P. 1987. The framing of buying decisions. *J. Consum. Res.* 14:301–15

Quiggin, J. 1982. A theory of anticipated utility. *J. Econ. Behav. Organ.* 3:323–43

Ranyard, R. 1989. Structuring and evaluating simple monetary risks. See Huber 1989, pp. 195–207

Ratneshwar, S., Shocker, A. D., Stewart, D. W. 1987. Toward understanding the attraction effect: the implications of product stimulus meaningfulness and familiarity. *J. Consum. Res.* 13:520–33

Ravinder, H. V., Kleinmuntz, D. N., Dyer, J. S. 1988. The reliability of subjective probabilities obtained through decomposition. *Manage. Sci.* 34:186–99

Redelmeir, D. A., Tversky, A. 1990. Discrepancy between medical decisions for individual patients and for groups. *New Engl. J. Med.* 322:1162–64

Ritov, I., Baron, J. 1990. Reluctance to vaccinate: omission bias and ambiguity. *J. Behav. Decis. Making* 3:263–78

Russo, J. E. 1977. The value of unit price information. *J. Mark. Res.* 14:193–201

Russo, J. E., Dosher, B. A. 1983. Strategies for multiattribute binary choice. *J. Exp. Psychol.: Learn. Mem. Cogn.* 9:676–96

Russo, J. E., Staelin, R., Nolan, C. A., Russell, G. J., Metcalf, B. L. 1986. Nutrition

information in the supermarket. *J. Consum. Res.* 13:48–70

Samuelson, W., Zeckhauser, R. 1988. Status quo bias in decision making. *J. Risk Uncertain.* 1:7–59

Schkade, D. A., Johnson, E. J. 1989. Cognitive processes in preference reversals. *Organ. Behav. Hum. Decis. Process.* 44:203–31

Schneider, S. L., Lopes, L. L. 1986. Reflection in preferences under risk: Who and when may suggest why. *J. Exp. Psychol.: Hum. Percept. Perform.* 12:535–48

Schoemaker, P. J. H. 1990. Are risk attitudes related across domains and response modes? *Manage. Sci.* 36:1451–63

Schulze, W., McClelland, G. 1990. The robustness of values from contingent valuation surveys. Paper presented at Meet. Soc. Judgment and Decision Making, New Orleans

Schwartz, S., Griffin, T. 1986. *Medical Thinking: The Psychology of Medical Judgment and Decision Making.* New York: Springer-Verlag

Segal, U. 1989. Axiomatic representation of expected utility with rank-dependent probabilities. *Ann. Oper. Res.* 19:359–73

Shafer, G. 1986. Savage revisited. *Stat. Sci.* 1:463–85

Shafer, G., Tversky, A. 1985. Languages and designs for probability judgment. *Cogn. Sci.* 9:309–39

Shafir, E. B., Osherson, D. N., Smith, E. E. 1989. An advantage model of choice. *J. Behav. Decis. Making* 2:1–23

Shanteau, J. 1988. Psychological characteristics and strategies of expert decision makers. *Acta Psychol.* 68:203–15

Shedler, J., Manis, M. 1986. Can the availability heuristic explain vividness effects? *J. Pers. Soc. Psychol.* 51:26–36

Shepard, R. N. 1964. On subjectively optimum selections among multi-attribute alternatives. In *Human Judgments and Optimality*, ed. M. W. Shelby, G. L. Bryan, pp. 257–81. New York: Wiley

Shields, M. D. 1983. Effects of information supply and demand on judgment accuracy: evidence from corporate managers. *Account. Rev.* 58:284–303

Siegel, S. 1957. Level of aspiration and decision making. *Psychol. Rev.* 64:253–62

Simon, H. A. 1955. A behavioral model of rational choice. *Q. J. Econ.* 69:99–118

Simon, H. A. 1978. Rationality as process and as product of thought. *Am. Econ. Rev.* 68:1–16

Simon, H. A. 1981. *The Sciences of the Artificial.* Cambridge, MA: MIT Press. 2nd ed.

Simonson, I. 1989. Choice based on reasons:

the case of attraction and compromise effects. *J. Consum. Res.* 16:158–74

Slovic, P. 1972. From Shakespeare to Simon: speculations and some evidence about man's ability to process information. *Oregon Res. Inst. Bull.* 12

Slovic, P. 1975. Choice between equally valued alternatives. *J. Exp. Psychol.: Hum. Percept. Perform.* 1:280–87

Slovic, P., Griffin, D., Tversky, A. 1990. Compatibility effects in judgment and choice. See Hogarth 1990, pp. 5–27

Slovic, P., Lichtenstein, S. 1968. The relative importance of probabilities and payoffs in risk taking. *J. Exp. Psychol. Monogr. Suppl.* 78: Part 2

Slovic, P., Lichtenstein, S., Fischhoff, B. 1988. Decision making. In *Stevens' Handbook of Experimental Psychology. Vol. 2: Learning and Cognition,* ed. R. D. Atkinson, R. J. Herrnstein, G. Lindzey, R. D. Luce, pp. 673–738. New York: Wiley

Smith, V. K., Desvousges, W. H., Fisher, A., Johnson, F. R. 1988. Learning about radon's risk. *J. Risk Uncertain.* 1:233–58

Staw, B. M. 1981. The escalation of commitment to a course of action. *Acad. Manage. Rev.* 6:577–87

Stevenson, M. K. 1986. A discounting model for decisions with delayed positive or negative outcomes. *J. Exp. Psychol.: Gen.* 115:131–54

Stevenson, M. K., Busemeyer, J. R., Naylor, J. C. 1990. Judgment and decision-making theory. In *Handbook of Industrial and Organizational Psychology,* ed. M. D. Dunnette, L. M. Hough, 1:283–374. Palo Alto: Consulting Psychologists Press. 2nd ed.

Stone, D. N., Schkade, D. A. 1991. Numeric and linguistic information representation in multiattribute choice. *Organ. Behav. Hum. Decis. Process.* 49:42–59

Sundstrom, G. A. 1987. Information search and decision making: the effects of information displays. *Acta Psychol.* 65:165–79

Svenson, O., Edland, A. 1987. Changes of preferences under time pressure: choices and judgments. *Scand. J. Psychol.* 28:322–30

Tetlock, P. E. 1985. Accountability: the neglected social context of judgment and choice. *Res. Organ. Behav.* 7:297–332

Thaler, R. H. 1985. Mental accounting and consumer choice. *Mark. Sci.* 4:199–214

Thaler, R. H., Johnson, E. J. 1990. Gambling with the house money and trying to break even: the effects of prior outcomes on risky choice. *Manage. Sci.* 36:643–60

Thuring, M., Jungermann, H. 1990. The conjunction fallacy: Causality vs. event probability. *J. Behav. Decis. Making* 3:61–74

Tversky, A. 1969. Intransitivity of preferences. *Psychol. Rev.* 76:31–48

Tversky, A. 1972. Elimination by aspects: a theory of choice. *Psychol. Rev.* 79:281–99

Tversky, A. 1988. Context effects and argument-based choice. Paper presented at the Assoc. Consum. Res. Conf., Maui, Hawaii

Tversky, A., Kahneman, D. 1981. The framing of decisions and the psychology of choice. *Science* 211:453–58

Tversky, A., Kahneman, D. 1983. Extensional versus intuitive reasoning: the conjunction fallacy in probability judgment. *Psychol. Rev.* 90:293–315

Tversky, A., Kahneman, D. 1986. Rational choice and the framing of decisions. *J. Bus.* 59:S251–78

Tversky, A., Kahneman, D. 1990. Cumulative prospect theory: an analysis of decision under uncertainty. Working paper, Stanford Univ.

Tversky, A., Kahneman, D. 1992. Loss aversion in riskless choice: a reference dependent model. *Q. J. Econ.* In press

Tversky, A., Sattath, S., Slovic, P. 1988. Contingent weighting in judgment and choice. *Psychol. Rev.* 95:371–84

Tversky, A., Slovic, P., Kahneman, D. 1990. The determinants of preference reversal. *Am. Econ. Rev.* 80:204–17

Viscusi, W. K., Magat, W. A., Huber, J. 1986. Informational regulation of consumer health risks: an empirical evaluation of hazard warnings. *Rand J. Econ.* 17:351–65

Von Neumann, J., Morgenstern, O. 1947. *Theory of Games and Economic Behavior.* Princeton, NJ: Princeton Univ. Press. 2nd ed.

Von Winterfeldt, D., Edwards, W. 1986. *Decision Analysis and Behavioral Research.* Cambridge: Cambridge Univ. Press

Waller, W. S., Mitchell, T. R. 1984. The effects of context on the selection of decision strategies for the cost variance investigation problem. *Organ. Behav. Hum. Perform.* 33:397–413

Wallsten, T. S. 1990. The costs and benefits of vague information. See Hogarth 1990, pp. 28–43

Wallsten, T. S., Barton, C. 1982. Processing probabilistic multidimensional information for decisions. *J. Exp. Psychol.: Learn. Mem. Cogn.* 8:361–84

Watson, S. R., Buede, D. M. 1987. *Decision Synthesis: The Principles and Practice of Decision Analysis.* Cambridge: Cambridge Univ. Press

Weber, E. U., Anderson, C. J., Birnbaum, M. H. 1992. A theory of perceived risk and attractiveness. *Organ. Behav. Hum. Decis. Process.* In press

Weber, E. U., Goldstein, W. M., Busemeyer,

J. R. 1991. Beyond strategies: implications of memory representations and memory processes for models of judgment and decision making. In *Relating Theory and Data: Essays on Human Memory in Honor of Bennett B. Murdock,* ed. W. E. Hockley, S. Lewandowsky. Hillsdale, NJ: Lawrence Erlbaum

Weber, M., Eisenfuhr, F., von Winterfeldt, D. 1988. The effects of splitting attributes on weights in multiattribute utility measurement. *Manage. Sci.* 34:431–45

Wedell, D. H., Bockenholt, U. 1990. Moderation of preference reversals in the long run. *J. Exp. Psychol.: Hum. Percept. Perform.* 16:429–38

Wells, G. L. 1985. The conjunction error and the representativeness heuristic. *Soc. Cogn.* 3:266–79

Yates, J. F., Carlson, B. W. 1986. Conjunction errors: evidence for multiple judgment procedures, including 'signed summation'. *Organ. Behav. Hum. Decis. Process.* 37: 230–53

Zakay, D. 1985. Post-decisional confidence and conflict experienced in a choice process. *Acta Psychol.* 58:75–80

Annu. Rev. Psychol. 1992. 43:133–68

INTERPERSONAL PROCESSES INVOLVING IMPRESSION REGULATION AND MANAGEMENT

Barry R. Schlenker

Department of Psychology, University of Florida, Gainesville, Florida 32611

Michael F. Weigold

Department of Advertising, University of Florida, Gainesville, Florida 32611

KEY WORDS: interpersonal processes, impression management, self-presentation, social
motivation, accounting

CONTENTS

0066-4308/92/0201-0133$02.00

INTRODUCTION

As social psychology has matured as a discipline, it has increasingly endorsed a more dynamic, purposeful, and strategic view of human behavior. It is now virtually axiomatic that people do not just passively react to their social environments; they try to structure and influence their environments so as to construct more beneficial, less threatening surroundings. People attempt to place themselves in beneficial circumstances through their selection of friends, mates, jobs, and hobbies; and try to rearrange the circumstances they encounter so as to aid in goal achievement, such as through attempts to influence the attitudes and behaviors of those with whom they interact. Strategic capabilities have even been included in recent conceptualizations of intelligence (Cantor & Kihlstrom 1987; Sternberg 1986) and are probably closely related to status and success in everyday life (Hogan & Hogan 1991).

Accompanying this dynamic view has been the acknowledgment that interpersonal communication involves more than expression or description. Words do not just describe; they "do things" (Austin 1962) such as influence the ideas and behaviors of others in ways that can have a substantial impact on the actor's fortunes and the relationship itself. Interpersonal communications are inherently instrumental, so the agendas of the participants must be considered in order to understand the communication process (Cody & McLaughlin 1990; Fleming et al 1990) and the interpersonal perception process (Jones 1990). A theme that emerges from these analyses is that at the heart of interpersonal processes is the witting or unwitting control of information about the identities of the participants, their relationship, and their activities together. Further, the control of information not only takes place in initial encounters or superficial relationships but also continues over the course of life-long relationships. For example, Bradbury & Fincham (1990) urged that attributions be studied as "public events" that have consequences for the processes and outcomes of long-term relationships. They noted that in marriages, the public attributions made by each party can facilitate or challenge the identity of the other and thereby promote or undermine the stability of the relationship.

This review focuses on interpersonal processes of impression management or, more broadly, impression regulation. The concept reflects the seminal idea that people attempt to regulate and control, sometimes consciously and sometimes without awareness, information they present to audiences, particularly information about themselves. It is assumed that people do not deal with information randomly or dispassionately. Instead, people's agendas systematically influence how they prefer to interpret events and how they package information for consumption by audiences. By *agenda,* we mean what people want to accomplish (i.e. their overt or covert interpersonal goals) and how they plan to go about doing so (i.e. their plans or scripts for goal achievement).

The chapter is organized around three central questions that have been driving research in the area. First, what motives underlie the control of information? In dealing with this question we focus on the types of identities people attempt to construct and the strategies they employ to do so. Second, how do public and private activities compare? This question addresses the similarities and differences between public and private experiences and their implications for interpersonal relations, including the role of real and imagined audiences in influencing self-regulation. Third, how do people attempt to explain or account for events that impede goal achievement, particularly when those events jeopardize their identities? In dealing with this question, we focus on the interpersonal implications of people's explanations. Before turning to these questions, we briefly consider the nature and scope of impression regulation and management.

Regulating Impressions: Nature and Scope

The conceptual roots of research on the regulation of social information can be traced to early symbolic interactionists (Cooley 1902; Mead 1934). They held that self-regulation involves imagining oneself in the role of others, anticipating others' likely reactions to various actions, and selecting conduct accordingly, ultimately shaping or reshaping how one views oneself and how one is viewed by others (see Scheibe 1985). These insights were expanded in Goffman's (1959, 1971) dramaturgical analysis of social behavior, which viewed people as actors on life's stage and viewed interpersonal conduct as performances by the participants. Goffman (1959:4) suggested that whenever "an individual appears in the presence of others, there will usually be some reason for him to mobilize his activity so that it will convey an impression to others which is in his interests to convey." Although Goffman's work has been criticized for deemphasizing the psychology of the individual and focusing on what often seemed to be illicit behaviors designed to manipulate others (Scheibe 1985; Schlenker 1980), his insights provided a springboard for current work.

Social psychologists prior to the 1980s generally regarded impression management as a peripheral concept. It was seen as either an annoying contaminant of the research process (e.g. subjects would sometimes experience evaluation apprehension or display social-desirability biases and thereby obscure the more "fundamental" processes the researcher was attempting to investigate) or an applied topic that was of interest primarily to devotees of advertising, business, or politics. It was rarely regarded as a fundamental interpersonal process in its own right. The 1980s brought significant change as a torrent of conceptual analyses appeared (Arkin & Baumgardner 1986;

Baumeister 1982; Cheek & Hogan 1983; Jones & Pittman 1982; Leary & Kowalski 1990; Schlenker 1980, 1985a; Snyder 1987; Tedeschi 1981; Tedeschi & Norman 1985; Tetlock & Manstead 1985). These analyses elevated the concept from the status of a curiosity to that of a fundamental and central interpersonal process that could and should be subjected to scientific analysis. Further, analysts began to apply the concept to a wide range of social phenomena, including aggression, helping behavior, social facilitation, self-serving attributional biases, justificatory attitude change, anticipatory attitude change, group polarization, reactance, behavioral consistency, nonverbal behaviors, self-handicapping, social anxiety, schizophrenic symptoms and other aberrant behaviors (see Baumeister 1982; Leary & Kowalski 1990; Schlenker 1980; Tetlock & Manstead 1985). Other recent applications have been to eating behavior (Chaiken & Pliner 1987; Pliner & Chaiken 1990), the reluctance to transmit bad news (Bond & Anderson 1987), appeals to fairness (Greenberg 1990), organizational behavior (Gardner & Martinko 1988; Giacalone & Rosenfeld 1989), responses to personal control (Burger 1987), personality theory (Hogan 1983), counseling processes (Friedlander & Schwartz 1985), depression (Hill et al 1986), criminal conduct (Hogan & Jones 1983), and even interaction patterns in kindergarten (Hatch 1987). While sometimes differing in specifics, these analyses shared the common idea that people attempt to control information for one or more salient audiences in ways that try to facilitate goal-achievement.

Impression Regulation: Restrictive and Expansive Positions

A continuing source of disagreement concerns the scope of impression management. Some analysts regard it (and self-presentation) as a type of behavior that occurs only under specific conditions or is employed primarily by certain types of people (Briggs & Cheek 1988; Buss & Briggs 1984; Jones & Pittman 1982; Snyder 1987). These restrictive views usually associate self-presentation with particular interpersonal motives (usually such selfish motives as gaining power or approval), suggest it involves pretense or even deceit, and view it as aimed at real audiences who are either present or about to be encountered.

Other analysts take a more expansive approach and view impression management (or self-presentation) as a ubiquitous feature of social behavior (Goffman 1959; Hogan 1983; Schlenker 1980, 1985b). Although Goffman recognized that self-presentations are instrumental in gaining approval and achieving valuable outcomes in life, he regarded self-presentation as a condition of interaction, one that is inherent in the fundamental structure of social life. In order to interact, people must define the situation (e.g. select the relevant cognitive scripts) and the roles each will play. Self-presentations serve the necessary function of communicating definitions of each person's identity and plans. Once identities are established, each participant has a moral obligation to behave congruently with the identity he or she has selected (the rule of self-respect: to maintain one's own face) and to accept and respect the identity selected by the others (the rule of considerateness: to help maintain the faces of others). Impression management activities thereby permit the participants to define who each will be and permit interactions to run smoothly and efficiently.

According to the expansivist view, there is nothing inherently nefarious or superficial about impression management. It involves packaging information in ways designed to lead audiences to a particular conclusion (Schlenker & Weigold 1989). Usually, the information presented is basically "true" but is fitted to the appropriate circumstances, including the actor's goals and the audience's expectations, values, and competencies. Just as a textbook writer must edit information to present it in a readable, concise fashion, so must people edit information about themselves in everyday life to provide the "best" descriptions possible. From this perspective, to ask when people will engage in self-presentation during social interaction is like asking when people will engage in cognition during social interaction. The process is always going on, but its character may change depending on the actor's goals and the circumstances.

Impression regulation can vary on dimensions including: (*a*) the amount of cognitive effort exerted by the actor in presenting information, (*b*) the extent to which the actor is conscious of trying to create particular impressions, (*c*) the extent to which the behavior is perceived as deceptive or authentic, (*d*) whether the behavior is automatic or controlled, (*e*) whether the behavior is seen as motivated by purer or baser objectives (e.g. to benefit or exploit others), and (*f*) the audience(s) to whom the behavior is addressed. Theory and research may fruitfully examine how impression regulation differs across these dimensions.

The restrictive and expansive positions differ at two levels, one conceptual and one terminological. Conceptually, the expansivists appear more sympathetic to the idea, developed by the early symbolic interactionists, that socialization involves internalizing a social matrix. In this conception, real or imagined audiences play a significant role in the regulation of social conduct, and people eventually come to observe, evaluate, and sanction themselves in ways analogous to the way they observe, evaluate, and sanction one another (i.e. interpersonal accountability provides the archetype for self-regulation).

The positions may seem more contradictory terminologically than they otherwise might because they attach different meanings to the same term, as when *self-presentation* is used variously to denote self-descriptive activities that validate one's self-conception (Swann 1983) or pretentious power-augmenting behaviors (Jones & Pittman 1982) is sometimes applied only to public activities designed to influence others (Leary & Kowalski 1990) and is sometimes expanded to consider the self as audience for one's own behavior (Greenwald & Breckler 1985; Schlenker 1980). The phenomena themselves are perhaps less disputed than are the terms used to describe them.

For the sake of clarity, we use the term *self-identification* to refer to the process, means, or result of showing oneself to be a particular type of person, thereby fixing and expressing one's identity for oneself and others (Schlenker 1985b). Here *self-presentation* denotes the activity of regulating identity primarily for real or imagined others. Although the terms *self-presentation* and *impression management* are often used interchangeably (Leary & Kowalski 1990), people can attempt to control information about objects and events that are only indirectly self-relevant, such as public relations efforts to influence the identity of a business organization or product. Thus, we use the term *impression regulation* to refer to the goal-directed activity of controlling information about some object or event, including self (subsuming the concept of self-identification); here *impression management* denotes the activity of regulating information primarily for real or imagined others (subsuming self-presentation).

WHAT MOTIVATES IMPRESSION REGULATION?

Whereas impression management was once associated largely with the attempt to maximize social approval and material outcomes, today the motives that have been proffered as energizing and guiding it are as varied as those postulated to underlie virtually any behavior. Because of space limitations, we focus on motives relevant to regulating information about oneself, and collapse these into three broad groupings: Self-glorification (self-esteem maintenance and enhancement), self-consistency (validating the self by confirming self-beliefs), and self-authentication (trying to learn the truth about self by pursuing diagnostic information). We do not include the need for control or effectance as a separate category because it has been cited as a basic need that could explain all of the other motives (Arkin & Baumgardner 1986; Steele 1988; Swann 1983).

Self-Glorification

SELF-ESTEEM MAINTENANCE AND ENHANCEMENT   The idea that people act to maximize their self-esteem is included as a cornerstone of many current theories of social behavior (Solomon et al 1991; Steele 1988; Tesser 1988) and is often cited as a key motive influencing the content of self-presentations (Brown & Gallagher 1991; Leary & Kowalski 1990; Tetlock 1985a). Self-glorifying illusions, at least in moderation, not only permit one to feel good and look good to others, but are also associated with psychological adjustment, mental health, and superior functioning (Brown 1991; Taylor & Brown 1988). Self-esteem needs have been cited as the basis for self-glorifying descriptions of self, self-serving attributional biases, self-flattering social comparisons, preferences for positive interpersonal evaluations, and self-justificatory activities (Brown & Gallagher 1991; Greenwald & Breckler 1985; Taylor & Lobel 1989; Tesser 1988; Steele 1988). In most of these areas, public and private facets of the motive usually have been treated as distinct but interrelated (e.g. maintaining self-esteem partly depends on being regarded favorably by significant others, and favorable regard boosts self-esteem). Differences between models exist when explaining why people want to maximize self-esteem (cf Solomon et al 1991; Tedeschi & Norman 1985) and whether people prefer to maintain or to boost current levels of self-evaluation (Tesser & Cornell 1991). Yet the models share the core idea that positive self-evaluations are preferred and sought.

Attributions that glorify the self usually generate positive affect, provided they do not commit the individual to perform at unrealistic levels; whereas attributions that diminish the self usually generate negative affect (Brown 1991; Baumgardner & Arkin 1987; Higgins 1989; Snyder & Higgins 1988). Because of these associations, self-esteem maintenance and affect regulation can be seen as interrelated processes. Baumgardner and her colleagues (1989) found support for the hypothesis that people attempt to regulate their affective state through self-presentation.

Despite the pervasiveness of egotistical activities, one problem for self-enhancement models has been to account for conditions under which people do not prefer self-glorification, as when they take responsibility for failure or seek out diagnostic information even if it may confirm their worst fears. Usually, these counterfindings are explained by arguing that there are cases where positive self-evaluations are not adaptive because they will produce poor decisions with costly consequences that ultimately lower self-evaluations (see Fiske & Taylor 1991). We return to this issue shortly.

SELF-CONSTRUCTION AND COMPENSATION   A relative of the self-esteem theme is the idea that people try to present their ideal selves (Baumeister 1982) or preferred "possible selves" while taking steps to avoid feared possible selves (Markus & Ruvolo 1989). In these models, ideal views of self act as guides or scripts for self-presentational activities, specifying what should and should not be done. In contrast to the preceding self-esteem models, these models focus on specific dimensions that comprise identities rather than on global self-evaluations.

Discrepancies between the real and ideal self-images are presumed to produce unpleasant affect and lead to increased cognitive and behavioral efforts to reduce the discrepancies (Baumeister & Tice 1986; Higgins 1989).

In his self-discrepancy theory, Higgins (1989:95) proposed that "people are motivated to reach a condition in which their self-concept matches their personally relevant self-guides," which consist of their ideal selves (attributes they would like to possess) and their "ought" selves (attributes they think they should possess). Discrepancies between the actual self and the ideal self generate dejection-related emotions (e.g. sadness, disappointment) whereas discrepancies between the actual self and the ought self generate agitation-related emotions (e.g. fear, anxiety, threat).

It also has been proposed that people are motivated to compensate for perceived shortcomings on important dimensions by bolstering some facet of self. Bolstering can occur on either the threatened dimension (e.g. the puny weakling whose physique has been the object of ridicule becomes a body builder) or on an unrelated but personally important dimension (e.g. the puny weakling studies hard and becomes a famous scientist). Several lines of research demonstrate compensation, as when (a) people who publicly fail elevate their self-ratings on unrelated dimensions (Baumeister 1982); (b) people who confront impediments to desired identity images (e.g. being denied credit for positive accomplishments) reaffirm their standing on the dimension by polarizing relevant attitudes and actions (Schlenker 1987); and (c) people who are committed to a particular goal for self (e.g. being a musician) strive toward completeness of their self-definition and, if they experience a shortcoming (e.g. few relevant accomplishments), engage in more dramatized and polarized actions to demonstrate their good standing (Gollwitzer & Wicklund 1985). Research is still needed to determine when people will try to bolster the threatened dimension versus irrelevant dimensions.

Self-Consistency

The preceding views share the idea that people prefer to construct somewhat glorified, larger-than-life identities. In contrast, Swann (1987, 1990) has proposed that people try to create environments, in their own minds and in the real world, that verify their existing self-conceptions, even if these are negative. People do so by employing an array of private and public strategies, including selective processing and recall of confirmatory information, selective affiliation with others who provide confirmatory feedback, and public self-presentations designed to evoke confirmatory responses from others. Swann's (see 1987, 1990) impressive research program has provided support for key tenets of self-verification theory.

One of the more controversial aspects of self-verification theory is the idea that people with negative self-beliefs will try to confirm these beliefs. How can self-verification theory be reconciled with the considerable empirical support for self-glorification? Swann (1990) suggests three points of reconciliation. First, self-verification occurs only when people are certain of their self-beliefs. Most people have positive self-conceptions, and when they do entertain a negative self-belief, they do so with little certainty. Thus, most of the time people appear to be seeking self-esteem gratification. Second, self-verification applies to specific characteristics, not to a global positive or negative impression. Even people with relatively low self-esteem want to receive favorable feedback on the many dimensions on which they hold positive self-beliefs. Third, Swann distinguishes between affective reactions, governed by self-enhancement principles, and cognitive reactions, governed by self-verification principles. Thus, a person with negative self-beliefs feels better upon receiving a favorable evaluation but cognitively rejects the evaluation as incorrect.

Even with these reconciliation attempts, questions remain about the existence of a self-verification motive. First, Swann suggests that self-verification occurs because people have a need for order; from order they gain a sense of predictability and control over their environment. However, needs for order and control do not lead only to the conclusion that people want to self-verify. These same needs have been used to explain preferences for self-enhancement (Arkin & Baumgardner 1986; Steele 1988) and for diagnostic information (Brown 1990; Trope 1986). Second, people may prefer information consistent with their self-beliefs for reasons other than a consistency motive. One such reason is that people with low self-evaluations on particular dimensions employ a self-protective rather than self-assertive interaction style (Arkin & Sheppard 1990; Baumeister et al 1989b; Schlenker 1987; Tedeschi & Norman 1985). The self-protective style is characterized by cautious, modest self-descriptions, actions that attempt to minimize evaluative scrutiny by audiences, and actions that attempt to reduce expectations about the caliber of future performance. These tendencies would produce "consistency-type" effects. Irrespective of how these questions are ultimately answered, Swann's research program has refocused attention on the issue of self-consistency and demonstrated that people's self-beliefs moderate their self-regulating activities.

Self-Authentication: The Quest for Accuracy

There are adaptive advantages to receiving feedback diagnostic of one's true abilities, irrespective of whether the feedback is flattering or consistent with prior self-beliefs (Brown 1990; Trope 1986). Trope (1986) has proposed that people are motivated to acquire diagnostic information that permits accurate self-knowledge; Trope reviews evidence indicating that the preference for diagnostic information is strongest when erroneous self-beliefs are likely to lead to important, adverse consequences. In a series of studies, Brown (1990) found that both self-enhancement and accuracy motives seemed to operate when people evaluated their abilities, although self-enhancement was the dominant force in the situations he examined.

Do people quest for accuracy, and how pervasive is such a motive? Because of criticisms of Trope's procedures, Fiske & Taylor (1991:212) have suggested that "the case for diagnosticity has not truly been made." According to Brown (1990), much of the time in everyday life people do not need accurate information about themselves. This is true particularly with respect to social abilities, because claims to many social qualities (e.g. kindness, generosity) are not subject to easy verification. Further, Brown has suggested that many life decisions are based on information not only about one's abilities, but also about one's values and tastes (e.g. choosing to become an artist depends not just on talent, but also on how much one enjoys the activity). People may therefore experience less motivation to acquire veridical knowledge than is often assumed.

What Is a Desirable Identity?

The preceding provides three different answers to the question of what constitutes a desirable identity: It is either primarily self-glorifying, consistent with self-beliefs, or accurate. These approaches focus on an individual motive and assume the motive applies broadly. Data that contradict the pervasiveness of the motive are accounted for by suggesting that certain conditions either weaken the motive or cause it to be overridden by competing motives. Self-identifications are seen as expressions of the motive.

Alternatively, self-identifications can be seen as goal-directed *activities* that occur in a particular social context and have expected consequences, for the actor and others, that influence the form and content of the activity. According to this view, self-identifications are constructed at the time they occur and represent a transaction among actor, audience, and situation; they are not simply expressions of the self-concept or faithful retrievals of information in memory. The form and content of self-identifications are affected by factors relevant to the actor (e.g. self-concept, values), the audience (e.g. expectations, reward-cost capabilities), and the situation (e.g. relevant social roles). Self-ider ification theory (Schlenker 1985b, 1986; Schlenker & Weigold 1989) iggests that these factors influence self-identifications because they affec the desirability of pertinent identity images.

When is a self-identification desirable? Two requirements seem essential. First, the self-identification should be *believable,* that is, it should be regarded as a reasonably accurate construal of the salient evidence (or the actor should perceive it as likely to be so regarded by the relevant audience). Second, it should be *beneficial,* that is, the actor should regard it as facilitating his/her goals and values relative to alternative claims. According to self-identification theory, these two elements are integrated components of all self-identifications [akin to the integration of expectations and values in decision models; an equation for representing desirability was suggested by Schlenker (1980)]; people are never solely concerned with accuracy (the believability component) or self-glorification (the beneficiality component). Schlenker & Weigold (1989) have reviewed the literature on the following proposition: The likelihood that a particular self-identification will occur is increased by factors that (a) increase the expected positive consequences if the identification is believed, (b) reduce the expected negative consequences if the identification is disbelieved, or (c) increase the likelihood that the salient audience will believe the self-identification.

BENEFICIALITY   An impressive amount of data indicates that people will present themselves in ways they associate with desired interpersonal outcomes (Baumeister 1982; Cody & McLaughlin 1990; Giacalone & Rosenfeld 1989; Jones 1990; Leary & Kowalski 1990; Schlenker 1980; Schlenker & Weigold 1989; Tedeschi 1981; Tedeschi & Norman 1985). As Jones (1990) has demonstrated in his pioneering research on ingratiation, (a) self-presentations are particularly likely to conform to the expectations of a target when actors are more dependent on the target, and (b) actors will attempt to camouflage their strategic activities by balancing self-servingly beneficial assertions on the most relevant dimensions with innocuously negative information on irrelevant dimensions. Impression management often appears to be directed toward improving the actor's power in social relationships, thereby making it more profitable (or less costly) for him or her to participate in social life (Jones & Pittman 1982; Schlenker 1980; Tedeschi & Norman 1985).

People can claim desirable attributes directly, by presenting information about their own qualities and accomplishments, or indirectly, by presenting information about the qualities and accomplishments of their associates (Cialdini et al 1990). In a series of studies, Cialdini and colleagues (see 1990) found that people will bask in the reflected glory of the accomplishments of others, distance themselves from unflattering people and events, denigrate the accomplishments of rivals, and boost their evaluations of otherwise unattractive people with whom they are already connected. These indirect self-presentation tactics are more pronounced after failure experiences and for people who are low in self-esteem. In fact, it has been suggested that low-self-esteem people are especially likely to use indirect modes of self-presentation because these involve mild assertions that avoid explicit claims about self that might be challenged by others (Brown et al 1988).

There is no single best image to cultivate in optimizing power or achieving goals; many different types of self-presentations can be effective depending on the actor's resources and the social context. The actor may attempt to be seen as likable, competent, moral, intimidating, or in need of assistance (Jones & Pittman 1982; Schlenker 1980). Research has shown that people will even present themselves negatively if it serves their purposes—e.g. if they believe a well-adjusted person will be assigned to perform an embarrassing task (Kowalski & Leary 1990), if they believe a self-glorifying claim will threaten the audience, or if they prefer to avoid excessive public expectations or onerous responsibilities (Baumeister & Scher 1988; Schlenker 1980). Self-promotion often backfires and produces negative evaluations (Godfrey et al 1986), especially if the actor volunteers such information without a specific request from the audience (Holtgraves & Srull 1989). Modesty results when the audience is already aware of an actor's superior achievement; the actor can then avoid the risk of seeming the braggart and be given credit for both the accomplishment and the humility (Baumeister 1982; Schlenker & Leary 1982b). Further, people will often incur short-term losses in order to build or protect a reputation that permits them to optimize their long-term outcomes (Baumeister & Scher 1988; Tedeschi & Norman 1985). Thus, people do not merely want to present themselves positively; people aim to accomplish goals, and these goals may involve modest or even unflattering self-presentations.

BELIEVABILITY   Indiscriminant self-glorification leads to numerous personal and interpersonal problems. It can generate unrealistically high expectations for performance that doom the actor to failure; it can generate anxiety caused by concerns about having to maintain an unrealistic facade; and it can mark the actor as an egotist, an irritant, and an uncooperative social participant (e.g. a ballplayer who takes personal credit for the team's success but blames teammates for failure). All such outcomes can harm the actor's reputation and produce negative sanctions. Self-presentations produce obligations for actors to be what they say they are or face personal and interpersonal repercussions (Goffman 1959; Tedeschi et al 1971). Indeed, it has been argued that self-enhancing illusions are most effective when they are only slightly more positive than can be unquestionably justified and documented (Baumeister 1989; Brown 1990).

One's self-identifications are held in check by their believability—by one's expectation that one's assertions can be justified and defended. Schlenker & Weigold (1989) have suggested that analyses of what constitutes a "good" (believable) scientific theory serve as a starting point for evaluating the believability of self-identifications. They considered the following factors as determinants of believability: (a) empirical consistency; (b) internal consistency; (c) simplicity and communicability (people think "truth" comes in tidy packages); (d) consistency with prevailing cultural assumptions, beliefs, and values; (e) consensual validation; and (f) the reputation, apparent confidence, and persuasive skills of the actor. Research indicates that these factors operate to facilitate or constrain an actor's claims. For example, discrepancies between an actor's descriptions and accomplishments produce negative responses from observers, and subjects present themselves less positively when boastful claims could be invalidated by publicly available information or an upcoming performance. People generally try to present themselves in ways they believe they can substantiate to observers (Arkin & Baumgardner 1986; Leary & Kowalski 1990; Schlenker 1980, 1986), going so far as to fail on tasks in order to lower high public expectations they fear they will be unable to meet (Baumeister & Scher 1988; Baumgardner & Brownlee 1987).

AUTHENTICITY REVISITED: DESIRABILITY IN CONTEXT   The desirability of a particular self-identification appears to vary based on the characteristics of the actor, situation, and audience. For example, being regarded as an outstanding salesperson is likely to be valued more when dealing with one's employer than when interacting with a casual acquaintance, and boasts to one's spouse of being the most talented salesperson in the company may give way to more discreet and justifiable claims when talking to coworkers who have made more sales. Because desirability varies, people can have as many "social selves" as there are audiences they encounter (James 1890). To the extent that personal, situational, and audience factors affect the beneficiality or believability of a self-identification, these factors will produce variations in behavior (Leary & Kowalski 1990; Schlenker 1980; Schlenker & Weigold 1989).

Is it appropriate to conclude, then, that people's identities are in constant flux? Some analysts have suggested that identity (or the self-concept) is more the product of social interaction than a determinant of it (Goffman 1959). However, more recent views have favored the existence of stable core components. Stability is fostered both by consistency in the situations and audiences one encounters (Swann 1983) and, perhaps more importantly, by the effect on identity of strong, central self-beliefs. Potent self-beliefs are those that are held with high certainty and are regarded by the actor as more important components of identity. Potent self-beliefs are relatively enduring and stable, and are more likely than weak self-beliefs to guide judgments and behaviors in social situations (Cheek & Hogan 1983; Leary & Kowalski 1990; Markus & Wurf 1987; Schlenker 1986; Swann 1990).

Self-beliefs can moderate self-presentations in at least three ways. First, potent self-beliefs are more accessible in memory—i.e. more likely to be primed or activated across situations and audiences (Fiske & Taylor 1991). Once primed, the relevant information may be more likely to be included in self-presentations and in reactions to others. For example, actors with stronger self-beliefs resist attempts by others to cast them in nonpreferred roles

(Swann 1987). Second, people regard their own attributes as more positive and beneficial than the attributes of others (Fiske & Taylor 1991); and people who believe an attribute is beneficial view themselves as having more of it than those who do not believe the attribute is beneficial (Kunda & Sanitioso 1989). Because people overvalue their own qualities, they may believe these qualities are more likely to create a good impression on others than qualities they do not think they possess. They may therefore be more likely to try to include the former in their self-presentations. Third, people's self-beliefs act as constraints on what they think they can credibly claim about themselves. People who regard themselves as lacking particular qualities are likely to doubt their ability to substantiate favorable claims to those qualities. People become more self-protective and cautious in their self-presentations when they fear challenge or invalidation (Schlenker 1987).

There are thus advantages to being viewed by others as one sees oneself. Presenting oneself "honestly" is the moral high ground, it minimizes anxiety about invalidation, and it reduces interpersonal stress arising from discrepancies between one's own self-appraisals and others' appraisals (Leary & Kowalski 1990; Schlenker 1980). Of course, people's honest self-appraisals are generally "too good to be true," representing reality-edited but self-glorifying images (Brown 1991; Greenwald & Breckler 1985); in our terms, self-beliefs integrate beneficiality and believability.

It may seem easy to be authentic—that is, to keep self-beliefs and public claims equivalent. However, translating the vast stores of information about oneself in memory into a compact form that seems to be representative of the whole and that others can comprehend and accept requires considerable skill in role taking and acting. Cheek & Hogan (1983) have suggested that it takes as much self-presentational skill to present an accurate portrait of self as it does to deceive. Cheek (1982) found that people who were most successful in getting friends to see them as they saw themselves were (a) high in acting skill (and hence better able to communicate effectively) and (b) high in private self-reflection (and hence more likely to have clearer self-images they could communicate). The discrepancies between self-beliefs and friends' beliefs about them were larger in people low in acting skill or self-reflection. To "be oneself" by communicating desired private conceptions of identity to others may involve considerable purposiveness, deliberation, and social skill. Even the self-presentations of low self-monitors, which are often characterized as spontaneous and expressive, may involve "as much deliberate, intentional, and motivational planning as the impression-managing activities of the high self-monitoring orientation" (Snyder 1987:57).

Finally, self-presentations that were once shaped by situational inducements and role expectations may later be regarded by the actor as authentic representations of self. Research indicates that people's public self-presentations can produce corresponding changes in their global self-evaluations (Jones et al 1981; Rhodewalt & Agustsdottir 1986) and their specific self-beliefs (Schlenker & Trudeau 1990). These changes appear to be maximized when (*a*) people feel personally responsible for the behavior and (*b*) the behavior receives approval from audiences (see Jones 1990; Schlenker 1986).

ACQUISITIVE AND PROTECTIVE STYLES   Distinctions have been drawn between acquisitive and protective self-presentation styles (Arkin 1981; Arkin & Sheppard 1990; Baumeister et al 1989b; Schlenker 1987; Tedeschi & Norman 1985; Wolfe et al 1986). The acquisitive style focuses on opportunities for gaining valued outcomes and regard, whereas the protective style focuses on avoiding dreaded outcomes and regard. Both styles can either be induced situationally or represent a chronic disposition.

The acquisitive style is characterized by more complete participation in social interaction (e.g. initiating discussions, talking more often) and the presentation of more distinctive and self-flattering qualities. People seem to employ the acquisitive style when they think it likely that they can create a preferred impression on others. The style is associated with such traits as high self-esteem, feelings of personal control, high self-confidence, low social anxiety, and nondepression.

In contrast, the protective style is characterized by defensive behaviors designed to avoid losses for identity. People seem to employ the protective style when they think it unlikely that they can create a preferred impression. The style is associated with actions that limit or reduce participation in social interaction (e.g. fewer initiated interactions, talking less during interactions); the avoidance of topics that might reveal ignorance or produce disagreements; less self-disclosure; and self-presentations that are cautious, modest, and designed to avoid attention (e.g. claims of being average, not unique). People who are low in self-esteem, high in fear of negative evaluations, socially anxious, shy, depressive, or low in personal control are more likely than others to employ the protective style. Although these individuals appear to want to be seen just as positively as their more confident counterparts, their self-doubts seem to require more substantiating information before they will take self-presentational risks.

AUTOMATIC OR CONTROLLED SELF-REGULATION   Impression management is sometimes described as a conscious, calculated behavior. However, analysts have distinguished between regulating activities that are deliberately and consciously selected and those that are relatively automatic, nonreflective, and habitual (Cheek & Hogan 1983; Jones 1990; Paulhus 1988; Schlenker 1980). Most of what is considered impression management is probably the result of habitual patterns of behavior triggered automatically and unthinkingly by situational cues.

When are people more likely to behave in automatic versus controlled ways? Controlled self-regulation appears more likely to occur either when the performance is more important to the actor (e.g. because it involves larger potential gains or losses) or when the actor encounters or anticipates impediments to desired self-identifications, as when an actor fears ridicule from critical others (Leary & Kowalski 1990; Schlenker 1985b). Research on social judgment and decision-making confirms that people will process information in a more thorough, intensive, controlled fashion when judgmental mistakes are costly and when people have the time to reflect without disruption (Fazio 1990; Fiske & Taylor 1991; Kruglanski 1990).

How do self-presentations change when they shift from controlled to automatic? Paulhus and his colleagues (1988; Paulhus & Levitt 1987; Paulhus et al 1989) have suggested that automatic self-presentations are often more self-flattering than controlled ones. When subjects are distracted, their self-descriptions are more positive than they otherwise are (Paulhus et al 1989; Paulhus & Levitt 1987), suggesting that egotistical responses are often automatic and not controlled or contrived. This automatic level acts as a default value and is rather high for most people. When people control their self-presentations, they can depart from this level in either direction depending on whether they are attempting to make an even better or a more modest impression on others.

Many discussions of self-presentation assume that when people act in a controlled fashion they try to contrive a more self-flattering impression than they privately hold. But Paulhus's findings indicate that deliberate control can make people more cautious, perhaps as they reflect about the believability of their claims and the embarrassing consequences of seeming immodest or suffering invalidation. Careful consideration of the situation, as compared to an initial global assessment, requires greater cognitive effort. People may therefore become more cautious and modest primarily when they can devote cognitive capacity to an assessment of self, audience, and situation. Swann et al's (1990) findings are consistent with this reasoning: Cognitively busy (distracted) subjects preferred a self-enhancing evaluator whereas nonbusy subjects preferred a self-verifying evaluator.

The actor's mode of thinking can also influence his or her perceptions about the audience. When people fail to concentrate during interactions, either because they approach the situation casually or because they are cognitively taxed by being preoccupied or socially anxious, they rely more heavily on schematic thinking and simple heuristics than they do otherwise (Fiske & Taylor 1991). This reliance can produce simplistic and erroneous perceptions of others, including an increased correspondence bias (Baumeister et al

1989a; Jones 1990), a tendency to confirm preconceptions about the other (Darley et al 1988), and a dependence on stereotypes (Wilder & Shapiro 1989). Thinking becomes less simplistic when the costs of being wrong are increased (Fiske & Taylor 1991). Research is needed on the ways these perceptions in turn influence the actor's subsequent self-presentations.

HOW EFFECTIVELY CAN PEOPLE CONTROL THEIR SELF-PRESENTA-TIONS?   When people try to control their self-presentations, do they perform better or worse than otherwise? Evidence indicates that devoting attention to the type of impression one is creating will sometimes improve and sometimes debilitate performance (Leary 1983; Pyszczynski & Greenberg 1987; Scheier & Carver 1988; Schlenker 1987). When people expect to perform well, attending to their self-presentations appears to improve performance. Confident people are better at deliberately conveying desired impressions to audiences through both verbal and nonverbal channels than are those who lack confidence or are not deliberately trying to create a particular impression (DePaulo 1991; DePaulo et al 1991). Improved performance appears to be due to greater expressive consistency across verbal and nonverbal communication channels (DePaulo 1991), better monitoring of one's own and others' behaviors (DePaulo 1991; Schlenker 1980), and more focused attempts to match one's behavior with appropriate standards for performance (Scheier & Carver 1988). Taking time to prepare and rehearse one's performance can also increase its caliber, and people who have better acting and communication skills are especially benefited by the opportunity to prepare (DePaulo 1991).

In contrast, when people expect to perform poorly, concentrating on the impression they are likely to make will interfere with performance (Schlenker 1987). Schlenker & Leary (1982a) have proposed that social anxiety is experienced when people are motivated to create a desired impression on others but doubt they can do so. Under these conditions, people become self-conscious in the everyday sense: They act in ways that seem awkward, labored, effortful, and inferior. Social anxiety is associated with nervous responses (e.g. fidgeting, self-manipulating), communication difficulties, the tendency to avoid or withdraw from social participation, and a protective self-presentational style, all of which generally create poor impressions on onlookers (Arkin & Sheppard 1990; DePaulo et al 1990). The performance of anxious people appears to be debilitated because of self-preoccupation, excessive worry, tendencies to escape psychologically, and emotionality, all of which interfere with successful self-regulation. People who are concerned with how they will be evaluated by others, including those who are socially anxious and low in self-esteem, are more likely than usual to blush, thereby signaling their social difficulties (Leary & Meadows 1991). Given their impaired social capabilities, it is not surprising that socially anxious people are less accurate at judging when other people are trying to deceive them (DePaulo & Tang 1991).

Self-presentational effectiveness seems to be influenced not only by whether people focus attention on their self-presentations, but also on which aspect of their behavior they bring into focus. In their action-identification theory, Vallacher & Wegner (1987) have proposed that actions can be identified (i.e. classified) at different levels in a hierarchy of abstraction. For example, the activity of conversing with another person can be identified at a high level of abstraction (the actor sees the task as "trying to make a good impression") or at a low level that designates the specifics of the behavior (the actor thinks of the task as that of "smiling, appearing to be attentive, nodding frequently"). Difficult tasks are performed better when they are identified at low levels, whereas easy tasks are performed better when they are identified at high levels (Vallacher et al 1989). Conversely, successful activities tend to be identified at higher levels whereas failures tend to be identified at lower levels (Vallacher et al 1987). Actions normally identified at a high level can be disrupted when people move to a lower level, as when people focus attention on the specifics of a well-learned sequence of behaviors (e.g. a skilled piano player is told to concentrate on each finger placement) (Vallacher & Wegner 1987). According to this analysis, people who have excellent skills will perform better when they focus on the type of impression they want to create, whereas people with poor social skills will do better if they focus on the specific activities that might lead to a desired impression.

DECEPTION   Research suggests that people are surprisingly effective, at least up to a point, at convincingly faking their emotional expressions, attitudes, and even personality characteristics (DePaulo 1991). In her excellent review of research on self-presentation through nonverbal behavior, DePaulo (1991) notes that virtually every relevant study shows "people can successfully convey to others the impression that they are experiencing something they are not.. . . Further, when people are deliberately trying to convey an impression of a state they are not really experiencing, their nonverbal behaviors convey that impression to others even more clearly and effectively than when they really are experiencing that state, but are not trying purposefully to communicate it to others."

When faking, people seem to do more of whatever it is they normally do when experiencing the state. For instance, when faking extroversion, subjects speak more quickly than do genuine extroverts (who speak more quickly than real introverts), and when feigning introversion, people speak even more slowly than genuine introverts. Indeed, subjects are so successful at faking introversion and extroversion that interviewers are unable to differentiate between genuine and faked displays (Toris & DePaulo 1984). Deceivers are aided, at least to some degree, by the everyday presumption of innocence: We tend to assume that others are telling the truth, and we even help them support their claims unless there is reason to suspect deceit (DePaulo et al 1985; Goffman 1959; Schlenker & Leary 1982b).

This is not to say that perceivers are unable to distinguish truth from lies. People can detect lies at better than chance levels, but accuracy rarely exceeds about 10% better than chance (DePaulo et al 1985). Consistent with research on social anxiety is the finding that the more motivated people are to create a desired impression and the less confident they are in their ability to do so, the easier it is for observers to detect their lies (DePaulo et al 1991). Further, when subjects have low outcome expectations, the more motivated they are to impress others, the better able observers are to detect deception (DePaulo et al 1988). The odds of successfully deceiving others seem to be increased by prior practice or experience telling lies, lack of guilt about lying, greater confidence in one's ability to deceive, and greater expressive skills (DePaulo 1991).

What of the opposite ideas, that people cannot keep a secret because their actions will inevitably betray them or that a personal style develops gradually and cannot be faked for very long? Because most research to date focuses on brief interactions, usually ones in which the target cannot interrogate the deceiver, the idea that people cannot long sustain a facade remains untested. Perhaps the idea that lies cannot be sustained successfully arises from our vivid memories of lies that have collapsed. People tell many "little white lies" to reduce interpersonal conflict or tension and to make others feel better (DePaulo 1991). However, we probably remember best those lies that were extremely important. These probably involve high motivation to succeed and high anxiety—the very circumstances in which people are poorest at deception. Our memories may be biased toward recall of lies that were the most difficult to tell and conceal. In any event, further research is needed to assess the boundaries of successful deception.

SELF-MONITORING AND OTHER PERSONALITY MEASURES   Snyder's (see 1987) concept of self-monitoring has stimulated more research on individual differences in impression management than any other personality measure. High self-monitoring reflects a sensitivity to cues about the situational appropriateness of one's social behavior and a willingness and ability to use these cues as guidelines for regulating and controlling self-presentations. Snyder (1987) reviews evidence indicating that high self-monitors are effective social participants who adapt their behavior to social expectations but pay the price of cross-situational inconsistency. Snyder's concept and scale have been critically analyzed, and several problem areas have been identified, including the following: (*a*) the scale is multidimensional and the sub-components are not conceptually or empirically consistent; (*b*) the sub-components sometimes display opposite correlations with variables that should be related to self-monitoring (e.g. role-taking ability); (*c*) low scores on the scale may reflect only an absence of a social orientation, and not the presence of a personal orientation; and (*d*) research support for the construct may be more inconsistent than previously believed (Briggs & Cheek 1988; Schwalbe 1991). The weight of the criticisms has led some to suggest that, although the concept of self-monitoring has been quite heuristic, it is time to rethink the key dimensions involved (Briggs & Cheek 1988). Nonetheless, the concept continues to stimulate research.

The Self-Monitoring Scale was developed specifically to deal with in-dividual differences in impression management. Many other measures have been related to impression management, but these were usually developed with some other purpose in mind. Relevant variables receiving recent atten-tion include self-consciousness (Scheier & Carver 1988), identity orientation (Hogan & Cheek 1983), social desirability (Paulhus 1991), self-esteem (Baumeister et al 1989b), and social anxiety (Leary 1983). Space limitations prohibit discussion of these measures here. Research on individual differences in impression regulation appears to be in its early stages, and we anticipate an increased volume of conceptual and empirical activity in the coming years.

FRONTSTAGE AND BACKSTAGE: AUDIENCES AND PUBLICITY

Goffman (1959) distinguished between the "frontstage," where one must regulate one's performance for the benefit of an immediate audience, and the "backstage," where one can relax without the same concerns for propriety and in-character actions. Social psychologists have tried to capture key aspects of this distinction with a public-vs-private dimension. Although there are several possible usages of the terms *public* and *private* (Tedeschi 1986), the distinc-tion usually reflects the extent to which behavior can be observed and evaluated by others or can be hidden from view. Manipulations of the public-vs-private nature of subjects' behavior have often been used to distin-guish intrapsychic from interpersonal processes, although serious questions have been raised about whether such manipulations really do so (Tetlock & Manstead 1985).

In general, when public is compared to private behavior, public behavior has been described (*a*) as more important, because it influences others' evaluations and expectations and therefore the actor's identity and in-terpersonal outcomes; (*b*) as more committing, because it can obligate the actor to behave in a consistent fashion in the future; (*c*) as more constraining, because the actor must be able to document and defend claims when challenged; (*d*) as more arousing physiologically; and (*e*) as a more authoritative source for defining social reality, because it offers the potential for consensual validation of one's opinions and qualities (Baumeister 1982; Schlenker 1980, 1986; Tetlock & Manstead 1985). Public behavior also offers opportunities that are not present privately, including being able to use secret agendas and to manipulate and deceive others (Tedeschi 1986). Of course, private parallels—unconscious motivation and self-deception—have been drawn to these public activities (Arkin & Baumgardner 1986; Fiske & Taylor 1991; Schlenker 1986). Even with these parallels, there are sufficient differences between public and private concerns that factor analyses of social desirability scales reveal two independent components: deceptive impression management, or the tendency to fake self-flattering responses to others, and self-deception, or the tendency to make self-flattering yet sincerely held assertions (Paulhus 1991; Paulhus & Reid 1991).

Analysts have specified many dimensions on which public and private behavior can differ, but it is difficult to draw invariant conclusions about resulting differences in specific behaviors, such as "people do more (or less) of behavior X in public than in private." For example, public conditions, as compared to private ones, have been found to increase egotistical claims, decrease egotistical claims, have no effect on egotistical claims, and increase egotism for high self-esteem subjects and decrease it for low self-esteem subjects (see Schlenker et al 1990). Manipulations of public-vs-private behavior produce few invariant main effects, and reactions appear to be moderated by other variables.

The concept of a desirable identity provides a framework for conceptualizing moderating variables because it focuses attention on the believability and beneficiality of self-identifications. First, an actor's perceptions of the believability of a particular self-identification are often affected by the public or private context of the activity. For example, actors' perceptions of how well they can substantiate and defend self-flattering claims may be higher in the presence of friendly and supportive audiences but lower in the presence of hostile and critical audiences than they are privately. In general, believability will be lower when the actor thinks the audience is aware of potentially contradictory information, the audience is seen as less supportive or trusting, the actor's self-confidence is lower because of low self-esteem or poor social skills, or the actor anticipates future public tests of the ability where failure is likely (Leary & Kowalski 1990; Schlenker & Weigold 1989). Lower believability translates into more cautious and protective self-identifications.

Second, public scrutiny can change the beneficiality of identity images. That is, it can alter the importance of the performance to the actor by making it potentially more rewarding to succeed but also more costly to fail. Reviews

(Schlenker 1980; Schlenker & Weigold 1989) suggest that people are more likely to present themselves positively when either the expected benefits of doing so increase (e.g. the audience can mediate more valuable rewards) or the expected costs of failing to do so decrease (e.g. there is little to lose). Similarly, public scrutiny can change the types of images and behaviors that are seen as beneficial. Public scrutiny increases the salience of applicable social norms and expectations of the observing audience, and therefore may alter the norms and roles that seem relevant (Greenwald & Breckler 1985; Leary & Kowalski 1990; Tetlock 1985a,b). For example, DePaulo (1991) concluded that people's nonverbal behaviors become more socially appropriate under public than under private conditions. If the situation calls for expressiveness, people become more expressive when their nonverbal acts are public (e.g. a teacher who praises a successful student face-to-face versus from behind a one-way mirror); if the situation calls for being less expressive, people become less expressive in public (e.g. suppressing delight at beating a rival who is in the same room).

Because of its potential impact, public scrutiny can intensify positive or negative reactions. When people are motivated to perform well but have low outcome expectations (expect failure), they perceive a threat to identity, and the perceived threat is greater when they are accountable to others (Schlenker et al 1991). Public threats create anxiety, procrastination, lower effort, an undermining of intrinsic interest in the task, task distraction, and protective self-presentations (Schlenker et al 1991). The anticipation of being unable to perform up to public expectations leads to "choking" (Baumeister & Scher 1988). When people lack the resources to accomplish tasks successfully yet nonetheless try to please those to whom they are accountable, compromises often replace good judgment and task performance suffers (Tetlock 1985b).

On the other hand, when people have higher outcome expectations (expect success), they perceive a challenge for identity that offers the opportunity to receive credit for competence; the perceived challenge is heightened when people are accountable to others (Schlenker et al 1991). Being publicly accountable can produce beneficial effects on task performance, including greater learning and subsequent recall of information, more cognitively complex decision strategies, data-driven rather than theory-driven processing, a greater awareness of decision strategies, and greater effort devoted to the task (Fiske & Taylor 1991; Schlenker et al 1991; Tetlock 1985b; Tetlock et al 1989). In short, public accountability can cause people to process information in a more thorough, less stereotyped fashion that minimizes the impact of preconceptions (Fiske & Taylor 1991). Research on social loafing provides an illustration of how public scrutiny is among the factors that mobilize effort and improve performance. Social loafing, which refers to a reduction of effort when one's performance in a group cannot be identified, is eliminated when personal performance is made publicly identifiable, people are highly involved in the task or otherwise given an incentive for good performance, and people can clearly evaluate their own performance, even in private (see Geen 1991).

Audiences

As important, if not more important, than the public or private nature of a performance is the audience that is salient to the actor at the time of the performance. The power of real and imagined audiences to shape people's beliefs and behaviors has been discussed by numerous analysts (Cheek & Hogan 1983; Jones 1990; Mead 1934; Schlenker 1980, 1986; Tetlock & Manstead 1985), and some have discussed the self as audience for one's own behavior (Greenwald & Breckler 1985; Schlenker 1980, 1985b; Snyder et al 1983; Tetlock & Manstead 1985). The self provides an evaluative orientation (Greenwald & Breckler 1985; Higgins 1989) that can be distinct from the evaluative orientation of specific other people. Yet the judgment process itself is similar for audiences of self and others in that it involves observing, evaluating, and sanctioning conduct in relation to a particular set of prescriptions and standards.

Traditional analyses have focused on the impact of immediate audiences, particularly as these affect the arousal of the actor and the possibilities of tangible and intangible outcomes (Baumeister 1982; Leary & Kowalski 1990; Schlenker 1980; Tedeschi & Norman 1985). In general, audiences have a greater impact on an actor's arousal and self-identifications when they are more significant (i.e. powerful, attractive, statused, and expert), greater in number, and more immediate psychologically (Leary & Kowalski 1990; Nowak et al 1990; Schlenker 1986). More recently, researchers have noted that audiences also have an impact on behavior by serving as targets of communication and by priming information about identity.

AUDIENCES AS COMMUNICATION TARGETS   In order to communicate, speakers and listeners must determine what constitutes their "common ground"—i.e. the knowledge, beliefs, and suppositions they share. Effective communication requires that information be tailored or fitted to the audience's knowledge and value systems, using terms, symbols, and evidence that will be readily understood and accepted without challenge (Clark 1985; Fussell & Krauss 1989; Schlenker 1986). This process requires role-taking skill in anticipating how an audience is likely to react and communication skill in tailoring one's communications to produce the desired effect. Audiences, then, may be viewed as templates, each with a different pattern of knowledge and values. Incoming communications must be fitted to these patterns if the actor is to communicate effectively and persuasively.

Research shows that people tailor their communications to accommodate the audience. DePaulo & Coleman (1986) found differences among the types of speech adults addressed to children, a retarded adult, a foreigner who spoke English as a second language, and a native adult. Speech to children, for instance, was clearer, simpler, more attention maintaining, and had longer pauses. The way women converse with men on the telephone differs depending on the intimacy levels of their past relationships (Montepare & Vega 1988), and judges' nonverbal behaviors are affected by the age and educational status of jurors (Blanck et al 1985). Fleming et al (1990) investigated how people deal with simultaneous viewing by multiple audiences, each with a different agenda. Subjects were able to include messages in their performances that could be decoded accurately by friends but not by strangers.

AUDIENCES AS CUES FOR IDENTITY INFORMATION AND EVALUATIVE ORIENTATION   Audiences—whether present or absent—can cue or prime identity-relevant information and a set of prescriptive standards for evaluating oneself. Audiences appear capable of activating relevant self-schemata and roles (e.g. the sight of her child activates a set of self-images and roles relevant to a mother's behavior), goals that can be satisfied and scripts that can be followed (e.g. the sight of an attractive member of the opposite sex primes a romantic-quest script), and standards for evaluating one's performance (e.g. the presence of a tolerant friend with a reputation for goofing off suggests lower standards for evaluating one's term paper than does the stern visage of a demanding parent). Once this information is activated, consciously or nonconsciously, actors can draw upon it in their subsequent self-presentations to that audience.

Baldwin and associates examined the capacity of imagined audiences to prime different experiences of self. Baldwin & Holmes (1987) found that women evaluated a sexually permissive piece of fiction more negatively after they had earlier visualized one of their parents, who might be expected to disapprove of the sexual content of the story, than when they had visualized a campus friend, who might be expected to be more permissive. Extending this work, Baldwin et al (1990) asked students to evaluate themselves or their ideas after unconscious exposure to slides of disapproving or approving others. Evaluations were more negative after exposure to the image of a disapproving significant other.

Audiences, even imagined ones, also influence people's emotional expressions. Fridlund (1991a,b) reviewed evidence that the presence or absence of other people has a pronounced effect on facial expressiveness (e.g. people are more expressive after bowling a strike when their faces are visible rather than hidden from audiences). Emotional expressions should be conceptualized not as pure indicants of covert activity but as tools for communication. Fridlund's (1991a) research shows that merely imagining a particular audience influences facial expressiveness. Subjects watched a pleasant videotape either alone, alone but with the belief a friend nearby was engaged in an irrelevant task, alone but with the belief the friend was watching the same tape in another room, or when the friend was physically present. Facial expressiveness varied monotonically with the sociality of the viewing situation, indicating that the imagined presence of the friend, especially when the friend was enjoying the same activity, mediated expressivity. Similarly, after controlling for happiness, Fridlund et al (1990) found that people smile more when they are imagining enjoyable situations in which they are with other people rather than alone.

Audiences affect self-identifications by providing an evaluative orientation (Greenwald & Breckler 1985; Schlenker 1986). Audiences can serve as a comparative standard for judgment and thereby influence self-evaluations. In a finding consistent with his self-evaluation maintenance theory, Tesser (1988) has shown that a superior performance by a close other increases an actor's self-evaluation if the performance occurs on a dimension that is of low personal relevance (e.g. a sibling performs superbly during a concert and is applauded by her sister, a professor of psychology, who bursts with pride) but decreases self-evaluation if the performance occurs on a dimension of high personal relevance (e.g. the sibling's superb musical performance diminishes feelings of self-worth by her other sister, the unemployed musician). More recently, Brown, Novick, Lord & Richards (unpublished) have shown that a salient audience can produce either a contrast effect (e.g. subjects rate themselves more positively after exposure to an unattractive other but less positively after exposure to an attractive other) or a carry-over effect (e.g. subjects associate themselves with the accomplishments of attractive others and dissociate themselves from the accomplishments of unattractive others).

Are Some People Oblivious to Social Pressures?

Two contrasting styles of self-regulation have been described in the literature (Buss & Briggs 1984; Scheier & Carver 1988). One style, epitomized by public self-consciousness, is characterized by concern about how one appears to others, sensitivity to the expectations of others, and tailoring of behaviors to create a desired impact on others. The second style, epitomized by private self-consciousness, is characterized by "tuning out" the social matrix, being oblivious to the expectations of others, and basing one's behavior on personal convictions. Buss & Briggs (1984) associated the former style with pretension and strategic impression management, the latter with authenticity and expressiveness. They concluded that impression-management interpretations have been overextended and should be applied only to certain situations (e.g. formal as compared to informal situations, or situations involving large economic profits) and certain types of people (e.g. those who are publicly self-conscious or high self-monitors).

In response, Schlenker & Weigold (1990) took the expansivist position and argued that the independence displayed by privately self-conscious people could be due either to their obliviousness to social concerns or to their desire to create the image, in their own minds and for others, of being autonomous and independent individuals. As predicted, the self-descriptions of people who were privately self-conscious were found to emphasize autonomy and personal identity. Further, an experiment found that both privately and publicly self-conscious subjects were highly responsive to the likely attributions of a partner, but in different ways. Privately self-conscious subjects publicly changed their attitudes if by so doing they protected the appearance of being autonomous (i.e. they publicly misrepresented their attitudes if the partner supposedly thought they were conformists and he could have misinterpreted their genuine attitudes as indicators of conformity). Publicly self-conscious subjects, in contrast, publicly changed their attitudes to conform to the expectations of their partner (i.e. they publicly presented attitudes that made them appear to be independent or conforming depending on what type of person the partner preferred them to be). Thus, publicly self-conscious subjects used the other person to tell them what they should be, and in this sense were other directed, whereas privately self-conscious subjects used the other person to tell them if they were creating the type of impression they wanted to create, that of being autonomous, and in this sense were inner directed. It is not whether people's self-presentations are influenced by others that differentiates these two styles of self-regulation, but how people are influenced.

ACCOUNTING: SELECTIVE EXPLANATIONS OF SOCIAL REALITY

As people go about the business of constructing desired identities in social life, they inevitably confront impediments and threats (e.g. accidents and mistakes, failed task performances, unwelcome feedback from others). People then mobilize their activities to deal with the problem, and as part of this mobilization, construct explanations for the difficulty. Explanations are required whenever people's activities violate personal or social prescriptions in ways that threaten identity (Goffman 1971; Schlenker 1980, 1982; Snyder et al 1983; Tedeschi & Riess 1981). People account for the problem, usually by proffering self-serving explanations that attempt to reconcile the conduct with the prescriptions that were violated.

The magnitude of the potential negative repercussions seems to be a monotonic function of (a) the importance of the prescription violated, including the amount of harm generated; and (b) the apparent linkage of the actor to the event, because of personal responsibility (e.g. freely and intentionally transgressing as opposed to transgressing due to accident or ignorance) or the possible involvement of central elements of self (e.g. task failure seems due to incompetence rather than task difficulty or lack of sleep) (Higgins & Snyder 1991; Schlenker 1980, 1982; Tedeschi & Riess 1981). As the importance of the event and the actor's linkage to it increase, so do the potential negative affect, the damage to identity, and the negative sanctions. People are then more likely to attempt self-serving accounts or apologies for their behavior.

From the actor's perspective, an account is effective to the extent it minimizes the negative repercussions, including damage to identity and negative sanctions. In order to reduce the potential repercussions, the actor can (*a*) proclaim innocence, claiming the event did not take place or the actor was in no way involved; (*b*) use an excuse that attempts to minimize personal linkage; (*c*) use a justification that tries to minimize the harm or show that, all things considered, the conduct was really advantageous, not harmful; or (*d*) offer an apology. Explanations of conduct are more desirable, from the actor's perspective, to the extent they are beneficial (e.g. eliminate or minimize the negative repercussions) and believable to the salient audience (Schlenker 1980, 1982). As with other types of impression regulation, accounts are directed at both external and internal audiences, self included (Schlenker 1980, 1982; Snyder et al 1983; Tetlock 1985a). Often, accounts are negotiated between actor and audience, as the participants try out and modify variations until they eventually construct an explanation of the event in question that is acceptable to both parties (Schlenker 1980; Snyder & Higgins 1988).

Defenses of Innocence

A defense of innocence (Schlenker 1980) or denial (Higgins & Snyder 1991) claims either that no transgression occurred (e.g. the "murder victim" committed suicide) or that the actor was not involved. Because such accounts offer total exoneration if they are accepted by audiences, they are ideal from the actor's perspective. Little research has been conducted on the use of these defenses. Higgins & Snyder (1991) noted that denials are sometimes used when an actor commits a transgression so heinous (e.g. incest or serial killing) that extenuating circumstances are unlikely to mitigate blame.

Excuses

Excuses attempt to attenuate the linkage between the actor and some undesired event. This is accomplished by trying to reduce personal responsibility or by shifting causal attributions from central elements of identity to peripheral or external elements (Higgins & Snyder 1991; Schlenker 1980, 1982; Tedeschi & Riess 1981). Research on self-serving attributional biases reveals a tendency to minimize personal responsibility for failure by blaming it on bad luck, task difficulty, lack of sleep, etc. Similarly, negative interpersonal evaluations can be excused by blaming them on undesirable traits of the evaluator, as in the case of stigmatized persons who attribute negative feedback to the prejudices of the source (Crocker et al 1991).

Excuses can protect actors from threatening attributions about their central characteristics. "Good" excuses, that is, ones that offer greater protection, attribute transgressions or failures to external, uncontrollable, or unintentional causes instead of internal, controllable, and intentional causes (Higgins & Snyder 1989, 1991; Weiner et al 1987, 1991). Such "good" excuses elicit less negative affect for the actor, lead to higher evaluations, and are more likely to be used (Weiner et al 1987). People will reconstruct their memory for past events in ways that excuse failure or misconduct, such as by simply forgetting about failed promises (Gentry & Herrmann 1990) and recalling their own transgressions as due to uncontrollable and unintentional factors while recalling others' transgressions as due to malice (Baumeister et al 1990). It has been suggested that when compared to justifications (which often challenge the audience's definition of the situation or its right to sanction), excuses are more "polite" (Gonzales et al 1990).

Excuses are desirable only to the extent they offer a believable explanation for the problem. People generally attempt to construct excuses that "fit the facts" (Schlenker 1980, 1982; Snyder & Higgins 1988; Tetlock 1985a). As examples, socially anxious people will use social anxiety as an excuse only when it is clear that anxiety might debilitate performance on the particular task (Snyder & Higgins 1988); and people are less likely to blame failure on task difficulty when they expect to discuss their performance with an informed audience who knows the nature of the task than when they do not anticipate discussion (Whitehead & Smith 1990). Further, people experience more negative affect after using excuses if they anticipate that their audience might challenge them (Snyder & Higgins 1988).

Snyder & Higgins (1988) have reviewed evidence supporting the idea that excuses have benefits for the excuse maker that go beyond simply reducing negative social sanctions. Excuses can increase positive affect and emotions, boost self-esteem, reduce anxiety and depression, aid health, and improve performance. On the other hand, excuses can generate problems if they are used too often or are not believed by significant others. Higgins & Snyder (1989) have proposed that excuses can undermine rewards and long-term esteem when they ignore the principles of good excuse-making and break social conventions, are phrased in ways that make them easy to disprove, involve pejorative labels (e.g. alcoholic), or fail to match the severity of the transgression. Further, at least one form of excuse—blaming others—appears to generate negative consequences. Tennen & Affleck's (1990) review of 22 studies found a reliable relationship between other-blame and poor psychological adjustment. Distressed spouses are especially likely to blame the other for problems, thereby intensifying conflict (Bradbury & Fincham 1990). Thus, self-blame, to the extent that it generates self-improvement, can produce positive consequences, including better personal adjustment and coping (Tennen & Affleck 1990).

Self-handicapping is a type of anticipatory excuse that paradoxically protects identity by giving the appearance of increasing the chances of failure. The concept has stimulated considerable research in the last decade because of its implications for impression regulation and its clinical application (Higgins et al 1990). Self-handicapping refers to the act of placing an obstacle in one's own path in order to obscure the evaluative implications of a performance (Jones & Berglas 1978). Subsequent failures can be discounted by blaming them on the obstacle instead of central components of identity, whereas subsequent successes are augmented because they occurred despite the debilitating factor. Self-handicapping seems most likely to occur when actors are uncertain how they will perform on a task that is relevant to central components of their self-conceptions (Snyder 1990). Researchers have studied a variety of obstacles that can be used as self-handicaps, including alcohol, debilitating drugs, distracting music, anxiety, bad moods, illness, reduced effort, sleeplessness, childhood traumas, and recent adversities (Baumgardner & Arkin 1987; Higgins et al 1990). Sheppard & Arkin (1991) have reported an interesting complement to self-handicapping: behavioral other-enhancement. Males who were uncertain how they would perform in competition with a rival gave the rival a performance advantage, thereby creating a plausible, less threatening, explanation for their own possible failure.

As research on self-handicapping suggests, people can reduce anxiety and stress from upcoming performances by preparing accounts of why they might perform poorly. The beneficial consequences of anticipatory excuses were demonstrated by Leary (1986), who found that socially anxious participants were more relaxed and performed better during a social interaction if a background noise was supposedly distracting and might harm their performance. Those without this excuse performed poorly. Of course, the chronic use of excuses, particularly those involving pejorative characteristics, can entail long-term costs (Baumeister & Scher 1988; Higgins & Snyder 1989).

Justifications

Justifications are aimed at altering the audience's interpretation of the event itself, either by minimizing the importance of the prescriptions that were violated (e.g. "Marijuana laws are ill-conceived and antiquated"), minimizing the amount of harm done (e.g. "The shocks I administered to him weren't very painful"), or appealing to an alternative set of prescriptions that might transform the act from bad to good (e.g. "I punished him for his own good; he'll thank me some day"). Literature reviews of the use of justifications are available (Higgins & Snyder 1991; Schlenker 1980, 1982; Tedeschi & Riess 1981).

Baumeister et al (1990) found that perpetrators and victims of transgressions usually have different interpretations of the event. Perpetrators usually minimize the harm they do, view expressions of anger as appropriate for the circumstances, and view events as having neat and tidy endings. In contrast, victims describe enduring negative consequences; view the perpetrator's anger as an overreaction; view the perpetrator's behavior as arbitrary, inconsistent, and immoral; and regard the perpetrator's conduct as senseless. A much-studied example of the use of justifications is found in the forced compliance literature (see Schlenker 1982). People who appear to be responsible for producing aversive consequences will change their attitudes to justify their behavior, thereby protecting their identities.

Apologies

Apologies are admissions of blameworthiness and regret for undesirable events. They serve the important social functions of acknowledging that prescriptions have been violated, reaffirming the value of the prescriptions, and recognizing interpersonal obligations. On the personal level they can minimize the negative repercussions for the actor, attenuating damage to identity and reducing negative sanctions (Goffman 1971; Scher & Darley, unpublished; Schlenker 1980). Apologies can range from perfunctory recognition that norms have been trivially violated (saying "Pardon me" after stepping one someone's toes in a theater line) to full blown expressions of apologetic intent, remorse, self-castigation, offers to make compensation, requests for forgiveness, and promises of better future conduct. The more severe the actor's transgression, the more of these elements are usually included in apologies (Schlenker & Darby 1981).

Apologies can improve a transgressor's lot. Apologetic actors are blamed less, forgiven more, liked better, and punished less than their unremorseful counterparts (Darby & Schlenker 1982, 1989; Ohbuchi et al 1989; Tedeschi & Norman 1985). Scher & Darley (unpublished) have proposed that apologies can communicate four important ideas about the actor: He or she accepts blame, feels remorse, promises not to commit the act again, and is willing to make compensation. They found all four contribute to the effectiveness of apologies, that the explicit inclusion of some components can lead to inferences about others, and that those who apologize in any form have an advantage compared to those who do not. Failing to apologize can elicit negative responses, including anger and aggression, from audiences and victims (Scher & Darley unpublished; Ohbuchi et al 1989). Failing to apologize may demean the victim by implying the victim is not worthy of respect and ordinary social courtesies.

Self-criticism often elicits support and reassurance from audiences (Goffman 1971; Jones & Pittman 1982), and apologies may similarly prompt audiences to offer public encouragement. However, apologies may create long-range drawbacks for the actor. Powers & Zuroff (1988) found that self-criticism elicited public support but private negative evaluations of the actor. Their data suggest a cycle in which those in need of support can elicit it by using self-castigating interpersonal strategies that give momentary public relief at the cost of long-run disrespect. Similarly, the protective self-presentational style of depressives may involve an overreliance on apologies as remedial behaviors (Schlenker et al 1991).

CONCLUSIONS

The last decade has brought a burgeoning interest in how people control and regulate information during social interactions. Along with this interest has come a conceptual expansion of the nature and functions of impression management. The traditional view saw such regulation as an immoral, pretentious, and circumscribed activity, employed primarily by professional politicians or salespersons and their amateur emulators. More recent conceptualizations describe it as a fundamental component of social interaction. In order to communicate, people must distill vast amounts of information about themselves into key elements relevant to particular relationships or situations. This packaging of information is influenced by people's agendas and by real and imagined audiences. It can comprise automatic or controlled activities involving varying levels of awareness, and it can entail assertions that are more or less "truthful." Impression regulation occurs at all stages of relationships, in first meetings as well as long-term relationships.

One of many potentially fruitful directions for theory and research concerns how people attempt to regulate information for the benefit of others, especially others with whom they are involved in close relationships. Besides advancing and protecting their own interests, people also regulate information in order to support and protect the identities of others, to make others feel good, to help them cope, and to inspire them to seek new goals and challenges. The literature relevant to these issues (e.g. social support) has usually examined the reactions of the recipient, not the use of the strategies. Work is also needed on the use of impression management over the course of long-term relationships. Research on these topics could begin to balance the abundance of research examining more short-lived and self-centered ploys.

164 SCHLENKER & WEIGOLD

Literature Cited

Arkin, R. 1981. Self-presentation styles. See Tedeschi 1981, pp. 311–33

Arkin, R. M., Baumgardner, A. H. 1986. Self-presentation and self-evaluation: Processes of self-control and social control. See Baumeister 1986, pp. 75–97

Arkin, R. M., Sheppard, J. A. 1990. Strategic self-presentation: an overview. See Cody & McLaughlin 1990, pp. 175–93

Austin, J. L. 1962. How to Do Things with Words. New York: Oxford

Baldwin, M. W., Carrell, S. E., Lopez, D. F. 1990. Priming relationship schemas: my advisor and the Pope are watching me from the back of my mind. J. Exp. Soc. Psychol. 26:435–54

Baldwin, M. W., Holmes, J. G. 1987. Salient private audiences and awareness of the self. J. Pers. Soc. Psychol. 52:1087–98

Baumeister, R. F. 1982. A self-presentational view of social phenomena. Psychol. Bull. 91:3–26

Baumeister, R. F. ed. 1986. Public Self and Private Self. New York: Springer-Verlag

Baumeister, R. F. 1989. The optimal margin of illusion. J. Soc. Clin. Psychol. 8:176–89

Baumeister, R. F., Tice, D. M. 1986. Four selves, two motives, and a substitute process self-regulation model. See Baumeister 1986, pp. 63–97

Baumeister, R. F., Scher, S. J. 1988. Self-defeating behavior patterns among normal individuals: review and analysis of common self-destructive tendencies. Psychol. Bull. 104:3–22

Baumeister, R. F., Hutton, D. G., Tice, D. M. 1989a. Cognitive processes during deliberate self-presentation: How self-presenters alter and misinterpret the behavior of their interaction partners. J. Exp. Soc. Psychol. 25:59–78

Baumeister, R. F., Tice, D. M., Hutton, D. G. 1989b. Self-presentational motivations and personality differences in self-esteem. J. Pers. 57:547–79

Baumeister, R. F., Stillwell, A., Wotman, S. R. 1990. Victim and perpetrator accounts of interpersonal conflict: autobiographical narratives about anger. J. Pers. Soc. Psychol. 59:994–1005

Baumgardner, A. H., Arkin, R. M. 1987. Coping with the prospect of social disapproval: strategies and sequelae. See Snyder & Ford 1987, pp. 323–46

Baumgardner, A. H., Brownlee, E. A. 1987. Strategic failure in social interaction: evidence for expectancy disconfirmation processes. J. Pers. Soc. Psychol. 52:525–35

Baumgardner, A. H., Kaufman, C. M., Levy,

P. E. 1989. Regulating affect interpersonally: when low esteem leads to greater enhancement. J. Pers. Soc. Psychol. 56: 907–21

Blanck, P. D., Rosenthal, R., Cordell, L. H. 1985. The appearance of justice: judges' verbal and nonverbal behavior in criminal jury trials. Stanford Law Rev. 38:89–164

Bond, C. F. Jr., Anderson, E. L. 1987. The reluctance to transmit bad news: private discomfort or public display? J. Exp. Soc. Psychol. 23:176–87

Bradbury, T. N., Fincham, F. D. 1990. Attributions in marriage: review and critique. Psychol. Bull. 107:3–33

Briggs, S. R., Cheek, J. M. 1988. On the nature of self-monitoring: problems with assessment, problems with validity. J. Pers. Soc. Psychol. 54:663–78

Brown, J. D. 1990. Evaluating one's abilities: shortcuts and stumbling blocks on the road to self-knowledge. J. Exp. Soc. Psychol. 26:149–67

Brown, J. D. 1991. Accuracy and bias in self-knowledge. See Snyder & Forsyth 1991, pp. 158–78

Brown, J. D., Collins, R. L., Schmidt, G. W. 1988. Self-esteem and direct versus indirect forms of self-enhancement. J. Pers. Soc. Psychol. 55:445–53

Brown, J. D., Gallagher, F. M. 1991. Coming to terms with failure: private self-enhancement and public self-effacement. J. Exp. Soc. Psychol. In press

Burger, J. M. 1987. Increased performance with increased personal control: a self-presentation interpretation. J. Exp. Soc. Psychol. 23:350–60

Buss, A. H., Briggs, S. R. 1984. Drama and the self in social interaction. J. Pers. Soc. Psychol. 47:1310–24

Cantor, N., Kihlstrom, J. 1987. Personality and Social Intelligence. Englewood Cliffs, NJ: Prentice-Hall

Chaiken, S., Pliner, P. 1987. Women, but not men, are what they eat: the effect of meal size and gender on perceived femininity and masculinity. Pers. Soc. Psychol. Bull. 13: 166–76

Cheek, J. M. 1982. Aggregation, moderator variables, and the validity of personality tests: a peer-rating study. J. Pers. Soc. Psychol. 43:1254–69

Cheek, J. M., Hogan, R. 1983. Self-concepts, self-presentations, and moral judgments. In Psychological Perspectives on the Self, ed. J. Suls, A. G. Greenwald, 2:249–73. Hillsdale, NJ: Erlbaum

Cialdini, R. B., Finch, J. F., DeNicholas, M. E. 1990. Strategic self-presentation: the indirect route. See Cody & McLaughlin 1990, pp. 194–206

Clark, H. H. 1985. Language use and language users. In *The Handbook of Social Psychology*, ed. G. Lindzey, E. Aronson, 2:179–231. New York: Random House. 3rd ed.

Cody, M. J., McLaughlin, M. L., eds. 1990. *The Psychology of Tactical Communication*. Bristol, PA: Multilingual Matters Ltd.

Cooley, C. H. 1902. *Human Nature and the Social Order*. New York: Scribner's

Crocker, J., Voelkl, K., Testa, M., Major, B. 1991. Social stigma: the affective consequences of attributional ambiguity. *J. Pers. Soc. Psychol.* 60:218–28

Darby, B. W., Schlenker, B. R. 1982. Children's reactions to apologies. *J. Pers. Soc. Psychol.* 43:742–53

Darby, B. W., Schlenker, B. R. 1989. Children's reactions to transgressions: effects of the actor's apology, reputation, and remorse. *Br. J. Soc. Psychol.* 28:353–64

Darley, J. M., Fleming, J. H., Hilton, J. L., Swann, W. B. Jr. 1988. Dispelling negative expectancies: the impact of interaction goals and target characteristics on the expectancy confirmation process. *J. Exp. Soc. Psychol.* 24:19–36

DePaulo, B. M. 1991. Nonverbal behavior and self-presentation. *Psychol. Bull.* In press

DePaulo, B. M., Coleman, L. M. 1986. Talking to children, foreigners, and retarded adults. *J. Pers. Soc. Psychol.* 51:945–59

DePaulo, B. M., Epstein, J. A., LeMay, C. S. 1990. Responses of the socially anxious to the prospect of interpersonal evaluation. *J. Pers.* 58:623–40

DePaulo, B. M., Kirkendo, S. E., Tang, J., O'Brien, T. P. 1988. The motivational impairment effect in the communication of deception: replications and extensions. *J. Nonverbal Behav.* 12:177–202

DePaulo, B. M., LeMay, C. S., Epstein, J. A. 1991. Effects of importance of success and expectations for success on effectiveness at deceiving. *Pers. Soc. Psychol. Bull.* 17:14–24

DePaulo, B. M., Stone, J. I., Lassiter, G. D. 1985. Deceiving and detecting deceit. See Schlenker 1985a, pp. 323–70

DePaulo, B. M., Tang, J. 1991. Social anxiety and social judgment: the example of detecting deception. *J. Anxiety.* In press

Fazio, R. 1990. Multiple processes by which attitudes guide behavior: the MODE model as an integrative framework. *Adv. Exp. Soc. Psychol.* 23:75–109

Feldstein, S., Sloan, B. 1984. Actual and stereotyped speech tempos of extroverts and introverts. *J. Pers.* 52:188–204

Fiske, S. T., Taylor, S. E. 1991. *Social Cognition.* New York: McGraw-Hill. 2nd ed.

Fleming, J. H., Darley, J. M., Hilton, J. L., Kojetin, B. A. 1990. Multiple audience problem: a strategic communication perspective on social perception. *J. Pers. Soc. Psychol.* 58:593–609

Fridlund, A. J. 1991a. The sociability of solitary smiling: potentiation by an implicit audience. *J. Pers. Soc. Psychol.* 60:229–40

Fridlund, A. J. 1991b. Evolution and facial action in reflex, social motive, and paralanguage. In *Advances in Psychophysiology*, ed. P. K. Ackles, J. R. Jennings, M. G. H. Coles, 4: In press. Greenwich, CT: JAI Press

Fridlund, A. J., Sabini, J. P., Hedlund, L. E., Schaut, J. A., Shenker, J. I., Knauer, M. J. 1990. Audience effects on solitary faces during imagery: displaying to the people in your head. *J. Nonverbal Behav.* 14:113–37

Friedlander, M. L., Schwartz, G. S. 1985. Toward a theory of strategic self-presentation in counseling and psychotherapy. *J. Consult. Psychol.* 32:483–501

Fussell, S. R., Krauss, R. M. 1989. The effects of intended audience on message production and comprehension: reference in a common ground framework. *J. Exp. Soc. Psychol.* 25:203–19

Gardner, W. L., Martinko, M. J. 1988. Impression management in organizations. *J. Manage.* 14:321–38

Geen, R. 1991. Social motivation. *Annu. Rev. Psychol.* 42:377–99

Gentry, M., Herrmann, D. J. 1990. Memory contrivances in everyday life. *Pers. Soc. Psychol. Bull.* 16:241–53

Giacalone, R. A., Rosenfeld, P., ed. 1989. *Impression Management in the Organization.* Hillsdale, NJ: Erlbaum

Godfrey, D., Jones, E. E., Lord, C. 1986. Self-promotion is not ingratiating. *J. Pers. Soc. Psychol.* 50:106–15

Goffman, E. 1959. *The Presentation of Self in Everyday Life.* Garden City, NY: Doubleday

Goffman, E. 1971. *Relations in Public.* New York: Basic Books

Gollwitzer, P. M., Wicklund, R. A. 1985. Self-symbolizing and the neglect of others' perspectives. *J. Pers. Soc. Psychol.* 48: 702–15

Gonzales, M. H., Pederson, J. H., Manning, D. J., Wetter, D. W. 1990. Pardon my gaffe: effects of sex, status, and consequence severity on accounts. *J. Pers. Soc. Psychol.* 58:610–21

Greenberg, J. 1990. Looking fair vs. being fair: managing impressions of organizational justice. *Res. Org. Behav.* 12:111–58

Greenwald, A. G., Breckler, S. J. 1985. To

whom is the self presented? See Schlenker 1985a, pp. 126-45

Hatch, J. A. 1987. Impression management in kindergarten classrooms: an analysis of children's face-work in peer interactions. *Anthropol. Educ. Q.* 18:100–15

Higgins, E. T. 1989. Self-discrepancy theory: What patterns of self-beliefs cause people to suffer? *Adv. Exp. Soc. Psychol.* 22:93–136

Higgins, R. L., Snyder, C. R. 1989. Excuses gone awry: an analysis of self-defeating excuses. In *Self-Defeating Behaviors: Experimental Research, Clinical Impressions, and Practical Implications*, ed. R. L. Curis, 99–130. New York: Plenum

Higgins, R. L., Snyder, C. R. 1991. Reality negotiation and excuse-making. See Snyder & Forsyth 1991, pp. 79–95

Higgins, R. L., Snyder, C. R., Berglas, S., eds. 1990. *Self-Handicapping: The Paradox That Isn't.* New York: Plenum

Hill, M. G., Weary, G., Williams, J. 1986. Depression: a self-presentation formulation. See Baumeister 1986, pp. 213–39

Hogan, R. 1983. A socioanalytic theory of personality. In *Nebraska Symposium on Motivation*, ed. M. M. Page, 29:55–89. Lincoln: Univ. Nebraska Press

Hogan, R., Cheek, J. M. 1983. Identity, authenticity, and maturity. In *Studies in Social Identity*, ed. T. R. Sarbin, K. E. Scheibe, pp. 339–57. New York: Praeger

Hogan, R., Hogan, J. 1991. Personality and status. In *Personality, Social Skills, and Psychopathology: An Individual Differences Approach*, ed. D. G. Gilbert, J. J. Conley. NY: Plenum. In press

Hogan, R., Jones, W. H. 1983. A role theoretical model of criminal conduct. In *Personality Theory, Moral Development and Criminal Behavior*, ed. W. S. Laufer, J. M. Days. Boston: Lexington

Holtgraves, T., Srull, T. K. 1989. The effects of positive self-descriptions on impressions: general principles and individual differences. *Pers. Soc. Psychol. Bull.* 15:452–62

James, W. 1890. *Principles of Psychology.* New York: Holt

Jones, E. E. 1990. *Interpersonal Perception.* New York: W. H. Freeman

Jones, E. E., Berglas, S. 1978. Control of attributions about the self through self-handicapping strategies: the appeal of alcohol and the role of underachievement. *Pers. Soc. Psychol. Bull.* 4:200–6

Jones, E. E., Pittman, T. S. 1982. Toward a general theory of strategic self-presentation. In *Psychological Perspectives on the Self*, ed. J. Suls, 1:231–62. Hillsdale, NJ: Erlbaum

Jones, E. E., Rhodewalt, F., Berglas, S., Skelton, J. A. 1981. Effects of strategic

self-presentation on subsequent self-esteem. *J. Pers. Soc. Psychol.* 41:407–21

Kowalski, R. M., Leary, M. R. 1990. Strategic self-presentation and the avoidance of aversive events: antecedents and consequences of self-enhancement and self-depreciation. *J. Exp. Soc. Psychol.* 26:322–36

Kruglanski, A. W. 1990. *Basic Processes in Social Cognition: A Theory of Lay Epistemology.* New York: Plenum

Kunda, Z., Sanitioso, R. 1989. Motivated changes in the self-concept. *J. Exp. Soc. Psychol.* 25:272–85

Leary, M. R. 1983. *Understanding Social Anxiety: Social, Personality, and Clinical Perspectives.* Beverly Hills, CA:Sage

Leary, M. R. 1986. The impact of interactional impediments on social anxiety and self-presentation. *J. Exp. Soc. Psychol.* 22:122–35

Leary, M. R., Kowalski, R. M. 1990. Impression management: a literature review and two-component model. *Psychol. Bull.* 107:34–47

Leary, M. R., Meadows, S. 1991. Predictors, elicitors, and concomitants of social blushing. *J. Pers. Soc. Psychol.* 60:254–62

Markus, H., Ruvolo, A. 1989. Possible selves: personalized representations of goals. See Pervin 1989, pp. 211–42

Markus, H., Wurf, E. 1987. The dynamic self-concept: a social psychological perspective. *Annu. Rev. Psychol.* 38:299–337

Mead, G. H. 1934. *Mind, Self, and Society.* Chicago: Univ. Chicago Press

Montepare, J. M., Vega, C. 1988. Women's vocal reactions to intimate and casual male friends. *Pers. Soc. Psychol. Bull.* 14:103–13

Nowak, A., Szamrej, J., Latané, B. 1990. From private attitude to public opinion: a dynamic theory of social impact. *Psychol. Rev.* 97:362–76

Ohbuchi, K., Kameda, M., Agarie, N. 1989. Apology as aggression control: its role in mediating appraisal of and response to harm. *J. Pers. Soc. Psychol.* 56:219–27

Paulhus, D. L. 1988. Automatic and controlled self-presentation. Presented at Annu. Meet. Am. Psychol. Assoc., Atlanta

Paulhus, D. L. 1991. Measurement and control of response biases. In *Measures of Personality and Social Psychological Attitudes*, ed. J. P. Robinson, P. R. Shaver, L. S. Wrightsman, 1:17–59. San Diego: Academic

Paulhus, D. L., Graf, P., Van Selst, M. 1989. Attentional load increases the positivity of self-presentation. *Soc. Cognit.* 7:389–400

Paulhus, D. L., Levitt, K. 1987. Desirable responding triggered by affect: automatic egotism? *J. Pers. Soc. Psychol.* 52:245–59

Paulhus, D. L., Reid, D. B. 1991. Enhancement and denial in socially desirable responding. *J. Pers. Soc. Psychol.* 60:307–17

Pervin, L. A., ed. 1989. *Goal Concepts in Personality and Social Psychology.* New York: Hillsdale, NJ: Erlbaum

Pliner, P., Chaiken, S. 1990. Eating, social motives, and self-presentation in women and men. *J. Exp. Soc. Psychol.* 26:240–54

Powers, T. A., Zuroff, D. C. 1988. Interpersonal consequences of overt self-criticism: a comparison with neutral and self-enhancing presentations of self. *J. Pers. Soc. Psychol.* 54:1054–62

Pyszczynski, T. A., Greenberg, J. 1987. Depression, self-focused attention, and self-regulatory perseveration. See Snyder & Ford 1987, pp. 105–29

Rhodewalt, F., Agustsdottir, S. 1986. The effects of self-presentation on the phenomenal self. *J. Pers. Soc. Psychol.* 50:47–55

Scheibe, K. E. 1985. Historical perspectives on the presented self. See Schlenker 1985a, pp. 33–64

Scheier, M. F., Carver, C. S. 1988. A model of behavioral self-regulation: translating intention into action. *Adv. Exp. Soc. Psychol.* 21:303–46

Schlenker, B. R. 1980. *Impression Management.* Monterey, CA: Brooks/Cole

Schlenker, B. R. 1982. Translating actions into attitudes: an identity-analytic approach to the explanation of social conduct. *Adv. Exp. Soc. Psychol.* 15:193–247

Schlenker, B. R., ed. 1985a. *The Self and Social Life.* New York: McGraw-Hill

Schlenker, B. R. 1985b. Identity and self-identification. See Schlenker 1985a, pp. 65–99

Schlenker, B. R. 1986. Self-identification: toward an integration of the private and public self. See Baumeister 1986, pp. 21–62

Schlenker, B. R. 1987. Threats to identity: self-identification and social stress. See Snyder & Ford 1987, pp. 273–321

Schlenker, B. R., Darby, B. W. 1981. The use of apologies in social predicaments. *Soc. Psychol. Q.* 44:271–78

Schlenker, B. R., Leary, M. R. 1982a. Social anxiety and self-presentation: a conceptualization and model. *Psychol. Bull.* 92:641–69

Schlenker, B. R., Leary, M. R. 1982b. Audiences' reactions to self-enhancing, self-denigrating, and accurate self-presentations. *J. Exp. Soc. Psychol.* 18:89–104

Schlenker, B. R., Trudeau, J. V. 1990. The impact of self-presentations on private self-beliefs: effects of prior self-beliefs and misattribution. *J. Pers. Soc. Psychol.* 58:22–32

Schlenker, B. R. Weigold, M. F. 1989. Goals and the self-identification process. See Pervin 1989, pp. 243–90

Schlenker, B. R., Weigold, M. F. 1990. Self-consciousness and self-presentation: being autonomous versus appearing autonomous. *J. Pers. Soc. Psychol.* 59:820–28

Schlenker, B. R., Weigold, M. F., Doherty, K. 1991. Coping with accountability: self-identification and evaluative reckonings. See Snyder & Forsyth 1991, pp. 96–115

Schlenker, B. R., Weigold, M. F., Hallam, J. R. 1990. Self-serving attributions in social context: effects of self-esteem and social pressure. *J. Pers. Soc. Psychol.* 58:855–63

Schwalbe, M. L. 1991. Role taking, self-monitoring, and the alignment of conduct with others. *Pers. Soc. Psychol. Bull.* 17:51–57

Sheppard, J. A., Arkin, R. M. 1991. Behavioral other-enhancement: strategically obscuring the link between performance and evaluation. *J. Pers. Soc. Psychol.* 60:79–88

Snyder, C. R. 1990. Self-handicapping processes and sequelae: on the taking of a psychological dive. See Higgins et al 1990, pp. 107–45

Snyder, C. R., Ford, C. eds. 1987. *Coping with Negative Life Events: Clinical and Social Psychological Perspectives.* New York: Plenum

Snyder, C. R., Forsyth, D. R., eds. 1991. *Handbook of Social and Clinical Psychology.* New York: Pergamon

Snyder, C. R., Higgins, R. L. 1988. Excuses: their effective role in the negotiation of reality. *Psychol. Bull.* 104:24–35

Snyder, C. R., Higgins, R. L., Stucky, R. J. 1983. *Excuses: Masquerades in Search of Grace.* New York: Wiley

Snyder, M. 1987. *Public Appearances/Private Realities: The Psychology of Self-Monitoring.* San Francisco: Freeman

Solomon, S., Greenberg, J., Pyszczynski, T. 1991. Terror management theory of self-esteem. See Snyder & Forsyth 1991, pp. 21–40

Steele, C. M. 1988. The psychology of self-affirmation: sustaining the integrity of the self. *Adv. Exp. Soc. Psychol.* 21:261–302

Sternberg, R. J. 1986. *Beyond IQ: A Triarchic Theory of Human Intelligence.* New York: Cambridge Univ. Press

Swann, W. B., Jr. 1983. Self-verification: bringing social reality into harmony with the self. In *Psychological Perspectives on the Self,* ed. J. Suls, A. Greenwald, 2:33–66. Hillsdale, NJ: Erlbaum

Swann, W. B. Jr. 1987. Identity negotiation: where two roads meet. *J. Pers. Soc. Psychol.* 53:1038–51

Swann, W. B. Jr. 1990. To be adored or to be known: the interplay of self-enhancement and self-verification. In *Handbook of Motivation and Cognition,* ed. R. M. Sorrentino, E. T. Higgins, 2:408–50. New York: Guilford

Swann, W. B. Jr., Hixon, G., Stein-Seroussi, A., Gilbert, D. T. 1990. The fleeting gleam of praise: cognitive processes underlying behavioral reactions to self-relevant feedback. *J. Pers. Soc. Psychol.* 59:17–26

Taylor, S. E., Brown, J. B. 1988. Illusion and well-being: a social psychological perspective on mental health. *Psychol. Bull.* 103:193–210

Taylor, S. E., Lobel, M. 1989. Social comparison activity under threat: downward evaluation and upward contacts. *Psychol. Rev.* 96:569–75

Tedeschi, J. T., ed. 1981. *Impression Management Theory and Social Psychological Research.* New York: Academic

Tedeschi, J. T. 1986. Private and public experiences and the self. See Baumeister 1986, pp. 1–20

Tedeschi, J. T., Norman, N. 1985. Social power, self-presentation, and the self. See Schlenker 1985a, pp. 293–321

Tedeschi, J. T., Riess, M. 1981. Verbal strategies in impression management. In *The Psychology of Ordinary Explanations of Social Behavior,* ed. C. Antaki, pp. 271–309. London: Academic

Tedeschi, J. T., Schlenker, B. R., Bonoma, T. V. 1971. Cognitive dissonance: private ratiocination or public spectacle? *Am. Psychol.* 26:685–95

Tennen, H., Affleck, G. 1990. Blaming others for threatening events. *Psychol. Bull.* 108:209–32

Tesser, A. 1988. Toward a self-evaluation maintenance model of social behavior. *Adv. Exp. Soc. Psychol.* 21:181–227

Tesser, A., Cornell, D. P. 1991. On the confluence of self processes. *J. Exp. Soc. Psychol.* In press

Tetlock, P. E. 1985a. Toward an intuitive politician model of the attribution process. See Schlenker 1985a, pp. 203–34

Tetlock, P. E. 1985b. Accountability: the neglected social context of judgment and choice. *Res. Org. Behav.* 9:279–332

Tetlock, P. E., Manstead, A. R. S. 1985.

Impression management versus intrapsychic explanations in social psychology: a useful dichotomy? *Psychol. Rev.* 92:59–77

Tetlock, P. E., Skitka, L., Boettger, R. 1989. Social and cognitive strategies for coping with accountability: conformity, complexity, and bolstering. *J. Pers. Soc. Psychol.* 57:632–40

Toris, C., DePaulo, B. M. 1984. Effects of actual deception and suspiciousness of deception on interpersonal perceptions. *J. Pers. Soc. Psychol.* 47:1063–73

Trope, Y. 1986. Self-enhancement, self-assessment, and achievement behavior. In *Handbook of Motivation and Cognition,* ed. R. M. Sorrentino, E. T. Higgins, pp. 350–78. New York: Guilford

Vallacher, R. R., Wegner, D. M. 1987. What do people think they're doing? Action identification and human behavior. *Psychol. Rev.* 94:3–15

Vallacher, R. R., Wegner, D. M., Frederick, J. 1987. The presentation of self through action identification. *Soc. Cogn.* 5:301–22

Vallacher, R. R., Wegner, D. M., Somoza, M. P. 1989. That's easy for you to say: action identification and speech fluency. *J. Pers. Soc. Psychol.* 56:199–208

Weiner, B., Amirkhan, J., Folkes, V. S., Verette, J. A. 1987. An attributional analysis of excuse giving: studies of a naive theory of emotion. *J. Pers. Soc. Psychol.* 52:316–24

Weiner, B., Figueroa-Munoz, A., Kakihara, C. 1991. The goals of excuses and communication strategies related to causal perceptions. *Pers. Soc. Psychol. Bull.* 17:4–13

Whitehead, G. I. III, Smith, S. H. 1990. The use of consensus-raising excuses as a function of the manipulation of publicness: the role of expectations of future interaction. *Pers. Soc. Psychol. Bull.* 16:562–72

Wilder, D. A., Shapiro, P. 1989. Effects of anxiety on impression formation in a group context: an anxiety-assimilation hypothesis. *J. Exp. Soc. Psychol.* 25:481–99

Wolfe, R. N., Lennox, R. D., Cutler, B. L. 1986. Getting along and getting ahead: empirical support for a theory of protective and acquisitive self-presentation. *J. Pers. Soc. Psychol.* 50:356–61

Annu. Rev. Psychol. 1992. 43:169–203

COMBINATORIAL DATA ANALYSIS

Phipps Arabie

Graduate School of Management, Rutgers University, Newark, New Jersey
07102-1895

Lawrence J. Hubert

Department of Psychology, University of Illinois, Champaign Illinois 61820

Dedicated to Ledyard Tucker

KEY WORDS: seriation, clustering, partitioning, additive trees, network models

CONTENTS

0066-4308/92/0201-0169$02.00

INTRODUCTION

Although the *Annual Review of Psychology* periodically offers chapters on topics in quantitative methodology (e.g. L. V. Jones & Appelbaum's 1989 chapter on psychometric methods), it occasionally allows reviews to herald new subareas of intense development (e.g. Smith's 1976 chapter on analysis of qualitative data). The present chapter is of the latter kind. There is thus no strong consensus on the boundaries of our area or even on when coverage in a review chapter should begin. There is, however, one enduring certainty: We lack adequate space to discuss all the meritorious and relevant work.

Combinatorial data analysis (CDA) concerns the *arrangement* of objects for which relevant data have been obtained. Stated more explicitly, CDA is involved either with (a) the location of arrangements that are optimal for the representation of a given data set (and thus is usually operationalized using a specific loss-function that guides the combinatorial search defined by some set of constraints imposed by the particular representation chosen) or with (b) trying to determine in a confirmatory manner whether a specific object arrangement given a priori reflects the observed data. CDA does not (cf Rouanet et al 1986) postulate strong stochastic models based on specific unknown parametric structures as underlying a given data set. Although CDA might use or empirically construct various weighting functions, the weights so obtained are not intended to be interpreted as parameter estimates in some presumed stochastic model viewed in turn as responsible for generating the data. In CDA, manifest data are emphasized, and the traditional concern for an assumed relationship between the data and a restrictively parameterized stochastic population model is essentially ignored.

Methods of CDA are generally organized around (a) the types of combinatorial structures we might use to represent a given data set (e.g. Guénoche & Monjardet 1987, Hubert 1987) and (b) the classes of combinatorial optimization methods used in solving problems of actually locating optimal arrangements rather than the (confirmatory) evaluation of a given one. The latter emphasis on computation may seem unusual, but such staples of combinatorial structures as the "traveling salesman problem," the "minimum spanning tree," and "additive trees" have been used to connect seemingly unrelated techniques of discrete data analysis (see respectively Hubert & Baker 1978; Hubert 1974a; Carroll 1976); similarly, explicit optimization techniques like "branch-and-bound" and "dynamic programming" have been used to suggest a general approach to broad classes of data analysis tasks (see respectively Hand 1981; Hubert & Golledge 1981).

The need for new techniques to answer questions that, for computational ease, had often been approached using restrictive parametric models (even when their underlying assumptions may be very unrealistic for the problem under study) has not always been acknowledged. According to personal communications, Lerman had considerable difficulty getting his (1980) programmatic statement published, and Edgington (1980) found a generally unreceptive audience for the randomization emphasis in his text. But the Zeitgeist has caught up with and vindicated those authors, as judged by the acclaim for their continuing contributions to the area (e.g. Edgington 1987; Lerman 1988) and by special issues of quantitative journals devoted entirely to combinatorial data analysis (e.g. Leclerc & Monjardet 1987a,b,c).

Most of the papers cited here were published after 1974. We avoid certain research areas here either because they rely implicitly on parameter estimation (e.g. classification decisions based on discriminant analysis) or because they merit their own review chapters (e.g. the related topics briefly mentioned in the section on Rankings, Relations, and Partially Ordered Sets, below). Our terminology for models and types of data follows that of an earlier *Annual Review* chapter by Carroll & Arabie (1980:609–12). We make extensive use of Tucker's (1964) terminology, distinguishing between "ways" (a matrix that has rows and columns is two-way) and modes: If the two ways both correspond to the same set of entities, as in a proximity matrix of n stimuli by n stimuli, the data are two-way one-mode; if the rows and columns correspond to disjoint sets (e.g. subjects by attributes), the data are two-way two-mode. We note that this terminology has found its way into relevant book titles (e.g. one dedicated to Tucker and edited by Law et al 1984; Coppi & Bolasco 1989).

SERIATION

Methods of seriation are, in effect, techniques for the unidimensional scaling or sequencing of a set of objects along a continuum. In the last several decades, these and other strategies of analysis have been developed most aggressively by archaeologists whose frequent concern is with a two-mode matrix of artifacts by sites which is typically converted to a one-mode matrix amenable to nonmetric multidimensional scaling (MDS) techniques. A review of this methodology may be found in Carroll & Arabie (1980:617; also see Lerman 1981: Ch. 8; Pliner 1984; Halperin 1989). The inherent problem is combinatorial in nature and can be characterized via the ordering of the objects defined by the one mode. Because the ostensible task is to place objects along a continuum so as to optimize an objective function, the problem seems to be one of location estimation along the real line. It is thus susceptible to the usual type of gradient-based optimization techniques (e.g. Kruskal 1964a,b). Such intuition conflicts with widespread observed failures (e.g. Shepard 1974:378–79) of gradient-based MDS algorithms when uni-dimensional solutions are sought. De Leeuw & Heiser (1977:740), however, noted that the one-dimensional MDS problem was in fact one of com-binatorial optimization and was thus reducible to the search for an ordering along a continuum, possibly with a secondary estimation of the actual coor-dinates if desired.

Hubert & Arabie (1986) demonstrated analytically why gradient-based MDS approaches fail for the unidimensional case. We have since provided a combinatorial algorithm that guarantees a global optimum and is compu-tationally feasible for medium-sized (e.g. $n = 20$) proximity matrices (Hubert & Arabie 1986). The difficulties with location estimation based on the usual gradient methods are not restricted to the unidimensional case, and we have shown that gradient-based MDS techniques will fail for identical technical reasons when city-block representations are sought in two or more di-mensions. As an alternative, combinatorial approaches to higher-dimensional city-block spaces are being developed (Hubert & Arabie 1988; Arabie et al 1989; Heiser 1989). These methods are in a tradition of combinatorial approaches to MDS (e.g. Hubert & Schultz 1976; Waller et al 1992).

CLUSTERING

Perhaps the most well-developed and commonly used form of combinatorial data analysis is clustering, which comprises those methods concerned in some way with the identification of homogeneous groups of objects, based on whatever data are available. The immensity of the literature on cluster analy-sis precludes our giving much space to applications; fortunately, the Classification Society of North America publishes an annual bibliography, *Classification Literature Automated Search Service,* based on citations to "classic" articles and books as compiled by the Institute for Scientific In-formation. The articles cited there are drawn primarily from the periodical literature on clustering and multidimensional scaling; there were 887 citations for 1990 (Volume 19; Day 1990).

Evidence of the activity propelling research in clustering is given by a selection of full-length texts devoted to the subject (Sneath & Sokal 1973; Bock 1974; Duran & Odell 1974; Hartigan 1975; Spaeth 1980, 1985; Gordon

1981; Lorr 1983; Murtagh 1985a; Godehardt 1988; Jain & Dubes 1988; Mandel 1988 [see Kamensky 1990]; McLachlan & Basford 1988) as well as a lengthy report commissioned by the US National Research Council (Panel on Discriminant Analysis, Classification, and Clustering 1988). This profusion of texts occasionally evinces a scholar's counterpart to Gresham's Law: The same publisher that took the English-language edition of Hartigan (1975) out of print released a second edition of Everitt (1980). The technique is mentioned in such potboilers as *Spycatcher* (Wright 1987:153), is central to *The Clustering of America* (Weiss 1988), and along with some other methodology suffers frequent misrepresentation in the literature on "artificial intelligence" (e.g. Denning 1989; and cf Dale's 1985 criticisms of Michalski & Stepp 1983). In addition to conference volumes largely devoted to clustering and closely related methods (e.g. Van Ryzin 1977; Felsenstein 1983a; Diday et al 1984; Diday et al 1986; Gaul & Schader 1986; Bock 1988), there have been some noteworthy reviews in such substantive areas as marketing (Wind 1978; Punj & Stewart 1983; Dickinson 1990; Beane & Ennis 1987; also see Green et al 1989: Section 7), experimental psychology (Luce & Krumhansl 1988; Shepard 1988), developmental psychology (K. Miller 1987), clinical psychology (Blashfield & Aldenderfer 1988), criminology (Brennan 1987), information retrieval (Willett 1988), biophysics (Hartigan 1973), image segmentation and related areas of computer science (Dubes & Jain 1979; Jain & Dubes 1988: Ch. 5) and phenetic taxonomy (Sokal 1986a, 1988a). More methodologically oriented review articles are cited below.

Formal Underpinnings

For many statisticians, the shady history of cluster analysis is an ongoing cause for suspicion. The early approaches to clustering (e.g. McQuitty 1960) were usually mere convenient algorithms devoid of any associated representational model or effort at optimizing a stated criterion. Subsequent remedies to this situation have taken two paths that with few exceptions (e.g. Ling 1973) are distinct.

The first is to note that the structures sought by many hierarchical clustering methods (whose output is often represented as an inverted tree diagram or dendrogram, as considered in Murtagh 1984a; see Gordon 1987a for an excellent, comprehensive review) conform to the ultrametric inequality

$$d_{ij} \leq \max (d_{ik}, d_{jk}) \text{ for all } k,$$

where i, j, and k are members of the stimulus set; d_{ij} is the distance between stimuli i and j predicted by the cluster analysis and corresponds to the observed dissimilarity measure that is input for the cluster analysis. The ultrametric inequality is to most forms of hierarchical cluster analysis what the triangle inequality is to two-way MDS (Shepard 1962a,b; Kruskal 1964a,b). That is, the predicted or reconstructed distances resulting from a relevant hierarchical cluster analysis conform to the ultrametric inequality, just as those from two-way MDS satisfy the triangle inequality. The ultrametric inequality was introduced independently into the literatures of biology, experimental psychology, and data analysis by C. J. Jardine et al (1967) and Johnson (1967; also see Hartigan 1967; and Lance & Williams 1967) in the same year; recognition of its importance in the physical sciences has been somewhat delayed (Rammal et al 1986) and apparently remains to be achieved in the neurosciences (e.g. Ambros-Ingerson et al 1990). A tradition of close inspection of its implications for clustering methods has led to a better understanding of how various hierarchical techniques are interrelated (Hubert & Baker 1976, 1979; Jambu 1978; Kim & Roush 1978; Leclerc 1979; Milligan 1979; Batagelj 1981; Leclerc 1981, 1986; Hubert 1983; Degens 1983, 1985; Herden 1984; Barthélemy & Guénoche 1988; Critchley & Van Cutsem 1989; Ohsumi & Nakamura 1989).

The second approach to providing a more defensible logical basis for clustering algorithms is to relate such algorithms to the vast literatures on graph theory (e.g. Monjardet 1978, 1981a; see reviews by Hubert 1974b and Guénoche & Monjardet 1987) and set and lattice theory (Barbut & Monjardet 1970a,b; Hubert 1977a; Janowitz 1978, 1979; Janowitz & Schweizer 1989). This strategy has yielded new insights about the results from cluster analyses (e.g. Ling 1975; Hubert & Baker 1976, 1979; Matula 1977; Frank 1978; Tarjan 1982; Godehardt 1988; Sriram 1990) and about the design of faster and more capacious algorithms (e.g. Hansen & Delattre 1978; Day 1984; Day & Edelsbrunner 1985; see reviews by Murtagh 1983, 1984b). Although much of this literature reaches a technical depth beyond the training of most psychologists (thus perhaps explaining why some of the field's most rudimentary aspects are continually reinvented—e.g. Cooke et al 1986), parts of it remain basic and highly applicable.

For example, a topic of considerable economic importance in graph theory is the *minimum spanning tree* (MST) problem, in which one employs a graph whose nodes correspond to stimuli and whose edges represent possible links, with weights typically used to predict or reconstruct the empirical dissimilarities data. The objective is to find that tree spanning the graph (so that there is a path between each pair of nodes, but without any cycles) for which the sum of the edge weights is a minimum/maximum for dis/similarities. Solving the MST problem is formally equivalent to performing single-link clustering (Gower & Ross 1969), and the connection between clustering and spanning trees has proven substantively useful (Hubert 1974a; Murtagh 1985a: Ch. 4). Although it is generally assumed that interest in the MST first arose in engineering (e.g. in the layout of telephone, powerline, and other types of networks), Graham & Hell's (1985) laudable and comprehensive history of the problem indicates that work by the anthropologist Czekanowski (1909) enabled Florek et al (1951) to devise single-link clustering before the appearance of the paper (Kruskal 1956) most heavily cited in the English literature on MST algorithms relevant to engineering. Thus, a formal problem first recognized in the behavioral sciences became one of enormous practical importance.

Lest our summary of these developments in clustering seem too optimistic, we should note the absence of progress in a few areas. For example, N. Jardine & Sibson (1971) introduced the useful distinction between methods of clustering versus algorithms for implementing them: "It is easy to show that the single-link method, for example, can be implemented by a divisive algorithm, an agglomerative algorithm, or by an algorithm which belongs to neither category" (p. 42). While this sensible recommendation has been endorsed by various leaders in the field (e.g. Rohlf 1982:267), there are still many authors whose writing would be much clearer if the distinction were respected in their papers. Another regrettable tendency is the occasional resurgence of a nostalgic preference for algorithms supported neither by optimization nor models (e.g. Whaley 1982:173) versus the more current approach outlined above.

We now consider some of the areas in which clustering has seen greatest development in recent years.

Clustering of Binary Data

As the limiting case of discreteness, binary (0, 1) data have often claimed a special place in the discussion of numerous forms of data analysis (Cox 1970; Tucker 1983), and clustering is no exception. Such input data are usually two-mode, and a selected list of clustering methods developed specifically for them includes Lerman et al (1980), Buser & Baroni-Urbani (1982), Brossier (1984), Guénoche (1985), Cliff et al (1986), Muchnik et al (1986), Govaert (1988), Barthélemy (1989), Li & Dubes (1989), and Mkhadri (1989). An especially elegant and model-based method is that of De Boeck & Rosenberg (1988; also see Van Mechelen & De Boeck 1990).

A closely related problem of data analysis, often omitted in surveys of methodology because of its nonprobabilistic basis, is the following: Devise a set of binary vectors or *keys* for optimally and parsimoniously classifying a set of objects, each represented itself as a binary vector (as in a two-mode matrix of objects by attributes). Results on this important problem are found largely in the biological literature (Barnett & Gower 1971; Gower 1973, 1974; Gower & Payne 1975; Payne & Preece 1980; Sackin & Sneath 1988).

Measures of Association or Dissimilarity Coefficients

Many methods of clustering (especially hierarchical ones) require two-way *one*-mode data, in the form of matrices variously gauging direct judgments of perceived similarity, brand switching among products, confusions, correlations, etc. But the data as they occur are often two-way *two*-mode (e.g. objects by attributes). As a step in preprocessing such data *prior* to performing a cluster analysis, the conversion from two- to one-mode data is such a common problem that it usually receives its own chapter in texts on clustering, and it is also relevant to MDS (Shepard 1972; Coxon 1982: Ch. 2) and related techniques of data analysis (see Gower 1985). Although the topic has traditionally seen greatest emphasis in biology (see references in Rao 1982), psychologists concerned with such substantive issues as content analysis (Krippendorf 1980, 1987), interrater agreement (Hubert 1977b; Hubert & Golledge 1983; Popping 1988), information retrieval (W. P. Jones & Furnas 1987), and choice processes (Doignon et al 1986) have recently begun contributing to the literature.

Such considerations as the scale type of the data—whether they are binary, more generally discrete, or continuous—have long been paid considerable attention, especially in biology. Gower (1971) and Lerman (1987), for example, devised general coefficients of similarity allowing for data where the "variables" (as in a two-mode matrix of objects by variables) were "mixed" among those different classes.

The case of binary data is of special interest. If we consider two binary-valued vectors **x** and **y**, then the element-by-element matches are of the four types labeled a, b, c, and d in Figure 1. For example, if **x** = (1, 1, 0, 0) and **y** = (1, 0, 1, 0), then the first entries (1, 1) in each vector are an a-type pair, the second (1, 0) are a b-type pair, etc. An endless number of coefficients of agreement can be written as a function of those four types; for example, Pearson product-moment correlation is given by $(ad - bc)/[(a + b)(a + c)(b + d)(c + d)]^{.5}$. Cheetham & Hazel (1969) were among the first to catalog the various coefficients published and based on the format of Figure 1, and their list had fewer than 25 entries, whereas Hubálek's (1982) had 43. The framework of Figure 1 is also useful for comparing pairs of partitions, as considered below in the section on Assessing and Comparing Structures, where a state of "1" corresponds to a pair of objects appearing in the same equivalence class or cluster in a partition, and "0" otherwise. The coefficients then can be used to gauge relatedness of pairs of partitions.

Given the plethora of such coefficients, several strategies of research have evolved to answer data analysts' questions concerning which coefficient(s) to use. For example, in research somewhat more relevant to MDS and related spatial models than to clustering, Gower (1971, 1986a,b), Critchley (1986b), Fichet (1986), Gower & Legendre (1986), and Zegers (1986) have studied those coefficients leading to one-mode matrices allowing the corresponding stimuli to be embedded perfectly in Euclidean spaces (see Heiser 1986 and Gower 1986b for a current summary of the main issues) by the fitting of various spatial models. W. P. Jones & Furnas (1987) have taken another type

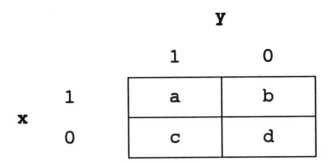

Figure 1   The four possible patterns resulting from matching elements of two binary-valued vectors **x** and **y**.

of geometric approach, leading to sophisticated visual portrayals of differential performance of such coefficients in the practice of information retrieval.

Another line of research has sought to fortify these descriptive statistics to sustain inferential statistical tests. This formidable task faces the immediate obstacle that many of the measures, as initially proposed, are not even bounded by the familiar limits of $[-1, +1]$ or $[0, 1]$. Determining the maximum value of such coefficients for a given set of data is often a computationally difficult problem of combinatorial optimization (cf Hubert & Arabie 1985:199). Impressive advances on this general problem have been made by Lerman (1983a,b, 1987), Giakoumakis & Monjardet (1987a,b), and Lerman & Peter (1988). For coefficients most commonly used in empirical studies, some important distributional results have recently been reported (Heltshe 1988, Snijders et al 1990).

It is not surprising that when confronted with such an abundance of coefficients, various investigators have taken *a priori* approaches, including emphasis upon patterns of sensitivity to certain aspects of data (Faith 1984), admissibility conditions (Hubálek 1982, Vegelius & Janson 1982, Gower & Legendre 1986, Zegers 1986), and formal axioms (Baulieu 1989). As an exemplar of the last approach, Baroni-Urbani & Buser (1976) began with a set of substantively motivated axioms and then derived a new measure satisfying them; the authors also simulated their coefficient's numerical behavior.

While some practitioners would no doubt agree with Proverbs 20:23 that "Divers weights [i.e. measures] are an abomination unto the Lord," we cannot improve upon the advice of Weisberg (1974:1652–1653): ". . . I would contend that analysts frequently should not seek a single measure and will never find a perfect measure. Different measures exist because there are different concepts to measure. . . . It is time to stop acting embarrassed about the supposed surplus of measures and instead make the fullest possible use of their diversity."

Mixture Models

No overview of recent developments in clustering would be complete without consideration of mixture models, in which an underlying continuum is assumed to give rise to distinct but continuous clusters or subpopulations. Sampling from such a space gives rise to a "mixture" from the clusters and to the problem of estimating parameters characterizing those clusters. Because this aspect of clustering relies heavily on parameter estimation (particularly by maximum likelihood), it is somewhat outside the declared scope of our chapter and will therefore receive only cursory treatment. Following in the tradition of J. H. Wolfe (1970), recent advances have appeared at an increasing rate (Hartigan 1975: Ch. 5; Marriott 1982; McLachlan 1982; Meehl & Golden 1982; Basford & McLachlan 1985; Windham 1985, 1987; Bryant 1988; Ganesalingam 1989; Govaert 1989), culminating in McLachlan & Basford's (1988) laudable *Mixture Models: Inference and Applications to Clustering* (see reviews by Windham 1988 and Morin 1990).

Overlapping Clustering

In the "modern" era of clustering, the first formalized approach to overlapping, instead of hierarchical or partitioning, clustering (N. Jardine & Sibson 1968) occasioned extensive rehearsals (in the form of algorithmic developments by Cole & Wishart 1970; Rohlf 1974, 1975), but to date only one performance (published analysis of empirical data with interpretation: Morgan 1973).

More recent times have been conducive to the developments of models, associated algorithms, and substantive applications. The ADCLUS model (Shepard & Arabie 1979), devised for fitting to a single (two-way one-mode) proximity matrix, has seen extensions to the three-way ("individual differences" or INDCLUS; Carroll & Arabie 1983) case, as well as other developments (DeSarbo 1982; Corter & Tversky 1986; Bandelt & Dress 1989), including linkage to latent class analysis (Grover & Srinivasan 1987). An important theoretical derivation of the relation between common and distinctive feature models, as represented by fitting the ADCLUS model, is given by Sattath & Tversky (1987). Algorithmic and software developments include those of Arabie & Carroll (1980a,b), DeSarbo (1982), Carroll & Arabie (1982, 1983), Hojo (1983), Mirkin (1987, 1989a,b, 1990), Imaizumi & Okada (1990).

For a list of published applications of overlapping clustering, see Arabie et al (1987a:57, 63; 1987b), as well as Faith (1985), Mirkin (1986, 1987, 1989b, 1990), Arabie & Maschmeyer (1988), Sabucedo et al (1990), and Walker (1989).

Partitioning

As an alternative both to hierarchical and to overlapping clustering, partitioning approaches assign each object to exactly one cluster. Described generically, the objective is to maximize similarity/cohesiveness/homogeneity within each cluster while maximizing heterogeneity among clusters. While the importance of partitioning approaches to data analysis has long been recognized in the behavioral and biological sciences (MacQueen 1967; Lee 1980; Lee & MacQueen 1980), it has recently enjoyed great emphasis in economics as well, in such applications as facility location (Klastorin 1982) and especially in the layout of computer circuitry (Barnes 1982). Because the number of distinct partitions of n objects into m clusters increases approximately as $m^n/m!$ (the printers' demons have conspired so successfully against this expression that its denominator is incomplete in Duran & Odell 1974:41 and missing altogether in Hartigan 1975:130), attempting to find a globally optimum solution (regardless of the measure of goodness-of-fit employed) is usually not computationally feasible.

Thus, a wide variety of heuristic approaches (capably reviewed both by Belbin 1987 and by Jain & Dubes 1988:89–117) have been developed to find local optima. Hartigan (1975:102) summarized differences among approaches as stemming from "(i) the starting clusters, (ii) the movement rule [i.e. transferring objects among clusters], and (iii) the updating [of goodness-of-fit] rule." In addition, the measure of goodness-of-fit should be consistent with the scale type of the data (see Hartigan 1975: Ch. 4, 6, 7). Not surprisingly, the scale type assumed often is interval or ratio, and the strongest results and most readily available software are for this case (Gordon & Henderson 1977; Spaeth 1980: Ch. 3; 1985, 1986a). Klein & Dubes (1989) have recently suggested that the simulated annealing approach to optimization (Kirkpatrick et al 1983; see Dubes 1988; Ripley 1990) might be useful for partitioning, in contrast to negative results for somewhat related problems of data analysis (De Soete et al 1988). In an interesting and novel development, Spaeth (1986b,c) has turned the traditional partitioning problem inside out with "anticlustering," which seeks maximal heterogeneity within clusters and minimal heterogeneity between clusters.

Constrained Clustering

The imposition of a priori constraints on a cluster solution generally makes both the description and implementation of a clustering algorithm more complicated but can sometimes confer major benefits. For example, if objects to be partitioned are already sequenced (i.e. placed on a line), so that all clusterings of them must respect this ordering, then the amount of computation is reduced enough to allow finding a global optimum in circumstances where an unconstrained global optimum would be inconceivable (Gordon 1973a; Hartigan 1975: Ch. 6; Spaeth 1980:61–64).

A commoner constraint is contiguity in a plane, with consequent difficulties in designing corresponding algorithms (as reviewed by Murtagh 1985b). The problem occurs frequently enough to have engendered an impressive literature within clustering (Gordon 1980b; 1981:61–69; Matula & Sokal 1980; Ferligoj & Batagelj 1982, 1983; Perruchet 1983a; DeSarbo & Mahajan 1984; Margules et al 1985; Finden & Gordon 1985; Legendre 1987).

Consensus Clustering

Inventors of spatial models have long disgreed over whether and how one should aggregate data and represent group structure or should instead portray individual differences (among subjects or other sources of data) (Tucker & Messick 1963; Ross 1966; Cliff 1968; Carroll & Chang 1970; Arabie et al 1987a; also see chapters in Law et al 1984 and Coppi & Bolasco 1989). But such discrete structures as dendrograms afford a different approach to this problem of data analysis: representation of the group structure as a consensus over the structures fitted to individuals' data (or dendrograms from other sources—such as different clustering procedures applied to the same data). That is, using the topology of the dendrograms for a common set of objects, and based on each source's data (and in general ignoring the ultrametric or other numerical values associated with levels of the dendrograms), highly formalized rules, often embodying classical approaches to voting and social choice (Mirkin 1979: Ch. 2; Day 1988), are used to construct a best-fitting consensus dendrogram. Excellent reviews and bibliographies of selected areas of this research are available (Barthélemy & Monjardet 1981, 1988; Day 1986b; Leclerc & Cucumel 1987; Barthélemy et al 1986; Leclerc 1988, 1989), and a special issue of the *Journal of Classification* (Day 1986a) was devoted to consensus classifications. In addition to empirically oriented developments (Gordon & Finden 1985; Gordon 1986, 1987b; Faith 1988; Leclerc 1988), numerous axiomatic frameworks have been devised for consensus structures (Barthélemy et al 1984; McMorris 1985; Day & McMorris 1985; Day et al 1986; Barthélemy & Janowitz 1990).

Cluster Validity

So long as the input data are of the appropriate number of modes, ways, etc, most methods of clustering will deterministically produce a clustering solution. Moreover, different methods will generally produce different solutions based on the same input data. The question naturally arises whether the clusters have "reality" or validity vis-à-vis the data (cf Hartigan 1975:202–203; Dubes & Jain 1979). Jain & Dubes (1988: Ch. 4) provide a useful summary of strategies for validation: "External criteria measure performance by matching a clustering structure to a priori information. . . . *Internal criteria* assess the fit between the structure and the data, using only the data themselves. . . . *Relative criteria* decide which of two structures is better in some sense, such as being more stable or appropriate for the data" (emphasis in the original, p. 161). Among the issues most commonly investigated are selection of indices of cluster structure and their distributions (Day 1977; Murtagh 1984c; Milligan & Cooper 1986; also see the section on practical advances, below) and determining the appropriate number of clusters (Dubes 1987; Cooper & Milligan 1988; Critchley 1988; Krzanowski & Lai 1988; Peck et al 1989).

Variable Selection and Weighting

Although we noted above in the section on dissimilarity coefficients that conversion of a two-mode to a one-mode matrix prior to clustering should be regarded as a step separate from the actual cluster analysis, some authors have sought to link the original two-mode matrix more directly to the mechanics of the cluster analysis. DeSarbo et al (1984) devised an approach for "synthesized clustering" in which the variables in a two-mode (objects by variables) matrix were iteratively and differentially weighted according to their relative importance to the emergent K-means (MacQueen 1967) cluster structure. This procedure was extended from partitions to ultrametric trees by De Soete et al (1985), who also sketched details for further extensions to additive, multiple, and three-way trees (discussed below), some of which were implemented later by De Soete & Carroll (1988). De Soete provided both an algorithm (1986) and software (1988) for optimal variable weighting in fitting either an ultrametric or an additive tree to a single two-mode matrix. Fowlkes et al (1988) devised a forward selection procedure for variables in a two-mode matrix intended for complete-link hierarchical clustering as well as other methods (1987).

The practical importance of such approaches quickly led to evaluations. Milligan (1989) reported positive results from a validation study of De Soete's (1986, 1988) techniques, whereas Green et al (1990) obtained disappointing results in evaluating algorithms of DeSarbo et al (1984) and De Soete et al (1985).

Computational Advances

Clustering was among the first areas of data analysis to be influenced by computer scientists' preoccupation with computational complexity (Day 1983a provides a nice overview), and efforts to design clustering algorithms for large data sets are ongoing. Relevant aspects of clustering comprise partitioning (Hansen & Jaumard 1987; Hansen et al 1989), complete-link (Defays 1977; Hansen & Delattre 1978), single-link (Rohlf 1973; Sibson

1973; Hansen & Lehert 1980; Hansen et al 1989), and other forms of hierarchical clustering (Morineau & Lebart 1986; Guénoche et al 1991), including by parallel algorithms (Lerman & Peter 1984).

Substantive Developments

We noted earlier that the enormous literature of applications of clustering could not be covered in this chapter, but we do want to mention two substantive areas that have been especially active in their use and advancement of clustering.

SOCIOMETRY AND SOCIAL PSYCHOLOGY   Many articles appearing in the journal *Social Networks* use and include discussions of clustering, even though methodological sophistication is sometimes lacking (e.g. Burt 1988), as Faust & Romney (1985) pointed out. Surveys of this area of research (e.g. Burt 1980; Knoke & Kuklinski 1982; Wasserman & Faust 1991) generally include sections on clustering techniques, and the contributors have greatly expanded the range of problems to which it is applied [e.g. to studying complex economic legislation (Boorman & Levitt 1983) or to legal precedents and structures of communication among state supreme courts (Caldeira 1988); also see abstracts collected in the bibliographic survey *Connections* (A. Wolfe 1990)]. Moreover, the area is increasingly quick to adopt recently developed combinatorial and statistical techniques (e.g. Feger & Bien 1982; Feger & Droge 1984; Noma & Smith 1985; Wasserman & Anderson 1987; Dow & de Waal 1989; Hummon & Doreian 1990).

In the area of social personality and autobiography, Rosenberg's innovative analyses (1988, 1989) of data meticulously extracted from the autobiographical novels of Thomas Wolfe coincide with a greater public demand for autobiographies. Such work might even provide a curative for psychobiographies.

EVOLUTIONARY TREES   When *Science* initiated its software review section, the first contribution (Fink 1986) compared programs for reconstructing phylogenetic trees, typically on the basis of molecular data. Further evidence of the surge of interest in the role of clustering in reconstructing evolutionary patterns is given by articles in the *Proceedings of the National Academy of Sciences* (e.g. Cavalli-Sforza et al 1988; Harding & Sokal 1988; Sokal 1988b) and attendant controversies (Cavalli-Sforza et al 1989; Bateman 1990). Methodological contributions from combinatorial data analysis to this substantive area include hierarchical clustering (Corpet 1988), additive trees (Dress et al 1986), computational complexity (Day et al 1986; Day & Sankoff 1986; Barthélemy & Luong 1987), graph theory (Mirkin & Rodin 1984; see Hubert 1984), lattice theory (Estabrook & McMorris 1980), sequence comparison (Kruskal 1983; Sankoff & Kruskal 1983), and statistical analysis

(Astolfi et al 1981; Felsenstein 1983b,c; Barry & Hartigan 1987). A general review is given by Sokal (1985), and numerous chapters in Felsenstein (1983a); Dress & von Haeseler (1990) and Luong (1989) provide a range of current topics of investigation. Holman (1985) provides an important psychological and methodological perspective on some of the basic issues of taxonomy.

ADDITIVE TREES AND OTHER NETWORK MODELS

In graph theory, a tree is a connected graph without cycles. As noted earlier when considering the MST problem, for representing psychological structure, the nodes of the graph correspond to stimuli and the links connecting them have weights whose numerical values are used to reconstruct or predict the input data so that goodness-of-fit can be gauged. In the subsections above concerned with hierarchical clustering, the metric used for predicting the data was usually based on the ultrametric. A different metric, based on a relaxation of the ultrametric inequality and often called the "four-points condition" is a popular alternative and gives representations variously known as free trees, path length trees, or additive trees. In general, we do not repeat the review of the topic given in Carroll & Arabie (1980:623–24) except to note general overviews by Carroll (1976) and Shepard (1980).

All subsections below, until the section on representations of two- and higher-mode data, assume a single input (one-mode two-way) proximities matrix.

Algorithms and Models

Considerable work on algorithms for fitting additive trees has been done recently (Abdi et al 1984; Brossier 1985; Guénoche 1986a; Barthélemy & Guénoche 1988); Guénoche (1987) has compared five algorithms. Some of the strategies of specialization used successfully for hierarchical clustering have also proved useful for additive trees. Specifically, there are versions for binary data (Guénoche 1986b) and for constrained representations (De Soete et al 1987).

Recent advances in devising and fitting more general graph-theoretic models are impressive (Orth 1988, 1989; Hutchinson 1989; Klauer 1989; Klauer & Carroll 1989, 1991). Some of these papers have also provided remarkable substantive results as well (e.g. Hutchinson 1989) while others (e.g. Cooke & McDonald 1987) have not.

Substantive Advances

Friendly (1977, 1979) pointed out the advantages of modeling structure of organization in free recall around the combinatorial framework of the MST (see Hubert 1974a). Combinatorial models have since been devised (Hubert &

Levin 1976, 1977, 1978; Levin & Hubert 1980; Pellegrino & Hubert 1982) to allow testing for a wide range of substantive structural predictions. Results from Hirtle and his colleagues (McKeithen et al 1981; Hirtle 1982; 1987; Hirtle & Crawley 1989) have demonstrated that a tree with seriated nodes can be reconstructed using replicated orderings of a set of objects, as in multi-trial free recall paradigms; Shiina (1986) has attempted the same feat for obtaining MDS solutions.

Representations Based on Two- and Higher-Mode Data

Although for many years ultrametric representations were limited to one mode, Furnas (1980) elegantly generalized the ultrametric inequality to two-mode data, and De Soete et al (1984a,b) provided least squares algorithms for fitting either ultrametric or additive trees to two-way two-mode data (also see contributions by Brossier 1986, 1990). De Soete et al (1986) have also devised an algorithm for fitting ultrametric or additive trees to two-mode data and simultaneously estimating optimal weights for the variables as well during the conversion to one-mode data. Finally, in a development that has seen rapid progress, two- or higher-mode preference data are now suitable for fitting stochastic tree unfolding models (Carroll et al 1988, 1989; Carroll & De Soete 1990).

ASSESSING AND COMPARING STRUCTURES

In our introductory characterization of what CDA might legitimately encompass, we mentioned the confirmatory comparison of two (or more) structures definable on some common set of objects. Usually, structures (e.g. input matrices, sequences, partitions, graphs, trees) to be compared are first represented in the form of matrices whose entries numerically gauge some relationship among the common objects; in the simplest case of two structures, one matrix is typically empirical and the second either posited theoretically or also generated empirically. The actual comparison strategy invariably relies on some correlational measure between the entries from the two given matrices (or their suitable transformations); a substantial literature illustrates the procedures using various types of descriptive measures. Depending on the objects and type of matrices involved, this work may be (a) axiomatic in attempting to characterize "good" measures in a particular context (Barthélemy 1979; Leclerc 1985a,b; Barthélemy et al 1986), (b) specific to certain types of structural representations (Day 1983b; Gower 1983; Leclerc 1982; Rohlf 1974, 1982; Gordon, 1980a, 1981:132–37), and (c) perhaps even dependent on solving certain initial (and possibly difficult) optimization tasks (Gordon 1973b, 1982, 1988; Delcoigne & Hansen 1975; Klastorin 1980; Lerman 1988; W. Miller & Myers 1988; ten Berge 1988; Gordon et al 1989).

The most active area of work involving the comparison of structures (through matrices) can be seen as extending a seminal paper by Mantel (1967), which suggests a particular randomization method that allows a correlational measure of association between matrix entries to be assessed for relative size, and does so through a significance test that maintains the integrity of the structures being compared. The actual evaluation is based on the conjecture of no relationship between matrices, and is operationalized by the explicit hypothesis of randomness in the pairing of the objects between the two structures.

The range of applications for this matrix comparison method and associated significance testing strategy is enormous; many of the possibilities, at least as of 1986, are documented by Hubert (1987). The encompassed topics include, among others, almost all methods encountered in classical nonparametric statistics (Hubert 1987), the assessment of spatial autocorrelation for variables observed over a set of geographical locations (Upton & Fingleton 1985; Sokal 1986b; Sokal et al 1987), multivariate analysis of variance (Mielke 1978, 1979; Mielke et al 1976), assessment techniques concerned with various conjectures of combinatorial structure that might be posited for an empirically determined measure of proximity (Dow & de Waal 1989), and the comparison of two empirically generated matrices that might contain rather general measures of proximity (Dow & Cheverud 1985; Cheverud et al 1989) or matrices with very restricted entries (e.g. binary) defining various combinatorial structures (Verhelst et al 1985; Lerman 1987, 1988; Lerman & Peter 1988).

The same general strategy for comparing two matrices has recently been extended to the comparison of sets of matrices through the use of optimally weighted composites. The case of particular interest in the literature thus far compares a single matrix to a set of matrices through the use of a multiple correlation coefficient between the corresponding matrix entries (Smouse et al 1986; Hubert & Arabie 1989)

NONDESTRUCTIVE DATA ANALYSIS

Murtagh (1989) contributed the engaging rubric of "nondestructive data analysis" to a particular class of matrix permutation strategies; we use it here to refer in general to matrix permutation approaches to data analysis. Such methods simply seek to find a permutation or reordering of the rows and columns of matrices so as to reveal interpretable patterns not otherwise apparent; historically these methods are linked to seriation (Katz 1947; see Hubert & Baker 1978; Hubert & Golledge 1981; and Hubert et al 1982). Perhaps because they have been orphaned in most overviews of data analysis, some of these techniques keep being reinvented (e.g. Beum & Brundage's 1950 approach by Deutsch & Martin 1971 and by Lingoes 1968).

Hartigan (1972, 1975: Ch. 14–15; 1976) has shown the advantages of "direct" clustering approaches that address two-mode data directly, without first converting them to a one-mode matrix (see also De Soete et al 1984a,b). Among the other strategies of matrix permutation and/or partitioning that have seen the most activity in recent years is the "bond energy" approach of McCormick et al (1972; also see Lenstra 1974). Reviews are given by Murtagh (1985a: Ch. 1) and Arabie & Hubert (1990). For a sampling of recent work on the problem, see Kusiak et al (1986), Marcotorchino (1986, 1987), Kusiak & Finke (1987), Hilger et al (1989), and Arabie et al (1990).

RELATIONSHIPS BETWEEN DISCRETE VERSUS SPATIAL STRUCTURES

C. J. Jardine et al (1967) provided a continuous transformation relating the triangle and ultrametric inequalities, somewhat in support of the common intuition that the Euclidean metric and ultrametric-based hierarchical clustering were highly compatible vehicles for representing structure in data. Holman's classic (1972; also see the appendix of Gower & Banfield 1975) result shattered this complacency by showing that data conforming perfectly to one metric were somewhat antithetical to the other. But because empirical data rarely ever fit either model without error, the folklore of compatibility between relevant discrete and spatial models is still empirically useful (see Kruskal 1977 for an excellent discussion). Critchley (1986a) aptly decried and undermined the "widespread myths surrounding the work [i.e. result] of Holman (1972)," which are still promulgated by some cognitive psychologists (e.g. McNamara 1990). Such misunderstandings can hardly be blamed on Holman, who stated his results concisely and elegantly.

Strategies of comparing the two classes of representations have included geometric analyses (Tversky & Hutchinson 1986) and computationally based comparative data analyses (Pruzansky et al 1982) which suggested that data from perceptual domains were more compatible with Euclidean spatial representations whereas data from conceptual domains were better suited to discrete representations. Furnas (1989) has provided an innovative graphical approach showing interrelations among families of relevant metrics. Critchley & Heiser (1988) showed that data perfectly conforming to hierarchical trees can also be represented without error unidimensionally, while Brossier (1984) and Diday (1986) have sought to generalize and exploit relationships between these different types of representations (Arabie 1986). Hybrid approaches seeking simultaneously to combine the advantages of MDS and clustering continue to be appealing (Carroll & Pruzansky 1980; Bock 1986; Mirkin 1989b).

REPRESENTATIONS OF THREE- AND HIGHER-WAY DATA

Carroll & Arabie (1980:638) noted that "we see a strong trend toward the development of three-way models with applications of three- and higher-way methods becoming almost as numerous as two-way applications." As reviewed by Arabie & Daws (1988), various substantive developments have helped assure the outcome of this prediction (Snyder et al 1984), and we noted earlier that some recent edited volumes (Law et al 1984; Coppi & Bolasco 1989) are exclusively concerned with representing higher-way data. In addition to the papers cited in the section above on additive trees, examples of such generalizations include hybrid models for three-way data (Carroll & Pruzansky 1983) and ultrametric representations for three-way two-mode (Carroll et al 1984) as well as three-mode data (De Soete & Carroll 1989).

RANKINGS, RELATIONS, AND PARTIALLY ORDERED SETS

As noted above, this congeries has demonstrated the signs of a mature subdiscipline, including its own specialized journal (*Order*, established in 1984), joining numerous others of relevance and amassing a burgeoning literature. We can give these topics only cursory consideration here—a constraint regrettable because too many psychologists are unaware of the enormous strides (some of them of eminently practical use) that have recently taken place in this area of research. For example, Cook and his collaborators (Armstrong et al 1982; Cook & Kress 1984; Cook et al 1986) have provided useful results for obtaining a consensus ordering from a set of ordinal rankings of n entities from a committee of *m* members. Other applications-oriented developments include those reported by Critchlow (1985) and Fligner & Verducci (1986).

Monjardet and his collaborators (Monjardet 1973, 1979a,b, 1981b; Barthélemy & Monjardet 1981; Barthélemy et al 1982, 1986) have capably surveyed the general area of partially ordered sets, ordered sets, and complete orderings, and have shown their relevance to combinatorial data analysis and the social sciences. Other especially noteworthy contributions include those of Marcotorchino & Michaud (1979), Michaud & Marcotorchino (1979, 1980), Schader (1979), Doignon & Falmagne (1984), Leclerc (1984, 1987, 1989), Gaul & Schader (1988), Saporta (1988), and Fishburn & Falmagne (1989).

PRACTICAL ADVANCES

A considerable lag will undoubtedly precede much of CDA's impact on workaday data analysis. We now wish to consider instead some results that should have more immediate impact. For example, we noted above that converting from a two- to a one-mode matrix is a common prerequisite for many cluster analyses. If the data are a matrix of objects by variables and the analyst wishes to compute Euclidean distances between all pairs of objects, a common problem is whether and how to standardize the variables, prior to using their entries as coordinates for computing inter-object distances. Milligan & Cooper (1988) have provided a result (the superiority of dividing by the range of a variable) that probably merits "written in stone" status.

Another practical problem on which Milligan and his collaborators have made progress is the question of which measure of relatedness between partitions is best for cluster validation. (As noted earlier, the framework of Figure 1 facilitates proliferation of such measures between partitions, just as it does for measures of association for paired variables.) Concluding a comparative study of the coefficients regarded for either theoretical or empirical reasons to be forerunners, Milligan & Cooper (1986:457) stated: "... it would appear that of the five indices the Hubert and Arabie [1985] adjusted Rand measure seems to be the index of choice for clustering validation research."

Most statistical consultants have at some time been badgered by users of clustering who feel unfulfilled and forlorn without some test of significance. This lacuna in general reflects no lack of interest in devising such tests (Perruchet 1983b; Bock 1985; Hartigan 1977, 1978, 1985) but rather the adamantine nature of the problems. It should be noted, however, that inferential procedures are available for testing significance for bimodality (Giacomelli et al 1971) as well as for multimodality (Hartigan & Hartigan 1985; Hartigan 1988; Hartigan & Mohanty 1992).

Another common problem arises as users of techniques try to compare the output from two or more analyses when in fact the substantive theory suggests that a correlation between the input proximity (or other types of) matrices is instead called for (cf Carroll & Arabie 1980:636). Although the inferential problem was solved over a decade ago (Hubert 1978, 1979), no general-purpose software is available for carrying out such analyses. Mehta (1990; personal communication) has informed us of the possibility of including such a capability in StatXact (Mehta 1990). StatXact runs as a stand-alone package but can also be invoked from SYSTAT (Wilkinson 1989). This development should undercut all excuses for doing the wrong analysis.

BIBLIOGRAPHIC CONSIDERATIONS

Authors of *Annual Review* chapters should be allowed the indulgence of observing what makes their work—and presumably that of others in the field—easy or difficult: We have already noted that much of the literature on CDA is found in conference proceedings and other edited volumes. These single volumes often cost three or more times the price of an annual subscription to the most relevant journals, and the chapters are generally not covered by indexing services like the Institute for Scientific Information or their publications. Reviewers' unhappiness has apparently become ritual: "In future publications, I hope editors can be prevailed upon to provide an index and the publisher can match price with quality of production and do greater justice to the contributors' work" (Coxon 1988:298), or "Finally, two 'classical' critical comments on such publications: unfortunately, this volume does not include a subject index and it is very expensive (US $136.75)" (Ferligoj 1990:158). Even when an index is included (Bock 1988), it is found inadequate (Okada 1989). Publishers' increasing reluctance to produce such volumes coincides with librarians' (not to mention private individuals') displeasure over the prices; the problem may be self-terminating.

PROSPECTS

Despite the disciplinary diversity of contributions (both negative and positive), it is clear that the field is coalescing around certain themes: (a) types of data and their implications for possible representations; (b) the relationships among algebraic, geometric, and logical structures; and (c) those relationships' implications for representations of structure in data. Such developments, however, are not buttressed by the software found in statistical packages, and the result is a widening gap between elegant developments in algorithms and models versus access to them by potential users.

ACKNOWLEDGMENTS

This research was supported in part by AT&T Information Systems' Industrial Affiliates Program at the University of Illinois. Of the many colleagues who helpfully pointed out references to us, we are especially indebted to J.-P. Barthélemy, J. Douglas Carroll, Geert De Soete, A. D. Gordon, John C. Gower, Steve Hirtle, Bruno Leclerc, I. C. Lerman, Jacqueline Meulman, Bernard Monjardet, Fionn Murtagh, and Akinori Okada. We are grateful to Francesca Lundström for editorial expertise. For bibliographic assistance, we are indebted to François Bronsard, Tom Merritt, and Nicole Sullivan.

Literature Cited

Abdi, H., Barthélemy, J.-P., Luong, X. 1984. Tree representations of associative structures in semantic and episodic memory research. In *Trends in Mathematical Psychology*, ed. E. Degreef, J. van Buggenhaut, pp. 3-31. Amsterdam: North-Holland

Ambros-Ingerson, J., Granger, R., Lynch, G. 1990. Simulation of paleocortex performs hierarchical clustering. *Science* 247:1344–48

Arabie, P. 1986. Comments on confounded experimental designs, pyramids, and seriation. In *Multidimensional Data Analysis*, ed. J. de Leeuw, W. Heiser, J. Meulman, F. Critchley, pp. 235–37. Leiden, The Netherlands: DSWO-Press

Arabie, P., Carroll, J. D. 1980a. MAPCLUS: a mathematical programming approach to fitting the ADCLUS model. *Psychometrika* 45:211–35

Arabie, P., Carroll, J. D. 1980b. *How To Use MAPCLUS, a Computer Program for Fit-*

ting the ADCLUS Model. Murray Hill, NJ: AT&T Bell Laboratories

Arabie, P., Carroll, J. D., DeSarbo, W. S. 1987a. *Three-way Scaling and Clustering.* Newbury Park, CA: Sage. Translated into Japanese by A. Okada and T. Imaizumi, 1990. Tokyo: Kyoritsu Shuppan

Arabie, P., Daws, J. 1988. The interface among data analysis, marketing, and knowledge representation. In *Data, Expert Knowledge and Decisions,* ed. W. Gaul, M. Schader, pp. 10–15. Berlin: Springer-Verlag

Arabie, P., Hubert, L. J. 1990. The bond energy algorithm revisited. *IEEE Trans. Syst. Man Cybern.* 20:268–74

Arabie, P., Hubert, L., Hesson-McInnis, M. 1989. Combinatorial optimization approaches to multidimensional scaling in city-block spaces. Paper presented at the 2nd Conf. Int. Fed. Classif. Soc., Univ. Virginia, Charlottesville

Arabie, P., Hubert, L., Schleutermann, S. 1990. Blockmodels from the bond energy algorithm. *Soc. Networks* 12:99–126

Arabie, P., Maschmeyer, C. J. 1988. Some current models for the perception and judgment of risk. *Organ. Behav. Hum. Decis. Process.* 41:300–29

Arabie, P., Maschmeyer, C. J., Carroll, J. D. 1987b. Impact scaling: method and application. *Technol. Forecast. Soc. Change* 32:245–72

Armstrong, R. D., Cook, W. D., Seiford, L. M. 1982. Priority ranking and consensus formation: the case of ties. *Manage. Sci.* 28:638–45

Astolfi, P., Kidd, K. D., Cavalli-Sforza, L. L. 1981. A comparison of methods for reconstructing evolutionary trees. *Syst. Zool.* 30:156–69

Bandelt, H.-J., Dress, A. 1989. Weak hierarchies associated with similarity measures—an additive clustering technique. *Bull. Math. Biol.* 51:133–66

Barbut, M., Monjardet, B. 1970a. *Ordre et Classification, Algèbre et Combinatoire,* Tome I. Paris: Hachette

Barbut, M., Monjardet, B. 1970b. *Ordre et Classification, Algèbre et Combinatoire,* Tome II. Paris: Hachette

Barnes, E. R. 1982. An algorithm for partitioning the nodes of a graph. *SIAM J. Algorithms Disc. Methods* 3:541–50

Barnett, J. A., Gower, J. C. 1971. Selecting tests in diagnostic keys with unknown responses. *Nature* 232:491–93

Baroni-Urbani, C., Buser, M. W. 1976. Similarity of binary data. *Syst. Zool.* 25:251–59

Barry, D., Hartigan, J. A. 1987. Statistical analysis of hominoid molecular evolution. *Stat. Sci.* 2:191–210

Barthélemy, J.-P. 1979. Caractérisations axiomatiques de la distance de la différence symétrique entre des relations binaires. *Math. Sci. hum.* 17(67): 85–113

Barthélemy, J.-P. 1989. Introduction: les arbres, de la matière pour bricoler. See Luong 1989, pp. 3–21

Barthélemy, J.-P., Flament, C., Monjardet, B. 1982. Ordered sets and social sciences. In *Ordered Sets,* ed. I. Rival pp. 721–58). Dordrecht: Reidel

Barthélemy, J.-P., Guénoche, A. 1988. *Les arbres et les représentations des proximités.* Paris: Masson. To be translated into English as *Tree Representation of Proximity Data,* and published by Wiley.

Barthélemy, J.-P., Janowitz, M. F. 1990. A formal theory of consensus. *SIAM J. Disc. Math.* In press

Barthélemy, J.-P., Leclerc, B., Monjardet, B. 1984. Ensembles ordonnées et taxonomie mathématique. *Ann. Disc. Math.* 23:523–48

Barthélemy, J.-P., Leclerc, B., Monjardet, B. 1986. On the use of ordered sets in problems of comparison and consensus of classifications. *J. Classif.* 3:187–224

Barthélemy, J.-P., Luong, X. 1987. Sur la topologie d'un arbre phylogénétique: aspects théoriques, algorithmes et applications à l'analyse de données textuelles. *Math. Sci. hum.* 25(100): 57–80

Barthélemy, J.-P., Monjardet, B. 1981. The median procedure in cluster analysis and social choice theory. *Math. Soc. Sci.* 1:235–67

Barthélemy, J.-P., Monjardet, B. 1988. The median procedure in data analysis: new results and open problems. See Bock 1988, pp. 309–16

Basford, K. E., McLachlan, G. J. 1985. The mixture method of clustering applied to three-way data. *J. Classif.* 2:109–25

Batagelj, V. 1981. Note on ultrametric hierarchical clustering algorithms. *Psychometrika* 46:351–52

Bateman, R. M. 1990. Balancing American linguists [Letter to editor]. *Science* 249:1228

Baulieu, F. B. 1989. A classification of presence/absence based dissimilarity coefficients. *J. Classif.* 6:233–46

Beane, T. P., Ennis, D. M. 1987. Market segmentation: a review. *Eur. J. Mark.* 21:20–42

Belbin, L. 1987. The use of non-hierarchical allocation methods for clustering large sets of data. *Aust. Comput. J.* 19:32–41

Beum, C. O., Brundage, E. G. 1950. A method for analyzing the sociomatrix. *Sociometry* 13:141–45

Blashfield, R. K., Aldenderfer, M. S. 1988. The methods and problems of cluster analysis. In *Handbook of Multivariate Experimental Psychology*, ed. J. R. Nesselroade, R. B. Cattell, pp. 447–73). New York: Plenum. 2nd ed.

Bock, H. H. 1974. *Automatische Klassifikation. Theoretische und praktische Methoden zur Gruppierung und Strukturierung von Daten (Clusteranalyse)*. Goettingen: Vandenhoeck Ruprecht

Bock, H. H. 1985. On some significance tests in cluster analysis. *J. Classif.* 2:77–108

Bock, H. H. 1986. Multidimensional scaling in the framework of cluster analysis. In *Die Klassifikation und Ihr Umfeld*, ed. P. O. Degens, H.-J. Hermes, O. Opitz, pp. 247–58. Frankfurt: Indeks Verlag

Bock, H. H., ed. 1988. *Classification and Related Methods of Data Analysis*. Amsterdam: North-Holland

Boorman, S. A., Levitt, P. R. 1983. Blockmodeling complex statutes: mapping techniques based on combinatorial optimization for analyzing economic legislation and its stress point over time. *Econ. Lett.* 13:1–9

Brennan, T. 1987. Classification: an overview of selected methodological issues. In *Prediction and Classification: Criminal Justice Decision Making*, ed. D. M. Gottfredson, M. Tonry, pp. 201–48. Chicago: Univ. Chicago Press

Brossier, G. 1984. Algorithmes d'ordonnancement des hiérarchies binaires et propriétés. *Rev. Stat. Appl. 23(3): 65–79*

Brossier, G. 1985. Approximation des dissimilarites par des arbres additifs. *Math. Sci. hum.* 23(91): 5–21

Brossier, G. 1986. Etude des matrices de proximité rectangulaires en vue de la classification. *Rev. Stat. Appl.* 25 (4):43–68

Brossier, G. 1990. Piecewise hierarchical clustering. *J. Classif.* 7:197–216

Bryant, P. 1988. On characterizing optimization-based clustering methods. *J. Classif.* 5:81–84

Burt, R. S. 1980. Models of network structure. *Annu. Rev. Sociol.* 6:79–141

Burt, R. S. 1988. Some properties of structural equivalence measures derived from sociometric choice data. *Soc. Networks.* 10:1–28

Buser, M. W., Baroni-Urbani, L. 1982. A direct nondimensional clustering method for binary data. *Biometrics* 38:351–60

Caldeira, G. A. 1988. Legal precedent: structures of communication between state supreme courts. *Soc. Networks* 10:29–55

Carroll, J. D. 1976. Spatial, non-spatial and hybrid models for scaling. *Psychometrika* 41:439–63

Carroll, J. D., Arabie, P. 1980. Multi-

dimensional scaling. *Ann. Rev. Psychol.* 31:607–49

Carroll J. D., Arabie, P. 1982. *How to Use INDCLUS, a Computer Program for Fitting the Individual Differences Generalization of the ADCLUS Model*. Murray Hill, NJ: AT&T Bell Laboratories

Carroll, J. D., Arabie, P. 1983. INDCLUS: an individual differences generalization of the ADCLUS model and the MAPCLUS algorithm. *Psychometrika* 48:157–69

Carroll, J. D., Chang, J. J. 1970. Analysis of individual differences in multidimensional scaling via an N-way generalization of "Eckart-Young" decomposition. *Psychometrika* 35:283–319

Carroll, J. D., Clark, L. A., DeSarbo, W. S. 1984. The representation of three-way proximities data by single and multiple tree structure models. *J. Classif.* 1:25–74

Carroll, J. D., De Soete, G. 1990. Fitting a quasi-Poisson case of the GSTUN (General Stochastic Tree Unfolding) model and some extensions. In *Knowledge, Data and Computer-Assisted Decisions*, ed. M. Schader, W. Gaul. Berlin: Springer-Verlag

Carroll, J. D., DeSarbo, W., De Soete, G. 1988. Stochastic tree unfolding (STUN) models: theory and application. See Bock 1988, pp. 421–30

Carroll, J. D., DeSarbo, W., De Soete, G. 1989. Two classes of stochastic tree unfolding models. In *New Developments in Psychological Choice Modeling*, ed. G. De Soete, H. Feger, C. Klauer, pp. 161–76. Amsterdam: North-Holland

Carroll, J. D., Pruzansky, S. 1980. Discrete and hybrid scaling models. In *Similarity and Choice*, ed. E. D. Lantermann, H. Feger, pp. 108–39. Bern: Hans Huber

Carroll, J. D., Pruzansky, S. 1983. Representing proximities data by discrete, continuous or "hybrid" models. See Felsenstein 1983a, pp. 229–48

Cavalli-Sforza, L. L., Piazza, A., Menozzi, P., Mountain, J. 1988. Reconstruction of human evolution: bringing together genetic, archaeological, and linguistic data. *Proc. Natl. Acad. Sci. USA* 85:6002–6

Cavalli-Sforza, L. L., Piazza, A., Menozzi, P., Mountain, J. 1989. Genetic and linguistic evolution [Letter to the editor]. *Science* 244:1128–29

Cheetham, H. L., Hazel, J. E. 1969. Binary (presence-absence) similarity coefficients. *J. Paleontol.* 43:1130–36

Cheverud, J. M., Wagner, G. P., Dow, M. M. 1989. Methods for the comparative analysis of variation patterns. *Syst. Zool.* 38:201–13

Cliff, N. 1968. The "idealized individual" interpretation of individual differences in multidimensional scaling. *Psychometrika* 33: 225–32

Cliff, N., McCormick, D. J., Zatkin, J. L., Cudek, R. A., Collins, L. M. 1986. BINCLUS: nonhierarchical clustering of binary data. *Multivar. Behav. Res.* 21:201–27

Cole, A. J., Wishart, D. 1970. An improved algorithm for the Jardine-Sibson method of generating overlapping clusters. *Computer J.* 13:156–63

Cook, W. D., Kress, M. 1984. Relationships between l^1 metrics on linear ranking spaces. *SIAM J. Appl. Math.* 44:209–20

Cook, W. D., Kress, M., Seiford, L. M. 1986. Information and preference in partial orders: a bimatrix representation. *Psychometrika* 51:197–207

Cooke, N. M., Durso, F. T., Schvaneveldt, R. W. 1986. Recall and measures of memory organization. *J. Exp. Psychol.: Learn. Mem. Cognit.* 12:538–49

Cooke, N. M., McDonald, J. E. 1987. The application of psychological scaling techniques to knowledge elicitation for knowledge-based systems. *Int. J. Man-Machine Stud.* 26:533–50

Cooper, M. C., Milligan, G. W. 1988. The effect of measurement error on determining the number of clusters in cluster analysis. See Arabie and Daws 1988, pp. 319–28

Coppi, R., Bolasco, S., eds. 1989. *Multiway Data Analysis.* New York: North-Holland

Corpet, F. 1988. Multiple sequence alignment with hierarchical clustering. *Nucleic Acids Res.* 16:10881–890

Corter, J., Tversky, A. 1986. Extended similarity trees. *Psychometrika* 51:429–51

Cox, D. R. 1970. *The Analysis of Binary Data.* London: Chapman & Hall

Coxon, A. P. M. 1982. *The User's Guide to Multidimensional Scaling.* Portsmouth, NH: Heinemann

Coxon, A. P. M. 1988. Review of *Classification as a Tool of Research,* edited by W. Gaul, M. Schader. *J. Classif.* 5:297–98

Critchley, F. 1986a. Dimensionality theorems in multidimensional scaling and hierarchical cluster analysis. See Diday et al 1986, pp. 45–70

Critchley, F. 1986b. Some observations on distance matrices. See Arabie 1986, pp. 53–60

Critchley, F. 1988. The Euclidean structure of a dendrogram, the variance of a node and the question: "How many clusters really are there?" See Bock 1988, pp. 75–84

Critchley, F., Heiser, W. 1988. Hierarchical trees can be perfectly scaled in one dimension. *J. Classif.* 5:5–20

Critchley, F., Van Cutsem, B. 1989. Predissimilarities, prefilters and ultrametrics on an arbitrary set. Res. Rep. No. 171. Univ. Warwick, Dept. Stat.

Critchlow, D. E. 1985. *Metric Methods for Analyzing Partially Ranked Data.* New York: Springer-Verlag

Czekanowski, J. 1909. Zur Differential diagnose der Neandertalgruppe. Korrspondenz-Blatt der Deutschen Gesellschaft für Anthroplogie. *Ethnol. Urgeschichte* 40:44–47

Dale, M. B. 1985. On the comparison of conceptual clustering and numerical taxonomy. *IEEE Trans. Pattern Anal. Machine Intell.* PAMI-7:241–44

Day, W. H. E. 1977. Validity of clusters formed by graph-theoretic cluster methods. *Math. Biosci.* 36:299–317

Day, W. H. E. 1983a. The relevance of computational complexity to classification research. Presented at Meet. Classif. Soc. N. Am., Philadelphia

Day, W. H. E. 1983b. The role of complexity in comparing classifications. *Math. Biosci.* 66:97–114

Day, W. H. E. 1984. Efficient algorithms for agglomerative hierarchical clustering methods. *J. Classif.* 1:7–24

Day, W. H. E., ed. 1986a. Consensus classification. *J. Classif.* 3(2) (Special issue)

Day, W. H. E. 1986b. Foreword: comparison and consensus of classifications. *J. Classif.* 3:183–85

Day, W. H. E. 1988. Consensus methods as tools for data analysis. See Bock 1988, pp. 317–24

Day, W. H. E., ed. 1990. *Classif. Lit. Automat. Search Serv.* 19

Day, W. H. E., Edelsbrunner, H. 1985. Investigation of proportional link linkage clustering methods. *J. Classif.* 2:239–54

Day, W. H. E., Johnson, D. S., Sankoff, D. 1986a. The computational complexity of inferring rooted phylogenies by parsimony. *Math. Biosci.* 81:33–42

Day, W. H. E., McMorris, F. R. 1985. A formalization of consensus index methods. *Bull. Math. Biol.* 47:215–29

Day, W. H. E., McMorris, F. R., Meronk, D. B. 1986b. Axioms for consensus functions based on lower bounds in posets. *Math. Soc. Sci.* 12:185–90

Day, W. H. E., Sankoff, D. 1986. Computational complexity of inferring phylogenies by compatibility. *Syst. Zool.* 35:224–29

De Boeck, P., Rosenberg, S. 1988. Hierarchical classes: model and data analysis. *Psychometrika* 53:361–81

Defays, D. 1977. An efficient algorithm for a complete link method. *Computer J.* 20:364–66

Degens, P. O. 1983. Hierarchical cluster methods as maximum likelihood estimators. See Felsenstein 1983a, pp. 249–53

Degens, P. O. 1985. Ultrametric approximation to distances. *Comput. Stat. Q.* 2:93–
101

Delcoigne, A., Hansen, P. 1975. Sequence
comparison by dynamic programming.
Biometrika 62:661–64

de Leeuw, J., Heiser, W. 1977. Convergence
of correction-matrix algorithms for multidimensional scaling. In *Geometric Representations of Relational Data: Readings in
Multidimensional Scaling* ed. J. C. Lingoes,
pp. 735–52. Ann Arbor, MI: Mathesis

Denning, P. J. 1989. The science of computing: Bayesian learning. *Am. Sci.* 77:216–
18

DeSarbo, W. S. 1982. GENNCLUS: new
models for general nonhierarchical clustering analysis. *Psychometrika* 47:446–49

DeSarbo, W. S., Carroll, J. D., Clark, L. A.,
Green, P.E. 1984. Synthesized clustering: a
method for amalgamating alternative
clustering bases with differential weighting
of variables. *Psychometrika* 49:57–78

DeSarbo, W. S., Mahajan, V. 1984. Constrained classification: the use of a priori
information in cluster analysis. *Psychometrika* 49:187–216

De Soete, G. 1986. Optimal variable weighting for ultrametric and additive tree clustering. *Qual. Quant.* 20:169–80

De Soete, G. 1988. Tree representations of
proximity data by least squares methods.
See Bock 1988, pp. 147–56

De Soete, G., Carroll, J. D. 1988. Optimal
weighting for one-mode and two-mode ultrametric tree representations of three-way
three-mode data. In *The Many Faces of
Multivariate Data Analysis,* ed. M. G. H.
Jansen, W. H. van Schuur, pp. 16–29. Gro-
ningen: RION

De Soete, G., Carroll, J. D. 1989. Ultrametric
tree representations of three-way three-
mode data. See Coppi & Bolasco 1989, pp.
415–26

De Soete, G., Carroll, J. D., DeSarbo, W. S.
1986. Alternating least squares optimal
variable weighting algorithms for ultrametric and additive tree representations. See
Gaul & Schader 1986, pp. 97–103

De Soete, G., Carroll, J. D., DeSarbo, W. S.
1987. Least squares algorithms for constructing constrained ultrametric and additive tree representations of symmetric proximity data. *J. Classif.* 4:155–73

De Soete, G., DeSarbo, W. S., Carroll, J. D.
1985. Optimal variable weighting for
hierarchical clustering: an alternating least-
squares algorithm. *J. Classif.* 2:173–92

De Soete, G., DeSarbo, W. S., Furnas, G.
W., Carroll, J. D. 1984a. The estimation of
ultrametric and path length trees from rectangular proximity data. *Psychometrika*
49:289–310

De Soete, G., DeSarbo, W. S., Furnas, G.
W., Carroll, J. D. 1984b. Tree representa-
tions of rectangular proximity matrices. See
Abdi et al 1984, pp. 377–92

De Soete, G., Hubert, L., Arabie, P. 1988.
On the use of simulated annealing for combinatorial data analysis. See Arabie & Daws
1988, pp. 329–40

Deutsch, S. B., Martin, J. J. 1971. An ordering algorithm for analysis of data arrays.
Oper. Res. 19:1350–62

Dickinson, J. R. 1990. *The Bibliography of
Marketing Research Methods.* Lexington,
MA: Lexington. (3rd ed.)

Diday, E. 1986. Orders and overlapping clusters by pyramids. See Arabie 1986, pp. 201–
34

Diday, E., Escoufier, Y., Lebart, L., Pagès,
J. P., Schektman, Y., Tomassone, R., eds.
1986. *Data Analysis and Informatics, IV.*
New York: North-Holland

Diday, E., Jambu, M., Lebart, L., Pagès, J.,
Tomassone, R., eds. 1984. *Data Analysis
and Informatics, III.* Amsterdam: North-
Holland

Doignon, J.-P., Falmagne, J.-C. 1984.
Matching relations and the dimensional
structure of social choices. *Math. Soc. Sci.*
7:211–29

Doignon, J.-P., Monjardet, B., Roubens, M.,
Vincke, P. 1986. Biorder families, valued
relations, and preference modelling. *J.
Math. Psychol.* 30:435–80

Dow, M. M., Cheverud, J. M. 1985. Comparison of distance matrices in studies of
population structure and genetic microdif-
ferentiation: quadratic assignment. *Am. J.
Phys. Anthropol.* 68:367–73

Dow, M. M., de Waal, F. B. M. 1989.
Assignment methods for the analysis of network subgroup interactions. *Soc. Networks*
11:237–55

Dress, A., von Haeseler, A., eds. 1990. *Trees
and Hierarchical Structures (Lecture Notes
in Biomathematics 84).* New York: Springer

Dress, A., von Haeseler, A., Krueger, M.
1986. Reconstructing phylogenetic trees using variants of the "four-point-condition."
See Bock 1986, pp. 299–305

Dubes, R. C. 1987. How many clusters are
best? —An experiment. *Pattern Recognit.*
20:645–63

Dubes, R. C. 1988. Review of *Simulated Annealing: Theory and Practice* by P. J. M.
van Laarhoven, E. H. L. Aarts. *J. Classif.*
5:126–28

Dubes, R., Jain, A. K. 1979. Validity studies
in clustering methodologies. *Pattern Recognit.* 11:235–54

Duran, B. S., Odell, P. L. 1974. *Cluster Analysis: A Survey.* New York: Springer-Verlag

Edgington, E. S. 1980. *Randomization Tests.*
New York: Marcel Dekker

Edgington, E. S. 1987. *Randomization Tests.* New York: Marcel Dekker. (2nd ed.)

Estabrook, G. F., McMorris, F. R. 1980. When is one estimate of evolutionary relationships a refinement of another? *J. Math. Biol.* 10:367–73

Everitt, B. 1980. *Cluster Analysis.* New York: Wiley-Halsted. (2nd ed.)

Faith, D. P. 1984. Patterns of sensitivity of association measures in numerical taxonomy. *Math. Biosci.* 69:1–9

Faith, D. P. 1985. A model of immunological distances in systematics. *J. Theor. Biol.* 114:511–26

Faith, D. P. 1988. Consensus applications in the biological sciences. See Bock 1988, pp. 325–32

Faust, K., Romney, A. K. 1985. Does STRUCTURE find structure? A critique of Burt's use of distance as a measure of structural equivalence. *Soc. Networks* 7:77–103

Feger, H., Bien, W. 1982. Network unfolding. *Soc. Networks* 4:257–83

Feger, H., Droge, U. 1984. Ordinale Netzwerkskalierung [Ordinal network scaling]. *Kölner Z. Soziol. Sozialpsychol.* 3:417–23

Felsenstein, J. , ed. 1983a. *Numerical Taxonomy.* Berlin: Springer-Verlag

Felsenstein, J. 1983b. Methods for inferring phylogenies: a statistical view. See Felsenstein 1983a, pp. 315–34

Felsenstein, J. 1983c. Statistical inference of phylogenies (with discussion). *J. R. Stat. Soc. Ser. A* 146:246–72

Ferligoj, A. 1990. Review of *Data Analysis and Informatics V*, edited by E. Diday. *J. Classif.* 7:153–58

Ferligoj, A., Batagelj, V. 1982. Clustering with relational constraint. *Psychometrika* 47:413–26

Ferligoj, A., Batagelj, V. 1983. Some types of clustering with relational constraints. *Psychometrika* 48:541–52

Fichet, B. 1986. Distances and Euclidean distances for presence-absence characters and their application to factor analysis. See Arabie 1986, pp. 23–46

Finden, C. R., Gordon, A. D. 1985. Obtaining common pruned trees. *J. Classif.* 2:255–76

Fink, W. L. 1986. Microcomputers and phylogenetic analysis. *Science* 234:1135–39

Fishburn, P. C., Falmagne, J.-C. 1989. Binary probabilities and rankings. *Econ. Lett.* 31:113–17

Fligner, M. A., Verducci, J. S. 1986. Distance based ranking models. *J. R. Stat. Soc. Ser. B* 48:359–69

Florek, K., Łukaszewicz, J., Perkal, J., Steinhaus, H., Zubrzycki, S. 1951. Sur la liaison et la division des points d'un ensemble fini. *Colloq. Math.* 2:282–85

Fowlkes, E. B., Gnanadesikan, R., Kettenring, J. R. 1987. Variable selection in clustering and other contexts. In *Design, Data, and Analysis,* ed. C. L. Mallows, pp. 13–34. New York: Wiley

Fowlkes, E. B., Gnanadesikan, R., Kettenring, J. R. 1988. Variable selection in clustering. *J. Classif.* 5:205–28

Frank, O. 1978. Inferences concerning cluster structure. In *COMPSTAT 1978 Proceedings in Computational Statistics,* ed. L. C. A. Corsten, J. Hermans, pp. 259–65) Vienna: Physica-Verlag

Friendly, M. L. 1977. In search of the M-gram: the structure of organization in free recall. *Cognit. Psychol.* 9:188–249

Friendly, M. L. 1979. Method for finding graphic representations of associative memory structures. In *Memory Organization and Structure,* ed. C. R. Puff, pp. 85–129. New York: Academic

Furnas, G. W. 1980. *Objects and their features: the metric analysis of two-class data.* PhD thesis. Stanford Univ., Stanford, CA

Furnas, G. W. 1989. Metric family portraits. *J. Classif.* 6:7–52

Ganesalingam, S. 1989. Classification and mixture approaches to clustering via maximum likelihood. *Appl. Stat. (J. R. Stat. Soc. Ser. C)* 38:455–66

Gaul, W., Schader, M., eds. 1986. *Classification as a Tool of Research.* Amsterdam: North-Holland

Gaul, W., Schader, M. 1988. Clusterwise aggregation of relations. *Appl. Stoch. Models Data Anal.* 4:273–82

Giacomelli, F., Wiener, J., Kruskal, J. B., Pomeranz, J. V., Loud, A. V. 1971. Subpopulations of blood lymphocytes demonstrated by quantitative cytochemistry. *J. Histochem. Cytochem.* 19:426–33

Giakoumakis, V., Monjardet, B. 1987a. Coefficients d'accord entre deux preordres totaux: comparaison ordinale des coefficients. *Math. Sci. hum.* 25(98):69–87

Giakoumakis, V., Monjardet, B. 1987b. Coefficients d'accord entre deux préordres totaux. *Stat. Anal. Données* 12:46–99

Godehardt, E. 1988. *Graphs as Structural Models: The Application of Graphs and Multigraphs in Cluster Analysis.* Wiesbaden: Vieweg

Gordon, A. D. 1973a. Classification in the presence of constraints. *Biometrics* 29:821–27

Gordon, A. D. 1973b. A sequence-comparison statistic and algorithm. *Biometrika* 60:197–200

Gordon, A. D. 1980a. On the assessment and comparison of classifications. In *Analyse de*

Données et Informatique, ed. R. Tomas-sone, pp. 149–60. Le Chesnay: Inst. Natl. Rech. Inform. Automat.

Gordon, A. D. 1980b. Methods of constrained classification. See Gordon 1980a, pp. 161–71

Gordon, A. D. 1981. *Classification.* London: Chapman and Hall

Gordon, A. D. 1982. An investigation of two sequence-comparison statistics. *Aust. J. Stat.* 24:332–42

Gordon, A. D. 1986. Consensus supertrees: the synthesis of rooted trees containing overlapping sets of labeled leaves. *J. Classif.* 3:335–48

Gordon, A. D. 1987a. A review of hierarchical classification. *J. R. Stat. Soc. Ser. A* 150:119–37

Gordon, A. D. 1987b. Parsimonious trees. *J. Classif.* 4:85–101

Gordon, A. D. 1988. Sequence comparison statistics. In *Encyclopedia of Statistical Sciences,* ed. S. Kotz, N. L. Johnson, C. B. Read, 8:375–77. New York: Wiley

Gordon, A. D., Finden, C. R. 1985. Classification of spatially-located data. *Comput. Stat. Q.* 2:315–28

Gordon, A. D., Henderson, J. T. 1977. An algorithm for Euclidean sum of squares classification. *Biometrics* 33:355–62

Gordon, A. D., Jupp, P. E., Byrne, R. W. 1989. The construction and assessment of mental maps. *Br. J. Math. Stat. Psychol.* 42:169–82

Govaert, G. 1988. Classification binaire et modéle. Rep. No. 949. Le Chesnay: Inst. Natl. Rech. Inform. Automat.

Govaert, G. 1989. Clustering model and metric with continuous data. In *Data Analysis, Learning Symbolic and Numeric Knowledge,* ed. E. Diday, pp. 65–71. Commack, NY: Nova Science

Gower, J. C. 1971. A general coefficient of similarity and some of its properties. *Biometrics* 27:857–71

Gower, J. C. 1973. Classification problems. *Bull. Int. Stat. Inst.* 45:471–77

Gower, J. C. 1974. Maximal predictive classification. *Biometrics* 30:643–54

Gower, J. C. 1983. Comparing classifications. See Felsenstein 1983a, pp. 137–55

Gower, J. C. 1985. Measures of similarity, dissimilarity and distance. In *Encyclopedia of Statistical Sciences,* ed. S. Kotz, N. L. Johnson, C. B. Read, 5:307–405). New York: Wiley

Gower, J. C. 1986a. Euclidean distance matrices. See Arabie 1986, pp. 11–22, 61–63

Gower, J. C. 1986b. Reply to discussants. See Arabie 1986, pp. 61–63

Gower, J. C., Banfield, C. F. 1975. Good-ness-of-fit criteria for hierarchical classification and their empirical distributions. In *Proc. 8th Int. Biometric Conference,* ed. L. C. A. Corsten, T. Dostelni-cu, pp. 347–61). Bucharest: Editura Academiei Republicii Socialiste Romania

Gower, J. C., Legendre, P. 1986. Metric and Euclidean properties of dissimilarity coefficients. *J. Classif.* 3:5–48

Gower, J. C., Payne, R. W. 1975. A comparison of different criteria for selecting binary tests in diagnostic keys. *Biometrika* 62:665–72

Gower, J. C., Ross, G. J. S. 1969. Minimum spanning trees and single linkage cluster analysis. *Appl. Stat.* 18:54–64

Graham, R. L., Hell, P. 1985. On the history of the minimum spanning tree problem. *Ann. Hist. Comput.* 7:43–57

Green, P. E., Carmone, F. J. Jr., Smith, S. M. 1989. *Multidimensional Scaling: Concepts and Applications.* Boston: Allyn and Bacon

Green, P. E., Carmone, F. J., Kim, J. 1990. A preliminary study of optimal variable weighting in k-means clustering. *J. Classif.* 7:271–85

Grover, R., Srinivasan, V. 1987. A simultaneous approach to market segmentation and market structuring. *J. Market. Res.* 24:139–53

Guénoche, A. 1985. Classification using dilemma functions. *Comput. Stat. Q.* 2:103–8

Guénoche, A. 1986a. Représentations arborées des classifications. *Rech. Opér./ Oper. Res.* 20:341–54

Guénoche, A. 1986b. Graphical representation of a Boolean array. *Comput. Hum.* 20:277–81

Guénoche, A. 1987. Cinq algorithmes d'approximation d'une dissimilarité par des arbres à distances additives. *Math. Sci. hum.* 25(98): 21–40

Guénoche, A., Monjardet, B. 1987. Méthodes ordinales et combinatoires en analyse des données. *Math. Sci. hum.* 25(100):5–47

Guénoche, A., Hansen, P., Jaumard, B. 1991. Efficient algorithms for divisive hierarchical clustering with the diameter criterion. *J. Classif.* 8:5–30

Halperin, D. 1989. Towards deciphering the Ugaritic musical notation. Tel-Aviv Univ., Dept. Musicol.

Hand, D. J. 1981. Branch and bound in statistical data analysis. *Statistician* 30:1–13

Hansen, P., Delattre, M. 1978. Complete-link cluster analysis of graph coloring. *J. Am. Stat. Assoc.* 73:397–403

Hansen, P., Jaumard, B. 1987. Minimum sum of diameters clustering. *J. Classif.* 4:215–26

Hansen, P., Jaumard, B., Frank, O. 1989.

Maximum sum-of-splits clustering. *J. Classif.* 6:177–93

Hansen, P., Lehert, P. 1980. Clustering by connected components large data sets with Minkowsky distances between entities. In *Data Analysis and Informatics,* ed. E. Diday, L. Lebart, J. P. Pagès, R. Tomassone, pp. 561–67. Amsterdam: North-Holland

Harding, M. R., Sokal, R. R. 1988. Classification of the European language families by genetic distance. *Proc. Natl. Acad. Sci. USA* 85:9370–72

Hartigan, J. A. 1967. Representation of similarity matrices by trees. *J. Am. Stat. Assoc.* 62:1140–58

Hartigan, J. A. 1972. Direct clustering of a data matrix. *J. Am. Stat. Assoc.* 67:123–29

Hartigan, J. A. 1973. Clustering. *Annu. Rev. Biophysics* 2:81–101

Hartigan, J. A. 1975. *Clustering Algorithms.* New York: Wiley

Hartigan, J. A. 1976. Modal blocks in dentition of West Coast mammals. *Syst. Zool.* 25:149–60

Hartigan, J. A. 1977. Distribution problems in clustering. See Van Ryzin 1977, pp. 45–71

Hartigan, J. A. 1978. Asymptotic distributions for clustering criteria. *Ann. Stat.* 6:117–31

Hartigan, J. A. 1985. Statistical theory in clustering. *J. Classif.* 2:63–76

Hartigan, J. A. 1988. The span test for unimodality. See Bock 1988, pp. 229–36

Hartigan, J. A., Hartigan, P. M. 1985. The dip test of unimodality. *Ann. Stat.* 13:70–84

Hartigan, J. A., Mohanty, S. 1992. The runt test for multimodality. *J. Classif.* 9

Heiser, W. J. 1986. Distances and their approximation. See Arabie 1986, pp. 47–52

Heiser, W. J. 1989. The city-block model for three-way multidimensional scaling. See Coppi & Bolasco 1989, pp. 395–404

Heltshe, J. F. 1988. Jackknife estimate of the matching coefficient of similarity. *Biometrics* 44:447–60

Herden, G. 1984. Some aspects of clustering functions. *SIAM J. Algorithms Disc. Methods* 5:101–16

Hilger, J., Harhalakis, G., Proth, J.-M. 1989. Generalized cross-decomposition method: algorithm and implementation Res. Rep. No. 1055. Le Chesnay: Inst. Natl. Rech. Inform. Automat.

Hirtle, S. C. 1982. Lattice-based similarity measures between ordered trees. *J. Math. Psychol.* 25:206–25

Hirtle, S. C. 1987. On the classification of recall strings using lattice-theoretic measures. *J. Classif.* 4:227–42

Hirtle, S. C., Crawley, E. 1989. The use of

ordered trees for uncovering strategies in free-recall. See Luong 1989, pp. 125–38

Hojo, H. 1983. A maximum likelihood method for additive clustering and its applications. *Jpn. Psychol. Res.* 25:191–201

Holman, E. W. 1972. The relation between hierarchical and Euclidean models for psychological distances. *Psychometrika* 37: 417–23

Holman, E. W. 1985. Evolutionary and psychological effects in pre-evolutionary classifications. *J. Classif.* 2:29–39

Hubálek, Z. 1982. Coefficients of association and similarity, based on binary (presence-absence) data: an evaluation. *Biol. Rev.* 57:669–89

Hubert, L. J. 1974a. Spanning trees and aspects of clustering. *Br. J. Math. Stat. Psychol.* 27:14–28

Hubert, L. J. 1974b. Some applications of graph theory to clustering. *Psychometrika* 39:283–309

Hubert, L. J. 1977a. A set-theoretical approach to the problem of hierarchical clustering. *J. Math. Psychol.* 15:70–88

Hubert, L. J. 1977b. Nominal scale response agreement as a generalized correlation. *Br. J. Math. Stat. Psychol.* 30:98–103

Hubert, L. J. 1978. Generalized proximity function comparisons. *Br. J. Math. Stat. Psychol.* 31:179–92

Hubert, L. J. 1979. Generalized concordance. *Psychometrika* 44:135–42

Hubert, L. J. 1983. Hierarchical cluster analysis. In *Encyclopedia of Statistical Sciences,* ed. S. Kotz, N. Johnson, C. Read, 3:623–30. New York: Wiley

Hubert, L. J. 1984. Review of *Graphs and Genes* by B. G. Mirkin and S. N. Rodin. *J. Classif.* 1:275–77

Hubert, L. J. 1987. *Assignment Methods in Combinatorial Data Analysis.* New York: Marcel Dekker

Hubert, L. J., Arabie, P. 1985. Comparing partitions. *J. Classif.* 2:193–218

Hubert, L. J., Arabie, P. 1986. Unidimensional scaling and combinatorial optimization. See Arabie 1986, pp. 181–96

Hubert, L. J., Arabie, P. 1988. Relying on necessary conditions for optimization: unidimensional scaling and some extensions. See Bock 1988, pp. 463–72

Hubert, L. J., Arabie, P. 1989. Combinatorial data analysis: confirmatory comparisons between sets of matrices. *Appl. Stoch. Models Data Anal.* 5:273–325

Hubert, L. J., Baker, F. B. 1976. Data analysis by single-link and complete-link hierarchical clustering. *J. Educ. Stat.* 1:87–111

Hubert, L. J., Baker, F. B. 1978. Applications of combinatorial programming to data analysis: the traveling salesman and related problems. *Psychometrika* 43:81–91

Hubert, L. J., Baker, F. B. 1979. Identifying a migration effect in complete-link hierarchical clustering. *J. Educ. Stat.* 4:74–92

Hubert, L. J., Golledge, R. G. 1983. Rater agreement for complex assessments. *Br. J. Math. Stat. Psychol.* 36:207–16

Hubert, L. J., Golledge, R. G. 1981. Matrix reorganization and dynamic programming: applications to paired comparison and unidimensional seriation. *Psychometrika* 46:429–41

Hubert, L. J., Golledge, R. G., Richardson, G. D. 1982. Proximity matrix reorganization and hierarchical clustering. *Environ. Plan. Ser. A* 14:195–203

Hubert, L. J., Levin, J. R. 1976. A general statistical framework for assessing categorical clustering in free recall. *Psychol. Bull.* 83:1072–80

Hubert, L. J., Levin, J. R. 1977. Inference models for categorical clustering. *Psychol. Bull.* 84:878–87

Hubert, L. J., Levin, J. R. 1978. Evaluating priority effects in free recall. *Br. J. Math. Stat. Psychol.* 31:11–18

Hubert, L. J., Schultz, J. R. 1976. Quadratic assignment as a general data analysis strategy. *Br. J. Math. Stat. Psychol.* 29:190–241

Hummon, N. P., Doreian, P. 1990. Computational methods for social network analysis. *Soc. Networks* 12:273–88

Hutchinson, J. W. 1989. NETSCAL: a network scaling algorithm for nonsymmetric proximity data. *Psychometrika* 54: 25–51

Imaizumi, T., Okada, A. 1990. *Three-way Scaling and Clustering: How to Use the Software.* Tokyo: Kyoritsu Shuppan

Jain, A. K., Dubes, R. C. 1988. *Algorithms for Clustering Data.* Englewood Cliffs, NJ: Prentice-Hall

Jambu, M. 1978. *Classification Automatique pour l'Analyse des Données,* Tome I. Paris: Dunod

Janowitz, M. F. 1978. An order theoretic model for cluster analysis. *SIAM J. Appl. Math.* 34:55–72

Janowitz, M. F. 1979. Monotone equivariant cluster methods. *SIAM J. Appl. Math.* 37:148–65

Janowitz, M. F., Schweizer, B. 1989. Ordinal and percentile clustering. *Math. Soc. Sci.* 18:135–86

Jardine, C. J., Jardine, N., Sibson, R. 1967. The structure and construction of taxonomic hierarchies. *Math. Biosci.* 1:173–79

Jardine, N., Sibson, R. 1968. The construction of hierarchic and non-hierarchic classifications. *Comput. J.* 11:177–84

Jardine, N., Sibson, R. 1971. *Mathematical Taxonomy.* London: Wiley

Johnson, S. C. 1967. Hierarchical clustering schemes. *Psychometrika* 32:241–54

Jones, L. V., Appelbaum, M. I. 1989. Psychometric methods. *Annu. Rev. Psychol.* 40:23–43

Jones, W. P., Furnas, G. W. 1987. Pictures of relevance: a geometric analysis of similarity measures. *J. Am. Soc. Inform. Sci.* 38:420–42

Kamensky, V. 1990. Review of *Klasternyi Analyz* by I. D. Mandel. *J. Classif.* 7:119–23

Katz, L. 1947. On the matric analysis of sociometric data. *Sociometry* 10:233–41

Kim, K. H., Roush, F. W. 1978. Ultrametrics and matrix theory. *J. Math. Psychol.* 18:195–203

Kirkpatrick, S., Gelatt, C. D. Jr., Vecchi, M. P. 1983. Optimization by simulated annealing. *Science* 220:671–80

Klastorin, T. D. 1980. Merging groups to maximize object partition comparison. *Psychometrika* 45:425–33

Klastorin, T. D. 1982. An alternative method for hospital partition determination using hierarchical cluster analysis. *Oper. Res.* 30:1134–47

Klauer, K. C. 1989. Ordinal network representation: representing proximities by graphs. *Psychometrika* 4:737–50

Klauer, K. C., Carroll, J. D. 1989. A mathematical programming approach to fitting general graphs. *J. Classif.* 6:247–70

Klauer, K. C., Carroll, J. D. 1991. A comparison of two approaches to fitting directed graphs to nonsymmetric proximity measures. *J. Classif.* 8

Klein, R. W., Dubes, R. C. 1989. Experiments in projection and clustering by simulated annealing. *Pattern Recognit.* 22:213–20

Knoke, D., Kuklinski, J. H. 1982. *Network Analysis.* Newbury Park, CA: Sage

Krippendorf, K. 1980. *Content Analysis, an Introduction to Its Methodology.* Newbury Park, CA: Sage

Krippendorff, K. 1987. Association, agreement, and equity. *Qual. Quant.* 21:109–23

Kruskal, J. B. 1956. On the shortest spanning subtree of a graph and the traveling salesman problem. *Proc. Am. Math. Soc.* 7:48–50

Kruskal, J. B. 1964a. Multidimensional scaling by optimizing goodness of fit to a nonmetric hypothesis. *Psychometrika* 29:1–27

Kruskal, J. B. 1964b. Nonmetric multidimensional scaling: a numerical method. *Psychometrika* 29:115–29

Kruskal, J. B. 1977. The relationship between

multidimensional scaling and clustering. See Van Ryzin 1977, pp. 17–44

Kruskal, J. B. 1983. An overview of sequence comparison. In *Time Warps, String Edits, and Macromolecules: The Theory and Practice of Sequence Comparison*, ed. D. Sankoff, J. B. Kruskal, pp. 1–44. Reading, MA: Addison-Wesley

Krzanowski, W. J., Lai, Y. T. 1988. A criterion for determining the number of groups in a data set using sum-of-squares clustering. *Biometrics* 44:23–4

Kusiak, A., Finke, G. 1987. Hierarchical approach to the process planning problem. *Disc. Appl. Math.* 18:145–84

Kusiak, A., Vannelli, A., Kumar, K. R. 1986. Clustering analysis: models and algorithms. *Control Cybern.* 15:139–54

Lance, G. N., Williams, W. T. 1967. A general theory of classificatory sorting strategies. I. Hierarchical systems. *Comput. J.* 9:373–80

Law, H. G., Snyder, C. W. Jr., Hattie, J. A., McDonald, R. P., eds. 1984. *Research Methods for Multimode Data Analysis*. New York: Praeger

Leclerc, B. 1979. Semi-modularité des treillis d'ultramétriques. *C. R. Acad. Sci.* 288:575–77

Leclerc, B. 1981. Description combinatoire des ultramétriques. *Math. Sci. hum.* 19 (73):5–37

Leclerc, B. 1982. Description, évaluation et comparaison de hiérarchies de parties. Cent. Anal. Math. Soc., Paris

Leclerc, B. 1984. Efficient and binary consensus functions on transitively valued relations. *Math. Soc. Sci.* 8:45–61

Leclerc, B. 1985a. La comparaison des hiérarchies: indices et metriques. *Math. Sci. hum.* 23(92):5–40

Leclerc, B. 1985b. Les hiérarchies de parties et leur demi-treillis. *Math. Sci. hum.* 23(89):5–34

Leclerc, B. 1986. Caractérisation, construction et dénombrement des ultramétriques supérieures minimales. *Stat. Anal. Données* 11(2):26–50

Leclerc, B. 1987. Arbres minimums communs et compatibilité de données de types variés. *Math. Sci. hum.* 23(98):41–67

Leclerc, B. 1988. Consensus applications in the social sciences. See Bock 1988, pp. 333–340

Leclerc, B. 1989. Consensus approaches for multiple categorical or relational data. See Coppi & Bolasco 1989, pp. 65–75

Leclerc, B., Cucumel, G. 1987. Consensus en classification: une revue bibliographique. *Math. Sci. hum.* 25(100):109–28

Leclerc, B., Monjardet, B. 1987a. Avant-propos. *Math. Sci. hum.* 25(98):5–7

Leclerc, B., Monjardet, B. 1987b. Combinatorics and data analysis, Part I *Math. Sci. hum.* 25(98) (Special issue)

Leclerc, B., Monjardet, B. 1987c. Combinatorics and data analysis, Part II *Math. Sci. hum.* 25(100) (Special issue)

Lee, H. B. 1980. A K-means cluster analysis computer program with cross-tabulations and next-nearest-neighbor analysis. *Educ. Psychol. Meas.* 40:133–38

Lee, H. B., MacQueen, J. B. 1980. Control parameters for program KMEANS. Program documentation, UCLA

Legendre, P. 1987. Constrained clustering. In *Developments in Numerical Ecology [NATO Adv. Stud. Inst. Ser. G (Ecol. Sci.)]*, ed. P. Legendre, L. Legendre, pp. 289–307. Berlin: Springer-Verlag

Lenstra, J. K. 1974. Clustering a data array and the traveling-salesman problem. *Oper. Res.* 22:413–14

Lerman, I. C. 1980. Combinatorial analysis in the statistical treatment of behavioral data. *Qual. Quant.* 14:431–69

Lerman, I. C. 1981. *Classification et analyse ordinale des données ata classification and ordinal analysis*. Paris: Dunod

Lerman, I. C. 1983a. Indices d'association partielle entre variables "qualitatives nominales". *Rech. Opér./Oper. Res.* 17:213–59

Lerman, I. C. 1983b. Indices d'association partielle entre variables "qualitatives" ordinales. *Publ. Stat. Univ. Paris* 28:7–46

Lerman, I. C. 1987. Construction d'un indice de similarité entre objets décrits par des variables d'un type quelconque. Application au problème du consensus en classification (1). *Rev. Stat. Appl.* 25(2):39–60

Lerman, I. C. 1988. Comparing partitions: mathematical and statistical aspects. See Bock 1988, pp. 121–31

Lerman, I. C., Hardouin, M., Chantrel, T. 1980. Analyse de la situation relative entre deux classifications floues. See Hansen & Lehert 1980, pp. 523–52

Lerman, I. C., Peter, P. 1984. Analyse d'un algorithme de classification hiérarchique "en parallele" pour le traitement de gros ensembles. Res. Rep. No. 339. Le Chesnay: Inst. Natl. Rech. Inform. Automat.

Lerman, I. C., Peter, P. 1988. Structure maximale pour la somme des carrés d'une contingence aux marges fixées; une solution algorithmique programmée. *Rech. Opér./Oper. Res.* 22:83–136

Levin, J. R., Hubert, L. J. 1980. Measuring clustering in free recall. *Psychol. Bull.* 87:59–62

Li, X., Dubes, R. C. 1989. A probabilistic measure of similarity for binary data in pattern recognition. *Pattern Recognit.* 22:397–409

Ling, R. F. 1973. A probability theory of cluster analysis. *J. Am. Stat. Assoc.* 68:159–64

Ling, R. F. 1975. An exact probability distribution on the connectivity of random graphs. *J. Math. Psychol.* 12:90–98

Lingoes, J. C. 1968. The multivariate analysis of qualitative data. *Multivar. Behav. Res.* 3:61–94

Lorr, M. 1983. *Cluster Analysis for Social Scientists.* San Francisco: Jossey-Bass

Luce, R. D., Krumhansl, C. L. 1988. Measurement, scaling, and psychophysics. In *Stevens' Handbook of Experimental Psychology,* ed. R. C. Atkinson, R. J. Herrnstein, G. Lindzey, R. D. Luce, pp. 3–74. New York: Wiley

Luong, X., ed. 1989. *Analyse arborée des Données textuelles [Tree Analysis of Textual Data].* Nice: Cent. Natl. Rech. Sci.

MacQueen, J. 1967. Some methods for classification and analysis of multivariate observations. In *Proceedings Fifth Berkeley Symposium on Mathematical Statistics and Probability,* ed. L. M. Le Cam, J. Neyman, 1:281–97). Berkeley: Univ. Calif. Press

Mandel, I. D. 1988. *Klasternyi analyz [Cluster Analysis].* Moscow: Finansy and Statistika

Mantel, N. 1967. The detection of disease clustering and a generalized regression approach. *Cancer Res.* 27:209–20

Marcotorchino, F. 1986. Cross association measures and optimal clustering. In *Compstat,* ed. F. DeAntoni, N. Lauro, A. Rizzi, pp. 188–94. Heidelberg: Physica-Verlag

Marcotorchino, F. 1987. Block seriation problems: a unified approach. *Appl. Stoch. Models Data Anal.* 3:73–91

Marcotorchino, F., Michaud, P. 1979. *Optimisation en Analyse ordinale des Données.* Paris: Masson

Margules, C. R., Faith, D. P., Belbin, L. 1985. An adjacency constraint in agglomerative hierarchical classifications of geographic data. *Environ. Plan. A* 17:397–412

Marriott, F. H. C. 1982. Optimization methods of cluster analysis. *Biometrika* 69:417–21

Matula, D. W. 1977. Graph theoretic techniques for cluster analysis algorithms. See Van Ryzin 1977, pp. 95–129

Matula, D. W., Sokal, R. R. 1980. Properties of Gabriel graphs relevant to geographic variation research and the clustering of points in the plane. *Geograph. Anal.* 12:205–22

McCormick, W. T. Jr., Schweitzer, P. J., White, T. W. 1972. Problem decomposition and data reorganization by a clustering technique. *Oper. Res.* 20:993–1009

McKeithen, K. B., Reitman, J. S., Rueter, H. R., Hirtle, S. C. 1981. Knowledge organization and skill differences in computer programmers. *Cognit. Psychol.* 13:307–25

McLachlan, G. J. 1982. Classification and mixture maximum likelihood approaches to cluster analysis. In *Handbook of Statistics 2: Classification, Pattern Recognition, and Reduction of Dimensionality,* ed. P. R. Krishnaiah, L. N. Kanal, pp. 199–208. Amsterdam: North-Holland

McLachlan, G. J., Basford, K. E. 1988. *Mixture Models: Inference and Applications to Clustering.* New York: Marcel Dekker

McMorris, F. R. 1985. Axioms for consensus functions on undirected phylogenetic trees. *Math. Biosci.* 74:17–21

McNamara, T. P. 1990. Memory's view of space. Paper presented at Dept. Psychol., Univ. Illinois, Champaign

McQuitty, L. L. 1960. Hierarchical syndrome analysis. *Educ. Psychol. Meas.* 20:293–304

Meehl, P. E., Golden, R. R. 1982. Taxometric methods. In *Handbook of Research Methods in Clinical Psychology.* ed. P. C. Kendall, J. N. Butcher, pp. 127–81. New York: Wiley

Mehta, C. R. 1990. StatXact: a statistical package for exact nonparametric inference. *J. Classif.* 7:111–4

Michalski, R. S., Stepp, R. E. 1983. Automated construction of classifications: conceptual clustering versus numerical taxonomy. *IEEE Trans. Pattern Anal. Mach. Intell.* PAMI-5:396–410

Michaud, P., Marcotorchino, F. 1979. Modéles d'optimisation en analyse des données relationnelles. *Math. Sci. hum.* 17(67):7–38

Michaud, P., Marcotorchino, F. 1980. Optimisation en analyse des données relationnelles: application à l'agrégation des préférences et à la recherche de partitions optimales. See Hansen & Lehert 1980, pp. 655–70

Mielke, P. W. 1978. Clarification and appropriate inference for Mantel & Valand's nonparametric multivariate analysis technique. *Biometrics* 34:277–82

Mielke, P. W. 1979. On asymptotic non-normality of null distributions of MRPP statistics. *Comm. Stat.: Theory and Methods* A8:1541–50. Errata: 1981. A10:1795 and 982. A11:847

Mielke, P. W., Berry, K. J., Johnson, E. S. 1976. Multi-response permutation procedures for a priori classifications. *Comm. Stat.: Theory and Methods* A5:1409–24

Miller, K. F. 1987. Geometric methods in developmental research. In *Formal Methods in Developmental Psychology,* ed. J.

Bisanz, C. J. Brainerd, R. Kail, pp. 216–62. New York: Springer-Verlag

Miller, W., Myers, E. W. 1988. Sequence comparison with concave weighting functions. *Bull. Math. Biol.* 50:97–120

Milligan, G. 1979. Ultrametric hierarchical clustering algorithms. *Psychometrika* 44:343–46

Milligan, G. 1989. A validation study of a variable weighting algorithm for cluster analysis. *J. Classif.* 6:53–71

Milligan, G. W., Cooper, M. C. 1986. A study of the comparability of external criteria for hierarchical cluster analysis. *Multivar. Behav. Res.* 21:441–58

Milligan, G. W., Cooper, M. C. 1988. A study of standardization of variables in cluster analysis. *J. Classif.* 5:181–204

Mirkin, B. G. 1979. Group Choice, ed. P. C. Fishburn, transl. Y. Oliker. Washington, DC: V. H. Winston. (Original work published 1974)

Mirkin, B. G. 1986. Additive clustering and qualitative factor analysis methods. See Diday et al 1986, pp. 71–82

Mirkin, B. G. 1987. Additive clustering and qualitative factor analysis methods for similarity matrices. *J. Classif.* 4:7–31 (Erratum, 1989, 6:271–72)

Mirkin, B. G. 1989a. Erratum. *J. Classif.* 6:271–72

Mirkin, B. G. 1989b. Bilinear clustering algorithms. See Govaert 1989, pp. 65–71

Mirkin, B. G. 1990. A sequential fitting procedure for linear data analysis models. *J. Classif.* 7:167–95

Mirkin, B. G., Rodin, S. N. 1984. *Graphs and Genes.* Heidelberg: Springer-Verlag

Mkhadri, A. 1989. Pondération des variables pour la classification binaire. Res. Rep. No. 1079. Le Chesnay: Inst. Natl. Rech. Inform. Automat.

Monjardet, B. 1973. Tournois et ordres médians pour une opinion. *Math. Sci. hum.* 11(43):55–70

Monjardet, B. 1978. *Théorie des Graphes et Classification: Bibliographie et Index matière.* Paris: Cent. Math. Soc. Univ. Paris-V

Monjardet, B. 1979a. Metriques et relations: avant-propos. *Math. Sci. hum.* 17(67):5–6

Monjardet, B. 1979b. Relations à "éloignement minimum" de relations binaires. Note bibliographique. *Math. Sci. hum.* 17(67):115–22

Monjardet, B. 1981a. Théorie des graphes et taxonomie mathématique. In *Regards sur la Théorie des Graphes*, ed. P. Hansen, D. de Werra, pp. 111–25. Lausanne: Presses Polytechniques Romandes

Monjardet, B. 1981b. Metrics on partially ordered sets: a survey. *Disc. Math.* 35:173–84

Morgan, B. J. T. 1973. Cluster analyses of two acoustic confusion matrices. *Percept. Psychophys.* 13:13–24

Morin, A. M. 1990. Review of *Mixture Models: Inferences and Applications to Clustering* by G. J. McLachlan, K. E. Basford. *Psychometrika* 55:167–68

Morineau, A., Lebart, L. 1986. Specific clustering algorithms for large data sets and implementation in SPAD software. See Gaul & Schader 1986, pp. 321–29

Muchnik, I. B., Chkuaseli, N. F., Shvartser, L. V. 1986. Modeling of behavior and intelligence: linguistic analysis of 0–1 matrices using monotone systems. *Automat. Remote Control* 4:533–60

Murtagh, F. 1983. A survey of recent advances in hierarchical clustering algorithms. *Comput. J.* 26:354–59

Murtagh, F. 1984a. Counting dendrograms: a survey. *Disc. Appl. Math.* 7:191–99

Murtagh, F. 1984b. Complexities of hierarchic clustering algorithms: state of the art. *Comput. Stat. Q.* 1:101–13

Murtagh, F. 1984c. An empirical study of coefficients for measuring the structure of hierarchic classifications. See Diday et al 1984, pp. 385–93

Murtagh, F. 1985a. *Multidimensional Clustering Algorithms.* Vienna: Physica-Verlag

Murtagh, F. 1985b. A survey of algorithms for contiguity-constrained clustering and related problems. *Comput. J.* 28:82–88

Murtagh, F. 1989. Review of *Data, Expert Knowledge and Decisions*, edited by W. Gaul, M. Schader. *J. Classif.* 6:129–32

Noma, E., Smith, D. R. 1985. Benchmark for the blocking of sociometric data. *Psychol. Bull.* 97:583–91

Ohsumi, N., Nakamura, N. 1989. Space distorting properties in agglomerative hierarchical clustering algorithms and a simplified method for combinatorial method. See Govaert 1989, pp. 103–8

Okada, A. 1989. Review of *Classification and Related Methods of Data Analysis*, edited by H. H. Bock. *J. Classif.* 6:121–25

Orth, B. 1988. Representing similarities by distance graphs: monotonic network analysis (MONA). See Bock 1988, pp. 489–94

Orth, B. 1989. Graph theoretical representations of proximities by monotonic network analysis (MONA). In *Mathematical Psychology in Progress*, ed. E. E. Roskam, pp. 299–308. New York: Springer-Verlag

Panel on Discriminant Analysis, Classification and Clustering. 1988. *Discriminant Analysis and Clustering.* Washington, DC: Natl. Academy Press

Payne, R. W., Preece, D. A. 1980. Identification keys and diagnostic tables: a review. *J. R. Stat. Soc. Ser. A* 143:253–92

Peck, R., Fisher, L., Van Ness, J. 1989. Approximate confidence intervals for the number of clusters. *J. Am. Stat. Assoc.* 84:184–91

Pellegrino, J., Hubert, L. J. 1982. The analysis of organization and structure in free recall. In *Handbook of Research Methods in Human Memory and Cognition*, ed. C. Richard Puff, pp. 129–72. New York: Academic

Perruchet, C. 1983a. Constrained agglomerative hierarchical classification. *Pattern Recognit.* 16:213–17

Perruchet, C. 1983b. Significance tests for clusters: overview and comments. See Felsenstein 1983a, pp. 199–208

Pliner, V. M. 1984. A class of metric scaling models. *Automat. Remote Control* 6:122–28

Popping, R. 1988. On agreement indices for nominal data. In *Sociometric Research*. Vol. 1. *Data Collection and Scaling*, ed. W. E. Saris I. N. Gallhofer, pp. 90–105. London: Macmillan

Pruzansky, S., Tversky, A., Carroll, J. D. 1982. Spatial versus tree representations of proximity data. *Psychometrika* 47:3–24

Punj, G., Stewart, D. W. 1983. Cluster analysis in marketing research: review and suggestions for application. *J. Market. Res.* 20:134–48

Rammal, R., Toulouse, G., Virasoro, M. A. 1986. Ultrametricity for physicists. *Rev. Mod. Phys.* 58:765–88

Rao, C. R. 1982. Diversity and dissimilarity coefficients: a unified approach. *Theor. Popul. Biol.* 21:24–43

Ripley, B. D. 1990. Review of *Simulated Annealing (SA) & Optimization* edited by M. E. Johnson *J. Classif.* 7:287–90

Rohlf, F. J. 1973. Hierarchical clustering using the minimum spanning tree. *Comput. J.* 16:93–5

Rohlf, F. J. 1974. Graphs implied by the Jardine-Sibson overlapping clustering models, B_k. *J. Am. Stat. Assoc.* 69:705–10

Rohlf, F. J. 1975. A new approach to the computation of the Jardine-Sibson B_k clusters. *Comput. J.* 18:164–68

Rohlf, F. J. 1982. Single-link clustering algorithms. See McLachlan 1982, pp. 267–84

Rosenberg, S. 1988. Self and others: studies in social personality and autobiography. *Adv. Exp. Soc. Psychol.* 21:57–95

Rosenberg, S. 1989. A study of personality in literary autobiography: an analysis of Thomas Wolfe's "Look Homeward, Angel". *J. Pers. Soc. Psychol.* 56 416–430

Ross, J. 1966. A remark on Tucker & Messick's "points of view" analysis. *Psychometrika* 31:27–31

Rouanet, H., Bernard, J.-M., Lecoutre, B. 1986. Nonprobabilistic statistical inference: a set-theoretic approach. *Am. Statistician* 40:60–65

Sabucedo, J., Ekehammar, B., Arce, C.,

Wendelheim, A. 1990. The cognitive representation of European countries: a comparison between Swedish and Spanish samples. Tech. Rep. No. 722. Univ. Stockholm, Dept. Psychol.

Sackin, M. J., Sneath, P. H. A. 1988. Choosing the smallest number of binary characters to distinguish the greatest number of OTUs. See Bock 1988, pp. 141–46

Sankoff, D., Kruskal, J. B., eds. 1983. *Time Warps, String Edits, and Macromolecules: The Theory and Practice of Sequence Comparison.* Reading, MA: Addison-Wesley

Saporta, G. 1988. About maximal association criteria in linear analysis and in cluster analysis. See Bock 1988, pp. 541–50

Sattath, S., Tversky, A. 1987. On the relation between common and distinctive feature models. *Psychol. Rev.* 94:16–22

Schader, M. 1979. Distance minimale entre partitions et préordonnances dans un ensemble fini. *Math. Sci. hum.* 17(67):39–48

Shepard, R. N. 1962a. The analysis of proximities: Multidimensional scaling with an unknown distance function. I. *Psychometrika* 27:125–40

Shepard, R. N. 1962b. Analysis of proximities: multidimensional scaling with an unknown distance function. II. *Psychometrika* 27:219–46

Shepard, R. N. 1972. A taxonomy of some principal types of data and of multidimensional methods for their analysis. In *Multidimensional Scaling: Theory and Applications in the Behavioral Sciences.* Vol. I: *Theory*, ed. R. N. Shepard, A. K. Romney, S. B. Nerlove, pp. 24–47. New York: Seminar Press

Shepard, R. N. 1974. Representation of structure in similarity data: problems and prospects. *Psychometrika* 39:373–421

Shepard, R. N. 1980. Multidimensional scaling, tree-fitting, and clustering. *Science* 210:390–98

Shepard, R. N. 1988. George Miller's data and the development of methods for representing cognitive structures. In *The Making of Cognitive Science: Essays in Honor of George A. Miller*, ed. W. Hirst, pp. 45–70. Cambridge: Cambridge Univ. Press

Shepard, R. N., Arabie, P. 1979. Additive clustering: representation of similarities as combinations of discrete overlapping properties. *Psychol. Rev.* 86:87–123

Shiina, K. 1986. A maximum likelihood nonmetric multidimensional scaling procedure for word sequences obtained in free-recall experiments. *Jpn. Psychol. Res.* 28(2):53–63

Sibson, R. 1973. SLINK: an optimally efficient algorithm for the single-link cluster method. *Comput. J.* 16:30–45

Smith, J. E. K. 1976. Analysis of qualitative data. *Annu. Rev. Psychol.* 27:487–99

Smouse, P. E., Long, J. C., Sokal, R. R. 1986. Multiple regression and correlation extensions of the Mantel test of matrix correspondence. *Syst. Zool.* 35:627–32

Sneath, P. H. A., Sokal, R. R. 1973. *Numerical Taxonomy.* San Francisco: W. H. Freeman

Snijders, T. A. B., Dormaar, M., van Schuur, W. H., Dijkman-Caes, C., Driessen, G. 1990. Distribution of some similarity coefficients for dyadic binary data in the case of associated attributes. *J. Classif.* 7:5–31

Snyder, C. W. Jr., Law, H. G., Hattie, J. A. 1984. Overview of multimode analytic methods. See Law et al 1984, pp. 2–35

Sokal, R. R. 1985. The continuing search for order. *Am. Nat.* 126:729–49

Sokal, R. R. 1986a. Phenetic taxonomy: theory and methods. *Annu. Rev. Ecol. Syst.* 17:423–42

Sokal, R. R. 1986b. Spatial data analysis and historical processes. See Diday et al 1986, pp. 29–43

Sokal, R. R. 1988a. Unsolved problems in numerical taxonomy. See Bock 1988, pp. 45–56

Sokal, R. R. 1988b. Genetic, geographic, and linguistic distances in Europe. *Proc. Natl. Acad. Sci. USA* 85:1722–26

Sokal, R. R., Lengyel, I. A., Derish, P. A., Wooten, M. C., Oden, N. L. 1987. Spatial autocorrelation of ABO serotypes in mediaeval cemeteries as an indicator of ethnic and familial structure. *J. Archaeol. Sci.* 14:615–33

Spaeth, H. 1980. *Cluster Analysis Algorithms,* transl. U. Bull. Chichester, England: Ellis Horwood. (Original work published 1977)

Spaeth, H. 1985. *Cluster Dissection and Analysis: Theory, FORTRAN Programs, Examples,* transl. J. Goldschmidt. Chichester: Ellis Horwood. (Original work published 1983)

Spaeth, H. 1986a. Maximizing partitioning cluster criteria for quantitative data. See Bock 1986, pp. 221–28

Spaeth, H. 1986b. Anticlustering: maximizing the variance criterion. *Control Cybern.* 15:213–18

Spaeth, H. 1986c. Homogenous and heterogeneous clusters for distance matrices. See Bock 1988, pp. 157–64

Sriram, N. 1990. Clique optimization: a method to construct parsimonious ultrametric trees from similarity data. *J. Classif.* 7:33–52

Tarjan, R. E. 1982. A hierarchical clustering algorithm using strong components. *Inf. Process. Lett.* 14:26–29

ten Berge, J. M. F. 1988. Generalized

approaches to the maxbet problem and the maxdiff problem, with applications to canonical correlations. *Psychometrika* 53:487–94

Tucker, L. R 1964. The extension of factor analysis to three-dimensional matrices. In *Contributions to Mathematical Psychology,* ed. N. Frederiksen, H. Gulliksen, pp. 109–27. New York: Holt, Rinehart, and Winston

Tucker, L. R 1983. Searching for structure in binary data. In *Principals of Modern Psychological Measurement.* ed. H. Wainer, S. Messick, pp. 215–35. Hillsdale, NJ: Erlbaum

Tucker, L. R, Messick, S. J. 1963. An individual difference model for multi-dimensional scaling. *Psychometrika* 28:333–67

Tversky, A., Hutchinson, J. W. 1986. Nearest neighbor analysis of psychological spaces. *Psychol. Rev.* 93:3–22

Upton, G., Fingleton, B. 1985. *Spatial Data Analysis by Example.* Vol. I. *Point Pattern and Quantitative Data.* New York: Wiley

Van Mechelen, I., De Boeck, P. 1990. Projection of a binary criterion into a model of hierarchical classes. *Psychometrika* 55:677–94

Van Ryzin, J., ed. 1977. *Classification and Clustering.* New York: Academic

Vegelius, J., Janson, S. 1982. Criteria for symmetric measures of association for nominal data. *Qual. Quant.* 16:243–50

Verhelst, N. D., Koppen, M. G. M., Van Essen, E. P. 1985. The exact distribution of an index of agreement between partitions. *Br. J. Math. Stat. Psychol.* 38:44–57

Walker, M. 1989. An analysis of auditory alphabet confusions. *Percept. Psychophys.* 45:315–22

Waller, N. G., Lykken, D. T., Tellegen, A. 1992. Occupational interests, leisure time interests and personality: three domains or one? Findings from the Minnesota Twin Registry. In *Assessing Individual Differences in Human Behavior: New Methods, Concepts, and Findings,* ed. R. V. Dawis, D. Lubinski. Minneapolis: Univ. Minnesota Press. In press

Wasserman, S., Anderson, C. 1987. Stochastic *a posteriori* blockmodels: construction and assessment. *Soc. Networks* 9:1–36

Wasserman, S., Faust, K. 1991. *Social Network Analysis: methods and Applications.* New York: Cambridge Univ. Press

Weisberg, H. F. 1974. Dimensionland: an excursion into spaces. *Am. J. Polit. Sci.* 18:743–76

Weiss, M. J. 1988. *The Clustering of America.* New York: Harper Row

Whaley, C. P. 1982. Interactive clustering. *Behav. Res. Meth. Instrument.* 14:170–75

Wilkinson, L. 1989. *SYSTAT: The System for Statistics*. Evanston, IL: Systat, Inc.

Willett, P. 1988. Recent trends in hierarchic document clustering: a critical review. *Inf. Process. Manage.* 24:577–97

Wind, Y. 1978. Issues and advances in segmentation research. *J. Market. Res.* 15:317–37

Windham, M. P. 1985. Numerical classification of proximity data with assignment measures. *J. Classif.* 2:157–72

Windham, M. P. 1987. Parameter modification for clustering criteria. *J. Classif.* 4:191–214

Windham, M. P. 1988. Review of *Mixture Models: Inference and Applications to Clustering* by G. J. McLachlan, K. E. Basford. *J. Classif.* 5:105–7

Wolfe, A. , ed. 1990. *Connections* 13

Wolfe, J. H. 1970. Pattern clustering by multivariate mixture analysis. *Multivar. Behav. Res.* 5:329–50

Wright, P. 1987. *Spycatcher*. New York: Viking

Zegers, F. E. 1986. Two classes of elementwise transformations preserving the psd nature of coefficient matrices. *J. Classif.* 3:49–53

Annu. Rev. Psychol. 1992. 43:205–34
Copyright © 1992 by Annual Reviews Inc. All rights reserved

MODELS FOR RECALL
AND RECOGNITION

Jeroen G. W. Raaijmakers

TNO Institute for Perception, 3769 ZG Soesterberg, The Netherlands

Richard M. Shiffrin

Department of Psychology, Indiana University, Bloomington, Indiana 47405

KEY WORDS: mathematical models, recall, recognition, connectionism, associative memory

CONTENTS

INTRODUCTION

Research on learning and memory has been driven by models since at least the
1940s. Over the years, the emphasis in mathematical modeling has shifted

0066-4308/92/0201-0205$02.00

from precise fitting of single experiments to what might be best described as semi-quantitative fitting of a wide variety of phenomena from a number of experimental paradigms [compare for instance Bower's one-element model (Bower 1961) to any of the current models such as ACT* (Anderson 1983b), SAM (Raaijmakers & Shiffrin 1981; Gillund & Shiffrin 1984) or TODAM (Murdock 1982)].

The complexities of recent models contributes to the apparent impossibility of deciding between them. Although couched in quite different terms, they often make very similar predictions, at least under appropriate choices of parameters. This makes it difficult to generate critical empirical tests. On the other hand, the similarity of predictions suggests real progress in theory development, forced by the necessity to account for a standard and agreed upon corpus of findings.

In this chapter, we review a number of the most important contemporary models of memory, trying to highlight the similarities and differences in the way they handle basic facts about recall and recognition. Space limitations prevent us from any attempt at exhaustive coverage. For the same reason, although a number of models can or do predict response latencies, we leave coverage of this important topic to a future chapter.

Theoretical Approaches

Although all classifications are to some degree unsatisfactory, we group current models into three categories: 1. separate-trace models involving spreading activation, or making no explicit activation assumptions—we term these *network models;* 2. separate-trace models involving parallel activation, here termed *episodic trace models;* and 3. *composite/distributed memory models.*

Network Models

Network models propose that long-term memory consists of a set of nodes with links connecting the nodes. The nodes represent concepts or cognitive units (Anderson 1983a,b), the links semantic or episodic relations. Whenever two items are studied together, a link between the nodes representing these items may be formed. In most of these models, a process of spreading activation determines the retrieval of information from memory. Basically, there are two types of network model: (*a*) the *all-or-none activation* model, and (*b*) the *continuous activation* model.

The all-or-none activation model assumes that network nodes are either active or inactive. The best known example is the ACTE model proposed by Anderson (1976). In such a model, the spreading of activation is determined by the (relative) strength of the nodes or the links. Suppose that two nodes, X and Y, are connected by a link l. If node X is active, the probability of activating Y in the next unit of time is a function of s/S, the relative strength of the link l compared to all other links emanating from X, or, alternatively, the relative strength of node Y compared to all other nodes linked to X. In such a model, the probability of retrieving Y, given that X is active, is equal to the likelihood that Y is activated before a specified cutoff time.

A continuous activation model was developed by Anderson (1983a,b) as an alternative to the all-or-none model. The basic difference is that network nodes now have a continuously varying activation strength. This means that one needs a different rule for determining whether a memory trace has been successfully retrieved. If a stimulus node X has an associative link to another node Y, some activation will spread from X to Y. The amount of activation of Y is determined by the relative strength of the link between X and Y (compared to all other links from X). In such a model it becomes more natural to assume that the probability and latency of retrieving the trace Y are a function of the amount of activation of Y. Thus, the notion of spreading activation has changed from gradually activating connected nodes (i.e. distant nodes take longer to activate) to a dynamic model in which the activation spreads rapidly over the network but in varying degrees (i.e. distant nodes have a lower level of activation).

As an example, in the most recent version of Anderson's ACT theory, the ACT* model (Anderson 1983b), it is assumed that during storage memory traces (called cognitive units) are formed. Traces vary in strength (a function of the number of presentations and the retention interval), and these strengths determine the amount of activation that converges on the trace from associated nodes (thus, in this model, it is relative node strength, not link strength, that determines the flow of activation; it is not evident whether this makes a difference). Thus, in a paired-associate recall situation, where the subject learns a list of pairs A-B, it is assumed that the trace (the cognitive unit) encodes the information that this pair was presented in this context. At test, the response will be retrieved if (a) such a trace has indeed been formed, and (b) it can be retrieved within the cutoff time.

Episodic Trace Models

The basic characteristic of episodic trace models is that they assume a set of separately stored memory traces that are activated in parallel. Such models are sometimes called "search models" because recall requires that some one of these traces must be "found" and output. In one subclass of models, recall of information from long-term memory involves sequential samples from a set of memory traces. The best-known example of such a model is the Search of Associative Memory (SAM) model proposed by Raaijmakers & Shiffrin (1980, 1981). In SAM the sampling probability of a particular trace depends on the relative strength of that trace compared to all other memory traces.

The SAM model assumes that during storage, information is represented in "memory images," which contain item, associative, and contextual information. The amount and type of information stored are determined by coding processes in short-term store (STS). In most (intentional) learning paradigms the amount of information stored is a function of the length of time that the item is studied while in STS. According to the SAM model, retrieval from long-term store (LTS) is based on cues (context, items, category names). Whether an image is retrieved or not depends on the associative strengths of the retrieval cues to that image. These strengths are a function of the overlap of the cue information and the information stored in the image.

An important property of the SAM model is that it incorporates a rule to describe the overall strength of a set of probe cues to a particular image: The overall activation strength $(A(i))$ is equal to product of the individual cue strengths (weighted if necessary for relative salience or importance). This multiplicative feature focuses the search process on those images that are strongly associated to all cues.

In recall tasks, the search process of the SAM model is based on a series of elementary retrieval attempts. Each attempt involves selecting or sampling one image based on the relative activation strengths. Sampling an image allows recovery of information from it. For simple recall tasks, the probability of successfully recovering the name of the encoded word is assumed to be a simple function of the weighted strengths.

Although the SAM model assumes that the process of activating information is basically the same in recall and recognition, it postulates some important differences between these two processes. It is assumed that recognition does not necessarily involve sequential sampling but is (mostly) based on a direct-access process involving a single retrieval step (Gillund & Shiffrin 1984:55–56). The recognition decision in this direct access process is based on the sum $(\Sigma\, A(k))$ of the activation strengths; if the same cues are used to probe memory for recall and recognition, the activations are the same in both cases, though used in different ways. As we shall see, the process of summing activations makes the SAM model for recognition remarkably similar in structure to models that appear quite different on the surface, even models (e.g. most composite, distributed models) that sum inputs at storage rather than retrieval.

Because an "old" response is made when $\Sigma\, A(k)$ is greater than a criterion value, the distribution of the sum determines performance. For this reason, SAM incorporates specific variance assumptions; in particular, the standard deviation of the distribution of a given strength is assumed to be proportional to the mean strength value (Gillund & Shiffrin 1984; Shiffrin et al 1990).

The SAM model assumes that for typical episodic-memory tasks, contextual information is always encoded in the memory image, and context is one of the retrieval cues. Mensink & Raaijmakers (1988, 1989) proposed an extension of the SAM model to handle time-dependent changes in context. The basic idea, adapted from Stimulus Sampling Theory (Estes 1955), is that a random fluctuation of elements occurs between two sets, a set of available context elements and a set of (temporarily) unavailable context elements. Performance is a function of the relationship between sets of available elements at different points in time (i.e. study and test trials).

Hintzman (1984, 1986, 1988) developed a model for episodic memory similar to Gillund & Shiffrin's SAM model for recognition. This model, MINERVA 2, has been applied primarily to category learning and recognition memory. It is assumed that each experience produces a separate memory trace. Both items and memory traces are represented as lists of features or vectors. In simulations of the model, it has been assumed that each feature is independently encoded with probability L, a learning rate parameter. When a probe cue is presented, all memory traces are activated in parallel. The amount of activation of any particular trace is a nonlinear function of the similarity to the probe cue.

As in the SAM model, recognition performance in MINERVA 2 depends on a single value, the summed activation of all traces. In order to allow recall to be carried out, the model also stipulates that a vector is retrieved. This vector (called the *echo*) is the sum of all trace vectors, each weighted by its activation value. Because of the weighting, and the nonlinear activation rule, the echo will contain a disproportional representation of those traces similar to the memory probe. Thus, if part of trace j is used as a probe, the echo will contain a strong representation from the entire trace j. For example, if a trace encodes a studied pair *A-B,* and *A* is used as a probe, the echo will contain something similar to *A-B,* allowing *B* to be recalled. Of course, the retrieved trace is actually a composite of many traces (unlike the SAM model), so some mechanism is needed to extract some particular item from the composite— Hintzman (1986, 1988) discusses several possibilities, such as comparing the echo to the stored traces, or repeating the retrieval process several times, each time using the retrieved echo as a probe, until the echo achieves a stable value (usually matching some stored trace). In any event, one basic difference between SAM and MINERVA 2 is that the latter model assumes that in recall a kind of composite memory trace is retrieved (at least initially), whereas the SAM model for recall holds that a specific memory trace is sampled (initially, though different traces may be sampled subsequently).

Distributed Memory Models

In recent years, composite/distributed memory models have enjoyed a rapidly growing popularity. [For additional discussion we refer the reader to a recent

Annual Review chapter by Hintzman (1990)]. These models fall in two related but somewhat different classes. In one class, items are represented by vectors (as in MINERVA 2) or matrixes of elementary features and the memory consists of a sum of the vectors or matrixes [e.g. TODAM (Murdock 1982), CHARM (Eich 1982; 1985), James Anderson's vector model (Anderson 1973), and the Matrix model (Pike 1984; Humphreys et al 1989); Kanerva's SDM model (Kanerva 1988) falls part way between this class and the separate storage class of the previous section]. In the second class, memory consists of nodes connected by weighted links; items are represented by a pattern or set of activations of the nodes, and long-term memory consists of the values of the weights on the links [e.g. Grossberg's ART model (Grossberg 1987; Grossberg & Stone 1986), James Anderson's BSB model (J. A. Anderson et al 1977), McClelland & Rumelhart's recurrent model, or any of the feedforward back-propagation models].

The basic difference between such models and the models discussed previously is that composite/distributed memory models assume that a memory trace is not a distinct, localized entity but rather part of a combination or superimposition of all traces input to the system. It is this aspect that has made many of these models seem both mysterious to the novice (who wonders how memory can be as good as it is) and attractive to many experts (who can explain why memory is as bad as it is, and how we can extract averages and prototypes from inputs, and who like the analogy to neuronal structures).

These composite/distributed storage assumptions can serve as a basis for a memory model because for each version there exists an appropriate retrieval operation. In some cases the cue will retrieve a noisy version of the original trace containing that cue; in other cases the cue will retrieve a noisy version of an item originally stored as an associate of the cue; in yet other cases the retrieval may be a clearly definable response, but with a type of noise determining the probability of reaching such a state, and determining whether the state would be the correct one. The retrieved information can be matched against the input to perform recognition, or if necessary can be "cleaned up" in some fashion to allow a response to be emitted.

As an example, consider one version of the Matrix model proposed by Anderson et al (1977; termed BSB for "brain state in a box"). Whenever two items (f_i, g_i) are associated, a matrix A_i is produced with cell elements $A_i(r,s)$ = $f_i(r)g_i(s)$. The composite memory (M) consists of the sum of all such association matrixes, $M = \Sigma\, A_i$. Ignoring for simplicity the details of the node activation process (such as its nonlinear limitations on activation growth), the retrieval of an associate (g_i) given a cue item (f_i) can be obtained by postmultiplying M with f_i: the result, Mf_i, is a noisy composite of those vectors that had been studied with both f_i and items similar to f_i (see Anderson et al 1977:417). Although this model is formulated specifically for paired-associate recall, a simple modification will handle recognition memory. The basic idea is that recognition involves a matching operation of the composite memory trace with the to-be-recognized item. In order for this to work, it must be assumed that the memory trace includes not only associative information but also item information.

Although we have ignored the short-term activation features of the BSB model, it is a member of our second class. We begin our discussion of the first class with a model closely related to Anderson's but without a node activation process (and its nonlinear limit on activation values). This is the Matrix model proposed by Pike (1984; see also Humphreys et al 1989a,b). Associations of item vectors are represented by matrixes to form a composite memory matrix. In recent versions of this model, context-to-item associations have been incorporated in the matrix model in order to account for the fact that memory of a to-be-memorized list is to some extent "isolated" from all other memories. Thus, instead of storing a two-way association between the members of a paired associate, a three-way association among the two items and the context is stored (in the form of a 3-dimensional matrix). In order to retrieve g_i the memory matrix (M) is multiplied in a specific way (see Humphreys et al 1989a) with the matrix obtained by multiplication of the context (x) and item (f_i) vectors. The latter product defines the "interactive" retrieval cue representing the association of context and stimulus item. This incorporation of contextual associations makes it possible to distinguish between episodic (list-specific) and semantic (preexisting) associations.

Related models have been proposed by Murdock (1982) and Eich (1982; 1985; see also Metcalfe & Murdock 1981). In both Murdock's Theory of Distributed Associative Memory (TODAM) and Metcalfe's Composite Holographic Associative Recall Model (CHARM),[1] the associative encoding and retrieval operations are the mathematical operations of convolution and correlation, respectively (see Eich 1982, 1985).

The TODAM model assumes that when each association A-B is studied, the vectors representing A and B, and the convolution vector representing A-B, are all added to a slightly decayed version of the single composite memory vector that contains all of episodic memory. In this model, recognition involves matching the to-be-recognized item vector to the memory vector (i.e. taking the dot product) and using the resulting scalar number as a measure of familiarity. Recall starts by correlating the cue item vector with the memory trace, producing a noisy vector containing components representing versions of all items associated to the cue vector during study. The noisy vector must

---

[1]The term "holographic" refers to the analogy between the properties of human associative memory and those of holograms (Pribram et al 1974; Willshaw 1981), in particular their resistance to local damage and the associative properties.

then be cleaned up to produce a response (say, by comparing the retrieved vector to a list of separately stored vectors representing items in semantic memory).

Rather than store vectors, CHARM (Eich 1985) stores autoconvolution vectors for each single item; these are stored along with the convolution vector for the association. For all studied pairs, these vectors are summed into a single composite memory vector. The retrieval operation is correlation, as in TODAM. In CHARM, a probe with A retrieves a composite noisy version of all items convolved with A, including A itself, so that item and associative information are not independently retrieved (as they are in TODAM). As usual, the trace must be cleaned up to generate a response in a recall task. Recognition can be accomplished by comparing the retrieved vector to the test vector.

The second class of composite/distributed model explicitly incorporates processes of node activation (often thought of as short-term memory) as well as weight modification (the set of weights representing long-term memory), both processes typically being nonlinear. The complexities introduced have led most investigators to explore these models in the form of computer simulations (with the notable exception of James Anderson and Steve Grossberg — see below). Such models are often described by the terms "connectionist" or "neural net." Most applications have been to learning phenomena, categorization and classification, or perceptual phenomena, but some discussion of applications to memory is useful.

Consider first a representative back-propagation model (Ackley et al 1985; Rumelhart et al 1986). This model assumes a 3-layer representation: a layer of input units or network nodes, a layer of output units, and a middle layer of so-called hidden units. Activation is fed from the input units to the hidden units (using a nonlinear transform) and from these to the output units. All connections between layers have weights that determine how much the activation of a particular, say, hidden unit depends on the activation of a particular input unit. The basic rule of the back-propagation model is that these weights are adjusted during training in order to optimize the correspondence between predicted and actual output vectors (the back-propagation algorithm performs a kind of least-squares fitting procedure). One can use such a model to perform recognition and recall in a number of ways; perhaps the simplest is to have each input association attempt to reproduce itself at the output layer. Then a subsequent test with an item will tend to produce a noisy version of the association containing that item at the output layer. Recognition can be accomplished by matching, and recall by cleaning up the trace in some fashion.

These networks can represent virtually any computable mapping from input to output layer (given enough hidden units). However, for our purposes the important issue is how such a mapping is learned and retained under various conditions. These aspects have been considered by McCloskey & Cohen (1989) and Ratcliff (1990).

McCloskey & Cohen (1989) showed that in two-list recall tasks the back-propagation model suffers from "catastrophic forgetting": The second list leads to almost complete forgetting of the first list. Similar problems were uncovered by Ratcliff (1990), who analyzed the model's predictions for recognition memory. This result is understandable if it is realized that these neural net models adjust the connection weights to fit the most recent stimuli, and that it is assumed that the inputs during the second list are of second-list items only. At the start of second-list learning, the weights will be configured optimally for the first list. However, there is no mechanism in the model that will keep the weights from obtaining completely different values, optimizing the "recall" of the second-list items. Hence, after a few training trials on the second list, the network will have "forgotten" the first-list items. Ratcliff (1990) also showed that this model fails to predict a positive effect of amount of learning on the d' measure for recognition. [Ratcliff also showed that several related models, including the auto-associative model proposed by McClelland & Rumelhart (1985)—see below, failed to resolve the problems. Research going on at the time of this writing suggests a number of new approaches that might work; e.g. Sloman & Rumelhart (1992); Kruschke (1992); Lewandowski (1992). Below we discuss Grossberg's ART model, which deals with the problem explicitly.]

The back-propagation models are "feedforward" networks: Activation flows only forward through the system (the amount of error is in a sense propagated backwards through the system in order to adjust the weights appropriately, but this should not be confused with the flow of activation). On the other hand, a number of models are recurrent: Activation that leaves a node can be fed back to that same node, possibly after flowing through a number of intermediate nodes, and the process typically continues until a stable pattern of activation results. (The BSB model has this character, though we did not discuss the dynamics of activation.)

Consider first the McClelland & Rumelhart (1985) model. In brief, a set of nodes accepts input from external sources and is fully interconnected (except that nodes do not directly activate themselves) by directional links having weights. Activation moves through the system driven by the sum of the external and internal inputs to a node, until a stable pattern is reached. Then weights are adjusted so as to reduce the difference between the internal and external input to each cell (so that the network will try to reproduce its external inputs). Recognition can be accomplished by matching an input to the stable pattern of activation it produces, and recall by cleaning up the same stable pattern in some fashion.

Finally, consider the recurrent ART models of Grossberg (e.g. Grossberg & Stone 1986, although the original models date back before 1970). We describe here a greatly simplified version of the theory to give the flavor of the approach. Memory consists of a series of ordered layers of nodes. Consider just two layers, with perceptual inputs to layer 1, (and, in general, top-down inputs to layer 2). In addition, weighted links exist in both directions between nodes in the two layers, and activations pass in both directions along these links. Within a layer, there may also be connections, but these are inhibitory and do not carry activations directly. The two layers pass activation rapidly back and forth until a stable result is achieved. Because of inhibition within layer 2, a single node will come to be active in this layer, in stable resonance with a pattern of activation on the nodes in layer 1. The stable pattern may be used for recognition or recall in ways similar to those we have discussed already.

A particularly noteworthy feature of the model is its method for picking the single active node in layer 2. The pattern of activations sent down from this node to layer 1 is compared with the pattern in layer 1. If these do not match well, the currently active layer 2 node is turned off, the system resets, and a new node in layer two wins the competition. This continues until a good match is found, until a node not yet used as a template for a pattern is found, or until no nodes are left, in which case all layer 2 nodes become inactive. The result is that different patterns are assigned new nodes, and new learning does not harm old learning in the destructive fashion of other models of this class.

The weights on the links change continuously also, but at a much slower rate than the activation changes. The upward weight changes are made so as to reduce the difference between a weight itself and the signal passed upward along that link. Thus a set of weights leading to a single active node comes to correlate with the activation pattern in the nodes. Also the downward links from the active node are adjusted to match the activation pattern in the layer 1 nodes, so that top-down templates of the presented patterns are learned. The weights leading to and from any one layer 2 node come to encode a set of highly similar patterns, so that each node in layer 2 can be thought of as a category prototype. A particularly noteworthy feature of this system is the fact that the system can have a distributed representation at some levels (e.g. level 1) and a potentially separate representation at other levels (e.g. layer 2).

Differences and Similarities

In this section we compare the various models on a number of important theoretical dimensions. Although the various approaches we have considered are superficially quite different, basic phenomena are often explained in a similar manner, albeit using different terminologies. Here we focus on the basic issues concerning the conceptualization of memory processes. The discussion deals with issues as if they were independent, but it is important to remember that no one of the hypotheses discussed below can be right or wrong in isolation; each must be analyzed in the context of the model in which it is embedded.

SEPARATE VS COMPOSITE MEMORY TRACES   The question here is whether the model assumes that different items are stored in separate traces or in one composite memory trace. Whether this is a meaningful theoretical distinction depends on a number of auxiliary assumptions in the models in question. For example, Shiffrin & Murnane (1991) showed that an arbitrary number of events can be stored in a single number on a single link in a way that allows each event to be retrieved without error. The method is not a physically realizable one, however. Plausible composite systems, incorporating the equivalent of neural noise, all seem to have at least one testable property: When the system is densely composite, then the storage of new inputs, or even the repetitions of old inputs, tends to degrade the representations of other old inputs. Ratcliff et al (1990) tested this notion empirically and found that repetitions of some list items did not reduce recognition performance for other list items (see also, Murnane & Shiffrin 1991).

Shiffrin et al (1990) looked at the implications for extant models. All then-current models were found wanting. They concluded that composite models dense enough to predict forgetting caused by the composition property could not predict the findings. They concluded that models positing separate traces had the potential to predict the results, and they developed a variant of the SAM model that did so. This variant assumed that repetitions were accumulated in a single trace (a kind of local composition hypothesis—see below). It also incorporated a "differentiation" hypothesis: Suppose two different items A and B were not rehearsed together. If B is stored in memory more strongly, then A used as a cue will tend to activate it less.

A more local composition issue concerns whether two separate pre-sentations of a given item are encoded separately or in the same trace. That is, if an item is repeated, does the second presentation lead to a strengthening of the originally formed trace, or will a new trace be formed?

MINERVA 2 assumes that each separate encoding of a single item (repetition) leads to a separate episodic memory trace, ACT* assumes that repetitions strengthen a given trace, and the early versions of SAM were somewhat ambiguous about this point. Recently (see Raaijmakers 1991), the SAM model has been extended to deal specifically with the effects of repetition and the spacing of repetitions. In this version, a kind of study-phase retrieval assumption has been added to the model. That is, on the second presentation an (implicit) retrieval attempt occurs. If the trace representing the first presentation is retrieved, it is assumed that the new information will be added to the "old" memory trace; otherwise, a new trace will be formed. In addition, Shiffrin et al (1990) had to assume a strengthened trace to explain the lack of a list-strength finding in recognition.

This view gained support from a study by Murnane & Shiffrin (1991). They tried to induce separate storage of a repeated word by embedding it in different sentence contexts; this manipulation produced the expected positive list-strength effect in recognition. Evidence of a different sort supporting this view arises from a study by Ross & Landauer (1978). They showed that the traditional spacing effect only occurs for the probability of recalling single items presented twice and not for the probability of recalling either one of two different items each presented once. This result seems to require that repetitions of an item should be treated differently from the case of multiple items, each presented once (although firm conclusions depend on the details of each model).

REPRESENTATIONAL ISSUES   We consider three representational aspects: 1. the nature of the information encoded in the memory trace, 2. whether links between memory traces are assumed, and 3. the representation of "associative strength."

The models we have considered differ in their assumptions about the information encoded in the memory trace. In the all-or-none activation model ACTE of Anderson (1976), storage of a simple pairwise association involves the formation of a new link between pre-existing network nodes. In the ACT* model, what is stored is a cognitive unit representing the episodic experience. It is assumed that such a new network node has associative links with nodes representing the constituent parts of the item—i.e. (in this case) stimulus, response, and list context. In ACT*, associative strength is represented simply by the strength of the memory traces. As described above, these strengths determine the amount of activation that spreads to the trace from associated nodes.

SAM and MINERVA 2 also assume that the trace represents the "episodic experience" but are less specific about the exact nature of what is stored. The original SAM model focused on the relation between cues and images: Associative relations are represented by a "retrieval structure" rather than the more traditional "storage structure." The model does not make use of explicit associative connections between images, though these are present implicitly in the following sense: Suppose two items are studied together; when one is used as a cue the retrieval strength to the image of the other is high. SAM was not entirely explicit concerning the nature of the "image," though for most verbal studies an image was based on the individual word. Shiffrin et al (1989) presented evidence that a good deal more flexibility is needed, and that a sentence is often a single image (and that, under some circumstances, a pair of words is a single image). Thus in principle a pair association could be stored in two ways: separate images governed by an implicit association that is represented in the retrieval structure, or a single combined image.

MINERVA 2 assumes that episodic experiences and memory traces can be represented as vectors of feature values. Since the nature of these features is left unspecified, this assumption does not really pose any restrictions. It is noteworthy that MINERVA represents pairs by encoding the component vectors back to back in a single stored vector. There is a nonlinear activation process during retrieval that lets the system distinguish whether two stored items are in the same or different traces.

Finally, what about the models with composite/distributed representations? The final representation is generally a vector or matrix; it is a composite of similar vectors or matrixes (or degraded forms of these) stored for individual items and pairs. The question is how associations and single items are handled during storage. TODAM has item vectors, and convolutions of item vectors for associations. Context information could in principle be part of each vector but in recent work has been treated as a separate vector. CHARM treats single items as autoconvolutions but is otherwise similar to TODAM in most respects. The Matrix model treats individual item vectors separately, and context as a separate vector. Single items are stored as an association matrix made from the item, context, and a unit vector. Pairs are matrixes made from the product of the two item vectors and the context vector. One issue left unresolved for these models is the basis on which some types of information are encoded in a given vector while other types are singled out for treatment as a separate vector. For example, how would category information be treated? (See Humphreys et al 1991 for one possible solution.)

A more general solution to this problem is possible if the various types of information, and various items to be associated, are all treated as components of a single vector, or single pattern of activation across a set of nodes. For example, in the McClelland & Rumelhart autoassociative recurrent model, and in Grossberg's ART models, all items to be associated, and related information, are encoded as a single vector or pattern of activation values sent to a set of nodes. Anderson's BSB model, and various versions of feedforward back-propagation models, use either of two methods. In one method, similar to those in the recurrent models just mentioned, items to be associated are encoded together in a single input vector [for example, the model of Ackley et al (1985) tries to reproduce at the output layer the vector presented to the input layer]. All such models use a pattern-completion property to retrieve associates. In the second method, the items to be associated are treated as separate vectors; for example, the input layer could encode one item and the output layer could encode the associated item (J. A. Anderson et al 1977).

218 RAAIJMAKERS & SHIFFRIN

CONTEXTUAL ENCODING   Any model that is designed to explain data from episodic memory experiments must somehow account for the fact that a paired associate item such as *apple-engine* can be learned despite the presence of strong competitive semantic associations (*apple-pear*). It seems highly unlikely that one or two presentations of a list would create such a strong association that it dominates the pre-experimental associations. Thus, subjects are able to learn different associative relationships in different situations. This contextual dependence is a fundamental property of episodic memory.

It therefore seems highly desirable for a model of memory to have some means of selectively accessing memory traces stored under particular temporal or contextual conditions. Note that a simple recency-based mechanism will not suffice—subjects can access information from contextually identifiable periods in the past. To give just one example, subjects are able to access selectively not the list learned most recently but the list learned prior to that (Shiffrin 1970; Anderson & Bower 1972).

Most models incorporate contextual associations as the means to focus retrieval processes in episodic memory, either by including the contextual information in the memory trace or by treating the contextual information as a separate item. Whether this alone will suffice is an open question. For example, ACT* and MINERVA 2 assume an additive rule for combining the associative strength due to context and item. Such a rule may not have a sufficiently strong focusing effect to eliminate strong interference by pre-experimental associations. The multiplicative combination rules used, for example, in SAM and the Matrix model are such that retrieval is focused on those traces (or those components of the composite trace) that are consistent with the context at test. Even a multiplicative rule may not, by itself, be sufficient to focus retrieval properly. For example, Humphreys et al (1989a) call attention to crossed-associates lists, in which the subject is asked to learn pairs like *doctor-king* and *queen-nurse*. Versions of the SAM model in which individual words (but not pairs) have a single (semantic) memory representation would not easily predict the learning seen in such cases. However, SAM models typically assume that images are episodic in nature, not semantic.

It should be no surprise that models that do not incorporate context will not fare well. For example, a model that does not include a way to reduce the effect of irrelevant associations will have serious problems explaining why the interfering effect of the number of items on a single experimental list is not completely swamped by the millions of previously acquired associations. A simple forgetting assumption, e.g. a reduction of strength for previous associations (as in TODAM), will not do the job without added assumptions about context: The strong empirical list-length effects would require too rapid and massive forgetting.

STORAGE   The issue we focus on here is the predicted effect of increasing study time for a list. TODAM, CHARM, and the Matrix model provide examples of models in which simply adding more copies of each trace to memory may not improve memory: Both the mean and standard deviation of the retrieved signal rise together in such a way that performance does not change (Murdock & Lamon 1988; Shiffrin et al 1990). At least two approaches have been used to solve this problem. Hintzman (1986, 1988) and Murdock & Lamon (1988; see also Murdock 1989) have proposed a probabilistic encoding assumption: Each feature of an item is encoded (stored) with a probability p that rises with presentation time. If not stored it is given a neutral value (or in a variant discussed by Shiffrin et al 1990, replaced by a random value). Eich (1985:28) proposes a variant in which all features of an item are either encoded or not (all-or-none encoding). In all these variants, both repetitions of an item and increased study time will improve storage relative to variance in the system, and therefore increase performance.

Shiffrin et al (1990) discuss an alternative way in which these models might show a learning or repetition effect. This alternative is based on the fact that performance in these models is related to the signal-to-noise ratio (or d'). Since d' measures the ratio of mean signal strength to the standard deviation, d' can show an increase with repetition if a constant is added to the standard deviation. The reason for this is that the standard deviation will no longer be completely proportional to the mean signal strength. It is natural to suppose that the constant represents activation of traces or trace components from lists other than the one being tested, or from extra-experimental memory. (More generally, this assumption may prove useful in all models because it lessens the effect of list variables like list length and study time in accord with the amount of extra-list activation).

The remaining models predict performance increases with repetitions or study time for fairly obvious reasons: storage of stronger associations in SAM or ACT*, or weight changes that produce better encoding in the neural net models.

RETRIEVAL   One of the major differences among the models discussed here concerns the manner in which the retrieval process produces a recalled item. In SAM separate traces are accessed separately, so the recovered information can be compared to a standard lexicon; SAM doesn't provide any details of this process but simply assumes the probability of successful recall rises with the strength of the cues to image relationship. The ACT models use similar probabilistic rules. MINERVA 2 also has separate storage but retrieves a composite. This composite could be compared with the individual stored traces, but this seems unsatisfactory because recognition is also assumed to be a composite process. Hintzman (e.g. 1988) proposes a somewhat more satisfactory solution in which the composite retrieved vector is used as a subsequent retrieval cue, the process continuing in this way until the retrieved vector comes to represent an unambiguous item. ART also has separate storage, and test probes come to activate some single node in at least one layer; this node sends down a pattern of activation that could itself produce a clear recall, or (if it is a category node rather than a single item node) could be compared to separately encoded patterns elsewhere in the system.

The models that assume composite storage and retrieval face a greater problem: How is the noisy retrieved trace cleaned up to allow an unambiguous recall? TODAM, CHARM, and the Matrix model assume a lexicon of separately stored items to which the retrieved trace can be compared. This solution tends to dilute the composite character of these models. The remaining connectionist and neural net models do not offer clear solutions for cases in which the retrieved trace is noisy enough to be ambiguous. Typically a probabilistic recall rule is adopted, based on the match of the retrieved trace to possible responses. If the model is fully composite, however, it is not entirely clear where the comparison stimuli lie.

A second issue involves whether the retrieval process is assumed to be probabilistic or not. Both ACT* and SAM assume a probabilistic retrieval process. In these models, an item that was not retrieved on a first retrieval attempt may still be retrieved if an additional attempt at retrieval is made. (In SAM it is usually assumed, however, that at least one new cue must be used for a subsequent retrieval to have a chance at success.) The other models, on the other hand, are such that a second attempt will always lead to the same result (unless the cues are changed, or have added noise (see McClelland 1991).

Finally, only a few models (namely SAM and the convolution/correlation model of Metcalfe & Murdock 1981) have been applied to extended search processes as in free recall, in which the subject uses a number of different retrieval cues in order to maximize recall. It might be argued that the search strategies that are probably involved in these paradigms are not part of the "basic" or "elementary" memory processes. However, such a viewpoint does not do justice to the fact that many real-life situations do involve this type of unstructured memory retrieval.

FORGETTING   Let us define forgetting as a failure to retrieve information from memory at time B when it was retrievable at an earlier time A, or as a decrease in the probability of retrieval. There seem to be three basic ways in which forgetting might occur: 1. a decrease in the "strength" of the memory trace—i.e. decay; 2. an increase in competition by other, interfering, traces (or items); and 3. a change in the nature of the cue between time A and time

B—i.e. a change in the (functional) stimulus. There does not seem to be any difference between the models with respect to the third aspect, although not all of them have explicitly dealt with it. Mensink & Raaijmakers (1988) have used this idea in their application of the SAM model to interference and forgetting. In this model, part of the forgetting was assumed to be caused by contextual changes—i.e. changes in the contextual cues between study and test.

MINERVA 2 (Hintzman 1988:532) and TODAM (Murdock 1989:77) both assume that trace information is subject to decay. In TODAM, this is built into the basic equation of the system (see Murdock 1982, Eq. 1). It should be noted, however, that this decay assumption differs somewhat from traditional decay conceptions in that it is related to the storage of new information in the memory trace: Each time a new item is added to the composite memory trace, a fixed proportion of what was there is lost, producing a strong recency effect with a geometric character. (It should be noted that this assumed decay is independent of the interference that is common to all of the composite storage models, including TODAM.) All the memory models considered in this chapter predict a decrease in performance due to learning other items, and to learning other pairs of items (in both *AB-AC* and *AB-CD* type tasks), the only general exception occurring when the other items are rehearsed or coded jointly with the items in question. In general, several mechanisms in each model help produce interference; these mechanisms may be different for different tasks (as in SAM), and the mechanisms may differ between models. We mention here a few of the more interesting differences among the models.

Most composite models incorporate explicit interference due to the superimposed storage assumptions. When vectors or matrixes are added together, or when a set of weights are jointly adjusted for each new input, the result tends to be degradation of the representations of each item. There are of course exceptions to this rule: If memory is large enough relative to the size of the inputs, then storage might be effectively separate (the amount of superimposition might be minimal; see Kanerva 1988), or if the inputs are orthogonal enough, or if the system orthogonalizes or separates the inputs (e.g. Grossberg's ART models), then interference would not be mandated by the factor of composite storage.

The remaining sources of forgetting are posited to arise during the course of retrieval (in SAM these are the only sources of forgetting). SAM assumes summation of activations at retrieval to accomplish recognition; as a consequence, extra items cause forgetting by increasing "noise." In MINERVA, composition during both recall and recognition causes interference due to increasing noise. One chief remaining cause of interference is based on the relative strength of storage of different items. For example, in SAM, sampling in recall is based on a ratio of activation strengths. Reduction in relative strengths of targets due to extra items also plays an important role in many of the models under discussion, especially the ACT models. This factor plays a chief role in accounting for list-length, fan, and cue-overload effects.

APPLICATIONS TO PARADIGMS

In this section, we compare the ways the various models predict certain basic findings in memory research, both qualitative and quantitative.

Cued Recall

Cued recall is the basic paradigm for associative memory, and the present set of models have been formulated so that cued-recall predictions can be made. ACT* and CHARM have been applied more or less exclusively to cued-recall data. In addition, ACT* and SAM have been shown to be able to account for both latency as well as accuracy data in cued recall (Anderson 1981; Mensink & Raaijmakers 1988).

List Length

All the models are capable of handling the basic list-length effect. However, in some models (TODAM, CHARM) no distinction is made between (a) the to-be-recalled list and (b) extra-list and extra-experimental information. When list length is predicted to have an effect, it does so because retrieval is restricted to the to-be-recalled list (without explanation). This seems un-satisfactory, and the natural way to resolve the difficulty would be the adoption of some form of contextual cuing (as is the case with other models).

However, whether a contextual cue is used may be less important than how it is used. A typical multiplicative rule for cue combination tends to focus access upon regions of memory in the intersection of the sets of memory traces evoked by each cue separately, whereas a typical additive rule tends to access traces in the union of these sets. Humphreys et al (1991) argue convincingly for the intersection approach, implying that "strengths" or "activations" should be acted upon in a way functionally equivalent to multi-plication (as in the SAM model, the Matrix model, etc) rather than addition (as in ACT*).

This type of explanation of list-length effects sees such effects as an example of a more general effect—i.e. that the efficacy of any probe cue is inversely related to the number of memory traces or items associated to that probe cue (which might be called the length of the list of associated items).

Interference and Forgetting

The basic issues here are the effects of different types of interference (i.e. AB-AC vs AB-CD), mechanisms for (relative) spontaneous recovery, single-list forgetting paradigms, and whether or not some sort of decay notion is used. ACT*, SAM, and CHARM have all been explicitly applied to such phenomena.

Anderson (1983a) and Mensink & Raaijmakers (1988) show that some results in this area necessitate the assumption that recall is based on both relative and absolute associative strengths. Relative strength is a function of the number and strength of other associations, while absolute strength is indexed by the amount of study time or the number of presentations of an item. In ACT*, absolute strength comes in through the assumption that trace formation is more likely as the total study time increases. In SAM, absolute strengths determine the probability of recovering enough information from the trace to give the name of the item as a response.

Mensink & Raaijmakers (1988) present a theoretical analysis of traditional interference phenomena. They show that modern memory models such as SAM can reconcile phenomena that have been problematic for traditional interference theories. Such analyses bring out a number of tacit assumptions in the typical verbal (i.e. nonquantitative) models that are not usually noted.

Free Recall

This paradigm is more complex than cued recall. This is due to the fact that it necessitates not only an exact formulation of the relation between STS/working memory and long-term memory but also a description of search/retrieval strategies. Only a few of the models have dealt explicitly with such data. We briefly discuss predictions by SAM (Raaijmakers & Shiffrin 1980) and an early version of the CHARM model (Metcalfe & Murdock 1981).

SAM assumes that contextual and inter-item associations are built up as a result of rehearsing the items in STS. A buffer process (Atkinson & Shiffrin 1968) is used to model the rehearsal process. Retrieval starts by outputting any items still in STS. Thereafter the retrieval process is modeled as a series of retrieval attempts either with the context cue alone or using both context and a previously retrieved item as probe cues. This process continues until the number of failed searches reaches a specific criterion.

One of the strong points of the SAM model is that it handles with a single set of parameter values data from lists with large variations in presentation rate and list length. The latter result is predicted because the search termination criterion is exceeded sooner for the longer lists, relative to list length: Relatively fewer samples are made from a longer list than from a shorter list. This prediction is characteristic of sampling-with-replacement search models with a fixed stop criterion. It also subsumes the cue-overload principle proposed by Watkins (1975; see also Mueller & Watkins 1977; Watkins & Watkins 1976). This principle states that the probability of recalling any particular item decreases with the number of instances associated to the retrieval cue.

Although the Metcalfe & Murdock (1981) free-recall model is described in the terminology of the convolution-correlation model, the actual simulation model does not in fact use the mathematical operations of convolution and correlation. Instead, all-or-none associations are stored between list items, and between list items and context (treated as a list item). When an item is used as a cue, a random choice is retrieved perfectly from the stored associates, if any.

The rehearsal process is conceptualized as a continuous cuing of the memory vector with the currently available item. Thus, when an item is presented, it is associated to the item that is currently available (context at the start of the list). Then the just-presented item is used as a cue to generate an item to which it has been associated, and then this item is used as a new cue, etc. This continues until the next item is presented, which is then associated to the item that is currently available.

At the time of recall, the last rehearsed item is recalled and used as a cue to generate another item; then this item is itself used as a cue, and this continues until a certain criterion period has passed without any new items being recalled. At that point, context is reinstated as a cue and the process begins anew and continues until the criterion period passes for the second time without any new recalls.

Each of these models predicts serial position effects. Since the SAM model is based on the two-store framework, it should not come as a surprise that it makes many of the same predictions as the classic two-store model (see Atkinson & Shiffrin 1971; Raaijmakers & Shiffrin 1980), and for the same reasons: Primacy is predicted because of the cumulative rehearsal assumption, while the output from STS leads to a recency effect. Although the two-store model is often described in textbooks as having problems handling data on levels-of-processing and recency effects, this is in fact not correct (see Raaijmakers 1991).

The Metcalfe-Murdock model has a quite different flavor. In this model, the shape of the serial-position curve is critically determined by the cues available at recall. Recency is predicted because the last-presented item is recalled first and then used as a cue. This item is assumed to be the optimum entry point into the end of the list. The disappearance of the recency effect by the introduction of a delay between presentation and test is explained by the assumption that rehearsal continues during the delay.

Hence, at the end of the delay the currently available item will most likely be some item other than the last item on the list. The optimum entry point for recall of the last few items is therefore lost. This explanation seems unlikely since providing the subject with the terminal item after the delay interval should reinstate the recency effect. (Another problematic aspect is the assumption that rehearsal continues during the delay filled with arithmetic.)

Primacy is predicted by this model because context is used as a retrieval cue (in the second phase of the recall process), and context is nearly always relatively strongly associated with the first item. Thus, this explanation is quite similar to the typical two-store explanation of primacy as being due to stronger traces for the initial items (in this case being more strongly associated to context).

One of the more important advantages of the recent work on models of memory is that it has led to model-based simulation programs for specific experimental tasks. These programs can then be used to see how the model behaves under specific experimental conditions. This is especially important in free recall since this paradigm does not lend itself easily to analytic approaches.

One aspect of the data where this has been proven helpful is in the analysis of the effects of various types of cuing manipulations of the likelihood of recall. We mention two: the (positive) effects of category cues and the (negative) effects of cuing with randomly selected list items (the so-called part-list cuing effect).

Raaijmakers & Shiffrin (1980) showed that typical effects of cuing with category names could be easily predicted by the SAM simulation model. These predictions do not greatly depend on the specific assumptions of SAM (vis-à-vis alternative models). Such analyses are, however, important to show that observed effects are indeed consistent with particular theoretical frameworks.

This is even more the case in the part-list cuing paradigm. In this paradigm subjects are given some randomly selected items from the list as cues for the remaining list items. The typical finding is that such cuing leads to a slight but unexpected decrease in the probability of recall for the remaining items. Raaijmakers & Shiffrin (1981) spent a good deal of effort analyzing this peculiar effect within their SAM simulation of free recall. They showed that this counterintuitive effect was in fact predicted by the model. In addition to the basic result, a number of related findings were predicted. These included the effect of the number of cues, the time at which the cues were given, and the effect of interpolated learning (between presentation and test). Raaijmakers (1991) shows that the model predicts a reversal of the cuing effect if a delayed testing procedure is used. This prediction is indeed borne out. This research has also shown that it is by no means easy to intuit the predictions of a relatively simple model such as SAM in a complicated experimental situation.

This part-list cuing effect has also been dealt with by Metcalfe & Murdock (1981). However, in their simulation it was assumed that the list cues were not actually used by the subject. This assumption makes it relatively easy to predict a negative effect of cuing but does not make much sense given the fact that most subjects will expect the cues to be helpful (as did most memory specialists). In addition, such an approach makes it impossible to predict a reversal of the cuing effect in delayed cuing.

Note, however, that these problems are not due to the basic structure of the convolution/correlation model (which was in fact put aside) but to the assumptions that are made concerning the subject's strategy. This illustrates that predictions for free-recall tasks depend critically on the strategy used— i.e. on the assumptions made concerning the sequence of cues to be used in retrieval. Gronlund & Shiffrin (1986) examined the effects of various retrieval strategies on recall from natural categories and categorized lists. They showed that different strategies indeed have an effect on recall performance. This result poses two problems for any model for free recall. First, it makes it problematic to apply a specific (arbitrary) version of the model to the data of a group of subjects, unless it can be shown that the result of interest is insensitive to the choice of strategy or that the subjects all use a similar strategy. Second, given a specification of retrieval strategies (i.e. in terms of the sequence of cues that are used), the model should be able to give a quantitative account of the resulting performance differences. Gronlund & Shiffrin (1986) show that a simple extension of SAM could account for the observed differences.

Recognition

Most current models of memory assume that simple recognition decisions are based on some sort of global familiarity value. By this we mean that the familiarity value is a kind of weighted, additive combination of the activation of all items in memory. This global familiarity value is determined by the match between the probe cues and the memory trace(s). This general type of model has been termed the General Global Matching Model (GGMM, Humphreys et al 1989b) or the Interactive Cue Global Matching (ICGM) model (Clark & Shiffrin, submitted). As these labels imply, such models differ from previous local matching models in that all items in memory are involved in the match, not just the representation of the tested item. In this section we consider some of the data used to test these models.

Pair Recognition

Pair recognition has been used as an experimental paradigm to test aspects of recognition models. Basically, the issue here is the way associative information is assumed to contribute to recognition decisions. In these experiments the subject first studies a list of word pairs $(A_1B_1, A_2B_2, \ldots)$. At test, intact pairs (A_iB_i) have to be discriminated from rearranged pairs (A_iB_j), mixed pairs

(A_iX), and/or new word pairs (XY). These results may be compared to those obtained in single item recognition $(A_i$ vs $X)$ and/or cued recognition $(A_iB_i$ vs A_iX where only the second item has to be judged; see Clark & Shiffrin submitted). Humphreys et al (1989b) show that all extant versions of the global matching model (SAM, MINERVA 2, Matrix, and TODAM) lead to similar equations for the mean matching strengths. This would seem to imply that it will be difficult to differentiate between these models. However, predictions for d' depend not only on the mean strengths but also on the variances. Furthermore, it may be possible to distinguish between the models if one also takes the predictions for single-item recognition and cued recognition into account.

Clark & Shiffrin (submitted) examined the predictions for all types of recognition tests. They show that the models differ with respect to whether they predict an advantage for cued recognition compared to single-item recognition. The results of their experiments were reasonably well predicted by TODAM and SAM, with TODAM producing the best fit. MINERVA 2 and the Matrix model did not fit the data well. One problem with such data, however, is that it might very well be the case that subjects make use of recall processes in addition to global matching. That is, the logic of the models allows subjects to supplement global matching with recall.

Gronlund & Ratcliff (1989) pointed to another problem for global matching models. They examined the time course of the availability of item and associative information using a response-signal procedure (Reed 1973, 1976; Dosher 1976). In this procedure, a recognition decision must be made at one of several predefined times after the onset of the test stimulus. With this procedure it is possible to determine the growth of accuracy as a function of processing time. Gronlund & Ratcliff showed that item information becomes available sooner than associative information. This poses a problem for global matching models since these treat these two types of information as inseparable. To accommodate the results, separate contributions of item and associative information are required, possibly by distinguishing between concurrent and compound usage of cues (see Gronlund & Ratcliff 1989). That is, it might be assumed that memory is probed in parallel with an interactive, compound cue and with the item cues separately. As an alternative, it might be the case that pair images are sometimes stored, and that the time course of pair-image activation differs from that of single-item image activation.

List Length vs List Strength

Recent research by Ratcliff et al (1990) has focused on the effects of the strength of other list items on the recall and recognition of target items. This so-called "list-strength effect" concerns the effects of strengthening (or weakening) some list items upon memory for other list items. Ratcliff et al (1990) showed that strengthening some items in the list decreases recall of the remaining list items but has no or even a positive effect on recognition performance. This contrasts with the list-length effect: Adding items to a list decreases both recall and recognition performance. Thus, the number of irrelevant items, but not their strength, affects recognition. This is true not only for strength variations due to amount of study time but also for variations due to spaced repetitions.

This peculiar result should have a number of consequences for models of recognition. In particular, it will be necessary to assume a structural difference between presentation of two different items and two presentations of a single item. Shiffrin et al (1990) showed that current memory models indeed cannot predict both the presence of a list-length effect and the absence (or reversal) of a list-strength effect.

Shiffrin et al (1990) also investigated whether the various models could be modified to enable prediction of these results. Such modification does not seem possible for models that assume items are stored in one composite memory trace. Even considering recognition only, these models cannot predict both a positive list-length effect and an absent or negative list-strength effect when strength variations are due to spaced repetitions. Models such as SAM and MINERVA 2 that assume separate storage are in principle better equipped to handle these results, although they too will have to be modified to enable prediction of negative list-strength effects.

Shiffrin et al (1990) show that a modification of SAM can handle these results. In this modified SAM model it is assumed that different items are stored in separate traces but repetitions of an item within a list are stored in a single memory trace. Second, the variance of activation of each separate trace, when the cue item is unrelated to the item(s) encoded in the trace, is constant regardless of the strength of the trace. The latter assumption is inconsistent with previous formulations of SAM but is defended using a differentiation argument: The better the image is encoded, the clearer are the differences between it and the test item, and hence the lower the activation. In this way, a constant or even decreasing variance may be predicted, depending on the weighting of context and item cues.

A crucial aspect of this explanation is that repetitions of an item are assumed to be stored in a single memory image. To evaluate it further, Murnane & Shiffrin (1991) tested whether a reversal of the list-strength effect in recognition occurs if repetitions are presented in such a way that they are likely to be encoded in separate images. They found that repetitions of words in different sentences produced a list-strength effect whereas repetitions of entire sentences did not. This demonstrates that the nature of the encoding of a repeated item is a crucial factor.

Evaluating the Models

In this chapter we have shown that current mathematical models of memory are capable of handling many classical and new findings in recall and recognition. We suggest that models of this type are superior to verbally stated theories of memory. Arguments in favor of the modeling approach include these: 1. the ability to predict the size (and not just the direction) of the effect of experimental factors, 2. the ability to predict the effect of combinations of experimental factors, 3. the ability to examine the combined result of theoretical assumptions, 4. the fact that a model (especially in the form of a simulation program) can be used to "experiment" with processing or strategy assumptions to determine the crucial variables that underlie a given prediction, and 5. the fact that models often demonstrate the limitations of more intuitive reasoning.

Such a conclusion is, however, often criticized on the ground that general models of memory of the type discussed in this chapter are too versatile. That is, the models usually incorporate a relatively large number of processes and parameters that seem to enable them to predict almost any type of empirical result. In addition, it is often difficult to intuit what a specific model will predict in a given situation. This contrasts with the simplicity of typical verbal, nonquantitative explanations of memory phenomena. In this section we argue that this difficulty is often more apparent than real.

First, quantitative models also make qualitative predictions that do not depend on parameter values. That is, in order to evaluate a model's ability to predict data, one should not only examine the phenomena that it can predict but also take into account whether it makes strong, parameter-free predictions about results that should not occur (no matter what parameter values are used). Second, if a particular prediction depends on the specific parameter values used, it should be possible to arrange the experimental situation in such a way that that particular result is reversed. Third, the argument may also be turned around: If the ability of a model to predict a particular phenomenon turns out to depend on parameter values one may well ask whether a corresponding qualitative explanation is in fact logically sufficient. Finally, some results are indeed complex (i.e. dependent on a number of interacting processes) whether we like it or not. In fact, one advantage of quantitative models of the type discussed in this chapter is that they may be used to see whether particular "verbal" explanations hold true when tested in the context of a comprehensive model of human memory. The next sections focus on specific aspects of this discussion.

Number of Parameters

Current quantitative models of memory frequently incorporate a dozen or so parameters. These parameters reflect both structural aspects of the memory system (decay rates, processing times) and task-related aspects (weighting of cues, stopping criteria, decision criteria). When a model is fitted to a set of data, these parameters usually have to be estimated from those data; that is, they are given values so as to optimize the fit to the data. Although this procedure can be rigorously defended on statistical grounds, it does seem to many to involve a bit of cheating. It is probably for this reason that the relatively large number of parameters in current models is frowned upon.

In many cases however, the number of parameters is not really an issue. That is, the qualitative nature of the predictions does not depend on the exact parameter values. Thus, many of the simulations are performed using a single set of parameter values (see, for example, Metcalfe & Murdock 1981; Mensink & Raaijmakers 1988; Hintzman 1988). In those cases where parameter values do reverse a particular prediction, empirical evidence should be obtainable concerning this prediction (see, for example, the prediction of a reversal of the part-list cuing effect as a function of the contextual strength parameter in the SAM model; Raaijmakers 1991). Another point is that nonquantitative models also include parameters—that is, degrees of freedom—although this is rarely realized. To put this in another way, most explanations for memory phenomena by models of memory might be formulated in a qualitative way. In this way, there would not be any basic difference between quantitative and qualitative models. However, the resulting theories would have lost most of their explanatory power.

Number of Processes

Most of the difficulties with well-specified quantitative models have to do with the relatively large number of processes that are usually proposed. This is especially the case when models attempt to be applicable to a large number of different experimental paradigms. As emphasized by Smith (1978), there is a tradeoff between generality and simplicity of theoretical models. The problem here is that due to the number of processes and the number of parameters (or quantitative relations) involved in complex memory models, it is often not possible to make predictions about the behavior of the model except through quantitative simulations.

An example (drawn from own experience) illustrates this point. When the SAM model was first applied to the part-list cuing paradigm (see Raaijmakers & Shiffrin 1981), it was not at all clear whether it would or would not predict this effect. Furthermore, even after the prediction turned out to be successful, it was not immediately clear (to say the least) what factors in the model were causing it.

What this shows is that it is not possible to make intuitive predictions about the behavior of a model under specific task conditions. However, it should be evident that a similar problem holds for "verbal" theories of memory. In such qualitative accounts it is not clear what the boundary conditions are that apply to a particular prediction. The lesson that can be drawn here is that much more effort should be invested in theoretical analyses of the factors involved in predicting empirical phenomena. Such analyses should focus on the role of each of the proposed processes in the explanation of a particular phenomenon.

Quantitative, Qualitative, and Semi-Quantitative Fits

Although all the models that we have considered are formulated in a quantitative manner, there is a tendency in current work to restrict the analysis to qualitative predictions; that is, one analyzes only whether a model predicts the general direction of an effect, rather than the exact magnitude. In contrast to the tradition of the 1960s and 1970s, typical goodness-of-fit measures such as the chi-square statistic do not figure prominently in the typical article that nowadays presents a formal model of memory.

This poses a problem. On the one hand, it can be defended that one does not want to focus too specifically on the exact numerical details of one particular experiment; on the other hand, it would be desirable at least to look at the relative magnitude of a particular effect (relative to other predicted effects). That is, suppose that there are two phenomena of interest, effect A and effect B, where A is a large effect and B a small (but consistent) one. It is conceivable that a model would be able to predict both A and B in a qualitative manner but that it would always predict either A and B both small or A and B both large. Such a "misfit" would not be detected if the analysis focuses only on the qualitative aspects.

Fortunately, most presentations of formal models of memory employ a strategy that falls between these two extremes. The typical approach is to use a single set of parameters to examine a set of data (or data patterns) that is representative of empirical findings. Although none of the actual data are really fitted in the traditional sense, the use of a single set of parameters makes it possible to verify that the model makes predictions in the right ballpark in terms of relative effect sizes.

Hence, we may distinguish among three degrees of comparing the model to actual data: qualitative, quantitative, and what might be called semi-quantitative analysis. The first involves only the direction of a difference between conditions; the second involves a direct comparison between the predicted and observed data using a goodness-of-fit measure; finally, the third does not involve a goodness-of-fit measure but does look at the sizes of the predicted and observed effects.

Although real quantitative fits remain a desirable feature, it might be argued that the proper approach is to aim first for a semi-quantitative prediction of the data. In this phase, the emphasis is on showing that a model can deal with a variety of findings from different task paradigms. At some point, a number of promising models will have been developed. At that stage, the time seems to be ripe for quantitative tests in which several models may be compared in terms of goodness-of-fit. We believe that the demonstrated potential of current models of memory justifies the expectation that future work in this area will involve more comparative, quantitative testing.

Quite recently, John Anderson (1990; see also Anderson & Milson 1989) has proposed a model that attempts, in a sense, to meld some of the best features of the two approaches we have been contrasting (detailed, formal, quantitative, process models vs general, verbal, descriptive models). His "Rational" model bypasses details of representation and process to the greatest possible degree, and instead is aimed at the general proposition that memory is organized so as to solve the memorizer's problems in an optimum fashion. In any given retrieval situation, it is assumed that each event stored in memory has a number assigned to it representing its probability of being relevant (containing the desired information). It is assumed that these events are searched in order of their relevance, either until a retrieval occurs or a stopping criterion is reached. The probabilities are based on two multiplicative factors: the past history of an event's usefulness (independent of the cues used to probe memory) and the likelihoods of relevance associated with the cues. So far only the barest hints of applications to memory paradigms are available. It is interesting that the model operates at a very abstract level and yet offers quantitative predictions for certain phenomena. Although initial results are intriguing, it is far too early to assess the long run usefulness of the approach.

ACKNOWLEDGMENTS

This research was supported in part by Grants NIMH 12717 and AFOSR 870089 to the second author.

Literature Cited

Ackley, D. H., Hinton, G. E., Sejnowski, T. J. 1985. A learning algorithm for Boltzmann machines. *Cogn. Sci.* 9:147–69

Anderson, J. A. 1973. A theory for the recognition of items from short memorized lists. *Psychol. Rev.* 86:417–38

Anderson, J. A., Silverstein, J. W., Ritz, S. A., Jones, R. S. 1977. Distinctive features, categorical perception, and probability learning: some applications of a neural model. *Psychol. Rev.* 84:413–51

Anderson, J. R. 1976. *Language, Memory, and Thought.* Hillsdale, NJ: Erlbaum

Anderson, J. R. 1981. Interference: the relationship between response latency and response accuracy. *J. Exp. Psychol.: Hum. Learn. Mem.* 7:326–43

Anderson, J. R. 1983a. A spreading activation theory of memory. *J. Verb. Learn. Verb. Behav.* 22:261–95

Anderson, J. R. 1983b. *The Architecture of Cognition.* Cambridge, MA: Harvard Univ. Press

Anderson, J. R. 1990. *The Adaptive Character of Thought.* Hillsdale, NJ: Erlbaum

Anderson, J. R., Bower, G. H. 1972. Recognition and retrieval processes in free recall. *Psychol. Rev.* 79:97–123

Anderson, J. R., Milson, R. 1989. Human memory: an adaptive perspective. *Psychol. Rev.* 96:703–19

Atkinson, R. C., Shiffrin, R. M. 1968. Human memory: a proposed system and its control processes. In *The Psychology of*

Learning and Motivation: Advances in Research and Theory, ed. K. W. Spence , J. T. Spence, 2:89–195. New York: Academic

Atkinson, R. C., Shiffrin, R. M. 1971. The control of short-term memory. *Sci. Am.* 224:82–90

Bower, G. H. 1961. Application of a model to paired-associate learning. *Psychometrika* 26:255–80

Clark, S. E., Shiffrin, R. M. 1992. Associations, retrieval capacity, and cued recognition. *J. Exp. Psychol.: Learn. Mem. Cogn.* submitted

Dosher, B. A. 1976. The retrieval of sentences from memory: a speed-accuracy study. *Mem. Cogn.* 8:291–310

Eich, J. M. 1982. A composite holographic associative recall model. *Psychol. Rev.* 89:627–61

Eich, J. M. 1985. Levels of processing, encoding specificity, elaboration, and CHARM. *Psychol. Rev.* 92:1–38

Estes, W. K. 1955. Statistical theory of spontaneous recovery and regression. *Psychol. Rev.* 62:145–54

Gillund, G., Shiffrin, R. M. 1984. A retrieval model for both recognition and recall. *Psychol. Rev.* 91:1–67

Gronlund, S. D., Ratcliff, R. 1989. The timecourse of item and associative information: implications for global memory models. *J. Exp. Psychol.: Learn. Mem. Cogn.* 15:846–58

Gronlund, S. D., Shiffrin, R. M. 1986. Retrieval strategies in recall of natural categories and categorized lists. *J. Exp. Psychol.: Learn. Mem. Cogn.* 12:550–61

Grossberg, S. 1987. Competitive learning: from interactive activation to adaptive resonance. *Cogn. Sci.* 11:23–63

Grossberg, S., Stone, G. 1986. Neural dynamics of word recognition and recall: attentional priming, learning, and resonance. *Psychol. Rev.* 93:46–74

Hintzman, D. L. 1984. MINERVA 2: a simulation model of human memory. *Behav. Res. Methods; Instrum. Comput.* 16:96–101

Hintzman, D. L. 1986. "Schema abstraction" in a multiple-trace memory model. *Psychol. Rev.* 93:411–28

Hintzman, D. L. 1988. Judgments of frequency and recognition memory in a multipletrace memory model. *Psychol. Rev.* 95: 528–51

Hintzman, D. L. 1990. Human learning and memory: connections and dissociations. *Annu. Rev. Psychol.* 41:109–39

Humphreys, M. S., Bain, J. D., Pike, R. 1989a. Different ways to cue a coherent memory system: a theory for episodic, semantic, and procedural tasks. *Psychol. Rev.* 96:208–33

Humphreys, M. S., Pike, R., Bain, J. D.,

Tehan, G. 1989b. Global matching: a comparison of the SAM, MINERVA II, Matrix, and TODAM models. *J. Math. Psychol.* 33:36–67

Humphreys, M. S., Wiles, J., Bain, J. D. 1991. Memory retrieval with two cues: Think of intersecting sets. In *Attention and Performance XIV: A Silver Jubilee,* ed. D. E. Meyer, S. Kornblum. Hillsdale, NJ: Erlbaum

Kanerva, P. 1988. *Sparse Distributed Memory.* Cambridge, MA: MIT Press

Kruschke, J. 1992. ALCOVE: an exemplarbased connectionist model of category learning. *Psychol. Rev.* In press

Lewandowski, S. 1991. Gradual unlearning and catastrophic interference: a comparison of distributed architectures. In *Relating Theory and Data: Essays on Human Memory and Learning in Honor of Bennet B. Murdock,* ed. W. E. Hockley, S. Lewandowski, pp. 445–76. Hillsdale, NJ: Erlbaum

McClelland, J. L. 1991. Stochastic interactive processes and the effect of context on perception. *Cogn. Psychol.* 23:1–44

McClelland, J. L., Rumelhart, D. E. 1985. Distributed memory and the representation of general and specific information. *J. Exp. Psychol.: Gen.* 114:159–88

McCloskey, M., Cohen, N. J. 1989. Catastrophic interference in connectionist networks: the sequential learning problem. *Psychol. Learn. Motiv.* 24:109–65

Mensink, G. J., Raaijmakers, J. G. W. 1988. A model for interference and forgetting. *Psychol. Rev.* 95:434–55

Mensink, G. J. M., Raaijmakers, J. G. W. 1989. A model of contextual fluctuation. *J. Math. Psychol.* 33:172–86

Metcalfe, J., Murdock, B. B. 1981. An encoding and retrieval model for single-trial free recall. *J. Verb. Learn. Verb. Behav.* 20:161–89

Mueller, C. W., Watkins, M. J. 1977. Inhibition from part-set cuing: a cue-overload interpretation. *J. Verb. Learn. Verb. Behav.* 16:699–709

Murdock, B. B. Jr. 1982. A theory for the storage and retrieval of item and associative information. *Psychol. Rev.* 89:609–26

Murdock, B. B. Jr. 1989. Learning in a distributed memory model. In *Current Issues in Cognitive Processes: The Tulane Flowerree Symposium on Cognition,* ed. C. Izawa, pp. 69–106. Hillsdale, NJ: Erlbaum

Murdock, B., Lamon, M. 1988. The replacement effect: repeating some items while replacing others. *Mem. Cogn.* 16:91–101

Murnane, K., Shiffrin, R. M. 1991. Word repetitions in sentence recognition. *Mem. Cogn.* 19:119–30

Murnane, K., Shiffrin, R. M. 1992. Interference and the representation of events in memory. *J. Exp. Psychol.: Learn. Mem. Cogn.* In press

Pike, R. 1984. A comparison of convolution and matrix distributed memory systems. *Psychol. Rev.* 91:281–94

Pribram, K., Nuwer, M., Baron, R. 1974. The holographic hypothesis of memory structure in brain function and perception. In *Contemporary Developments in Mathematical Psychology,* ed. R. C. Atkinson, D. Krantz, R. D. Luce, P. Suppes, pp. 416–57. San Francisco: Freeman

Raaijmakers, J. G. W. 1991. The story of the two-store model: past criticisms, current status, and future directions. See Humphreys et al 1991. In press

Raaijmakers, J. G. W., Shiffrin, R. M. 1980. SAM: A theory of probabilistic search of associative memory. *Psychol. Learn. Motiv.: Adv. Res. Theory* 14:207–62

Raaijmakers, J. G. W., Shiffrin, R. M. 1981. Search of associative memory. *Psychol. Rev.* 88:93–134

Ratcliff, R. 1990. Connectionist models of recognition memory: constraints imposed by learning and forgetting functions. *Psychol. Rev.* 97:285–308

Ratcliff, R., Clark, S., Shiffrin, R. M. 1990. The list-strength effect. I. Data and discussion. *J. Exp. Psychol.: Learn. Mem. Cogn.* 16:163–78

Reed, A. V. 1973. Speed-accuracy trade-off in recognition memory. *Science* 181:574–76

Reed, A. V. 1976. List length and the time course of recognition in immediate memory. *Mem. Cogn.* 4:16–30

Ross, B. H., Landauer, T. K. 1978. Memory for at least one of two items: test and failure of several theories of spacing effects. *J. Verb. Learn. Verb. Behav.* 17:669–80

Rumelhart, D. E., Hinton, G. E., Williams, R. J. 1986. Learning internal representations by error propagation. In *Parallel Distributed Processing: Explorations in the Microstructures of Cognition. Vol. 1: Foundations,* ed. D. E. Rumelhart, J. L. McClelland, pp. 216–71. Cambridge, MA: MIT Press

Shiffrin, R. M. 1970. Forgetting: trace erosion or retrieval failure? *Science* 168:1601–3

Shiffrin, R. M., Murnane, K. 1991. Composition, distribution, and interference in memory. See Lewandowski 1991, pp. 331–46

Shiffrin, R. M., Murnane, K., Gronlund, S., Roth, M. 1989. On units of storage and retrieval. In *Current Issues in Cognitive Processes: The Tulane Flowerree Symposium on Cognition,* ed. C. Izawa, pp. 25–68. Hillsdale, NJ: Erlbaum

Shiffrin, R. M., Ratcliff, R., Clark, S. 1990. The list-strength effect. II. Theoretical mechanisms. *J. Exp. Psychol.: Learn. Mem. Cogn.* 16:179–95

Sloman, S., Rumelhart, D. E. 1992. Reducing interference in distributed memory through episodic gating. In *From Learning Theory to Cognitive Processes: Essays in Honor of William K. Estes,* ed. A. F. Healy, S. M. Kosslyn, R. M. Shiffrin. Hillsdale, NJ: Erlbaum

Smith, E. E. 1978. Theories of semantic memory. In *Handbook of Learning and Cognitive Processes. Vol. 6.: Linguistic Functions in Cognitive Theory,* ed. W. K. Estes. Hillsdale, NJ: Erlbaum

Watkins, M. J. 1975. Inhibition in recall with extralist "cues". *J. Verb. Learn. Verb. Behav.* 14:294–303

Watkins, M. J., Watkins, O. C. 1976. Cue-overload theory and the method of interpolated attributes. *Bull. Psychonom. Soc.* 7:289–91

Willshaw, D. 1981. Holography, associative memory, and inductive generalization. In *Parallel Models of Associative Memory.,* ed. G. E. Hinton, J. A. Anderson, pp. 33–104. Hillsdale, NJ: Erlbaum

Annu. Rev. Psychol. 1992. 43:235–67

COGNITIVE-BEHAVIORAL APPROACHES TO THE NATURE AND TREATMENT OF ANXIETY DISORDERS

Richard E. Zinbarg, David H. Barlow, Timothy A. Brown, and Robert M. Hertz

Center for Stress and Anxiety Disorders, University at Albany, State University of New York, Albany, New York 12203

KEY WORDS: relation between anxiety and depression, relation between anxiety and fear, etiology of anxiety, maintenance of anxiety, anxiety and fear reduction

CONTENTS

In an important volume on anxiety and the anxiety disorders, Tuma & Maser (1985) observed that the 1980s have been called the decade of anxiety. Indeed, in the past 10 years investigators of the nature and treatment of anxiety disorders have made major advances, both theoretical and empirical.

235

0066-4308/92/0201-0235$02.00

The theoretical advances have produced novel hypotheses about the etiology and maintenance of anxiety disorders. In addition, there now exist controlled studies examining the efficacy of new cognitive-behavioral treatment packages for almost all of the anxiety disorders. While the specific interventions designed for each anxiety disorder differ considerably across the disorders, some important common elements can be identified. These common elements appear to target mechanisms that have been identified as playing crucial roles in the etiology and maintenance of anxiety disorders.

This chapter has four goals. We begin with a brief discussion of the progress made toward understanding the nature of anxiety disorders. Given this background on the hypothesized core elements of anxiety, we suggest essential targets for therapeutic intervention. We then review recent evidence on the effects of cognitive-behavioral treatments across the variety of anxiety disorders. Finally, we conclude with suggestions for future research in this area.

THE NATURE OF ANXIETY

What is anxiety? Because anxiety and depression are closely related constructs, more specific versions of this question ask in what ways do anxiety and depression overlap, and how does anxiety differ from depression?

The Relation between Anxiety and Depression

Many different points of view on the distinction between anxiety and depression have appeared (e.g. Kendall & Watson 1989). A number of theorists have suggested that anxiety and depression are variable expressions of the same pathology, while others hypothesize that the two differ fundamentally. Clark & Watson (1991) reviewed the relevant psychometric evidence and concluded that both views are correct: The pattern of convergent and divergent validity coefficients suggests both considerable overlap and significant differentiability between anxiety and depression.

To reconcile the evidence for both substantial overlap and differentiability, Clark & Watson (1991) proposed a tripartite model of the relationship between anxiety and depression—an elaboration of Tellegen's (1985; Watson & Tellegen 1985; Zevon & Tellegen 1982) earlier work on Positive Affect (PA) and Negative Affect (NA). Clark & Watson (1991) suggested that anxiety and depressive syndromes share a nonspecific component of generalized affective distress which, following Tellegen (1985; Zevon & Tellegen 1982), they labeled NA. The other two elements in the tripartite model are: (a) physiological symptoms of hyperarousal, a factor containing features specific to anxiety; and (b) lack of PA, a factor specific to depression.

The general distress factor of NA accounts for the moderate to high

ANXIETY DISORDERS   237

correlations that are consistently found between symptom measures of anxiety and depression. In addition, given the substantial heritability estimates and trait-like temporal consistency for NA (Watson & Tellegen 1985; Tellegen et al 1988), NA may account for the data from family studies suggesting that anxiety and depression share a common genetic vulnerability (e.g. Puig-Antich & Rabinovitch 1986; Weissman 1985; Leckman et al 1983). That is, the temperamental variable of negative affectivity may be an expression of a genetic diathesis common to anxiety and depression.

In interpreting the factors that differentiate anxiety and depression, we find it useful to consider a framework suggested by Tellegen (1985) in which PA is linked to Gray's (1982) construct of the Behavioral Activating System (BAS). One of the functions of the BAS is to regulate active coping responses to threat (Gray 1982). From this point of view, fundamental differences between depression and anxiety may be found in action tendencies. Depression suggests loss of hope of actively coping with stress (low PA/BAS activity); anxiety implies efforts to actively cope with stress (moderate to high PA/BAS activity). The physiological hyperarousal factor specific to anxiety may then be seen as representing preparation for coping—that is, activation of the underlying physiology necessary to support active coping (Barlow 1988; Fowles 1986; Fridlund et al 1986).

The Relation between Anxiety and Fear

Similarly, there has been some recent theoretical debate over the relationship between anxiety and a fight-or-flight mechanism labeled as either fear (e.g. Barlow 1988; 1991a,b) or panic (e.g. Gray 1991). On the one hand, some theorists, such as Barlow (1988, 1991a,b), suggest that fear is clearly distinct from anxiety. Others, such as Rachman (1991), find this distinction to be unnecessary and view anxiety and fear as essentially equivalent. Of course, both of these views may be correct. In fact, psychometric and physiological data suggest both considerable overlap and differentiability between anxiety and fear. As an example of the psychometric evidence, Tellegen and his colleagues (1985; Watson & Tellegen 1985; Watson & Clark 1991) have identified a hierarchical structure of mood in which fear is a distinct primary factor that loads on the higher-order factor of NA. The loading of fear on the second-order factor of NA suggests substantial overlap with anxiety, while the identification of fear as a distinct first-order factor suggests reliable variance in fear that is unrelated to anxiety.

Analysis of physiological evidence marshaled by Gray (1982) also supports the conclusion of both considerable overlap and differentiation between anxiety and fear. Through a review of an enormous literature of lesion, stimulation, and pharmacological studies, Gray concludes that anxiety is based physiologically on a system comprising the hippocampal area, the septal area, their interconnections, and the afferent and efferent pathways that connect them to other parts of the brain. One of the most important afferent projections to the septo-hippocampal system, a noradrenergic pathway originating in the locus coeruleus, also sends an excitatory projection to the hypothalamus, which Gray (1982) identifies as the physiological substrate of the fight-or-flight response. It is important to note the existence of an inhibitory efferent projection from the lateral septal area to the hypothalamus and a serotonergic pathway originating in the raphe nuclei that sends excitatory projections to the septal area and hippocampus.

According to Gray (1982), information about signals that threat may be imminent is carried by both the noradrenergic pathway originating in the locus coeruleus and the serotonergic pathway originating in the raphe nuclei. On the other hand, information about threat itself is carried by the ascending noradrenergic pathway but not by the ascending serotonergic pathway. Thus, in response to threat itself, the fight-or-flight response is triggered via the noradrenergic pathway. On the other hand, in response to signals of threat, the fight-or-flight response is simultaneously primed via the noradrenergic pathway and inhibited via the inhibitory pathway from the septo-hippocampal system to the hypothalamus. Thus, anxiety and fear overlap, in that anxiety involves a priming of the fight-or-flight response. On the other hand, the two are differentiable in that anxiety also involves a simultaneous inhibition of the fight-or-flight response.

Fear suggests a discharging of the fight-or-flight mechanism; anxiety implies preparation for discharging the fight-or-flight mechanism; depression implies a lack of arousal of the fight-or-flight response and other active coping responses. Fear says, "A terrible event is happening and I need to take action right now to stop it." Anxiety says, "A terrible event may happen; I may not be able to deal with it, but I've got to be ready to try." Depression says, "A terrible event may happen; I won't be able to cope with it, so I won't bother trying."

Considerations of anxiety's relationships with both depression and fear, then, converge on emphasizing the role of action tendencies in defining anxiety. That is, a core element of anxiety is preparation for fight or flight. To be more precise, anxiety is associated with a conflict between discharging the fight-or-flight response and inhibiting it.

Etiology of Anxiety

As suggested above, anxiety and depression may share a common genetic vulnerability. In addition, several theorists, including Barlow (1988), have suggested that early experiences with controllability may comprise a psychological vulnerability to anxiety (and depression). Obviously, understanding the etiological role of uncontrollability in the anxiety disorders has been hindered by the same constraints that impede the study of the etiology of any disorder. On the one hand, ethics constrain experimental manipulation of such variables as uncontrollable trauma, thought to produce the full-blown manifestation of the disorder. On the other hand, enormous quantities of time and money are needed to conduct longitudinal investigations of individuals at high risk. For these reasons, laboratory analog studies and animal models represent important tools in the investigation of etiology.

Indeed, animal models have made important contributions to recent theories about the etiology of anxiety disorders. Much of the impetus for these developments has stemmed from the seminal work of Susan Mineka and her colleagues in reinterpreting the importance of the variables of unpredictability and uncontrollability in the early experimental neurosis literature (Mineka 1985; Mineka & Kihlstrom 1978; Mineka & Henderson 1985). While uncontrollability was implicated in models of depression that were prominent in the 1970s, the relationship of uncontrollability to anxiety had been often overlooked until Mineka & Kihlstrom (1978) revived interest in it.

Since the time of Mineka & Kihlstrom's (1978) important review, several theorists have emphasized these variables in models of the etiology of anxiety disorders (e.g. Barlow 1988; Foa, Olasov-Rothbaum & Zinbarg, submitted for publication; Mineka 1985; Mineka & Henderson 1985; Mineka & Zinbarg 1991; Zinbarg & Mineka 1991). Indeed, many animal studies have shown that uncontrollable and/or unpredictable aversive events, as compared with controllable, predictable aversive events of the same duration and intensity, produce a wide range of disturbances in animals, including intense and persistent fear and physiological arousal (see Foa et al, submitted for publication; Mineka 1985; Mineka & Henderson 1985; Minor et al 1989 for recent reviews of the animal literature).

Some recent experimental investigations of individuals with panic disorder have provided support for the notion that unpredictability and uncontrollability play a role in the processes underlying anxiety disorders. Here, work on cognitive mechanisms in laboratory-provoked panic (through induction procedures such as CO_2 inhalation) is relevant. Rapee et al (1986) arranged for panic disordered patients to inhale a 50% CO_2 mixture. Half of the subjects received instructions on what somatic symptoms to expect as a result of the CO_2 inhalation, while the other half did not. Subjects in the latter group reported significantly more intense somatic symptoms, more catastrophic thoughts, and greater similarity of the experience to naturally occurring panics than did the subjects who were told what symptoms to expect. These results are consistent with the hypothesis that the predictability of somatic sensations moderates the affective reaction to the sensations in panic disordered patients.

Sanderson et al (1988) administered 5.5% CO_2 to patients with panic disorder. Half of the subjects were led to believe that they could regulate the flow of CO_2 they received by manipulating a dial; the other half were led to believe that they could not regulate the flow of CO_2 in this manner. The group who did not have the perception of control over CO_2 flow experienced significantly more anxiety and panic, and rated their panics as more similar to naturally occurring panic. These results support the hypothesis that perceptions of control over the source of somatic symptoms moderate the affective reaction to somatic symptoms in panic disordered patients.

Such theoretical approaches to uncontrollability and unpredictability are not without their shortcomings. For example, the hypothesis that uncontrollability plays a role in the development of phobias and anxiety states involves an apparent contradiction. On the one hand, Seligman and his colleagues have argued that uncontrollable shock leads to "learned helplessness" characterized by escape and avoidance deficits (Seligman 1975; Maier & Seligman 1976). Yet on the other hand, excessive avoidance is a prominent feature in many of the anxiety disorders. This apparent mismatch between the animal model and human anxiety disorders may explain in part why uncontrollability has received more emphasis in the literature on depression than in that on anxiety.

A careful analysis of the animal literature, however, distinguishing between active and passive avoidance, suggests a potential resolution of the contradiction (Foa et al submitted, Zinbarg & Mineka in preparation). Some evidence suggests that while uncontrollability impairs active avoidance and escape, it actually facilitates passive avoidance (see Foa et al submitted, Rush et al 1982 for reviews of this evidence). This conclusion leads to novel predictions of dissociations between the strength of active avoidance tendencies and that of passive avoidance tendencies among anxiety disordered individuals.

For example, to the degree that uncontrollability plays a role in the etiology of agoraphobia, agoraphobics should display strong passive avoidance tendencies but weak active avoidance and escape tendencies (Zinbarg & Mineka 1991). Though this prediction has not yet been tested empirically, it appears consistent with clinical observations. Many agoraphobics avoid entering certain situations because they fear that they will experience the urge to escape and that escape from the situations will be difficult or humiliating. Avoiding such situations altogether seems to demonstrate strong passive avoidance tendencies, whereas the belief that escape from these situations would be difficult or humiliating demonstrates weak active avoidance tendencies.

Maintenance of Anxiety

Recent models of anxiety disorders have emphasized the role of attentional biases as maintanence factors. One of the most widely used strategies for examining these attentional biases has been the adaptation of various dual-task paradigms, such as the Stroop color naming task (Stroop 1938). In a typical experiment of this type, subjects are asked to perform a task and are simultaneously presented with task-irrelevant information that is either anxiety-relevant (most often threatening words presented either aurally or visually) or anxiety-irrelevant (most often words that are affectively neutral or positive). The interpretation of results from these paradigms usually rests on the following two assumptions: (*a*) the task-relevant and task-irrelevant materials are processed by a common pool of attentional resources, and (*b*) this pool of attentional resources is limited. Thus, interference with task performance is seen as an indication of the extent to which processing resources are devoted to task-irrelevant rather than task-relevant stimuli.

The modal finding from these studies is that threatening distractors interfere with task performance more than anxiety-irrelevant distractors do, to a greater degree among anxiety disordered patients than among normal controls. This selective interference effect has been demonstrated among patients with simple phobia (Watts et al 1986a), panic disorder (Ehlers et al 1988; McNally et al 1990b), generalized anxiety disorder (Mathews & MacLeod 1985; 1986; Mogg et al 1989), social phobia (Hope et al 1990), and posttraumatic stress disorder (Foa 1989; McNally et al 1990a). These findings have been widely interpreted to mean that the patients allocate more of their attentional resources to the task-irrelevant threatening materials than do controls.

While the interference effects cited above are certainly consistent with the hypothesis that anxiety disordered patients allocate more resources to processing threat words, it is important to note that alternative explanations are possible. For example, MacLeod et al (1986) suggested that anxious subjects may process the threat-related distractor material to the same degree as controls but experience a greater increase in negative affect, which then impairs performance. To address this issue, MacLeod et al (1986) designed an elegant experiment that allowed for more direct measurement of the distribution of attention. Subjects were presented with a pair of words, one threatening and one neutral, simultaneously on a visual display unit (VDU); presentation was followed occasionally by a visual reaction-time probe that was presented in the same location on the VDU as either the threatening or neutral word.

MacLeod et al (1986) found facilitation of reaction times among a group of clinically anxious patients when the reaction-time probe appeared in the same location (VDU) as a threat word; normal control subjects were slightly slower to respond to the probe when it appeared in the vicinity of a threat word. These results provide unambiguous support for the notion that clinically anxious subjects are more likely than normals to shift attention toward threat cues.

In a related series of experiments, anxiety disordered patients have been shown to be biased toward interpreting ambiguous situations as threatening. Mathews et al (1989b) found that generalized anxiety disorder patients were more likely than normal controls to use the threatening spelling (e.g. die) of homophones that have both threatening and nonthreatening meanings (e.g. die, dye). An increased tendency to make threatening interpretations of ambiguous scenarios (e.g. you are walking in a park and see a dog running toward you) relative to normal controls has been demonstrated in patients with generalized anxiety disorder (Butler & Mathews 1983) and panic disorder with agoraphobia (McNally & Foa 1987).

Recent data suggest that the attentional scanning for threat cues characteristic of clinical anxiety and high trait anxiety takes place at an automatic level of processing, outside of awareness (MacLeod & Rutherford 1990; Mathews & MacLeod 1986; Mathews et al 1989a). On the other hand, strategic processing, associated with awareness and mediated by conscious intent, appears to restrict (Mathews and MacLeod 1985; Mathews et al 1989a—cued recall test) or even reverse (MacLeod & Rutherford 1990; Mathews et al 1989a—word completion test; Mogg et al 1987; Watts et al 1986b) the automatic biases favoring the processing of threat observed in anxious individuals. For example, relatively poor recall and recognition memory for threatening stimuli have been observed in spider phobics (Watts et al 1986b) and generally anxious patients (Mogg et al 1987). Thus, Mogg et al (1987) have suggested that clinical anxiety is characterized by scanning the environment for potentially threatening events that occurs automatically followed by subsequent active efforts to avoid processing these stimuli further.

It is interesting to note that the attentional scanning for threat and tendency to favor threatening interpretations of ambiguous events observed in clinically anxious groups are also associated with high trait anxiety in normal controls (Broadbent & Broadbent 1988; Eysenck et al 1987; MacLeod & Mathews 1988; Mogg et al 1990—experiment 1; Zinbarg & Revelle 1989). Given the close relationship between neuroticism and trait anxiety (Eysenck & Eysenck 1985; Zinbarg & Revelle 1989), the finding reported by Levenson et al (1988) that neuroticism accounts for almost 25% of the variance in self-reported psychological symptoms 10 years later suggests that highly trait-anxious individuals may be at elevated risk for developing anxiety disorders. If this is true, then the attentional scanning found in highly trait-anxious individuals may mediate this vulnerability to the development of anxiety disorders. Evaluation of this intriguing hypothesis will obviously require large-scale prospective studies.

A strong argument can be made for the role of a scanning-avoidance pattern of processing in maintaining anxiety disorders (Mogg et al 1987). Because of their attentional scanning for threat and bias toward threatening interpretations of ambiguous events, anxiety disordered individuals would be more likely to identify mildly threatening stimuli and encode ambiguous stimuli as threatening. However, subsequent efforts to avoid elaborative processing would prevent more accurate evaluation of those events. Anxiety disordered individuals would thus experience anxiety in response to cues that others do not find threatening, and these threat cues would then retain their anxiety-provoking properties.

ANXIETY AND FEAR REDUCTION

In this section, we review recent evidence on the effects of cognitive-behavioral interventions for each of the anxiety disorders. The procedures have common elements. At their heart is the arrangement or encouragement of exposure to the anxiety-provoking stimuli. In addition, almost all approaches involve a restructuring of beliefs, cognitions, and images associated with the anxiety-provoking stimuli. Other common procedures include relaxation and biofeedback.

Despite enormous strides, development of effective psychological treatments of anxiety has not, by and large, been guided by theories about the nature of anxiety. Most treatments have been developed serendipitously. Of course, influential theorists such as Wolpe and Beck have made important contributions to our knowledge of anxiety and anxiety reduction, and the major empirically supported therapeutic approaches to anxiety disorders are outgrowths of their pioneering procedures. Nevertheless, our knowledge of the mechanisms of action involved in the modification of intense anxiety is rudimentary at best.

The numerous competing theories of anxiety reduction put forward over the years have recently shown signs of convergence. Before reviewing the efficacy of treatments for each of the anxiety disorders, we identify the converging theoretical trends and, based on the models of anxiety and fear described earlier, specify the essential therapeutic targets and mechanisms

Converging Theoretical Trends

Cognitive-behavioral therapists know which therapeutic techniques are efficacious, but their mechanisms of action are still in dispute. For example, exposure to fearful or anxiety-producing cues is an integral part of anxiety reduction procedures when treating phobic disorders. However, treatment programs differ tremendously in how exposure is arranged (in vivo vs imaginal, flooding vs gradual, therapist-assisted vs self-directed) and in the additional procedures implemented (e.g. modeling, relaxation, strong suggestion, etc). Furthermore, while some in the past have held that exposure helps to explain anxiety reduction, exposure is now more widely treated simply as a set of procedures.

At present, no single theory of anxiety reduction is preeminent. A detailed comparison of how well the competing theories account for the empirical evidence on anxiety reduction is beyond the scope of this paper (see Barlow 1988 for a discussion of five distinct theories of anxiety reduction).

One dimension along which the traditional theories differ is that of cognitive mediation. For example, traditional models of extinction minimized the role of cognitive mediation whereas Bandura's self-efficacy theory (1984, 1986), Lang's emotional processing model (Lang 1977, 1985), and models proposed by Beck & Emery (1985) and Clark (1988) place heavy emphasis on cognitive-mediational constructs.

Recent developments in conditioning theory have implications that begin to blur the cognitive vs noncognitive distinction among theories of anxiety reduction (see Rapee 1991 and Zinbarg 1990 for detailed discussions of these developments). Many contemporary theorists suggest that conditioning is mediated by information-processing mechanisms such as covariation detection (Alloy & Tabachnik 1984), expectancies (Grossberg 1982; Reiss 1980; Rescorla & Wagner 1972; Seligman & Johnston 1973), attention (Mackintosh 1975), and short-term memory and rehearsal (Wagner 1978; 1981). At a general level, the implication of these informational models of conditioning is that the label "cognitive-behavioral" contains redundant information. Behavioral techniques, such as exposure, may be viewed as one particularly effective way to alter the meaning and cognitive representations of stimuli and responses (Zinbarg 1990).

Essential Targets for Change

The core of anxiety disorders (see above) is negative affect accompanied by high arousal (which prepares the organism for active coping) and a diminished sense of control or mastery. The cognitive processes of attentional scanning for threat, followed by avoidance of elaboration, are also part of the core of anxiety, perhaps as etiological and almost certainly as maintenance factors. The essential targets for therapeutic action are thus (a) preparation for coping with threat, including the emergency action tendencies associated with fear; (b) a sense of lack of control; and (c) information processing mechanisms such as hypervigilance for threat and cognitive avoidance.

A comprehensive therapy should target all three essential components. Barlow (1988) has identified other useful, but not essential, targets for therapy. While we suggest that therapy will not be successful without marked change in each of the essential components, it is important to note that individual therapeutic procedures are not necessarily associated with one component of anxiety or another. For example, exposure techniques may have effects through altering fight-or-flight action tendencies, increasing a sense of control, and fostering elaboration rather than cognitive avoidance.

ACTION TENDENCIES   We have suggested that a core element of anxiety is the preparation for coping, and more specifically, preparation for fight or flight. This preparation consists of the simultaneous priming and inhibition of the fight-or-flight mechanism. This reasoning implies that altering the action tendencies associated with anxiety is essential in modifying anxiety. Thus, in our view the priming of the fight-or-flight mechanism and its accompanying subjective experience of the urge to escape or avoid are important targets for change.

For years, therapists of various schools of thought have encouraged phobics into contact with the feared object or situation. In discussing the treatment of phobics, Freud (1919:165–66) observed that "one succeeds only when one can induce them through the influence of the analysis . . . to go about alone and struggle with the anxiety while they make the attempt." Bandura, an influential proponent of cognitive explanations of behavior change, has stated that "the treatments implemented through actual performance achieve results consistently superior to those in which fears are eliminated to cognitive representations of threat" (1977:78). Thus, while various explanations of exposure-based treatments have been offered by theorists, exposure to feared situations has become a central component of many treatment approaches.

From the perspective of the model of anxiety outlined earlier, the crucial function of exposure may be the alteration of the action tendencies associated with fear and anxiety. It appears to be crucial to counter directly the escapist and avoidant action tendencies associated with fear, and to replace them with approach tendencies.

It is also possible to interpret the role of non-exposure based treatments in terms of their effects on action tendencies. Thus, procedures such as relaxation and biofeedback may be effective, at least in part, to the extent that they alter the action tendencies associated with fear through undermining the supportive physiology. On the other hand, relaxation may be useful not because of activation-reducing properties but because it directly substitutes a different action tendency for the chronic priming of the fight-or-flight response. Paradoxical intention may be effective not because of changes in self statements, as is often assumed. Rather, laughter and humor induced during successful paradoxical intention (Frankl 1960) may prevent behavioral responses associated with fear and substitute alternative action tendencies.

CONTROLLABILITY   We have also suggested that a sense of uncontrollability is a core element of anxiety. A reliable finding in the animal literature is that uncontrollable shock is associated with more fear than controllable shock of the same duration and intensity (Brennan & Riccio 1975; Cook et al 1987; Desiderato & Newman 1971; Mineka et al 1984; Osborne et al 1975; Starr & Mineka 1977). Similarly, Sanderson et al (1988) demonstrated that panic disordered patients who did not believe they could control CO_2 administration reported more anxiety than patients who had an illusion of control during this panic induction. Thus, it appears that altering perceptions of control is important for anxiety reduction.

Clearly, altering action tendencies may be a good beginning to altering a sense of control. Replacing the fight-or-flight action tendency with an approach tendency should be associated with an increased sense of mastery. On the other hand, it might be possible to instill a sense of control without reducing escapist tendencies. Indeed, our analyses of the nature of anxiety and of the experimental effects of uncontrollability suggest that it may be possible to instill a sense of control and reduce anxiety by strengthening (or disinhibiting) escapist and active avoidance tendencies. For example, reducing an agoraphobic's fear that escape from a public situation would be humiliating should reduce both his anxiety in that situation and his passive avoidance of it. A similar enhanced sense of control may account for a series of studies demonstrating that anxiety reduction can occur even though subjects are allowed to escape from the feared situation early in an exposure trial, before reaching maximum anxiety (e.g. Agras et al 1968; Emmelkamp 1982; Rachman et al 1986).

Various relaxation and biofeedback techniques can also be interpreted in terms of altering a sense of control. Here it may be useful to distinguish between control over one's own emotions and control over the environment. Procedures such as relaxation and biofeedback may be effective only to the extent that they enhance the sense that the aversive somatic and affective components of anxiety can be controlled.

ATTENTION   Clinical anxiety is associated with a pattern of information processing characterized by initial scanning for threat at a relatively automatic level, followed by avoidance of elaboration and processing of threatening stimuli at a strategic level. Cognitive restructuring techniques target these information-processing biases. At a general level, these techniques encourage elaboration of threatening stimuli and discourage cognitive avoidance. Some cognitive techniques, such as considering alternative explanations and examining the evidence regarding catastrophic thinking, directly target particular processing mechanisms such as the tendencies to interpret ambiguous stimuli as being threatening and to scan the environment for threatening information.

It is also possible to interpret the effects of exposure-based interventions in terms of information-processing mechanisms. Clinical observations have implied the importance of targeting cognitive avoidance in exposure therapy (e.g. Borkovec & Grayson 1980; Foa & Kozak 1986; Rachman 1980). Indeed, some evidence suggests that distraction, one form of cognitive avoidance, during exposure procedures interferes with anxiety reduction (Grayson et al 1982; Sartory et al 1982). In addition, Watts et al (1986b) observed a tendency for exposure to improve recognition memory for spider stimuli among spider phobics. From this perspective, exposure is effective because in addition to altering action tendencies it replaces cognitive avoidance with further processing and elaboration.

Treatment of DSM-III-R Anxiety Disorders

PANIC DISORDER WITH AND WITHOUT AGORAPHOBIA

Treating avoidance behavior   Since the late 1960s, a wealth of evidence has demonstrated that exposure in vivo is an effective treatment for agoraphobia and is substantially more effective than a number of credible psychotherapeutic procedures (Emmelkamp 1982; Leitenberg et al 1970; Mathews et al 1981; Mavissakalian & Barlow 1981). In the few studies where this was not the case, either exposure in vivo was not the primary treatment modality (Klein et al 1983) or treatment comparisons were confounded because patients were systematically encouraged to expose themselves in vivo in their home environment between sessions in all groups (Mathews et al 1976). In fact, given the wide publicity that exposure-based treatments have received, Barlow (1988) has suggested that the only methodologically sound way to evaluate the effects of exposure is to prevent exposure in the comparison groups.

When exposure is precluded in comparison groups, the efficacy of exposure is even more apparent. For example, Telch et al (1985) treated a group of agoraphobics with imipramine, telling subjects not to confront their feared situations until blood levels of the medication were in a therapeutic range. Two other groups received intensive in vivo exposure with either imipramine (IMI) or placebo. After the first eight weeks of treatment, the group that received anti-exposure instructions showed little or no improvement in panic attacks, phobic avoidance, or anxiety, despite the presence of imipramine. On the other hand, patients receiving exposure therapy with or without imipramine displayed substantial improvements on these measures. Taken together with the earlier research cited above, these results indicate the importance of exposure as a basic therapeutic ingredient in the treatment of agoraphobia. In fact, 60–70% of agoraphobics who complete exposure therapy have shown some improvement, and follow-up studies reveal these effects have been maintained for periods of four years or more (Barlow 1988).

Several recent studies have investigated the comparative and combined efficacy of exposure therapy and pharmacotherapy in the treatment of panic disorder with substantial agoraphobic avoidance (e.g. Mavissakalian &

Michelson 1986; Telch et al 1985). In the Telch et al (1985) study cited above, IMI had little impact on outcome assessed after the first eight weeks of treatment. However, by the time treatment was over, IMI combined with in vivo exposure did seem to lead to greater improvement than in vivo exposure alone.

In the most recent report from this line of research, Agras et al (submitted for publication) treated 100 PDA patients with IMI or placebo combined with either programmed in vivo self-paced exposure practice (PP) or anti-exposure instructions. After an eight-week trial, subjects were reassigned to eight-week trials of PP or intensive group exposure (GE) while maintaining their original medication condition. In a final eight-week phase, all subjects received PP and continued with their original medication assignment. After the initial eight-week phase, PP was significantly superior to anti-exposure instructions on several outcome measures. On the other hand, IMI had little impact on outcome at this assessment, which the authors attributed to the gradual dosing regimen performed in this phase. A very different pattern of results emerged by the end of the third phase. At this time, using a global index of outcome (involving measures of panic, agoraphobic avoidance, and depression), 59% of subjects who received IMI and PP only improved substantially, compared with 28% of the subjects who received IMI and GE, 36% of the subjects who received placebo and GE, and 14% of the subjects who received placebo and PP only. These results demonstrate an interaction between the pharmacotherapy and exposure type. Agras et al (submitted) concluded that the combination of IMI and PP was the most effective of the approaches they examined for treating PDA.

Despite the many successes of exposure therapy, the approach has limitations. The best estimates of the efficacy of exposure therapy indicate that 90% of clients completing treatment are not completely symptom free, and 30–40% fail to receive any benefit whatsoever. Recent conceptualizations of agoraphobia suggest at least one reason for the limitations of traditional exposure treatments. The essence of this conceptualization is that panic attacks are seen as the central feature of PDA and that avoidance behavior is a subsequent complication of initial panic. Following this logic, the direct treatment of panic should be a primary goal of treatment. While in vivo exposure to feared situations reduces panic to some extent (e.g. Barlow et al 1984b; Chambless et al 1986), most exposure-based programs have concentrated on avoidance behavior rather than on panic.

Treating panic   During the past few years, successes have been reported from around the world for several cognitive-behavioral treatment packages aimed at reducing or eliminating panic (e.g. Barlow et al 1984a; Barlow et al 1989; Clark et al 1985; Craske et al 1991; Haslam 1974; Michelson et al 1990;

Öst 1988; Rapee 1985; Salkovskis et al 1986; Sokol et al 1989). Among the interventions included in these treatment packages are breathing retraining to correct hyperventilatory breathing patterns, cognitive restructuring to correct catastrophic misinterpretations of benign somatic sensations, and exposure to somatic cues (also called interoceptive exposure) through the use of any of a number of provocation procedures (e.g. hyperventilation, CO_2 inhalation, running in place, spinning in a chair).

It is currently difficult to determine which of these three treatment components is responsible for the success of treatment. To date, panic treatment studies advocating one or the other of these approaches have typically included at least one of the other components. Even in our own center, past treatment protocols for panic have deliberately included a combination of breathing retraining, cognitive therapy, and interoceptive exposure (e.g. Barlow et al 1984a; Craske et al 1991). Little data are yet available from dismantling designs that would allow the identification of the essential components of cognitive-behavioral treatments for panic.

Researchers have begun to compare cognitive-behavioral treatments for panic to pharmacological treatments such as imipramine and alprazolam. For example, Klosko et al (1990) recently reported the results of a study comparing the efficacy of their panic control treatment (PCT; consisting of cognitive restructuring, breathing retraining, relaxation, and exposure to somatic cues) to alprazolam, placebo, and a waiting list control (WLC) in 57 patients with PD. At posttreatment, 87% of PCT patients were panic free, compared with 50% for alprazolam, 36% for placebo, and 33% for the WLC.

Clark et al (1990) are currently examining the efficacy against panic of cognitive therapy, imipramine (IMI), applied relaxation (AR), and a WLC in 64 patients with PD or PD with agoraphobia (PDA). The three treatments were delivered across 12 sessions in conjunction with self-exposure assignments. All three active treatments appeared to be effective when compared with the WLC. However, at posttreatment, cognitive therapy was significantly more effective on several measures than either IMI or AR, which did not differ from each other. At a three-month follow-up assessment, cognitive therapy remained more effective than AR on several measures. However, by this time, the IMI group (which had not yet begun tapering off IMI) tended to catch up with those treated with cognitive therapy. Clark et al (1990) are now collecting 12- and 24-month follow-up data on these subjects. Given the paucity of data pertaining to the long-term functioning of treated PD patients, the results from these follow-up assessments will be particularly valuable.

New directions Because data isolating the essential components of panic control-treatments are few, it is important to begin using dismantling strategies. Data have been collected using such a strategy for the past few years at the Center for Stress and Anxiety Disorders at the State University of New York at Albany in a large clinical trial supported by the National Institutes of Mental Health. The four treatment conditions in this study are cognitive restructuring only, cognitive restructuring plus breathing retraining, cognitive restructuring plus interoceptive exposure, and cognitive restructuring plus breathing retraining plus interoceptive exposure. The last few patients are being enrolled as we write this chapter, so the posttreatment comparisons with the full sample should be available soon.

We also need far more data comparing the efficacies of panic control treatments, pharmacological treatments, and their combinations. To address this need, a large-scale collaborative study also sponsored by the National Institutes of Mental Health has been recently initiated. The four sites collaborating on this project are the Center for Stress and Anxiety Disorders (David H. Barlow, PI), the Department of Psychiatry at Columbia University and Hillside Hospital (Jack M. Gorman, PI), the Department of Psychiatry at Yale University (Scott W. Woods, PI), and the Payne Whitney Clinic at Cornell University (M. Katherine Shear, PI). The following five conditions are being evaluated: PCT only, PCT and IMI, PCT and placebo, IMI only, and placebo only. The collaborative nature of this project allows for the collection of a large sample size (480), providing power to detect subtle yet potentially important effects that may predict outcome—effects such as subject variables or interactions between subject variables and treatment condition. In addition, the examination of differences between sites will provide important information about the general applicability of treatment procedures.

GENERALIZED ANXIETY DISORDER   In considering new developments in the treatment of generalized anxiety disorder (GAD), it is useful to keep in mind recent changes in the criteria for the diagnosis itself. When the DSM-II category of anxiety neurosis was split into a number of subcategories in the DSM-III—including, most importantly, panic disorder—GAD was considered residual. If individuals were anxious but did not present with a particularly salient symptom such as panic or phobic avoidance, they would meet the criteria for GAD.

In DSM-III-R, however, the criteria for GAD were revised. A key symptom was identified as defining this disorder: chronic unrealistic or excessive worry focused on two or more life circumstances (Barlow et al 1986). Many individuals experience chronic anxiety without unrealistic or excessive worry. The relationship between GAD, chronic anxiety, and mixed anxiety depression is discussed in some length by Rapee & Barlow (1991).

Early studies evaluating cognitive-behavioral treatments can be grouped into two types according to whether they targeted somatic or cognitive manifestations of generalized anxiety. The most common techniques aimed at reducing somatic symptoms were biofeedback and relaxation (including meditation techniques). With few exceptions, these early studies treated only mildly anxious college students. Two general conclusions emerge from the few early studies that examined relaxation or biofeedback techniques in clinical populations (Brown et al 1991). First, while an occasional study suggests superiority of biofeedback training (e.g. Canter et al 1975), various forms of relaxation and biofeedback were most often comparable in their effects (Barlow 1988). Second, as noted by Raskin et al (1980), relaxation techniques appear to be insufficient by themselves in treating chronic generalized anxiety.

Data on treatment approaches to GAD using DSM-III-R criteria to classify subjects are scarce. A few controlled studies have begun to appear, however, evaluating cognitive-behavioral approaches to GAD as defined by the DSM-III-R.

Recent studies have typically utilized combinations of procedures (including cognitive, relaxation, and other components). For example, Barlow et al (1984a) evaluated the effectiveness of a package combining cognitive and relaxation procedures for patients with GAD. Compared to a WLC group, treated patients improved, not only on clinical ratings but also on psychophysiological measures, daily self-monitoring measures of background anxiety, and questionnaire measures of anxiety. At follow-up assessments averaging 6 months posttreatment, the treated group showed additional improvement. This pattern suggests that these patients had learned skills during treatment that they continued to master and apply after treatment ended.

Preliminary results are also available from a study in progress at the Center for Stress and Anxiety Disorders comparing three different treatment programs to a WLC group for subjects meeting DSM-III-R criteria for GAD (R. M. Rapee and D. H. Barlow, unpublished). The three treatment conditions included relaxation only, cognitive restructuring only, and a combination of the relaxation and cognitive strategies. Preliminary results indicate that all three treatments are more beneficial than the WLC—the cognitive procedures seeming to produce the greatest improvement and the relaxation alone condition producing the highest rate of dropouts. A full analysis of the data including a 24-month follow-up assessment should be completed shortly.

Butler and her colleagues at Oxford have also reported an important series of studies in this area (Butler et al 1987; Butler et al 1991). Butler et al (1987) compared an anxiety-management package for GAD to a WLC condition, excluding subjects who suffered substantial anxiety for more than two years. Although the Research Diagnostic Criteria were used to classify patients as having GAD, this definition, as modified by the investigators, comes extremely close to the DSM-III-R definition. Their treatment package included self-administered relaxation procedures and, to deal with cognitive aspects of anxiety, patients were taught distraction procedures and the control of upsetting thoughts. Subtle types of avoidance of both somatic and situational cues were also addressed. Patients were also encouraged to schedule positive activities and note areas in their life in which they were functioning well.

The results from this first study indicated that the treatment package led to significantly more improvement than the WLC on all the measures of anxiety used in the study. At a six-month follow-up assessment, all the measures indicated either maintanence of improvement or further improvement. To give one an idea of the size of these gains, scores on the Hamilton Anxiety Scale, a measure well known to many clinicians and researchers alike, decreased from a pretreatment mean of 16 to a mean of 6.6 immediately posttreatment, and to a mean of 5 by the six-month follow-up.

In a follow-up study, Butler et al (1991) compared a more extensive cognitive therapy based on the work of Beck & Emery (1985) with a version of their earlier anxiety management package devoid of any cognitive therapy. Treatment consisted of weekly sessions lasting up to 12 weeks. Booster sessions were provided at two, four, and six weeks after treatment. In general, the findings revealed that cognitive therapy produced significantly more improvement on most measures. A six-month follow-up assessment indicated maintenance of the treatment gains. In this study, Hamilton Anxiety Scale scores decreased from a mean of 16.4 at pretreatment to 7.9 at both posttreatment and follow-up. Of the patients receiving cognitive therapy 42% had achieved an end-state functioning status essentially equivalent to "cured" by the six month follow-up assessment. Thus despite significant gains associated with treatment, much room remains for improving and refining our current techniques.

The finding that a treatment approach combining cognitive therapy and relaxation is effective when compared to a WLC group has been replicated (e.g. Blowers et al 1987), but the degree of improvement reported by Butler et al (1987, 1991) exceeds that found in other studies (e.g. Blowers et al 1987; Durham & Turvey 1987). Furthermore, it has been more difficult to replicate the finding that any specific cognitive-behavioral treatment is more effective than a comparison treatment. For example, Blowers et al (1987) failed to find differences between a nondirective counseling approach and a combined cognitive and relaxation therapy. Similarly, Borkovec & Mathews (1988) failed to find differences among a cognitive therapy, a coping desensitization treatment including relaxation, and a nondirective therapy.

New directions   We are just beginning to develop effective cognitive-behavioral treatments for GAD. However, even the most optimistic estimates of treatment effects (Butler et al 1987, 1991) indicate that our current treatments need refining and improving. As noted above, we have recently suggested that perceptions of uncontrollability may be a core element of anxiety and that correction of this basic deficit will be crucial to any attempt at intervention. In addition, the recent changes in the definition of GAD suggest worry is the central or most salient feature of the disorder. Thus, greater attention to the worry component also appears to be warranted. Preliminary results with our newest protocol for GAD, which incorporates innovative procedures to deal with chronic worry and to instill a greater sense of control, are encouraging (Craske & Barlow 1991).

More attention must be paid to evaluating long-term outcome. One of the proposed advantages of cognitive-behavioral approaches over benzodiazepine therapy and other commonly used pharmacotherapies is that patients will learn coping skills and a sense of control so that therapeutic gains may be maintained and improved. Unfortunately, few follow-up data beyond six months are available.

Finally, it is important to begin to compare directly the efficacy of cognitive-behavioral approaches, pharmacological approaches, and their combinations. Although it is possible that these approaches may exert synergistic, or at least additive, effects when combined, they may also interfere with each other (Barlow 1988).

SIMPLE PHOBIA   While most cognitive-behavior therapists and researchers would agree that some form of exposure therapy is effective in treating simple phobias, some debate still remains regarding the relative efficacy of the various types of exposure (e.g. in vivo, imaginal, participant modeling). Earlier reviews have generally found no particular advantage for one type of exposure over another (Barlow 1988; Linden 1981). For example, Bourque & Ladouceur (1981) compared five different exposure-based treatments for height phobics, including participant modeling and self-initiated, self-paced exposure, and found no differences among them. Öst and his colleagues have demonstrated essentially equivalent benefits from several exposure-based treatments for thunder-and-lightning phobics (Öst 1978) as well as blood phobics (Öst et al 1984).

Some researchers have recently suggested that there may be heterogeneity in the etiology and expression of simple phobias that has important implications for treatment outcome. For example, blood/injury phobias are distinguishable from other specific phobias in regard to their unique psychophysiological response, age of onset, and strong familial tendency (Himle et al 1989; Kleinknecht & Lenz 1989; Öst et al 1984). Unlike other sufferers from simple phobias, blood phobics tend to display a vasovagal slowing of heart rate (sometimes even to the point of brief asystole and fainting), after an initial brief increase in heart rate and blood pressure (Öst et al 1989).

The distinctiveness of the physiological response in blood phobia has led to modifications of the traditional in vivo exposure therapy used for the other simple phobias. Öst and his colleagues have devised and evaluated several treatment strategies for blood/injury phobia. One technique, applied tension (AT), has been designed to counter fainting by teaching the phobic to tense gross body muscles at the early signs of hypotension (Öst & Sterner, 1987). In the most comprehensive study of treatments for blood phobia to date, Öst et al (1989) compared applied relaxation (AR) with AT and their combination in 30 blood/injury phobics. All groups improved, and these improvements were maintained at a six-month follow-up. No significant differences were found between the groups but a trend indicated superiority of the AT approach. Despite the lack of statistical significance, the superiority of the AT group's results is noteworthy because AT was applied in only 5 sessions, in contrast to 9 and 10 sessions for the AR and combined conditions, respectively. On this basis, the authors concluded that AT should be considered the treatment of choice for blood/injury phobia.

That variability in the etiology and expression of phobias may have important implications for treatment is further suggested by the observation that "situational" simple phobias (e.g. fears of driving, flying, enclosed places), unlike other specific phobias (e.g. animals, choking), resemble PDA in such diverse features as age and manner of onset, phenomenology, and in some cases (e.g. claustrophobia) predictability of panic (Craske 1990; Himle et al 1989; Munjack 1984; Öst 1987). Some recent findings suggest that many situational phobics are concerned primarily with panicking in their phobic situations (Craske 1990; Munjack 1984). Thus panic-control techniques may be helpful in the treatment of situational phobias and may be more effective for situational phobics than for other phobics.

In another innovation in exposure-based treatments for specific phobias, Öst (1989) has presented data on the efficacy of one-session treatments of simple phobias. Rather than gradually presenting elements of the hierarchy of feared stimuli over multiple sessions, the entire hierarchy is presented during a single session with an average session duration of 2.1 hr. Of 20 consecutive patients that he treated in this fashion, Öst reported that 90% were much improved or completely recovered at follow-up assessments after an average of 4 years. Moreover, Öst reported only 3 of 23 original patients refused the one-session treatment, with no dropouts among the 20 who accepted treatment.

New directions   We have begun to match specific cognitive-behavioral treatments to salient individual differences among patients with simple phobias. This trend is most clearly evidenced in the work of Öst and his colleagues in developing AT to target hypotension among blood/injury phobics. The initial results with this technique are promising. Further research is necessary, comparing AT with other credible treatments using the same number of sessions across each of the treatments, to provide a more sensitive test of AT's superiority.

The evidence on situational simple phobias suggests they may share important features with PDA. These similarities and their implications for treatment must be explored further. Current research at our Center has begun to investigate these issues and has revealed that some simple phobics do report fear and demonstrate avoidance in response to panic-like sensations (e.g. tachycardia, paresthesia, dizziness) provoked by various physical activities (e.g. jogging in place, hyperventilation, spinning). We have begun to use exposure to these somatic cues as part of the treatment for situational simple phobias. All patients treated with interoceptive exposure have shown decreases in fear and avoidance of their target simple phobic situation (Zarate et al 1989).

Finally, another innovation introduced by Öst, single-session treatment, promises to increase cost-effectiveness in the treatment of at least some simple phobias. Initial results indicate that single-session treatment is effective. Öst (personal communication) is currently comparing the efficacy of the one-session treatment with that of a five-session protocol.

SOCIAL PHOBIA   Earlier reviews have concluded that research on the treatment of social phobia is still in its infancy (Barlow 1988; Heimberg 1989). Interventions such as imaginal and in vivo exposure, social skills training, relaxation techniques, and cognitive restructuring have been the focus of initial research efforts. Though the preliminary findings with many of these interventions appear promising, the literature is relatively small, and Heimberg (1989) has noted several methodological weaknesses in many studies that prevent firm conclusions. According to Heimberg, future studies of cognitive-behavioral treatments for social phobia must (a) provide increased experimental control through the use of WLC or attention placebo controls, (b) track long-term outcome, (c) compare the efficacy of such treatments to that of leading pharmacological approaches, and (d) explain the therapeutic mechanisms at work. Results from more recent studies bear on many of the important issues Heimberg (1989) raised.

Cognitive factors such as the fear of negative evaluation may do more to cause and maintain the social phobias than the other phobias (Butler 1985; Heimberg 1989). Cognitive restructuring may therefore help more against social phobias than against other phobias. Recent attempts to identify active therapeutic mechanisms have compared treatments involving exposure with those involving cognitive restructuring. For example, Mattick & Peters (1988) compared therapist-assisted exposure (EXP) to exposure plus cognitive restructuring (EXP+CR) in a sample of 51 social phobics. The EXP+CR group fared significantly better at posttreatment on measures of behavioral approach, self-rated avoidance, and proportion achieving high end-state functioning. At a three-month follow-up, the EXP+CR group showed further improvement while the EXP group did not.

In another study comparing exposure and cognitive restructuring, Mattick et al (1989) compared EXP, cognitive restructuring (CR), and EXP+CR to a WLC in a sample of 43 social phobics. All three active treatments resulted in significant improvement compared to the WLC. Comparisons among the three active treatments were complex, as the pattern varied across different outcome measures. The CR and EXP+CR groups improved on all outcome measures, including attitudinal measures, whereas the EXP group did not show improvement on the attitudinal measures. On the other hand, the CR group showed significantly less improvement at posttreatment on a behavioral approach test (BAT) than did the two groups receiving exposure. At the three month follow-up, however, the pattern of results changed. The CR group showed continued improvement on all measures, including the BAT, compared to the two groups that received exposure. In both of the studies conducted by Mattick and colleagues changes in Fear-of-Negative-Evaluation scores accounted for most of the variance in treatment-induced change, further supporting the importance of cognitive variables in the treatment of social phobia.

Heimberg et al (1990) recently compared their cognitive-behavioral group treatment (CBGT) to a credible placebo treatment, educational-supportive psychotherapy (ES), thus controlling for a variety of nonspecific effects such as therapist attention, treatment credibility, and client expectancies. CBGT included a combination of exposure exercises (both within the sessions and between sessions for homework) and cognitive restructuring. CBGT led to significantly more improvement on several measures at posttreatment and at three- and six-month follow-up assessments. Many of the benefits seen in the ES group at posttreatment were not maintained at the six-month follow-up, whereas scores on virtually every measure for the CBGT group remained significantly better than at pretreatment. Greater improvement in CBGT patients was associated with cognitive changes.

New directions   Researchers have begun to address many of the questions and methodological weaknesses identified by Heimberg (1989). Controlled studies using WLC or credible placebo controls have begun to demonstrate the efficacy of cognitive-behavorial interventions. Investigations of the cognitive factors hypothesized to mediate these treatment gains are under way.

Assessments of long-term outcome are still needed. Meanwhile Richard Heimberg (Center for Stress and Anxiety Disorders in Albany) and Michael Liebowitz (New York State Psychiatric Institute at Columbia University) are currently collaborating on a study comparing cognitive-behavioral treatments with the leading pharmacological approaches. They are randomly assigning each of 320 social phobic patients to one of the following four conditions: CBGT, ES, phenelzine (PZ), and pill placebo. Not only will this study compare the efficacy of CBGT and PZ, but the large sample size should also afford sufficient power to detect predictors of treatment response. Variables that have been implicated as predictors of outcome in the past include social phobia subtype (generalized vs discrete), level of depression, and presence of a personality disorder. Preliminary evidence suggests that the two social phobia subtypes may respond differently to both cognitive-behavioral treatments (Heimberg 1989; Heimberg et al 1990) and pharmacological interventions (Levin et al 1989). Thus, the study in progress may provide evidence that will have important implications for patient–treatment matching in the treatment of social phobia.

POSTTRAUMATIC STRESS DISORDER   While initial investigations of the efficacy of cognitive-behavioral treatments for posttraumatic stress disorder (PTSD) consisted of mostly single-case experimental designs, reports from several controlled group outcome studies have emerged within the past two years. Reviewers (e.g. Brown et al 1991; Keane et al 1991) have tended to classify behavioral interventions for PTSD as either direct therapeutic exposure (DTE), including both prolonged imaginal exposure and in vivo exposure, or stress management, including such techniques as cognitive restructuring, relaxation, problem solving, and anger management. Evidence from recent controlled group outcome studies suggests that both approaches are associated with positive outcome in both combat- and rape-related PTSD (Boudewyns & Hyer 1990; Cooper & Clum 1989; Foa et al submitted for publication; Frank et al 1988; Keane et al 1989; Resick et al 1988).

The results from one of the group outcome studies examining DTE are particularly important because they indicate that this treatment may be effective for only some of the symptoms of PTSD. In this study, Keane et al (1989) randomized 24 Vietnam veterans to either a 14–16-session implosive therapy condition (IT) or a WLC group. The IT group exhibited fewer reexperiencing symptoms, less hyperarousal, anxiety, and depression; these improvements were maintained at a 6-month follow-up assessment. On the other hand, members of this group did not improve on measures of numbing and social avoidance.

In the only controlled study to date directly comparing DTE and stress management approaches, Foa et al (submitted for publication) randomly assigned 45 rape victims diagnosed with PTSD to one of four conditions: stress inoculation training (SIT), prolonged exposure (PE), supportive counseling (SC), and a WLC. All four groups (including WLC) showed improvement across the active treatment phase, although SIT was most effective in reducing PTSD symptoms immediately after treatment. At a 3.5-month follow-up, PE emerged as the most effective treatment; the subjects in this condition continued to improve while SIT and SC subjects showed no further improvement. SIT and PE were superior to the other conditions only on measures of PTSD symptomatology; no group differences were found on other measures of psychopathology, such as depression. In contrast to the findings of Keane et al (1989), in this study PE was associated with improvement on measures of numbing and social avoidance. Foa et al (submitted for publication) speculated that the long-term superiority of PE reflected permanent changes in the processes producing PTSD symptoms whereas the techniques introduced in SIT may produce more transient or state-like effects and require continued applications to maintain their efficacy.

New directions   Development of a comprehensive treatment for PTSD requires identification of the factors that account for the discrepancy between the findings of Keane et al (1989) and those of Foa et al (submitted for publication) on how exposure treatment affects numbing and social avoidance. One important procedural difference between these two studies is that Foa et al embellished their exposure condition with in vivo exercises whereas Keane et al did not. On the other hand, individual differences, as yet unidentified, may have moderated the impact of treatment on these measures. Thus, it will be important to search for predictors of outcome on measures of numbing symptoms and social avoidance, and to examine whether in vivo exposure is necessary for improvement on these measures. Alternatively, including communication training or problem-solving packages in treatment may be useful for treating certain interpersonal aspects of PTSD.

Several researchers have called for the evaluation of multicomponent treatments for PTSD since, to date, exposure and stress-management approaches have been delivered separately. Future research should evaluate the efficacy of exposure-based approaches in tandem with stress-management and pharmacological approaches.

Finally, associated features of PTSD have often been overlooked in PTSD treatment outcome studies. Problems such as substance abuse, marital conflict, and vocational difficulties are often seen among patients with PTSD. A recent study has focused on the treatment of combat veterans diagnosed as having both PTSD and alcohol dependence or abuse (Abueg et al 1989). Using a modification of the 12-session relapse prevention training program developed by Marlatt & Gordon (1985), Abueg et al found that, compared with untreated controls, the patients receiving this package had longer latencies to return to drinking and a lower severity of relapse (operationalized as amount of alcohol consumed) at a 9-month follow-up. However, these authors also observed high rates of relapse between the 9- and 12-month follow-up in both groups and concluded that much work remains to be done in this area.

OBSESSIVE-COMPULSIVE DISORDER   Cognitive-behavioral treatments for obsessive-compulsive disorder (OCD) most commonly involve some combination of graduated prolonged exposure to feared situations (either in vivo or imaginal) and prevention of ritualistic behavior. Recent reviews of outcome studies have generally concluded that treatment packages incorporating exposure and response prevention are effective (Foa et al 1985; Beck & Bourg 1991; Christensen et al 1987). For example, Foa et al (1985) reviewed 18 controlled studies involving a total of some 200 patients and found that 51% were much improved (they experienced at least a 70% reduction of symptoms), whereas only 10% failed to benefit from treatment. Moreover, several studies have demonstrated the importance of both exposure and response-prevention procedures (e.g. Steketee et al 1982).

Christensen et al (1987) conducted a meta-analysis of 38 studies published between 1961 and 1984 examining either behavioral or pharmacological approaches to treating OCD. They observed that few follow-up data were available for pharmacological trials, whereas the improvements associated with behavior therapy trials have been maintained at follow-up assessments. They concluded that while tricyclic antidepressant and exposure-based treatments are significantly superior to nonspecific treatment programs, the effects of these two forms of treatment appear to be essentially equivalent when assessed immediately after treatment. At the same time, Christensen et al (1987) noted that this conclusion must be tempered by the fact that there were no large-scale, randomized trials comparing the leading pharmacological [i.e. clomipramine (CMI)] and behavioral treatments at the time of their review.

Marks et al (1988) addressed this deficiency in the literature by randomly assigning 49 OCD patients to treatment in a study comparing CMI, pill placebo, self-guided exposure (SE), and therapist-aided exposure (TE). SE consisted of homework assignments involving graduated exposure and response prevention to anxiety- and ritual-evoking stimuli. SE appeared to be the most effective of the three active treatments. CMI, relative to placebo, had a limited and transient effect when delivered together with SE. TE also had negligible effects; however, this component was not introduced until after eight weeks of SE treatment had been administered. Thus, the lack of incremental efficacy of TE may have been due to a ceiling effect on improvement. The finding that SE is effective has important implications for clinical practice: Minimizing therapist contact reduces the cost of treatment and is less likely to foster patient dependence.

Some evidence indicates that exposure-based treatment has not been as successful for patients who have obsessions without overt compulsions as for patients who do perform overt compulsions (e.g. Christensen et al 1987). However, Salkovskis & Westbrook (1989) hypothesized that poor outcome in these patients may reflect inadequate conceptualization and implementation of effective cognitive-behavioral principles and techniques. Salkovskis & Westbrook observed that "cognitive rituals"—voluntarily initiated thoughts to reduce anxiety—often accompany obsessional thoughts (defined as intrusive thoughts that increase anxiety). They suggested that prior therapeutic attempts with patients who have obsessions without overt compulsions failed because the cognitive rituals were not addressed. They described a series of single-case studies demonstrating the effectiveness of a treatment involving both exposure to obsessional thoughts and response prevention of cognitive rituals. This package warrants further research attention; however, as far as we know a controlled evaluation of this package has not yet been published.

Some earlier studies suggested that depression is another variable that is associated with poor outcome in the treatment of OCD (e.g. Foa et al 1985). However, more recent studies have not replicated this finding (Basoglu et al 1988; Foa et al submitted for publication). In the most recent of these studies, Foa et al (submitted for publication) assessed both symptoms of OCD and level of depression. They found that imipramine reduced depression among a group of OCD patients with initially high levels of depression. However, on measures of OCD symptoms, imipramine did not augment the effects of behavior therapy (exposure and response prevention), and depression did not moderate the effects of treatment. Basoglu et al (1988) also found no relationship between treatment response and level of depression and concluded that severity of the OCD, rather than depression per se, is associated with treatment response.

New directions   Randomized evaluations are needed, similar to that conducted by Marks et al (1988) comparing the efficacy of cognitive-behavioral treatment, pharmacological treatment, and their combination. Edna Foa and Michael Liebowitz are currently conducting a large-scale study of this type. They are evaluating CMI, exposure plus response prevention, CMI plus exposure plus response prevention, and a pill placebo. They will also be able to evaluate potential predictors of treatment response such as initial severity and level of depression.

CONCLUSIONS AND FUTURE DIRECTIONS

Major advances in our understanding of the processes underlying anxiety and in the development of specific cognitive-behavioral treatments for the anxiety disorders have occurred in the last 10 years. Analyses of the convergent and divergent validity of anxiety vis-à-vis the constructs of depression and fear suggest that the core of anxiety disorders is negative affect accompanied by a prepatory set for active coping, including the physiological arousal necessary to support such coping efforts. Experimental evidence from human analog studies has begun to provide support for the hypothesis derived from animal models that a diminished sense of control is also at the core of the anxiety disorders. Attentional scanning for threat followed by avoidance of elaborative processing may be another risk factor and is almost certainly a maintenance factor for anxiety disorders. Following this reasoning, the essential targets for treating anxiety disorders are (a) action tendencies associated with coping with threat, (b) a sense of lack of control, and (c) a scanning-avoidance pattern of processing threatening information.

For each of the anxiety disorders, controlled studies demonstrate the effectiveness of cognitive-behavioral treatments. Almost all of these treatment packages have at least two common elements: exposure to the anxiety-provoking stimuli and restructuring of cognitions associated with the anxiety-provoking stimuli. The efficacy of these common elements can be seen as being due to their effects on the three essential target mechanisms identified above.

Despite the advances documented in this chapter, several important questions still confront us. First, the tripartite model of anxiety and depression proposed by Clark & Watson (1991) suggests that there may be many patients whose predominant symptoms are nonspecific complaints of high negative affect with neither marked physiological arousal nor anhedonia. Preliminary evidence indicates that such cases exist and are highly prevalent in primary care settings (Katon & Roy-Byrne, 1989). Currently, we are collaborating with Eugene Broadhead (Duke University), Michael Liebowitz (New York State Psychiatric Institute), and Wayne Katon and Peter Roy-Byrne (University of Washington) in the DSM-IV mixed anxiety-depression field trial to investigate whether a new diagnostic category needs to be created to include these cases (see Zinbarg & Barlow 1991 for a detailed description of this project). Research illuminating the nature of mixed anxiety-depression will be needed to develop effective treatments for this proposed category if it is added to the nomenclature.

Second, greater attention must be paid to the variability among individuals presenting with the same disorder. While the creation of detailed therapeutic protocols has been a major methodological advance for studying therapeutic outcome, such protocols infrequently allow sufficient flexibility in matching specific interventions to a particular patient's clinical presentation. For example, in our evaluation of the essential components of the Panic Control Treatment developed in Albany, patients assigned to the cognitive-restructuring-plus-breathing retraining group receive the breathing retraining even if they do not experience hyperventilatory symptoms. Conversely, patients assigned to the cognitive- restructuring-only group do not receive breathing retraining even if they do experience hyperventilatory symptoms. Large-scale comparative studies are needed to identify individual differences that predict response to different treatments.

Finally, we are on the verge of being able to determine the separate and interactive effects of pharmacotherapy and cognitive-behavioral therapy.At least three large collaborative studies of this type, targeting PD, social phobia, and OCD, are currently under way (described above). Several beneficial consequences arise from the collaborative nature of these studies. First, pharmacological and cognitive-behavioral researchers have been forced to agree on common measures for evaluating the efficacy of their respective treatments, allowing for more direct and convincing comparisons of the efficacy of these treatments than has been possible in the past. Second, it will be possible to evaluate the effects of various patient or setting variables on the efficacy of the different treatments, enabling even further tailoring of treatment to match specific patient (and perhaps therapist) characteristics. These developments suggest that the field is ready to move beyond the simple question of what works best; we may now begin to answer the more important question of what works best for whom. This shift in the questions we ask of our data should result in even more treatment effectiveness than is currently achieved.

Literature Cited

Abueg, F. R., Kriegler, J. A., Falcone, H., Dondershine, H. E., Gusman, F. D. 1989. Relapse prevention training with PTSD-alcoholics: a treatment outcome study with one-year follow-up. Symposium on comorbidity in traumatic stress disorders with special attention to substance abuse and dependence, presented at the Annu. Meet. Assoc. Adv. Behav. Ther., Washington, DC

Agras, W. S., Leitenberg, H., Barlow, D. H. 1968. Social reinforcement in the modification of agoraphobia. Arch. Gen. Psychiatr. 19:423–27

Alloy, L., Tabachnik, N. 1984. Assessment of covariation by humans and animals: the joint influence of prior expectations and current situational information. Psychol. Rev. 91:112–49

Bandura, A. 1977. Self-efficacy: toward a unifying theory of behavioral change. Psychol. Rev. 84:191–215

Bandura, A. 1984. Recycling misconceptions of perceived self-efficacy. Cognit. Ther. Res. 8:231–55

Bandura, A. 1986. Social Foundations of Thought and Action: A Social Cognitive Theory. Englewood Cliffs, NJ: Prentice-Hall

Barlow, D. H. 1988. Anxiety and Its Disorders: The Nature and Treatment of Anxiety and Panic. New York: Guilford

Barlow, D. H. (1991a). Disorders of emotion. Psychol. Inq. In press

Barlow, D. H. (1991b). Disorders of emotion: clarification, elaboration, and future directions. Psychol. Inq. In press

Barlow, D. H., Blanchard, E. B., Vermilyea, J. A., Vermilyea, B. B., Di Nardo, P. A. 1986. Generalized anxiety and generalized anxiety disorder: description and reconceptualization. Am. J. Psychol. 143:4–44

Barlow, D. H., Cohen, A. S., Waddell, M., Vermilyea, J. A., Klosko, et al. 1984a. Panic and generalized anxiety disorders: nature and treatment. Behav. Ther. 15:431–49

Barlow, D. H., O'Brien, G. T., Last, C. G. 1984b. Couples treatment of agoraphobia. Behav. Ther. 15:41–58

Barlow, D. H., Craske, M. G., Cerny, J. A., Klosko, J. S. 1989. Behavioral treatment of panic disorder. *Behav. Ther.* 20:261–82

Basoglu, M., Lax, T., Kasvikis, Y., Marks, I. M. 1988. Predictors of improvement in obsessive-compulsive disorder. *J. Anxiety Dis.* 2:299–317

Beck, A. T., Bourg, W. 1991. Obsessive-compulsive disorder in adults. In *Handbook of Behavior Therapy with Children and Adults: A Longitudinal Perspective,* ed. R. M. Ammerman, M. Hersen. New York: Pergamon. In press

Beck, A. T., Emery G. 1985. *Anxiety Disorders and Phobias: A Cognitive Perspective.* New York: Basic Books

Blowers, C., Cobb, J., Mathews, A. 1987. Generalized anxiety: a controlled treatment study. *Behav. Res. Ther.* 25:493–502

Borkovec, T. D., Grayson, J. B. 1980. Consequences of increasing the functional impact of internal emotional stimuli. In *Advances in the Study of Communication and Affects,* ed. K. Blankstein, P. Pliner, L. H. Polivey, 3:117–37. New York: Plenum

Borkovec, T. D., Mathews, A. M. 1988. Treatment of nonphobic anxiety disorders: a comparison of nondirective, cognitive, and coping desensitization therapy. *J. Consult. Clin. Psychol.* 56:877–84

Boudewyns, P. A., Hyer, L. 1990. Physiological response to combat memories and preliminary treatment outcome in Vietnam veteran PTSD patients treated with direct therapeutic exposure. *Behav. Ther.* 21:63–87

Bourque, P., Ladouceur, R. 1981. An investigation of various performance-based treatments with agoraphobics. *Behav. Res. Ther.* 18:161–70

Brennan, J. F., Riccio, D. C. 1975. Stimulus generalization of suppression in rats followed by aversively motivated instrumental or Pavlovian training. *J. Compar. Physiol. Psychol.* 88:570–79

Broadbent, D., Broadbent, M. 1988. Anxiety and attentional bias: state and trait. *Cognit. Emot.* 2:165–83

Brown, T. A., Abueg, F. R., Fairbank, J. A. 1991. Patterns of adjustment following exposure to extreme events: psychological aftermath of combat and sexual assault. In *Community Psychology and Mental Health,* ed. M. S. Gibbs, J. R. Lachenmeyer, J. Sigal. New York: Gardner. In press

Brown, T. A., Hertz, R. M., Barlow, D. H. 1992. New developments in cognitive-behavioral treatment of anxiety disorders. *Annu. Rev. Psychiatry.* In press

Butler, G. 1985. Exposure as a treatment for social phobia: some instructive difficulties. *Behav. Res. Ther.* 23:651–57

Butler, G., Cullington, A., Hibbert, G., Klimes, I., Gelder, M. 1987. Anxiety management for persistent generalized anxiety. *Br. J. Psychol.* 151:535–42

Butler, G., Fennell, M., Robson, P., Gelder, M. 1991. A comparison of behavior therapy and cognitive-behavior therapy in the treatment of generalized anxiety disorder. *J. Consult. Clin. Psychol.* In press

Butler, G., Mathews, A. 1983. Cognitive processes in anxiety. *Adv. Behav. Res. Ther.* 5:51–62

Canter, A., Kondo, C. Y., Knott, J. R. 1975. A comparison of EMG feedback and progressive muscle relaxation training in anxiety neurosis. *Br. J. Psychol.* 127:470–77

Chambless, D. L., Goldstein, A. A., Gallagher, R., Bright, P. 1986. Integrating behavior therapy and psychotherapy in the treatment of agoraphobia. *Psychother. Theor. Res. Prac.* 23:150–59

Christensen, H., Hadzi-Pavlovic, D., Andrews, G., Mattick, R. 1987. Behavior therapy and tricyclic medication in the treatment of obsessive-compulsive disorder: a quantitative review. *J. Consult. Clin. Psychol.* 55:701–11

Clark, D. M. 1988. A cognitive model of panic attacks. In *Panic: Psychological Perspectives,* ed. S. Rachman, J. D. Maser, pp. 71–89. Hillside, NJ: Erlbaum

Clark, D. M., Gelder, M. G., Salkovskis, P. M., Hackman, A., Middleton, H., et al. 1990. Cognitive therapy for panic: comparative efficacy. Presented at Annu. Meet. Am. Psychol. Assoc., New York

Clark, D. M., Salkovskis, P. M., Chalkey, A. J. 1985. Respiratory control as a treatment for panic attacks. *J. Behav. Ther. Exp. Psychol.* 16:23–30

Clark, L. A., Watson, D. 1991. A tripartite model of anxiety and depression: psychometric evidence and taxometric implications. *J. Abnorm. Psychol.* In press

Cook, M., Mineka, S., Trumble, D. 1987. The role of response-produced and exteroceptive feedback in the attenuation of fear over the course of avoidance learning. *J. Exp. Psychol.: Anim. Behav. Proc.* 13:239–49

Cooper, N. A., Clum, G. A. 1989. Imaginal flooding as a supplementary treatment for PTSD in combat veterans: a controlled study. *Behav. Ther.* 20:381–91

Craske, M. 1990. Phobic fear and panic attacks: the same or different? Rep. DSM-IV Workgroup on Simple Phobia

Craske, M. G., Barlow, D. H. 1991. *Mastery of Your Anxiety and Worry.* New York: Graywind Publications

Craske, M. G., Brown, T. A., Barlow, D. H. 1991. Behavioral treatment of panic: a two-year follow-up. *Behav. Ther.* In press

Desiderato, O., Newman, A. 1971. Conditioned suppression produced in rats by tones paired with escapable or inescapable shock. *J. Compar. Physiol. Psychol.* 77:427–31

Durham, R. C., Turvey, A. A. 1987. Cognitive therapy vs. behaviour therapy in the treatment of chronic general anxiety: outcome at discharge and at six-month follow-up. *Behav. Res. Ther.* 25:229–34

Ehlers, A., Margraf, J., Davies, S., Roth, W. T. 1988. Selective processing of threat cues in subjects with panic attacks. *Cognit. Emot.* 2:201–19

Emmelkamp, P. M. G. 1982. *Phobic and Obsessive-Compulsive Disorders: Theory, Research and Practice.* New York: Plenum

Eysenck, H. J., Eysenck, M. W. 1985. *Personality and Individual Differences: A Natural Science Approach.* New York: Plenum

Eysenck, M. W., MacLeod, C., Mathews, A. 1987. Cognitive functioning and anxiety. *Psychol. Res.* 49:189–95

Foa, E. B. 1989. Processing of rape-related information and post-traumatic stress disorder. Presented at the World Cong. Cognit. Ther., Oxford

Foa, E. B., Grayson, J. B., Steketee, G. 1982. Depression, habituation, and treatment outcome in obsessive-compulsives. In *Practical Applications of Learning Theories in Psychiatry,* ed. J. C. Boulougouris, pp. 129–42. New York: Wiley

Foa, E. B., Kozak, M. S. 1986. Emotional processing of fear: exposure to corrective information. *Psychol. Bull.* 99:20–35

Foa, E. B., Steketee, G. S., Ozarow, B. 1985. Behavior therapy with obsessive-compulsives: From theory to treatment. In *Obsessive-Compulsive Disorder: Psychological and Pharmacological Treatment,* ed. M. Mavissakalian. New York: Plenum

Fowles, D. C. 1986. The psychophysiology of anxiety and hedonic affect: motivational specificity. In *Anxiety disorders: Psychological and biological perspectives,* ed. B. F. Shaw, Z. V. Segal, T. M. Vallis, E. F. Cashman. New York: Plenum

Frank, E., Anderson, B., Stewart, B. D., Dancu, C., Hughes, C. et al. 1988. Efficacy of cognitive behavior therapy and systematic desensitization in the treatment of rape trauma. *Behav. Ther.* 19:403–20

Frankl, V. E. 1960. Paradoxical intention: a logotherapeutic technique. *Am. J. Psychother.* 14:520–35

Freud, S. 1919. Turnings in the ways of psycho-analytic therapy (transl. J. Riviere). Reprinted 1959 in *The Collected Papers of Sigmund Freud,* Vol. 2. New York: Basic Books

Fridlund, A. J., Hatfield, M. E., Cottam, G. L., Fowler, J. C. 1986. Anxiety and striate-muscle activation: evidence from electromyographic pattern analysis. *J. Abnorm. Psychol.* 95:228–36

Gray, J. A. 1982. *The Neuropsychology of Anxiety: An Enquiry into the Functions of the Septo-Hippocampal System.* New York: Oxford Univ. Press

Gray, J. A. 1991. Fear, panic and anxiety: What's in a name? *Psychol. Inq.* In press

Grayson, J. B., Foa, E. B., Steketee, G. 1982. Habituation during exposure treatment: distraction versus attention-focusing. *Behav. Res. Ther.* 20:323–28

Grossberg, S. 1982. Processing of expected and unexpected events during conditioning and attention: a psychophysiological theory. *Psychol. Rev.* 89:529–72

Haslam, M. T. 1974. The relationship between the effect of lactate infusion on anxiety states and their amelioration by carbon dioxide inhalation. *Br. J. Psychol.* 51:171–82

Heimberg, R. G. 1989. Cognitive and behavioral treatments for social phobia: a critical analysis. *Clin. Psychol. Rev.* 9:107–28

Heimberg, R. G., Dodge, C. S., Hope, D. A., Kennedy, C. R., Zollo, L. J., et al 1990. Cognitive-behavioral group treatment for social phobia: comparison with a credible placebo control. *Cognit. Ther. Res.* 14:1–23

Himle, J. A., McPhee, K., Cameron, O. G., Curtis, G. C. 1989. Simple phobia: evidence for heterogeneity. *Psychol. Res.* 28:25–30

Hope, D. A., Rapee, R. M., Heimberg, R. G., Dombeck, M. 1990. Representations of the self in social phobia: vulnerability to social threat. *Cognit. Ther. Res.* 14:177–89

Katon, W., Roy-Byrne, P. 1989. Mixed anxiety and depression. Rep. DSM-IV Subgroup on GAD and Mixed Anxiety Depression

Keane, T. M., Fairbank, J. A., Caddell, J. M., Zimering, R. T. 1989. Implosive (flooding) therapy reduces symptoms of PTSD in Vietnam combat veterans. *Behav. Ther.* 20:245–60

Keane, T. M., Gerardi, R. J., Quinn, S. J., Litz, B. T. 1991. Behavioral treatment of post-traumatic stress disorder. In *Handbook of Behavior Therapy,* ed. S. M. Turner, K. S. Calhoun, H. E. Adams. New York: Wiley. 2nd ed. In press

Kendall, P. C., Watson, D., eds. 1989. *Anxiety and Depression: Distinctive and Overlapping Features.* New York: Academic

Klein, D. G., Zitrin, C. M., Woerner, M. G., Ross, D. C. 1983. Behavior therapy and supportive psychotherapy: Are there any specific ingredients? *Arch. Gen. Psychiatr.* 40:139–53

Kleinknecht, R. A., Lenz, J. 1989. Blood/

injury fear, fainting, and avoidance of medically related situations: a family correspondence study. *Behav. Res. Ther.* 27:537–47

Klosko, J. S., Barlow, D. H., Tassinari, R., Cerny, J. A. 1990. A comparison of alprazolam and behavior therapy in treatment of panic disorder. *J. Consult. Clin. Psychol.* 58:77–84

Lang, P. J. 1977. Imagery in therapy: an information processing analysis of fear. *Behav. Ther.* 8:862–86

Lang, P. J. 1985. The cognitive psychophysiology of emotion: fear and anxiety. See Tuma & Maser 1985, pp. 131–70

Leckman, J. F., Weissman, M. M., Merikangas, K. R., Pauls, D. L., Prusoff, B. A. 1983. Panic disorder and major depression. *Arch. Gen. Psychiatr.* 40:1055–60

Leitenberg, H., Agras, W. S., Edwards, J. A., Thompson, L. E., Wincze, J. 1970. Practice as a psychotherapeutic variable: an experimental analysis within single cases. *J. Psychol. Res.* 7:215–25

Levenson, M. R., Aldwin, C. M., Bosse, R., Spiro, A. 1988. Emotionality and mental health: longitudinal findings from the normative aging study. *J. Abnorm. Psychol.* 97:94–96

Levin, A. P., Schneier, F. R., Liebowitz, M. R. 1989. Social phobia: biology and pharmacology. *Clin. Psychol. Rev.* 9:129–40

Linden, W. 1981. Exposure treatments for focal phobias. *Arch. Gen. Psychiatr.* 38:769–75

Mackintosh, N. 1975. A theory of attention: variation in the associability of stimuli with reinforcement. *Psychol. Rev.* 82:276–98

MacLeod, C., Mathews, A. 1988. Anxiety and the allocation of attention to threat. *Q. J. Exp. Psychol.* 40A:653–70

MacLeod, C., Mathews, A., Tata, P. 1986. Attentional bias in emotional disorders. *J. Abnorm. Psychol.* 95:15–20

MacLeod, C., Rutherford, E. M. 1990. Anxiety and the selective processing of emotional information: mediating roles of awareness, trait and state variables, and personal relevance of stimulus materials. Presented at the Annu. Meet. Assoc. Adv. Behav. Ther., 24th, San Francisco

Maier, S. F., Seligman, M. E. P. 1976. Learned helplessness: theory and evidence. *J. Exp. Psychol.: Gen.* 105:3–46

Marks, I. M., Lelliott, Basoglu, M., Noshirvani, H., Monteiro, W., et al. 1988. Clomipramine, self-exposure, and therapist-aided exposure for obsessive-compulsive rituals. *Br. J. Psychol.* 152:522–34

Marlatt, G. A., Gordon, J. R., eds. 1985. *Relapse Prevention.* New York: Guilford

Mathews, A., MacLeod, C. 1985. Selective

processing of threat cues in anxiety states. *Behav. Res. Ther.* 23:563–69

Mathews, A., MacLeod, C. 1986. Discrimination of threat cues without awareness in anxiety states. *J. Abnorm. Psychol.* 95:131–38

Mathews, A. M., Gelder, M. G., Johnston, D. W. 1981. *Agoraphobia: Nature and Treatment.* New York: Guilford

Mathews, A. M., Johnston, D. W., Lancashire, M., Munby, M., Shaw, P. N., et al. 1976. Imaginal flooding and exposure to real phobic situations: treatment outcome with agoraphobic patients. *Br. J. Psychol.* 129:362–71

Mathews, A., Mogg, K., May, J., Eysenck, M. 1989a. Implicit and explicit memory bias in anxiety. *J. Abnorm. Psychol.* 98:236–40

Mathews, A., Richards, A., Eysenck, M. 1989b. Interpretation of homophones related to threat in anxiety states. *J. Abnorm. Psychol.* 98:31–34

Mattick, R. P., Peters, L. 1988. Treatment of severe social phobia: effects of guided exposure with and without cognitive restructuring. *J. Consult. Clin. Psychol.* 56:251–60

Mattick, R. P., Peters, L., Clarke, J. C. 1989. Exposure and cognitive restructuring for social phobia: a controlled study. *Behav. Ther.* 20:3–23

Mavissakalian, M., Barlow, D. H. 1981. *Phobia: Psychological and Pharmacological Treatment.* New York: Guilford

Mavissakalian, M., Michelson, L. 1986. Agoraphobia: relative and combined effectiveness of therapist-assisted in vivo exposure and imipramine. *J. Clin. Psychol.* 47:117–22

McNally, R. J., Foa, E. B. 1987. Cognition and agoraphobia: bias in the interpretation of threat. *Cognit. Ther. Res.* 11:567–81

McNally, R. J., Kaspi, S. P., Riemann, B. C., Zeitlin, S. B. 1990a. Selective processing of threat cues in posttraumatic stress disorder. *J. Abnorm. Psychol.* 99:398–402

McNally, R., Rieman, B., Kim, E. 1990b. Selective processing of threat cues in panic disorder. *Behav. Res. Ther.* 28:407–12

Michelson, L., Marchione, K., Greenwald, M., Glanz, L., Testa, S., et al. 1990. Panic disorder: cognitive-behavioral treatment. *Behav. Res. Ther.* 28:141–51

Mineka, S. 1985. Animal models of anxiety disorders: their usefulness and limitations. See Tuma & Maser 1985, pp. 199–244

Mineka, S., Cook, M., Miller, S. 1984. Fear conditioned with escapable and inescapable shock: the effects of a feedback stimulus. *J. Exp. Psychol.: Anim. Behav. Proc.* 10:307–23

Mineka, S., Henderson, R. 1985. Controllability and predictability in acquired motivation. *Annu. Rev. Psychol.* 87:256–71

Mineka, S., Kihlstrom, J. 1978. Unpredictable and uncontrollable aversive events. *J. Abnorm. Psychol.* 87:256–71

Mineka, S., Zinbarg, R. 1991. Animal models of psychopathology. In *Clinical Psychology: Historical and Research Foundations,* ed. C. E. Walker, pp. 51–86. New York: Plenum

Minor, T., Dess, N., Overmier, J. B. 1989. Inverting the traditional view of "learned helplessness": a reinterpretation in terms of anxiety and modulator operations. In *Aversive Events and Behavior,* ed. M. R. Denny. Hillsdale, NJ: Erlbaum

Mogg, K., Mathews, A., Bird, C., Macgregor-Morris, R. 1990. Effects of stress and anxiety on the processing of threat stimuli. *J. Per. Soc. Psychol.* 59:1230–37

Mogg, K., Mathews, A., Weinman, J. 1987. Memory bias in clinical anxiety. *J. Abnorm. Psychol.* 96:94–98

Mogg, K., Mathews, A., Weinman, J. 1989. Selective processing of threat cues in anxiety states: a replication. *Behav. Res. Ther.* 27:317–23

Munjack, D. J. 1984. The onset of driving phobias. *J. Behav. Ther. Exp. Psychol.* 15:305–8

Osborne, F. H., Mattingly, B. A., Redmon, W. K., Osborne, J. S. 1975. Background stimuli and the inter-stimulus interval during Pavlovian conditioning. *Q. J. Exp. Psychol.* 27:387–92

Öst, L. G. 1978. Fading vs. systematic desensitization in the treatment of snake and spider phobia. *Behav. Res. Ther.* 16:379–89

Öst, L. G. 1987. Age of onset of different phobias. *J. Abnorm. Psychol.* 96:223–29

Öst, L. G. 1988. Applied relaxation in the treatment of panic disorder. *Behav. Res. Ther.* 26:13–22

Öst, L. G. 1989. One-session treatment for specific phobias. *Behav. Res. Ther.* 27:1–7

Öst, L. G., Sterner, U. 1987. Applied tension: a specific behavioral method for treatment of blood phobia. *Behav. Res. Ther.* 25:25–29

Öst, L. G., Sterner, U., Fellenius, J. 1989. Applied tension, applied relaxation, and the combination in the treatment of blood phobia. *Behav. Res. Ther.* 27:109–21

Öst, L. G., Sterner, U., Lindahl, I. L. 1984. Physiological responses in blood phobics. *Behav. Res. Ther.* 22:109–17

Puig-Antich, J., Rabinovitch, H. 1986. Relationship between affective and anxiety disorders in childhood. In *Anxiety Disorders of Childhood,* ed. R. Gittelman. New York: Guilford

Rachman, S. J. 1980. Emotional processing. *Behav. Res. Ther.* 18:51–60

Rachman, S. 1991. Disorders of emotion: a critique. *Psychol. Inq.* In press

Rachman, S. J., Craske, M., Tallman, K., Solyom, C. 1986. Does escape behavior strengthen agoraphobic avoidance? A replication. *Behav. Ther.* 17:467–78

Rapee, R. M. 1985. A case of panic disorder treated with breathing retraining. *J. Behav. Ther. Exp. Psychol.* 16:63–65

Rapee, R. M. 1991. The conceptual overlap between cognition and conditioning in clinical psychology. *Clin. Psychol. Rev.* 11: 193–203

Rapee, R. M., Barlow, D. H., eds. 1991. *Chronic Anxiety, Generalized Anxiety Disorder, and Mixed Anxiety Depression.* New York: Guilford. In press

Rapee, R., M.,Mattick, R., Murrell, E. 1986. Cognitive mediation in the affective component of spontaneous panic attacks. *J. Behav. Ther. Exp. Psychol.* 17:245–53

Raskin, M., Bali, L. R., Peeke, H. V. 1980. Muscle biofeedback and transcendental meditation. *Arch. Gen. Psychiatr.* 37:309–19

Reiss, S. 1980. Pavlovian conditioning and human fear: an expectancy model. *Behav. Ther.* 11:380–96

Rescorla, R., Wagner, A. 1972. A theory of Pavlovian conditioning: variations in the effectiveness of reinforcement and nonreinforcement. In *Classical Conditioning II: Current Research and Theory,* ed. A. H. Black, W. F. Prokasy, pp. 64–99. New York: Appleton-Century-Crofts

Resick, P. A., Jordan, C. G., Girelli, S. A., Hutter, C. K., Marhoefer-Dvorak, S. 1988. A comparative outcome study of behavioral group therapy for sexual assault victims. *Behav. Ther.* 19:385–401

Rush, D. K., Mineka, S., Suomi, S. J. 1982. The effects of control and lack of control on active and passive avoidance in rhesus monkeys. *Behav. Res. Ther.* 20:135–52

Salkovskis, P. M., Jones, D. R. O., Clark, D. M. 1986. Respiratory control in the treatment of panic attacks: replication and extension with concurrent measurement of behavior and pCO_2. *Br. J. Psychol.* 148:526–32

Salkovskis, P. M., Westbrook, D. 1989. Behavior therapy and obsessional ruminations: Can failure be turned into success? *Behav. Res. Ther.* 27:149–60

Sanderson, W. C., Rapee, R. M., Barlow, D. H. 1988. The influence of an illusion of control on panic attacks induced via inhalation of 5.5% CO_2 enriched air. *Arch. Gen. Psychiatr.* 46:157–64

Sartory, G., Rachman, S., Grey, S. J. 1982.

Return of fear: the role of rehearsal. *Behav. Res. Ther.* 20:123–33

Seligman, M. E. P. 1975. *Helplessness: On Depression, Development and Death.* San Francisco: W. H. Freeman

Seligman, M. E. P., Johnston, J. 1973. A cognitive theory of avoidance learning. In *Contemporary Approaches to Conditioning and Learning.* New York: Wiley

Sokol, L., Beck, A. T., Clark, D. A. 1989. A controlled treatment trial of cognitive therapy for panic disorder. Presented at the World Cong. Cognit. Ther., Oxford, England

Starr, M. D., Mineka, S. 1977. Determinants of fear over the course of avoidance learning. *Learn. Motiv.* 8:3332–50

Steketee, G. S., Foa, E. B., Grayson, J. B. 1982. Recent advances in the behavioral treatment of obsessive-compulsives. *Arch. Gen. Psychiatr.* 39:1365–71

Stroop, J. R. 1938. Factors affecting speed in serial verbal reactions. *Psychol. Monogr.* 50:38–48

Telch, M. J., Agras, W. S., Taylor, C. B., Roth, W. T., Gallen, C. C. 1985. Combined pharmacological and behavioral treatment for agoraphobia. *Behav. Res. Ther.* 23:325–35

Tellegen, A. 1985. Structures of mood and personality and their relevance to assessing anxiety, with an emphasis on self-report. See Tuma & Maser 1985a, pp. 681–706

Tellegen, A., Lykken, D. T., Bouchard, T. J., Wilcox, K. J., Segal, N. L., et al. 1988. Personality similarity in twins reared apart and together. *J. Per. Soc. Psychol.* 54:1031–39

Tuma, A. H., Maser, J. D. eds. 1985. *Anxiety and the Anxiety Disorders.* Hillsdale, NJ: Erlbaum

Wagner, A. 1978. Expectancies and the priming of STM. In *Cognitive Processes in Animal Behavior.*, ed. S. H. Hulse, H. Fowler, W. K. Honig, pp. 177–209. Hillside, NJ: Erlbaum

Wagner, A. 1981. SOP: a model of automatic memory processing in animal behavior. In *Information Processing in Animals: Memory Mechanisms,* ed. N. E. Spear, R. R. Miller, pp. 5–47. Hillside, NJ: Erlbaum

Watson, D., Clark, L. A. 1991. Self- versus peer ratings of specific emotional traits: evidence of convergent and discriminant validity. *J. Pers. Soc. Psychol.* 60:927–40

Watson, D., Tellegen, A. 1985. Toward a consensual structure of mood. *Psychol. Bull.* 98:219–35

Watts, F. N., MacKenna, F. P., Sharrock, R., Trezise, L. 1986a. Color naming of phobia-related words. *Br. J. Psychol.* 77:97–108

Watts, F. N., Trezise, L., Sharrock, R. 1986b. Processing of phobic stimuli. *Br. J. Clin. Psychol.* 25:253–59

Weissman, M. M. 1985. The epidemiology of anxiety disorders: rates, risks and familial patterns. See Tuma & Maser 1985, 275–96

Zarate, R., Craske, M. G., Rapee, R. M., Barlow, D. H. 1989. The effectiveness of interoceptive exposure in the treatment of simple phobia. Presented at the Annu. Meet. Assoc. Adv. Behav. Ther., Washington, DC

Zevon, M. A., Tellegen, A. 1982. The structure of mood change: idiographic/nomothetic analysis. *J. Pers. Soc. Psychol.* 43:111–22

Zinbarg, R. E. 1990. Animal research and behavior therapy, part I: Behavior therapy is not what you think it is. *Behav. Ther.* 13:171–75

Zinbarg, R. E., Barlow, D. H. 1991. Mixed anxiety depression: a new diagnostic category? See Rapee & Barlow 1991

Zinbarg, R. E., Mineka, S. 1991. Animal models of psychopathology: II. Simple phobia. *Behav. Ther.* 14:61–65

Zinbarg, R., Revelle, W. 1989. Personality and conditioning: a test of four models. *J. Pers. Soc. Psychol.* 57:301–14

Annu. Rev. Psychol. 1992. 43:269–302

PSYCHOLOGICAL DIMENSIONS OF GLOBAL ENVIRONMENTAL CHANGE

Paul C. Stern

Commission on Behavioral and Social Sciences and Education, National Research Council, 2101 Constitution Avenue, NW, Washington, DC 20418

KEY WORDS: conservation, pollution, energy consumption, energy conservation, natural resource conservation

CONTENTS

In recent years, scientists have come to realize that human activities are changing the natural environment on a global scale. By such actions as burning fossil fuels, clearing great forests, manufacturing and consuming chemical products, and farming marginal lands, all at unprecedented rates, humans are changing the very face of the earth and modifying the natural cycles of water, minerals, and nutrients, and the ecological relationships among living things (Turner et al 1991a). Human action is causing many

0066-4308/92/0201-0269$02.00

global environmental changes at once. It is changing the earth's radiative balance, thus altering its climate (the so-called global warming phenomenon; Schneider 1989); causing species extinctions at a rate 10,000 times as fast as in the period before the emergence of humans (Wilson 1988); damaging the ozone layer that shields living things from harmful ultraviolet radiation (Silver & DeFries 1990); polluting the oceans with oil, heavy metals, fertilizers, and trash (la Riviere 1989); and making other alterations in the earth's life support systems, some known, some suspected, and probably others yet unrecognized. This review examines the contributions that psychological research has made and might make to understanding the human behavior that has these effects and to understanding—and possibly changing—the ways humans respond in the face of potential environmental disaster.

WHAT IS GLOBAL ENVIRONMENTAL CHANGE?

Environmental changes are called "global" when their impacts cannot be localized. This attribute differentiates global change from the more familiar, localized environmental problems, such as waste disposal, pollution of rivers and local airsheds, or loss of wilderness areas to agricultural or industrial development. Human activities can have global environmental effects in two ways. They can alter systems that flow throughout the earth, such as the oceans or atmosphere. Or, an accretion of localized changes can become global cumulatively, such as when the deforestation of areas that provide habitat for large numbers of species results in the extinction of a considerable proportion of all the species on earth (for further exposition of the concepts of systemic and cumulative global change, see Turner et al 1991b).

Over the past decade, natural scientists have become concerned about global environmental change because of its unprecedented rate. Life did not evolve in such a rapidly changing environment, so no one knows which species or ecosystems can survive in one. The Ice Ages, for example, advanced and retreated over millennia. By contrast, methane concentration in the atmosphere has doubled in the past century, and chlorofluorocarbons (CFCs), which together accounted for one quarter of the anthropogenic contribution to the "greenhouse effect" in the 1980s, were not present in the atmosphere before the 1930s (Houghton et al 1990). Changes this rapid in the earth's atmosphere can alter climate much more rapidly than during the Ice Ages. Over only the next few centuries accumulation of carbon dioxide, methane, CFCs, and other greenhouse gases may raise temperatures sufficiently to melt glaciers and crack icecaps, thereby raising sea levels worldwide and threatening the capacity of some plants and animals to survive in a rapidly changing biosphere (Warrick & Oerlemans 1990).

Particularly worrisome is the long time lag inherent in many processes of environmental change. Many of the chlorofluorocarbons that deplete stratospheric ozone continue to do so for many decades after they are released by human action. With such long lags, global changes may be impossible to control once they get started; by the time a catastrophe is foreseen, it may already be too late to prevent it. Humanity is conducting a grand experiment on its natural environment, and cannot afford to fail. We have only one earth on which to experiment.

Psychology is relevant to global environmental change because the current changes are largely anthropogenic in origin. No longer do large-scale environmental changes result from forces beyond human control. Instead, it is human behavior itself that must be controlled to ameliorate or redirect global change.

Scientists have embarked on a serious international, interdisciplinary effort to understand global environmental change. The International Geosphere-Biosphere Programme is a multinational effort coordinating global-change research around the world. Its main focus is on climate change—the so-called global warming phenomenon—but it includes attention to other global environmental processes, such as depletion of stratospheric ozone and loss of biological diversity. Its goal is to gain understanding of how the global environment works, in the hope that by understanding the processes, humans can take action to protect ourselves and the natural phenomena we value from irreparable damage. The United States has played a leading role in research. The US Global Change Research Program (USGCRP) budget approached \$1 billion in fiscal 1991, and \$1.2 billion in expenditures were proposed for 1992. The money is being spent to monitor change in the earth's biogeochemical cycles with space-based and ground-based measurement, study the processes involved, and model climatic processes. A much smaller US research effort, called Mitigation and Adaptation Research Strategies, has been proposed to coordinate federal government research aimed at developing techniques and practices that could either slow the pace of global change or improve society's ability to cope with it.

The Place of Psychology

The scientific effort began among atmospheric chemists, ecologists, and other natural scientists whose expertise was relevant to understanding changes in the earth, oceans, atmosphere, and biosphere. Early on, however, broad-thinking natural scientists realized that because of the anthropogenic nature of current global change, social and behavioral science expertise would be necessary both to understand the causes and to bring about the changes in human behavior necessary to forestall, slow, or respond to global change. The National Research Council's Committee on Global Change Research, which advises the government concerning its program, has consistently recommended an increased effort to understand human interactions with the global environment (National Research Council 1988, 1990). In the 1991 budget, the USGCRP included Human Interactions as one of its seven program elements, funded at $28 million.

The current chapter defines a place for psychology in research on global change, mitigation, and adaptation; reviews relevant existing knowledge; and identifies key research opportunities for the next 5–10 years. In my conceptualization of the issue, I draw heavily on the work of the National Research Council's Committee on the Human Dimensions of Global Change (Stern et al 1991).

It is useful to imagine the relationship between human interaction and the global environment in terms of the schematic diagram in Figure 1. People affect the global environment through a subset of activities that directly alter significant environmental conditions: global flows of water and nutrients, atmospheric gases and particulates, the stability of ecosystems, and so forth. These activities are proximate causes of global change. The global environment affects people through a subset of events that directly change things people value: the viability of food crops, the frequency of storms and droughts, the incidence of disease, the survival of endangered species, and so forth. These events are proximate effects of global change. The role of social and behavioral science in the global-change research agenda is to improve understanding of how human systems produce the proximate causes, how changes in human systems might change the rate at which people alter the environment, how people perceive changes in the global environment, how people respond to the anticipation of global environmental change and are affected by experienced change, and how changes in human systems might make people less susceptible to the effects of global environmental change. The role of psychology is to improve understanding of the function of individual and interpersonal behavior in all these human-environment relationships. Over the past decade several efforts have been made to sketch research agendas for the human dimensions of global change (Chen et al 1983; Kates et al 1985; Stern et al 1991), including some focused on the possible contributions of psychology (Fischhoff & Furby 1983; Sjöberg 1989).

Psychological research may be relevant at three levels of generality. Basic research may yield relevant theory, concepts, or hypotheses; research on human-environment relations below the global level may refine theory and generate important conditional generalizations; and research on human-environment relations at the global level can yield directly applicable knowledge. The current review draws on concepts from basic psychological research, including attitude theory, the theory of social dilemmas, applied behavior analysis, the theory of altruistic behavior, and the cognitive psychology of judgment and choice, as applied to the study of environmentally

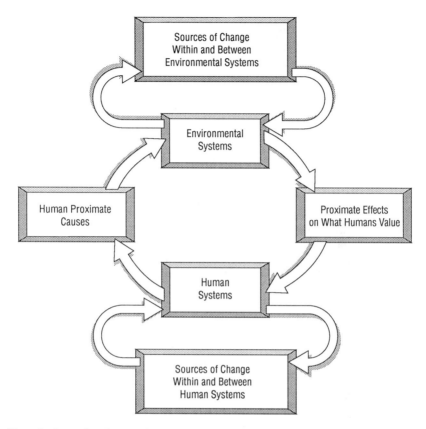

Figure 1 Interactions between human and environmental systems. Source: Stern et al 1991

relevant attitudes, beliefs, and actions. Most of the research concerns human interactions with local environmental problems, although some, such as on energy conservation, concerns human activities that affect the global environment as a system.

I focus here first on research on the human causes of global environmental changes, including broad assessments of environmental attitudes and behavior, and research on specific human activities, such as energy use and conservation or participation in environmental movement organizations, through which individuals can participate in causing or altering the causes of global change. I then examine research on the ways people may perceive, respond to, or be affected by global environmental changes, including studies of interventions to change behavior and of the psychological aspects of environmental activism and conflict. I only cover studies focused narrowly on local environmental issues, such as littering, recycling behavior, and behavior in relation to toxic waste or nuclear energy facilities when the issues they raise seem likely to apply to global as well as local environmental problems. Owing primarily to space limitations, I also exclude studies of fertility decisions and other population-related behavior, in spite of their obvious relevance to the global environment. I emphasize recent research; reviews of earlier work are available (e.g. Geller et al 1982; Stern & Oskamp 1987; Geller 1987; Katzev & Johnson 1987). Finally, the review is restricted to research from Western industrialized countries.

THE HUMAN CAUSES OF GLOBAL CHANGE

Each type of anthropogenic global change has distinctive causes. Analysis of the place of psychological research must begin by identifying the human behaviors that are the most potent proximate causes of whatever type of global change is under investigation.

Identifying the Important Proximate Causes

In the past, psychologists have often tended to study what their theories, methods, or intuition suggested rather than the behaviors with the greatest environmental impact. For example, much of the early psychological research on energy use, air pollution, and solid-waste generation focused on the daily behaviors of individuals, even though investment decisions by households and corporations generally have much greater impact on the environment (Stern & Gardner 1981a,b).

An analysis of global climate change illustrates a way to identify high-impact behaviors (see Stern et al 1991). The human effect on climate depends largely on releasing gases that alter the ability of the atmosphere to transmit and reflect infrared radiation, and thus change the heat balance of earth. The most important radiatively active gases, in terms of their current contributions to the total anthropogenic global warming effect during the 1980s, are carbon dioxide (55%), chlorofluorocarbons (25%), methane (11%), and nitrous oxide (6%) (their relative contributions in the future are likely to be somewhat different owing to chemical reactions in the atmosphere) (Shine et al 1990). Thus, the activities that do the most to release these greenhouse gases are the most important proximate human causes of climate change.

Table 1 identifies these activities. The impact of each activity is roughly equal to its contribution of each greenhouse gas times the gas's effect on the earth's radiative balance. The table clearly shows fossil energy use to be the single largest contributor of greenhouse gases, with several other activities significantly implicated.

Fossil fuel burning is so important that it is worthy of more detailed behavioral analysis to clarify the key actors and their purposes. For example,

Table 1 Estimated Composite Relative Contributions of Human Activities to Global Warming, 1980s

Activity	Gases (Percent of total anthropogenic contribution)					
	CO_2	CH_4	CFCs	N_2O	Other	Total
Fossil fuel use	42	3		1.5		46.5
CFC use			25			25
Biomass burn	13	1		1		15
Paddy rice		3				3
Cattle		3				3
Nitrogen fertilization				2		2
Landfills		1				1
Other				1.5	4	5.5
Total	55	11	25	6	4	101

These estimates are of "radiative forcing" by greenhouse gases, that is, the change they produce in the earth's radiative balance that in turn changes global temperature and climate. Radiative forcing is calculated from current gas concentrations in the atmosphere, which include gases remaining in the atmosphere from all emissions since the beginning of the industrial era, set here at 1765. It is not identical to the "global warming potential" of gasses emitted by human activity, a property that integrates the effects of gas emissions over future time. Global warming potential is affected by the different rates of breakdown of greenhouse gasses and chemical conversion of some radiationally inactive compounds into greenhouse gases over time, so that global warming potential depends on the future date to which effects are estimated. The global warming potential of currently emitted gasses is quite uncertain due to incomplete knowledge of the relevant atmospheric chemistry. An early estimate of the 100-year global warming potential of gas emissions in 1990 allocates it as follows: CO_2, 61%; CH_4, 15%; CFCs, 12%; N_2O, 4%; other gases (NO_x, non-methane hydrocarbons, carbon monoxide), 8% (Shine et al, 1990). Although these estimates differ from the radiative forcing estimates in the table, the differences are not great in terms of the relative importance of the gases for the global warming phenomenon. My analysis uses the estimates of radiative forcing because they are far less uncertain.

Source: Stern et al 1991; data from Shine et al 1990.

it may be subdivided by type of user (residences, industries, etc), purpose (transportation, space heating, etc), or type of decision determining the activity (e.g. design vs purchase vs utilization of equipment). The most important subclasses call for more detailed subdivision and study. Fuel consumption for personal transportation, for example, accounts for over 20% of US carbon dioxide emissions (US Congress 1991). It can be further analyzed as the product of number of automobiles, average fuel efficiency of automobiles, and miles driven per automobile. Such analysis can tell the relative importance of each behavior that might become a target of research. For example, a single class of behavior in one country—automobile purchase decisions in the United States—has a noticeable effect on the global climate: If the fuel efficiency of the US passenger vehicle fleet were to double—a technically and politically realistic possibility—worldwide carbon dioxide emissions would fall by about 2.5% (calculation based on US Congress 1991).

Conducting this sort of analysis enables a psychologist to direct research attention to behaviors that can produce important environmental effects. For maximal practical importance, the analysis and research effort should be detailed in proportion to the potential impact of the behavior to be studied—in terms of the tree-structured representation of Figure 2, in proportion to the thickness of the branches.

The behaviors responsible for global warming have been specified better than those implicated in other global changes. For example, ozone depletion is caused, so far as currently known, mainly by the release of a number of synthetically produced, halogenated hydrocarbon gases, including CFCs. At present, these compounds are used mainly in refrigeration and air-conditioning, electronics production, foam packaging, and as industrial solvents. The effects of each gas on the ozone layer can be estimated, and the current uses of each gas can be learned from sales figures. Therefore, it is possible to analyze in some detail the effects of past behavior on the ozone layer. However, because new uses and substitutes for ozone-depleting gases are continually being found and the environmental effects of many substitutes are yet unknown, it is difficult to know which future behaviors will have the greatest effect. For another example, species extinction is believed to occur most rapidly where the concentration of species is greatest, namely in moist tropical forests. Thus, the main human activities responsible are those resulting in the loss of these tropical habitats. They include ranching, lumbering, and fuelwood gathering, but the relative importance of these activities varies greatly from one tropical forest to another.

Explaining the Proximate Causes

It is easier to identify the major proximate causes of global change than to explain them. They result from a complex of so-called driving forces, including population growth, economic growth, technological change, political-economic institutions, and values and attitudes. The roles of these forces are difficult to determine, however, because different disciplines offer expertise on different driving forces and because forces operate in combination and in interaction, rather than additively (Stern et al 1991). For example, the impact of economic growth on climate change depends on consumer values. If people use their increased income on travel or indoor climate control, they release more greenhouse gases than if they buy more personal services. Therefore, when materialist values are strong, higher income may be more harmful to the environment than when other values predominate. But a shift to "postmaterialist" values may do little to halt damage to the global environment if economic conditions, government policies, and technological limitations make it difficult to convert attitudes into action. In the United States of the 1990s, for example, people who might prefer to travel by foot or bicycle usually find themselves constrained to use automobiles.

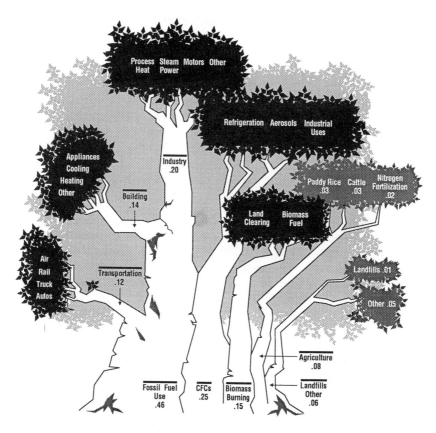

Figure 2   A representation of relative contributions of human activities in the late 1980s to global warming. Source: Stern et al 1991

To understand how the driving forces work, the relevant disciplines must listen to each other. Psychology has something to say about each of the driving forces of global change, but it can do little by itself to illuminate or modify the proximate causes. It is central to understanding values and attitudes, and also relevant to population growth (fertility behavior), economic growth (saving and investment behavior), technological change (diffusion of innovation through social networks), and political-economic institutions (compliance with laws; public support for environmental policies). But because of the interactions among the driving forces, psychologists must determine how psychological variables fit among the many other causal factors of anthropogenic global change if their concepts are to be used effectively.

LEVELS OF ORGANIZATION   The human actions that drive global change are only partly the acts of individuals. Not only individuals, but firms, communities, governments, and international organizations make relatively autonomous choices about how energy and land are used and CFCs are produced. Individual choices account for a minority of the proximate causes of global change. Of US energy, for example, only about one third is consumed directly by households, and two thirds by commercial, industrial, and governmental organizations. Consequently, the study of consumer behavior— that is, individual choices affecting resource use—can yield only partial knowledge about the causes of global change. Psychologists can contribute by learning what determines individual resource use and also by studying how individual actions influence resource choices made by organizations and governments.

TYPES OF BEHAVIOR   Researchers concerned with energy conservation and other environmentally relevant behavior distinguish among investment decisions, management, and daily operation of the buildings and equipment that consume fossil fuels—for example, among purchasing an energy-efficient furnace, keeping it running efficiently, and setting the level of heat it produces (Kempton et al 1992). These types of behavior are different along many dimensions: the amount of time involved, the amount of money, the ease with which one can know the effects of one's behavior, and the amount of difference each action can make in energy use. Generally, the decisions with the greatest long-term impact are purchase decisions, because they have a continuing effect for the life of the equipment (Stern & Gardner 1981a). One-time and repeated behaviors may need to be investigated with different methods, and they appear to have different determinants (see below).

ACTION AND CONTEXT   It is useful to think of other driving forces as creating the context for individual behavior. For example, the purchase of automobiles depends on the price of gasoline, government emissions regulations, and the marketing strategies of manufacturers, as well as the preferences of the purchasers. Some of these contextual influences can have more effect than any choice at the individual level. The decision by the US government to require automobile manufacturers to achieve a certain average fuel economy among their products is a good case in point. Because contextual factors are so important, psychologists must be interdisciplinary even in explaining individual behavior. But context also opens a major research opportunity for psychologists. They can explore the role of individuals in influencing the policy context of resource-using behavior: the enactment and implementation of environmental policies and programs.

TIME SCALES   Global environmental change is a process that operates on the time scale of decades to centuries. Consequently, to understand the driving forces, it may be useful for psychologists to give special consideration to behavioral processes that operate, or change, on that time scale. Among the behavioral variables that may affect the global environment and that operate on that scale are the socialization of attitudes; fertility decisions; and the purchase of buildings, vehicles, and major household appliances.

Areas of Psychological Research

Three main areas of psychological research can significantly illuminate the causes of global environmental change: the study of environmental attitudes; the analysis of individual actions that, in aggregate, have a high impact on important global changes; and the study of individual effects on collective action, including organizational resource consumption and policies that set the context for resource use.

ENVIRONMENTAL ATTITUDES   Attitudes are likely to affect behavior when other factors do not constrain their expression. Consequently, environmental attitudes can influence global change by affecting individual consumer and political behavior; they are less likely to influence organizational behavior, because role demands typically dominate the expression of individual attitudes. A decade ago, Heberlein (1981) concluded that research on environmental attitudes had not been cumulative, and this remains true for the most part today. Nevertheless, an assessment of the research can prepare the ground for conceptual and methodological progress.

The nature of environmental attitudes   Concern about the environment, as measured by the single-item indicators typically used in public opinion polls, has remained at a high level in the US population for two decades (Dunlap 1985, 1991). However, the nature and structure of these attitudes are not yet well understood. It is still unclear, for instance, whether environmental attitudes are one thing or many. The statement that "there is some evidence for a construct of general environmental attitudes" (Stern & Oskamp 1987:1051) is still as strong a conclusion as can be justified. It reflects the evidence that attitudes about pollution, resource use, and environmental regulation (but not population) share significant common variance (Van Liere & Dunlap 1981). Although one of the early general-attitude scales is probably the most frequently used (e.g. Dunlap & Van Liere 1978), no measuring instrument has emerged as standard in the field.

The anarchy of measurement reflects theoretical ambiguity about the nature of environmental concern. At least four concepts can be found—often conflated—in the literature and the measuring instruments. In one concept, environmental concern reflects a new way of thinking—an ecological awareness or New Environmental Paradigm (NEP) that some investigators claim is replacing the older, anthropocentric Human Exceptionalism Paradigm in people's thinking (Dunlap & Van Liere 1978; Catton 1980). The NEP reflects a "land ethic" (Leopold 1948; Heberlein 1972)—a concern for maintaining the balance of nature as an end in itself or as a spiritual value. The NEP scale developed by Dunlap & Van Liere (1978) measures this concept of environmental concern with such items as "the balance of nature is very delicate and easily upset."

In a second concept, environmental concern is tied to anthropocentric altruism: People care about environmental quality not mainly for its own sake, but because they believe its loss threatens to harm the health or well-being of large numbers of people. In this view, environmental concern is an outgrowth of the Golden Rule (Dunlap & Van Liere 1977; Heberlein 1977). This concept is reflected in research that applies Schwartz's (1977) norm-activation model of altruistic behavior to environmental problems (e.g. Van Liere & Dunlap 1978; Black et al 1985; Stern et al 1986b). In this research, general concern about environmental problems is measured by statements of belief that these problems are serious or important; general concern is held to predict action only among people who believe the environmental problems have adverse consequences for humans.

In a third concept, environmental concern is a function of egoism: People care about environmental quality only to the extent they believe it may affect their own well-being or that of their close kin. This utilitarian concept is implicit in some research that correlates opposition to hazardous technologies, particularly in local contexts, with belief about the level or type of personal risk or benefit those technologies present (e.g. Hughey et al 1985; Van der Pligt et al 1986a,b). It is also evident in studies that treat egoistic concerns such as expected personal costs and benefits of resource conservation (e.g. Black et al 1985) or the perceived difficulty of pro-environmental activity (e.g. DeYoung 1989) as intervening variables between environmental attitudes and behavior. In research using utility or value-expectancy frameworks, values or preferences are typically integral to attitudes, but the theory does not specify whether the values are egocentric, altruistic, or ecological (e.g. Gill et al 1986; Slovic 1987; Gould et al 1988; Jones 1990).

In a fourth concept, environmental concern is a function of some deeper cause, such as Rokeach's "terminal values" (Rokeach 1967; Dunlap et al 1983; Neuman 1986), underlying religious beliefs (White 1967; Eckberg & Blocker 1989), or a shift from materialist to postmaterialist cultural values (Inglehart 1990). The interrelationships among these deeper causes are not clearly established (Pierce et al 1987; Steger et al 1989), nor is the strength of their effect on environmentally relevant behavior (Dunlap et al 1983; Neuman 1986).

It is possible, of course, that several concepts of environmental concern apply simultaneously. Some models of attitude-behavior relationships postulate specific connections between them. For example, Schwartz-model studies treat altruistic concerns and an egocentric cost-benefit calculus as intervening variables between general environmental concern and more situation-specific personal norms (e.g. Black et al 1985). Other studies, by separately measuring different aspects of concern, address the relationships as an empirical question (e.g. DeYoung 1989; Vining & Ebreo 1990). Research on these relationships seems worthwhile because, especially in relation to political behavior, it may make a considerable difference whether an individual's environmental concern is basically ecological, altruistic, egoistic, or religious/ideological in nature. It is also important to learn how these orientations toward the environment are acquired and transmitted, because over the time scale of generations, change in these orientations may be a critical factor determining the pace of global change.

Correlates of environmental attitudes   Researchers continue to produce a stream of articles—generally atheoretical—reporting sociodemographic, personality, or attitudinal correlates of one or another measure of environmental attitude. The observed relationships are generally weak (the significant correlations are typically below 0.2); the variables most consistently correlated with measures of environmental concern are education (Van Liere & Dunlap 1980), age or cohort (e.g. Mohai & Twight 1987), political liberalism (e.g. Samdahl & Robertson 1989), and internal-external locus of control (e.g. Pettus & Giles 1987). Women show up as more environmentally concerned in studies that focus on nuclear power (Farhar et al 1980; Longstreth et al 1989), but gender is not a consistent correlate of more general measures of environmental concern.

INDIVIDUAL BEHAVIORS DIRECTLY AFFECTING THE GLOBAL ENVIRONMENT   Table 1 identifies the most important human activities affecting global warming. The most significant by far are actions that control demand for fossil energy, but other individual actions are also important. As already noted, purchase decisions (such as those affecting the size of housing units; the fuel efficiency of automobiles, furnaces, and major appliances; and ownership of air-conditioning and refrigeration equipment) are particularly important. The most important management decisions include maintaining the energy-efficient operation of automobiles and furnaces and choosing a method of fertilizing crops with nitrogen; the most important daily behavioral choices include amount of recreational travel and level of cooling or heating provided to living spaces. Some behaviors with climatic impacts— specifically, those that affect demand for refrigeration and air-conditioning— also affect ozone depletion through demand for CFCs. In addition, purchases of products that use CFCs in the packaging process may have a significant impact. Individual actions that can affect the rate of loss of biodiversity are those that alter demand for products and services that depend on endangered species or the disruption of their habitats.

Almost all these actions are consumer behaviors. For the purpose of developing generalizations, I examine here the determinants of such behaviors without regard to their environmental importance. I include studies of behaviors that produce local environmental effects, such as solid waste and pollutants, when these behaviors are affected by factors, such as general environmental attitudes, that are also implicated in behaviors with global consequences. For future research, of course, an importance criterion should guide the choice of behaviors to investigate.

Individual behavior is potentially a function of psychological variables (e.g. attitudes, beliefs, motives), interpersonal variables (e.g. communication, social norms), situational structure (e.g. the size or level of solidarity of a community facing a commons dilemma), and various contextual factors (e.g. demographic background, household size and equipment ownership, incomes and prices, government regulations). Psychologically oriented research has addressed all these variable types, although not in equal detail.

Psychological determinants   Environmentally significant behavior may be affected by individuals' values, attitudes, beliefs, and knowledge, as well as by personality variables. Stern & Oskamp (1987) concluded that behavior tended to correlate with attitudes (see also Hines et al 1987), although they offered some qualifications: Relationships are stronger when attitudes and behavior are measured at the same level of specificity and when behaviors are easy to perform; environmentally relevant behaviors often do not correlate well with each other; and self-reported behaviors, which are not always reliable indicators of actual behavior, may correlate more strongly with attitudes than actual behavior does. They proposed a multi-stage causal model of environmentally relevant behavior (see Table 2) that attempted to account for the imperfection of attitude-behavior relationships by postulating a causal chain in which background variables (including sociodemographics and personality) influence general attitudes and beliefs, which in turn influence specific attitudes and beliefs, behavioral commitment and intention, resource-using and resource-saving behavior, and finally resource use. In the model, behavior and its direct effects (e.g. energy savings) can feed back into the system by changing specific knowledge and beliefs through mechanisms such as learning and the minimal-justification effect, which changes attitudes when an individual acts without clear external motives (Katzev & Johnson 1983, 1984; Kahle & Beatty 1987). The model is generally compatible with the theoretical analyses of Schwartz (1977) and of Ajzen & Fishbein (1980).

Table 2 An approximate causal model of resource use with examples from residential energy conservation.[a]

	Level of Causality	Type of Variable	Examples
	8	Background factors	Income, education, number of household members, local temperature conditions
	7	Structural factors	Size of dwelling unit, appliance ownership
		Institutional factors	Owner/renter status, direct or indirect payment for energy
	6	Recent events	Difficulty paying energy bills, experience with shortages, fuel price increases
	5	General attitudes	Concern about national energy situation
		General beliefs	Belief households can help with national energy problems
	4	Specific attitudes	Sense of personal obligation to use energy efficiently
Self-Justification		Specific beliefs	Belief that using less heat threatens family health
		Specific knowledge	Knowledge that water heater is a major energy user
	3	Behavioral commitment	Commitment to cut household energy use 15%
Learning		Behavioral intention	Intention to install a solar heating system
	2	Resource-using behavior	Length of time air conditioner is kept on
		Resource-saving behavior	Insulating attic, lowering winter thermostat setting
	1	Resource use	Kilowatt-hours per month
	0	Observable effects	Lower energy costs, elimination of drafts, family quarrels over thermostat

[a] Source: Stern & Oskamp 1987

Consistent with this model, it is easier to find significant zero-order relationships between variables closer together in the causal chain. Also, causal-modeling studies investigating variables at several points along the causal chain have tended to be supportive (Verhallen & van Raaij 1981; Macey & Brown 1983; Black et al 1985; Balderjahn 1988; Jones 1990). Studies confirm the direct effects on self-reported behavior of specific personal norms (Black et al 1985; Hines et al 1987), with other psychological variables having indirect effects (Black et al 1985; Jones 1990).

Independently of attitudes, studies demonstrate effects on environmentally

relevant behavior of knowledge about the monetary costs of different behaviors (Byrne et al 1985, Archer et al 1987), perceived difficulty of relevant
behaviors (DeYoung 1989, 1990; Vining & Ebreo 1990), and a person's
perceived knowledge or skill in performing the behaviors (Sia et al 1986;
Archer et al 1987; Sivek & Hungerford 1990). Knowledge about which
actions have the greatest effect also seems to affect action (Kempton &
Montgomery 1982), although at least for energy-using behaviors (Kempton et
al 1985) this type of knowledge is faulty among many individuals. In addition, several variables from attitude theory moderate the attitude-behavior
relationship, including issue involvement (Verplanken 1989), issue salience
(Cialdini et al 1990), instrumentality to personal values (Neuman 1986), and
the presence of intrinsic motives or satisfactions (DeYoung 1986; 1990;
DeYoung & Kaplan 1986). Personality variables rarely show systematic
relationships to environmentally relevant behavior, with the exception of
locus of control and related variables (Hines et al 1987; Pettus & Giles 1987).

Interpersonal variables   Environmentally relevant individual actions are influenced by other people through perceived social norms (Black et al 1985;
Kahle & Beatty 1987; Jones 1990; but see Vining & Ebreo 1990). In addition,
one of the few consistent predictors of adoptions of costly energy conservation and renewable energy technologies is personal contact with individuals
who have already adopted the technology (Darley 1978; Archer et al 1987).
Interpersonal influences are also important to behavior change, as noted
below.

Situational structure   The theory of collective action and commons dilemmas (Olson 1965; G. Hardin 1968; Dawes 1980; R. Hardin 1982) has
generated a number of propositions about how rational consumers respond to
the structure of a shared resource. For example, resource-conserving behavior
is predicted to be greater in smaller user groups, with the identification of
private property rights, and with increased solidarity within the user group.
The postulated solidarity effect has been demonstrated in laboratory simulations of local resource crises (Samuelson & Messick 1986) and in real-
world crises such as drought (e.g. Agras et al 1980; Berk et al 1980), as well
as in studies demonstrating correlations between energy-conserving behavior
and integration into community activities (e.g. Neuman 1986).

Contextual factors   Behavior can be affected by a wide range of contextual
factors usually ignored in psychological research but potentially important to
human-environment interaction. They include sociodemographic status (e.g.
education, gender, income, family size), control of environmentally significant technology (e.g. ownership of home heating equipment, automobiles,

appliances), geographic/meterological context (e.g. number of annual heating or cooling degree days in one's home locale), economic incentives (e.g. prices of fuels or of environmentally benign products), institutional arrangements (e.g. laws or customs governing access to water or sunlight), and policy context (including government regulations, tax structures, and policy decisions by manufacturers that bound consumer choice). According to the causal model in Table 2, such factors are antecedent variables that may condition attitudes and behavior. That is, these nonpsychological factors are important to psychological research because they interact with psychological ones (Stern et al 1991), so that in some contexts, attitudes, beliefs, and knowledge may exercise great control over behavior, while in others, context may effectively constrain choice so that psychological factors matter little. Psychologists should also consider and assess the role of contextual factors to make their work credible. Nonpsychologists, including economists, engineers, and policy makers will need to be shown that psychological factors make a difference after context is taken into account. The challenge for psychology is to build understanding of the interactions between contextual and psychological variables, in order to identify the conditions under which the latter make a practical difference as determinants of global change.

Research has begun to illuminate the interactions. For instance, psychological variables such as attitudes and personal norms appear to have more effect on relatively inexpensive, easy-to-perform energy-saving actions than on major household investments in energy efficiency (Stern et al 1983; Heberlein & Warriner 1983; Black et al 1985; Neuman 1986; Balderjahn 1988; however, see Palmborg 1987). Availability of financial resources and knowledge (income and education) seem to be important mediators of the attitude-behavior link for expensive or difficult behaviors (Stern et al 1983; Archer et al 1987; Lynne & Rola 1988). Where environmental concern is high, as is sometimes the case with voluntary recycling programs, a combination of the physical difficulty of pro-environmental action and lack of specific information on how to act may effectively prevent the expression of pro-environmental attitudes (DeYoung 1989, 1990). And the greater the financial stake in an energy choice, the more difference the consumer's level of information appears to make (Stern 1986). Multivariate econometric techniques are appropriate for further analysis of such interactions among psychological and contextual variables, and they are commonly used to study energy consumption, but typically not by psychologists and not with psychological variables in the mix (exceptions include Stern et al 1983; Heberlein & Warriner 1983; Byrne et al 1985).

INDIVIDUAL BEHAVIORS AFFECTING COLLECTIVE ACTION   A neglected, but potentially important area for psychological research concerns the role of individuals in determining what firms, communities, and governments do to the global environment. The behavior of firms is influenced, of course, by the demand of individuals for their products or services; this sort of consumer behavior is addressed in the previous section. It may also be influenced by the choices of managers, by the presence of individuals who persistently raise environmental concerns within the firm (Goitein 1989), and by various aspects of organizational process (Stern & Aronson 1984: Ch. 5). Although these factors are probably less influential than pressures in an organization's decision environment, little systematic research has been done on how the values and decision rules of managers and organizational routines, structures, and change affect resource use by organizations.

Communities and governments are also affected by individual action, both through leadership and, perhaps more importantly, by pressures that individuals put on leaders through public opinion and lobbying. If government action sets the context for individual choices, the attitudes and beliefs of individuals, when effectively aggregated, set a context for the behavior of government officials. The process is complex; it is most often studied by political scientists and sociologists who work on the "mobilization" of social movement organizations and political interest groups. But the factors that lead individuals to support such groups or demand environmental protection policies are a legitimate subject for psychological research (e.g. McAdam et al 1988).

Political behavior includes support for governmental action, an attitude that is potentially convertible into overt action; voting; and political participation or activism, which ranges from signing petitions to participating in demonstrations and financial or personal involvement in politically active organizations. Many attitude-behavior studies combine political and consumer behaviors within a single scale, thereby begging the question of whether political behaviors about the environment have the same psychological basis as consumer behaviors. Even review articles and meta-analyses do not always make a scrupulous distinction. The question deserves explicit attention.

Support for governmental action on the environment appears to fit the same causal model of determination as other environmental attitudes. Support for regulation of hazardous technology is related to attitudes toward the technology to be regulated (Verplanken 1989); to specific beliefs about the technology, such as about its potential risks and often its benefits (e.g. Hughey et al 1985; Van der Pligt et al 1986a,b; Gould et al 1988); and to the factors that activate relatively specific altruistic norms (Stern et al 1986b). It is only weakly related to general environmental attitudes (Gould et al 1988) or to sociodemographic and personality variables, although to the same familiar ones (education, age, and sometimes gender) (Buttel & Flinn 1978; Van Liere & Dunlap 1980; Pettus & Giles 1987; Gould et al 1988; Samdahl & Robertson 1989). From the limited evidence, environmental voting is similarly determined. Votes appear to be influenced by general environmental attitudes indirectly, with value-expectancy factors and perceived social norms acting as intervening variables (Gill et al 1986).

Activism, however, seems to be somewhat more complex, with attitudinal factors being a necessary but insufficient determinant. Activists may be differentiated from other concerned individuals by higher levels of environmental concern (Prester et al 1987; Steger et al 1989), greater personal exposure to the environmental problems they act on (Prester et al 1987; Manzo & Weinstein 1987), greater general political interest (Prester et al 1987), or social contacts with other activists (Manzo & Weinstein 1987). However, the most important factors differentiating activists and nonactivists appear to be personal resources such as knowledge about the particular issues and how to participate effectively (Mohai 1985; Prester et al 1987), and the presumably related variable of subjective sense of political efficacy (Mohai 1985; Manzo & Weinstein 1987). Apparently, attitudes determine the direction of political interest but resources determine the level of activity (Mohai 1985). Political behavior appears to be analogous to consumer behaviors in one sense: Complex or difficult behaviors (consumer investment and political activism) are strongly dependent on resources or abilities, whereas less effortful behaviors (daily consumption changes, expressions of political support, and voting choices) tend to be more attitude-determined.

HUMAN CONSEQUENCES OF AND RESPONSES TO GLOBAL CHANGE

Global environmental change matters to people because it has the potential to harm what they value (Stern et al 1991). Psychology is relevant because values have a psychological component, because some of the harm may be psychological, because anticipatory responses depend on perceptions of the environment, and because behavioral change is necessary for preventing or slowing global change and limiting the damage it may cause. The key behavioral questions include these: What values shape human responses, and how? Will humans take effective action to stop or slow the activities that harm environmental systems such as the climate and the ozone layer? What actions would be effective in changing behavior? Are there behavioral changes that would make it easier to adapt to possible future changes in the global environment? And how will people be affected by any global changes that ultimately occur?

The Range of Consequences and Responses

Global change does not have "impacts" on an inert population the way a meteorite has an impact on the earth. The consequences of global change depend on how society changes while its environment is changing, and on what responses people may make in anticipation of environmental change. Whatever global changes occur will affect people who live differently from the way they live now. If in two or three generations, sea level rises by one meter, it will not necessarily flood those homes now situated less than one meter above sea level. In the interim, "people may migrate, build dikes, or buy insurance, and the society and economy may have changed so that people's immediate responses— and therefore, the costs of global change—are different from what they would be in the present" (Stern et al 1991:102–3).

Even though it is not possible to forecast human society generations into the future, useful behavioral analyses can be done. They can focus on how people and societies are affected by environmental stresses as experienced and on how they make anticipatory responses. But because the effects of global change will mostly be decades in the future, the stresses experienced are conditional on the anticipatory responses that precede them. Consequently, analysis of responses is the first priority.

People may respond in many ways to anticipated global change, but it is worth distinguishing two main classes of response. *Mitigation* "includes all actions that prevent, limit, delay, or slow the rate of undesired impacts by acting directly or indirectly on environmental systems" (Stern et al 1991:105). Mitigations come in many varieties. Consider the problem of global warming, which is the direct reflection of a change in the earth's radiative balance. Humans can mitigate global warming by intervening directly in the natural environment—for example, by blocking incident solar radiation with orbiting particles or enhancing the ocean sink for carbon dioxide by adding nutrients. They can intervene directly in the proximate causes by regulating automobile use or engine design to cut carbon dioxide emissions or limiting the use of certain nitrogen fertilizers to reduce nitrous oxide emissions. And they can intervene in human systems in ways that control the proximate causes in-directly—for example, by investing in research on renewable energy tech-nologies to replace fossil fuel or providing tax incentives for more compact settlements to lower demand for transportation.

Adaptations are responses that do not alter the rate of environmental change but limit the effects on what people value. Adaptations also come in various types. People may intervene to break the link between environmental change and what they value. An example is the use of drought-resistant crops or crop strains so that if climate change produces drought, crop failure and famine do not result. They may intervene to prevent or compensate for losses of welfare that would otherwise result from global change. Examples include evacuation from areas stricken with flood or drought, food shipments or financial assis-tance to those remaining in such areas, and systems of insurance against crop failures or floods caused by climatic change. People may also make "an-ticipatory adaptations" by improving the robustness of social systems, so that an unchecked environmental change would produce less reduction of values than would otherwise be the case. An example is diversification in agricultural systems. Farmers, regions, and countries that rely on a range of crops with different requirements for growth may or may not produce smaller volumes of greenhouse or ozone-depleting gases than monoculturists. But polycultures are more robust in the face of drought, acid deposition, and ozone depletion because they will not be wiped out by a failure of any one crop. (The above distinctions are taken from Stern et al 1991: Ch. 4).

To the extent that human efforts to mitigate or adapt are unsuccessful or incomplete, global changes may create environmental stresses for future populations, and the psychological consequences are worthy of study.

Areas of Psychological Research

In this section I review psychological knowledge on the following issues concerning the human consequences of global environmental change: the processes by which lay and expert observers identify and anticipate global change, the problem of changing environmentally destructive behaviors, the causes of change in levels of political support for environmental protection, processes of conflict as they concern environmental policy, and response to environmental stressors. These issues must be considered in terms of processes that may change on the time scale of decades to centuries, during which human responses to global change might be made. Some of the topics have received much more research attention than others; none has been seriously studied with respect to long time scales.

PERCEPTION AND GLOBAL ENVIRONMENTAL CHANGE   Considerable basic research exists on human cognition and judgment processes, but the insights have only been applied in a preliminary way to responses to global change. It is difficult to improve on the analysis and detailed research agenda developed a decade ago by Fischhoff & Furby (1983). Defining response to climate change as a decision problem, they identified four important groups of research questions relevant to perceptions. First, what are the psychological determinants of expert judgment about climate change, and how can experts gain a better appreciation of the limits of their abilities? The relevant knowledge concerns sources of expert error and overconfidence (Lichtenstein et al 1982). Second, how do nonexperts interpret information from experts, what kinds of information are particularly hard to interpret, and how can the problems be remedied? Relevant knowledge concerns understanding of probability (Lichtenstein et al 1978) and uncertainty (e.g. Kahneman & Tversky 1973) and the effects on understanding of "framing" information (Tversky & Kahneman 1981). An extensive literature on "risk communication" is relevant to the problem (National Research Council 1989; Mileti & Fitzpatrick 1991).

Third, how do people judge and misjudge the range of available options? Relevant knowledge concerns the possibility that both experts and nonexperts may believe, prematurely, that all options have been identified. Fourth, how do people combine information on the risks and benefits of various options into a decision, and how can these judgments be elicited accurately? Relevant analytic methods exist (e.g. Keeney & Raiffa 1976), and they might be applicable to judgments about the possible consequences of global change.

Research on environmental perception is relevant to climate change (Whyte 1985; Taylor et al 1988), but only recently have researchers begun to explore nonexperts' perceptions of global climatic change directly (Kempton 1991; Doble et al 1990). As of 1990, samples of American lay people were aware of and concerned about the global warming phenomenon but had not differentiated it clearly from other environmental problems, such as air pollution and ozone depletion. Their understanding, as well as their opinions on a number of policy options, was open to change as a result of a modest amount of increased information (Doble et al 1990).

CHANGING ENVIRONMENTALLY DESTRUCTIVE BEHAVIOR   A large literature through the 1970s and 1980s focused on interventions to alter behaviors that produced solid waste or consumed energy, water, and other natural resources. Of this research, the studies of energy conservation are most directly relevant to global change because of the direct effect of fossil energy use on global climate; they are also among the most thoroughly reviewed (for a recent review, see Stern 1992). The research can be classified by the type of intervention used. It includes both small, controlled field-experimental studies and evaluations of large-scale interventions.

Information, feedback, and persuasive communication   A common policy intervention is to provide how-to information for individuals who may desire to decrease resource use. Mere provision of information, such as with pamphlets, slogans, or instructions, has typically been ineffective (Ester & Winett 1982; Condelli et al 1984; Stern & Aronson 1984; Costanzo et al 1986; Dennis et al 1990). However, greater success has been achieved by applying more aggressive techniques that rely on using clear language, vivid and personalized presentation of information, appropriate framing of alternatives, concrete recommendations, and credible sources (for reviews, see Stern & Aronson 1984; Coltrane et al 1986; Stern 1986; Dennis et al 1990).

Two informational approaches based on psychological principles have been particularly successful in changing daily energy-using behaviors: regular feedback about energy use (Seligman et al 1981; Dennis & Soderstrom 1988) and exposure to models who demonstrate effective conservation behaviors on videotaped presentations (Winett et al 1982; 1985; Syme et al 1987). In

GLOBAL ENVIRONMENTAL CHANGE   291

addition, techniques of minimal justification have been effective in small-scale experiments (Katzev & Johnson 1983, 1984), and elicited commitment to conserve has been effective, especially when combined with feedback (Becker 1978; Pallak et al 1980; Van Houwelingen & Van Raaij 1989). Programs that combine a range of enhanced informational techniques have proven more successful than traditional informational efforts (Heberlein & Baumgartner 1985). However, these more complex interventions tend to be difficult or expensive to implement on a large scale. Moreover, their conservation potential is limited because of their focus on the utilization of equipment already in place.

Some informational techniques have been applied successfully to the more environmentally significant behaviors that determine investments in energy efficiency. These include framing energy conservation as avoiding the prospect of a financial loss (Yates 1982), providing information from credible sources (Polich 1984; Miller & Ford 1985), and using information providers trained in communications techniques (Gonzales et al 1988). The successes indicate significant untapped potential to apply psychological knowledge to strengthen government informational programs directed at purchase decisions, including energy-efficiency labeling of automobiles, appliances, and homes, and energy auditing programs (Stern & Aronson 1984; Robinson 1989; Dennis & Soderstrom 1988; Kushler 1989; Dennis et al 1990). The effectiveness of such programs varies widely as a function of implementation (Vine & Harris 1988; Berry 1990), and the means of delivering information may be a significant explanatory factor.

Altering rewards and costs   Another common policy intervention is to use financial incentives, such as taxes, interest subsidies, credits, and rebates, to encourage resource-conserving behavior. The experimental literature by psychologists demonstrates the effectiveness of incentives, mostly with daily behaviors, but has been insufficiently sensitive to the problem of cost-effectiveness (Geller et al 1982; Geller 1987). More important in practical terms have been the evaluation studies of government and utility-company incentive programs aimed at influencing investments in home insulation, energy-efficient appliances, and renewable energy systems (for reviews, see Stern et al 1986a; Berry 1990). These studies reveal, not surprisingly, that larger incentives are more effective than smaller ones. The surprise is the importance of nonfinancial factors: Incentives with the same financial value have widely different effects as a function of the form in which they are presented (e.g. low-interest loans tend to be less effective than grants); the strength of the marketing effort, particularly the effort to make the intended audience aware of the incentive being offered; and the credibility and motivation of the sponsoring organization. With any given incentive, the most successful program is typically at least ten times as effective as the least, and "the stronger the financial incentive, the more a program's success depends on nonfinancial factors" (Stern 1986:211). Thus, psychological variables may be even more powerful levers in incentive-based conservation programs than in informational ones.

Regulation and technological development   Governments can mitigate global change by imposing desired behavior on citizens. Examples include the US Corporate Average Fuel Economy standards for automobiles, the 55 mile per hour speed limit on US highways, and the energy-efficiency standards sometimes imposed on appliance manufacturers and builders. They can also invest in developing new technologies, such as solar energy or agroforestry, that cause less harm to the global environment than conventional methods of energy or crop production. Psychologists have done little work in these areas of behavior change, even though there are important behavioral issues: The success of regulations and new technology depends on people's willingness to support and comply with regulations and to adopt the new technologies (see Stern et al 1987).

Combinations of techniques   The most effective practical programs to change resource-using behavior often rely on a combination of the above types of interventions, even adding supplementary techniques (see Stern & Aronson 1984; Coltrane et al 1986; Hirst 1987; Geller 1989; Robinson 1989; Olsen & Harris 1991). This is so because it may be necessary simultaneously to overcome a number of barriers, any one of which may prevent action: lack of knowledge, money, and attention; mistrust of experts (e.g. the energy auditors who estimate what an expensive action will save); difficulty or inconvenience of taking the necessary action; and lack of social support (Stern & Aronson 1984). Energy conservation programs have been most effective when they address all these barriers—that is, when they market intelligently and aggressively (Vine & Harris 1988; Berry 1990). For instance, it may be critical to involve organizations that have good communication and trust with the program's intended audience, such as community organizations (Coltrane et al 1986; Stern et al 1987), local governments (Miller & Ford 1985; Egel 1987), or professional communities of builders or lenders (Stern & Aronson 1984). The reviews in the field offer a useful practical guide to the design of residential energy conservation programs; although many of the lessons seem likely to be transferable to other behaviors affecting the global environment, there are probably also important behavior-specific differences.

Behavior change in institutional settings   Psychologists have worked on resource use in certain institutional settings that structure the problem as one of collective action—for instance, apartment buildings or college dormitories where energy costs are not billed directly to individual users. Effective interventions have included individual metering (McClelland 1980), cash rewards to individuals (Walker 1979), prizes to groups for reaching a conservation target (McClelland & Cook 1980), and appointing energy monitors (DeYoung 1989–1990). The interventions work by inducing changes in behavior rather than investments in equipment.

Evaluation of interventions   Conservation programs pose significant problems for evaluation. First, their success seems to depend on a conjunction of factors at the individual and organizational levels, making it difficult or prohibitively expensive to assess the value of each program element or combination of elements separately. Second, programs that effectively improve the efficiency of resource use often have smaller-than-expected effects on total resource use (Gonzales et al 1988; Hirst 1990). This discrepancy has a behavioral component: Consumers may "take back" some of what they save by improving efficiency in the form of increased comfort (warmer homes in winter; larger, although more fuel-efficient, automobiles, and so forth). Such behavior raises questions about the criterion of success. How should one judge a conservation program that instead of slowing the rate of global change improves well-being while holding environmental change constant? Third, evaluations need to control for economic and technical factors unfamiliar to most psychologists, such as resource prices, household incomes, appliance ownership, and weather. Methods of evaluation are being developed to deal with these issues (Hirst 1990). Fourth, program evaluations are conducted in a social and political context in which psychologists must be sophisticated not only about the behavior of energy users but about that of the institutions that have sponsored and may make use of evaluation results (Kushler 1989; Archer et al 1992; Kempton et al 1992). Moreover, it is difficult to get sufficient funds for evaluation research and to get the results used, especially to modify ongoing programs (Kushler 1989). Despite these difficulties, the evaluation of energy conservation programs may be the area in which psychology has made its greatest practical contribution to date in mitigating global change.

CHANGES IN SUPPORT FOR ENVIRONMENTAL PROTECTION   Over the decades-to-centuries time scale of global environmental change, human response will depend on the rate of change of attitudes and political behavior toward the environment. Relatively little research exists on the causes of change in environmental attitudes and activism. However, some mechanisms are known.

Cognitive dissonance theory suggests conditions under which small behavioral changes can, by altering attitudes, produce larger changes. The phenomenon has been demonstrated in small-scale experiments (e.g. Katzev & Johnson 1983, 1984), but such attitude change would be more important if it also occurs on a longer time scale and in response to policies. One recent study suggests that just such long-term attitudinal changes may be attributable to "growing up with the bottle bill," which induces individuals to engage in habitual recycling for the "minimal justification" of 5 cents per container (Kahle & Beatty 1987).

Sociological work on resource mobilization by social-movement organizations suggests that environmental organizations (and their opponents) can elicit support and reshape policy debates by framing issues so as to arouse sentiments and engage individuals and organizations that would not otherwise become involved (e.g. Snow et al 1986; Gunter & Finlay 1988; Dietz et al 1989). Further work on this process may illuminate the processes by which environmental policies change (Stern et al 1986b; Dietz et al 1989).

Public opinion and activism can also be mobilized when a community experiences a serious threat (e.g. Edelstein & Wandersman 1987) or perceives a technological hazard (Kroll-Smith et al 1991). These processes may generate activism around global change if well-publicized threats or hazards come to be seen as related to such change.

ENVIRONMENTAL CONFLICT AND CONFLICT MANAGEMENT   Policy responses to global change, like other environmental policy choices, will be controversial, with prospective winners opposing prospective losers and proponents of conservation opposing proponents of development (Rayner 1991). Even though global environmental change may pose a threat to everyone on earth, and thus present a classic superordinate goal, it may not be perceived this way. Not only may it be treated as a collective-action problem, with each actor motivated to "free ride" on the efforts of others, but its mixed-motive aspects may become a basis for competition. Global climate change will not be uniform around the world, so that some regions and countries may expect to be in a better comparative position afterward than they are now. Ozone depletion poses a cancer threat mainly to fair-skinned people, so it may be of little concern to African governments. The tremendous scientific uncertainty concerning projections of the global environment will engender conflicts about how to interpret knowledge and about which responses most appropriately take uncertainty into account (Fischhoff & Furby 1983; Stern 1991). Psychologists have long studied the cognitive and other roots of conflict, and have investigated techniques of conflict resolution; global-change phenomena may give them a new context in which to pursue their research (Stern et al 1991).

INDIVIDUAL RESPONSE TO ENVIRONMENTAL STRESSORS   Global changes that result in environmental catastrophes (more frequent floods, droughts, or storms, for example) will create stress on individuals and communities. A large body of literature has examined the human effects of environmental stressors (Evans & Cohen 1987) and of natural disasters (Mileti & Nigg 1991) and technological hazards (Kroll-Smith et al 1991). The effect of a stressor may well depend on whether or not it is perceived as anthropogenic (Kroll-Smith et al 1991); moreover, the anticipation of an anthropogenic hazard may produce stress (Freudenburg & Jones, In press), mistrust of information (Stern & Aronson 1984: Ch. 6), or behavior counterproductive to wise resource management (Rutte et al 1987). Analysis of these issues in the context of global change is difficult because of uncertainties about catastrophies in the distant future and about the characteristics of the human populations they may affect.

MAJOR RESEARCH OPPORTUNITIES AND CHALLENGES

Understanding the human causes and consequences of global environmental change requires problem-oriented, interdisciplinary research. The problems of global change generate important substantive research needs. The most important ones for psychology include improved analysis of the determinants of global change–producing behavior and of changes in such behavior, analysis of the barriers to adoption of technologies and practices to mitigate global change, identification of cost-effective interventions by government and other actors, and improved analysis of the bases for individual support for change in environmental policy. These research problems require psychologists to draw on concepts and theories from unfamiliar or unfashionable subfields. For example, energy demand depends more on one-time household investments and on organizational decisions than on everyday behaviors; therefore, the concepts of consumer and organizational psychology may deserve increased attention, supplementing the concepts of experimental social psychology and applied behavior analysis, which have been more prominent in research but have been used mainly for explaining frequently repeated individual behaviors. Practical research questions also require psychologists to demonstrate the relevance of their knowledge in field settings using accepted techniques of evaluation. Psychologists have much to learn and to contribute to the field of environmental policy evaluation.

Research must be interdisciplinary because human-environment relations are natural and technological as well as behavioral and because the relevant human actions are those not only of individuals, but also of communities, organizations, and political-economic institutions. At the frontier of research is the problem of analyzing environmentally significant behavior as a joint function of psychological, social-structural, economic, technological, and other variables. For example, the relationship between environmental attitudes and behavior is stronger when action is easier to take; consequently, policies or price structures that discourage conservation may lower attitude-behavior correlations. They may also decrease the potential impact of consumer behavior relative to that of political behavior. For practical purposes, what matters is not to show that psychological variables are significant in a statistical sense but to assess their importance in the context of other factors, and particularly the importance of psychological variables that are subject to deliberate control by individuals or via policy changes. Progress requires that psychological concepts of the determination of behavior be integrated with engineering concepts of energy use, economic concepts of decision making, sociological concepts of mobilization, and techniques of policy analysis.

Another frontier research area concerns the connections between individual behavior and the actions of entities at higher levels of analysis. When analyzed over the long time scales of global change, individual attitudes and beliefs may have their greatest effect by changing organizations and governments, even as they are influenced by them.

The global-change research agenda challenges behavioral scientists to think on a much longer time scale than they typically do, because the consequences of global change will depend on changes in human behavior on the scale of decades to centuries. Psychological concepts apply to such important topics as the transmission of environmental attitudes between generations; the causes of long-term change in public opinion, environmental activism, and consumer behavior; the determinants of decisions to adopt renewable energy or other environmentally benign technological systems; and the role of interpersonal influence in changing social norms about resource use.

Finally, global-change research challenges psychologists to find an appropriate balance between basic and policy-oriented research. Several areas of basic psychology offer important concepts for global-change research, so furthering such work can improve understanding of global change. However, the transfer of broad theoretical concepts to a practical domain is not direct or straightforward; it requires reinterpretation for a context in which variables outside psychological theory play important roles. Attempts to make direct application may be wrongheaded and embarrassing to the discipline. Policy research also can teach lessons to basic researchers, particularly about the boundary conditions within which psychological variables are effective. A healthy interplay between basic psychological research and studies of the human dimensions of global change stands to benefit both lines of work.

ACKNOWLEDGMENTS

I wish to thank Gerald Gardner and Thomas Dietz for comments on an earlier version of this chapter.

Literature Cited

Agras, W. S., Jacob, R. G., Lebedeck, M. 1980. The California drought: a quasi-experimental analysis of social policy. *J. Appl. Behav. Anal.* 13:561–70

Ajzen, I., Fishbein, M. 1980. *Understanding Attitudes and Predicting Behavior.* Englewood Cliffs, NJ: Prentice-Hall

Archer, D., Aronson, E., Pettigrew, T. 1992. Making research apply: high stakes public policy in a regulatory environment. *Am. Psychol.* In press

Archer, D., Pettigrew, T., Costanzo, M., Iritani, B., Walker, I., et al. 1987. Energy conservation and public policy: the mediation of individual behavior. In *Energy Efficiency: Perspectives on Individual Behavior,* ed. W. Kempton, M. Neiman, pp. 69–92. Washington: Am. Counc. Energy-Efficient Economy

Balderjahn, I. 1988. Personality variables and environmental attitudes as predictors of ecologically responsible consumption patterns. *J. Bus. Res.* 17:51–56

Becker, L. J. 1978. The joint effect of feedback and goal setting on performance: a field study of residential energy conservation. *J. Appl. Psychol.* 63:428–33

Berk, R. A., Cooley, T. F., LaCivita, C. J., Parker, S., Sredl, K., et al. 1980. Reducing consumption in periods of acute scarcity: the case of water. *Soc. Sci. Res.* 9:99–120

Berry, L. 1990. *The Market Penetration of Energy-Efficiency Programs.* ORNL/CON-299. Oak Ridge, TN.: Oak Ridge Natl. Lab.

Black, J. S., Stern, P. C., Elworth, J. T. 1985. Personal and contextual influences on household energy adaptations. *J. Appl. Psychol.* 70:3–21

Buttel, F. H., Flinn, W. L. 1978. Social class and environmental beliefs: a reconsideration. *Environ. Behav.* 10:433–50

Byrne, J., Rich, D., Tannian, F. X., Wang, Y.-D. 1985. Rethinking the household energy crisis: the role of information in household energy conservation. *Marriage Fam. Rev.* 9:83–113

Catton, W. R. Jr. 1980. *Overshoot: The Ecological Basis of Revolutionary Change.* Urbana: Univ. Illinois Press

Chen, R. S., Boulding, E., Schneider, S. H., eds. 1983. *Social Science Research and Climate Change.* Dordrecht, Netherlands: Reidel

Cialdini, R. B., Reno, R. R., Kallgren, C. A. 1990. A focus theory of normative conduct: recycling the concept of norms to reduce littering in public places. *J. Pers. Soc. Psychol.* 58:1015–26

Coltrane, S., Archer, D., Aronson, E. 1986. The social-psychological foundations of successful energy conservation programmes. *Energy Policy* 14:133–48

Condelli, L., Archer, D., Aronson, E., Curbow, B., McLeod, B., et al. 1984. Improving utility conservation programs: outcomes, interventions, and evaluations. *Energy* 9:485–94

Costanzo, M., Archer, D., Aronson, E., Pettigrew, T. 1986. Energy conservation behavior: the difficult path from information to action. *Am. Psychol.* 41:521–28

Darley, J. M. 1978. Energy conservation techniques as innovations and their diffusion. *Energy Build.* 1:339–43

Dawes, R. M. 1980. Social dilemmas. *Annu. Rev. Psychol.* 31:169–93

Dennis, M. L., Soderstrom, E. J. 1988. Application of social psychological and evaluation research: lessons from energy information programs. *Eval. Prog. Plan.* 11:77–84

Dennis, M. L., Soderstrom, E. J., Koncinski, W. S. Jr., Cavanaugh, B. 1990. Effective dissemination of energy-related information: applying social psychology and evaluation research. *Am. Psychol.* 45:1109–17

DeYoung, R. 1986. Some psychological aspects of recycling: the structure of conservation satisfactions. *Environ. Behav.* 18:435–49

DeYoung, R. 1989. Exploring the difference between recyclers and non-recyclers: the role of information. *J. Environ. Syst.* 18:341–51

DeYoung, R. 1989–1990. Promoting conservation behavior in shared spaces: the role of energy monitors. *J. Environ. Syst.* 19:265–73

DeYoung, R. 1990. Recycling as appropriate behavior: a review of survey data from selected recycling education programs in Michigan. *Resour. Conserve Recyc.* 3:1–13

DeYoung, R., Kaplan, S. 1986. Conservation behavior and the structure of satisfactions. *J. Environ. Syst.* 15:233–42

Dietz, T., Stern, P. C., Rycroft, R. W. 1989. Definitions of conflict and the legitimation of resources: the case of environmental risk. *Sociol. Forum* 4:47–70

Doble, J., Richardson, A., Danks, A. 1990. *Science and the Public: A Report in Three Volumes.* Vol. 3. *Global Warming Caused by the Greenhouse Effect.* New York: Public Agenda Found.

Dunlap, R. E. 1985. Public opinion: behind the transformation. *EPA J.* 11(July-Aug.):15–17

Dunlap, R. E. 1991. Trends in public opinion toward environmental issues: 1965–1990. *Soc. Nat. Resour.* 4. In press

Dunlap, R. E., Grieneeks, J. K., Rokeach, M. 1983. Human values and pro-environmental behavior. In *Energy and Material Resources: Attitudes, Values, and Public Policy,* ed. W. D. Conn. Boulder, CO: Westview

Dunlap, R. E., Michelson, W., eds. 1991. *Handbook of Environmental Sociology.* Greenwich, CT: Greenwood

Dunlap, R. E., Van Liere, K. D. 1977. Land ethic or golden rule. *J. Soc. Issue* 33(3):200–7

Dunlap, R. E., Van Liere, K. D. 1978. The "new environmental paradigm": a proposed measuring instrument and preliminary results. *J. Environ. Educ.* 9:10–19

Eckberg, D. L., Blocker, T. J. 1989. Varieties of religious involvement and environmental concerns: testing the Lynn White thesis. *J. Sci. Stud. Relig.* 28:509–17

Edelstein, M. R., Wandersman, A. 1987. Community dynamics in coping with toxic environments. *Hum. Behav. Environ.: Adv. Theory Res.* 9:69–112

Egel, K. 1987. Evaluation of an alternative home energy audit program. *Eval. Rev.* 11:116–30

Ester, P. A., Winett, R. A. 1982. Toward more effective antecedent strategies for environmental programs. *J. Environ. Syst.* 11:201–21

Evans, G. W., Cohen, S. 1987. Environmental stress. In *Handbook of Environmental Psychology,* ed. D. Stokols, I. Altman, pp. 571–610. New York: Wiley

Farhar, B. C., Unseld, C. T., Vories, R., Crews, R. 1980. Public opinion about energy. *Annu. Rev. Energy* 5:141–72

Fischhoff, B., Furby, L. 1983. Psychological dimensions of climatic change. In *Social Science Research and Climate Change: An Interdisciplinary Appraisal,* ed. R. S. Chen, E. Boulding, S. H. Schneider, pp. 180–203. Doredrecht: Reidel

Freudenburg, W. R., Jones, T. R. 1991. Attitudes and stress in the presence of technological risk: a test of the Supreme Court hypothesis. *Soc. Forces* 69:1143–68

Geller, E. S. 1987. Environmental psychology and applied behavior analysis: from strange bedfellows to a productive marriage. In *Handbook of Environmental Psychology,* ed. D. Stokols, I. Altman, pp. 361–88. New York: Wiley

Geller, E. S. 1989. Applied behavior analysis and social marketing: an integration for environmental preservation. *J. Soc. Issues* 45(1):17–36

Geller, E. S., Winett. R. A., Everett, P. B. 1982. *Preserving the Environment: Strategies for Behavior Change.* New York: Pergamon

Gill, J. D., Crosby, L. A., Taylor, J. R. 1986. Ecological concern, attitudes, and social norms in voting behavior. *Pub. Opin. Q.* 50:537–54

Goitein, B. 1989. Organizational decision-making and energy conservation investments. *Eval. Prog. Plan.* 12:143–51

Gonzales, M. H., Aronson, E., Costanzo, M. A. 1988. Using social cognition and persuasion to promote energy conservation: a quasi-experiment. *J. Appl. Soc. Psychol.* 18:1049–66

Gould, L. C., Gardner, G. T., DeLuca, D. R., Tiemann, A. R., Doob, L. W., et al. 1988. *Perceptions of Technological Risks and Benefits.* New York: Russell Sage Foundation

Gunter, V. J., Finlay, B. 1988. Influences on group participation in environmental conflicts. *Rural Sociol.* 53:498–505

Hardin, G. 1968. The tragedy of the commons. *Science* 162:1243–48

Hardin, G. 1982. *Collective Action.* Baltimore, MD: Johns Hopkins Univ. Press

Heberlein, T. A. 1972. The land ethic realized: some social psychological explanations for changing environmental attitudes. *J. Soc. Issues* 28(4):79–87

Heberlein, T. A. 1977. Norm activation and environmental action. *J. Soc. Issues* 33(3):207–11

Heberlein, T. A. 1981. Environmental attitudes. *Z. Umweltpolit.* 2:241–70

Heberlein, T. A., Baumgartner, R. M. 1985. Changing attitudes and electricity consumption in a time-of-use experiment. Presented at Int. Conf. Consum. Behav. Energy Policy, Versailles, April

Heberlein, T. A., Warriner, G. K. 1983. The influence of price and attitude on shifting residential electricity consumption from on to off-peak periods. *J. Econ. Psychol.* 4:107–30

Hines, J. M., Hungerford, H. R., Tomera, A. N. 1987. Analysis and synthesis of research on responsible environmental behavior: a metaanalysis. *J. Environ. Educ.* 18:1–8

Hirst, E. 1987. *Cooperation and Community Conservation: The Hood River Conservation Project.* ORNL/CON-235: DOE/BP-11287–16. Oak Ridge, TN: Oak Ridge Natl. Lab.

Hirst, E. 1990. Progress and potential evaluating energy efficiency programs. *Eval. Rev.* 14:192–205

Houghton, J. T., Jenkins, G. J., Ephraums, J. J., eds. 1990. *Climate Change: The IPCC Scientific Assessment.* Cambridge: Cambridge Univ. Press

Hughey, J. B., Sundstrom, E., Lounsbury, J. W. 1985. Attitudes toward nuclear power: a longitudinal analysis of expectancy-value models. *Basic Appl. Soc. Psychol.* 6:75–91

Inglehart, R. 1990. *Culture Shift in Advanced Industrial Society.* Princeton, NJ: Princeton Univ. Press

Jones, R. E. 1990. Understanding paper recycling in an institutionally supportive setting: an application of the theory of reasoned action. *J. Environ. Syst.* 19:307–21

Kahle, L. R., Beatty, S. E. 1987. Cognitive consequences of legislating postpurchase behavior: growing up with the bottle bill. *J. Appl. Soc. Psychol.* 17:828–43

Kahneman, D., Tversky, A. 1973. On the psychology of prediction. *Psychol. Rev.* 80:237–51

Kates, R. W., Ausubel, J., Berberian, M., eds. 1985. *Climate Impact Assessment: Studies of the Interaction of Climate and Society.* New York: Wiley

Katzev, R. D., Johnson, T. R. 1983. A social-psychological analysis of residential electricity consumption: the impact of minimal justification techniques. *J. Econ. Psychol.* 3:267–84

Katzev, R. D., Johnson, T. R. 1984. Comparing the effects of monetary incentives and foot-in-the-door strategies in promoting residential energy conservation. *J. Appl. Soc. Psychol.* 14:12–27

Katzev, R. D., Johnson, T. R. 1987. *Promoting Energy Conservation: An Analysis of Behavioral Research.* Boulder, CO: Westview

Keeney, R. L., Raiffa, H. 1976. *Decisions with Multiple Objectives: Preferences and Value Tradeoffs.* New York: Wiley

Kempton, W. 1991. Lay perspectives on global climate change. *Glob. Environ. Change* 1:183–208

Kempton, W., Darley, J. M., Stern, P. C. 1992. Psychological research for the new energy problems. *Am. Psychol.* In press

Kempton, W., Montgomery, L. 1982. Folk quantification of energy. *Energy* 7:817–27

Kempton, W., Harris, C. K., Keith, J. G., Weihl, J. S. 1985. Do consumers know what works in energy conservation? *Marriage Fam. R.* 9:115–33

Kroll-Smith, J. S., Couch, S. R., Levine, A. G. 1991. Technological hazards and disasters. See Dunlap & Michelson, 1991

Kushler, M. G. 1989. Use of evaluation to improve energy conservation programs: a review and case study. *J. Soc. Issues* 45(1):153–68

la Riviere, J. W. M. 1989. Threats to the world's water. *Sci. Am.* 261(3):80–94

Leopold, A. 1948. *A Sand County Almanac.* New York: Oxford

Lichtenstein, S., Slovic, P., Fischhoff, B., Layman, M., Combs, B. 1978. Judged frequency of lethal events. *J. Exp. Psychol.: Hum Learn. Mem.* 4:551–78

Lichtenstein, S., Fischhoff, B., Phillips, L. D. 1982. Calibration of probabilities: the state of the art. In *Judgment Under Uncertainty: Heuristics and Biases,* ed. D. Kahneman, P. Slovic, A. Tversky. New York: Cambridge

Longstreth, M., Turner, J., Topliff, M. L., Iams, D. R. 1989. Support for soft and hard path American energy policies: Does gender play a role? *Women's Stud. Int. Forum* 12:213–26

Lynne. G. D., Rola, L. R. 1988. Improving attitude-behavior prediction models with economic variables: farmer attitudes toward soil conservation. *J. Soc. Psychol.* 128:19–28

Macey, S. M., Brown, M. A. 1983. Residential energy conservation: the role of past experience in repetitive household behavior. *Environ. Behav.* 15:123–41

McAdam, D., McCarthy, J. D., Zald, M. N. 1988. Social movements. In *Handbook of Sociology,* ed. N. J. Smelser. Newbury Park, CA: Sage

Manzo, L. C., Weinstein, N. D. 1987. Behavioral commitment to environmental protection: a study of active and nonactive members of the Sierra Club. *Environ. Behav.* 19:673–94

McClelland, L. 1980. Encouraging energy conservation in multi-family housing: RUBS and other methods of allocating energy costs to residents. Executive summary and list of contents. Boulder, CO: Univ. Colo., Inst. Behav. Sci.

McClelland, L., Cook, S. W. 1980. Promoting energy conservation in master-metered apartments through financial incentives. *J. Appl. Soc. Psychol.* 10:19–31

Mileti, D. S., Fitzpatrick, C. 1991. Communication of public risk: its theory and its application. *Sociol. Pract. Rev.* 2(1):20–28

Mileti, D. S., Nigg, J. M. 1991. Natural hazards and disasters. 1991. See Dunlap & Michelson 1991

Miller, R. D., Ford, J. M. 1985. *Shared Savings in the Residential Market: A Public/Private Partnership for Energy Conservation.* Baltimore, MD: Energy Task Force, Urban Consortium for Technology Initiatives

Mohai, P. 1985. Public concern and elite involvement in environmental-conservation issues. *Soc. Sci. Q.* 66:820–38

Mohai, P., Twight, B. W. 1987. Age, social integration, and concern for the environment. Presented at Annu. Meet. Rural Sociol. Soc.

National Research Council. 1988. *Toward an Understanding of Global Change: Initial Priorities for U. S. Contributions to the International Geosphere-Biosphere Program.* Washington DC: Natl. Acad. Press

National Research Council. 1989. *Improving Risk Communication.* Washington DC: Natl. Acad. Press

National Research Council. 1990. *Research Strategies for the U. S. Global Change Research Program.* Washington DC: Natl. Acad. Press

Neuman, K. 1986. Personal values and commitment to energy conservation. *Environ. Behav.* 18:53–74

Olsen, M., Harris, C. 1991. Energy in society. See Dunlap & Michelson 1991

Olson, M. 1965. *The Logic of Collective Action.* Cambridge, MA: Harvard Univ. Press

Pallak, M. S., Cook, D. A., Sullivan, J. J. 1980. Commitment and energy conservation. In *Applied Social Psychology Annual,* ed. L. Beckman, 1:235–53. Beverly Hills, CA: Sage

Palmborg, C. 1987. Social habits and energy consumption in single-family homes. *Energy* 11:643–50

Pettus, A. M., Giles, M. B. 1987. Personality characteristics and environmental attitudes. *Popul. Environ.* 9:127–37

Pierce, J. C., Lovrich, N. P. Jr., Tsurutani, T., Abe, T. 1987. Environmental belief systems among Japanese and American elites and publics. *Polit. Behav.* 9:139–59

Polich, M. D. 1984. Minnesota RCS: the myths and realities. In *Doing Better: Setting an Agenda for the Second Decade, American Council for an Energy-Efficient Economy,* G:141–51. Washington DC: Author

Prester, G., Rohrmann, B., Schellhammer, E. 1987. Environmental evaluations and participation activities: a social psychological field study. *J. Appl. Soc. Psychol.* 17:751–87

Rayner, S., ed. 1991. Managing the global commons. *Eval. Rev.* 15(1):1–170

Robinson, J. B. 1989. The proof of the pudding: policy and implementation issues associated with increasing energy efficiency. Dept. Environ. Resour. Stud., Univ. Waterloo

Rokeach, M. 1967. *Value Survey.* Sunnyvale, CA: Hallgren Tests

Rutte, C. G., Wilke, H. A. M., Messick, D. 1987. Scarcity or abundance caused by people or the environment as determinants of behavior in the resource dilemma. *J. Exp. Soc. Psychol.* 23:208–16

Samdahl, D. M., Robertson, R. 1989. Social determinants of environmental concern: specification and test of the model. *Environ. Behav.* 21:57–81

Samuelson, C. D., Messick, D. M. 1986. Alternative structural solutions to resource dilemmas. *Organ. Behav. Hum. Decis. Proc.* 37:139–55

Schneider, S. H. 1989. *Global Warming: Are We Entering the Greenhouse Century?* San Francisco: Sierra Club Books

Schwartz, S. H. 1977. Normative influences on altruism. In *Adv. Exp. Soc. Psychol.* 10:221–79

Seligman, C., Becker, L. J., Darley, J. M. 1981. Encouraging residential energy conservation through feedback. In *Advances in Environmental Psychology,* ed. A. Baum, J. E. Singer, 3:93–113. Hillsdale, NJ: Erlbaum

Shine, K. P., Derwent, R. G., Wuebbles, D. J., Morcrette, J.-J. 1990. Radiative forcing of climate. In *Climate Change: The IPCC Assessment,* ed. J. T. Houghton, G. J. Jenkins, J. J. Ephraums, pp. 41–68. Cambridge: Cambridge Univ. Press

Sia, A. P., Hungerford, H. R., Tomera, A. N. 1986. Selected predictors of responsible environmental behavior: an analysis. *J. Environ. Educ.* 17:31–40

Silver, C. S., DeFries, R. S. 1990. *One Earth, One Future.* Washington DC: Natl. Acad. Press

Sivek, D. J., Hungerford, H. R. 1990. Predictors of responsible behavior in members of three Wisconsin conservation organizations. *J. Environ. Educ.* 21:35–40

Sjöberg, L. 1989. Global change and human action: psychological perspectives. *Int. Soc. Sci. J.* 41:413–32

Slovic, P. 1987. Perception of risk. *Science* 236:280–85

Snow, D. A., Rochford, E. B. Jr., Worden, S. K., Benford, R. D. 1986. Frame alignment processes, micromobilization and movement participation. *Am. Sociol. R.* 51:464–81

Steger, M. A. E., Pierce, J. C., Steel, B. S., Lovrich, N. P. 1989. Political culture, post-material values, and the new environmental paradigm: a comparative analysis of Canada and the United States. *Polit. Behav.* 11:233–54

Stern, P. C. 1986. Blind spots in policy analysis: What economics doesn't say about energy use. *J. Policy Anal. Manage.* 5:200–27

Stern, P. C. 1991. Learning through conflict: a realistic strategy for risk communication. *Policy Sci.* 24:99–119

Stern, P. C. 1992. What psychology knows about energy conservation. *Am. Psychol.* In press

Stern, P. C., Aronson, E., eds. 1984. *Energy Use: The Human Dimension.* New York: Freeman

Stern, P. C., Aronson, E., Darley, J. M., Hill, D. H., Hirst, E., et al. 1986a. The effectiveness of incentives for residential energy conservation. *Eval. Rev.* 10:147–76

Stern, P. C., Aronson, E., Darley, J. M., Hill, D. H., Hirst, E., et al. 1987. Answering behavioral questions about energy conservation in buildings. *Energy* 12:339–53

Stern, P. C., Black, J. S., Elworth, J. T. 1983. Adaptations to changing energy conditions among Massachusetts households. *Energy* 8:515–23

Stern, P. C., Dietz, T., Black, J. S. 1986b. Support for environmental protection: the role of moral norms. *Popul. Environ.* 8:204–22

Stern, P. C., Gardner. G. T. 1981a. Psychological research and energy policy. *Am. Psychol.* 36:329–42

Stern, P. C., Gardner, G. T. 1981b. The place of behavior change in the management of environmental problems. *Z. Umweltpolit.* 2:213–39

Stern, P. C., Oskamp, S. 1987. Managing scarce environmental resources. In *Handbook of Environmental Psychology,* ed. D. Stokols, I. Altman, 2:1043–88. New York: Wiley

Stern, P. C., Young, O. R., Druckman, D., eds. 1991. *Global Environmental Change: The Human Dimensions.* Washington DC: Natl. Acad. Press

Syme, G. J., Seligman, C., Kantola, S. J., Macpherson, D. K. 1987. Evaluating a television campaign to promote petrol conservation. *Environ. Behav.* 19:444–61

Taylor, J. J., Stewart, T. R., Downton, M. 1988. Perceptions of drought in the Ogallala aquifer region. *Environ. Behav.* 20:150–75

Turner, B. L. II, Clark, W. C., Kates, R. W.,

Richards, J. F., Mathews, J. T. et al, eds. 1991a. *The Earth as Transformed by Human Action.* New York: Cambridge Univ. Press

Turner, B. L. II, Kasperson, R. E., Meyer, W. B., Dow, K., Golding, D. et al. 1991b. Two types of global environmental change: definitional and spatial scale issues in their human dimensions. *Global Environ. Change* 1:14–22

Tversky, A., Kahneman, D. 1981. The framing of decisions and the rationality of choice. *Science* 211:453–58

US Congress, Office of Technology Assessment. 1991. *Changing by Degrees: Steps to Reduce Greenhouse Gases.* Washington DC: USGPO

Van der Pligt, J., Eiser, J. R., Spears, R. 1986a. Attitudes toward nuclear energy: familiarity and salience. *Environ. Behav.* 18:75–93

Van der Pligt, J., Eiser, J. R., Spears, R. 1986b. Construction of a nuclear power station in one's locality: attitudes and salience. *Basic Appl. Soc. Psychol.* 7:1–15

Van Houwelingen, J. H., Van Raaij, W. F. 1989. The effect of goal-setting and daily electronic feedback on in-home energy use. *J. Consum. Res.* 16:98–105.

Van Liere, K. D., Dunlap, R. E. 1978. Moral norms and environmental behavior: an application of Schwartz's norm-activation model to yard burning. *J. Appl. Soc. Psychol.* 8:174–88

Van Liere, K. D., Dunlap, R. E. 1980. The social bases of environmental concern: a review of hypotheses, explanations, and empirical evidence. *Publ. Opin. Q.* 44:43–59

Van Liere, K. D., Dunlap, R. E. 1981. Environmental concern: Does it make a difference how it's measured? *Environ. Behav.* 13:651–76

Verhallen, T. M. M., van Raaij, W. F. 1981. Household behavior and the use of natural gas for home heating. *J. Consum. Res.* 8:253–57

Verplanken, B. 1989. Involvement and need for cognition as moderators of beliefs-attitude-intention consistency. *Brit. J. Soc. Psychol.* 28:115–22

Vine, E., Harris, J. 1988. *Planning for an Energy-Efficient Future: The Experience with Implementing Energy Conservation Programs for New Residential and Commercial Buildings,* Vols. 1, 2. LBL-25525. Berkeley, CA: Lawrence Berkeley Lab.

Vining, J., Ebreo, A. 1990. What makes a recycler? A comparison of recyclers and nonrecyclers. *Environ. Behav.* 22:55–73

Walker, J. M. 1979. Energy demand behavior in a master-metered apartment complex: an experimental analysis. *J. Appl. Psychol.* 64:190–96

Warrick, R. A., Oerlemans, H. 1990. Sea level rise. See Houghton et al 1990, pp. 257–81

White, L. 1967. The historical roots of our ecological crisis. *Science* 155:1203–7

Whyte, A. V. T. 1985. Perception. See Kates et al 1985, pp. 403–36

Wilson, E. O., ed. 1988. *Biodiversity.* Washington DC: Natl. Acad. Press

Winett, R. A., Hatcher, J. W., Fort, T. R., Leckliter, E. N., Love, S. Q., et al. 1982. The effects of videotape modeling and daily feedback on residential electricity conservation, home temperature and humidity, perceived comfort, and clothing worn: winter and summer. *J. Appl. Behav. Anal.* 15:381–402

Winett, R. A., Leckliter, I. N., Chinn, D. E., Stahl, B., Love, S. Q. 1985. Effects of television modeling on residential energy conservation. *J. Appl. Behav. Anal.* 18:33–44

Yates, S. 1982. *Using prospect theory to create persuasive communications about solar water heaters and insulation.* PhD thesis, Univ. Calif., Santa Cruz

Annu. Rev. Psychol. 1992. 43:303–336

SCHIZOPHRENIA: DIATHESIS-STRESS REVISITED

D. C. Fowles

Department of Psychology, University of Iowa, Iowa City, Iowa 52242

KEY WORDS: dopamine, polygenic models, schizoaffective disorders, positive & negative symptoms, appetitive & aversive motivation

CONTENTS

The diathesis-stress model of schizophrenia has been with us for many years (Rosenthal 1970), yet there have been few attempts to address its full im-

0066-4308/92/0201-0303$02.00

plications. Specifically, the categorical or disease-model approach to psychopathology and the current interest in molecular biology have combined to produce a strong focus on single-gene models of schizophrenia with little attention to environmental variables or to nonspecific modifier genes. For example, recent major reviews in the *British Journal of Psychiatry* (Mullan & Murray 1989) and the *American Journal of Psychiatry* (Pardes et al 1989) focused on single-gene models of psychopathology. Reiss et al (1991) criticized these reviews as being distinctly one-sided, neglecting polygenic models and environmental contributions, and Risch (1990) similarly criticized single-gene approaches as being incompatible with a substantial body of evidence. It is appropriate, therefore, to offer an alternative neurobehavioral model for the etiology of schizophrenia, with an eye toward accounting for some of the major phenomena seen in the literature on schizophrenia.

This approach to schizophrenia has been encouraged by several recent developments. Plomin (1990) argued that a behavior genetics perspective strongly supports environmental contributions. A 1989 *Annual Review* chapter by Wise & Rompre explicated the behavioral functions of the neurotransmitter dopamine, which is the focus of pharmacological theories of schizophrenia. Similarly, in the most recent *Annual Review* chapter on biological approaches to psychopathology, Depue & Iacono (1989) complained that current neuro*biological* models focus almost exclusively on biological variables and called on psychologists to develop more truly integrative frameworks. They offered their own neuro*behavioral* theory of bipolar affective disorder (also implicating dopamine). Other developments that stimulated the present review include the current distinction between positive and negative symptoms in schizophrenia, the continuing challenge to the disease model presented by the schizoaffective disorders, the acknowledgement of problems of comorbidity that also challenge the disease model, a growing body of evidence implicating life events and aversive psychosocial stimulation in symptom onset in schizophrenia, the increasing recognition among psychopathologists of the relevance of Gray's (e.g. 1982) motivational theory, Tellegen's (e.g. 1985) development of personality dimensions related to motivational constructs, and a continuing defense of the multifactorial polygenic model by Gottesman and his colleagues. The starting point for the present review is a summary of the evidence for a genetic contribution to schizophrenia, because these data provide the most informative framework for understanding the etiology of schizophrenia.

GENETIC FACTORS

The Diathesis-Stress Model

Taken together, the family, twin, and adoption studies—all of which have been well replicated—show that genetic factors are important in the familial risk for schizophrenia: Schizophrenia runs in families largely for genetic reasons. On this basis, Rosenthal (1970) proposed that the etiology of schizophrenia should be conceptualized in the context of the diathesis-stress model. In this model, the environmental factors are not specific to schizophrenia, whereas the genetic (diathesis) factors are. That is, genetic factors predict a specific risk of schizophrenia. Environmental stress, in contrast, is common to many disorders and is not specific to schizophrenia—i.e. the environmental component is not "schizophrenogenic."

Current Data and Genetic Models

Gottesman et al (1987) reviewed the current status of research on genetic factors in schizophrenia. Their summary (Gottesman et al 1987: Table 2, p. 29) was drawn from a large data base of all Western European family and twin studies, 1920–1978. For a relatively broad concept of schizophrenia (definite + probable schizophrenia), there is an orderly decrease in risk for schizophrenia as one goes from monozygotic (MZ) twins (45.6%) to first-degree relatives (9.26–13.7%) to second-degree relatives (3.46–5.99%) and, finally, to third-degree relatives (2.44%). These risks are to be compared with a population risk of 0.99%. The risk of schizophrenia among the offspring of dual matings (both parents are schizophrenic) is 46%, a greater risk than that of having a single schizophrenic parent (Gottesman & Shields 1982:48).

Because of the large data base for genetic studies, schizophrenia provides an excellent opportunity to examine genetic models for the mode of transmission of the vulnerability or liability to schizophrenia. The two major alternatives are the monogenic-biochemical (Rosenthal 1970:187) or single-major-locus (Faraone & Tsuang 1985) model versus multifactorial polygenic inheritance. In spite of the attractiveness of the single-major-locus model with *high penetrance,* the data are so strongly against it that the model has repeatedly been found not to fit the data (e.g. Faraone & Tsuang 1985; McGue & Gottesman 1989; Risch 1990). A variation on the single-major-locus model is to assume a small number of loci (e.g. two loci with two alleles each)—what Faraone & Tsuang call the limited-loci-polygenic model. However, genetic factors account for a relatively small portion of phenotypic variance in these models, meaning that most individuals with genetic vulnerability do not develop schizophrenia—i.e. are phenotypically normal (Faraone & Tsuang 1985). The same conclusion applies to mixed models, in which there is either (*a*) a single gene with high penetrance (e.g. 0.6) and low frequency (e.g. 20% of schizophrenics) or (*b*) a common single gene with low penetrance (Gottesman & McGue 1991). An advocate of a model embracing a small number of loci, then, is forced to accept that nongenetic factors—either physical or psychosocial environmental—play a major role in whether schizophrenia develops in a person with genotypic vulnerability, a position consistent with the diathesis-stress model.

Gottesman & Shields (1967) first applied the multifactorial polygenic model (adopted from Falconer 1965) to schizophrenia. This model assumes that a large number of genes contribute in an additive fashion to the overall liability for schizophrenia and that phenotypic schizophrenia is seen when the liability exceeds a given threshold. Familial and nonfamilial environmental influences are included in the model and are assumed to combine additively with genetic influences.

In general, multifactorial polygenic models with a threshold are consistent with the genetic data for schizophrenia (e.g. Faraone & Tsuang 1985; Gottesman et al 1987; Risch 1990).

The polygenic model is not only consistent with the genetic data, it is also likely to be the correct model on other grounds (Plomin 1990). Widely ranging studies of animal behavior have converged to show that the contribution of genetic factors to the phenotypic variability almost always appears to be less than 50%. Additionally, these studies show that many genes affect the behavior, each contributing a small effect. Although there may be isolated single-gene effects, these account for only a small portion of the overall behavioral variability. Plomin specifically includes schizophrenia and the affective disorders as involving behavior that is likely to reflect polygenic influences (see also Reiss et al 1991).

Another important question regarding the genetic contribution to schizophrenia concerns the portion of patients to whom the genetic model applies. That is, are there large numbers of patients who develop schizophrenia without a genetic diathesis? At present, the alternative etiologic pathway is often assumed to be physical environmental. In the context of a genetic perspective, these nongenetic etiologies are called "phenocopies"—i.e. manifesting a similar phenotype but without the (expected) genetic etiology. Murray et al (1985) proposed that "sporadic" (nongenetic) forms of schizophrenia are quite common and suggested further that the absence of a family history of any major psychiatric disorder (including schizophrenia) is indicative of a possible sporadic schizophrenia. Additionally, they suggested that the afflicted twin in discordant MZ twin pairs might reflect sporadic schizophrenia, possibly reflecting early trauma such as birth injury. Reveley et al (1984) reported an association among a negative family history, a positive history of early cerebral insults, and enlarged cerebral ventricles.

Gottesman et al (1987) have criticized this position on a number of grounds: Negative family histories are to be expected from all plausible genetic models, the use of negative family history of any major psychiatric disorder is flawed for several reasons, and studies of the relationship between family history of psychiatric disorders and cerebral ventricular size have yielded inconsistent results. Perhaps most important, Fischer (1971) reported the risk of schizophrenia among the offspring of the healthy twin in discordant

MZ pairs to be comparable to that for the afflicted MZ twins and, more generally, to that for children of schizophrenic probands. This finding has been confirmed and extended by Gottesman & Bertelsen (1989), and similar results have been reported by Kringlen & Gunnar (1989). Thus the healthy twin in discordant MZ twins conveys as much genetic vulnerability to offspring as the afflicted twin, strongly implying that discordant MZ twin pairs are to be counted among those with a genetic etiology, as opposed to a nongenetic etiology such as birth trauma.

The point is not that phenocopies with a physical environmental etiology do not occur but that the multifactorial polygenic model applies to most patients with a diagnosis of schizophrenia. There undoubtedly are physically produced phenocopies (e.g. Faraone & Tsuang 1985; Gottesman 1991:28–31) and, possibly, rare single genes with large effects (high penetrance) and/or a common single gene with greatly reduced penetrance. It seems likely, however, that a simple multifactorial polygenic model applies to most cases; in addition, the alternative genetic models require a contribution of nonspecific genetic and environmental factors that makes them similar to the polygenic model.

The Multifactorial Polygenic Model

Gottesman & Shields (1982:63–69, 220–29) present the major features of a polygenic model: (a) a liability to the development of schizophrenia, derived from both genetic and environmental sources; (b) continuous and normal distribution of this liability in the population; and (c) a liability threshold for the development of schizophrenia, such that individuals whose liability exceeds the threshold develop (phenotypic) schizophrenia. The sources of liability include *specific* genetic liability, *general* genetic liability, and *general* environmental liability. The term specific genetic liability refers to the genetic contribution that conveys a specific risk for schizophrenia. The general sources of liability have nothing to do with schizophrenia per se, but represent *modifiers* or *potentiators* of the specific liability—i.e. they are nonspecific contributors to etiology. The sources of these general genetic and environmental liabilities have been somewhat neglected in the literature on schizophrenia, and they include the components that mediate the effects of stress in the diathesis-stress model. Also, the general genetic liability constitutes a component of the genetic contribution to etiology in estimates of heritability and could be quantitatively important.

Estimates of heritability tend to be high in the polygenic model. Path analytic multifactorial polygenic models estimate the overall genetic contribution to be 60–70% (Faraone & Tsuang 1985). However, even a small environmental contribution can be important.

It is an obvious inference from the polygenic model that the role of the environment varies with the magnitude of the genetic liability (Gottesman & Shields 1982:63–69, 220–21; Zubin & Spring 1977). To clarify this point, it is useful to divide the continuum of liability arbitrarily into a number of segments or categories. At the "upper extreme" lies the theoretical possibility that a small number of individuals are *genetically above threshold*—i.e. that the environment plays no significant role in causing their chronic schizophrenia. A larger number of individuals will have a genetic liability that is *near threshold*. Given the additional liability in *most* environments, these individuals are likely to reach threshold (develop schizophrenia); and they are, for that reason, likely to be chronic. A third group will have a genetic liability great enough (close enough to threshold) to be at risk but low enough to require a significant environmental contribution. If they are in chronically harsh environments, they might also be chronic, but often they will show episodes in response to an increase in environmental liability. As the genetic liability decreases even more, a fourth group might be said to be at *minimal risk,* meaning that schizophrenic symptoms could develop in response to very severe but infrequently encountered environments. They might well develop a brief reactive psychosis in response to major stressors. Finally, many individuals will have such a low genetic liability that they are *not at risk.* Phenotypic outcome for the first (genetically above threshold) and last (not at risk) groups is not dependent upon an environmental contribution; such individuals may be thought of as either genetically schizophrenic or genetically not schizophrenic. For the minimal-risk group the environmental contribution is large on an individual basis (i.e. adds a lot of liability), but the infrequency of these severe life events reduces their contribution to population phenotypic variance. Further, such schizophrenic reactions are likely to be dismissed as unrelated to "true" schizophrenia because they remit rapidly and because the genetic contribution is so small as to fail to show statistically significant effects in family risk studies. For the near-threshold group the environmental contribution adds only a small amount to the total liability, and it can involve stressors so mild that they are difficult to recognize. *Thus, only for the at-risk group would one expect to see an appreciable contribution of recognizable life events among patients conventionally seen as schizophrenic.*

Since the addition of environmental liability is critical for the development of schizophrenia in only a small portion of the population, the total contribution of environmental liability to population phenotypic variance need not be large to contribute importantly to etiology. This environmental contribution exerts its greatest effect in the population of most interest—those who are genetically at risk for schizophrenia and, to a lesser extent, those near threshold. In contrast, much of the genetic contribution to population phenotypic variance is to the absence of schizophrenia—i.e. a large portion of the population is not at risk or minimally at risk for schizophrenia, because they have so little genetic liability that environmental liability is unlikely to bring them above threshold.

Given the potential importance of general genetic and environmental liability, what can be said about their nature? The diathesis-stress model suggests that any variables that increase the stressfulness of the environment can be expected to facilitate the development of schizophrenia. These variables can act both directly and indirectly. Any genetic factor that increases stress reactivity (e.g. anxiety-proneness, depression-proneness) will lead directly to the experience of greater stress. Indirect contributors would include those that make the environment objectively more stressful. For example, low IQ, with its subsequent educational and occupational disadvantages will, on the average, increase environmental aversiveness (e.g. Wing 1978). Similarly, any temperament factors that interfere with one's ability to reach an adequate social and occupational adjustment will have pervasive effects on social and occupational success—e.g. such behavioral deficit traits as anhedonia, shyness, social withdrawal, etc. At the environmental level, the host of factors that make the environment more aversive are likely candidates. These factors are considered below, but first it is necessary to consider other aspects of schizophrenia.

IMPORTANT SUBTYPES AND BOUNDARIES

Subtype Heterogeneity vs a Continuum of Severity

The familial-risk data can be used to examine the question of whether phenotypic heterogeneity among diagnosed schizophrenics reflects etiologic heterogeneity. The etiologic-heterogeneity model hypothesizes that qualitatively different genetic factors underlie different subtypes of schizophrenia. This model predicts that subtypes will "breed true"—i.e. family studies will show the same subtype in all family members. In contrast, it may be hypothesized that there is only a single genetic etiology but that the genetic contribution to etiology varies in severity. In this continuum-of-severity model, phenotypic heterogeneity is attributed to quantitative differences in severity of the overall liability, but all (genetically based) schizophrenia shares a common etiology. Although there is a noteworthy degree of subtype specificity within families, the range of subtypes seen within families is so great that one can reject the hypothesis of qualitatively distinct subtypes (Gottesman & Shields 1982:89–92; Gottesman et al 1987). Moreover, there is not enough subtype specificity to reject the simple hypothesis of a single dimension of severity of genetic liability.

Thus, these data lead to the important conclusion that the more severe forms of schizophrenia are associated with greater risk to offspring. Although these forms are, therefore, considered to represent a quantitatively more severe genetic loading (e.g. Rosenthal 1970:144; Gottesman & Shields 1982:90; Gottesman et al 1987), they are on an etiologic continuum with the less severe forms. Exactly which less severely affected patients are to be considered schizophrenic (based on family and twin studies) is not altogether clear, but schizoaffective and borderline or latent schizophrenics are included (Gottesman et al 1987:28). Gottesman (1991:36) continues to argue (based on twin concordance data) for a "middle-of-the-road" diagnosis. These data clearly support the inclusion of nonchronic forms of schizophrenia, with the result that the most salient feature of differences in severity is the degree of chronicity.

Prognosis and the Positive vs Negative Symptom Distinction

Although underlying differences in genetic liability are likely to contribute strongly to differences in chronicity, these genetic influences are not necessarily due to specific genetic liability, nor do they preclude environmental effects. Consequently, it is worth examining the features associated with the dimension of severity, with an eye toward identifying differences that may relate to multiple etiologic factors.

Information on this point comes from literature on the distinction between process vs reactive schizophrenics, on the dimension of activity vs withdrawal, and on positive vs negative symptoms. The process-reactive distinction is strongly correlated with prognosis (Chapman & Chapman 1973:28). The process schizophrenic shows a poor premorbid adjustment, with little interest in people or other activities (anhedonia), an insidious onset without an identifiable precipitating stress, affective flattening, and a poor prognosis (including a chronic course). The reactive schizophrenic shows a normal premorbid adjustment, a rapid onset in response to severe stress, marked affective symptoms, and a better prognosis with possible recovery. Three aspects of these characteristics are important. First, the picture of the reactive schizophrenic fits the "at risk" zone of the continuum of liability. In contrast, the process schizophrenic fits the "near threshold" and the "genetically above threshold" zones. Second, process schizophrenics appear to exemplify *anhedonia*—a classic feature of schizophrenia (Carpenter et al 1988). Third, the presence of affective symptoms is a good prognostic sign—so much so that there is "a very great overlap" between schizoaffective disorder and good-prognosis schizophrenia (Kendler et al 1986:1102). The combination of schizophrenic and affective symptoms is discussed below.

The activity–withdrawal dimension was the focus of a series of studies of chronic schizophrenics in England by Venables and Wing. Activity–withdrawal is assessed by ward ratings on ten items (Venables 1957). Individuals assessed at the active end of the dimension are characterized as restless, loud, overtalkative, overactive, and having many friends and interests. Withdrawn patients showed an absence of these features. Although the withdrawn patients were behaviorally inactive, among nonparanoid schizophrenics (see Wing 1961) withdrawal was strongly associated with "arousal" on the basis of three measures: palmar skin potential, two flash fusion threshold, and two click fusion threshold (Venables & Wing 1962; Venables 1963a,b, 1967). Skin potential most likely reflects (sympathetically innervated) palmar sweat gland activity. The two perceptual measures assessed the time interval at which two closely spaced stimuli fuse and were introduced as indexes of cortical reactivity. Thus, the active schizophrenics showed a pattern of behavioral activation, reward-seeking, and (in some sense) low arousal, whereas the withdrawn schizophrenics showed anhedonia, behavioral inactivity, and high arousal.

Depue (1976) confirmed the presence of the activity–withdrawal dimension among American schizophrenics and found that withdrawn patients tended to avoid stimulation, become even more withdrawn under disorganized ward conditions, exhibit flat affect, be anhedonic (lack of interest in pleasurable activities), be first hospitalized at an earlier age than actives, remain in the hospital longer than actives, be less likely to be married or to have supporting friends or relatives, experience financial difficulties due to their poorer vocational skill level and employment history, and have fewer social contacts throughout the premorbid period. Overall, Depue concluded that there is a close congruence between activity–withdrawal and the good–poor premorbid adjustment distinction.

Several conclusions may be reached from these data. First, withdrawn patients show an uncoupling between some type of physiological arousal and motor activation. Second, these severely disabled, classical schizophrenics show greatly diminished motor activity. Third, withdrawn schizophrenics appear to include a substantial portion of patients exhibiting poor premorbid adjustment. Fourth, among British-diagnosed chronic schizophrenics are a group exhibiting high levels of activity and reward-seeking, reminiscent of mania. Indeed, Klein (1982) found that manics (Research Diagnostic Criteria) scored high on activity, suggestive of behavioral similarities to Venables & Wing's active schizophrenics.

In recent years there has been much interest in the distinction between positive and negative symptoms, introduced by Strauss et al (1974). Which symptoms are to be called negative and which positive is subject to debate (Crow 1985; Sommers 1985). By *negative symptoms* we commonly mean the absence or quantitative insufficiency of normal functioning (e.g. emotional and social withdrawal, blunted affect, apathy, and poverty of thought or speech); by *positive symptoms* is meant the presence of abnormal functioning (e.g. hallucinations, delusions, and excited catatonic motor behavior) (Sommers 1985). Thus, the negative symptoms almost perfectly describe the features of withdrawn schizophrenics. Indeed, Crow (1985) relates negative symptoms to Wing's concept of the clinical poverty syndrome, which in turn appears to be an outgrowth of his earlier work on withdrawn schizophrenics. Negative symptoms are also strongly associated with chronicity (e.g. Carpenter et al 1988; Crow 1980). Additionally, Andreasen et al (1990) found a strong association between positive symptoms and good premorbid adjustment assessed with the Phillips scale. The term "negative symptoms" may only be a new name for well-established phenomena such as process schizophrenia and chronic schizophrenia (Lewine 1985).

A prominent aspect of the positive/negative symptom literature is Crow's (1980, 1985) Type I and Type II distinction. Crow holds that two independent dimensions or pathological processes underlie schizophrenic symptomatology. Type I schizophrenia is characterized by positive symptoms (e.g. delusions, hallucinations), acute onset, an episodic course, good premorbid adjustment, and good response to antipsychotic medication. Type II schizophrenia is characterized by negative symptoms, insidious onset, intellectual deterioration, poor premorbid functioning, a chronic course, and a poorer response to antipsychotic medication. Crow further proposes that Type I schizophrenia primarily reflects a neurochemical disturbance involving the neurotransmitter dopamine, whereas Type II schizophrenia primarily reflects structural brain changes (e.g. enlarged cerebral ventricles as assessed by computed tomographic studies). Since these are independent processes, individual patients may exhibit only Type I or Type II symptoms or a mixture of the two. Pure negative symptom patients are rare (Andreason et al 1990; Gottesman et al 1987).

The better response of positive than negative symptoms to antipsychotics is widely accepted (e.g. Andreasen 1985; Losonczy et al 1987; Lydiard & Laird 1988; Reynolds 1989), although negative symptoms appear to respond to some extent (Lydiard & Laird 1988; Meltzer et al 1986). The presumed association between negative symptoms and ventricular enlargement is more controversial (Andreasen et al 1990; Gottesman & Bertelsen 1989). In addition, it is well established that more chronic patients—including negative symptom patients (Gottesman et al 1987)—seem to carry a greater genetic liability, suggesting a strong genetic contribution to etiology rather than a nongenetic etiology due to structural brain changes. It has been suggested that negative symptoms are associated with insufficient dopamine activity (e.g. Heritch 1990; Meltzer 1985, 1989). The positive/negative symptom literature appears to form a strong link between pharmacological theories of schizophrenia (the dopamine hypothesis) and positive symptoms. In contrast, the stronger genetic effects are seen with the more chronic, poor premorbid, negative symptom group of patients. Thus, the cornerstones of the biological approaches to schizophrenia—pharmacological and genetic theories—do not mesh very well, implying a need for a more complex model of the processes underlying schizophrenia. It is clear that those who would see only the chronic, negative symptom patients as "true" schizophrenia would have difficulty incorporating pharmacological theories into their view of schizophrenia (see Carpenter et al 1985 for a criticism of attempts to narrow the construct of schizophrenia).

The Boundary with Affective Disorders

As noted above, affective symptoms are associated with a better prognosis. Much debate has centered on whether schizoaffective disorder represents a variant of schizophrenia, a variant of affective disorders, the joint occurrence of schizophrenia and affective disorder, a mixture of a variant of schizophrenia and a variant of affective disorder, or a separate psychosis (Meltzer 1984; Procci 1989). In the context of the disease model, the joint-occurrence hypothesis is clearly wrong, since schizoaffective disorder is far more common than predicted by the joint occurrence of two independent diseases with low incidence (Procci 1989). Abrams (1984) rejects the separate-psychosis hypothesis, on the grounds that schizoaffective disorder does not breed true in family risk studies. Attempts to treat schizoaffective disorder as a simple variant of schizophrenia and/or affective disorder are challenged by the failure to find a bimodal distribution when patients are arranged along the continuum from schizophrenia to affective disorders. Kendell (1982) refers to this as the fundamental problem and notes that the distribution is unimodal—i.e. patients with schizoaffective symptoms *actually outnumber* those with purely affective or purely schizophrenic symptoms. Although the variant-of-affective-disorders hypothesis is popular (e.g. Meltzer 1984; Procci 1989), the evidence is not consistent (Procci 1989). Moreover, most recent studies (on which this popularity is based) have selected patients for more prominent affective than schizophrenic symptomatology (Williams & McGlashan 1987).

There is an obvious danger of circularity when a stronger association is found with affective disorders when diagnostic approaches that emphasize affective symptoms are employed in making the initial schizoaffective diagnosis (Procci 1989). For example, the Research Diagnostic Criteria (RDC) divide the schizoaffective continuum into those patients with mainly affective symptoms and those with mainly schizophrenic symptoms. Patients with schizoaffective mania, mainly affective subtype, show more characteristics of bipolar disorder, whereas those with schizoaffective mania, mainly schizophrenic subtype, have more familial schizophrenia and less familial affective disorder (Levinson & Levitt 1987). Other investigators have also found that the symptoms of RDC schizoaffective, mainly schizophrenic patients are related to schizophrenia (Kendler et al 1986; Kendler & Gruenberg 1984). When the diagnosis of schizoaffective disorder requires both the full schizophrenic syndrome and the full affective disorder syndrome, follow-up data suggest a closer relationship to schizophrenia (Williams & McGlashan 1987). Thus, the degree of association with schizophrenia or affective disorders depends on the diagnostic criteria used to define the initial group.

In view of the fusion of the boundary between affective disorders and schizophrenia and the evidence in favor of the multifactorial polygenic model for psychopathology, one should seriously consider a dimensional hypothesis, in which there are (separate) continua of liability for schizophrenia and affective disorders. At least under some circumstances, these separate dimensions of liablity could combine additively to produce a mixture of schizophrenic and affective symptoms in proportion to the underlying contribution of each type of liability (i.e. the greater the relative contribution of affective disorder to the liability, the more prominent are the affective symptoms). If each type of liability is normally distributed, the threshold will be reached more often from a combination of moderate liability from both dimensions than from more extreme liability from only one dimension, forming a unimodal distribution. This suggestion is not entirely novel. Meltzer (1984:12) noted, as the most interesting hypothesis, that "an interacting group of biological vulnerabilities, environmental insults, or ensuing psychological reactions produces the spectrum of clinical states from 'pure' schizophrenia to 'pure' affective psychosis."

PHARMACOLOGICAL APPROACH

The Dopamine Hypothesis of Schizophrenia

The dopamine hypothesis of schizophrenia derives from three observations. First, the therapeutic efficacy of the antipsychotic drugs relates especially to their ability to block dopamine receptors, especially D-2 receptors (e.g. Snyder 1978; Haracz 1982; Losonczy et al 1987). Second, large doses of drugs that increase dopamine activity (e.g. amphetamine) can produce a clinical syndrome indistinguishable from paranoid schizophrenia in otherwise nonschizophrenic individuals (Snyder 1978). Third, small doses of the same drugs exacerbate schizophrenic symptoms in a patient who is actively schizophrenic at the time (Andreasen 1985; Davis 1978) or produce transient symptoms in schizophrenic patients in remission (Losonczy et al 1987). These findings converge to suggest that dopaminergic activity contributes in some way to the production of schizophrenic symptoms. In view of the comments above concerning the link between positive symptoms and response to medication, dopamine is likely to contribute especially to the development of positive symptoms.

The Behavioral Functions of Dopamine

Much has been learned about the behavioral functions of dopaminergic pathways in the central nervous system. Of particular importance are the mesolimbic (projecting from the ventral tegmental area to the nucleus accumbens) and the mesocortical (projecting from the ventral tegmental area to the frontal cortex) systems, which have been strongly implicated in the incentive/ reward effects of stimulants and opioids, as well as in the effects of naturally occurring rewards (e.g. Stewart et al 1984; Willner 1985:147–55; Wise 1988; Wise & Bozarth 1987; Wise & Rompre 1989). A third dopaminergic pathway, the nigrostriatal system, has been viewed classically as important in the regulation of movement but not so central to motivated behavior. However, Wise (1988) suggests that the dopaminergic cells of the substantia nigra and the ventral tegmental area may be parts of a common physiological mechanism, and Willner (1985:148) also notes the close connection between the two. Thus, the role of the nigrostriatal pathway in mechanisms of reward is uncertain.

Dopamine blockers, including the antipsychotics, reduce the rewarding impact of stimulation of the reward pathways in proportion to their affinity for the D-2 dopamine receptor (Wise & Rompre 1989:210). Since it is the mesolimbic and/or mesocortical dopamine pathways that are implicated in the dopamine theory of schizophrenia, these findings strongly suggest that dopamine's incentive/reward-mediating effects underlie the production of schizophrenic symptoms and that blockage of these effects is important to the efficacy of the antipsychotics. Thus activity in the system associated with the behavioral response to incentive/reward cues may be involved in the etiology of a disorder classically seen as characterized by anhedonia. The resolution of this seeming contradiction probably lies in the observation that the antipsychotics seldom produce complete remission of all symptoms and that a substantial number of patients fail to respond to them at all (Losonczy et al 1987). That is, the dopamine hypothesis only relates to a portion of symptoms in a portion of patients, leaving considerable room for other factors to contribute to the development of schizophrenia. In particular, (as noted above) deficient rather than excessive dopamine activity may be implicated in the negative symptoms associated with anhedonia.

The concept of reward as Wise and his colleagues use it includes two components: an increased probability of the response that is rewarded and an energizing or *psychomotor activation* of approach behavior in response to *incentive cues* (Wise & Bozarth 1987; Wise & Rompre 1989). Incentive motivation refers to the ability of *conditioned* stimuli or the expectation of receiving a reward to motivate behavior, not to the unconditioned effects of rewards themselves (Willner 1985:153–54). This incentive/behavioral activation component to dopaminergic activity provides a link to observable behavior, as well as a link to behavioral theories of motivation (see below).

Parkinsonian symptoms, attributed to an antidopaminergic effect on the nigrostriatal pathway, are obvious consequences of neuroleptic use. Since the nigrostriatal pathway is traditionally seen as involving only the regulation of movement, Parkinsonian symptoms have not been of great theoretical interest. In the present context, a more interesting, but less obvious, "side effect" of neuroleptics is the induction of akinesia in some patients. Akinesia (broadly defined) involves a range of negative symptoms—e.g. lack of emotional reactivity, lack of goal-directedness, reduced or retarded speech, diminished social and vocational initiative, etc (Sommers 1985). The similarity of the akinesia syndrome to naturally occurring negative symptoms has made this effect of neuroleptics less obvious clinically. With the recent interest in assessing negative symptoms, however, concern about akinesia has increased (e.g. Carpenter et al 1988; Sommers 1985). This pharmacologically induced anhedonia in some patients is to be expected from attenuation of incentive/ reward functions of the mesolimbic and mesocortical dopamine systems and is, therefore, consistent with the hypothesis that neuroleptics attenuate the response to rewards. In those patients whose symptoms are due to high levels of dopamine activity, antipsychotics will normalize function. In patients whose symptoms result from an unusual vulnerability to moderate levels of dopamine activity, antipsychotics risk overshooting normal function and producing anhedonia.

Dopamine and Bipolar Affective Disorder

Depue and his colleagues (e.g. Depue et al 1989; Depue & Iacono 1989) have described a behavioral facilitation system (BFS) that depends critically on the mesolimbic and mesocortical dopamine pathways; they have incorporated the BFS into a neurobehavioral theory of bipolar affective disorder. The following summary is based on Depue & Iacono's (1989) *Annual Review* chapter.

The BFS has two major components: the initiation of locomotor activity and incentive/reward motivation (cf Wise's view of the function of the dopamine systems). The BFS facilitates two broad categories of behavior: 1. positive engagements with the environment (approach responses) under the control of stimuli for social, sexual, consummatory, and achievement related rewards and 2. responses to environmental threat, especially active avoidance responses and irritative aggression. The BFS is said to facilitate both conditioned and unconditioned behavior. In both types of behavior, the incentive and locomotor components of the BFS are activated by inherently rewarding stimuli or conditioned signals of these stimuli. In active avoidance, the cues in the safe compartment are viewed as conditioned stimuli for reward. In irritative aggression in response to frustrative nonreward, the BFS is activated by the expectation of rewards following removal of the stimuli that block access to the reward. Depue & Iacono comment that the BFS is activated during stress and defensive aggression, but they do not consider those stimulus contexts further.

The first link to bipolar affective disorder is a consideration of the symptoms of hypomania/mania and bipolar depression, which appear to represent extreme state alterations in BFS functioning. Although Depue & Iacono's description of the clinical symptoms is too extensive to describe fully, some of the most obvious parallels can be described. The motor symptoms of hyperactivity and rapid pressured speech appear to reflect extreme behavioral activation, whereas retardation represents deficient behavioral activation. The manic's excessive interest and pleasure reflect the hedonic component of incentive/reward activation, whereas loss of interest or pleasure (pervasive anhedonia) is the opposite extreme. Elation and euphoria are manifestations of the mood component of the response to reward; they stand in contrast the depressed patient's lack of emotional reactivity. The manic's self-confidence and decreased estimation of the likelihood of negative outcomes appear to result from strong expectations that his/her behavior will be rewarded. In contrast, the depressive's pessimism and hopelessness about future outcomes result from a failure to expect rewards as a result of effortful striving. The functions of the BFS and the symptoms of hypomania/mania and bipolar depression thus match well.

Depue & Iacono review an extensive literature suggesting that dopamine in the mesolimbic and mesocortical systems provides affective/motivational input to the motor system in the form of initiation of locomotor activity and mediates incentive/reward motivation. They also review evidence more directly implicating dopamine in at least a portion of bipolar patients. The success of selective dopamine antagonists in reducing manic symptoms and the precipitation of mania in bipolar patients by dopamine agonists implicate dopamine in bipolar affective disorder (Jimerson 1987).

There are two points to be underscored here. First, the juxtaposition of dopamine theories of both schizophrenia and mania raises interesting theoretical issues about how to reconcile a contribution to both disorders. An obvious hypothesis is that excessive dopamine activity is not the primary problem in schizophrenia but rather contributes to overall liability, eliciting schizophrenic (florid) symptoms in vulnerable individuals. Thus, the excessive dopaminergic activity in mania adds to the liability for schizophrenia, producing a schizomanic disorder. Second, some types of depression (bipolar depressions with retardation and severe loss of interest) show deficit or negative symptoms attributable to diminished dopamine activity (see also Willner 1985:147–92, for a similar view).

PSYCHOSOCIAL APPROACHES

The genetic literature discussed above offers the strongest evidence available of environmental influences. This evidence is, however, neutral with respect to whether the environmental contribution is physical or psychosocial in nature. Evidence that psychosocial stressors probably are implicated has been forthcoming in recent years, especially with respect to identifiable environmental stressors (life events) and aversive family interactions.

Life Events

Brown & Birley (1968; Birley & Brown 1970) reported the classic life-event study, based on retrospective reports at the time of admission. Their sample was restricted to those patients with a diagnosis of schizophrenia whose onset (or exacerbation) of symptoms could be dated to within a week. For those patients, they found an increased number of life events in the three weeks prior to onset, compared to three earlier three-week periods (i.e. 3–6, 6–9, and 9–12 weeks prior to onset) in the same patients and compared to community controls for all four three-week periods. These results held both for clearly independent events (i.e. could not be secondary to symptoms) and for all events (including events that were possibly but not certainly independent of the illness).

These results supported the role of life events in precipitating psychotic episodes, but there were no successful replications for almost 20 years. Other studies had not, however, used the same methodology—e.g. different time periods were used, or patients were not restricted to those with a datable onset. Recently, a World Health Organization–sponsored cross-national study explicitly attempted to replicate the Brown & Birley methodology at eight field research centers located in developed and developing countries (Day et al 1987), with the (unfortunate) exception that community controls were not available. Thus, the focus of the analyses was on the expected increase in life events in the three weeks prior to the onset of symptoms. The analysis of all events (separately for each center) yielded a significant difference at six centers and strong trends at the remaining two centers. The analysis of independent events yielded a significant difference at five centers and strong trends at the remaining three centers. An analysis with all eight centers included did not show an interaction between center and period, indicating that the pattern of life events did not differ across centers. From this perspective, the Brown & Birley results were replicated at all eight centers. The authors comment that they considered their results to be "a rather remarkable replication" (p. 180) of the Brown & Birley results.

Both the original Brown & Birley study and the WHO replication study depended on retrospective reports. To eliminate possible weaknesses associated with retrospective reports, Ventura et al (1989) conducted a one-year prospective, longitudinal study of relapse in 30 recent-onset schizophrenic patients. As anticipated, they found a higher number of independent life events in the month preceding relapse for those patients who relapsed than for an analogous "nonrelapse" month for the same patients or for the average events per month for nonrelapsing patients. It does not appear, therefore, that biases in retrospective reports account for the association between symptom onset and life events.

These results are consistent with expectations from the polygenic model, in which nonchronic but vulnerable individuals will develop symptoms of schizophrenia as a result of a sudden increase in environmental liability. The requirement of a datable onset in the studies just reviewed serves to select for reactive schizophrenics and to select against the chronic, insidious-onset, process schizophrenic patients. The latter can be viewed as having sufficient liability that life events are not required to reach the threshold for schizophrenia.

An older paper on life events should not go unnoticed. Dohrenwend & Egri (1981) addressed the question of whether life events can produce schizophrenia in individuals with no obvious vulnerability. They cited reports of transient battlefield psychoses whose symptom pattern was indistinguishable from schizophrenia, occurring in the absence of any prior evidence of incipient psychopathology. Although most investigators would argue that these psychoses are not schizophrenia, because they remit within a few days, such an assertion misses the point: An extreme life event *can* produce a schizophrenia-like psychosis. The amphetamine psychoses are said not to be true schizophrenia, but they are important because they demonstrate that extreme doses of dopamine agonists produce schizophrenia-like symptoms in apparently nonschizophrenic individuals. The theory is then extended to more modest dopamine activity in vulnerable individuals or, in the current version, to extreme sensitivity to ordinary amounts of dopamine activity. The battlefield psychoses are important in the same way: They demonstrate the potency of life events, from which we may infer that less extreme life events may have a similar effect in vulnerable individuals. Especially when seen in combination with the life-event studies above, this is an important demonstration.

Life events can be seen to be potent in a different context—the induction of depression (see below). This observation has three implications. First, to the extent that a depressive reaction documents the ability of life events to elicit a *stress response,* the life-events/depression literature supports the potency of life events. Second, to the extent that life events produce *syndromal depression* and to the extent that syndromal depression adds to liability for schizophrenia, the (schizoaffective) continuum from schizophrenia to depression reflects the additive impact of life events on vulnerability to schizophrenia. Third, the same argument applies to a gene-based tendency to respond to life events with strong depressive reactions—i.e. a genetic tendency to develop a strong depressive reaction would add to general genetic liability in an episodic fashion.

The ability of life events, in the form of the loss of a loved one, to induce depression (uncomplicated bereavement) is recognized in DSM-III-R (American Psychiatric Association 1987:222) and is well documented (Clayton 1982). In a longitudinal study with a representative community sample as part of the New Haven Epidemiological Catchment Area Program, Bruce et al (1990) reported that 30.8% of newly widowed respondents met diagnostic criteria for DSM-III major depressive episode (ignoring the exclusion criterion for bereavement); only 3.2% of married controls did so. When compared with nonbereaved respondents who met diagnostic criteria for major depressive episode, the bereaved group did not differ on neurovegetative symptoms, psychomotor disturbance, and suicidal ideation. The two groups differed only on feelings of guilt or worthlessness (fewer for bereaved respondents). The depression seen in this group was not related to past depressive episodes, since none of the newly bereaved subjects reported a prior depressive episode, demonstrating the strong contribution of the life event. Parallel results were reported by Dura et al (1990) in a study of dementia care givers. Compared with controls, these care givers had an increased risk of major depressive disorder (8:1), dysthymic disorder (10:0), and depression not otherwise specified (8:0). Depression in care givers was not even weakly related to vulnerability to depression, as indicated by a family history of depressive disorders, nor was it related to a history of depressive disorders prior to care giving. These studies confirm that severe life events can produce the *syndrome of depression* in individuals with no detectable prior vulnerability, indicating that life events are potent contributors to episodes of depression.

This argument can be extended to the concept of secondary depression (Weissman et al 1977). For example, following amputation of a leg the causal chain to depression must involve the psychological reaction secondary to the medical problem (American Psychiatric Association 1987:221). As with bereavement, the symptom picture in secondary depression resembles that in primary depression (Weissman et al 1977). Thus, the ability of psychosocial stressors to produce syndromal depression is seen in a range of contexts. Because there are individual differences in the magnitude of the depressive response to depressogenic life events, both environmental and genetic factors can be expected to contribute to the development of schizoaffective disorder with depression.

Finally, Day et al (see also Dohrenwend & Egri 1981) argue that the life-event studies underestimate the contribution of psychosocial factors on two counts. First, out of the methodological concern to establish the direction of causality, many life events are excluded from consideration as illness-related. However, even life events that are illness related contribute to the final appearance of florid symptoms. Making the same argument, Lukoff et al

(1984) found evidence that schizophrenics experience a high rate of nonin-dependent life stressors, suggesting the quantitative importance of this source of liability. Second, life events constitute only one category of environmental stressor. They are conceptualized as being datable, relatively nonrepetitive, and requiring a change in the subject's daily routine. These requirements exclude "ongoing noxious environmental factors which are a commonplace and repetitive feature of the subject's routine life world" (Day et al 1987, p. 194). The point of the life-event studies is to establish that the environmental stress hypothesis is credible. Once that hypothesis is supported, it is plausible to expect more subtle stressors to contribute to liability.

Family Interactions

Family interactions comprise an important source of stress that cannot be documented as a life event; they contribute nonspecifically to liability in already vulnerable individuals. An active literature on what are called "high-expressed-emotion families" had been summarized by Leff & Vaughn (1985). These studies are concerned with predicting relapse over a nine-month period among schizophrenic patients after they are discharged from the hospital and return to live with their families. On the basis of an interview at the time of hospitalization with the relatives with whom the patient lived (spouse or parents), the relatives' attitudes toward the patient are rated for expressed emotion. High-EE relatives are those who criticize and/or are emotionally overinvolved with the patient. The primary finding is an increased rate of symptomatic relapse among patients discharged to high-EE families com-pared to those discharged to low-EE families. Among patients returning to high-EE homes, relapse was more frequent if they spent more than 35 hours per week in face-to-face contact than if they had less contact with their family, supporting the notion that aversive family interaction produces relapse.

An obvious question is whether the relatives' negative attitudes are secon-dary to the patient's symptomatology, which also predicts relapse—i.e. the third-variable problem. However, the finding holds up even when attempts are made to correct for any effects of the patient's disturbed behavior. Perhaps more persuasively, a therapeutic intervention with high-EE families that reduced the family's expressed emotion and/or the contact between the family and the patient eliminated relapse in all nine families in which this reduction was achieved (Leff et al 1982). Other interventions aimed at reducing the family's expressed emotion have also been successful (Tarrier et al 1988).

These studies were all conducted in England. An important replication study conducted in California (Vaughn et al 1984) also found significant differences in relapse between high- and low-EE families. Among patients living with high-EE relatives, there was a trend toward lower relapse rates with lower face-to-face contact, but the difference was not statistically significant. The effects of EE could not be explained by the severity of the patient's clinical condition at admission.

The basic finding of a difference in relapse rates between high- and low-EE families has been widely replicated (e.g. see Barrelet et al 1990) although there have been a few negative results, as well. The preponderance of positive findings suggests that something of importance has been demonstrated, and the negative findings may reflect methodological factors and differences in conditions at different sites (Barrelet et al 1990).

Subtler Environmental Factors

Life events and aversive family interactions are obvious sources of stress. Subtler psychosocial variables that influence symptom development among schizophrenic patients have been summarized by Wing (1978), who argued that the course of schizophrenia is influenced by what he called extrinsic disadvantages and secondary handicaps. Extrinsic disadvantages include such handicaps as poor education, lack of vocational skills, low intelligence, and the absence of social support. The stress associated with these extrinsic disadvantages may well be more chronic than that due to life events. Some portion of chronicity may reflect chronic environmental liability.

Secondary handicaps are the consequence of having a chronic disorder that makes it difficult to follow an ordinary domestic and working life—e.g. altered self-attitudes and expectations and the development of maladaptive traits associated with long-term hospitalization ("institutionalism"). Again, this source of liability may contribute to chronicity and may also contribute, in some cases, to the acute-to-chronic transition. That is, a person whose total liability is brought above threshold by some life event might then remain above threshold as a result of secondary handicaps.

Wing & Brown (1970) found that psychosocial factors were important in the development of the "clinical poverty" syndrome. This syndrome consists of negative symptoms associated with social withdrawal: slowness, underactivity, blunting of affect, and poverty of speech. Across time and hospitals, the clinical poverty syndrome increased on wards that placed many restrictions on patients and provided few opportunities for positive activities, whereas it was minimized on wards that placed fewer restrictions and required more socially positive activities. These observations suggest that even the negative symptoms so strongly related to chronicity are responsive to psychosocial factors.

Finally, it is of special interest that Wing (1978) attributes these negative symptoms to "a protective reaction against the painful effects of social interaction when one has inadequate equipment for communication" (p. 606). That is, some negative symptoms can be seen as a form of passive or active avoidance. Carpenter et al (1985) also comment that in some cases social withdrawal may be a reaction to the development of positive symptoms and to aversive environments (including stigma), as well as reflecting diminished social drive. The thrust of all of these observations is that some aspects of chronicity and negative symptoms are not simply hard-wired manifestations (symptoms) of a genetic disease but rather are influenced by psychosocial sources of liability.

The Invisible Gene

These attempts to link life events and other stressors with the timing of the onset of episodes have met with some success, but the results are often less than dramatic. The explanation offered here is that only a portion of patients are in the "at risk" zone of liability that will allow additional *identifiable* stress to precipitate schizophrenia, and that many sources of stress are too subtle to measure with current methods. Lest this argument be dismissed too easily, a comparison with the alternative genetic explanation is useful.

Some genetic disorders first manifest their effects in adulthood. It is therefore not illogical to think that genetic differences present at birth can produce a disorder like schizophrenia during adulthood. It is important to note, however, that *no* clear genetic explanation for the *timing* of schizophrenic episodes has yet appeared. The genetic liability is invisible: Inferred from family risk studies, it cannot at present be measured. Similarly, the complex biological changes presumed to transform genetic vulnerability into an episode of schizophrenia have not yet been elucidated. Even an increase in neurotransmitter activity, proposed as preceding an episode, may be secondary to psychosocial stress. For example, it has been argued that increased norepinephrine activity is associated with increases in both positive and negative symptoms of schizophrenia (van Kammen et al 1990). Since norepinephrine level appears strongly responsive to stress (e.g. Glavin 1985; Panksepp 1986), a role of this transmitter in relapse could reflect the effect of environmental, rather than genetic, factors. Even though the evidence for psychosocial contributors to the onset of symptoms is often circumstantial, it is stronger than is the evidence that gene-controlled biochemical changes contribute to the time of onset of symptoms. A similar argument applies to physical environmental hypotheses, such as pregnancy and birth complications, structural damage to the brain, and infections: No positive evidence links these factors to the onset of episodes. Overall, the evidence for a physical environmental etiology of schizophrenia is equivocal (Mesulam 1990). Thus, the inclusion of episodic schizophrenia as "true" schizophrenia and the finding that aversive life events occur during the three weeks prior to an episode in rapid-onset schizophrenia argue strongly that psychosocial contributions may serve as nonspecific contributors to liability.

CONCEPTUALIZATION OF THE DIMENSIONS OF STRESS

Let us now consider the nature of stress in the diathesis-stress model. A behavioral theory of motivation will aid this discussion, because it contains two motivational systems that relate to the constructs reviewed above and has much to say about behavioral activation.

Gray's Motivational Theory

Although this motivational theory reflects a broad literature and is not attributable to any one person, Gray's (e.g. 1982, 1987b) presentation of it is especially well known and has the advantage of attempting to delineate a neurobiological substrate. Gray's model includes an appetitive motivational system, an aversive motivational system, and a nonspecific arousal system (Gray 1987b:246–47). Nonspecific arousal receives inputs from both the appetitive and the aversive motivational systems—i.e. arousal is increased by activation of either motivational system. Arousal has the effect of increasing behavioral vigor for those responses that occur (e.g. increased running speed). Gray has focused particulary on the aversive motivational system, which he calls the behavioral inhibition system (BIS). The present author (Fowles 1980) introduced the parallel term behavioral activation system (BAS) to describe the appetitive motivational system. These names underscore the behavioral effects of these two systems: inhibition and activation. Both systems respond to conditioned, not unconditioned, stimuli.

The BAS activates instrumental behavior in response to conditioned stimuli for reward (simple reward paradigm) or for the relief associated with the absence of an expected punishment (active avoidance paradigm). The BIS inhibits instrumental behavior (that would otherwise occur) in response to conditioned stimuli for punishment (passive avoidance or conflict paradigm) or frustrative nonreward (frustration or extinction paradigm). In the simple reward paradigm, the BAS activates an approach response (e.g. running down an alleyway) in response to cues for reward; the BIS is not involved. If response-contingent punishment is superimposed on the reward paradigm (e.g. requiring the animal to cross an electrified grid in order to reach the reward), conflict is induced: The BAS activates approach tendencies, whereas the BIS inhibits approach tendencies in response to cues for punishment. If the threat of punishment is sufficiently great, the BIS will dominate and passive avoidance will result—i.e. the animal will not approach. The extinction paradigm resembles the conflict paradigm in that there is an approach motivation for rewards and a BIS-induced aversive motivation to inhibit the approach. In this case, the aversive motivation derives from the frustration associated with failure to receive an expected reward. The BIS is activated by the anticipation of frustrative nonreward. In the active avoidance paradigm, an impending punishment can be avoided by making a response (e.g. jumping over a barrier to a "safe" compartment). The cues for safety are viewed as the functional equivalent to conditioned stimuli for rewards. Similarly, the cues for frustration in the extinction paradigm are seen as functionally equivalent to conditioned stimuli for punishment.

BAS activity is associated with a positive affective state (hope, relief), whereas BIS activity is associated with a negative affective state (fear or anxiety, frustration). One of Gray's major contributions (e.g. Gray 1977, 1982, 1987b) has been to show that drugs with anxiolytic effects (alcohol, barbiturates, minor tranquilizers) share a common property of diminishing the efficacy of the BIS—e.g. they disinhibit behavior in extinction and conflict paradigms. Because it is activated by threats of aversive outcomes and weakened by anxiolytic drugs, Gray concludes that the BIS is the neurobiological substrate for anxiety.

Elucidating the nature of this neurobiological substrate has been the object of much of Gray's work. In his current view (Gray 1987a), the BIS includes the septo-hippocampal system and the closely related Papez loop, noradrenergic pathways that ascend from the locus coeruleus to the septo-hippocampal system, and neocortical structures (entorhinal, prefrontal, and cingulate cortex) with two-way communication with the septo-hippocampal system. Although Gray has not been strongly concerned with the BAS, he does note consistent evidence that the mesolimbic dopaminergic pathway that ascends from the A10 nucleus in the ventral tegmental area to the nucleus accumbens and the ventral striatum plays a key role in incentive motivation and, therefore, in the BAS. It will not have escaped the attentive reader that there are more similarities than differences between Gray's concept of the BAS and Depue's concept of the behavioral facilitation system.

Tellegen's Personality Dimensions

Individual differences in the strengths of the BAS and BIS should be reflected in personality and current mood. The BAS should be related to a dimension of positive affect and active engagement of the environment, and the BIS should be related to negative affect and passive avoidance of aversive outcomes.

Tellegen's (1985) work most directly bears on this expectation. Tellegen concluded that self-report ratings of current mood are dominated by two large dimensions (second-order factors), Positive Affect and Negative Affect. Thus, self-reported mood is consistent with expectations from Gray's theory. Self-report ratings of personality, however, yielded three trait dimensions: Positive Emotionality, Negative Emotionality, and Constraint. The mood dimensions of positive affect and negative affect are correlated with the personality dimensions of Positive Emotionality and Negative Emotionality, respectively, as might be expected. Constraint was not correlated with the two mood dimensions. There is a substantial genetic influence on the personality dimensions (Tellegen et al 1988).

At first glance, one would expect that Positive Affect and Positive Emotionality would relate directly to the BAS and that Negative Affect and Negative Emotionality would relate to the BIS; Constraint would be a third dimension of personality unrelated to the BAS and BIS. The data are consistent with the Positive Affect/Positive Emotionality association with the BAS, but not with the other relationships. In addition to its positive affect component, Positive Emotionality is described as being associated with the primary factors of Well-Being, Social Potency, and Achievement, the last two of which appear to imply efficacious behavior. Moreover, Tellegen (1985:695) says that high scores on Positive Emotionality imply "an appraisal of oneself as pleasurably and effectively engaged interpersonally and through achievement, as active and generally self-efficacious in Bandura's sense." Thus, Positive Emotionality appears to represent positive affect and behavioral activation, especially reward-seeking behavior. In an assertion consistent with this conclusion, Depue et al (1987) argued that Positive Emotionality is the personality expression of individual differences in the strength of the behavioral facilitation system.

With respect to the BIS, the Negative Emotionality dimension appears to focus more exclusively on emotional *experience* in the form of negative affect, whereas Constraint appears to reflect the *behavioral* dimension of the BIS. The Negative Emotionality factor is said to reflect a description of oneself "as unpleasurably engaged, as stressed by one's own and others' actions and attitudes"; it is characterized by an inclination "to worry, to be anxious, to feel victimized and resentful, and to appraise generally in ways that foster negative emotional experiences" (p. 696). Constraint is associated with the primary factors of Control-vs-Impulsiveness, Harm Avoidance-vs-Danger Seeking, and Traditionalism. High scores on Constraint reflect a portrayal of oneself as "cautious, restrained, as refraining from risky adventures, and as accepting the strictures of conventional morality" and as showing "avoidant, timid, anancastic (obsessive-compulsive-phobic) patterns" (p. 696); low scores indicate a self-description as "impulsive, adventurous, and inclined to reject conventional restrictions on behavior" (p. 696). These descriptions of Constraint are precisely what one would expect *at the behavioral level* from individual differences in the strength of the BIS, but the negative affect component expected from the BIS is split off as an orthogonal dimension, Negative Emotionality. I (1987) have argued that Constraint may be more closely related to individual differences in BIS functioning than is Negative Emotionality.

This personality perspective, then, raises the question whether the application of a motivational approach to schizophrenia should involve two dimensions or three. This question cannot be answered on the basis of the data reviewed here, but the issue is critical for future research.

Overall, the evidence supports a dimension of appetitive motivation involving positive affect, behavioral activation, and an important contribution from dopaminergic pathways. This dimension is involved with reward-seeking and with active responding to cope with threats. There is also strong evidence for an aversive motivational system involving behavioral inhibition in response to threats, but it is less clear how tightly associated negative affect will be with activity in this system. In considering applications to schizophrenia, this perspective suggests that (*a*) positive affect/behavioral activation/high dopaminergic activity, (*b*) negative affect, and (*c*) behavioral inhibition might all be found among the nonspecific genetic and environmental contributors to phenotypic variance.

The Nature of Stress in Diathesis-Stress: Negative Affect

Traditional views of the aversive nature of stress in the diathesis-stress model would emphasize activation of the aversive motivational system (anxiety, frustration) in Gray's theory or a high degree of negative affect in Tellegen's work. In the life-events literature, only negative events have been associated with stress (Blaney 1985), and they can be expected to elicit negative affect. The inclusion of anxiety in negative affect is obvious, especially in view of Gray's interpretation of the aversive motivational system as the neurophysiological substrate for anxiety. The inclusion of depression is more complicated and requires discussion from a number of perspectives.

At an empirical level, it is difficult to separate anxiety and depression. Beck Depression Inventory scores are highly correlated with scores on anxiety scales and load on the same factor (Watson & Clark 1984). The difficulty of separating anxiety and depression clinically (especially of finding depressed patients without anxiety) has long been recognized (e.g. Barlow 1988:279; Swinson & Kirby 1986) and has resulted in the recent emphasis on the comorbidity of anxiety and depression (e.g. Maser & Cloninger 1990) and even in suggestions that anxiety and depression share a common diathesis (Barlow 1988:278; Kendler et al 1987). The onset of depression is associated with negative life events (Paykel 1982), as is anxiety. This considerable overlap between anxiety and depression suggests that both are forms of the negative affect that contributes to the liability for schizophrenia.

Theories of depression emphasize a disruption of appetitive motivation as the disorder's core feature, but negative affect is highly likely to be present (Fowles 1988, in press). From a motivational perspective, depression may involve negative affect from two sources: frustration over the loss of rewards due to bereavement, loss, failure, etc; and anxiety over uncontrollable punishment. Both empirically and theoretically, therefore, one should expect that many instances of depression will include a component of negative affect (frustration or anxiety), although reduced appetitive motivation (and a reduction in behavioral activation) is a more essential feature.

According to the diathesis-stress model of schizophrenia, negative affect (and its biological concomitants) in the form of anxiety and/or depression contributes to nonspecific liability. The inclusion of depression in this model is particularly important, since it relates to the contribution of depression to the development of schizophrenic symptoms in schizoaffective depressed patients, as argued above. If this view is correct, the frequent association of schizophrenic and depressive symptoms can be attributed to a role of depression in raising the liability for schizophrenia above threshold. The depressive reaction in these instances could reflect environmental factors [including familial environment (McGuffin & Katz 1989)] and/or genetic influences. Thus, both genetic and psychosocial environmental factors associated with depression probably contribute to nonspecific liability for schizophrenia.

The Nature of Stress in Diathesis-Stress: Positive Affect/Behavioral Activation

The dopamine hypothesis of schizophrenia, combined with the conclusion that dopamine activity contributes strongly to appetitive motivation and behavioral activation, implicates appetitive motivation and behavioral activation as contributors to the liability for schizophrenia. Depue's dopamine/behavioral facilitation theory of mania, combined with the dopamine hypothesis of schizophrenia, also suggests that manic symptoms contribute to the liability for schizophrenia.

A case can be made that dopaminergic activity is involved in mediating the response to stressful life events. In Gray's theory, the BAS mediates active coping in the face of threats. Similarly, Depue's BFS facilitates responses to environmental threat. Animal studies have implicated dopamine in the response to stressful stimuli (Braden 1984), especially including active avoidance responding (Willner 1985:155–56). Thus, one can view the appetitive motivational system as a component of the stress reaction in the diathesis-stress model. In the traditional view of stress, however, only the active avoidance or active coping aspect of this system would be included. The reward-seeking aspect of appetitive motivation, so prominent in mania, contributes to liability but is less obviously part of a response to stressful environments.

In the present context, note should be taken of Braden's (1984) two-factor theory of the etiology of mixed schizophrenic and manic symptoms in schizoaffective psychoses. In Braden's usage, "cognitive symptoms" are schizophrenia-like symptoms, such as hallucinations, delusions, Schneiderian experiences (e.g. delusions of thought broadcasting), and disorganized speech and thinking; "activated symptoms" are mania-like symptoms, such as motor excitement and insomnia. Braden hypothesized two types of vulnerabilities. The first factor is vulnerability to episodes of psychosis. This factor involves an increased level of behavioral activation as a result of activity in the dopaminergic mesolimbic pathways, producing characteristics of the manic state. The second type of vulnerability is to schizophrenia-like disorganization and cognitive disturbance, which can be triggered by the first factor. That is, an episode of the first factor can induce schizophrenic symptoms in individuals with the second type of vulnerability. Braden's first factor resembles the BAS or BFS, and the second factor is strongly suggestive of a schizophrenia diathesis—i.e. a specific vulnerability to schizophrenia.

Although Braden's theory was primarily concerned with the development of schizophrenia-like symptoms in connection with the severe behavioral activation seen in mania, he explicitly proposed that there are individual differences in the threshold for the severity of (behavioral) activation required to trigger cognitive disorganization. As the vulnerability increases, the threshold is lowered into a range where less dramatic activation of appetitive motivation will trigger schizophrenic symptoms. In that case, the contribution of mania will be less obvious, consistent with the traditional dopamine hypothesis (which says nothing about the presence of manic symptoms). Braden also distinguished between his own concept of (behavioral) activation and "arousal," citing Venables & Wing (1962) as showing high levels of autonomic arousal in withdrawn schizophrenics. In his view, then, withdrawn, negative-symptom schizophrenics do not suffer from excessive behavioral activation associated with dopamine activity, but from another type of arousal. From the reasoning above, it can be suggested that this other type of arousal involves negative affect and activation of the aversive motivational system.

Thus behavioral activation/dopamine activity may represent an important nonspecific contributor to liability for schizophrenia. In part, this dimension can be seen as mediating the response to stressful stimuli, but there is a more purely appetitive contribution associated with manic symptoms that accounts for the continuum of schizoaffective manic symptoms.

APPETITIVE AND AVERSIVE MOTIVATION AND PHENOTYPIC HETEROGENEITY

Schizophrenics exhibit a considerable range of behavioral activation, as indicated by the activity-withdrawal dimension and by comparisons of schizoaffective manic patients with predominantly negative-symptom patients. The discussion above suggests that appetitive and aversive motivational systems contribute to the nonspecific liability for schizophrenia and that the balance between these two systems influences the degree of activity or withdrawal. Predictions are clearest when one system dominates. In view of the many influences on these motivational systems, the behavioral outcome (activity/withdrawal) should be seen as a *final common pathway*.

A number of factors push the balance between BAS and BIS responding in the direction of the inactivity and social withdrawal seen in negative-symptom schizophrenics. First, there may be trait-like or *temperament* variables. In terms of Tellegen's personality dimensions, low Positive Emotionality and high Constraint should be associated with withdrawal and poor premorbid adjustment. To the extent that Gray's model is correct (at least for many patients) in combining negative affect and behavioral inhibition, high Negative Emotionality will also be associated with withdrawal. Similarly, the finding that withdrawn schizophrenics are more aroused suggests a contribution of aversive motivation to their inactivity—i.e. high negative affect and behavioral inhibition. The anhedonia seen in poor premorbid adjustment and negative-symptom schizophrenia suggests a particular deficit in appetitive motivation. This deficit could be due to a temperament of low Positive Emotionality, which would have pervasive negative influences on social and occupational adjustment, accompanied by many failure experiences.

Second, *affective disorder* can have a profound influence on activity-withdrawal. Mania produces high levels of behavioral activation. Depression can be associated with behavioral inactivity either as a result of a more or less primary reduction in dopaminergic activity (manifested as retardation and loss of interest) or as a result of such cognitive factors as hopelessness and demoralization (negative expectancies that undermine appetitive motivation). Increased aversive motivation will also be seen in many depressed patients.

Third, *situational factors* may tend to reduce approach response rates. The literature on institutionalism links hospital environments to social withdrawal. Similarly, Wing's conclusion that extrinsic disadvantages and secondary handicaps promote chronicity (see the discussion above on subtler environmental factors) is consistent with the importance of situational factors, and some of these disadvantages and handicaps may facilitate extinction or passive avoidance.

Fourth, the genetics literature suggests that negative-symptom, chronic schizophrenia has a *greater genetic component* than other forms of the disorder. Such schizophrenia may involve a smaller contribution from dopaminergic behavioral activation than other kinds—i.e. forms of schizophrenia with a smaller genetic component require more dopamine activity to elicit symptoms, and this high level of behavioral activation precludes a negative-symptom pattern. In contrast, those whose disorder has a larger genetic component may develop schizophrenia in the absence of behavioral activation. Another possible explanation is that the temperament variables associated with withdrawal have a substantial genetic component that combines with specific genetic liability to schizophrenia.

Still another explanation is that social withdrawal is secondary to the chronic symptomatology associated with a strong genetic liability—i.e. the withdrawal is a protective reaction against the difficulties of social interaction when one is handicapped by chronic schizophrenia (see the discussion above on subtler environmental factors). A modification of this perspective makes it a more powerful explanation for withdrawal. Wing (1978) found that withdrawn schizophrenics suffer relapse if exposed to too much stimulation, and Depue (1976) found that they avoided stimulation and became even more withdrawn under disorganized ward conditions. These phenomena would make sense if the strong diathesis for schizophrenia makes these patients more vulnerable to aversive arousal (i.e. aversive arousal brings the liability above threshold) and if demanding and disorganized environments elicit aversive arousal. If so, the withdrawal is a protection against stimulation that would exacerbate schizophrenic symptoms and is, therefore, more strongly linked to a great than to a small genetic liability. This explanation accords with traditional views that social withdrawal is a core feature of chronic schizophrenia.

The traditional diathesis-stress model emphasizes aversive motivation and negative affect as contributors to schizophrenic symptomatology, but the literature on the behavioral functions of dopamine suggests that certain positive symptoms are associated with dopamine activity and appetitive motivation. What role does aversive motivation play in the production of schizophrenic symptoms? A case has been made that the behavioral inhibition associated with aversive motivation can contribute to passive avoidance and, therefore, to negative symptoms. However, it would be surprising to find that the aversive motivation in the traditional diathesis-stress model contributes *only* to deficit symptoms. One should take seriously the possibility that aversive motivation and negative affect contribute to certain positive or florid symptoms as well, as suggested in the preceding paragraph. An attractive hypothesis is that aversive motivational states involve an arousal component (distinct from behavioral activation)—e.g. the increased nonspecific arousal associated with BIS activity in Gray's model—that adds to the liability for schizophrenia. Thus, negative symptoms would be related to behavioral inhibition, whereas some florid symptoms would be related to nonspecific arousal/negative affect. As suggested by Tellegen's work, these two aspects of aversive motivation may show a considerable degree of independence.

With respect to florid symptoms and the two motivational systems, there are three possibilities: Aversive arousal and (dopaminergic) appetitive behavioral activation might elicit the *same* florid symptoms in vulnerable individuals, they might elicit *different* symptoms, or they might elicit partially *overlapping* sets of symptoms. Dopaminergic activity seems likely to produce specific symptoms, making the first alternative improbable. Of the other two, the partial-overlap hypothesis seems preferable. In Gray's model, both types of motivation increase nonspecific arousal. That assumption would suggest that appetitive motivation might produce some symptoms due to dopamine activity and other symptoms due to nonspecific arousal. The latter symptoms would also be associated with aversive motivational states. Empirically, florid symptoms are not limited to Crow's Type I schizophrenia. For example, cognitive or intellectual impairments are associated with negative symptoms, and the appearance of thought disorder is a component of the chronic syndrome (Crow 1985). Similarly, Depue (1976) reported a high incidence of delusions and hallucinations in withdrawn patients, and patients who exhibit only negative symptoms are rare (Andreasen et al 1990; Gottesman et al 1987). It is at least a plausible hypothesis, therefore, that the aversive arousal seen in withdrawn schizophrenics may contribute to florid symptomatology via nondopaminergic pathways.

The traditional neuroleptics appear to exert their therapeutic effects via a reduction in dopaminergic activity and thus, by implication, a reduction in appetitive motivation. Such treatment may be less than optimal in several respects. First, if some florid symptoms result from aversive motivation, neuroleptics may not relieve them. Second, unless the patient's dopamine activity is at a high level that is normalized by treatment, administration of neuroleptics may increase his/her anhedonia (reduce his/her appetitive motivation). For example, if a diathesis to schizophrenic symptoms makes the patient vulnerable to normal levels of dopaminergic activity, neuroleptics will reduce positive symptoms at the cost of producing negative ones (i.e. as a result of reducing appetitive motivation to a subnormal level). Third, the argument presented here assumes that the primary diathesis in schizophrenia does not take the form of excessive dopamine activity, but rather is a separate vulnerability that interacts with dopamine activity (cf Reynolds 1989). This perspective, then, suggests that drugs having more complex effects than traditional neuroleptics may yield greater clinical efficacy. For example, clozapine appears to affect both dopamine and serotonin activity and to be superior in the treatment of schizophrenia (Meltzer 1989). Perhaps an optimal combination of pharmacological effects can be achieved in the future.

COMMENT

Owing to limitations of knowledge and the complexity of the topic, any attempt to organize many of the major features of schizophrenia into an integrated model is inherently speculative and simplistic. The primary point of the present attempt to do so is to call attention to the potential value of examining the full implications of the genetic data in the form of a polygenic model and to the value of viewing appetitive and aversive motivational systems as important nonspecific sources of liability. Given the longstanding view that emotional disturbance is central to functional psychiatric disorders, the central role of these motivational systems in emotion and mood makes them likely contributors to theories of psychopathology. Additionally, these motivational systems have neurochemical substrates that permit a link to genetic, pharmacological, and environmental influences. Only dopamine pathways were considered here because their behavioral functions and relation to psychopathology are more obvious than those of other neurotransmitters. With the rapid increases in our knowledge of behavioral neurochemistry, it should be possible to expand this model to include other neural pathways, providing a more comprehensive model and possibly guiding the development of more effective pharmacological treatments.

Literature Cited

Abrams, R. 1984. Genetic studies of the schizoaffective syndrome: A selective review. *Schizophr. Bull.* 10:26–29

American Psychiatric Association. 1987. *Diagnostic and Statistical Manual of Mental Disorders* Washington, DC: Author. 3rd ed., rev.

Andreasen, N. C. 1985. Positive vs. negative schizophrenia: a critical evaluation. *Schizophr. Bull.* 11:380–89

Andreasen, N. C., Flaum, M., Swayze, V. W. II, Tyrell, G., Arndt, S. 1990. Positive and negative symptoms in schizophrenia: a critical reappraisal. *Arch. Gen. Psychiatry* 47:615–21

Barlow, D. H. 1988. *Anxiety and Its Disorders.* New York: Guilford Press

Barrelet, L., Ferrero, F., Szigethy, L., Giddey, C., Pellizzer, G. 1990. Expressed emotion and first-admission schizophrenia. Nine-month follow-up in a French cultural environment. *Br. J. Psychiatry* 156:357–62

Birley, J., Brown, G. W. 1970. Crisis and life changes preceding the onset or relapse of acute schizophrenia: clinical aspects. *Br. J. Psychiatry* 16:327–33

Blaney, P. H. 1985. Stress and depression in adults: a critical review. In *Stress and Coping,* ed. T. Field, P. McCabe, N. Schneiderman, pp. 263–83. Hillsdale, NJ: Earlbaum

Braden, W. 1984. Vulnerability and schizoaffective psychosis: a two-factor model. *Schizophr. Bull.* 10:71–86

Brown, G. W., Birley, J. L. T. 1968. Crisis and life change and the onset of schizophrenia. *J. Health and Social Behav.* 9:203–14

Bruce, M. L., Kim, K., Leaf, P. J., Jacobs, S. 1990. Depressive episodes and dysphoria resulting from conjugal bereavement in a prospective community sample. *Am. J. Psychiatry* 147:608–11

Carpenter, W. T. Jr., Heinrichs, D. W., Wagman, A. M. I. 1985. On the heterogeneity of schizophrenia. In *Controversies in Schizophrenia: Changes and Constancies,* ed. M. Alpert, pp. 38–47. New York: Guilford Press

Carpenter, W. T. Jr., Heinrichs, D. W., Wagman, A. M. I. 1988. Deficit and nondeficit forms of schizophrenia: the concept. *Am. J. Psychiatry* 145:578–83

Chapman, L. J., Chapman, J. P. 1973. *Disordered Thought in Schizophrenia,* Ch.1–6, 12–13, and Conclusions, pp. 1–138, 243–85, 345–47. Englewood Cliffs, NJ: Prentice-Hall

Clayton, P. J. 1982. Bereavement. In *Handbook of Affective Disorders,* ed. E. Paykel, pp. 403–15. New York: Guilford Press

Crow, T. 1980. Molecular pathology of schizophrenia: more than one disease process? *Br. Med. J.* 180:66–68

Crow, T. J. 1985. The two-syndrome concept: origins and current status. *Schizophr. Bull.* 11:471–86

Davis, J. M. 1978. Dopamine theory of schizophrenia: a two-factor theory. In *The Nature of Schizophrenia: New Approaches to Research and Treatment,* ed. L. Wynne, R. L. Cromwell, S. Matthyse, pp. 105–15. New York: John Wiley

Day, R., Nielsen, J. A., Korten, A., Ernberg, G., Dube, K. C., Gebhart, J., et al. 1987.

334   FOWLES

Stressful life events preceding the acute onset of schizophrenia: a cross-national study from the World Health Organization. *Cult. Med. Psychiatry* 11:123–205

Depue, R. A. 1976. An activity-withdrawal distinction in schizophrenia: behavioral, clinical brain damage, and neurophysiological correlates. *J. Abnorm. Psychol.* 85:174–85

Depue, R. A., Arbisi, P., Spoont, M. R., Leon, A., Ainsworth, B. 1989. Dopamine functioning in the Behavioral Facilitation System and seasonal variation in behavior: normal population and clinical studies. In *Seasonal Affective Disorder*, ed. N. H. Rosenthal, M. Blehar. New York: Guilford Press

Depue, R. A., Iacono, W. G. 1988. Neurobehavioral aspects of affective disorders. *Annu. Rev. Psychol.* 40:457–92

Depue, R. A., Krauss, S. P., Spoont, M. R. 1987. A two dimensional model of seasonal bipolar affective disorder. In *Psychopathology: An Interactive Perspective.*, ed. D. Magnusson, A. Ohman. New York: Academic

Dohrenwend, B. P., Egri, G. 1981. Recent stressful life events and episodes of schizophrenia. *Schizophr. Bull.* 7:12–23

Dura, J. R., Stukenberg, K. W., Kiecolt-Glaser, J. K. 1990. Chronic stress and depressive disorders in older adults. *J. Abnorm. Psychol.* 99:284–90

Falconer, D. S. 1965. The inheritance of liability to certain diseases estimated from the incidence among relatives. *Ann. Hum. Genet.* 29:51–76

Faraone, S. V., Tsuang, M. T. 1985. Quantitative models of the genetic transmission of schizophrenia. *Psychol. Bull.* 98:41–66

Fischer, M. 1971. Psychoses in the offspring of schizophrenic monozygotic twins and their normal co-twins. *Br. J. Psychiatry* 115:981–90

Fowles, D. C. 1980. The three arousal model: implications of Gray's two-factor learning theory for heart rate, electrodermal activity, and psychopathy. *Psychophysiology* 17:87–104

Fowles, D. 1987. Application of a behavioral theory of motivation to the concepts of anxiety and impulsivity. *J. Res. Pers.* 21:417–35

Fowles, D. C. 1988. Psychophysiology and psychopathology: a motivational approach. *Psychophysiology* 25:373–91

Fowles, D. C. 1992. Biological variables in psychopathology: a psychobiological perspective. In *Comprehensive Handbook of Psychopathology*, ed. P. Sutker, H. Adams, 2. New York: Plenum. In press

Glavin, G. B. 1985. Stress and brain noradrenalin: a review. *Neurosci. Biobehav. Rev.* 9:233–43

Gottesman, I. I. 1991. *Schizophrenia Genesis.* New York: W. H. Freeman

Gottesman, I. I., Bertelsen, A. 1989. Confirming unexpressed genotypes for schizophrenia. *Arch. Gen. Psychiatry* 46:867–72

Gottesman, I. I., McGue, M. 1991. Mixed and mixed-up models for the transmission of schizophrenia. In *Thinking Clearly about Psychology: Essays in Honor of Paul E. Meehl*, ed. D. Cichetti, W. Grove. Minneapolis: Univ. Minnesota Press

Gottesman, I. I., McGuffin, P., Farmer, A. E. 1987. Clinical genetics as clues to the "real" genetics of schizophrenia (a decade of modest gains while playing for time). *Schizophr. Bull.* 13:23–47

Gottesman, I. I., Shields, J. A. 1967. A polygenic theory of schizophrenia. *Proc. Natl. Acad. Sci.* 58:199–205

Gottesman, I. I., Shields, J. 1982. *Schizophrenia: The Epigenetic Puzzle*, Ch. 3–7, pp. 37–148. New York: Cambridge Univ. Press

Gray, J. A. 1977. Drug effects on fear and frustration: possible limbic site of action of minor tranquilizers. In *Handbook of Psychopharmacology: Drugs, Neurotransmitters, and Behavior*, ed. L. Iversen, S. Iversen, S. Snyder, 8:433–529. New York: Plenum

Gray, J. A. 1982. *The Neuropsychology of Anxiety: An Enquiry into the Functions of the Septo-Hippocampal System.* Oxford: Oxford Univ. Press

Gray, J. A. 1987a. Perspectives on anxiety and impulsivity: a commentary. *J. Res. Pers.* 21:493–509

Gray, J. A. 1987b. *The Psychology of Fear and Stress.* Cambridge, England: Cambridge Univ. Press. 2nd ed

Haracz, J. L. 1982. The dopamine hypothesis: an overview of studies with schizophrenic patients. *Schizophr. Bull.* 8:438–69

Harrow, M., Grinker, R. R. Sr., Holzman, P. S., Kayton, L. 1977. Anhedonia and schizophrenia. *Am. J. Psychiatry* 134:794–97

Heritch, A. J. 1990. Evidence for reduced and dysregulated turnover of dopamine in schizophrenia. *Schizophr. Bull.* 16:605–15

Jimerson, D. C. 1987. Role of dopamine mechanisms in the affective disorders. In *Psychopharmacology: The Third Generation of Progress*, ed. H. Meltzer, pp. 505–12. New York: Raven Press

Kendell, R. E. 1982. The choice of diagnostic criteria for biological research. *Arch. Gen. Psychiatry* 39:1334–339

Kendler, K. S., Gruenberg, A. M. 1984. An independent analysis of the Copenhagen sample of the Danish adoption study of schizophrenia: VI. The relationship between psychiatric disorders as defined by DSM-III in the relatives and adoptees. *Arch. Gen. Psychiatry* 41:555–64

Kendler, K. S., Gruenberg, A. M., Tsuang, M. T. 1986. A DSM-III family study of the nonschizophrenic psychotic disorders. *Am. J. Psychiatry* 143:1098–105

Kendler, K., Heath, A. C., Martin, N. G., Eaves, L. J. 1987. Symptoms of anxiety and symptoms of depression; same genes, different environments? *Arch. Gen. Psychiatry* 43:923–29

Klein, D. N. 1982. Activity-withdrawal in the differential diagnosis of schizophrenia and mania. *J. Abnorm. Psychol.* 91:157–64

Kringlen, E., Gunnar, C. 1989. Offspring of monozygotic twins discordant for schizophrenia. *Arch. Gen. Psychiatry* 46:873–77

Leff, J. P., Kuipers, L., Berkowitz, R., Eberlein-Vries, R., Sturgeon, D. 1982. A controlled trial of social intervention in the families of schizophrenic patients. *Br. J. Psychiatry* 141:121–34

Leff, J. P., Vaughn, C. E. 1985. Expressed emotion in families: Its significance for mental illness. New York: Guilford Press

Levinson, D. F., Levitt, M. E. M. 1987. Schizoaffective mania reconsidered. *The Am. J. Psychiatry* 144:415–25

Lewine, R. R. J. 1985. Negative symptoms in schizophrenia: editor's introduction. *Schizophr. Bull.* 11:361–63

Losonczy, M. F., Davidson, M., Davis, K. L. 1987. The dopamine hypothesis of schizophrenia. In Psychopharmacology: The third generation of progress, ed. H. Meltzer, pp. 715–26. New York: Raven Press

Lukoff, D., Snyder, K., Ventura, J., Nuechterlein, K. H. 1984. Life events, familial stress, and coping in the developmental course of schizophrenia. *Schizophr. Bull.* 10:258–92

Lydiard, R. B., Laird, L. K. 1988. Prediction of response to antipsychotics. *J. Clin. Psychopharmacol.* 8:3–13

Maser, J. D., Cloninger, C. R. 1990. Comorbidity of anxiety and mood disorders: introduction and overview. In *Comorbidity of Mood and Anxiety Disorders,* ed. J. Maser, C. Cloninger, pp. 3–12. Washington, DC: Am. Psychiatr. Press

McGue, M., Gottesman, I. I. 1989. Genetic linkage in schizophrenia: perspectives from genetic epidemiology. *Schizophr. Bull.* 15:453–64

McGuffin, P., Katz, R. 1989. The genetics of depression and manic-depressive disorder. *Br. J. Psychiatr.* 155:294–304

Meltzer, H. Y. 1984. Schizoaffective disorder; editor's introduction. *Schizophr. Bull.* 10:11–13

Meltzer, H. Y. 1985. Dopamine and negative symptoms in schizophrenia: critique of the Type I-II hypothesis. In *Controversies in Schizophrenia: Changes and Constancies,* ed. M. Alpert, pp. 110–36. New York: Guilford Press

Meltzer, H. Y. 1989. Clinical studies on the mechanism of action of clozapine: the dopamine-serotonin hypothesis of schizophrenia. *Psychopharmacology* 99:S18-S27

Meltzer, H. Y., Sommers, A. A., Luchins, D. J. 1986. The effect of neuroleptics and other psychotropic drugs on negative symptoms in schizophrenia. *J. Clin. Psychopharmacol.* 6:329–38

Mesulam, M. 1990. Schizophrenia and the brain. *New Engl. J. Med.* 311:842–45

Mishlove, M., Chapman, L. J. 1985. Social anhedonia in the prediction of psychosis proneness. *J. Abnorm. Psychol.* 94:384–96

Mullen, M. J., Murray, R. M. 1989. The impact of molecular genetics on our understanding of the psychoses. *Br. J. Psychiatry* 154:591–95

Murray, R. M., Lewis, S., Reveley, A. M. 1985. Towards an aetiological classification of schizophrenia. *Lancet* I:1023–26

Panksepp, J. 1986. The neurochemistry of behavior. *Annu. Rev. Psychol.* 37:77–107

Pardes, H., Kaufmann, C. A., Pincus, H. A., et al. 1989. Genetics and psychiatry: past discoveries, current dilemmas, and future directions. *Am. J. Psychiatry* 146:435–43

Paykel, E. S. 1982. Life events and early environment. In *Handbook of Affective Disorders,* ed. E. Paykel, pp. 146–61. New York: Guilford Press

Plomin, R. 1990. The role of inheritance in behavior. *Science* 248:183–88

Procci, W. R. 1989. Psychotic disorders not elsewhere classified. In *Comprehensive Textbook of Psychiatry/V,* ed. H. Kaplan, B. Sadock, pp. 830–42. Baltimore: Williams & Williams

Reiss, D., Plomin, R., Hetherington, E. M. 1991. Genetics and psychiatry: an unheralded window on the environment. *Am. J. Psychiatry* 148:283–91

Reveley, A. M., Reveley, M. A., Murray, R. M. 1984. Cerebral ventricular enlargement in nongenetic schizophrenia: a controlled twin study. *Br. J. Psychiatry* 144:89–93

Reynolds, G. P. 1989. Beyond the dopamine hypothesis: the neurochemical pathology of schizophrenia. *Br. J. Psychiatry* 155:305–16

Risch, N. 1990. Genetic linkage and complex diseases, with special reference to psychiatric disorders. *Genet. Epidemiol.* 7:3–16

Rosenthal, D. 1970. *Genetic Theory and Abnormal Behavior.* New York: McGraw-Hill

Snyder, S. H. 1978. Dopamine and schizophrenia. See Davis 1978, pp. 87–94

Sommers, A. A. 1985. "Negative symptoms":

conceptual and methodological problems. *Schizophr. Bull.* 11:364–79

Stewart, J., de Witt, H., Eikelboom, R. 1984. Role of unconditioned and conditioned drug effects in the self-administration of opiates and stimulants. *Psychol. Rev.* 91:251–68

Strauss, J., Carpenter, W. T. Jr., Bartko, J. 1974. The diagnosis and understanding of schizophrenia: Part III. Speculations on the processes that underlie schizophrenic symptoms and signs. *Schizophr. Bull.* 1:61–69, Exp. Issue 11

Swinson, R. P., Kirby, M. 1986. The differentiation of anxiety and depressive syndromes. In *Anxiety Disorders: Psychological and Biological Perspectives*, ed. B. Shaw, Z. Segal, T. Vallis, F. Cashman, pp. 21–34. New York: Plenum

Tarrier, N., Barrowclough, C., Vaughn, C., Bamrah, J. S., Porceddu, K., et al. 1988. The community management of schizophrenia: a controlled trial of a behavioural intervention with families to reduce relapse. *Br. J. Psychiatry* 153:532–42

Tellegen, A. 1985. Structures of mood and personality and their relevance to assessing anxiety, with an emphasis on self-report. In *Anxiety and the Anxiety Disorders*, ed. A. Tuma, J. Maser, pp. 681–706. Hillsdale, NJ: Lawrence Erlbaum

Tellegen, A., Lykken, D. T., Bouchard, T. J. Jr., Wilcox, K. J., Segal, N. L., Rich, S. 1988. Personality similarity in twins reared apart and together. *J. Pers. Soc. Psychol.* 54:1031–39

van Kammen, D. P., Peters, J. L., van Kammen, W. B., Neylan, T., Yao, J. K., et al. 1990. Noradrenalin, state dependency and relapse prediction in schizophrenia: a hypothesis. In *International Perspectives in Schizophrenia: Biological, Social and Epidemiological Findings*, ed. M. Weller, pp. 253–68. London: John Libbey

Vaughn, C. E., Snyder, K., Jones, S., Freeman, W. B., Falloon, I. R. H. 1984. Family factors in schizophrenic relapse. *Arch. Gen. Psychiatry* 41:1169–77

Venables, P. H. 1957. A short scale for rating "activity-withdrawal" in schizophrenics. *J. Mental Sci.* 103:197–99

Venables, P. H. 1963a. Selectivity of attention, withdrawal, and cortical activation. *Arch. Gen. Psychiatry* 9:74–78

Venables, P. H. 1963b. The relationship between level of skin potential and fusion of paired light flashes in schizophrenic and normal subjects. *J. Psychiatr. Res.* 1:279–87

Venables, P. H. 1967. The relation of two flash and two click thresholds to withdrawal in paranoid and non-paranoid schizophrenics. *Br. J. Soc. Clin. Psychol.* 6:60–62

Venables, P. H., Wing, J. K. 1962. Level of arousal and the subclassification of schizophrenia. *Arch. Gen. Psychiatry* 7:114–19

Ventura, J., Nuechterlein, K. H., Lukoff, D., Hardesty, J. P. 1989. A prospective study of stressful life events and schizophrenic relapse. *J. Abnorm. Psychol.* 98:407–11

Watson, D., Clark, L. A. 1984. Negative affectivity: the disposition to experience aversive emotional states. *Psychol. Bull.* 96:465–90

Weissman, M. M., Pottenger, M., Kleber, H., Ruben, H. L., Williams, D., Thompson, W. D. 1977. Symptom patterns in primary and secondary depression. *Arch. Gen. Psychiatry* 34:854–62

Williams, P. V., McGlashan, T. H. 1987. Schizoaffective psychosis. *Arch. Gen. Psychiatry* 44:130–37

Wilner, P. 1985. *Depression: A Psychobiological Synthesis*. New York: John Wiley & Sons

Wing, J. K. 1961. A simple and reliable subclassification of chronic schizophrenia. *J. Mental Sci.* 107:862–75

Wing, J. K. 1978. Social influences on the course of schizophrenia. See Davis 1978, pp. 599–616

Wing, J. K., Brown, G. W. 1970. *Institutionalism and Schizophrenia*. London: Cambridge Univ. Press

Wise, R. A. 1988. The neurobiology of craving: implications for the understanding and treatment of addiction. *J. Abnorm. Psychol.* 97:118–32

Wise, R. A., Bozarth, M. A. 1987. A psychomotor stimulant theory of addiction. *Psychol. Rev.* 94:469–92

Wise, R. A., Rompre, P.-P. 1989. Brain dopamine and reward. *Annu. Rev. Psychol.* 40:191–225

Zubin, J., Spring, B. 1977. Vulnerability—a new view of schizophrenia. *J. Abnorm. Psychol.* 86:103–26

Annu. Rev. Psychol. 1992. 43:337–75

COGNITIVE DEVELOPMENT: FOUNDATIONAL THEORIES OF CORE DOMAINS

Henry M. Wellman and Susan A. Gelman

Department of Psychology, University of Michigan, Ann Arbor, Michigan 48109

KEY WORDS: concepts, conceptual development, commonsense, infancy and early childhood

Contents

Cognitive development has been reviewed twice in this series in the last ten years: The first of these reviews concerned stages of cognitive development (Fischer & Silvern 1985), the second mechanisms of cognitive change (Siegler 1989). These topics reflect only two of many important themes in the field. For example, over the past ten years research with infants has increasingly

0066-4308/92/0201-0337$02.00

revealed a rich set of early cognitive capacities. There has been renewed interest in instruction, including such new or reinvigorated topics as emergent literacy in the preschool years (Teale & Sulzby 1986), science understandings, and academic achievement across different nations and cultures (Stevenson et al 1986). More generally, cross-cultural studies of cognitive development (Stigler et al 1990) are of increasing importance. Cognition, intelligence, and learning in the elderly have dramatically increased their research presence with topics such as wisdom and late-life potential (Baltes & Baltes 1990), complementing earlier concern with loss of function. Reflecting increasing interdisciplinary research in psychology generally, there has been a blurring of traditional disciplinary lines in research on cognitive development. In the past several years the problematic boundaries between cognition, instruction, development, and acculturation have begun to crumble.

Two further trends in the field stand out in our minds and figure prominently in our review, namely contemporary concern with domains of cognition and with naive theories. These two topics represent a recent revolution in the study of cognitive development.

DOMAINS AND THEORIES

It is increasingly accepted that cognition may differ substantially in different areas or domains (Chomsky 1975; Fodor 1983; Gallistel 1990). Recently, arguments have been made for each of the following: a unique language-learning faculty; distinctive neuronal substrates for cognizing about space; predispositions in infancy to attend to numbers versus faces versus speech; a highly evolved primate social intelligence; specific islands of expertise, such as about dinosaurs, physics, and chess. The general claim is that the mind is in some sense compartmentalized or "modularized"; that is, that human conceptual understanding of one sort (e.g. about space) is likely to be quite different in character, structure, and development from understanding of another sort (e.g. about language).

Complementarily, investigators in disciplines such as anthropology, cognitive science, education, and developmental psychology increasingly discuss folk, naive, lay, or commonsense theories (Berlin et al 1973; Carey 1985; Karmiloff-Smith & Inhelder 1975; Murphy & Medin 1985; see Harold Kelley's chapter in this volume). Commonsense theories are nonscientists' everyday understandings of certain bodies of information such as folk zoology or naive astronomy. Various serious claims have been advanced: that human concepts are entrenched in larger naive theories; that conceptual change and thus important aspects of cognitive development are akin to theory change in science; that cultural world views are instantiated in folk theories; and that theories supplant similarity-based conceptions both in current scientific thinking and in the individual's own learning or development.

A classic question in psychology is to what extent the mind develops in a general as opposed to a specific fashion. Concern with domains and concern with theories reflect increased interest in the development of systems of cognition specific to some bodies of information and not others. This represents a contrast to several earlier domain-general approaches to cognitive development. For example, as it is generally understood (but see Chapman 1988), Piaget's standard theory describes general stages of thought (sensori-motor cognition, preoperational thought, concrete operational thought, and formal operational thought) that apply across widely varying content areas. For example, concrete-operational thinking similarly structures such disparate conceptions as the child's understanding of number, time, weight, morality, classification, and causality, or so the theory goes. In this sense Piagetian cognitive structures are content independent and also domain general.

Similarly, despite many contrasts with Piagetian theory, information processing views of development have, until recently, concerned themselves with general processes or architectures said to characterize cognitive development broadly. For example, the cognitive system's basic representational format was hypothesized to change with development from enactive, to iconic, to symbolic (Bruner 1964). Or, certain general parameters such as speed of processing or size of working memory were seen as increasing developmentally, and influencing all of cognition (Case 1985). Thus, studies of such basic information processes as storage and retrieval, for example, characterized memory development as a general improvement in capacity, strategies, and performance with age (see Kail & Hagen 1977).

The appeal of domain-general approaches is their ability to account for a broad range of phenomena with a relatively small set of principles. These approaches are thus parsimonious and powerful. However, in the last ten years or so a domain-general, content-independent picture of cognitive development has become increasingly problematic. At least some, and perhaps most, conceptual abilities seem specialized for, or first specifically developed for, particular types of contents. For example, memory skills and capacities were shown to be determined substantially by specific content and thus did not necessarily exhibit a developmental advantage for adults or older children over younger ones. In a seminal study of this sort (Chi 1978), children who were chess experts vastly outperformed adults who were chess novices on memory for chess board positions. This did not reflect better overall memory in these children, because the adults were better on standard memory tasks such as digit span—the classic developmental finding. Memory was not simply developing in some domain-general fashion but was tied, in part, to different contents, stemming from different domains of expertise.

Similarly, research on Piagetian topics such as classification and conservation seemed to show that the child "works out concepts in separate domains without using the kinds of integrative structures that would be required by a general stage theory" (Gelman & Baillargeon 1983:214). As Gelman & Baillargeon concluded in their review of the development of Piagetian concepts, this suggests "the possibility that there are domain-specific structures rather than domain-independent structures" (p. 210).

Although it is now widely acknowledged that domain-specific content has profound implications for human cognition, the term *domain* is used in several separable senses: 1. innately given, modular abilities, including for example a specialized faculty for language and language acquisition (Fodor 1983); 2. modes of processing tied to particular sensory modalities, such as verbal versus visual domains; 3. areas of knowledge that have special properties because of highly prolonged and intensive experience and expertise, including for example chess (Chase & Simon 1973); 4. Piaget-inspired partitionings of cognitive tasks such as the "domains of classification, seriation, and conservation" (Gelman & Baillargeon 1983:172); and 5. naive theories that carve phenomena into differing organized systems of knowledge and belief, such as biology (Carey 1985) or psychology (Wellman 1990). While these differing perspectives share a dissatisfaction with traditional views that cognition is domain general, they encompass distinctly different claims about domains: where they come from, what are prototypic examples, how many there would be, how they might be structured, and how and whether they would undergo developmental change. Innate modules, for example, can be assumed to be least open to change or individual variation; expert systems would be most open to change and variation (though they might be characterized more by learning than by development); and theories may entail a mixture of some unchanging core beliefs as well as a periphery of changing specifics.

Similarly, the term *theory* has been used to describe a great variety of specific conceptual understandings. These range from the very specific [e.g. a boy's assertion of a relation between eating sugary foods such as cake and catching colds (Kuhn 1989:676)] to global but still content-dependent bodies of knowledge [e.g. everyday understanding of biological phenomena such as life, death, digestion, and reproduction (Carey 1985)]. The term has been used to refer to concatenations of empirical generalizations—"a loose-knit network of largely tacit principles, platitudes, and paradigms which constitute a sort of folk theory" (Stitch 1983:1)—as well as to coherent, well-organized systems of explanatory beliefs (Murphy & Medin 1985).

We will not argue that any one usage is correct; current discussion points to several topics for further research and analysis. Instead, we examine a topic that lies at the intersection of a concern with theories and domains: the early development of foundational human knowledge systems. It has been proposed that infants and young children rapidly acquire certain bodies of knowledge that in turn frame or launch most later conceptual acquisitions. If this is so, then characterizing such conceptual structures would prove central to any understanding of domain-specific cognitive development. We concentrate on research that addresses this topic—a substantial portion of contemporary cognitive development research. Three features characterize this research and its theoretical significance: 1. a focus on knowledge (foundational human abilities could be content-free processes or architecture, such as memory buffers or rates of processing; in contrast the focus here is on bodies of knowledge that gain structure from the nature of their contents); 2. a focus on core understandings (some knowledge is more powerful, enabling, seminal, constituitive than other knowledge—knowledge of objects may be an apt example; how we understand physical objects figures in our understanding of measurement, astronomy, economics, geography, human artifacts, and so on); and 3. a focus on development (foundational knowledge constrains the path of conceptual acquisition, enabling learners to fill the gaps in underdetermined observations).

In what follows we sketch an emerging picture of several foundational knowledge systems. We begin with a brief presentation of a conceptual framework for construing some of the issues and for posing critical questions of the research; this revolves around the notion of framework theories that constitute domains of phenomena. Then we review research on what may well be three early-developing framework theories.

Framework Theories

A quick look at scientific theories shows that it is important to distinguish two different sorts of theories—foundational or framework theories vs specific theories. Specific theories are detailed scientific formulations about a delimited set of phenomena. To use psychological examples, theories at this level would include the Rescorla-Wagner theory of classical conditioning, Piaget's theory of object permanence, and Freud's theory of the Oedipal complex. On the other hand, there are also more global theoretical traditions. Examples in psychology include behaviorism, psychodynamics, and connectionism. Such framework theories constrain and guide the development of specific theories.

Philosophers of science have called framework theories paradigms (Kuhn 1962), research programs (Lakatos 1970), or research traditions (Laudan 1977). There are important differences in these writers' characterizations, but for our purposes there are basic commonalities. Specifically, framework theories outline the ontology and the basic causal devices for their specific theories, thereby defining a coherent form of reasoning about a particular set of phenomena.

A research tradition provides a set of guidelines for the development of specific theories. Part of those guidelines constitute an ontology which specifies, in a general way, the types of fundamental entities which exist in the domain or domains within which the research tradition is embedded. The function of specific theories within the research tradition is to explain all the empirical problems in the domain by "reducing" them to the ontology of the research tradition. . . . Moreover, the research tradition outlines the different modes by which these entities can interact. Thus, Cartesian particles can only interact by contact, not by action-at-a-distance. Entities within a Marxist research tradition can only interact by virtue of the economic forces influencing them (Laudan 1977:79).

Framework theories define domains; they coherently parse phenomena into bodies of different specific contents. But such domains outline areas for discovery—that is, research programs—rather than finished bodies of understanding. Framework theories are, therefore, both open-ended and constraining; they allow and inspire the development of more specific theories but do so by defining the domain of inquiry in the first place.

This sort of analysis represents an attempt by philosophers of science to characterize an intriguing epistemological structure, framework understandings that predate and constitute, but at the same time are themselves further articulated in, more specific understandings of phenomena. Framework understandings of this sort could exist within individuals as well as in scientific communities, constituting areas of human thinking for further conceptual development. Indeed, in what follows, we review emerging research on the development of three possible commonsense framework theories: naive physics, naive psychology, and naive biology. A priori these seem to be three major sorts of understandings in that they encompass most of the external world with which we interact. When we consider that early humans were a distinctly social species evolved to use objects as tools and to hunt and forage within their natural environment, then it is hard to imagine any more fundamental cognitive tasks than knowing about people, about plants and animals, and about the physical world of objects.

Could these areas of thought even constitute foundational theories; could they represent everyday domains of thought organized around distinctive ontological categories and causal reasoning frameworks? Some sense that distinctive understandings may be involved can be seen by contrasting a material solid object (say, a billiard ball), an animate living organism (say, a butterfly), and a sentient human person (say, yourself). In our everyday thinking, these are three very different sorts of things engaging in very different forms of causal interactions. Consider the actions or movements of these three things. The ball moves if driven by some external force transmitted directly to it (e.g. another ball striking it), evidencing characteristic mechanical motion. The butterfly is self-propelled; it moves because of an inner biological "engine," evidencing characteristic biomechanical movements. A human engages in intentional action based on psychological reasons; the act of voting, for example, based on the belief that one candidate is best and on the desire to see him or her elected. Alternatively, consider three different human movements, as seen from the three contrasting perspectives: 1. physical forces—the wind buffets a human across the street; 2. biological forces—a human shivers in response to cold; 3. mental forces—the human imagines herself in a different place, decides to go, and persuades a friend to provide a ride.

These examples suggest the existence of three domains of reasoning constituted by three different ontological, causal-explanatory understandings; that is, three different naive foundational theories. Do humans develop such framework theories? If so, do they distinguish these three possible domains? And when: late in life as the product of many other developments, or early in development as the framework for further acquisitions? In what follows we assess contemporary cognitive development research that addresses these questions, we more precisely characterize the nature of these three kinds of knowledge, and begin to answer the questions of whether, when, and how they develop in childhood.

NAIVE PHYSICS

Partly because of Piaget's (1954) discussion of the object concept, students of cognitive development are accustomed to thinking of certain conceptions as providing a foundational framework for later cognitions. The object concept is an organism's knowledge that physical objects exist within a space encompassing self and object, but are independent of self in that they continue to exist when not in view. Imagine the worldview and actions of an organism without such an understanding, who instead "lives in an ever-changing world where objects are continually made and unmade" (Harris 1983:716).

An understanding of the existence of objects seems ontologically central to anything like our everyday physics— our ordinary understanding of the world of middle-sized objects and their interactions. Furthermore, everyday understanding of physical causality would seem to require some understanding of object dynamics—the force-transmissions that influence the position and movement of objects, for example that one ball colliding with another sets the second one rolling unless impeded. The two core framework notions here— physical objects and physical-mechanical causes—can become quite complex. After all, physical entities in the broadest sense encompass not only solid objects but unbounded masses like sand and snow, liquids like water, gases like air, and the insides of objects (the crystals inside a geode) as well as their material solidity; and physical causal-transformations include not only the dynamics of object contact but processes like flight, wave action, combustion, and melting.

Infants

Piaget (1954) concluded that the object concept was acquired late in infancy as an end-product of sensorimotor development. It was an insight based on, and manifest in, the infant's manipulation and practical experience with objects, especially searching for visible, then invisible, then invisibly moved objects. Recently these conclusions have been challenged because of Piaget's reliance on search tasks (e.g. Wellman 1986). Studies utilizing preferential-looking paradigms suggest a rather different developmental story.

For example, Baillargeon et al (1985) first habituated infants to a display of a rectangular screen, hinged at its base, that moved back and forth through a 180-degree arc—a "flapping panel." Infants viewed this display from the front, the panel flipping first forward and then away from them. After habituation, a box was positioned behind the panel, and infants were shown two test events, one a possible event and one an anomalous event. In the former, the panel swung to the front and then to the back, stopped appropriately when it touched the hidden box, and then swung forward again. In the anomalous case, it swung through the complete 180 degrees as if the hidden box were not there. Note that this anomalous event is superficially most similar to the habituation event, because in it the panel continues to flap through 180 degrees. Infants looked significantly longer at the anomalous (but similar) event than at the dissimilar but possible event. This suggests that infants were puzzled when the screen did not stop on expected contact with the box and thus believed the hidden box continued to exist. Baillargeon's many experiments (reviewed in Baillargeon 1992) contain a variety of converging controls and provide evidence that infants as young as 3–4 months represent the continued existence of an object that is currently invisible. The results also suggest that infants believe material objects to be solid and substantial (e.g. not simply compressed or scattered by the panel), and to remain stationary.

What about object dynamics? Infants' perception of physical causality has been the focus of recent research (Leslie 1982; Leslie & Keeble 1987; Oakes & Cohen 1990). As a specific example, Leslie showed 6-month-olds either (a) a film of one object colliding with and launching a second object, (b) or control events such as a first object making contact with a second one that only began to move after a considerable delay (violating temporal aspects of the causal dynamics). Leslie reasoned that since the control events do not specify causal connections, then an infant habituated to one of those events should be unsurprised if the event was reversed (since the reversal, too, provides no causal regularity). For the target event, however, reversal of the sequence specifies a real reversal of causal roles: The cause is now the effect. Thus, if infants understand the object dynamics, dishabituation should occur upon reversal only in the causally determined case. In several converging studies (reviewed in Leslie 1988), Leslie found dishabituation only upon reversing the causally proper sequence, suggesting an early appreciation of at least some aspects of mechanical causation.

Of course, infants could perceptually discriminate between causal and noncausal sequences without necessarily interpreting such events within a physical-causal understanding—that is, without representing physical causality conceptually (see Mandler 1988). Spelke has been especially concerned with the issue of whether infants' understanding of objects represents perceptual mechanisms or conceptual understandings, and with the timing involved (e.g. Spelke 1988). She argues that infants' understanding of physical objects and their spatiotemporal properties constitutes an early theory of objects, rather than merely a perceptual organization of current sensory experiences. Here she cites especially research like Baillargeon's above, demonstrating that infants' understanding of objects is apparent even in their reactions to invisible—not currently perceivable—objects. In her latest research (Spelke 1991), she extends such reasoning and methods to further investigate infants' understanding of object substantiality as well as object movements.

For example, in one study with 4-month-olds, infants were habituated to a sequence in which a ball fell behind a screen and then the screen was removed to show the ball at rest on the floor of the apparatus. Two test events then followed, in which an intermediate ledge was put in place behind the screen creating a shelf above the floor of the apparatus. In the plausible test event, the ball fell behind the screen, and when the screen was removed, the ball was on the shelf. In the anomalous test event, the ball fell, and when the screen was removed the ball was at rest below the shelf on the original floor of the apparatus. (This anomalous event, in which the ball somehow moves through the intervening shelf, was actually superficially most similar to the habituation event because the ball is seen at the same resting place when the screen is removed.) Four-month-olds looked considerably longer at the anomalous than the plausible test event. In this and further studies, Spelke showed that young infants expect invisible objects to continue at rest or motion, unless impeded by solid obstacles. At the same time, infants do not understand other ubiquitous physical events, such as the constant downward pull of gravity.

Later Developments

Little research exists characterizing the expanding understanding of objects in older infants and toddlers, but by age 3 or 4 years children evidence considerable understanding of physical objects and physical causality.

OBJECTS   Not all understanding of objects involves their mere existence, solidity, and rigidity. As one recently researched aspect of this sort, consider children's understanding of the insides of objects. The insides of objects (the gears of a watch, the crystals within a geode) comprise the matter lying interior to the outer surfaces. Insides are often unobserved (though in principle observable), and they are often particularly important for understanding and explaining what items are and how they function (e.g. the gears of a watch vs its glass crystal). More generally, as adults we appeal to a variety of less obvious theoretical constructs to explain and make sense of the physical world—for example, an object's center of balance, mass, or its molecular composition—and insides may constitute an early analog for other theoretical constructs.

Recent work demonstrates that children know a significant amount about the insides of familiar objects by age 3 years. If asked to report the contents of various objects, 3-year-olds offer different answers for animate and inanimate things, typically reporting that animates have blood, bones, and internal organs (such as hearts or muscles), whereas inanimates have either nothing or have material such as cotton, paper, hair, or "hard stuff" (Gelman 1987). By age 4 years, children seem ready to assume that members of a particular category are likely to have the same internal parts and substance as one another, claiming, for example, that all dogs have "the same kinds of stuff inside" (Gelman & O'Reilly 1988).

These kinds of responses may represent nothing more than reports of common associates—responding "skin" or "shell" to questions about outsides and "stuffing"or "blood" to questions about insides, or reporting that since all watches are similar, their insides are similar. However, in a different sort of task, we asked chidlren to reason about triads of objects such as an almond, a very similar-looking rock, and a dissimilar-looking peanut (Gelman & Wellman 1991). Children were asked which two items looked most alike and which had the same kinds of insides. To answer correctly about insides, children had to select two items that looked very different on the outside. Even 3-year-olds were significantly correct at distinguishing insides and outsides. In a second study 4- and 5-year-olds judged that nonobvious insides were often essential to an object's identity or function. If asked, for example, would an egg still be an egg, or a turtle still a turtle, if its outside (shell) vs insides (white and yolk, or blood and bones) were removed, 4- and 5-year-olds affirmed that insides were more essential than outsides.

Objects such as eggs have distinct insides; in contrast a rubber ball is one kind of material throughout. Smith et al (1985) showed that even 4-year-olds understand that objects of this sort are composed of material substances and that such material kinds are different from object kinds. For example, they showed several items (e.g. a paper cup, a wooden airplane) to 4-, 5- 7-, and 9-year-olds who judged what they were and what they were made of. Then the items were cut into small pieces as the children watched and the child was asked whether it was still the same kind of object and whether it was still the same kind of stuff. At all ages children knew that the cut-up bits were no longer the same kinds of objects but that they were the same material kinds (e.g. still paper but not still a cup). Thus, at this age children already evidence a conception of matter in the sense of the kinds of materials out of which physical objects are composed. Additional research by Carey (1991) and her colleagues shows several ways in which children's conception of matter and object substances significantly develop beyond the preschool years. For example, preschool children judge that visible large pieces of Styrofoam, or very small but obvious objects such as a single grain of rice, weigh nothing at all. Thus having weight, having matter, and occupying space are not coextensive aspects of objects for young children, as they are for adults.

CAUSALITY   One can think of causality either (a) as entrenched in different domains of content (the physical causes of object movements vs the psychological causes of human actions) or (b) as requiring only content-independent logical reasoning. Following Hume, for example, a causal inference might be induced whenever events (of whatever sort) exhibit requisite patterns of temporal and spatial contiguity and covariation. Developmental research on children's understanding of causality, following Piaget, began by documenting children's developing ability to make logical causal inferences in cases of isolated covariation. One conclusion of such research concerned preschoolers' consistent failures to reason causally in these logical ways (see Shultz & Kestenbaum 1985). In the 1980s, however, researchers questioned this conclusion, sensing that a Humean analysis missed an essential content-dependent aspect of human thinking about physical causal events, namely that we ordinarily assume and reason about specific causal mechanisms (Bullock et al 1982; Shultz 1982). In physical systems in particular we reason to and from assessment of specific mechanisms whereby some cause produces some effect by transmitting a force or restraint to it, or some set of forces causes trajectories, accelerations, and so on. Young children evidence several proficiencies at understanding the transmission and outcome of mechanical forces of this sort.

For example, a recent literature has tackled adults' and older children's understanding of naive physics by examining their understanding of classical mechanics (see Proffitt et al 1990). In these studies, people must predict, for example, the trajectories of balls rolling out of curved tubes or the weight or direction of movement of colliding balls. These studies show that adults' naive understanding of such motions is coherent, indeed theoretical (McCloskey 1983), although not always accurate with respect to scientific physics. Proffitt & Kaiser, who have contributed extensively to this literature, conclude that adults and children are relatively competent with "simple" problems as opposed to "extended body" problems to be discussed next— that is, problems where motions and force transmission involve essentially simple symmetrical objects whose action can be adequately seen in terms of a single particle of mass.

> We take this to be the case for four reasons. First, whereas early studies highlighted the tendency of college student populations to err on these problems, we note that typically the majority of subjects give correct responses. Second, when asked to reason about these problems in a familiar context, very few people make erroneous predictions (Kaiser, McCloskey & Proffitt 1986). Third, and of special significance, people demonstrate an excellent appreciation of particle dynamics when making judgments about ongoing events (Kaiser, Proffitt, & Anderson 1985; Kaiser & Proffitt 1986). . . .. Finally, it should be noted that the events used in the intuitive mechanics studies are fairly complex exemplars of particle motions: external forces are applied and removed. The only experiments that have involved simple particle motions were developmental studies in which simple motions were used to ensure that young children understood the task (Kaiser et al 1986). Here, it has been found that even a child of 4 years of age realizes that a ball exiting a straight tube rolls straight, and a dropped object falls straight down (Proffitt et al 1990:347).

However, what Proffitt et al (1990) call extended body problems— problems that require an understanding of more than point masses—are typically poorly understood even by adults. By studying peoples' understanding of the dynamics of wheels, where, for example, both a center of gravity and a distribution of mass or a set of rotational forces are involved, they show that even very familiar events (such as rotating wheels) whose understanding falls outside the core notions of our intuitive physics may be completely misunderstood.

Perhaps children merely "see" or recognize familiar kinds of physical sequences of simple events. What of children's ability to reason inferentially about physical causality? Hume seems at least partly right: Understanding causality requires the ability to infer effects or causes from properly structured causal information. If knowledge about physical objects and physical causal mechanisms constitutes a domain of understanding, and if children are early acquiring a rich understanding of that domain, then they might evidence abilities to make appropriate logical inferences in that domain, although not more generally. Bullock et al (1982) tackled this question in a series of experiments with the following domino-like device. A stuffed rabbit sat on a platform. A series of domino-like blocks were lined up in front of the platform such that if the first block fell over it caused the others to topple over in series, and when the last block fell over it caused the rabbit to tumble from its platform. A device with a rod through a hole preceded the first block; when the rod was pushed through the hole it toppled the first block. In one study, 3- and 4-year-olds first saw the toppling sequence and then were asked to predict the as-yet-unviewed effect of 23 different relevant or irrelevant modifications to the device. Relevant changes included using a rod too short to hit the first block, and removing intermediate blocks. Irrelevant modifications included changing the material of the initial rod (from wood to glass) or wrapping a cloth around an intermediate block. Three-year-olds' predictions ranged from 78–91% correct, 4-year-olds' from 70–100% correct. This, and similar research by Shultz et al (1982) with a very different design, demonstrates young children's ability to reason correctly about physical causation mediated by a series of connected mechanical steps.

Shultz (1982) has demonstrated that by preschool age children reason sensibly not only about mechanically mediated causal sequences but also about immediate causal results, for several sorts of causal transmissions. In several ingeniously controlled situations, preschoolers attributed the snuffing out of a candle to a blower that was on rather than to one that was off, or the appearance of a spot of light to a lamp that was on as opposed to one that was off. The spotlight effect, for example, was instantaneous, not temporally prior, and involved no mechanical-spatial contiguity. Shultz thus demonstrated that young children are busily figuring out specific causal mechanisms and often reasoning properly about them, not noticing (or failing to notice) raw patterns of temporal sequence and covariation and deducing causes for them.

Finally, Goswami & Brown (1989) considered the possibility that when it comes to physical causality young children (3–6 years) might be able to engage in very sophisticated reasoning indeed—specifically, analogical reasoning. Piagetian theory suggests that analogical reasoning of the classical a : b : : c : d form is very difficult for children before the age of formal operations, and considerable research supports the claim that such reasoning becomes apparent only late in middle childhood (Goswami 1991). However, the analogies used in these studies rely on relations such as semantic opposites (black : white : : hard : ?) or biological habitat (bird : air : : fish : ?). What if children's analogical reasoning were tested instead using physical causal mechanisms that they understand? Goswami & Brown first tested 3- to 6-year-olds' understanding of such familiar causal acts or transformations as cutting (a knife cutting bread) or melting. Causal reasoning about such transformations was typically very good, even for 3-year-olds; they knew, for example, that a knife cutting through a whole loaf of bread yields cut-up bread. Then Goswami & Brown tested children's ability to reason analogically about such relations via analogies such as, Playdoh : cut-up Playdoh : : apple : ?. After being presented the first three terms in this problem, children had to choose the correct answer for the missing last term of the analogy from several carefully composed alternatives: 1. a correct choice (cut-up apple); 2. a correct object but wrong physical change (bruised apple); 3. a wrong object but correct physical change (cut-up bread); 4. a mere appearance match for the third term (red ball); 5. a semantic associate of the third term (banana). Even 3-year-olds' analogical reasoning was significantly correct for these sorts of problems. Goswami & Brown conclude that "as long as the child understands the causal relation, he or she can solve an analogy based on that relation" (1989:79).

Conclusions

Understanding physical objects and understanding physical causes are complex endeavors: Witness the complexity of scientific physics. Still, an understanding of solid objects and mechanical dynamics seems central to understanding physics more generally. Indeed, certain core beliefs about the nature and causal interactions of the everyday world of physical objects seems a domain of early foundational human knowledge and reasoning. A developing naive physics makes its early appearance in an infant's understanding of solid, cohesive, physical objects and certain causal regularities among them. The infant's understanding becomes rapidly enriched to include a deeper understanding of objects (for example their insides) and of physical causality (for example, object dynamics and causal mechanisms).

In order to claim that young children have a naive physics, however, we need to ask if the understandings we have reviewed function as a distinct domain for children. Specifically, is this sort of knowledge and reasoning separable from other domains of knowledge? We address this question in the next section where we describe a potential alternate domain, naive psychology. We ask, first, do children make a fundamental ontological distinction between the two domains—for example between physical objects (e.g. rocks) and psychological entities (e.g. thoughts about rocks); and, second, do children distinguish and reason differently about mechanical and psychological causation?

NAIVE PSYCHOLOGY

As outlined earlier, persons may be construed in several ways. Here are two: as physical objects (material bodies) mechanically interacting with other physical bodies, or as psychological beings whose actions are caused and explained by psychological forces and states. Adult naive psychology adheres to this second sort of construction. We construe people's actions as resulting from such internal mental states as their hopes, wishes, beliefs, and doubts. If any two domains of thought could be considered distinct, mentality and mechanics could.

What characterizes naive mentalistic psychology? Consider two of its central components: the ontological and causal aspects of mind. The ontological aspect concerns the existence and nature of mental contents, states, and processes as and distinguished from the real world of physical objects, material states, and mechanical or behavioral processes. Contents and states of the mind are internal, mental, and subjective, whereas the contents and states of the world are external, substantial, and objective.

Thoughts, beliefs, and ideas are distinct from the physical world of objects and behavior, but they are causally related to that physical-behavioral world. Mind causes action; the world shapes mind. A useful shorthand for characterizing psychlogical causation is to divide causal mental states into two sorts: beliefs and desires. Causal reasoning based on beliefs and desires then produces such accounts as the following: *Why did Jill go to that restaurant? She* wanted *to eat quickly and* thought *that it was a fast-food place.* Thus an essential causal idea is that people engage in actions because they believe those actions will fulfill certain desires. Under the heading of "theory of mind," recent research has documented the emergence of our everyday understanding of such mental states and reasoning.

Theory of Mind

Current research reveals sophisticated reasoning about the mental states of self and others in 3- to 5-year-olds. This contemporary consensus overthrows earlier assertions that young children were ignorant about the mind, misconstruing internal mental states and contents as external physical ones until 6 or 7 years of age (e.g. Piaget 1929; Keil 1979). We begin by considering 3- and 4-year-olds and then move backwards to infancy.

ONTOLOGY   Children as young as 3 years firmly distinguish the mental and physical worlds. For example, if told about one boy who has a dog and another one who is thinking about a dog, they correctly judge which "dog" can be seen, touched, and petted, and which not (Harris et al 1991; Wellman & Estes 1986). Moreover, if told about someone who has a dog that has run away and about someone who is thinking of a dog, 3-year-olds know that although neither "dog" can be seen or petted, one is mental ("just in his mind," "only imagination") whereas the other is physically real but unavailable (Estes et al 1989). By 3 years children know that physical force is necessary to manipulate physical objects (e.g. to open and close a real pair of scissors) but that "just thinking" is sufficient to affect mental changes (e.g. to open and close the image of a pair of scissors in your mind) (Estes et al 1989).

Young children also understand something of the subjectivity of thoughts. In appropriately simple tasks they are able to state, for example, that they can "see" their own mental images but that others cannot (Estes et al 1989), or that while they think a particular cookie tastes yummy, someone else could think it's yucky (Flavell et al 1990).

BELIEF   What about the causal aspect of mind? Investigators have studied extensively what young children understand about the beliefs of other persons and what they know about how beliefs guide behavior. Beliefs are central to our everyday grasp both of the way the mind influences action (*Jane takes her umbrella because she believes it is raining*) and of the way the mind reflects the world (*Jane believes it is raining because she saw rain outside*). To understand mental causation children must recognize that people behave in response to their beliefs about the world, not in response to "objective" facts. For this reason, children's understanding of false beliefs (*Jane believes it is raining, but it is not*) provides especially intriguing and useful evidence about how they understand causal mental states more generally. Many studies now show that by 4 years children reason proficiently about false beliefs (see e.g. Perner et al 1987). For example, if shown a candy box they will predict it contains candy. If then shown it holds pencils, they can correctly predict that a naive viewer of the box will falsely believe it contains candy instead (Gopnik & Astington 1988). Some studies show an even earlier understanding of belief in 3-year-olds via their understanding of true beliefs (Wellman & Bartsch 1988) and their use of common terms such as think and know (Shatz et al 1983). Indeed several recent studies show an initial understanding of false beliefs in 3-year-olds (Bartsch & Wellman 1989; Siegal & Beattie 1992; Lewis & Osbourne 1990; Moses 1990; Hala et al 1991; Wellman & Banerjee 1991).

The status of 3-year-olds' understanding of belief and false belief remains controversial. But a substantial consensus remains wherein 4-year-olds, if not 3-year-olds, are characterized as belief-desire reasoners. Indeed by 4 years, normal children's understanding of the mental mediation of experience and behavior is robust enough that they understand the existence not only of false beliefs but also of false perceptions (Flavell et al 1986).

COHERENCE   As discussed above, by age 3 children seem to recognize a domain of mental-psychological entities and processes distinct from a contrasting domain of physical objects and mechanical processes. To count as a framework theory, however, more is needed: some degree of coherence among children's beliefs. "Not any collection of beliefs forms a theory. The unity of a theory . . . is something that most sets of assertions cannot have. Number all the commonly held beliefs, and take the theory consisting of the prime numbered ones. . . It couldn't evolve as a unit or be criticized as one" (Morton 1980:6).

It may be impossible to tackle the question of coherence in the abstract, to specify the sort of coherence required for all theories. However, it is possible to assess whether children grasp the sort of coherence entailed by a particular theory; as for example our everyday mentalistic naive psychology. Briefly, according to this everyday theory, physiological states and basic emotions underlie one's desires. Beliefs, on the other hand, are often derived from perceptual experiences. Moreover, one's actions lead to outcomes in the world, and these outcomes lead to emotional reactions of predictable sorts, such as disappointment, happiness, and surprise. Thus various constructs within a naive psychology make reference to one another. Accounts of coherent everyday belief-desire reasoning are elaborated more fully by D'Andrade (1987) and Wellman (1990:Ch. 4).

By 3 or 4 years of age young children demonstrate that they understand this larger interelated system of constructs and reasoning. Recent research shows that young children can reason forward from beliefs and desires to predict a person's actions (e.g. Wimmer & Perner 1983; Wellman & Bartsch 1988). They can also reason backwards (Bartsch & Wellman 1989): If asked about an action (*Why is Jane looking under the piano for her kitten?*) they explain it by appeal to beliefs (*She thought it was there.*) and desires (*She wanted her kitty.*).

By age 4 or 5 children understand that perception is instrumental in the acquisition of beliefs (Wimmer et al 1988; Taylor 1988). Again, recent studies suggest that some initial understanding of the links between perception and belief are understood in significant initial forms by 3- as well as 4- and 5-year-olds (Pillow 1989; Pratt & Bryant 1990).

According to our everyday theory, emotions are also entangled in this web of causal mental states. Some emotional reactions, for example, depend predominantly on the person's desire, others on the person's beliefs. If an actor desires something and then gets it (or fails to get it) he is likely to feel happy (or sad or mad). If he believes something will happen but it does not, he is likely to feel surprise or puzzlement. The causal understanding of emotional events is, in this fashion, mentalistically dependent not just on situations but on beliefs and desires (Stein & Levine 1987). By 3 years, preschoolers seem to understand the causal organization of emotions such as happiness, sadness, and anger (Stein & Levine 1989; Yuil 1984). Indeed even 2-year-olds begin to do so (Wellman & Woolley 1990). More recent research on children's understanding of surprise shows that preschoolers' organization of emotional understanding encompasses belief as well as desire states, although there is controversy about whether understanding of surprise appears at about 3 years with the first understanding of belief (Wellman & Banerjee 1991) or later, in the preschool years (Hadwin & Perner 1991).

By age 3 or 4, it can be argued, children's naive psychology evidences the character of a naive framework theory with a content and coherence that is quite different from that of a contrasting naive physics.

Earlier Developments

Where might the mentalistic framework psychology of 3- and 4-year-olds come from? A plausible hypothesis is that it is related to, although importantly distinct from, infant social discriminations. Even in the first months of life, infants are complex social creatures. They cry, smile, attend to faces, imitate others, become attached, and interact in dyadic face-to-face routines. If framework theories are manifest in (*a*) an ontological aspect that picks out certain entities for consideration and (*b*) a causal aspect that frames explanations about how such entities interact, then infant social understanding could encompass two parallel precursory aspects—mechanisms for picking out social objects for special processing, and early discrimination of human movements and causation.

The young infant seems to be specially prepared to attend to and interact with social objects. Infants preferentially attend to faces (or, at first, arrays with face-like configurations and features) (Sherrod 1981); they discriminate facial expression of emotion at an early age (Nelson 1987); and they imitate human actions (Meltzoff & Moore 1983). Infants find bodily contact with and being held by others desirable, and they seek out such contacts with the onset of voluntary movement. Infants attend preferentially to human speech over other sounds—especially female speech and even specifically their own mother's voice (DeCasper & Fifer 1980). Theories and research on parent-infant attachment (e.g. Bowlby 1969) and interaction (e.g. Stern 1985) amply document certain proclivities that help infants attend to and represent people as special, significant, and information laden.

Similarly, there is evidence of early infant attention to human movement. Young infants discriminate animate-biological motions vs random or artificial ones (Bertenthal et al 1985), and older infants (by 13 to 16 months, for example) seem able to distinguish between (*a*) the sorts of internally generated and self-propelled movements possible to people and (*b*) the transmission of external forces necessary for movement of physical objects such as balls and rocks (Poulin-Dubois & Shultz 1988; Golinkoff 1983). Indeed, Premack (1990) has recently argued that infants probably evidence a rich biologically prepared tendency to discriminate animate self-propelled movements in contrast to inanimate externally caused physical ones. However, it is important to point out that while preference for faces and attention to self-propelled motions may lead the infant to study human conspecifics, such competencies do not indicate a specifically mentalistic psychological understanding of any sort.

A conception of mental states and mentally caused actions requires something more. A critical step in this direction would be something like an understanding of intentionality, as philosophers use that term (not intentional in the narrower everyday sense of "on purpose"). The hallmark of intentionality in this sense, is "aboutness," or object-directedness. Consider a desire for an apple or a belief that something is an apple; such desires and beliefs are object specific; they are *about* an apple. Attributing intentionality therefore requires attributing internal states (or attitudes) directed toward (or about) specific objects (or contents). Many who study infancy describe a transition in infant social interaction first evident in the period from 9 to 12 months wherein the infant seems to see self and others in notably different terms. This change has been termed the advent of a sense of subjectivity (Stern 1985), triadic awareness (Adamson & Bakeman 1985), and even an implicit theory of mind (Bretherton et al 1981). It can be argued that the older infant manifests a transition to understanding people (self and others) as intentional in the very rudimentary but significant sense of having certain experiences *about* or *of* external objects or events (Wellman, in press).

Consider, for example, early understanding of others' perception or attention. Gestures such as pointing and showing emerge between 9 and 13 months or so (Butterworth 1991; Lempers et al 1977; Zinober & Martlew 1985). Some early sorts of pointing could be simple actions of the infant toward the object itself (something like attenuated poking or reaching). But research consistently documents pointing and showing in the child's second year directed at getting others to attend *to something*. For example, if the other's eyes are covered by his or her hands, 1.5- and 2-year-olds will move the hands or try to place a to-be-shown object between the hands and eyes (Lempers et al 1977). In the second year the infant points at an object but also in increasingly sophisticated ways looks at the other to check that person's gaze as well (Masur 1983). In compelling cases the infant will begin to point only when the other is attending to him or her, execute the point, check the other's visage, keep pointing or augment the behavior if the other is not correctly directed, and quit if the other orients or comments on the object (Bates et al 1979; Butterworth 1991). Findings such as these document a simple intentional understanding of perception, that people can be perceptually directed toward certain objects or events.

An understanding of intentionality must go beyond an understanding of reference, however; it must include an understanding of internal psychological experiences. Research on social referencing in infants suggests that in the second year infants know not only that persons are oriented to objects in the world, but also that they experience them—e.g. as pleasing or scary, desired or undesired (Walden & Ogan 1988). Of course, simple attention or even reaction to others' emotional displays would not necessarily imply an intentional understanding. Referencing a mother's frown or smile could simply and directly alter the baby's mood (Feinman 1985) or action (perhaps the infant sees the mother's fear expression and simply freezes). However, social referencing could work through the infant's reading the other's emotional expression as indicating an emotional reaction about a particular situation or object. Indeed, Hornick et al (1987) seem to have demonstrated this sort of intentional understanding by 1-year-olds. In that research, mothers posed expressions of delight or disgust toward a particular toy in a situation containing several alternative toys. The 12-month-olds in that study were selective in reaction, interpreting mother's expression as about a particular toy. For example, they avoided a toy toward which the mother expressed disgust but showed no change in overall mood and approached and played with other nontarget toys.

Note that while understanding people as having certain inner experiences (happiness, fear) of external objects, actions, or situations qualifies as an impressive understanding of intentionality, it does not mean that children construe people as having all the sorts of inner experiences encompassed by belief-desire understanding. In particular, a simple understanding of intentionality does not encompass internal *representations* of the world, such as images or beliefs. In this regard, consider that simple desires can be construed as an internal experience (or longing) for external objects (he wants that apple). Beliefs, however, require an understanding of mental representations (he thinks that that is an apple). Thus it is of import that 2.5-year-olds understand simple desires but fail to understand comparable beliefs (Wellman & Woolley 1990).

To summarize, by age 3 or 4, young children see people as possessing beliefs as well as desires; as having ideas, thoughts, and images as well as emotional reactions. This achievement of a belief-desire understanding is preceded by earlier phases. There is a phase of infant attention to people as entities and to personal-human causation as different from physical-mechanical causation. More important, with regard to specifically psychological conceptions there is a phase evident at least in later infancy of simple intentional understanding of action and experience, evident in construing people as gazing at, seeking to attain, and emotionally reacting to real-world objects and actions. This constitutes first evidence of a rapidly developing understanding of people as having the intentional subjective experiences of seeing, desiring, and emotionally experiencing the world.

Autism

If a mentalistic construction of persons constitutes a distinct domain of human thinking, then it may be possible to find people who evidence distinctive impairment of this sort of reasoning. Recently, researchers have proposed that autistic persons lack a "theory of mind" or are severely delayed or impaired in everyday mentalistic psychology (Baron-Cohen et al 1985). A provocative initial case has been made: Autistics can reason about physical causation but are impaired specifically with regard to understanding mental causation, even in comparison to retarded controls of the same mental age (see Baron-Cohen 1990 for a review). These data suggest that mentalistic naive psychology may well be a distinct domain of human thought.

Conclusions

Our discussion is by no means a complete summary of children's understanding of naive psychology. Naive psychology includes or overlaps with children's understanding of moral issues, kinship relations, social roles, and so on. Many of these topics are currently receiving vigorous research. For example, there is an extensive current literature on preschool and school age children's understanding of emotion (see Harris 1989) and of personality traits (see Rholes et al 1990). Such research falls under the heading of social cognition and social cognitive development. The research we have reviewed can be seen as attempting to base social cognition in a mentalistic belief-desire psychology. The foundational core of this domain seems to be understood and used by children quite early in development.

NAIVE BIOLOGY

Everyday notions of biology encompass such processes as organic growth, reproduction, and inheritance; such animal functions as eating and sleeping; and such outcomes as illness and death. The study of biology enables us to see the important commonalities between humans and other species (including plants), as well as the critical ways that species differ in their solutions to important evolutionary problems. Indeed, we humans have been fascinated by our relationship to other species, sometimes viewing ourselves as part of the animal and natural world, sometimes as standing apart from it (Thomas 1983).

Do children show evidence of a framework biological understanding distinct from naive physics and psychology? There are at least two plausible ways in which they may not. First, biology could be confused in children's minds with psychology (internal motivations, feelings, beliefs on the one hand; beliefs about human social interaction on the other). Particularly given the power of psychological causes, detailed above, children may explain biological processes in terms of psychological ones (people grow because they want to get bigger) as hypothesized by Carey (1985). Second, biology could also fail to function as a distinct domain if domain-general principles govern children's understandings. For example, children may classify animals and plants using domain-general principles of similarity (e.g. classifying objects by overall color and shape), failing to attend to any specifically biological features (e.g. presence of eyes, particular types of limbs, blowholes). This possiblity has been explicitly articulated by Keil (1989) and by Gelman & Coley (1991).

Again these issues require us to address, first, whether children have a sensible, separate ontology of biological kinds, and second, whether children hold beliefs about distinctly biological causal laws and principles. If we can establish that children refer to specifically biological ontologies and laws, then we must also consider coherence: whether these laws or principles are theoretically organized with respect to one another. We argue that children have at least the outline for a biological theory by preschool age.

Ontology: Living Things

ANIMATE/INANIMATE DISTINCTION   Piaget's (1930) account of animism would argue against children's making a clear ontological distinction between biological and nonbiological kinds of objects. On this account, children attribute animate properties to inanimate objects (e.g. a bicycle is alive; rocks can feel pain). The evidence, typically based on the clinical interview method, suggested that until school age children were not at all clear on the distinction between animals (e.g. elephants, fish, insects) and inanimate objects (e.g. desks, houses, pencils).

In contrast, a rich body of research using more sensitive measures demonstrates that young children make a firm ontological distinction between animate and inanimate objects. This distinction does not map directly onto the biological/nonbiological distinction (because although plants are alive, since they cannot move on their own, children consider them inanimate). Nonetheless, the animate/inanimate distinction may be the beginning of the grasp of biological kinds as a distinct domain.

Golinkoff et al (1984) review a variety of evidence that children distinguish animate and inanimate in their language comprehension and production (e.g. in their early production of sentences, most syntactic subjects are animate; see Brown 1973). Golinkoff & Markessini (1980) devised a simple pointing task in which children were asked to respond to various possessor-possessed relations. When the questions involved an animate possessor ("Where's the boy's flower?"), children performed quite well; in contrast, they often refused to answer when the possessor was "inanimate" ("Where's the flower's boy?"). Golinkoff et al (1984) found that by 24 months of age children typically show surprise when a chair moves forward on its own. By that age they are therefore sensitive to one of the most important criteria distinguishing animate from inanimate objects (capacity for self-generated movement).

Gelman & Spelke (1981) map out a variety of criteria that children could use to distinguish animate and inanimate objects (e.g. capacity to grow; capacity to move and initiate actions without external force) and suggest that this distinction may be among the first that children honor. Gelman et al (1983) argue that Piaget's methods biased children toward supplying animistic answers. In their own tasks, involving simple yes/no questions about actions, parts, and states (e.g. "Can a person (rock, doll) feel sad?"), they find that children as young as age 3 clearly distinguish animate from inanimate items (e.g. animates but not inanimates have feelings and autonomous movement, and can reciprocate actions; see also Dolgin & Behrend 1984 for related findings). With slightly older children, Keil finds that children distinguish animals from inanimate objects, for example, reporting that a porcupine cannot be transformed into a cactus (1989) and that the predicates that apply to animals do not apply to inanimates (1979).

Clearly, then, even young children honor a distinction between animate and inanimate. Are they using domain-general principles on which to do so (e.g. a simple similarity metric)? Apparently not. According to Carey (1985), children report that a mechanical monkey is highly similar to a person but unlikely to have properties attributed to people (e.g. eating, sleeping, having babies). Thus, children distinguish animates from inanimates in ways that cannot be reduced to domain-general principles of similarity. In a more in-depth look at this question, Massey & Gelman (1988) found that preschool children can classify unfamiliar animate and inanimate objects on the basis of very subtle cues. For example, highly realistic statues of animals were grouped with other inanimates (i.e. were judged to be unable to move up a hill by themselves); highly atypical animals (e.g. porcupines) were grouped with other animals.

Similarly, a recent study by Jones et al (1992) showed that young children extended novel labels (e.g. "dax") differently depending on whether the objects being named had eyes or not. Apparently, the information that something is an animal (conveyed by the presence of eyes) led to a shift in the properties children attended to. These studies demonstrate that a simple notion of domain-general similarity cannot account for the animate-inanimate distinction children make.

INFANCY   The data so far available from infants suggest that babies are specially attuned to humans and other animals—i.e. are particularly interested in faces and eyes, respond to emotional expression in faces from an early age, and attempt to communicate with other humans and not with inanimate objects. Although not constituting an appreciation for the biological domain per se, this argues against a domain-general understanding of the biological world.

Some recent evidence suggests that infants distinguish animates more generally from inanimates. In a habituation study with 12-month-old infants, Smith (1989) found that subjects treated toy versions of artifacts and animals as falling into separate classes. Infants saw a series of toy objects of one type (e.g. all animals) until their attention waned. They then saw a new toy object, either of the same ontological type (e.g. another animal: an elephant) or of a different ontological type (a toy vehicle: a boat). Of interest was how long children gazed at the new object. Children's attention increased when the novel object was of a different ontological category (e.g. when the experiment switched from artifacts to an animal or vice versa). Moreover, this discrimination could not be attributed to the mere presence of distinguishing parts such as eyes and mouths (for animals) vs wheels and windshields (for vehicles).

CLASSIFICATION OF PLANTS   The above evidence supports the view that children are not animistic, and that they honor an ontological distinction between animate and inanimate objects—perhaps even in infancy. However, this distinction might be rooted in an understanding of psychology rather than of biology per se. That is, children might distinguish animals from inert physical objects on the basis of motivations and mental states that animals such as humans (but not other biological beings, such as plants) could have. Thus, an intriguing issue is how children classify plants, which fall within the domain of biology but not psychology.

Carey (1985) finds that children below age 10 show confusion about what it means to be "alive" (see also Piaget 1929; Laurendeau & Pinard 1962). The confusion arises, she argues, from their not understanding how animals and plants can be grouped together to form a coherent category. Richards & Siegler (1984, 1986) find that plants are rarely classed as "alive" until age 8 or 9 (see Stavy & Wax 1989 for errors continuing till age 12). Clearly this is an area of important developmental change. However, by themselves these findings do not address directly the question of whether children conceive of a distinctively biological domain. Children may simply not understand that the biological domain, for adults, includes plants. The question is better addressed by looking more closely at children's beliefs about biological kinds.

Beliefs about Biological Kinds

ATTRIBUTION OF PROPERTIES   In an extensive series of studies, Carey (1985) demonstrates that how children attribute properties (e.g. eating, sleeping, breathing, having babies) to other animals reflects not an adult-like biological model but the approximation of those animals to humans. That is, living things are not seen as categorically alike in having biological functions—not even all animals are assumed to require food, air, and sleep—but are graded in terms of their similarity to humans. Moreover, when taught new properties about a novel living thing (e.g. that a certain animal has "golgi" inside), children generalize the property only to other animals (again, using humans as the prototypical haver-of-things) and not to plants. And when supplied with two examples of things that have the new property—examples that for adults would span the category "living thing" (e.g. dogs and flowers)—children are prone subsequently to generalize the property to inanimate objects (implying that they see nothing common to dogs and flowers aside from being physical objects).

Carey uses these findings to argue that children do not have a theory of biology, and that they understand what for adults are biological functions in terms of anthropocentric psychological principles. However the evidence is quite indirect. Again, children may indeed treat biology as a distinct domain but fail to grasp either the scope of the domain (excluding plants, for example) or how it is organized (e.g. that vertebrates form a subclass within animals) for adults.

With a more direct examination of the issue, Inagaki & Hatano (1988; Inagaki 1990) have challenged the view that psychology and biology are inseparable for young children. They have asked whether children realize that psychological laws operate independently of biological laws and vice versa. In one study, they presented 4- and 5-year-old children with three different kinds of tasks: differentiation, controllability, and conflict. Differentiation tested whether children could distinguish among hereditary, bodily, and mental characteristics with respect to their modifiability (e.g. *Could a boy change his eye color if he wants to?*). Children reported distinctly different means of modifying mental vs bodily characteristics (e.g. intentions vs physical practice, respectively). Controllabilty measured whether children believe that bodily functions can be controlled by intentions (e.g. *Can you stop your heartbeat?*). According to Inagaki & Hatano, "both 4- and 5-year-olds understand that there are things going on inside the body which are not fully subject to our intention" (1988:5).

Finally, the conflict task examined whether the children thought biological or intentional forces are more effective in modifying physiological features. For example, subjects were asked to predict who will become fatter, a girl who wants to get fat but who eats less or one who wants to get slim but eats more. If psychological laws dominate, then wanting to get fat should prevail. If psychological and biological laws are confused, then children should guess randomly. But if biological laws are understood as existing and potentially conflicting with psychological ones, then children should report that the first girl will not get fat. Indeed this is what 90% of the 4-year-olds and 95% of the 5-year-olds reported. Inagaki & Hatano point out that children of this age still do not understand in detail how biological processes (such as digestion) work, although appreciating biology as separate from psychology.

Gelman & Kremer (1991) similarly find that preschool children have a grasp of biological causation that does not involve human intention or human action (for example, children realize that leaves turn color because of intrinsic, innate forces rather than human ones). This is at least a step toward distinguishing biological from psychological cause. If children were restricted to thinking about psychological or mechanical causes, they should be unable to grasp the idea of nonhuman nonmechanical causation. Children also distinguish intended actions from reflexes by age 5 (Shultz et al 1980). Thus, they do not apply a psychological model of causation indiscriminately, even in cases that might easily be confused with such a model.

CONCEPTS OF IDENTITY   The nature of identity—what properties make something the individual or category member that it is (e.g. what makes Joe a unique person, a male, or a mammal)—varies importantly as a function of domain (Schwartz 1977). Keil (1986, 1989) points out that, for adults, dramatic changes in appearance can affect the identity of artifacts but not of living kinds (e.g. alterations can change a coffeepot into a birdfeeder but cannot change a horse into a zebra). Children grasp this insight by second grade (Keil 1986, 1989). In contrast, according to Keil, kindergarten children fail to grasp the distinction, treating the identity of both living kinds and artifacts as changed. However, a possible source of their confusion at this younger age is that the transformations probed by Keil were nonnatural, for example, surgery.

For living kinds, both personal and species identities are maintained across the dramatic but nonetheless natural changes that occur with growth. Recently, Rosengren et al (in press) pointed out that adults have three conceptual insights about such natural changes (such as an egg hatching into a tadpole and becoming a frog). First, real-life transformations are predictable and nonrandom (e.g. animals can increase but not decrease in size, as they grow). Second, the kinds of transformations possible are domain and mechanism specific (e.g. growth applies to animals and plants but not chairs). Third, identity is maintained across even striking appearance changes, such as the transformation from infancy to adulthood. In a series of experiments, Rosengren et al demonstrated that children as young as age 3 years appreciate the first two insights about growth: They realize that animals increase (but do not decrease) in size as they mature and that growth does not apply to artifacts. (The third insight was not tested directly in these studies.) When judging natural but radical transformations children do not accept just any change as possible, nor do they assume that transformations necessarily lead to changed identities.

Gender identity is of specific interest in this context because it readily lends itself to being construed in multiple ways: as a social, psychological, or biological construct. Based on research on gender constancy (Kohlberg 1966; Liben & Signorella 1987), Carey (1985) suggests that children construe gender as a social construct. According to Carey, changes in social roles (e.g. change in behavior or play pattern) are enough to cause children to judge that sex has changed. However, the gender constancy task may not be an appropriately sensitive measure. Siegal & Robinson (1987) argue that the task itself is pragmatically odd and that minor modifications (e.g. reversing the order of the questions) result in vastly improved performance. Gelman et al (1986) also point out that the gender constancy task requires children to construct a gender classification on the basis of conflicting cues (e.g. when shown a child who used to be a boy but now looks like a girl). Even for adults, classifying ambiguous entities is difficult (cf Mayr 1988). In contrast, when children are explicitly given the gender identity of an ambiguous individual (e.g. they are told that a long-haired child is a boy), even 4-year-olds infer sex-appropriate properties about that child (e.g. he will play with trucks and grow up to be a daddy) (Gelman et al 1986). Finally, even 4-year-olds treat gender like a biological construct in the sense of having innate potential that is largely unaffected by environmental influences (Taylor & Gelman 1991; see also Smith & Russell 1984 with evidence from older children).

Biologically Specific Causal Processes

If naive biology functions as a separate domain of reasoning for children, they should understand something about biologically specific causal transformations—causal processes that dictate how and why characteristically biological events unfold. Maturational growth, as discussed above, is an example of exactly this sort. There are other important instances as well—e.g. inheritance, disease transmission and contagion, and biological potential. In each case what counts as an effective cause, and the consequence of that cause, cannot be translated into any other domain. For example, the laws of inheritance cannot apply to inanimate objects (40-watt light bulbs do not beget other light bulbs). Such specifically biological processes begin to pinpoint areas in which naive biology might approximate a coherent theory.

INHERITANCE AND INNATE POTENTIAL   The concept of inheritance is specifically biological, in that only and all living things have mechanisms for transmitting features from one generation to the next. Most research on conceptions of inheritance focus on children with at least some schooling (Clough & Wood-Robinson 1985; Deadman & Kelly 1978; Kargbo et al 1980). In contrast, Springer & Keil (1989) recently examined models of inheritance in children as young as preschool age. Children heard stories about parent animals that possessed a certain abnormal feature (e.g. "Mr. and Mrs. Bull . . . were both born with pink hearts inside their chests instead of normal-colored hearts"). They were then asked to predict whether their offspring would be born with a normal form of the feature or an abnormal form (e.g. a normal-colored heart or an odd pink-colored one). Preschoolers were most likely to consider features as inherited when they had biological consequences (e.g. born with a white stomach inside so they could eat a lot and stay strong) rather than social or psychological consequences (e.g. born with a white stomach inside that made them feel angry a lot). As Springer & Keil report, "our subjects demonstrated a consistent, implicit belief that alterations leading to functional consequences for animals are inherited, while other sorts of alterations are not. . . . this belief is limited to biological rather than social or psychological consequences. This seems to implicate a biological theory of inheritance" (1989:647).

Closely related to the notion of inheritance is that of innate potential. In particular, biological entities—but not other kinds of objects—manifest predictable features that are dictated by their innate potential. For example, a newborn tiger is neither large nor fierce, yet it inevitably comes to exhibit those traits. Adult naive biological thinking accounts for these phenomena by considering them as part of an animal's innate potential. To test children's grasp of innate potential, we presented 4-year-olds with a series of stories describing a seed from a plant or a newborn animal that was reared with plants or animals of a different species (Gelman & Wellman 1991). For example, a newborn cow was taken to a pig farm and raised with other pigs, never seeing another cow. Children saw realistic pictures of the newborn (which did not resemble the adult form of its parents or foster parents) and of the rearing environment. They were then asked to judge what behaviors and physical attributes the plant or animal would manifest when grown to adulthood. For animals, both younger and older 4-year-olds consistently reported that the infants would grow to have the innate potential characteristic of their species (e.g. the baby cow will moo and have a straight tail, despite being raised with pigs). For plant seeds, older 4-year-olds showed the same pattern of response, although younger 4-year-olds were performing at chance levels. Thus, a specific belief about biology (a belief in innate potential) is found even in young 4-year-olds.

CONTAGION AND ILLNESS   Contagion is an interesting belief to examine from the perspective of biological theory. In adult form, it is a domain-specific causal notion, in three senses. First, it provides a causal analysis of disease that applies to biological entities only: A car cannot "catch" a flat tire from another car. Second, only certain bodily illnesses are contagious—not accidental mishaps such as a bruised knee, nor even other bodily pains such as toothaches. Third, for adults in our culture illnesses are spread by biological means and cannot be explained by appeal to other causal domains (e.g. as the result of immanent justice, in which illness is the inevitable consequence of moral transgressions). Adult understanding of contagion is specific to the domain of biology. It would be easy, however, for children to construe contagion in a wholly domain-general manner, operating on the basis of domain-general principles such as contiguity and similarity. On this view, illness could be transmitted between any two things as long as they are near one another, or as long as they are similar. It would also be easy to construe contagion on psychological terms alone, as the immanent justice example demostrates.

Some intriguing studies in the literature have suggested that children at first understand contagion in terms of domain-general principles: A variety of illnesses or accidents—including toothaches or scraped knees, for example—are viewed as contagious (Kister & Patterson 1980; Piaget 1932). Kister & Patterson (1980) and Bibace & Walsh (1981) also found children adhering to immanent justice explanations—reporting, for example, that moral transgressions could be the cause of various ailments (a cold, a toothache, a scraped knee).

Using a simpler task, however, Siegal (1988) has found that preschool children evidence more knowledge about contagion and contamination than previously suspected. Children were asked to evaluate explanations provided by others (namely, puppets suffering from colds and toothaches). Even preschoolers realized that contagion is domain specific (e.g. scraped knees are not contagious) and that immanent justice cannot explain why people get colds. Thus, even early understandings of the transmission of certain sorts of illness may honor domain-specific boundaries.

Summary

Children treat biology as a distinct domain in the sense of having an ontology of biological kinds (at least including animals) and having biologically specific causal beliefs that apply to members of that ontology. There is as yet, however, no research that attempts to describe something like a coherent naive biological theory and to determine whether young children's biological understanding is theory-like in this final sense. In the absence of such research, current studies suggest that naive biology may not be a highly developed domain. It may not be as coherently developed or organized as naive psychology, for example, in the preschool years. Nonetheless, preschoolers' biological reasoning cannot be reduced to domain-general principles (such as similarity) and seems clearly distinguished from psychology as a domain.

CONCLUSIONS

Infants and children rapidly acquire several framework theories of core domains—certain foundational understandings of the world that in turn frame further conceptual acquisitions. This proposal has generated exciting new research, some of it reviewed here. This perspective also raises several fundamental questions deserving further discussion. One particularly critical question is, how would one test and therefore potentially disconfirm the hypothesis that early understandings develop within distinct domains of thought?

This is a complicated question; a number of broad and complex claims are involved, and no proposal of this scope is confirmed or disconfirmed alone, but competes with alternative frameworks. The question of confirmation thus intimately includes the question of what this position tells us that is novel, and not discernible from Piagetian or information-processing views. Although the issues are complex, one can still test major assumptions and compare alternative hypotheses. Three assumptions to be tested emerge if we consider foundational knowledge as something like commonsense framework theories. These assumptions are the ones noted throughout the chapter: (*a*) Children honor core ontological distinctions; (*b*) children use specific causal principles in reasoning about particular domains; and (*c*) children's causal beliefs cohere and form a larger interconnected framework. These assumptions guide but also find support in the research we have reviewed; consequently the findings contrast with those expected from Piagetian or domain-general information-processing approaches.

As described in our introduction, Piaget's standard theory characterizes cognition in terms of increasingly content-free logical structures. The findings here argue instead for content-specific systems of knowing—forms of reasoning and knowledge acquisition tailored to specific objects of thought. The studies document impressive reasoning in young children, but limited to certain contents only. Concern with the specific contents of children's knowledge was apparent in Piaget's earlier research, albeit de-emphasized in his later theory. In his early writings Piaget (1929, 1930) described the content of young children's knowledge of the world as simultaneously animistic, realistic, artificialistic, and impervious to causal reasoning. Piaget's claims here are complex, but the essence is that until age 6 or 7 children fail to distinguish among three domains of thought that adults categorically separate—naive mechanics, psychology, and biology. The research we reviewed, however, documents young children's firm distinctions among these foundational systems of thought. Well before the start of formal schooling, children distinguish the physical world, the animate world, and the mental world and begin to reason appropriately about these three quite different realms of explanation.

An alternative explanation for these findings might be that apparently knowledgeable answers result from domain-general information-processing procedures. What look like ontological distinctions could reflect similarity-based categorizations summing over clusters of similar and dissimilar features. But research that we reviewed (especially in the section on naive biology) demonstrates that such domain-general similarity reasoning inadequately accounts for children's judgments. Similarly, what looks like causal reasoning specific to physical dynamics, for example, might reflect some domain-general Humean reasoning procedures for detecting continuities, contiguities, and covariations. But research that we reviewed (especially in the section on physical causality) documents that general causal reasoning schemes fail to account for young children's abilities to reason about specific causal mechanisms. Indeed across the three sections children exhibit three very different forms of causal reasoning, involving in the case of naive physics a kernel sense of mechanical forces; in the case of naive psychology a kernel sense of belief-desire causation; and in the case of naive biology a kernel sense of biological functions.

While we have focused on children's understanding of core distinctions, it would be incorrect to conclude that children honor all major distinctions that adults do. In fact the opposite seems true. Young children's early understanding of mental states, for example, includes desire, perception, and emotion but does not include belief. Their early understanding of biology includes animals but tends to exclude plants. Such findings do not argue against the notion that children have framework theories; they argue instead that children's frameworks differ substantially from those of adults. It would be troubling for a domain-specific foundational-knowledge position, however, if when probing for children's ontologies we found that they collapsed every important distinction. If children collapsed mental and physical, living and nonliving, animate and inanimate, perception and desire, there would be no firm ground on which to build content-specific frameworks and theories. The picture of the child as confusing these fundamental distinctions is close to Piaget's characterization; that is why research continues to test itself against Piaget's claims.

A description of young children as knowledgeable about several core domains has important implications for research methodology, implications that provide further tests of the general approach. Specifically, research of the sort reviewed here is often summarized as documenting early competence—unexpected understandings in young children and infants. A typical description of the methodological successes of such research is that investigators have succeeded in simplifying assessment tasks by making them easier, stripping away unnecessary processing demands, and removing complexity. This leads to a concomitant description of the nature of early development itself: Initial developments constitute first fragile, almost ephemeral understandings that are strengthened and consolidated as children become increasingly consistent in the face of more difficult task demands. Surely these descriptions are partly correct: Good experimental methods require removing unnecessary noise and achieving more accurate assessments; part of development entails increasing information processing fluency and consolidating initial partial understandings.

However, we believe it is misleading to characterize investigators' more sensitive tasks and methods as merely reducing task demands. Instead, if we assume that children are acquiring core understandings of certain domains, then experimenters succeed only when they tap into those core understandings. The investigator's ingenuity is needed not so much for sim-

plification in a domain-neutral information-processing sense, as for simplification in the sense of accommodating more precisely to infants' and
children's core understandings. Such core understandings can often be different from our own (e.g. an understanding of desires without a concomitant
understanding of beliefs), and hence tasks require considerable calibration to
the child's world. But our tasks need not be simple or easy in some theory-
free sense. In our estimation, for example, Goswami & Brown's (1989)
analogical reasoning tasks reveal competence in young children not because
they are simple or stripped down but because they target children's core
understandings of certain physical-causal events; Estes et al's (1989) tasks for
probing children's understanding of mental entities are not less demanding
than Piaget's clinical interviews; rather, they more precisely help children
focus on the core distinctions in question; Rosengren et al's (in press)
questions about growth and metamorphosis are not just simple, they tap
children's understanding of natural biological transformations.

When, if ever, do children's early conceptualizations cohere into sensible
theory-like systems of understanding? The charge of coherence is perhaps the
most difficult one to assess empirically. Without it, however, we would not
wish to ascribe foundational frameworks to children. Coherence is sometimes
confused with consistency, but the two are distinct in an important way.
Coherence refers to whether different beliefs make reference to or depend on
one another; consistency refers to whether different beliefs contradict one
another. One can have consistency without coherence, by holding noncontra-
dictory beliefs that are unrelated. (We thank Doug Medin for calling our
attention to this point.) For example, the beliefs "2 + 2 = 4" and "Earth is
round" are consistent with one another but not coherent. Likewise, one can
have coherence without full (global) consistency. That is, one can hold beliefs
that make reference to other beliefs (i.e. that are not just isolated facts)
but allow for some contradictions. In such cases, consistency might be only
local.

In the present context, the distinction between coherence and consistency is
particularly important when trying to assess whether children's belief systems
are coherent. We need to examine whether children's beliefs cross-reference
one another, and not whether contradictory beliefs are held. Wellman (1990)
claims to show, for example, that children's reasoning about the mind coheres
in a rich network of interwoven terms and inferences. Similarly, Keil (1989)
has proposed that everyday theories entail a "causal homeostasis," in which
causal links mutually reinforce other causal links. Still, in much of the
research we reviewed, the question of coherence remains unaddressed.

However, several attacks on the problem seem possible. For example,
patterns of inductive inference may be a useful guide to the degree of
coherence in a domain. To the extent that a new piece of knowledge in-

troduced in one part of the domain has ramifications for beliefs in a very different part of the domain, we have positive evidence for some coherence among concepts in the domain. If such evidence cannot be found, then children's beliefs may not have the status of framework theories. Similarly, if children are embracing framework theories of understanding then, paradoxically, they might do better on certain tasks that are made deliberately complex, enriched, and elaborated. We owe this suggestion to Karen Bartsch (see Bartsch 1991). A task that has much information to process, but information that rests on the coherent complexity central to the framework in question, may prove easier for a young child to understand and hence perform well on than a stripped down, bare-bones, and in that sense simplified version of the same task. Detailed presentations may aid rather than confuse young children by helping them recognize the elaborated domain of reasoning involved.

Similarly, if children first acquire *framework* understandings rather than specific knowledge of concrete phenomena, then we could expect children's understandings and beliefs to appeal to the framework involved even in the absence of specific knowledge. That is, their conceptualization may be sensible before being accurate. Sensitivity to larger forms of thinking in the absence of detailed information seems to us to be evident in much of the research we have reviewed. For example, 3- and 4-year-olds appear to know that various objects have insides and that such insides are important to identity and function, while at the same time being inaccurate or vague about just what those insides are (Gelman 1987; Gelman & Wellman 1991). Three-year-olds, like adults, tend to explain human action by appeal to the beliefs and desires of the actor; however, their sense of what the actor's beliefs and desires really are is often vague ("she just wanted to"), distorted, or wrong (Bartsch & Wellman 1988). Children appear to understand the animate-inanimate distinction, in essence, at an early age (Gelman et al 1983) but often do not know where various entities, such as plants, fall with regard to that distinction (Richards & Siegler 1986). In short, young children often seem to invoke a larger domain of understanding before evidencing accurate or detailed understandings of the specifics of that domain (see also Mandler et al 1991).

A similar sort of conclusion is found in R. Gelman's (1990) description of "skeletal principles" that define domains of cognitive development. For example, in her research on early understanding of numbers, she concludes that several counting principles define the child's early sense of numerosity and thereby shape a domain of number understanding for further exploration, development, and articulation. Gelman characterizes such formative domains "in terms of a set of interrelated principles that define entities and operations on them" (p. 81). This parallels the way we construe framework understandings that specify ontologies and modes of reasoning. Early cognitive development, we believe, requires description in terms of foundational frameworks; foundational frameworks that shape acquisition of a rich set of specific understandings rather than resulting from abstraction off of such specifics.

If such foundational theories of core domains are apparent by age 2, 3, or 4, a set of intriguing and as yet unanswered questions arise. One concerns the course of conceptual development. Infants, we now know, make many sophisticated perceptual discriminations and probably possess a representational system that allows conceptualization about the products of such perceptual analyses (Mandler 1988). Research and theory are only beginning to consider the nature of the infant conceptualizations that lead to the foundational theories of 3-year-olds and have only begun to glimpse how such early conceptual development proceeds. At what points and how is foundational knowledge dependent on perceptual analyses evident in young infants; how is early conceptual knowledge represented; how do different core domains of thinking change, restructure, and differentiate (cf. Mandler, 1988; Carey & Gelman 1991)?

Another set of questions concerns how foundational understandings influence and are influenced by cultural systems (including science itself). How are the belief systems of young children across a variety of cultures related? Currently, the evidence draws from a range of countries in North America, Western Europe, and Asia; however, these questions are only beginning to be explored in any detail in societies with more divergent, less industrial, less literate cultures and beliefs. The story here is bound to be complex; it is extremely unlikely that these conceptions are either simply innate or entirely learned, either simply universal or entirely culture-specific. Consider early acquisition of a theory of mind. Some initial social understandings are necessary for infants to enter into the complex and instructive social life of their family and culture. According to initial framework hypotheses, the infant embarks on a *collaborative* research program, the results of which are proximally the 3-year-old's theory of mind (or of biology or physics) and distally the adult's folk psychology (biology, physics) of his or her culture.

Although we have referred to these understandings as naive theories, they need not be influenced by scientific theories. Thus, our view of framework theories does not derive from claims in philosophy of language that scientific knowledge fixes or underwrites everyday knowledge or reference. If anything, we propose that the weightier influence is likely to be the other way around—naive frameworks may prime or motivate scientific theory-making, at least until scientific theories develop and break away from commonsense on their own. Thus, observations that children are poor scientific reasoners (Kuhn 1989), or that many cultures do not formulate scientific theories (Atran 1990), do not imply that children cannot have or develop framework theories. Children and lay adults are nonscientists (see Strauss 1988); nonetheless, their thinking appears to be framed by initial hypotheses or modes of construal that function for them as framework theories function for scientists. Such initial frameworks establish informal research programs that constrain and enable children to search for and acquire further information about the world. Indeed, historically the first framework theories in a science may well grow directly out of these naive framework theories, before the processes of explicit scientific formulation, test, and revision take hold.

Several questions remain with regard to domains, theories, and domain-specific cognitive development; we do not contend that a concern with foundational domains and framework theories resolves them all. However, we do contend that a central mechanism of cognitive development is the early acquisition of foundational theories of core domains of human understanding.

ACKNOWLEDGMENTS

This chapter was written while the first author was a Fellow at the Center for Advanced Study in the Behavioral Sciences. We acknowledge support from the Center, from the McArthur Foundation, and from NICHD grants HD-22378 and HD-22149. We especially wish to thank Marilyn Shatz, John Flavell, Ed Smith, Alison Gopnik, Margaret Evans, and John Coley for their helpful comments on an earlier draft.

Literature Cited

Adamson, L. B., Bakeman, R. 1985. Affect and attention: infants observed with mothers and peers. *Child Dev.* 56:582–93

Atran, S. 1990. *Cognitive Foundations of Natural History.* Cambridge: Cambridge Univ. Press

Baillargeon, R. 1992. The object concept revisited. In *Visual Perception and Cognition in Infancy. Carnegie-Mellon Symposia on Cognition,* Vol. 23. Hillsdale, NJ: Erlbaum. In press

Baillargeon, R., Spelke, E. S., Wasserman, S. 1985. Object permanence in five-month-olds. *Cognition* 20:191–208

Baltes, P. B., Baltes, M. M. 1990. *Successful Aging.* Cambridge: Cambridge Univ. Press

Baron-Cohen, S. 1990. Autism: a specific cognitive disorder of "mind-blindness." *Int. Rev. Psychiatry* 2:81–90

Baron-Cohen, S., Leslie, A. M., Frith, U. 1985. Does the autistic child have a "theory of mind?" *Cognition* 21:37–46

Bartsch, K. 1991. Children's reasoning about beliefs in the context of desires. Paper presented at the Bienn. Meet. Soc. Res. Child Dev., Seattle

Bartsch, K.,Wellman, H. M. 1989. Young children's attribution of action to beliefs and desires. *Child Dev.* 60:946–64

Bates, E., Bonigni, L., Bretherton, I.,

Camaioni, L., Volterra, V. 1979. *The Emergence of Symbols: Cognition and Communication in Infancy.* New York: Academic

Berlin, B., Breedlove, D., Raven, P. 1973. General principles of classification and nomenclature in folk biology. *Am. Anthropol.* 75:212–42

Bertenthal, B. I., Proffitt, H. D. R., Spetner, N. B., Thomas, M. A. 1985. The development of infant sensitivity to biomechanical motions. *Child Dev.* 56:531–43

Bibace, R., Walsh, M. E. 1981. Children's conceptions of illness. In *New Directions for Child Development: Children's Conceptions of Health, Illness, and Bodily Functions,* ed. R. Bibace, M. E. Walsh, No. 14, pp. 31–48. San Francisco: Jossey-Bass

Bowlby, J. 1969. *Attachment and Loss.* Vol. 1. *Attachment.* New York: Basic Books

Bretherton, I., McNew, S., Beeghly-Smith, M. 1981. Early person knowledge as expressed in gestural and verbal communication: When do infants acquire a "theory of mind?" In *Social Cognition in Infancy,* ed. M. Lamb, L. Sherrod, pp. 333–73. Hillsdale, NJ: Erlbaum

Brown, R. 1973. *A First Language.* Cambridge, MA: Harvard Univ. Press

Bruner, J. S. 1964. The course of growth. *Am. Psychol.* 19:1–15

Bullock, M., Gelman, R., Baillargeon, R. 1982. The development of causal reasoning. In *The Developmental Psychology of Time*, ed. W. J. Friedman, pp. 209–54. New York: Academic

Butterworth, G. E. 1991. The ontogeny and phylogeny of joint visual attention. In *Natural Theories of Mind*, ed. A. Whiten, pp. 223–32. Oxford: Basil Blackwell

Carey, S. 1985. *Conceptual Change in Childhood*. Cambridge, MA: MIT Press

Carey, S. 1991. Knowledge acquisition: enrichment or conceptual change? In *The Epigenesis of Mind: Essays on Biology and Cognition*, ed. S. Carey, R. Gelman, pp. 257–91. Hillsdale, NJ: Erlbaum

Carey, S., Gelman, R. 1991. *The Epigenesis of Mind: Essays on Biology and Cognition*. Hillsdale, NJ: Erlbaum

Case, R. 1985. *Intellectual Development: Birth to Adulthood*. New York: Academic

Chapman, M. 1988. *Constructive Evolution: Origins and Development of Piaget's Thought*. New York: Cambridge Univ. Press

Chase, W. G., Simon, H. A. 1973. Perception in chess. *Cogn. Psychol.* 4:55–81

Chi, M. T. H. 1978. Knowledge structure and memory development. In *Children's Thinking: What Develops?*, ed. R. Siegler, pp. 73–96. Hillsdale, NJ: Erlbaum

Chomsky, N. 1975. *Reflections on Language*. New York: Random House

Clough, E. E., Wood-Robinson, C. 1985. Children's understanding of inheritance. *J. Biol. Educ.* 19:304–10

D'Andrade, R. 1987. A folk model of the mind. In *Cultural Models in Language and Thought*, ed. D. Holland, N. Quinn, pp. 112–48. Cambridge: Cambridge Univ. Press

Deadman, J. A., Kelly, P. J. 1978. What do secondary school boys understand about evolution and heredity before they are taught the topics? *J. Biol. Educ.* 12:7–15

DeCasper, A. S., Fifer, W. P. 1980. Of human bonding: Newborns prefer their mothers' voices. *Science* 208:1174–76

Dolgin, K., Behrend, D. 1984. Children's knowledge about animates and inanimates. *Child Dev.* 55:1646–50

Estes, D., Wellman, H. M., Woolley, J. D. 1989. Children's understanding of mental phenomena. *Adv. Child Dev. Behav.* 22:41-87

Feinman, S. 1985. Emotional expression and preparedness for learning in infancy. In *Development of Expressive Behavior: Biology-Environment Interaction*, ed. G. Zivin, pp. 291–318. New York: Academic

Fischer, K. W., Silvern, L. 1985. Stages and individual differences in cognitive development. *Annu. Rev. Psychol.* 36:613–48

Flavell, J. H., Flavell, E. R., Green, F. L., Moses, L. J. 1990. Young children's understanding of fact beliefs versus value beliefs. *Child Dev.* 61:915–28

Flavell, J. H., Green, F. L., Flavell, E. R. 1986. *Development of Knowledge about the Appearance-Reality Distinction*. Monogr. Soc. Res. Child Dev. 51(212). Chicago: Univ. Chicago Press

Fodor, J. A. 1983. *Modularity of Mind*. Cambridge MA: MIT Press

Gallistel, C. R. 1990. *The Organization of Learning*. Cambridge, MA: MIT Press

Gelman, R. 1987. "Cognitive development: Principles guide learning and contribute to conceptual coherence." Invited address to Am. Psychol. Assoc. Meet., NY

Gelman, R., Baillargeon, R. 1983. A review of some Piagetian concepts. In *Handbook of Child Psychology,*, ed. J. H. Flavell, E. M. Markman, 3:167–230. New York: John Wiley

Gelman, R., Spelke, E. 1981. The development of thoughts about animate and inanimate objects: implications for research on social cognition. In *Social Cognitive Development*, ed. J. H. Flavell, L. Ross, pp. 43–66. Cambridge: Cambridge Univ. Press

Gelman, R., Spelke, E. S., Meck, E. 1983. What preschoolers know about animate and inanimate objects. In *The Acquisition of Symbolic Skills*, ed. D. Rogers, J. A. Sloboda, pp. 297–324. New York: Plenum

Gelman, S. A., Coley, J. D. 1991. Language and categorization: the acquisition of natural kind terms. In *Perspectives on Language and Thought: Interrelations in Development*, ed. S. A. Gelman, J. P. Byrnes. Cambridge: Cambridge Univ. Press. In press

Gelman, S. A., Collman, P., Maccoby, E. E. 1986. Inferring properties from categories versus inferring categories from properties: the case of gender. *Child Dev.* 57:396–404

Gelman, S. A., Kremer, K. E. 1991. Understanding natural cause: children's explanations of how objects and their properties originate. *Child Dev.* 62:396–414

Gelman, S. A., O'Reilly, A. W. 1988. Children's inductive inferences within superordinate categories. *Child Dev.* 59:876–87

Gelman, S. A., Wellman, H. M. 1991. Insides and essences: early understandings of the non-obvious. *Cognition* 38:213–44

Golinkoff, R. M. 1983. Infant social cognition: self, people, and objects. In *Piaget and the Foundations of Knowledge*, ed. L. Liben, pp. 179–200. Hillsdale, NJ: Erlbaum

Golinkoff, R. M., Harding, C. G., Carlson, V., Sexton, M. E. 1984. The infant's perception of causal events: the distinction between animate and inanimate objects. In *Advances in Infancy Research*, ed. L. L. Lipsitt, C. Rovee-Collier, Vol. 3. pp. 146–65. Norwood, NJ: Ablex

Golinkoff, R. M., Markessini, J. 1980. "Mommy sock": the child's understanding of possession as expressed in two-noun phrases. *J. Child Lang.* 7:119–36

Gopnik, A., Astington, J. W. 1988. Children's understanding of representational change and its relation to the understanding of false belief and the appearance-reality distinction. *Child Dev.* 59:26–37

Goswami, U. 1991. Analogical reasoning: What develops? A review of research and theory. *Child Dev.* 62:1–22

Goswami, U., Brown, A. L. 1989. Melting chocolate and melting snowmen: analogical reasoning and causal relations. *Cognition* 35:69–95

Hadwin, J., Perner, J. 1991. Pleased and surprised: children's cognitive theory of emotion. *Br. J. Dev. Psychol.* 9:215–34

Hala, S., Chandler, M., Fritz, A. S. 1991. Fledgling theories of mind: deception as a marker of 3-year-olds' understanding of false belief. *Child Dev.* 62:83–97

Harris, P. L. 1983. Infant Cognition. In *Handbook of Child Psychology.* Vol. 2. *Infancy and Developmental Psychobiology,* ed. M. Haith, J. Campos, pp. 699–782. New York: Wiley

Harris, P. L. 1989. *Children and Emotion.* Oxford: Basil Blackwell

Harris, P. L., Brown, E., Marriot, C., Whithall, S., Harmer, S. 1991. Monsters, ghosts and witches: testing the limits of the fantasy-reality distinction in young children. *Br. J. Dev. Psychol.* 9:105–23

Hornick, R., Risenhoover, N., Gunnar, M. 1987. The effects of maternal positive, neutral, and negative affective communications and infant responses to new toys. *Child Dev.* 58:937–44

Inagaki, K. 1990. Young children's everyday biology as the basis for learning school biology. *Bull. Faculty Educ., Chiba Univ.* 38:177–84

Inagaki, K., Hatano, G. 1988. Young children's understanding of the mind-body distinction. Paper presented at the Meet. Am. Educ. Res. Assoc., New Orleans

Jones, S. S., Smith, L. B., Landau, B. 1992. Object properties and knowledge in early lexical learning. *Child Dev.* In press

Kail, R., Hagen, J. 1977. *Perspectives on the Development of Memory and Cognition.* Hillsdale, NJ: Erlbaum

Kaiser, M. K., Proffitt, D. R., Anderson, K. 1985. Judgments of natural and anomalous trajectories in the presence and absence of motion. *J. Exp. Psychol.: Learn., Mem., Cogn.* 11:795–803

Kaiser, M. K., Proffitt, P. G. 1986. Swingtime: observers' sensitivity to the dynamics of pendulums. Paper presented at the Annu. Meet. Psychonom. Soc., New Orleans

Kaiser, M. K., McCloskey, M., Proffitt, D. R. 1986. Development of intuitive theories of motion. *Dev. Psychol.* 22:67- 71

Kargbo, D., Hobbs, E., Erickson, G. 1980. Children's beliefs about inherited characteristics. *J. Biol. Educ.* 14:137–46

Karmiloff-Smith, A., Inhelder, B. 1975. If you want to get ahead, get a theory. *Cognition* 3:195–212

Keil, F. C. 1979. *Semantic and Conceptual Development.* Cambridge, MA: Harvard Univ. Press

Keil, F. C. 1986. The acquisition of natural kind and artifact terms. In *Language Learning and Concept Acquisition,* ed. W. Demopoulos, A. Marras, pp. 133–53. Norwood, NJ: Ablex

Keil, F. C. 1989. *Concepts, Kinds, and Cognitive Development.* Cambridge, MA: MIT Press

Kister, M. C., Patterson, C. J. 1980. Children's conceptions of the causes of illness: understanding of contagion and use of immanent justice. *Child Dev.* 51:839–49

Kohlberg, L. 1966. A cognitive-developmental analysis of children's sex-role concepts and attitudes. In *The Development of Sex Differences* ed. E. E. Maccoby, pp. 82–173. Stanford, CA: Stanford Univ. Press

Kuhn, D. 1989. Children and adults as intuitive scientists. *Psychol. Rev.* 96:674–89

Kuhn, T. 1962. *The Structure of Scientific Revolutions.* Chicago: Univ. Chicago Press

Lakatos, I. 1970. Falsification and the methodology of scientific research programmes. In *Criticism and the Growth of Knowledge,* ed. I. Lakatos, I. Musgrave, pp. 91–196. Cambridge: Cambridge Univ. Press

Laudan, L. 1977. *Progress and Its Problems: Towards a Theory of Scientific Growth.* Berkeley: Univ. Calif. Press

Laurendeau, M., Pinard, A. 1962. *Causal Thinking in the Child: A Genetic and Experimental Approach.* New York: International Universities Press

Lempers, J. D., Flavell, E. R., Flavell, J. H. 1977. The development in very young children of tacit knowledge concerning visual perception. *Gen. Psychol. Monogr.* 95:3–53

Leslie, A. M. 1982. The perception of causality in infants. *Perception* 11:173–86

Leslie, A. M. 1988. The necessity of illusion: perception and thought in infancy. In *Thought without Language,* ed. L. Weiskrantz, pp. 185–210. Oxford: Clarendon Press

Leslie, A. M., Keeble, S. 1987. Do six-month-old infants perceive causality? *Cognition* 25:265–88

Lewis, C., Osbourne, A. 1990. Three-year-olds' problems with false belief: conceptual deficit or linguistic artifact? *Child Dev.* 61:1514–19

Liben, L. S., Signorella, M. L., eds. 1987. *New Directions for Child Development:*

Children's Gender Schemata, No. 38. San Francisco: Jossey-Bass

Mandler, J. 1988. How to build a baby: on the development of an accessible representational system. *Cogn. Dev.* 3:113–36

Mandler, J. M., Bauer, P. J., McDonough, L. 1991. Separating the sheep from the goats: differentiating global categories. *Cognit. Psychol.* 23:263–98

Massey, C. M., Gelman, R. 1988. Preschooler's ability to decide whether a photographed unfamiliar object can move itself. *Dev. Psychol.* 24:307–17

Masur, E. F. 1983. Gestural development, dual-directional signaling, and the transition to words. *J. Psycholinguist. Res.* 12:93–109

Mayr, E. 1988. *Toward a New Philosophy of Biology: Observations of an Evolutionist.* Cambridge, MA: Harvard Univ. Press

McCloskey, M. 1983. Naive theories of motion. In *Mental Models,* ed. D. Gentner, A. Stevens, pp. 299–324. Hillsdale, NJ: Erlbaum

Medin, D. 1989. Concepts and conceptual structure. *Am. Psychol.* 44:1469–81

Meltzoff, A. N., Moore, M. K. 1983. Newborn infants imitate adult facial gestures. *Child Dev.* 54:702–19

Morton, A. 1980. *Frames of Mind.* Oxford: Clarendon Press

Moses, L. J. 1990. *Young children's understanding of intention and belief.* PhD thesis, Stanford Univ.

Murphy, G. L., Medin, D. L. 1985. The role of theories in conceptual coherence. *Psychol. Rev.* 92:284–316

Nelson, L. A. 1987. The recognition of facial expressions in the first two years of life: mechanisms of development. *Child Dev.* 58:889–909

Oakes, L. M., Cohen, L. B. 1990. Infant perception of a causal event. *Cogn. Dev.* 5:193–207

Perner, J., Leekam, S. R., Wimmer, H. 1987. Three-year-olds' difficulty with false belief. *Br. J. Dev. Psychol.* 5:125–37

Piaget, J. 1929. *The Child's Conception of the World.* London: Routledge & Kegan Paul

Piaget, J. 1930. *The Child's Conception of Physical Causality.* London: Routledge & Kegan Paul

Piaget, J. 1932. *The Moral Judgment of the Child.* London: Routledge & Kegan Paul

Piaget, J. 1954. *The Construction of Reality in the Child.* Basic Books

Pillow, B. H. 1989. Early understanding of perception as a source of knowledge. *J. Exp. Child Psychol.* 47:116–29

Poulin-Dubois, D., Shultz, T. R. 1988. The development of the understanding of human behavior: from agency to intentionality. In *Developing Theories of Mind,* ed. J. Astington, P. Harris, D. Olson, pp. 109–25. New York: Cambridge Univ. Press

Pratt, C., Bryant, P. E. 1990. Young children understand that looking leads to knowing (so long as they are looking into a single barrel). *Child Dev.* 61:973–82

Premack, D. 1990. The infant's theory of self-propelled objects. *Cognition* 36:1–16

Proffitt, D. R., Kaiser, M. K., Whelan, S. M. 1990. Understanding wheel dynamics. *Cogn. Psychol.* 22:342–73

Rholes, W. S., Newman, L. S., Ruble, D. N. 1990. Understanding self and other: developmental and motivational aspects of perceiving persons in terms of invariant dispositions. In *Handbook of Motivation and Cognition: Foundations of Social Behavior,* ed. E. Higgins, R. Sorrentino, 2:369–407. New York: Guilford

Richards, D. D., Siegler, R. S. 1984. The effects of task requirements on children's abilities to make life judgments. *Child Dev.* 55:1687–96

Richards, D. D., Siegler, R. S. 1986. Children's understandings of the attributes of life. *J. Exp. Child Psychol.* 42:1–22

Rosengren, K. S., Gelman, S. A., Kalish, C. W., McCormick, M. 1992. As time goes by: children's early understanding of growth in animals. *Child Dev.* In press

Schwartz, S. P. 1977. Introduction. In *Naming, Necessity, and Natural Kinds,* ed. S. P. Schwartz, pp. 13–41. Ithaca, NY: Cornell Univ. Press

Shatz, M., Wellman, H. M., Silber, S. 1983. The acquisition of mental verbs: a systematic investigation of first references to mental state. *Cognition* 14:301–21

Sherrod, L. R. 1981. Issues in cognitive-perceptual development: the special case of social stimuli. In *Infant Social Cognition: Empirical and Theoretical Considerations,* ed. M. Lamb, L. Sherrod, pp. 11–36. Hillsdale, NJ: Erlbaum

Shultz, T. R. 1982. *Rules of Causal Attribution.* Monogr. Soc. Res. Child Dev. 194. Chicago: Univ. Chicago Press

Shultz, T. R., Kestenbaum, N. R. 1985. Causal reasoning in children. In *Annals of Child Development,* ed. G. Whitehurst, Vol. 2. pp. 195–244. Greenwich, CT: JAI Press

Shultz, T. R., Pardo, S., Altman, E. 1982. Young children's use of transitive inference in causal chains. *Br. J. Psychol.* 73:235–41

Shultz, T. R., Wells, D., Sarda, M. 1980. Development of the ability to distinguish intended actions from mistakes, reflexes, and passive movements. *Br. J. Soc. Clin. Psychol.* 19:301–10

Siegal, M. 1988. Children's knowledge of contagion and contamination as causes of illness. *Child Dev.* 59:1353–59

Siegal, M., Beattie, K. 1992. Where to look first for children's understanding of false beliefs. *Cognition.* In press

Siegal, M., Robinson, J. 1987. Order effects

in children's gender constancy response. *Dev. Psychol.* 23:283–86

Siegler, R. S. 1989. Mechanisms of cognitive development. *Annu. Rev. Psychol.* 40:353–79

Smith, C., Carey, S., Wiser, M. 1985. On differentiation: a case study of the development of the concepts of size, weight, and density. *Cognition* 21:177–237

Smith, J., Russell, G. 1984. Why do males and females differ? Children's beliefs about sex differences. *Sex Roles* 11:1111–20

Smith, L. B. 1989. In defense of perceptual similarity. Paper presented at the Meet. Soc. Res. Child Dev., Kansas City

Smith, L. B., Heise, D. 1992. Perceptual similarity and conceptual structure. In *Percepts, Concepts, and Categories: The Representation and Processing of Information*, ed. B. Burns. New York: Elsevier. In press

Spelke, E. S. 1988. Where perceiving ends and thinking begins: the apprehension of objects in infancy. *Minn. Symp. Child Psychol.* 20:197–234

Spelke, E. S. 1991. Physical knowledge in infancy. In *The Epigenesis of Mind: Essays on Biology and Cognition*, ed. S. Carey, R. Gelman, pp. 133–69. Hillsdale, NJ: Erlbaum

Springer, K., Keil, F. C. 1989. On the development of biologically specific beliefs: the case of inheritance. *Child Dev.* 60:637–48

Stavy, R., Wax, N. 1989. Children's conceptions of plants as living things. *Hum. Dev.* 32:88–94

Stein, N. L., Levine, L. J. 1987. Thinking about feelings: the development and organization of emotional knowledge. In *Aptitude, Learning, and Instruction*. Vol. 3. *Cognition, Conation, and Affect*, ed. R. Snow, M. Farr, pp. 165–98. Hillsdale, NJ: Erlbaum

Stein, N. L., Levine, L. J. 1989. The causal organization of emotional knowledge: a developmental study. *Cogn. Emot.* 3:343–78

Stern, D. N. 1985. *The Interpersonal World of the Infant*. New York: Basic Books

Stevenson, H. W., Lee, S. Y., Stigler, J. W. 1986. Mathematics achievement of Chinese, Japanese, and American children. *Science* 231:693–99

Stigler, J. W., Shweder, R. A., Herdt, G. 1990. *Cultural Psychology: Essays on Comparative Human Development*. Cambridge: Cambridge Univ. Press

Stitch, S. P. 1983. *From Folk Psychology to Cognitive Science: The Case Against Belief.* Cambridge, MA: MIT Press

Strauss, S. 1988. *Ontogeny, Phylogeny, and Historical Development*. Norwood, NJ: Ablex

Taylor, M. G., Gelman, S. A. 1991. Children's beliefs about sex differences: the role of nature vs. nurture. Paper presented at the Meet. Soc. Res. Child Dev., Seattle

Taylor, M. 1988. Conceptual perspective taking: children's ability to distinguish what they know from what they see. *Child Dev.* 59:703–18

Teale, W., Sulzby, E. 1986. *Emergent Literacy: Reading and Writing*. Norwood, NJ: Ablex

Thomas, K. 1983. *Man and the Natural World*. New York: Pantheon Books

Walden, T. A., Ogan, T. A. 1988. The development of social referencing. *Child Dev.* 59:1230–40

Wellman, H. M. 1990. *The Child's Theory of Mind*. Cambridge, MA: M. I. T. Press

Wellman, H. M. 1992. Early understanding of mind: the normal case. In *Understanding Other Minds: Perspectives from Autism*, ed. S. Baron-Cohen, H. Tager-Flusberg, D. Cohen, In press

Wellman, H. M., Bannerjee, M. 1991. Mind and emotion: children's understanding of the emotional consequences of beliefs and desires. *Br. J. Dev. Psychol.* 9:191–214

Wellman, H. M., Bartsch, K. 1988. Young children's reasoning about beliefs. *Cognition* 30:239–77

Wellman, H. M., Cross, D., Bartsch, K. 1986. Infant search and object permanance: a meta-analysis of the A-not-B error. *Monogr. Soc. Res. Child Dev.* 51(3)

Wellman, H. M., Estes, D. 1986. Early understanding of mental entities: a reexamination of childhood realism. *Child Dev.* 57:910–23

Wellman, H. M., Woolley, J. D. 1990. From simple desires to ordinary beliefs: the early development of everyday psychology. *Cognition* 57:245–75

Wimmer, H., Hogrefe, J., Sodian, B. 1988. A second stage in children's conceptions of mental life: understanding sources of information. In *Developing Theories of Mind*, ed. J. Astington, P. Harris, D. Oleson, pp. 173–92. New York: Cambridge Univ. Press

Wimmer, H., Perner, J. 1983. Beliefs about beliefs: representation and constraining function of wrong beliefs in young children's understanding of deception. *Cognition* 13:103–28

Yuill, N. 1984. Young children's coordination of motive and outcome in judgments of satisfaction and morality. *Br. J. Dev. Psychol.* 2:73–81

Zinober, B., Martlew, M. C. 1985. Developmental changes in four types of gesture in relation to acts and vocalizations from 10 to 21 months. *Br. J. Dev. Psychol.* 3:293–306

Annu. Rev. Psychol. 1992. 43:377–98

THE NEUROBIOLOGY
OF FILIAL LEARNING

Michael Leon

Department of Psychobiology, University of California, Irvine, CA 92717

KEY WORDS: development, imprinting, behavioral development, neural plasticity

CONTENTS

Neonates must form a bond with their mothers if they are to receive the sustenance, protection, and comfort they require to grow and develop. Learning is the means by which they establish this bond, as various characteristics of the mother are identified and preferred after early postnatal or even prenatal experience. Neonates may use various means to maintain contact with their mothers. The different sensory modalities that are involved in this process have been studied separately rather than as complementary and perhaps interacting mechanisms. Moreover, the possibility that shared mechanisms are involved in developing attractions in different sensory modalities has not received much attention. While I cannot present new data integrating these areas of research, I can present the existing evidence and point out the possibility of similar neural mechanisms.

In the context of this discussion, filial learning means any experience-induced preference for the mother. Here I discuss preferences acquired during fetal life, postnatal preferences induced by what has been called "imprinting,"

377

0066-4308/92/0201-0377$02.00

as well as other preferences that arise through stimulus exposure or associative learning. Though much has been made of the uniqueness of each of these forms of learning in the visual, auditory, and olfactory modalities, a case may be made for their common function, mechanisms, and classification.

The neural mechanisms underlying such learning may be more accessible to investigation than adult forms of learning. Young animals appear to learn about relatively few things, but must learn them very well; the neonate that does not learn to be attracted to its mother is unlikely to survive. Developing brains may therefore be prepared for the stimuli that must be learned and stored, and the mechanisms may lack the subtlety that has characterized neural changes following learning in the adult. Redundant systems may exist that assure learning even in a degraded nervous system or in a situation when degraded stimuli are available to the neonate. Finally, the growth and development of the brain at the time of learning may amplify any changes that are produced by the learning. That is, a small change induced in a developing brain may become a large, observable change as the developing systems commit to different courses.

Early Olfactory Preference Learning

HUMAN INFANTS   Neonates who depend on their mothers for nurturing typically have a means of staying with them or remaining in a nest. Olfactory cues may play a particularly important role in maintaining mother-young interactions in a wide range of species. The role of such cues might be particularly important for species that interact at night or underground. Additionally, olfactory cues may be important in neonates whose auditory and visual systems function poorly.

Human mothers produce odors that preferentially attract their own infants. Macfarlane (1975) tested the preference of infants to the breast odor of their own mothers when compared to either a clean gauze pad or the odor of another mother within the first week of life. For the test, each infant was placed alone on its back with two gauze pads near either cheek and allowed to turn toward either one during two videotaped 1-min periods. The position of the pads was reversed for the second test period. Own mother's breast odor was preferred over either alternative stimulus. This ability to identify and move toward the maternal breast odor may help infants to localize the nipple of the mother in the dark.

At six weeks of age, infants will both orient toward the maternal breast odor and produce sucking movements in response to it, in contrast to their lack of response to the odor of another mother or to cow's milk (Russell 1976). The breast odor of their own mothers, but not that of a stranger, also appears to calm infants by decreasing their movements (Schaal et al 1980).

Infants who are bottle-fed may have a different olfactory experience from infants who are breast-fed. Since the bottle-fed infants are less likely to be exposed to the breast odor of the mother, comparisons between breast odors would not constitute a fair comparison. However, breast-fed infants preferred their mothers' axillary or neck odor to that of another woman (Cernoch & Porter 1985; Schaal et al 1980). Bottle-fed babies, on the other hand, did not exhibit this preference (Cernoch & Porter 1985). The axillary odors of their fathers, with which they were unlikely to have had much direct contact, were not preferred by breast-fed infants (Cernoch & Porter 1985). These data suggest that specific experience with maternal odors can induce a subsequent preference for them. Moreover, the data suggest that a variety of maternal odors can become attractive to the infants.

If experience with any of a variety of maternal odors can shift odor preference behavior in infants, it seemed possible that experience with arbitrarily selected nonmaternal odors would also produce such preferences. Differential experience with one of two neutral nonmaternal odors was given to newborn infants for almost a full day by taping a scented gauze pad to their bassinets (Balogh & Porter 1986). Each infant was then exposed to the two odors on a gauze pad on either side of its head while it was in an active sleep state and then tested for its preference. After a forced sampling of the two odors, the infant's head was centered and a choice allowed. The female but not the male infants exhibited a clear preference for the experienced odor whether they received breast or bottle feeding.

These data, however, did not directly address the question of whether odor familiarity alone was sufficient to produce the preference. Indeed, one might predict that continued exposure to an odor in the absence of reinforcing stimulation from the mother would cause the infants to habituate to the odor (Engen et al 1963). However, during the period when the babies were exposed to the neutral odor, they also received maternal care. Perhaps the association between the odor and the mother was critical for the development of the early preference by the babies. Alternatively, both familiarity and associative responses could be involved independently or in concert to produce the observed preferences for both natural and artificial odors.

To determine whether preferences could be developed for odors familiarized during suckling, Schleidt & Genzel (1990) allowed newborn infants to be nursed by mothers who routinely applied a perfume to their breasts (though not to their nipples). After two weeks of this olfactory experience, the infants were tested in a bassinet for their preferences to scented gauze pads. Twenty one of twenty two infants preferred the odor that had been associated with their mother at both one and two weeks of age. During the test, the infants turned their heads almost constantly, as they do when searching for the breast. The preference demonstrated for the perfume was comparable to that previously reported for maternal breast odor (Macfarlane 1975). There was no sex difference observed in this study. Mothers then refrained from applying the perfume for the next two weeks, at which time the infants were retested.

The data indicated that the preference for the perfume waned by the time the infants were four weeks old. Occasional use of the perfume during that period, however, appeared to maintain the olfactory preference by the infants.

These data raise the possibility that the infants develop an attraction to the odor because they associate the odor with the reinforcing aspects of maternal care. Of course, the data still do not rule out the possibility that odor familiarity alone is sufficient to produce an early attraction to such odors. To assess the possibility that some associative process was involved in the development of an early odor attraction, an odor would have to be presented in the absence of maternal care; exposure to the odor would of necessity have to be relatively brief. Newborn infants in a quiet alert state were therefore presented with a neutral odor as they lay in a bassinet in a room isolated from their mothers (Sullivan et al 1991b). Another group of infants was presented with the same odor but with concurrent tactile stimulation, given by rubbing their torsos, to mimic maternal care. The tactile stimulation was suffucient to evoke an increase in body movement by the infants. A third group was given the tactile stimulation followed by odor stimulation. This group therefore received the same amount of both odor and tactile stimulation, but received them unpaired. Finally, a group of infants received only tactile stimulation. The stimuli were presented 10 times for 30 sec with a 1-min intertrial interval. The odor was delivered on a cotton swab held laterally and 10 cm from the infant's head. Following training, the infants were placed in a clean bassinet and clean clothing.

On the second day of life, the infants were brought back to the training room to be tested for their response to the trained odor. The test consisted of five 3-sec exposures to the trained odor. Head turns toward and away from the odor were scored, as was the activity of the infants in response to the odor. Only those infants given paired odor and tactile stimulation preferred the conditioned odor, and only those infants exhibited a conditioned increase in activity. The increase in head turns toward the odor was not due to a general increase in activity, since the number of head turns away from the odor did not increase among those infants.

This type of learning appears to be odor specific, since babies given paired exposures to one odor with tactile stimulation did not have a differential response to another odor on the test day. These data indicate that the babies do not learn a generalized response to olfactory stimulation during training.

Brief odor exposure unpaired with tactile stimulation did not alter the behavior of the infants. These data suggest that at least brief odor exposures must be accompanied by reinforcing tactile stimulation to evoke odor prefer-ences. It is also possible that long-term odor exposure would be sufficient to produce such preferences in the absence of other stimuli. It is also possible that the tactile stimulus simply aroused the infants in the presence of olfactory cues, thus allowing them to become familiar with the odor; but this interpretation is unlikely for several reasons. First, the presentation of the odor itself is arousing, causing an increase in the respiration of these infants. Second, if familiarity alone were responsible for the change in behavior then one would not expect to observe the similar response of the control groups, some of which had odor exposure and some of which did not. Third, the infants who received unpaired odor and tactile stimulation received the tactile stimulation just before the onset of the odor exposure; the infants presumably experienced the attentional effects of the tactile stimulation while the odor was experienced. Finally, Engen et al (1963) have shown that continued odor exposure to infants produces habituation to the odor. Since the question of the nature of reinforcement—particularly the role of arousal in both adults and infants—is still unanswered, both familiarity and associative processes may be involved in the development of early odor preferences.

Similar odor preference conditioning can be shown with brief pairings of odor and breast feeding or bottle feeding (Sullivan 1990). Again, the preferential response was odor specific. These data suggest that several aspects of the mother-young interaction may be reinforcing to the infants. Moreover, in previous infant studies prolonged, familiarizing odor exposure would have been paired with such reinforcement. Thus, while the normal mechanism for odor preference acquisition may not be completely clear from the available data, what does emerge from these studies is the remarkably robust nature of the development of early olfactory preferences. Indeed, there may be alternate, redundant means by which the critical information concerning the mother can be acquired by the infant.

OTHER SPECIES   Olfactory learning early in life has been linked to parental care in a variety of other species: young rats (Leon 1974), mice (Breen & Leshner 1977), deer (Müller-Schwarze & Müller-Schwarze 1971), hamsters (Devor & Schneider 1974), crayfish (Little 1975), cichlid fish (Barnett 1977), lambs (Vince & Ward 1984), guinea pigs (Pettijohn 1979), spiny mice (Porter & Ruttle 1975), squirrel monkeys (Kaplan & Cubiciotti 1980), and gerbils (Yahr & Anderson-Mitchell 1983). Similar responses can be seen after experience with nonmaternal odors (Carter 1972; Mainardi et al 1965; Leon et al 1984; Cornwell 1976; Porter & Etscorn 1976; Redican & Kaplan 1978).

Young rats learn to approach the odor of their mothers' nipples and must use this ability to attach to their only source of food. Pups made anosmic are not able to find and attach to their mothers' nipples (Singh et al 1976). Similarly, 4-day-old neonates are unable to suckle at the washed nipples of anesthetized dams, even when the pups are held to the nipple (Teicher & Blass 1976). Application to the nipple of saliva taken from other pups allowed pups to attach and suckle at the nipple. Since pup saliva cannot be present for the initial attachment to the nipples, however, another factor must be involved in initiating this behavior. Amniotic fluid applied to the nipple successfully brought pups to the nipple (Teicher & Blass 1977), suggesting that the amniotic fluid licked by dams before licking their nipples may control the first nipple attachment.

The data also raised the possibility that the pups learn to become attracted to that odor in utero. If that were the case, one might predict that fetal exposure to a nonmaternal odor would allow that odor to direct the initial neonatal nipple attachment. Pedersen & Blass (1982) introduced either an odor or saline into the amniotic sacs containing fetal rats on the 20th day of embryogenesis. Two days later, at the time of natural birth, the pups were removed by cesarean section and given tactile stimulation in the presence of either the odor or saline. If pups experienced the odor both prenatally and postnatally, they subsequently attached to washed nipples that had been painted with that odor. These pups did not attach to nipples coated with amniotic fluid. All other pups attached to the maternal odor and not to the nonmaternal odor. Therefore, the dominant odor experienced in the perinatal period appears to determine nipple attachment behavior, a behavior of obvious critical importance for the early survival of newborn rats.

There is also direct evidence for the kind of fetal learning that could underlie immediate olfactory preferences at birth. Specifically, pups exposed to an odor in utero preferred as adults to drink water scented with that odor (Smotherman 1982).

After suckling is established, the young must maintain contact with the mother. In rats, this is accomplished by remaining in the nest for the return of the mother and moving toward her when she arrives (Leon et al 1990). This behavior is also facilitated by a learned attraction to a maternal olfactory cue. Rat pups will come to approach the odor of their mothers (Leon 1974), but since mothers can produce different odors (Leon 1975), the young must acquire this preference postnatally. This kind of olfactory preference can be seen when pups are given either (a) prolonged exposure to a nonmaternal odor (Leon et al 1977) or (b) brief odor exposure in the presence of reinforcing tactile stimulation (Coopersmith & Leon 1984; Sullivan et al 1986; Sullivan & Leon 1986; Sullivan et al 1989a; Sullivan & Hall 1988), intraoral milk infusion (Johanson & Hall 1979; Johanson & Teicher 1980; Johanson & Hall 1982; Johanson et al 1984; Sullivan & Hall 1988; Brake 1981), tail pressure (Sullivan et al 1986), high humidity (Do et al 1988), warmth (Alberts & May 1984), or suckling (Amsel et al 1976; Kenny & Blass 1977).

One common aspect of these learning situations is that the mother provides all of this stimulation to the young; another is that these stimuli are all arousing to young pups. There may be a special kind of relationship between filial cues and the arousing nature of maternal stimulation that induces preferences and approach behavior (Hall 1987). It is not clear whether the arousal has its effects by activating reinforcement mechanisms or by allowing attention to be paid to the olfactory cues.

One might expect that when the pups are aroused their respiration would increase and thereby increase olfactory stimulation. Do et al (1988) monitored the respiratory patterns of pups during training stimulation and observed such an increase in respiration; but this increase is not critical to the change in neurobehavioral response to the trained odor. When pups were trained to prefer an odor by pairing it with high humidity, they developed the preference and the enhanced olfactory bulb response without increasing their respiration during training (Do et al 1988). The suppression of the neurobehavioral changes in response to the learned odor when it had been paired with both tactile stimulation and humidity suggested that the humidity was arousing and that the combined stimulation blocked the learning.

NEURAL CHANGES DURING PREFERENCE LEARNING   This common arousing feature of early olfactory learning may have a noradrenergic basis. Blocking the beta noradrenergic receptors in young rats blocks the acquisition of an olfactory preference (Lin et al 1990; Sullivan et al 1989b, 1991a). Conversely, pairing the catecholaminergic agonist amphetamine (Pedersen et al 1983) or the beta noradrenergic agonist isoproterenol (Sullivan et al 1989b; Sullivan et al 1989b, 1991a) with an odor early in life induces olfaction-guided nipple attachment and an olfactory preference, respectively. Direct measurement of norepinephrine in the olfactory bulbs of young rats indicates that tactile stimulation causes a rise in norepinephrine level (Coopersmith et al 1990). It seems plausible that all these kinds of stimulation evoke a similar increase in bulb levels of this neurotransmitter. Other forms of neonatal learning and plasticity also appear to depend on noradrenergic mechanisms (Saiers & Campbell 1990; Bear & Singer 1986; Gordon et al 1988; Kasamatsu & Pettigrew 1979; Loeb et al 1986).

There appears to be a sensitive period for the development of the olfactory preference in young rats. That period extends through the first week of life for tactile stimulation (Woo & Leon 1987). These data match reasonably well with the period during which the noradrenergic locus coeruleus neurons, which are present and functional in the olfactory bulb during the first postnatal week (Shipley et al 1985; McLean & Shipley 1991; Sullivan et al 1989b), are also sensitive to the kind of tactile stimulation that will produce an olfactory preference during that period (Nakamura et al 1987). Other stimuli may have different developmental periods during which they can evoke an increase in norepinephrine. Indirect evidence for this possibility comes from the finding that intraoral milk infusions extended the period during which pairing with an olfactory cue would result in an olfactory preference (Sullivan & Wilson

1990). One might predict either that milk infusions after the second week would evoke an increase in bulb norepinephrine or that such learning would have a different mechanism for its establishment.

Stimulation of the medial forebrain bundle, when paired with an olfactory cue on postnatal day (PND) 12 will produce a preference for that odor (Wilson & Sullivan 1990). Random presentations of brain stimulation and odor did not evoke an olfactory preference on the following day. The stimulation itself produced a dramatic, long-lasting depression of the neurophysiological activity of a subset of responses of the olfactory bulb output neurons. Perhaps this kind of change in neural activity accompanies other kinds of reinforcing stimulation and is normally involved in the neural mechanisms underlying early learning. While stimulation of the medial forebrain bundle arouses pups (Moran et al 1983), it is not clear whether its impact on learning occurs through its effect on arousal or through a direct reinforcement system. Evidence for the latter comes from a study showing that self-stimulation of the medial forebrain bundle leads to increased responding by PND 3 pups (Moran et al 1981).

A particularly interesting aspect of this notion of noradrenergic mediation of arousal/reinforcement is that high levels of stimulation or a combination of reinforcing stimuli actually block early olfactory learning. For example, Pedersen et al (1983) found interactions among odor concentration, ambient temperature, tactile stimulation, and dose of amphetamine indicating that high levels of stimulation in rat pups suppress preferential attachment to maternal nipples. Similarly, the combination of odor, tactile stimulation, and isoproterenol suppressed olfactory preference learning (Sullivan et al 1989b; Sullivan et al 1991a). Again, odor paired with tactile stimulation and high humidity did not result in the formation of an olfactory preference, although either stimulus alone paired with the odor did (Do et al 1988). The endogenous increase in norepinephrine presumably added to the exogenous increase in adrenergic activity produced by the agonist to block preference formation. Indeed, decreasing the endogenous levels by halving the amount of tactile stimulation and decreasing the exogenous levels of the agonist by half restored the development of olfactory preference (Sullivan et al 1991).

Dopaminergic as well as noradrenergic modulation may be important for development of odor preferences. In the olfactory bulb, dopamine is found only in juxtaglomerular cells (Davis & Macrides 1983; Gall et al 1987; Halasz et al 1981). During olfactory preference training, a large and prolonged increase in extracellular dopamine occurs (Coopersmith et al, in press). On PND 3, odor stimulation alone or tactile stimulation alone presented within a 10-min period increases extracellular dopamine levels by about 200%, a change lasting over 50 min. The combined odor and stroking stimulation that induces olfactory preference learning increases dopamine levels by about

400%, a change that also persists past 50 min. The importance of this increase in dopamine level for early olfactory learning is not yet clear, but it may reflect a special potentiation of neural activity in the bulb that could provoke the changes in cell development described below.

Dopamine action has been manipulated in the developing rat during olfactory preference training in which intraoral milk delivery has been used as a reinforcer. PND 5 pups were either injected with saline or treated with desmethylimipramine and 6-hydroxydopamine to deplete the brain of dopamine (Weldon et al 1982; Wool et al 1987). On PND 7, these pups were given odor-milk pairings and then tested for their odor preference. Dopamine-depleted pups did not acquire an odor preference. The deficit was not due to changes in olfactory sensitivity or to differential arousal. Amphetamine blocked learning in controls, as would be expected if there was an over-stimulation effect, but that drug reversed the deficit observed in dopamine-depleted pups, indicating the specificity of the response.

While these data suggest a role for dopamine in early olfactory learning, other data suggest that the locus of influence may not be in the olfactory bulb. Weldon et al (1991) found that they could block a preference for an odor after odor-tactile pairings if the pups were injected with a dopamine D1 receptor blocker, but not with a dopamine D2 receptor blocker. Since D2 receptors are the dominant receptor subtype in the olfactory bulb (Guthrie et al 1991; Bouthenet et al 1987), it seems unlikely that dopamine plays a critical role in the establishment of olfactory preferences. Rather, an increase in the activity of the dopaminergic neurons may reflect other, critical changes occurring in the bulb during early learning. It is also possible that the D1, but not the D2 receptor blocker, reached the brain after systemic injection or that peripheral mechanisms mediated the effects of these drugs.

The D1 receptor blocker was effective when given just after training, rather than just before the conditioning trial. These data suggest that a prolonged increase in dopamine in the posttraining period may be critical for the consolidation and/or expression of odor preference memories. It is also the case that dopamine agonists are effective during the training period, rather than after it. There is likely an optimal stimulation level for the dopaminergic receptors both during and after training.

Differential cellular metabolism has been studied in young rats during conditioning by assessing the uptake of radiolabeled 2-deoxyglucose (2-DG), a glucose analogue that is incompletely metabolized in cells. Increased 2-DG uptake suggests increased cellular glucose utilization and therefore increased cellular activity. Uptake patterns of 2-DG determined while pups were given odor-milk pairings differed from those of controls (Hall 1987). Among the areas that differed in 2-DG uptake were the olfactory tubercle, hippocampus, and the central amygdaloid nucleus, which are part of the olfactory projection system, and the pontine reticular nucleus, which is associated with arousal. The effects of dopamine may be mediated within the olfactory tubercle, an area rich in dopamine D1 receptors (Wamsley et al 1989).

NEURAL CONSEQUENCES OF EARLY OLFACTORY PREFERENCE LEARN-ING   A unique glomerular grouping arises by embryonic day 19 (Friedman & Price 1984) and is clearly visible two days later (Pedersen et al 1983). This group appears to be more mature than other glomeruli and has been called the modified glomerular complex (Greer et al 1982). This area is activated during suckling (Greer et al 1982; Teicher et al 1980), raising the possibility that this area may play a special role in the development of preferences for the maternal nipple odor. In addition, perinatal learning with a nonmaternal odor evokes an increased uptake of 2-DG in focal regions of the olfactory bulb in response to the preferred odor (Pedersen et al 1982).

Uptake of 2-DG in PND 19 pups increases in response to the preferred odor of their mother (Sullivan et al 1990). Allowing a nonmaternal odor to be present continuously during the first 18 days of maternal care allows the development of an attraction to that odor and an increased glomerular re-sponse to it (Sullivan et al 1990). The combination of continued odor expo-sure and the pairing of maternal care with the odor presumably forms the subsequent attraction.

Coopersmith & Leon (1984) found an increased uptake of 2-DG in specific focal regions of the olfactory bulb glomerular layer in response to the learned odor when pups were given odor-tactile stimulation from PND 1–18 and presented with the trained odor on PND 19. This kind of training continues to evoke an increased uptake of 2-DG in rats tested at 90 days of age (Cooper-smith & Leon 1986). Such early olfactory learning may also form the basis for adult mating preferences (Fillion & Blass 1986).

The neurobehavioral response to the trained odor is specific to that odor (Coopersmith et al 1986; Wilson et al 1987) since training with one odor does not increase the 2-DG uptake for another odor. Other odors, however, will evoke increased responses in their specific regions of the glomerular layer after early learning (Coopersmith et al 1986; Frazier-Cierpial & Hall 1989). The odor preference and 2-DG response can also be specific to the trained odor concentration (Carmi & Leon, in press). Early olfactory learning also determines the subsequent response to odors of different concentrations (Car-mi & Leon, in press). That is, pups trained with a high odor concentration will subsequently have a greater 2-DG response to both high and low odor concentrations than will control pups. Early experience therefore may set the "gain" on future responses to odors.

A sensitive period for development of both the olfactory preference and increased olfactory bulb response extends through the first week of life (Woo

& Leon 1987). Odor-tactile training in the second week of life does not increase the neurobehavioral response (Woo & Leon 1987), although odor-milk pairings continue to do so (Sullivan & Wilson 1990). The behavioral and neural changes can also be seen on the day after a single pairing of odor and tactile stimulation during the first week of life (Sullivan & Leon 1987).

Pairing odor and tactile stimulation in a classical conditioning paradigm also induces the odor preference and increased 2-DG uptake. Concurrent odor-tactile stimulation produces the neurobehavioral response, whereas either odor alone or sequential presentation of tactile and odor stimulation is ineffective in that regard (Sullivan & Leon 1986; Sullivan et al 1989b). The behavioral and neural responses in odor-conditioned pups can be extinguished by repeatedly exposing the trained pups to the odor without tactile stimulation (Sullivan & Wilson 1991). Concurrent presentations of an odor with medial forebrain bundle stimulation subsequently evoke the increased 2-DG response to that odor, whereas random presentations of odor and brain stimulation do not (Wilson & Sullivan 1990). At the same time, under certain conditions, odor exposure alone can produce olfactory attractions (Leon et al 1977; Caza & Spear 1984; Janus 1989). The odor itself may be arousing or reinforcing if it is experienced for long periods or at high concentrations, thereby allowing an attraction to develop.

When young rats come to prefer the odor, they might increase their respiration of that odor and thereby increase the stimulation of the olfactory bulb glomerular foci; such a mechanism might underlie the observed increase in 2-DG uptake. Monitoring the respiration of pups during the uptake of 2-DG on PND 19, however, revealed no differences in respiration that could account for the increased uptake (Coopersmith & Leon 1984; Woo & Leon 1987; Sullivan & Leon 1986; Sullivan et al 1988). Neither number of respirations nor the distribution of respiratory frequencies differed across groups. However, although there were no overall differences, or even differences in respiration during briefer periods within the test, there might have been a special pattern of respiration that induced an increased uptake of 2-DG in the olfactory bulb. We therefore removed control of respiration by the pups via tracheotomy and imposed the same number of respirations on trained pups and their controls (Sullivan et al 1988). Only those pups that had been trained to prefer the odor had an increased uptake of 2-DG, despite the absence of differential respiration. These data indicate that the increased uptake of 2-DG does not arise from a self-induced increase in stimulus availability to the olfactory system.

If the increased metabolic response of the olfactory bulb is not due to a change in the amount of stimulus sampled by the pups, perhaps an intrinsic change in the bulb could underlie the increased pattern of 2-DG uptake. In an effort to address this question, we determined first whether the size and/or number of glomeruli changed within the increased 2-DG focus (Woo et al 1987). The 2-DG autoradiographs of trained and control pups were aligned with adjacent bulb sections that had been stained to reveal individual glomeruli. The trained pups and controls had the same number of glomeruli within the 2-DG focus, but both the width of the glomerular layer and the size of individual glomeruli were greater in trained pups. No differences were observed between groups in the nonfocal regions of the glomerular layer.

Thus early learning actually changes the morphology of the developing olfactory system. The increased glomerular size may be explained in one of two ways: either by an increase in the size of cellular processes within the glomerular layer or by an increase in the number of cells with processes in the glomeruli. The second possibility was evaluated by aligning 2-DG autoradiographs with adjacent bulb sections stained to reveal cell bodies in trained and control pups (Woo & Leon 1991). There was a striking increase in the number of neurons within the 2-DG foci of trained than of control pups. Again, no difference in cell number was found in the regions of the glomerular layer outside the 2-DG focus for the trained odor. Enrichment of neonatal olfactory experiences by daily exposure to a variety of odors during maternal care also increases the number of mitral and granule cells in the developing olfactory bulb (Rosselli-Austin & Williams 1990). The pups probably develop attractions to these odors, although the the number of attractions that can be acquired is not known.

If this increase in glomerular-layer cells were composed, at least in part, of periglomerular cells, a subpopulation of which are thought to be inhibitory (Getchell & Shepherd 1975), the altered neural organization might suppress the output signal from the mitral/tufted cells emanating from the bulb. Mitral/tufted cells were therefore recorded in response to the trained odor in the region associated with the 2-DG focus for that odor (Wilson et al 1985; Wilson et al 1987; Wilson & Leon 1988). In these output neurons the proportion of excitatory responses decreased and the proportion of suppressive responses increased relative to untrained controls. This suppression could be seen on the first inhalation of the trained odor, was specific to the trained odor, and was specific to the region of the bulb associated with the 2-DG focus. The structural changes in the bulb induced by early learning may therefore affect the function of the bulb.

The precise function of these neural changes has not yet been defined. The memory of the preferred odor is likely stored in circuits that include areas away from the olfactory bulb, since elimination of the trained bulb did not affect memory of an olfactory preference when accessed through untrained bulb (Kucharski & Hall 1987; Kucharski & Hall 1988). The olfactory bulb, though, is clearly required for the establishment of the memory. There is also reason to believe that the altered signal from the bulb indicates the special nature of an olfactory stimulus, the other aspects of which appear to be extracted by other brain areas. Evidence for this notion comes from the finding that aversive conditioning produces the same increase in 2-DG and the same suppression of the output signal as olfactory preference conditioning does (Sullivan & Wilson 1991).

The fact that olfactory preference and avoidance behaviors, increased 2-DG uptake, and suppression of neurophysiological changes in the bulb can be reversed with extinction (Sullivan & Wilson 1991) has interesting implications for the function of the structural changes induced by early learning. One possibility is that the increase in cell number plays no critical role in the neural or behavioral changes that develop as a result of early learning. Another possibility is that the extinction activates a neural system that suppresses the activity of these cells. Still another possibility is that the juxtaglomerular cells withdraw their processes or reduce their synaptic contacts with extinction. Finally, a conditioned increase in a neurotransmitter in the bulb may be evoked by the trained odor and may be required to activate the cells. Extinction may eliminate that neurotransmitter peak and thereby prevent the activation of the juxtaglomerular cells by the trained odor. Indeed, the trained odor elicits a conditioned increase in norepinephrine. Norepinephrine, however, may not be the critical conditioned factor, since blocking its beta receptors does not block the expression of either the behavior or the 2-DG response (Lin et al 1990). Alpha receptor activation may be involved in the expression of the behavior, however, as it is in other forms of neonatal learning (Saiers & Campbell 1990).

A fascinating aspect of this neurobehavioral response to the preferred odor is that it continues to elicit a response after weeks of virtually constant exposure. The function of the changes in the bulb and of the conditioned increase in norepinephrine may be to prevent habituation to the preferred odor and allow continued responsiveness to it throughout early life.

Early Auditory Preference Learning

HUMAN INFANTS   Just as they show early olfactory learning, human infants come to recognize the sound of their mother shortly after birth, and a portion of that learning may be accomplished prenatally. The human fetus develops a functional auditory system in utero (Pujol & Hilding 1973), and the uterine environment allows the effective transmission of maternal and external sounds to the fetus (Armitage et al 1980). The sound frequencies associated with the human voice appear to be transmitted particularly well within the uterine environment (Armitage et al 1980; Aslin et al 1983).

The sensitivity of newborn infants to sound may also be biased toward human speech (Hutt & Hutt 1970; Aslin et al 1983), and this bias may determine the infant preference for speech over nonspeech sounds (Eisenberg

1976). More important for our discussion is the observation that neonates develop an early preference for their mothers' voices (DeCasper & Fifer 1980). When 2–3 day-old infants were allowed to control the duration of the sound of their mothers' or a stranger's voice by sucking on a nonnutritive nipple, they increased their exposure to their mother's voice during the test period.

Mothers who read aloud the same story each day of the last six months of pregnancy gave birth to infants who preferred to listen to that passage over an unfamiliar one (DeCasper & Fifer 1980). These data lend credence to the notion that prenatal auditory experience alone can affect the preferences of newborns. It is again unclear whether familiarity or an associative response underlies the development of even the prenatal experience. For example, the fetus may be aroused and/or reinforced by the movement of the maternal muscles involved in speech production, allowing an association to be developed prenatally.

OTHER SPECIES   Much of the research on filial auditory learning has been done with young birds during a process called imprinting. Young birds will come to approach the sounds of their mothers (Gottlieb 1965). Guinea chicks also can learn to approach preferentially a nonmaternal sound after postnatal exposure (Fischer 1972).

The sound was presented initially to the young while the chicks were with their siblings in a nest in the presence of a stuffed hen. The pairing of the sound with the rewarding combined presence of mother-surrogate, siblings, and nest may have provoked an association that induced the subsequent preference for the sound. Continued response to the preferred sound could be maintained only when the stuffed hen was present in the arm of the Y maze from which the preferred sound emanated. The diminution of the auditory preference in the absence of maternal stimulation may reflect an extinction of the learned preference in the absence of maternal reinforcement. Chicks also learn to prefer a nonmaternal sound when it is paired with a mother surrogate in one arm of a Y maze (Maier & Scheich 1987). There is a sensitive period, ending on the fourth day of life, during which chicks can learn this auditory preference (Maier & Scheich 1983).

NEURAL CONSEQUENCES OF EARLY AUDITORY PREFERENCE LEARNING
To examine the neural correlates of early auditory learning, Maier & Scheich (1983) trained chicks with either a 1.8 kHz or a 2.5 kHz sound that was presented while the chicks were in the nest on the first day of life. The chicks were then tested repeatedly in the Y maze for their auditory preference in the following days. On the seventh day, the chicks were injected with

radiolabeled 2-DG and presented with the 1.8 kHz tone. The auditory cortex analogue in birds is field L, in which isolaminar stripes of 2-DG uptake are evoked by different sounds for single "best" frequencies at which there is a maximal neural response (Heil & Scheich 1986; Theurich et al 1984). The investigators found no difference in 2-DG uptake within the uptake focal stripes in this region or in other auditory regions in chicks with different early auditory experience.

While the auditory regions demonstrated no systematic differences after differential auditory experience, regions of the rostral forebrain did (Maier & Scheich 1983). The composite forebrain areas of chicks, referred to as the hyperstriatum accessorium (HAD), lateral neostriatum (LNH), and medial neostriatum/hyperstriatum ventrale (MNH), showed dense 2-DG uptake in response to the 1.8 kHz sound if the chick had learned to prefer it, had an intermediate response if it had been trained to prefer a 2.5 kHz sound (perhaps because the sounds shared a common rhythm), and had a relatively low response if the chick was naive with respect to the test sound. The change in auditory preference behavior precedes the development of the increased 2-DG uptake in these regions, as chicks trained for one day and then tested on the next preferred the sound but did not exhibit the change in 2-DG (Maier & Scheich 1987). This pattern of increased 2-DG labelling paralleled that observed in chicks when they were separated from their mother (Müller & Scheich 1986). The behavior of such chicks is similar to the aroused searching behavior observed when they are seeking out maternal or other preferred stimuli.

The development of the increased 2-DG response is somewhat delayed relative to the development of the auditory preference (Maier & Scheich 1987). Specifically, 2-day-old chicks approached the sound but did not have the increased 2-DG response, which did not develop fully until day 7, the end of the sensitive period. The sensitive period could be extended if the chicks were reared in isolation (Scheich 1987).

When chicks were separated from their mother and placed in the dark with just the sound of their siblings, the high 2-DG uptake in HAD and LNH was much reduced, relative to controls, while the MNH continued to have a high 2-DG uptake (Scheich 1987). These data suggest that the MNH is particularly sensitive to species-typical auditory preferences, or that the other two areas had reduced activity, perhaps owing to the calming influence of the familiar sounds. However, blindfolding one eye in the presence of the sounds reduced activity in HAD and LNH in just the side to which its connections projected. HAD and LNH are therefore likely to be involved in visual aspects of early preference learning and are stimulated in tandem with the auditory areas of the brain.

Deafening of the birds, however, did not decrease the activity of MNH (Scheich 1987), suggesting that this area may not be activated solely by auditory cues but may also receive input from regions aroused in the absence of the mother. That auditory cues do affect this area was shown by the presence of neurons highly tuned to specific frequencies in MNH (Scheich 1987). Lesions of this area after early auditory preference formation blocked the expression of the preference for the familiar sound (Scheich 1987).

The increase in 2-DG uptake may be due to an increase in the number, activity, or size of the cells. However, a Golgi analysis of this region in isolated chicks trained to prefer a sound indicated a large decrease in the number of dendritic spines in one of the neural populations in MNH (Wallhäusser & Scheich 1987). Since the dendritic spines are the site of synaptic contacts on such cells, these data suggest that a decrease in synaptic density occurs in this region after early auditory preference learning. While these data do not account for the increase in 2-DG, they indicate that early auditory learning may select a subpopulation of synapses to survive during the postnatal period. This differential cell survival may form the basis for the development of a unique organization for the MNH as a consequence of early learning.

Early Visual Preference Learning

HUMAN INFANTS   Infants can learn to prefer the faces of their mothers to those of strangers when they are presented either live (Carpenter 1974; Masi & Scott 1983; Field et al 1984) or in a photograph (Barrera & Maurer 1981). This preference is present by the second day of life (Field et al 1984) and is also present after one (Barrera & Maurer 1981) and two months of age (Masi & Scott 1983). In the cases cited here, however, the visual information about the mother was accompanied by either her voice (Carpenter 1974; Masi & Scott 1983) or odor (Field et al 1984). Since infants learn to prefer both auditory and olfactory aspects of their mothers, there is no convincing evidence that young infants learn to prefer the sight of their mothers.

OTHER SPECIES   Studies of early preferences for visual cues have largely focused on the ability of members of avian species to learn to prefer their mothers or nonmaternal objects. The mobile young of a number of avian species begin to approach and follow their mothers shortly after hatching (Sluckin 1972). These birds also will come to approach a stuffed adult or a nonmaternal object (Sluckin 1972).

NEURAL CONSEQUENCES OF EARLY VISUAL PREFERENCE LEARNING   To examine the neural consequences of early visual learning, Kohsaka et al

(1979) exposed domestic chicks that had been kept in the dark after hatching to a moving red balloon for 45 min on each of the first three days of life. On the following day, the chicks were exposed to the balloon after injection of radiolabeled 2-DG. Compared to those of controls, the brains of these chicks exhibited increased 2-DG uptake in the medial hyperstriatum ventrale (MHV) and the lateral neostriatum. Early visual preference learning also increases the incorporation of radiolabeled lysine into protein and radiolabeled uracil into ribonucleic acid within a similar region of the brain, referred to as the intermediate portion of the medial hyperstriatum ventrale (IMHV; Bateson et al 1969, 1972; Horn et al 1979). The strength of the approach response to the preferred stimulus is correlated with the level of neural uracil incorporation in the IMHV (Bateson et al 1972). This region overlaps with the brain area of guinea fowl chicks that increases 2-DG uptake after early auditory learning (Maier & Scheich 1983).

Lesions of the IMHV block the development and the expression of learned visual preferences in chicks, while their sensorimotor functions remain intact (McCabe et al 1981, 1982; Takamatsu & Tsukada 1985). This region therefore appears to serve a critical role in this type of learning.

Accompanying these changes in cellular activity are changes in the synaptic makeup of the IMHV. Specifically, postsynaptic densities in the left brain hemisphere are longer in trained chicks than in undertrained or dark-reared controls (Horn et al 1985). An increase in the density of N-methyl-D-aspartate receptors in the IMHV of chicks also emerges about 8.5 hr after training (Horn 1990; McCabe & Horn 1988). A positive correlation was found between the strength of the visual preference and receptor density.

Summary

Early filial learning evokes clear neural changes in the developing brain. Anatomy and function in the developing olfactory, auditory, and visual systems change following early learning. Since this type of learning seems critical for the survival of the young, the mechanisms of such plasticity should be clear and reliable. In each sensory modality examined, both distinct changes in the brain and the reliable nature of learning through early experience have become evident with experimental analysis.

ACKNOWLEDGMENTS

This chapter has been prepared with support from grants MH45353 from NIMH, HD24236 from NICHD, and a grant from the Pew Charitable Trusts. M. L. holds Research Scientist Development Award 00371.

Literature Cited

Alberts, J. R., May, B. 1984. Nonnutritive, thermotactile induction of filial huddling in rat pups. *Dev. Psychobiol.* 17:161–81

Amsel, A., Burdette, D. R., Letz, R. 1976. Appetitive learning, patterned alteration and extinction in 10-day-old rats with non-lactating suckling as reward. *Nature* 262:816–18

Armitage, S. E., Baldwin, B. A., Vince, M. A. 1980. Fetal response to extrauterine sounds in sleep. *Science* 208:1173–74

Aslin, R. N., Pisoni, D. B., Jusczyk, P. W. 1983. Auditory development and speech perception in infancy. In *Carmichael's Manual of Child Psychology. 2. Infancy and the Biology of Development*, ed. P. Mussen pp. 573–687. New York: Wiley. 4th ed.

Balogh, R. D., Porter, R. H. 1986. Olfactory preference resulting from mere exposure in human neonates. *Infant Behav. Dev.* 9:395–401

Barnett, C. 1977. Chemical recognition of the mother by the young of the cichlid fish, *Cichlasoma citrinellum*. *J. Chem. Ecol.* 3:463–68

Barrera, M. E., Maurer, D. 1981. Recognition of mother's photographed face by the three-month-old infant. *Infant Behav. Dev.* 52:714–18

Bateson, P. P. G., Horn, G., Rose, S. P. R. 1969. The effects of an imprinting procedure on regional incorporation of tritiated lysine into protein of chick brain. *Nature* 223:534–35

Bateson, P. P. G., Horn, G., Rose, S. P. R. 1972. Effects of early experience on regional incorporation of precursors into RNA and protein in the chick brain. *Brain Res.* 39:449–65

Bear, M. F., Singer, W. 1986. Modulation of visual cortical plasticity by acetylcholine and noradrenaline. *Nature* 320:172–76

Bouthenet, M. L., Martres, M. P., Sales, N., Schwartz, J. C. 1987. A detailed mapping of dopamine D-2 receptors in rat central nervous system by autoradiography with U21 25IIodosulpride. *Neuroscience* 20:117–55

Brake, S. C. 1981. Suckling infant rats learn a preference for a novel olfactory stimulus paired with milk delivery. *Science* 211:506–8

Breen, M. F., Leshner, A. I. 1977. Maternal pheromone: a demonstration of its existence in the mouse (*Mus musculus*). *Physiol. Behav.* 18:527–29

Carmi, O., Leon, M. Neurobehavioral responses of neonatal rats to previously experienced odors of different concentrations. *Dev. Brain Res.* In press

Carpenter, G. 1974. Mother's face and the newborn. *New Sci.* 61:742–44

Carter, C. S. 1972. Effects of olfactory experience on the behavior of the guinea pig (*Cavia porcellus*). *Anim. Behav.* 20:54–60

Caza, P. A., Spear, N. E. 1984. Short-term exposure to an odor increases its subsequent preference in preweanling rats: a descriptive profile of the phenomenon. *Dev. Psychobiol.* 17:407–22

Cernoch, J. M., Porter, R. H. 1985. Recognition of maternal auxillary odors by infants. *Child Dev.* 56:1593–98

Coopersmith, R., Henderson, S. R., Leon, M. 1986. Odor specificity of the enhanced neural response following early odor experience in rats. *Devel. Brain Res.* 27:191–97

Coopersmith, R., Leon, M. 1984. Enhanced neural response to familiar olfactory cues. *Science* 225:849–51

Coopersmith, R., Leon, M. 1986. Enhanced neural response by adult rats to odors experienced early in life. *Brain Res.* 371:400–3

Coopersmith, R., Weihmuller, F., Kirstein, C. L., Marshall, J. F., Leon, M. 1991. Extracellular dopamine increases in the neonatal olfactory bulb during odor preference training. *Brain Res.* In press

Coopersmith, R., Weihmuller, F., Marshall, J., Leon, M. 1990. Odor and tactile stimulation each increase olfactory bulb catecholamine release in rat pups. *Soc. Neurosci. Abstr.* 16:102

Cornwell, C. A. 1976. Selective olfactory exposure alters social and plant odor preferences of immature hamsters. *Behav. Biol.* 17:131–37

Davis, B. J., Macrides, F. 1983. Tyrosine hydroxylase-immunoreactive neurons and fibers in the olfactory system of the hamster. *J. Comp. Neurol.* 214:427–40

DeCasper, A. J., Fifer, W. P. 1980. Of human bonding: Newborns prefer their mothers' voices. *Science* 208:1174–76

Devor, M., Schneider, G. E. 1974. Attraction to home-cage odor in hamster pups: specificity and changes with age. *Behav. Biol.* 10:211–21

Do, J. T., Sullivan, R. M., Leon, M. 1988. Behavioral and neural correlates of postnatal olfactory conditioning. II. Respiration during conditioning. *Dev. Psychobiol.* 21:591–600

Eisenberg, R. B., ed. 1976. *Auditory Competence in Early Life: The Roots of Communicative Behavior*. Baltimore: University Park Press

Engen, T., Lipsitt, L. P., Kaye, H. 1963.

Olfactory responses and adaptation in the human neonate. *J. Physiol. Psychol.* 56:73–77

Field, T. M., Cohen, D., Garcia, R., Greenberg, R. 1984. Mother-stranger face discrimination by the newborn. *Infant Behav. Dev.* 7:19–25

Fillion, T. J., Blass, E. M. 1986. Infantile experience with suckling odors determines sexual behavior in male rats. *Science* 231:729–31

Fischer, G. J. 1972. Sound stimuli and following in the domestic fowl. *J. Comp. Physiol. Psychol.* 81:183–90

Frazier-Cierpial, L., Hall, W. G. 1989. Changes in neural activity after unilateral odor preference conditioning in 6-day-old rats. *Assoc. Chemorecept. Sci. Abstr.* 11, 50

Friedman, B., Price, J. L. 1984. Fiber systems in the olfactory bulb and cortex: a study in adult and developing rats, using the Timm method with the light and electron microscope. *J. Comp. Neurol.* 223:88–109

Gall, C. M., Hendry, S. H. C., Seroogy, K. B., Jones, E. G., Haycock, J. W. 1987. Evidence for coexistence of GABA and dopamine in neurons of the rat olfactory bulb. *J. Comp. Neurol.* 266:307–18

Getchell, T. V., Shepherd, G. M. 1975. Short-axon cells in the olfactory bulb: dendrodendritic synaptic interactions. *J. Physiol.* 251:523–48

Gordon, E., Allen, E. E., Trombley, P. Q. 1988. The role of norepinephrine in plasticity of visual cortex. *Prog. Neurobiol.* 30:171–91

Gottlieb, G. 1965. Imprinting in relation to parental and species identification by avian neonates. *J. Comp. Physiol. Psychol.* 59: 345–56

Greer, C. A., Stewart, W. B., Teicher, M. H., Shepherd, G. M. 1982. Functional development of the olfactory bulb and a unique glomerular complex in the neonatal rat. *J. Neurosci.* 2:1744–59

Guthrie, K. M., Pullara, J. M., Marshall, J. F., Leon, M. 1991. Olfactory deprivation increases dopamine D2 receptor density in the rat olfactory bulb. *Synapse* 8:61–70

Halasz, N., Johansson, O., Hokfelt, T., Ljungdahl, A., Goldstein, M. 1981. Immunohistochemical identification of two types of dopamine neuron in the rat olfactory bulb as seen by serial sectioning. *J. Neurocytol.* 10:251–59

Hall, W. G. 1987. Early motivation, reward, learning and their neural bases: developmental revelations and simplifications. In *Perinatal Development: A Psychological Approach,* ed. N. A. Krasnegor, E. M. Blass, M. A. Hofer, W. P. Smotherman, pp. 169–93. New York: Academic

Heil, P., Scheich, H. 1986. Effects of unilateral and bilateral cochlea removal on 2-deoxyglucose patterns in the chick auditory system. *J. Comp. Neurol.* 252:279–301

Horn, G. 1990. Neural bases of recognition memory investigated through an analysis of imprinting. *Philos. Trans. R. Soc. London Ser. B* 329:133–42

Horn, G., Bradley, P., McCabe, B. J. 1985. Changes in the structure of synapses associated with learning. *J. Neurosci.* 5:3161–68

Horn, G., Mc Cabe, B. J., Bateson, P. P. G. 1979. An autoradiographic study of the chick brain after imprinting. *Brain Res.* 168:361–73

Hutt, S. J., Hutt, C., 1970. *Direct Observation and Measurement of Behavior.* Springfield, IL: Thomas

Janus, C. 1989. The development of olfactory preferences for artificial odors briefly experienced by the precocial spiny mouse young. *Behav. Neural Biol.* 52:430–36

Johanson, I. B., Hall, W. G. 1979. Appetitive learning in 1-day-old rat pups. *Science* 205:419–21

Johanson, I. B., Hall, W. G. 1982. Appetitive conditioning in neonatal rats: conditioned orientation to a novel odor. *Dev. Psychobiol.* 15:379–97

Johanson, I. B., Poleferone, J. M., Hall, W. G. 1984. Appetitive conditioning in neonatal rats: conditioned ingestive responding to stimuli paired with oral infusions of milk. *Dev. Psychobiol.* 17:357–81

Johanson, I. B., Teicher, M. 1980. Classical conditioning of an odor preference in 3-day-old rats. *Behav. Neural Biol.* 29:132–36

Kaplan, J. N., Cubicciotti D. D. III. 1980. Early perceptual experience and social preferences in squirrel monkey. In *Maternal Influences and Early Behavior,* ed. W. P. Smotherman, R. W. Bell, pp. 253–70. New York: Spectrum Publication

Kasamatsu, T., Pettigrew, J. D. 1979. Preservation of binocularity after monocular deprivation in the striate cortex of kittens treated with 6-hydroxydopamine. *J. Comp. Physiol. Psychol.* 93:752–50

Kenny, J. T., Blass, E. M. 1977. Suckling as incentive to instrumental learning in preweanling rats. *Science* 196:898–99

Kosaka, S., Takamatsu, K., Aoki, E., Tsukada, Y. 1979. Metabolic mapping of chick brain after imprinting using $^{14}C_2$-deoxyglucose technique. *Brain Res.* 172:539–44

Kucharski, D. A., Hall, W. G. 1988. Developmental changes in the access to olfactory memories. *Behav. Neurosci.* 102:340–48

Kucharski, D., Hall, W. G. 1987. New routes to old memories. *Science* 238:786–88

Leon, M. 1974. Maternal pheromone. *Physiol. Behav.* 13:441–53

Leon, M. 1975. Dietary control of maternal pheromone in the lactating rat. *Physiol. Behav.* 8:683–86

Leon, M., Coopersmith, R., Beasley, L. J., Sullivan, R. M. 1990. Thermal aspects of parenting. In *Mammalian Parenting*, ed. N. A. Krasnegor, R. S. Bridges, pp. 400–415. New York: Oxford Univ. Press

Leon, M., Coopersmith, R., Ulibarri, C., Porter, R. H., Powers, J. B. 1984. Development of olfactory bulb organization in precocial and altricial rodents. *Dev. Brain Res.* 12:45–53

Leon, M., Galef, B. G., Behse, J. H. 1977. Establishment of pheromonal bonds and diet choice in young rats by odor pre-exposure. *Physiol. Behav.* 18:387–91

Lin, W., Wilson, D. A., Sullivan, R. M. 1990. Olfactory bulb norepinephrine may be required for early olfactory learning. *Soc. Neurosci. Abstr.* 16:1236

Little, E. E. 975. Chemical communication in maternal behavior of crayfish. *Nature* 255:400–1

Loeb, E. R., Chang, F. L. F., Greenough, W. 1986. Effects of neonatal 6-hydroxydopamine treatment on morphological organization in the posteromedial barrel subfield in the mouse somatosensory cortex. *Brain Res.* 403:113–20

Macfarlane, A. J. 1975. Olfaction in the development of social preferences in the human neonate. *Ciba Found. Symp.* 33:103–17

Maier, V., Scheich, H. 1983. Acoustic imprinting leads to differential 2-deoxy-D-glucose uptake in the chick forebrain. *Proc. Natl. Acad. Sci. USA* 80:3860–64

Maier, V., Scheich, H. 1987. Acoustic imprinting in Guinea fowl chicks: age dependence of 14-C-deoxyglucose uptake of relevant forebrain areas. *Dev. Brain Res.* 31:15–28

Mainardi, D., Marsan, M., Pasquali, A. 1965. Causation of sexual preferences of the house mouse. The behaviour of mice reared by parents whose odour was artificially altered. *Attiv. Soc. Ital. Sci. Nat. Mus. Civ. Storia Nat.* 104:325–38

Masi, W., Scott, K. 1983. Preterm and full-term infant's visual responses. In *Infants Born at Risk: Physiological, Perceptual and Cognitive Processes*, ed. T. F. Sostek, A. Sostek, pp. 173–79. New York: Grune and Stratton

McCabe, B. J., Cipolla-Neto, J., Horn, G., Bateson, P. 1982. Amnesic effects of bilateral lesions in the hyperstriatum ventrale of the chick after imprinting. *Exp. Brain Res.* 48:13–21

McCabe, B. J., Horn, G. 1988. Learning and memory: regional changes in N-methyl-D-aspartate receptors in the chick brain after imprinting. *Proc. Natl. Acad. Sci. USA* 85:2849–53

McCabe, B. J., Horn, G., Bateson, P. P. G. 1981. Effects of restricted lesions of the chick forebrain on the acquisition of filial preferences during imprinting. *Brain Res.* 205:29–37

McLean, J. H., Shipley, M. T. 1991. Postnatal development of the noradrenergic projection from locus coeruleus to the olfactory bulb in the rat. *J. Comp. Neurol.* 304:467–77

Moran, T. H., Lew, M. F., Blass, E. M. 1981. Intracranial self stimulation in 3 day old rats. *Science* 214:1366–68

Moran, T. H., Schwartz, G. J., Blass, E. M. 1983. Organized behavioral responses to lateral hypothalamic electrical stimulation in infant rats. *J. Neurosci.* 3:10–19

Müller, S. C., Scheich, H. 1986. Social stress increases 14-C-2-deoxyglucose incorporation in three rostral forebrain areas of the young chick. *Behav. Brain Res.* 19:93–98

Müller-Schwarze, D., Müller-Schwarze, C. 1971. Olfactory imprinting in a precocial mammal. *Nature* 229:55–56

Nakamura, S., Kimuar, F., Sakaguchi, T. 1987. Postnatal development of electrical activity in the locus coeruleus. *J. Neurophysiol.* 58:510–24

Pedersen, P. E., Blass, E. M. 1982. Prenatal and postnatal determinants of the first suckling episode in albino rats. *Dev. Psychobiol.* 15:349–56

Pedersen, P. E., Greer, C. A., Stewart, W. B., Shepherd, G. M. 1982. A 2DG study of behavioral plasticity in odor dependent suckling. *Assoc. Chemorecept. Sci. Abstr.* 22

Pedersen, P. E., Stewart, W. B., Greer, C. A., Shepherd, G. M. 1983. Evidence for olfactory function in utero. *Science* 221:478–80

Pettijohn, T. F. 1979. Social attachment of the infant guinea pig to its parents in a two-choice situation. *Anim. Learn. Behav.* 7(2):263–66

Porter, R. H., Etscorn, F. 1976. A sensitive period for the development of olfactory preference in *Acomys cahirinus*. *Physiol. Behav.* 17:127–30

Porter, R. H., Ruttle, K. 1975. The responses of one-day-old *Acomys cahirinus* pups to naturally occurring chemical stimuli. *Z. Tierpsychol.* 38:154–62

Pujol, R., Hilding, D. 1973. Anatomy and physiology of the onset of auditory function. *Acta Oto-Laryngol.* 76:1–10

Redican, W. K., Kaplan, J. N. 1978. Effects of synthetic odors in filial attachment in infant squirrel monkeys. *Physiol. Behav.* 320:79–85

Rosselli-Austin, L., Williams, J. 1990. Enriched neonatal odor exposure leads to increased numbers of olfactory bulb mitral and granule cells. *Dev. Brain Res.* 51:135–37

Russell, M. J. 1976. Human olfactory communication. *Nature* 260:520–22

Saiers, J. A., Campbell, B. A. 1990. Disruption of noradrenergic, but not serotonergic or opiate, functioning blocks both cardiac and behavioral components of the orienting response in preweanling rats. *Behav. Neur. Biol.* 54:254–70

Schaal, B., Montagner, H., Hertling, E., Bolzoni, D., Moyse, A., et al. 1980. Les stimulations olfactives dans les relation entre l'enfant et lat mére. *Reprod. Nutr. Dév.* 20:843–58

Scheich, H. 1987. Neural correlates of auditory filial imprinting. *J. Comp. Physiol. A.* 161:605–19

Schleidt, M., Genzel, C. 1990. The significance of mother's perfume for infants in their first weeks of life. *Ethol. Sociobiol.* 11:145–54

Shipley, M. T., Halloran, F. J., De la Torre, J. 1985. Surprisingly rich projection from locus coeruleus to the olfactory bulb in the rat. *Brain Res.* 329:294–99

Singh, P. J., Tucker, A. M., Hofer, M. A. 1976. Effects of nasal ZnSO₄ irrigation and olfactory bulbectomy on rat pups. *Physiol. Behav.* 17:373–82

Sluckin, W. 1972. *Imprinting and Early Learning.* London: Methuen

Smotherman, W. P. 1982. Odor aversion learning by the rat fetus. *Physiol. Behav.* 29:769–71

Sullivan, R. M. 1990. Newborn human infants exhibit CR's to an odor previously paired with either breast or bottle feeding. *Int. Soc. Dev. Psychobiol. Abstr.*

Sullivan, R. M., Hall, W. G. 1988. Reinforcers in infancy: classical conditioning using stroking or intraoral infusions of milk as a UCS. *Dev. Psychobiol.* 21:215–23

Sullivan, R. M., Hofer, M. A., Brake, S. C. 1986. Olfactory-guided orientation in neonatal rats is enhanced by a conditioned change in behavioral state. *Dev. Psychobiol.* 19:615–23

Sullivan, R. M., Leon, M. 1986. Early olfactory learning induces an enhanced olfactory bulb response in young rats. *Dev. Brain Res.* 27:278–82

Sullivan, R. M., Leon, M. 1987. One-trial olfactory learning enhances olfactory bulb responses to an appetitive conditioned odor in 7-day-old rats. *Dev. Brain Res.* 35:301–11

Sullivan, R. M., McGaugh, J., Leon, M. 1991a. Norepinephrine induced plasticity and one-trial olfactory learning in neonatal rats. *Dev. Brain Res.* 60:219–28

Sullivan, R. M., Taborsky-Barbar, S., Mendoza, R., Itino, A., Leon, M., et al. 1991b. Olfactory classical conditioning in neonates. *Pediatrics* 87:511–18

Sullivan, R. M., Wilson, D. A. 1990. Plasticity in the reinforcement system of infant rats. *Soc. Neurosci. Abstr.* 16:917

Sullivan, R. M., Wilson, D. A. 1991. Neural correlates of conditioned odor avoidance in infant rats. *Behav. Neurosci.* 105:307–12

Sullivan, R. M., Wilson, D. A., Leon, M. 1989a. Associative processes in early olfactory preference acquisition: neural and behavioral consequences. *Psychobiology* 17:29–33

Sullivan, R. M., Wilson, D. A., Leon, M. 1989b. Norepinephrine and learning-induced plasticity in infant rat olfactory system. *J. Neurosci.* 9:3998–4006

Sullivan, R. M., Wilson, D. A., Wong, R., Correa, A., Leon, M. 1990. Modified behavioral and olfactory responses to maternal odors in preweanling rats. *Dev. Brain Res.* 53:243–47

Sullivan, R. M., Wilson, D., Kim, M.-H., Leon, M. 1988. Behavioral and neural correlates of postnatal olfactory conditioning. I. Effect of respiration on conditioned neural responses. *Physiol. Behav.* 44:85–90

Takamatsu, K., Tsukada, Y. 1985. Neurobiological basis of imprinting in chick and duckling. In *Perspectives on Neuroscience from Molecule to Mind,* ed. Y. Tsukada, pp. 187–206. Berlin: Springer-Verlag

Teicher, M. H., Blass, E. M. 1976. Suckling in newborn rats: eliminated by nipple lavage, reinstated by pup saliva. *Science* 193:422–25

Teicher, M. H., Blass, E. M. 1977. First suckling response of the newborn albino rat: the roles of olfaction and amniotic fluid. *Science* 198:635–36

Teicher, M. H., Stewart, W. B., Kauer, J. S., Shepherd, G. M. 1980. Suckling pheromone stimulation of a modified glomerular region in the developing rat olfactory bulb revealed by the 2-deoxyglucose method. *Brain Res.* 194:530–35

Theurich, M., Müller, C. M., Scheich, H. 1984. 2-deoxyglucose accumulation parallels extracellularly recorded spike activity in the avian auditory neostriatum. *Brain Res.* 322:157–61

Vince, M. A., Ward, T. M. 1984. The responsiveness of newly born clun forest lambs to odour sources in the ewe. *Behavior* 89–1/2:117–27

Wallhäuβer, E., Scheich, H. 1987. Auditory

imprinting leads to differential 2-deoxyglu-cose uptake and dendritic spine loss in the chick rostral forebrain. *Dev Brain Res.* 31:29–44

Wamsley, J. K., Gehlert, D. R., Filloux, F. M., Dawson, T. M. 1989. Comparison of the distribution of D-1 and D-2 dopamine receptors in the rat brain. *J. Chem. Neuroanat.* 2:119–37

Weldon, D. A., Travis, M. L., Kennedy, D. A. 1991. Posttraining D1 receptor blockade impairs odor conditioning in neonatal rats. *Behav. Neurosci.* 105:450–58

Weldon, D. A., Wool, R. S., Teicher, M. H., Shaywitz, B. A., Cohen, D. J. et al. 1982. Effects of apomorphine on appetitve conditioning in 6-hydroxydopamine-treated rat pups. *Pharmacol. Biochem. Behav.* 17:1281–84

Wilson, D. A., Leon, M. 1988. Spatial patterns of olfactory bulb single-unit responses to learned olfactory cues in young rats. *J. Neurophysiol.* 59:1770–82

Wilson, D. A., Sullivan, R. M. 1990. Olfactory associative conditioning in infant rats with brain stimulation as reward. I. Neurobehavioral consequences. *Devel. Brain Res.* 53:215–21

Wilson, D. A., Sullivan, R. M., Leon, M. 1985. Odor familiarity alters mitral cell response in the olfactory bulb of neonatal rats. *Dev. Brain Res.* 22:314–17

Wilson, D. A., Sullivan, R. M., Leon, M. 1987. Single unit analysis of postnatal learning: modified olfactory bulb output response patterns to learned attractive odors. *J. Neurosci.* 7:3154–62

Woo, C. C., Coopersmith, R., Leon, M. 1987. Localized changes in olfactory bulb morphology associated with early olfactory learning. *J. Comp. Neurol.* 263:113–25

Woo, C. C., Leon, M. 1987. Sensitive period for neural and behavioral response development to learned odors. *Dev. Brain Res.* 36:309–13

Woo, C. C., Leon, M. 1991 Increase in a focal population of juxtaglomerular cells in the olfactory bulb associated with early learning. *J. Comp. Neurol.* 305:49–56

Wool, R. S., Weldon, D. A., Shaywitz, B. A., Anderson, G. M., Cohen, D. J. et al. 1987. Amphetamine reverses learning deficits in 6-hydroxydopamine-treated rat pups. *Dev. Psychobiol.* 20:219–23

Yahr, P., Anderson-Mitchell, K. 1983. Attraction of gerbil pups to maternal nest odors: duration, specificity and ovarian control. *Physiol. Behav.* 32:241–47

Annu. Rev. Psychol. 1992. 43:399–441

TRAINING AND DEVELOPMENT IN WORK ORGANIZATIONS

Scott I. Tannenbaum and Gary Yukl

Management Department, State University of New York at Albany, Albany, New York 12222

KEY WORDS: management development, training design, training evaluation, simulation, team training

CONTENTS

0066-4308/92/0201-0399$02.00

INTRODUCTION

This is the fourth review of training and development to appear in the *Annual Review of Psychology*. The earlier reviews were by Campbell (1971), Goldstein (1980), Wexley (1984), and Latham (1988). Our review focuses on the scientific literature on training and development in an organizational context during the years from 1987 through February, 1991. We describe current practices and emerging trends in training in work organizations. We describe continuing trends and prevailing approaches but pay special attention to new concepts and methods. Our review is selective rather than comprehensive. We do not attempt to review literature on some of the subjects emphasized four years ago by Latham (1988), including the historical background of training, training in other cultures, training of raters, and leadership training. We focus on training design, selected training methods, trainee characteristics, the pretraining and posttraining environments, and to a lessor extent, on training needs analysis and evaluation. Recent developments that receive special attention include cognitive learning theories, high technology training methods, team training, and on-the-job managerial development.

Following Latham's (1988) example, we do not attempt to make a systematic review of the voluminous literature in practitioner-oriented publications. Nor do we review the literature on related but distinct subjects such as organizational development, socialization in organizations, motivational interventions to change behavior, and training administration. Literature in instructional psychology, management education, and motor skill training is cited when especially relevant, but we do not examine the literature in those related disciplines in detail.

Our review is primarily descriptive regarding current training theory and research, but it is prescriptive regarding future training research. Whenever appropriate, we identify research gaps and highlight issues that need more research or a different research orientation.

TRAINING NEEDS ANALYSIS

The importance of conducting a thorough needs analysis is well accepted in the training literature. A properly conducted needs analysis yields information helpful to the development of instructional objectives and training criteria. Unfortunately, only 27% of companies surveyed by Saari et al (1988) reported having procedures for determining the training and educational needs of their managers. A thorough description of training needs–assessment methodology can be found in Goldstein et al (1991). Only a limited amount of empirical work on training needs analysis has appeared in the last several years, although research in job analysis (e.g. Cranny & Doherty 1988) and performance assessment (e.g. Sackett et al 1988) has implications for assessing training needs. The most prevalent framework for considering training needs continues to be McGehee & Thayer's (1961) categorization of organizational, task, and person analysis. In a conceptual development, Ostroff & Ford (1989) suggested extending McGehee & Thayer's framework to incorporate different levels of analysis explicitly. Their extension provides ideas to guide future research, but for purposes of summarizing the recent research on training needs analysis we rely on McGehee & Thayer's original categorization.

Organizational Analysis

The original purpose of organizational analysis as described by McGehee & Thayer (1961) was to provide information about where and when training was needed in an organization. Over the last several years, organizational analysis has been reconceptualized as an examination of systemwide components that determine whether a training program can yield behavior change back on the job (Goldstein 1991). Along these lines, Rouillier & Goldstein (1991) have conducted research on assessing an organization's or unit's transfer climate. Their work is discussed in the section below on the posttraining environment.

One recurring theme, particularly in the practitioner literature, is the need to link training and organizational strategy (see Sonnenfeld & Peiperl 1988; Schuler & Jackson 1987). Training courses should support the strategic direction of the organization, and training objectives should be aligned with organizational goals. For example, an organization undergoing downsizing should have a different training and development focus than an organization actively involved in geographic expansion, product development, or quality enhancement (see London 1987). The American Society for Training and Development (ASTD) and the Work in America Institute completed projects that examined the link between training and company strategy in many organizations. Examples and case descriptions can be found in Carnevale et al (1990b), Casner-Lotto and Associates (1989), and Rosow & Zager (1988).

As more organizations assume global strategies and operate in international arenas, the need for effective cross-cultural development continues to grow (Ronen 1989; Tung 1988; Von Glinow & Milliman 1990). Research has shown that employees who receive overseas assignments often return prematurely or show low levels of effectiveness (e.g. Black 1988). However, the use of cross-cultural training and development in US organizations has been limited (Finney & Von Glinow 1988; Tung 1988). Black & Mendenhall (1990) reviewed the empirical research on cross-cultural training and concluded that it can be effective in developing skills, facilitating cross-cultural adjustment, and enhancing job performance. Noting that most of the previous research has lacked theoretical grounding, they presented a framework based on social learning theory to guide future research efforts.

Task Analysis

A task analysis identifies the nature of the tasks to be performed on the job and the knowledge, skills, and abilities (KSAs) needed to perform these tasks. Increasingly rapid technological changes can modify task requirements, which in turn can influence knowledge, skill, and ability requirements. Staying ahead of the technology curve can be difficult. Schneider & Konz (1989) described a procedure for anticipating future training needs by having subject matter experts project how the job will change and how KSA requirements will be affected. Campbell (1988) suggested collecting hypothetical critical incidents that might be expected under future conditions. He noted that this approach would require judges to express desired and undesired performance in concrete terms. While the logic behind future-oriented job analysis is clear, its applicability and usefulness are still untested.

Rapid changes in job requirements are increasing the importance of cross-job retraining. Lance and his associates (e.g. Lance et al 1991) examined methods for estimating cross-job retraining times for different tasks. Mumford et al (1987) examined the validity of a measure of occupational learning difficulty. Sparrow (1989) reported on the use of a measure of Position Analysis Questionnaire (PAQ) profile similarity to predict the transfer of learning across jobs. Each of these methods is designed to facilitate planning by assessing how easily employees can be trained to assume new responsibilities.

Howell & Cooke (1989:123) noted that work requirements at all levels are becoming cognitively more demanding. "What were once highly structured tasks may now call for inference, diagnosis, judgment, and decision-making." Howell & Cooke called for an expanded view of task analysis to include an examination of the cognitive processing and learning requirements necessary to perform job tasks. Some authors have even suggested that the Instructional System Development (ISD) methodology so prevalent in the military should be modified to reflect what is known about changing cognitive demands (Ryder et al 1987).

Campbell (1988) emphasized the need for a better understanding of what is meant by competent or expert performance. Identifying differences in the way experts and novices approach a task and process information could yield insights valuable in determining what to include in training and how it should be presented (Kraiger 1988). The most common methods used in the cognitive psychology and artificial intelligence literatures for eliciting this information from experts are the analysis of "think-aloud" verbal protocols and psychometric scaling techniques (e.g. Cooke & Schvaneveldt 1988). Green & Gilhooly (1990) studied how novices learned to use a statistical software package. They used verbal protocols to identify differences in learning strategies employed by fast and slow learners. A group trained to use the "effective" learning strategy performed better and retained more information than an alternate training group or a control group. The application and translation of cognitive-task analysis concepts for training purposes are not as well developed as traditional methods. However, this approach holds great promise as a supplemental tool for training analysts.

Person Analysis

Person analysis focuses on identifying who should be trained and what training is needed by an individual. Inadequate person analysis can result in training targeted to an inappropriate level or to the wrong people. Ford & Noe (1987) studied self-assessed training needs and found small but significant differences for managers with different job levels, functions, and attitudes towards the utility of training. Lower-level managers reported higher needs for administrative skills than did middle managers. Managers who perceived training to be worthwhile reported greater need for training in quality-control skills.

The training needs of older employees have received more attention lately. Sterns & Doverspike (1988, 1989) reviewed the literature on training and retraining of older employees. They identified some of the factors that seem to result in better performance for older individuals and suggested areas for further research. Similarly, London & Bassman (1989) examined the retraining of midcareer workers, including those experiencing career plateauing, midlife crisis, and job loss.

New employees also have unique training needs, and formal training programs for new employees often fail to present material at the appropriate level of difficulty and job specificity (Feldman 1988). When the diagnosis of recruits' strengths and weaknesses is inadequate, many organizations will provide training at the lowest common denominator, resulting in suboptimization of training effectiveness (Feldman 1989).

Finally, in addition to determining who needs training, person analysis can be used to assess whether employees have the prerequisite attitude, knowledge, and motivation to benefit from training. Individuals who lack basic skills or motivation prior to training are less likely to succeed and may require remedial preparation prior to entering a specific training program.

DESIGN OF TRAINING

After the training needs analysis is complete and training objectives have been identified, the next step is to determine how training will be accomplished. Design of training should take into account learning objectives, trainee characteristics, current knowledge about learning processes, and practical considerations such as constraints and costs in relation to benefits.

In a comprehensive review of the organizational training literature, Bald-

win & Ford (1988) found that much of the research on learning principles
(e.g. identical elements, stimulus variability, conditions of practice) was done
with college students on short-term memory tasks and simple motor tasks. As
a result, these learning principles have limited utility for designing training to
develop the complex skills required in most organization jobs. Likewise,
Campbell (1988) concluded that the current state of the art regarding training
principles does not provide precise guidelines for design of training. However, he noted that even the consistent use of the guidelines we already have
would contribute significantly to training effectiveness. The following guidelines appear most useful:

1. The instructional events that comprise the training method should be
consistent with the cognitive, physical, or psychomotor processes that lead to
mastery. For example, the training method should guide the learner to the
most appropriate encoding operations for storing information in memory.

2. The learner should be induced to produce the capability actively (e.g.
practice behaviors, recall information from memory, apply principles in doing
a task). The more active the production the greater the retention and transfer
(e.g. restating or applying principles rather than just recalling them, adapting
behavior to varying situations rather than just imitating it repeatedly in the
same situation.)

3. All available sources of relevant feedback should be used, and feedback
should be accurate, credible, timely, and constructive.

4. The instructional processes should enhance trainee self-efficacy and
trainee expectations that the training will be successful and will lead to valued
outcomes. For example, training should begin with simple behaviors that can
be mastered easily, then progress to more complex behaviors as trainees
become more confident.

5. Training methods should be adapted to differences in trainee aptitudes
and prior knowledge.

Our knowledge about training design has been advanced by recent developments in the fields of cognitive psychology (Anderson 1985) and instructional psychology (Gagne & Glaser 1987; Pintrich et al 1986). Cognitive
approaches to learning supplement behavioral approaches and provide additional insights into the way trainees acquire knowledge and learn skills
(Howell & Cooke 1989). Ackerman & Kyllonen (1991) summarized the work
of Anderson (1985, 1987) and others on the stages of skill acquisition,
highlighting the progression through declarative knowledge (knowledge about
facts and things, "what to do"), knowledge compilation (integration of facts)
and procedural knowledge (knowledge about "how to do things"). Others
have addressed the importance of conditional or tacit knowledge (knowledge
about when and why to do things) which should facilitate application of
training back on the job (Cassidy-Schmitt & Newby 1986). Research on a

taxonomy of learning skills has been conducted by Kyllonen & Shute (1989). Other writers have described research on metacognition, a term that refers to mental processes involved in acquiring knowledge, interpreting feedback, and learning from experience (Clark 1988; Kanfer & Ackerman 1989, Swanson 1990). In reviewing the developments in the field Thayer (1989:461) stated that "it will be hard to write training texts in the future without the use of such cognitive expressions as declarative knowledge, procedural knowledge, automaticity, schema, scripts, and frames."

The cognitive approaches are especially useful for guiding the design of training on tasks involving cognitive processes such as monitoring, problem solving, and decision making. Howell & Cooke (1989) described some of the insights for training design gained from understanding the nature of cognitive processes involved in learning complex tasks.

AUTOMATIC PROCESSING   Performance in a complex task with a mix of routine and nonroutine elements can be enhanced by having a trainee initially overlearn the routine task elements. Repeated practice of only these elements under conditions that ensure a correct response causes the behavior to shift from conscious to automatic control, thereby conserving mental capacity to perform the nonroutine tasks that require more mental capacity and cannot be automated easily. If the routine elements are not initially automatized, they will compete for attention with the complex elements and inhibit learning of these elements. If the routine elements are automatized early but are learned incorrectly ("bad habits"), they will likewise inhibit development of competence in performing the task.

MENTAL MODELS AND SCHEMATA   Learning of a complex task can be facilitated by helping the learner develop an accurate and efficient mental conceptualization of the material that must be understood before the task can be performed correctly. Retention can be facilitated by use of encoding methods such as mnemonics, imagery, and cues that relate information to the learner's existing knowledge. Conceptual learning can be increased by providing relevant category systems, coding guidelines, diagrams, analogies, and conceptual models. The manner in which material is presented can foster the formation of appropriate mental models (e.g. Caplan & Schooler 1990; Zeitz & Spoehr 1989).

METACOGNITION AND LEARNING SKILLS   Learning of tasks that require analytical processing is facilitated by helping learners monitor their own progress and evaluate what they know and don't know. An important discovery of the research on metacognition is that feedback about performance outcomes may be of little value if the learner is using an inappropriate mental model and the feedback does not provide guidance for recognizing why it is inappropriate and developing a better one. Learning can be facilitated by showing learners how to seek and utilize relevant feedback about their strategy for doing a task (e.g. what strategy was used, what was done correctly and what mistakes were made, what might have been done instead). Meta-cognitive skills, along with other learning strategies (e.g. if-then rules, working backwards) distinguish proficient from nonproficient learners. There is some evidence that these skills can be taught or that learning can be facilitated by embedding within the training diagnostic probes and clues to help the learner analyze and interpret performance feedback (Clark 1988; Derry & Murphy 1986). Additional work is needed to examine the utility of cognitive concepts for facilitating transfer of training in addition to skill acquisition.

Training design is advanced by continuing developments in learning theories of all types, and these developments have been reviewed in detail by Weiss (1991). Research on motor skills has continued to investigate the traditional design parameters (e.g. distribution of practice, knowledge of results, conditions facilitating retention and transfer), and a detailed review of this literature can be found in Adams (1987). Our knowledge has been advanced also by the ongoing work in the military on design of training systems. An example is the work by Morrison & Holding (1990), who described recent efforts to refine design instructional guidelines developed for the military in the 1970s. Morrison & Holding reviewed theory and research, including cognitive psychology, relevant to several design issues such as identification of relationships among training objectives, sequencing of training components, selection of training methods, and allocation of training time to various training activities. Tentative design guidelines based on the current state of knowledge were offered as hypotheses to guide future research.

The effectiveness of different forms and amounts of learner self-control over training is an issue that has become increasingly important owing to the growing interest in self-management (Frayne & Latham 1987; Kanfer & Hagerman 1987; Latham & Frayne 1989; Manz & Sims 1989) and the availability of interactive training methods that allow individualized instruction and increased trainee control over learning. Kinzie (1990) noted that significant questions have emerged about the capability of learners to manage their own learning in an effective way. (Will they make good choices, will they be motivated to learn?) Kinzie reviewed the limited research relevant to this question and identified areas where more research is needed.

TRAINING METHODS

A major question in the design of training is the selection of training methods. The literature on evaluation of training methods continues to increase. As

Campbell (1988) noted recently, by far the largest category of studies involves comparison of a single training method to another method or to a control condition with no training. The purpose of such studies is usually to demonstrate that a particular method "works" or that it is "superior" to another method. We agree with Campbell that research of this type has only marginal utility for improving our understanding of training. All of the well-known training methods have been shown to be effective for some learning objectives, but "demonstration" studies do not reveal why a particular method or combination of methods facilitates learning or how the method can be used more effectively. Even a study that pits one method against another can be inconclusive as it is likely that the relative effectiveness of different methods will depend on the purpose and objective of the training, the attributes of the trainees, and the effectiveness criteria selected. Here we briefly review research on training methods that have received the most attention in the past few years, namely simulations and games, high technology methods, and behavioral role modeling.

Simulations and Games

Faria (1989) found in a survey of training managers, consulting firms, and business schools that simulations and games are now widely used as a training method. Simulations are also a popular training method in the armed services. Thornton & Cleveland (1990) pointed out that simulations vary widely in complexity of issues and number of participants, ranging from relatively simple simulations for an individual (e.g. in-basket, some computerized business games) or small group (e.g. dyadic role play, leaderless group discussion, group problem-solving exercises), to moderately complex computerized business games, combat simulations, and large-scale simulations of a particular type of organization. Looking Glass (McCall & Lombardo 1982; Van Velsor et al 1989) is the best known of the large-scale behavior simulations, but the development of industry-specific simulations has increased in recent years. There are now simulations for a wide variety of industries (Keys 1987; Lepsinger et al 1988; Stumpf & Dunbar 1990).

The amount of research on simulations and games has increased dramatically in the last several years. Research on simulations and games used for management education has been reviewed by Hsu (1989), Keys & Wolfe (1990), Thornton & Cleveland (1990), and Wolfe (1990). Aspects of simulations that may influence the success of the training include the complexity of the simulation, scope of functional and environmental activities, size and composition of teams, scheduling of activities (e.g. concentrated in a 2–3 day period versus 1–2 hour sessions distributed over several weeks), type of preliminary preparation and conceptual learning, type of feedback and debriefing, use of decision support systems and tutoring aids based on expert systems, and the quality of game administration.

Despite the growing research literature on simulations, many important research questions remain unresolved. More research is needed to determine what types of learning occur and the conditions that facilitate it. Hsu (1989) reanalyzed the simulation research and concluded that most studies of multi-team and large-scale behavioral simulations fail to evaluate the types of learning for which these simulations are most appropriate, namely problem solving and interpersonal skills. Furthermore, because simulations are typically used together with other training methods such as reading materials, lecture-discussion, and demonstrations, it is difficult to disentangle their unique contribution to trainee learning (Thornton & Cleveland 1990).

Evaluation is complicated also by the fact that simulations often have multiple learning objectives, some of which are general and long-term rather than specific and immediate. There is little evidence that simulation training results in long-term improvements in managerial effectiveness. A study by Wolfe & Roberts (1986) found that performance in a single-person game predicted career success as a manager five years later, but the study did not assess what, if anything, trainees learned in the game. Keys & Wolfe (1990) pointed out that game performance is not equivalent to learning; a team that experiences difficulties and setbacks may learn more about interpersonal processes and problem solving than a team for which financial success is easy. There is clearly a need for more longitudinal research on how simulation training affects immediate learning and longer-term performance.

Because management games have become something of a fad, some writers have urged caution in their use (Jacobs & Baum 1987). Although it was assumed initially that learning would occur automatically as a result of the game experience, we are coming to realize that extensive preparation, planning, and debriefing are needed to realize the potential benefits from simulations (Keys & Wolfe 1990). Thornton & Cleveland (1990) recommended that complex simulations should be used only within a carefully planned sequence of developmental experiences. In addition, the training should include presentation of an appropriate model of effective management with clear descriptions of relevant managerial skills, there should be an adequate debriefing of the simulation experience, and there should be opportunities for coaching, feedback, reinforcement, and practice of skills on the job.

High-Technology Methods

This section deals with a variety of high-technology training methods such as computer-aided instruction, interactive videodisc instruction, and equipment simulators. As development of technology proceeds at a rapid pace and the cost of computers continues to decline, these high-technology training methods are finding increasing use in industry, academia, and the military (Lippert 1989; London 1989; Pursell & Russell 1991). Moreover, innovative media such as teleconferencing and satellite television networks are being used increasingly to provide training to widely separated sites in a cost-effective manner (see London 1989).

Computer aided instruction (CAI) allows individualized instruction with the advantages of self-pacing by trainees, active practice or rehearsal, immediate feedback, continuous monitoring and assessment of learning, diagnosis of learning problems, and remedial assistance when needed. One major disadvantage of CAI is the extensive development time and expense, but computer software has been developed to simplify and speed up the design process and facilitate programming (e.g. CASE technology). Eberts & Brock (1987) described recent developments in CAI. They cautioned that computers will not automatically improve training because success depends upon the adequacy of the needs assessment and instructional design, as well as on the technology for delivering instruction. Eberts & Brock noted that improvement of computer aided instruction depends heavily upon research in cognitive processes.

Some progress is being made in improving computer-aided instruction, particularly with respect to incorporating artificial intelligence, but it is too early to reach any firm conclusions about its effectiveness (Lippert 1989). Fletcher (1988) reviewed developments in the use of intelligent computer-aided instruction (ICAI) by the military. He found almost no data on training effectiveness for the nine ICAI systems he reviewed, and he urged more evaluation of ICAI, not only to determine its effectiveness, but also to discover why and how it facilitates learning. Despite the lack of rigorous evaluation studies Fletcher, like most other writers who have examined ICAI, is optimistic about its potential to improve training.

As new technology continues to be developed, progress has been made also in linking various types of instructional technology. One promising innovation of the 1980s is the linking of videodisc players with microcomputers to create interactive videodisc instruction. Videodisc players present information in the form of text, still photographs, videotaped pictures, computer graphics, and multi-track sound recordings. The simpler versions of videodisc training have a menu that allows the trainee to select the type of information desired; the more sophisticated versions permit an interactive experience with diagnosis, feedback, and remedial coaching for the trainee. Touch screens, voice recognition, and optical readers provide promising alternatives to the keyboard as a medium of interaction with the computer-tutor (De Bloois 1988; Pursell & Russell 1991). An example of the flexibility of interactive videodisc training is provided by Alliger et al (1989), who described a successful interactive videodisc training program that included behavior modeling to train entry-level sales personnel at IBM.

Fletcher (1990) conducted a comprehensive review and meta-analysis of 47 studies evaluating interactive videodisc instruction in the military, industry, and higher education. The training content in these studies was very diverse, including instruction in equipment maintenance, equipment operation, medical procedures, military operations, science education, and interpersonal skills. Videodisc instruction was substantially more effective than conventional instruction (e.g. lecture, videotaped demonstration, text, programmed text, on-the-job training) with respect to both knowledge acquisition and job performance. The more the videodisc instruction included interactive features such as tutorials, the greater its effectiveness. Within-group variability in criterion scores was lower for videodisc instruction than for conventional instruction, which indicates that the benefits were widespread rather than attributable to large improvement in a few "star" trainees. However, Fletcher (1990) noted that aside from the question of interactivity, the studies provide little insight into the relative contribution of the various features of interactive videodisc technology to learning. He concluded that more research is needed to identify design alternatives that contribute to various learning objectives.

Equipment simulators based on computers have been used extensively for training aircraft pilots, and Jacobs et al (1990) conducted a meta-analysis of this research. Their analysis indicated that simulator training combined with training on the actual aircraft was more effective than training on the aircraft by itself. Simulator training was more effective when pacing was based on each trainee's individual progress as compared to having all trainees proceed at the same pace. Progress in understanding how to use simulators effectively requires evaluation of simulators in relation to specific learning objectives. An example of this kind of research is a study by Drucker & Campshure (1990) on army tank operations. A computer-based simulation was compared to a table-top simulation with respect to their utility for training a variety of skills needed by tank platoon officers. The computer simulation was superior for some tasks but not for others.

The realism of simulators is being enhanced greatly by continuing developments in videodisc technology, speech simulation, and speech recognition. For example, Hamel et al (1989) found that realism could be increased in microcomputer-based training for air controllers by using "off the shelf" automated voice recognition and speech generation technology.

Advancements in networking technology in the last few years have opened up new possibilities for large-scale simulator networking (SIMNET). Although simulators have been used in the past for training of small teams in the military, simulator networking allows large groups of military trainees to practice their skills in an interactive simulation of combat conditions (Thorpe 1987; Alluisi 1991). Since under these circumstances the opponent is not just a computer but another military team, trainees are highly motivated by the competition. As in real combat, the chain of command for each side plans operations, logistics, and combat support; issues commands; receives reports; and reacts to unpredictable, rapidly changing developments. Learning occurs at all levels, from the operators of several different weapon simulators (e.g. tanks, helicopters, aircraft) to the commanders who plan and coordinate the operations. Just as in the case of field simulations with real weapons, learning is facilitated by feedback received in detailed "after action reviews" during which actions and decisions taken during the simulation are analyzed to discover what was done well, what mistakes were made, and how perform-ance could be improved. A thorough history of the development of SIMNET technology is provided by Alluisi (1991).

Behavior Modeling

Interest in behavioral role modeling has continued to be strong since the pioneering research by Goldstein & Sorcher (1974). A meta-analysis by Burke & Day (1986) of studies evaluating behavior modeling found that it was one of the most effective training methods. Subsequent reviews continue to support the utility of this training method (Latham 1989; Mayer & Russell 1987; Robertson 1990). However, several writers (e.g. Mayer & Russell 1987; Parry & Reich, 1984; Robertson 1990; Russell et al 1984) have expressed concerns about the conclusions drawn from the research. One concern is that claims for the superiority of behavior modeling are exagger-ated and unsubstantiated (Mayer & Russell 1987). Mayer & Russell found little evidence that role modeling is more cost effective than other methods, and they noted that most studies on behavior modeling examined only im-mediate learning, not the application of the learned behaviors back on the job or the effects on job performance. Another concern involves the type of training for which behavior modeling is appropriate. Behavior modeling appears useful for teaching concrete behaviors that are clearly optimal for a particular type of task (e.g. operate equipment, assemble a machine, perform a surgical procedure). However, it is not clear how effective behavior model-ing is for teaching flexible adaptive behaviors or cognitive knowledge (Robertson 1990). More research is needed to determine the types of tasks and skills that can be trained effectively through behavior modeling.

For some types of learning, the effectiveness of behavior modeling may be increased by using a modified form of the typical training method. Gist (1989) found that a variation called "cognitive modeling" may be useful for training people to increase idea generation. Parry & Reich (1984) suggested a varia-tion of the usual procedure of presenting concrete behavioral guidelines for training interpersonal skills that require flexible, adaptive behavior. They proposed that the training should emphasize general principles, and trainees should be encouraged to devise alternative ways to apply the principles in various situations.

Some of the most useful research on behavior modeling examines how learning is affected by different aspects of the training, such as characteristics of the modeling demonstration, the way behavior is practiced or rehearsed, and the type of feedback provided to participants (e.g. Hogan et al 1986; Mills & Pace 1989). One important question about model characteristics is whether trainees should be exposed to a variety of models of varying competence. Baldwin (1991) found that exposing trainees to models of varying competence and models in varying situations increased generalization of skills. However, Trimble et al (1989) found that showing both positive and negative models, as compared to showing only positive models, did not result in greater recall or performance of the guideline behaviors. A negative model alone was less effective than either a positive model or a combination of positive and negative models. Results from the two studies appear contradictory, and it is not clear yet whether model variability improves discrimination of appropriate behavior or increases ability to apply a general principle to varying conditions.

Some progress has been made in understanding the conditions that facilitate learning in behavior modeling, but more research is needed both on the learning process and on the motivational process. The theoretical basis for behavioral role modeling is Bandura's (1986) social learning theory. Robertson (1990) noted that prior role modeling studies do not test all aspects of the theory. For example, the motivational aspects of the theory, such as level of trainee self-efficacy and perceived instrumentality of applying learned behaviors on the job, are rarely explored (Robertson 1990; Mayer & Russell 1987). More research is needed to identify characteristics of the training that increase trainee self-efficacy. Some of the recent research on self-management (e.g. Latham & Frayne 1989; Frayne & Latham 1987) suggests that it would be feasible to measure changes in self-efficiency during behavior modeling training.

In summary, some of the same concerns can be expressed regarding the research on simulations, high-technology methods, and behavior modeling. Each training method has demonstrated some utility, but more research is needed to determine the types of content for which a training method is appropriate and to discover how different aspects of the training method affect training outcomes.

TRAINEE CHARACTERISTICS

Training effectiveness is determined in part by the thoroughness of the needs analysis and the quality of the training design, but other factors also contribute to training effectiveness, including the attributes of trainees. Historically, research on trainee characteristics has focused more on selecting trainees who will pass training and less on placing individuals into appropriate training programs, revising training to match trainee attributes, or understanding how trainee characteristics influence training effectiveness. Empirical investigation of trainee characteristics in organizational settings is still limited, but there appears to be a recent increase in research on the implications of trainee characteristics for improving training effectiveness. In the next few sections we summarize literature on trainee characteristics, including trainee abilities and skills; trainee motivation, attitudes, and expectations; and aptitude treatment interactions.

Trainee Abilities and Skills

Trainability testing attempts to predict whether a person will successfully complete training. An example of this method is the minicourse approach used in the AT&T system (Reilly & Israelski 1988). In a minicourse, a candidate is given a standardized sample of programmed training material followed by a knowledge test to measure learning of the material. A similar method is the work-sample test of trainability. In this method the period of instruction is followed by a work sample test to predict subsequent trainee performance. Unlike standard work samples, these can be used with inexperienced applicants because they include a structured training experience. The rationale behind these approaches is that a trainee's ability to learn material can be assessed by placing the person in a context that approximates the training setting. Robertson & Downs (1989) conducted a meta-analysis of studies on work-sample trainability tests and found that they predict subsequent training and job performance in most situations. Although the relationship was positive for all subsets of validity coefficients, the greater the interval between the work sample test and the criterion, the weaker the relationship. In other words, trainability tests predict short-term training success better than longer-term training success or subsequent job performance. In general, trainability testing research has value from a selection perspective but does not shed much light on why training works or how to improve training. Moreover, it is unclear whether trainability tests provide any useful incremental gain over the use of cognitive ability tests in predicting training success and subsequent job performance (Robertson & Downs 1989).

There is an ongoing debate among researchers about whether certain abilities are more important at various points during the skill acquisition process, and if so, which ones and under what circumstances (see Ackerman 1989; Barrett et al 1989; Fleishman & Mumford 1989a,b; Henry & Hulin 1987; Murphy 1989). For example, Ackerman (1988) found that for novel, moderately complex, but consistent psychomotor tasks, initial performance is best predicted by general and broad content abilities; intermediate levels of skilled performance are best predicted by perceptual speed abilities; and late, asymptotic performance levels are best predicted by psychomotor abilities.

Trainee Motivation, Attitudes, and Expectations

As Noe (1986) suggested, a variety of factors besides ability can influence training effectiveness, including trainee motivation, attitudes, and expectations. Some conceptual development has been done recently on the effects of trainee characteristics. Kanfer & Ackerman (1989) presented a theoretical framework for integrating ability and motivation, and this theory has important implications for the study of skill acquisition and training performance. Their framework (based on Kahneman 1973) depicts performance as a joint function of the trainee's relative attentional capacity (cognitive ability) and the proportion of the trainee's total capacity actually devoted to the task (motivation). The model also differentiates distal (i.e. antecedent to task engagement) and proximal motivational processes (i.e. distribution of effort during task engagement). Empirical work focusing on simulated air traffic control tasks provided some support for their model. Mathieu et al (1990) presented and tested a model that hypothesized linkages between trainee characteristics and training outcomes based on the work of Noe (1986). Additional attention should be given to understanding the relationships among trainee characteristics and their relative contribution in facilitating learning, skill acquisition, and transfer.

MOTIVATION   It is widely accepted that learning and transfer will occur only when trainees have both the ability ("can do") and volition ("will do") to acquire and apply new skills (Wexley & Latham 1991; Noe 1986). Yet until recently there was only a limited amount of research on the "will do" factors in the training context.

Baldwin & Ford (1988) and Noe (1986) suggested the use of an expectancy framework for studying training motivation. Mathieu et al (1990) used expectancy-type motivation measures in a study of proofreading training for clerical employees. As predicted, they found that trainees with higher pre-training motivation demonstrated greater learning and more positive reactions to training, even after controlling for educational differences. Williams et al (1991), Tannenbaum et al (1991b), and Baldwin et al (1991) all provided additional empirical evidence for a positive relationship between trainee motivation and training outcomes. Kanfer (1991) reviewed and summarized developments in motivation theory as they pertain to individuals in organizations. The application of motivation theory to the training environment could enhance our understanding of training effectiveness. In an effort to clarify what trainees believe are the rewards of training, Nordhaug (1989) conducted interviews with Norwegian employees and asked whether their participation in training had contributed to certain outcomes. Factor analysis identified three dimensions of payoffs from training including "motivation to learn" (e.g. increased interest in the subjects of the course), "career development" (e.g. increased autonomy, promotion), and "psychosocial development" (e.g. increased self-confidence). Although based strictly on retrospective recall, this exploratory study provides some information on employee perceptions about the instrumentality of training. However, Nordhaug did not assess what trainees expect or desire from the training.

Feldman (1989) noted that "the whole issue of expectations about training itself has to be explored more fully" (1989:381). Tannenbaum et al (1991b) examined the expectations and desires of naval recruits regarding their upcoming training experience (e.g. degree of challenge, opportunity to practice). They found that trainees who had their pretraining expectations and desires met (referred to as "training fulfillment") developed greater posttraining commitment, self-efficacy, and motivation even after controlling for pretraining attitudes and ability, training performance, and trainee reactions. Eden (1990) summarized the research on the Pygmalion and Galatea effects and concluded that enhancing a trainee's performance expectations can have an impressive effect on trainee achievement. In fact, this research showed that trainee achievement can be increased by heightening the trainer's expectations (e.g. telling the trainer that a trainee has superior capabilities).

SELF-EFFICACY   Self-efficacy is another important trainee construct that has received increased attention in the training literature. Self-efficacy refers to a belief in one's ability to perform a specific task, and it is a central concept in social learning theory (Bandura 1986). Self-efficacy can be considered a potential antecedent of training effectiveness, because individuals with high self-efficacy tend to outperform individuals with low self-efficacy (Taylor et al 1984; Bouffard-Bouchard 1990). That is, individuals who enter training believing they are capable of mastering the training content are likely to learn more during the training. Gist et al (1989) studied managers and administrators undergoing two types of training in the use of computer software. Trainees with higher self-efficacy prior to training and those who reported higher self-efficacy at the midpoint of training performed better than their low-self-efficacy peers on a timed computer task at the end of training.

Individuals who leave training with the belief that they can successfully perform the task they have been trained to do should be more resilient when they encounter obstacles in the transfer environment (Marx 1982) and more willing to try new things (Hill et al 1987). As noted earlier, increased self-efficacy is probably one reason for the effect of behavior modeling on trainee behavior. Thus, self-efficacy can be regarded as a predictor of training success, as a process variable during training, or as a desirable outcome of training.

OTHER TRAINEE CHARACTERISTICS   Other trainee characteristics that may have relevance for understanding the training process include problem solving style (e.g. Basadur et al 1990), action orientation (Kuhl 1985), openness to experience (Barrick & Mount 1991), trainee attributions of success and failure (Campbell 1988), need for achievement, and goal orientation (See Dweck 1986; Elliott & Dweck 1988). The last characteristic is a concept in the educational literature that can be applied to the training context. Elliott & Dweck (1988) proposed that individuals can pursue two different types of goals in achievement situations: (*a*) performance goals, in which individuals seek to maintain positive judgments about their ability; and (*b*) learning goals, in which individuals seek to increase their ability or to master new tasks. Although most of the research on goal orientation has been conducted with school children, it is reasonable to assume that trainees with a learning goal orientation will approach training quite differently from trainees with a performance orientation. Research is needed on the influence of goal orientation with adult trainees.

In sum, trainee self-efficacy, motivation, and expectations appear to be central constructs in understanding training effectiveness, and other trainee characteristics (e.g. goal orientation) hold promise as well. Dynamic trainee characteristics that can be influenced before, during, or after the training process should receive particular attention because these have the greatest potential for enhancing our understanding of how and why training works. However, measures of these constructs should be refined to fit the training context. For example, self-efficacy and trainee motivation must be operationalized more clearly, and distinctions must be made between motivation to attend, motivation to learn, and motivation to transfer, with the latter perhaps focusing on behavioral intentions (see Tubbs & Ekeberg 1991). Additional research on motivational antecedents to training is needed. We agree with Campbell (1988) that "we have barely scratched the surface here, and much more remains to be done" (p. 209).

Aptitude-Treatment Interactions

An aptitude-treatment interaction occurs when one training program is not uniformly superior to another, but instead the programs have a differential impact on trainees of different aptitudes. In this context, an aptitude can be broadly defined as any characteristic of trainees that determines their ability to profit from instruction, including abilities, skills, knowledge, and even previous achievement (Cronbach & Snow 1977). Aptitude-treatment interactions have important implications for the design of training. In order to adapt training methods to differences in trainee aptitudes and prior knowledge, it is necessary to understand the interactions between training methods and aptitudes. In addition, aptitude-treatment interactions provide information for placing people into training conditions that will maximize training effectiveness. For example, Savage et al (1982) found the use of regression-based techniques to assign trainees to one of two training programs reduced training time by 50% over random assignment of trainees.

Aptitude-treatment interactions have received considerable attention in the instructional and education psychology literatures (Pintrick et al 1986; Ackerman et al 1989; Snow 1989), but they have not been studied extensively in organizational settings. Overall, the empirical support for consistent interaction effects has been limited. For the training context, one of the most promising interactions may be between general academic ability and the complexity or structure of the instructional program. According to Snow & Lohman (1984), high-ability students tend to benefit more from programs with less structure (e.g. emphasizing independent acquisition of knowledge) and greater complexity, whereas low-ability students benefit more from explicit, structured instruction. Campbell (1988) suggested that within organizational contexts, trainee achievement and experience may also interact with training complexity or difficulty. As he noted, if this is true, we should pay more attention to measuring the existing achievement level of potential trainees and tailoring the training accordingly during the design process.

In sum, although aptitude-treatment interactions may have important implications for personnel training, little empirical research has been conducted in organizational settings. To date, the potential of aptitude-treatment interactions to be useful in organizational training applications remains unfulfilled.

PRETRAINING ENVIRONMENT

Accumulating evidence suggests that events prior to training (i.e. the pretraining environment) can influence training effectiveness. Management actions provide cues and signals that influence employee motivation. The pretraining environment contains many cues about training; some are conveyed by managers but others are conveyed by peers or reflected in organizational policies and practices. Employees start to learn about the way training is viewed in the organization early in the socialization process (Feldman 1989) and continue to gather information with each course they attend. Some actions signal to trainees whether training is important (e.g. supervisory and peer support, resource availability, and posttraining follow-up). Other actions reveal to employees the amount of control, participation, or input they have in the training process (e.g. advance notification, participation in needs assessment, and degree of choice in attendance).

Environmental Cues and Signals

In a study across five companies, Cohen (1990) found that trainees with more supportive supervisors entered training with stronger beliefs that training would be useful. Supervisors can show their support for an upcoming training course by discussing the training with the employee, establishing training goals, providing release time to prepare, and generally encouraging the employee. Cohen also found that trainees who set goals prior to training entered training with higher levels of motivation to learn. Unfortunately, the cross-sectional nature of the study makes it impossible to determine whether setting goals enhanced motivation to learn or whether the highly motivated trainees were more likely to set goals.

Baldwin & Magjuka (1991) found that trainees who entered training expecting some form of follow-up activity or assessment afterward reported stronger intentions to transfer what they learned back to the job. The fact that their supervisor would require them to prepare a posttraining report or undergo an assessment meant that they were being held accountable for their own learning and apparently conveyed the message that the training was important. The pretraining environment can act also as an inhibitor of training effectiveness. Mathieu et al (1990) found that trainees who reported many situational constraints in their job (e.g. lack of time, equipment, and resources) entered training with lower motivation to learn. These trainees had little incentive to learn new skills in an environment where the skills could not be applied.

A clearer distinction is needed between effects of cues associated with a particular training course (e.g. Did my manager meet with me to develop goals?) and effects of cues associated with the overall training culture (e.g. Does my company tend to promote from within; is training considered a reward or a punishment?). Future research should examine the relative importance of specific and global cues on trainee motivation.

Trainee Input and Choice

Wlodkowski (1985) suggested that involving employees in decisions about the training process could enhance their motivation to learn. In the pretraining context participation may include informing trainees about training content in advance, soliciting trainee preferences for training content and methods, and/or allowing trainees to decide which courses to attend.

Saari et al (1988) reported that about half to three quarters of all managers who attend training are briefed prior to training. However, the depth and nature of the pretraining information can vary. Baldwin & Magjuka (1991) found that those trainees who had received information about the training ahead of time reported a greater intention than others to apply what they learned back on the job. In an interesting study of race relations training, Alderfer et al (1991) found that trainees who had received more information prior to the training had more positive reactions at the conclusion of the training. In a study of supervisory training, Hicks & Klimoski (1987) manipulated the information trainees received prior to training and found that trainees who received a realistic description of the training reported more motivation to learn than trainees who received a traditional positive portrayal of the training. However, no difference was found in actual learning. In general, it appears that providing trainees with advance notification may be helpful, but it is not clear whether notification enhances feelings of involvement, creates realistic expectations, indicates importance, or allows time for trainees to align their personal goals with the training goals.

Wlodkowski (1985) suggested that trainee participation in the training needs–assessment process should enhance motivation to learn, but we know of no research that has examined this proposition directly. Noe (1986) and Campbell (1988) proposed that trainees will be more motivated if they believe that the assessment of their strengths and weaknesses is accurate. Noe & Schmitt (1986) tested this proposition and found a weak relationship between perceived assessment accuracy and pretraining motivation. In contrast, Williams et al (1991) reported a strong link between perceived assessment accuracy and posttraining motivation to transfer.

An important question with respect to participation is whether trainees can choose which training they attend. Voluntary participation has been shown to be related to higher motivation to learn, greater learning, and more positive trainee reactions than mandatory attendance (Cohen 1990; Hicks & Klimoski 1987; Mathieu et al 1990). In contrast, Baldwin & Magjuka (1991) found that engineers who perceived training to be mandatory reported greater intentions to apply what they learned back on the job than engineers who viewed their attendance as voluntary. One explanation for the discrepancy in results between this study and the others may be the different attitudes towards training in the various companies. Over 80% of the engineers reported that their previous training experiences with the company had been favorable or very favorable. Baldwin & Magjuka suggested that by making training mandatory the company was signaling to the employees which courses were most important. In the study by Hicks & Klimoski only 17% of the employees who were given a choice whether to attend the training actually did so, suggesting that employees in that organization perceived training to be of low value. When training is not valued, mandatory attendance may be demoralizing.

Baldwin et al (1991) showed that there is a clear difference between soliciting a trainee's opinion and taking that opinion into account. In a lab experiment, they found that allowing trainees to specify what training they wanted increased their motivation to learn, provided they were given the training of their choice. However, trainees who were allowed to "choose" a course but were then assigned to a different course were less motivated and learned less than the trainees who did not participate at all in the choice of training. Baldwin et al explained their findings based on procedural justice concepts of "fair process" and "frustration effects".

Pretraining Preparation

In addition to the signals provided to trainees in the pretraining environment, specific preparatory activities may also occur. Trainee deficiencies in self-efficacy, learning skills, or reading skills can create problems during training (Mumford et al 1988). As an alternative to selecting only trainees with the necessary aptitudes or designing training to the lowest common denominator, pretraining activities can be used to enhance self-efficacy or prepare trainees with the necessary learning, reading, meta-cognitive, or other basic skills (Carnevale et al 1990a).

POSTTRAINING ENVIRONMENT

The effectiveness of a training program can be influenced by events that occur after a trainee returns to the job. Some employees leave training with new skills and with strong intentions to apply those skills to their job, but limitations in the posttraining environment interfere with the actual transfer of training. As Ajzen (1985) noted, the degree to which intentions are converted into acts and products is partially determined by various inhibiting and facilitating control factors. The personal skills, ability, and willpower that trainees possess at the conclusion of training are potential determinants of transfer. In addition, elements of the posttraining environment can encourage (e.g. rewards, job aids), discourage (e.g. ridicule from peers), or actually prohibit the application of new skills and knowledge on the job (e.g. lack of necessary equipment). In this section we examine developments regarding the influence of the posttraining environment.

Transfer Environment

Transfer of training can be defined as the extent to which trainees effectively apply the knowledge, skills, and attitudes gained in a training context back to the job. Several writers have discussed conceptual issues in understanding transfer of training. Baldwin & Ford (1988) emphasized the distinction between (*a*) generalization, or the extent to which trained skills and behaviors are exhibited in the transfer setting, and (*b*) maintenance, or the length of time that trained skills and behaviors continue to be used on the job. They presented several hypothetical maintenance or decay curves that illustrate the changes that can occur in the level of knowledge, skills, and behaviors exhibited on the job as a function of the time elapsed since the completion of training.

Laker (1990) suggested that the concept of transfer distance, prevalent in the educational literature (e.g. Butterfield & Nelson 1989), may be useful for examining generalization in organizational settings. Transfer distance refers to the extent to which a trainee applies what is learned to job situations similar to the training situation (near transfer) or different from it (far transfer). Ford (1990) noted that Laker did not consider other aspects of generalization that might be equally valuable in examining transfer, such as lateral and vertical transfer, literal and figural transfer, and specific and nonspecific transfer. Increased conceptual clarity regarding transfer can help us understand how to modify the work environment to facilitate transfer of training.

While practitioners acknowledge that transfer is dependent on the posttraining environment, little empirical research is available to guide practice. Baldwin & Ford (1988) found only seven studies that examined the influence of the work environment on transfer of training and none that attempted to change the work environment. In particular, they noted that supervisory support is considered a key environmental factor that can affect the transfer process. In the posttraining environment, supervisor support could include reinforcement, modeling of trained behaviors, and goal-setting activities. Baldwin & Ford called for better identification and operationalization of key work-environment variables that affect trainee perceptions and influence transfer of training.

Along these lines, Rouillier & Goldstein (1991) presented an encouraging study that examined the organizational climate for transfer of training. They identified transfer climate components and classified them into situational cues and consequences, based on an organizational behavior model proposed by Luthans & Kreitner (1985). Situational cues in the work environment included (a) goal cues that serve to remind trainees to use their training; (b) social cues, including the behavior and influence processes exhibited by supervisors, peers and/or subordinates; and (c) task and structural cues, including the design and nature of the job itself. Consequences included positive and negative feedback and punishment. Trainees were assistant managers who completed a week-long training program and were then randomly assigned to one of 102 organizational units. In units with a more positive transfer climate, trainees demonstrated significantly more trained behaviors even after controlling for learning and for unit performance. Situational cues and consequences each contributed additional explained variance over and above the other. This study highlights the importance of assessing transfer climate during the needs-analysis process and suggests the potential benefits of manipulating the work environment to support subsequent transfer.

Another factor that could influence transfer is the extent to which the posttraining environment provides opportunities for trainees to apply what they have learned. Ford et al (1991) studied Air Force technical trainees after they completed training and found significant differences in opportunity to apply the training and wide variations in the length of time before trainees first performed the tasks for which they had been trained. Supervisor and peer support were related to the extent to which airmen had opportunities to perform trained tasks. In a study of IRS managers, Pentland (1989) found that attempts to practice trained computer skills immediately upon returning to the job had a major impact on long-term retention. Clearly, opportunity to apply and practice trained skills is an important construct worthy of further attention.

Situational constraints in the posttraining work environment can impede transfer of training (Noe 1986). Goodman & Miller (1990) described several facilitators and inhibitors of training in a high-tech manufacturing environment. Schoorman & Schneider's book (1988) contains a great deal of useful information about the nature and influence of environmental facilitators and situational constraints—as does the work of Peters and his associates (e.g. Peters et al 1988).

Posttraining Activities

Baldwin & Ford (1988) noted that the counseling and psychotherapy literatures are potentially rich sources of ideas for creating conducive transfer environments. They mentioned the applicability of buddy systems, booster sessions, and relapse-prevention programs to an organizational context. A few recent empirical studies utilized aspects from related fields.

Fleming & Sulzer-Azaroff (1990) conducted a study of paraprofessionals at a facility for the disabled. After training, peers were paired and instructed to provide feedback and reinforcement to each other. Fleming & Sulzer-Azaroff reported that this peer management approach increased the maintenance of training behaviors.

Several studies have examined whether transfer is facilitated by relapse-prevention training, an approach derived from research on physical addictions (Marx 1982). Relapse-prevention training is designed to prepare trainees for the posttraining environment and to anticipate and cope with "high risk" situations. Marx & Karren (1988) found that trainees who received relapse-prevention training after a regular training seminar demonstrated more of the trained behaviors than trainees without relapse training. Gist et al (1990) found that relapse prevention training that incorporated self-management and goal-setting techniques yielded higher rates of skill generalization and better overall performance than training that used only goal-setting. Although this approach holds promise, the research on relapse prevention training in organizational settings has been mixed (cf Wexley & Baldwin 1986; Marx & Karren 1990).

As we noted earlier, trainees who expected some form of posttraining follow-up left training with stronger intentions to transfer (Baldwin & Magjuka 1991). Nevertheless, most companies report conducting no specific follow-up of participants after program attendance (Saari et al 1988). Marx & Karren (1990) found that trainees were more likely to apply time management skills when follow-up occurred three weeks after a time management course. In this study, follow-up consisted of either a re-examination of high-risk situations (for those who had also undergone relapse-prevention training) or a discussion of long- and short-term career goals. Neither follow-up was specifically related to the time management training per se, yet both improved transfer. Thus, it appears that posttraining follow-up can be helpful. However, this study, like the one by Wexley & Baldwin (1986), was conducted with college students, and follow-up was conducted by a trainer and not a supervisor. Future research should examine the impact of engaging the trainee's supervisor in follow-up activities. For example, a supervisor could examine a summary developed by the trainee, discuss the relevance of the training, or review posttraining action plans with the trainee in order to signal that transfer of training is important and that the trainee is accountable for it.

In summary, although research has not been plentiful, it appears that limitations in the posttraining environment may inhibit the application of skills acquired during training. Furthermore, supervisory actions taken after one training course may become pretraining cues for subsequent training courses. As such they can influence employee attitudes upon entering the next program. To optimize training effectiveness we must consider some of the diagnostic concerns expressed in the organizational development and sociotechnical literatures. We should examine the transfer environment carefully, identify situational facilitators and inhibitors, and propose means either to prepare trainees to deal with the inhibitors or to modify the posttraining environment to encourage transfer.

TRAINING EVALUATION

As was the case with training-needs analysis, researchers generally agree that training evaluation is an important part of the training system (Goldstein & Gilliam 1990). Unfortunately, although a great deal of information exists regarding various evaluation designs (e.g. Cook et al 1991; Goldstein 1991) application still lags, and employee reactions are too frequently relied upon to determine training effectiveness (Brinkerhoff 1989; Saari et al 1988). The American Society of Training and Development (1990) examined the evaluation practices of several large organizations in detail. Almost all of the companies reported that they evaluated trainee reactions, but only 10% reported evaluating behavior change on the job. In this section we present recent developments regarding training evaluation.

Evaluation Design and Analysis

Arvey & Cole (1989) examined the power of posttest only, gain score, and analysis of covariance (ANCOVA) options for analyzing classic experimental designs for training evaluation, and they concluded that ANCOVA is at least as powerful as the other options under most conditions. They also reiterated some concerns regarding the use of nonequivalent control groups. They suggested use of an alternative-ranks procedure when sample sizes are small, and use of latent-variable models when pretest differences are exhibited. Maxwell et al (1991) compared two methods for increasing power in randomized between-subject designs. They recommended using analysis of variance (ANOVA) with a lengthened posttest in situations where pretest sensitization or an inability to administer a posttest prohibit the traditional ANCOVA approach. Additional studies that compare the tradeoffs in using various analyses would be beneficial. Although our knowledge about randomized evaluation designs continues to improve, organizational constraints often limit the applicability of such designs (Brinkerhoff 1989). Research on the usefulness of alternative, quasi-experimental designs is sorely needed (Goldstein & Gessner 1988). Latham (1989) advocated the use of multiple-baseline designs to assess training effectiveness. Woods & Tannenbaum (1990) presented an application of a "multiple cohort design" in a large financial organization, comparing learning and performance changes both within and across groups of trainees. The measurement of change across nonequivalent groups remains a complex problem (Arvey & Cole 1989). However, because it is unlikely that organizational realities will allow for extensive use of experimental designs, we must continue to explore alternatives more consistent with typical constraints.

The collection of pre- and posttraining self-report data is common in evaluating training effectiveness. Concerns about response-shift bias have prompted researchers to consider the use of retrospective pretest measures (sometimes called a "then score") (Howard & Dailey 1979). Most studies have shown that change scores based on retrospective pretest measures are more in agreement with objective indications of change than change scores based on more traditional pre-test measures (Sprangers & Hoogstraten 1989), but retrospective recall measures may entail potential biases (Sprangers & Hoogstraten 1988).

The few evaluation studies that examined transfer tended to focus on initial generalization to the job, not long-term retention or behavior maintenance. However, initial retention is not necessarily equivalent to longer-term retention (Fendrich et al 1988). Longitudinal follow-up, such as that done by Latham & Frayne (1989), provides additional information about the maintenance of trained skills. Pellum & Teachout (1990) presented a longitudinal evaluation of training Air Force jet engine mechanics. They collected work samples and learning measures after introductory training, after advanced training, and again after on-the-job training.

Despite the importance of assessing maintenance of skills there are no guidelines for determining the appropriate length of time to wait before collecting posttraining measures. Research that collects outcome measures over several points in time would allow us to understand skill decay better and could help clarify when follow-up measures should be collected and refresher training offered.

Criterion Issues

Kirkpatrick's (1976) typology remains the prevalent framework for categorizing training criteria. His typology includes four levels of training effectiveness: reactions, learning, behavior and organizational results. As trainee reactions remain the most commonly used training criterion, it is important to understand the extent to which positive reactions are indicative of the other three types of criteria. In a meta-analysis of previous training studies, Alliger & Janak (1989) examined the correlations among the four levels of training effectiveness. They found virtually no relationship among trainee reactions and the other levels, but slightly higher correlations among the other levels. However, Alliger & Janak noted that their findings were based on a small number of studies. A few recent studies add related information. Mathieu et al (1990) reported a significant relationship between learning and subsequent performance (a proofreading work sample). They also found that training motivation was positively related to learning among those individuals who reacted positively to the training; that is, trainee reactions moderated the relationship between motivation and learning. In a study of interview-skills training, Campion & Campion (1987) found positive indications of trainee reactions and learning, but no differences were observed between the trained group and nonparticipants with regard to their interview behaviors or outcomes.

In sum, these studies fail to support the direct causal relationship among levels often assumed in Kirkpatrick's typology. In particular, trainee learning appears to be a necessary but not sufficient prerequisite for behavior change. As discussed earlier, the posttraining environment can play an important role in determining whether transfer occurs. Furthermore, reactions do not appear to be directly related to the other criteria. In other words, liking does not imply learning, a finding that highlights the problem of using trainee reactions as the sole criterion of training effectiveness. Future research could examine whether trainee reactions that focus on the utility or applicability of training (as opposed to assessing whether trainees liked the training) are related to any of the other effectiveness criteria. At this point, however, we conclude that reaction measures are not a suitable surrogate for other indexes of training effectiveness.

The selection and development of appropriate criterion measures remains a critical component of training evaluation. Goldstein (1991) has reminded us that the issues of criterion relevance, deficiency, and contamination are as applicable to measuring training effectiveness as they are to any other performance evaluation context. Furthermore, the most convenient or easily accessible measures of performance may prove to be inappropriate for assessing training effectiveness. Campbell (1988) noted problems with the use of global measures of performance. Since training is but one of many factors that contribute to overall performance, global measures of performance can easily suffer from criterion contamination. Campbell advocated the use of targeted measures based on specific training objectives.

Sackett et al (1988) found low correlations between measures of typical and maximum performance across two samples, suggesting that the two indexes measure distinct phenomena. Maximum performance is characterized by: (*a*) an explicit awareness of being evaluated, (*b*) an acceptance of explicit instructions to maximize effort, and (*c*) a short enough measurement period to allow focused attention on the goal. Although Sackett et al's study was not conducted in a training context it does have implications for evaluating training effectiveness. For example, in a training context, a role-play conducted at the end of training approximates a maximum performance measure and indicates how well a trainee "can" exhibit the trained behavior, but it does not indicate that the trainee "will" typically perform at that level.

Although skill development is often the primary goal of training, it is not necessarily the sole purpose (Marx & Hamilton 1991; Brinkerhoff 1989). Marx & Hamilton (1991) noted that training can also contribute to team building, coalition building, and culture building outcomes. Under certain circumstances, variables such as self-efficacy (Latham 1989) and organizational commitment (Tannenbaum et al 1991b) may be valuable outcomes in their own right. For example, socialization training may be designed both to transmit knowledge and to affect attitudes (Feldman 1989). Thus, it is important to establish clear training objectives and develop outcome measures that assess these objectives.

According to an ASTD study, approximately two thirds of training managers felt they were coming under additional pressure to show that their programs produce "bottom-line" results (Carnevale & Schulz 1990). Methods for estimating "bottom-line" impact continue to be refined. Mathieu & Leonard (1987) applied utility concepts to examine the effectiveness of training bank supervisors. They included estimates of decay and employee flow as well as economic parameters and break-even analyses to project the cost effectiveness of the training over a 20-year period. Cascio (1989) presented guidelines for assessing the economic impact of training, incorporating net present value adjustments, and explaining breakeven analysis. Finally, Deitchman (1990) attempted to quantify the military value of training expenditures in comparison to equipment improvements. He found that training and equipment improved force effectiveness by comparable amounts, but training cost the same or less than most equipment improvements. Deitchman explained that his findings only pertained to specific cases but demonstrated the feasibility of the approach for military planning purposes.

TRAINING FOR SPECIFIC POPULATIONS

In the next two sections, we discuss the application of training to two unique and especially important populations of trainees: managers and teams.

Management Development

Training and development of managers continues to be a multi-billion dollar business. Two recent articles report the results of large surveys on the amount and types of management training in companies (Gordon 1988; Saari et al 1988). Saari et al surveyed a representative sample of 611 companies of different sizes and types to identify the type of management development activities they use, the reasons for using them, procedures for selecting managers to participate in training activities, demographic characteristics of the participants, preparation of managers prior to program attendance, and procedures for evaluating training effectiveness. The percentage of companies that reported using various types of training was 93% for on-the-job training, 90% for external short courses, 80% for special projects or task forces, 57% for mentoring, 40% for job rotation, 31% for university residential programs, and 25% for executive MBA programs. Significant differences in training practices were found among various industries and between large and small companies.

An extensive literature on management development within the discipline of management education includes considerable theory and research on the skills relevant for managers and the effectiveness of different approaches in teaching these skills (see review by Keys & Wolfe 1988). For example, a recent special issue of the *Journal of Management Development* contained articles on a variety of training methods, including cases (Osigweh 1989), lecture and discussion (Griffin & Cashin 1989), and simulations (Faria 1989). A current concern in management education is to identify the skills and competencies needed by managers and evaluate the capacity of MBA programs to teach these skills (Porter & McKibbin 1989).

NEEDS ASSESSMENT FOR MANAGERS   Assessment of training needs for managers is more difficult than for most jobs owing to the complexity of managerial work. Identification of competencies likely to be relevant for a particular type of managerial position is facilitated by continuing progress in the research on managerial skills, activities, and behavior. This research is reviewed in leadership books by Bass (1990) and Yukl (1989), and additional findings are reported in recent articles (e.g. Jonas et al 1990; Kraut et al 1989).

Needs assessment should be based on accurate measures of managerial behavior and skills. A recent book edited by Clark & Clark (1990) includes reports on the development and validation of several measures useful for assessing training needs of managers. For example, Compass is a set of three types of questionnaires used to provide managers with information about their managerial behavior and the developmental needs related to this behavior (Yukl et al 1990; Yukl & Lepsinger 1991). Subordinates and peers describe how much a manager uses each of fourteen managerial practices, and they recommend whether the manager should do more, the same amount, or less of each behavior. Managers compare this feedback to their own self-assessment of behavior and to norms for similar managers. Ratings of the importance of each type of behavior for the manager's job provide additional information for selecting relevant training.

Another example of a needs-assessment instrument is Benchmarks (McCauley et al 1989), a rating form developed to measure relevant skills and traits identified in research on managerial experiences and managerial derailment. Self-ratings and ratings made by subordinates, peers, and superiors are used to assess a manager's strengths and weaknesses and identify developmental needs.

Streufert et al (1988) described research on assessment of managerial skills with two computer-based simulations (Woodline County Disaster Control Coordinator, and Governor of Shamba). The simulations are designed for a single individual (like an in-basket) rather than a group in order to regulate the information available to each participant. Managerial behavior and skills in handling crises can be assessed under standardized conditions. In other business games, by contrast, each player faces a unique situation determined by the joint actions of all the players and the parameters of the industry model used in the simulation software.

LEADERSHIP TRAINING PROGRAMS   An extensive review of leadership training programs was done by Latham (1988) in the last *Annual Review* chapter on training, and that review is updated in the new edition of the training book by Wexley & Latham (1991). Leadership training is also reviewed by Bass (1990) and by Tetrault et al (1988). Most of the training studies described in these reviews examined whether managerial effectiveness is improved by training based on a particular leadership theory. The typical design of these studies is to show improvement in performance ratings after training, or to compare ratings for managers who receive the training to ratings for untrained managers. It is difficult to interpret positive results in this type of study, since a number of rival hypotheses are plausible (e.g. criterion contamination, increased self-confidence), and these rival hypotheses may explain improved performance even though trainees did not learn the leadership theory showcased in the training, or did not behave back on the job in ways prescribed by the theory. Future research on the effects of leadership training should be designed to evaluate rival hypotheses and to determine how training affects managerial behavior as well as job performance.

DEVELOPMENTAL EXPERIENCES AND MENTORING   In recent years, researchers have paid increasing attention to management development that occurs on the job. Much of this development is informal and unplanned. Most organizations do not use developmental assignments and other forms of on-the-job training for managers in a systematic way. Even when there is a program of job rotation or developmental assignments, it is usually not linked to specific learning objectives or assessment of individual training needs (Ruderman et al 1990).

Efforts to improve management development have focused on identifying the types of experiences that facilitate development and the processes by which managers are able to learn from these experiences. Research conducted at the Center For Creative Leadership (McCall et al 1988) found that growth and learning were greatest when challenging situations or adversity forced a manager to come to terms with his or her limitations and overcome them. Challenging situations likely to encourage development included conflict with the boss, problem subordinates, a forced merger or reorganization, problems inherited from a predecessor, intense pressure from a difficult assignment with high visibility, a job for which the manager lacks experience and credibility, unfavorable business conditions or unusual external threats, and turning around a weak unit. A study by Kelleher et al (1986) examined personal and organizational variables that jointly affect learning from experience by managers. A study by Dechant (1990) investigated the process by which managers diagnose their learning needs and develop strategies to meet them.

Ruderman et al (1990) described a new questionnaire called the Job Challenge Profile (JCP) designed to measure the potential of a job for management development. In contrast to traditional job analysis, which focuses on duties and responsibilities, the JCP focuses on demands and challenges in a job. The JCP could be useful for determining which job rotation assignments, special projects, or job changes have the greatest developmental potential for a manager.

Kaplan et al (1987) found that self-development becomes more difficult at high-level executive positions in the organization. Several obstacles inhibit learning from experience by executives: the hectic pace and unrelenting demands of the job make introspection difficult, success fosters resistance to changing behavior or recognizing personal weaknesses, executives tend to become isolated, and executives are insulated from criticism from people reluctant to risk offending them. Thus, even if an executive wants to discover his or her weaknesses, it is difficult to do so. Kaplan et al (1987) suggested ways to develop sources of accurate feedback and identify developmental needs.

Interest continues in mentoring as a method for facilitating management development (London & Mone 1987; Noe 1991). Many organizations rely on informal mentoring, although without any formal structure some managers who need mentors are unlikely to establish a mentoring relationship. In most formal programs individuals are assigned a mentor. However, problems such as personality conflicts and lack of mentor commitment are more likely to occur with assigned mentors than with informal mentors unless the assigned mentors are carefully selected and trained. Zey (1988) recommended greater use of mentors to facilitate adjustment during difficult job transitions, such as with newly hired employees, employees transferred or promoted to a different unit in the organization, employees in newly merged companies, and employees with a job assignment in a foreign country. Noe (1988a) developed a questionnaire to measure mentor behavior and found that mentors provide two functions similar to those found in Kram's (1985) research based on interviews: a psychosocial function (acceptance, encouragement, coaching, counseling) and a career facilitation function (sponsorship, protection, challenging assignments, exposure and visibility). People with assigned mentors reported receiving psychosocial benefits but only limited career benefits. Noe (1988b) and Ragins (1989) examined the difficulties encountered by female managers in mentoring relationships. Willbur (1987) found that career advancement and success were predicted by several aspects of mentoring, including number of mentors and the functions provided by mentors. Unfortunately, there has been little empirical research on the ways mentors facilitate managerial development, as opposed to their influence on job satisfaction and career advancement.

Action learning is an approach widely used in Europe for combining formal management training with learning from experience (Revans 1982). A typical program is conducted over a period of from 6 to 9 months and includes field project work interspersed with skill training seminars. Teams of managers with diverse backgrounds conduct field projects on complex organizational problems requiring use of skills learned in the formal training sessions. The teams meet periodically with a skilled facilitator to discuss, analyze, and learn from their experiences (Marsick 1990).

Team Training

As organizations rely more on the use of teams to attain organizational goals the need to enhance team effectiveness has increased (Hackman 1989). Two methods designed to enhance team effectiveness are team training and team building. Although team building and team training interventions often focus on similar concerns (e.g. enhancing communication, decision making, coordination) the means of approaching the concerns differ (Tannenbaum et al 1991a). In team training, the specific knowledge, skills, and attitudes to be developed are determined prior to the start of training, and learning objectives are established. In contrast, team building is more of a process intervention, aimed at helping individuals and groups examine and act upon their behavior and relationships. Recent reviews concluded that team building appears to have a positive effect on the perceptions and attitudes of team members although results for behavioral outcomes were more equivocal (Sundstrom et al 1990; Tannenbaum et al 1991a,b). A meta-analysis of team performance research found few empirical studies of team training through the mid-1980s (Salas et al 1991b). Interest in team training has recently increased, and this section focuses on developments in the area.

Several writers have noted that an obstacle to developing an effective team training program is a lack of methods for analyzing team tasks, behaviors, and skills (Modrick 1986; Morgan & Salas 1988). Earlier research on task analysis has typically focused on the individual level of analysis, aggregated to the job level (Ostroff & Ford 1989). Recently, Levine & Baker (1991) presented a methodology to analyze team tasks, and Bowers et al (1991) presented preliminary work on assessing the coordination requirements of team tasks. Glickman et al (1987) studied military command and control teams in training and reported that two separate tracks of behavior evolve during team training: taskwork, involving the development of skills related to execution of the task; and teamwork, focusing on the behaviors required to function effectively as a team member. Teamwork behaviors that differentiate effective teams include effective communication, coordination, compensatory behavior, mutual performance monitoring, exchange of feedback, and adaption to varying situational demands (Oser et al 1989). Other developments include Fleishman & Zaccaro's (1991) team-oriented taxonomy of performance, and Franz et al's (1990) identification of seven categories of team skills to be included in aircrew coordination training.

Although preliminary progress has been made in the analysis of team tasks and skills, little research has been done on the design of team training. Salas et al (1991a) raised a number of questions about the applicability of traditional learning principles to the team training context. Swezey & Salas (1991a,b) examined the related research and presented a series of learning and instructional guidelines for use in developing team training. In one of the few empirical studies comparing team training methods, Lassiter et al (1990) found that teams trained in a skill-oriented training program demonstrated better communication skills than those in a lecture-based program or a control group. A number of commercial airlines have established team training programs for their aircrews, but the preliminary results on training effectiveness have been mixed (cf Cannon-Bowers et al 1989; Helmreich & Wilhelm 1989; Helmreich et al 1990).

The examination of mental models has particular relevance in the team training context. Cannon-Bowers et al (1990) suggested that shared or overlapping mental models among team members should enhance the use of implicit coordination strategies by enabling team members to anticipate behavior and information needs more accurately. Thus, training efforts to enhance the development of common and accurate mental models (e.g. crosstraining) should improve team effectiveness. Additional research is also needed on team task analysis, the nature of team performance, and the applicability of traditional learning principles to team training. Finally, research is needed to determine the optimal configuration of individual and team training to enhance team effectiveness.

CONCLUDING COMMENTS

In closing, we highlight a few general trends in the field and offer a few general suggestions about future research. The practice of training continues to grow, with employers spending approximately $30 billion on formal training and approximately $180 billion on informal on-the-job training each year (Carnevale et al 1990b). Along with the growth in practice, the quantity and quality of research related to training have increased during the last several years. There appears to be increased cross-pollination with other disciplines, most notably cognitive, instructional, and social psychology. Training researchers are drawing upon related conceptual work, including social learning theory and self-efficacy (e.g. Gist et al 1989), cognitive or attentional resources (Kanfer & Ackerman 1989), realistic job previews (Hicks & Klimoski 1987), relapse prevention (Marx & Karren 1988), situational cues and reinforcers (e.g. Rouillier & Goldstein 1991), and procedural justice (e.g. Baldwin et al 1991). The signs of improving integration and conceptual development are encouraging, but a great deal more is possible and desirable.

For many years writers have discussed training as a system embedded within an organizational context (e.g. Hinrichs 1976). During the last few years, researchers have begun to pay more attention to the pre- and posttraining environments as important determinants of training effectiveness. Researchers are starting to consider trainees as active participants in the system who interact with the environment before training, during training, and after training. This trend is encouraging, and more research with a systems perspective is clearly desirable.

A recurring theme in several recent reviews and overviews of training is the need for a paradigm shift from research designed to show that a particular type of training "works," to research designed to determine why, when, and for whom a particular type of training is effective. Furthermore, we must do a better job of describing the nature and purpose of the training being studied. Researchers have tended to consider all training the same, without regard to the purpose of the training or the type of learning involved. We need to be clear not only about the training method(s) employed but also about the basic content and purpose of the training. Making these distinctions should greatly enhance the ability to compare studies in future reviews.

One of the most important changes in the field is the increased attention being given to cognitive concepts. As the kinds of tasks performed by humans in organizations become more complex owing to technological change, internationalization, and other significant developments (Goldstein & Gilliam 1990), cognitive models of learning are becoming increasingly important. Cognitive developments have already made some contributions to training-needs analysis and training design. Cognitive approaches hold great promise for the field of training, but we should be careful they do not become the latest research fad. Cognitive models only supplement existing behavioral training models, they do not replace them. Although significant work remains in applying and evaluating cognitive concepts in organizational settings, the prospects are exciting.

Improvements in high-technology training methods such as intelligent computer-aided instruction, interactive-videodisc instruction, and equipment simulators, continue at a rapid pace. It is now possible to link several different training methods into an integrative, technology-based, training program with the capacity to provide the benefits of self-pacing, active involvement and expert tutoring for each trainee. The new developments promise to revolutionize the practice of training and education in the next century. Unfortunately, empirical research to determine how different features of the high-technology methods facilitate training has lagged far behind development of the technology itself.

The distinction between on-the-job training and off-site training is becoming blurred. New technology allows training to occur "on-line" as expert systems provide diagnostic clues and feedback to workers operating sophisticated equipment, monitoring operations, and troubleshooting problems. As organizations decentralize to become "closer to their customers," training responsibilities often become decentralized as well. Approaches that integrate on-the-job practice with formal training are becoming more popular. Research on the developmental experiences of managers is providing information with which to improve on-the-job learning of relevant skills and allow better integration of developmental experiences and formal training.

In general we are optimistic about the field of training. In the past, the field has been labeled faddish and atheoretical and it is still prone to those tendencies. Nevertheless, progress during the past decade has been encouraging. Several areas of current research hold particular promise for improving our understanding of training effectiveness, and the field appears poised to move forward rapidly.

ACKNOWLEDGMENTS

Lisa Dupuree-Bruno and Bruce Tracey, doctoral students at the University of Albany's Organizational Studies Program, provided valuable assistance in conducting the literature search for this chapter. We also wish to thank George Alliger, Irv Goldstein, John Mathieu, Eduardo Salas, and Tom Taber for their helpful comments and suggestions on an earlier draft of this chapter.

Literature Cited

Ackerman, P. L. 1988. Determinants of individual differences during skill acquisition: cognitive abilities and information processing. *J. Exp. Psychol.: Gen.* 117:288–318

Ackerman, P. L. 1989. Within-task intercorrelations of skilled performance: implications for predicting individual differences? (A comment on Henry and Hulin, 1987). *J. Appl. Psychol.* 74:360–64

Ackerman, P. L., Kyllonen, P. C. 1991. Trainee characteristics. In *Training for Performance: Principles of Applied Human Learning,* ed. J. E. Morrision, 193–230. West Sussex, England: John Wiley & Sons

Ackerman, P. L., Sternberg, R. J., Glaser, R., ed. 1989. *Learning and Individual Differences: Advances in Theory and Research.* New York: W. H. Freeman

Adams, J. A. 1987. Historical review and appraisal of research on the learning, retention, and transfer of human motor skills. *Psychol. Bull.* 101:41–74

Ajzen, I. 1985. From intentions to actions: a theory of planned behavior. See Kuhl & Beckman 1985, pp. 11–39

Alderfer, C. P., Tucker, R. C., Alderfer, C. J., Tucker, L. M. 1991. The race relations competence workshop: an intergroup educational procedure. *Hum. Relat.* In press

Alliger, G. M., Janak, E. A. 1989. Kirkpatrick's levels of training criteria: thirty years later. *Pers. Psychol.* 42:331–42

Alliger, G. M., Serbell, C. V., Vadas, J. E. 1989. Computer-based simulation for soft skills training. *J. Interact. Instr. Dev.* 4:8–15

Alluisi, E. A. 1991. The development of technology for collective training: SIMNET, a case history. *Hum. Factor.* In press

Anderson, J. R. 1985. *Cognitive Psychology and its Implications.* New York: Freeman. 2nd ed

Anderson, J. R. 1987. Skill acquistion: compilation of work-method problem solutions. *Psychol. Rev.* 94:192–210

Arvey, R. D., Cole, D. A. 1989. Evaluating change due to training. See Goldstein 1989, pp. 89–118

Baldwin, T. T. 1991. Effects of alternative modeling strategies on outcomes of interpersonal skills training. *J. Appl. Psychol.* In press

Baldwin, T. T., Ford, J. K. 1988. Transfer of training: a review and directions for future research. *Pers. Psychol.* 41:63–105

Baldwin, T. T., Magjuka, R. J. 1991. Organizational training and signals of importance: effects of pre-training perceptions on intentions to transfer. *Hum. Res. Dev.* 2(1):25–36

Baldwin, T. T., Magjuka, R. J., Loher, B. T. 1991. The perils of participation: effects of choice on training on trainee motivation and learning. *Pers. Psychol.* 44: 51–66

Bandura, A. 1986. *Social Foundations of Thought and Action.* Englewood Cliffs, NJ: Prentice-Hall

Barrett, G. V., Caldwell, M. S., Alexander, R. A. 1989. The predictive stability of ability requirements for task performance: a critical reanalysis. *Hum. Perform.* 2:167–81

Barrick, M. R., Mount, M. K. 1991. The big five personality dimensions and job performance: a meta-analysis. *Pers. Psychol.* 44:1–26

Basadur, M. S., Wakabayashi, M., Graen, G. B. 1990. Individual problem solving styles and attitudes toward divergent thinking before and after training. *Creat. Res. J.* 3:22–32

Bass, B. M. 1990. *Handbook of Leadership:*

Theory, Research and Managerial Implications. New York: Free Press. 3rd ed

Black, J. S. 1988. Work role transitions: a study of American expatriate managers in Japan. *J. Int. Bus. Stud.* 19:277–94

Black, J. S., Mendenhall, M. 1990. Cross-cultural training effectiveness: a review and a theoretical framework for future research. *Acad. Manage. Rev.* 15:113–36

Bouffard-Bouchard, T. 1990. Influence of self-efficacy on performance in a cognitive task. *J. Soc. Psychol.* 130: 353–63

Bowers, C. A., Morgan, B. B., Salas, E. 1991. The assessment of aircrew coordination demand for helicopter flight requirements. Paper presented at the Int. Symp. Aviation Psychol.

Brinkerhoff, R. O. 1989. *Evaluating Training Programs in Business and Industry.* San Francisco: Jossey-Bass

Burke, M. J., Day, R. R. 1986. A cumulative study of the effectiveness of managerial training. *J. Appl. Psychol.* 71:232–45

Butterfield, E. C., Nelson, G. D. 1989. Theory and practice of teaching for transfer. *Educ. Technol. Res. Dev.* 37:5–38

Campbell, J. P. 1971. Personnel training and development. *Annu. Rev. Psychol.* 22:565–602

Campbell, J. P. 1988. Training design for performance improvement. In *Productivity in Organizations,* ed. J. P. Campbell, R. J. Campbell, and Associates, pp. 177–216. San Francisco: Jossey-Bass

Campion, M. A., Campion, J. E. 1987. Evaluation of an interview skills training program in a natural field setting. *Pers. Psychol.* 40:675–91

Cannon-Bowers, J., Prince, C., Salas, E., Owens, J., Morgan, B. B., Gonos, G. H. 1989. Determining aircrew coordination training effectiveness. Presented at the 11th Interserv./Indust. Conf., Fort Worth, TX

Cannon-Bowers, J. A., Salas, E., Converse, S. A. 1990. Cognitive psychology and team training: training shared mental models of complex systems. *Hum. Factor. Soc. Bull.* 33(12):1–4

Caplan, L. J., Schooler, C. 1990. Problem-solving by reference to rules or previous episodes: the effects of organized training, analogical models, and subsequent complexity of experience. *Mem. Cognit.* 18: 215–27

Carnvevale, A. P., Gainer, L. J., Meltzer, A. S. 1990a. *Workplace Basics.* San Francisco: Jossey-Bass

Carnevale, A. P., Gainer, L. J., Villet, J. 1990b. *Training in America: The Organization and Strategic Role of Training.* San Francisco: Jossey-Bass

Carnevale, A. P., Schulz, E. R. 1990. Evaluation practices. *Train. Dev. J.* 44:S-23–S-29

Cascio, W. F. 1989. Using utility analysis to assess training outcomes. See Goldstein 1989, pp. 63–88

Casnier-Lotto, J. and associates. 1989. *Successful Training Strategies.* San Francisco: Jossey-Bass

Cassidy-Schmitt, M. C., Newby, T. J. 1986. Metacognition: relevance to instructional design. *J. Instr. Dev.* 9:20–33

Clark, R. C. 1988. Metacognition and human performance improvement. *Perform. Improve. Q.* 1:33–45

Clark, K. E., Clark, M. B. 1990. *Measures of Leadership.* West Orange, NJ: Leadership Library of America

Cohen, D. J. 1990. What motivates trainees. *Train. Dev. J.* Nov.:91–93

Cook, T. D., Campbell, D., Peracchio, L. 1991. Quasi-experiments. See Dunnette & Hough 1991, pp. 491–576

Cooke, N. M., Schvaneveldt, R. W., 1988. Effects of computer programming experience on network representations of abstract programming concepts. *Int. J. Man-Mach. Stud.* 29:533–50

Cranny, C. J., Doherty, M. E. 1988. Importance ratings in job analysis: notes on the misinterpretation of factor analysis. *J. Appl. Psychol.* 73:320–22

Cronbach, L. J., Snow, R. E. 1977. *Aptitudes and Instructional Methods: A Handbook for Research on Interactions.* New York: Irvington

DeBlois, M. L. 1988. *Use and Effectiveness of Videodisc Training.* Falls Church, VA: Future Systems Inc.

Dechant, K. 1990. Knowing how to learn: the "neglected" management ability. *J. Manage. Dev.* 9:40–49

Deitchman, S. J. 1990. Further explorations in estimating the military value of training. IDA Paper P-2317. Alexandria, VA: Inst. Defense Anal.

Derry, S. J., Murphy, D. A. 1986. Designing systems that train learning ability: from theory to practice. *Rev. Educ. Res.* 56:1–39

Drucker, E. H., Campshure, D. A. 1990. An analysis of tank platoon operations and their simulation on simulation networking (SIMNET). ARI Res. Prod. 90–22. Alexandria, VA: US Army Res. Inst. Behav. Soc. Sci.

Dunnette, M. D., Hough, L. M., eds. 1991. *Handbook of Industrial and Organizational Psychology,* Vol. 1. Palo Alto, CA: Consulting Psychologists Press. 2nd ed.

Dweck, C. S. 1986. Motivational processes affecting learning. *Am. Psychol.* 41:1040–48

Eberts, R. E., Brock, J. F. 1987. Computer-assisted and computer-managed instruction. In *Handbook of Human Factors,* ed. G. Salvendy, pp. 976–1011. New York: Wiley-Interscience

Eden, D. 1990. *Pygmalion in Management.* Lexington, MA: Lexington Books

Elliott, E. S., Dweck, C. S. 1988. Goals: an approach to motivation and achievement. *J. Pers. Soc. Psychol.* 54:5–12

Faria, A. J. 1989. Business gaming: current usage levels. *J. Manage. Dev.* 8:59–65

Feldman, D. 1988. *Managing Careers in Organizations.* Glenview, IL: Scott Foresman

Feldman, D. C. 1989. Socialization, resocialization, and training: reframing the research agenda. See Goldstein 1989, pp. 376–416

Fendrich, D. W., Healy, A. F., Meiskey, L., Crutcher, R. J., Little, W., Bourne, L. E. 1988. Skill maintenance: literature review and theoretical analysis. Air Force Hum. Res. Lab. Tech. Rep. 87–73. Brooks, AFB, TX: Air Force Systems Command

Finney, M., Von Glinow, M. A. 1988. Integrating academic and organizational approaches to developing the international manager. *J. Manage. Dev.* 7:16–27

Fleishman, E. A., Mumford, M. D. 1989a. Abilities as causes of individual differences in skill acquistion. *Hum. Perform.* 2:201–23

Fleishman, E. A., Mumford, M. D. 1989b. Individual attributes and training performance. See Goldstein 1989, pp. 183–225

Fleishman, E. A., Zacaro, S. J. 1991. Toward a taxonomic classification of team performance functions: initial considerations, subsequent evaluations, and current formulations. See Swezey & Salas. In press

Fleming, R. K., Sulzer-Azaroff, B. 1990. Peer management: effects on staff teaching performance. Presented at the 15th Annu. Convent. Assoc. Behav. Anal., Nashville

Fletcher, J. D. 1988. Intelligent training systems in the military. In *Defense Applications of Artificial Intelligence: Progress and Prospects,* ed. S. J. Andriole, G. W. Hopple, pp. 33–59. Lexington, MA: Lexington Books

Fletcher, J. D. 1990. Effectiveness and cost of interactive videodiscs in defense training and education. Alexandria, VA: Inst. Defense Anal.

Ford, J. K. 1990. Understanding training transfer: the water remains murky. *Hum. Resour. Dev. Q.* 1:225–29

Ford, J. K., Noe, R. A. 1987. Self-assessed training needs: the effects of attitudes toward training, managerial level, and function. *Pers. Psychol.* 40:39–53

Ford, J. K., Quinones, M., Sego, D., Speer, J. 1991. Factors affecting the opportunity to use trained skills on the job. Presented at the 6th Annu. Conf. Soc. Indust. Org. Psychol., St. Louis

Franz, T. M., Prince, C., Cannon-Bowers, J. A., Salas, E. 1990. The identification of aircrew coordination skills. *Proc. Dept. Defense Symp.* 12:92–96

Frayne, C. A., Latham, G. P. 1987. The application of social learning theory to employee self management of attendance. *J. Appl. Psychol.* 72:387–92

Gagne, R. M., Glaser, R. 1987. Foundations in learning research. In *Instructional Techniques: Foundations,* ed. R. Glaser, pp. 49–83. Hillsdale, NJ: Erlbaum

Gist, M. E. 1989. The influence of training method on self-efficacy and idea generation among managers. *Pers. Psychol.* 42:787–805

Gist, M. E., Bavetta, A. G., Stevens, C. K. 1990. Transfer training method: its influence on skill generalization, skill repetition, and performance level. *Pers. Psychol.* 43:501–23

Gist, M. E., Schwoerer, C., Rosen, B. 1989. Effects of alternative training methods on self-efficacy and performance in computer software training. *J. Appl. Psychol.* 74:884–91

Glickman, A. S., Zimmer, S., Montero, R. C., Guerette, P. J., Campbell, et al. 1987. The evolution of teamwork skills: an empirical assessment with implications for training. Tech Rep. NTSC 87–016. Arlington, VA: Office of Naval Research

Goldstein, A. P., Sorcher, M. 1974. *Changing Supervisor Behavior.* NY: Pergamon

Goldstein, I. L. 1980. Training in work organizations. *Annu. Rev. Psychol.* 31:229–72

Goldstein, I. L., ed. 1989. *Training and Development in Organizations.* San Francisco: Jossey-Bass

Goldstein, I. L. 1991. Training in organizations. In *Handbook of Industrial/Organizational Psychology,* ed. M. D. Dunnette, L. M. Hough, Vol. 2. 2nd ed. In press

Goldstein, I. L., Braverman, E. P., Goldstein, H. W. 1991. The use of needs assessment in training systems design. In *ASPA/BNA Handbook of Human Resource Management,* Vol. 5. *Developing Human Resources,* ed. K. Wexley, pp. 5-35–5-75. Washington, DC:BNA Books

Goldstein, I. L., Gessner, M. J. 1988. Training and development in work organizations. In *International Review of Industrial and Organizational Psychology,* ed. C. L. Cooper, I. Robertson, pp. 43–72. London: Wiley

Goldstein, I. L., Gilliam, P. 1990. Training system issues in the year 2000. *Am. Psychol.* 45:134–43

Goodman, P. S., Miller, S. M. 1990. Designing effective training through the technical life cycle. *Natl. Prod. Rev.* 9:169–77

Gordon, J. 1988. Who is being trained to do what? *Train. Mag.* Oct:51–60
Green, A. J. K., Gilhooly, K. J. 1990. Individual differences and effective learning procedures: the case of statistical computing. *Int. J. Man-Mach. Stud.* 33:97–119
Griffin, R. W., Cashin, W. E. 1989. The lecture and discussion method for management education: pros and cons. *J. Manage. Dev.* 8:25–32
Hackman, J. R. 1989. *Groups That Work (And Those That Don't).* San Francisco: Jossey-Bass
Hamel, C. J., Kotick, D., Layton, M. 1989. Microcomputer system integration for air control training Spec Rep. SR89–01. Orlando, FL: Naval Training Systems Center
Helmreich, R. L., Wilhelm, J. A. 1989. When training boomerangs: negative outcomes associated with cockpit resource management programs. In *Proceedings of the Fifth Symposium on Aviation Psychology*, ed. R. S. Jensen, pp. 692–97. Columbus, OH: Ohio State Univ.
Helmreich, R. L., Wilhelm, J. A., Gregorich, S. E., Chidester, T. R. 1990. Preliminary results from the evaluation of cockpit resource management training: performance ratings of flightcrews. *Aviation, Space, Environ. Med.* 61:576–79
Henry, R. A., Hulin, C. I. 1987. Stability of skilled performance across time: some generalizations and limitations on utilities. *J. Appl. Psychol.* 72:457–62
Hicks, W. D., Klimoski, R. J. 1987. Entry into training programs and its effects on training outcomes: a field experiment. *Acad. Manage. J.* 30:542–52
Hill, T., Smith, N. D., Mann, M. F. 1987. Role of efficacy expectations in predicting the decision to use advanced technologies: the case of computers. *J. Appl. Psychol.* 72:307–13
Hinrichs, J. R. 1976. Personnel training. In *Handbook of Industrial and Organizational Psychology*, ed. M. D. Dunnette, pp. 829–60. Chicago: Rand-McNally
Hogan, P. M., Hakel, M. D., Decker, P. J. 1986. Effects of trainee-generated versus trainer-provided rule codes on generalization in behavior-modeling training. *J. Appl. Psychol.* 71:469–73
Howard, G. S., Dailey, P. R. 1979. Response-shift bias: a source of contamination of self-report measures. *J. Appl. Psychol. Meas.* 64:144–50
Howell, W. C., Cooke, N. J. 1989. Training the human information processor: a review of cognitive models. See Goldstein 1989, pp. 121–82
Hsu, E. 1989. Role-event gaming and simulation in management education: a conceptual framework. *Simul. Games* 20:409–38

Jacobs, J. W., Prince, C., Hays, R. T., Salas, E. 1990. A meta-analysis of the flight simulator training research. NAVTRASYSCEN TR-89–006. Orlando, FL: Naval Training Systems Center
Jacobs, R. L., Baum, M. 1987. Simulation and games in training and development. *Simul. Games* 18:385–94
Jonas, H. S. III, Fry, R. E., Srivasta, S. 1990. The office of the CEO: understanding the executive experience. *Executive* 4:36–47
Jones, J. W., Steffy, B. D., Bray, D. W. eds. 1991. *Applying Psychology in Business.* Lexington, MA: Lexington Books
Kahneman, D. 1973. *Attention and Effort.* Englewood Cliffs, NJ: Prentice Hall
Kanfer, F. H., Hagerman, S. 1987. A model of self regulation. In *Motivation, Intention, and Volition*, ed. F. Halish, J. Kuhl, pp. 297–307. New York: Springer-Verlag
Kanfer, R. 1991. Motivation theory and industrial and organizational psychology. See Dunnette & Hough 1991, pp. 75–170
Kanfer, R., Ackerman, P. L. 1989. Motivation and cognitive abilities: an integrative/ aptitude-treatment interaction approach to skill acquisition. *J. Appl. Psychol. Monogr.* 74:657–90
Kaplan, R. E., Kofodimos, J. R., Drath, W. H. 1987. Development at the top: a review and a prospect. In *Research on Organizational Change and Development*, ed. W. Pasmore, R. W. Woodman, pp. 229–73. Greenwich, CT: JAI Press
Kelleher, D., Finestone, P., Lowry, A. 1986. Managerial learning: first notes from an unstudied frontier. *Group Org. Stud.* 11:169–202
Keys, B. 1987. Total enterprise business games. *Simul. Games* 18:225–41
Keys, B., Wolfe, J. 1988. Management education and development: current issues and emerging trends. *J. Manage.* 14:205–29
Keys, B., Wolfe, J. 1990. The role of management games and simulation in education and research. *J. Manage.* 16:307–36
Kinzie, M. B. 1990. Requirements and benefits of effective interactive instruction: learner control, self-regulation and continuing motivation. *Educ. Tech. Res. Dev.* 38:1–21
Kirkpatrick, D. L. 1976. Evaluation of training. In *Training and Development Handbook*, ed. R. L. Craig, pp. 18-1–18-27. New York: McGraw-Hill. 2nd ed
Kraiger, K. 1988. Implications of research on expert/novice differences for training assessment and design. Paper presented at the Annu. Meet. Soc. Indust. Org. Psychol.
Kram, K. E. 1985. *Mentoring and Work: Development Relationships in Organizations.* Greenview, IL: Scott Foresman

Kraut, A. I., Pedigo, P. R., McKenna, D. D., Dunnette, M. D. 1989. The role of the manager: what's really important in different managerial jobs. *Acad. Manage. Exec.* 3:286–93

Kuhl, J. 1985. Volitional mediators of cognition-behavior consistency: self-regulatory processes and action versus state orientation. See Kuhl & Beckman 1985, pp. 11–39

Kuhl, J., Beckman, J. eds. 1985. *Action Control: From Cognition to Behavior.* Berlin: Springer-Verlag

Kyllonen, P. C., Shute, V. J. 1989. A taxonomy of learning skills. See Ackerman et al 1989, pp. 117–63

Laker, D. R. 1990. Dual dimensionality of training transfer. *Hum. Resour. Dev. Q.* 1:209–23

Lance, C. E., Mayfield, D. L., Gould, R. B., Lynskey, M. C. 1991. Global versus decomposed estimates of cross-job retraining time. *Hum. Perform.* Vol. 4:71–88

Lassiter, D. L., Vaughn, J. S., Smaltz, V. E., Morgan, B. B. 1990. A comparison of two types of training interventions on team communication performance. Presented at the Meet. Hum. Factors Soc.

Latham, G. P. 1988. Human resource training and development. *Annu. Rev. Psychol.* 39: 545–82

Latham, G. P. 1989. Behavioral approaches to the training and learning process. See Goldstein 1989, pp. 256–95

Latham, G. P., Frayne, C. A. 1989. Self-management training for increasing job attendance: a follow-up and replication. *J. Appl. Psychol.* 74:411–16

Lepsinger, R., Mullen, T. P., Stumpf, S. A., Wall, S. J. 1988. Large scale management simulations: a training technology for assessing and developing strategic management skills. In *The Practice of Management Development,* ed. S. Mailick, S. Hoberman, S. J. Wall, pp. 173–83. New York: Praeger

Levine, E. L., Baker, C. V. 1991. Team task analysis: a procedural guide and test of a methodology. Paper presented at Annu. Meet. Soc. Indust. Org. Psychol.

Lippert, R. C. 1989. Expert systems: tutors, tools and tutees. *J. Computer-Based Instr.* 16:11–19

London, M. 1987. Employee development in a downsizing organization. *J. Bus. Psychol.* 2:60–73

London, M. 1989. *Managing the Training Enterprise.* San Francisco: Jossey-Bass

London, M., Bassman, E. 1989. Retraining midcareer workers for the future workplace. See Goldstein 1989, pp. 333–75

London, M., Mone, E. M. 1987. *Career Management and Survival in the Workplace:*

Helping Employees Make Tough Career Decisions. San Francisco: Jossey-Bass

Luthans, F., Kreitner, R. 1985. *Organizational Behavior Modification and Beyond.* Illinois: Scott, Foresman & Co

Manz, C., Sims, H. 1989. *Superleadership: Leading Others to Lead Themselves.* New York: Simon & Schuster

Marx, R. D. 1982. Relapse prevention for managerial training: a model for maintenance of behavior change. *Acad. Manage. Rev.* 7:433–41

Marx, R. D., Hamilton, E. E. 1991. Beyond skill building: a multiple perspective view of personnel training. *Issues Trends Bus. Econ.* In press

Marx, R. D., Karren, R. K. 1988. The effects of relapse prevention training and interactive followup on positive transfer of training. Paper presented at the Natl. Acad. Manage. Meet.

Marx, R. D., Karren, R. J. 1990. The effects of relapse prevention and post-training followup on time management behavior. Presented at the Annu. Meet. Acad. Manage., San Francisco

Marsick, V. 1990. Experience-based learning: executive learning outside the classroom. *J. Manage. Dev.* 9:50–60

Mathieu, J. E., Leonard, R. L. 1987. Applying utility concepts to a training program in supervisory skills: a time based approach. *Acad. Manage. J.* 30:316–35

Mathieu, J. E., Tannenbaum, S. I., Salas, E. 1990. A causal model of individual and situational influences on training effectiveness measures. Presented at the 5th Annu. Conf. Soc. Indust. Org. Psychol., Miami

Maxwell, S. E., Cole, D. A., Arvey, R. A., Salas, E. 1991. A comparison of methods for increasing power in randomized between-subjects designs. *Psychol. Bull.* In press

Mayer, S. J., Russell, J. S. 1987. Behavior modeling training in organizations: concerns and conclusions. *J. Manage.* 13:21–40

McCall, M. W. Jr., Lombardo, M. M. 1982. Using simulation for leadership and management research: through the Looking Glass. *Manage. Sci.* 28:533–49

McCall, M. W. Jr., Lombardo, M. M., Morrison, A. M. 1988. *The Lessons of Experience.* Lexington, MA: Lexington Books

McCauley, C. D., Lombardo, M. M., Usher, C. J. 1989. Diagnosing management development needs: an instrument based on how managers develop. *J. Manage.* 15: 389–403

McGehee, W., Thayer, P. W. 1961. *Training in Business and Industry.* New York: Wiley

Mills, G. E., Pace, R. W. 1989. What effects

do practice and video feedback have on the development of interpersonal communication skills. *J. Bus. Commun.* 26:159–76

Modrick, J. A. 1986. Team performance and training. In *Human Productivity Enhancement*, Vol. 1: *Training and Human Factors in Systems Design*, ed. J. Zeidner, pp. 130–66. New York: Praeger

Morgan, B. B., Salas, E. 1988. A research agenda for team training and performance: issues, alternatives, and solutions. *Proc. Interserv./Indust. Train. Sys. Conf.* 10:560–65

Morrison, J. E., Holding, D. H. 1990. Designing and gunnery training strategy. ARI Tech. Rep. 899. Alexandria, VA: Army Res. Inst. Behav. Soc. Sci.

Mumford, M. D., Weeks, J. L., Harding, F. D., Fleishman, E. A. 1987. Measuring occupational difficulty: a construct validation against training criteria. *J. Appl. Psychol.* 72:578–87

Mumford, M. D., Weeks, J. L., Harding, F. D., Fleishman, E. A. 1988. Relations between student characteristics, course content, and training outcomes: an integrative modeling effort. *J. Appl. Psychol.* 72:578–87

Murphy, K. R. 1989. Is the relationship between cognitive ability and job performance stable over time? *Hum. Perform.* 2:183–200

Noe, R. A. 1986. Trainees' attributes: neglected influences on training effectiveness. *Acad. Manage. Rev.* 11:736–49

Noe, R. A. 1988a. An investigation of the determinants of successful assigned mentoring relationships. *Pers. Psychol.* 41:457–79

Noe, R. A. 1988b. Women and mentoring: a review and research agenda. *Acad. Manage. Rev.* 13:65–78

Noe, R. A. 1991. Mentoring relationships for employee development. See Jones et al 1991, pp. 475–82

Noe, R. A., Schmitt, N. 1986. The influence of trainee attitudes on training effectiveness: test of a model. *Pers. Psychol.* 39:497–523

Nordhaug, O. 1989. Reward functions of personnel training. *Hum. Relat.* 42:373–88

Oser, R., McCallum, G. A., Salas, E., Morgan, B. B. 1989. Toward a definition of teamwork: an analysis of critical team behaviors. Tech Rep. TR-89–004. Orlando, FL: Naval Training Systems Center

Osigweh, C. A. B. 1989. Casing the case approach in management development. *J. Manage. Dev.* 8:41–57

Ostroff, C., Ford, J. K. 1989. Assessing training needs: critical levels of analysis. See Goldstein 1989, pp. 25–62

Parry, S. B., Reich, L. R. 1984. An uneasy look at behavioral modeling. *Train. Dev. J.* Mar.:57–62

Pellum, M. W., Teachout, M. S. 1990. A longitudinal evaluation of training effectiveness using multiple levels of information. Presented at the Annu. Meet. Soc. Indust. Org. Psychol.

Pentland, B. T. 1989. The learning curve and the forgetting curve: the importance of time and timing in the implementation of technological innovations. Presented at the 49th Annu. Meet. Acad. Manage., Washington, DC

Peters, L. H., O'Connor, E. J., Eulberg, J. R., Watson, T. W. 1988. An examination of situational constraints in Air Force work settings. *Hum. Perform.* 1:133–44

Pintrich, P. R., Cross, D. R., Kozma, R. B., McKeachie, W. J. 1986. Instructional psychology. *Annu. Rev. Psychol.* 37:611–51

Porter, L. W., McKibbin, L. 1989. *Future of Management Education and Development.* New York: McGraw-Hill

Pursell, E. D., Russell, J. S. 1991. Employee development. In *ASPA/BNA Handbook of Human Resource Management.* Vol. 5. *Developing Human Resources*, ed. K. Wexley, pp. 5-76–5-119. Washington, DC: BNA Books

Ragins, B. R. 1989. Barriers to mentoring: the female manager's dilemma. *Hum. Relat.* 42:1–22

Reilly, R. R., Israelski, E. W. 1988. Development and validation of minicourses in the telecommunication industry. *J. Appl. Psychol.* 73:721–26

Revans, R. W. 1982. *The Origin and Growth of Action Learning.* Hunt, England: Chatwell-Bratt, Bickley

Robertson, I. T. 1990. Behavior modelling: its record and potential in training and development. *Br. J. Manage.* 1:117–25

Robertson, I. T., Downs, S. 1989. Work sample tests of trainability: a meta-analysis. *J. Appl. Psychol.* 74:402–10

Ronen, S. 1989. Training the international assignee. See Goldstein 1989, pp. 417–53

Rosow, J. M., Zager, R. 1988. *Training-The Competitive Edge.* San Francisco: Jossey-Bass

Rouillier, J. Z., Goldstein, I. L. 1991. Determinants of the climate for transfer of training. Presented at the Meet. Soc. Indust. Org. Psychol.

Ruderman, M. N., Ohlott, P. J., McCauley, C. D. 1990. Assessing opportunities for leadership development. See Clark & Clark 1990, pp. 547–62

Russell, J. S., Wexley, K. N., Hunter, J. E. 1984. Questioning the effectiveness of behavior modeling training in an industrial setting. *Pers. Psychol.* 37:465–81

Ryder, J. M., Redding, R. E., & Beckschi, P. F. 1987. Training development for complex cognitive tasks. *Proc. 31st Annu. Meet. Hum. Factors Soc.* 2:1261–65

Saari, L. M., Johnson, T. R., Mclaughlin, S. D., Zimmerle, D. M. 1988. A survey of management training and education practices in U. S. companies. *Pers. Psychol.* 41:731–43

Sackett, P. R., Zedeck, S., Fogli, L. 1988. Relations between measures of typical and maximum job performance. *J. Appl. Psychol.* 73:482–86

Salas, E., Dickinson, T. L., Converse, S. A., Tannenbaum, S. I. 1991a. Toward an understanding of team performance and training. In *Teams: Their Training and Performance,* ed. R. W. Swezey & E. Salas. New Jersey: Ablex. In press

Salas, E., Dickinson, T. L., Tannenbaum, S. I., Converse, S. A. 1991b. A meta-analysis of team performance and training. Tech. Rep. Orlando, FL. Naval Training System Center. In press

Savage, R. E., Williges, B. H., Williges, R. C. 1982. Empirical prediction models for training group assignment. *Hum. Factor.* 24:417–26

Schneider, B., Konz, A. 1989. Strategic job analysis. *Hum. Resour. Manage.* 28:51–63

Schoorman, F. D., Schneider, B. 1988. *Facilitating Work Effectiveness.* Lexington, MA: Lexington Books

Schuler, R. S., Jackson, S. E. 1987. Organizational strategy and organizational level as determinants of human resource management practices. *Hum. Resour. Plan.* 10: 123–41

Snow, R. E. 1989. Cognitive-conative aptitude interactions in learning. In *Abilities, Motivation, and Methodology: The Minnesota Symposium on Learning and Individual Differences,* ed. R. Kanfer, P. L. Ackerman, R. Cudeck, pp. 435–74. Hillsdale, NJ: Erlbaum

Snow, R. E., Lohman, D. F. 1984. Toward a theory of cognitive aptitude for learning from instruction. *J. Educ. Psychol.* 76:347–76

Sonnenfeld, J. A., Peiperl, M. A. 1988. Staffing policy as a strategic response: a typology of career systems. *Acad. Manage. Rev.* 13:588–600

Sparrow, J. A. 1989. The measurement of job profile similarity for the prediction of transfer of learning: a research note. *J. Occup. Psychol.* 62:337–41

Sprangers, M., Hoogstraten, J. 1988. On delay and reassessment of retrospective ratings. *J. Exp. Educ.* 56:148–53

Sprangers, M., Hoogstraten, J. 1989. Pretesting effects in retrospective pretest-posttest designs. *J Appl. Psychol.* 74:265–72

Sterns, H. L., Doverspike, D. 1988. Training

and developing the older worker: implications for human resource management. In *14 Steps to Managing an Aging Workforce,* ed. H. Dennis. Lexington, NY

Sterns, H. L., Doverspike, D. 1989. Aging and the training and learning process. See Goldstein 1989, pp.299–332

Streufert, S., Pogash, R., Plasecki, M. 1988. Simulation-based assessment of managerial competence: reliability and validity. *Pers. Psychol.* 41:537–57

Stumpf, S. A., Dunbar, R. L. M. 1990. Using behavioral simulations in teaching strategy implementation. *Organ. Behav. Teach. Rev.*

Sundstrom, E., DeMeuse, K. P., Futrell, D. 1990. Work teams: applications and effectiveness. *Am. Psychol.* 45:120–33

Swanson, H. L. 1990. Influence of metacognitive knowledge and aptitude problem solving. *J. Educ. Psychol.* 82:306–14

Swezey, R. W., Salas, E., eds. 1991a. *Teams: Their Training and Performance.* Norwood, NJ: Ablex. In press

Swezey, R. W., Salas, E. 1991b. Guidelines for use in team training development. See Swezey & Salas 1991a. In press

Tannenbaum, S. I., Beard, R. L., Salas, E. 1991a. Team building and its influence on team effectiveness: an examination of conceptual and empirical developments In *Issues, Theory, and Research in Industrial/ Organizational Psychology,* ed. K. Kelley. Amsterdam: Elsevier. In press

Tannenbaum, S. I., Mathieu, J. E., Salas, E., Cannon-Bowers, J. A. 1991b. Meeting trainees' expectations: the influence of training fulfillment on the development of commitment, self-efficacy, and motivation. *J. Appl. Psychol.* In press

Taylor, M. S., Locke, E. A., Lee, C., Gist, M. E. 1984. Type A behavior and faculty research productivity: What are the mechanisms? *Organ. Behav. Hum. Perform.* 34:402–18

Tetrault, L. A., Schrieshiem, C. A., Neider, L. L. 1988. Leadership training interventions: a review. *Organ. Dev. J.* Fall:77–83

Thayer, P. W. 1989. A historical perspective on training. See Goldstein 1989, pp. 457–68

Thornton, G. C. III, Cleveland, J. N. 1990. Developing managerial talent through simulation. *Am. Psychol.* 45:190–99

Thorpe, J. A. 1987. The new technology of large scale simulation networking: implications for mastering the art of nonfighting. Proc. 9th Interserv./Indust. Train. Syst. Conf.

Trimble, S. K., Decker, P. J., Nathan, B. R. 1989. Effect of positive and negative models on learning in behavior modeling training. Presented at the 4th Annu. Conf. Soc. Indust. Org. Psychol., Boston

Tubbs, M. E., Ekeberg, S. E. 1991. The role of intentions in work motivation: implications for goal-setting theory and research. *Acad. Manage. Rev.* 16:180–99

Tung, R. 1988. *The New Expatriates: Managing Human Resources Abroad.* Cambridge, MA: Harper & Row

Van Velsor, E., Ruderman, M., Phillips, A. D. 1989. The lessons of the Looking Glass. *Leader. Org. Dev. J.* 10:27–31

Von Glinow, M. A., Milliman, J. 1990. Developing strategic international human resource management: prescriptions for multinational company success. *J. Manage. Issues* 2:91–104

Weiss, H. M. 1991. Learning theory and industrial and organizational psychology. See Dunnette & Hough 1991, pp. 171–222

Wexley, K. N. 1984. Personnel training. *Annu. Rev. Psychol.* 35:519–51

Wexley, K. N., Baldwin, T. T. 1986. Posttraining strategies for facilitating positive transfer: an empirical exploration. *Acad. Manage. J.* 29:503–20

Wexley, K. N., Latham, G. 1991. *Developing and Training Human Resources in Organizations.* Glenview, IL: Scott-Foresman. 2nd ed

Willbur, J. 1987. Does mentoring breed success? *Train. Dev. J.* Nov.:38–41

Williams, T. C., Thayer, P. W., Pond, S. B. 1991. Test of a model of motivational influences on reactions to training and learning. Presented at the 6th Annu. Conf. Soc. Indust. Org. Psychol., St. Louis

Wlodkowski, R. J. 1985. *Enhancing Adult Motivation to Learn.* San Francisco: Jossey-Bass

Wolfe, J. 1990. The evaluation of computer-based business games. Methodology, findings and future needs. In *ABSEL Guide to Experiential Learning and Simulation Gaming,* ed. J. W. Gentry. New York: Nichols Publishing

Wolfe, J., Roberts, C. R. 1986. The external validity of a business management game: a five year longitudinal study *Simul. Games* 17:45–59

Woods, S., Tannenbaum, S. I. 1990. Evaluating supervisory training: a case study. Presented at the Conf. Soc. Indust. Org. Psychol.

Yukl, G. 1989. *Leadership in Organizations.* Englewood Cliffs, NJ: Prentice-Hall

Yukl, G., Lepsinger, R. 1991. An integrative taxonomy of managerial behavior: implications for improving managerial effectiveness. See Jones et al 1991, pp. 563–72

Yukl, G., Wall, S., Lepsinger, R. 1990. Preliminary report on validation of the managerial practices survey. See Clark & Clark 1990, pp. 223–37

Zeitz, C. M., Spoehr, K. T. 1989. Knowledge organization and the acquisition of procedural expertise. *Appl. Cogn. Psychol.* 3:313–36

Zey, M. G. 1988. A mentor for all reasons. *Pers. J.* Jan.:46–51

Annu. Rev. Psychol. 1992. 43:443–471

THE PSYCHOBIOLOGY OF REINFORCERS

Norman M. White and Peter M. Milner

Department of Psychology, McGill University, Montreal, Quebec H3A 1B1 Canada

KEY WORDS: learning and memory, reward, self-stimulation, posttraining effects, conditioned motivation

CONTENTS

INTRODUCTION

B. F. Skinner (1938) defined a reinforcer as an event that follows a response and changes the probability that the response will be emitted in the future. As a consequence of Skinner's radical behaviorism the definition contains no information whatsoever about how reinforcers cause changes in future behavior. Apparently without thinking about the matter too carefully, most people refer to this process as "reinforcement." Walker (1969) was so irritated by what he considered to be the misuse of this ill-defined concept that he

443

0066-4308/92/0201-0443$02.00

likened reinforcement to J. R. R. Tolkien's (1964) all-powerful, all-corrupting "One Ring," suggesting that it had been inflicted on psychologists by an evil sorcerer. Although we doubt that its origins are quite so sinister, we do agree that the term generally obscures more than it explains.

It is, of course, possible to imagine a number of different mechanisms by which reinforcers could produce changes in behavior. A general feature of all such mechanisms is that they must explain how an event can change behavior when the new behavior occurs in the absence of the event. The obvious way to deal with this requirement is to explain the action of reinforcers in the context of learning and memory. Thus, an understanding of how reinforcers change behavior can be had by investigating the mechanism by which these events promote the acquisition (learning) and/or storage (memory) of information.

When the term "reinforcement" was first introduced into psychology [probably by G. V. Anrep, in his translation of Pavlov's *Conditioned Reflexes* (1927)] it was used in its ordinary, nontechnical sense to suggest strengthening; that is, the strengthening of synaptic connections. Thorndike (1898) and Hull (1943) also used concepts of this general type. In this sense reinforcers are events that enhance the storage of information about situations in which they are encountered. This enhanced storage increases the probability that the behavior leading to the reinforcer will be repeated in the future, even in the absence of the reinforcer. Note that this concept of the action of reinforcers does not require that the animal learn anything about the reinforcing event itself; it is simply a description of the tendency of an event to enhance information storage. A line of evidence beginning at least at the start of this century supports the idea that reinforcers have this type of action, which we refer to here as the *enhancing function* of reinforcers.

The role of reinforcers contemplated by the so-called "cognitive" learning theories (e.g. Tolman et al 1932; Tolman 1948) is quite different. First, these theories view reinforcers primarily as motivators: events or objects that elicit behavior. Second, such theories postulate that learning in general consists of the formation of representations of the relationships among objects and events. An encounter with a reinforcer leads to the formation of a representation of that event and of its relationship to other objects and events. As representations of reinforcers can also act as motivators of behavior, when the representation of a reinforcer is aroused by one of these associations, it results in a behavior appropriate to the situation in the absence of the reinforcer itself. We review evidence concerning the physiological basis of this function of reinforcers under the heading of *conditioned motivation*.

ENHANCING FUNCTION

Thorndike's (1911) notion of the enhancing action of reinforcers was called the *Law of Effect*. In "A proof of the law of effect" (Thorndike 1933), he described a phenomenon called "spread of effect." Human subjects were asked to free associate to each word in a list and were verbally reinforced for their response to a randomly chosen word. Upon later testing, recall was better for reinforced than unreinforced responses. Furthermore, recall of responses to words immediately before and after the reinforced word was also improved, showing a spreading of the effect of the reinforcer. Thus, a temporally contiguous but unrelated reinforcer was sufficient to increase the probability of observing those responses.

More recently, Huston et al (1974) trained mice on a passive avoidance task in which the animals were shocked for stepping down from a platform. When tested the next day, the mice remained on the platform for some time, their latency to step down being a measure of their memory for their experience on the previous day. Some of the mice were fed in their home cages immediately after stepping down and receiving shock; when tested they remained on the platform longer than those that had not been fed. This finding is interpreted as improved retention of the consequences of stepping down produced by the occurrence of an unrelated but contiguous reinforcer.

There were actually two reinforcers in this experiment: shock and food, and both had motivating as well as enhancing properties. The fact that the animals remained on the platform longer on the test day than on the training day suggests that they had formed a representation of the contingent relationship between stepping down and the aversive motivating property of the shock. The enhancing property of the shock may also have acted to strengthen the memory of this relationship and increase the animal's step-down latency; however, it was impossible to detect any such effect because it could not be separated from the effect of the shock's motivating property. This was not the case for the food, however. The fact that the animals that were fed after the training trial remained on the platform longer than those that were not fed shows two things: 1. that the enhancing property of the food reinforcer influenced the animals' behavior by strengthening their representations of the contingent relationship between stepping down and shock; and 2. that the animals learned nothing about the rewarding motivating property of the food. If the fed animals had formed a representation of the contingent relationship between stepping down and the rewarding motivating property of the food they would have stepped down sooner than the unfed animals on the test trial.

Because it will inevitably be obscured by a reinforcer's motivating property, the effect of the enhancing property on a given behavior generally cannot be observed in experimental paradigms in which the reinforcer is contingent upon that behavior. It can only be observed when reinforcers are presented noncontingently, so that animals do not learn about contingent relationships involving their motivating properties. Such demonstrations show that the enhancing property of reinforcers is independent of their motivating properties. Operationally, this usually means presenting the reinforcer within a few minutes after the end of an acquisition trial, in a venue different from the one in which the learning took place.

Memory Consolidation

A complete understanding of the enhancing property of reinforcers and of the paradigm that is used to demonstrate it requires a consideration of some ideas developed during the investigation of memory processes. Memory consolidation refers to an hypothetical process [usually attributed to Müller and Pilzecker (1900)] by which the labile neural representation of a memory that exists immediately after it is formed changes over time into a relatively permanent representation. As proposed by Hebb (1955), by Milner (1957), and by McGaugh and his coworkers (McGaugh & Herz 1972; Gold & McGaugh 1975) it is thought that both the labile and permanent forms of representation are instantiated in the same neurons, that the memory is represented by a change in the relationship among these neurons, and that consolidation involves a change in the way these altered relationships are stored, from self-re-excitation (reverberation) of neural activity during the labile phase, to altered synaptic function after consolidation.

According to this theory, events occurring during the labile period, immediately after acquisition, can affect the representation of the memory and, therefore, behaviors that are dependent on that representation. Certain posttraining events can disrupt the representation of a memory, resulting in impairment of any dependent behavior. Other posttraining events might affect the consolidation process, either hindering or promoting it. In the case of hindrance, future dependent behavior would be impaired; in the case of promotion, future behavior would be affected by the presence of a representation that is more accurate and more resistant to extinction than the representation of an unenhanced memory.

Several lines of evidence support these ideas. A number of publications over the past 95 years (Dana 1894; Burnham 1903; Ewert et al 1989; Russell & Nathan 1946) describe how individuals sustaining concussion often lose their memories for events that occurred during some period immediately prior to the trauma but retain normal memory for events that occurred earlier in time (retrograde amnesia). Patients receiving electro-convulsive shock (ECS) for therapeutic purposes also sustain memory loss for the events that immediately precede their treatments but retain normal memory for earlier events (Zubin & Barrera 1941). These observations are consistent with consolidation theory: Memories still in the labile state may be lost following concussion or ECS. Older memories, which have (in theory) undergone consolidation and become relatively permanent, are unaffected by these events.

In studies with animals, ECS, anoxia, and anesthetization, among other treatments, have been used to test consolidation theory (Duncan 1949; Pearlman et al 1961; Chorover & Schiller 1965; McGaugh 1966; McGaugh & Herz 1972; Bloch 1970; Hayes 1953; Thompson & Pryer 1956). When given immediately after training on a wide variety of tasks these treatments disrupt retention tested one or more days later. When the same treatments are delayed for 45 minutes or more after training they have little or no effect on retention, suggesting that the representation of the memory undergoes a change in form, from labile to permanent, during the immediate posttraining period.

Local electrical stimulation of the caudate nucleus, the amygdala, and the hippocampus also impairs performance on tasks requiring memory when applied immediately after training but not when applied later (see Kesner & Wilburn 1974, for review, and Gold et al 1977; Liang & McGaugh 1983; Kapp et al 1978; Collier et al 1982; Berman & Kesner 1976), suggesting the possibility that these brain structures may be involved in the neural representation of memories. Furthermore, electrical stimulation of the reticular formation (Glickman 1961; Kesner & Conner 1973; Kesner & Berman 1977; Hennevin et al 1989; Deweer 1970; Bloch 1970) and the hypothalamus (Kesner & Berman 1977; Mondadori et al 1976; Mueller et al 1977; Berman & Kesner 1976; Destrade & Cardo 1975; Destrade & Cazala 1979; Destrade & Jaffard 1978; Huston et al 1977) improve performance when given immediately after training on such tasks but not when applied after a delay. These findings suggest that neural representations of memories are also susceptible to enhancement during the labile phase and raise the possibility that these brain structures may be involved in the consolidation process.

Bloch et al (1970) studied the interaction of the disruptive effect of posttraining anesthetization and the enhancing action of posttraining reticular stimulation on memory. Rats were trained on a black-white discrimination for water reward. When each rat had learned which color led to water it was given a single reversal trial followed by administration of a fast-acting anesthetic or 30 sec of electrical stimulation of the reticular formation. Animals tested after the former treatment exhibited amnesia; those tested after the latter treatment exhibited enhanced performance of the reversal task compared to untreated animals.

The rats in another group received reticular stimulation followed by the anesthetic treatment, both immediately after training. These animals behaved in the same way as untreated control animals. This finding suggests that the two treatments acted on the same substrate: The stimulation may have promoted the consolidation process, making the representation of the memory more permanent and protecting it from the disruptive effect of the anesthetic. This in turn implies the possibility that the reverberatory phase itself causes the process known as consolidation. Prolonging or intensifying this phase may potentiate consolidation; shortening it may impair consolidation. Alternatively, posttraining memory-enhancing events may act on some other stage of the consolidation process, possibly at the synapses that are thought to change when representations of memories are stored.

These data and concepts from the area of memory consolidation provide a theoretical context in which to understand the memory-enhancing action of reinforcers. This property of reinforcers modulates, or modifies the consolidation process so as to enhance the representation of memories. The manifestation of such an enhanced memory depends upon the nature of the behavioral test. The behavior may be more accurate, quicker, or more resistant to extinction, compared to behavior based on a similar but unenhanced memory. Such alterations in behavior are among the effects of reinforcers described by Skinner's definition.

Posttraining Electrical Stimulation of the Brain

Several early experiments reported facilitation of memory with electrical stimulation of various brain structures (Kesner & Wilburn 1974), but the first investigators to appreciate the necessity of providing contiguous, noncontingent stimulation by delivering it after training in a different venue appear to have been Bloch and his colleagues (Bloch 1970; Bloch et al 1966; see also Denti et al 1970). Using stimulation of the midbrain reticular formation, these workers demonstrated enhanced retention of both appetitive and aversive multi- and single-trial learning tasks. Tests for electrical self-stimulation with the same electrodes and current intensities were negative, leading to the conclusion that the stimulation lacked motivating properties.

Two other sets of experiments on the enhancing action of rewarding posttraining electrical stimulation of the lateral hypothalamus were designed to rule out the possibility that the behavioral changes observed were due to learning about the motivating effects of the stimulation. Huston and coworkers (Huston et al 1977) trained rats on a black-white discrimination in a T-maze. Correct responses were rewarded with food in the goal box. Following each incorrect response the rats were removed from the empty goal box and placed into a stimulation chamber. Animals in the experimental group were given 30 sec of intermittent stimulation of the lateral hypothalamus; control animals were not stimulated. No stimulation was given to any animals following correct responses. Rats in the experimental group learned the discrimination faster than rats in the control group, strongly suggesting that the former did not learn a contingent relationship between the incorrect response and the rewarding stimulation. Rather, the finding suggests, the stimulation acted to enhance the animals' retention of the negative contingency of the incorrect (and possibly also the positive contingency of the correct) responses. Similar posttraining enhancement effects were observed using both passive (Huston et al 1977) and active (Mondadori et al 1976) avoidance tasks.

Huston and his coworkers interpret these enhancement effects in terms of experiments showing that neural activity can be facilitated by reward in operant conditioning paradigms (e.g. Olds 1962; Fox & Rudell 1968; Rosenfeld & Hetzler 1973). They suggest that these demonstrations model the effect of posttraining reward on the neural activity that is thought to represent memories during the labile period immediately after acquisition. If reward does in fact prolong this activity it would, according to an hypothesis already described, potentiate consolidation, resulting in an enhanced memory. Evidence that "rewarded" increases in firing rates can result from the direct iontophoretic application of cocaine, dopamine, and dynorphin A to hippocampal pyramidal cells contingently upon increases in their "operant" rates of firing has recently been summarized (Stein & Belluzzi 1989). Such an effect could constitute a physiological basis for this hypothesis.

White and his coworkers examined the effects on retention of posttraining electrical self-stimulation of the brain with electrodes located in the far-lateral part of the lateral hypothalamic area (FLHA). Since the animals bar-pressed avidly for the stimulation, it is clear that the posttraining event in these experiments had rewarding motivating properties. In one series of studies, (Coulombe & White 1980, 1982a,b) posttraining self-stimulation with electrodes in the FLHA improved retention of a tone-shock association (conditioned emotional response), a tone-water association (conditioned licking for water), and a tone-light association (sensory preconditioning). In all of these studies the animals were removed from the training apparatus immediately after exposure to the training stimuli and placed into a self-stimulation chamber for 20 min where they were allowed to bar-press for brain stimulation. Retention testing was conducted 24 hr later. In each case control groups in which the training stimuli were presented in an unassociated manner (Rescorla & Wagner 1972) showed that the behavioral change produced by the posttraining stimulation depended upon a contingent relationship between those stimuli but explicitly did not depend upon any learned relationship between the stimuli and the rewarding motivating properties of the posttraining self-stimulation. In other control groups the animals were allowed to self-stimulate 2 hr after training; no effects on retention were observed in these animals.

In another series of studies (Major & White 1978; White & Major 1978a) thirsty rats in an open field found a drinking tube that contained water for some rats and was dry for others. After taking a few licks, all rats were removed from the open field and allowed to bar-press for self-stimulation with electrodes located in the FLHA. When tested the next day, rats that had found water and then self-stimulated approached the drinking tube faster than those that had not self-stimulated. Rats that had found a dry drinking tube and then self-stimulated took much longer to approach the tube than rats that had not self-stimulated. The behavior of the animals in the latter groups shows that they did not learn a contingent relationship between the response of approaching the tube and the rewarding effects of the self-stimulation. Rather, the self-stimulation acted to enhance retention of the animals' experiences in the open field.

In other groups of rats, posttraining self-stimulation with electrodes located in the substantia nigra enhanced memory, but no such effect was observed when the electrodes were located in the medial part of the lateral hypothalamus or in the preoptic area, even though the animals' rates of bar-pressing suggested that stimulation of these areas was just as rewarding as stimulation of the effective areas. This finding shows that reward is not a sufficient condition for producing the memory-enhancement effect with brain stimulation. Rather, the stimulation must have acted on some process that is specific to consolidation. This could have been the prolongation or intensification of the labile phase or an action on some other stage of consolidation. On the basis of the fact that nigro-striatal dopamine-containing neurons traverse the effective but not the ineffective stimulation sites (Fallon & Moore 1978), White and his coworkers suggested that this process might involve the stimulation-induced release of dopamine from the terminals of these neurons in the dorsal striatum (caudate nucleus). This hypothesis was supported by the finding that administration of the dopamine receptor blocker pimozide blocked the posttraining memory-enhancing effect of self-stimulation of the FLHA (White & Major 1978b).

Post-Training Administration of Drugs and Endogenous Substances

The earliest reports of memory enhancement following posttraining injection of drugs appear to have been for strychnine (McGaugh et al 1962; McGaugh & Thomson 1962; Hudspeth 1964), and pentylenetetrazol (Grossman 1969). The effect of both of these drugs on the nervous system is excitatory, but there is no evidence that either of them has rewarding properties. This is consistent with the electrical stimulation data in two respects: 1. Reward is neither necessary nor sufficient to produce memory enhancement; and 2. the occurrence of a generally excitatory or arousing event during the posttraining period can enhance retention, possibly by prolonging or intensifying the neural activity representing the memory (McGaugh 1966; Gold & McGaugh 1975; Huston et al 1977).

Amphetamine is another excitatory drug that enhances retention when administered during the posttraining period (Doty & Doty 1966; Krivanek & McGaugh 1969; Evangelista & Izquierdo 1971), and there is considerable evidence from self-administration (Pickens & Thompson 1971; Hoebel et al 1983; Piazza et al 1989) and conditioned place preference (Reicher & Holman

1977; Spyraki et al 1982; Carr et al 1988) studies that this drug also has rewarding properties. Martinez et al (1980) reported that adrenal demedullation eliminated the posttraining memory-enhancing action of peripherally injected amphetamine, suggesting that the effect may be mediated by some peripheral action of the drug. White (1988) reported that posttraining injections of amphetamine failed to improve retention of a conditioned emotional response in rats with 6-OHDA lesions of the substantia nigra that reduced striatal dopamine to 12.2% of normal. This finding suggests that one of amphetamine's memory-enhancing actions is probably mediated by its dopamine-releasing action on these neurons (Biel & Bopp 1978; Romo et al 1986). This conclusion is consistent with reports that posttraining intracerebroventricular injections of both dopamine and norepinephrine improve retention (Haycock et al 1977), and that similar effects are observed following posttraining intracranial microinjections of amphetamine (Carr & White 1984) and of the direct dopamine receptor agonists quinpirole (LY-171555) (Packard & White 1991a; White & Viaud 1990) and SKF-38393 (Packard & White 1990a) into the dorsolateral part of the caudate nucleus, the site of termination of nigro-striatal neurons.

Injection of amphetamine into the dorsolateral caudate sites that enhance memory has no effect in the conditioned place preference (CPP) paradigm (Carr & White 1983), suggesting that this site does not mediate the drug's rewarding properties. Conversely, posttraining injection of amphetamine into the nucleus accumbens has no memory-enhancing effect (Carr 1981) but produces a conditioned place preference (Carr & White 1983), suggesting that this site mediates the rewarding, but not the memory-enhancing action of amphetamine. This dissociation between the sites at which the drug produces its memory-enhancing and rewarding actions is consistent with the notion that these two functions are independent.

Several other substances have both memory-enhancing and rewarding properties. Posttraining systemic (Staubli & Huston 1980) and intracerebroventricular (White et al 1978) injections of morphine enhance retention. It has also been reported that morphine impairs retention (Messing et al 1981; Introini-Collison et al 1985) and that the opiate antagonists, naloxone (Gallagher et al 1983; Messing et al 1979; Messing et al 1983; Tomaz et al 1990) and naltrexone (Introini-Collison et al 1985; Canli et al 1990; Castellano et al 1989b; Messing et al 1983) enhance retention. No explanation for these contradictory results is presently available. Morphine is self-administered (Woods & Schuster 1971), and systemic injections produce CPPs (Mucha et al 1982; Beach 1957; Hasenohrl et al 1989), suggesting that the drug has rewarding properties. Posttraining injections of endogenous peptides also have memory-enhancing effects (Baratti et al 1984; Flood & Morley 1988; Flood & Morley 1989; Itoh & Lal 1990; Introini-Collison et al

1985), and there is evidence that some of these substances also have reward-ing properties (Phillips et al 1982; Phillips & LePaine 1982; Croeders et al 1984; Heinrichs & Martinez 1986). Although there is some evidence concern-ing the physiological basis of the rewarding action of opiates (see Wise 1989 for a review), the basis of the memory-related effects of these substances is still in an early stage of investigation (McGaugh 1989). There is some evidence that the endogenous opiates and peptides interact with dopaminergic mechanisms in the striatum (see White 1989 for review).

Low doses of substance P injected either peripherally or centrally also produce both rewarding motivating and posttraining memory-enhancement effects; these data have recently been reviewed by Huston & Oitzl (1989). According to Huston's view, described above, substance P enhances memory because its motivating effects contingently reward the neural activity representing the memory, and the resulting increase in activity promotes consolidation. Substance P also interacts with dopamine in the nigro-striatal system (Waldmeier et al 1978; Elliott et al 1986; Sonsalla et al 1986; Cruz & Beckstead 1989; Tamiya et al 1990; Reid et al 1990).

There have been several demonstrations of posttraining memory-enhancing effects of picrotoxin, a gamma-amino-butyric acid (GABA) receptor an-tagonist (Breen & McGaugh 1961; Castellano & McGaugh 1989), and disrup-tion of retention by baclofen, a GABA receptor agonist (Castellano et al 1989a). Although there is no direct evidence that this substance has rewarding properties, it has been implicated in the control of the rewarding effects of electrical self-stimulation of the brain via its action on dopaminergic cell bodies in substantia nigra (Rompré & Wise 1989). By increasing dopamine release, this drug could affect retention in the same way amphetamine and other dopamine agonists do. Some of this evidence also implicates the amygdala in the memory-enhancing action of posttraining picrotoxin (McGaugh et al 1990).

Another well-documented posttraining, memory-enhancing effect is observed with epinephrine (Gold & van Buskirk 1975, 1976, 1978; Gold et al 1977). In an inhibitory (passive) avoidance paradigm with mild footshock, Gold and his coworkers observed that an optimum dose of epinephrine injected immediately after training, but not 2 hr later, enhanced retention; lower and higher doses were ineffective (Gold et al 1982; McCarty & Gold 1981). In the inhibitory avoidance paradigm with strong footshock the same dose of epinephrine impaired retention. The strong footshock alone increased plasma epinephrine and glucose levels. The mild footshock alone had no effect on epinephrine or glucose levels; however, the mild footshock followed by epinephrine (at the dose that enhanced retention) raised both plasma epinephrine and glucose levels by about the same amount as the strong footshock alone (Hall & Gold 1986). Gold and his coworkers determined that

100 mg/kg of glucose produced a rise in plasma glucose comparable to that produced by strong footshock alone or mild footshock followed by epinephrine.

These workers then reported that posttraining injection of 100 mg/kg of glucose enhanced retention of mild-shock inhibitory avoidance and impaired retention of strong-shock inhibitory avoidance (Gold 1986). Moreover, the adrenergic receptor blockers propranalol and phenoxybenzamine blocked the effects of posttraining epinephrine on memory but had no effect on the posttraining enhancement of memory by glucose (Gold et al 1986). This observation suggested that the hepatic glucose releasing action of epinephrine (Gorbman et al 1983) may mediate its memory-enhancing effect. Finally, these workers demonstrated that posttraining intracerebroventricular injections of glucose enhanced retention of the mild-shock inhibitory avoidance response (Lee et al 1988). This finding suggests that increases in plasma glucose, which could be produced by eating or by stressful events, may act on a central substrate to enhance retention.

Another approach to the investigation of the effect of glucose on memory has been taken by Messier & White (1984, 1987). Based on the finding that post-training self-stimulation at some brain sites failed to enhance retention even though it was rewarding, they compared the rewarding and memory-enhancing effects of post-training consumption of sucrose and saccharine solutions that were equated for their rewarding properties. Sucrose enhanced retention of a conditioned emotional response, while saccharine had no significant effect. This finding constitutes a further demonstration of the independence of reward and memory enhancement. More recently it has also been demonstrated that posttraining consumption of about 150 mg of saccharin in a highly concentrated solution enhances retention by an unknown mechanism (Stefaruk & van der Kooy 1989).

Posttraining injections of glucose, in amounts comparable to those voluntarily ingested by the rats during the posttraining period in the drinking study (2 g/kg), also enhanced retention for the conditioned emotional response. The dose of glucose used in these studies was considerably higher than that used by Gold and his coworkers. However, it has been shown that posttraining injection of both the 2 g/kg and 100 mg/kg doses can improve retention of the conditioned emotional response (White 1991) and of certain appetitive tasks (Messier & Destrade 1988; Packard & White 1990b). Doses below 100 mg/kg, above 2 g/kg, and between the two effective doses failed to affect retention of the conditioned emotional response, suggesting that the two values may be the optimally effective doses for two independent memory-enhancement mechanisms. This suggestion is supported by the fact that fructose, a sugar that does not enter the brain, is effective at 2 g/kg but not at 100 mg/kg (White 1991). Thus the low dose of glucose may affect memory consolidation by acting on a central substrate, while the high dose may have a similar effect by acting on a peripheral substrate.

Investigations of the peripheral substrate of the enhancing action of glucose have tended to eliminate the involvement of the adrenal medulla (White & Messier 1988) and insulin (Messier & White 1987). Lesions of the celiac ganglion, through which pass most of the autonomic afferents from liver to brain, block the enhancing action of glucose (Sawchenko & Friedman 1979), suggesting that the liver may mediate this effect in its capacity as a sensory organ. Several authors have speculated that the central enhancing action of glucose may be mediated by its potentiating effect on acetylcholine function (Stone et al 1988a,b, 1990; Messier et al 1990); and it can also be noted that blood glucose interacts with dopamine function (see White & Blackburn 1986 for review).

Summary

A wide variety of different treatments that undoubtedly act on an even larger array of both central and peripheral substrates have memory-enhancing properties, as demonstrated in posttraining paradigms. Many memory-enhancing substances also have rewarding motivational properties, but several lines of evidence from studies using self-stimulation, central injections of amphetamine, and consumption of sucrose and saccharin lead to the conclusion that the mechanisms of enhancement and motivation are independent. This means that the process by which the consolidation of a memory may be promoted is independent, in both the physiological and informational senses, of the representation of the memory itself. One idea concerning the enhancement phenomenon is that reverberatory activity by the neurons representing the memory may promote consolidation. Any process that prolongs or potentiates this activity by rewarding it or by directly increasing the excitability of the neurons involved might therefore enhance the memory. The other possibility is that an enhancing event may initiate a process that acts directly on some later stage of consolidation, possibly by promoting the synaptic change that is thought to be the basis of the consolidation process. Several lines of evidence suggest that dopamine may be one endogenous substance with this type of effect.

CONDITIONED MOTIVATION

Certain words—e.g. the name of a lover, or a cry of "Fire!"—cause changes in heart-rate, blood-pressure, skin-resistance, and other physiological measures in the hearer (Waller 1918); but not all words produce these effects. The autonomic responses produced by some words must therefore be the result of learned connections. This is acknowledged by the name given to the phenomenon: "conditioned emotional response." Autonomic responses are not the only responses that can be elicited by conditioned stimuli. A convincing cry of "Fire!" can cause you to leave a building in a hurry, perhaps through a window or other unusual exit. When animals make responses to a nonreinforcing stimulus that has become associated with a reinforcer, the stimulus is called a secondary (or conditioned) reinforcer; but because reinforcers are usually motivating, secondary reinforcement might be referred to more precisely as conditioned motivation, by analogy with conditioned emotional responses. Thus, one effect of introducing a reinforcer into a learning situation is to confer motivating power on previously nonmotivating stimuli. In this section we review physiological data that offer clues to the brain structures and mechanisms that participate in this sort of association.

Self-Stimulation Experiments

One approach to the study of biological mechanisms of reinforcement derives from the discovery that electrical stimulation of parts of the brain can be rewarding (Olds & Milner 1954). Soon after its discovery, Olds (Olds & Travis 1960; Olds et al 1956) found that brain-stimulation reward (BSR) is strongly attenuated by drugs that block catecholamine transmission, and shortly afterwards he identified the medial forebrain bundle (MFB) in the region of the lateral hypothalamus as a highly effective locus for BSR (Olds & Olds 1963). Subsequent research has indicated that dopamine is the most important catecholamine involved in the reward produced by MFB stimulation. (These experiments were extensively reviewed by Wise & Rompré 1989.) The main evidence for this conclusion is that specific antagonists of dopamine (e.g. α-flupenthixol) eliminate the effect. There are two major dopaminergic paths in the MFB, the nigro-striatal path, terminating in the caudate-putamen, and the mesolimbic path, which innervates several forebrain regions including the nucleus accumbens, the olfactory tubercle, the ventral pallidum, and part of the frontal cortex (Ungerstedt 1971a). Microinjections of neuroleptics into various sites have shown that for self-stimulation the relevant site of dopaminergic action is the nucleus accumbens (Mogenson et al 1979; Robertson & Mogenson 1978; Stellar et al 1983; Stellar & Corbett 1989; Nakajima 1989; Broekkamp 1976; Phillips et al 1989; Hunter et al 1988; Nakajima 1988; Mora et al 1975; Kurumiya & Nakajima 1988; Yim & Mogenson 1983; Robbins et al 1990). Furthermore, rats can learn to microinject dopamine agonists or potentiators into the nucleus accumbens (Dworkin et al 1986; Hoebel et al 1983) and to stimulate dopaminergic tissue grafted onto the striatum after the original dopaminergic afferents have been destroyed by 6-OHDA (Fray et al 1983).

When the presence of the dopaminergic pathways in the MFB first became known (Andén et al 1964; Hillarp et al 1966), many investigators assumed that they must be the paths fired by rewarding MFB stimulation. However, they consist of unmyelinated axons; and although the stimulation most frequently used in self-stimulation experiments at the time was a 60 Hz sine-wave current, which is capable of firing unmyelinated fibers, it was already known that animals self-stimulate for pulses 0.1 msec or shorter, and refractory period measurements (Deutsch 1964; Gallistel et al 1969) indicated that such short pulses stimulate mostly myelinated fibers. More recently Millar et al (1985) have shown that when the MFB is stimulated using 0.1 msec pulses the release of dopamine in the striatum is too small to be detected, though release can easily be demonstrated when pulses longer than 0.5 msec are used. To save the dopamine hypothesis, it has been proposed that directly stimulated myelinated fibers synapse with dopamine neurons in the tegmentum, thereby firing the ascending dopamine pathways indirectly (Bozarth 1987; Wise & Rompré 1989). This idea gained credence from the discovery that the directly stimulated myelinated fibers conduct impulses in the caudal direction (Bielajew & Shizgal 1986). The fact that microinjections of opiate in the vicinity of the ventral tegmentum are rewarding (Bozarth & Wise 1981) has also been interpreted as supporting the dopamine theory of reward, because dopaminergic cells in the ventral tegmental area are known to have opiate receptors (Bozarth 1986). Phillips et al (1989) found a high correlation between bar-pressing rate and voltammetrically measured dopamine activity in the nucleus accumbens. Unfortunately the only type of stimulation they used was a 60 Hz sine-wave, which stimulates unmyelinated fibers well, so it is not possible to say from these results whether the correlation would hold for stimulation that does not directly fire the dopamine path.

Although the effectiveness of MFB stimulation varies with the level of dopamine released in the striatum, several experiments indicate that other input is also important. For example, the failure of Millar et al (1985) to detect any change in dopamine level during self-stimulation in the experiment just described argues against the reward's being due to the indirect firing of dopaminergic paths. Nor can the dopamine theory explain Gallistel's (1986) inability to detect any change in nucleus accumbens activity, as measured by uptake of labeled 2-deoxyglucose (2-DG), during self-stimulation with 0.1 msec pulses, though changes were seen either when longer pulses were used or when amphetamine or a neuroleptic was administered. Even using 60 Hz sine-wave stimulation Druhan et al (1987) found that when stimulation of the ventral tegmental area was brief and presented at short intervals, rats' ability to discriminate between strong and weak stimulation was unaffected by administration of amphetamine or haloperidol, whereas if less-frequent but longer-lasting stimulation was used their ability to discriminate intensity was impaired by the drugs, indicating that, depending on the parameters of stimulation, the discriminations were, or were not, based on dopamine release.

Hand & Franklin (1985) found that 6-OHDA lesions of the dopamine cells of the ventral tegmental area, the source of the mesolimbic path, had little effect on MFB self-stimulation. Amphetamine increased the rate of bar-pressing as much in the lesioned rats as in controls. In another experiment K. B. J. Franklin and A. Robertson (unpublished) found that 6-OHDA lesions of the nucleus accumbens had no effect on either the rate of MFB self-stimulation or the increase in self-stimulation rate produced by amphetamine, though the lesion did reduce the effect of amphetamine on locomotion. It is clear that chronic lesions produced by 6-OHDA have less effect than acute blocking of dopamine transmission by neuroleptics. At present it seems safe to assume that reward from MFB stimulation is modulated by dopamine level, probably in both the dorsal and ventral striatum, but it would be a mistake to jump to the conclusion that the dopamine paths are the main input for reward signals (Milner 1991).

Conventional Rewards

In view of the similarities in behavior produced by brain-stimulation reward and conventional rewards such as food and water, the suggestion was put forward that conventional rewards also involve the release of dopamine in the striatum (e.g. Beninger 1983; Wise 1982), and a number of experiments have investigated this possibility. It has long been known that bilateral lesions of the lateral hypothalamus produce transient aphagia in rats (Anand & Brobeck 1951), and it was later found that 6-OHDA lesions of the ascending dopaminergic pathways in the same region produce a similar eating disorder (Ungerstedt 1971b; Marshall et al 1974). Several studies (Wise et al 1978; Beninger et al 1987; Nakajima 1986; Wise & Colle 1984) have shown that neuroleptics reduce feeding; and Ettenberg & Camp (1986) found that haloperidol administered before some trials during training of a food-rewarded task produced a partial reinforcement extinction effect (this *should*, of course, be "partial *reward* extinction effect") like that produced by with-holding food on some trials. These data tend to confirm the hypothesis that some conventional primary rewards such as food owe their motivating effect to dopaminergic activity. When a dopamine block is confined to the mesolimbic system, however, no changes are seen in eating (Wise & Rompré 1989). These authors suggest that the nigro-striatal bundle is the path that modulates eating and drinking.

Attempts have been made to measure levels of dopamine activity directly, either biochemically, by determining the ratios of dopamine metabolic pro-ducts to dopamine, or electrochemically by voltammetry. Heffner et al (1980) found that an hour after the onset of feeding there was an increase in dopamine metabolism in the hypothalamus, the nucleus accumbens, and the amygdala of rats. Blackburn et al (1986) also found that eating pellets or a liquid diet increased the turnover of dopamine in the nucleus accumbens and striatum. Both these experiments used biochemical methods to determine the increase in dopamine release, and thus the time relation between feeding and dopamine release could not be precisely determined. Later, however, Blackburn et al (1989) found that the turnover of dopamine in the nucleus accumbens was associated with the presence of conditioned reinforcers and that bouts of feeding a few minutes long had no effect on the ratio of metabolites to dopamine. This observation was in keeping with an earlier experiment in which Blackburn et al (1987) found that pimozide impaired conditioned responses to food but did not have any effect on feeding once the food was delivered. It is difficult to reconcile the finding that striatal dopamine increases only during conditioned reward, and not during primary reward with food, with the common view that the effects of primary reward are produced by dopamine release. These experiments should be repeated using a faster method of measuring the rate of dopamine release, such as differential ramp voltammetry (Millar & Williams 1990).

As in the case of MFB self-stimulation, there is ample evidence that dopamine plays a role in at least some types of conventional reward. At the same time, there is little evidence that an increase in dopamine release is necessary for reward to occur. The data persistently point to the involvement of alternative reward paths, apparently modulated by dopamine but not themselves dopaminergic. It is conceivable that in the absence of this alternative activity dopamine release in the striatum would not have any rewarding effect. A possible relay for this nondopaminergic input to the striatum is the amygdala. We review data supporting this view in the next section.

Amygdala

Brown & Schäfer (1888) observed monkeys whose temporal lobes had been removed and were impressed by their insatiable curiosity, remarkable loss of aggressiveness, and indiscriminate feeding. These results were replicated by Klüver and Bucy (1939) half a century later and were subsequently shown to depend mainly on damage to the amygdala (Rosvold et al 1951; Rosvold et al 1954). More formal testing of amygdalectomized animals revealed deficits in avoidance learning and conditioned emotional response (Pribram & Weiskrantz 1957; Brady et al 1954; Horvath 1963; Weiskrantz 1956). Weiskrantz & Wilson (1958) found that amygdaloid lesions raised avoidance thresholds; there is also a report (Milner et al 1968) of elevated pain threshold in a patient with medial temporal lobe lesions (which include amygdala and hippocampus). Goddard (1964) found that weak electrical stimulation of the amygdala immediately after pairing sound with shock interfered with the consolidation of a conditioned emotional response. He concluded that "Both the present investigation and the majority of lesion studies appear to suggest that one of the major functions of the amygdala is the consolidation of the association of a neutral stimulus with an aversive stimulus" (p. 30).

The role of the amygdala in conditioned fear is also illustrated in a number of experiments using the fear-potentiated startle response (Brown et al 1951). Hitchcock & Davis (1986) found that bilateral lesions of the central nucleus of the amygdala eliminated the potentiation of startle by a conditioned fear stimulus. The startle response itself was also attenuated to some extent by the lesion. The same investigators (Hitchcock & Davis 1987) later found that the lesion also eliminated the potentiation of startle by an auditory cue conditioned to foot-shock. Electrical stimulation of the central nucleus of the amygdala markedly increases the startle response in intact rats (Davis 1986). Potentiation of the startle response depends on a pathway from the amygdala to the substantia nigra (Mondlock & Davis 1985).

Although Goddard (1964) found no effect of amygdaloid stimulation on the learning of a response rewarded by food, it does appear that the amygdala plays an important role in feeding. Amygdalectomy greatly reduces neophobia in general, and particularly gustatory neophobia (Nachman & Ashe 1974; Rolls & Rolls 1973; Sutherland & McDonald 1990), suggesting that the amygdala is part of a system that inhibits basic appetitive responses in the presence of novel sensory input. Schwartzbaum (1965) noted severe impairment on discrimination reversals and learning-set problems for food reward in amygdalectomized monkeys. Jones & Mishkin (1972), in a series of experiments expressly designed to localize stimulus-reward association, confirmed the impairment of food-rewarded learning in reversal problems. Gaffan & Harrison (1987) trained monkeys on learning-set problems using secondary reinforcement only. The monkeys had previously been trained to make visual discriminations for food reward. During an intermediate period, correct responses were rewarded by a positive sound which was followed half the time by food; incorrect responses were followed by a different sound and no reward. Finally the monkey made visual discriminations with no other reinforcement than the positive sound for correct responses and the negative sound for errors. When the monkeys had acquired the learning-set using only secondary reinforcement, bilateral amygdalectomy severely impaired the performance. Lesions that disconnected the amygdala from the auditory input had a similar effect, but disconnection of the amygdala from the visual input had no effect. The interpretation was that the amygdala was responsible for associating neutral stimuli with the primary reinforcing effect of food.

These results are in keeping with the generally held view that the limbic system is responsible for emotional and motivational expression and that to acquire emotional or secondary reinforcing properties sensory input must therefore acquire an association with the limbic system (Spiegler & Mishkin 1981); but the question then arises, how does the limbic system influence responses? There are important pathways from the amygdala to the hypothalamus (see Gloor 1960) and to the ventral striatum (Kelley et al 1982; Swanson & Mogenson 1981), the hypothalamic projections probably subserve the autonomic "emotional" responses, and the connections to the striatum and nucleus accumbens are well directed to influence learned skeletal responses (Mogenson 1984). Everitt et al (1989) trained male rats to bar-press for the secondary reinforcement of a light that had been associated with the appearance of an estrous female. The bar-pressing response was attenuated by neurotoxic lesions of the basolateral amygdalae, though the lesions did not affect sexual behavior. Infusion of D-amphetamine into the nucleus accumbens reversed the effect of the lesions. In a parallel experiment Cador et al (1989) conditioned a stimulus to water and then measured the preference of thirsty rats for a lever that delivered the stimulus in a 2-lever box. The preference for the lever delivering secondary reinforcement was reduced after neurotoxic lesions of the basolateral amygdalae. Injections of D-amphetamine into the nucleus accumbens increased the rate of responding of both amygdalectomized and sham-operated rats.

Further evidence for the participation of the amygdala (more specifically, the lateral nucleus of the amygdala) is provided by an experiment in which lesions of that nucleus attenuated a conditioned place preference produced by administration of D-amphetamine (Hiroi & White 1991). Lesions of other nuclei of the amygdala or of the fornix had no effect on the preference. Hiroi & White (1990) had previously shown that expression of the conditioned place preference induced by D-amphetamine is blocked by bilateral micro-injection of the neuroleptic α-flupenthixol into the accumbens, indicating that the association of the preferred compartment with amphetamine reward takes place via a pathway that involves the amygdala and the nucleus accumbens. These experiments are consistent with the idea that the ventral striatum is an interface between the limbic system and the motor system, as suggested by Mogenson et al (1980), Mogenson (1984), and Milner (1977). The lateral nucleus of the amygdala has strong reciprocal connections with the cortex, thalamus, and hypothalamus; it also projects to the striatum, especially the nucleus accumbens, as well as having direct connections to the primary motor cortex (De Olmos et al 1985).

Striatum

In order to motivate, a stimulus must influence the motor system. In keeping with the anatomy of the day, Pavlov (1927) assumed that during conditioning the motor cortex acquired direct connections from analyzers in the sensory cortex. Subsequent research points to the importance of the striatum as the important link between motivating stimuli, conditioned as well as un-conditioned, and motor activation. The caudate-putamen receives much of its input from the neocortex; the nucleus accumbens receives a comparable input from the hippocampus and amygdala. The main efferents from the striatum are to the pallidum, which provides a major relay to the motor cortex via the thalamus, as well as more direct paths to brainstem motor nuclei (Graybiel 1990; Alexander & Crutcher 1990). A simple way in which reward input to the striatum could influence responses is by "gating," or modulating, the ongoing motor activity. Increased dopaminergic activity, induced by large doses of amphetamine, for example, undoubtedly lowers the threshold for responding, maintaining an ongoing response in much the way a contingent reward would do (Ettenberg & Milner 1977; Randrup & Munkvad 1970; Robbins 1976; Valenstein 1980; White 1986). Milner (1977) has suggested that this gating function of the striatum becomes conditioned to brain activity (representing stimuli and planned responses) frequently occurring before a reward. The presence of dopamine likely enhances this association. Thus, the plan to make a response that has previously led to a reward in a particular situation is more likely to be executed in a similar situation than plans less strongly associated with reward.

On the basis of experiments demonstrating that caudate nucleus lesions disrupt acquisition of a conditioned emotional response, and that posttraining microinjections of amphetamine into the striatum improve memory (Carr & White 1984; Viaud & White 1989), White recently (1989) suggested that some learning may involve direct association between sensory input and the striatal motor path. This theory is supported by a number of experiments in rats and monkeys showing that discrimination learning, but not short-term recognition memory (e.g. "working memory" in the radial maze), is impaired by caudate-putamen lesions (Packard et al 1989; Wang et al 1990), while discrimination learning is spared by hippocampal ablation that abolishes short-term recognition. Although these results have been interpreted as supporting the thesis of Hirsh (1974), Mishkin & Petri (1984), and others that simple discrimination learning, especially in the absence of the hippocampus, must take the form of classical S-R association, other interpretations are possible. "Expectancies" may be acquired by neocortical association, and they could then facilitate or inhibit responses via the striatum in a typical cognitive way. The difference between neocortical motivating associations and limbic ones is that cortical associations require multiple presentations to become effective (Milner 1989); thus such tasks as remembering which alleys have been entered in the radial maze, or which objects were recently presented in the matching-to-sample task, would be severely impaired in the absence of the hippocampus and amygdala, structures that are assumed to acquire effective (but transient) associations in one trial. It is less easy to explain why caudate lesions selectively impair simple discriminations unless such discriminations depend on cortical input to the caudate-putamen, whereas more complex ("cognitive") learning may be acquired via limbic-accumbens routes.

Summary

In the normal animal an important function of rewards and punishments is to condition their motivating effects to other brain activity present at the time. Data from brain-stimulation reward experiments point to the nucleus accumbens as an important site at which rewards influence responses, and (with the rest of the striatum) it is probably the structure in which neutral stimuli are associated with rewards. Increased striatal dopamine certainly enhances reward, though it seems likely that the true reward inputs to the striatum are not dopaminergic; they probably arrive via the amygdala, hippocampus, or neocortex. We speculate that the striatum serves a dual role. In conjunction with other parts of the motor system it controls specific responses such as grooming, licking, walking, etc, and is involved in associating these responses with specific sensory inputs; but it also has a gating function, facilitating or inhibiting incipient responses in response to unconditioned or conditioned (i.e. expected) motivating input. These two functions may correspond in part to the division of the striatum into patches (or striosomes) and matrix (White 1989).

CONCLUSION

This review began with the question of how reinforcers change the probability of responding. The evidence reviewed suggests that they do this in at least two ways. First, they enhance retention of learned behaviors and of information acquired through experience. This mechanism does not involve learning: The effect on the neural representation of memory is purely one of enhancement. The second function of reinforcers involves their motivating properties, which may be rewarding or aversive. Animals learn about these motivating properties; they become associated with neutral stimuli of various kinds, and the presence of these associations influences behavior when the stimuli are encountered on future occasions. In these two general ways, reinforcers change the probability of occurrence of a response, as described by Skinner.

On the physiological level, the evidence reviewed suggests that striatal dopamine function is central to both of the behavioral processes described. Although the enhancing function can be produced by a number of different events, both natural and experimental, two processes may account for most of them. All of the enhancing events interact with dopamine systems in some way. A large number of different kinds of events affect blood glucose, and the evidence presented suggests that this parameter of the internal environment can affect memory by actions on both central and peripheral substrates.

Other evidence reviewed implicates the ventral part of the striatum (nucleus accumbens) in both the acquisition of associations involving the motivating properties of reinforcers and in the mechanism whereby these associations influence ongoing behavior. The connections of the nucleus accumbens with limbic (amygdala, hippocampus) and cortical structures provide the basis for a neural system that can interact with dopamine to produce behavior based on previously experienced rewarding and aversive events.

The findings reviewed here suggest that future research should take into account more explicitly than has often been the case the fact that reinforcers affect behavior by their action on learning and memory mechanisms. Moreover, the two independent actions of reinforcers on these mechanisms should also be considered in interpreting the results of experiments.

Physiological systems suggested for future study by the evidence reviewed include the nigro-striatal dopamine system; the striatal patch/matrix anatomy and its associated neurochemicals, acetylcholine, opiate peptides, and GABA; acetylcholine function in other parts of the brain; and the interaction of hippocampus, amygdala, and cerebral cortex with the striatal system. In the periphery, the role of epinephrine, glucose, corticosteroids, and other substances that appear to affect memory will also be the subjects of further study.

ACKNOWLEDGMENTS

Preparation of this manuscript was supported by grants from the Natural Sciences and Engineering Council of Canada, and from Fonds FCAR, province de Québec.

Literature Cited

Alexander, G. E., Crutcher, M. D. 1990. Functional architecture of basal ganglia circuits: neural substrates of parallel processing. *Trends Neurosci.* 13:266–71

Anand, B. K., Brobeck, J. R. 1951. Hypothalamic control of food intake in rats and cats. *Yale J. Biol. Med.* 23:124–40

Andén, N.-E., Carlsson, A., Dahlström, A., Fuxe, K., Hillarp, N. A., Larsson, K. 1964. Demonstration and mapping out of nigro-striatal dopamine neurons. *Life Sci.* 3:523–30

Baratti, C. M., Introini, I. B., Huygens, P. 1984. Possible interaction between central cholinergic muscarinic and opioid peptidergic systems during memory consolidation in mice. *Behav. Neural Biol.* 40:155–69

Beach, H. D. 1957. Morphine addiction in rats. *Can. J. Psychol.* 11:104–12

Beninger, R. J. 1983. The role of dopamine in locomotor activity and learning. *Brain Res. Rev.* 6:173–96

Beninger, R. J., Cheng, M., Hahn, B. L., Hoffman, D. C., Mazurski, E. J., et al. 1987. Effects of extinction, pimozide, SCH 23390, and metoclopramide on food-rewarded operant responding of rats. *Psychopharmacology* 92:343–49

Berman, R. F., Kesner, R. P. 1976. Posttrial hippocampal, amygdaloid, and lateral hypothalamic electrical stimulation: effects on short- and long-term memory of an appetitive experience. *J. Comp. Physiol. Psychol.* 90:260–67

Biel, J. H., Bopp, B. A. 1978. Amphetamines: structure-activity relationships. In *Handbook of Psychopharmacology,* ed. L. L. Iversen, S. D. Iversen, S. H. Snyder, 11:1–39. New York: Plenum

Bielajew, C., Shizgal, P. 1986. Evidence implicating descending fibers in self-stimulation of the medial forebrain bundle. *J. Neurosci.* 6(4):919–29

Blackburn, J. R., Phillips, A. G., Fibiger, H. C. 1987. Dopamine and preparatory behavior: I. Effects of pimozide. *Behav. Neurosci.* 101:352–60

Blackburn, J. R., Phillips, A. G., Jakubovic, A., Fibiger, H. C. 1986. Increased dopamine metabolism in the nucleus accumbens and striatum following consumption of a nutritive meal but not a palatable nonnutritive saccharin solution. *Pharmacol. Biochem. Behav.* 25:1095–1100

Blackburn, J. R., Phillips, A. G., Jakubovic, A., Fibiger, H. C. 1989. Dopamine and preparatory behavior. II. A neurochemical analysis. *Behav. Neurosci.* 103:15–23

Bloch, V. 1970. Facts and hypotheses concerning memory consolidation processes. *Brain Res.* 24:561–75

Bloch, V., Denti, A., Schmaltz, G. 1966. Effets de la stimulation réticulaire sur la phase de consolidation de la trace amnésique. *J. Physiol. (Paris)* 58:469–70

Bloch, V., Deweer, B., Hennevin, E. 1970. Suppression de l'amnésie rétrograde et consolidation d'un apprentissage à essai unique par stimulation réticulaire. *Physiol. Behav.* 5:1235–41

Bozarth, M. A. 1986. Neural basis of psychomotor stimulant and opiate reward: evidence suggesting involvement of a common dopaminergic system. *Behav. Brain Res.* 22:107–16

Bozarth, M. A. 1987. Ventral tegmental reward system. In *Brain Reward Systems and Abuse,* ed. J. Engel, L. Oreland, pp. 1–17. New York: Raven Press

Bozarth, M. A., Wise, R. A. 1981. Intracranial self-administration of morphine into the ventral tegmental area in rats. *Life Sci.* 28:551–55

Brady, J. V., Schreiner, L., Geller, I., Kling, A. 1954. Subcortical mechanisms in emotional behavior: the effect of rhinencephalic injury upon the acquisition and retention of a conditioned avoidance response in cats. *J. Comp. Physiol. Psychol.* 47:179–86

Breen, R. A., McGaugh, J. L. 1961. Facilitation of maze learning with posttrial injections of picrotoxin. *J. Comp. Physiol. Psychol.* 54:498–501

Broekkamp, C. L. E. 1976. The effects of manipulations with the dopaminergic system on self-stimulation behavior. In *Brain-Stimulation Reward,* ed. A. Wauquier, E. T. Rolls, pp. 194–95. Amsterdam: North Holland

Brown, J. S., Kalish, H. I., Farber, I. E. 1951. Conditioned fear as revealed by magnitude of startle response to an auditory stimulus. *J. Exp. Psychol.* 41:317–28

Brown, S., Schäfer, E. A. 1888. An investigation into the functions of the occipital and temporal lobes of the monkey's brain. *Philos. Trans. R. Soc. London Ser. B* 179:303–27

Burnham, W. H. 1903. Retroactive amnesia: illustrative cases and a tentative explanation. *Am. J. Psychol.* 14:382–96

Cador, M., Robbins, T. W., Everitt, B. J. 1989. Involvement of the amygdala in stimulus-reward associations: interaction with the ventral striatum. *Neuroscience* 30:77–86

Canli, T., Cook, R. G., Miczek, K. A. 1990. Opiate antagonists enhance the working memory of rats in the radial maze. *Pharmacol. Biochem. Behav.* 36:521–25

Carr, G. D. 1981. *Relationships among amphetamine-induced locomotor activity, stereotypy, memory-facilitation and conditioned taste aversion.* Masters Thesis. McGill Univ.

Carr, G. D., Phillips, A. G., Fibiger, H. C. 1988. Independence of amphetamine reward from locomotor stimulation demonstrated by conditioned place preference. *Psychopharmacology* 94:221–26

Carr, G. D., White, N. M. 1983. Conditioned place preference from intra-accumbens but not intracaudate amphetamine injections. *Life Sci.* 33:2551–57

Carr, G. D., White, N. M. 1984. The relationship between stereotypy and memory improvement produced by amphetamine. *Psychopharmacology* 82:203–9

Castellano, C., Brioni, J. D., Nagahara, A. H., McGaugh, J. L. 1989a. Posttraining systemic and intra-amygdala administration of the GABA-B agonist baclofen impair retention. *Behav. Neural Biol.* 52:170–79

Castellano, C., Introini-Collison, I. B., Pavone, F., McGaugh, J. L. 1989b. Effects of naloxone and naltrexone on memory consolidation in CD1 mice: involvement of GABAergic mechanisms. *Pharmacol. Biochem. Behav.* 32:563–67

Castellano, C., McGaugh, J. L. 1989. Retention enhancement with post-training picrotoxin: lack of state-dependency. *Behav. Neural Biol.* 51:165–70

Chorover, S. L., Schiller, P. H. 1965. Short-term retrograde amnesia in rats. *J. Comp. Physiol. Psychol.* 59:73–78

Collier, T. J., Miller, J. S., Travis, J., Routtenberg, A. 1982. Dentate gyrus granule cells and memory: electrical stimulation disrupts memory for places rewarded. *Behav. Neural Biol.* 34:227–39

Coulombe, D., White, N. M. 1980. The effect of post-training lateral hypothalamic self-stimulation on aversive and appetitive classical conditioning. *Physiol. Behav.* 25:267–72

Coulombe, D., White, N. M. 1982a. Post-training self-stimulation and memory: a study of some parameters. *Physiol. Psychol.* 10:343–49

Coulombe, D., White, N. M. 1982b. The effect of post-training lateral hypothalamic self-stimulation on sensory pre-conditioning in rats. *Can. J. Psychol.* 36:57–66

Croeders, M. E., Lande, J. D., Smith, J. E. 1984. Self-administration of methionine enkephalin into the nucleus accumbens. *Pharmacol. Biochem. Behav.* 20:451–55

Cruz, C. J., Beckstead, R. M. 1989. Nigrostriatal dopamine neurons are required to maintain basal levels of substance P in the rat substantia nigra. *Neuroscience* 30:331–38

Dana, C. L. 1894. The study of a case of amnesia or 'double consciousness'. *Psychol. Rev.* 1:570–80

Davis, M. 1986. Pharmacological and anatomical analysis of fear conditioning using the fear-potentiated startle paradigm. *Behav. Neurosci.* 100:814–24

Denti, A., McGaugh, J. L., Landfield, P. W., Shinkman, P. G. 1970. Effects of posttrial electrical stimulation of the mesencephalic reticular formation on avoidance learning in rats. *Physiol. Behav.* 5:659–62

De Olmos, J., Alheid, G. F., Beltramino, C. A. 1985. Amygdala. In *The Rat Nervous System*, ed. G. Paxinos, 1:223–34. Sydney: Academic

Destrade, C., Cardo, B. 1975. Amélioration de la reminiscence par stimulation postessai de l'hypothalamus latéral chez la souris BALB/c. *C. R. Acad. Sci. Paris* 280:1401–4

Destrade, C., Cazala, P. 1979. Aversive and appetitive properties of lateral hypothalamic stimulation in mice. *Behav. Neural Biol.* 27:398–412

Destrade, C., Jaffard, R. 1978. Post-trial hippocampal and lateral hypothalamic electrical stimulation. *Behav. Biol.* 22:353–74

Deutsch, J. A. 1964. Behavioral measurement of the neural refractory period and its application to intracranial self-stimulation. *J. Comp. Physiol. Psychol.* 58:1–9

Deweer, B. 1970. Accélération de l'extinction d'un conditionnement par stimulation réticulaire chez le rat. *J. Physiol. (Paris)* 62:270–71

Doty, B., Doty, L. 1966. Facilitating effects of amphetamine on avoidance conditioning in relation to age and problem difficulty. *Psychopharmacology* 9:234–41

Druhan, J. P., Martin-Iverson, M. T., Wilkie, D. M., Fibiger, H. C., Phillips, A. G. 1987. Dissociation of dopaminergic and non-dopaminergic substrates for cues produced by electrical stimulation of the ventral tegmental area. *Pharmacol. Biochem. Behav.* 28:251–59

Duncan, C. P. 1949. The retroactive effect of electroshock on learning. *J. Comp. Physiol. Psychol.* 42:32–44

Dworkin, S. I., Goeders, N. E., Smith, J. E. 1986. The reinforcing and rate effects of intracranial dopamine administration. In *Problems of Drug Dependence*, ed. L. S.

Harris, pp. 242–48. Washington, DC: USGPO

Elliott, P. J., Nemeroff, C. B., Kilts, C. D. 1986. Evidence for a tonic facilitatory influence of substance P on dopamine release in the nucleus accumbens. *Brain Res.* 385:379–82

Ettenberg, A., Camp, C. H. 1986. Haloperidol induces a partial reinforcement extinction effect in rats: implications for a dopamine involvement in food reward. *Pharmacol. Biochem. Behav.* 25:813–21

Ettenberg, A., Milner, P. M. 1977. Effects of dopamine supersensitivity on lateral hypothalamic self-stimulation in rats. *Pharmacol. Biochem. Behav.* 7:507–14

Evangelista, A. M., Izquierdo, I. 1971. The effect of pre- and post-trial amphetamine injections on avoidance responses in rats. *Psychopharmacology* 20:42–47

Everitt, B. J., Cador, M., Robbins, T. W. 1989. Interactions between the amygdala and ventral striatum in stimulus-reward associations: studies using a second-order schedule of sexual reinforcement. *Neuroscience* 30:63–75

Ewert, J., Levin, H. S., Watson, M. G., Kalisky, Z. 1989. Procedural memory during posttraumatic amnesia in survivors of severe closed head injury: implications for rehabilitation. *Arch. Neurol.* 46:911–16

Fallon, J. H., Moore, R. Y. 1978. Catecholamine innervation of the basal forebrain. IV Topography of the dopamine projection to the basal forebrain and neostriatum. *J. Comp. Neurol.* 180:545–79

Flood, J. F., Morley, J. E. 1988. Effects of systemic pancreastatin on memory retention. *Peptides* 9:1077–80

Flood, J. F., Morley, J. E. 1989. Cholecystokinin receptors mediate enhanced memory retention produced by feeding and gastrointestinal peptides. *Peptides* 10:809–13

Fox, S. S., Rudell, A. P. 1968. Operant controlled neural event: formal and systematic approach to electrical coding of behavior in man. *Science* 162:1299–302

Fray, P. J., Dunnett, S. B., Iversen, S. D., Björklund, A., Stenevi, U. 1983. Nigral transplants reinnervating the dopamine-depleted neostriatum can sustain intracranial self-stimulation. *Science* 219:416–19

Gaffan, D., Harrison, S. 1987. Amygdalectomy and disconnection in visual learning for auditory secondary reinforcement by monkeys. *J. Neurosci.* 7:2285–92

Gallagher, M., King, R. A., Young, N. B. 1983. Opiate antagonists improve spatial memory. *Science* 221:975–76

Gallistel, C. R. 1986. The role of the dopaminergic projections in MFB self-stimulation. *Behav. Brain Res.* 22:97–105

Gallistel, C. R., Rolls, E., Greene, D. 1969. Neuron function inferred from behavioral and electrophysiological estimates of refractory period. *Science* 166:1028–30

Glickman, S. E. 1961. Perseverative neural processes and consolidation of the memory trace. *Psychol. Bull.* 58:218–33

Gloor, P. 1960. Amygdala. In *Handbook of Physiology, Section 1: Neurophysiology,* ed. J. Field, 2:1395–1420. Washington, DC: Am. Physiol. Soc.

Goddard, G. V. 1964. Amygdaloid stimulation and learning in the rat. *J. Comp. Physiol. Psychol.* 58:23–30

Gold, P. E. 1986. Glucose modulation of memory storage processing. *Behav. Neural Biol.* 45:342–49

Gold, P. E., Hankins, L. L., Rose, R. P. 1977. Time-dependent post-trial changes in the localization of amnestic electrical stimulation sites within the amygdala in rats. *Behav. Biol.* 20:32–40

Gold, P. E., McCarty, R., Sternberg, D. B. 1982. Peripheral catecholamines and memory modulation. In *Neuronal Plasticity and Memory Formation,* ed. C. Ajimone-Marsan, H. Matthies, pp. 327–38. New York: Raven

Gold, P. E., McGaugh, J. L. 1975. A single trace, two process view of memory storage processes. In *Short Term Memory,* ed. D. Deutsch, J. A. Deutsch. New York: Academic

Gold, P. E., van Buskirk, R. B. 1975. Facilitation of time-dependent memory processes with posttrial epinephrine injections. *Behav. Neural Biol.* 13:145–53

Gold, P. E., van Buskirk, R. B. 1976. Effects of post-trial hormone injections on memory processes. *Horm. Behav.* 7:509–17

Gold, P. E., van Buskirk, R. B. 1978. Posttraining brain norepinephrine concentrations: correlation with retention performance of avoidance training and with peripheral epinephrine modulation of memory processing. *Behav. Biol.* 23:509–20

Gold, P. E., van Buskirk, R. B., Haycock, J. W. 1977. Effects of posttraining epinephrine injections on retention of avoidance training in mice. *Behav. Neural Biol.* 20:197–204

Gold, P. E., Vogt, J., Hall, J. L. 1986. Glucose effects on memory: behavioral and pharmacological characteristics. *Behav. Neural Biol.* 46:145–55

Gorbman, A., Dickhoff, W. W., Vigna, S. R., Clark, N. B., Ralph, C. L. 1983. *Comparative Endocrinology.* New York: Wiley

Graybiel, A. M. 1990. Neurotransmitters and neuromodulators in the basal ganglia. *Trends Neurosci.* 13:244–54

Grossman, S. P. 1969. Faciliatation of learning following intracranial injections of pentylenetetrazol. *Physiol. Behav.* 4:625–28

Hall, J. L., Gold, P. E. 1986. The effects of training, epinephrine and glucose injections on plasma glucose levels in rats. *Behav. Neural Biol.* 46:156–67

Hand, T. H., Franklin, K. B. J. 1985. 6-OHDA lesions of the ventral tegmental area block morphine-induced but not amphetamine-induced facilitation of self-stimulation. *Brain Res.* 328:233–41

Hasenohrl, R. U., Oitzl, M.-S., Huston, J. P. 1989. Conditioned place preference in the corral: a procedure for measuring reinforcing properties of drugs. *J. Neurosci. Methods* 30:141–46

Haycock, J. W., van Buskirk, R. B., Ryan, J. R., McGaugh, J. L. 1977. Enhancement of retention with centrally administered catecholamines. *Exp. Neurol.* 54:199–208

Hayes, K. J. 1953. Anoxic and convulsive amnesia in rats. *J. Comp. Physiol. Psychol.* 46:216–17

Hebb, D. O. 1955. Drives and the C. N. S. (conceptual nervous system). *Psychol. Rev.* 62:243–54

Heffner, T. G., Hartman, J. A., Seiden, L. S. 1980. Feeding increases dopamine metabolism in the rat brain. *Science* 208:1168–70

Heinrichs, S. C., Martinez, J. L. 1986. Modification of place preference conditioning in mice by systemically administered [leu]enkephalin. *Behav. Brain Res.* 22:249–55

Hennevin, E., Hars, B., Bloch, V. 1989. Improvement of learning by mesencephalic reticular stimulation during postlearning paradoxical sleep. *Behav. Neural Biol.* 51:291–306

Hillarp, N. A., Fuxe, K., Dahlström, A. C. 1966. Demonstration and mapping of central neurons containing dopamine, noradrenaline, 5-hydroxytryptamine and their reactions to psychopharmaca. *Pharmacol. Rev.* 18:727–41

Hiroi, N., White, N. M. 1990. The reserpine-sensitive dopamine pool mediates (+)-amphetamine- conditioned reward in the place preference paradigm. *Brain Res.* 510:33–42

Hiroi, N., White, N. M. 1991. The lateral nucleus of the amygdala mediates expression of the amphetamine conditioned place preference. *J. Neurosci.* 11:2107–16

Hirsh, R. 1974. The hippocampus and contextual retrieval of information from memory: a theory. *Behav. Biol.* 12:421–44

Hitchcock, J. M., Davis, M. 1986. Lesions of the amygdala, but not of the cerebellum or red nucleus, block conditioned fear as measured with the potentiated startle paradigm. *Behav. Neurosci.* 100:11–22

Hitchcock, J. M., Davis, M. 1987. Fear-potentiated startle using an auditory conditioned stimulus: effect of lesions of the amygdala. *Physiol. Behav.* 39:403–8

Hoebel, B. G., Monaco, A. P., Hernandez, L., Aulisi, E. F., Stanley, B. G., Lenard, L. G. 1983. Self-injection of amphetamine directly into the brain. *Psychopharmacology* 81:158–63

Horvath, F. E. 1963. Effects of basolateral amygdalectomy on three types of avoidance behavior in cats. *J. Comp. Physiol. Psychol.* 56:380–89

Hudspeth, W. J. 1964. Strychnine: its facilitating effect on the solution of a simple oddity problem by the rat. *Science* 145:1331–33

Hull, C. L. 1943. *Principles of Behavior.* New York: Appleton-Century-Crofts

Hunter, G. A., Hernandez, L., Hoebel, B. G. 1988. Microdialysis shows increased dopamine turnover in the nucleus accumbens during lateral hypothalamic self-stimulation. *Soc. Neurosci. Abstr.* 14:1100

Huston, J. P., Mondadori, C., Waser, P. G. 1974. Facilitation of learning by reward of post-trial memory processes. *Experientia* 30:1038–40

Huston, J. P., Mueller, C. C., Mondadori, C. 1977. Memory facilitation by posttrial hypothalamic stimulation and other reinforcers: a central theory of reinforcement. *Biobehav. Rev.* 1:143–50

Huston, J. P., Oitzl, M.-S. 1989. The relationship between reinforcement and memory: parallels in the rewarding and mnemonic effects of the neuropeptide substance P. *Neurosci. Biobehav. Rev.* 13:171–80

Introini-Collison, I. B., McGaugh, J. L., Baratti, C. M. 1985. Pharmacological evidence of a central effect of naltrexone, morphine, and beta-endorphin and a peripheral effect of met- and Leu-enkephalin on retention of an inhibitory avoidance response in mice. *Behav. Neural Biol.* 44:434–46

Itoh, S., Lal, H. 1990. Influences of cholecystokinin and analogues on memory processes. *Drug Dev. Res.* 21:257–76

Jones, B., Mishkin, M. 1972. Limbic lesions and the problem of stimulus-reinforcement associations. *Exp. Neurol.* 36:362–77

Kapp, B. S., Gallagher, M., Holmquist, B. K., Theall, C. L. 1978. Retrograde amnesia and hippocampal stimulation: dependence upon the nature of associations formed during conditioning. *Behav. Biol.* 24:1–23

Kelley, A. E., Domesick, V. B., Nauta, W. J. H. 1982. The amygdalo-striatal projection in the rat- an anatomical study by anterograde and retrograde tracing methods. *Neuroscience* 7:615–30

Kesner, R. P., Berman, R. F. 1977. Effects of

midbrain reticular formation, hippocampal, and lateral hypothalamic stimulation upon recovery from neophobia and taste aversion learning. *Physiol. Behav.* 18:763–68

Kesner, R. P., Conner, H. S. 1973. Effects of electrical stimulation of limbic system and midbrain reticular formation upon short and long term memory. *Physiol. Behav.* 9:271–79

Kesner, R. P., Wilburn, M. W. 1974. A review of electrical stimulation of the brain in the context of learning and retention. *Behav. Biol.* 10:259–92

Klüver, H., Bucy, P. C. 1939. Preliminary analysis of functions of the temporal lobe in monkeys. *Arch. Neurol. Psychiatr.* 42:979–1000

Krivanek, J., McGaugh, J. L. 1969. Facilitating effects of pre- and post-training amphetamine administration on discrimination learning in mice. *Agents Actions* 1:36–42

Kurumiya, S., Nakajima, S. 1988. Dopamine D1 receptors in the nucleus accumbens: involvement in the reinforcing effect of tegmental stimulation. *Brain Res.* 448:1–6

Lee, M. K., Graham, S. N., Gold, P. E. 1988. Memory enhancement with posttraining intraventricular glucose injections in rats. *Behav. Neurosci.* 102:591–95

Liang, K. C., McGaugh, J. L. 1983. Lesions of the stria terminalis attenuate the amnestic effect of amygdaloid stimulation on avoidance responses. *Brain Res.* 274:309–18

Major, R., White, N. M. 1978. Memory facilitation by self-stimulation reinforcement mediated by the nigro-neostriatal bundle. *Physiol. Behav.* 20:723–33

Marshall, J. F., Richardson, J. S., Teitelbaum, P. 1974. Nigrostriatal bundle damage and the lateral hypothalamic syndrome. *J. Comp. Physiol. Psychol.* 87:808–30

Martinez, J. L., Vasquez, B. J., Rigter, H., Messing, R. B., Jensen, R. A., et al. 1980. Attenuation of amphetamine-induced enhancement of learning by adrenal demedullation. *Brain Res.* 195:433–43

McCarty, R., Gold, P. E. 1981. Plasma catecholamines: effects of footshock level and hormonal modulators of memory storage. *Horm. Behav.* 15:168–82

McGaugh, J. L. 1966. Time dependent processes in memory storage. *Science* 153:1351–58

McGaugh, J. L. 1989. Dissociating learning and performance: drug and hormone enhancement of memory storage. *Brain Res. Bull.* 23:339–45

McGaugh, J. L., Herz, M. J. 1972. *Memory Consolidation.* San Francisco: Albion

McGaugh, J. L., Introini-Collison, I. B., Nagahara, A. H., Cahill, L., Brioni, J. D., Castellano, C. 1990. Involvement of the amygdaloid complex in neuromodulatory influences on memory storage. *Neurosci. Biobehav. Rev.* 14:425–31

McGaugh, J. L., Thomson, C. W. 1962. Facilitation of simultaneous discrimination learning with strychnine sulphate. *Psychopharmacology* 3:166–72

McGaugh, J. L., Thomson, C. W., Westbrook, W. H., Hudspeth, W. J. 1962. A further study of learning facilitation with strychnine sulphate. *Psychopharmacology* 3:352–60

Messier, C., Destrade, C. 1988. Improvement of memory for an operant response by posttraining glucose in mice. *Behav. Brain Res.* 31:185–91

Messier, C., Durkin, T., Mrabet, O., Destrade, C. 1990. Memory-improving action of glucose: indirect evidence for a facilitation of hippocampal acetylcholine synthesis. *Behav. Brain Res.* 39:135–43

Messier, C., White, N. M. 1984. Contingent and non-contingent actions of sucrose and saccharin reinforcers: effects on taste preference and memory. *Physiol. Behav.* 32:195–203

Messier, C., White, N. M. 1987. Memory improvement by glucose, fructose and two glucose analogs: a possible effect on peripheral glucose transport. *Behav. Neural Biol.* 48:104–27

Messing, R. B., Jensen, R. A., Martinez, J. L., Spiehler, V. R., Vasquez, B. J., et al. 1979. Naloxone enhancement of memory. *Behav. Neural Biol.* 27:266–75

Messing, R. B., Jensen, R. A., Vasquez, B. J., Martinez, J. L., Spiehler, V. R., McGaugh, J. L. 1981. Opiate modulation of memory. In *Endogenous Peptides in Learning and Memory Processes,* ed. J. L. Martinez, R. A. Jensen, R. B. Messing, H. Rigter, J. L. McGaugh, pp. 431–43. New York: Academic

Messing, R. B., Rijk, H., Rigter, H. 1983. Facilitation of hot plate response learning by pre- and post-training naltrexone administration. *Psychopharmacology* 81:33–36

Millar, J., Stamford, J. A., Kruk, Z. L., Wightman, R. M. 1985. Electrochemical, pharmacological, and electrophysiological evidence of rapid dopamine release and removal in the rat caudate nucleus following electrical stimulation of the medial forebrain bundle. *Eur. J. Pharmacol.* 109:341–48

Millar, J., Williams, G. V. 1990. Fast differential ramp voltammetry: a new voltammetric technique designed specifically for use in neuronal tissue. *J. Electroanal. Chem.* 282:33–49

Milner, B., Corkin, S., Teuber, H.-L. 1968. Further analysis of the hippocampal amnesic syndrome: 14-year follow-up study of H. M. *Neuropsychologia* 6:215–34

Milner, P. M. 1957. The cell assembly: mark II. *Psychol. Rev.* 64:242–52

Milner, P. M. 1977. Theories of reinforcement, drive and motivation. In *Handbook of Psychopharmacology. Principles of Behavioral Pharmacology,* ed. L. L. Iversen, S. D. Iversen, S. H. Snyder, 7:181–200. New York: Plenum

Milner, P. M. 1989. A cell assembly theory of hippocampal amnesia. *Neuropsychologia* 27:23–30

Milner, P. M. 1991. Brain stimulation reward: a review. *Can. J. Psychol.* 45:1–36

Mishkin, M., Petri, H. L. 1984. Memories and habits: some implications for the analysis of learning and retention. In *Neuropsychology of Memory,* ed. L. R. Squire, N. Butters, pp. 287–96. New York: Guilford Press

Mogenson, G. J. 1984. Limbic-motor integration—with emphasis on initiation of exploratory and goal-directed locomotion. In *Modulation and Sensorimotor Activity During Alterations in Behavioral States,* pp. 121–37. New York: Alan R. Liss, Inc.

Mogenson, G. J., Jones, D. L., Yim, C. Y. 1980. From motivation to action: functional interface between the limbic system and the motor system. *Prog. Neurobiol.* 14:69–97

Mogenson, G. J., Takigawa, M., Robertson, A., Wu, M. 1979. Self-stimulation of the nucleus accumbens and ventral tegmental area of Tsai attenuated by microinjections of spiroperidol into the nucleus accumbens. *Brain Res.* 171:247–59

Mondadori, C., Ornstein, K., Waser, P. G., Huston, J. P. 1976. Post-trial reinforcing hypothalamic stimulation can facilitate avoidance learning. *Neurosci. Lett.* 2:183–87

Mondlock, J. M., Davis, M. 1985. The role of various amygdala projection areas (bed nucleus of stria terminalis, rostral lateral hypothalamus, substantia nigra) in fear-enhanced acoustic startle. *Soc. Neurosci. Abstr.* 2:331

Mora, F., Sanguinetti, A. M., Rolls, E. T., Shaw, S. G. 1975. Differential effects on self-stimulation and motor behaviour produced by microintracranial injections of a dopamine-receptor blocking agent. *Neurosci. Lett.* 1:179–84

Mucha, R. F., van der Kooy, D., O'Shaughnessy, M., Bucenieks, P. 1982. Drug reinforcement studied by the use of place conditioning in rat. *Brain Res.* 243:91–105

Mueller, C., Huston, J. P., Mondadori, C. 1977. Passive avoidance learning improved with intermittent but not continuous trains of post-trial rewarding hypothalamic stimulation. *Neurosci. Lett.* 6:279–81

Müller, G. E., Pilzecker, A. 1900. Experimentelle Beiträge zur Lehre vom Gedächtnis. *Z. Psychol. Physiol.* 1:1–288

Nachman, M., Ashe, J. H. 1974. Effects of basolateral amygdala lesions on neophobia, learned taste aversions, and sodium appetite in rats. *J. Comp. Physiol. Psychol.* 87:622–43

Nakajima, S. 1986. Suppression of operant responding in the rat by dopamine D1 receptor blockade with SCH 23390. *Physiol. Psychol.* 14:111–14

Nakajima, S. 1988. Involvement of dopamine D2 receptors in the reinforcement of operant behavior. *Soc. Neurosci. Abstr.* 14:1101

Nakajima, S. 1989. Effects of dopamine antagonists injected into the ventral tegmental area on lateral hypothalamic self-stimulation. *Soc. Neurosci. Abstr.* 15:34

Olds, J. 1962. Hypothalamic substrates of reward. *Psychol. Rev.* 42:554–604

Olds, J., Killam, K. F., Bach-y-Rita, P. 1956. Self-stimulation of the brain used as a screening method for tranquilizing drugs. *Science* 124:265–66

Olds, J., Milner, P. M. 1954. Positive reinforcement produced by electrical stimulation of septal area and other regions of rat brain. *J. Comp. Physiol. Psychol.* 47:419–27

Olds, J., Travis, R. P. 1960. Effects of chlorpromazine, meprobamate, pentobarbital and morphine on self-stimulation. *J. Pharmacol. Exp. Ther.* 128:397–404

Olds, M. E., Olds, J. 1963. Approach-avoidance analysis of rat diencephalon. *J. Comp. Neurol.* 120:259–95

Packard, M. G., Hirsh, R., White, N. M. 1989. Differential effects of fornix and caudate nucleus lesions on two radial maze tasks: evidence for multiple memory systems. *J. Neurosci.* 9:1465–72

Packard, M. G., White, N. M. 1990a. Dissociation of hippocampal and caudate nucleus memory systems by post-training intracerebral injection of dopamine agonists. *Behav. Neurosci.* 105:295–306

Packard, M. G., White, N. M. 1990b. Memory improvement produced by post-training glucose injections in two appetitive learning tasks. *Psychopharmacology* 18:282–86

Pavlov, I. P. 1927. *Conditioned Reflexes.* Oxford: Oxford Univ. Press

Pearlman, C. A., Sharpless, S. K., Jarvik, M. E. 1961. Retrograde amnesia produced by anesthetic and convulsant agents. *J. Comp. Physiol. Psychol.* 54:109–12

Phillips, A. G., Blaha, C. D., Fibiger, H. C. 1989. Neurochemical correlates of brain-stimulation reward measured by ex vivo and in vivo analyses. *Neurosci. Biobehav. Rev.* 13:99–104

Phillips, A. G., LePaine, F. G. 1982. Reward produced by microinjection of (D-

ala2),met5-enkephalinamide into the ventral tegmental area. *Behav. Brain Res.* 5:225–29

Phillips, A. G., Spyraki, C., Fibiger, H. C. 1982. Conditioned place preference with amphetamine and opiates as reward stimuli: attenuation by haloperidol. In *The Neural Basis of Feeding and Reward,* ed. B. G. Hoebel, D. Novin, pp. 455–64. Brunswik, ME: Haer Inst.

Piazza, P. V., Deminière, J.-M., Le Moal, M., Simon, H. 1989. Factors that predict individual vulnerability to amphetamine self-administration. *Science* 245:1511–13

Pickens, R., Thompson, T. 1971. Characteristics of stimulant drug reinforcement. In *Stimulus Properties of Drugs,* ed. T. Thompson, R. Pickens, pp. 177–92. New York: Appleton-Century-Crofts

Pribram, K. H., Weiskrantz, L. 1957. A comparison of the effects of medial and lateral cerebral resections on conditioned avoidance behavior in monkeys. *J. Comp. Physiol. Psychol.* 50:74–80

Randrup, A., Munkvad, I. 1970. Biochemical, anatomical and psychological investigations of stereotyped behavior induced by amphetamines. In *Amphetamines and Related Compounds,* ed. E. Costa, S. Garattini, pp. 695–713. New York: Raven

Reicher, M. A., Holman, E. W. 1977. Location preference and flavor aversion reinforced by amphetamine in rats. *Anim. Learn. Behav.* 5:343–46

Reid, M. S., Herrera-Marschitz, M., Hökfelt, T., Ohlin, H., Valentino, K. L., Ungerstedt, U. 1990. Effects of intranigral substance P and neurokinin A on striatal dopamine release. I. Interactions with substance P antagonists. *Neuroscience* 36:643–58

Rescorla, R. A., Wagner, A. R. 1972. A theory of Pavlovian conditioning: variations in the effectiveness of reinforcement and non-reinforcement. In *Classical Conditioning II: Current Research and Theory,* ed. A. H. Black, W. F. Procasy. New York: Appleton-Century-Crofts

Robbins, T. W. 1976. Relationship between reward-enhancing and stereotypical effects of psychomotor stimulant drugs. *Nature* 264:57–59

Robbins, T. W., Giardini, V., Jones, G. H., Reading, P., Sahakian, B. J. 1990. Effects of dopamine depletion from the caudate-putamen and nucleus accumbens septi on the acquisition and performance of a conditional discrimination task. *Behav. Brain Res.* 38:243–61

Robertson, A., Mogenson, G. J. 1978. Evidence for a role for dopamine in self-stimulation of the nucleus accumbens of the rat. *Can. J. Psychol.* 32:67–76

Rolls, E. T., Rolls, B. J. 1973. Altered food

preferences after lesions in the basolateral region of the amygdala in the rat. *J. Comp. Physiol. Psychol.* 83:218–59

Romo, R., Cheramy, A., Godeheu, G., Glowinski, J. 1986. In vivo presynaptic control of dopamine release in the cat caudate nucleus. 1. Opposite changes in neuronal activity and release evoked from thalamic motor nuclei. *Neuroscience* 19:1067–79

Rompré, P.-P., Wise, R. A. 1989. Behavioral evidence for midbrain dopamine depolarization inactivation. *Brain Res.* 477:152–56

Rosenfeld, J. P., Hetzler, B. E. 1973. Operant controlled evoked responses: discrimination of conditioned and normally occurring components. *Science* 181:767–70

Rosvold, H. E., Fuller, J. L., Pribram, K. H. 1951. Ablation of pyriform, amygdala, hippocampal complex in genetically pure strain cocker spaniels. In *Frontal Lobotomy and Affective Behavior: A Neurophysiological Analysis*, ed. J. F. Fulton, pp. 80–82. New York: Norton

Rosvold, H. E., Mirsky, A. F., Pribram, K. H. 1954. Influence of amygdalectomy on social behavior in monkeys. *J. Comp. Physiol. Psychol.* 47:173–78

Russell, W. R., Nathan, P. W. 1946. Traumatic amnesia. *Brain* 69:280–300

Sawchenko, P. E., Friedman, M. I. 1979. Sensory functions of the liver—a review. *Am. J. Physiol.* 236:R5–R20

Schwartzbaum, J. S. 1965. Discrimination behavior after amygdalectomy in monkeys: visual and somesthetic learning and perceptual capacity. *J. Comp. Physiol. Psychol.* 60:314–19

Skinner, B. F. 1938. *The Behavior of Organisms.* New York: Appleton-Century-Crofts

Sonsalla, P. K., Gibb, J. W., Hanson, G. R. 1986. Nigrostriatal dopamine actions on the D2 receptors mediate methamphetamine effects on the striatonigral substance P system. *Neuropharmacology* 25:1221–30

Spiegler, B. J., Mishkin, M. 1981. Evidence for the sequential participation of inferior temporal cortex and amygdala in the acquisition of stimulus-reward associations. *Behav. Brain Res.* 3:303–17

Spyraki, C., Fibiger, H. C., Phillips, A. G. 1982. Dopaminergic substrates of amphetamine-induced place preference conditioning. *Brain Res.* 253:185–93

Staubli, U., Huston, J. P. 1980. Avoidance learning enhanced by post-trial morphine injection. *Behav. Neural Biol.* 28:487–90

Stefaruk, T. L., van der Kooy, D. 1989. The kinetics of the motivational property of saccharin: measurement of rewarding and reinforcing effects. *Soc. Neurosci. Abstr.* 15:56

Stein, L., Belluzzi, J. D. 1989. Cellular investigations of behavioral reinforcement. *Neurosci. Biobehav. Rev.* 13:69–80

Stellar, J. R., Corbett, D. 1989. Regional neuroleptic microinjections indicate a role for nucleus accumbens in lateral hypothalamic self-stimulation reward. *Brain Res.* 477:126–43

Stellar, J. R., Kelley, A. E., Corbett, D. 1983. Effects of peripheral and central dopamine blockade on lateral hypothalamic self-stimulation: evidence for both reward and motor deficits. *Pharmacol. Biochem. Behav.* 18:433–42

Stone, W. S., Cottrill, K. L., Walker, D. L., Gold, P. E. 1988a. Blood glucose and brain function: interactions with CNS cholinergic systems. *Behav. Neural Biol.* 50:325–34

Stone, W. S., Croul, C. E., Gold, P. E. 1988b. Attenuation of scopolamine-induced amnesia in mice. *Psychopharmacology* 96:417–20

Stone, W. S., Rudd, R. J., Gold, P. E. 1990. Glucose and physostigmine effects on morphine- and amphetamine-induced increases in locomotor activity in mice. *Behav. Neural Biol.* 54:146–55

Sutherland, R. J., McDonald, R. J. 1990. Hippocampus, amygdala and memory deficits in rats. *Behav. Brain Res.* 37:57–79

Swanson, L. W., Mogenson, G. J. 1981. Neural mechanisms for functional coupling of autonomic, endocrine and skeletomotor responses in adaptive behavior. *Brain Res. Rev.* 3:1–34

Tamiya, R., Hanada, M., Kawai, Y., Inagaki, S., Takagi, H. 1990. Substance P afferents have synaptic contacts with dopaminergic neurons in the ventral tegmental area of the rat. *Neurosci. Lett.* 110:11–15

Thompson, R., Pryer, R. S. 1956. The effect of anoxia on the retention of a discrimination habit. *J. Comp. Physiol. Psychol.* 49: 297–300

Thorndike, E. L. 1898. Animal intelligence. An experimental study of the associative processes in animals. *Psychol. Monogr.* 2(4):1–109

Thorndike, E. L. 1911. *Animal Intelligence.* New York: Macmillan

Thorndike, E. L. 1933. A proof of the law of effect. *Science* 77:173–75

Tolkien, J. R. R. 1964. *The Lord of the Rings.* New York: Ballantine. Three parts

Tolman, E. C. 1948. Cognitive maps in rats and men. *Psychol. Rev.* 56:144–55

Tolman, E. C., Hall, C. S., Bretnall, E. P. 1932. A disproof of the law of effect and a substitution of the laws of emphasis, motivation and disruption. *J. Exp. Psychol.* 15:601–15

Tomaz, C., Aguiar, M. S., Nogueira, P. J. C. 1990. Facilitation of memory by peripheral administration of substance P and naloxone using avoidance and habituation learning tasks. *Neurosci. Biobehav. Rev.* 14:447–53

Ungerstedt, U. 1971a. Stereotaxic mapping of the monoamine pathways in the rat brain. *Acta Physiol. Scand. Suppl.* 367:1–48

Ungerstedt, U. 1971b. Adipsia and aphagia after 6-hydroxydopamine induced degeneration of the nigro-striatal dopamine system. *Acta Physiol. Scand. Suppl.* 367:95–122

Valenstein, E. S. 1980. Stereotypy and sensory-motor changes evoked by hypothalamic stimulation: possible relation to schizophrenic behavior patterns. In *Biology of Reinforcement: Facets of Brain-Stimulation Reward,* ed. A. Routtenberg, pp. 39–52. New York: Academic

Viaud, M. D., White, N. M. 1989. Dissociation of visual and olfactory conditioning in the neostriatum of rats. *Behav. Brain Res.* 32:31–42

Waldmeier, P. C., Kam, R., Stocklin, K. 1978. Increased dopamine metabolism in rat striatum after infusions of substance P into the substantia nigra. *Brain Res.* 159:223–27

Walker, E. L. 1969. Reinforcement-"The One Ring". In *Reinforcement and Behavior,* ed. J. T. Tapp, pp. 47–62. New York: Academic

Waller, A. D. 1918. The galvanometric measurement of "emotive" physiological changes. *Proc. R. Soc. London Ser. B* 90: 214–17

Wang, J., Aigner, T., Mishkin, M. 1990. Effects of neostriatal lesions on visual habit formation in rhesus monkeys. *Soc. Neurosci. Abstr.* 16:617

Weiskrantz, L. 1956. Behavioral changes associated with ablation of the amygdaloid complex in monkeys. *J. Comp. Physiol. Psychol.* 49:381–91

Weiskrantz, L., Wilson, W. A. Jr. 1958. The effect of ventral rhinencephalic lesions on avoidance thresholds in monkeys. *J. Comp. Physiol. Psychol.* 51:167–71

White, N. M. 1986. Control of sensori-motor function by dopaminergic nigrostriatal neurons: influence on eating and drinking. *Neurosci. Biobehav. Rev.* 10:15–36

White, N. M. 1988. Effect of nigrostriatal dopamine depletion on the post-training, memory improving action of amphetamine. *Life Sci.* 43:7–12

White, N. M. 1989. A functional hypothesis concerning the striatal matrix and patches: mediation of S-R memory and reward. *Life Sci.* 45:1943–57

White, N. M. 1991. Peripheral and central memory enhancing actions of glucose. In

Peripheral Signalling of the Brain: Neural, Immune and Cognitive Function, ed. R. C. A. Frederickson, J. L. McGaugh, D. L. Felten. Toronto: Hogrefe and Huber

White, N. M., Blackburn, J. 1986. Effects of glucose on amphetamine induced-motor behavior. *Life Sci.* 38:2255–62

White, N. M., Major, R. 1978a. Facilitation of retention by self-stimulation and by experimenter-administered stimulation. *Can. J. Psychol.* 32:116–23

White, N. M., Major, R. 1978b. Effect of pimozide on the improvement in learning produced by self stimulation and by water reinforcement. *Pharmacol. Biochem. Behav.* 8:565–71

White, N. M., Major, R., Siegel, J. 1978. Effect of morphine on one-trial appetitive learning. *Life Sci.* 23:1967–72

White, N. M., Messier, C. 1988. Effects of adrenal demedulation on the conditioned emotional response and on the memory improving action of glucose. *Behav. Neurosci.* 102:499–503

White, N. M., Viaud, M. D. 1991. Localized intracaudate dopamine D2 receptor activation during the post-training period improves memory for visual and olfactory conditioned emotional responses. *Behav. Neural Biol.*55:255–69

Wise, R. A. 1982. Neuroleptics and operant behavior: the anhedonia hypothesis. *Behav. Brain Sci.* 5:39–87

Wise, R. A. 1989. Opiate reward: sites and substrates. *Neurosci. Biobehav. Rev.* 13: 129–33

Wise, R. A., Colle, L. M. 1984. Pimozide attenuates free feeding: best scores analysis reveals a motivational deficit. *Psychopharmacology* 84:446–51

Wise, R. A., Rompré, P.-P. 1989. Brain dopamine and reward. *Annu. Rev. Psychol.* 40:191–225

Wise, R. A., Spindler, J., Legault, L. 1978. Major attenuation of food reward with performance-sparing doses of pimozide in the rat. *Can. J. Psychol.* 32:77–85

Woods, J. H., Schuster, C. R. 1971. Opiates as reinforcing stimuli. In *Stimulus Properties of Drugs,* ed. T. Thompson, R. Pickens, pp. 163–75. New York: Appleton-Century-Crofts

Yim, C. Y., Mogenson, G. J. 1983. Response of ventral pallidal neurons to amygdala stimulation and its modulation by dopamine projections to nucleus accumbens. *J. Neurophysiol.* 50:148–61

Zubin, J., Barrera, S. E. 1941. Effect of electric convulsive therapy on memory. *Proc. Soc. Exp. Biol. Med.* 48:596–97

Annu. Rev. Psychol. 1992. 43:473–504

PERSONALITY: STRUCTURE AND ASSESSMENT

Jerry S. Wiggins and Aaron L. Pincus

Department of Psychology, University of British Columbia, Vancouver, British Columbia, Canada V6T 1Z4

KEY WORDS: traits, study of lives, perception of traits, five-factor-model, interpersonal psychology

CONTENTS

INTRODUCTION

Although conceived in different ways by different investigators, the concept of *trait* is the central concern of the fields of personality structure and personality assessment. Investigators of personality structure are concerned with providing multivariate representations of the organization of traits, from both nomothetic and idiographic perspectives, and with the consistency and change of these structures over the lifespan. Investigators of personality assessment are concerned with the development and evaluation of procedures for the measurement of traits, within both nomothetic and idiographic testing

473

paradigms, and with the forecasting of significant life events from the information provided by these measurement procedures. For some of us, these are heady enterprises that enrich our lives and work. For others, they are less so. Much may depend upon one's early experiences in graduate school.

As McAdams (1990) notes, the budding personologist is likely to find both villains and heroes in forging his or her own professional identity (Erikson 1980). For McAdams, and likely for many of his generation, the early heroes were Henry Murray and Gordon Allport, and the first villain was Walter Mischel (p. 284). However, with the passage of time since Mischel's (1968) first formulation of the person-situation issue, at least some personologists have come to view the debate "as an intellectually stimulating chapter in the history of the discipline, replete with useful lessons for professionals who include assessment in their repertoire" (Kenrick & Funder 1988:23). It is clear from the literature reviewed here that there has also been a strong "back to basics" trend that reaffirms the centrality of trait psychology in the study of lives.

BACK TO BASICS

The Concept of Trait

One might easily conclude from Kenrick & Funder's (1988) evenhanded historical analysis of the highly polarized trait controversy that in future personality psychologists will seek truth "somewhere in the less striking gray area" (p. 31) between the hyperskeptical position (traits are in the eye of the beholder) and the pure-trait position ["people show powerful, unmodulated consistencies in their behavior across time and diverse situations" (p. 24)]. Not so. Tellegen (1991), for one, would like to consider "the nature and viability of a *strong,* rather than straw-man, trait position" (p. xx, italics added). He does so in a carefully reasoned and documented defense of the realist view of the trait concept as "an inferred organismic structure underlying an extended family of consequential behavioral dispositions" (p. xx). The implications of this strong position are explored in detail for such topics as the nature of traits, traits as dispositions, trait-situation matching, situational constraints, aggregation, person-situation interactions, and "traitedness." Tellegen's chapter is a sharply focused and modern exposition of the "basics" found in the writings of Allport, Cattell, Murray, and Thurstone.

On another front, McCrae & Costa (1990) are seeking to reestablish a strong trait psychology within the pantheon of classical theories of personality (psychoanalysis, behaviorism, humanism): "from the beginning trait psychology has been regarded as a relatively minor part of personality theory: not as a fourth school, but only a set of personality measures, a few isolated studies, an appendix to one of the "true schools" (p. 21). Although their case for trait psychology as a major theory of personality originally rested largely on studies of the longitudinal stability of personality dimensions, their more recent studies of the prediction of major life outcomes, such as occupational change (McCrae & Costa 1985), life satisfaction (Costa & McCrae 1984), and coping with a nuclear accident (Costa & McCrae 1989a) attest to what Tellegen calls the "response penetration" of traits.

On still a different front, Arnold Buss (1989) makes it clear that "If there is to be a specialty called personality, its unique and therefore defining characteristic is traits" (p. 1378). In an invited article meant to describe personality psychology to psychologists in other specialties, Buss captures many of the central issues in a strong trait psychology with gratifying clarity. In contrasting the work of trait psychologists with that of others who study the impact of experimental manipulations on specific responses, he discusses laboratory procedures that tend to increase or decrease the importance of traits (see Table 1). This discussion is meant to discourage those who would attempt to establish the relative importance of traits or manipulations in a single experiment.

And for those who are still not convinced that personality psychology has taken a decided swing back to fundamentals, consider Funder's (1991) observation that "As it turns out, Allport's basic ideas look remarkably sound even with 53 years of hindsight, and yield a large number of implications for conceptualization and research in modern personality psychology" (p. 32). Although Funder's brief outline of a "Neo-Allportian" theory of global traits is informed by the results of contemporary empirical research, it is unmistakably Allportian in its fundamental assertion that "Traits are real" (p. 32). That this return to roots may continue for some time is suggested by John & Robins' (1992) forthcoming chapter, "Gordon Allport: Father and critic of the five-factor model."

Personality Language and Trait Taxonomies

Within the field of personality structure, it is convenient to distinguish between: 1. the development of multivariate models for representing latent variables underlying individual differences in personality structure and 2. the

Table 1 Manipulations and traits

	Manipulations become important	Traits become important
context	novel, formal, public	familiar, informal, private
instructions	detailed, complete	general or none
choice	little or none	considerable
duration	brief	extensive
response	narrow	broad

development of taxonomies of trait-descriptive terms that provide a representation of how personality attributes are encoded in ordinary language. The latter, long-standing, lexical approach to the study of personality (John et al 1988) constitutes an important area of inquiry in its own right (Goldberg 1981b). It is also of central importance to the development of multivariate models of personality structure for those who subscribe to Cattell's (1946) dictum that an analysis of the "language personality sphere" must precede scale construction. Recent overviews of both of these traditions have emphasized their convergence within a common framework provided by the five-factor model of human characteristics (John 1990a,b; Wiggins & Trapnell 1992).

Personality language was recently the topic of a special issue of the *European Journal of Personality* that provides an interesting cross-section of current taxonomic research in several countries (Hofstee & Van Heck 1990). Reading these articles, one can still detect some of the enthusiasm that accompanied earlier proposals for transcultural taxonomies: "In our most grandiose moments, my colleagues and I see our scientific task as one of discovering the basic elements that underlie the personality compounds found in the various natural languages" (Goldberg 1981a:44). Overall, the tone of these recent articles is soberer, and the focus is upon the difficult obstacles that must be overcome before trait taxonomies can be considered to have a firm scientific basis (e.g. Hofstee 1990). Although the superordinate dimensions of the five-factor model are discernible across cultures and between taxonomies developed within the same language groups, "convergence on a set of specific 'middle level' categories or facets (Briggs 1989) is nowhere in sight" (Angleitner et al 1990:115). And it may be that complex dimensions, such as openness to experience, cannot be represented at even a superordinate level by single trait-descriptive adjectives (McCrae 1990).

Those not directly familiar with this work may not appreciate the magnitude or the labor-intensive nature of these taxonomic enterprises. Consider, to take a single example, the procedures whereby judges classified 5,092 German adjectives in the research of Angleitner et al (1990): "To ensure that they would work as carefully as possible, the judges were given no time limit. As a consequence, the categorization of the entire pool of adjectives by each of the 10 judges required almost four years" (p. 107).

Personality Structure

Digman's (1990) *Annual Review* chapter provided a thoughtful overview of the five-factor model of personality structure that serves as an excellent introduction to what is still the most noteworthy topic in the literature. Although sharing the enthusiasm of some of the more "bullish" investors in this enterprise, Digman notes that the model is not without its critics. In particular, Waller & Ben-Porath (1987), in response to an article by McCrae & Costa (1986) suggesting that clinical assessment could benefit from the five-factor model, argued that "the field of clinical psychology, as well as personality, should refrain from prematurely jumping onto a 'big-five' bandwagon" (p. 888). Their major reservations may be summarized as follows:

1. Many of the studies cited in support of the five-factor model were based on variants of Cattell's (1943) original rating scales, and hence "are better thought of as replications, rather than conceptual validations of the five-factor model" (p. 887).
2. Claims for the comprehensiveness of the model are premature because "we are aware of several well-articulated models of personality structure (e.g. Jackson's 1967 work on Murray's needs; Gough's 1969 catalog of folk concepts; Tellegen's 1992 three-factor temperament model) that have yet to be incorporated into the five-factor model" (p. 887).
3. It is premature to stress the inadequacies of the MMPI as a measure of critical dimensions and to advocate "inclusion of standardized measures of the five factors in clinical assessment so that practitioners will be able to take advantage of state-of-the-art personality assessment strategies" (p. 887).

These reservations, if well founded, should be taken seriously, and they may be thought of as raising issues related to 1. structure, 2. assessment, and 3. applications, respectively. In the three sections that follow, we emphasize recent work relevant to each of these issues.

THE FIVE-FACTOR MODEL

Structural issues   In response to the first reservation stated above, Goldberg (1990) sought evidence for a five-factor structure in a comprehensive set of common English trait adjectives that were assembled independently of the Cattell tradition. Previously, Norman (1967) selected 2,800 trait terms from an unabridged dictionary and reduced the list to 1,431 relatively familiar terms. He later classified these terms into 75 fine-grained categories within the framework of the five-factor model. In factoring these 75 scales formed by summing within categories, Goldberg (1990) found a clear five-factor structure that was virtually invariant under different methods of factor extraction, different methods of rotation, and different numbers of factors rotated.

To demonstrate the generalizability of this structure beyond Norman's initial classifications, Goldberg developed a new set of 133 synonym clusters from 479 commonly used terms that were independently judged by lexicographers as similar in meaning. When scale versions of these clusters were factored, a clear five-factor structure emerged in both peer- and self-ratings. *Conclusion:* The five-factor model has substantial generalizability across different sets of representative English adjectives.

Angleitner et al (1990) went to even greater lengths to avoid any possible "prestructuring" of terms that might be biased toward a five-factor solution. From a pool of more than 5,000 German trait-descriptive terms they selected 430 adjectives that judges agreed were clearly dispositional in nature. Instead of grouping terms into synonym clusters, Ostendorf (1990) then factored self- and peer-ratings of the items in the entire pool and obtained a clear five-factor structure that was invariant across different methods of rotation and different numbers of factors rotated. *Conclusion:* The five-factor model has substantial generalizability to sets of representative German adjectives.

The Ostendorf (1990) study is also noteworthy for its inclusion of marker variables from previous studies so as to facilitate factor interpretation. External markers of the five factors were provided by translations of bipolar adjective marker scales employed by previous investigators, by prototypicality ratings for all adjectives, and by a translation of the NEO Personality Inventory (NEO-PI; Costa & McCrae 1985). The importance of including appropriate external markers in exploratory studies of the five-factor model cannot be overemphasized (Goldberg 1990), and studies that fail to do so (e.g. Livneh & Livneh 1989) are inherently ambiguous.

Marker variables may also serve to highlight cultural *differences* in content within five-factor structures. Yang & Bond (1990) employed a Chinese translation of the 20 bipolar rating scales of Tupes & Christal (1958) along with a set of 150 frequently used Chinese trait adjectives selected from a pool of 557 terms (Yang & Lee 1971). When subjects rated themselves and significant others on both sets of rating scales, five-factor solutions were obtained for both the imported (Tupes-Christal) and indigenous (Chinese) instruments. However, as the authors noted, "there is no one-to-one correspondence between the local and imported factors. All five indigenous factors show significant beta weights with at least two and sometimes four of the imported factors" (Yang & Bond 1990:1093), suggesting a possible difference in structure between the two sets of factors. The lesson here is that "If only these indigenous materials had been used, many cross-culturalists would probably have detected some apparent universals" (p. 1094).

Most structural investigations of the five-factor model have employed single adjectives as stimuli (e.g. Brand & Egan 1989) or scales from personality inventories (e.g. Conn & Ramanaiah 1990). Recently, however, Borkenau & Ostendorf (1989) and Ostendorf & Angleitner (1990) investigated the structure of questionnaire items taken from four widely used instruments: the Personality Research Form (PRF; Jackson 1967), the Freiberg Personality Inventory (FPI; Fahrenberg & Selg 1970), the Eysenck Personality Inventory (EPI; Eysenck & Eysenck 1968), and the NEO-PI (Costa & McCrae 1985).

Factor analysis of the 576 items from these inventories revealed the expected five-factor structure, which was interpreted with reference to appropriate marker variables.

Assessment   Waller & Ben-Porath's (1987) second reservation concerned the comprehensiveness of the five-factor model. Since that critique, the specific assessment traditions they mentioned have indeed been incorporated within the model: Jackson's scales for Murray's needs (Costa & McCrae 1988a), Gough's catalog of folk concepts (McCrae et al 1992), and Tellegen's temperament model (McCrae & Costa 1991; Watson & Clark 1992). The Myers-Briggs Type Indicator has also been evaluated from a five-factor perspective (McCrae & Costa 1989b). More generally, the NEO-PI has been systematically related to measures derived from virtually all of the major research traditions in personality assessment (Wiggins & Trapnell 1992). In this context, McCrae & Costa (1989a) note that "We should make it clear that we do not think of the five-factor model as a replacement for other personality systems, but as a *framework* for interpreting them" (p. 451, italics added).

The framework employed by McCrae & Costa is not the only theoretical perspective on the five-factor model, however. Wiggins & Trapnell (1992) distinguish four major contemporary perspectives: the enduring-dispositional (Costa & McCrae), the dyadic-interactional (Wiggins), the social-competency (Hogan), and the lexical (Goldberg). These perspectives differ in their foci of convenience, theoretical orientations, universes of content, assessment instruments, and representative applications (Wiggins & Pincus 1992). Collectively, these perspectives, and the empirical work conducted within them, demonstrate the *comprehensiveness* of the five-factor model.

Different assessment instruments are associated with the theoretical perspectives just enumerated: the NEO-PI (Costa & McCrae 1985), the extended Interpersonal Adjective Scales (IASR-B5; Trapnell & Wiggins 1990), the Hogan Personality Inventory (HPI; Hogan 1986), and the standard marker scales of the Big Five structure (SMS; Goldberg 1992). A convenient 60-item short-form version of the NEO-PI is now available (NEO-FFI; Costa & McCrae 1989b), and a revision that includes facet scales for all five domains is in the works (Costa et al 1992). The Act Report measure of Buss & Craik (1984) has recently been extended from the original dimensions of dominance and nurturance to include the three additional dimensions of the five-factor model (AR-B5; Botwin & Buss 1989). When choosing an assessment instrument, an investigator who contemplates research within the five-factor framework is faced with an embarrassment of riches. Fortunately, Briggs's (1992) comprehensive review of available measures offers sound advice on selecting an instrument that is suited to the particular interests of the investigator.

Applications   The third reservation of Waller & Ben-Porath involved the use of five-factor measures in clinical assessment. It is noteworthy that the most recent applications of the five-factor model appear to have taken just that direction. The interest of personality psychologists in clinical assessment was stimulated by the appearance of the Diagnostic and Statistical Manual (DSM-III) of the American Psychiatric Association (APA 1980), which defined personality disorders (Axis II) in terms of *personality traits* (p. 305). A number of self-report instruments were developed to discriminate among these categories of personality disorder (e.g. Hyler et al 1989; Millon 1983, 1987; Morey et al 1985; Strack 1987, 1990); and these scales were subsequently found to be substantially and meaningfully related to the five-factor model of personality (e.g. Costa & McCrae 1990; Lyons et al 1990; Wiggins 1987; Wiggins & Pincus 1989, 1992).

The use of the five-factor model in clinical assessment has been the topic of several recent symposia (e.g. Shea 1989; McCrae 1989), the focus of a special section of the *Journal of Personality Assessment* (Costa 1992), and the topic of a forthcoming edited book (Costa & Widiger 1992). Many of these reports are concerned with the application of the five-factor model to the personality disorders described in Axis II of DSM-III, a concern stimulated in part by current deliberations about the role of dimensional assessment in the personality disorders section of the forthcoming DSM-IV (Widiger 1989). As a consequence, the conceptual context in which the five-factor model is embedded has been broadened to include psychiatric and biological perspectives (Costa & Widiger 1992). Within this broadened context, there is evidence that practitioners are in fact availing themselves of state-of-the-art five-factor assessment strategies.

Timothy R. Miller (1992), a clinical psychologist in full-time private practice, has presented a fascinating and highly personal account of the manner in which the five-factor model (as implemented by the NEO-PI) may facilitate the practice of psychotherapy. The recommendations made by Miller do not strike us as premature; they suggest the possibility of more rational assignment of patients to treatments on the basis of well-established dimensions of personality.

THE STRUCTURE OF INTERPERSONAL BEHAVIOR   "If I were to bet on what sort of 'basic dimensions' we will eventually settle on in personality research," wrote Carson in his recent *Annual Review* chapter on personality psychology (1989), "I would *still* (Carson 1969) expect variables with an interpersonal referent to provide a large share of the successful candidates" (p. 232). Examination of the recent literature on personality structure suggests that Carson might well win his wager on a number of grounds: 1. There is increasing agreement on the appropriate structural model (namely, the circumplex—see below) for representing the dimensions of interpersonal be-havior; 2. the theoretical, geometric, and psychometric bases of this model have been clarified; 3. the model has been operationalized in a number of different assessment instruments; and 4. the model has been applied to diverse substantive topics.

Structural issues   Until the recent resurgence of interest in the five-factor model there was general agreement that the appropriate structural model for representing interpersonal dispositions was a two-dimensional circumplex in which variables are ordered in a circular arrangement around the orthogonal dimensions of dominance (vs submission) and nurturance (vs hostility) (e.g. Benjamin 1974; Kiesler 1983; Leary 1957; Lorr & McNair 1963; Wiggins 1979). The five-factor model provides a comprehensive superordinate taxon-omy of individual differences that includes a simple-structure representation of the interpersonal dimensions of surgency/extraversion and agreeableness. The recent recognition that the circumplex and five-factor representations are *complementary* rather than competing (McCrae & Costa 1989a; Trapnell & Wiggins 1990) has led to an increased interest in the structural relations between the two models.

McCrae & Costa (1989c) have addressed a number of methodological issues pertinent to such an integration by jointly factoring self-reports on the revised Interpersonal Adjective Scales (IAS-R; Wiggins et al 1988) and self-, peer-, and spouse-ratings on the extraversion and agreeableness scales of the NEO-PI. Their results provide cross-observer validation of the circumplex structure of interpersonal traits. These findings, together with the ongoing research of Gifford (1992; Gifford & O'Connor 1987), suggest that the circumplex structure reflects behavioral consistencies rather than artifacts (cf Jackson & Helmes 1979). McCrae & Costa also addressed the major structu-ral issue between the two models, that of factor rotation. The NEO-PI model provides a simple-structure representation of the factors of extraversion and aggreeableness that differs by approximately 30 degrees from the orientation of the IAS-R dimensions of dominance and nurturance. The authors suggest that the dimensions of extraversion and agreeableness may be more stable and cross-situationally consistent, and that the circumplex dimensions of domi-nance and nurturance may be more fruitful for the study of interpersonal interactions. In the end, they conclude that "The five-factor model provides a larger framework in which to orient and interpret the circumplex, and the interpersonal circle provides a useful elaboration about aspects of two of the five factors—Extraversion and Agreeableness—and their combinations" (p. 593).

Lorr & Strack (1990) suggest that circumplex and factor-analytic views of the first two factors of the five-factor model may be reconciled by focusing on the first-order factors *within* the interpersonal domain. They demonstrated that the first four oblique factors extracted from the IAS-R item pool correspond directly to the four bipolar radii of the Interpersonal Circle (e.g. gregarious-extraverted vs aloof-introverted) that are subsumed by the "higher-order" factors of dominance and nurturance. Because this result follows necessarily from the manner in which IAS-R was constructed (Wiggins et al 1988), it may be viewed as additional evidence of the structural validity of IAS-R. The authors emphasize that scales constructed at this level, such as those in the Interpersonal Style Inventory (ISI; Lorr & Youniss 1986), may be of considerable importance and may lead to increased predictiveness (see also Strack & Lorr 1990).

   Wiggins and his colleagues (Trapnell & Wiggins 1990; Wiggins & Pincus 1992; Wiggins & Trapnell 1992) have proposed a dyadic-interactional perspective on the five-factor model that supplements circumplex classifications of interpersonal behaviors with reference to the additional dimensions of conscientiousness, neuroticism, and openness to experience. Wiggins & Pincus (1992) investigated the empirical relations between the traditional interpersonal circumplex dimensions of dominance and nurturance and the interpersonal dimensions of both the NEO-PI (extraversion and agreeableness) and the Hogan Personality Inventory (ambition/sociability and likeability). Their results demonstrate that the issue is one of rotation rather than discrepancies regarding the domain of interpersonal traits. In this context, Wiggins (1991) argues that evidence spanning the social sciences and humanities (e.g. world views and philosophies, theories of personality, the study of language, and the study of sex roles) supports the argument that Agency (dominance) and Communion (nurturance) should serve as the conceptual coordinates for the measurement of interpersonal behavior.

Assessment   Over the years a number of self-report and observer-rating instruments have been developed to assess interpersonal behavior (Kiesler 1991). Often, these instruments are theoretically associated with the interpersonal circumplex, although some do not meet the strong geometric and psychometric assumptions required to represent circumplex structure (Wiggins et al 1989). For example, the FIRO-B scales (Schutz 1958) appear to be almost completely unrelated to the two generally accepted interpersonal dimensions (Hurley 1990). Lorr & Youniss's ISI appears to be overinclusive with regard to dimensions of interpersonal behavior (Lorr & Suziedelis 1990; Strack & Lorr 1990), and the circumplex properties of the ISI items have not been investigated. A recent circumplex modification of the Inventory of Interpersonal Problems (IIP; L. Horowitz 1979; L. Horowitz et al 1988) appears to meet the strong assumptions of circumplex structure. Alden et al (1990) have developed precise circumplex scales (IIP-C) based on a subset of the original IIP items. The IIP items were originally derived from transcripts of presenting complaints made by psychotherapy patients. As such, the instrument is clinically useful, both for assessing the interpersonal style of a client and for identifying specific behavioral difficulties at the item level.

Gurtman (1992) reports the results of a principal components analysis of a subset of items from Kiesler's (1983) 1982 Interpersonal Circle. His results provide initial support for a circumplex structure underlying Kiesler's theoretically derived items. Gurtman's work also presents additional guidelines for evaluating the "interpersonalness" of scales and inventories, and he offers three reasons why an interpersonal taxonomy of personality constructs is important: 1. it is important to know what a scale measures, specifically what it shares with other broad factors of individual differences; 2. objective data concerning interpersonal content are important in establishing construct validity; and 3. many constructs are assumed to be interpersonal on an a priori basis, without regard to their relations with the established interpersonal dimensions of personality. Gurtman illustrates these points by using the interpersonal circumplex as an objective criterion to evaluate the "interpersonalness" of a number of *purportedly* interpersonal scales.

When the geometric and psychometric assumptions of circumplexity are met, two long-standing issues in interpersonal assessment may be resolved by empirical investigation: the circumplex representation of interpersonal deviance referred to as *vector length* (Gurtman 1992; Wiggins et al 1989), and the concept of interpersonal *complementarity* (Carson 1969; Kiesler 1983; Leary 1957; Orford 1986). In the interpersonal system of personality diagnosis, an individual may be classified as falling within one of the 8 (or 16) sectors of the Interpersonal Circle with reference to his or her average profile of scores on the constituent variables of the system. An individual's location within a sector of the circle may be further characterized in terms of the distance of his or her location from the center of the circle (i.e. vector length). Vector length has been considered a measure of "deviance" in a psychiatric as well as statistical sense (e.g. Leary 1957). However, vector length is not, in itself, considered to be a general measure of psychopathology. Rather, vector length *within* a particular sector of the circle is taken to be an index of the intensity or extremity with which that particular *pattern* of interpersonal dispositions is expressed.

In testing this assumption of interpersonal theory (e.g. Carson 1969; Kiesler 1983; Leary 1957), Wiggins et al (1989) examined the correlations between vector length and measures of psychological dysfunction in a sample of undergraduates and in eight subgroups of the same sample, formed by classification of IAS-R profiles. They found that, within the total sample, vector length was unrelated to general measures of psychopathology [Lanyon's (1973) Psychological Screening Inventory] and to more specific measures of interpersonal problems [circumplex scales from Horowitz et al's (1988) IIP]. However, meaningful patterns of correlations were found between vector length and scales from the aforementioned inventories within groups of subjects classified as falling in particular sectors of the Interpersonal Circle.

An interpersonal relationship is considered to be complementary if the behaviors of the two participants endorse and confirm each other's self-presentations with respect to both dominance and nurturance. On the Interpersonal Circle, complementarity occurs on the basis of "reciprocity" in regard to dominance (dominance pulls submission, submission pulls dominance) and of "correspondence" in regard to nurturance (hostility pulls hostility, friendliness pulls friendliness). Empirical demonstrations of this interpersonal proposition have been equivocal at best. Orford (1986) concluded that research has generally supported the correspondence hypothesis, but findings regarding the reciprocity of dominance have been inconsistent.

Bluhm et al (1990) investigated whether individual differences in dominance and nurturance mediate the influence of interpersonal impact on the elicitation of complementary responses. Using both self- and observer-ratings of an experimental interaction, they found evidence supporting both correspondence on the nurturant axis of the circumplex and reciprocity on the dominance axis. However, the latter effect disappeared when subjects' initial differences on dominance were taken into account. Although these results are again consistent with Orford's review, no adequate explanation is provided for the fact that dominant/submissive behaviors are more influenced by individual differences than are nurturant/hostile behaviors. Two additional studies also suggest that the hypothesized complementarity on the nurturance axis of the Interpersonal Circle is more clearly supported than is reciprocity on the dominance axis. Kiesler & Watkins (1989) demonstrated that complementarity on the nurturance axis is important in establishing a positive therapeutic working alliance, but "total complementarity" (referring to both axes) showed no relations with the therapeutic alliance. Benjamin's (1989) study of the interpersonal relationships between chronic schizophrenics and their auditory hallucinations indicated that complementarity between patients and their hallucinated voices occurred on the nurturance axis, but again the trends toward reciprocity on the dominance axis were less marked.

In perhaps the most important study of interpersonal complementarity in recent years, L. Horowitz et al (1991) provide the only recent experimental evidence for "reciprocity" on dominance and propose a number of methodological and theoretical hypotheses of importance to interpersonal theory and complementarity research. Based on their studies of semantics and on the interpersonal impact of self- and other-derogations, they concluded that: 1. judgments of nurturance are not independent of judgments of dominance—

people seen as friendly or hostile are more apt to seem self-assured or assertive, whereas people who seem submissive, helpless, or passive are more apt to be seen as neutral in nurturance; 2. previous research has often forced individuals to rate the two interpersonal dimensions independently, thus obscuring the rating dependency they discovered; 3. interpersonal theory does not claim that every reaction to a given behavior is complementary—rather, it claims that when the interactants' behaviors are not complementary, the discrepancy needs to be resolved through further negotiation; and finally, 4. noncomplementary responses (particularly on the dominance axis) seem to occur as opening moves under certain conditions, implying a need to negotiate power or status.

Applications   The original focus of convenience of interpersonal theory and the Interpersonal Circle involved dyadic interactions in psychotherapeutic settings (Freedman et al 1951). Hence, it is not surprising that most applications of interpersonal constructs and of the Interpersonal Circle continue to involve psychotherapy and psychopathology.

L. Horowitz's conception of interpersonal problems has been applied to both of these domains. The IIP has been found useful in predicting problems that would become the focus of psychotherapy, even when judges' IIP ratings were based on independently formulated case summaries (L. Horowitz et al 1989). This report also provided important evidence indicating that patients with primarily interpersonal (as opposed to symptomatic) problems are better candidates for brief dynamic psychotherapy. Similarly, Mohr et al (1990) reported that the IIP was useful in discriminating nonresponders from positive and negative responders in psychotherapy. They concluded that interpersonal problems and distress activate the individual to seek change in psychotherapy. Pincus & Wiggins (1990a,b) demonstrated that a subset of the DSM-III personality disorders are systematically related to the interpersonal-problems circumplex and proposed that interpersonal problems are a useful way of operationalizing maladaptive and inflexible trait expression. Finally, Alden & Phillips (1990) used the interpersonal-problems circumplex to differentiate socially anxious depressives from pure depressives, suggesting that subtypes of depression may involve the presence or absence of interpersonal problems.

A number of recent studies have investigated the utility of the Interpersonal Circle in discriminating and describing DSM-III, Axis II personality disorders. These studies are noteworthy for the range of methodologies and variety of assessment instruments that have been brought to bear on this topic. Strack et al (1990) conducted principal components analyses of Millon's MCMI-II and Strack's PACL personality disorder scales and concluded that the interpersonal dimensions of personality can be identified in instruments operationalizing Millon's personality theory. Wiggins & Pincus (1989) used principal components analyses to demonstrate the relations between the IAS-R and a number of self-report personality disorder scales. Romney & Bynner (1989) used structural equations to reanalyze a number of previously published sets of correlational data involving personality disorder diagnoses. Kiesler et al (1990) provided interpersonal behavior profiles for eight personality-disordered patients based on ratings of multiple judges who viewed videotaped psychotherapy sessions. Sim & Romney (1990) used multidimensional scaling techniques to investigate the relations between the Interpersonal Circle and personality disorders. Their results and the results of DeJong et al (1989) are less clear, and may be limited by the structural shortcomings of the Interpersonal Check List (see Paddock & Nowicki 1986). Given the general consistency of the other results, however, we would conclude that interpersonal dysfunction seems central to histrionic, narcissistic, dependent, avoidant, schizoid, and antisocial personality disorders.

Applications of the Interpersonal Circle to the practice of psychotherapy have led to direct intervention models (e.g. Anchin & Kiesler 1982). Kiesler's (1988) contribution to interpersonal psychotherapy is seminal. The therapeutic relationship is viewed by Kiesler as a microcosm of the "maladaptive transaction cycle" in which the patient pulls a restricted range of responses from significant others, which in turn tends to reinforce the patient's rigidly held self-view. Kiesler's intervention model relies heavily on metacommunicative feedback to the patient concerning the interpersonal impact he/she is having on the therapist. Kiesler uses the Interpersonal Circle and the principles of complementarity to structure and systematize his intervention strategies. Benjamin (1992) also uses the Interpersonal Circle, as operationalized by the Structural Analysis of Social Behavior (SASB; Benjamin 1974, 1984), to systematize "brief SASB-directed reconstructive learning therapy." The key proposition is that each of the mental disorders in the DSM-III-R is hypothetically associated with specific SASB-codable interpersonal and intrapsychic patterns. The SASB model also provides hypotheses about specific associated interpersonal learning experiences presumed to contribute to a disorder; the analysis has specific implications for learning experiences needed to change the patterns characteristic of the respective disorders (p. xx). In a different vein, Andrews (1989) uses the Interpersonal Circle in an especially imaginative way to systematize the existential philosophies underlying various schools of psychotherapy, in the hope of facilitating integration among the schools. He assigns an existential "vision of reality," or "*Weltanschauung* that underlies the values and theoretical models inherent in psychotherapeutic schools" (p. 803), corresponding to each of the eight octants of the Interpersonal Circle.

A section on applications of the Interpersonal Circle would not be complete without additional consideration of the diverse and often fascinating research using Benjamin's SASB. Benjamin has operationalized the interpersonal dimensions of personality to include three circumplex surfaces, corresponding to transitive interpersonal behaviors directed toward others, intransitive interpersonal behaviors focused on the self, and introjected intrapsychic aspects of interpersonal relationships. Over the years, operationalization of this model has been modified. Currently the long and short versions of the INTREX questionnaire seem to reflect the state-of-the-art (Benjamin 1988). In addition to the SASB-based brief psychotherapy mentioned above, Tunis et al (1990) used the SASB to validate other clinical methods for identifying a phobic patient's dysfunctional schemas. They concluded that "The three methods together paint a convergent picture that provides extensive insight into how various self-schemas are organized and how they may relate to conflictual situations such as the phobic situation" (p. 1285). Johnson et al (1989) use the SASB as a component of their "Cyclical Maladaptive Pattern" assessment in psychotherapy. Their results support the use of this SASB-based procedure as a clinically relevant means of quantifying psychotherapeutic transference and rigidity of interpersonal style. Talley et al (1990) used the INTREX to test hypotheses regarding therapist-client matching in psychotherapy. Their findings suggest that treatment outcome differs as a function of patients' and therapists' self-concepts as assessed by the Interpersonal Circle. Based on the principles of complementarity, they also found that greater degrees of noncomplementarity between the therapist's self-concept and the therapist's perception of patient behaviors is associated with less clinical improvement. Conversely, greater degrees of noncomplementarity between the patient's self-concept and the patient's perception of therapist's behaviors is associated with the patient's perceptions of therapeutic gain. The authors conclude that "The more noncomplementary a behavior is to one's self-concept, the more likely it is to disrupt the self-system. With therapists it seems undesirable to have such disruptions occurring, but with patients, it is generally regarded as a necessary part of change" (p. 187). Finally, the SASB has been applied to helpful and unhelpful instances of emotional catharsis in psychotherapy (Benjamin 1990), to analyses of chronic schizophrenics' relationships with their hallucinated voices (Benjamin 1989), and to differentiation of interaction patterns among families of anorexic, bulimic, and patients with mixed eating disorders (Humphrey 1989).

The Study of Lives

PSYCHOBIOGRAPHY   Some personality psychologists appear to be returning to even deeper disciplinary roots—the study of persons. In an integrative and informative introduction to a special issue of the *Journal of Personality* on "Psychobiography and Life Narratives," Dan McAdams (1988) observed that "Once again, it is okay to study the 'whole person'. Better, contemporary personologists insist, as did pioneers like Gordon Allport and Henry Murray, that such an endeavor is the personologist's *raison d'être*" (p. 1). McAdams also emphasizes that, in its most recent reincarnation, psychobiography is considerably more methodologically rigorous and more conceptually pluralistic than it was in the days of the pioneers. The *Journal's* special issue reflects this diversity in several autobiographical accounts, and biographical reconstructions, of persons who are "famous, enigmatic, or paradigmatic" (p. 2). Thus, Elms (1988) presents a psychobiographical account of the psychological factors in Freud's own life that contributed to the major psychobiographical errors committed in Freud's classic study of Leonardo da Vinci (1957 [1910]). Stewart et al (1988) demonstrate the utility of Erikson's (1980) theory of personality development in providing an increased understanding of the life of Vera Britten (a British feminist and pacifist). Winter & L. A. Carlson (1988) analyze the motives of Richard Nixon by coding his first inaugural address for themes of achievement, intimacy, and power. R. Carlson (1988) analyzes biographies of Nathaniel Hawthorne and Eleanor Marx (social activist and daughter of Karl) from the perspective of Tomkins's (1979) script theory. Anderson (1988) draws upon his own extensive interviews with Henry Murray to add to our growing knowledge of Murray's life and work (see also Elms 1987). And elsewhere Rosenberg (1989) sheds light on the personality of Thomas Wolfe through a multidimensional scaling analysis of trait terms appearing in *Look Homeward, Angel*.

The most recent volume from the Henry A. Murray Lecture Series at Michigan State University is *Studying Persons and Lives* (Rabin et al 1990), and is dedicated to the memory of Murray, who died in 1988 at the age of 95. In that volume, Runyan (1990) attempts to place the study of individual lives within the broader "structure of personality psychology." He relates the former to the major theoretical traditions, core conceptual issues, different methodological traditions, and empirical research on substantive processes that constitute the field of personality psychology. It is clear from his review that many traditions have advanced our understanding of individual lives, including the individual differences tradition (pp. 30–31). In fact, the boundaries between psychobiography and traditional personality assessment become indistinct in the procedures described by Craik (1988) for assessing the personalities of historical figures. In this paradigm, experts (e.g. present-day editors of targets' correspondence) or created experts (teams that review source materials) provide judgments of historical figures (e.g. Woodrow Wilson) on traditional assessment instruments, such as rating scales, adjective check lists, and Q-sorts (assignment of a target's personality characteristics within a forced normal or near-normal distribution from least accurate to most accurate). Although this is clearly "assessment at a distance" (pp. 201–2), the findings are comparable in reliability to those of more traditional assessment programs.

Alexander (1990) has provided a thoughtful and perceptive account of method and content in personality assessment and psychobiography, one that is deeply rooted in the personological traditions of Henry Murray and Silvan Tomkins. His arguments are richly illustrated with material from both the lives and theories of Freud, Jung, and Sullivan. Alexander's reconstruction of the "missing years" of Sullivan's life (1909–1911) is nothing short of spellbinding. If, as seems likely, Alexander's work will serve to introduce many graduate students to the personological tradition, McAdam's (1990) unusual introductory textbook on personality psychology may serve the same purpose for some undergraduate students. This textbook is unusual in at least two respects: 1. It adopts the person as the unit of study in personality psychology in an uncompromising exposition of the traditions of Murray and Allport, and 2. it does so within the context of the more traditional textbook topics of classical theories and contemporary empirical research. This is one to watch—it could produce some changes in undergraduate personality psychology course syllabi in the coming years.

STUDYING PERSONALITY STABILITY AND PERSONALITY CHANGE   The methodological sophistication and conceptual pluralism McAdams notes regarding psychobiography are also evident in new approaches to the study of personality development, and in the descriptions and explanations of long-term stability and change. In another special issue of the *Journal of Personality,* West & Graziano (1989) bring together personality, social, and developmental psychologists, along with sociologists and psychometricians, to consider topics in the study of personality stability and change. The empirical papers in this collection focus on stability in children, personality change as a consequence of important life events, and the processes that influence both change and stability.

Of the four studies of personality stability in children, Digman's (1989) is the only one cast within the framework of the five-factor model. Although the stability of these factors over a seven-year period was lower than that usually found for adult samples (e.g. Costa & McCrae 1988b), the correlations between more closely adjacent periods were generally high. It seems likely that "personality structure may be less set during the childhood years than it is in later life" (p. 206). An alternative approach to the issue of stability in childhood is illustrated by Mathaney's (1989) multimeasure-multioccasion assessment of the trait of behavioral inhibition in monozygotic (MZ) and dizygotic (DZ) twins at 12, 18, 24, and 30 months. MZ twins were found to be more concordant than DZ twins for each of the measures of behavioral inhibition employed at each of the ages studied. The results of this study support the hypotheses that trait manifestations "include both the flow and stasis of behavior" (p. 217) and that "It is the coordination of the MZ twin pairs' changes in behavioral patterns that informs us that there is a semblance of a trait that regulates behavior" (p. 233). Rubin et al (1989) found moderate consistency for the related construct of social withdrawal across grades 2, 3, 4, and 5. Moreover, children identified as withdrawn in kindergarten and grade 2 were more likely to suffer from internalizing problems (anxiety, insecurity, negative self-regard, depression) in grades 4 and 5.

Renken et al (1989) investigated the early childhood antecedents of aggression and passive-withdrawal within the framework of attachment theory (Ainsworth et al 1978; Bowlby 1973). According to the authors, this conceptual framework maintains that "continuity in individual adaptation is not due so much to the presence of static traits in the child as to a transactional process guided by experience" (p. 260). The alternative to "static trait" predictions in this context were the differential predictions that: 1. children who developed avoidant attachments would become aggressive; 2. children who developed resistant attachments would become passive; and 3. children who developed secure attachments would become neither. The results of zero-order correlations between attachment styles (assessed at 12 and 18 months) and teacher ratings (in first through third grades) did not sustain this distinction. Avoidant attachment was correlated with both aggressive ($r = .23$) *and* passive ($r = .29$) outcomes, in boys only. Resistant attachment was unrelated to outcome.

Two of the studies in the *Journal's* special issue are concerned with important life events that may be associated with personality change. Eccles et al (1989) focus on the salient life-transition from grade school to junior high school, as it affects the adolescent's self-concept. They found that although overall self-esteem was lowest immediately after this transition, it recovered during seventh grade. In addition, "Children's self-concepts of ability for math and English became less stable across the junior high transition, whereas beliefs about other activities and general self-esteem were more stable in seventh grade" (p. 284). Elder & Clipp (1989) investigated personality change induced by exposure to the extreme life event of heavy combat in World War II and the Korean war. A sample of veterans from the Institute of Human Development longitudinal study were assessed by Q-sort ratings at adolescence, age 30, and age 40, and by interviews in 1985. Those veterans who were experiencing at least one symptom of posttraumatic stress disorder in 1985 were found to have ranked below average on *ego resilience* (Block & Block 1980) when they were adolescents. However, there were also positive changes in personality characteristics from adolescence to midlife following exposure to combat. Q-sorts at age 40 revealed that combat veterans were more goal oriented, assertive, and less helpless than they were during adolescence. The authors concluded that, when other factors were statistically controlled, exposure to heavy combat increased the likelihood of ego resilient behavior at midlife.

Caspi et al (1989) distinguish between two kinds of person-environment interaction that serve to sustain behavioral patterns across the life course. *Cumulative continuity* occurs when a person's interactional style directs or channels that person into particular kinds of environments that themselves are supportive of that style, and hence sustain the pattern over the life course (e.g. Snyder & Ickes 1985). *Interactional continuity* occurs when a person's interactional style itself tends to evoke reciprocal responses from others that sustain that style across replications of this type of ongoing social interaction (e.g. Carson 1969). Convincing evidence is presented for the operation of these two kinds of sustaining processes in longitudinal studies of ill-tempered, shy, and dependent children (see also Caspi et al 1987, 1988).

METHODOLOGICAL ISSUES IN THE STUDY OF LIVES   One of the methodological innovations included in Block's (1971) classic book *Lives Through Time* was the classification of subjects into homogeneous groups of personality "types," which had been identified by transposed factor analysis of clinicians' Q-sort ratings of data from both adolescent and adult samples. Continuity and change in subjects' lives were then evaluated with respect to a variety of data sources not involved in typological classification. Stokes et al (1989) have described a variant of this strategy in which typological categories were constructed directly from subjects' responses to biographical questionnaires. Stokes et al's subjects were university students who were first assessed during freshman orientation and assessed again 6–8 years following graduation. At the initial assessment, subjects completed the Biographical Questionnaire (BQ), an instrument designed to measure significant prior experiences and behaviors during childhood and adolescence. At Time 2, subjects completed the Post College Experiences Inventory (PCEI), an instrument designed to assess significant aspects of life history during the decade following college. Separate factor analyses of these two inventories yielded dimensional profiles for describing individuals in terms of their patterns of life history during adolescence (BQ) and young adulthood (PCEI).

Typological groups were formed separately within the BQ and PCEI data by assessing individual's component profile similarities with reference to a generalized distance function (D^2). This permitted the examination of individual subject's developmental pathways from adolescent life-history subgroups (e.g. Business-Oriented "Fraternity Joe") to young adult life-history subgroups (e.g. Contented Affluent Conservative). The percentage of persons entering each young-adult subgroup from each adolescent subgroup was calculated and corrected for the base rate of all adolescent subgroups who entered each young-adult group. Thus, for example, 22% of "Fraternity Joes" entered the young-adult subgroup of Conservatives. Some of the paths taken could clearly be interpreted as continuity whereas others just as clearly suggested discontinuity. Although attempts to predict path-follower vs non-path-follower status from BQ factor scores were largely unsuccessful, some of the trends found were consistent with Block's findings for "changers" and "non-changers" discussed below.

Another methodological contribution of the *Lives Through Time* project was the emphasis given to both variables and persons in the study of personality consistency and change (Block 1971, pp. 9–13). The consistency of *variables* is typically evaluated with reference to correlations between measures administered at different periods to the same group of subjects. A consistent variable is one on which individuals maintain their relative positions within a group over time. The consistency of *persons* may be evaluated with reference to the correlation across a wide variety of attributes between two assessments of the same person at different periods. A consistent individual is one whose attributes on different occasions are highly correlated. Block (1971) emphasized the typically neglected notion of person stability by evaluating personality types and by examining the personality characteristics of "changers" and "non-changers" (1971: Ch. 6).

Ozer & Gjerde (1989) have extended Block's analysis of "changers" and "nonchangers" by employing a "person-centered" approach that permitted the separate and independent assessment of consistency and change for each person studied. Their subjects were drawn from the longitudinal study of Block & Block (1980), and they were assessed at five different periods between the ages of 3 and 18. For each subject, the correlations between consecutive Q-sorts were obtained, the median values of which ranged from moderate to large (.52–.71). A stability "profile" was formed for each subject, based on the four test-retest correlations between Q-sorts obtained at different periods. A cluster analysis of the similarity among subjects' profiles identified four clusters for males and five clusters for females. Ozer & Gjerde (1989) emphasize that "*there is no necessary link between cluster membership and Q-item content*" (pp. 495–96; italics in original). Substantively dissimilar subjects could have highly similar patterns of consistency. For that reason, Q-items were regressed on cluster membership in order to identify the contents that distinguished the cluster groups from one another. A large number of these multiple correlations were significant. The strongest finding was the striking resemblance in personality characteristics between Ozer & Gjerde's largest cluster of consistent males and Block's earlier sample of male "non-changers."

Studies of individual lives often rely heavily upon the accuracy with which subjects can recall and formulate their early attributes and those of significant others. Ross (1989) has recently argued that deviations from accurate recall in such studies may be reliable and systematic across a variety of content domains. In particular, he proposed that subjects' recollections of their earlier attributes are guided by implicit theories of personal change or stability over the lifespan. To illustrate this possibility, Ross asked university students to draw graphs of how they expected attributes (traits, abilities, opinions) of target persons (self, best friend, average student) to change or remain constant across their lifetimes. Independent raters were able to classify almost 74% of these plots into four prototype categories: 1. stability across the lifetime, 2. a U-shaped curve, 3. an inverted U-shaped curve, and 4. an early rise followed by stability. Ross explored the implications of the possibility that personal recall is influenced by a few relatively simple implicit theories of lifespan development with reference to previous studies in cognitive and social psychology.

Some recent work on attributional style may also increase our understanding of factors that influence the manner in which subjects construct life narratives. Burns & Seligman (1989) have demonstrated that the attributional style of viewing negative life events as caused by internal, stable, and global factors is consistent over the life-span. They recruited older subjects who had saved diaries or letters they had written when they were adolescents or young adults. Thirty subjects whose average age was 72 were asked to provide descriptions of positive and negative events that had occurred in the last year. These narratives, together with letters or diaries written an average of 52 years earlier, were rated for explanatory style. A composite index of explanatory style was stable ($r = .54$) over this 50-year period for negative life events. In contrast, essentially no stability was found for attributions made to *positive events*.

The focus of attributional style research has for the most part been on depression, and the relation between pessimistic attributional style and depression is well documented (e.g. Sweeny et al 1986). Perhaps for this reason, there has been little interest in explanatory styles for positive events that might be of considerable personal significance. In the Burns & Seligman (1989) study, for example, the positive events suggested to subjects (e.g. birthdays, holiday dinners) do not appear to have emotional significance comparable to that for suggested negative events (e.g. an illness or accident, a financial problem). A notable exception to this trend is found in a recent study by Needles & Abramson (1990). These authors have demonstrated the importance both of the occurrence of positive events and of an optimistic or enhancing style of interpreting these events in recovery from depression. It seems likely that optimistic explanatory styles, as well as "positive illusions" (Taylor 1989), may be important in understanding the life narratives of highly effective persons.

The Perception of Traits

In reflecting on his own wide-ranging studies of the accuracy of personality judgments and the ability to perceive traits in others, David Funder (1989) observed, "Somebody once said that what makes a dancing bear so impressive is not that it dances well, but that it dances at all. I am impressed by human judgments of personality for roughly the same reason—not because judgments are perfect, but because in the face of enormous difficulties it seems remarkable they manage to have any accuracy at all" (p. 212). The study of trait perception and personality judgments is becoming increasingly analytic; rather than simply demonstrating accuracy in terms of interjudge agreement, the goal is to understand "what kind of target, judge, relationship between judge and target, setting of interaction, or dimension of judgment makes accuracy most likely" (Funder 1989:219).

The acquaintance level of judges and targets has been a continuing topic of investigation. Using an unusually rich data set generated by self-reports, peer-ratings (by friends and strangers), and videotaped interactions, Funder & Colvin (1988) found that Q-sort judgments by close acquaintances were in greater agreement with each other and with the self-ratings of targets than were judgments of strangers who viewed a videotaped interaction. Although the correlation was smaller, strangers' judgments agreed with each other and with the self-ratings of targets beyond a chance level. Greater agreement was also found for traits rated as more observable. The authors conclude that "agreement among acquaintances' judgments must derive at least partly from experience with and observation of the person who is judged" (p. 149).

Paunonen (1989) framed the variables of target-rater acquaintanceship and trait observability within the context of Brunswick's (1955) lens model and reasoned that length of acquaintanceship per se may not lead to increased accuracy of ratings because "situational or social constraints may not allow for a wide latitude in behavior, and hence target cues may be highly redundant" (p. 825). He asked judges and targets to rate how well they knew each other on a 9-point scale, and then examined the effects of acqaintanceship and trait observability on personality judgments based on Jackson's PRF. Using moderated multiple-regression techniques, the acquaintanceship effect was replicated, and level of acquaintanceship was found to interact with trait observability such that, at low to moderate levels of acquaintanceship, agreement improved as trait observability increased. This effect gradually diminished as target-rater acquaintanceship increased, and no overall main effect for trait observability was found. Paunonen concluded that as acquaintanceship increases, knowledge of a target's behavior predispositions broadens to include less-observable trait domains, and hence the correlation between accuracy and observability found by Funder & Colvin might be attributable to the employment of a less well-acquainted set of participants.

Colvin & Funder (1991) reframed the acquaintanceship-accuracy problem within the set of procedures that Cronbach & Meehl (1955) recommended for establishing the construct validity of psychological tests. They argued that interjudge agreement cannot serve as the ultimate criterion of judgmental accuracy, because both judges and raters may agree but be innaccurate, for a number of reasons. Considerations of construct validity would require that the additional criterion of *behavioral prediction* be investigated. In so doing, Colvin & Funder required targets to participate in three videotaped interactions (coded by Q-sorts of six observers) and to fill out personality measures. Predictions of strangers' personality characteristics and videotaped interactions were based solely on exposure to a different videotape of the target in a highly similar interaction. Predictions of acquaintances' personalities and interactions relied solely on prior knowledge of the target. Although acquaintances predicted general personality characteristics more accurately than strangers, acquaintances and strangers were approximately equal in their prediction of situation-specific behavior. The authors concluded that situational similarity is a boundary condition on the acquaintanceship-accuracy relationship.

Frequency counts of uncontextualized behaviors may not provide a meaningful unit of analysis for the study of trait perception and personality consistency. Shoda et al (1989) have developed an elegant paradigm for studying the effects of situation-behavior relations on judgments of personality dispositions (see also Wright 1989). Within this paradigm, situation-behavior contingencies may be manipulated with reference to normative data established by naturalistic observation. Over the course of a 6-week summer camp, observers recorded 19 childrens' specific behaviors (e.g. "the child hit") in relation to antecedent situations (e.g. "when a peer teased"). For 19 "targets" these data permitted the construction of statements describing established conditional probabilities between situations and behaviors. These targets were presented to judges in "intact" form, with "altered" relations between situations and behaviors, and with uncontextualized behaviors alone. When camp counselors were presented with a series of veridical situation-behavior descriptions of a previously observed child, their judgments of aggression were highly related ($r = .84$) to total aggression scores based on six weeks of observation in a summer camp. When behaviors were presented without a situational context, predictive accuracy decreased significantly; and when veridical situation-behavior relations were extensively altered, targets were viewed as strange and implausible, rather than aggressive.

Funder & Colvin (1991) make a similar point, albeit from a quite different theoretical perspective:

> Research has focused on the consistency of *behavior*. Intuition focuses on the consistency of *personality*. The two are related, but they are not exactly the same thing. When we regard an acquaintance as consistently fearful, or awkward, or cheerful, we are not necessarily expressing an intuition that all the behaviors by which one might manifest these dispositions will be consistent across all situations of the acquaintance's life. Rather, we are expressing a belief that in any situation in which these behaviors are relevant, our acquaintance will manage to exhibit fearfulness, awkwardness, or cheerfulness in some way or another (p. 790).

Funder & Colvin videotaped the interactions of targets in three laboratory situations and obtained personality descriptions of targets from friends and acqaintances. They found that behaviors coded for *social effect* or *psychological meaning* (Cairns & Green 1979) exhibited "impressive consistency" across situations.

Moskowitz (1990) found some limited support for the more traditional frequency-count method. The traits of dominance and friendliness were coded in six different laboratory situations, by direct behavior counts and by global ratings made at the end of each session. Target self-reports of the same two traits were obtained from adjective ratings (e.g. "dominant") and from situationally contextualized questionnaire statements (e.g. "how friendly and outgoing you would be with a close male friend"). The behavior-count method had the highest convergent validity with other measures of dominance and was highly correlated with global ratings of friendliness. However, neither behavior counts nor global ratings were correlated with self-report measures of friendliness.

Basic research on impression formation and trait attribution continues to enrich long-standing areas of inquiry. Topics include: agreement among observers on initial impressions of where targets stand on trait dimensions (Park & Judd 1989); assimilation and contrast effects in spontaneous trait inference (Newman & Uleman 1990); and processing of congruent and incongruent information in impression formation (Casselden & Hampson 1990; Hampson 1990). We are also pleased to note the continuing influence of George Kelly (1955), the first truly cognitive personologist, on contemporary research in the perception of personality characteristics (see Benesch & Page 1989).

PERSONALITY STRUCTURE: THEN AND NOW

Kenneth Craik (1986) has observed that the history of personality research methods is not "cumulative" in the ordinary usage of that term but rather is characterized by a variety of continuous, arrested, and interrupted trajectories of development (much like the human lives to which these methods are applied). To the extent that the current status of personality research reflects an "identity achieved," some sense of this may be conveyed by comparing the research described in the present review with that covered by an *Annual Review* chapter on personality structure written almost 25 years ago (Wiggins 1968). Any such attempt to discern continuities and discontinuities from this comparison is, of course, necessarily subjective and vulnerable to many sources of error (much like the retrospective process involved in the study of the development of personal identity).

The bulk of the literature reviewed in 1968 was concerned with two rather different kinds of "styles": *response styles* (e.g. social desirability and acquiescence) and *cognitive styles* (e.g. field dependence and cognitive complexity). The earlier concern with the "problem" of response styles appears to have diminished considerably; much of that concern has been redirected into more fruitful substantive topics, such as the distinction between self-deception and impression management (e.g. Paulhus 1991)—although there are still holdouts (e.g. Edwards 1991). Similarly, a constructive obituary for the once viable area of cognitive styles has been provided by Cantor & Kihlstrom (1987). They observe that despite the conceptual and empirical shortcomings of the earlier work on cognitive styles, we should acknowledge "the precedent set by this tradition for placing interpretive and reasoning processes at the center of a theory of personality" (p. 13).

The personality dimensions underlying the concept of *psychopathy* were of considerable interest in the 1960s, as is evident from the research programs reviewed in the 1968 chapter. There is still an active interest in this topic (e.g. Hare et al 1991), although current interpretations of dimensions are somewhat different, and in the case of one dimension (neuroticism), reversed. These recent interpretations have benefited from the recognition that dimensions of psychopathy may be related to both the interpersonal circumplex (Harpur et al 1989) and the five-factor model (Widiger & Trull 1992).

The current widespread interest in *trait stability* over the lifespan contrasts with the few earlier studies, which were mainly methodological or short term in nature. In the earlier review, the serious student of personality structure was urged to consider more carefully the voluminous writings of *Raymond B. Cattell,* who was then, it appeared, at the height of his ill-deserved unpopularity. Although Cattell is now often cited in the context of the origins of the five-factor model, it is not as widely recognized that he has been generally opposed to that paradigm (Cattell 1973; Wiggins & Trapnell 1992).

Two sections of the earlier review may be related directly to the present one: "The Big Two: Extraversion and Anxiety" and "The Structure of Interpersonal Behavior." In the former section, we find this statement: "If consensus exists within the realm of temperament structure, it does so with respect to the importance of the large, ubiquitous, and almost unavoidable dimensions of extraversion and anxiety (neuroticism)" (p. 309). In the latter section appears this conclusion: "Of all domains of personality study, the interpersonal sphere has recently enjoyed the most active explication of the substantive and structural components of construct validity" (p. 322). If we add three more dimensions to the first quotation and the *external* component of construct validity to the second, we can discern a clear cumulative trend from then to now, despite the intervening "era of challenge and stock-taking" (1968–1980) described by Craik (1986:23).

The preceding trip down memory lane may have provided less nostalgia than anticipated. Current research appears, in comparison, to be more coherent, purposive, and promising. The back-to-basics movement we have described *may* reflect a renewed sense of continuity within a broader context of change, a clearer identification with certain intellectual forebears, and a more confident commitment to a particular direction of research. These characteristics of a maturing identity (see Stewart et al 1988), if indeed they are present, have been achieved not through a return to basics per se, but through a deeper appreciation of their contemporary implications.

ACKNOWLEDGMENTS

Preparation of this chapter was facilitated by Social Sciences and Humanities Research Council of Canada Grant 410-90-1374 awarded to the first author and by a UBC Killam Predoctoral Fellowship to the second author. We are greatly indebted to Leslie Reilly for her help in locating and assembling reference material. We would also like to thank Lorna S. Benjamin, Lewis R. Goldberg, Oliver P. John, Robert R. McCrae, Delroy L. Paulhus, William McKinley Runyan, and Candace Taylor Wiggins for their comments on an earlier version of this chapter.

Literature Cited

Ainsworth, M., Bleahar, M., Waters, E., Wall, S. 1978. *Patterns of Attachment.* Hillsdale, NJ: Erlbaum

Alden, L. E., Phillips, N. 1990. An interpersonal analysis of social anxiety and depression. *Cognit. Ther. Res.* 14:499–513

Alden, L. E., Wiggins, J. S., Pincus, A. L. 1990. Construction of circumplex scales for the Inventory of Interpersonal Problems. *J. Pers. Assess.* 55:521–36

Alexander, I. E. 1990. *Personology: Method and Content in Personality Assessment and Psychobiography.* Durham: Duke Univ. Press

American Psychiatric Association. 1980. *Diagnostic and Statistical Manual of Mental Disorders* Washington DC: Author. 3rd ed.

Anchin, J. C., Kiesler, D. J., eds. 1982. *Handbook of Interpersonal Psychotherapy.* New York: Pergamon

Anderson, J. W. 1988. Henry A. Murray's early career: a psychobiographical exploration. *J. Pers.* 56:139–71

Andrews, J. D. W. 1989. Integrating visions of reality: interpersonal diagnosis and the existential vision. *Am. Psychol.* 44:803–17

Angleitner, A., Ostendorf, F. 1989. Personality factors via self- and peer-ratings based on a representative sample of German trait descriptive terms. Paper presented at the 1st Eur. Congr. Psychol., Amsterdam

Angleitner, A., Ostendorf, F., John, O. P. 1990. Towards a taxonomy of personality descriptors in German: a psycho-lexical study. *Eur. J. Pers.* 4:89–118

Benesch, K. F., Page, M. M. 1989. Self-construct systems and interpersonal congruence. *J. Pers.* 57:139–73

Benjamin, L. S. 1974. Structural analysis of social behavior. *Psychol. Rev.* 81:392–425

Benjamin, L. S. 1984. Principles of prediction using structural analysis of social behavior. In *Personality and the Prediction of Behavior,* ed. R. A. Zucker, J. Aronoff, A. J. Rabin, pp. 121–73. New York: Academic

Benjamin, L. S. 1988. *Intrex Shortform Users Manual.* Madison, WI: Intrex Interpersonal Institute

Benjamin, L. S. 1989. Is chronicity a function of the relationship between the person and the auditory hallucination? *Schizophren. Bull.* 15:291–310

Benjamin, L. S. 1990. Interpersonal analysis of the cathartic model. *Emotion* 5:209–29

Benjamin, L. S. 1992. Brief SASB-directed reconstructive learning therapy. In *Handbook of Short-Term Dynamic Therapy,* ed. P. Crits-Christoph, J. Barber. New York: Guilford. In press

Block, J. 1971. *Lives Through Time.* Berkeley, CA: Bancroft

Block, J. H., Block, J. 1980. The role of ego-control and ego-resiliency in the organization of behavior. *Minn. Symp. Child Psychol.* 13:39–101

Bluhm, C., Widiger, T. A., Miele, G. M. 1990. Interpersonal complementarity and individual differences. *J. Pers. Soc. Psychol.* 58:464–71

Borkenau, P., Ostendorf, F. 1989. Descriptive consistency and social desirability in self- and peer-reports. *Eur. J. Pers.* 3:31–45

Botwin, M. D., Buss, D. M. 1989. Structure of act-report data: Is the five-factor model of personality recaptured? *J. Pers. Soc. Psychol.* 56:988–1001

Bowlby, J. 1973. *Attachment and Loss.* Vol. 2. *Separation: Anxiety and Anger.* London: Hogarth Press

Brand, C. R., Egan, V. 1989. The "Big Five" dimensions of personality? Evidence from ipsative, adjectival self-attributions. *Pers. Individ. Differ.* 10:1165–71

Briggs, S. R. 1989. The optimal level of measurement for personality constructs. In *Personality Psychology: Recent Trends and Emerging Directions,* ed. D. M. Buss, N. Cantor, pp. 246–60. New York: Springer-Verlag

Briggs, S. R. 1992. Assessing the five factor model of personality description. *J. Pers.* In press

Brunswick, E. 1955. Representative design and probabalistic theory in a functional psychology. *Psychol. Rev.* 62:193–217

Burns, M. O., Seligman, M. E. P. 1989. Explanatory style across the life span: evidence for stability over 52 years. *J. Pers. Soc. Psychol.* 56:471–77

Buss, A. H. 1989. Personality as traits. *Am. Psychol.* 44:1378–88

Buss, D. M., Craik, K. H. 1984. Acts, dispositions, and personality. *Progr. Exp. Pers. Res.: Norm. Pers. Process.* 13:241–301

Cairns, R. B., Green, J. A. 1979. How to assess personality and social patterns: observations or ratings? In *The Analysis of Social Interactions: Methods, Issues, and Illustrations,* pp. 209–26. Hillsdale, NJ: Erlbaum

Cantor, N., Kihlstrom, J. F. 1987. *Personality and Social Intelligence.* Englewood Cliffs, NJ: Prentice-Hall

Carlson, R. 1988. Exemplary lives: the uses of psychobiography for theory development. *J. Pers.* 56:105–38

Carson, R. C. 1969. *Interaction concepts of personality.* Chicago: Aldine

Carson, R. C. 1989. Personality. *Annu. Rev. Psychol.* 40:227–48

Caspi, A., Bem, D. J., Elder, G. H. Jr. 1989. Continuities and consequences of interactional styles across the life course. *J. Pers.* 57:375–406

Caspi, A., Elder, G. Jr., Bem, D. J. 1987. Moving against the world: life-course patterns of explosive children. *Dev. Psychol.* 23:308–13

Caspi, A., Elder, G. Jr., Bem, D. J. 1988. Moving away from the world: life course patterns of shy children. *Dev. Psychol.* 24:824–31

Casselden, P. A., Hampson, S. E. 1990. Forming impressions from incongruent traits. *J. Pers. Soc. Psychol.* 59:353–62

Cattell, R. B. 1943. The description of personality: basic traits resolved into clusters. *J. Abnorm. Soc. Psychol.* 38:476–506

Cattell, R. B. 1946. *The Description and Measurement of Personality.* Yonkers-on-Hudson, NY: World Book

Cattell, R. B. 1973. *Personality and Mood by Questionnaire.* San Francisco, CA: Jossey-Bass

Colvin, C. R., Funder, D. C. 1991. Predicting personality and behavior: a boundary on the acqaintanceship effect. *J. Pers. Soc. Psychol.* 60:884–94

Conn, S. R., Ramanaiah, N. V. 1990. Factor structure of the Comrey Personality Scales, The Personality Research Form-E, and the five-factor model. *Psychol. Rep.* 67:627–32

Costa, P. T. Jr., ed. 1992. Clinical use of the five-factor model. *J. Pers. Assess.* (Special Section) In press

Costa, P. T. Jr., McCrae, R. R. 1984. Personality as a lifelong determinant of well-being. In *Affective Processes in Adult Development and Aging,* ed. C. Malatesta, C. Izard, pp. 141–57. Beverly Hills, CA: Sage

Costa, P. T. Jr., McCrae, R. R. 1985. *The NEO Personality Inventory Manual.* Odessa, FL: Psychological Assessment Resources

Costa, P. T. Jr., McCrae, R. R. 1988a. From catalogue to classification: Murray's needs and the five-factor model. *J. Pers. Soc. Psychol.* 55:258–65

Costa, P. T. Jr., McCrae, R. R. 1988b. Personality in adulthood: a six-year longitudinal study of self-reports and spouse ratings on the NEO Personality Inventory. *J. Pers. Soc. Psychol.* 54:853–63

Costa, P. T. Jr., McCrae, R. R. 1989a. Personality, stress, and coping: some lessons from a decade of research. In *Aging, Stress, Social Support, and Health,* ed. K. S. Markides, C. L. Cooper, pp. 267–83. New York: Wiley

Costa, P. T. Jr., McCrae, R. R. 1989b. *The NEO-PI/NEO-FFI Manual Supplement.* Odessa, FL: Psychological Assessment Resources

Costa, P. T. Jr., McCrae, R. R. 1990. Personality disorders and the five-factor model of personality. *J. Pers. Disord.* 4:362–71

Costa, P. T. Jr., McCrae, R. R., Dye, D. A. 1992. Facet scales for Agreeableness and Conscientiousness: a revision of the NEO

Personality Inventory. *Pers. Individ. Differ.* In press

Costa, P. T. Jr., Widiger, T. A., eds. 1992. *Personality Disorders and the Five-Factor Model of Personality.* Washington, DC: Am. Psychol. Assoc. In press

Craik, K. H. 1986. Personality research methods: an historical perspective. *J. Pers.* 54:18–51

Craik, K. H. 1988. Assessing the personalities of historical figures. In *Psychology and Historical Interpretation,* ed. W. M. Runyan, pp. 196–218. New York: Oxford Univ. Press

Cronbach, L. J., Meehl, P. E. 1955. Construct validity in psychological tests. *Psychol. Bull.* 52:177–93

DeJong, C. A. J., van den Brink, W., Jansen, J. A. M., Schippers, G. M. 1989. Interpersonal aspects of DSM-III Axis II: theoretical hypotheses and empirical findings. *J. Pers. Disord.* 3:135–46

Digman, J. M. 1989. Five robust trait dimensions: development, stability, and utility. *J. Pers.* 57:195–214

Digman, J. M. 1990. Personality structure: emergence of the five-factor model. *Annu. Rev. Psychol.* 41:417–40

Eccles, J. S., Wigfield, A., Flanagan, C. A., Miller, C., Reuman, D. A., Yee, D. 1989. Self-concepts, domain values, and self-esteem: relations and changes at early adolescence. *J. Pers.* 57:283–310

Edwards, A. L. 1991. Social desirability and ego resiliency. *Am. Psychol.* 46:250–51

Elder, G. E. Jr., Clipp, E. C. 1989. Combat experience and emotional health: impairment and resilience in later life. *J. Pers.* 57:311–41

Elms, A. C. 1987. The personalities of Henry A. Murray. In *Perspectives in Personality,* ed. R. Hogan, W. H. Jones, 2:1–14. Greenwich, CT: JAI Press

Elms, A. C. 1988. Freud as Leonardo: Why the first psychobiography went wrong. *J. Pers.* 56:19–40

Erikson, E. H. 1980. *Identity and the Life Cycle.* New York: Norton

Eysenck, H. J., Eysenck, S. B. G. 1968. *Manual for the Eysenck Personality Inventory.* San Diego, CA: Educational and Industrial Testing Service

Fahrenberg, J., Selg, H. 1970. *Das Freiburger Persönlichkeits-Inventar (FPI)—Handanweisung.* Göttingen: Hogrefe

Freedman, M. B., Leary, T. F., Ossorio, A. G., Coffey, H. S. 1951. The interpersonal dimension of personality. *J. Pers.* 20:143–61

Freud, S. 1957. Leonardo da Vinci and a memory of his childhood. In *The Standard Edition of the Complete Psychological*

Works of Sigmund Freud, 11:59–137. London: Hogarth Press

Funder, D. C. 1989. Accuracy in personality judgment and the dancing bear. See Briggs 1989, pp. 210–23

Funder, D. C. 1991. Global traits: a neo-Allportian approach to personality. *Psychol. Sci.* 2:31–39

Funder, D. C., Colvin, C. R. 1988. Friends and strangers: acquaintanceship, agreement, and the accuracy of personality judgment. *J. Pers. Soc. Psychol.* 55:149–58

Funder, D. C., Colvin, C. R. 1991. Explorations in behavioral consistency: properties of persons, situations, and behaviors. *J. Pers. Soc. Psychol.* 60:773–94

Gifford, R. 1992. Mapping nonverbal behavior on the Interpersonal Circle. *J. Pers. Soc. Psychol.* In press

Gifford, R., O'Connor, B. 1987. The interpersonal circumplex as a behavior map. *J. Pers. Soc. Psychol.* 52:1019–26

Goldberg, L. R. 1981a. Developing a taxonomy of trait-descriptive terms. In *New Directions for Methodology of Social and Behavioral Sciences: Problems with Language Imprecision,* ed. D. W. Fiske, 9:43–66. San Francisco, CA: Jossey Bass

Goldberg, L. R. 1981b. Language and individual differences: the search for universals in personality lexicons. In *Review of Personality and Social Psychology,* ed. L. Wheeler, 2:141–65. Beverly Hills, CA: Sage

Goldberg, L. R. 1990. An alternative "description of personality": the Big Five factor structure. *J. Pers. Soc. Psychol.* 59:1216–29

Goldberg, L. R. 1992. The development of markers of the Big Five factor structure. *Psychol. Assess.: A J. Consult. Clin. Psychol.* In press

Gough, H. 1969. *Manual for the California Psychological Inventory.* Palo Alto, CA: Consulting Psychologists Press

Gurtman, M. B. 1992. Evaluating the interpersonalness of personality scales. *Pers. Soc. Psychol. Bull.* In press

Hampson, S. E. 1990. Reconciling inconsistent information: impressions of personality from combinations of traits. *Eur. J. Pers.* 4:157–72

Hare, R. D., Hart, S. D., Harpur, T. J. 1991. Psychopathy and the DSM-IV criteria for Antisocial Personality Disorder. *J. Abnorm. Psychol.* 100:391–98

Harpur, T. J., Hare, R. D., Hakstian, A. R. 1989. Two-factor conceptualization of psychopathy: construct validity and assessment implications. *Psychol. Assess.: A J. Consult. Clin. Psychol.* 1:6–17

Hofstee, W. K. B. 1990. The use of everyday

personality language for scientific purposes. *Eur. J. Pers.* 4:77–88

Hofstee, W. K. B., Van Heck, G. L., eds. 1990. Personality language. *Eur. J. Pers.* 4:75–173 (Special Issue).

Hogan, R. 1986. *Hogan Personality Inventory Manual.* Minneapolis, MN: National Computer Systems

Horowitz, L. M. 1979. On the cognitive structure of interpersonal problems treated in psychotherapy. *J. Consult. Clin. Psychol.* 47:5–15

Horowitz, L. M., Locke, K. D., Morse, M. B., Waikar, S. V., Dryer, D. C. 1991. Self-derogations and the interpersonal theory. *J. Pers. Soc. Psychol.* 61:68–79

Horowitz, L. M., Rosenberg, S. E., Baer, B. A., Ureno, G., Villasenor, V. S. 1988. Inventory of Interpersonal Problems: psychometric properties and clinical applications. *J. Consult. Clin. Psychol.* 56:885–92

Horowitz, L. M., Rosenberg, S. E., Ureno, G., Kahlehzan, B. M., O'Halloran, P. 1989. Psychodynamic formulation, consensual response method, and interpersonal problems. *J. Consult. Clin. Psychol.* 57: 599–606

Humphrey, L. L. 1989. Observed family interactions among subtypes of eating disorders using Structural Analysis of Social Behavior. *J. Consult. Clin. Psychol.* 57:206–14

Hurley, J. R. 1990. Does FIRO-B relate better to interpersonal or intrapersonal behavior? *J. Clin. Psychol.* 46:454–59

Hyler, S. E., Rieder, R. O., Williams, J. B. W., Spitzer, R. L., Hendler, J., Lyons, M. 1989. A comparison of self-report and clinical diagnosis of DSM-III personality disorders in 552 patients. *Compr. Psychiatr.* 30:170–78

Jackson, D. N. 1967. *Personality Research Form Manual.* Goshen, NY: Research Psychologists Press

Jackson, D. N., Helmes, E. 1979. Personality structure and the circumplex. *J. Pers. Soc. Psychol.* 37:2278–85

John, O. P. 1990a. The "Big Five" factor taxonomy: dimensions of personality in the natural language and in questionnaires. In *Handbook of Personality: Theory and Research,* ed. L. A. Pervin, pp. 66–100. New York: Guilford

John, O. P. 1990b. The search for basic dimensions of personality: a review and critique. In *Advances in Psychological Assessment,* ed. P. McReynolds, J. C. Rosen, G. J. Chelune, 7:1–37. New York: Plenum

John, O. P., Robins, R. W. 1992. Gordon Allport: father and critic of the five factor model. In *Fifty Years of Personality Psychology,* ed. K. H. Craik, R. T. Hogan, R. N. Wolfe. New York: Plenum

John, O. P., Angleitner, A., Ostendorf, F. 1988. The lexical approach to personality: a historical review of trait taxonomic research. *Eur. J. Pers.* 2:171–203

Johnson, M. E., Popp, C., Schacht, T. E., Mellon, J., Strupp, H. H. 1989. Converging evidence for identification of recurrent relationship themes: comparison of two methods. *Psychiatry* 52:275–88

Kelly, G. A. 1955. *The Psychology of Personal Constructs.* New York: Norton

Kenrick, D. T., Funder, D. C. 1988. Profiting from controversy: lessons from the person-situation debate. *Am. Psychol.* 43:23–34

Kiesler, D. J. 1983. The 1982 Interpersonal Circle: a taxonomy for complementarity in human transactions. *Psychol. Rev.* 90:185–214

Kiesler, D. J. 1988. *Therapeutic Metacommunication: Therapist Impact Disclosure as Feedback in Psychotherapy.* Palo Alto, CA: Consulting Psychologists Press

Kiesler, D. J. 1991. Interpersonal methods of assessment and diagnosis. In *Handbook of Social and Clinical Psychology: The Health Perspective,* ed. C. R. Snyder, D. R. Forsyth, pp. 438–68. Elmsford, NY: Pergamon

Kiesler, D. J., Watkins, L. M. 1989. Interpersonal complementarity and the therapeutic alliance: a study of relationship in psychotherapy. *Psychotherapy* 26:183–94

Kiesler, D. J., Van Denburg, T. F., Sikes-Nova, V. E., Larus, J. P., Goldston, C. S. 1990. Interpersonal behavior profiles of eight cases of DSM-III personality disorder. *J. Clin. Psychol.* 46:440–53

Lanyon, R. I. 1973. *Psychological Screening Inventory Manual.* Goshen, NY: Research Psychologists Press

Leary, T. 1957. *Interpersonal Diagnosis of Personality.* New York: Ronald Press

Livneh, H., Livneh, C. 1989. The five-factor model of personality: Is evidence of its cross-measure validity premature? *Pers. Individ. Differ.* 10:75–80

Lorr, M., McNair, D. M. 1963. An interpersonal behavior circle. *J. Abnorm. Soc. Psychol.* 67:68–75

Lorr, M., Strack, S. 1990. Wiggins Interpersonal Adjective Scales: a dimensional view. *Pers. Individ. Differ.* 11:423–25

Lorr, M., Suziedelis, A. 1990. Distinctive personality profiles of the Interpersonal Style Inventory. *J. Pers. Assess.* 54:491–500

Lorr, M., Youniss, R. P. 1986. *The Interpersonal Style Inventory.* Los Angeles, CA: Western Psychological Service

Lyons, M. J., Merla, M. E., Ozer, D. J.,

502 WIGGINS & PINCUS

Hyler, S. E. 1990. Relationship of the "Big-Five" factors to DSM-III personality disorders. Paper presented at the Annu. Meet. Am. Psychol. Assoc., Boston

Mathaney, A. P. Jr. 1989. Children's behavioral inhibition over age and across situations: genetic similarity for a trait during change. *J. Pers.* 57:215–35

McAdams, D. P. 1988. Biography, narrative, and lives: an introduction. *J. Pers.* 56:1–18

McAdams, D. P. 1990. *The Person: An Introduction to Personality Psychology.* San Diego, CA: Harcourt Brace Jovanovich

McCrae, R. R. (Chair). 1989. Personality disorders from the perspective of the five-factor model. Symp. presented at the Meet. Am. Psychol. Assoc., New Orleans

McCrae, R. R. 1990. Traits and trait names: How well is openness represented in natural languages? *Eur. J. Pers.* 4:119–29

McCrae, R. R., Costa, P. T. Jr. 1985. Openness to experience. In *Perspectives in Personality*, ed. R. Hogan, W. H. Jones, 1:145–72. Greenwich, CT: JAI Press

McCrae, R. R., Costa, P. T. Jr. 1986. Clinical assessment can benefit from recent advances in personality psychology. *Am. Psychol.* 41:1001–3

McCrae, R. R., Costa, P. T. Jr. 1989a. More reasons to adopt the five-factor model. *Am. Psychol.* 44:451–52

McCrae, R. R., Costa, P. T. Jr. 1989b. Reinterpreting the Myers-Briggs Type Indicator from the perspective of the five-factor model of personality. *J. Pers.* 57:17–40

McCrae, R. R., Costa, P. T. Jr. 1989c. The structure of interpersonal traits: Wiggins' circumplex and the five-factor model. *J. Pers. Soc. Psychol.* 56:586–95

McCrae, R. R., Costa, P. T. Jr. 1990. *Personality in Adulthood.* New York: Guilford

McCrae, R. R., Costa, P. T. Jr. 1991. Adding Liebe und Arbeit: the full five-factor model and well-being. *Pers. Soc. Psychol. Bull.* 17:230–35

McCrae, R. R., Costa, P. T. Jr., Piedmont, R. L. 1992. Folk concepts, natural language, and psychological constructs: the California Psychological Inventory and the five-factor model. *J. Pers.* In press

Miller, T. R. 1992. The psychotherapeutic utility of the five-factor model of personality: a clinician's experience. *J. Pers. Assess.* In press

Millon, T. 1983. *Millon Clinical Multiaxial Inventory.* Minneapolis, MN: National Computer Systems, Inc.

Millon, T. 1987. *Manual for the MCMI-II.* Minneapolis, MN: National Computer Systems, Inc. 2nd ed.

Mischel, W. 1968. *Personality and Assessment.* New York: Wiley

Mohr, D. C., Beutler, L. E., Engle, D., Shohan-Solomon, V., Bergan, J., et al. 1990. Identification of patients at risk for nonresponse and negative outcome in psychotherapy. *J. Consult. Clin. Psychol.* 58:622–28

Morey, L. C., Waugh, M. H., Blashfield, R. K. 1985. MMPI scales for DSM-III personality disorders: their derivation and correlates. *J. Pers. Assess.* 49:245–51

Moskowitz, D. S. 1990. Convergence of self-reports and independent observers: dominance and friendliness. *J. Pers. Soc. Psychol.* 58:1096–1106

Needles, D. J., Abramson, L. Y. 1990. Positive life events, attributional style and hopefulness: testing a model of recovery from depression. *J. Abnorm. Psychol.* 99:156–65

Newman, L. S., Uleman, J. S. 1990. Assimilation and contrast effects in spontaneous trait inference. *Pers. Soc. Psychol. Bull.* 16:224–40

Norman, W. T. 1967. *2800 Personality Trait Descriptors: Normative Operating Characteristics for a University Population.* Ann Arbor, MI: Dept. Psychol., Univ. Michigan

Orford, J. 1986. The rules of interpersonal complementarity: Does hostility beget hostility and dominance, submission? *Psychol. Rev.* 93:365–77

Ostendorf, F. 1990. Sprache und Persönlichkeitsstruktur: Zur Validät des Fünf-Faktoren-Modells der Persönlichkeit [Language and Personality Structure: Toward the Validation of the Five-Factor Model of Personality]. Regensburg: S. Roderer

Ostendorf, F., Angleitner, A. 1990. On the comprehensiveness of the five-factor model of personality: some more evidence for the five robust rating factors in questionnaire data. Paper presented at the 5th Eur. Conf. Pers., Rome, Italy

Ozer, D. J., Gjerde, P. F. 1989. Patterns of personality consistency and change from childhood through adolescence. *J. Pers.* 57:483–507

Paddock, J. R., Nowicki, S. Jr. 1986. An examination of the Leary Circumplex through the Interpersonal Check List. *J. Res. Pers.* 20:107–44

Park, B., Judd, C. M. 1989. Agreement on initial impressions: differences due to perceivers, trait dimensions, and target behaviors. *J. Pers. Soc. Psychol.* 56:493–505

Paulhus, D. L. 1991. Measurement and control of response bias. In *Measures of Personality and Social Psychological Attitudes*, ed. J. P. Robinson, P. Shaver, L. S. Wrightsman, pp. 17–59. San Diego, CA: Academic

Paunonen, S. V. 1989. Consensus in personality judgments: moderating effects of target-rater acquaintanceship and behavior observability. *J. Pers. Soc. Psychol.* 56:823–33

Pincus, A. L., Wiggins, J. S. 1990a. Interpersonal problems and conceptions of personality disorders. *J. Pers. Disord.* 4:342–52

Pincus, A. L., Wiggins, J. S. 1990b. Interpersonal traits, interpersonal problems, and personality disorders: dual circumplex analyses. Paper presented at the Annu. Meet. Am. Psychol. Assoc., Boston, MA

Rabin, A. I., Zucker, R. A., Emmons, R. A., Frank, S., eds. 1990. *Studying Persons and Lives.* New York: Springer

Renken, B., Egeland, B., Marvinney, D., Mangelsdorf, S., Sroufe, L. A. 1989. Early childhood antecedents of aggression and passive-withdrawal in early elementary school. *J. Pers.* 57:257–81

Romney, D. M., Bynner, J. M. 1989. Evaluation of a circumplex model of DSM-III personality disorders. *J. Res. Pers.* 23:525–38

Rosenberg, S. 1989. A study of personality in literary autobiography: an analysis of Thomas Wolfe's *Look Homeward, Angel. J. Pers. Soc. Psychol.* 56:416–30

Ross, M. 1989. Relation of implicit theories to the construction of personal histories. *Psychol. Rev.* 96:341–57

Rubin, K. H., Hymel, S., Mills, R. S. L. 1989. Sociability and social withdrawal in childhood: stability and outcomes. *J. Pers.* 57:237–55

Runyan, W. M. 1990. Individual lives and the structure of personality psychology. In *Studying Persons and Lives,* ed. A. I. Rabin, R. A. Zucker, R. A. Emmons, S. Frank, pp. 10–40. New York: Springer

Schutz, W. C. 1958. *FIRO: A Three Dimensional Theory of Interpersonal Behavior.* New York: Reinhart

Shea, T. (Chair). 1989. Personality dimensions and personality disorders. Symp. conducted at the Soc. for Pers. Assess. Midwinter Meet., New York

Shoda, Y., Mischel, W., Wright, J. C. 1989. Intuitive interactionism in person perception: effects of situation-behavior relations on dispositonal judgments. *J. Pers. Soc. Psychol.* 56:41–53

Sim, J. P., Romney, D. M. 1990. The relationship between a circumplex model of interpersonal behaviors and personality disorders. *J. Pers. Disord.* 4:329–41

Snyder, M., Ickes, W. 1985. Personality and social behavior. In *Handbook of Social Psychology,* ed. G. Lindzey, E. Aronson, 2:883–947. New York: Random House

Stewart, A. J., Franz, C., Layton, L. 1988. The changing self: using personal documents to study lives. *J. Pers.* 56:41–74

Stokes, G. S., Mumford, M. D., Owens, W.

A. 1989. Life history prototypes in the study of human individuality. *J. Pers.* 57:510–45

Strack, S. 1987. Development and validation of an adjective checklist to assess the Millon personality types in a normal population. *J. Pers. Assess.* 51:572–87

Strack, S. 1990. *Manual for the Personality Adjective Check List (PACL).* Richland, WA: Pacific Psychological

Strack, S., Lorr, M. 1990. Three approaches to interpersonal behavior and their common factors. *J. Pers. Assess.* 54:782–90

Strack, S., Lorr, M., Campbell, L. 1990. An evaluation of Millon's circular model of personality disorders. *J. Pers. Disord.* 4:351–64

Sweeny, P. D., Anderson, A., Bailey, S. 1986. Attributional style in depression: a meta-analytic view. *J. Pers. Soc. Psychol.* 50:974–91

Talley, P. F., Stupp, H. H., Morey, L. C. 1990. Matchmaking in psychotherapy: patient-therapist dimensions and their impact on outcome. *J. Consult. Clin. Psychol.* 58:182–88

Taylor, S. 1989. *Positive Illusions.* New York: Basic Books

Tellegen, A. 1992. Tellegen, A. 1992. *The Multidimensional Personality Questionnaire.* Minneapolis: Natl. Comput. Serv.

Tellegen, A. 1991. Personality traits: issues of definition, evidence and assessment. In *Thinking Clearly about Psychology: Essays in Honor of Paul Everett Meehl,* ed. D. Cicchetti, W. Grove. Minneapolis, MN: Univ. Minnesota Press. In press

Tomkins, S. S. 1979. Script theory: differential magnification of affects. In *Nebraska Symposium on Motivation,* ed. H. E. Howe, R. E. Dienstbier, 26:201–36. Lincoln: Univ. Nebraska Press

Trapnell, P. D., Wiggins, J. S. 1990. Extension of the Interpersonal Adjective Scales to include the Big Five dimensions of personality. *J. Pers. Soc. Psychol.* 59:781–90

Tunis, S. L., Fridhandler, B. M., Horowitz, M. J. 1990. Identifying schematized views of self with significant others: convergence of quantitative and clinical methods. *J. Pers. Soc. Psychol.* 59:1279–86

Tupes, E. C., Christal, R. E. 1958. Stability of personality trait rating factors obtained under diverse conditions (USAF WADC Tech. Note, No. 58–61

Waller, N. G., Ben-Porath, Y. 1987. Is it time for clinical psychology to embrace the five-factor model of personality? *Am. Psychol.* 42:887–89

Watson, D., Clark, L. A. 1992. On traits and temperament: general and specific factors of emotional experience and their relation to the five-factor model. *J. Pers.* In press

West, S. G., Graziano, W. G., eds. 1989. Special Issue: long-term stability and change in personality. *J. Pers.* 57(2):175–545

Widiger, T. A. 1989. *Personality Disorder Dimensional Models for DSM-IV.* DSM-IV Work Group on Personality Disorders, Cornell Univ. Medical College

Widiger, T. A., Trull, T. J. 1992. Personality and psychopathology: an application of the five-factor model. *J. Pers.* In press

Wiggins, J. S. 1968. Personality structure. *Annu. Rev. Psychol.* 19:293–350

Wiggins, J. S. 1979. A psychological taxonomy of trait-descriptive terms: the interpersonal domain. *J. Pers. Soc. Psychol.* 37:395–412

Wiggins, J. S. 1987. How interpersonal are the MMPI personality disorder scales? In *Current Research on MMPI Personality Disorder Scales.* Symp. conducted at the Meet. Am. Psychol. Assoc., New York

Wiggins, J. S. 1991. Agency and communion as conceptual coordinates for the understanding and measurement of interpersonal behavior. See Tellegen 1991, pp. 89–113

Wiggins, J. S., Phillips, N., Trapnell, P. 1989. Circular reasoning about interpersonal behavior: evidence concerning some untested assumptions underlying diagnostic classification. *J. Pers. Soc. Psychol.* 56:296–305

Wiggins, J. S., Pincus, A. L. 1989. Conceptions of personality disorders and dimensions of personality. *Psychol. Assess. : A J. Consult. Clin. Psychol.* 1:305–16

Wiggins, J. S., Pincus, A. L. 1992. Personality structure and the structure of personality disorders. See Costa & Widiger 1992

Wiggins, J. S., Trapnell, P. D. 1992. Personality structure: the return of the Big Five. In *Handbook of Personality Psychology,* ed. S. R. Briggs, R. Hogan, W. H. Jones. Orlando, FL: Academic

Wiggins, J. S., Trapnell, P., Phillips, N. 1988. Psychometric and geometric characteristics of the revised Interpersonal Adjective Scales (IAS-R). *Multivar. Behav. Res.* 23:517–30

Winter, D. G., Carlson, L. A. 1988. Using motive scores in the psychobiographical study of an individual: the case of Richard Nixon. *J. Pers.* 56:75–103

Wright, J. C. 1989. An alternative paradigm for studying the accuracy of person perception: simulated personalities. See Briggs 1989, pp. 61–81

Yang, K. S., Bond, M. H. 1990. Exploring implicit personality theories with indigenous or imported constructs: the Chinese case. *J. Pers. Soc. Psychol.* 58:1087–95

Yang, K. S., Lee, P. H. 1971. Likeability, meaningfulness and familiarity of 557 Chinese adjectives for personality trait description. *Acta Psychol. Taiwan* 13:36–37 (In Chinese)

Annu. Rev. Psychol. 1992. 43:505–29

PSYCHOLOGY IN BELGIUM

M. Richelle

Laboratory of Experimental Psychology, University of Liège, B-4000 Liège, Belgium

P. Janssen

Center for School Psychology, Catholic University of Leuven, B-3000 Leuven, Belgium

S. Brédart

Laboratory of Social Psychology, University of Liège, B-4000 Liège, Belgium

KEY WORDS: Belgium, history, psychological profession, International Congress of Psychology

CONTENTS

A BRIEF RETROSPECT[1]

Historico-Geographical Keys to Belgian Psychology

The geographical distribution of universities, and of their faculties of psychology, is, in part, linked to the present political configuration of the country. Belgium is a recent entity in European history, emerging from a short local revolution against the Dutch rulers in 1830, after 15 years of a rather artificial state created by the Congress of Vienna. The country has evolved, in the last decades, into a quasi-federal system, whose organization aims to solve complex linguistic issues. Belgium has three official languages : French, Flemish (similar to Dutch), and German. To oversimplify, French is spoken in the southern half of the country, Flemish in the northern part, and German in a small territory in the East. The large Brussels area is bilingual.

Seven universities have faculties of psychology and education (under various labels) offering a full range of subject areas in psychology. Four of them are French-speaking (Brussels, Liège, Louvain-la-Neuve, and Mons); three are Flemish (Brussels, Ghent and Leuven).[2] The two universities in Brussels were born from a single institution, formerly teaching in both languages. This has been the case also for the universities of Leuven/Louvain, but the French-speaking university moved from the city of Leuven to a new site in the southern part of the country, called Louvain-la-Neuve (New Leuven).[3] As these changes do not go back more than 25 years or so, in the cases of both the Brussels and Leuven/Louvain universities, the now separate institutions, including their psychology faculties, share the same history.

Three periods can be distinguished in the historical development of scientific psychology in Belgium: the 19th century only highlights a few forerunners and pioneers; in the first half of the 20th century, psychology entered the academic institutions with the creation of laboratories and the development of curricula, usually with an emphasis on applied fields; from the 1950s on, full and diversified curricula were created, distinct faculties were eventually established, and research expanded.

---

[1]For more historical information, see Nuttin (1961), Montpellier (1971), and Bertelson (1984).

[2]The complete names labeling of these institutions are as follow: Université Libre de Bruxelles, Université de Liège, Université de Mons, Université catholique de Louvain à Louvain-la-Neuve, Vrije Universiteit Brussels, Rijk Universiteit Gent, Katholieke Universiteit te Leuven. Liège, Mons, and Ghent depend on public administration, now at the level of linguistically defined communities. The universities of Leuven/Louvain and of Brussels are private institutions, the first two, as the name indicates, depending on the Catholic religious authorities, the other two originally on nonreligious groups. For most practical purposes, all are now financially supported by public sources, and they share equal access to research funding.

[3]With the exception of the Medical School, which moved to the Brussels area.

Some Pioneers

Psychology textbooks mention the names of a few Belgian scientists who contributed directly or indirectly to the progress of psychological science in the 19th century. The names of Quételet (1796–1874), Plateau (1801–1883) and Delboeuf (1831–1896) are especially salient.

An astronomer and mathematician in Brussels, Quételet made important contributions to statistical methods and to the theory of normal distribution; he had the idea of putting them to work in measuring mental faculties in humans, opening the way to the quantified approach to interindividual differences that Galton was to develop later in the century (Quételet 1869, 1870).

Plateau, a physicist who taught at the university of Ghent, was an expert in vision, especially in color vision, a field he went on studying after he became blind in his forties. He published an essay on a general theory of vision, and his experimental contributions include empirical data on color mixing and studies of stroboscopic movement (Plateau 1834).

Delboeuf's name is best known now in relation with the visual illusion named after him. He was affiliated with the department of philosophy at the University of Liège, where he taught logic as well as psychology. His contributions to both fields have been highly praised. He performed experiments of his own in sensation and perception, and wrote extensively in the field of psychophysics, discussing the conflicting theories of his day (Delboeuf 1883a,b). Freud came across his work and occasionally discussed his views. William James visited him when traveling in Belgium and reported in a letter to his brother Henry how much the man and his scientific achievements impressed him.[4] Delboeuf had been an active participant in the first two Congresses of Psychology, in Paris (1889) and London (1892). Although he had been involved in the preparation of the 1896 Munich meeting, he could not attend for health reasons, and he died shortly after it took place. His work in Liège was discontinued, presumably because he had not established a group of followers, and for reasons of local institutional policy.

The Growth of Academic Psychology

Scientific psychology found its place, with a better prospect of lasting, with the foundation of the Laboratory of Experimental Psychology at the University of Louvain in 1892. The laboratory's establishment was due to the initiative of D. Mercier (later a Cardinal of the Roman Church), then the head of a recently created Institute of Philosophy. One of his students, A. Thiéry,

---

[4]James's letter is dated November 2, 1882. The document is part of the important Delboeuf archives, deposited at the philosophy department of the University of Liège. The information is reproduced by courtesy of F. Duyckaerts, who has been exploring Delboeuf's papers for some years (Duyckaerts 1989a, 1990).

who had studied with Wundt in Leipzig, was appointed as the first director. He had worked on optical illusions. He was succeeded in 1906 by A. Michotte (1881–1965), his student, who also spent some time at Leipzig and later developed close relationships with Külpe in Würzburg. Michotte's contributions to experimental psychology have been many and diverse, but he is best known for his often quoted work on perception of movement and of phenomenal causality (1954). Michotte has played an important role, at the international level, in making Belgian psychology visible. He was President of the International Union of Psychological Science (1957–1960).

The Louvain laboratory was to develop, not only along the lines that Michotte had developed in the field of perception with A. Fauville (1946, 1948) and G. Thinès (1961), but in new areas as well. Fauville is to be credited for making early use of information theory (1963), Thinès initiated a research group in animal behavior (Thinès 1966), while J. Nuttin engaged in personality and motivation research (1953a,b, 1980) and G. de Montpellier developed animal learning studies (1950) before turning to experimental social psychology. Much current research at both Catholic universities has its roots in such developments, which were due to Michotte's impetus.

In other universities psychology did not so quickly achieve its due place; as a rule, applications were emphasized initially. This was the case at the University of Brussels, where psychology was linked with psychopathology—for example in the work of A. Ley (1946, 1948) and R. Nyssen (1946, 1948)—and with child and educational psychology—in the work of O. Decroly; the same assessment applies to the State Universities of Ghent and Liège, where programs of vocational and work psychology were organized.

The Postwar Period: Laying the Foundation of the Present

After the Second World War, the rapid growth of scientific psychology, resulting in the organization of full and varied university curricula, in the creation of laboratories and research groups, and in increased interactions with psychologists outside the country and outside Europe, was essentially the work of dynamic individuals, of high scientific status and committed to the progress of their field as well as to the development of their own academic institutions. The names of these men of transition deserve mention in the present historical survey because the current scene of psychology in Belgium is clearly a consequence of their decisive action, sometimes carried out at the expense of their own careers as scientists.

In Brussels, A. Ombredane (1898–1958), a French psychologist and physician, was in charge of the chair of psychology from 1948 until his untimely death. He promoted research in various directions of basic psychology— laying the foundations for the later development by P. Bertelson of current experimental cognitive psychology in Brussels—as well as of applied psychology, be it clinical, industrial, or child psychology—work associated with the names of F. Robaye, J. M. Faverge, and P. A. Osterrieth, respectively.

In Ghent, L. Coetsier (1912–1968) and W. De Coster (1920–), beside developing their own fields of expertise—applied psychology and developmental psychology, respectively—promoted new domains of experimental, theoretical and mathematical psychology.

In Leuven, J. Nuttin (1909–1988), besides being active for many years as an officer and president (1972–1976) of the International Union of Psychological Science, also developed a laboratory with various research orientations in human social and individual psychology—a laboratory that was full-fledged when the two universities separated. A similar role was played in what was to become the University of Louvain-la-Neuve by Montepellier and Thinès.

J. Paulus (1909–) was a former student of Pierre Janet, and was well known for his synthesis of the various European and American traditions (Paulus 1965). This background was reflected in the impetus he gave, during the 1950s and early 1960s, at the University of Liège, to the development of complementary branches of psychology and closely related fields, ranging from psychoanalysis and psychodynamics, represented by F. Duyckaerts (1954, 1964), to cultural anthropology; from psychophysiology to ethology; and from clinical to experimental psychology—the latter field being developed after 1960 by M. Richelle, who started the first operant conditioning laboratory on the European continent (Richelle 1991a). The study of animal behavior, carried out since then in the psychological laboratory and in the ethology laboratory (the latter at the Science Faculty), reinstated work initiated in the 1920s and 1930s by L. Verlaine (1889–1939) at the zoology department but interrupted for two decades. Verlaine performed a number of insightful and well-designed experiments and produced important writings on animal cognition; among other things, he pioneered in the study of counting capacities in monkeys (Verlaine 1935–1936, 1938).

These men who shaped contemporary Belgian psychology had in common their strategy of encouraging bright young students to complete their training abroad, a policy that was continued and, of course, largely facilitated by increasing international university exchanges. This has been the source of the diversification in backgrounds that can be noticed among Belgian psychologists of the generations now active.

The 1950s and early 1960s have also been marked by research activities in the field of cross-cultural psychology, carried out in the territory of Zaire, until 1960 a Belgian colony. This research was supported by each of the Belgian universities, and some of the psychologists whose names have been mentioned above have been engaged in it personally at one time or another (Ombredane 1954; Ombredane et al 1957; Richelle 1961, 1966).

A significant event for Belgian psychology in that period was the organization of the 15th International Congress of Psychology in Brussels in 1957. Michotte was the president, and Paulus the acting president of the Belgian Psychology Society, created in 1947.

CURRENT RESEARCH—AN OVERVIEW

The period that follows, extending roughly from 1965 to the present, cannot possibly be described in full detail. The field of psychology has been expanding tremendously, as evidenced by the number of students (which jumped from 2000 in 1965 to 6000 in 1990), the size of faculties, the number of PhDs granted (estimated at about 300 in the last 25 years), and the number of publications at the international level. Belgian psychologists participate in international scientific associations and programs; in addition, professional associations have arisen alongside the Belgian Psychological Society, which has retained essentially its scientific raison d'être.

The following survey of current research does not claim, of course, to be exhaustive; it presents a sample of psychological research activities in Belgium today, based on information provided on request by most Belgian research teams. We illustrate most of the areas referred to below with only one or two printed references, using two main criteria: First, we gave priority to papers written in English because we assumed they are accessible to most readers of the *Annual Review of Psychology*. This is not to say that excellent work has not been reported in Dutch or French by Belgian psychologists. Second, most of the illustrative references we chose were published after 1986.

Cognitive Psychology

In Belgium, as everywhere else, the cognitive psychologists' main fields of research deal with attentional processes (Soetens et al 1985); perception, especially visual perception (Verfaillie & d'Ydewalle 1991) including the developmental approach (Kolinsky 1989); memory—some more specific topics being mood and memory (Peeters & d'Ydewalle 1987; Ucros 1989), hypermnesia (Hoentjens & d'Ydewalle 1987), implicit memory, memory for faces (Bruyer 1986) and proper names (Brédart 1989), and memory for schemata (Vandierendonck & Van Damme 1988); concept learning and categorization (Thibaut 1986; Vandierendonck 1988); reasoning—for instance, syllogistic reasoning (Costermans & Heuschen 1990); and problem solving, with special interest in the role of decision processes in such complex problem-solving domains as chess (Lories 1987), genetic counseling (Huys et al 1990), and the control of dynamic systems (De Keyser 1990).

Psycholinguistics is the favorite topic of several groups. Three main lines of research can be mentioned. Reading processes have received much attention. Researchers investigated the relationship between alphabetic literacy training and phonological awareness (Morais et al 1987; Bertelson & De Gelder 1990), Braille reading (Mousty & Bertelson 1985), and reading among deaf people (Alegria & Leybaert 1991). Research in pragmatics is also active in both psychology departments (Hupet & Tilmant 1986) and departments of linguistics. It is worth noting that the "Pragmatic Documentation Center" of the International Pragmatics Association is located in Belgium (Antwerp). A third important research topic is first-language acquisition, particularly syntactic development in normal and handicapped children (Rondal 1985, 1988).

Apart from these classical "macro areas" of cognitive psychology, it is worth noticing some examples of other, more specific, topics in which some Belgian psychologists are currently engaged: music perception (Deliège 1989; Peretz & Morais 1989), number processing (Deloche & Seron 1987), gesture production and recognition (Feyereisen 1988; Feldman & Rimé 1990), software psychology (Vandierendonck et al 1988), and cognitive aspects of time estimation (Soffie & Lejeune 1991a). More epistemological works about cognitivism and its relationships with other theoretical frameworks of psychology have also been published (Richelle 1987, 1990). As elsewhere, computer modeling has become more and more appealing to cognitive psychologists in Belgium, many of them showing a strong interest in connectionist and hybrid models (Content 1991; Defays 1990; Lamberts 1990). Finally, thanks to recent financial support, psychology departments have been engaged in research on artificial intelligence in several universities.

Developmental Psychology

During the 1960s and 1970s, Belgian developmental psychology was strongly influenced by the Piagetian tradition, with the consequence that cognitive development in childhood and early adolescence was the main topic of research. During the 1980s, interest expanded to include other research topics. For instance, social development during childhood and adolescence (Marcoen & Brumagne 1985; Van den Plas-Holper & Jenart 1989) but also in adulthood (Verhofstadt-Denève 1985) has drawn the attention of several teams. Recently aging, especially its cognitive aspects, has received much attention from cognitive psychologists and neuropsychologists (Van der Linden 1990; Schweich et al 1991). Emotional changes (Hulbert & Lens 1988) and existential problems (Marcoen 1991) related to aging have also been investigated. Other groups are currently working on psychological aspects of pre- and neo-natology (Gillot-Devries 1988a; Van den Bergh 1988).

Cognitive development proper, in childhood and adolescence, is still studied, not only in the framework of perception and language, as already mentioned, but also with emphasis on conceptual development, development of mental imagery, or development of scientific reasoning (Goosens et al 1987).

Social Psychology and Personality

Research in social cognition began to develop primarily at the end of the 1970s. This development was influenced by the social information processing approach originated in the United States as well as by a more European tradition of socio-cognitive research (see Leyens & Codol 1988). Preferred topics in this field currently include social hypothesis testing (Van Avermaet 1988a) with a particular interest in intuitive personality testing (Yzerbyt & Leyens 1991), estimation bias (Peeters 1987), impression formation (Leyens & Fiske 1991), and relationships between social schemata and emotions (Rimé et al 1990).

Group processes, in a broad sense, comprise another important topic of research in Belgium. Investigators study social influence in small groups (Van Avermaet 1988b), the processes of group membership identification and group discrimination (Vanbeselaere 1987; Marques et al 1988), and the history of group dynamics (De Visscher 1991).

The famous "name letter effect" (a letter is judged more attractive if it occurs in one's own name than if it does not) is a more specific issue recently investigated by several Belgian social psychologists (e.g. Nuttin 1987). Certain aspects of applied research in social psychology are mentioned below.

Research in the psychology of personality deals with theoretical problems—for instance the development of the phenomenal/dialectal model of personality (Verhofstadt-Denève 1988) and the study of relationships between personality and person perception (Mervielde & Pot 1989)—as well as with the improvement and evaluation of personality assessment tools (De Boeck & Van Mechelen 1990; Sloore & Rouckhout 1989), including computerized assessment (Mervielde 1988). The consequences of brain damage for personality have also been investigated (Seron & Van der Linden 1988; Thiery 1988).

Other aspects of the research on personality are mentioned below in the section devoted to clinical psychology.

Neuropsychology and Psychobiology

The interest of some neuropsychologists in the study of cognitive aging has already been mentioned.

Laterality and hemispheric specialization remain important research topics in our country. Recent papers concern the lateral differences in visual processing (Bruyer & Caruso 1988), laterality of language processing in illiterates (Castro & Morais 1987), hemispheric differences in emotional language processing (Morais & Ladavas 1987), and methodological aspects of the assessment of laterality (Brysbaert & d'Ydewalle 1990). Neurolinguistics, and particularly aphasiology, is almost a traditional issue. Recent studies have investigated the pragmatic abilities of aphasics (Feyereisen et al 1988) and assessed fluency (Feyereisen et al 1991) or anosognosia in aphasia (Lebrun 1987). Language disorders in epilepsy (Lebrun 1988) and Alzheimer's disease (Wens et al 1989) have also been examined. Interesting work has also been done on mathematical abilities in brain-damaged patients, with a focus on number-transcoding mechanisms (Deloche & Seron 1987).

The cognitive approach in neuropsychology became popular in the 1980s. This trend resulted in a revival of interest in in-depth single case studies involving the collaboration of specialists from different subdisciplines of neuropsychology, neurology, speech therapy, and cognitive sciences. For instance, such single case studies have been successfully carried out with cases of visual neglect of objects, impairment of working memory, and visual agnosia (Grailet et al 1990).

Of course, neuropsychological rehabilitation (Seron & Deloche 1989) is also an important field of research as it deals, for example, with the rehabilitation of memory impairments (Van der Linden & Van der Kaa 1989).

Several departments of psychology are active in psychopharmacological research. The addictive properties of drugs, and more specifically the modulation of tolerance of and dependence on psychoactive drugs (morphine, ethanol, benzodiazepines) by environmental cues, have been studied (Jodogne & Tirelli 1990). The developmental approach in psychopharmacology has also received attention, and studies of age-related effects of drugs on behavior have been carried out (Soffie & Bronchart 1988; Tirelli & Jodogne 1990). The effects of hormones on performance and fatigue (Hueting et al 1988), of drugs in sleep research (De Roeck & Cluydts 1989), and of neuropeptides on behavior (Heidbreder et al 1989) form the focus of other lines of research.

Continuing a long tradition of research on temporal regulation (Richelle et al 1985), recent research has been bearing essentially upon comparative cross-species aspects (Lejeune 1990; Lejeune & Richelle 1991; Lejeune & Wearden 1991) and upon life-span developmental aspects (Soffie & Lejeune 1991a,b). Behavioral variability is another actively studied issue (Richelle 1997b; Machado 1989).

Clinical Psychology

The family approach to clinical questions became ever more popular during the 1980s. Family psychology and family therapy are now main issues for several clinical research centers. The family approach to psychosomatic problems (Kog et al 1987) and to eating disorders like anorexia and bulimia (Kog, Vandereycken & Vertommen 1989) has been investigated. Family and more widely systemic approaches to the rehabilitation of institutionalized children, autistic or psychotic children, for instance, have also received much attention.

Client-centered psychotherapy and counseling is a third important line of research in clinical psychology. A good presentation of this trend can be seen in Lietaer et al (1990). For instance, helping and hindering processes in experiential psychotherapy have been examined (Lietaer 1990). This approach is also applied to a wide range of specific questions—for example, the counseling of patients with cancer (Willemaers 1987).

The more traditional psychoanalytical perspective is of course still well represented among Belgian researchers in clinical psychology. Reports of case studies and theoretical essays on neurotic and psychotic personality structures are regularly published. Other directions include research on Freudian epistemology (Quackelbeen 1987), historical research (Duyckaerts 1989b; Valcke & Corveleyn 1989), and reflections on the relationships between psychoanalysis and such other disciplines as education (Verhaeghe 1987). The psychodynamic perspective has also been applied to analyze the emotional consequences of current human practices like transsexuality (Desmit & Corveleyn 1990).

Research in behavior therapy is also done (Eelen & Fontaine 1986). The behavioral approach to depression (Eelen & Van den Bergh 1986) and to management of fear (Van den Bergh et al 1989) or stress has developed. Recently, special attention has been given to evaluative conditioning (Baeyens et al 1989, 1990). Finally, behavioral medicine and social psychophysiology seem to be more and more appealing to researchers, particularly to psychologists concerned with cardiovascular diseases (Vinck et al 1988; Rimé et al 1989; Janne et al 1991) and patients' emotional responses to painful medical procedures like surgery or chemotherapy (Fontaine 1987; Fontaine & Salah 1990). Huber (1987) has focused on research comparing the validity of various types of psychotherapies, and on the current status of clinical psychology.

Industrial Psychology and Ergonomics

Industrial psychology and work psychology comprise an active field. It includes ergonomics, with a strong interest in cognitive ergonomics—e.g. control of continuous processes by operators (De Keyser 1987) or cognitive factors in human-computer interaction (Vandierendonck et al 1988; Karnas et al 1988); organizational psychology applied to work situations—e.g. the organizational approach to personnel training (De Cock 1990), the construction of grievances (Bouwen & Salipante 1991), and the occurrence of occupational accidents (Janssens et al 1989), but also analyses of organizational problems in such particular work settings as hospitals (Coetsier & Claes 1988); and the psychology of professional life, including studies of job satisfaction (Lagrou & De Witte 1990) and of work motivation (Coetsier & Claes 1990) in young people.

Other Topics

Research in mathematical psychology engages issues such as hierarchical classes (De Boeck & Rosenberg 1988; Van Mechelen & De Boeck 1990), tree models (De Soete 1988), and the construction of procedures for assessing the state of systems (Falmagne & Doignon 1988). Another facet of this field involves psychological choice modeling (De Soete et al 1989).

Research in educational and school psychology deals with such topics as educational practices in families, including the investigation of parental didactics (Vyt 1989); stimulation of cognitive development in classrooms (De Coster et al 1990); motivation and school performance (Lens 1987); studying processes (Janssen 1989; Van Overwalle 1991); the modeling of individual differences in academic performance of university students (Decruyenaere & Janssen 1989); and students' causal attributions with respect to their academic performance (Van Overwalle 1989).

A good part of clinical and psychosocial applied research is also devoted to other issues of immediate concern to society. These include delinquency and youth criminology (Born 1987), drug addiction (Born & Schaber 1987), analysis of violence in soccer stadia (Rimé & Leyens 1988), psychological consequences of stress in children living in war areas (Mahjoub et al 1989), unemployment (Salengros et al 1989), the evolution of religious behavior (Jaspard 1987), and the consequences of the methods of procreation on parenthood (Gillot-DeVries 1988b).

THE PSYCHOLOGICAL PROFESSION

At present, more than 5000 university-trained psychologists actively practice the psychological profession in Belgium. They share this work with at least two other groups of people, who in public—improperly according to the university graduates—also call themselves psychologists. One group apparently uses this title to justify the work they are doing without formal qualifications. As the title is not yet officially protected, no one in Belgium can legally prevent this use of the term. The second group is more homogeneous: After a three-year technical course in non-university higher education, one can obtain the degree of "Assistant in Psychology." This certificate allows one to perform technical tasks under the direct supervision of a psychologist who has obtained the degree of "Licentiate in Psychology" after at least four, but most often five, years of university training. The training spheres of psychological activities and organizations for these licentiates are described below.

Training in Psychology

Unlike many other countries, Belgium has two forms of higher education. The university form is characterized by direct interaction with science and the conduct of scientific research. University students are first introduced to a scientific discipline; their professional training, being of secondary importance for the university, only starts in the second cycle of the study program. Non-university higher education is characterized by technical training from the very beginning in the practice of the skill for which it prepares its students.

INSIDE UNIVERSITIES   University education is organized in three cycles: the candidature, the licentiate, and the doctorate. The certificate issued at the end of the second cycle enables the licentiate to practice the profession. Only a few students go through the last stage and complete their university training with the doctoral degree, which is required for the autonomous practice of science within a university. Each of these three stages is described here with respect to psychology. As such, this program fulfills almost all the requirements of the European Federation of Professional Psychologists' Associations (EFPPA). The only one it fails to meet is the number of years to be spent in university (one fewer than the six proposed by the EFPPA).

The candidature consists of broad basic training in the science of psychology, its methodology, and the so-called auxiliary sciences of biology, physiology, philosophy, sociology, and so on. It takes two years to obtain the candidature certificate, which is roughly equivalent to the bachelor's degree. In Belgium the first year in higher education generally serves a selective purpose: More than half of the freshmen enrolled do not pass. There are three reasons for this high casualty rate. In Belgium, everyone who completes general secondary education (with the exception of those applying for faculties of engineering) may enter university. There are no entrance examinations and no restrictions on the numbers that can be admitted. Second, the universities, like all other educational institutions, are subsidized on the basis of student enrollment, so every freshman is welcome at the beginning of a new academic year. Finally, there is the general feeling that such a selection method is the most democratic of all the selection methods in use in higher education throughout the world. Psychological methods could contribute to selection of secondary school graduates for admission to the university, but admission tests or procedures are, as yet, politically unacceptable, although the scientific competence has been available for many years. After the successful completion of his or her second year, the student is officially proclaimed a "Candidate in Psychology."

With this certificate, the student may enter the license program, the second study cycle in psychology training at the university. It will take the student three years to achieve the cycle's two main objectives: deepening the scientific basic training and starting a specialization within a freely chosen domain in applied or basic psychology. The student composes, within well-defined "majors," a personal study program. Within the universities, these majors in psychology may have specific names. In the main, four can be identified. The three applied majors are developmental, social-industrial, and clinical psychology, and the fourth is basic psychology, which also involves a further choice of the specific area the student wants to specialize in as a potential researcher. Important components of this second-cycle training are the thesis prepared during these three years under the direction of a member of the academic staff and the internship (outside the university for applied psychology) during the fifth year. The thesis is a scientific report of personal research on a self-selected psychological problem. It must be presented at the end of the program. The time spent on the internship varies from university to university. In Leuven, for instance, it occupies four days a week for at least seven months of the fifth year.

Most students leave university after completion of their second cycle; only a few remain in order to prepare their doctorate under the direction of a member of the academic staff. Sometimes they do this as a temporary member of the scientific staff, in which case they are appointed for two years; every two years their scientific progress is evaluated, and this appointment can be renewed twice. Two thirds of their time is available for research. It is also possible to obtain a scholarship, which enables them to complete their doctoral studies in four years of full-time research.

OUTSIDE UNIVERSITIES   Professional psychology training in universities was formally instituted in Belgium only after the Second World War. Before that, one could only study psychology in the university as a major in philosophy or education. At that time in Belgium, there were already specific study programs in psychology outside of the universities. Two types deserve mention here because they are at the root of the problem of professional qualifications. The first consisted of an examination, and the part-time preparation for it, for the certificate of "Assistant in Vocational Guidance." Its main objective was to offer teachers and social workers an opportunity to prepare themselves for part-time jobs in services to assist 14-year-old school-leavers in their vocational choice. Expansion of these services had increased to such an extent under the impetus of the Catholic Workers Union, especially in the Dutch-speaking part of the country, that by 1936 this measure was required.

The second type of study program was provided by the "Ecole d'Ergologie," which was founded in 1927 in Brussels. This "School of Labor Science" had three divisions: vocational guidance, psychotechnics (personnel selection), and scientific organization of labor. To meet the remaining demand for such assistants, other schools were founded in Antwerp, Brussels, Kortrijk, and elsewhere. They currently offer a full-time three-year program leading to the certificate of "Assistant in Psychology." Their trainees are highly valued employees in psychological services where most of them work—for instance, in taking care of the administration of standard group and individual tests—under the direct supervision of a university-trained psychologist. After completion of their three-year program, some of these assistants go to a university. They sometimes then have to pass an entrance examination (combining the main parts of the university's first-cycle program in psychology into a special one-year program) before entering the three years of second-cycle training. Thus the two types of training in Belgian higher education must be clearly distinguished. Although understandable in some respects, the claim of these assistants that they should be called psychologists is ill founded.

Spheres of Activity

The employment of university-trained psychologists is sensitive to economic trends. There have been periods in which these licentiates could find a job immediately after graduation. In other times, they have had great difficulty finding employment at their level of competence (Lagrou & De Witte 1990). The present seems relatively favorable. Each period of economic recovery creates new demand for psychologists, directly—for instance, in industrial psychology and related fields—as well as indirectly—e.g. in school and in clinical psychology. A recession almost immediately results in a contraction of the professions in the so-called soft sector because most of them are subsidized by the government. The three domains of applied psychology are described below. Some information about scientific research as a sphere of psychological activity is also provided.

SCHOOL PSYCHOLOGY   School psychology is the oldest and perhaps best known form of the profession in Belgium. Almost everyone under the age of 45 has come in personal contact with it in the one way or another. School psychology gradually developed from vocational guidance, which was introduced immediately after the First World War to help 14-year-old school-leavers find employment and additional training in industry. After the Second World War, as soon as the state of the economy permitted secondary education for every youngster, and after compulsory education was extended, this work increasingly became educational guidance. Around 1960, a new infrastructure was created in which the Psycho-Medical-Social Centers occupy a central position. Here the psychological, medical, and social disciplines work together as a team to provide every child constant guidance from the beginning of preschool kindergarten (at the age of two and a half years old) to the end of secondary education (officially at 18 years old). Within the discipline of psychology, the original emphasis on guidance has been broadened to all relevant aspects of school psychology: academically trained psychologists and technically trained assistants in psychology work together with nurses, welfare workers, and school doctors. These teams provide for prevention, relief, and first-level therapy of learning difficulties and developmental disorders. Vocational counseling is also given. For many years, the expansion of these centers was frozen for budgetary reasons, but the restrictions on staff recruitment have recently been removed.

INDUSTRIAL PSYCHOLOGY   Around 1800, the first "modern" industrial area on the European continent came into being in the French-speaking part of Belgium, with the exploitation of iron ore and pit coal. The industrialization of Flanders came about much later, which is why industrial psychology started earlier in the Walloon provinces. At present, this psychological activity is equally well developed in both parts of the country, within industry itself as well as in independent centers. The latter take care of recruitment, selection, out-placement, and training and also provide managerial consulting. Recent technological innovations in information processing and automation have created a demand for experts in occupational resettlement and in-service training. Psychologists, more explicitly than in the past, are becoming involved in human resources management, as this, following the Japanese model, has come to the fore as a means of raising the motivation and commitment of workers. The marketing sector is also relatively well established. Many young industrial psychologists start their career in this field.

CLINICAL PSYCHOLOGY   The introduction of clinical psychology within the second cycle of the university programs in about 1965 responded to a real need in Belgian society. Until the beginning of 1982, alumni with a major in clinical psychology could easily find work in therapeutic services all over the country. Under government sponsorship, psychiatric centers, mental health services, rehabilitation centers, family therapy centers and, last but not least, psychiatric wards in general hospitals were established. At present, it is difficult for young clinical psychologists to find employment in this sector: The small number of positions that become vacant are occupied immediately by clinical psychologists who have been holding temporary and part-time jobs or who have specialized in psychotherapy in postgraduate university programs. In the near future, however, new career opportunities will open up because government plans now require clinical psychologists on basic health teams. The ex-psychiatric patient living in small-scale residences must also be served. In hospital wards for physical illnesses, the clinical psychologist can provide counseling during illness, can contribute to the improvement of the patient's quality of life, and can assist in the treatment of functional complaints. In geriatric and psycho-geriatric hospitals, the clinical psychologist has to perform typical tasks in assessment, counseling, therapy, and management. Collaboration with the family doctor has to be intensified in the care of patients with psychosocial problems and psychophysiological complaints. Clinical and health psychologists have to be involved in specialized rehabilitation centers for sufferers of coronary and vascular diseases and patients in traumatological and orthopedic wards. Both have a role to play in the development of health-promoting campaigns on smoking, alcohol abuse, drugs, eating habits, stress management, etc. The necessary and sufficient condition for promoting these clinical psychological activities in Belgium would imply either the repayment of the costs of the client by the national health insurance system or the subsidizing of such centers by that system. Here again, economic forces are determining the development of the psychological profession.

RESEARCH   Research is a relatively small sphere of psychological activity and is situated mostly within the universities. Where funding has to be managed by the universities themselves, research opportunities are directly related to enrollment numbers and the student-staff ratio. The latter is small for the human sciences, which include psychology: For every 14 students only one staff member (academic and scientific) is financed. In natural science faculties this ratio is more favorable, and in the faculties of medicine and its associated disciplines (such as physical education), this ratio is much more advantageous. This is why the future PE teacher in this country is better "supported" during his university training than the would-be psychologist. Given that the average member of the academic staff has a high teaching load, research in universities is executed mainly by members of the temporary scientific staff during the preparation of their doctorates under the supervision of a lecturer or professor. Successful completion of the PhD does not automatically imply an appointment in the university, however; gradually more and more doctors in psychology are having to find work outside the universities.

Although placement opportunities for licentiates with a major in scientific research are few, their prospects for finding an appropriate job are not unfavorable. The fact that they are methodologically better trained than their colleagues gives them an advantage when they apply for functions that require such training. Sometimes, too, they can easily find employment in other than specifically psychological areas.

Organizations of Psychologists

Only a few of the many organizations of psychologists in this country are really Belgian both in name and in bilingual functioning. The two most important "Belgian" associations are the Belgian Psychological Society (Belgische Vereniging voor Psychologie/Société Belge de Psychologie; BVP/SBP) and the Belgian Federation of Psychologists (Fedération Belge des Psychologues/Belgische Federatie van Psychologen; FBP/BFP). Both maintain the usual international relations. Most other organizations are active in only one of the two linguistic communities and almost all of them—including the Belgian Society—are grouped together in the Federation. The latter has taken on the responsibility for the promotion of the interests of all psychologists with respect to the Belgian government.

BVP/SBP   The Belgian Psychological Society was founded in 1947. Its objectives are threefold: to promote scientific contacts among university-trained psychologists in Belgium, to coordinate their activities, and to promote their professional interests. At present the Society has about 400 members and is a member society of the International Union of Psychological Science (IUPsyS). The Belgians Albert Michotte van den Berck and Jozef R. Nuttin served this Union as Presidents; Géry van Outrive d'Ydewalle is presently the Union's Deputy Secretary-General. The Society, then chaired by Jean Paulus, organized the 15th International Congress of Psychology in 1957 and it is now preparing, also in Brussels, the 25th International Congress for 1992.

In the 1960s, the Society tried, in line with its third objective and in cooperation with associations of psychological practitioners, to define an ethical code of conduct for psychologists and to take measures to obtain the legal status for the psychological profession. It did not succeed. In 1975, the Society concluded that a more appropriate organizational infrastructure had to be composed in collaboration with other Belgian associations of psychologists. Four years later the "Belgian Federation" was founded (see below).

The Society decided, in line with its first and second objectives, to concentrate on such tasks as the scientific organization of Belgian psychology. It founded discipline-based working groups in the universities and still takes great pains in the publication of its scientific journal *Psychologica Belgica*. Four times a year, a bilingual *Information Bulletin* is issued. In April or May of each year, a one-day workshop is held during which members present and discuss their latest findings (psychology departments act as host in turn).

FBP/BFP   The "Belgian Federation" was founded in 1979 and coordinates 15 associations of university-trained psychologists in both parts of the country. On the Dutch-speaking side, the three major spheres of psychological activities as described above are represented by as many Flemish organizations: the VOCAP (Vlaamse Vereniging voor Organisatie-, Consumenten- en Arbeidspsychologen) for organizational, consumer, and industrial psychologists, the VVKP (Vlaamse Vereniging voor Klinische Psychologen) for clinical psychologists, and the VWPP (Vlaamse Wetenschappelijke Vereniging voor Psychologen van PMS-Centra) for school psychologists. The French-speaking side has many relatively small associations, most of them for clinical psychologists and each reflecting a specific therapeutic orientation. An association of industrial psychologists is being formed. The Belgian Federation is a member of the European Federation of Professional Psychologists' Associations (EFPPA).

The Belgian Federation has set itself the goal of uniting Belgian licentiates and doctors in psychology in a well-structured professional community. It wishes to promote and (when and where necessary) to defend the professional, socioeconomic, and moral interests of Belgian psychologists, representing them to governmental officials and in the media on the local, European, and world levels. Between its members and colleagues from abroad, the FBP/BFP wants to stimulate a spirit of collegiality, to promote professional contacts and the exchange of information, to develop an adequate ethical code, and to promote the growth and application of psychology as a science.

The Federation's board of directors is composed of representatives of the associations and elected members for each of the four spheres in which psychologists are active. The executive committee, assisted by a permanent secretariat, coordinates the activities. The Federation has four permanent committees and ad hoc task forces. Four times a year, two *Bulletins*—Dutch and French, each having its own editorial board—are published. When information must be given quickly to the members, the Executive Committee uses *News Flashes*. At present, the associations of the Federation have about 1200 members, a relatively small number, considering there are some 5000 "licentiates" active in the profession.

In the past decade, the Federation has devoted considerable effort to achieving its first objective, the legal protection of the title of psychologist in the interest of potential clients—an issue that owes its significance not least to the forthcoming political unification of Europe. One of the major problems to be solved is that of "acquired rights," a central concept in Belgian social law. People who, according to their personal view, have the right to call themselves psychologists—as some educationalists and assistants in psychology do—claim the right to continue to do so, even though they are not psychologists in the way psychologists themselves, being university-trained "licentiates," want to see their own competence defined. Therefore, many compromises have to be worked out in parallel with the preparation of legislation in parliament. As the history of other European countries teaches, the realization of such an initiative can take a decade or more. Other matters have the undivided attention of the Federation, such as the definition of the task of clinical psychologists in dialog with the national Ministry of Public Health and the work of the industrial psychologist in employment agencies in discussion with the Flemish Ministry of Labor. Such tasks turn out to be extremely difficult as long as the title of psychologist is not adequately protected. Another difficult circumstance is that the Federation is still too small to be able to afford a full-time professional manager to carry out its tasks. It seems to be caught in a vicious circle.

1992: THE TURNING POINT?

In 1992, many European countries will commemorate a century of scientific research in psychology. Belgium will do the same. This was one of the arguments used by the Belgian Psychological Society in 1984 when it applied for the honor of organizing the 25th International Congress of Psychology of 1992 in Brussels. Other arguments were based on the scientific and social development of psychology in this country. A better insight into the essence of psychology as a science may stimulate more appropriate funding of psychological faculties within the Belgian university system. For the further development of psychology in Belgium, it is essential that its real psychologists receive the right to exclusive use of their title, which may help them to create the place they deserve in a better-developed national health service.

To the degree that the 25th International Congress of Psychology promotes these domestic objectives, the year 1992 will, indeed, be remembered as a historical turning point in the development of "Psychology in Belgium."

ACKNOWLEDGMENTS

Thanks to Marc Lejeune for his help in gathering bibliographical data and preparing the manuscript and to Andrée Houyonx for her technical assistance. We also thank the Fonds National de la Recherche Scientifique for its financial support.

Literature Cited

Alegria, J., Leybaert, J. 1991. Méchanismes d'identification de mots chez le sourd. In *La reconnaissance de mots: Etudes psycholinguistiques,* ed. R. Kolinsky, J. Morais, J. Segui, pp. 277–304. Paris: Presses Universitaires de France

Baeyens, F., Eelen, P., Van den Bergh, O., Crombez, G. 1989. Acquired affective-evaluative value: conservative but not unchangeable. *Behav. Res. Ther.* 27:279–87

Baeyens, F., Eelen, P., Van den Bergh, O. 1990. Contingency awareness in evaluative conditioning: a case for unaware affective-evaluative learning. *Cognit. Emot.* 4:3–18

Bertelson, P. 1984. La Faculté des sciences psychologiques et Pédagogiques. In *Les cent cinquante ans de l'Université Libre de Bruxelles (1834–1984).* Brussels: Presses de l'Université Libre de Bruxelles

Bertelson, P., De Gelder, B. 1990. Learning about reading from illiterates. In *From Reading to Neurons,* ed. A. M. Galaburda. Cambridge, MA: MIT Press

Bouwen, R., Salipante, P. 1991. A multi perspective view on the social reality of construction of grievances. *Hum. Relat.* In press

Born, M. 1987. L'adolescence au carrefour de la déviance et de la délinquance. *Méd. Travail Méd. Lég.* 44:157–66

Born, M., Schaber, G. 1987. Risque de consommation de drogues et perception des risques á l'adolescence. *Nouv. Sci. Technol.* 5:45–48

Brédart, S. 1989. Categorization of familiar persons from their names: a case of interference. *Br. J. Psychol.* 80:273–83

Bruyer, R., ed. 1986. *The Neuropsychology of Face Perception and Facial Expression.* Hillsdale, NJ: Lawrence Erlbaum

Bruyer, R., Caruso, A. 1988. Relative vs absolute right hemisphere superiority from lateral differences in visual processing in normals: an example of uncertainty in experimental neuropsychology. *Int. J. Psychol.* 23:461–70

Brysbaert, M., d'Ydewalle, G. 1990. Tachistoscopic presentation of verbal stimuli for assessing cerebral dominance: reliability data and some practical recommendations. *Neuropsychologia.* 28:443–55

Castro, S. L., Morais, J. 1987. Ear differences in illiterates. *Neuropsychologia* 25:409–17

Coetsier, P., Claes, R. 1988. Organization and participation in Belgian hospitals. In *Stress and Organizational Problems in Hospitals,* ed. D. Wallis, Ch. de Wolff. London: Crook Helm

Coetsier, P., Claes, R. 1990. Work motivation of youngsters entering the labour market. In *Work Motivation,* ed. U. Kleinbeck. Hillsdale, NJ: Erlbaum

Content, A. 1991. La reconnaissance des mots écrits: approche connexioniste. See Alegria & Leybaert 1991, pp. 237–75

Costermans, J., Heuschen, V. 1990. Syllogistic reasoning with probabilities and continuous truth values. In *Cognitive Biases,* ed. J. P. Caverni. Amsterdam: North Holland

De Boeck, P., Rosenberg, S. 1988. Hierarchical classes: model and data analysis. *Psychometrika* 53:361–81

De Boeck, P., Van Mechelen, I. 1990. Traits and taxonomies: a hierarchical classes approach. *Eur. J. Pers.* 4:147–56

De Cock, G. 1990. Personnel training, an organizational approach. In *Methodology in Work and Organizational Psychology: European Perspectives,* ed. R. A. Roe, E. Spaltro. Paris: ENOP

De Coster, W., De Meyer, A., Parmentier, R. 1990. Practical perspectives on changing schools to stimulate cognitive development. In *Promoting Cognitive Growth Over the Life Span,* ed. M. Schwebel, C. Maher, N. Fagley. Hillsdale, NJ: Erlbaum

Decruyenaere, M., Janssen, P. 1989. A structural model for individual differences in academic performance of freshmen. In *Learning and Instruction: European Re-*search *in an International Context,* ed. H. Mandl, E. De Corte, N. Bennett & H. F. Friedrich, Vol. 2. Oxford: Pergamon

Defays, D. 1990. Numbo: a study in cognition and recognition. *C. C./A. I.* 7:217–43

De Keyser, V. 1987. Structuring of knowledge of operators in continuous process: a case study of a continuous casting plant start-up. In *Human Error and New Technology,* ed. J. Rasmussen, J. Leplat, K. Duncan. London: John Wiley & Sons

De Keyser, V. 1990. Temporal decision making in complex environments. *Philos. Trans. R. Soc. London* B327:569–76

Delboeuf, J., ed. 1883a. *Elements de psychophysique générale et spéciale.* Paris

Delboeuf, J., ed. 1883b. *Examen critique de la loi psychophysique.* Paris

Deliège 1. 1989. A perceptual approach to contemporary musical forms. *Contemp. Music Rev.* 4:213–30

Deloche, G., Seron, X. 1987. *Mathematical Disabilities: A Cognitive Neuropsychological Perspective.* Hillsdale, NJ: Lawrence Erlbaum

Desmit, F., Corveleyn, J. 1990. Psychodynamische hypothesen omtrent transseksualiteit. *Tijdschr. Seksuol.* 14:239–55

De Soete, G. 1988. Tree representations of proximity data by least squares methods. In *Classification and Related Methods of Data Analysis,* ed. H. M. Bock. Amsterdam: North Holland

De Soete, G., Feger, H., Klauer, K. C. eds. 1989. *New Developments in Psychological Choice Modeling.* Amsterdam: North Holland

De Roeck, J., Cluydts, R. 1989. Effects of zopiclone and triazolam on nighttime learning and recall. In *Sleep Research,* ed. N. Chase. Los Angeles: B. I. S.

De Visscher, P. 1991. *Us, avatars et métamorphoses de la dynamique des groupes: La brève histoire des groupes restreints.* Grenoble: Presses Universitaires de Grenoble

Duyckaerts, F, ed. 1954. *La notion de normal en psychologie clinique.* Paris: Vrin

Duyckaerts, F, ed. 1964. *La formation du lien sexuel.* Bruxelles: Dessart

Duyckaerts, F. 1989a. Sigmund Freud: lecteur de Joseph Delboeuf. *Frénésie, Hist. Psychiatr. Psychoanal.* 11(8):71–88

Duyckaerts, F. 1989b. 1889: un congrès houleux sur l'hypnotisme. *Arch. Psychol.* 57:53–68

Duyckaerts, F. 1990. Delboeuf-Ladame: un conflit paradigmatique! *Rev. Int. Hist. Psychoanal.* 3:25–37

Eelen, P., Fontaine, O., eds. 1986. *Behavior Therapy: Beyond the Conditioning Framework.* Hillsdale, NJ: Lawrence Erlbaum

Eelen, P., Van den Bergh, O. 1986. Cognitive-behavioral models of depression. *Acta Psychiatr. Belg.* 86:748–59

Falmagne, J. C., Doignon, J. P. 1988. A Markovian procedure of assessing the state of a system. *J. Math. Psychol.* 33:91–98

Fauville, A. 1946. Le travail du psychologue au service de l'orientation professionnelle. *Nouv. Rev. Pédag. Belg.* 1:314–24

Fauville, A. 1948. La psychologie néothomiste. *Rev. Philos. Louvain* 46:42–56

Fauville, A. 1963. *Perception tachistoscopique et communication*. (Studia Psychologics). Louvain: Publ. Univ. Louvain

Feldman, R., Rimé, B. eds. 1990. *Fundamentals of Nonverbal Behavior*. Cambridge: Cambridge Univ. Press

Feyereisen, P. 1988. Non verbal communication. In *Aphasia*, ed. F. C. Rose, R. Whurr, M. A. Wyke. London: Whurr

Feyereisen, P., Barter, D., Goossens, M., Clerebaut, N. 1988. Gestures and speech in referential communication by aphasic subjects: channel use and efficiency. *Aphasiology* 2:21–32

Feyereisen, P., Pillon, A., de Partz, M. P. 1991. On the measures of fluency for the assessment of spontaneous speech in aphasia. *Aphasiology* 5:1–21

Fontaine, O. 1987. La Psychologie du patient multi-opéré. Assoc. Sci. Méd. d'Assurance. Cycle de Perfectionnement 86-87. Ed. Ecoles de Santé Publique et Fac. Méd. U. C. L.-U. Lg.

Fontaine, O., Salah, D. 1990. Stress d'origine médicale et éducation du patient. *Rev. Méd. Liège* 45:422–32

Gillot-deVries, F. 1988a. Social and psychological research methods in the evaluation of prenatal screening procedures. *Eur. J. Obstet. Gynecol. Reprod. Biol.* 28:93–103

Gillot-deVries, F. 1988b. Impact de l'insémination artificielle sur le vécu de la parentalité. In *Les thématiques en éducation familiale*, ed. J. P. Pourtois. Brussels: De Boeck

Goosens, L., Marcoen, A., Vandenbroecke, G. 1987. Availability of the control-of-variables strategy in early adolescence: elicitation techniques revisited. *J. Early Adolesc.* 4:453–62

Grailet, J. M., Seron, X., Bruyer, R., Coyette, F., Frederix, M. 1990. Case-report of a visual integrative agnosia. *Cogn. Neuropsychol.* 7:275–309

Heidbreder, C., De Witte, P., Rogues, B. P. 1989. Similar potencies of CCK-8 and its analogue BOC deNle (28,31) CCK27–33 on the self stimulation both are antagonized by a new cyclic CCK analogue. *Neuropeptides* 13:89–94

Hoentjens, G., d'Ydewalle, G. 1987. Why do Socratic stimuli produce hypermnesia? *Psychol. Res.* 49:169–72

Huber, W., ed. 1987. *La psychologie clinique aujourd'hui*. Brussels: Mardaga

Hueting, J. E., Soetens, E., Wauters, F. 1988. Influence of ACT-hormones on maximal performance and fatigue. *Bull. Psychonom. Soc.* 26:413

Hulbert, R., Lens, W. 1988. Time and self-identity in later life. *Int. J. Aging Hum. Dev.* 27:293–303

Hupet, M., Tilmant, B. 1986. What are cleft good for? Some consequences for comprehension. *J. Mem. Lang.* 25:419–30

Huys, J., Evers, G., d'Ydewalle, G. 1990. Framing biases in genetic risk perception. In *Cognitive Biases*, ed J. P. Caverni. Amsterdam: North Holland

Janne, P., Reynaert, C., De Coster, P. 1991. Denial and silent ischemia: which comes first? *J. Am. Med. Assoc.* 265:213

Janssen, P. J. 1989. Task, development and process in student learning: towards an integrative model of studying. *Eur. J. Psychol. Educ.* 4:469–88

Janssens, L., Grotenhuis, H., Michiels, H., Verhaegen, P. 1989. Social organizational determinants of safety in nuclear power plants: operator training in the management of unforeseen events. *J. Occup. Accidents* 11:121–29

Jaspard, J. M. 1987. Va-t-on vers une sécularisation de la conscience morale chez les jeunes? *Eglise d'aujourd'hui* 487:214–27

Jodogne, C., Tirelli, E. 1990. Modulation of tolerance of the GABA agonist THIP by environmental cues. *Behav. Brain Res.* 36:33–40

Karnas, G., Salengros, P., Van de Leemput, C. 1988. Experimental study of the effects of spatial and chromatic structuration, and of the role of training on file consulting. *C. C. -A. I.* 5:263–73

Kog, E., Vertommen, H., Vandereycken, W. 1987. Minuchin's psychosomatic family model revised: a concept-validation study using a multitrait-multimethod approach. *Family Process* 26:235–53

Kog, E., Vandereycken, W., Vertommen, H. 1989. Multimethod investigation of eating disorder families. In *The Family Approach to Eating Disorders: Assessment and Treatment of Anorexia Nervosa and Bulimia*, ed. W. Vandereycken, E. Kog, J. Vanderlinden. New York: P. M. A.

Kolinsky, R. 1989. The development of separability in visual perception. *Cognition* 33:243–84

Lagrou, L., De Witte, H. 1990. The quality of employment in the career of young psychologists and their job-and life satisfaction. *Psychol. Belg.* 30:1–22

Lamberts, K 1990. A hybrid model of learning to solve physics problems. *Eur. J. Cogn. Psychol.* 2:151–70

Lebrun, Y. 1987. Agnosia in aphasics. *Cortex* 23:251–63

Lebrun, Y. 1988. Language and epilepsy: a review. *Br. J. Disord. Commun.* 23:97–110

Lejeune, H. 1990. Timing: generality beyond differences or differences in continuity? In *Behavior Analysis in Theory and Practice: Contributions and Controversies,* ed. D. Blackman and H. Lejeune, pp. 53–90. Hove/London: Lawrence Erlbaum Assoc.

Lejeune, H., Richelle, M. 1991. Time estimation: animals and human compared. *Int. J. Compar. Psychol.* In press

Lejeune, H., Wearden, J. 1991. The comparative psychology of fixed-interval responding: some quantitative analyses. *Learn. Motiv.* 22:84–111

Lens, W. 1987. Future time perspective, motivation and school performance. In *Learning and Instruction: European Research in an International Context,* ed. E. De Corte, J. Lodewijks, R. Parmentier, P. Span, 1:181–89. Oxford: Pergamon

Ley, A., Wauthier, M., eds. 1946. *Etudes de psychologie instinctive et affective.* Paris: Presses Universitaires de France

Ley, A., Wauthier, M., eds. 1948. *L'instinct de propriété.* Paris: Masson & Cie

Leyens, J. P., Codol, J. P. 1988. Social cognition. In *Introduction to Social Psychology: A European Perspective,* ed. M. Hewstone, W. Stroebe, J. P. Codol, G. Stephenson. Cambridge: Cambridge Univ. Press

Leyens, J. P., Fiske, S. T. 1991. Impression formation: something old, something new and something borrowed. In *Social Cognition: Contributions to Classic Issues in Social Psychology,* ed. P. Devine, D. Hamilton, T. Ostrom. New York: Springer

Lietaer, G. 1990. Helping and hindering in client-centered/experiential psychotherapy: a content analysis of client and therapist post-session perceptions. In *Psychotherapeutic Change: Theory-Guided and Descriptive Research Strategies,* ed. S. G. Toukmanian, D. L Rennie. Toronto: Wall & Thompson

Lietaer, G., Rombauts, J., Van Balen, R., eds 1990. *Client-Centered and Experiential Psychotherapy in the Nineties.* Leuven: Leuven Univ. Press

Lories, G. 1987. Effect of context on the decision processes of chess players. *Eur. Bull. Cogn. Psychol.* 7:75–86

Machado, A. 1989. Operant conditioning of behavioral variability using a percentile

reinforcement schedule. *J. Exp. Anal. Behav.* 52:155–66

Mahjoub, A., Leyens, J. P., Yzerbyt, V., Di Giacomo, J. P. 1989. War stress and coping modes: representations of self-identity and time among Palestinian children. *Int. J. Mental Health* 18:44–62

Marcoen, A. 1991. Ageing and the search for meaning: reflections on theory and methodology. In *The Ultimate Meaning of Our Existence,* ed. R. Macken, J. Van der Vecken. Leuven: Leuven Univ. Press. In press

Marcoen, A., Brumagne, M. 1985. Loneliness among children and young adolescents. *Dev. Psychol.* 21:1025–1031

Marques, J., Yzerbit, V., Leyens, J. P. 1988. The "Black Sheep Effect": extremity of judgments towards in-group members as a function of group identification. *Eur. J. Psychol.* 18:1–18

Mervielde, I. 1988. Cognitive processes and computerized personality assessment. *Eur. J. Pers.* 2:97–111

Mervielde, I., Pot, E. 1989. Perceiver and target effects in person perception. *Eur. J. Pers.* 3:1–13

Michotte, A, ed. 1954. *La perception de la causalité.* (Studia Psychologica). Louvain: Publications Universitaires de Louvain

Montpellier, G. de. 1950. Réflexe conditionné, apprentissage et dressage. *Ann. Psychol.* VOL?? 325–339

Montpellier, G. de. 1971. La psychologie en Belgique: historique. *Psychol. Belg.* X1–2:165–71

Morais, J., Alegria, J., Content, A. 1987. The relationship between segmental analysis and alphabetic literacy: an interactive view. *Eur. Bull. Cogn. Psychol.* 7:415–38

Morais, J., Ladavas, E. 1987. Hemispheric interactions of the recognition of words and emotional intonations. *Cogn. Emot.* 1:89–100

Mousty, P., Bertelson, P. 1985. A study of Braille reading: reading speed as a function of hand usage and context. *Q. J. Exp. Psychol.* 37A:217–234

Nuttin, J, ed. 1953a. *Psychoanalysis and Personality.* New York: Sheed & Ward

Nuttin, J. 1953b. *Tâche, réussite et échec. Théorie de la conduite humaine.* (Studia Psychologica). Louvain: Publications Universitaires de Louvain

Nuttin, J. 1961. *Psychology in Belgium.* (Studia Psychologica) Louvain: Publications Universitaires de Louvain

Nuttin, J, ed. 1980. *Théorie de la motivation humaine.* Paris: Presses Universitaires de France

Nuttin, J. M. Jr. 1987. Affective consequences of mere ownership: the name letter effect in twelve European languages. *Eur. J. Soc. Psychol.* 17:381–402

Nyssen, R. 1946. Le problème de l'examen analytique de l'intelligence. *J. Belge Neurol. Psychiatr.* 44–5–6 réunis: 297–309

Nyssen, R. 1948. Le problème de la constitution et du caractère hystérique. *Act. Neurol. Psychiatr. Belg.* 48:47–56

Ombredane, A. 1954. *L'exploration de la mentalité des Noirs congolais au moyen d'une épreuve projective: le Congo TAT.* Bruxelles: Lamertin

Ombredane, A., Robaye, F., Robaye, E. 1957. *Etude psychotechnique des Baluba application expérimentale du test d'intelligence Matrix 38 e 485 noirs Baluba.* Bruxelles: Lamertin

Paulus, J., ed. 1965. *Les fondements théoriques et méthodologiques de la psychologie.* Bruxelles: Dessart

Peeters, G. 1987. The Benny Hill Effect: switching cognitive programmes underlying subjective estimations of the outcomes of bargains concerning distributions of rewards. *Eur. J. Soc. Psychol.* 17:465–481

Peeters, R., d'Ydewalle, G. 1987. Influences of emotional states upon memory: the state of the art. *Commun. Cogn.* 20:171–90

Peretz, I., Morais, J. 1989. Music and modularity. *Contemp. Music Rev.* 4:279–93

Plateau, J. 1834. *Essai d'une théorie générale comprenant l'ensemble des apparences visuelles qui succèdent à la contemplation des objets colorés et de celles qui accompagnent cette contemplation.* Bruxelles: Hayez

Quackelbeen, J. 1987. De Freudiaanse epistemologische coupure en haar effecten voor de pedagogic. *Rondzendbrief Freudiaanse Veld* 26:3–22

Quételet, A, ed. 1869. *Sur l'homme et le développement de ses facultés, ou essai de physique sociale.* Paris: Bachelier. 2 vols. 2nd ed.

Quételet, A, ed. 1870. *L'anthropométrie, ou mesure des différentes facultés de l'homme.* Bruxelles

Richelle, M. 1961. *Aspects psychologiques de l'acculturation* Liège: FULREAC. 217 pp.

Richelle, M. 1966. Etude génétique de l'intelligence manipulatoire chez des enfants africains à l'aide des dispositifs de Rey. *Int. J. Psychol.* 1:273–87

Richelle, M. 1987. Les cognitivismes: progrès, régression ou suicide de la psychologie? In *Comportement, cognition, conscience: la psychologie à la recherche de son objet,* ed. M. Siguan. Paris: Presses Universitaires de France

Richelle, M. 1990. Behavior, past and future. See Lejeune 1990

Richelle, M. 1991a. Behavioral pharmacology in continental Europe: a personal account of its origin and development. *J. Exp. Anal. Behav.* In press

Richelle, M. 1991b. Reconciling views on intelligence? In *Intelligence: Reconceptualization and Measurement.* Hove/London: Lawrence Erlbaum Assoc.

Richelle, M., Lejeune, H., Perikel, J. J., Fery, P. 1985. From biotemporality to nootemporality: toward an integrative and comparative view of time in behavior. In *Time, Mind and Behavior,* ed. J. Michon, J. Jackson, pp. 75–99. Berlin-Heidelberg: Springer

Rimé, B., Leyens, J. P. 1988. Violence dans les stades: la réponse des psychologues. *La Recherche* 19:528–31

Rimé, B., Ucros, C., Bestgen, Y., Jeanjean, M. 1989. Type A behavior pattern. Specific coronary risk factor or general disease-prone condition? *Br. J. Med. Psychol.* 62:229–40

Rimé, B., Philipott, P., Cisamolo, D. 1990. Social schemata of peripheral changes in emotion. *J. Pers. Soc. Psychol.* 59:39–49

Rondal, J. A. 1985. *Adult-Child Interaction and the Process of Language Acquisition.* New York: Praeger Press

Rondal, J. A. 1988. Positive and negative evidence in first language acquisition. *Eur. Bull. Cogn. Psychol.* 8:383–98

Salengros, P., Van de Leemput, C., Mubikangiey, L. 1989. Psychological and sociological perspectives on precarious employment in Belgium. In *Precarious Job in Labour Market Regulation. The Growth of Atypical Employment in Western Europe,* ed. G. J. Rodgers, pp. 197–223. Geneva: I. L. S.

Schweich, M., Van der Linden, M., Brédart, S., Bruyer, R., Nelles, B., Schils, J. P. 1991. Daily-life difficulties in face recognition reported by young and elderly subjects. *Appl. Cogn. Psychol.* In press

Seron, X., Deloche, G. 1989. *Cognitive Approaches in Neuropsychological Rehabilitation.* Hillsdale, NJ: Erlbaum

Seron, X., Van der Linden, M. 1988. Aphasia and personality. *Acta Neurochir.* 44:113–17

Sloore, H., Rouckhout, D. 1989. The MMPI critical item pool. Paper presented at the 24th Annu. Symp. Recent Dev. Use of MMPI, Honolulu

Soetens, E., Boer, L. E., Hueting, J. E. 1985. Expectancy or automatic facilitation? Separating sequential effects in two-choice reaction time. *J. Exp. Psychol.: Human Percept. Perform.* 11:598–616

Soffie, M., Bronchart, M. 1988. Age-related scopolamine effects on social and individual behaviour in rats. *Psychopharmacology* 95:344–51

Soffie, M., Lejeune, H. 1991a. Approche des fonctions cognitives chez l'animal âgé l'espace et le temps. In *Le vieillissement*, ed. C. Bastien, J. Montangero. Paris: Presses Universitaires de France. In press

Soffie, M., Lejeune, H. 1991b. Acquisition and long-term retention of a two-lever DRL schedule: comparison between mature and aged rats. *Neurobiol. Aging* 12:25–30

Thibaut, J. P. 1986. Classification et représentativité d'objets: rôle des attributs constitutifs. *Cah. Psychol. Cogn.* 6:41–60

Thiery, E. 1988. Personality traits after prolonged vegetative state. In *Neurosurgery and Personality*, ed. J. Brihaye, L. Calliauw, R. Van den Bergh. New York: Springer

Thinès, G. 1961. *Contribution 6, a la théorie de la causalité perceptive.* (Studia psychologica). Louvain: Publications Universitaires de Louvain

Thinès, G, ed. 1966. *Psychologie des animaux.* Bruxelles: Dessart

Tirelli, E., Jodogne, C. 1990. Dopamine-GABAergic mechanisms of rearing and locomotion in infant and weanling mice. *Psychobiology* 18:443–50

Ucros, C. 1989. Mood state-dependent memory: a metaanalysis. *Cogn. Emot.* 3:139–67

Valcke, K, Corveleyn, J. 1989. Honderd jaar psychoanalyse in Frankrijk. *Psychol. Maatschappij* 13:179–86

Van Avermaet, E. 1988a. Testing hypotheses about other people confirmatory and diagnostic strategies. *Commun. Cogn.* 21: 179–89

Van Avermaet, E. 1988b. Social influence in small groups. In *Introduction to Social Psychology*, ed. J. P. Codol, G. Stephenson. Oxford: Blackwell

Vanbeselaere, N. 1987. The effects of dichotomous and crossed social categorizations upon intergroup discrimination. *Eur. J. Soc. Psychol.* 17:143–56

Van den Bergh, B. 1988. The relationship between maternal emotionality during pregnancy and the behavioural development of the fetus and neonatus. In *Prenatal Psychology: Encounter with the Newborn*, ed. F. Freybergh. Carnforth: Parthenon

Van den Bergh, B., Eelen, P., Baeyens, F. 1989. Brief exposure to fear stimuli; imagery ability as a condition of fear enhancement or fear decrease. *Behav. Ther.* 20: 563–72

Van den Plas-Holper, C., Jenart, A. 1989. Children's recall of familiar and discrepant adult-child relations. *Arch. Psychol.* 57:33–51

Van der Linden, M. 1990. Troubles de la mémoire et vieillissement normal. In *Interdisciplinarité en gérontologie*, ed. R. Hébert, pp. 134–48. Montréal: St Hyacinthe-Maloine

Van der Linden, M., Van der Kaa, M. 1989. Reorganization therapy for memory impairments. In *Cognitive Approaches in Neuropsychological Rehabilitation*, ed. X. Seron, G. Deloche. Hillsdale, NJ: Erlbaum

Vandierendonck, A. 1988. Typicality gradient in well-defined artificial categories. *Acta Psychol.* 69:61–81

Vandierendonck, A., Van Damme, R. 1988. Schema anticipation in recall: memory process or report strategy? *Psychol. Res.* 47:116–22

Vandierendonck, A., Van Hoe, R., De Soete, G. 1988. Menu search as a function of menu organization, categorization and experience. *Acta Psychol.* 69:231–48

Van Overwalle, F. 1989. Structure of freshmen's causal attributions for exam performance. *Br. J. Educ. Psychol.* 81:400–7

Van Overwalle, F. 1991. The effects of attribution-based intervention and study strategy training on academic performance in college freshmen. *Br. J. Educ. Psychol.* In press

Van Mechelen, I., De Boeck, P. 1990. Projection of a binary criterion into a model of hierarchical classes. *Psychometrika* 55:677–94

Verfaillie, K., d'Ydewalle, G. 1991. Representational momentuum and event course anticipation in the perception of implied periodical motions? *J. Exp. Psychol.: Learn., Mem. Cogn.* 17:302–13

Verhaeghe, P. 1987. Psychoanalytische en pseudopsychoanalytische impact op de pedagogiek: de verborgen meester. *Rondzendbrief Freudiaanse Veld* 26:33–44

Verhofstadt-Denève, L. 1985. Crises in adolescence and psycho-social development in young adulthood: a seven-year follow-up study from a dialectal viewpoint. In *Developmental Psychology*, ed. C. J. Brainerd, V. F. Reyna, pp. 509–22. Amsterdam: Elsevier

Verhofstadt-Denève, L. 1988. The phenomenal-dialectic personality model. *J. Group Psychother. Psychodrama Sociometry* 41: 3–20

Verlaine, L, ed. 1935–1936. *Histoire naturelle de la connaissance chez le singe inférieur.* Paris: Hermann. 3 Vols.

Verlaine, L. 1938. La notion de nombre chez le macaque. *Bull. Soc. Roy. Liège*, Vols. 1, 2, 3, 4

Vinck, J., Arickx, M., Hongenaert, M., Vertommen, H., Beckers, J. 1988. Can psychophysiological changes explain the blood pressure lowering effects of relaxation training? In *Behavioral Medicine in Cardiovascular Disorders*, ed. T. Elbert, W.

Langosch, A. Steptoe, D. Vaitl, pp. 91–100. New York: Wiley

Vyt, A. 1989. The second year as developmental turning point: implications for sensitive caretaking. *Eur. J. Psychol. Educ.* 4:145–58

Willemaers, H. 1987. Counseling cancer patients: enhancing quality of life. *Challenge* 8:9–10

Wens, L., Baro, F., d'Ydewalle, G. 1989. The information processing approach in clinical memory assessment. In *Classification and Diagnosis of Alzeimer Disease*, ed. T. Houaguimian, S. Henderson, Z. Khatchaturian, J. Orley, pp. 103–12. Toronto: hogrefe

Yzerbyt, V., Leyens, J. P. 1991. Dispositional inference and intuitive personality testing: the impact of evaluative valence and confirmatory status. *J. Exp. Soc. Psychol.* In press

Annu. Rev. Psychol. 1992. 43:531–82

NEGOTIATION AND MEDIATION

Peter J. Carnevale

Department of Psychology, University of Illinois at Urbana-Champaign, Champaign, Illinois 61820

Dean G. Pruitt

Department of Psychology, State University of New York at Buffalo, Buffalo, New York 14260

KEY WORDS: bargaining, conflict, disputes, third party intervention, problem solving

CONTENTS

INTRODUCTION

This chapter presents an overview of the behavioral literature on negotiation and mediation. Negotiation and mediation are procedures for resolving opposing preferences between parties. Negotiation involves discussion between the parties with the goal of reaching agreement. There is no limit to the number of parties ("disputants") who can take part in negotiation, but two-party negotiations are the kind most often studied. Mediation is a variation on negotiation in which one or more outsiders ("third parties") assist the parties in their discussion. Since mediation is a special case of negotiation, and since the negotiation literature is more voluminous, we treat the topic of negotiation first.

Opposing preferences are found in all social arenas, from relations between children on the playground to international relations. Hence a theory of negotiation and mediation is essential for understanding topics as diverse as marital decision making, industrial relations, interoffice coordination, corporate mergers, group decision making, and international relations.

Other Procedures for Dealing with Opposing Preferences

Negotiation and mediation are two of four main procedures for dealing with opposing preferences. A third procedure is struggle—which can take the form of physical combat (military battles, strikes), wars of words (shouting matches), political contest (vying for allies), or taking unilateral advantage (theft, slipping out of the house unobserved by one's spouse). Struggle sometimes culminates in an agreement of sorts, in which the parties accommodate to each other without discussion of the issues. Schelling (1960) calls the process of moving to such an agreement "tacit bargaining." The fourth procedure is arbitration (adjudication, decision by the boss), in which a third party makes a binding decision about the controversy.

How do these procedures compare with one another? Negotiation has two main advantages over struggle as a means of resolving opposing preferences. One is that it is usually less costly. Struggle often requires heavy expenditure of resources (e.g. bombs, wear and tear on the vocal cords, embarrassment) and endangers the relationship between the parties; negotiation is usually more benign. The other advantage is that negotiation makes it easier to find and adopt a mutually acceptable solution and thus to end the controversy. Words are flexible and subtle and allow joint projection into the future, while struggle followed by tacit bargaining is often a clumsy procedure.

Given these advantages of negotiation, why is struggle so popular? There are several reasons. Communication may be difficult, because the parties cannot meet or do not understand each other when they do. Trust levels may be so low that the parties dare not enter into an explicit agreement. One party may be too proud to concede or too angry to do anything that favors the other's welfare. It takes two to negotiate, but either party can decide to go the route of struggle, forcing the other to adopt the same approach.

In addition, it is common for one or both parties to believe that they can achieve more through struggle than through negotiation. This outlook often produces alternation between negotiation and struggle. For example, a labor negotiation may fail, leading to a strike in which the two parties test their relative strengths, followed by more negotiation. The first negotiation fails because each party believes that it can succeed in a manner that will allow it to dictate the terms. The second negotiation succeeds because the struggle phase has clarified the two parties' relative capacity to withstand a strike. The option agreed upon in the second negotiation is likely to reflect this relative capacity.

Negotiation also has some distinct advantages over arbitration. Arbitrators often fail to find mutually acceptable solutions, thereby endangering the relationship between the parties. Furthermore, arbitration (e.g. court) tends to be expensive and risky. Nevertheless, people often opt for arbitration, because they view their cause as just and believe that the arbitrator will rule in their favor.

Part of the job of the mediator is to make negotiation more viable and thus reduce the likelihood that the parties will turn to struggle or arbitration (Ury et al 1988). Among the tools of successful mediators are procedures for correcting the defects just mentioned: shuttling between parties who cannot or will not meet, interpreting statements made by parties who do not understand each other, encouraging trust or suggesting agreements that do not require trust, allowing a proud party to concede to the mediator instead of the other party, reminding the parties about the costs of struggle or adjudication, and casting doubt on the likelihood that the other party can be pushed into further concession or that a judge will rule in one's favor.

THE STUDY OF NEGOTIATION

There are three main traditions in the study of negotiation. The first consists of books of advice to negotiators, which have been written for many centuries. Earlier books addressed international (de Callières 1716; Nicolson 1964) or industrial (Peters 1955) negotiators. More recent books have targeted managers (Lax & Sebenius 1986) or negotiators in general (Filley 1975; R. Fisher & Ury 1981; Lewicki & Litterer 1985; Murnighan 1991; Zartman & Berman 1982). A second, rather different tradition has involved the construction of mathematical models of rational negotiation and mediation by economists and game theorists (Harsanyi 1956; Nash 1950; Zeuthen 1930; see Young 1975; Roth 1985, and Kagel & Roth 1991). These models are both descriptive, in the sense of specifying the parameters within which negotiators operate or some of the dynamics of negotiation behavior, and prescriptive, in the sense of recommending rational policies. Many of them are provocative; but they also tend to be narrow, involving only a few variables and making highly restrictive assumptions. Two theorists in the same tradition have retained the careful rational analysis but have taken a broader and more realistic view of the task of negotiators and the options open to them (Raiffa 1982; Schelling 1960).

The third or behavioral tradition, which has its theoretical roots in the mathematical model tradition, began with three analyses of the behavior of labor negotiators (Douglas 1962; Stevens 1963; Walton & McKersie 1965). This tradition has placed a heavy emphasis on empirical research in both the laboratory and the field. The first general overview of this research was published by Rubin & Brown (1975), and a number of summaries and books of readings have appeared more recently (Bazerman & Lewicki 1983; Druckman 1977; Kremenyuk 1991; Lewicki et al 1986; Lewicki et al 1991; Morley & Stephenson 1977; Neale & Bazerman 1991; Pruitt 1981; Putnam & Pool 1987; Putnam & Roloff 1991; Sheppard et al 1990; Smith 1987; Thompson 1990b; Wall 1985; Zartman 1978). Unlike those in the other two traditions, writers in the behavioral tradition have emphasized description (including explanation and prediction) rather than prescription. However, their theories and findings are rich enough to yield many prescriptions (Pruitt 1986), which we highlight throughout this chapter and comment on in a special section at the end.

In addition to the behavioral studies of negotiation, there have been studies of two other settings that involve opposing preferences: the prisoner's dilemma (see Pruitt & Kimmel 1977) and several varieties of social dilemmas (see Messick & Brewer 1983). The subjects have usually not been allowed to communicate in these studies; hence, they have usually engaged in struggle and tacit bargaining. But a few studies have examined the effect of communication, i.e. of negotiation (Brechner 1977; Dawes et al 1977; Deutsch 1958; Edney & Harper 1978; Voissem & Sistrunk 1971; Wichman 1972). These studies show, in support of a point made earlier, that negotiation encourages the development and implementation of mutually acceptable options.

ISSUES, LIMITS, AND OUTCOMES IN NEGOTIATION

The Nature of Issues

The topics under consideration in negotiation can usually be divided into one or more issues requiring separate decisions by the parties. When several issues are related, they are often discussed at the same time, in what can be called an "issue group."

There is nothing sacred about the issues with which a negotiation starts; indeed, it is often necessary to reconceptualize the initial issues to reach agreement. For example, an issue between Production and Sales of whether to alter the production schedule to accommodate an impatient customer might be reconceptualized as the issue of how to preserve the integrity of the production schedule while accommodating the customer.

When there are a large number of interrelated issues, as in many international negotiations, it is often expedient to negotiate an abstract formula or thumbnail sketch of the overall agreement first and later fill in the details (Zartman 1977). The formula provides order and coherence to discussions of the specific issues, which might otherwise be examined sequentially with little attention to their interrelationships. Specialized subcommittees are often involved in negotiating the finer details.

Options, Limits, and Outcomes

The possible outcomes of a negotiation can be understood in terms of the joint utility space shown in Figure 1a. (A similar diagram is used in most mathematical models of negotiation.) The points in this space correspond to the options available for settling an issue or issue group, the solid points referring to options that are known at the beginning of negotiation and the hollow points to options that can be devised with some creative thinking. The axes give the utility (e.g. monetary value, level of happiness) to each party of the options shown. Assume that at the start of negotiation, party Y is advocating option 1 while X is advocating option 5. An example might be a negotiation over a new car with the dealer (X) asking a price of $12,000 and the customer (Y) offering $10,000. Options 2, 3, and 4 are various prices between these two figures. Options 6, 7, and 8 are possible mutually beneficial solutions in which the dealer adds extras (accessories, treatments, or maintenance policies, etc) that benefit the customer more than they cost the dealer.

The negotiation can end in four possible ways: 1. No agreement. The utility of this to each party is shown by the point marked "NA." 2. Victory for one party, either option 1 or option 5. 3. A simple compromise (options 2, 3, or 4). A compromise is defined as some middle ground on an obvious dimension connecting the two parties' initial offers (Pruitt 1981). 4. A win-win ("integrative") agreement (options 6, 7, or 8) in which the parties achieve higher

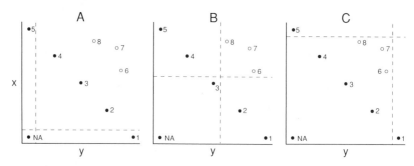

Figure 1 Three contrasting joint utility spaces.

joint benefit than they could with a compromise agreement (see Follett 1940; Pruitt 1981; Walton & McKersie 1965). It is generally believed (e.g. Pruitt 1981) that win-win agreements are longer lasting and more beneficial for the relationship between the parties than simple compromises. However, a recent study of community mediation (Pruitt et al 1991b) found no correlation between level of joint benefit and the extent of compliance with the agreement or improvement in the parties' relationship.

The dashed lines in Figure 1a stand for the two parties' limits (also called "reservation prices"), those levels of benefit below which they will not concede. Options that are above and to the right of these lines are said to be "viable" in the sense of being mutually acceptable. Figure 1a shows a situation in which several known alternatives are viable. Agreement is likely to be reached in such a situation (Ben-Yoav & Pruitt 1984a; Carnevale & Lawler 1986; Pruitt & Lewis 1975); but it is not inevitable, because one or both parties may become locked into an unrealistic demand through a defect in strategy or understanding of the other party's constraints (Bartos 1974).

Figure 1b shows a contrasting situation in which the limits are so high that none of the obvious options are viable; but there are some viable win-win options just over the horizon if the parties will use their imaginations. In our example, the customer is not willing to pay the dealer's minimal price; but there are two possible packages of extras that are sufficiently attractive to the customer to warrant paying a price that will give the dealer an acceptable profit. Such situations are said to have "integrative potential" (Pruitt & Rubin 1986; Walton & McKersie 1965).

Research (Bazerman et al 1985; Ben-Yoav & Pruitt 1984a; Carnevale & Lawler 1986; Huber & Neale 1986; Neale & Bazerman 1985; Pruitt & Lewis 1975) shows that when the negotiators are motivated by self-interest, agreement is less likely to be reached in the situation shown in Figure 1b than in that shown in Figure 1a; apparently creativity is not always forthcoming in negotiation. The likelihood of agreement may also increase in situation 1b if the parties are motivated by a concern about both parties' outcomes, and if agreement is reached, higher limits may produce greater joint benefit (Carnevale & Lawler 1986; Pruitt & Lewis 1975; Ben-Yoav & Pruitt 1984b).

Figure 1C shows a situation in which the parties' limits are so high that there are no viable options. The only way to reach agreement in such a situation is for limits to decline on one or both sides.

Determinants of Limits

It is usually asserted (e.g. R. Fisher & Ury 1981; Neale & Bazerman 1991; Raiffa 1982) that rational negotiators will place their limits at the value of no agreement—i.e. will concede no lower than the best alternative to negotiated agreement (sometimes called the "BATNA"). Limits are indeed influenced by the value of no agreement (Kelley et al 1967; Smith et al 1982), but there are many other influences as well, including instructions from constituents (Ben-Yoav & Pruitt 1984a).

Ethical principles and principles of fairness are important sources of limits. Such principles can be either helpful or harmful with respect to reaching agreement, depending on whether they are shared by the negotiating parties. If the parties share the same principle of fairness and it is clearly applicable to the situation, agreement should be particularly easy to reach, for two reasons: (a) both sides are likely to view the same option as correct; and (b) both sides are likely to view that option as inevitable, since the other side cannot be expected to accept anything less (Schelling 1960). Research supports this reasoning. Faster and/or more reliable agreements have been shown in settings where one option clearly provided equal outcome to the two parties (Benton & Druckman 1973; Lamm & Rosch 1972; Liebert et al 1968; Pruitt & Syna 1985) or was equidistant from their starting point so that they would reach it through equal concessions (Joseph & Willis 1963). These findings suggest that the principles of equal division and equal concession have broad appeal to negotiators. Another principle that structures negotiation agreements is that pay should be proportional to the amount of work done (Messe 1971)—a variant of the equity principle (Deutsch 1975).

However, negotiators often disagree about the proper principles or how to apply them. This is likely to make it hard to reach agreement, because each party digs in its heels to defend its own interpretation. The situation is likely to resemble that shown in Figure 1c, with neither party willing to concede to an option acceptable to the other. The disruptive impact of principles has been shown in an experiment by Druckman et al (1988), in which negotiators became rigid when they were shown how to derive their positions from principles espoused by their groups, and in a field study on community mediation by Pruitt et al (1991b), which found that parties who prominently mentioned principles tended to be hostile and rigid and to fail to reach agreement. Such dynamics have led Kolb & Rubin (1991) to advise mediators to "be wary when matters of principle, not pragmatics, are the central issues."

Disagreements about principles are particularly likely to occur when two (or more) universally acceptable principles point to different options. What typically happens is that each party shows a partisan bias toward the principle(s) that favor(s) its own interests, creating or reinforcing a clash. Such dynamics have been demonstrated in negotiation settings where principles of equal outcome and equity point in different directions (Komorita 1984; Lamm & Kayser 1978) and those where principles of equal outcome and equal concession do the same (Hamner & Baird 1978). The interpretation of the equal concession principle is also subject to a partisan bias, since negotiators tend to view the other party's concessions as smaller than their own.

MOTIVATION AND STRATEGY IN NEGOTIATION

Two traditions of thought underlie most empirical research on negotiation. One is a motivation and strategy tradition, which predicts the outcomes of negotiation from the strategies chosen by the negotiators and predicts strategic choice from negotiator motivation. The other is a cognitive tradition, which predicts negotiation outcomes from the negotiators' perceptions and their information-processing procedures. We discuss the motivation and strategy tradition first because it is the earlier and more voluminously reported approach.

Strategic Choice

Three main strategies have attracted the most attention in this research:

1. Concession making (also called "yielding") involves reducing one's demands or aspirations to accommodate the other party.
2. Contending involves trying to persuade the other party to yield. Specific tactics that implement this strategy include threats and commitments not to concede.
3. Problem solving involves trying to locate options that satisfy both parties' goals. The host of problem-solving tactics includes active listening, providing information about one's own priorities, and brainstorming in search of solutions. Problem solving is a major route—though not the only route—to the development of win-win solutions.

These strategies are somewhat incompatible because they require different mind-sets and may have contradictory effects on the other party (Kelley 1966; Lax & Sebenius 1986; Pruitt 1991). Nevertheless, all three strategies are often needed to achieve agreement. This creates a dilemma, which is resolved by various methods of isolating the strategies from each other (Pruitt 1991;

Putnam 1990). These include rapid sequencing (e.g. concede-contend-concede-contend), moving through stages (e.g. contending followed by problem solving), arena shielding (e.g. contending at the negotiation table while problem solving in unofficial meetings on the side), personnel shielding (e.g. the black-hat/white-hat routine in which one team member takes a contentious approach while the other engages in problem solving), and issue shielding (e.g. standing firm on some issues while showing a willingness to problem-solve on others).

The three strategies are alternative ways of moving toward agreement. Hence (assuming that agreement is sought) if conditions reduce the likelihood of using one strategy, the other two become more likely. If two of these strategies are ruled out, the use of the third becomes virtually certain.

The three strategies just listed will be taken up one by one after discussing motivational orientations and the dual-concern model, which is the chief theory of negotiator motivation.

Motivational Orientations

It is possible to distinguish four mutually exclusive "motivational orientations" that appear to have a large impact on negotiator behavior (see Deutsch 1958; Kuhlman et al 1986; Messick & McClintock 1968): 1. Individualistic orientation—exclusive concern about one's own outcomes; 2. altruistic orientation—exclusive concern about the other parties' outcomes; 3. cooperative orientation—concern about both parties' outcomes; 4. competitive orientation—desire to do better than the other party.

The individualistic orientation has tended to dominate research and thinking on negotiation. All of the mathematical models of negotiation assume an individualistic orientation, and in much of the experimental research subjects have been instructed to be concerned only with their own outcomes. This has led to the development of a one-sided theory, because many negotiators in reality are cooperatively or competitively oriented. An altruistic orientation is probably less common.

The Dual Concern Model

Three of the orientations just listed occupy regions in a two-dimensional diagram, the "dual-concern" model, which makes predictions about strategic choice. This model, which is shown in Figure 2, is an extension of Blake & Mouton's (1979) conflict grid (see also Filley 1975; Rahim 1986; Thomas 1976). It views self-concern (concern about own outcomes) and other-concern (concern about the other party's outcomes) as dimensions that run from weak to strong. These dimensions are regarded as independent, rather than as opposite ends of the same dimension as was previously thought (Thomas 1976).

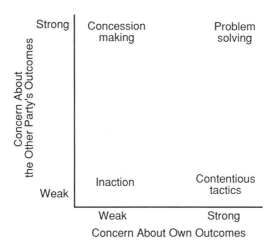

Figure 2   The dual-concern model.

High self-concern coupled with low other-concern—the individualistic orientation—is assumed to produce use of a contentious strategy. High other-concern and low self-concern is assumed to produce concession making. High self-concern and high other-concern is assumed to produce problem solving. Low self-concern and low other-concern is assumed to produce inaction, the absence of strategy.

PSYCHOMETRIC EVIDENCE   The dual-concern model fits data from both psychometric and experimental studies. The psychometric tradition views strategic preferences as individual differences in "conflict style." The studies in this tradition, which begin with Ruble & Thomas (1976), typically factor-analyze self-reports about the use of various strategies in conflict situations. As predicted by the model, a two-dimensional solution is always found, with the largest distances between contending and yielding and between problem solving and avoidance (van de Vliert & Prein 1989). The only consistent discrepancy from the model is that yielding and inaction are closer to each other than shown in Figure 2.

These studies often include a "compromise" strategy, which seeks a solution in which both parties make concessions. In Blake & Mouton's (1979) original formulation, compromise was in the middle of the figure, equidistant from the other four strategies. But factor analysis usually locates it between yielding and problem solving, at a considerable distance from contending and inaction (van de Vliert & Prein 1989). This suggests that a preference for compromise results from moderate self-concern coupled with high other-concern.

EXPERIMENTAL EVIDENCE   Four experiments on negotiation behavior show the value of the dual-concern model for understanding the effects of environmental variables (Carnevale & Keenan 1990; Pruitt et al 1983; Ben-Yoav & Pruitt 1984a,b). All employed a 2×2 design in which self-concern and other-concern were independently manipulated. High self-concern was produced either by giving the negotiators a negative rather than a positive frame (Study 1), requiring them to achieve an ambitious profit target (Studies 2 and 3), or making them accountable to powerful constituents (Study 4). High other-concern was produced either by telling the bargainers that they would have to cooperate on a future task (Studies 3 and 4), giving them instructions to care about the other's outcomes (Study 1), or giving them a gift and thus putting them in a positive mood (Study 2). Similar results were achieved in all four studies. The combination of high self-concern and low other-concern (the individualistic orientation) produced heavy use of contentious tactics (threats, positional commitments, and strong arguments for one's own advantage). The combination of high self-concern and high other-concern produced high levels of joint benefit (i.e. win-win solutions), suggesting that some form of problem solving was prominent in that condition. Both results are implied by the dual-concern model. However, there was no evidence of greater concession making under the combination of low self-concern and high other-concern.

PERSPECTIVE ON THE DUAL CONCERN MODEL   Thompson (1990b) has criticized the dual-concern model (and the evidence supporting it) on six points. The first is that "its predictions are limited to situations in which negotiators have the same bargaining orientation" (p. 524). While this is true of all the experiments supporting this model, the model itself concerns the origins of a single disputant's behavior. The second criticism is that the model does not specify the nature of the problem solving that occurs under high self-concern and high other-concern. While this is true, a study by Carnevale & Isen (1986) suggests that this problem solving takes the form of systematic trial and error. All subjects in this study were given ambitious profit targets producing high self-concern, and mood was manipulated. Subjects who were in a good mood (and hence presumably had high concern for the other party) proposed more new ideas, conceded more often on low-priority items, and more often asked the other party to react to their proposals than those who were not in a good mood. The result was the discovery of win-win solutions. Thompson's third criticism is that the model fails to explain "how negotiators who are presumably highly concerned with their opponents' welfare (e.g. partners in romantic relationships) fail to reach mutually beneficial outcomes" (p. 524). The model actually does explain this phenomenon, arguing that high concern with the other's welfare in the absence of self-concern leads to rapid concession making and failure to find win-win solutions. Self-concern is sometimes low in romantic relationships because of fear that conflict will hurt the relationship (Fry et al 1983). The fourth criticism is that the "experimental manipulations used to induce concern for the other party also contain unintentional cues about the variable-sum structure of the task" (pp. 523–24). It is hard to see how giving the negotiators a gift before the negotiation or telling them that they will be cooperating in a future task can provide such structural information. Thompson's fifth criticism is that the model fails to account for the fact that negotiators sometimes develop win-win solutions when they have little or no concern with the other party's outcomes, and the sixth criticism is that the model ignores important negotiator goals such as the "desire to reach a fair outcome" (p. 524).

The latter two criticisms say in sum that the dual-concern model is not a comprehensive theory of strategic choice. This is a valid point. The model was designed as a heuristic device rather than as a comprehensive theory, and there are many relevant phenomena it does not cover. For example, the model ignores the competitive motive altogether. No research on the impact of the competitive motivation on negotiation has been reported, but evidence from prisoner's dilemma research (Kuhlman & Marshello 1975) suggests that this orientation encourages a contentious strategy.

The dual-concern model also fails to explain how and why people so often shift from one strategy to another during negotiation. It is our view that the dual-concern model indicates a negotiator's preferred strategy but that practical considerations often deflect negotiators from their preferences. An example would be two negotiators who are cooperatively oriented but, after a bit of exploration, conclude that there is no integrative potential in their situation. Problem solving is impractical so they must turn to either contending or concession making if they wish to reach agreement. Pruitt (1991) has postulated that cooperatively oriented negotiators in such a situation will compare needs with one another, and the one with the stronger needs will hold firm (contending) while the one with the weaker needs will concede. Such a policy will lead to high joint benefit across a series of negotiations in which there is variety in the relative strengths of the two parties' needs. Evidence supporting these postulates was found by Beggs et al (1989).

In addition, individualistically oriented subjects may prefer a contentious approach, but they are often pushed into concession making by contentious behavior from the other party or by a recognition that the other party cannot possibly accept what they are demanding. They may be pushed instead into problem solving if they cannot concede and the other party will not budge. In such a situation, neither contending nor yielding is feasible, and the only strategy left is problem solving, which will be embraced out of practical necessity rather than concern about the other party's outcomes.

The latter reasoning may underlie a progression of two stages that has often been observed in real-life negotiations (Douglas 1962; Morley & Stephenson 1977). The first stage involves a combination of contending and concession making, while the second stage involves heavy problem solving. What may happen in the first stage is that the parties—both individualistically oriented— use contentious tactics effectively enough to persuade each other to make all of the easy concessions. By the end of this stage, concession making and contending are no longer viable strategies. The only remaining strategy is problem solving, which is adopted in desperation, for strictly individualistic reasons. The transition between these stages may well involve a sense of "hurting stalemate" (Touval & Zartman 1985).

Research on Concession Making

Much of the early research on negotiation concerned the antecedents and consequences of various patterns of concession making. Most studies were laboratory experiments on negotiation about a single issue (e.g. options 1–5 in Figure 1) by subjects with an individualistic orientation. Underlying this research was a demand-concession model that viewed negotiators as starting at a particular level of demand and then conceding (reducing their demand) more or less rapidly until they reached one another's positions or negotiation was broken off. For example, the dealer in Figure 1a might start at $12,000 (option 1) and then concede after a considerable period of time to $11,500 (option 2) and eventually to $11,000 (option 3), stopping there. In the context of the options shown in Figure 1a, this would be a "high" initial demand and a "slow" rate of concessions.

CONCESSION PATTERNS AND NEGOTIATION OUTCOMES   This research supports three reasonable conclusions about the effect of a single party's demand level and rate of concession on the outcome of negotiation. One is that higher initial demands and slower concessions make agreement less likely and less rapidly reached (Bartos 1974; Benton et al 1972; Hamner 1974; Harnett & Vincelette 1978). The second conclusion is that lower initial demands and faster concessions produce smaller outcomes for the party employing them and larger outcomes for the other party, if agreement is reached (Bartos 1974; Benton et al 1972; Chertkoff & Conley 1967). The third conclusion, which can be derived from the first two, is that there is an inverted U-shaped relationship between level of demand and level of outcome. Negotiators who start with high demands and concede slowly often fail to reach agreement, which usually leads to inferior outcomes. Those who start with low demands and concede rapidly usually reach agreement on the other party's terms, also yielding inferior outcomes. Those between these extremes ordinarily achieve better outcomes. Three studies have shown this curvilinear relationship (Benton et al 1972; Hamner 1974; Harnett & Vincelette 1978). A fourth study (Bartos 1974) failed to find it, probably because most negotiators reached agreement.

ANTECEDENTS OF CONCESSION PATTERNS   Research on the impact of negotiator limits has shown that higher limits produce higher initial demands and slower concession making (Holmes et al 1971; Kelley et al 1967; Schoeninger & Wood 1969; Smith et al 1982; Yukl 1974a,b). As mentioned earlier, this leads to slower agreements and fewer agreements (Bazerman et al 1985; Ben-Yoav & Pruitt 1984a; Huber & Neale 1986; Neale & Bazerman 1985; Pruitt & Lewis 1975). One qualification on this finding is that a limit has greater impact on demand the closer it is to demand. Thus, an increase in a seller's limit from $8,000 to $9,000 will have more impact on his or her demand if that demand is in the $10,000 range than if it is in the $12,000 range. This means that limit has a larger impact on demand at later stages of negotiation, when enough concessions have been made to bring demand level into the range of limit (Holmes et al 1971; Kelley et al 1967; Yukl 1974b).

Findings on negotiator *aspirations*—i.e. goals—are similar to those on limits. Higher aspirations produce higher demands (Hamner & Harnett 1975; Holmes et al 1971; Yukl 1974a,b), smaller concessions (Hamner & Harnett 1975), and slower agreements (Kahan 1968). Furthermore, when agreement is reached, higher aspirations produce larger profits for the individual negotiator (Holmes et al 1971; Siegel & Fouraker 1960). Level of aspiration interacts with limit, in that limit has a larger impact on demand when aspirations are lower (Smith et al 1982). This is probably because lower aspirations mean that limit and demand are closer to each other.

Yielding is also affected by time pressure. Time pressure may be due to the cost or risk involved in continued negotiation or the closeness of a perceived deadline at which negotiation must terminate. In negotiation about a single issue, time pressure produces lower demands, faster concessions, and faster agreement (Hamner 1974; Hamner & Baird 1978; Komorita & Barnes 1969; Pruitt & Drews 1969; Pruitt & Johnson 1970; Smith et al 1982; Yukl 1974a). Evidence gathered by Yukl (1974a) suggests that these effects may be mediated by level of aspiration. Time pressure also interacts with limit, in that limit has a larger impact on demand under greater time pressure (Pruitt & Drews 1969). This is probably because limit and demand are closer to each other under greater time pressure.

Negotiator *hostility* tends to constrain yielding and make it hard to reach agreement (Pruitt et al 1991b). This is particularly common when the hostility is based on a perception that the other party has acted unfairly or exploitatively, violating our rights (Gruder 1971; Michener et al 1975). This may be because yielding is seen as rewarding a disliked other or because hostility produces a competitive orientation.

Negotiators often represent other people, who can be called their "constituents." Their aim, in such roles, is ordinarily to please these constituents (Gruder & Rosen 1971; Wall 1975). Hence, if they believe that their constituents are anxious to win, they will tend to be unyielding and take a long time to reach agreement; but if they believe that their constituents stress cooperation and agreement, they will tend to be yielding and move quickly toward agreement (Benton & Druckman 1974; Tjosvold 1977). In the absence of information about constituent preferences, representatives tend to view their constituents as more anxious to win than they themselves are (Gruder 1971; Pruitt et al 1978), a belief that is often accurate (Walton & McKersie 1965). Such representatives are usually less yielding and take longer to reach agreement than do individual negotiators (Benton 1972; Benton & Druckman 1973; Druckman et al 1972).

Representatives are especially anxious to please their constituents when they are either accountable to these constituents or feel insecure about their standing in the group. Such circumstances lead them to be unyielding and make it harder to reach agreement. Accountability was produced in these studies by giving the constituents power over negotiators' outcomes (Bartunek et al 1975; Benton 1972; Ben-Yoav & Pruitt 1984b; Carnevale et al 1981; Neale 1984) or by making it clear that the constituents would receive information about the outcome of the negotiation (Gruder 1971; Klimoski 1972; Klimoski & Ash 1974). Insecurity was produced by giving the negotiators low status in their organizations (Hermann & Kogan 1968; Kogan et al 1972) or making them feel distrusted by their constituents (Frey & Adams 1972; Wall 1975, 1976). Two studies in which accountability effects were not shown (Frey & Adams 1972; Gruder & Rosen 1971) employed what appeared to be weak manipulations.

Constituent surveillance of the negotiation also tends to reinforce perceived constituent preferences. If negotiators think their constituents favor conciliation, surveillance will push them toward concession making (Organ 1971; Pruitt et al 1986). But surveillance is more likely to enhance negotiator toughness (Benton 1975; Carnevale et al 1979; Druckman et al 1972; Klimoski & Ash 1974), especially under conditions of high negotiator accountability (Sharma et al 1991). Indeed, with constituents (or journalists reporting to them) in the room, negotiators tend toward heroic grandstanding. Hence, to reach agreement, it is often necessary to move into executive session with only the chief negotiators in attendance.

The effects described in this section are compelling and consistent, but their generality must be called into question. Many appear specific to conditions in which the negotiators seek to maximize their own interests—i.e. are individualistically oriented. Four studies have shown that these effects disappear when negotiators are concerned about the other party's welfare as well as their own—i.e. are cooperatively oriented. The tendency for high limits to induce rigidity disappeared when the negotiators were married to each other (Schoeninger & Wood 1969) or expected to have to work together in the future (Ben-Yoav & Pruitt 1984a); time-pressure effects disappeared when negotiators were cooperatively oriented (Carnevale & Lawler 1986); and accountability effects disappeared when negotiators expected to have to work together in the future (Ben-Yoav & Pruitt 1984b). Thus the demand-concession model with which we started this section may be inappropriate when there is a cooperative orientation. Rather than starting at a particular level of demand and gradually conceding toward the other party, cooperatively oriented negotiators tend to seek options that maximize both parties' gains. In other words, they engage in problem solving, as predicted by the dual-concern model.

REACTIONS TO THE OTHER PARTY'S CONCESSION PATTERNS   There are two opposing reactions to the other party's demands and concessions: matching and mismatching. Matching occurs when one demands more if the other's demands are larger or concedes more rapidly the faster the other concedes. Mismatching occurs when one demands more if the other's demands are smaller or concedes more rapidly the slower the other concedes.

These reactions tend to be found at different points in the negotiation cycle. Mismatching is found at the beginning of negotiation. People tend to respond with moderate demands when the other is initially tough and to demand a lot if the other is initially conciliatory (Chertkoff & Conley 1967; Liebert et al 1968; Pruitt & Syna 1985; Yukl 1974b). This pattern can be interpreted as "tracking" behavior (Pruitt 1981)—an effort to place one's demands at a reasonable distance from the other's limit, so that they are realistic but do not give the other too much hope. In this interpretation, the other party's initial demand is assumed to provide information about the location of his or her limit. There are two kinds of evidence for this interpretation. One is direct evidence that tracking occurs: The other party's limit, if known, has a large impact on demand level (Chertkoff & Baird 1971). The other evidence is the finding that initial mismatching disappears when sounder information is available about the location of the other party's limit (Liebert et al 1968; Pruitt & Syna 1985; Yukl 1974a).

Matching is common in the *middle* of negotiation. Negotiators hold firm if the other holds firm and concede if the other concedes. The evidence is clearest for matching the frequency of the other party's concessions (Bartos 1974; Chertkoff & Conley 1967; Esser & Komorita 1975; Hopmann & Smith 1977; Kelley et al 1967; Pruitt & Johnson 1970; Yukl 1974b). Partial matching of the other's concession size was also found in four studies (Benton et al 1972; Esser & Komorita 1975; Komorita & Esser 1975; Smith et al 1982), though no matching at all was found in two others (Pruitt & Drews 1969; Pruitt & Syna 1985). Matching of concession sizes and degree of contentious rhetoric has also been found in studies of real-life international negotiation (Beriker & Druckman 1991; Druckman 1986; Druckman & Harris 1990; Stoll & McAndrew 1986). Matching is probably motivated by a principle of reciprocity or a desire to reinforce the other for cooperative behavior. One element of matching, failing to concede when the other fails to concede, may also be motivated by a desire to avoid looking like a sucker (Kerr 1986).

Mismatching is found again at the end of negotiation if, as is commonly the case, a deadline is looming (Carnevale & Lawler 1986; Druckman et al 1972; Smith et al 1982; Yukl 1974b, but not Benton et al 1972). Tough opponents can often pull substantial concessions out of negotiators who are facing a deadline, because the latter will move to fill the gap. However, negotiators will not move beyond their limits; hence, opponents who are too tough simply consign the negotiation to an outcome of no agreement. Though mismatching is common at this stage, the forces that push toward matching are probably also present. It follows that parties who face a tough opponent at the end of negotiation will often be in severe conflict between mismatching to fill the gap and matching to even up the score and to avoid looking like a sucker. The result is variability in response; most subjects mismatch, but a few match (Yukl 1974a).

If mismatching is found at the beginning of negotiation and matching in the middle, it should be possible to get maximal concessions from the other party by starting with a high level of demand and then conceding regularly. Such a "reformed sinner" strategy has been shown to be more effective than a strategy that starts with a moderate level of demand and makes few additional concessions (Bartos 1974; Benton et al 1972; Hamner 1974). The latter strategy is likely to mislead the other party into setting unrealistically high aspirations, making agreement hard to reach (Bartos 1974; Hamner 1974). A related finding is that a negotiator who takes a tough approach to one negotiation and a soft approach to the next will elicit more concessions in the second negotiation than one who is soft in both (Hilty & Carnevale 1992). In addition, Hilty & Carnevale (1992) showed that a shift from a soft to a tough approach, a "lapsed saint" strategy, also elicited cooperation.

Research has also been done on the impact of a matching or "tit-for-tat" strategy on the other party—that is, of conceding when the other concedes and failing to concede when the other fails to concede. This contingent strategy elicits more concessions than are found in free negotiation (Wall 1977b). It is also more effective than a strategy of conceding on every trial, never conceding, or conceding only one-half or one-quarter of the times when the other concedes (Komorita 1973; Komorita & Esser 1975). There are two possible explanations for the success of the matching strategy (Pruitt et al 1987). One

(Wall 1977b) involves learning: The other party discovers that the only way to get the strategist to concede is to concede first. The second (Komorita & Esser 1975) involves labeling: The other party comes to see the strategist as both "firm" (because he or she fails to cooperate when the target fails to cooperate) and "fair" (because he or she cooperates when the target cooperates). Firmness means that the strategist cannot be exploited, while fairness implies that he or she can be trusted to equalize the two parties' outcomes. Hence, it makes no sense to hold out in an effort to persuade the other to mismatch and makes a lot of sense to concede in the expectation of further reciprocity. Evidence compatible with the firm-fair interpretation comes from a study in which opponents who followed a matching strategy were rated as "stronger" than those who followed a noncontingent strategy involving many concessions and "fairer" than those who followed a noncontingent strategy involving few concessions (McGillicuddy et al 1984).

Many of the findings on reactions to the other party's concession patterns may be specific to individualistically oriented negotiators who are taking a demand-concession approach to bargaining. Indirect evidence of this can be seen in a study of the prisoner's dilemma (Kuhlman & Marshello 1975). Individualistically oriented subjects showed the same pattern that has been found for negotiation: A tit-for-tat strategy elicited C-playing (cooperation) more than a consistently cooperative strategy; but cooperatively oriented subjects showed a high level of C-playing in response to both strategies. These subjects were ready to cooperate regardless of whether their opponent was contingently or noncontingently cooperative.

Research on Contending

Contending is a strategy aimed at pushing the other party in the direction of one's wishes. It can be regarded as an open-ended script (Abelson 1981) that prescribes one or another contentious tactic depending on the circumstances. Among the most common contentious tactics are persuasive arguments (designed to convince the other that concession making is in his or her best interest), threats (designed to reduce the value of no agreement for the other and thus lower the other's limit), and positional commitments (designed to make it necessary for the other to concede in order to reach agreement). Other contentious tactics build on the antecedents of concession making mentioned in the last section. For example, efforts are sometimes made to put time pressure on the other party or to persuade the other party to send a representative with enough freedom of action to make concessions.

EFFECTS OF CONTENDING   The prisoner's dilemma literature on the effects of threats on the other party's behavior is probably relevant to negotiation. Threats are more effective at getting the other to concede the larger the penalty threatened and the more credible it is that this penalty will actually be delivered (Tedeschi et al 1973). Threat credibility is enhanced by consistent enforcement of past threats (Horai & Tedeschi 1969) and diminished if fulfilling the threat is costly to the threatener (Mogy & Pruitt 1974). Threats are also more effective when they come from high-status people (Faley & Tedeschi 1971) and from people who are viewed negatively (Schlenker et al 1970), probably because such threats are more credible.

Positional commitments are more credible if they are made publicly (Schelling 1960) or are backed up by evidence that the strategist cannot concede beyond them—for example, that the strategist faces high limits (Chertkoff & Baird 1971) or constituent pressures (Wall 1977). However, credibility is not always a key to success, because a commitment to an option that is outside the other's limit is bound to fail. Hence, negotiators often hedge their commitments, leaving a small path for graceful exit, even though this may dilute the credibility of these commitments (Iklé 1964). Another way to avoid an unwise commitment is to wait until the end of negotiation when maximal information is available about the other party's limits. Kelley (1966) has found that repeated experience with negotiation leads people to learn to delay their commitments, presumably for this reason.

Unequal use of contentious tactics leads to an agreement favoring the heavier user (Williams & Lewis 1976). But such agreements are likely to be Pyrrhic in situations with integrative potential, because contentious tactics are associated with low joint benefit and, when limits are high, with failure to reach agreement (Pruitt 1981; Pruitt et al 1991b). This is probably because contending blocks creativity and makes it hard to accept new alternatives, especially if these alternatives seem to benefit the other party.

Most contentious tactics have another pitfall: They are often imitated by the other party for defensive reasons (Hornstein 1965; Kimmel et al 1980). Arguments produce counterarguments, positional commitments encourage countercommitments, threats elicit counterthreats (Deutsch & Krauss 1962). Such imitation can lead to failure of the tactic, and to conflict escalation (Pruitt & Rubin 1986). Research on marriage (Gottman 1979) and roommate pairs (Sillars 1981) shows that such imitation is more common in distressed than in happy relationships.

ANTECEDENTS OF CONTENDING   Many of the conditions that discourage yielding tend to incline people toward contending. This is true of hostility (Pruitt et al 1991b), high limits (Ben-Yoav & Pruitt 1984a), high accountability to constituents (Ben-Yoav & Pruitt 1984b; Carnevale et al 1981), and surveillance by male (though not by female) constituents (Pruitt et al 1986). In addition, there is a tendency to prefer contending when the parties' aspirations seem far apart, presumably because it is hard to believe that the other party will agree with one's demands voluntarily (Thompson & Hastie 1990). These perceptions are heightened by high time pressure (Carnevale & Lawler 1986).

Putting a physical barrier between negotiators, so that they can hear but not see each other, tends to reduce contending under conditions that ordinarily produce such behavior (Carnevale & Isen 1986; Carnevale et al 1981; Lewis & Fry 1977). As a result, win-win agreements are more often found with the barrier in place. This unusual but reliable effect is probably due to two nonverbal elements of contending, staring at the other party and moving into the other's territory (Lewis & Fry 1977). With the barrier in place, people cannot see their opponents doing these things and hence are less defensive.

POWER DIFFERENCES AND CONTENDING   Power can be thought of as the capacity to put effective pressure on the other party. Power takes many forms, the most commonly studied being reward and threat capacity. In negotiation, it is possible for either party or both parties to have substantial power. Hence, the effects of both relative and absolute power can be examined (Bacharach & Lawler 1981; Habeeb 1988).

An experiment by Hornstein (1965) showed an inverted U-shaped relationship between relative threat capacity and several indexes of contending (counterthreats, penalty use, unwillingness to yield to a threat). Contending was more prominent when there was a mild discrepancy in threat capacity than when there was equal or highly unequal threat capacity. As a result, there were fewer agreements and less money was made in the mild discrepancy condition. There was evidence that this might have been because the low-power negotiator was unwilling to accept lower status in the mild discrepancy condition, and fought for equal treatment. Hornstein's results are similar to findings by Vitz & Kite (1970) in an experiment where the negotiators differed in their capacity to contribute to a pool of resources that was useful to both parties. The most severe conflicts occurred when there was a mild, as opposed to a large, discrepancy in this capacity. A possible generalization from these two studies is that contentious tactics and escalation are more likely when there is a mild power discrepancy between the two parties than when the parties are equal or highly unequal in power.

Two studies also looked at the impact of absolute threat capacity (Hornstein 1965; Lawler et al 1988). The first showed that fewer threats were made and more agreements were reached when both parties had high threat capacity than when they had moderate or low capacity. The second showed that high mutual threat capacity lowered the temptation to use coercion and the expectation that the other party would use coercion.

Research on Problem Solving

The third strategy available to negotiators is problem solving, which involves efforts to locate and adopt a win-win solution—i.e. a solution that satisfies both parties' goals. Problem solving is not absolutely necessary for achieving win-win solutions. Kelley & Schenitzki (1972) have shown that such solutions can emerge when negotiators engage in "systematic concession making," starting with a high level of aspiration and lowering their aspirations slowly, proposing all options they can think of at each successive level of aspiration. But problem solving increases the likelihood of win-win solutions.

Most laboratory experiments on problem solving have used a multiple-issue negotiation task developed by Kelley (1964, 1966) and Pruitt & Lewis (1975), which involves two or more issues of different priority to the disputants. Win-win solutions are achieved by means of logrolling, each party winning on the issues it finds important. This task also allows the parties to adopt a compromise on each issue, producing agreements like those at points 2, 3, and 4 in Figure 1. But logrolling yields solutions like 6, 7, and 8 that are better for the parties collectively, and often better for both parties individually.

Logrolling is not the only route to win-win solutions. There are four others (Pruitt 1981; Pruitt & Rubin 1986): expanding the pie, compensating the loser, cutting the loser's costs, and "bridging," which involves constructing new options that have not previously been considered. To enable bridging, someone (one or both disputants or a third party) must analyze the interests (goals, values, needs) that underlie one or both parties' overt positions and reconceptualize the issues as achieving these underlying interests (R. Fisher & Ury 1981; Pruitt & Rubin 1986).

THE NATURE AND IMPACT OF PROBLEM SOLVING   Problem solving is a strategy available to either party separately or the two parties working together in joint session. Like contending, it can be regarded as an open-ended script prescribing one or another specific tactic depending on the circumstances. Effective problem solving requires that negotiators be both firm and flexible (R. Fisher & Ury 1981; Pruitt & Rubin 1986). They must be firm about their basic interests, adopting high aspirations and maintaining these aspirations long enough to determine whether they can be achieved. The importance of firmness can be seen in a negotiation study in which pairs of strangers achieved higher joint benefit than dating couples because they were less afraid of conflict and hence maintained their aspirations longer (Fry et al 1983). But negotiators must also be flexible about the means to achieve these interests, seeking options that are acceptable to the other party as well as themselves.

Problem solving often involves information exchange, in which one or both parties provide information about their priorities (promoting the development of logrolling solutions) or the interests underlying their positions (promoting the development of bridging solutions). There is both correlational (Pruitt 1981) and experimental (Thompson 1991) evidence that information exchange promotes the development of win-win solutions. Negotiators tend to believe that unilateral provision of such information will put them in a weak position that the other party can exploit. Hence trust is a prerequisite for information exchange (Kimmel et al 1980). However, Thompson (1991) did not find that providing such information unilaterally actually puts a negotiator's outcomes in jeopardy.

Certain forms of problem solving do not involve information exchange—for example, Carnevale & Isen's (1986) tactic of systematic trial and error, described in the section above on the dual-concern model. Books of advice to negotiators (e.g. Filley 1975; R. Fisher & Ury 1981) recommend many other kinds of problem-solving tactics: brainstorming, avoiding personal attacks on the other, posing a problem before stating an answer, putting oneself in the other's shoes, and active listening. Active listening involves checking one's understanding of the other's position with the other party. Johnson (1967, 1971a,b) has shown that this tactic fosters understanding of the other's position, improves the other's attitude toward oneself, and increases the other's willingness to concede. However, if active listening is done too warmly, it runs the risk of signaling weakness and thus diminishing the other's willingness to concede (Johnson 1971b).

SOURCES OF PROBLEM SOLVING   According to the dual-concern model, problem solving is encouraged by a combination of concern about the other party's outcomes and concern about one's own outcomes. Concern about the other party's outcomes can be genuine—one likes the other party, one feels responsible for the other party, or one is in a good mood (Carnevale & Isen 1986; Pruitt et al 1983); or the concern can be strategic—one depends on the other and hence seeks the other's good will (Ben-Yoav & Pruitt 1984a,b; Pruitt et al 1991b) or one benefits from the other's good fortune (Schultz & Pruitt 1978).

The dual-concern model predicts that concern about the other party's outcomes moderates the impact of concern about one's own outcomes. When concern about the other's outcomes is low, concern about one's own outcomes should encourage contending—behavior aimed at winning. This should diminish the likelihood of achieving a win-win solution. But when concern about the other's outcomes is high, concern about one's own outcomes should encourage problem solving. This should enhance the likelihood of achieving a win-win solution. Several studies support these predictions. Two studies show that when there is low concern for the other, high aspirations encourage contending and low joint benefit; but when there is high concern for the other, high aspirations encourage problem solving and high joint benefit (Ben-Yoav & Pruitt 1984a; Pruitt et al 1983). Another study showed the same effects for accountability to constituents (Ben-Yoav &

Pruitt 1984b). These studies indicate, as suggested above, that the laws governing negotiation are different under individualistic and cooperative orientations.

Problem solving can also emerge from a strictly individualistic orientation if it becomes clear that contending will be ineffective. Negotiators often realize that they do not have the power to force the other party to concede. Hence, if they are unwilling to capitulate, they must engage in problem solving to achieve agreement. In short, they see that they can only get what they want if the other party also gets what it wants. As mentioned above, this realization probably accounts for the progression from contending to problem solving that is often observed in negotiation (Douglas 1962; Morley & Stephenson 1977). However, several studies have shown that time pressure can interfere with the development of problem solving when negotiators adopt an individualistic orientation (Carnevale & Lawler 1986; Yukl et al 1976).

Problem solving is more likely to develop and persist if negotiators perceive that there is integrative potential in their situation, that options other than compromise are possible (Pruitt & Rubin 1986). One example of perceived integrative potential is the belief that the two parties have different priorities among the issues, which implies that logrolling is possible. There is correlational evidence that this belief encourages problem solving (Thompson & Hastie 1990).

Conclusions about Motivation and Strategy

In the past, most research has assumed that negotiators have an individualistic orientation. But what is emerging from recent research is that reactions to a number of conditions change markedly if negotiators are concerned about the other party's outcomes in addition to their own. When they are only concerned about their own outcomes, high limits, accountability to constituents, and negative framing of the issues lead to slow concession making and contentious behavior; time pressure interferes with problem solving; and barriers separating the negotiators diminish contentious behavior. But when they are also concerned about the other party's outcomes, these effects disappear; and contentious behavior is often replaced by problem solving, leading to the development of high joint benefit. The dual-concern model is useful for understanding these effects.

COGNITIVE PROCESSES IN NEGOTIATION

The current emphasis on cognitive mechanisms in negotiation extends theory and research in social cognition (Sherman et al 1989), information processing in cognitive psychology (Anderson 1985), and decision theory (Dawes 1988) to negotiation. Researchers in this tradition tend to adopt one of two perspectives that are not necessarily in opposition. The first stems directly from Tversky & Kahneman's (1974) notions about cognitive heuristics and biases, which are mental shortcuts that can produce erroneous judgments. In negotiation, research shows that these shortcuts sometimes produce poor outcomes and sometimes good outcomes. The second perspective emphasizes *schematic information processing* and the construction of mental models. These are organized knowledge structures that guide and potentially distort the acquisition, storage, and recall of information (see Beach 1990; Deutsch 1982; Fiske & Taylor 1984; Hastie 1981, 1991).

The two perspectives—heuristics and biases and schematic information processing—differ on several dimensions. These include the manner in which experiments are designed and the nature of the response measures. Researchers who adopt the former perspective emphasize the normative theory of rational belief and choice (Dawes 1988). Typically, they identify a variable that, given the predictions of a normative model, should not affect negotiation outcome; they then conduct an experiment to show that it does. Deviations from the normative model are labeled "irrational." Researchers who focus on schematic information processing shun this label and argue that testing null hypotheses derived from normative models produces unimportant results (see Hastie 1991:138). These researchers aim to develop and test theories about the underlying cognitive processes that mediate negotiation behavior (cf Thompson & Hastie 1990).

Heuristics and Biases

Negotiators are assumed to have limited attention and limited capacity to store and retrieve information from memory. As a result, they consciously or unconsciously use heuristics—shortcuts and other simplifying strategies—that help manage information. There are numerous heuristics that negotiators may adopt, including availability, representativeness, and anchoring and adjustment. In addition, research has shown that negotiator judgment is susceptible to bias due to the framing of outcomes in terms of gain and loss, and also to overconfidence.

AVAILABILITY AND REPRESENTATIVENESS   Availability is the decision maker's reliance on the ease of recall of information as a cue for judgments about frequency or likelihood of occurrence (Tversky & Kahneman 1974). In negotiation, availability can lead negotiators to rely too much on salient information and therefore produce biased negotiator judgment (Neale & Bazerman 1991). Representativeness involves making judgments on the basis of seemingly relevant characteristics that in fact belie the true state of affairs (Tversky & Kahneman 1974). Both heuristics can translate into the tendency of negotiators to rely too much on historical analogies. A well-known example of this comes from international negotiation: The statement "If this aggression goes unchecked it will be another Munich" is sometimes used to justify the choice of struggle over negotiation. The statement refers to the sham agreement that was reached in negotiations between Neville Chamberlain and Adolph Hitler in 1938 with calamitous consequences. In this example, an historical negotiation is seen as representative of the current negotiation, when the current negotiation may in fact be quite different (see Gilovich 1981, Jönsson 1991).

ANCHORING AND ADJUSTMENT   Anchoring and adjustment is a simplifying strategy in which an arbitrarily chosen reference point has an inordinate influence on judgments (see Dawes 1988 for examples). Anchoring and adjustment may account for the large influence that initial offers have in negotiation, a phenomenon mentioned above. It also may explain the unusual impact of prior information about pricing in buyer-seller negotiations (Northcraft & Neale 1987). Evidence that anchoring and adjustment can play an important role in negotiation was obtained in an interesting study by Fobian & Christensen-Szalanski (1992). These authors simulated a medical-liability negotiation to examine the effects of ambiguity about the likelihood of winning in adjudication if there was no agreement in negotiation. They found the use of an anchoring and adjustment heuristic was particularly likely to occur when negotiators experienced high ambiguity. High ambiguity increased the likelihood of agreement and the parties' cooperativeness. Use of this heuristic thus had a beneficial effect on negotiation. The data in this study were consistent with a model of ambiguity developed by Einhorn & Hogarth (1985).

BIAS DUE TO FRAMING OF OUTCOMES   In an application of Kahneman & Tversky's (1979) prospect theory to negotiation, Neale & Bazerman (1985) and Bazerman et al (1985) used a task that was either positively framed or negatively framed. With a positive frame, negotiators viewed prospective outcomes as gains and saw the negotiation as an effort to maximize net profit. With a negative frame, negotiators viewed prospective outcomes as losses and saw the negotiation as an effort to minimize expenses. Net outcomes were formally identical in both cases. Bazerman et al (1985) showed that when the task was positively framed, subjects were more likely to reach agreements than when the task was negatively framed. This finding was replicated by Bottom & Studt (1990), who also looked at a condition in which one negotiator had a positive frame and the other a negative frame. If negative framing produces resistance to concession, one can predict that in this condition the negotiator with the negative frame should do substantially better in an agreement than the negotiator with the positive frame. This is exactly what they found. These findings imply that a negative frame can be an asset if the opponent has a positive frame.

Carnevale & Keenan (1990) and Bottom (1989) argued that rather than affecting attitude toward risk, a positive or negative decision frame affects the negotiators' concern for their own outcomes. These authors argue that the risk-seeking/risk-aversion formulation from prospect theory is unnecessary, and that the frame effect in negotiation is a simple matter of the greater significance of loss than of gain. That is, negotiators find it harder to concede when this means "loss" rather than "failure to gain." Based on the dual-concern model presented in Figure 2, these authors argued that decision frame can thus act as a two-edged sword, depending on the negotiators' concern about the other party's outcomes. When there is low concern about the other party's outcomes, a negative frame on both sides should lead to little concession making and thus less frequent agreement, as found by Bazerman et al and Bottom & Studt. But in the context of high concern about the other party's outcomes, a negative frame should encourage the development of a win-win agreement, assuming that the situation has integrative potential. Carnevale & Keenan's (1990) evidence supports this prediction, showing that a negative frame can be an asset for negotiators when they have a high concern for the other party's outcomes. Similarly, Neale et al (1987) found that a negative frame led to improved outcomes when negotiators were given fictitious role labels.

Research has uncovered other moderators of the frame effect in negotiation. These include negotiator mood (Hollingshead & Carnevale 1990) and whether the negotiation task is segregated or integrated (Bontempo 1990). In addition, Carnevale & Mead (1990) found that the effects of negotiator frame extended to perceptions by a mediator. The subjects were mediators who observed bargainers who had either a positive frame (the bargaining involved profits) or a negative frame (the bargaining involved expenses). Mediators who saw a concession by bargainers who had a negative frame viewed them as more cooperative than mediators who saw a concession by bargainers who had a positive frame. This occurred despite the fact that in both conditions the bargainers made *equivalent concessions*. The finding is consistent with the assumption that disutility for loss is greater than the utility for gain; hence, a third party will view concessions that increase loss as more significant than concessions that decrease gain. Recent research has also addressed the important role of communication processes in the development and revision of negotiator frames (de Dreu et al 1991; cf Putnam 1990).

BIAS DUE TO OVERCONFIDENCE   Another source of bias in negotiation stems from the beliefs that negotiators have about their likelihood of success. Negotiators sometimes believe that their opponent will make greater concessions than they will (Stevens 1963; Kochan & Jick 1978). Neale &

Bazerman (1985) reported that negotiators tend to be overly optimistic about how well they will do in arbitration when negotiation ends in nonagreement. This overoptimism obviously can interfere with the likelihood of agreement in negotiation and also can interfere with the efforts of mediators (Kochan & Jick 1978). Carnevale and Keenan (1990) found that such overoptimism only occurred when negotiators had low concern for each others' outcomes. Pruitt et al (1991a) reported that disputants were overly optimistic about the success of struggle tactics involving the use of threats without negotiation. A study by Rothbart & Hallmark (1988) suggests that the latter effect is more likely when negotiations are between people from different groups rather than the same group.

Schematic Information Processing

Negotiation researchers who emphasize schematic information processing focus on how individual negotiators acquire and use knowledge in negotiation. The basic idea is that cognitive factors—the perception of intentions, attitudes and beliefs about the other, the perception of the situation—in short, a person's construction of social reality, determines negotiation behavior (Abric 1982; Deutsch 1982; Brodt 1990). Norms of behavior and the relevance of information are determined by the way the parties develop a cognitive interpretation of the context, the issues, and the negotiation task. As with all knowledge, negotiator knowledge is represented in schemata. Schemata are hypothesized cognitive structures that contain information about the negotiation and that guide negotiation behavior (Bar-Tal et al 1989; Carroll & Payne, 1991; see especially Deutsch 1982). Schemata are thought to develop from frequent processing of different instances of items or material in memory (Taylor & Crocker 1981).

One way in which schemata can influence information processing is through selective attention and memory, which can perpetuate and exacerbate conflict. Pinkley (1990) has argued that two disputants can see the same conflict differently, and possibly in contradictory terms, as a result of differing schemata. Vallone et al (1985), found that both sides in a conflict perceived that the news media were against them. Hammond & Grassia (1985) developed a theory of cognition that explains how peoples' judgments of the same circumstances can differ. One problem arises when different people base their judgments on different cues, or when individuals weight the same cues differently and therefore reach different judgments that lead to a quarrel. There is evidence that each side in a conflict tends to remember more facts that support its own position (Grzelak 1982). Pruitt & Rubin (1986) have argued that the relationship between negative attitudes toward the other party and contentious behavior are perpetuated by selective perception and memory.

Researchers have examined the influence of various schemata, treated in the following sections, on information processing in negotiation.

THE FIXED-PIE PERCEPTION   An example of a schema in negotiation is the assumption some negotiators make that "your win is my loss." This fixed-pie—i.e. zero-sum or win/lose—perception has implications for future action. For example, in multiple-issue negotiation tasks the fixed-pie perception occurs when negotiators believe that the other negotiator's interests are directly opposed to their own—i.e. that the other has the same priorities on the issues as the self (Pruitt 1981; Thompson & Hastie 1990). This is a faulty judgment when negotiation situations provide the opportunity for joint gain (Follett 1940; Schelling 1960). The fixed-pie perception is an instance of the false consensus effect, where people tend to believe that others share the same views as themselves, more than the others actually do (see Sherman et al 1989).

Pruitt & Lewis (1975), Lewis & Fry (1977), Kimmel et al (1980), and Carnevale & Isen (1986) had negotiators indicate their perceptions of the opposing negotiator's priorities on the issues just after negotiation. Negotiators who realized that the other negotiator had different priorities on the issues also attained higher joint outcomes than those who did not. Using a related measure, Thompson & Hastie (1990) found that most of the negotiators entered with a fixed pie perception of the task but became more accurate as negotiation proceeded. Accurate judgments about the other party's interests led to higher joint outcomes and higher individual profits.

There is evidence that schemata tend to persist from one negotiation to the next. Thompson (1990a) found that early experience with a negotiation task that did not allow win-win agreements led negotiators to assume that later negotiations also did not allow win-win agreements, when in fact the task was changed and win-win agreements were available.

ILLUSORY CONFLICT   Sometimes disputes involve issues where the parties want the same thing but fail to realize it. Lax & Sebenius (1986:107) refer to these issues as "common value." Rubin et al (1990) refer to the failure to see common value issues, to perceive opposing interests when no opposition exists, as "illusory conflict." It has been called "incompatibility error" by Thompson & Hastie (1990). Thompson & Hastie (1990) used a multiple-issue negotiation task that included an issue on which the subjects had completely compatible interests. At first, most negotiators failed to realize that they had compatible interests. As time went on, some of them discovered their error; but misperceptions were still substantial at the end of negotiation.

REACTIVE DEVALUATION   Stillinger et al (submitted) found that proposals and offers suggested by opponents tend to be devalued in negotiation, simply on the basis of knowledge that the adversary has offered them. In one study, some negotiators rated the value of an opponent's concession before it was actually made, and others rated the concession after it was offered. The results indicated that negotiators tend to denigrate and misconstrue concessions offered by their opponent. Apparently, negotiators reason that whatever is good for the other must be bad for the self. This is the other side of the same coin as illusory conflict, which assumes that whatever is good for the self is bad for the other.

ATTRIBUTIONS AND BEHAVIOR   The attributions negotiators make about the causes of the opposing negotiator's behavior are an important determinant of their reactions to that behavior (Bar-tal & Geva 1986; Hewstone 1988; Kelley & Stahelski 1970). In several studies, Baron (1985, 1988) found that confrontational negotiation behaviors induced less retribution when they were attributed to sincerely held beliefs. Other research suggests that negative attributions about the partner's behavior can both stem from and contribute to marital unhappiness (Fincham 1985; Holtzworth-Munroe & Jacobson 1985) and roommate disaffection (Sillars 1981). Hammond & Grassia (1985) argue that in social conflict, people attribute disagreement to erroneous causes, including ill-will, or hidden agendas.

NEGOTIATION SCRIPTS   Assumptions about the procedures one goes through in any situation are "scripts" (Abelson 1981) or "event schemas" (Hastie 1981). Among other features, scripts usually include assumptions about behavior that is fair or appropriate to expect from oneself and other parties. Negotiation is often guided by highly stylized and detailed scripts (Carroll & Payne 1991)—for example, not withdrawing a concession once it has been made (Pruitt 1981).

POSITIVE AFFECT   Positive affect, pleasant feelings that are typically induced by commonplace events such as reading a cartoon, hearing a joke, or getting a small gift or piece of candy, can have important effects in negotiation. Professional mediators know this when they tell humorous stories prior to and during negotiation in an effort to improve cooperation (Kressel & Pruitt 1989). Positive affect can lessen anger and overt hostility (Baron 1984), and it can encourage cooperative behavior and creative problem solving in negotiation (Baron et al 1990; Carnevale & Isen 1986; Hollingshead & Carnevale 1990).

Perspective on the Cognitive Approach

The cognitive approach to negotiation has numerous strengths. These include the use of process-tracing methods for direct analysis of information-processing strategies. A fine example is the talk-aloud procedure used by

Carroll et al (1988) and Thompson & Hastie (1990), and efforts to relate measures of information exchange in negotiation to measures of perceptions (Lewis & Fry 1977; Thompson & Hastie 1990).

Another potential strength of the cognitive approach is its emphasis on information gathering prior to decision. For example, building on a concept developed by Simon (1957), Pruitt (1981) postulated that negotiators employ a search model, a set of goals and requirements that are used for generating and screening alternatives. Search models often include insights into the other negotiator's goals, priorities, and constraints as well as one's own. Once an alternative is found that fits a negotiator's search model, it must be submitted to the opposing negotiator as a proposal. If the other rejects it, the search is resumed with the same or a modified model. Carroll & Payne (1991) present a useful overview of rule-based evaluation strategies for processing information about offers and alternatives in negotiation.

Perhaps the most surprising conclusion from recent research on negotiator cognition is evidence that the use of heuristics can produce positive, win-win negotiation outcomes. This was seen in studies by Fobian & Christensen-Szalanski (1992) for use of the anchoring-and-adjustment heuristic, and in studies by Bottom (1989), Bottom & Studt (1990), Carnevale & Keenan (1990), and Neale et al (1987) on framing. This conclusion contrasts with the assertion that heuristics and biases in negotiation are a prime cause of poor negotiation outcomes. The finding points to a criticism of the biases-and-heuristics approach: the failure to acknowledge that simplifying strategies can have a positive impact on handling information and decision making in negotiation (see Lopes & Oden 1991; Hogarth 1981; Taylor & Brown 1988).

Carroll & Payne (1991) and Thompson (1990b) provide other criticisms of the heuristics-and-biases perspective. They argue that it falls short of a full analysis of information processing since suboptimal strategies are inferred rather than observed. Thompson (1990b) further argues that the term "bias" is overused in this research and should not be used when the negotiators simply lack relevant information or have been misled by the opposing negotiator.

A challenge for future research on negotiator cognition is the development of unified models that can tie together the various cognitive processes that have been uncovered. Lack of attention to the underlying cognitive mechanisms and processes may produce a disorganized field, with long lists of cognitive effects but little understanding either of what causes them or of the circumstances in which they are manifested and attenuated. Moreover, the preoccupation in this literature with the attainment of win-win agreements should be reexamined in the light of evidence that such agreements are not necessarily good predictors of long-term success (Pruitt et al 1991b).

Future research should link cognition and motivation in negotiation (cf Carnevale & Keenan 1990; Kramer 1990; Thompson 1990b). It is unreasonable to assume that cognitive processes operate in a vacuum and reasonable to assume that most of them are influenced by or actually operate through motivational processes (see Burton 1969; Grzelak 1982; Kramer 1990; Rubin et al 1990; Sorrentino & Higgins 1986). A case in point is the escalation of commitment to a previous decision in negotiation (Neale & Bazerman 1991), which likely has a strong motivational basis. Another case in point is the common observation that competitively oriented conflict promotes "black and white thinking," which involves a tendency to dichotomize information, to assign extreme values to objects or items, and not to see relationships among concepts in memory (Deutsch 1973, 1982; Judd 1978; White 1984). There is evidence that black and white thinking inhibits creativity and effective problem solving in negotiation. Carnevale (1991) found that subjects in a competitive negotiation were less likely than those in a cooperative negotiation to see relationships among items in a categorization task that was unrelated to the negotiation. This finding is consistent with recent theoretical work by Bar-Tal et al (1989), Kramer (1990), and Thompson (1990b) showing that goals and other motivational forces are important determinants of the accessibility of conflict schemata in memory.

MEDIATION

History and Literature

Research on mediation has increased dramatically in the past ten years, which is probably a reflection of the rapid proliferation of mediation in practice. Mediation has long been an important part of industrial relations and international negotiation. One of the earliest recorded mediations occurred more than four thousand years ago in Mesopotamia when a Sumarian ruler helped avert a war and develop an agreement in a dispute over land (Kramer 1963). Mediation is now found in realms as diverse as neighborhood feuds (Duffy et al 1991; McGillis 1981), civil and criminal litigation (Folberg & Taylor 1984; Wall & Rude 1985, 1987, 1991), police interventions (Palenski 1984), family disputes and divorce (Donohue 1991; Emery & Wyer 1987; Rubin 1985), public disputes, environmental planning and siting (Susskind & Cruikshank 1987; Susskind & Ozawa 1985), and decision making in organizations (Karambayya & Brett 1989; Kolb 1986; Sheppard 1984; Thomas 1982).

This field of research is remarkably interdisciplinary, involving important contributions by psychologists, economists, political scientists, sociologists, anthropologists, and scholars in the fields of communications, industrial relations, law, and organizational behavior. Most of the early theoretical and empirical pieces on mediation dealt with international conflicts, including works by Burton (1969), Campbell (1976), Doob (1970), Edmead (1971), R. Fisher & Ury (1978), Frei (1976), Hill (1982), Jackson (1952), Kelman &

Cohen (1979), Rubin (1981), Touval (1975), Touval & Zartman (1985), and Young (1967, 1972). Studies dealing with labor-management conflict include Kerr (1954), Landsberger (1955a,b), Douglas (1962), Stevens (1963), Kochan & Jick (1978), Brett & Goldberg (1983), Kolb (1983), Kressel (1972), Maggiolo (1985), Peters (1952, 1955), Rehmus (1965), and Walton (1969). Laboratory researchers have often used this literature to develop and test propositions about (*a*) the effects of mediation on negotiation (Bartunek et al 1975; Bigoness 1976; Brookmire & Sistrunk 1980; Hamilton et al 1981; Harris & Carnevale 1990; Hiltrop & Rubin 1982; Johnson & Pruitt 1972; Johnson & Tullar 1972; Podell & Knapp 1969; Pruitt & Johnson 1970; Ross et al 1990; Vidmar 1971; Wall 1979) and (*b*) the antecedents of mediator behavior (Carnevale & Conlon 1988; Carnevale & Henry 1989; Harnett & Wall 1983).

Practitioner manuals (e.g. Keltner 1987; Kessler 1978; Underhill 1981) and books of advice to mediators (Moore 1986) have proliferated. A literature has also sprung up, that espouses (Wahrhaftig 1981, 1982) or criticizes (Tomasic 1982) one or another aspect of mediation (see also R. J. Fisher & Keashly 1988; Murnighan 1986).

Much of the best recent empirical work is represented in the edited volume by Kressel & Pruitt (1989), and these authors provide a comprehensive review in their concluding chapter. Other recent reviews include Duffy et al (1991), Kressel & Pruitt (1985), Bercovitch (1984), Smith (1987), Wall & Lynn (unpublished), Lewicki et al (1991), and the excellent interdisciplinary overview by Kolb & Rubin (1991). Earlier reviews include R. J. Fisher (1983), Pruitt (1981), Rubin (1980, 1981), and Wall (1981).

In the present review of the literature we focus on the overall effectiveness of mediation, the structure of mediator behavior, the effectiveness of specific mediator behaviors, and the antecedents of mediator behavior.

Mediation Effectiveness

GENERAL EVALUATION   Most of the research suggests that mediation is effective in general—agreements are usually reached, participants are ordinarily satisfied, and compliance is high—though a number of these studies have methodological problems (see Kressel & Pruitt 1989; Vidmar 1985). The question of overall effectiveness is clearly too broad. More interesting research questions are, "Under what circumstances is mediation effective?" and "What mediation tactics are effective under various circumstances?"

WHEN MEDIATION IS EFFECTIVE   Mediation is more effective when conflict is moderate rather than intense (Glasl 1982), and when the parties are highly motivated to reach settlement, as they are in a "hurting stalemate" (Touval & Zartman 1985). Mediation is also more effective when the parties are committed to mediation (Hiltrop 1989), when there is not a severe resource shortage (Kochan & Jick 1978), when the issues do not involve general principles (Bercovitch 1989; Pruitt et al 1989), and when the parties are relatively equal in power (Bercovitch 1989; Kelly & Gigy 1989; Raymond & Kegley 1985; see Ippolito & Pruitt 1990 for a failure to find this effect).

Mediation has also been shown to be more effective when arbitration is threatened as a next step. In a field experiment at a community mediation center, McGillicuddy et al (1987) compared mediation to two forms of mediation-arbitration: 1. "med-arb(same)," where the mediator becomes an arbitrator and issues a binding decision if agreement is not reached during mediation, and 2. "med-arb(diff)," where a fourth party, not present during mediation, becomes an arbitrator. The results indicated that the med-arb(same) condition produced the highest levels of problem solving and the lowest levels of hostility, although there were no differences in the likelihood of settlement.

Mediator Behavior and Effectiveness

CLASSES OF MEDIATOR BEHAVIOR   Much of the research on mediator behavior attempts to identify specific behaviors, i.e. "tactics," and to organize them into categories or "strategies" (Kressel 1972; Kressel & Pruitt 1985; Lim & Carnevale 1990; McLaughlin et al 1991; Wall 1981; Touval & Zartman 1985). In this section we categorize mediator behaviors on the basis of four distinct components of mediation: 1. the relationship between the mediator and the disputants, 2. the relationship between the parties during mediation, 3. the issues, and 4. the individuals (or groups) on each side of the dispute and their motivation to reach agreement.

Mediator-disputant relationship   Certain mediator behaviors are designed to improve acceptance of mediation by establishing trust in the mediator and confidence in the mediation process [see Kressel (1972) and Kressel & Pruitt's (1985, 1989) discussion of the use of "reflexive tactics"]. Several studies have shown that trust in the mediator is an important predictor of settlement (Carnevale & Pegnetter 1985; Pruitt et al 1989).

The parties' relationship in mediation   Mediators can control the communication between the parties and can help the parties understand one another's positions. Hiltrop (1985, 1989) reports that such efforts are positively related to settlement in labor mediation. Perhaps the most widely used technique for controlling communication in mediation is the caucus, where the mediator separates the parties and meets privately with each side. Caucuses are usually called when the parties are showing high levels of hostility toward one another and little joint problem solving (Pruitt et al 1989).

Research suggests that caucuses become an alternative location of problem solving involving a single disputant and the mediator subtly taking the other party's perspective (Pruitt et al 1989). However, caucus sessions can be misleading to the mediator since disputants can make derogatory statements about the other party, who is not present to make disclaimers (Pruitt et al 1989; Welton et al 1988).

The issues   Dealing with the issues is central to mediation. This process includes identifying the issues, uncovering underlying interests and concerns, setting an agenda, packaging, sequencing and prioritizing the issues, interpreting and shaping proposals, and making suggestions for possible settlement. Pruitt et al (1991b) and Lim & Carnevale (1990) found that structuring the issue agenda led to greater short-term success. Because they have greater access to the parties' underlying interests and aspirations, mediators can serve in an "analytic" capacity and help foster negotiator rationality by uncovering efficient options (Lax & Sebenius 1986; Raiffa 1982, 1983; Kolb & Rubin 1991). Mediators can help overcome the problem of reactive devaluation, advancing as their own proposal a position that is acceptable to the other party but would be rejected if the other party put it forward (Stillinger et al, submitted). Mediators also can reduce negotiator optimism about gaining a favorable outcome (Kochan & Jick 1978) and can arrange the agenda so that early agreements on simple issues produce momentum for achieving agreement on later more difficult issues (Pruitt 1981).

The parties   Some mediator behaviors are designed to reduce a party's reluctance to make concessions or reach agreements by, for example, helping them save face when making concessions (Podell & Knapp 1969; Pruitt & Johnson 1970; Stevens 1963), helping them resolve internal disagreements (Lim & Carnevale 1990), or helping them deal with constituents (Wall 1981). In addition, mediators can influence the parties' motivation to reach agreement by adding positive incentives for agreement or concession making, or applying negative sanctions, threats, and arguments (Bercovitch 1989; Carnevale 1986; Lovell 1952; Touval & Zartman 1985).

   These four categories of action are by no means mutually exclusive. Several of them can occur at the same time. For example, conducting a caucus may simultaneously allow the mediator to develop rapport with one party, enhance that party's understanding of the other's position, and allow the mediator an opportunity to offer to one side, in private, a positive incentive for concession making.

   The few empirically based taxonomies of mediator behavior have certain dimensions in common—e.g. the degree of forcefulness of tactics (Lim & Carnevale 1990; McLaughlin et al 1991; Wall & Rude 1985). Differences between these taxonomies suggest that context plays an important role in shaping the character of mediation (Kolb 1989). Wall & Rude (1985) identify mediation tactics that are unique to judicial mediation, and Wall & Blum (1991) identify tactics that seem unique to community mediation in China.

EFFECTIVENESS   Some kinds of mediator behavior appear to be effective regardless of the dispute situation. Lim & Carnevale (1990), for example, found that mediator efforts to control the agenda and to help the parties establish priorities among the issues were positively associated with settlement regardless of the nature of the dispute. Similarly, Pruitt et al (1990) reported that creating an agenda was positively related to the extent of joint benefit in the final agreement. Prein (1984) found that a mediation strategy that emphasized control over the process was positively associated with settlement in a variety of disputes. Ross et al (1990) reported that a friendly style of mediation was effective regardless of the time pressure on the disputants.

The effectiveness of other kinds of mediator tactics seems to be contingent on the dispute circumstances (Shapiro et al 1985). Donohue (1989) reported that an active mediator strategy is useful when there is high conflict intensity but is counterproductive when conflict intensity is low. Hiltrop (1985, 1989) found similarly that in British labor disputes, the use of forceful, substantive mediator tactics was positively associated with settlement when there were high levels of hostility, but when hostility was low the use of these tactics was negatively associated with settlement. In a survey of professional mediators in the United States, Lim & Carnevale (1990) found that the use of pressure tactics (e.g. mentioning to the parties that their positions were unrealistic) was positively associated with settlement when conflict was intense, but when hostility between the parties was low the use of pressure tactics was negatively associated with settlement.

In addition, Zubek et al (1989) found that when there was high hostility and little joint problem solving by the disputants, agreement was more likely to be reached if the mediator stimulated thought by posing problems to be solved, challenging the parties to come up with ideas, suggesting new ideas, and requesting reactions to new ideas. But when the level of joint problem solving effort was high, agreement was more likely to be reached if the mediator refrained from such actions.

These findings suggest that when disputants are able to resolve the dispute themselves, mediator intrusiveness gets in the way (Rubin 1980, 1981); but when conflict intensity is high, directive, forceful intervention is effective. Such intervention allows the parties to make concessions while preserving their sense of personal strength, because the impetus for the concessions can be attributed to the mediator. This is sometimes referred to as the "face saving" function of mediation (Bartunek et al 1975; Pruitt & Johnson 1970; Stevens 1963).

ACTUAL VERSUS ANTICIPATED INTERVENTION   An interesting parallel effect is observed with anticipated forceful mediation. Hiltrop & Rubin (1982) studied the interaction between level of conflict and actual-vs-anticipated third party intervention. High conflict encouraged cooperation among bargainers who did not anticipate third party intervention, whereas low conflict encouraged cooperation when a third party was expected to intervene. Actual intervention produced the opposite results: Bargainers under high conflict were closer to agreement when a third party had actually intervened, whereas bargainers under low conflict moved closer to agreement when there was no actual third party intervention.

Taken together with the findings mentioned earlier, these results suggest that potential mediators in low-intensity conflicts should create an expectation of heavy-handed intervention; but when mediation begins, they should not actually apply a heavy hand unless the discussions are going poorly (see Rubin 1980, 1981; Kolb & Rubin 1991).

LONG-TERM SUCCESS   The research cited so far is characteristic of most in the field in dealing with the antecedents of short-term mediation success, such as agreement and immediate satisfaction. One exception to this trend is a study by Pruitt et al (1990, 1991b) that focused on the determinants of long-term success in community mediation: compliance with the terms of the agreement, improvement in the relationship between the parties, and the absence of new problems. Surprisingly, no relationship was found between short-term and long-term success; agreements that achieved the disputant's goals were no more effective in the long run than those that did not. The best predictors of long-term success were joint problem solving during the discussion and procedural justice, the disputant's perceptions that fair procedures were used in the mediation hearing (cf Tyler 1987).

Antecedents of Mediator Behavior

A central concern of mediators is what to do in a given situation. How are these decisions made?

CONTINGENT BEHAVIOR   Several studies indicate that mediators become more active as the level of conflict increases (Landsberger 1955a,b; Carnevale & Pegnetter 1985; Donohue 1989; Gerhart & Drotning 1980). As they become more active or use more mediation tactics, they perceive that their efforts are more effective (Wall & Rude 1991). Also, Carnevale & Pegnetter (1985) have found that professional labor mediators tend to use issue-related tactics, such as devising a framework for negotiations and creating priorities among the issues, when bargainers bring many issues to the negotiation. Sheppard et al (1989) have shown that mediators tend to emphasize fact finding and clarification of the issues when the disputants are interdependent and the issues are complex; mediators tend to emphasize solution identification when they are concerned about efficiency or are in a position of authority over the disputants.

CONCERN-LIKELIHOOD MODEL   Carnevale (1986) has developed a strategic choice model to predict mediator behavior. It postulates two antecedent variables that interact to predict mediator behavior: 1. the mediator's likelihood estimate of a win-win agreement ("perceived common ground"); and 2. the mediator's level of concern that the parties achieve their aspirations. Mediators are predicted to emphasize a problem-solving strategy aimed at discovering win-win solutions when they have high concern for the parties' aspirations and perceive the likelihood of a win-win agreement to be high. They are predicted to use compensation to entice the parties into concessions and agreements when they have high concern for the parties' aspirations and perceive the likelihood of a win-win agreement to be low. They are predicted to employ pressure to force the parties to reduce their aspirations and make concessions when they have little concern for the parties' aspirations and perceive the likelihood of a win-win agreement to be low. Finally, they are predicted to be inactive—letting the parties handle the dispute on their own—when they have low concern for the parties' aspirations and perceive that the likelihood of a win-win agreement is high. Research has supported and extended parts of this model (Carnevale & Conlon 1988; Carnevale & Henry 1989; Chaudhry & Ross 1989; Conlon 1988; Harris & Carnevale 1990; Lim 1990).

PHASES OF MEDIATION   Pruitt et al (1989) have developed a three-stage descriptive model of mediation. Stage 1 is "setting the stage," which includes clarifying the ground rules and gathering information. Stage 2 is "problem solving," which includes posing issues and generating alternatives. Stage 3 is "achieving a workable agreement," which includes pressing the parties to reach agreement. A similar model was reported by Shaw et al (1973) and Landsberger (1955b). Carnevale & Conlon (1988) reported findings consistent with these models: that mediators were less directive at first but shifted in the direction of pressure tactics and compensation tactics as time progressed and as time pressure increased. Wall & Rude (1991) found a similar effect for assertiveness in judicial mediation.

MEDIATOR COGNITION   Several studies suggest that mediators are susceptible to overconfidence and other cognitive biases of the kinds discussed above. In an early study, Shaw et al (1973) found that third-party preconceptions were positively associated with the conduct and outcome of negotiation. Carnevale & Conlon (1988) reported that mediators in a laboratory study were poor judges of win-win potential. Mediators only made win-win recommendations when the negotiators' offers were already win-win.

Carnevale & Pegnetter (1985) found that professional labor mediators were overconfident about the likelihood that they could resolve a dispute. This may be due in part to the third party's inclination to underestimate the negotiators' aspirations.

Research derived from prospect theory (Kahneman & Tversky 1979) suggests that mediators work harder to avoid a loss than to achieve a gain. Carnevale & Mead (1990) gave mediators either a positive decision frame (i.e. the mediators would gain money if the bargainers reached agreement) or a negative frame (i.e. they would lose money if the bargainers did not reach agreement). In a manner consistent with prospect theory, the mediators who had something to lose adopted a more forceful strategy than mediators who had something to gain, even though the money they could earn in each case was identical.

MEDIATOR POWER   Mediator power sometimes stems from reputation and authority and sometimes from the capacity to reward or punish the disputants (Kressel & Pruitt 1989; Carnevale 1986; Touval & Zartman 1985). Power has been found to encourage mediators to use more forceful tactics. For example, community mediators who had the capacity to arbitrate were especially likely to use threats and heavy advocacy (McGillicuddy, Welton, & Pruitt 1987). This observation is consistent with the finding that judges who mediate often use strong-arm tactics (Wall & Rude 1987). Welton & Pruitt (1987) found that disputants who had higher power over a mediator were more accepting of the mediator and behaved less contentiously, but they were less influenced by the mediator.

MEDIATOR BIAS   The traditional view of mediation is that, to be effective, the mediator must be impartial and have no stake in the outcome of negotiation (Young 1967, 1972). There is no question that neutrality often contributes to successful mediation. Welton & Pruitt (1987) found that disputants who perceived the mediator as neutral were more receptive to mediation than those who perceived the mediator as biased against their side. However, the absolute necessity of mediator neutrality has been challenged by several authors (Brookmire & Sistrunk 1980; Smith 1985; Touval 1975; Touval & Zartman 1985), who argue that a biased mediator is sometimes the only available alternative and is often the person with the greatest influence over the party that most needs to change (see Kressel 1972 for an example of this in labor mediation). Wittmer et al (1991) and Carnevale & Conlon (1990) examined the combined impact of two forms of mediator bias on negotiator receptivity to mediation: the mediator's general alignment with one side versus the mediator's overt support for one side. Negotiators were receptive to a mediator who was biased against them, i.e. who was unfavorably aligned, but only when the mediator acted in an overtly evenhanded manner.

NEGOTIATOR BEHAVIOR TOWARD MEDIATORS   Several studies indicate that negotiators use concession making in an effort to influence the mediator's choice of strategy. Negotiators sometimes make concessions to avoid the intervention of a potentially coercive mediator (Hiltrop & Rubin 1982; Harris & Carnevale 1990). By contrast, they tend to reduce their concession making when faced with a mediator who can provide rewards in the future (Harris & Carnevale 1990; Idaszak & Carnevale 1989), perhaps with the thought of later trading their concessions for rewards. Rubin (1981) and Touval & Zartman (1985) cite instances of this practice in international mediation.

CONCLUSIONS: CHALLENGES FOR FUTURE RESEARCH

Negotiation Teams

Negotiation often occurs between teams of negotiators, as is true in collective bargaining and international negotiation, and what happens within the team may have important consequences for the between-group negotiation. Although Walton & McKersie (1965) drew attention to the importance of within-group negotiation more than 25 years ago, little is known about these effects (R. Fisher 1989; Stephenson 1981; Pruitt 1990). Research by Insko et al (1987, 1988) suggests that negotiation teams are more competitive than individuals in between-group negotiation, and a study by Keenan & Carnevale (1989) indicates that within-group conflict carries over to between-group negotiation. Rothbart & Hallmark (1988) showed that coercion is seen as more effective for dealing with out-group members, and conciliation is seen as more effective for dealing with in-group members. In another study that points to the importance of within-group processes, Lim & Carnevale (1990) found that mediator suggestions made when there were internal disagreements within a negotiation team decreased the likelihood of agreement in the between-group negotiation. The importance of within-group communication processes for between-group interaction in a social-dilemma paradigm has been shown recently by Bornstein et al (1989). This is likely a fruitful area for further research.

Working Relationships

Fisher & Brown (1988), Pruitt (1990, 1991), and Greenhalgh (1987) have argued that negotiation is more efficient (more rapid, more likely to reach agreement) and more likely to produce win-win agreements, when the parties have positive working relationships. The most important prerequisite for such working relationships is that both sides have a sense of mutual dependence, in which each will depend on the other for help across a number of separate issues and opportunities for action. Various strategies can contribute to the development of relationships (Fisher & Brown 1988; Pruitt 1991). Where relationships are strained, problem-solving workshops (Kelman & Cohen 1979) can contribute to their development. The development of working relationships and their impact on negotiation comprise an important research frontier.

Procedural Choice

Negotiation and mediation are often chosen from a broader set of procedures, including arbitration and struggle. Inaction, the absence of a procedure, is of course a fifth option. A few early studies treated choices among these options (see Lind & Tyler 1988; Thibaut & Walker 1975), and this field of study has shown some recent signs of revival (Heuer & Penrod 1986; Leung 1987; Pruitt et al 1991a). More research is needed on the conditions under which people will enter negotiation and mediation and the conditions under which they will take other routes when faced with a conflict.

Cultural Differences

There is evidence of cultural differences in negotiation behavior (Adler 1986; Gulliver 1979, 1988; Leung & Wu 1989; Roth et al 1991) and in preferences among dispute resolution procedures (Leung 1987). Mediation has a long history in some cultures (Cohen 1966), and its nature can change from one cultural context to another (Merry 1982; Wall & Blum 1991). Hence cultural differences in negotiation and mediation will likely become more important as countries become increasingly multicultural and increasingly interrelated. One perspective on cultural differences derives from the distinction between collectivism and individualism (Triandis 1989). Chan (1991) had subjects in Hong Kong and in the United States negotiate with a friend or a stranger in an integrative bargaining task, showing that negotiators in the collectivist culture (Hong Kong) were more sensitive to in-group/out-group differences than were negotiators in the United States.

Individual Differences

The study of personality and other individual differences in negotiation has had a mixed history. Earlier efforts to relate broad personality variables to negotiation behavior yielded a confusing and inconsistent pattern (Pruitt 1981; Rubin & Brown 1975). However, research on the prisoner's dilemma (e.g. Kuhlman & Marshello 1975) suggests that direct measures of motivational orientation are related to negotiation behavior, and studies should begin to incorporate these measures (see Rahim 1986; van de Vliert & Prein 1989). The results on gender differences are also inconsistent. Some studies show that men are more likely than women to adopt a forceful style in both negotiation and mediation (Kimmel et al 1980; Lim & Carnevale 1990) and that negotiation is likely to produce better outcomes for men than for women (Gerhart & Rynes 1991). Other studies show no differences between men and women in negotiation behavior and outcome (Pruitt et al 1986). The theoretical variables underlying gender differences are unclear, but we suspect that interaction effects involving personality or gender variables and situational variables will be found. For example, Williams & Lewis (1976) found that women who held traditional sex-role attitudes did worse in negotiation with their romantic partners when they had low than when they had high aspirations.

Computer-Assisted Negotiation and Mediation

The use of computers in the conduct of negotiation and mediation is an exciting recent development. Papers by Pool et al (1990) and Nyhart & Samarasan (1989) on negotiation support systems (NSS) extend concepts from Group Decision Support Systems (GDSS) to negotiation (see Hollingshead & McGrath 1992 for a review of research on GDSS). Arunachalam (1991) reported that computer-mediated negotiations took longer to complete, were more hostile, and led to poorer outcomes than face-to-face negotiation, although negotiators with a computer-based medium showed marked improvement in outcomes over repeated negotiations.

ACKNOWLEDGMENTS

Preparation of this chapter was supported in part by National Science Foundation grants BNS-8809263 to Peter Carnevale and SES-8520084 to Dean Pruitt. The authors are grateful to Boris Kabanoff, Deborah Kolb, Keith Murnighan, and Leigh Thompson for their helpful comments.

Literature Cited

Abel, R., ed. 1982. *The Politics of Informal Justice*. New York: Academic

Abelson, R. P. 1981. The psychological status of the script concept. *Am. Psychol.* 36:715–29

Abric, J. C. 1982. Cognitive processes underlying cooperation: the theory of social representation. See Derlega & Grzelak 1982, pp. 73-94

Adler, N. J. 1986. *International Dimensions of Organizational Behavior*. Boston: Kent

Anderson, J. 1985. *Cognitive Psychology and Its Implications*. New York: W. H. Freeman

Arunachalam, V. 1991. *Decision aiding in multi-party transfer negotiation: the effects of computer-mediated communication and structured interaction*. PhD thesis. Univ. Illinois, Urbana. 236 pp.

Austin, W. G., Worchel, S., eds. 1979. *The Social Psychology of Intergroup Relations*. Monterey, CA: Brooks/Cole

Bacharach, S. B., Lawler, E. J. 1981. *Bargaining: Power, Tactics, and Outcomes*. Greenwich, CT: JAI

Baron, R. A. 1984. Reducing organizational conflict: an incompatible response approach. *J. Appl. Psychol.* 69:272–79

Baron, R. A. 1985. Redᵉcing organizational

conflict: the role of attributions. *J. Appl. Psychol.* 70:434–41

Baron, R. A. 1988. Attributions and organizational conflict: the mediating role of apparent sincerity. *Org. Behav. Hum. Perform.* 41:111–27

Baron, R. A., Fortin, S. P., Frei, R. L., Hauver, L. A., Shack, M. L. 1990. Reducing organizational conflict: the role of socially-induced positive affect. *Int. J. Confl. Manage.* 1:133-52

Bar-Tal, D., Geva, N. 1986. A cognitive basis of international conflicts. In *Psychology of Intergroup Relations*, ed. S. Worchel, W. G. Austin, pp. 118–33. Chicago: Nelson-Hall

Bar-Tal, D., Kruglanski, A. W., Klar, Y. 1989. Conflict termination: an epistemological analysis of international cases. *Polit. Psychol.* 10:233–55

Bartos, O. J. 1974. *Process and Outcome in Negotiation.* New York: Columbia Univ. Press

Bartunek, J., Benton, A., Keys, C. 1975. Third party intervention and the behavior of group representatives. *J. Confl. Resolut.* 19:532–57

Bazerman, M. H., Lewicki, R. J., eds. 1983. *Negotiating in Organizations.* Newbury Park, CA: Sage

Bazerman, M. H., Lewicki, R. J., Sheppard, B. H., eds. 1991. *Research on Negotiation in Organizations,* Vol. 3. Greenwich, CT: JAI. In press

Bazerman, M. H., Magliozzi, T., Neale, M. A. 1985. Integrative bargaining in a competitive market. *Org. Behav. Hum. Dec. Proc.* 35:294–313

Beach, L. R. 1990. *Image theory: Decision making in personal and organizational contexts.* Chichester, England: Wiley

Beggs, R. J., Brett, J. M., Weingart, L. R. 1989. The impact of decision aids and motivational orientation on group negotiations. Dispute Resol. Res. Cent. Work. Pap. 48, Kellogg Grad. Sch. Manage., Northwestern Univ., Evanston, IL

Benton, A. A. 1972. Accountability and negotiations between group representatives. In Proc. 80th Annu. Conf. Am. Psychol. Assoc., pp. 227–28

Benton, A. A. 1975. Bargaining visibility and the attitudes and negotiation behavior of male and female group representatives. *J. Pers.* 43:661–75

Benton, A. A., Druckman, D. 1973. Salient solutions and the bargaining behavior of representatives and nonrepresentatives. *Int. J. Group Tensions* 3:28–39

Benton, A. A., Druckman, D. 1974. Constituent's bargaining orientation and intergroup negotiations. *J. Appl. Soc. Psychol.* 4:141–50

Benton, A. A., Kelley, H. H., Liebling, B. 1972. Effects of extremity of offers and concession rate on the outcomes of bargaining. *J. Pers. Soc. Psychol.* 24:73–83

Ben-Yoav, O., Pruitt, D. G. 1984a. Accountability to constituents: a two-edged sword. *Org. Behav. Hum. Perform.* 34: 283–95

Ben-Yoav, O., Pruitt, D. G. 1984b. Resistance to yielding and the expectation of cooperative future interaction in negotiation. *J. Exp. Soc. Psychol.* 34:323–35

Bercovitch, J. 1984. *Social Conflicts and Third Parties: Strategies of Conflict Resolution.* Boulder, CO: Westview

Bercovitch, J. 1989. Mediation in international disputes. See Kressel & Pruitt 1989, pp. 284–99

Beriker, N., Druckman, D. 1991. Models of responsiveness: the Lausanne Peace Negotiations (1922–1923). *J. Soc. Psychol.* 131:297-300

Bigoness, W. J. 1976. The impact of initial bargaining position and alternative modes of third party intervention in resolving bargaining impasses. *Org. Behav. Hum. Perform.* 17:185–98

Blake, R. R., Mouton, J. S. 1979. Intergroup problem solving in organizations: from theory to practice. See Austin & Worchel 1979

Bomers, G. B. J., Peterson, R. B., eds. 1982. *Conflict Management and Industrial Relations.* Boston: Kluwer Nijhoff

Bontempo, R. 1990. *Behavioral decision theory and the negotiation process: effects of agenda and frame.* PhD thesis. Univ. Illinois, Urbana. 129 pp.

Bornstein, G., Rapoport, A., Kerpel, L., Katz, T. 1989. Within and between group communication in intergroup competition for public goods. *J. Exp. Soc. Psychol.* 25:422–36

Bottom, W. P. 1989. *A theory of adaptive reference points in decision making and negotiation.* PhD thesis. Univ. IL, Urbana, 154 pp.

Bottom, W. P., Studt, A. 1990. The nature of risk and risk preference in bargaining. Presented at 3rd Annu. Meet. Int. Assoc. Conflict Manage., Vancouver, British Columbia

Brechner, K. C. 1977. An experimental analysis of social traps. *J. Exp. Soc. Psychol.* 13:552–64

Brett, J. M., Goldberg, S. B. 1983. Mediator-advisors: a new third-party role. See Bazerman & Lewicki 1983, pp. 165–76

Brodt, S. E. 1990. Inside information and negotiator decision behavior. Presented at 3rd Annu. Meet. Int. Assoc. Conflict Manage., Vancouver, British Columbia

Brookmire, D., Sistrunk, F. 1980. The effects

of perceived ability and impartiality of mediators and time pressure on negotiation. *J. Confl. Resolut.* 24:311–27

Burton, J. W. 1969. *Conflict and Communication: The Use of Controlled Communication in International Relations.* London: Macmillan

Campbell, J. C. 1976. *Successful Negotiation: Trieste 1954.* Princeton, NJ: Princeton Univ. Press

Carnevale, P. J. 1986. Strategic choice in mediation. *Negot. J.* 2:41–56

Carnevale, P. J. 1991. Cognition and affect in cooperation and conflict. Presented at 4th Annu. Meet. Int. Assoc. Confl. Manage., Ernst Sillem Hoeve, Den Dolder, The Netherlands

Carnevale, P. J., Conlon, D. E. 1988. Time pressure and strategic choice in mediation. *Org. Behav. Hum. Dec. Proc.* 42:111–33

Carnevale, P. J., Conlon, D. E. 1990. Effects of two forms of bias in the mediation of disputes. Presented at 3rd Annu. Meet. Int. Assoc. Confl. Manage., Vancouver, British Columbia

Carnevale, P. J., Henry, R. 1989. Determinants of mediator behavior: a test of the strategic choice model. *J. Appl. Soc. Psychol.* 19:481–98

Carnevale, P. J., Isen, A. M. 1986. The influence of positive affect and visual access on the discovery of integrative solutions on bilateral negotiation. *Org. Behav. Hum. Dec. Proc.* 37:1–13

Carnevale, P. J., Keenan, P. A. 1990. Decision frame and social goals in integrative bargaining: the likelihood of agreement versus the quality. Presented at 3rd Annu. Meet. Int. Assoc. Confl. Manage., Vancouver, British Columbia

Carnevale, P. J., Lawler, E. J. 1986. Time pressure and the development of integrative agreements in bilateral negotiation. *J. Confl. Resolut.* 30:636–59

Carnevale, P. J., Mead, A. 1990. Decision frame in the mediation of disputes. Presented at Annu. Meet. Judgment Decis. Making Soc., New Orleans

Carnevale, P. J., Pegnetter R. 1985. The selection of mediation tactics in public-sector disputes: a contingency analysis. *J. Soc. Issues* 41:65–81

Carnevale, P. J., Pruitt, D. G., Britton, S. D. 1979. Looking tough: the negotiator under constituent surveillance. *Pers. Soc. Psychol. Bull.* 5:118–21

Carnevale, P. J., Pruitt, D. G., Seilheimer, S. 1981. Looking and competing: accountability and visual access in integrative bargaining. *J. Pers. Soc. Psychol.* 40:111–20

Carroll, J. S., Bazerman, M. H., Maury, R. 1988. Negotiator cognitions: a descriptive approach to negotiators' understanding of their opponents. *Org. Behav. Hum. Dec. Proc.* 41:352–70

Carroll, J. S., Payne, J. 1991. An information processing approach to two-party negotiations. See Bazerman et al 1991

Chan, D. K. S. 1991. *Effects of concession pattern, relationship between negotiators, and culture on negotiation.* MA thesis. Univ. Illinois, Urbana. 54 pp.

Chaudhry, S. S., Ross, W. R. 1989. Relevance trees and mediation. *Negot. J.* 5:63–73

Chertkoff, J., Baird, S. L. 1971. Applicability of the big-lie technique and the last clear choice doctrine to bargaining. *J. Pers. Soc. Psychol.* 20:298–303

Chertkoff, J. M., Conley, M. 1967. Opening offer and frequency of concessions as bargaining strategies. *J. Pers. Soc. Psychol.* 7:181–85

Cohen, D. 1966. Chinese mediation on the eve of modernization. *Calif. Law Rev.* 54:1201–26

Conlon, D. 1988. *Mediator behavior and interest: effects on mediator and disputant perceptions.* PhD thesis. Univ. Illinois, Urbana. 85 pp.

Dawes, R. M. 1988. *Rational Choice in an Uncertain World.* San Diego: Harcourt Brace Jovanovich

Dawes, R. M., McTavish, J., Shaklee, H. 1977. Behavior, communication, and assumptions about other people's behavior in a commons dilemma situation. *J. Pers. Soc. Psychol.* 35:1–11

de Callières, F. 1716 (reissued in 1976). *On the Manner of Negotiating with Princes,* transl. A. F. Whyte. Notre Dame, IN: Notre Dame Univ. Press

de Dreu, C. K. W., Emans, B. J. M., van de Vliert, E. 1991. Other's decision frame in negotiation behavior: an exploration of frame exchange. Presented at 4th Annu. Meet. Int. Assoc. Conflict Manage., Ernst Sillem Hoeve, Den Dolder, The Netherlands

Derlega, V. J., Grzelak, J., eds. 1982. *Cooperation and Helping Behavior: Theories and Research.* New York: Academic

Deutsch, M. 1958. Trust and suspicion. *J. Confl. Resolut.* 2:265–79

Deutsch, M. 1973. *The Resolution of Conflict.* New Haven, CT: Yale Univ. Press

Deutsch, M. 1975. Equity, equality, and need: What determines which value will be used as the basis of distributive justice? *J. Soc. Issues* 31:137–50

Deutsch, M. 1982. Interdependence and psychological orientation. See Derlega & Grzelak 1982, pp. 15-42

Deutsch, M., Krauss, R. M. 1962. Studies of interpersonal bargaining. *J. Confl. Resolut.* 6:52–76

Donohue, W. A. 1989. Communicative competence in mediators. See Kressel & Pruitt, pp. 322-43

Donohue, W. A. 1991. *Communication, Marital Dispute and Divorce Mediation.* Hillsdale, NJ: Lawrence Erlbaum.

Doob, L. W. 1970. *Resolving Conflict in Africa: The Fermeda Workshop.* New Haven, CT: Yale Univ. Press

Douglas, A. 1962. *Industrial Peacemaking.* New York: Columbia Univ. Press

Druckman, D. 1986. Stages, turning points, and crisis: negotiating military base rights, Spain and the United States. *J. Confl. Resolut.* 30:327-60

Druckman, D., Harris, R. 1990. Alternative models of responsiveness in international negotiation. *J. Confl. Resolut.* 34:234-52

Druckman, D., Broome, B. J., Korper, S. H. 1988. Values differences and conflict resolution. *J. Confl. Resolut.* 32:489-510

Druckman, D. ed. 1977. *Negotiations: Social Psychological Perspectives.* Beverly Hills, CA: Sage

Druckman, D., Solomon, D., Zechmeister, K. 1972. Effects of representative role obligations on the process of children's distributions of resources. *Sociometry* 35:387-410

Duffy, K. G., Grosch, J. W., Olczak, P. W., ed. 1991. *Community Mediation: A Handbook for Practitioners and Researchers.* New York: Guilford. 355 pp.

Edmead, F. 1971. *Analysis and Prediction in International Mediation.* New York: UNITAR, Study PS-2

Edney, J. J., Harper, C. S. 1978. The commons dilemma: a review of contributions from psychology. *Environmental Manage.* 2:491-507

Einhorn, H. J., Hogarth, R. M. 1985. Decision making under ambiguity. *Psychol. Rev.* 92:433-61

Emery, R. E., Wyer, M. M. 1987. Child custody mediation and litigation: an experimental evaluation of the experience of parents. *Journal of Consulting and Clinical Psychology* 55:179-86

Esser, J., Komorita, S. S. 1975. Reciprocity and concession making in bargaining. *J. Pers. Soc. Psychol.* 31:864-72

Faley, T. E., Tedeschi, J. T. 1971. Status and reactions to threats. *J. Pers. Soc. Psychol.* 17:192-99

Filley, A. C. 1975. *Interpersonal Conflict Resolution.* Glenville, IL: Scott, Foresman

Fincham, F. D. 1985. Attributions in close relationships. In *Contemporary Attribution Theory and Research,* ed. J. H. Harvey, G. Weary. New York: Academic

Fisher, R. 1989. Negotiating inside out: What are the best ways to relate internal negotiations with external ones? *Negot. J.* 5:33-41

Fisher, R., Brown, S. 1988. *Getting Together: Building a Relationship that Gets to YES.* Boston: Houghton Mifflin

Fisher, R., Ury, W. 1978. *International Mediation: Ideas for the Practitioner.* New York: International Peace Academy

Fisher, R., Ury, W. 1981. *Getting to YES: Negotiating Agreement Without Giving In.* Boston: Houghton Mifflin

Fisher, R. J. 1983. Third party consultation as a method of intergroup conflict resolution: a review of studies. *J. Confl. Resolut.* 27: 301-34

Fisher, R. J., Keashly, L. 1988. Third party interventions in intergroup conflict: consultation is not mediation. *Negot. J.* 4:381-93

Fiske, S. T., Taylor, S. E. 1984. *Social Cognition.* New York: Random House

Fobian, C. S., Christensen-Szalanski, J. J. J. 1992. Ambiguity and liability negotiations: the effects of the negotiators' role and the sensitivity zone. *Org. Behav. Hum. Dec. Proc.* In press

Folberg, J., Taylor, A. 1984. *Mediation: A Comprehensive Guide to Resolving Conflicts Without Litigation.* San Francisco, CA: Jossey-Bass

Follett, M. P. 1940. Constructive conflict. In *Dynamic Administration: The Collected Papers of Mary Parker Follett,* ed. H. C. Metcalf, L. Urwick, pp. 30-49. New York: Harper and Row

Frei, D. 1976. Conditions affecting the effectiveness of international mediation. *Peace Sci. Soc.* 26:67-84

Frey, R. L., Adams, J. S. 1972. The negotiator's dilemma: simultaneous in-group and out-group conflict. *J. Exp. Soc. Psychol.* 8:331-46

Fry, W. R., Firestone, I. J., Williams, D. L. 1983. Negotiation process and outcome of stranger dyads and dating couples: Do lovers lose? *Basic Appl. Soc. Psychol.* 4:1-16

Gerhart, B., Rynes, S. 1991. Determinants and consequences of salary negotiations by male and female MBA graduates. *J. Appl. Psychol.* 76:256-62

Gerhart, P. F., Drotning, J. E. 1980. Dispute settlement and the intensity of mediation. *Indust. Rel.* 19:352-59

Gilovich, T. 1981. Seeing the past in the present: the effect of associations to familiar events on judgments and decisions. *J. Pers. Soc. Psychol.* 40:797-808

Glasl, F. 1982. The process of conflict escalation and roles of third parties. See Bomers & Peterson 1982, pp. 119-40

Gottman, J. M. 1979. *Marital Interaction: Experimental Investigations.* New York: Academic

Greenhalgh, L. 1987. Relationships in negotiations. *Negot. J.* 3:325-45

Gruder, C. 1971. Relationship with opponent and partner in mixed-motive bargaining. *J. Confl. Resolut.* 15:403–16

Gruder, C. L., Rosen, N. 1971. Effects of intergroup relations on intergroup bargaining. *Int. J. Group Tensions* 1:301–17

Grzelak, J. L. 1982. Preferences and cognitive processes in interdependence situations: a theoretical analysis of cooperation. See Derlega & Grzelak 1982, pp. 95–122

Gulliver, P. H. 1979. *Disputes and Negotiation: A Cross-Cultural Perspective.* New York: Academic

Gulliver, P. H. 1988. Anthropological contributions to the study of negotiations. *Negot. J.* 4:247–55

Habeeb, W. M. 1988. *Power and Tactics in International Negotiation: How Weak Nations Bargain with Strong Nations.* Baltimore, Maryland: The Johns Hopkins Univ. Press

Hamilton, T. P., Swap, W. C., Rubin, J. Z. 1981. Predicting the effects of anticipated third party intervention: a template matching approach. *J. Pers. Soc. Psychol.* 41:1141–52

Hammond, K. R., Grassia, J. 1985. The cognitive side of conflict: from theory to resolution of policy disputes. In *Applied Social Psychology Annual*, ed. S. Oskamp, 6:233–54. Beverly Hills: Sage

Hamner, W. C. 1974. Effects of bargaining strategy and pressure to reach agreement in a stalemated negotiation. *J. Pers. Soc. Psychol.* 30:458–67

Hamner, W. C., Baird, L. S. 1978. The effect of strategy, pressure to reach agreement and relative power on bargaining behavior. See Sauermann 1978

Hamner, W. C., Harnett, D. L. 1975. The effects of information and aspiration level on bargaining behavior. *J. Exp. Soc. Psychol.* 11:329–42

Harnett, D. L., Vincelette, J. P. 1978. Strategic influences on bargaining effectiveness. See Sauermann 1978

Harnett, D. L., Wall, J. A. Jr. 1983. Aspiration/competitive effects on the mediation of bargaining. See Tietz 1983

Harris, K. L., Carnevale, P. J. 1990. Chilling and hastening: the influence of third-party power and interests on negotiation. *Org. Behav. Hum. Dec. Proc.* 47:138–60

Harsanyi, J. 1956. Approaches to the bargaining problem before and after the theory of games: a critical discussion of Zeuthen's, Hick's, and Nash's theories. *Econometrica* 24:144–57

Hastie, R. 1981. Schematic principles in human memory. See Higgins et al 1981, pp. 39–88

Hastie, R. 1991. A review from a high place: the field of judgment and decision making as revealed in its current textbooks. *Psychol. Sci.* 2:135–38

Hermann, M. G., Kogan, N. 1968. Negotiation in leader and delegate groups. *J. Confl. Resolut.* 12:332–44

Heuer, L. B., Penrod, S. 1986. Procedural preference as a function of conflict intensity. *J. Pers. Soc. Psychol.* 51:700–10

Hewstone, M. 1988. Attributional bases of intergroup conflict. In *The social Psychology of Intergroup Conflict: Theory, Research, and Applications*, ed. W. Stroebe, A. W. Kruglanski, D. Bar-Tal, M. Hewstone, pp. 47–72. New York: Springer-Verlag

Higgins, E. T., Heiman, C. P., Zanna, M. P., eds. 1981. *Social Cognition: The Ontario Symposium.* Hillsdale, NJ: Erlbaum

Hill, B. J. 1982. An analysis of conflict resolution techniques: from problem-solving workshops to theory. *J. Confl. Resolut.* 26:109–38

Hiltrop, J. M. 1985. Mediator behavior and the settlement of collective bargaining disputes in Britain. *J. Soc. Issues* 41:83–99

Hiltrop, J. M. 1989. Factors associated with successful labor mediation. See Kressel & Pruitt 1989, pp. 241–62

Hiltrop, J. M., Rubin, J. Z. 1982. Effects of intervention conflict of interest on dispute resolution. *J. Pers. Soc. Psychol.* 42:665–72

Hilty, J., Carnevale, P. J. 1992. Black-hat/White-hat strategy in bilateral negotiation. *Org. Behav. Hum. Dec. Proc.* In press.

Hogarth, R. 1981. Beyond discrete biases: functional and dysfunctional aspects of judgmental heuristics. *Psychol. Bull.* 90:197–217

Hollingshead, A. B., Carnevale, P. J. 1990. Positive affect and decision frame in integrative bargaining: a reversal of the frame effect. *Proc. Annu. Conf. Acad. Manage.*, 50th, pp. 385-89

Hollingshead, A. B., McGrath, J. E. 1992. The whole is less than the sum of its parts: a critical review of research on computer-aided groups. In *Team Decision and Team Performance in Organizations*, ed. R. A. Guzzo, E. Salas. San Francisco: Jossey-Bass

Holmes, J. G., Throop, W. F., Strickland, L. H. 1971. The effects of prenegotiation expectations on the distributive bargaining process. *J. Exp. Soc. Psychol.* 7:582–99

Holtzworth-Munroe, A., Jacobson, N. S. 1985. An attributional approach to marital dysfunction and therapy. In *Social Processes in Clinical and Counseling Psychology*, ed. J. E. Maddux, C. D. Stoltenberg, R. Rosenwein, pp. 153–69. New York: Springer-Verlag

Hopmann, P. T., Smith, T. C. 1977. An application of a Richardson process model: soviet-American interactions in the Test Ban Negotiations 1962–3 *J. Confl. Resolut.* 21:701–26

Horai, J., Tedeschi, J. 1969. Effects of credibility and magnitude of punishment on compliance to threats. *J. Pers. Soc. Psychol.* 12:164–9

Hornstein, H. A. 1965. Effects of different magnitudes of threat upon interpersonal bargaining. *J. Exp. Soc. Psychol.* 1:282–93

Huber, V. L., Neale, M. A. 1986. Effects of cognitive heuristics and goals on negotiator performance and subsequent goal setting. *Org. Behav. Hum. Perform.* 38:342–65

Idaszak, J. R., Carnevale, P. J. 1989. Third party power: some negative effects of positive incentives. *J. Appl. Soc. Psychol.* 19:499–516

Iklé, F. 1964. *How Nations Negotiate.* New York: Harper

Insko, C., Hoyle, R. H., Pinkley, R. L., Hong, G., Slim, R. M. 1988. Individual-group discontinuity: the role of a consensus rule. *J. Exp. Soc. Psychol.* 24:505–19

Insko, C. A., Pinkley, R. L., Hoyle, R. H., Dalton, B., Hong, G., et al 1987. Individual versus group discontinuity: the role of intergroup contact. *J. Exp. Soc. Psychol.* 23:250–67

Ippolito, C. A., Pruitt, D. G. 1990. Power balancing in mediation: outcomes and implications of mediator intervention. *Int. J. Confl. Manage.* 1:341–56

Jackson, E. 1952. *The Meeting of Minds: A Way to Peace Through Mediation.* New York: McGraw-Hill

Johnson, D. F., Pruitt, D. G. 1972. Pre-intervention effects of mediation versus arbitration. *J. Appl. Psychol.* 56:1–10

Johnson, D. F., Tullar, W. L. 1972. Style of third party intervention, face saving, and bargaining behavior. *J. Exp. Soc. Psychol.* 6:319–30

Johnson, D. W. 1967. The use of role reversal in intergroup competition. *J. Pers. Soc. Psychol.* 7:135–41

Johnson, D. W. 1971a. The effectiveness of role reversal: the actor or the listener. *Psychol. Reports* 28:275–82

Johnson, D. W. 1971b. The effects of warmth of interaction, accuracy of understanding, and the proposal of compromises on the listener's behavior. *J. Counsel. Psychol.* 18:207–16

Jönsson, C. 1991. Cognitive theory and international negotiation. See Kremenyuk 1991

Joseph, M. L., Willis, R. H. 1963. An experiment analog to two party bargaining. *Behav. Sci.* 8:117–27

Judd, C. M. 1978. Cognitive effects of attitude conflict resolution. *J. Confl. Resolut.* 22:483–98

Kahan, J. P. 1968. Effects of level of aspiration in an experimental bargaining situation. *J. Pers. Soc. Psychol.* 8:154–59

Kahneman, D., Knetsch, J. L., Thaler, R. H. 1990. Experimental tests of the endowment effect and the Coase theorem. *J. Polit. Econ.* 98:1325–48

Kahneman, D., Tversky, A. 1979. Prospect theory: an analysis of decision under risk. *Econometrica* 47:263–91

Kagel, J., Roth, A. E., eds. 1991. *Handbook of Experimental Economics.* Princeton, NJ: Princeton Univ. Press

Karambayya, R., Brett, J. M. 1989. Managers handling disputes: third party roles and perceptions of fairness. *Acad. Manage. J.* 32:687–704

Keenan, P. A., Carnevale, P. J. 1989. Positive effects of within-group cooperation on between-group negotiation. *J. Appl. Soc. Psychol.* 19:977–92

Kelley, H. H. 1964. Interaction process and the attainment of maximum joint profit. In *Decision and Choice,* ed. J. Messick, A. H. Brayfield. New York: McGraw-Hill

Kelley, H. H. 1966. A classroom study of the dilemmas in interpersonal negotiations. In *Strategic Interaction and Conflict: Original Papers and Discussion,* ed. K. Archibald. Berkeley, CA: Inst. Int. Stud.

Kelley, H. H., Beckman, L. L., Fischer, C. S. 1967. Negotiating the division of reward under incomplete information. *J. Exp. Soc. Psychol.* 3:361–98

Kelley, H. H., Schenitzki, D. P. 1972. Bargaining. In *Experimental Social Psychology,* ed. C. G. McClintock, pp. 298–337. New York: Holt

Kelley, H. H., Stahelski, A. J. 1970. Social interaction basis of cooperators' and competitors' beliefs about others. *J. Pers. Soc. Psychol.* 16:190–97

Kelly, J. B., Gigy, L. 1989. Divorce mediation: characteristics of clients and outcomes. See Kressel & Pruitt, pp. 263-83

Kelman, H. C., Cohen, S. P. 1979. Reduction of international conflict: an interactional approach. See Austin & Worchel 1979, pp. 288–303

Keltner, J. 1987. *Mediation: Toward a Civilized System of Dispute Resolution.* Urbana, IL: ERIC Clearinghouse on Reading and Communication Skills

Kerr, C. 1954. Industrial conflict and its mediation. *Am. J. Sociol.* 60:230–45

Kerr, N. L. 1986. Motivational choices in task groups: a paradigm for social dilemma research. See Wilke et al 1986, pp. 1–27

Kessler, S. 1978. *Creative Conflict Resolu-*

NEGOTIATION & MEDIATION 577

tion: Mediation Leader's Guide. Atlanta, GA: Natl. Inst. Prof. Train.

Kimmel, M., Pruitt, D. G., Magenau, J., Konar-Goldband, E., Carnevale, P. J. 1980. The effects of trust, aspiration, and gender on negotiation tactics. J. Pers. Soc. Psychol. 38:9–23

Klimoski, R. J. 1972. The effect of intragroup forces on intergroup conflict resolution. Org. Behav. Hum. Perform. 8:363–83

Klimoski, R. J., Ash, R. A. 1974. Accountability and negotiation behavior. Org. Behav. Hum. Perform. 11:409–25

Kochan, T. A., Jick, T. A. 1978. The public sector mediation process: a theory and empirical examination. J. Confl. Resolut. 22:209–40

Kogan, N., Lamm, H., Trommsdorff, G. 1972. Negotiation constraints in the risk-taking domain: effects of being observed by partners of higher or lower status. J. Pers. Soc. Psychol. 23:143–56

Kolb, D. 1983. The Mediators. Cambridge, MA: MIT Press

Kolb, D. 1986. Who are organizational third parties and what do they do? See Lewicki et al 1986

Kolb, D. 1989. Labor mediators, managers, and ombudsmen: roles mediators play in different contexts. See Kressel & Pruitt, pp. 91–114

Kolb, D., Rubin, J. Z. 1991. Mediation from a disciplinary perspective. See Bazerman et al 1991

Komorita, S. S. 1973. Concession making and conflict resolution. J. Confl. Resolut. 17:745–62

Komorita, S. S. 1984. Coalition bargaining. In Advances in Experimental Social Psychology, ed. L. Berkowitz, Vol. 18. New York: Academic

Komorita, S. S., Barnes, M. 1969. Effects of pressures to reach agreement in bargaining. J. Pers. Soc. Psychol. 13:245–52

Komorita, S. S., Esser, J. K. 1975. Frequency of reciprocated concessions in bargaining. J. Pers. Soc. Psychol. 32:699–705

Kramer, S. 1963. The Summarians: Their History, Culture, and Character. Chicago: Univ. Chicago Press

Kramer, R. M. 1990. Cooperative and competitive decision making in organizations: a social identity framework. Presented at 3rd Annu. Meet. Int. Assoc. Conflict Manage., Vancouver, British Columbia

Kremenyuk, V., ed. 1991. International Negotiation: Analysis, Approaches, Issues. San Francisco: Jossey-Bass

Kressel, K. 1972. Labor Mediation: An Exploratory Survey. Albany, NY: Assoc. Labor Mediation Agencies

Kressel, K., Pruitt, D. G. 1985. Themes in the mediation of social conflict. J. Soc. Issues 41:179–98

Kressel, K., Pruitt, D. G., eds. 1989. Mediation Research. San Francisco: Jossey-Bass. 457 pp.

Kuhlman, D. M., Camac, C. R., Cunha, D. A. 1986. Individual differences in social orientation. See Wilke et al 1986, pp. 151–76

Kuhlman, D. M., Marshello, A. 1975. Individual differences in game motivation as moderators of preprogrammed strategic effects in prisoner's dilemma. J. Pers. Soc. Psychol. 32:922–31

Lamm, H., Kayser, E. 1978. An analysis of negotiation concerning the allocation of jointly produced profit or loss: the role of justice norms, politeness, profit maximization, and tactics. Int. J. Group Tensions 8:64–80

Lamm, H., Rosch, E. 1972. Information and competitiveness of incentive structure as factors in two-person negotiation. Eur. J. Soc. Psychol. 2:459–62

Landsberger, H. A. 1955a. Interaction process analysis of professional behavior: a study of labor mediators in twelve labor-management disputes. Am. Sociol. Rev. 20:566–75

Landsberger, H. A. 1955b. Interaction process analysis of the mediation of labor-management disputes. J. Abnorm. Soc. Psychol. 51:552–59

Lawler, E. J., Ford, R. S., Blegen, M. A. 1988. Coercive capability in conflict: a test of bilateral deterrence versus conflict spiral theory. Soc. Psychol. Q. 51:93–107

Lax, D. A., Sebenius, J. K. 1986. The Manager as Negotiator. New York: Free Press

Leung, K. 1987. Some determinants of reactions to procedural models for conflict resolution: a cross national study. J. Pers. Soc. Psychol. 53:898–908

Leung, K., Wu, P. 1989. Dispute processing: a cross-cultural analysis. Presented at the Workshop on Textbooks in Cross-Cult. Psychol., East-West Center, Honolulu, Hawaii

Lewicki, R. J., Litterer, J. 1985. Negotiation. Homewood, IL: Richard D. Irwin

Lewicki, R. J., Weiss, S. E., Lewin, D. 1991. Models of conflict, negotiation and third party intervention: a review and synthesis. J. Organ. Behav. In press

Lewicki, R. J., Sheppard, B. H., Bazerman, M. H., eds. 1986. Research on Negotiation in Organizations, Vol. 1. Greenwich, CT: JAI Press

Lewis, S. A., Fry, W. R. 1977. Effects of visual access and orientation on the discovery of integrative bargaining alternatives. Org. Behav. Hum. Perform. 20:75–92

578 CARNEVALE & PRUITT

Liebert, R. M., Smith, W. P., Hill, J. H., Keiffer, M. 1968. The effects of information and magnitude of initial offer on interpersonal negotiation. *J. Exp. Soc. Psychol.* 4:431–41

Lim, R. G. 1990. *Framing mediator decisions through the development of expectations: a range-frequency explanation.* PhD thesis. Univ. Illinois, Urbana. 114 pp.

Lim, R. G., Carnevale, P. J. 1990. Contingencies in the mediation of disputes. *J. Pers. Soc. Psychol.* 58:259–72

Lind, E. A., Tyler, T. R. 1988. *The Social Psychology of Procedural Justice.* New York: Plenum

Lopes, L. L., Oden, G. C. 1991. The rationality of intelligence. In *Rationality and Reasoning*, ed. E. Eells, T. Maruszewski. Amsterdam: Rodopi

Lovell, H. 1952. The pressure lever in mediation. *Indust. Labor Relat. Rev.* 6:20–33

Maggiolo, W. A. 1985. *Techniques of Mediation.* New York: Oceana Publications

McGillicuddy, N. B., Pruitt, D. G., Syna, H. 1984. Perceptions of firmness and strength in negotiation. *Pers. Soc. Psychol. Bull.* 10:402–9

McGillicuddy, N. B., Welton, G. L., Pruitt, D. G. 1987. Third party intervention: a field experiment comparing three different models. *J. Pers. Soc. Psychol.* 53:104–12

McGillis, D. 1981. Conflict resolution outside the courts. In *Applied Social Psychology Annual*, ed. L. Bickman. Beverly Hills, CA: Sage

McLaughlin, M., Carnevale, P. J., Lim, R. 1991. Professional mediators judgments of mediation tactics: MDS and clustering analyses. *J. Appl. Psychol.* 76:465–72

Merry, S. E. 1982. The social organization of mediation in nonindustrial societies. See Abel 1982

Messé, L. A. 1971. Equity in bilateral bargaining. *J. Pers. Soc. Psychol.* 17:287–91

Messick, D. M., Brewer, M. B. 1983. Solving social dilemmas: a review. In *Review of Personality and Social Psychology*, ed. L. Wheeler, P. Shaver, 4:11–44. Beverly Hills: Sage

Messick, D. M., McClintock C. G. 1968. Motivational bases of choice in experimental games. *J. Exp. Soc. Psychol.* 4:1–25

Michener, H. A., Vaske, J. J., Schleiffer, S. L., Plazewski, J. G., Chapman, L. J. 1975. Factors affecting concession rate and threat usage in bilateral conflict. *Sociometry* 38:62–80

Mogy, R. B., Pruitt, D. G. 1974. Effects of a threatener's enforcement costs on threat credibility and compliance. *J. Pers. Soc. Psychol.* 29:173–80

Moore, C. W. 1986. *The Mediation Process: Practical Strategies for Resolving Conflict.* San Francisco: Jossey-Bass

Morley, I. E., Stephenson, G. M. 1977. *The Social Psychology of Bargaining.* London: Allen and Unwin

Murnighan, J. K. 1986. The structure of mediation and intravention: comments on Carnevale's strategic choice model. *Negot. J.* 2:351–56

Murnighan, J. K. 1991. *The Dynamics of Bargaining Games.* Englewood Cliffs, NJ: Prentice Hall

Nash, J. F. 1950. Equilibrium points in n-person games. *Proc. Natl. Acad. Sci.* 36:48–49

Neale, M. A. 1984. The effect of negotiation and arbitration cost salience on bargainor behavior: the role of arbitrator and constituency in negotiator judgment. *Org. Behav. Hum. Perform.* 34:97–111

Neale, M. A., Bazerman, M. H. 1985. The effects of framing and negotiator overconfidence on bargaining behaviors and outcomes. *Acad. Manage. J.* 28:34–49

Neale, M. A., Bazerman, M. H. 1991. *Negotiator Cognition and Rationality.* Free Press: New York

Neale, M. A., Huber, V. L., Northcraft, G. B. 1987. The framing of negotiations: contextual versus task frames. *Org. Behav. Hum. Dec. Proc.* 39:228–41

Nicolson, H. 1964. *Diplomacy.* New York: Oxford

Northcraft, G. B., Neale, M. A. 1987. Experts, amateurs, and real estate: an anchoring and adjustment perspective on property pricing decisions. *Org. Behav. Hum. Perform.* 39:84–97

Nyhart, J. D., Samarasan, D. K. 1989. The elements of negotiation management: using computers to help resolve conflict. *Negot. J.* 5:43–62

Organ, D. W. 1971. Some variables affecting boundary role behavior. *Sociometry* 34:524–37

Palenski, J. 1984. The use of mediation by police. *Mediat. Q.* 5:31–38

Peters, E. 1952. *Conciliation in Action.* New London, CT: Natl. Foremen's Inst.

Peters, E. 1955. *Strategy and Tactics in Labor Negotiations.* New London, CT: Natl. Foremen's Inst.

Pinkley, R. 1990. Dimensions of conflict frame. *J. Appl. Psychol.* 75:117–26

Podell, J. E., Knapp, W. M. 1969. The effect of mediation on the perceived firmness of the opponent. *J. Confl. Resolut.* 13:511–20

Poole, M. S., Zappa, J., DeSanctis, G., Shannon, D., Dickson, G. 1990. A theory and design for negotiation support systems. Presented at Annu. Meet. Acad. Manage., San Francisco

Prein, H. 1984. A contingency approach for conflict intervention. *Group Org. Stud.* 9:81–102

Pruitt, D. G. 1981. *Negotiation Behavior.* New York: Academic

Pruitt, D. G. 1986. Trends in the scientific study of negotiation and mediation. *Negot. J.* 2:237–44

Pruitt, D. G. 1990. Organizational negotiators as intermediaries. Presented at 3rd Annu. Meet. Int. Assoc. Confl. Manage., Vancouver, British Columbia

Pruitt, D. G. 1991. Strategy in negotiation. See Kremenyuk 1991

Pruitt, D. G., Carnevale, P. J., Ben-Yoav, O., Nochajski, T. H., Van Slyck, M. 1983. Incentives for cooperation in integrative bargaining. See Tietz 1983, pp. 22–34

Pruitt, D. G., Carnevale, P. J., Forcey, B., Van Slyck, M. 1986. Gender effects in negotiation: constituent surveillance and contentious behavior. *J. Exp. Soc. Psychol.* 22:264–75

Pruitt, D. G., Crocker, J., Hanes, D. L. 1987. Matching in social influence. In *Enhancing Human Performance: Issues, Theories, and Techniques,* ed. D. Druckman, J. Swets. Washington, DC: Natl. Academy Press

Pruitt, D. G., Drews, J. L. 1969. The effect of time pressure, time elapsed, and the opponent's concession rate on behavior in negotiation. *J. Exp. Soc. Psychol.* 5:43–60

Pruitt, D. G., Johnson, D. F. 1970. Mediation as an aid to face-saving in negotiation. *J. Pers. Soc. Psychol.* 14:239–46

Pruitt, D. G., Kimmel, M. J. 1977. Twenty years of experimental gaming: critique, synthesis, and suggestions for the future. *Annu. Rev. Psychol.* 28:363–92

Pruitt, D. G., Kimmel, M., Britton, S., Carnevale, P. J., Magenau, J., et al. 1978. The effect of accountability and surveillance on integrative bargaining. See Sauermann 1978

Pruitt, D. G., Lewis, S. A. 1975. Development of integrative solutions in bilateral negotiation. *J. Pers. Soc. Psychol.* 31:621–33

Pruitt, D. G., Pierce, R. S., Czaja, S. J., Keating, M. 1991a. Procedural choice in social conflict. Presented at 4th Annu. Meet. Int. Assoc. Confl. Manage., Ernst Sillem Hoeve, Den Dolder, The Netherlands

Pruitt, D. G., Pierce, R. S., Zubek, J. M., Welton, G. L., Nochajski, T. H. 1990. Goal achievement, procedural justice and the success of mediation. *Int. J. Confl. Manage.* 1:33–45

Pruitt, D. G., Pierce, R. S., Zubek, J. M., McGillicuddy, N. B., Welton, G. L., 1991b. Determinants of short-term and long-term success in mediation. In *Conflict Between People and Peoples,* ed. S. Wor-

chel, J. A. Simpson. Chicago: Nelson Hall. In press

Pruitt, D. G., Rubin, J. Z. 1986. *Social Conflict: Escalation, Stalemate, and Settlement.* New York: Random House

Pruitt, D. G., Syna, H. 1985. Mismatching the opponent's offers in negotiation. *J. Exp. Soc. Psychol.* 21:103–13

Pruitt, D. G., Welton, G. L., Fry, W. R., McGillicuddy, N. B., Castrianno, L., Zubek, J. M. 1989. The process of mediation: caucusing, control, and problem solving. See Rahim 1989

Putnam, L. L. 1990. Reframing integrative and distributive bargaining: a process perspective. See Sheppard et al 1990, pp. 3–30

Putnam, L. L., Poole, M. S. 1987. Conflict and negotiation. In *Handbook of Organizational Communication,* ed. F. M. Jablin, L. L. Putnam, K. H. Roberts, L. W. Porter, pp. 549–99. Beverly Hills, CA: Sage

Putnam, L. L., Roloff, M. E., eds. 1991. *Communication Perspectives on Negotiation.* Newbury Park, CA: Sage

Rahim, M. A., ed. 1986. *Managing Conflict in Organizations.* New York: Praeger

Rahim, M. A., ed. 1989. *Managing Conflict: An Interdisciplinary Approach.* New York: Praeger

Raiffa, H. 1982. *The Art and Science of Negotiation.* Cambridge, MA: Harvard Univ. Press

Raiffa, H. 1983. Mediation of conflicts. *Am. Behav. Sci.* 27:195–210

Raymond, G. A., Kegley, C. W. Jr. 1985. Third party mediation and international norms: a test of two models. *Confl. Manage. Peace Sci.* 9:33–51

Rehmus, C. M. 1965. The mediation of industrial conflict: a note on the literature. *J. Confl. Resolut.* 9:118–26

Ross, W. H. Jr., Conlon, D. E., Lind, E. A. 1990. The mediator as leader: effects of behavioral style and deadline certainty on negotiator behavior. *Group Org. Stud.* 15:105–24

Roth, A. E., ed. 1985. *Game-Theoretic Models of Bargaining.* Cambridge: Cambridge Univ. Press

Roth, A. E., Prasnikar, V., Okuno-Fujiwara, M., Zamir, S. 1991. Bargaining and market behavior in Jerusalem, Ljubljana, Pittsburgh, and Tokyo: an experimental study. *Am. Econ. Rev.* In press

Rothbart, M., Hallmark, W. 1988. Ingroup-outgroup differences in the perceived efficacy of coercion and conciliation in resolving social conflict. *J. Pers. Soc. Psychol.* 55:248–57

Rubin, J. Z. 1980. Experimental research on third-party intervention in conflict: toward some generalizations. *Psychol. Bull.* 87:379–91

Rubin, J. Z. 1981. Introduction. In *Dynamics of Third Party Intervention: Kissinger in the Middle East*, ed. J. Z. Rubin, pp. 3–43. New York: Praeger

Rubin, J. Z. 1985. Third party intervention in family conflict. *Negot. J.* 1:363–72

Rubin, J. Z., Brown, B. 1975. *The Social Psychology of Bargaining and Negotiations*. New York: Academic

Rubin, J. Z., Kim, S. H., Peretz, N. M. 1990. Expectancy effects and negotiation. *J. Soc. Issues* 46:125–39

Ruble, T. L., Thomas, K. W. 1976. Support for a two-dimensional model of conflict behavior. *Org. Behav. Hum. Perform.* 16: 143–55

Sauermann, H., ed. 1978. *Contributions to Experimental Economics*. Mohr: Tubingen

Schelling, T. 1960. *The Strategy of Conflict*. Cambridge: Harvard Univ. Press

Schlenker, B. R., Bonoma, T. V., Tedeschi, J. T., Pivnick, W. P. 1970 Compliance to threats as a function of the wording of the threat and the exploitativeness of the threatener. *Sociometry* 33:394–408

Schoeninger, D. W., Wood, W. D. 1969. Comparison of married and ad hoc mixed-sex dyads negotiating the division of a reward. *J. Exp. Soc. Psychol.* 5:483–99

Schulz, J. W., Pruitt, D. G. 1978. The effects of mutual concern on joint welfare. *J. Exp. Soc. Psychol.* 14:480–91

Shapiro, D., Driegh, R., Brett, J. M. 1985. Mediator behavior and the outcome of mediation. *J. Soc. Issues* 41:101–14

Sharma, A., Shapiro, D., Kesner, I. 1991. Targets of mergers: what factors predict their resistance. Presented at Annu. Meet. Acad. Manage., Miami

Shaw, J. I., Fischer, C. S., Kelley, H. H. 1973. Decision making by third parties in settling disputes. *J. Appl. Soc. Psychol.* 3: 197–18

Sheppard, B. H. 1984. Third party conflict intervention: a procedural framework. In *Research in Organizational Behavior*, ed. B. M. Staw, L. L. Cummings, 6:141–90. Greenwich, CT: JAI

Sheppard, B. H., Bazerman, M. H., Lewicki, R. J., eds. 1990. *Research on Negotiation in Organizations*, Vol. 2. Greenwich, CT: JAI

Sheppard, B. H., Blumenfold-Jones, K., Roth, J. 1989. Informal thirdpartyship: studies of everyday conflict intervention. See Kressel & Pruitt 1989, pp. 166–89

Sherman, S. J., Judd, C. M., Park, B. 1989. Social Cognition. *Annu. Rev. Psychol.* 40: 281–326

Siegel, S., Fouraker, L. E. 1960. *Bargaining and Group Decision Making: Experiments in Bilateral Monopoly*. New York: McGraw-Hill

Sillars, A. L. 1981. Attributions and interpersonal conflict resolution. In *New Directions in Attribution Research*, ed. J. H. Harvey, W. Ickes, R. F. Kidd, 3:279–305. Hillsdale, NJ: Lawrence Erlbaum

Simon, H. A. 1957. *Models of Man: Social and Rational*. New York: Wiley

Smith, D. L., Pruitt, D. G., Carnevale, P. J. 1982. Matching and mismatching: the effect of own limit, other's toughness, and time pressure on concession rate in negotiation. *J. Pers. Soc. Psychol.* 42:876–83

Smith, W. P. 1985. Effectiveness of the biased mediator. *Negot. J.* 1:363–72

Smith, W. P. 1987. Conflict and negotiation: trends and emerging issues. *J. Appl. Soc. Psychol.* 17:641–77

Sorrentino, R. M., Higgins, E. T. 1986. *Handbook of Motivation and Cognition: Foundations of Social Behavior*. New York: Guilford

Stephenson, G. M. 1981. Intergroup bargaining and negotiation. In *The Social Psychology of Intergroup Behavior*, ed. J. C. Turner, H. Giles, pp. 168–98. Oxford: Blackwell

Stevens, C. M. 1963. *Strategy and Collective Bargaining Negotiation*. New York: McGraw-Hill

Stoll, R. J., McAndrew, W. 1986. Negotiating strategic arms control, 1969–1979. *J. Confl. Resolut.* 30:315–26

Susskind, L., Cruikshank, J. 1987. *Breaking the Impasse*. New York: Basic Books

Susskind, L., Ozawa, C. 1985. Mediating public disputes: obstacles and possibilities. *J. Soc. Issues* 41:145–59

Taylor, S. E., Brown, J. D. 1988. Illusion and well being: a social-psychological perspective on mental health. *Psychol. Rev.* 103: 193–210

Tedeschi, J. T., Schlenker, B. R., Bonoma, T. V. 1973. *Conflict, Power, and Games*. Chicago: Aldine

Thibaut, J., Walker, L. 1975. *Procedural Justice: A Psychological Analysis*. Hillsdale, NJ: Erlbaum

Thomas, K. W. 1976. Conflict and conflict management. In *Handbook of Industrial and Organizational Psychology*, ed. M. Dunnette, pp. 889–935. Chicago: Rand McNally

Thomas, K. W. 1982. Manager and mediator: a comparison of third-party roles based upon conflict-management goals. See Bomers & Peterson 1982, pp. 119–40

Thompson, L. L. 1990a. The influence of experience on negotiation performance. *J. Exp. Soc. Psychol.* 26:528–44

Thompson, L. L. 1990b. Negotiation behavior and outcomes: empirical evidence and theoretical issues. *Psychol. Bull.* 108:515–32

Thompson, L. L. 1991. Information exchange in negotiation. *J. Exp. Soc. Psychol.* 27:161-79

Thompson, L. L., Hastie, R. 1990. Social perception in negotiation. *Org. Behav. Hum. Dec. Proc.* 47:98–123

Tietz, R., ed. 1983. *Aspiration Levels in Bargaining and Economic Decision Making.* Berlin: Springer

Tjosvold, D. 1977. Commitment to justice in conflict between unequal persons. *J. Appl. Soc. Psychol.* 7:149–62

Taylor, S. E., Crocker, J. 1981. Schematic bases of social information processing. See Higgins et al 1981, pp. 89–134

Tomasic, R. 1982. Mediation as an alternative to adjudication: rhetoric and reality in the neighborhood justice movement. In *Neighborhood Justice: an Assessment of an Emerging Idea,* ed. R. Tomasic, M. Feeley. New York: Longman

Touval, S. 1975. Biased intermediaries: theoretical and historical considerations. *Jerusalem J. Int. Relat.* 1:51–69

Touval, S. 1982. *The Peace Brokers: Mediators in the Arab-Israeli Conflict 1948–1979.* Princeton, NJ: Princeton Univ. Press

Touval, S., Zartman, I. W. 1985. *International Mediation in Theory and Practice.* Boulder, CO: Westview Press

Triandis, H. C. 1989. The self and social behavior in different cultural contexts. *Psychol. Rev.* 96:506–20

Tversky, A., Kahneman, D. 1974. Judgement under uncertainty: heuristics and biases. *Science* 185:1124–31

Tyler, T. R. 1987. The psychology of disputant concerns in mediation. *Negot. J.* 3:367–74

Underhill, C. I. 1981. *A Manual for Community Dispute Settlement.* Buffalo, NY: Better Business Bureau of Western New York

Ury, W., Brett, J. M., Goldberg, S. 1988. *Getting Disputes Resolved.* San Francisco: Jossey-Bass

Vallone, R. P., Ross, L., Lepper, M. R. 1985. The hostile media phenomenon: biased perception and perceptions of media bias in coverage of the Beirut massacre. *J. Pers. Soc. Psychol.* 49:577–85

van de Vliert, E., Prein, H. C. M. 1989. The difference in the meaning of forcing in the conflict management of actors and observers. See Rahim 1989

Vidmar, N. 1971. Effects of representational roles and mediators on negotiation effectiveness. *J. Pers. Soc. Psychol.* 17:48–58

Vidmar, N. 1985. An assessment of mediation in a small claims court. *J. Soc. Issues* 41:127–44

Vitz, P. C., Kite, W. R. 1970. Factors affecting conflict and negotiation within an alliance. *J. Exp. Soc. Psychol.* 5:233–47

Voissem, N. H., Sistrunk, F. 1971. Communication schedule and cooperative game behavior. *J. Pers. Soc. Psychol.* 19:160–67

Wahrhaftig, P. 1981. Dispute resolution retrospective. *Crime and Delinquency* 27:99–105

Wahrhaftig, P. 1982. An overview of community-oriented citizen dispute resolution programs in the United States. See Abel 1982

Wall, J. A. Jr. 1975. Effects of constituent trust and representative bargaining orientation on intergroup bargaining. *J. Pers. Soc. Psychol.* 31:1004–12

Wall, J. A. Jr. 1976. Effects of sex and opposing representative's bargaining orientation on intergroup bargaining. *J. Pers. Soc. Psychol.* 33:55–61

Wall, J. A. Jr. 1977a. Intergroup bargaining: effects of opposing constituents' stance, opposing representative's bargaining, and representatives' locus of control. *J. Confl. Resolut.* 21:459–74

Wall, J. A. Jr. 1977b. Operantly conditioning a bargainer's concession making. *J. Exp. Soc. Psychol.* 13:431-40

Wall, J. A. Jr. 1979. The effects of mediator rewards and suggestions upon negotiations. *J. Pers. Soc. Psychol.* 37:1554–60

Wall, J. A. Jr. 1981. Mediation: an analysis, review, and proposed research. *J. Confl. Resolut.* 25:157–80

Wall, J. A. Jr. 1985. *Negotiation: Theory and Practice.* Glenview, IL: Scott, Foresman

Wall, J. A. Jr., Blum, M. 1991. Community mediation in the People's Republic of China. *J. Confl. Resolut.* 35:3–20

Wall, J. A. Jr., Rude, D. E. 1985. Judicial mediation: techniques, strategies, and situational effects. *J. Soc. Issues* 41:47–63

Wall, J. A. Jr., Rude, D. E. 1987. Judge's mediation of settlement negotiations. *J. Appl. Psychol.* 72:234–39

Wall, J. A. Jr., Rude, D. E. 1991. The judge as mediator. *J. Appl. Psychol.* 76:54–59

Walton, R. E. 1969. *Interpersonal Peacemaking: Confrontations and Third-Party Consultation.* Reading, MA: Addison-Wesley

Walton, R., McKersie, R. 1965. *A Behavioral Theory of Labor Negotiations: An Analysis of a Social Interaction System.* New York: McGraw-Hill

Welton, G. L., Pruitt, D. G. 1987. The mediation process: the effects of mediator bias and disputant power. *Pers. Soc. Psychol. Bull.* 13:123–33

Welton, G. L., Pruitt, D. G., McGillicuddy, N. B. 1988. The role of caucusing in community mediation. *J. Confl. Resolut.* 32:181–202

582   CARNEVALE & PRUITT

White, R. K. 1984. *Fearful Warriors: A Psychological Profile of U. S.-Soviet Relations.* New York: The Free Press

Wichman, H. 1972. Effects of communication on cooperation in a 2-person game. In *Cooperation and Competition,* ed. L. Wrightsman, J. O'Connor, N. Baker. Belmont, CA: Brooks/Cole

Wilke, H. A. M., Messick, D. M., Rutte, C. G., eds. 1986. *Experimental Social Dilemmas.* New York: Lang. 235 pp.

Williams, D. L., Lewis, S. A. 1976. The effects of sex-role attitudes on integrative bargaining. Presented at the 84th Annu. Meet. Am. Psychol. Assoc., Washington, DC

Wittmer, J., Carnevale, P. J., Walker, M. 1991. General alignment and overt support in biased mediation. *J. Confl. Resolut.* In press

Young, O. R. 1967. *The Intermediaries: Third Parties in International Crises.* Princeton, NJ: Princeton Univ. Press

Young, O. R. 1972. Intermediaries: additional thoughts on third parties. *J. Confl. Resolut.* 16:51–65

Young, O. R., ed. 1975. *Bargaining: Formal Theories of Negotiation.* Urbana: Univ. Illinois Press

Yukl, G. A. 1974a. The effects of situational variables and opponent concessions on a bargainer's perception, aspirations, and concessions. *J. Pers. Soc. Psychol.* 29:227–36

Yukl, G. A. 1974b. Effects of opponents initial offer, concession magnitude, and concession frequency on bargaining behavior. *J. Pers. Soc. Psychol.* 30:332–35

Yukl, G. A., Malone, M. P., Hayslip, B., Pamin, T. A. 1976. The effects of time pressure and issue settlement order on integrative bargaining. *Sociometry* 39:277–81

Zartman, I. W. 1977. Negotiation as a joint decision-making process. *J. Confl. Resolut.* 21:619–38

Zartman, I. W. ed. 1978. *The Negotiation Process.* Beverly Hills, CA: Sage

Zartman, I. W., Berman, M. R. 1982. *The Practical Negotiator.* New Haven, CN: Yale Univ. Press

Zeuthen, F. 1930. *Problems of Monopoly and Economic Warfare.* London: Routledge and Kegan Paul

Zubek, J. M., Pruitt, D. G., Peirce, R. S., Iocolano, A. 1989. Mediator and disputant characteristics and behavior as they affect the outcome of community mediation. Presented at 2nd Annu. Meet. Int. Assoc. Confl. Manage., Athens, GA

Annu. Rev. Psychol. 1992. 43:583–626

INSTRUCTIONAL PSYCHOLOGY: APTITUDE, ADAPTATION, AND ASSESSMENT

Richard E. Snow and Judy Swanson

School of Education, Stanford University, Stanford, California 94305

KEY WORDS: learning and individual differences, tutoring, grouping for instruction

CONTENTS

INTRODUCTION

Instructional psychology narrowly defined is the science of human learning in situations explicitly designed to promote it; its goals are to understand knowledge and skill acquisition and to devise principles of effective instructional

583

treatment. Broadly defined, the field becomes educational psychology, including learner cognitive, conative, and affective development across learning situations; individual differences in these functions; the structure of knowledge in different domains; the nature of teachers and teaching; the social organization of learning; and the measurement and evaluation of all these factors. But the deepest issues in instructional psychology—what it means to learn, know, and be skilled in a domain of knowledge—are one with those of cognitive science. This convergence became obvious in the 1980s, as instructional psychology clearly joined the mainstream of theory and research on human learning, cognition, and development. Cognitive scientists now see understanding performance on instructional tasks as crucial to improving basic theory, and instructional scientists now see that improving such performance requires basic theory. Increasingly, also, cognitive scientists and instructional scientists are the same people.

To grasp the field's advance in breadth and depth, one reads the 1980s reviews (Resnick 1981; Gagné & Dick 1983; Pintrich, et al 1986; Glaser & Bassok 1989). But one must now also review work on cognitive science (Hunt 1989; Simon 1990), the social contexts of instruction (Sarason & Klaber 1985; Weinstein 1991), and the range of related topics appearing in new European as well as US sources (e.g. DeCorte et al 1987; Mandl et al 1990). We choose references to identify new sources where possible. It is hoped that the forthcoming *Handbook of Educational Psychology* (being edited by Berliner & Calfee) will provide a comprehensive listing.

This chapter uses the taxonomic structure of 1980s reviews, and a first section notes theoretical issues in general terms. But only parts of that structure are then sampled. Given the new thematic emphasis in the *Annual Review,* we devote our space to work on individual differences in learning and adaptive instructional design, with notes also on assessment. Our choice should complement Glaser & Bassok's (1989) coverage of learning and achievement theory in particular instructional programs and Weinstein's (1991) emphasis on classroom teaching.

THEORETICAL PROBLEMS

Components of Instructional Theory

Building on Glaser's (1976, 1977) views, we distinguish five essential components of an instructional theory: (*a*) description of desired end states or goals of instruction in a domain; (*b*) description of goal-relevant initial states of learners prior to instruction; (*c*) explication of the transition processes from initial to desired states; (*d*) specification of instructional conditions that promote this transition; and (*e*) assessment of performance and instructional effects. For short, we refer to these components as achievement, aptitude, learning, treatment design, and assessment theories, respectively.[1] For any given instructional domain, then, one could lay out a taxonomy of the important aptitude, learning, and achievement constructs, the major instructional treatment designs, and the approaches to assessment used to study the complex of effects observed. Instructional theories might then be fashioned to link constructs and designs across categories for particular purposes.

Glaser & Bassok (1989) were able to identify several such linkages of learning, achievement, and treatment design constructs that have been developed in recent years. However, issues concerning aptitude, assessment, and adaptive instruction were largely ignored in these developments. Furthermore, the construction of theory on the full framework faces several unresolved tensions. Some of these problems were noted by Glaser & Bassok (1989) as agenda for future research.

Current Tensions

Current research seems to be fragmented and specialized, with programs focusing on different aptitude, learning, and achievement constructs, levels of analysis, subject matter domains, student populations, and instructional methods; their results lead to different learning and instructional theories, and some of these seem incompatible. While divergent thinking can be healthy for a field, a growing implication is that no unified theory of learning from instruction is possible. Glaser & Bassok (1989) urge research aimed at testing integrative approaches before accepting this conclusion. Iran-Nejad et al (1990) also argue that the multisource nature of learning demands integrative process constructs as the focus of new research. But there are many directions in which to seek integration, each involves complicated issues, and many of these hinge on how learner aptitude differences are handled. We treat these issues in two groups; those that seem to make general theory local by specialization within boundaries of some sort, and those that concern choices of theoretical units, levels, and goals.

GENERAL VS LOCAL THEORY   Theories may be specialized for different types of learning, knowledge domains, and instructional treatments, but also for different learning situations and populations. These facets may also interact.

Types of tasks and processes   The problem of taxonomy for different learning tasks goes back decades, but some modern reviews provide new twists.

---

[1]The fifth component could be termed evaluation theory, to include assessment methodology and instructional evaluation design and interpretation more generally (as in Cronbach 1982). But this goes beyond our boundaries here.

Kyllonen & Shute (1989) considered the integration of taxonomies of learning skills based on correlational constructs vs computer models for use in describing and comparing adaptive tutoring systems. They make connections between particular ability and learning constructs that deserve research attention, and also distinguish knowledge type, subject-matter domain, and learning strategy as facets in the taxonomy. Strategy distinctions in particular link learner differences to differences in instructional environments. Ryan's (1981) framework brought back the importance of learner intentions in comparing kinds of learning and memory, and included affective learning as a kind. This helps integrative thinking about cognition and motivation; it recognizes as well that intentions vary across learners (Bereiter & Scardamalia 1989). Greeno & Simon (1988) identified several kinds of cognitive processes and structures in analyses of problem solving. They contrast well- vs ill-structured problems that do vs do not involve domain- specific knowledge, and are novel vs familiar, for novices vs experts. Novices attempting novel, knowledge-lean tasks rely on flexible general-purpose abilities and strategies. As knowledge-relevance and expertise increase, there are shifts to domain-specialized mental representations and processing strategies, and then to automatic recognition and solution processes, at least for well-structured problems. With difficult, ill-structured, or novel problems, however, experts revert to the general, weak methods of novices. We do not yet understand these shifts, upward or downward, on the expert-novice continuum, nor have we studied individual differences in this respect. There may be thresholds for problem difficulty and learner ability, within problem types, that separate heuristic from algorithmic processing; only in zones around these thresholds may learning and problem solving be optimal (Elshout 1987).

In short, the kind of information processing one expects in an instructional situation depends on the match between task demands and learner abilities, the learning strategies a situation affords the learner, and learner intentions in the situation. The question of general vs special theory rests in part on whether or not process models for each of these person-situation interfaces are compatible.

Specialization by knowledge domain   Another old issue made new is whether special theories are needed for different subject matter domains. Two questions are: (*a*) to what degree are different domains characterized by unique knowledge structure and procedure, and (*b*) to what degree does learner progress in a domain depend on mastery of this knowledge?

On the second question, much research has shown that knowledge is highly domain specialized and a prime source of cognitive development, from child to adult and from novice to expert (Carey 1988; Chi et al 1988; Vosniadou & Brewer 1987). However, this conclusion can be criticized (Peverly 1991;

Sternberg 1989). Clearly, knowledge is acquired through active use in problem solving toward specific goals within a domain, but domain-general principles and strategies interact with domain-specific principles and strategies in this process (Perkins & Simmons 1988; Pressley et al 1989; Resnick 1987; Resnick & Neches 1984; Schneider & Pressley 1989). Also, the mix of general and special may vary across domains and across learners within a domain.

The first question is epistemological; to address it, psychologists must read curriculum theorists as well as domain experts. This is happening, especially in research on mathematics and science learning (Gardner et al 1990; Nesher & Kilpatrick 1990; Schoenfeld 1987; Shulman & Ringstaff 1989). But the answer may mean adopting a viewpoint alien to many instructional psychologists. As Shulman (1990:307) put it:

> Different texts from different disciplines call for quite different forms of reading. We do not learn that from psychology; we learn it from the discipline itself.... We put the content first and then ask . . . psychology . . . to adapt to the subject matter.. . . This represents a real challenge to the hegemony of a certain kind of information-processing model in accounting for human cognition.

As research expands into other instructional domains, such as art (Eisner 1987; Jackson 1987; Somerville & Hartley 1986), computer programming (Mayer 1988), engineering (Vincenti 1990), history (Wineburg 1991), music (Hargreaves 1986; Serafine 1986; Sloboda 1985), and social studies (Voss 1986; Voss et al 1989), this issue must be faced. Research on school tasks that reflect ability with different kinds of symbol systems may also contribute here (Hatch & Gardner 1990). In short, different domains may promote the development of different kinds of aptitude; in each, experts become adapted to its specialized styles of learning and thinking. Acquiring expertise means becoming more and more different from novices, but also more and more different from experts in other domains.

Specialization by instructional treatment   Different treatment designs may also promote specialized learning styles adapted to their characteristics. As with content domains, some students adapt to and adopt these styles more readily than others (Kyllonen & Shute 1989). Glaser & Bassok (1989) summarized work on two kinds of treatment design, termed here "mastery" and "guided discovery." Mastery imposes specific transition paths through progressive curriculum units that represent sequenced subgoals. It is relatively structured, explicit, and complete, with substantial system control over feedback and correction. Discovery provides a learning environment to explore with guidance and assistance as needed. It represents an end goal in itself, and places more responsibility on learners for structuring and controlling instruction; it is thus less structured and complete, relative to mastery instruction. The dichotomy oversimplifies, glossing over other treatment variations. But as prototypes the two represent different treatment design theories relying on different assumptions about optimum learning. As these two major kinds of instructional treatment fit different knowledge domains, and different kinds of learners, rather different learning and achievement theories seem required.

Specialization by situation   The situation in which learning occurs is also an inherent part of the learning experience (Brown et al 1989; Greeno 1989a,b; Lave 1988; Rogoff 1990). If learning is adaptation to a situation, then it is situated in some sense; it exists in the person-situation interaction, not solely in the learner's head (Snow 1991). The special features of particular domains and treatment designs are part of the situation, but so are other features of the physical-ecological (Gibson 1979; McCabe & Balzano 1986) and social-historical (Vygotsky 1978; Moll 1990) environment. If the concept of situated cognition interprets learning and thinking processes as relative to particular person-situation interactions, then these processes might be seen as specialized for and limited to these interactions. Situated learning over long development, as in apprenticeships, may produce situation-limited expertise—i.e. transfer only within a situation type (Palincsar 1989; Wineburg 1989). However, general as well as special abilities do develop, and learners learn how to learn, think, and reason from one situation to another; the issue then is finding an integrative theory of transfer that accounts for generalization, specialization, and situated processes. Recent work confronts this problem from several perspectives (Greeno et al 1992; Perkins & Salomon 1989; Salomon & Perkins 1989; Singley & Anderson 1989; Vosniadou & Ortony 1989).

Specialization by population   Just as different domains, treatments, and learning situations may define boundaries wherein different theories apply, so may differences among human populations. Indeed, the sociocultural perspective noted above sees other persons in the social ecology as significant features of the learning situation for each individual. One hypothesis is that instructional theories need to be specialized to fit different ethnic and cultural styles of social interaction (Cole 1985; Tharp 1989). An older question concerns whether different instructional theories are needed for qualitatively distinct stages and domains of child development (Case 1985; Siegler 1986). Such hypotheses have been expressed at one time or another regarding gender differences, socioeconomic differences, and even national differences. International comparisons of achievement in elementary mathematics, for example, suggest that qualitatively different configurations of home and school factors account for learning variations in different cultural contexts (Stigler et al 1990; Stevenson et al 1992).

THEORETICAL UNITS, LEVELS, AND GOALS   The other group of tensions concerns what units and levels of analysis seem most useful for what theoretical and instructional goals. This "grain size" problem arises because instruction requires analysis simultaneously on minute-to-minute, day-to-day, month-to-month, and year-to-year scales, yet theoretical units come in different sizes from different parts of the taxonomy; aptitude, learning, achievement, treatment design, and assessment constructs are often nonconformable.

The need for small units   Molar aptitude, treatment, and achievement constructs need to be decomposed into components of knowledge and skill that can usefully guide instructional and assessment design (Snow & Lohman 1989). Rejecting behavioral objectives as units (Case & Bereiter 1984) still leaves a range of alternatives. Several kinds of information-processing components have been defined and used in both test and training design (Sternberg 1985, 1986). Units based on analyses of learner actions with content, such as remembering or applying rules or concepts, and connected to specific test items, form the basis for a variety of prescriptive instructional designs (Gagné et al 1988; Reigeluth 1987). But other instructional tasks and situations seem to call for quite different psychological units.

At a finer grain, designers of computerized instruction identify "just learnable units," to fit psychological and engineering constraints (Wenger 1987). For example, a learnable unit might be constrained to present no more than one branch of a decision tree in procedural learning, and not to exceed one frame on the computer screen. Presumably, the size of instructional increments is limited by the learner's working memory capacity, by how well developed the knowledge structure already is when a new unit is incorporated into it, and by how coherent that unit is with existing structure. Thus, the learnable unit size varies with age, ability, and prior knowledge of the learner. Still another small unit is needed for assessment in computerized instruction. Burton's (1982) criterion of diagnostic discernability defines the unit of knowledge as the smallest that can be individually mislearned, and detected as such. Complete understanding, then, is the avoidance of all possible errors on all possible problems. Such small units may be useful in particular contexts; but much current controversy about achievement tests vs instructional goals concerns mismatch of unit sizes and levels of description (Frederiksen 1984; Nitko 1989).

The need for large units   To represent instructional goals in larger units, cognitive theorists have used several kinds of knowledge structure and phase distinctions (Anderson 1987; Norman 1982; Shuell 1990). Semantic networks, schemas, production systems, scripts, prototypes, images, and mental models are examples; so are the learning phases of accretion, structuring, and tuning, or alternatively, of declarative knowledge acquisition, compilation, proceduralization, and automatization. Each such unit has advantages and disadvantages, fitting some tasks or domains but not others. None seems to capture the multivariate, person-situation interactive nature of complex learning, or the sense of coordinated, adaptive whole performance exhibited by able learners or experts. Similarly, the catalog of aptitude constructs describing learner differences is only a list of distinct, static variables. Larger theoretical units seem needed.

Part of the problem is attacked when multiple aptitude constructs are combined with situational features to form "aptitude complexes" (Snow 1987, 1992). But a more complete solution may come from Bereiter's (1990) notion of "acquired contextual modules" as the appropriate unit for educational learning theory. Such a unit addresses a level distinct from extant theories; it describes adaptation via learning over significant time blocks of a whole complex of knowledge, skills, goals, feelings, and their interrelations. The adaptation is to a distinctive situational context, involving a network of relations among parts not reducible to parts alone. Bereiter's examples are modules for public speaking, schoolwork, and intentional learning.

Adaptation and instructional goals   Ideally, instruction should promote learner acquisition of new and improved contextual modules, in part by adapting to individual differences that otherwise impede learning. But research on adaptive instruction is divided among several approaches. Some work aims at macroadaptive decisions, perhaps on a month-to-month scale, whereas other research concerns the microadaptive decisions needed to steer instruction on a minute-to-minute scale. Some work attempts to remediate detected weaknesses in initial states directly, whereas some seeks to circumvent weaknesses that cannot easily be removed. Also, alternative instructional routes toward common goals can be fit to capitalize on learner strengths, or learners can be given control of choices among optional routes. Although there are theoretical and practical tensions among these approaches, too, they are not really alternatives; the problem is finding integrations (Corno & Snow 1986; Tobias 1987, 1989; Wang & Lindvall 1984). Unfortunately, most recent work has sought direct remediation, microadaptation, or learner control of options, not integration.

Conclusion

A basic issue for theory and taxonomy in instructional psychology is "carving to find the joints." The matrix of aptitudes × learning types × content domains × instructional designs × situations × populations must be partitioned into regions within which coherent descriptions and common principles apply. And these must be stated, for each region, in units and levels that are both theoretically and instructionally tractable. To reach this goal, research must find ways to integrate across rows and columns in this matrix where possible and identify boundary conditions in it where necessary. The sections below review research that moves toward these ends, with particular reference to the adaptation of learners to instruction and vice versa.

APTITUDES FOR LEARNING

Aptitudes are initial states reflecting the learning history of each student that then influence learning from present instruction. Momentary states that are easily changed, such as knowing a specific fact, are excluded. The concept of aptitude, in both origin and recent usage, is not limited to cognitive abilities; it covers conative and affective characteristics, prior differences in relevant knowledge and skill, personal beliefs about self and world, and characteristic styles and strategies that affect learning in one or another situation (Snow 1989b,c). Analyses of these initial states should help suggest ways to design adaptive instruction by capitalizing on individual strengths to circumvent weaknesses, or to remove weaknesses by direct aptitude training.

Whenever instruction aims at transfer, furthermore, the desired end states are also aptitudes for further learning, so education is largely an aptitude-development program (Cronbach & Snow 1977; Glaser 1977). Bereiter's (1990) acquired modules are aptitude constructs in this sense. Ultimately, understanding aptitude development through education requires longitudinal research on individual differences in development, transfer, and ability organization. Although some work in this direction is noted initially, we focus here on understanding aptitudes for learning cross-sectionally.

Cognitive Aptitudes

ABILITY ORGANIZATION AND DEVELOPMENT   Carroll's (1989, 1992) massive reanalysis of previous factor analytic evidence yields an integrated hierarchical model with first-order abilities incorporated into the second-order domains of fluid reasoning, crystallized language, visual perception, auditory perception, memory, speed, and idea production, under a third-order general intelligence (G). A similar list comes from Horn's (1989) extensive work. Furthermore, Gustafsson (1984, 1988, 1989) demonstrated that fluid reasoning ability can be equated with G, that residualizing crystallized and visualization ability for G then reproduces Vernon's (1950) hierarchical model, and that both broad and narrow abilities are needed in studying individual differences in learning from instruction; the two levels can relate differently to achievement, within or between treatments, and the presence of each level is needed to clarify the influence of the other.

Expanding research on individual differences in development is now bringing differential, developmental, and instructional psychology into intersection. Two programs serve as examples. In one, longitudinal patterns of ability differences (Demetriou & Efklides 1987) are related to differences in learning activities and interests (Undheim & Gustafsson 1989), to direct training and transfer effects (Gustafsson et al 1989) and to different domains of educational achievement (Balke-Aurell 1982; Gustafsson & Balke-Aurell 1989). The results, though complicated, support Ferguson's (1954, 1956) theory of differential ability development through specialization of learning and transfer over time, and seem also akin to Bereiter's (1990) view. G is here interpreted as reflecting cognitive processing complexity, a view consistent with other developmental and differential theory (Case 1985; Snow & Lohman 1984). The other program studies cognitive, motivational, and social development and individual differences longitudinally across initial school entry (Weinert & Schneider 1991; Weinert & Perlmutter 1988). Although general results are not yet available, particular findings of interest below concern interactions of aptitudes, knowledge, and strategies within particular instructional contexts (Schneider & Weinert 1990; Weinert 1989).

ABILITY AND KNOWLEDGE CONSTRUCTS   Old and new theory and research on particular cognitive aptitudes is reviewed elsewhere (Lohman 1989a; Thorndike & Lohman 1989; Snow & Lohman 1989; Tobias 1987, 1989). Here we merely update these summaries.

Fluid analytic reasoning ability (G_f) G_f is interpreted as facility in assembly and control of processing strategies needed for flexible adaptation of learning and problem solving, particularly in novel situations. Instruction that aims at novel, complex, or abstract learning goals and is relatively inductive, indirect, incomplete, or unstructured is thought to place heavy demands on G_f and thus to produce strong correlations of G_f with learning. Most discovery treatments, for example, require students to analyze puzzling situations, generate inferences about them, and keep track of their own progress through the problem, without strong support from the instructional program or teacher. But teacher-controlled instruction often requires student G_f also, if it is complex, confusing, or incomplete, leaving key concepts or relations to be inferred by learners.

G_f is represented by inductive reasoning tasks, such as analogies and series completions. Componential analyses have identified encoding, inference, application, and evaluation processes in performance on these tasks. These components have been used to trace ability development (Pellegrino 1985; Sternberg 1984, 1985), to target direct training (Sternberg 1986), and to combine with other resources in describing creativity (Sternberg & Lubart 1991).

New work examines Raven Progressive Matrices as perhaps the best measure of G_f; Raven items require rule discovery and use in a two-way matrix of abstract figures to decide which response figure completes the matrix. Tullos (1987) studied high school students, concluding that rule inference and application components were central; errors involved inferring wrong rules or omitting rules. Results supported previous findings that high-scoring students tend to construct answers analytically before searching response alternatives to find a match, whereas lower-scoring students more often use response-elimination strategies (Bethell-Fox et al 1984). Carpenter et al (1990), furthermore, presented a computer simulation theory that Raven measures "the common ability to decompose problems into manageable segments and iterate through them, the differential ability to manage the hierarchy of goals and subgoals generated by this problem decomposition, and the differential ability to form higher level abstractions" (p. 429). On this view, discovery instruction requires G_f primarily because it demands rule and subgoal analysis and management in working memory. The model is based on college student performance and leaves out visual encoding, strategic assembly, and rule induction processes as sources of individual differences. The Tullos study and other prior work would emphasize rule induction and assembly.

Further work is needed to bridge the ability and education levels contrasted in these studies, but Carpenter et al note that direct training to promote analytic strategy use and reduce response elimination and other extraneous processes could make the measure and their theory more valid. They cite evidence that such training can increase correlations of Raven with other tests; presumably, training constrains individual differences in Raven performance to those sources represented in the computer model. This assumes that sources of variance thus eliminated are irrelevant to understanding the correlation of G_f with learning from instruction.

Research on G_f as aptitude for learning also needs to compare such models with the sorts of informal reasoning and knowledge used by beginners in a new domain (Voss et al 1989). Studies contrasting G_f and domain knowledge differences have begun to show some instances where low G_f is unimportant relative to prior knowledge (Schneider et al 1990) and others where G_f is more important than prior knowledge (Langstaff 1989). But most interaction questions remain unaddressed (Schneider & Weinert 1990).

New demonstrations that G_f can be trained are plentiful (Budoff 1987; Campione & Brown 1987, 1990; DeLeeuw et al 1987; Feuerstein et al 1987; Klauer 1990). Training research on related thinking and reasoning skills is covered by Baron & Sternberg (1987), Segal et al (1985), Chipman et al (1985b), Nickerson et al (1985), and Resnick (1987).

Visual spatial abilities (G_v) G_v stands for facility in visualization of figural-spatial situations and mental operations applied to them (e.g. rotation, reflection, analysis, and synthesis). Also included are skill in imagining spatial situations seen from different perspectives, remembering and controlling visual images, and identifying figures or objects in fragmented or degraded form. G_v and G_f are hard to distinguish empirically; their measures allow both analytic and spatial solution strategies, and adaptive strategy shifting is a mark of able performance on both (Lohman 1988).

G_v abilities relate to learning and performance in some vocational, industrial, and military training domains, and in aspects of art, architecture, dentistry, engineering, and medicine. Depending on topic, treatment design, and grade level, G_v differences can be important to learning in mathematics (Ben-Chaim et al 1989; Bishop 1989; Hershkowitz 1989) and science (Pribyl & Bodner 1985). Several new studies show G_v skills to be trainable (Ben-Chaim 1988; Schiano & Kahleifeh 1988); computer graphic techniques appear particularly useful here (Lajoie 1986; Zavotka 1987). Since gender differences appear on some spatial tasks (Baenninger & Newcombe 1989; Linn & Petersen 1985; Lord 1987), G_v training may help more female students advance in mathematics and science.[2]

Improved methods for diagnostic assessment of G_v are now appearing (Bejar 1986; Embretson 1987; Ohlsson 1990). But much deeper analysis of spatial thinking in domains such as geometry or mechanics is required for both assessment and instructional design; Soviet work seems particularly advanced here (Yakimanskaya 1991). Instructional improvement depends on knowing when and how to capitalize on G_v for some students while circumventing it for others. Some learners and some learning tasks require the invention of strategies that circumvent the process of visualization (Rock et al 1989).

Crystallized verbal abilities (G_c) G_c denotes crystallized abilities centered on vocabulary and reading comprehension, but including related language skills and verbal knowledge. Process analytic research is summarized by Hunt (1985), Perfetti (1985), Sternberg (1987), and Lohman (1989a). Both improved assessment and direct training of component reading skills based on these process models are demonstrable (Calfee 1982; Frederiksen & Warren 1987). Also, verbal deficiencies can be helped by capitalizing on other aptitudes (Byrd Smith 1989).

Perfetti (1989) argues that reading comprehension is a general ability impenetrable by knowledge influences from outside the module in which its linguistic components reside. Word identification, sentence parsing, and propositional encoding are encapsulated components that produce text models of meaning (Kintsch 1988). When differential prior knowledge influences text comprehension, this reflects text interpretation (and Kintsch's situation mod-

---

[2]Regarding research on gender, mathematics, and science in general, see Chipman et al (1985a); Harding (1986); Hyde & Linn (1986); Hyde et al (1990).

els), not text meaning. Thus, instruction can provide practice with texts in different knowledge domains to develop skills and strategies of reading to learn. But learning to read means learning to achieve meaning from print— i.e. modular coordination of coding, parsing, and meaning identification skills. Thus, phonics and look-say treatment designs should not be separated and contrasted; instruction should be engineered to integrate the two.

The Just & Carpenter (1992) theory of differential working memory capacity also applies to the computational and storage demands of language comprehension. For individuals with larger capacities, syntactic processing is not encapsulated but can use pragmatic knowledge; such persons can also maintain multiple interpretations, keep track of syntactic complications, and more readily meet other demands of complex verbal processing. Componential theories are accommodated by assuming that each inefficient component robs some working memory capacity, but individual differences in overall capacity is the central issue. Thus, treatment designs should fit the working memory capacities of targeted learners.

Mathematical abilities   Factor models usually list mathematical ability as a mixture of crystallized knowledge, fluid reasoning, and numerical speed. Correspondingly, Mayer (1985) summarized task analyses of mathematical problem-solving performance showing individual differences in knowledge related to problem representation, translation, and schema identification, then strategy differences in solution planning, and then computation automaticity in reaching solutions. Resnick & Omanson (1987) reviewed research on arithmetic understanding to emphasize the complex interplay between reflection on principles and automatization of procedure.

Gelman & Greeno (1989; Greeno 1989b, 1992) have now analyzed early mathematical competence to suggest that children bring implicit principles as initial states to instruction. Although components of mathematical performance usually are regarded as skills to be trained onto a blank slate, children have at least intuitive concepts of counting, number, and sets even before school begins; this early principled knowledge tunes selective attention and allows learning to be generative, rather than just receptive, from the start. In effect, early principles are constraints that help learners assemble and monitor successful plans for performance, including novel plans. New meanings and principles are built onto this basic structure, allowing broader transfer as new tasks appear in the domain. It follows that assessment of initial states in mathematics should be geared to detect understanding of these principles, and new instruction should relate to them meaningfully. Such assessment and instruction concerns not just what students "already know"; it also addresses what students can perceive in novel situations and generate as mental models for reasoning therein. Along similar lines, Soviet work has identified the sensory and perceptual skills involved in such situations (Leushina 1991).

Early growth in mathematical ability, and in science and other subject matters, may be thought of as development in central conceptual structures (Case 1985, 1992; Case & Griffin 1989; Case & McKeough 1989). A major feature of the development of these structures is the number of dimensions children can operate with simultaneously, which is constrained by working memory capacity as it varies within as well as across ages. So again minute-to-minute instruction must be adapted to working memory differences. But Case and his coworkers have also designed macro-level treatments for conceptual and strategic development.

Other knowledge and beliefs   Knowledge organization and content differences form parts of many aptitude constructs, beyond G_c and mathematical ability. Work on central conceptual structures just noted may help define just how many such domain-specialized aptitude constructs are needed. But even more specific knowledge differences, personal beliefs and preconceptions can influence learning.

Specific knowledge differences can function in relation to instructional treatments just as G_c does (Tobias 1987); indeed, domain knowledge and G_c are usually correlated. Strong prior knowledge is an asset to be capitalized upon, especially in some instructional treatments (Whitener 1989).

Some learner preconceptions offer alternative creditable ideas that may conflict with a teacher's concepts, and some may be wrong or misleading. Some may be tightly organized into naive theories that resemble the theories of earlier centuries—in science for example (see Marton 1983; McCloskey & Kargon 1988; Wiser 1988). All can be serious impediments to learning if not detected and dealt with. Clearly, adaptation here involves unlearning and relearning. Instruction may need to recapitulate theoretical transitions in history to help learners escape their naive theories. Conceptual recapitulation is a means of remediating learning problems by retracing instructionally what should have been naturally occurring developmental stages (Case et al 1986); it might fit the historical recapitulation hypothesis as well. Given the research on early mathematical understanding, however, what learners bring to instruction should not be regarded as simply misconceived; there may be primitive principles to detect and build upon, rather than erase (diSessa 1983).

Research on assessing prior knowledge as aptitude now extends to possibilities beyond conventional pretests (Snow & Lohman 1989). For example, Marshall (1988, 1990) devised procedures for identifying nodes and arcs in mathematical knowledge schemas. Different kinds of semantic structures in memory produce different patterns and sequences of recall, and kinds of errors (Mandler 1984). A variety of word association, graphing, card sorting, interview, and questionnaire techniques have also been tried with some success (McKeachie et al 1986; Naveh-Benjamin et al 1986; Pines et al

1978; Renstrom et al 1990). Further, research on learning strategies suggests methods for assessing knowledge structuring as well as student strategies.

Memory space and mental speed Although listed as distinct, working memory capacity and speed of mental processing are seen as two faces of one aptitude that also underlies many other aptitude differences. Lohman (1989a,b) reviewed the speed aspect in detail, showing the importance of the speed-accuracy tradeoff in interpreting results. Just & Carpenter (1992) see memory capacity as the basic aptitude because it more easily accounts for present evidence. But speed and capacity are not mutually exclusive alternatives. Limitations in one can constrain the other. Some tasks may be better understood in speed terms, others in capacity terms (Halford 1989; Jensen 1989).

Using measures based on Baddeley's (1986) theory of working memory, Kyllonen & Christal (1990) suggest that memory capacity differences underlie performance on a variety of reasoning ability tests (consistent with Carpenter et al 1990); speed and knowledge factors were not important. Working-memory differences also accounted for individual differences in skill acquisition in electronics (Kyllonen & Stephens 1990; Woltz 1988). On the other hand, breadth of knowledge and memory search speed were critical aptitudes in associative learning (Kyllonen et al 1992); speed of processing also related to individual differences in forgetting (Kyllonen & Tirre 1988). Other work implicates working-memory differences in mathematical problem solving (Cooney & Swanson 1990).

The Kyllonen group has proposed that four basic aptitudes (processing speed, memory capacity, declarative and procedural knowledge) work in concert to account for individual differences in learning. Each of the four has important subdivisions. For example, Kyllonen & Woltz (1989) summarize work on a distinction between attention capacity (how many items can be held in working memory simultaneously) and activation capacity (how long can an item be held without rehearsal). Results indicate that attention capacity and verbal knowledge differences govern acquisition and proceduralization phases of rule learning, whereas the later phases of composing and strengthening combinations of rules may depend more on activation capacity and speed. The emerging model elaborates Anderson's (1987, 1990) theory and suggests that different kinds of learner differences need attention in different phases of instruction based on that theory.

The results also correspond to Ackerman's (1989) model of individual differences in skill learning, where early phases depend more on G_f and G_c and later phases depend on perceptual speed and other specialized abilities. In the Kyllonen framework, G_f and G_c become memory capacity and verbal knowledge, respectively, and perceptual speed connects with processing speed or efficiency measures. Ackerman's results for task complexity, memory load, and transfer manipulations are also consistent with the framework.

Learning strategies and styles   Deep-seated ability and knowledge differences of the above sorts are presumably manifested in observable differences in learning strategies and tactics. Thus, when direct training supplants ineffective strategies with effective ones, the hope is that deeper inaptitudes, or at least their effects, are being removed. Dozens of learning strategy constructs have now been defined (Weinstein & Mayer 1986; Weinstein et al 1988). Most reflect activities of rehearsal, elaboration, organization, monitoring, or motivation during learning or studying. Some concern use of global planning, heuristic, or mnemonic devices; some are mapping and structuring tactics using cues detected in reading or listening; and some promote metacognitive processes of comprehension monitoring or hypothesis generating and testing while learning. Combinations of these activities distinguish good vs poor student self-explanations while studying (Chi et al 1989). A particularly important general distinction concerns whether such strategies lead to deep vs surface processing during learning (Marton et al 1984; Entwistle 1987; Ferguson-Hessler & deJong 1990). Depth of processing may be a core construct to which many other strategies connect.

There is much evidence that strategies can be directly trained. Unfortunately, such training can be situation or treatment specific. It also can be dysfunctional; for learners with some ability profiles, the new strategy being learned (at least temporarily) conflicts with strategies already automatic. Lohman (1986) explained these interference effects using a production-system account of skill acquisition consistent with previous discussion. He predicts failure for skill and strategy training whenever it ignores the particulars of G_f or G_c strengths.

It is clear that training design requires careful analysis of poor learning strategies in comparison with more able learners to allow point by point incrementation toward more effective performance (Case & Bereiter 1984). Metacognitive strategies also need attention. Learners can be helped through a graduated scaffold of tutorial hints and demonstrations to model and eventually internalize the performance of able performers (Campione & Brown 1990). The result should be a repertoire of strategies, skill in their use, and flexibility in adaptation to instructional opportunities and demands. Research also shows that learners devise multiple strategies for a task and shift among them during performance (Kyllonen et al 1984; Ohlsson 1984a,b). Flexible strategy shifting seems to be a hallmark of able learning, whereas rigid strategies or random shifting suggest low ability. A simulation model of children's strategies for arithmetic (Siegler & Campbell 1990) further suggests that confidence in retrieved answers is a key individual difference controlling strategy use. The model distinguishes good, perfectionist, and not-so-good problem-solvers as an initial state construct and suggests instructional adaptations for each. It also shows how assessment of a conative aptitude (i.e. confidence) may clarify cognitive aptitude effects.

When strategic differences appear deeply rooted in learner personality, they may be conceptualized as more pervasive learning or cognitive styles (Schmeck 1988). Some style constructs may capture important ability-personality interactions (Messick 1987). Some also appear to reflect cognitive organizational differences between subject-matter domains. For example, Pask (1976; Pask & Scott 1972; Lindstrom 1983) distinguishes holist and serialist styles of knowledge organization; although persons habitually prefer one or the other style, it also seems that domains like physics and mathematics call for serialist structure, whereas history is better served by holist structure.

Current lists of style constructs and associated assessment instruments are lengthy and unorganized (Keefe 1987, 1988; Schmeck 1988); they include many hypothesized habits and preferences as distinct styles but also include traditional ability and personality characteristics. To date, research evidence is inadequate to judge their validity or usefulness in adapting instruction to individuals; some have been called seriously into question (Tiedeman 1989).

Conative and Affective Aptitudes

Adding style constructs as aptitudes for learning opens a Pandora's Box of personality differences. Even though hundreds of personality constructs can now be organized into a neat taxonomy (Digman 1990), most of these have not yet been connected to learning differences in instruction. Also, the taxonomy omits or glosses over motivational and volitional aptitudes that clearly are connected to instruction. We note here only the most obviously relevant constructs; this topic really deserves its own chapter. For broader reviews, see Lepper (1988), Heckhausen et al (1985), Kanfer et al (1989), and the series by Ames & Ames (1984, 1985, 1989).

MOTIVATIONAL CONSTRUCTS   There are new attempts to bring disparate aspects of motivational differences together, consider them jointly with cognitive abilities in learning, and derive instructional design implications. In relation to adaptive instruction, most notable are the programs by Lepper (1988; Lepper & Malone 1987; Lepper & Chabay 1988; Lepper et al 1992) and by Kanfer & Ackerman (1989; Kanfer 1990). Lepper has integrated various contrasting student orientations under the general heading of intrinsic vs extrinsic motivation and devised principles for promoting intrinsic motivation for learning. Of particular interest are findings that expert tutors use these principles subtly and adaptively while preserving the student's sense of control. Lepper (1988) also reviews some attempts at remediating dysfunctional orientations directly. The Kanfer-Ackerman work builds a model of ability-motivation task interaction centered on attention-resource capacity differences. Results indicate that motivational interventions can impede learning by diverting attention to self-regulatory activities in early stages of skill acquisition, depending on ability; in later stages the same interventions can facilitate performance. Much new work also focuses on separate constructs.

Anxiety and achievement motivation   Anxiety is the most studied motivational aptitude. Its interaction with instructional treatment seems similar to that of G; high teacher structure is best for more anxious students; low teacher structure is best for less anxious students (Tobias 1985). But ability and anxiety also interact (Snow 1989a). Research continues to elaborate the information-processing model of anxiety effects in learning (Naveh-Benjamin 1991), the development of anxiety, and its amelioration by direct intervention (Wigfield & Eccles 1989).

As Rand et al (1989) point out, however, anxiety is but half of the traditional theory of achievement motivation; it ought to be studied together with need for achievement as well as ability measures. Lens (1983) has shown that need for achievement and anxiety measures both yield curvilinear relations with instructional achievement. Lens & DeCruyenaere (1991) have also shown that measures derived from theories emphasizing achievement motivation, anxiety, intrinsic motivation, and causal attribution, and expectancy-value instrumentality all yield similar and strong relations to teacher ratings of school motivation. Boekaerts (1987) shows, however, that general measures can miss important situation and task differences.

Also significant in this category are differences in goal orientations and attitudes toward the future. Van Calster et al (1987) found complex interactions suggesting that achievement and study motivation depend on future attitudes about goals as well as perceived instrumentality of performance for goals. And Dweck & Leggett (1988) have shown that learners differ in their prior conceptions about ability development, which then influence motivational orientation to learning; mastery-oriented students believe ability improves with learning and direct their actions toward this end, whereas performance-oriented students think of ability as fixed and direct their actions toward teacher evaluations. Performance goal orientation limits achievement, particularly for learners with low self-perceived ability.

Intrinsic motivation and interests   Beyond work noted above, academic intrinsic motivation is now known to be assessible as aptitude and related to achievement and ability in young children (Gottfried 1990). A closely related new line focuses on interest as both aptitude and task characteristic, studied at levels ranging from subject-matter domains to text sentences and paragraphs.

Some effects of interest differences on learning rival those of ability differences. There are also qualitative differences in cognitive processing in learning that accrue from interest (see Hidi 1990; Nenniger 1987; Renninger et al 1992).

VOLITIONAL CONSTRUCTS   Volition is action control. But the category includes other meta-motivational constructs reflecting mindfulness, purposive striving, and persistence.

Self efficacy and effort investment   Self-perceptions of ability are known to influence choice of learning acitivities and effort investment as well as achievement in the short term (Schunk 1989); but new results show that such differences in self-efficacy have direct effects on effort investment across semester-long courses (MacIver et al 1991). Other work shows long-range relations of self-concept to ability, effort, and achievement (Boekaerts 1988; Helmke 1989). Self-concept also may differ in different instructional domains (Skaalvik & Rankin 1990); much old and new work here ought to be integrated with the construct of self-efficacy.

Metacognitive strategy in learning implies awareness or mindfulness; mindful learning in turn requires the investment of mental effort (Salomon 1983; Salomon & Globerson 1987). Individual differences in effort investment can appear in the extreme as pathological effort avoidance (Rollett 1987).

Self-regulation and action control   Some learners display state-orientation, wherein attention perseverates on internal or external concerns; failures lead to an inability to concentrate on continuing intentions to perform well. The contrast is action-orientation, in which attention is focused on strong intention-action relationships. Action-oriented learners use control strategies to protect their intention-action sequence from competing tendencies; they persist in learning despite momentary difficulties and distractions (Kuhl 1986, 1990; Kuhl & Kraska 1989).

Self regulation has become the new place to bring cognitive, motivational, and volitional views of instruction together. Much work is in progress, and an array of distinctive advances are in hand, even if integration is not (see Corno 1986; McCombs & Whisler 1989; Simons & Beukhof 1987; Higgins & Sorrentino 1990; Zimmerman & Schunk 1989; as well as Glaser & Bassok 1989).

Conclusion

Unfortunately, reviews of aptitude research still result in a list. Yet much progress has identified structures and processes that comprise major cognitive aptitude constructs and designed training interventions that promote improvement in such performance. Important new work also brings conative and affective aptitudes into this picture. Hypotheses have even been offered to explain some cognitive and conative aptitude constructs, and their relations, in the common process terms of attentional memory capacity. Initial attempts have been made to combine some cognitive and conative constructs into complexes.

Beyond continuance of this program, two steps seem crucial. One seeks to connect analyses of aptitude to analyses of instruction redesigned toward adaptive improvement; unfortunately, as seen below, most research on treatment design still makes minimal use of aptitude information beyond the record of previous learning in the program at hand. The other seeks to learn how best to synthesize aptitude and treatment constructs to promote understanding of education and development beyond the level of instructional design.

ADAPTIVE INSTRUCTION

In contrast to earlier work on large-scale adaptive instructional programs (Corno & Snow 1986; Wang & Lindvall 1984), recent research has concentrated on microadaptation of instruction in computerized or human tutoring, or in small-group teaching. This section begins with microadaptation and then moves toward selected forms of macroadaptation, considering some questions about assessment and evaluation at both levels along the way.

Microadaptation through Tutoring

COMPUTERIZED TUTORING   Intelligent tutoring systems (ITS) promise diagnosis to guide moment-to-moment adaptation of instruction to individual learner needs. ITS designs include four components, each with a role in adaptation: expert knowledge, learner modeling, tutorial planning, and communication (Mandl & Lesgold 1988). But ITS research so far also makes two assumptions (VanLehn 1988): (*a*) modeling student knowledge acquisition within the specific domain being taught allows feedback adequate to correct any misconceptions or missteps that result in error (Anderson 1988); and (*b*) beyond error correction, such diagnosis provides interpretations of student knowledge and thinking at a level that supports pedagogical decisions about the organization of further instruction. Research is needed to justify this position.

Expert knowledge   In this component, facts and rules of the domain are explicitly represented in a goal structure. To build it, task analyses are conducted to capture the details of expert knowledge and skill; this provides an instructional content organization, a standard for evaluating student performance, and a basis for explanation and error correction (Wenger 1987). In a domain with alternative expert viewpoints, all are represented in a way that avoids inconsistency (Lesgold 1988). However, constructing such a system poses problems because domain-specific expertise is built into the heads of tutors through long experience in abstracted but not necessarily accessible form (Sleeman & Brown 1982). Articulateness is not a trait of expertise, but it is crucial for instructional design (Wenger 1987).

How complete the expert knowledge component must be depends on the treatment design adopted. More directive, mastery instruction permits simpler expert systems. In guided discovery, however, the expert system must include content knowledge plus a complete guide for student exploration. The role of guide (vs provider of information) requires not only an explicit curriculum (Lesgold 1988) but also an understanding of student reasoning processes and the means to detect different student approaches to the task; this is beyond the capabilities of current systems because aptitude information outside of content knowledge is not used. Also, expert knowledge structures may not provide the most useful models for teaching. McArthur et al (1988) found that students learning algebra do not readily generalize equivalent procedures, as do experts. Task sequencing required steps smaller than those of an ideal problem solver to represent accurately the skills of students still learning to solve equations. Roschelle's (1990) work with physics simulations suggested that epistemic fidelity (Wenger 1987), or the quality of the denotational relationship between external visual displays and the expert's mental representations, may actually interfere with some students' comprehension. Roschelle found that students often do not know what to do, where to look, or how to make sense of a display in order to interpret the denoted relationships correctly. ITS designers as experts themselves often assume novices will make appropriate interpretations if material is accurately portrayed. They forget that seeing epistemic correspondences requires knowledge and experience.

Learner model   An updatable representation of the developing knowledge of each student is needed to choose what to teach next and how to teach it. For many reasons, the learner model is only an approximation. Student performance is rarely consistent; there are lucky guesses and careless mistakes. Some systematic and domain-specific errors occur frequently, others are rare, but either may be multiply determined. Student actions reflect many different personal background factors and momentary states that are not represented in the model. Learning itself introduces noise; hypotheses about the student that were accurate in one knowledge state may be incorrect when the student's knowledge structures change as learning continues. The computer's restricted communication channel limits the ability to update the student model rapidly (Wenger 1987). The tasks of diagnosis and student modeling are even difficult for human tutors, who can use richer conative, affective, and cognitive background information, as well as present sources such as voice intonations, hesitations, or facial expressions.

Existing student models are insensitive to the intricacies of particular student misconceptions. Strategies for tracing errors back to deeper misconceptions are extremely important pedagogically, but few systems address this need. Currently, there are two major techniques (with numerous variations) used to represent differences between student and expert.

The overlay model evaluates the presence or absence of single units of knowledge. The student is represented as a subset of the expert—i.e. the expert model and a list of missing units of knowledge that the expert has but the student does not (VanLehn 1988). It thus maintains only one perspective of the subject matter and evaluates each student's understanding from that perspective only. Examples of ITS that use this technique are WUSOR II (Carr 1977) and the LISP Tutor (Anderson 1987). The other approach represents both missing conceptions and misconceptions (units that the student has but the expert does not). The common program here employs a library of predefined bugs and procedures to test which one or combination produced the observed error. Examples of ITS that use bug libraries are BUGGY (Brown & Burton 1978) and DEBUGGY (Burton 1982). A system called PIXIE generates new bugs (or malrules) when it cannot account for errors with existing bugs (Sleeman 1987).

When learning failures occur in either approach, the system can only reteach the same material in the same way that was ineffective the first time (Lesgold 1988). Truly adaptive ITS would detect the weakness in the first presentation and choose an alternative treatment to help students work through the error. Sleeman et al (1989) has investigated one such remediation procedure compared with simple reteaching. In algebra tutoring the two methods did not differ, but student aptitudes were not studied; the enhanced program (TPIXIE) did help teachers improve their ability to diagnose student errors. Most ITS continue to rely on simple exposition to explain errors and correct solutions.

Tutorial planning   This component regulates instructional presentation in relation to the learner model and its own goal structure. Little research to date has focused on alternative teaching strategies in this connection (Ohlsson 1986). The linear plan of pre-assembled units of instruction used in most ITS severely limits tutor adaptation to individual learners. The strategy distinction given most attention is the degree of learner control over instructional activities the ITS allows. Some systems monitor student activity closely, adapting their actions to student responses but never relinquishing control. An example is the LISP tutor; Anderson et al (1984) argue that the system should prevent students from floundering off the optimal solution path. Diagnosis is immediate as the student works. The resulting student model may be a close approximation to what the student actually does, but the directiveness of instruction is best suited for beginners in well-structured domains. Tutor directiveness did not disturb complete novices but produced impatience in experienced students (Anderson & Skwarecki 1986). The LISP Tutor does not adapt to these initial state differences.

Some ITS are designed to share control with students by exchanging questions and answers. The system responds to questions but also asks questions; answers help assess what the student knows or is trying to do. To be effective, the system needs to anticipate all possible answers and questions. SCHOLAR (Carbonell 1970) attempted to employ this mixed-initiative tutorial strategy. Although SCHOLAR had interesting capabilities, it was unable to do the kind of plausible reasoning that people rely on to cope with incomplete knowledge, so its ability to answer questions as a human tutor would was extremely limited. The WHY project attempted to overcome these problems with a Socratic-dialog design (Stevens & Collins 1977). WHY uncovered many difficult issues for research; in particular, it showed the need to understand adaptive interactions between teaching strategies and knowledge representations.

At the other extreme, discovery environments give students primary control of learning activities. Various forms of interactive learning environments, microworlds, and simulations fit this category. Discovery environments are said to allow learners to construct new knowledge from immediate experience, using concepts and capabilities they already possess. Leading proponents (Papert 1980) aim to help learners develop and debug their own theories rather than teach them theories others consider correct; in LOGO, students use computers as experimental simulators to explore concepts.

However, diagnostic functions are more difficult to design as the degree of student control increases. Also, some degree of structure is seen as characteristic of good tutoring (Collins et al 1975). Recent work suggests that many students need additional guidance to take advantage of discovery treatments. Pea & Sheingold (1987) found students needing a structure to think about what to do on computers; fully self-directed learning worked well for only a few. As already noted, previous research shows able students doing well in discovery and less able students doing poorly, relative to other treatments. In research on computer-aided instruction (Steinberg 1989), students with little prior knowledge are also likely to perform poorly under conditions of learner control.

Guided discovery programs like WEST (Burton & Brown 1979) and WHY (Stevens & Collins 1977) introduce a goal structure and various forms of assistance as needed. For example, Collins & Stevens (1982) start with a question; instruction then attempts to help students to an understanding of the answer to that question. An interesting new example is Smithtown (Shute & Glaser 1990). Its primary goal is to develop scientific inquiry skills in the context of supply and demand economics. Even though no economic principles are directly taught, tutoring on inquiry skills resulted in learning domain knowledge as a by-product.

Communication   The need to communicate knowledge with explicit representations has led ITS research into questions about the nature of knowledge and the characteristics that make it communicable (Wenger 1987); communication and knowledge interact in deep ways. Leinhardt & Ohlsson (1989) observed that ITS concerns instruction one step at a time, but successful human teaching has a global organization that is communicated to students in meta-level statements about instruction and content. Communication is structured to help students set up successive learning tasks in a way coherent with several goal levels. Unlike ITS, expert teachers do much more than simply provide information and tell students what to learn (Lepper & Chabay 1988; Putnam 1987; Shulman 1986).

Newman et al (1989) also identify a process of appropriation, in which teachers interpret learner responses using their own analysis of the task; goals emerge in the course of interaction. Students begin by working within the social constraints of the tutorial and only later come to understand the tutor's goal for the learner.

Tutors must be problem solvers (Leinhardt & Greeno 1986; Ohlsson 1986) that can compute means-ends relations between goals and alternative instructional actions in the current model of each student. Such microadaptation requires a large repertoire of teaching tactics, so that tutors can choose actions that benefit each student at each moment. This requires research on alternative instructional strategies and their orchestration. In general, taking advantage of emergent properties in the student-tutor interaction to steer instructional interventions tailored to the needs of individual students requires adaptability that is beyond the capabilities of current ITS. Wenger (1987) summarized as follows: "Admittedly, adaptability in the best systems is rather coarse when compared to the way human teachers can weave diagnosis and didactics tightly together. The ability of teachers to move back and forth between compiled and articulate knowledge, in both diagnosis and didactics, also contrasts strikingly with current systems in which diagnosis in terms of compiled knowledge is the norm (p. 426)." Deeper studies of communication, diagnosis, and adaptation processes in human tutoring and teaching are clearly needed. It is noteworthy that significant improvements in ITS projects (e.g. WHY, PROUST, GUIDON) have often resulted when ITS researchers paused to study adaptation in human tutoring (Littman et al 1987).

Computer systems as adjuncts   There is growing concern that investment in ITS development may not be worth it (Lippert 1989). Most ITS remain as prototypes, although notable exceptions are PROUST (Johnson & Soloway 1985) and Anderson's mathematics and LISP tutors. Attention recently has turned to the development of expert systems as adjuncts to instruction. Expert systems are not designed as adaptive tutors, so they are cheaper to produce; with involvement of an instructor they are also more versatile.

One innovation switched tutor and student roles (Lippert 1989). Knowledge engineers probe experts, to get them to indicate what is needed to improve a computational model of the domain. When students used knowledge engineering techniques to build an expert system on a subject of their own choosing, they developed improved understanding of the domain problems and heuristics, skill at detecting erroneous or incomplete data, and ideas about promising instructional approaches and methods.

GUIDON2 (Clancey 1988) is based on the same notion: students actively direct the tutoring program through dialog, just as knowledge engineers direct experts to reveal their knowledge. GUIDON2 is an expert system for medical diagnosis; student learning proceeds by critiquing, improving, and applying medical hypotheses. Learning is failure driven. When a hypothesis is not substantiated, the student must search for alternative explanations and missing data, to understand how the misdiagnosis was arrived at and how to avoid future failures.

Computer-simulations, such as GUIDON2 are well suited for teaching or coaching the development of knowledge in situations where it will be used. This type of apprenticeship seems a natural way to learn (Collins et al 1989); it was the medium for vocational and professional training before there was formal education, and it is how specialized training is still delivered in medicine. Computer simulations can allow teachers to give personal attention to individual students, to provide the adaptive coaching and scaffolding of apprentice-style learning. This process of learning through interaction in the context of ongoing work Schon (1987) is called "reflective practice." For example, computer simulations of velocity and acceleration (Roschelle 1990) and light refraction (Pea et al 1990) have enabled students to understand complex scientific concepts by participating in the activity and the corresponding discussions between teacher and students, as they reason together about observed phenomena.

An example of a computer simulation used successfully this way is IN-COFT (Newman 1989), for training soldiers who monitor the Patriot missile system. INCOFT has no tutoring component to regulate feedback or task sequencing; its use is supervised by instructors. The simulation enables trainees to observe how the system's decision logic works, and interactions with the machine and instructor lead to student understanding and sensitivity to the context and goals of the task. INCOFT may not be an advance in artificial intelligence, but as an instructional design this simplification of the ITS model has proved effective in use.

Whether ITS are designed as adjuncts to human teachers or as independent providers, they require more in-depth study of skilled human tutors. The aim is to identify adaptive instructional strategies and teaching tactics for different domains and different kinds of students.

HUMAN TUTORING   Research on human tutoring is a recent development. In earlier times, individual tutoring was viewed as an exception—a privilege of wealth or a remedial, last resort for students who had failed in other settings.

In today's schools, students are usually tutored by peers, older students, or teacher aides, not by professionals. Recent dramatic increases in the use of tutoring has introduced wide variability among programs but also some notable effects. Cohen et al (1982), reviewing 65 evaluations of school tutoring programs, reported positive effects on both achievement and attitudes. Also, tutoring experience had positive effects on students who served as tutors; like those they helped, tutors gained better understanding and more positive attitudes in the subject they tutored.

Tutoring has been found the most effective treatment for at-risk elementary school children (Slavin & Madden 1989), more effective than lengthening the school day, reducing class size, or adding CAI (Niemic & Walberg 1987). Increasingly, tutoring is used to avoid early reading failure; Wasik & Slavin (1990) reviewed five programs using adult reading tutors for first graders that produced significant reading gains beyond controls. Such programs vary considerably in tutoring methods, curriculum, degree of integration with regular instruction, and amount and kind of tutor training. However, even when classmates tutor each other, impressive gains have occurred and been sustained for years (Greenwood et al 1989; Fantuzzo et al 1989). The results suggest that the one-to-one human interaction in tutoring is an important factor. Two components seem critical; cognitive instruction focused on building competence, and motivational influences on student attitudes toward the subject matter and themselves as learners (Lepper & Chabay 1988). It remains unclear how these components actually work and interact in effective tutoring.

Although little is known about the process, tutoring presumably succeeds because it provides opportunity for constant tailored attention, explanation, demonstration, and immediate personal feedback and reinforcement of each particular student's questions and responses (Cohen 1986). Bloom (1984) studied tutoring as the "ideal" standard against which the effectiveness of other, presumably less optimal, group treatments could be assessed. Unfortunately, most studies have been simple comparisons that failed to identify the aspects of tutoring process that make it effective as instruction.

Theoretical research on tutoring has used some concepts derived from developmental perspectives on learning. Vygotsky's (1978) idea that learning occurs first in social interaction and then is internalized inspired Bruner and his colleagues to develop the notion of scaffolding, based initially on studies of interaction between parents and their young children in informal teaching situations (Bruner 1978; Wood et al 1976, 1978). Tutoring in this view involves a scaffolding process in which the tutor controls those aspects of the task that are initially too difficult for the child, thereby permitting the child to concentrate upon and complete those aspects that the child is able to perform. By adapting the task demands, keeping them within the child's zone of proximal development (Vygotsky 1978), the tutor not only helps the child complete the task at hand but also gradually promotes the additional skill and strategy development that will enable the child to accomplish similar tasks alone.

According to Bruner (1966; also Case 1992), learning something in a domain requires that one already understands the nature of what is to be learned. An important function of adult-child interaction is to create links between the goal and context of a novel problem and more familiar problems, allowing the child to apply skills and knowledge previously acquired (Rogoff & Gardner 1984). There is a parallel also between this kind of tutoring and learning in apprenticeships; novices are responsible for simple aspects of the task while they observe experts modeling the goal and the more difficult aspects of reaching it. Novices learn at their own rate, participating only at a level they are capable of fulfilling, until they too have mastered the whole task (Greenfield 1984; Lave 1988; Wertsch & Stone 1985).

Based on further studies, Wood (1980; Wood et al 1986) concluded that tutor effectiveness depended on the tutor scaffolding being contingent upon the interaction of task demands and student performance. As defined by Wood, contingent instruction requires that tutorial interventions are inversely related to the student's level of competence. The more difficulty a student has with a task, the more directive the tutor. The more success the student experiences, the more the tutor encourages the student to work independently. To make tutoring interventions contingent, the tutor must understand what the student is attempting to achieve, and be able to diagnose degrees and kinds of success and failure. Assessing while teaching is a subtle, difficult process.

In these studies, the more contingent was the mother's instruction, the more the child learned. Wood replicated these results in a second study that examined tutorial interaction not only between mothers and their own children but also between the mothers and children they did not know. The instructional strategy seemed a more powerful determinant of learning than the relationship between a mother and her own child. Wood et al (1978) also compared the contingency rule with other tutorial strategies. Children taught contingently learned much more than children taught by other methods, so this strategy seems to be a crucial part of effective tutoring.

Swanson (1990) compared contingent tutoring with two other strategies in teaching optics to college undergraduates who varied in G_c aptitude. A "lecture" condition gave tutors full control and a "discovery" condition gave students full control; in a contingent condition, tutor control varied to adapt to individual student needs and progress. Results showed that discovery was good for the most able students, but it was particularly ineffective with low-ability students, who benefited most from contingent tutoring. Lecture produced intermediate results. When correctly applied, contingent instruction produced the highest learning outcomes across the ability range, but this strategy did prove difficult for one tutor to use.

FURTHER RESEARCH ON TUTORING   A range of issues for further research are suggested above. Some concern the evaluation and improvement of tutoring. More generally, however, deeper work on tutoring could provide some of the integrative concepts called for earlier.

Aptitude treatment interaction (ATI)   In effect, the Swanson (1990) result is a macro-level aptitude-treatment interaction (ATI) used to evaluate a microadaptation of instruction. Tutoring that is contingent on learner performance should provide more scaffolding for less able learners and less scaffolding for more able learners. In the extreme the tutor is ranging between mastery-style direct instruction and guided discovery, the treatment contrast emphasized by Glaser & Bassok (1989). Here then is a suggestion for integration of instructional theory across treatments, conditioned on learner differences. But the tutors seem to be adapting not only to the student's domain-specific responses but also to behavioral correlates of more general aptitude differences. That is, human tutors seem to integrate domain-general and domain-specific learner characteristics in their adaptations. Further research is needed to explain how this is done.

Unfortunately, computer tutors have not been evaluated using student aptitudes outside of the confines of their domain-specific student and expert models. But preliminary studies by Shute (1989, 1990a-c) used measures of ability and knowledge, as well as working memory and speed, in evaluations of ITS for computer programming and electricity. She also fashioned indexes to reflect student differences in exploratory behavior during performance and included macro-adaptive experimental contrasts, such as inductive vs deductive feedback, in the treatment design. Some initial ATI results suggest that the more structured, deductive condition is better for learners showing low exploratory behavior; others imply that abilities and the feedback treatment interact in different ways depending on outcome measures. It seems clear that the ATI framework is useful for evaluation studies of ITS.[3]

Learning assessment Tutoring affords assessment of learning strategy and style differences such as Shute's exploratory behavior index (see also Kyllonen & Shute 1989). But it also permits integration of instruction and assessment. Campione & Brown (1987, 1990; Brown & Reeve 1987) capitalized on this possibility by designing scripted tutoring that incorporates a hierarchical hint structure; the depth of help needed by a student is an inverse learning efficiency measure. A structured continuum of transfer tasks provides a transfer distance measure. Campione & Brown's research has shown that the graduated scaffolding of the hint structure builds skill in the domain but also aids in developing more general self-regulatory strategies. Beyond this, the learning and transfer assessments offer better prediction of later performance than do conventional ability and knowledge measures.

Much new research on aptitude and learning assessment is now emerging, in human and computer tutoring but also in other instructional contexts. For a sampling, see Frederiksen et al (1990), Frederiksen et al (1992), Lidz (1987), Palincsar & Winn (1990), Ruijssenaars & Hamers (1990), and Sternberg & Davidson (1990).

Distributed aptitude Adaptive instruction has long been described, in part, as designing treatments to include prosthetic devices, to do for learners what learners cannot yet do for themselves (Cronbach & Snow 1977). Contingent tutoring and scaffolding, as described above, similarly involve in a more dynamic way the distributing of task components between tutor and learner as a function of what the learner can and cannot do at the moment. New perspectives on situated cognition (Greeno 1989a,b, 1991) and on ATI (Snow 1991, 1992) also place aspects of performance not in the person or the situation alone, but in the relation between them.

Given this trend, dispute arises over how much aptitude for learning should be designed into the instructional treatment and how much should be required of the student, in any given instance (e.g. contrast discussions by Pea 1990; Perkins 1990; Salomon 1990). A closely related problem is how to design diagnostic assessment to decide this question dynamically. Again,

---

[3]This is not the place for a detailed review of ATI research. For examples of advances on several fronts, see Peterson (1988) and associated commentaries, Snow (1989) and Weinert et al (1990).

research on human and computer tutoring may be the best avenue through which to confront this concern. Some ITS researchers are now studying means by which the computer can tailor tasks to circumvent weaknesses in particular learners while noting the weakness for later, more direct attention. The best example so far is Lesgold's (1988; Lesgold et al 1989) electricity tutor, which uses multivariate information about student present state to decide next steps. To advance a student's problem-solving skill (e.g. with voltage measurement) the program might select a next set of challenging problems; because it has recognized this student as weak in arithmetic skills, however, it designs the new problems to avoid taxing the student with complex computations. Later having built problem-solving skill, it can use this strength to work back on removing computational weakness. Of course, the aptitude functions could also be designed into the program temporarily, as computational scaffolding. Aptitude information from sources external as well as internal to the ITS could be used this way. The basic research question is: What is the optimal tradeoff for each learner at each step between challenge and circumvention?

ITS seems to provide an ideal laboratory for studying different teaching strategies and tradeoffs in relation to different learner aptitudes. The machine would guarantee that each teaching strategy is consistently executed. This provides the necessary controls for experimental evaluations (Ohlsson 1988). More importantly, it would allow integrated study of macro- and microadaptation, domain-general and domain-specific aptitudes, and strategy and style differences in student activities during learning.

Teaching and Learning in Groups

COOPERATIVE SMALL GROUPS   Another rapid expansion of research concerns cooperative learning in small groups as an adaptive teaching medium. Students work together on tasks in heterogeneous ability groups of four to six. Usually, teacher-structured instruction precedes the cooperative learning activity, and evaluation and feedback follow it. The evidence clearly shows its effectiveness in achieving cognitive goals, but the methods also promote more positive attitudes toward school, improved student self-esteem, and improved relations among different types of students (Johnson et al 1981; Sharan 1980; Slavin 1983, 1987, 1990a).

Unfortunately, most studies have been simple comparisons that do not help explain how the process works. Slavin (1990a) hypothesizes two essential features for effective cooperative learning: incentive to cooperate and individual accountability. Group reward or recognition for group academic performance is believed to provide the incentive for students to work together. But cooperative incentives alone seem insufficient to increase student

INSTRUCTIONAL PSYCHOLOGY   613

achievement; group performance needs to depend on the performance of each student in the group.

Studies of communication during cooperative activities show a consistent relationship between student talk and achievement if the interactions are focused on learning (Cohen et al 1989; Ross & Raphael 1990; Webb 1982, 1983, 1989; Webb et al 1986). Both lower- and higher-ability students profit in heterogeneous groups when the former ask questions and the latter provide explanations; however, the dynamics of uniform-ability groups seem not to promote learning this way (Webb 1982). Extroverted, moderately anxious students seem to benefit most in cooperation (Hall et al 1990). Students who give or receive explanations outperform those who simply receive correct answers from their peers (Webb 1983). Groups in which students spend more time discussing substantive facts and concepts outperform other groups, even when there are no differences in reward structures (Ross & Raphael 1990). Thus, the importance of reward structure is debatable. Slavin (1990a) emphasizes manipulation of reward structures, but his research has not analyzed interactions among participants. For Sharan (1984), what counts is mutual helping behavior; group rewards encourage the kind of collaborative activity that prompts students to reflect on their knowledge and make generalizations and elaborations that they can convey to their peers.

Palincsar & Brown's (1984) reciprocal teaching procedure is one small-group method where the process has received research attention. It provides a structure for teaching students the process of collaboration, giving them strategies to acquire knowledge from text and from peers. Students of different levels of competence and an adult teacher take turns "being the teacher," leading discussion on a segment of text. Discussion is structured by practicing four strategies: questioning, clarifying, summarizing, and predicting. The dialog leader begins by asking a question on the main idea of the text, invites clarification and discussion of any points of confusion, then summarizes the gist of the passage and asks for predictions about future content. The strategies provide specific heuristics for students to use, the reciprocal nature of the procedure forces student engagement, and the teacher models expert performance (Brown & Palincsar 1989).

Substantial evidence now supports the effectiveness and efficiency of reciprocal teaching (Brown & Palincsar 1987, 1989; Brown et al 1992; Palincsar 1986; Palincsar & Brown 1984). New research seeks to incorporate reciprocal teaching into the repertoires of classroom teachers. Even with variations in teacher skill, experience, and enthusiasm, significant improvements in individual student achievement have been obtained. Further steps involve adapting the procedures for use in whole-class discussion and training peer tutors to serve as teachers to train other students (Brown & Palincsar 1989; Palincsar et al 1989). Heterogeneous cooperative learning groups may also provide an alternative to traditional homogeneous ability groups.

ABILITY GROUPING   Some recent research on this controversial practice suggests that the effects of ability grouping and tracking are essentially zero at both the elementary and secondary levels. Slavin (1987, 1990b) found no clear trend indicating that students in high-track classes learn more than high-achieving students in heterogeneous classes, or that students in low-track classes learn less than low-achieving students in heterogeneous classes. But this conclusion is contrary to a substantial literature indicating the low quality of instruction in low groups and the negative impact of ability grouping on the motivation and self-esteem of students assigned to low groups (Sharan 1980; Oakes 1987; Webb 1982; Wilkinson 1988). Large-scale survey studies have also found that high-track placement has a positive effect on achievement and low-track placement has a negative effect, after controlling for ability and socioeconomic differences (Hoffer 1991). Statistical controls, however, are not sufficient to partial out other factors such as differential course taking. Perhaps the inconsistencies are partly due to methodology. Experimental studies often artificially control factors that have real effects in natural settings, and few experiments or correlational studies examine actual classroom practices (Hallinan 1990). Unfortunately most research on ability grouping still leaves the nature of instruction in different groups out of consideration (Cronbach & Snow 1977).

Conclusion

Research on the adaptive processes of human tutoring and learning in small groups is a rich new vein for the development of instructional theory. Deeper investment in research here may provide solid payoff across a much broader front. Expert teaching in such situations can be a standard against which all other forms of instruction are evaluated, since these other forms are in a real sense compromises on the ideal of individual tutoring made for economic reasons. Computerized instructional designs, then, may be judged in either of two ways: how well they approximate the effects of expert tutoring and small-group teaching directly, and how well they complement human classroom teaching to reach such effects. Two rather different design goals are implied for further research.

ASSESSMENT: A PROSPECTUS

An undercurrent in this review is the need for improved assessment. Some developments in this direction were noted in passing, but an attempt at full review was judged premature. We thus conclude with a plea for more and better research on this aspect in particular and for broad agenda setting for the new decade's research toward this goal (Snow & Mandinach 1991). The key to combining information on cognitive, conative, and affective aptitude with information on knowledge and skill acquisition in the progress of instruction lies in new assessment design. The key to steering individuals toward optimal learning based on such information lies in assessment designs integrated with instruction, at both micro and macro levels. The theoretical tensions listed at the outset, as well as the issues of aptitude and adaptive instruction then addressed, become explicit when the concrete problem of assessment in an actual instructional situation is faced. One can study only what one can measure. New measuring instruments and techniques are needed. Much more than that, however, instructional psychologists should take seriously the need for a theory of assessment that completes and coordinates Glaser's (1976) list of components of instructional theory.

Literature Cited

Ackerman, P. 1989. Individual differences and skill acquisition. See Ackerman et al 1989, pp. 164–217

Ackerman, P. L., Sternberg, R. J., Glaser, R., eds. 1989. *Learning and Individual Differences* New York: Freeman

Ames, R. E., Ames C., eds. 1984. *Research on Motivation in Education. Vol. 1: Student Motivation*. Orlando: Academic

Ames, R. E., Ames C., eds. 1985. *Research on Motivation in Education. Vol. 2: The Classroom Milieu*. Orlando: Academic

Ames, R. E., Ames C., eds. 1989. *Research on Motivation in Education. Vol. 3: Goals and Cognitions*. Orlando: Academic

Anderson, J. R. 1987. Skill acquisition: compilation of weak-method problem solutions. *Psychol. Rev.* 94:192–210

Anderson, J. R. 1988. The expert model. In *Foundations of Intelligent Tutoring Systems*, ed. M. C. Polson, J. J. Richardson, pp. 21–54. Hillsdale, NJ: Erlbaum

Anderson, J. R. 1990. *The Adaptive Character of Thought*. Hillsdale, NJ: Erlbaum

Anderson, J. R., Boyle, C. F., Farrell, R. G., Reiser, B. J. 1984. Cognitive principles in the design of computer tutors. *Proc. 6th Cogn. Sci. Soc. Conf., Boulder*, pp. 2–8

Anderson, J. R., Skwarecki, E. 1986. The automated tutoring of introductory programming. *Commun. Assoc. Comput. Mach.* 29:842–49

Baddeley, A. 1986. *Working Memory*. Oxford: Oxford Univ. Press

Baenninger, M., Newcombe, N. 1989. The role of experience in spatial test performance: a meta-analysis. *Sex Roles* 20(5–6):327–44

Balke-Aurell, G. 1982. *Changes in Ability as Related to Educational and Occupational Experience*. Goteborg, Sweden: Acta Univ. Gothoburgensis

Baron, J., Sternberg, R. J. 1987. *Teaching Thinking Skills*. New York: Freeman

Bejar, I. I. 1986. Adaptive assessment of spatial abilities. Final report. Princeton, NJ: Educational Testing Service

Ben-Chaim, D. 1988. The effect of instruction on spatial visualization skills of middle school boys and girls. *Am. Educ. Res. J.* 25:51–71

Ben-Chaim, D., Lappan, G., Houang, R. T. 1989. The role of visualization in the middle school mathematics curriculum. *Focus Learn. Probl. Math.* 11(1):49–60

Bereiter, C. 1990. Aspects of an educational learning theory. *Rev. Educ. Res.* 60:603–24

Bereiter, C., Scardamalia, M. 1989. Intentional learning as a goal of instruction. See Resnick 1989, pp. 361–92

Bethell-Fox, C. E., Lohman, D. F., Snow, R. E. 1984. Adaptive reasoning: componential and eye movement analysis of geometric analogy performance. *Intelligence* 8:205–38

Bishop, A. J. 1989. Review of research on visualization in mathematics education. *Focus Learn. Probl. Math.* 11(1):7–16

Bloom, B. S. 1984. The 2-Sigma problem: the search for methods of group instruction as effective as one-to-one tutoring. *Educ. Res.* 13:4–16

Boekaerts, M. 1987. Situation-specific judgments of a learning task versus overall measures of motivational orientation. See De-Corte et al 1987, pp. 169–79

Boekaerts, M., ed. 1988. Emotion, motivation, and learning. *Int. J. Educ. Res.* 12:227–345

Brophy, J. E., Good, T. L. 1986. Teacher behavior and student achievement. See Wittrock 1986, pp. 328–75

Brown, A. L., Campione, J. C., Reeve, R. A., Ferrara, R. A., Palincsar, A. S. 1992. Interactive learning and individual understanding: the case of reading and mathematics. In *Culture, Schooling and Psychological Development*, ed. L. T. Landsmann. Hillsdale, NJ: Erlbaum. In press

Brown, A. L., Palincsar, A. S. 1987. Reciprocal teaching of comprehension strategies: a natural history of one program for enhancing learning. In *Intelligence and Exceptionality: New Directions for Theory, Assessment, and Instructional Practice*, ed. J. D. Day, J. Borkowski, pp. 81–132. Norwood, NJ: Ablex

Brown, A. L., Palincsar, A. S. 1989. Guided, cooperative learning and individual knowledge acquisition. See Resnick 1989, pp. 393–451

Brown, A. L., Reeve, R. A. 1987. Bandwidths of competence: the role of supportive contexts in learning and development. In *Development and Learning: Conflict or Congruence?*, ed. L. S. Liben, pp. 173–223. Hillsdale, NJ: Erlbaum

Brown, J. S., Burton, R. R. 1978. Diagnostic models for procedural bugs in basic mathematical skills. *Cogn. Sci.* 2:155–91

Brown, J. S., Collins, A., Duguid, P. 1989. Situated cognition and the culture of learning. *Educ. Res.* 18(1):32–42

Bruner, J. S. 1966. *Toward a Theory of Instruction*. Cambridge, MA: Harvard Univ. Press

Bruner, J. S. 1978. The role of dialogue in language acquisition. In *The Child's Conception of Language*, ed. A. Sinclair, R. J. Jarvell, W. J. M. Levelt, pp. 241–56. New York: Springer

Budoff, M. 1987. The validity of learning potential assessment. See Lidz 1987, pp. 52–81

Burton, R. R. 1982. Diagnosing bugs in simple procedural skill. In *Intelligent Tutoring Systems*, ed. D. H. Sleeman, J. S. Brown, pp. 157–84. London: Academic

Burton, R. R., Brown, J. S. 1979. An investigation of computer coaching for informal learning activities. *Int. J. Man-Machine Stud.* 11:5–24

Byrd Smith, L. 1989. Average nonverbally oriented adolescents an at risk population in our schools: Implications for teachers of black students. Presented at Am. Educ. Res. Assoc., San Francisco

Calfee, R. C. 1982. Cognitive models of reading: implications for assessment and treatment of reading disability. In *Reading Disorders: Varieties and Treatments*, ed. R. N. Malatesha, P. G. Aaron. New York: Academic

Campione, J. C., Brown, A. L. 1987. Linking dynamic assessment with school achievement. See Lidz 1987, pp. 82–115

Campione, J. C., Brown, A. L. 1990. Guided learning and transfer: Implications for approaches to assessment. See Frederiksen et al 1990, pp. 141–72

Carbonell, J. R. 1970. *Mixed initiative mancomputer instructional dialogues*. PhD thesis. MIT

Carey, S. 1988. Reorganization of knowledge in the course of acquisition. In *Ontogeny, Phylogeny, and Historical Development*, ed. S. Strauss. Norwood, NJ: Ablex

Carpenter, P. A., Just, M. A., Shell, P. 1990. What one intelligence test measures: a theoretical account of the processing in the Raven Progressive Matrices Test. *Psychol. Rev.* 97:404–31

Carr, B. 1977. Wusor-II: a computer-aided instruction program with student modeling capabilities. AI Lab. Memo 417 (Logo Memo 45). Cambridge, MA: MIT

Carroll, J. B. 1989. Factor analysis since Spearman: Where do we stand? What do we know? See Kanfer et al 1989, pp. 43–67

Carroll, J. B. 1992. *Human Cognitive Abilities*. New York: Cambridge Univ Press. In press

Case, R. 1985. *Intellectual Development*. Orlando: Academic

Case, R., ed. 1992. *The Mind's Staircase: Stages in the Development of Human Intelligence*. Hillsdale, NJ: Erlbaum. In press

Case, R., Bereiter, C. 1984. From behaviorism to cognitive behaviorism to cognitive development: steps in the evolution of instructional design. *Instruct. Sci.* 13:141–58

Case, R., Griffin, S. 1989. Child cognitive development: The role of central conceptual structures in the development of scientific thought. In *Developmental Psychology: Cognitive, Perceptual, Motor, and Neurological Perspectives*, ed. C. A. Havert. Amsterdam: North Holland

Case, R., McKeough, A. 1989. Schooling and the development of central conceptual structures: an example from the domain of children's narrative. *Int. J. Educ. Res.* 13:835–55

Case, R., Sandieson, R., Dennis, S. 1986. Two cognitive-developmental approaches to the design of remedial instruction. *Cogn. Dev.* 1:293–333

Chi, M. T. H., Bassok, M., Lewis, M. W., Reimann, P., Glaser, R. 1989. Self-explanations: How students study and use examples in learning to solve problems. *Cog. Sci.* 13:145–82

Chi, M. T. H., Glaser, R., Farr, M. J., eds. 1988. *The Nature of Expertise*. Hillsdale, NJ: Erlbaum

Chipman, S. F., Brush, L. R., Wilson, D. M., eds. 1985a. *Women and Mathematics: Balancing the Equation*. Hillsdale, NJ: Erlbaum

Chipman, S. F., Segal, J. W., Glaser, R., eds. 1985b. *Thinking and Learning Skills*, Vol. 2. Hillsdale, NJ: Erlbaum

Clancey, W. J. 1988. The knowledge engineer as student: Metacognitive bases for asking good questions. See Mandl & Lesgold 1988, pp. 80–113

Cohen, E. G., Lotan, R. A., Leecer, C. 1989. Can classrooms learn? *Sociol. Educ.* 62:75–94

Cohen, J. 1986. Theoretical considerations of peer tutoring. *Psychol. Sch.* 23:175–86

Cohen, P. A., Kulik, J. A., Kulik, C. C. 1982. Educational outcomes of tutoring: a meta-analysis of findings. *Am. Educ. Res. J.* 19:237–48

Cole, M. 1985. Mind as a cultural achievement: Implications for IQ testing. In *Learning and Teaching the Ways of Knowing*, ed. E. Eisner, pp. 218–49. Chicago: Natl. Soc. Stud. Educ.

Collins, A., Brown, J. S., Newman, S. E. 1989. Cognitive apprenticeship: teaching the craft of reading, writing, and mathematics. See Resnick 1989, pp. 453–94

Collins, A., Stevens, A. L. 1982. Goals and strategies of inquiry teachers. In *Advances in Instructional Psychology*, ed. R. Glaser, 2:65–119. Hillsdale, NJ: Erlbaum

Collins, A., Warnock, E. H., Passafiume, J. J. 1975. Analysis and synthesis of tutorial dialogues. *Psychol. Learn. Motiv.* 9:49–87

Cooney, J. B., Swanson, H. L. 1990. Individual differences in memory for mathematical story problems: Memory span and problem perception. *J. Educ. Psychol.* 82: 570–77

Corno, L. 1986. The metacognitive control components of self-regulated learning. *Contemp. Educ. Psychol.* 11:333–46

Corno, L., Snow, R. E. 1986. Adapting teaching to individual differences among learners. See Wittrock 1986, pp. 605–29

Cronbach, L. J. 1982. *Designing Evaluations of Educational and Social Programs*. San Francisco: Jossey-Bass

Cronbach, L. J., Snow, R. E. 1977. *Aptitudes and Instructional Methods: A Handbook for Research on Interactions*. New York: Irvington

DeCorte, E., Lodewijks, H., Parmentier, R., Span, P., eds. 1987. *Learning and Instruction: European Research in an International Context*, Vol. 1. Leuven/Belgium/Oxford: Leuven Univ. Press/Pergamon Press

DeLeeuw, L., Van Daalen, H., Beishuizen, J.

J. 1987. Problem solving and individual differences: Adaptation to and assessment of student characteristics by computer-based instruction. See DeCorte et al 1987, pp. 99–110

Demetriou, A., Efklides, A. 1987. Towards a determination of the dimensions and domains of individual differences in cognitive development. See DeCorte et al 1987, pp. 41–52

Digman, J. M. 1990. Personality structure: Emergence of the five-factor model. *Annu. Rev. Psychol.* 41:417–40

diSessa, A. A. 1983. Phenomenology and the evolution of intuition. In *Mental Models*, ed. D. Gentner, A. Stevens, pp. 15–33. Hillsdale, NJ: Erlbaum

Dweck, C. S., Leggett, E. L. 1988. A social-cognitive approach to motivation and personality. *Psychol. Rev.* 95:256–73

Eisner, E. W. 1987. Discipline-based art education: A reply to Jackson. *Educ. Res.* 16(9):50–52

Elshout, J. J. 1987. Problem solving and education. See DeCorte et al 1987, pp. 259–73

Embretson, S. E. 1987. Improving the measurement of spatial aptitude by dynamic testing. *Intelligence* 11:333–58

Entwistle, N. 1987. Explaining individual differences in school learning. See DeCorte et al 1987, pp. 69–88

Fantuzzo, J. W., Riggio, R. E., Connelly, S., Dimeff, L. A. 1989. Effects of reciprocal tutoring on academic achievement and psychological adjustment: A component analysis. *J. Educ. Psychol.* 81:173–77

Ferguson, G. A. 1954. On learning and human ability. *Can. J. Psychol.* 8:95–112

Ferguson, G. A. 1956. On transfer and the abilities of man. *Can. J. Psychol.* 10:121–31

Ferguson-Hessler, M. G. M., deJong, T. 1990. Studying physics texts: Differences in study processes between good and poor performers. *Cogn. Instruc.* 7:41-54

Feuerstein, R., Rand, Y., Jensen, M. R., Kaniel, S., Tzuriel, D. 1987. Prerequisites for assessment of learning potential: The LPAD model. See Lidz 1987, pp. 35–81

Frederiksen, J. R., Warren, B. M. 1987. A cognitive framework for developing expertise in reading. See Glaser 1987, pp. 1–39

Frederiksen, N. 1984. The real test bias: influences on teaching and learning. *Am. Psychol.* 39:193–202

Frederiksen, N., Glaser, R., Lesgold, A., Shafto, M., eds. 1990. *Diagnostic Monitoring of Skill and Knowledge Acquisition*. Hillsdale, NJ: Erlbaum

Frederiksen, N., Mislevy, R., Bejar, I., eds.

1992. *Test Theory for a New Generation of Tests.* Hillsdale, NJ: Erlbaum. In press

Gagne, R. M., Briggs, L. J., Wager, W. W. 1988. *Principles on Instructional Design.* New York: Holt, Rinehart & Winston. 3rd ed.

Gagne, R. M., Dick, W. 1983. Instructional psychology. *Annu. Rev. Psychol.* 34:261–95

Gardner, M., Greeno, J. G., Reif, F., Schoenfeld, A. H., diSessa, A. A., Stage, E., eds. 1990. *Toward a Scientific Practice of Science Education.* Hillsdale, NJ: Erlbaum

Gelman, R., Greeno, J. G. 1989. On the nature of competence: Principles for understanding in a domain. See Resnick 1989, pp. 125–86

Gibson, J. J. 1979. *The Ecological Approach to Visual Perception.* Boston: Houghton Mifflin

Glaser, R. 1976. Components of a psychology of instruction: toward a science of design. *Rev. Educ. Res.* 46:1–24

Glaser, R. 1977. *Adaptive Education: Individual Diversity and Learning.* New York: Holt, Rinehart & Winston

Glaser, R., ed. 1987. *Advances in Instructional Psychology.* Vol. 3. Hillsdale, NJ: Erlbaum

Glaser, R., Bassok, M. 1989. Learning theory and the study of instruction. *Annu. Rev. Psychol.* 40:631–66

Gottfried, A. E. 1990. Academic intrinsic motivation in young elementary school students. *J. Educ. Psychol.* 82:525–38

Greenfield, P. M. 1984. A theory of the teacher in the learning activities of everyday life. In *Everyday Cognition: Its Development in Social Context,* ed. B. Rogoff, J. Lave, pp. 117–38. Cambridge, MA: Harvard Univ. Press

Greeno, J. G. 1989a. Situations, mental models, and generative knowledge. In *Complex Information Processing: The Impact of Herbert A. Simon,* ed. D. Klahr, K. Kotovsky. Hillsdale, NJ: Erlbaum

Greeno, J. G. 1989b. Mathematical and scientific thinking in classrooms and other situations. Presented at Am. Assoc. Adv. Sci., January

Greeno, J. G. 1991. A view of mathematical problem solving in school. In *Toward a Unified Theory of Problem Solving,* ed. M. U. Smith, pp. 69–98. Hillsdale, NJ: Erlbaum

Greeno, J. G. 1992. Number sense as situated knowing in a conceptual domain. *J. Res. Math. Educ.* In press

Greeno, J. G., Smith, D. R., Moore, J. L. 1992. Transfer of situated learning. In *Transfer on Trial,* ed. D. Detterman, R. Sternberg. In press

Greeno, J. G., Simon, H. A. 1988. Problem

solving and reasoning. In *Stevens' Handbook of Experimental Psychology,* ed. R. C. Atkinson, R. Herrnstein, G. Lindzey, R. D. Luce. New York: John Wiley & Sons. Revised ed.

Greenwood, C. R., Delquadri, J. C., Hall, R. V. 1989. Longitudinal effects of classwide peer tutoring. *J. Educ. Psychol.* 81:371–83

Gustafsson, J.-E. 1984. A unifying model for the structure of intellectual abilities. *Intelligence* 8:179–203

Gustafsson, J.-E. 1988. Hierarchical models of the structure of cognitive abilities. In *Advances in the Psychology of Human Intelligence,* ed. R. J. Sternberg, 4:35–71. Hillsdale, NJ: Erlbaum

Gustafsson, J.-E. 1989. Broad and narrow abilities in research on learning and instruction. See Kanfer et al 1989, pp. 203–37

Gustafsson, J.-E., Balke-Aurell, G. 1989. General and special abilities in the prediction of school achievement. Rep. Dept. Educ., Univ. Goteborg, Sweden

Gustafsson, J.-E., Demetriou, A., Efklides, A. 1989. Organization of cognitive abilities: training effects. Presented at the Eur. Assoc. Res. Learn. Instruct., Madrid, Spain, September 4–7

Halford, G. S. 1989. Cognitive processing capacity and learning ability: An integration of two areas. *Learn. Individ. Differ.* 1:125–53

Hall, R. H., Dansereau, D. F., Skaggs, L. P. 1990. The cooperative learner. *Learn. Individ. Differ.* 2:327–36

Hallinan, M. T. 1990. The effects of ability grouping in secondary schools: A response to Slavin's best-evidence synthesis. *Rev. Educ. Res.* 60:501–4

Harding, J., ed. 1986. *Perspectives on Gender and Science.* New York: Falmer Press

Hargreaves, D. J. 1986. *The Developmental Psychology of Music.* Cambridge, UK: Cambridge Univ. Press

Hatch, T., Gardner, H. 1990. If Binet had looked beyond the classroom: The assessment of multiple intelligences. *Int. J. Educ. Res.* 14:415–29

Heckhausen, H., Schmalt, H. D., Schneider, K. 1985. *Achievement Motivation in Perspective.* Orlando: Academic

Helmke, A. 1989. Affective student characteristics and cognitive development: Problems, pitfalls, perspectives. *Int. J. Educ. Res.* 13:915–32

Hershkowitz, R. 1989. Visualization in geometry—two sides of the coin. *Focus Learn. Probl. Math.* 11(1):61–76

Hidi, S. 1990. Interest and its contribution as a mental resource for learning. *Rev. Educ. Res.* 60:549-71

Higgins, E. T., Sorrentino, R. M., eds. 1990. *Handbook of Motivation and Cognition:*

Foundations of Social Behavior, Vol. 2. New York: Guilford

Hoffer, T. B. 1991. The effects of ability grouping in middle school science and mathematics on student achievement. Public Opinion Laboratory, Northern Illinois Univ., Dekalb, IL

Horn, J. L. 1989. Cognitive diversity: a framework of learning. See Ackerman et al, 1989, pp. 61–116

Hunt, E. 1985. Verbal ability. In *Human Abilities: An Information-Processing Approach*, ed. R. J. Sternberg, pp. 31–58. New York: Freeman

Hunt, E. 1989. Cognitive science: Definition, status, and questions. *Annu. Rev. Psychol.* 40:603–29

Hyde, J. S., Fennema, E., Lamon, S. J. 1990. Gender differences in mathematics performance: A meta-analysis. *Psychol. Bull.* 107:139-55

Hyde, J. S., Linn, M. C., eds. 1986. *The Psychology of Gender: Advances Through Meta-Analysis*. Baltimore: Johns Hopkins Univ. Press

Iran-Nejad, A., McKeachie, W. J., Berliner, D. C., eds. 1990. Toward a unified approach to learning as a multisource phenomenon. *Rev. Educ. Res.* 60:590–626

Jackson, P. W. 1987. Mainstreaming art: An essay on discipline-based art education. *Educ. Res.* 16(6):39–43

Jensen, A. 1989. The relationship between learning and intelligence. *Learn. Individ. Differ.* 1:37-62

Johnson, D., Marayama, G., Johnson, R., Nelson, D., Skon, L. 1981. Effects of cooperative, competitive, and individualistic goal structures on achievement: A meta-analysis. *Psychol. Bull.* 89:193

Johnson, W. L., Soloway, E. 1985. PROUST: An automatic debugger for Pascal programming. *Byte* 10:179–90

Just, M. A., Carpenter, P. A. 1992. A capacity theory of comprehension: Individual differences in working memory. *Psychol. Rev.* In press

Kanfer, R. 1990. Motivation and individual differences in learning: An integration of developmental, differential, and cognitive perspectives. *Learn. Individ. Differ.* 2:221–39

Kanfer, R., Ackerman, P. L. 1989. Motivation and cognition abilities: An integrative/aptitude-treatment interaction approach to skill acquisition. *J. Appl. Psychol-Monogr.* 74:657–90

Kanfer, R., Ackerman, P. L., Cudeck, R., eds. 1989. *Abilities, Motivation, and Methodology: The Minnesota Symposium on Learning and Individual Differences*. Hillsdale, NJ: Erlbaum

Keefe, J. W. 1987. *Learning Style Theory and Practice*. Reston, VA: Natl. Assoc. Secondary School Principals

Keefe, J. W., ed. 1988. *Profiling and Using Learning Style*. Reston, VA: Natl. Assoc. Secondary School Principals

Kintsch, W. 1988. The role of knowledge in discourse comprehension: A construction-integration model. *Psychol. Rev.* 95:163–82

Klauer, K. J. 1990. Paradigmatic teaching of inductive thinking. See Mandl et al 1990, pp. 23–45

Kuhl, J. 1986. Motivation and information-processing: A new look at decision-making, dynamic change, and action control. In *The Handbook of Motivation and Cognition: Foundations of Social Behavior*, ed. R. M. Sorrentino, G. T. Higgins, pp. 404–34. New York: Guilford Press

Kuhl, J. 1990. Self-regulation: A new theory for old applications. Invited address to Intl. Congr. Appl. Psychol., Kyoto, Japan, July

Kuhl, J., Kraska, K. 1989. Self-regulation and metamotivation. See Kanfer et al 1989, pp. 343–74

Kyllonen, P. C., Christal, R. E. 1990. Reasoning ability is (little more than) working-memory capacity? *Intelligence* 14:389–433

Kyllonen, P. C., Lohman, D. F., Woltz, D. J. 1984. Componential modeling of alternative strategies for performing spatial task. *J. Educ. Psychol.* 76:1325–45

Kyllonen, P. C., Shute, V. J. 1989. A taxonomy of learning skills. See Ackerman et al 1989, pp. 117–63

Kyllonen, P. C., Stephens, D. L. 1990. Cognitive abilities as determinants of success in acquiring logic skill. *Learn. Individ. Differ.* 2:129–60

Kyllonen, P. C., Tirre, W. C. 1988. Individual differences in associative learning and forgetting. *Intelligence* 12:393-421

Kyllonen, P. C., Tirre, W. C., Christal, R. E. 1992. Knowledge and processing speed as determinants of associative learning. *J. Exp. Psychol.: Gen.* In press

Kyllonen, P. C., Woltz, D. J. 1989. Role of cognitive factors in the acquisition of cognitive skill. See Kanfer et al 1989, pp. 239–80

Lajoie, S. P. 1986. *Individual differences in spatial ability: A computerized tutor for orthographic projection tasks*. PhD thesis. Stanford Univ.

Langstaff, J. J. 1989. *Problem representation and achievement in computer programming: the differential effects of inductive reasoning skills and computer programming experience*. PhD thesis. Univ. Iowa

Lave, J. 1988. *Cognition in Practice: Mind, Mathematics and Culture in Everyday Life*. Cambridge: Cambridge Univ. Press

Leinhardt, G., Greeno, J. G. 1986. The cognitive skill of teaching. *J. Educ. Psychol.* 78:75–95

Leinhardt, G., Ohlsson, S. 1989. Tutorials on the structure of tutoring form teachers. Tech. Rep. No. CLIP-89-03 & No. KUL-89-05. Cent. Stud. Learn., LRDC Univ. Pittsburgh

Lens, W. 1983. Achievement motivation, test anxiety, and academic achievement. Psychol. Rep., Univ. Leuven, Belgium

Lens, W., DeCruyenaere, M. 1991. Motivation and de-motivation in secondary education: Student characteristics. Learn. Instruc. 1:145-59

Lepper, M. R. 1988. Motivational considerations in the study of instruction. Cogn. Instruct. 5:289-309

Lepper, M. R., Aspinwall, L., Mumme, D., Chabay, R. W. 1992. Self-perception and social perception processes in tutoring: Subtle social control strategies of expert tutors. In Self Inference Processes: The Sixth Ontario Symposium in Social Psychology, ed. J. Olson, M. P. Zanna. Hillsdale, NJ: Erlbaum

Lepper, M. R., Chabay, R. W. 1988. Socializing the intelligent tutor: Bringing empathy to computer tutors. See Mandl & Lesgold 1988, pp. 242-57

Lepper, M. R., Malone, T. W. 1987. Intrinsic motivation and instructional affectiveness in computer-based education. See Snow & Farr 1987, pp. 255-86

Lesgold, A. 1988. Toward a theory of curriculum for use in designing intelligent tutoring systems. See Mandl & Lesgold 1988, pp. 114-37

Lesgold, A., Ivill-Friel, J., Bonar, J. 1989. Toward intelligent systems for testing. See Resnick 1989, pp. 337-60

Leushina, A. M. 1991. Soviet Studies in Mathematics Education, Vol. 4: The Development of Elementary Mathematical Concepts in Preschool Children. Reston, VA: Natl. Council Teachers Math.

Lidz, C. S., ed. 1987. Dynamic Assessment. New York: Guilford Press

Lindstrom, B. 1983. Learning styles and learning strategies. I. Conversation theory-the work of Gordon Pask. Rep., Dept. Educ., Univ. Goteborg, Sweden

Linn, M. C., Petersen, A. C. 1985. Emergence and characterization of sex differences in spatial ability: a meta-analysis. Child Dev. 56(6):1479-98

Lippert, R. C. 1989. Expert systems: Tutors, tools, and tutees. J. Comput.-Based Instruct. 16:11-19

Littman, D., Pinto, J., Soloway, E. 1987. The knowledge required for tutorial planning: An empirical analysis. Presented at 3rd Annu. Conf. Artif. Intell. Educ., Pittsburgh

Lohman, D. F. 1986. Predicting mathematic effects in the teaching of higher-order thinking skills. Educ. Psychol. 21:191-208

Lohman, D. F. 1988. Spatial abilities as traits, processes, and knowledge. In Advances in the Psychology of Human Intelligence, ed. R. J. Sternberg, 4:181-248. Hillsdale, NJ: Erlbaum

Lohman, D. F. 1989a. Human intelligence: An introduction to advances in theory and research. Rev. Educ. Res. 59:333-73

Lohman, D. F. 1989b. Individual differences in errors and latencies on cognitive tasks. Learn. Individ. Differ. 1:179-202

Lohman, D. F., Nichols, P. D. 1990. Training spatial abilities: Effects of practice on rotation and synthesis tasks. Learn. Individ. Differ. 2:67-93

Lord, T. R. 1987. A look at spatial abilities in undergraduate women science majors. J. Res. Sci. Teach. 24:757-67

MacIver, D. J., Stipek, D. J., Daniels, D. H. 1991. Explaining within-semester changes in student effort in junior high school and senior high school courses. J. Educ. Psychol. 83:201-11

Mandl, H., DeCorte, E., Bennett, S. N., Friedrich, H. F., eds. 1990. Learning and Instruction: European Research in an International Context. Vol. 2:1. Social and Cognitive Aspects of Learning and Instruction. Vol. 2:2. Analysis of Complex Skills and Complex Knowledge Domains. Oxford: Pergamon

Mandl, H., Lesgold, A. 1988. Learning Issues for Intelligent Tutoring Systems. New York: Springer-Verlag

Mandler, J. M. 1984. Stories, Scripts, and Scenes: Aspects of Schematic Theory. Hillsdale, NJ: Erlbaum

Marshall, S. P. 1988. Assessing Schema Knowledge. Tech. Rep. San Diego, CA: San Diego State Univ., Cent. Res. Math. Sci. Educ.

Marshall, S. P. 1990. Generating good items for diagnostic tests. See Frederiksen et al 1990, pp. 433-52

Marton, F. 1983. Beyond individual differences. Educ. Psychol. 3:289-304

Marton, F., Hounsell, D., Entwistle, N. 1984. The Experience of Learning. Edinburgh, Scotland: Scottish Academic

Mayer, R. E. 1985. Mathematical ability. In Human Abilities: An Information Processing Approach, ed. R. J. Sternberg, pp. 127-50. New York: Freeman

Mayer, R. E., ed. 1988. Teaching and Learning Computer Programming. Hillsdale, NJ: Erlbaum

McArthur, D., Stasz, C., Hotta, J., Peter, O., Burdorf, C. 1988. Oriented task sequencing in an intelligent tutor for basic algebra. Instruct. Sci. 17:281-307

McCabe, V., Balzano, G. J. 1986. *Event Cognition: An Ecological Perspective.* Hillsdale, NJ: Erlbaum

McCloskey, M., Kargon, R. 1988. The meaning and use of historical models in the study of intuitive physics. In *Ontogeny, Phylogeny, and Historical Development,* ed. S. Strauss. Norwood, NJ: Ablex

McCombs, B. L., Whisler, J. S. 1989. The role of affective variables in autonomous learning. *Educ. Psychol.* 24:277–306

McKeachie, W. J., Pintrich, P. R., Lin, Y. G., Smith, D. A. F. 1986. *Teaching and Learning in the College Classroom: A Literature Review.* Ann Arbor: Univ. Michigan

Messick, S. J. 1987. Structural relationships across cognition, personality, and style. See Snow & Farr 1987, pp. 35–75

Moll, L. C., ed. 1990. *Vygotsky and Education.* New York: Cambridge Univ. Press

Naveh-Benjamin, M. 1991. A comparison of training programs intended for different types of test-anxious students: Further support for an information processing model. *J. Educ. Psychol.* 83:134–39

Naveh-Benjamin, M., McKeachie, W. J., Lin, Y. G., Tucker, D. G. 1986. Inferring students' cognitive structures and their development using the "Ordered Tree Technique." *J. Educ. Psychol.* 78:130–40

Nenniger, P. 1987. How stable is motivation by contents? See DeCorte et al 1987, pp. 159–68

Nesher, P., Kilpatrick, J., eds. 1990. *Mathematics and Cognition: A Research Synthesis by the International Group for the Psychology of Mathematics Education.* Cambridge: Cambridge Univ. Press

Newman, D. 1989. Application of intelligent tutoring technology to an apparently mechanical task. Presented at Annu. Meet. Am. Educ. Res. Assoc., San Francisco

Newman, D., Griffin, P., Cole, M. 1989. *The Construction Zone: Working for Cognitive Change in School.* Cambridge: Cambridge Univ. Press

Nicholls, J., Cheung, P. C., Lauer, J., Patashnick, M. 1989. Individual differences in academic motivation: Perceived ability, goals, beliefs, and values. *Learn. Individ. Differ.* 1:63–84

Nickerson, R., Perkins, D. N., Smith, E. 1985. *The Teaching of Thinking.* Hillsdale, NJ: Erlbaum

Niemic, R., Walberg, H. J. 1987. Comparative effects of computer-assisted instruction: a synthesis of reviews. *J. Educ. Comp. Res.* 3:19–37

Nitko, A. J. 1989. Designing tests that are integrated with instruction. In *Educational Measurement,* ed. R. L. Linn, pp. 447–74. New York: Macmillan. 3rd. ed.

Norman, D. 1982. *Learning and Memory.* San Francisco: Freeman

Oakes, J. 1987. Tracking in secondary schools: A contextual perspective. *Educ. Psychol.* 22:129–53

Ohlsson, S. 1984a. Attentional heuristics in human thinking. Proc. 6th Conf. Cogn. Sci. Soc., Boulder

Ohlsson, S. 1984b. Induced strategy shifts in spatial reasoning. *Acta Psychol.* 57:47–67

Ohlsson, S. 1986. Some principles of intelligent tutoring. *Instruct. Sci.* 14:293–326

Ohlsson, S. 1988. Computer simulation and its impact on educational research and practice. *Int. J. Educ. Res.* 12:5–34

Ohlsson, S. 1990. Trace analysis and spatial reasoning: an example of intensive cognitive diagnosis and its implications for testing. See Frederiksen et al 1990, pp. 251–96

Palincsar, M. S. 1986. The role of dialogue in providing scaffolded instruction. *Educ. Psychol.* 21:73–98

Palincsar, M. S. 1989. Less charted waters. *Educ. Res.* 18:5–7

Palincsar, M. S., Brown, A. L. 1984. Reciprocal teaching of comprehension—fostering and monitoring activities. *Cogn. Instruct.* 1:117–75

Palincsar, M. S., Ransom, K., Derber, S. 1989. Collaborative research and development of reciprocal teaching. *Educ. Leadership* 46(4):37–40

Palincsar, M. S., Winn, J., eds. 1990. Assessment models focused on new conceptions of achievement and reasoning. *Int. J. Educ. Res.* 14:409–83

Papert, S. 1980. *Mindstorms: Children, Computers, and Powerful Ideas.* New York: Basic Books

Pask, G. 1976. Styles and strategies of learning. *Br. J. Educ. Psychol.* 46:128–48

Pask, G., Scott, B. C. E. 1972. Learning strategies and individual competence. *Int. J. Man-Machine Stud.* 4:217–53

Pea, R. D. 1990. Distributed intelligence and education. Presented at Annu. Meet. Am. Educ. Res. Assoc., Boston, April

Pea, R. D., Sheingold, K., eds. 1987. *Mirrors of Minds: Patterns of Experience in Educational Computing.* Norwood, NJ: Ablex

Pea, R., Sipusic, M., Allen, S., Reiner, M. 1990. Dynagrams for reasoning about light. Presented at Annu. Meet. Am. Educ. Res. Assoc., Boston

Pellegrino, J. W. 1985. Inductive reasoning ability. In *Human Abilities: An Information-Processing Approach,* ed. R. J. Sternberg, pp. 195–225. San Francisco: Freeman

Perfetti, C. A. 1985. *Reading Ability.* New York: Oxford Univ. Press

Perfetti, C. A. 1989. There are generalized abilities and one of them is reading. See Resnick 1989, pp. 307–35

Perkins, D. N. 1990. Person plus: A distributed view of thinking and learning. Presented at Annu. Meet. Am. Educ. Res. Assoc., Boston, April

Perkins, D. N., Salomon, G. 1989. Are cognitive skills context-bound? *Educ. Res.* 18(1):16–25

Perkins, D. N., Simmons, R. 1988. An integrative model of misconceptions. *Rev. Educ. Res.* 58:303–26

Peterson, P. L. 1988. Selecting students and services for compensatory education: Lessons from aptitude-treatment interaction research. *Educ. Psychol.* 23:313–52

Peverly, S. T. 1991. Problems with the knowledge-based explanation of memory and development. *Rev. Educ. Res.* 61:71–93

Pines, A. L., Novak, J. D., Posner, G. J., Van Kirk, J. 1978. *The Clinical Interview: A Method for Evaluating Cognitive Structure.* Res. Rep. 6. Ithaca, NY: Cornell Univ. Dept. Educ.

Pintrich, P. R., Cross, D. R., Kozma, R. B., McKeachie, W. J. 1986. Instructional psychology. *Annu. Rev. Psychol.* 37:611–51

Polson, M. C., Richardson, J. J., eds. 1988. *Foundations of Intelligent Tutoring Systems.* Hillsdale, NJ: Erlbaum

Pressley, M., Borkowski, J. G., Schneider, W. 1989. Good information processing: What it is and how education can promote it. *Int. J. Educ. Res.* 13:857–97

Pribyl, J. R., Bodner, G. M. 1985. The role of spatial ability and achievement in organic chemistry. Presented at 58th Annu. Meet. Natl. Assoc. Res. Sci. Teach., French Lick Springs, IN

Putnam, R. T. 1987. Structuring and adjusting content for students: A study of live and simulated tutoring addition. *Am. Educ. Res. J.* 24:13–48

Rand, P., Lens, W., Decock, B. 1989. Negative motivation is half the story: Achievement motivation combines positive and negative motivation. Rep. 2. Inst. Educ. Res., Univ. Oslo, Norway

Reigeluth, C. M., ed. 1987. *Instructional Theories in Action: Lessons Illustrating Selected Theories and Models.* Hillsdale, NJ: Erlbaum

Renninger, K. A., Hidi, S., Krapp, A., eds. 1992. *The Role of Interest in Learning and Development.* Hillsdale, NJ: Erlbaum. In press

Renstrom, L., Andersson, B., Marton, F. 1990. Student's conceptions of matter. *J. Educ. Psychol.* 82:555–69

Resnick, L. B. 1981. Instructional psychology. *Annu. Rev. Psychol.* 32:659–704

Resnick, L. B. 1987. *Education and Learning to Think.* Washington, DC: Natl. Acad. Press

Resnick, L. B., ed. 1989. *Knowing, Learning, and Instruction: Essays in Honor of Robert Glaser.* Hillsdale, NJ: Erlbaum

Resnick, L. B., Neches, R. 1984. Factors affecting individual differences in learning ability. In *Advances in the Psychology of Human Intelligence,* ed. R. J. Sternberg, 2:275–323. Hillsdale, NJ: Erlbaum

Resnick, L. B., Omanson, S. F. 1987. Learning to understand arithmetic. See Glaser 1987, pp. 41–95

Rock, I., Wheeler, D., Tudor, L. 1989. Can we imagine how objects look from other viewpoints? *Cogn. Psychol.* 21:185–210

Rogoff, B. 1990 *Apprenticeship in Thinking.* New York: Oxford Univ. Press

Rogoff, B., Gardner, W. 1984. Adult guidance of cognitive development. In *Everyday Cognition: Its Development in Social Context,* ed. B. Rogoff, J. Lave, pp. 95–116. Cambridge, MA: Harvard Univ. Press

Rollett, B. A. 1987. Effort avoidance and learning. See DeCorte et al 1987, pp. 147–57

Roschelle, J. 1990. Designing for conversations. Presented at Annu. Meet. Am. Educ. Res. Assoc., Boston

Ross, J. A., Raphael, D. 1990. Communication and problem solving achievement in cooperative learning groups. *J. Curric. Stud.* 22:149–64

Ruijssenaars, W., Hamers, J. 1990. Assessment of learning ability: Learning ability tests and the analysis of learning processes. See Mandl et al 1990, pp. 547–59

Ryan, T. A. 1981. Intention and kinds of learning. In *Cognition in Human Motivation and Learning,* ed. G. d'Ydewalle, W. Lens, pp. 59–85. Leuven, Belgium/Hillsdale, NJ: Leuven Univ. Press/Erlbaum

Salomon, G. 1983. The differential investment of mental effort in learning from different sources. *Educ. Psychol.* 18:42–50

Salomon, G. 1990. If intelligence is distributed—what about the cultivation of individuals' abilities? Presented at Annu. Meet. Am. Educ. Res. Assoc., Boston, April

Salomon, G., Globerson, T. 1987. Skill may not be enough: The role of mindfulness in learning. *Int. J. Educ. Res.* 11:623–37

Salomon, G., Perkins, D. N. 1989. Rocky roads to transfer: Rethinking mechanisms of a neglected phenomenon. *Educ. Psychol.* 24:113–42

Sarason, S. B., Klaber, M. 1985. The school as a social situation. *Annu. Rev. Psychol.* 36:115–40

Schiano, D. J., Kahleifeh, B. 1988. Spatial aptitude as expertise: A training study. Presented at Am. Psychol. Assoc., Atlanta

Schmeck, R. R., ed. 1988. *Learning Strategies and Learning Styles.* New York: Plenum

Schmeck, R. R., Geisler-Brenstein, E. 1989. Individual differences that affect the way students approach learning. *Learn. Individ. Differ.* 1:85–124

Schneider, W., Korkel, J., Weinert, F. E. 1990. Expert knowledge, general abilities, and text processing. See Schneider & Weinert 1990, pp. 235–51

Schneider, W., Pressley, M. 1989. *Memory Development Between 2 and 20.* New York: Springer-Verlag

Schneider, W., Weinert, F. E., eds. 1990. *Interactions Among Aptitudes, Strategies, and Knowledge in Cognitive Performance.* New York: Springer-Verlag

Schoenfeld, A. H., ed. 1987. *Cognitive Science and Mathematics Education.* Hillsdale, NJ: Erlbaum

Schon, D. A. 1987. *Educating the Reflective Practitioner.* San Francisco, CA: Jossey Bass

Schunk, D. H. 1989. Self-efficacy and cognitive skill learning. See Ames & Ames 1989, pp. 13–44

Segal, J. W., Chipman, S. F., Glaser, R., eds. 1985. *Thinking and Learning Skills,* Vol. 1. Hillsdale, NJ: Erlbaum

Serafine, M. L. 1986. Music. In *Cognition and Instruction,* ed. R. F. Dillon, R. J. Sternberg, pp. 299–341. Orlando: Academic

Sharan, S. 1980. Cooperative learning in small groups: Recent methods, and effects on achievement, attitudes, and ethnic relations. *Rev. Educ. Res.* 50:241–72

Sharan, S. 1984. Cooperative and traditional teaching: An overview of results. In *Cooperative Learning in the Classroom: Research in Desegregated Schools,* ed. S. Sharan, P. Kussell, R. Hertz-Lazarowitz, Y. Bejarno, S. Ravi, Y. Sharan, T. Brosh, R. Peleg. Hillsdale, NJ: Erlbaum

Shuell, T. J. 1990. Phases of meaningful learning. *Rev. Educ. Res.* 60:531–47

Shulman, L. S. 1986. Those who understand: Knowledge growth in teaching. *Educ. Res.* 15:4–14

Shulman, L. S. 1990. Reconnecting foundations to the substance of teacher education. *Teach. Coll. Rec.* 91:300–10

Shulman, L. S., Ringstaff, C. 1989. Current research on the psychology of learning and tutoring. In *Designing Computer-Based Learning Material,* ed. A. Bork, H. Weinstock. New York: Springer-Verlag

Shute, V. J. 1989. Individual differences in learning from an intelligent tutoring system.

Presented at Meet. Am. Educ. Res. Assoc., March

Shute, V. J. 1990a. A comparison of inductive and deductive learning environments: Which is better for whom and why? Presented at Meet. Am. Educ. Res. Assoc., April

Shute, V. J. 1990b. Aptitude-treatment interactions and cognitive skill diagnosis. Brooks AFB, TX: Air Force Hum. Resourc. Lab.

Shute, V. J. 1990c. Modeling individual differences in programming skill acquisition. Brooks AFB, TX: Air Force Hum. Resourc. Lab.

Shute, V. J., Glaser, R. 1990. A large-scale evaluation of an intelligent discovery world: Smithtown. *Interact. Learn. Environ.* 1:51–77

Siegler, R. S. 1986. *Children's Thinking.* Englewood Cliffs, NJ: Prentice-Hall

Siegler, R. S., Campbell, J. 1990. Diagnosing individual differences in strategy choice procedures. See Frederiksen et al 1990, pp. 113–39

Simon, H. A. 1990. Invariants of human behavior. *Annu. Rev. Psychol.* 41:1–19

Simons, P. R. J., Beukhof, G., eds. 1987. *Regulation of Learning.* Den Haag, Netherlands: Inst. Onderzoek Het Onderwijs S. V. O.

Singley, M. K., Anderson, J. R. 1989. *The Transfer of Cognitive Skill.* Cambridge, MA: Harvard Univ. Press

Skaalvik, E. M., Rankin, R. J. 1990. Math, verbal and general academic self-concept: The internal/external frame of reference model and gender differences in self-concept structure. *J. Educ. Psychol.* 82: 546–54

Slavin, R. E. 1983. When does cooperative learning increase student achievement? *Psychol. Bull.* 94:429–45

Slavin, R. E. 1987. Ability grouping and student achievement in elementary schools: A best-evidence synthesis. *Rev. Educ. Res.* 57:293–336

Slavin, R. E. 1990a. *Cooperative Learning: Theory, Research, and Practice.* Englewood Cliffs, NJ: Prentice-Hall

Slavin, R. E. 1990b. Achievement effects of ability grouping secondary school: A best-evidence synthesis. *Rev. Educ. Res.* 60:471–99

Slavin, R. E., Madden, N. A. 1989. What works for students at risk: A research synthesis. *Educ. Leadership* 46:4–13

Sleeman, D. 1987. PIXIE a shell for developing intelligent tutoring systems. In *Artificial Intelligence and Education,* ed. R. W. Lawler, M. Yazdani, 1:239–65. Norwood, NJ: Ablex

Sleeman, D. H., Brown, J. S., eds. 1982. *Intelligent Tutoring Systems.* London: Academic

Sleeman, D., Kelly, A. E., Martinak, R., Ward, R. D., Moore, J. L. 1989. Studies of diagnosis and remediation with high school algebra students. *Cogn. Sci.* 13:551–68

Sloboda, J. A. 1985. *The Musical Mind: The Cognitive Psychology of Music.* Oxford, UK: Oxford Univ. Press

Snow, R. E. 1987. Aptitude complexes. See Snow & Farr 1987, pp. 11–34

Snow, R. E. 1989a. Aptitude-treatment interaction as a framework of research in individual differences in learning. See Ackerman et al 1989, 13–59

Snow, R. E. 1989b. Cognitive-conative aptitude interactions in learning. See Kanfer et al 1989, pp. 435–74

Snow, R. E. 1989c. Toward assessment of cognitive and conative structures in learning. *Educ. Res.* 18(9):8–14

Snow, R. E. 1991. The concept of aptitude. In *Improving Inquiry in Social Science,* ed. R. E. Snow, D. F. Wiley, pp. 249–84. Hillsdale, NJ: Erlbaum

Snow, R. E. 1992. Aptitude theory: yesterday, today, and tomorrow. *Educ. Psychol.* In press

Snow, R. E., Farr, M. J., eds. 1987. *Aptitude, Learning, and Instruction.* Vol. 3: *Conative and Affective Process Analyses.* Hillsdale, NJ: Erlbaum

Snow, R. E., Lohman, D. F. 1984. Toward a theory of cognitive aptitude for learning from instruction. *J. Educ. Psychol.* 76:347–76

Snow, R. E., Lohman, D. F. 1989. Implications of cognitive psychology for educational measurement. In *Educational Measurement,* ed. R. L. Linn, pp. 263–331. New York: Macmillan. 3rd ed

Snow, R. E., Mandinach, E. B. 1991. Integrating assessment and instruction: A research and development agenda. Res. Rep. RR-91-8. Educ. Test. Serv., Princeton, NJ

Somerville, S. C., Hartley, J. L. 1986. Art. In *Cognition and Instruction,* ed. R. F. Dillon, R. J. Sternberg, pp. 241–98. Orlando: Academic

Speece, D. L., Cooper, D. H. 1990. Dynamic assessment, individual differences, and academic achievement. *Learn. Individ. Differ.* 2:113–27

Steinberg, E. R. 1989. Cognition and learner control: A literature review, 1977–1988. *J. Comput.-Based Instruct.* 16:117–21

Sternberg, R. J., ed. 1984. *Mechanisms of Cognitive Development.* San Francisco: Freeman

Sternberg, R. J. 1985. *Beyond IQ: A Triarchic Theory of Human Intelligence.* Cambridge: Cambridge Univ. Press

Sternberg, R. J. 1986. *Intelligence Applied.* Orlando: Harcourt Brace Jovanovich

Sternberg, R. J. 1987. The psychology of verbal comprehension. See Glaser 1987, pp. 97-151

Sternberg, R. J. 1989. Domain-generality versus domain-specificity: The life and impending death of a false dichotomy. *Merrill-Palmer Q.* 35:115–30

Sternberg, R. J., Davidson, J. E. 1990. Special issue: Intelligence and intelligence testing. *Educ. Psychol.* 25:173–358

Sternberg, R. J., Lubart, T. I. 1991. An investment theory of creativity and its development. *Hum. Dev.* 34:1–31

Stevens, A. L., Collins, A. 1977. The goal structure of a Socratic tutor. *Proc. Natl. ACM Conf.,* pp. 256–63, Seattle, WA

Stevenson, H. W., Lee, S.-Y., Chen, C., Stigler, J. W., Hsu, C.-C., Kitamura, S. 1992. Contexts of achievement: A study of American, Chinese, and Japanese children. *Monogr. Soc. Res. Child Dev.* Chicago: Univ. Chicago Press. In press

Stigler, J., Lee, S.-Y., Stevenson, H. W. 1990. *Mathematical Knowledge of Japanese, Chinese, and American Elementary School Children.* Reston, VA: Natl. Counc. Teach. Math.

Swanson, J. H. 1990. *One-to-one instruction: an experimental evaluation of effective tutorial strategies.* PhD thesis. Stanford Univ.

Tharp, R. G. 1989. Psychocultural variables and constants: effects on teaching and learning in schools. *Am. Psychol.* 44:349–59

Thorndike, R. M., Lohman, D. F. 1989. *A Century of Ability Testing.* Chicago: Riverside

Tiedeman, J. 1989. Measures of cognitive styles: A critical review. *Educ. Psychol.* 24:261–75

Tobias, S. 1985. Test anxiety: interference, defective skills, and cognitive capacity. *Educ. Psychol.* 20:135–42

Tobias, S. 1987. Learner characteristics. In *Instructional Technology: Foundations,* ed. R. M. Gagne, pp. 207–31. Hillsdale, NJ: Erlbaum

Tobias, S. 1989. Another look at research on the adaptation of instruction and student characteristics. *Educ. Psychol.* 24:213–27

Tullos, D. 1987. *Individual differences in reasoning: An analysis of solution processes in figural matrix problems.* PhD thesis. Stanford Univ.

Undheim, J. O., Gustafsson, J.-E. 1989. Development of broad and narrow factors of intelligence as a function of verbal interests and activities. Presented at the Eur. Assoc.

Res. Learn. Instruct., Madrid, Spain, September 4–7

Van Calster, K., Lens, W., Nuttin, J. 1987. Affective attitude toward the personal future: Impact on motivation in high school boys. Am. J. Psychol. 100:1–13

VanLehn, K. 1988. Student modeling. In Foundations of Intelligent Tutoring Systems, ed. M. C. Polson, J. J. Richardson, pp. 55–78. Hillsdale, NJ: Erlbaum

Vernon, P. E. 1950. The Structure of Human Abilities. London: Methuen

Vincenti, W. G. 1990. What Engineers Know and How They Know It: Analytical Studies from Aeronautical History. Baltimore, MD: The Johns Hopkins Press

Vosniadou, S., Brewer, W. F. 1987. Theories of knowledge restructuring in development. Rev. Educ. Res. 57:51–67

Vosniadou, S., Ortony, A. eds. 1989. Similarity and Analogical Reasoning. New York: Cambridge Univ. Press

Voss, J. F. 1986. Social studies. In Cognition and Instruction, ed. R. F. Dillon, R. J. Sternberg, pp. 205–39. Orlando: Academic

Voss, J. F., Blais, J., Means, M. L., Greene, T. R., Ahwesh, E. 1989. Informal reasoning and subject matter knowledge in the solving of economics problems by naive and novice individuals. See Resnick 1989, pp. 217–49

Vygotsky, L. S. 1978. Mind in Society: The Development of Higher Psychological Processes. Cambridge, MA: Harvard Univ. Press

Wang, M. C., Lindvall, C. M. 1984. Individual differences and school learning environments. Rev. Res. Educ. 11:161–225

Wasik, B. A., Slavin, R. E. 1990. Preventing early reading failure with one-to-one tutoring: a best-evidence synthesis. Presented at Annu. Meet. Am. Educ. Res. Assoc., Boston

Webb, N. M. 1982. Student interaction and learning in small groups. Rev. Educ. Res. 52:421–45

Webb, N. M. 1983. Predicting learning from student interaction: Defining the interaction variables. Educ. Psychol. 18:33–41

Webb, N. M. 1989. Peer interaction and learning in small groups. Int. J. Educ. Res. 13:21–39

Webb, N. M., Ender, P., Lewis, S. 1986. Problem-solving strategies and group process in small group learning computer programming. Am. Educ. Res. J. 23:243–61

Weinert, F. E., ed. 1989. The relation between education and development. Int. J. Educ. Res. 13:827–948

Weinert, F. E., Helmke, A., Schneider, W. 1990. Individual differences in learning performance and in school achievement: Plaus-

ible parallels and unexplained discrepancies. See Mandl et al 1990, pp. 461–79

Weinert, F. E., Perlmutter, M., eds. 1988. Memory Development: Universal Changes and Individual Differences. Hillsdale, NJ: Erlbaum

Weinert, F. E., Schneider, W., eds. 1991. The Munich Longitudinal Study on the Genesis of Individual Competencies (LOGIC) Rep. 7: Assessment Procedures and Results of Wave Four. Munich: Max-Planck-Inst. Psychol. Res.

Weinstein, C. E., Goetz, E. T., Alexander, P. A., eds. 1988. Learning and Study Strategies. San Diego, CA: Academic

Weinstein, C. E., Mayer, R. E. 1986. The teaching of learning strategies. See Wittrock 1986, pp. 315–27

Weinstein, C. E., Mayer, R. E. 1986. The teaching of learning strategies. See Wittrock 1986, pp. 315–27

Weinstein, C. S. 1991. The classroom as a social context for learning. Annu. Rev. Psychol. 42:493–525

Wenger, E. 1987. Artificial Intelligence and Tutoring Systems. Los Altos, CA: Morgan Kaufmann Publ.

Wertsch, J. V., Stone, C. A. 1985. The concept of internalization in Vygotsky's account of the genesis of higher mental functions. In Culture, Communication, and Cognition: Vygotskian Perspectives, ed. J. V. Wertsch, pp. 162–79. New York: Cambridge Univ. Press

Whitener, E. M. 1989. A meta-analytic review of the effect on learning of the interaction between prior achievement and instructional support. Rev. Educ. Res. 59:65–86

Wigfield, A., Eccles, J. S. 1989. Test anxiety in elementary and secondary school students. Educ. Psychol. 24:159–83

Wilkinson, L. C. 1988. Grouping children for learning: Implications for kindergarten education. Rev. Res. Educ. 15:203–23

Wineburg, S. S. 1989. Remembrance of theories past. Educ. Res. 18:7–10

Wineburg, S. S. 1991. Historical problem solving: A study of the cognitive processes used in the evaluation of documentary and pictorial evidence. J. Educ. Psychol. 83:73–87

Wiser, M. 1988. The differentiation of heat and temperature: History of science and expert-novice shift. In Ontogeny, Phylogeny, and Historical Development, ed. S. Strauss. Norwood, NJ: Ablex

Wittrock, M. C., ed. 1986. Handbook of Research on Teaching. New York: Macmillan. 3rd ed.

Woltz, D. J. 1988. An investigation of the role of working memory in procedural skill acquisition. *J. Exp. Psychol.: Gen.* 117: 319–31

Wood, D. J. 1980. Teaching the young child: Some relationships between social interaction, language, and thought. In *The Social Foundation of Language and Thought*, ed. D. R. Olson, pp. 280–96. New York: Norton

Wood, D. J., Bruner, J. S., Ross, G. 1976. The role of tutoring in problem solving. *J. Child Psychol. Psychiatry* 17:89–100

Wood, D. J., Wood, H., Griffiths, A., Howarth, I. 1986. *Teaching and Talking with Deaf Children*. New York: John Wiley

Wood, D. J., Wood, H., Middleton, D. 1978. An experimental evaluation of Four Face-To-Face Teaching Strategies. *Int. J. Behav. Dev.* 1:131–47

Yakimanskaya, I. S. 1991. *Soviet Studies in Mathematics Education*, Vol. 3: *The Development of Spatial Thinking in School Children*. Reston, VA: Natl. Counc. Teach. Math.

Zavotka, S. L. 1987. Three-dimensional computer animated graphics: A tool for spatial skill instruction. *Educ. Commun. Technol. J.* 35(3):133–44

Zimmerman, B., Schunk, D., eds. *Self-Regulated Learning and Academic Achievement*. New York: Springer-Verlag

Annu. Rev. Psychol. 1992. 43:627–70

PERSONNEL SELECTION

Frank L. Schmidt and Deniz S. Ones

Department of Management and Organization, College of Business, University of Iowa, Iowa City, Iowa 52242

John E. Hunter

Department of Psychology, Michigan State University, East Lansing, Michigan 48823

KEY WORDS: validity, validity generalization, predictors, selection utility, test fairness

---

CONTENTS

INTRODUCTION

This review covers the years 1989 and 1990 but cites earlier studies where appropriate. It does not purport to be comprehensive but rather is selective

0066-4308/92/0201-0627$02.00

and critical, emphasizing what we consider to be the more important developments. Much good research in personnel selection appears in unpublished technical reports—e.g. in the case of military and government research, which is sometimes the best supported in terms of resources, sample sizes, and other critical factors. We include such research whenever appropriate. We do not attempt to cover item response theory and its application in computer adaptive testing, nor do we cover such selection-related topics as recruitment, retention, and turnover.

VALIDITY GENERALIZATION AND META-ANALYSIS

Validity generalization (VG) continues to be a focal point for progress, discussion, and debate. Dunnette (1989) reported on a major consortium study of electrical power plant operators that employed VG methods; validities were found to generalize across plants and organizations. In Chapter 6 of its report, the National Research Council Committee on the General Aptitude Test Battery (GATB) of the US Employment Service examined in detail the statistical and measurement procedures of VG and pronounced them scientifically sound (Hartigan & Wigdor 1990). On the other hand, it was widely believed among industrial/organizational (I/O) psychologists and others that a major purpose of some of the language in the proposed Civil Rights Acts of 1990 and 1991 was to prevent or reduce the use of VG in US industry. The US Department of Labor (1990) announced its intention to suspend the GATB VG program for two years because of controversy over adjustments made to test scores to eliminate score differences among whites, blacks, and Hispanics (see the section below on fairness). The stakes here are major: to the extent that widespread use of VG leads to increased validity of selection, the economic gains will be large (see the section below on utility analysis); prevention of such use would forego those gains.

The methods of VG are widely applied to research literatures other than selection. A new book has appeared that explicates these meta-analysis methods in detail (Hunter & Schmidt, 1990a) and discusses most criticisms of VG and meta-analysis. Wanous et al (1989) showed that, in nonselection areas, differing decisions by meta-analysts (e.g. about which studies to include) can result in somewhat different final numerical results (correlation and effect-size estimates). Correcting for these different decisions eliminates these differences in results. However, most differences are not in numerical results but in the substantive *interpretations* of results, a domain outside of meta-analysis. Whetzel & McDaniel (1988) presented evidence that in VG studies, intercoder agreement is virtually perfect, because study coding is more factual and straightforward than in most other research areas. Callender & Osburn (1988) empirically and rationally examined Spector & Levine's surprising conclusion (1987) that the standard formula for the sampling error variance of the correlation coefficient was substantially positively biased and demonstrated that this was not the case. The considerations are complex, but the traditional statistical formula proves accurate. Kemery et al (1989) examined the 90% credibility value (CV) under unrealistic simulation conditions in which some percentage of the population correlations were zero and the rest were all some single nonzero value. Not surprisingly, they found that the 90% CVs based on the normality assumptions were not accurate in an artificial dichotomous condition. This study, along with their previous study, is critiqued by Hunter & Schmidt (1990a:222–23).

Osburn & Callender (1990) examined the critique by Thomas (1988) of the basic VG subtractive model, $S^2_\rho = S^2_r - S^2_e$. Thomas concluded that an anomaly existed such that the expected value of S^2_ρ computed using this equation can be larger when its true value is zero than when the true value is greater than zero. Osburn & Callender showed that this phenomenon was due to an unrealistic assumption made by Thomas and does not occur in real data. They also addressed other objections raised by Thomas. In another article, Thomas (1990) proposed a new, somewhat different validity generalization model [explained in more detail by Thomas (1989)]. The major current weakness of this model is that it is not applicable if there is any variation across studies in reliability, range restriction levels, dichotomization cut points, or other artifacts; this appears to rule out its use with real data. In this vein, Raju et al (1989) presented and compared VG models for regression slopes and covariances (in addition to the usual model for correlations). Although their simulation studies showed these methods can be accurate, they can be used only when the studies in the meta-analysis all use the same measurement scales for both variables—something that is very rare indeed.

Other problems with these methods are discussed in Hunter & Schmidt (1990a:202–6). However, Raju et al (1991) have presented a modified procedure for meta-analysis of correlations that takes into account sampling error in reliability coefficients; simulation results indicate the procedure is quite accurate. Millsap (1988) correctly noted that 90% CVs are subject to second-order sampling error and presented adjustments for this. However, Hunter & Schmidt (1991) showed there are errors in Millsap's formulas, and when these are corrected, the resulting values are only slightly different from those given by the conventional method.

The formula for sampling error variance of a correlation assumes that the variables correlated are both at least approximately normal. Direct range restriction violates this assumption. Millsap (1989) used computer simulation to show that in the presence of direct range restriction, correlations have larger sampling variances than indicated by the standard formula, causing VG methods to undercorrect for sampling error and making generalizability conclusions conservative. There is no known alternative formula for use in the presence of range restriction and thus no way to make the additional correction needed. Alexander et al (1989a) tabulated empirical distributions of range restriction values from a large employment data set and found the distribution for cognitive tests to be similar to those used in most published VG studies. They recommended use of their distributions in VG studies but concluded that generalizability conclusions are not likely to change as a result. Hedges (1989) presented corrections for the tiny downward statistical bias in the usual correction for sampling error variance but concluded that the correction was so small as to be unnecessary in most real VG studies. Linearity of ability-performance relations is a major assumption in all validity studies based on the Pearson correlation and is therefore critical to VG. Coward & Sackett (1990) report a large sample reconfirmation of earlier findings of linearity, using somewhat more powerful tests. The frequent practice of dichotomizing continuous measures and variables causes bias in meta-analytic estimates of means (downward) and variances (upward). Hunter & Schmidt (1990b) present methods for correcting for these neglected biases in VG and other meta-analyses.

Whitener (1990) addressed the distinction in meta-analysis between credibility intervals and confidence intervals, about which there has been considerable confusion in the literature. In credibility intervals, the effects of sampling error have been removed, whereas confidence intervals are *based on* the amount of (second-order) sampling error in the mean observed r (or d) statistic. W. G. Osburn & J. Callender (unpublished) offer slightly different formulas for confidence intervals. Confidence intervals have been used primarily as tests of statistical significance of the mean observed r (by examining whether its lower bound includes zero), thus raising the question of whether significance tests should be used in meta-analysis. Hunter & Schmidt (1990a, Ch. 2 and Ch. 11) argue that use of significance tests is the major cause of the interpretational errors that meta-analysis is designed to correct, and thus should not be introduced into meta-analysis. Related to this question, Alexander et al (1989c) argue that the chi-square test of homogeneity should not be applied directly to correlations but only to Fisher's z transforms of correlations. This is a moot point if significance tests should generally not be used at all, as contended by Hunter & Schmidt (1990a:483–84). Alexander et al (1989c) reported a typically small Type I bias when untransformed r are used; this bias may be less than the Type I bias in real data due to excess variance (beyond sampling variance) caused by variations across studies in reliabilities and range restriction levels. They did not examine this ubiquitous Type I bias. Earlier research has shown that different computational formulas for VG yield similar results. Burke & Doran (1989) reported a similar study with similar findings, and then went on to show that the resulting dollar utility figures were also similar.

Overall, VG continues to generate much research, but the questions studied are becoming more micro and less macro; many articles are examinations of potential fine tunings. The larger questions appear to be in areas of application of meta-analysis outside of personnel selection (Hunter & Schmidt 1990a). However, this is a positive development, indicating the maturing of what was viewed 10 years ago as an abrupt paradigm shift in personnel selection. The big questions in VG today appear to be not in the scientific but in the applications domain. For example, will the Supreme Court's Wards Cove decision mean increased use of VG by employers? What are the implications of the Civil Rights Bill of 1991 and of the US Department of Labor's proposed two-year suspension of the GATB? The answers to these questions will depend on the societal struggle to balance the competing values of economic efficiency and competitiveness, on the one hand, and equality, on the other.

PREDICTORS

Ability and Aptitude Tests

Aptitude and ability tests continue to be a major focus of research in personnel selection. Anastasi (1989) presents an overview of some major trends in ability and aptitude testing, including the increasing emphasis on theory and construct validation, item response theory, validity generalization, and the responsibilities of test users. An informative book-length integrative review of validity studies conducted on the Armed Services Vocational Aptitude Battery (ASVAB) is now available (Welsh et al 1990). This is accompanied by an extensive annotated bibliography of ASVAB studies, with abstracts of each study. The importance of these two documents is enhanced by the fact that most of the studies covered are not in the published literature but are available as technical reports to the researcher who knows what to ask for.

An attempt to validate the ASVAB for civilian occupations (Armstrong et al 1988) was crippled when the Office of Management and Budget (OMB) refused to allow gathering of criterion data; as a result the criterion used was *membership* in occupations rather than performance. However, Hunter (1986) had previously shown that several of the key constructs in the ASVAB are identical to their counterparts in The General Aptitude Test Battery (GATB), thus making GATB validity evidence relevant. Also, Austin & Hanisch (1990) found in a large-sample longitudinal study using Project Talent data that mental-ability scores obtained by high school sophomores were the best predictor of occupational attainment 11 years later. Research relating the general mental ability component of the ASVAB to hands-on performance measured by job sample tests in the three armed services has found substantial validity that is stable over the four years of the enlistment period (Office of the Assistant Secretary of Defense, Force Management and Personnel 1990).

Although people at all levels of aptitude improved with job experience, differences between higher- and lower-aptitude personnel persisted, replicating earlier findings (Schmidt et al 1988b).

For some years the Army has conducted a major research effort (Project A) to validate predictors of hands-on performance measures and other criteria for Army jobs. A special issue of *Personnel Psychology* (J. P. Campbell 1990) devotes nine articles to describing Project A. "Core job performance" (technical proficiency and general soldiering proficiency) was best predicted by general cognitive ability (assessed by the ASVAB), while ratings of effort and leadership, personal discipline, and physical fitness were best predicted by personality measures (McHenry et al 1990; see also the section below on personality). Other cognitive and noncognitive predictors produced only small increments in validity over general cognitive ability in predicting core job performance. Increments for personality measures were substantial for the three ratings-based secondary criteria. (All ASVAB validities were predictive; other validities were concurrent.)

Project A, conducted at a cost of approximately $25 million, is probably the largest and most expensive selection research project in history. The availability of money, time, talent, and large samples made possible state of the art thoroughness throughout the research. It is a major contribution to personnel psychology substantively, conceptually, and methodologically. Yet in the area of cognitive abilities and aptitudes, Project A reconfirms previous findings rather than reporting new findings.

A major event in the area of ability testing was the release of the National Research Council report on the GATB (Hartigan & Wigdor 1990), mentioned above. Key questions for this panel were "Is the GATB valid?" and "Does the validity generalize?" The Committee answered both these questions positively, but estimated the magnitude of validity at a lower level than had Hunter (1983). This was due partly to the availability of new studies not included in the original analysis; but it was also the result of the committee's overestimating the interrater reliability of ratings by a single rater (.80 vs the actual value of about .55; see Rothstein 1990), thus undercorrecting for measurement error, and to the failure of the committee to make any correction at all for range restriction (on grounds that precise estimates of applicant SDs were not available). The result was a lower bound mean validity estimate of about .30, versus the original .50. However, the committee concluded that .30 was sufficient to produce substantial utility.

In May 1990, the US Office of Personnel Management introduced a new nationwide examination for college graduates seeking government careers. For each of six job families, tests of verbal and quantitative reasoning abilities have been developed that are cast in terms of concrete tasks appearing on those jobs. The tests are unique in that they are constructed using the principles of Logic Based Measurement (Colberg & Nestor 1987; Colberg

1985), which ensure that 1. all relevant facets of deductive and inductive reasoning are covered, and 2. the keyed correct answers are logically correct. The exam also includes a biodata component (discussed below). Initial validity findings for the exam have been encouraging.

The use of meta-analysis to calibrate the absolute and relative validities of selection procedures more precisely requires the availability of validity studies. But journals have become increasingly reluctant to publish standard validity studies. One solution to this problem is the new *Test Validity Yearbook*, edited by Professor Frank Landy of Pennsylvania State University. Some 35 manuscripts have been accepted, and Volume I is expected in 1991. Ash et al (1990) reported a survey of selection methods used by urban and state police. The percentages of forces using the various methods were: cognitive ability, 92%; personality tests, 68%; biodata, 35%; and physical strength and agility, 80%. Based on a sample of almost 300 managers, Schippmann & Prien (1989) reported an uncorrected correlation of .35 between general mental ability and rate of managerial progression (age-corrected managerial rank). Most studies relating ability to managerial success have used ratings, making this study an improvement. Campion (1989) reported evidence that designing or redesigning jobs to increase their motivating potential (motivational attributes) may also increase the levels of general mental ability required, and hence could affect selection and compensation practices.

Prediger (1989) challenged the conclusion (Hunter 1986; Jensen 1986; Thorndike 1986) that general ability is more important in determining occupational level and job performance than specific abilities, but he presented no data on validity or incremental validity. His conclusion that specific aptitudes are important in performance was based on data showing distinct patterns of specific-aptitude means across occupations, both among incumbents and among high school students who later entered specific occupations. However, validities can be equal for different occupations when means are different. Prediger seems to have overlooked the possibility, predicted by the investment theory of ability, that interests determine both (*a*) the specific skills (e.g. mechanical) that the individual "invests" his general ability in developing, and (*b*) job choice. If interests determine both relative standing on specific aptitudes (within the individual) and job choice, this would explain why specific aptitudes contribute little beyond general ability to prediction of job *performance*.

Avolio & Waldman (1990) hypothesized a stronger negative correlation between age and mental ability in low- than in high-complexity jobs, but this hypothesis was not supported. The variation across occupations in the small negative r's was not interpretable and may be due to statistical and measurement artifacts. Answering the question of whether high-complexity jobs prevent mental-ability declines with age will probably require longitudinal data. Carretta (1989) found that psychomotor tests produced incremental validity over use of general cognitive ability alone in predicting success in pilot training. Sperl et al (1990) showed that the key cognitive ability constructs measured by the Air Force Officer Qualifying Test (AFOQT) and the ASVAB (used only with enlisted personnel) were identical. This study is an example of the increasing recognition that the critical sources of validity and the important constructs tend to be similar across different cognitive batteries. Incremental validity over general mental ability appears to require measurement outside the strictly cognitive domain—e.g. psychomotor ability, social skills, perceptual speed, or personality. However, some studies purporting to study the validity of measures other than general mental ability are probably not doing so. For example, Arthur et al (1990) used the Rod and Frame Test and the Group Embedded Figures Test, which Cronbach (1970) had earlier shown to measure aspects of general mental ability. The pattern of test intercorrelations found in the Arthur et al study (1990) supports Cronbach's interpretation.

Fiedler and his coworkers have reported initial findings on the relation between leader mental ability and *group* performance that are provocative (Fiedler 1989; F. E. Fiedler & F. W. Gibson, unpublished; Gibson et al 1990; S. E. Murphy et al 1990). They find that when leaders are directive, high ability in leaders is conducive to high group performance. But among non-directive leaders, group performance is better on average when leaders have lower ability (and this is especially true if group support for the leader is low or the leader is in conflict with his/her boss). These researchers suggest that group members react negatively to an obviously intelligent leader who refuses to tell people what to do but more positively to nondirectiveness when they can see that the leader is in need of group input. They also report some evidence that under conditions of stress or conflict with higher-level managers (the leader's boss), higher-ability leaders talk too much, making it difficult for group members to offer suggestions and ideas. These findings are based on small samples and are in need of replication. If they are upheld in future research, the implications will obviously be important, perhaps as much so for training as for selection.

Stone et al (1990) found that people with higher cognitive ability produce responses to *noncognitive* measures (e.g. measures of job satisfaction) that are more reliable than those of lower-ability people, supporting the notion that higher ability means reduced noise in the general information processing system. Pooling across a wide variety of jobs, Avolio & Waldman (1990) found a correlation of .36 *for individuals* between the complexity of their jobs and their general mental ability. Following earlier research (Nevo & Jager 1987), Arvey et al (1990) began a research program on the attitudes and reactions of employment applicants to the tests they take. Most of the relationships obtained between their nine attitude scales and test scores were small, but some were substantial (e.g. $r = -.47$ between reported test anxiety and scores on an arithmetic reasoning test). A meta-analysis by Hembree (1988) also found substantial negative associations between test anxiety and test scores. In the Arvey et al study, partialing out self-reported motivation in taking the tests led to slightly reduced mean racial differences. However, it is difficult in this research to disentangle cause and effect in interpreting findings.

Assessment Centers

An earlier meta-analysis (Gaugler et al 1987) found that assessment center validities generalize with a corrected mean validity of .37 and that assessment center ratings predict candidates' ratings of potential better than they do performance. Assessment center research has since focused on three main areas: additional evidence for validity and validity generalizability, construct validity of the ratings, and mechanical vs judgmental combining of scores.

Schmitt et al (1990) applied validity generalization methods to ratings from a single assessment center administered at multiple sites. The mean uncorrected validity in this study (.14) was considerably lower than in Gaugler et al's (1987) meta-analysis (.25). Schmitt et al's moderator analysis may have been affected by capitalization on chance; a total of 23 moderators were tested via regression with a sample size of 16 (16 assessment sites). The major conclusion of the Schmitt et al (1990) study is that assessment center validities deteriorate if the centers are not implemented as intended. Dobson & Williams (1989) reported the results of a large-scale validation study of assessment center board ratings for selection of British Army officers. The meta-analysis results estimated the operational validity of the selection procedure for predicting job performance at .33, and for predicting specialized Army training grades at .31. Three studies investigated the validity of the assessment center ratings for law enforcement personnel. Feltham (1988), in a 19-year longitudinal study in Britain, found that overall assessment ratings predict job performance ratings better than they do ratings of potential or rank attained (uncorrected values were: r = .18 vs r = .11 and r = .00, respectively). This result, counter to previous findings, may be due to the fact that British assessment centers resemble extended interviews rather than assessment centers in the American sense. Pynes & Bernardin (1989) studied police recruits and found lower observed validities with training performance (.14) and job performance (.20) than found in the earlier meta-analysis of Gaugler et al (1987). Consistent with past research findings (Hunter & Hunter 1984), Pynes & Bernardin (1989) concluded that cognitive ability tests are superior to assessment center ratings in validity, and cost less as well. Finally, in a seven-year predictive validity study of assessment centers for law enforcement agency managers, McEvoy & Beatty (1989) confirmed earlier findings that assessment center ratings predict promotions better than they do supervisory performance ratings. They also found that longer time intervals between assessment and performance measurement yielded higher validities.

A second group of studies on assessment centers dealt with the construct validity issue, the question of why assessment centers work. Schippmann et al (1990) summarized the literature on the in-basket exercise used in personnel assessment, noting that reliability and validity information on this exercise was fragmentary. Brannick et al (1989), using the multitrait-multimethod matrix to investigate the construct validity of in-basket scores, found exercise factors rather than dimension factors. They found that convergent validity was low and that there was method variance within each in-basket exercise, reflected in much higher correlations within exercises than between exercises. This finding is similar to those of Sackett & Harris (1988) in an extension of an earlier paper which concluded that factors underlying ratings were exercises and not dimensions (Sackett & Dreher 1982). Application of confirmatory factor analysis provided *some* evidence for *some* dimension factors (Sackett & Harris 1988), but the overall conclusion was that the constructs underlying assessment center ratings did not reflect assessment center dimensions. In all datasets where the correlations between summated exercise ratings can be estimated, there is considerable correlation across exercises as well, indicating a dominant single factor. Shore et al (1990) claimed to have found confirmatory evidence for two factor categories: an interpersonal and a performance category. Their results do not contradict the findings of others: They found one dominant factor in the performance dimension. Their interpersonal style dimension seems to have been a result of some *new* (i.e. nonperformance) categories of behavior they asked the observers to rate at the assessment center. Their results suggested that performance-style category ratings are closely associated with several cognitive ability measures and later promotion performance, while some interpersonal style category ratings are related to personality factors. Given the limitations of human information processing capabilities, it is probably unrealistic to expect assessors to differentiate among many dimensions. However, if primary dimensions other than performance are measured, raters can generate more than a single dimension factor. Gaugler & Thornton (1989) have found that evaluators who are asked to rate a small number of dimensions make more accurate classifications and ratings. On the other hand, since the single exercise reliability in assessment centers is typically low (e.g. see Sackett & Harris 1988), it might be best to have assessors rate many short *exercises* measuring the same overall general *factor dimension* than a few long ones. Crawley et al (1990) administered aptitude tests and personality inventories to two samples of assessment center participants. Assessment center ratings were found to be highly related to scores on aptitude tests. There was no evidence that specific aptitudes correlated differentially with specific assessment center dimension ratings.

Other research addressed the question whether assessment center scores should be mechanically or judgmentally combined. Lowry (1988) concluded that rankings in assessment centers are similar when assessor judgments are combined judgmentally and mechanically. Feltham (1988) and Pynes et al (1988) concluded that mechanically derived assessment center ratings produce at least as valid if not more valid predictions.

Biodata

Despite the cumulative evidence for substantial validity, biodata scales are still infrequently used. In a survey of 248 firms, Hammer & Kleiman (1988) found that only 6.8% of firms stated that they had ever used biodata in employment decisions, and only .4% indicated they currently use biodata scales. The most frequent reasons for not using it were (*a*) lack of knowledge, (*b*) lack of methodological expertise, and (*c*) lack of personnel, money, and time. Large minorities of respondents also expressed concerns about Equal Employment Opportunity and invasion of privacy risks. Clearly, human resource managers could benefit from education about biodata.

Many of these reservations stem from the belief that biodata scales must be validated in each organization. Rothstein et al (1990) reported a large-sample study showing that the validity of the biodata portion of the Supervisor Profile Record generalizes across organizations, age levels, sexes, levels of education, supervisory experience, and tenure with the organization. Items were initially selected for job relevance, keying was based on samples from multiple organizations, and only items showing validity across organizations were retained. The validity generalization results reported were for a cross-validation sample of 11,000 supervisors in new organizations. Validities averaged in the low to mid .30s. The advantages of biodata scales with generalizable validity are obvious for organizations that do not have the necessary large sample, the expertise, and the resources to develop their own biodata scales. Finally, this study found the generalizability of this biodata scale to be comparable to that found for cognitive ability measures in previous research, indicating that biodata scales developed in this manner need not be situationally specific. Methodological considerations in applying meta-analysis to biodata validities are discussed by Schmidt & Rothstein (in press). As noted earlier, the new nationwide examination by the US Office of Personnel Management includes a biodata scale. This scale was developed in a similar manner, and analysis of (concurrent) validity studies shows that its validity generalizes across both occupations and government agencies (Gandy et al 1989). Uncorrected validity averaged .30.

A key assumption in biodata is that past behaviors—often behaviors far in the past: e.g. high school achievements—are good predictors of future behaviors. However, Kleiman & Faley (1990) found biodata items inquiring about *present* behaviors were just as valid as those focusing on past behaviors in predicting intention to re-enlist in the Air National Guard. If this finding holds for other criteria, some rethinking of a basic assumption will be required. Russell et al (1990) found that retrospective life-history essays could serve as the source of valid biodata items, and Russell (1990) found some suggestions that structured interviews could also serve as such a source. McDaniel (1989) examined the validity of biodata scales derived from background investigations used by government agencies to determine applicant "suitability" (e.g. drug use, delinquency, school suspension). His samples were large, but the measures were all self-report, unlike most background investigations. His seven scales yielded a multiple R of .19 for the criterion of unsuitability discharges from the Armed Services. The two most valid scales were School Suspension (.14) and Quitting High School (.17).

The potential of biodata has not yet been fully realized. Now that we know that biodata scales with substantial generalizable validity can be constructed, the next major need is research that explicates the constructs underlying such generalizable scales. That is, as we focus increasing research effort on construct explication, it may be profitable, at least initially, to focus on item sets known to be correlated with success in the world of work, thus reducing the biodata domain to its most relevant components and to manageable proportions. One potentially interesting question is the extent to which biodata scales are measuring the personality trait of conscientiousness (see next section).

Personality and Related Predictors

There has been a revival of interest in recent years in the potential validity of personality measures, stimulated in part by advances in basic research in personality (e.g. Eaves et al 1989). Also, to the extent that differential aptitudes theory has been disconfirmed in the cognitive domain (see the section below on technical and theoretical aspects of validity), the noncognitive domain has assumed increased relative importance.

Digman (1990) summarized considerable current evidence supporting the five-factor theory of personality: Extraversion/Introversion, Agreeableness, Conscientiousness (also called Will to Achieve), Neuroticism, and Intellect. In particular, Conscientiousness has been shown to correlate substantially with academic performance and occupational level achieved. Goldberg (1990) presented additional evidence supporting the five-factor theory. Barrick & Mount (1991) meta-analyzed available personality test validities for overall job performance using the five-factor model. They found consistent moderate true score correlations (.20–.25) for conscientiousness measures in all job families, while the other factors showed generally smaller and more variable mean correlations. S. W. Kobs & R. D. Arvey (unpublished) also found validity for this factor. Hough (1988) and Hough et al (1990) meta-analyzed validity for five criterion types in addition to job proficiency, based on a six-factor modification of the five-factor theory. Although exact comparisons are difficult for technical reasons, results for job proficiency are roughly comparable, with Dependability and Achievement (both aspects of

Conscientiousness) showing some validity. Some of the other constructs were found to predict other criteria, such as training performance and nondelinquency. A separate meta-analysis for predictive validities obtained results similar to the overall analysis; however, it is not clear that all predictive studies were begun with applicants. Hough et al (1990) developed multiple scales for four of the factors in the five-factor theory and found that Achievement and Dependability were among the best predictors of ratings of Effort and Leadership, Personal Discipline, and Physical Fitness and Military Bearing in a large-sample military study that was part of the Army's Project A. Other factors also showed some validity, but none of the personality scales predicted core job proficiency. Another study (McHenry et al 1990) reported that personality measures produced incremental validity over a measure of general cognitive ability for the three criteria described above, although not for the two measures of core job proficiency. Hough et al (1990) found that intentional distortion of responses in a socially desirable direction was not a major problem, although careless responding was. However, it was not clear how those detected as careless responders (using their response validity scale) were to be evaluated for selection. Overall, the Project A research on the validity of personality and temperament measures is a major step forward, both conceptually and methodologically, and to some extent it sets the agenda for future research in the domain of noncognitive predictors.

In another study, Hansen (1989) tested a complex causal model of industrial accidents and found evidence that both distractibility (essentially neuroticism) and general social maladjustment (which appears to be the extreme opposite end of the conscientiousness dimension) contribute to accident frequency. This finding may be important because many other variables, including age, general mental ability, and accident risk exposure, were controlled for. A study by Day & Silverman (1989) examined eight predictors, including six personality variables, on a sample of only 43. In addition, stepwise multiple regression was employed. Such small-sample studies cannot support even tentative conclusions, although they can have value when they are included as part of a meta-analysis.

An increasingly important area of research in the noncognitive domain concerns written integrity tests. Ash (1991) details the history and current status of integrity tests. Since the Federal Employee Polygraph Protection Act banned most uses of the polygraph testing in employment selection in December 1988, employers have shown increased interest in these tests. O'Bannon et al (1989) provide a good overview of the characteristics of currently used integrity tests. An excellent current source of research information on integrity tests is the review by Sackett et al (1989). They point out that one of the major developments since the earlier review by Sackett & Harris (1984) is the emergence of two distinct types of tests: overt integrity tests and personality-oriented measures. Overt tests inquire directly about job applicants' attitudes toward theft, while personality-based tests attempt to measure poor impulse control, lack of conscientiousness, disregard of rules and regulations, and general organizational delinquency (e.g. see Hogan & Hogan 1989). Sackett et al state that the four major personality-based integrity tests on the market are similar in content and would probably correlate highly. We would add that they all appear to assess the extreme lower range of the conscientiousness factor studied by Barrick & Mount (1991), indicating a potentially important construct link between the personality and integrity domains. In addition, the construct validity evidence indicates that people who score very high on this factor may prefer tasks requiring conformity rather than creativity (Hogan & Hogan 1989), raising the question of selection tradeoffs in this area.

Overt integrity tests have been validated mostly against measures of employee theft, either applicant admissions of theft or detected thefts, while criteria for the broader personality-based tests are often measures of "counter-productive behavior," such as excessive absences, tardiness, malingering, equipment damage, drug abuse, and disciplinary infractions. However, both types of tests appear to be valid for both theft and counterproductive behaviors (Ones et al 1991). New studies, such as that of Rafilson & Frost (1989), are contributing to this data base. A second major development in this area has been a substantial increase in the amount of validity evidence based on external (nonself-report) criteria, including detected thefts, absences, turn-over, and supervisor ratings. Sackett et al conclude that support for the validity of integrity tests has been strengthened. There is also considerable evidence that scores differ little by race and sex, and that the correlation with general cognitive ability is quite low [although some studies (e.g. Werner et al 1989) have used questionable measures of ability, such as education]. Research continues to accumulate indicating that applicants view integrity testing as legitimate and appropriate and do not resent it (Jones & Joy 1989; Ryan & Sackett 1987). The legal considerations surrounding integrity testing were explored by Jones et al (1990a). There are now written guidelines for the use of integrity tests in employment (Association of Personnel Test Publishers 1990; Jones et al 1990b).

Some psychologists continue to be skeptical about integrity test research, in large part because most of it has been conducted by the test publishers. However, many of these researchers are I/O psychologists in good standing, and no evidence has been produced to indicate that negative findings have been withheld. Another reason for skepticism is that integrity testing is not a traditional topic for personnel psychologists (Sackett et al 1989), who do, however, study personality measurement. Thus research on the newer personality based integrity tests may lead to some integration in this respect. Integrity tests have also been criticized for high false positive rates (Murphy 1987). As pointed out by Sackett et al (1989), Manhardt (1989), and Martin & Terris (1991), this criticism is conceptually flawed. All selection procedures have false positives, and the alternative of using a less valid procedure for the same selection decisions yields a *higher* false positive rate. Thus attempts to reduce the false positive rate, such as that of Martin (1989), are as applicable to all predictors as to integrity tests.

The Congressional Office of Technology, after two years of study, released a "background paper" on integrity testing (Office of Technology Assessment 1990). The study is superficial and in part clearly erroneous, but its tone is neutral to only mildly critical. In early 1991, a task force of the American Psychological Association released a report (Goldberg et al 1991) on research and practice in integrity testing that was on balance favorable. Although integrity testing, for reasons that are not entirely clear, remains controversial, the APA report may lead to greater acceptance. The present authors' hope is that future research on integrity tests will lead to fundamental advances in understanding of the role of personality in the various aspects of job performance. From a theoretical point of view, this is the real potential of the integrity testing movement.

Interviews

A narrative review of the literature summarized research findings between 1982 and 1989 (Harris 1989). Two meta-analyses indicate that interviews can have higher average validities than researchers have traditionally believed, and the validities are generalizable (McDaniel et al 1990; Wiesner & Cronshaw 1988). The mean corrected validity across all interview types is .45 (McDaniel et al 1990); even for unstructured interviews the operational validity is surprisingly high at .40 (McDaniel et al 1990). Wright et al (1989) meta-analyzed structured interview validities and confirmed earlier findings that structured interviews yield higher validities. For employment interviews with job performance criteria, meta-analysis results indicate residual standard deviations smaller than those for ability tests. Despite differences in jobs, constructs measured, and other factors, there appears to be little room for moderators to operate. Two additional studies have lent support to the proposition that there is no evidence of sex discrimination in interviewer evaluations of applicant qualifications (Gardner & Discenza 1988; Graves & Powell 1988).

Dreher et al (1988) examined traditional research design for interview validation and concluded that flawed methodology may have produced the traditional low validities cited in the literature. They argue that "even the most favorable review to date (McDaniel et al 1990) is likely to underestimate the validity of the typical employment interview" (Dreher et al 1988:323). Again on a methodological note, Maurer & Fay (1988) found that the interrater reliability of applicant suitability assessments is higher using the situational interview format than it is using other formats. Dipboye et al (1990) investigated individual differences between interviewers in incremental validity above and beyond ability tests. They found large variability in incremental validities of different interviewers. Some or all of this variability is sampling error, but it is possible that more intelligent interviewers could be making more incrementally valid judgments, although Dipboye et al (1990) do not report any data to confirm or refute this hypothesis. Kinicki et al (1990) found that résumés are weighted less than interview information in making hiring recommendations. But these results could be due to the authors' operationalization of "résumé information" as only "education and experience levels." Macan & Dipboye (1990) found that preinterview impressions of applicants were highly related to the post interview impressions (uncorrected r = .53; a correlation equal to the mean of all such correlations in the literature). Campion et al (1988) found a strong cognitive component in structured interviews and virtually no incremental validity of the structured interview over ability tests.

Alternative ways of conducting the interviews have been studied. Motowidlo et al (1989) found that a paper and pencil situational inventory for entry-level management positions correlated from .28 to .37 (uncorrected) with job performance ratings. However, the authors acknowledged that the situational inventory was essentially a test of "practical intelligence." Martin & Nagao (1989) compared face to face, paper and pencil, and computerized versions of the interview and found there was less social desirability in responses when impersonal modes of interviewing were used but that applicants to high-status jobs resented impersonal interviews.

Tullar (1989) found that successful applicants are given longer interviews and dominate the conversation more. Phillips & Dipboye (1989) found that if the preinterview impressions are favorable, then interviewers attribute poor performance in the interview to external factors. Their results also confirmed the finding that ability test scores are the most valid predictors of job performance. Rynes & Gerhart (1990) examined assessments of employability as reflected in two components: general employability and firm-specific employability (fit). They claim that these components are distinct from idiosyncratic interviewer preferences. One important question is the predictive validity of the judgements of fit. In a study of realistic job previews (RJPs), Vandenberg & Scarpello (1990) found that Wanous' (1980) matching model was generally an accurate description of new workers' adjustment to the organization. Despite earlier meta-analyses indicating very small effect sizes for RJPs, Wanous (1989) has compiled a "how to" guide discussing ten issues to be considered when implementing a realistic job preview.

Additional Predictors

In this section, we review predictors not covered elsewhere. A qualitative review by Ash et al (1989) of methods for evaluation of job applicant training and work experience confirmed the meta-analysis finding of McDaniel et al (1988) that the behavioral consistency method had higher validity than other methods. However, research is needed to determine what *constructs* are measured by different training and experience rating methods. Robertson & Downs (1989) conducted a meta-analysis of work-sample tests of trainability, which differ from regular work-sample tests in being designed for untrained people and thus including a learning period. Work-sample tests of trainability typically yield two scores: a rating of predicted performance in training and an error score (the number of errors made during the test). Results indicate that work-sample ratings and error scores have mean uncorrected validities of .41 and .48, respectively, in predicting training performance. The observed correlation with job performance ratings was smaller (.24). Robertson & Downs (1989) found some evidence that validity for predicting training success declined over time. The authors labeled the construct measured by trainability tests as "trainee's capacity to learn" (Robertson & Downs 1989:407). However, it probably is better considered a measure of initial training performance, which would explain the apparent decline in validity over time (see the discussion on the simplex matrix in the section below on technical and theoretical aspects of validity).

Graphology is utilized as a selection device in 85% of European firms (Levy 1979) and in at least 3000 US firms (Klimoski & Refaeli 1983), with these figures increasing over time (Ben-Shakhar 1989). A meta-analysis by Neter & Ben-Shakhar (1989) found that when neutral (noncontent-laden) scripts are used, the validity of graphologists' inferences is virtually zero. Any predictive validity that graphological inference has (no larger than .21) stems from the content of the written text. Even in that case, nongraphologists (i.e. psychologists) are able to make predictions at least as valid.

Unconventional selection techniques received some attention. Hurd (1990) reviewed issues related to genetic testing, and Bosshardt et al (1989) reviewed research on the investigative background interview. During the period covered by this review, several alternative management-selection procedures were developed and validated. Motowidlo et al (1990) investigated the validity of a "low-fidelity" simulation for management selection that described several hypothetical work situations and asked the respondents to choose the course of action they would take from among several options presented to them. Results suggest that responses about hypothetical work situations predict ratings of overall job performance (observed predictive validities of .30 and .32 in two samples). Although correlations with cognitive ability were low, they write that "we cannot absolutely rule out the possibility that scores on our simulation can vary significantly with cognitive ability . . ." (Motowidlo et al 1990:645). In a small-scale validation study using performance appraisal ratings, Molcan & Orban (1989) found an uncorrected concurrent validity of .37 for the Management Readiness Profile (MRP), a paper and pencil inventory designed to assess management potential of job candidates without any previous managerial experience. The MRP contains an interest subscale, several personality subscales, and a cognitive subscale. Shechtman & Sansbury (1989) evaluated the validity of a structured group assessment (peer assessment) of personality factors along with a test of cognitive ability for selection of teacher-education candidates and concluded that the structured group assessment predicts success in training.

Pre-employment drug testing received extensive attention in the literature. McDaniel (1988) investigated the validity of self-reported pre-employment drug use for a sample of 10,188 military service young adults and found that a frequency-of-drug-use composite covering several drugs had a predictive validity of .08 for employment "suitability" in the military. Normand, Salyards & Mahoney (1990) reported a blind longitudinal study of physiological pre-employment drug testing of 5,465 postal service job applicants. Drug test results correlated .33 with absenteeism and .22 with involuntary separation. However, these validities may be range-restricted values because the prior selection procedure included medical examinations and separate drug screenings in some cases. Normand et al (1990), in a utility analysis, estimated that substantial cost savings would result from reduced absenteeism and turnover if pre-employment drug testing were used in selection. Their estimates provide a partial response to the hypothesis of Fraser & Kroeck (1989) that the value of drug screening in selection may be low. However, drug screening cannot be expected to replace other valid predictors of job performance, and selection utility will be suboptimal if organizations emphasize drug testing too heavily in relation to other predictors of job performance that may be more valid. Stone & Kotch (1989) found that advance notice of drug testing and less severe consequences for detected drug use cause blue-collar workers to have more favorable attitudes toward drug testing. Murphy et al (1990), using college student samples, found that individual drug use and self-reported frequency of drug use are consistently correlated with disapproval of employee drug testing. They did not find any evidence of association between acceptability of drug testing, on one hand, and employment experience, qualifications, or political inclinations, on the other.

TECHNICAL AND THEORETICAL ASPECTS OF VALIDITY

One of the major problems in personnel selection is that all observed estimates of operational (true) validities are biased (usually downward), and statistical methods must be used to correct these biases. Until recently, there was no known method for correcting for range restriction when *both* variables have been restricted. As reviewed by Alexander et al (1989b), the research program headed by Ralph Alexander has developed an accurate procedure (described more fully in Alexander et al 1987). Hunter & Schmidt (1990a:50–52) found this procedure to be accurate for both direct and indirect restriction. Burke et al (1989) examined a different procedure from this program—one designed to estimate unrestricted means and SDs from restricted data only—and found it to be only moderately accurate in their data sets. Estimated true or operational validity is observed validity corrected for both criterion unreliability and range differences between the incumbent group and the *full applicant pool* for a particular job (e.g. see J. P. Campbell 1990). Therefore, whether selection procedures are administered sequentially using a multiple-hurdle approach or all procedures are administered to all applicants has no effect on true validity estimates. True validity is not incremental validity relative to other procedures; it is validity in the full applicant pool. Based on a misunderstanding of this fact and unrealistic assumptions about applicant self-selection, Sackett & Larson (1990) argued against the concept of true validity as a parameter to be estimated. Their argument is based in part on a hypothetical example in which the norm group predictor SD is 20, while the applicant group SD is only 15. The evidence is strong that applicant self-selection substantially affects mean test scores; Sackett & Larson (and many others) assume a comparably large effect on the SD of test scores. As part of our research program in validity generalization we have repeatedly compared norm group and applicant pool predictor SDs; differences are either nonexistent or very small (as would be predicted from the relevant variance theorem from ANOVA). Thus there is not one true validity for applicant pools and another for the general population; the two are typically essentially the same.

The important question of the stability of test validities continues to be debated (Austin et al 1989; Barrett & Alexander 1989). Ackerman (1989) critiqued the study by Henry & Hulin (1989), who concluded there was strong evidence for decline of validities over time. Ackerman noted that a simplex matrix of criterion correlations across time does not imply that validities decline and cited considerable empirical evidence to the contrary. Drawing on his earlier work (Ackerman 1987), he reviewed recent theoretical and empirical developments that offer explanations for stability, decline, and *increases* under different circumstances. Schmidt et al (1988b) also discussed this question and presented empirical evidence showing the stability of cognitive test validities out to five years. A later larger-sample independent military study, which also employed job-sample performance measures, found stable validities over the four-year period studied (Office of the Assistant Secretary of Defense, Force Management and Personnel 1990). Additional evidence that cognitive ability validities do not decline was presented by Deadrick & Madigan (1990). Weiss et al (1988) reported substantial validities for an achievement test in predicting medical school performance out to six years. Henry & Hulin (1990) responded to Ackerman's critique but do not appear to have fully addressed the issues it raised. Hulin et al (1990) presented an extended literature review, but many of the tasks they examined, both as predictors and criteria, are narrow and appear remote from test or job performance. G. V. Barrett, R. A. Alexander, and D. Doverspike (unpublished) extensively analyzed the Hulin et al (1990) review and found no support for its conclusions. They found that many studies had been classified inappropriately (i.e. were not really predictive), that errors were made in the interpretation of lagged correlations, that many relevant studies had been omitted, and that corrections for range restriction and unreliability were applied inappropriately.

Based on Ackerman's (1987) model, and in particular on his distinction between automatic vs controlled information processing, K. Murphy (1989) developed a theory that predicts instability over time in the validity of cognitive ability for overall job performance. The theory posits "maintenance stages" during which job tasks are well learned and can be performed with minimal mental effort (automatic information processing), resulting in low or zero validities. We believe the evidence indicates that when the criterion is overall job performance, the "task" remains complex enough that it is not "automatable;" it continues to require "controlled information processing" and hence to correlate with general cognitive ability. There may be a tendency in this research area to generalize inappropriately from narrow and automatable tasks to broader, more complex, and less automatable real-world job performance composites, which are the meaningful variables in selection and employment. This question will continue to be practically important because declining validities would imply lower utility for selection programs, and vice versa for increasing validities. It is also of paramount importance theoretically in understanding the nature of human performance.

Recent findings in validity generalization research (e.g. Hunter 1986) have challenged the notion that prediction can be enhanced by differential weighting of cognitive aptitudes rather than use of measures of general ability alone. Based on 24,482 people and 37 Air Force jobs, G. E. Jones (1988) found an (uncorrected) correlation of .72 between the average validity of the 10 subtests of the Armed Services Vocational Aptitude Battery (ASVAB) for predicting training performance and the general ability ("g") saturation of the subtests. Ree & Earles (1990a) examined 89 Air Force jobs using 10 principle components derived from the ASVAB; they found that the mean increase in the squared multiple R from adding components beyond the general ability component was .02, a small increase but large enough to have practical value. However, they employed stepwise regression with no cross-validation (or formula-based shrinkage adjustment), and Ns were often in the 200–300 range. Thus their small gains may have been due to capitalization on chance. A second study (Welsh et al 1990) obtained similar results, although more samples and jobs were used and the minimum sample was larger (min = 550). A third study (Ree & Earles 1990b) based on the same data but using simultaneous rather than stepwise regression found somewhat smaller validity gains; however, this study was also affected to some extent by capitalization on chance. Schmidt et al (1988b) discuss some of the difficult technical problems inherent in researching this important question. (See also Lautenschlager 1990.) Differential aptitude theory continues to enjoy credence among some practitioners, but accumulating evidence appears to be increasingly restricting its potential effectiveness. This is similar to the process that occurred earlier in the case of the theory of situational specificity of test validities. Finally, Ree & Earles (1990c) found that 14 different estimates of general mental ability derived from the ASVAB all correlated highly—from .93–.99, with most in the .97–.99 range.

In other technical developments, McIntyre (1990) presented useful partial-correlation formulas that yield unbiased estimates of validity in pooled samples in which some of the pooled groups show spurious mean differences on the predictor, the criterion, or both. However, judgment is required in determining whether such differences are spurious. Turban et al (1989) present methods for determining whether two tests measure the same construct and hence are substitutable. Their approach includes not only traditional corrections for attenuation but also structural equation modeling and analysis of resulting hiring decisions. Using a large sample of validation data from the US Employment Service, Waldman & Avalio (1989) found that the predictive accuracy of three aptitudes for supervisory ratings of job performance was similar at all aptitude levels, contrary to the conclusions of Lee & Foley (1986) and Brown et al (1988). Along with that of Coward & Sackett (1990) discussed above, this study provides additional support for the basic linear homoscedastic model in validation research. Binning & Barrett (1989) examined in some detail broader conceptual issues related to both the validation of selection measures and the construction of theories. They present a conceptual framework designed to integrate content, construct, and criterion-related validity evidence into a unified view of validity. Finally, Carrier et al (1990) attempted to correlate observed validities of individual items with their Content Validity Ratios (CVRs; Lawshe 1975). The CVRs were reliably measured, but sampling error in the empirical validities made them unreliable, and this was probably one reason for the mixed results. Another possible reason is that many items that are not superficially content valid are empirically valid—because they tap general mental ability.

FAIRNESS IN SELECTION PROCEDURES

Fairness

A special issue of the *Journal of Vocational Behavior* dated 1988 but appearing in 1989 was devoted to scientific and legal issues in fairness (Gottfredson & Sharf 1988). The various contributors covered the issue thoroughly but could not resolve the dilemma, which is as follows. Measures of ability, achievement, and knowledge (especially general mental ability) are probably the most valid and useful predictors of performance in most jobs. Yet blacks, and to a lesser extent Hispanics, have lower average scores, and hence lower hiring rates. But these differences are not due to any bias in the tests as predictors of job performance; research evidence is strong that tests are predictively fair for minorities (and that validity coefficients are comparable, too). Failure to use such tests would cause great productivity losses to employers and the economy, losses we can ill afford in today's competitive international economy. But increasing use of such tests could mean fewer minorities hired in the more desirable jobs, or at least could make it difficult to increase current minority representation. Most economic gains (utility) from testing can be maintained by hiring top down within white, black, and Hispanic groups, while still eliminating hiring rate differences. However, this approach can be criticized as reverse discrimination. A similar dilemma exists in Israel (Zeidner 1988) and many other countries (Klitgaard 1986).

This was the problem that faced a National Research Council (NRC) Committee (Hartigan & Wigdor 1990). The US Employment Service, in its General Aptitude Test Battery (GATB) job referral system, had opted for "within group norming" and had been charged with reverse discrimination by the US Department of Justice. The blue-ribbon NRC committee of social scientists, statisticians, and lawyers carefully reviewed existing research and concluded that validities were comparable for minorities and the majority and that GATB scores did not underpredict minority job performance, thus supporting past research findings (and another, earlier NRC report). However, they concluded that there was a "scientific basis" for adjusting minority test scores upward, and recommended this be done. The basis was the long-rejected (Peterson & Novick 1976; Hunter & Schmidt 1976) Cole-Darlington model of test fairness. The committee noted that by this concept of fairness, GATB (and other) test scores are biased against low scorers, not against minorities per se. Yet they called for adjustments to be made only to minority scores, and to *high* as well as low minority scores. Many personnel psychologists and others were unimpressed with this as a scientific rationale (Blits & Gottfredson 1990; Tenopyr 1990; see also Hartigan & Wigdor 1990). (The GATB system of score adjustment had been based on no rationale other than the sheer desire to equalize referral rates.) After studying this report for over a year, the US Department of Labor announced in July 1990 its intention to suspend use of the GATB nationwide for at least two years, pending research designed to improve the test. Since such research is unlikely to resolve this dilemma, these recent events raise the question of whether it will be politically and legally possible to employ valid ability tests as selection procedures, with or without adverse impact, in a complex, litigious, multi-cultural society. The Civil Rights Bills of 1990 and 1991 raise the same question. If the answer is negative, the implications for US economic efficiency will also be negative.

Although the fairness dilemma had major social effects during the period of this review, the issue is essentially resolved as a research topic in personnel psychology. Because of this consensus, few new studies are being conducted. Major findings and conclusions were summarized by Schmidt (1988). Steffy & Ledvinka (1989) used computer simulation to show that the long-range impact of the regression definition of test fairness, the most widely accepted definition, was limited minority hiring; however, as expected, this model produced the largest productivity (output) gains, highlighting the dilemma discussed above. Finally, in a little-noticed article, Lawshe (1987) critiqued the legal concept of adverse impact and illustrated many important deficiencies. To his list we would add one more. The term adverse impact implies that the test *creates* a discriminatory impact. But research indicates that the observed differences were created years earlier and are merely *revealed* in selection (Schmidt 1988). Thus both the connotations of the term and its use as a trigger for discrimination are no longer plausible. New, more relevant concepts and indicators of discrimination are needed.

Legal and Social Considerations

Spencer (1989) provides a summary of recent Supreme Court rulings on preferential hiring and reverse discrimination and identifies properties she feels are necessary to make affirmative action plans (AAPs) legally defensible. The tradeoffs for using AAPs are usually viewed as between economic efficiency and social equity. However, the adverse political reactions of nonpreferred groups must also be considered. Warner & Steele (1989) report the results of three Gallup Polls in which the public was asked to choose between selection based on "preferential treatment" as a remedy for past discrimination and selection "as determined by ability test scores." In all the polls approximately 10% chose preferential treatment and more than 80% chose selection based on ability test scores. Sowell (1989) pointed out that the public supports special educational and vocational courses for minority groups, and stated "The issue is not simply whether one is for or against the advancement of particular groups or is willing to see transfers of resources for their betterment. The method by which their betterment is attempted matters greatly . . .". Affirmative Action Plans that result in lowering of valid standards in selection are unacceptable to many people.

In 1989, the Supreme Court issued two important decisions regarding employment discrimination. In Wards Cove Packing Company v. Atonio (109 S. Ct. 3115, 1989), the Supreme Court ruled that mere statistical racial imbalance in the work force is not sufficient to establish a prima facie case of disparate impact. Where the plaintiff *is* able to establish disparate impact, the Wards Cove decision reduces the employer's burden from the Griggs requirement of demonstrating job relatedness (usually in the form of validity evidence) to one of merely "articulating a legitimate business purpose." This is a significant easing of the employer's burden. Under the Wards Cove decision, the burden of proof remains with the plaintiff at all times, as has long been the case in other areas of civil law. One result of the Wards Cove decision is probably that validity generalization can now be more widely used as an alternative to local validation. Taken in its entirety, the Wards Cove decision seems to be favorable to employers (Potter 1989) and to the increased use of more valid selection methods. In Watson v. Fort Worth Bank & Trust (108 S. Ct. 2177, 1988), the Supreme Court concluded that job relatedness (validation) requirements should be the same for subjective and objective procedures. But the court then stated that even objective procedures such as tests do not require technical validity studies. This was a major development, and was later reaffirmed in the Wards Cove decision, which held that employers need only articulate a legitimate business purpose.

These 1988–1989 Supreme Court rulings, along with some previous decisions, stimulated the passage by Congress of the Civil Rights Bill of 1990. The President vetoed this bill, but it was then reintroduced as the Civil Rights Bill of 1991. This bill would overturn several Supreme Court rulings and ostensibly return the courts to the Griggs v. Duke Power Co. (1971) standards. In actuality, it would place heavy new burdens on employers that go far beyond Griggs. Under the Griggs standards, if a selection procedure is found to result in adverse impact, the employer must justify its use by demonstrating job-relatedness. If enacted, the present bill would impose a requirement to demonstrate that the challenged practice or practices have a "substantial and demonstrable relationship to effective job performance" (see below). The Bill would also allow punitive damages and jury trials in employment discrimination cases. In addition, employers would more frequently have to pay the legal costs of those challenging selection procedures. Parts of the Civil Rights Bill of 1990 drew opposition from the professional community, scientific circles, and employers. These groups especially objected to the words "substantial and demonstrable relationship to effective job performance." The word "effective" implies that performance is a dichotomous variable. The Society for Industrial-Organizational Psychology, the American Psychological Society, and the American Psychological Association pointed out in several letters to the Congress that job performance is a continuous variable; there is no "minimal" level of job performance beyond which different levels of performance are equally economically valuable to the employer. This definition is objectionable also because of the implication that "job performance" is the only acceptable criterion, seemingly ruling out other important criteria such as turnover, absenteeism, violence on the job, theft, and even accidents (see the Personality Measures and Additional Predictors sections of this chapter). Finally, by most interpretations, the Bill would require a local validation study for each job in each company, eliminating by legal fiat transportability and validity generalization, as noted in letters to Congress from the Society for Industrial-Organizational Psychology. Thus the label "Civil Rights Bill" appears to be a misnomer in this case: The Bill would clearly be an attempt to replace the scientific process with the legislative process as the determiner of scientific facts. It would also cause substantial economic losses in the form of reduced productivity and output—and corresponding loss of jobs to foreign competitors.

An important bill that did become law is the 1990 Americans with Disabilities Act. Tenopyr (1990) stated that this law requires establishing an "essential link" between the selection device and job performance on an individual basis. As a result, traditional validation studies conducted on "jobs," and also validity generalization studies, may not constitute defense in lawsuits. However, the interpretation of the Act will depend critically on regulations now being written. At the present time, the real implications of this law for personnel selection are not known.

In a meta-analysis of experimental studies, Olian et al (1988) found no evidence of discrimination against females in hiring recommendations; applicant qualifications rather than gender appear to account for the variability in hiring recommendations observed across studies. Social acceptability affects selection research. In recent years, there seems to be a trend toward use of the term "literacy" in preference to "ability" (e.g. Squires & Ross 1990; Anderson & Stewart 1989). However, literacy, defined as reading comprehension (Baker 1989) and mathematics skills (Glaser 1989), reflects cognitive ability as evidenced by the high correlation between literacy measures and cognitive ability tests (Squires & Ross 1990).

UTILITY ANALYSIS

Important research during the past decade has concerned methods for determining the economic value of valid selection procedures. Different initial assumptions yield somewhat different dollar values, but all approaches lead to the conclusion that the economic impact is large—a fact that has sustained interest in this topic. Dunnette (1989) reported large utility gains from improved selection of electrical power plant operators. Sadacca et al (1990) explored the special problems in scaling selection and classification utility in the Army's Project A. The NRC Committee on the GATB (Hartigan & Wigdor 1990) devoted considerable attention to the economic value of that testing program and concluded that utility is substantial for individual employers and is probably large for the economy as a whole (although it is more difficult to assess the economy-wide gains in output). This suggests that the losses from the 2-year suspension of the GATB proposed by the US Labor Department (1990) would be economically significant. Likewise, the proposed Civil Rights Bill of 1991, by making the use of valid selection methods more difficult, would also cause major losses in output and productivity if enacted.

Interest in utility methods and their implications has expanded into other nations. A book extensively applying these methods in a British context has appeared (Cook 1988), as has a research article (Smith 1989). Klitgaard (1986) applied these methods to the problem of university admissions in developing countries and related the results to expected rates of economic growth. Zeidner & Johnson (1989a) have prepared a comprehensive book-length review of selection utility models and research, a unique and informative document. These authors have prepared equally detailed reviews and analyses of job assignment (classification) methods as used in the military (Johnson & Zeidner 1989b, 1990; Johnson et al 1990). In the latter three documents, the authors argue that the potential utility gain from cognitive test–based classification, over and above the utility of selection, is larger than is suggested by the dominance of validities by general ability. Their basis for this conclusion is technically complex and will require close examination for an adequate evaluation.

Although the basic regression-based utility model is well established, issues and controversies continue. There is a long tradition of belief in nonlinear predictor-performance relations. Linearity of this relationship is the only major statistical assumption of the basic utility model. As noted earlier, Coward & Sackett (1990) presented considerable new empirical evidence that linearity can safely be assumed. Hunter et al (1988) presented examples showing that use of capital budgeting and financial accounting techniques can be conceptually and logically inappropriate in utility analysis. In reply, Cascio & Morris (1990) and Cronshaw & Alexander (1991) argued the opposite, primarily on grounds that potential investments in personnel pro-grams should be evaluated using the same methods applied to other potential investments an organization might make. Most utility studies have employed an estimate of the dollar standard deviation of job performance (SD_y) that is calculated from estimates provided by supervisors (e.g. Barrick et al 1990). Raju et al (1990) presented an alternative approach that does not require these estimates. However, M. K. Judiesch, F. L. Schmidt, and J. E. Hunter (unpublished) showed that this procedure simply shifts the judgment problem to the subjective estimation of the coefficient of variation of job performance ($SD_y/\bar{Y}$). Their ostensibly objective procedure is just as dependent on sub-jective estimates as the standard procedure.

There is also continuing discussion of the appropriate units for expressing utility gains. The major dichotomy is between utility as the dollar value of increased output as sold vs utility as the reduction in costs of production (Hunter et al 1988; Cascio & Morris 1990). Although both figures are usually large, increases in dollar value as sold are larger than cost reductions. The CREPID method of estimating SD_y is based on labor costs (Edwards et al 1988). The earlier method of estimating SD_y (Schmidt et al 1979) is ostensi-bly based on dollar value as sold and therefore should yield utility estimates in that metric. However, Judiesch et al (in press) presented evidence that supervisors using the Schmidt et al (1979) method base their estimates of the dollar value of various percentile points of performance more on employee earnings than on output as sold, thus underestimating SD_y. A study by Mathieu & Tannenbaum (1989) provides additional evidence for this conclusion. Judiesch et al also presented evidence that such supervisory estimates can be used to compute accurate estimates of SD_p, the coefficient of variation of job performance ($SD_y/\bar{Y}$). They advocate that these SD_p estimates be multiplied by available objective estimates of the *average* value of employee output for any given job, to yield a more accurate estimate of SD_y. These SD_y estimates are larger, and thus utility estimates are larger. Orr et al (1989) presented evidence that supervisors using the Schmidt et al method do consider and weight "citizenship behaviors," over and above formally prescribed job behaviors, in making their estimates of dollar value of different percentile points of performance. However, this fact is insufficient, both empirically and logically, to overcome the downward bias identified by Judiesch et al in the resulting SD_y estimates. Roth (in press) presented evidence that the general literature on human decision-making is relevant to understanding how supervisors make dollar estimates and suggested ideas for future research. Campbell (1990) also called for such research.

As an alternative to dollar value units, utility gains can be expressed as percentage increases in output. Doing so requires estimates of SD_p. Hunter et al (1990) analyzed available studies on actual employee output and found that SD_y varied with the cognitive complexity of jobs: 19% for low-complexity, 32% for medium-complexity, and 48% for high-complexity jobs. The SD_p values for sales jobs were larger. These findings indicate that, other things equal, percentage-output increases resulting from better selection are greater in medium- and high-complexity jobs than in low-complexity jobs, and the SD_p values from this study can be used in making these estimates. One of the mysteries in the area of utility has been the relative neglect of the percentage increase in output metric in actual applications. In our experience, economists are impressed with output gains of 8–15%, but I/O psychologists are not. I/O psychologists often appear not to realize that such output increases imply large dollar values, and tend to regard dollar estimates as indicating greater utility than the percentage-increase estimates. This is unfortunate, because percentage increases in output can probably be more accurately estimated than dollar utilities.

Becker (1989) criticized utility research on grounds that it has ignored the effects of the external labor market, and concluded that utility gains have been generally overstated as a result. However, his analysis is based solely on theory, and no empirical evidence is presented for either the conclusions deduced from theory or the assumptions underlying the theory. Hunter et al (1990) present empirical evidence that appears to contradict some of Becker's assumptions. Becker seems to assume levels of rationality and optimization among human resource managers that many would judge to be highly unrealistic, based on both field observations and available data.

JOB ANALYSIS

Ghorpade (1988) summarized different techniques of job analysis and their applications for human resource practitioners. Kleiman & Biderman (1989) described the requirements they believe are necessary for conducting legally defensible job analyses for development of managerial selection tests. The most comprehensive summary of job analysis to date is Gael's (1988) two-volume book on the subject. In recent years, attempts have again been made to use job analysis to identify the ability requirements for jobs via synthetic validity methods. Sparrow (1989) investigated use of the Position Analysis Questionnaire (PAQ) to estimate the ability requirements of jobs. He operationalized these requirements as the mean Differential Aptitude Test Battery scores of incumbents for each job investigated, a dubious procedure [see the section above on ability and aptitude tests in connection with the Prediger (1989) study]. He concluded that a method that focuses on the range (rather than the frequency) of behaviors performed yielded the most accurate synthetic validity results. He also concluded that validity generalizes across jobs with similar ability profiles on the PAQ. McCormick et al (1989) reported synthetic validity results they interpret as indicating that PAQ job-dimension scores also have potential for deriving estimates of personality requirements for jobs. Jeanneret (1988) concluded that ability/aptitude requirements for the jobs of space station personnel can be determined in advance using PAQ dimensions. Arvey et al (1989) used task-oriented job-analytic information to predict abilities needed for eight skilled trade occupations as part of a test-validation study. They argued that their analyses indicated which tasks predict which ability requirements for the jobs investigated.

Much current job analysis research, including research in synthetic validity, is based on the assumption that specific job tasks can be used to identify specific ability requirements of jobs. There are three major criticisms of this assumption. First, weighted combinations of specific aptitudes do not predict overall job performance better than general mental ability, and do not predict specific dimensions of jobs differentially (Hunter 1986). Therefore, using job analysis to identify specific abilities to use in selection may not be a wise use of resources. Second, the notion of "job requirements" tends to perpetuate the use of "minimum requirements" for selection. When minimum qualifications are used, selection utility losses are sizable when compared to top-down selection. Finally, validity generalization research has established the validity of all cognitive ability tests for all jobs, in all settings. Therefore, efforts to use synthetic validity methods to establish generalizability, and efforts to create a matrix of tasks and abilities necessary to perform those tasks, appear to be problematic. Validity generalization appears to be a less costly, more accurate, and more efficient way of demonstrating the validity of cognitive abilities across different jobs (Schmidt et al 1985; Schmidt 1988). Also, as noted earlier, the practice of using the *mean* trait level of job incumbents as an index of the *validity* of that trait for that job is problematic. J. P. Campbell (1990) has proposed a different approach to synthetic validity to be used for noncognitive and cognitive traits: Validity estimates for major job components are based on estimates by experienced personnel psychologists. This approach was employed in Project A, discussed above. Applied to general mental ability, perceptual speed, psychomotor ability, and temperament constructs, this approach has promise. It is unlikely to work if applied to specific cognitive aptitudes (e.g. verbal, quantitative, spatial, etc).

Cunningham & Scott (1988) compared the dimensionality of the US Employment Service worker-oriented job analysis ratings and the ratings from the Occupation Analysis Inventory, another worker-oriented job analysis instrument. Dimensionality of both closely paralleled the three aptitude factors derived by Hunter (1983b) for the GATB: cognitive ability, psychomotor ability, and perceptual ability. Hughes & Prien (1989) discussed and illustrated the use of job analysis judgments by subject matter experts to identify skills/abilities necessary for job performance. Geyer et al (1989) investigated the interrater reliabilities of ratings that job analysts make for the *Dictionary of Occupational Titles*. All single-rater reliabilities for data, people, and things scales are above .80, although some other dimensions of DOT ratings had lower interrater reliability. The reliability of a job-complexity scaling using paired comparisons was .98! This finding is important since both ability-test validities and the coefficient of variation of worker output (SD_p) vary as a function of job complexity. If ratings of individual differences in job performance could be as reliable as ratings of jobs, problems in conducting validity studies would be reduced.

Schmitt & Cohen (1989) evaluated the effect of incumbent characteristics (race, sex, and job experience) on responses to a job analysis inventory and found differences between men and women in the same jobs. There were also differences by occupational type, but there were no racial group differences. However, none of the differences detected were large enough to warrant different test specifications for different subgroups.

For ability and aptitude constructs, the evidence is strong that differences in tasks performed do not produce variation in validities for jobs comparable in overall complexity (Ackerman & Humphreys 1990). Therefore, task-oriented job analysis is not of much value for selection using measures of those constructs as predictors. However, for noncognitive constructs, the evidence is less complete; and for job knowledge or work-sample tests, task-oriented job analysis is important in achieving content validity.

656   SCHMIDT ET AL

PERFORMANCE MEASUREMENT AND CRITERION ISSUES

Criterion measures have long been considered critical because of the assumption that the nature of the criterion measure determines which predictors will be deemed valid and which invalid. It is now clear that for criteria of overall job performance (whether measured using one global dimension or as a composite of multiple dimensions) and tests of cognitive abilities, this assumption is incorrect. All cognitive tests are valid, in varying degrees, for all such measures; there are no documented cases of an aptitude or ability test being valid for one such criterion measure but not for another (i.e. zero validity).

Nathan & Alexander (1988) used meta-analysis to demonstrate that supervisory ratings, supervisory rankings, work samples, production quantity, and production quality are all validly predicted by tests of cognitive abilities. They found that average correlations are higher for work-sample criteria than for supervisory ratings (.60 vs .44, respectively), and that validities for work-sample criteria are as large as those found in the previous literature for training performance measures. They also found that validities for supervisory *rankings* of overall job performance are similar to those for work-sample performance. One unexpected finding was that validities for objective measures of production quality were lower and not generalizable. This result may be due to inability to correct appropriately for criterion unreliability; objective quality measures may be less reliable than the other criteria. Another question that merits investigation is whether appropriate measures of conscientiousness predict quality of work better than do ability measures.

Carey (1990) compared the validities of cognitive tests for six "surrogate" measures of job performance (supervisory ratings, training GPA, task proficiency ratings, conduct ratings, video simulation grades, and job knowledge tests). Validities were sizable for all criteria investigated. Hattrup & Schmitt (1990) found that validities for aptitude tests against job-sample performance criteria in a skilled trades apprenticeship training program are high (averaging .52, corrected only for range restriction), confirming the meta-analysis results of Hunter & Hunter (1984).

Considerable attention in the literature continues to be devoted to errors and biases in ratings. Nathan & Tippins (1990) investigated the effects of halo on the accuracy of performance ratings and validity coefficients. In a validation of clerical-ability tests, they found that ratings with greater halo (greater dimension intercorrelations) produced more accurate estimates of validity. They also found that when the general factor is statistically removed from ratings, validities are lowered. They conclude that halo is not a contaminant in supervisory ratings of job performance but rather a source of true variance in overall ratings. A similar perspective is expressed in the Project A research (e.g. see McHenry et al 1990). Murphy & Balzer (1989), in a meta-analytic investigation of the relationship between rater errors (halo and leniency) and rating accuracy, concluded that presence of halo "tends to indicate accuracy rather than inaccuracy in rating" (p. 622). In a similar vein, Gomez-Mejia (1988) compared halo, test-retest reliability, and criterion-related validity for be- haviorally anchored rating scales and global rating scales. Global rating scales were found to result in slightly greater validity, and the behaviorally anchored rating scales had no scale properties superior to the global rating scales.

In much applied selection research, the purpose of performance measure- ment is essentially to rank order individuals correctly on the basis of their overall performance, in order to determine the relative importance of different predictors for overall performance (Schmidt & Kaplan 1971). Also, utility analysis as usually conducted requires a measure of overall job performance, because the standard deviation of job performance typically refers to the job as a whole, not to components of job performance. The weight of the evidence in personnel selection indicates that "sophisticated" multi- dimensional approaches to performance measurement ratings are often not desirable or needed in selection research.

Pulakos et al (1989) report large-sample evidence that race and gender biases, job type, and rater source have only small effects on performance ratings when ability is controlled, suggesting that any race and gender effects on performance evaluations probably result from true performance differ- ences. Kraiger & Ford (1990) present evidence that job-performance and job-knowledge criteria correlate positively with supervisory ratings of job performance for both blacks and whites. P. R. Sackett & C. L. Z. DuBois (unpublished) present results from two large-sample data sets that failed to support the hypothesis that raters generally give more favorable ratings to members of their own race. J. Lefkowitz & M. Battista (unpublished) report failure to detect any evidence of sex bias in performance ratings in a predic- tive criterion-related test validation study. They found only a slight tendency for supervisors to give higher ratings to members of their own race (average r = .11). They reported that supervisors' liking for the employee correlated with supervisory job performance ratings, but failed to note that employee performance may cause liking. Previous research also shows that when friendship, likability, and similarity between supervisor and employee are partialed out of ratings, validity estimates for predictors change little. Ratings criteria may differ somewhat in levels of halo, deficiency, leniency, and race and gender bias, but none of these errors and biases appears per se to result in different conclusions about the presence of criterion-related validity of ability/ aptitude tests. However, it remains to be determined whether the same holds for noncognitive measures.

Rothstein (1990) investigated the interrater reliability of multi-scale com- posite job performance ratings. Across ratings of 9975 employees participating in validity studies, she found mean interrater agreement (reliability for one rater) of .48. Reliability increased fastest with length of supervisory exposure to the ratee during the first 12 months of exposure and reached an asymptote level of .60 after 20 years of opportunity to observe. Since .60 is the reliability that can be expected under optimal opportunity to observe, Schmidt et al's (1985) suggestion that .48 is the best estimate for a single rater is supported by the Rothstein (1990) results. Hence the use of .60 as the average criterion reliability to correct for attenuation in previous validity generalization studies may have resulted in *undercorrection* of the validities. Rothstein's (1990) findings obviously call into question the interrater reliability estimate of .80 assumed by the National Academy of Sciences panel (Hartigan & Wigdor 1990).

Weekly & Gier (1989) investigated the ceiling on the reliability for one type of rating under ideal conditions. Interrater agreement of ratings given by world-class professional expert judges in the figure-skating competition at the 1984 Olympics suggested .81 as the maximum average reliability of performance ratings by one rater. These professional judges each had at least 15 years of experience as expert judges; they were extensively trained to use a shared frame of reference; they all used the same clear set of performance dimensions; and their evaluations were under constant public scrutiny. In addition, they rated performance within a short time in two particular events, not performance over a year or more in many performance areas, as would be the case with job performance. The unusually high single-rater reliability in this study is probably due to all these factors; interrater agreement this high cannot be expected in typical work performance settings.

C. H. Campbell et al (1990), using Project A data, reported that the median single-rater reliability for ratings of overall effectiveness was .66, and for individual behaviorally anchored rating scales the mean single-rater reliabilities ranged between .51 and .68 for supervisors trained in the use of these scales. The similarity of these values to the Rothstein (1990) results is noteworthy. Finally, Schmidt & Hunter (1989) critiqued the erroneous practice of attempting to compute reliability coefficients for ratings when only one stimulus (e.g. one employee) is rated.

The issue of whether job performance is stable across time is extremely important. The value of different selection devices depends on their ability to predict job performance at all points in time, and in particular in the long term. Austin et al (1989) and Barrett & Alexander (1989) continued the earlier debate (Barrett et al 1985; Henry & Hulin 1987) on the degree to which criteria are dynamic. Austin et al (1989) claimed that there is considerable temporal unreliability in job performance and that it reflects changes in the rank order of employees on *true performance*. They also argued that data show that past levels of employee output do not predict future output well. Barrett & Alexander (1989) responded by presenting evidence from several areas of psychology casting serious doubt on the universal presence of the simplex matrix of performance measures. They also noted that several studies have found that validities do not decline over time (e.g. Schmidt et al 1988b), discounting the position that ability levels change over time. The literature appears to indicate that the simplex phenomenon does not necessarily result in decline of validity over time (see the section above on technical and theoretical aspects of validity). Support for this was found by Deadrick & Madigan (1990) in a two-year longitudinal study. Their results indicated that performance-stability coefficients declined as the time interval between the measurements increased but that the validity of cognitive ability for predicting job performance actually increased with tenure, while the validity of psychomotor ability remained constant (and the validity of job experience declined). Hanges et al (1990) found evidence for stability of student ratings of faculty performance over 6.5 years. In addition, their results indicated that criterion stability is a function of the faculty member's performance attributes and not the course being taught.

Many articles on performance measurement and criteria state that too little is known about constructs underlying job performance (e.g. J. P. Campbell et al 1990; J. P. Campbell 1990). Researchers in Project A addressed this issue by developing multidimensional performance measures, with two major categories: organization-wide dimensions and job-specific dimensions. Each category in turn had several scales, tests, questionnaires, and rating scales designed to measure different subdimensions. The five factors that emerged from factor analysis were (a) core (job) technical proficiency, (b) general soldiering proficiency, (c) effort and leadership, (d) personal discipline, and (e) physical fitness and military bearing. Project A results indicate that the latent structure of the five factors is consistent across different job categories for the population of jobs investigated. One may question, however, whether all criterion measures that an employer may be interested in are components of job performance (e.g. military bearing and appearance in the Project A studies). If not, we must distinguish between criteria that are part of job performance and those that are *valued by management* but are not components of job performance. Although this may appear to be merely an issue of semantics, it is an important theoretical question. J. P. Campbell et al (1990) note that, to the extent that validities are not the same across criterion dimensions, different performance constructs will be best predicted by different predictors. It is clear in the Project A data that some dimensions of job behavior, such as physical fitness and military bearing (which may not be part of job performance per se), are better predicted by noncognitive than cognitive predictors, and are better predicted by some noncognitive predictors than by others. Other evidence suggests that some dimensions of job behavior (counterproductivity; theft) can be predicted well by personality measures (Hogan & Hogan 1989; Ones et al 1991).

In the last few years considerable progress has been made toward explaining why particular predictors work. Most recently Vance et al (1989) used path analysis to investigate the construct validity of *task* performance and its proposed antecedents: mental ability, job experience, and the contextual variable of supervisor support. Supervisor support did not have an impact on task performance. In general, the Vance et al (1989) findings are similar to the Schmidt et al (1986) results even though the former concentrated on performance task subdomains and the latter on global job performance. Job experience and ability were found to have a strong impact on task proficiency. Both studies found mental ability/aptitude and job experience to be virtually uncorrelated.

BOOKS, REVIEWS, AND THE WIDER CONTEXT OF SELECTION

Books relevant to particular selection topics are included in the appropriate sections of this review. Here we cover some recent books that encompass a wide variety of topics in selection. Volume 1 of the long awaited *Handbook for Industrial and Organizational Psychology* edited by Dunnette & Hough appeared in 1990. This volume includes chapters on performance measurement and methodology in I/O psychology, some of which were cited earlier in this review. Smith & Robertson (1989) edited a book emphasizing the integration of selection topics into an overall process model of selection. They stated that the recent research summarized in the book indicates a "Renaissance" in selection. Gatewood & Field (1990) authored a comprehensive text summarizing current research and covering selection devices increasing in popularity, such as drug and honesty testing. Schmitt & Klimoski (1991) authored a book on research methods in human resource management. J. P. Campbell & R. J. Campbell (1988) edited a volume presenting the contributions of I/O psychology to understanding and improving productivity in organizations.

Dachler (1989) related selection to the wider organizational context and provided an innovative perspective on current epistemology in selection. Giffin (1989) reviewed personnel testing, selection, and performance appraisal techniques as they apply to the public sector, nominating validity generalization and the quantification of selection utility as the most important research advances of the last 25 years. Cronshaw (1988), in a review article on future directions for industrial psychology research in Canada, indicated that validity generalization is useful in transporting validity evidence from the United States to Canada. Windolf & Wood (1988), in a short book, compared selection practices in Great Britain and West Germany; the heavy use of biodata and personality variables in these two countries may represent a contrast to the US case. R. D. Arvey, R. S. Bhagat, and E. Salas (unpublished) discussed selection in the international and cross-cultural environment. Their review found differences in average weights given in hiring to predictors in different countries. They also argued that *international* generalizability of validities of construct-equivalent predictors is highly probable, although empirical support for this position is still limited. We would add that ability and some personality-based predictors used in *expatriate selection* (selection of overseas assignees) may prove to be valid and generalizable across cultures as well (D. S. Ones & F. L. Schmidt 1991, unpublished).

SUMMARY OF MAJOR TRENDS

Meta-analytic methods and findings have now become well established in validity generalization, and have been extended beyond ability and aptitude tests to biodata, assessment centers, interviews, integrity tests, and other predictors. Fine tuning of methods continues, and a *Test Validity Yearbook* has been established to collect primary validity studies for future meta-analyses. Progress has also occurred in research on selection utility methods, and new research indicates that individual variability in output is large at all levels of the occupational spectrum, suggesting substantial potential selection utilities.

Research evidence against differential aptitude theory mounts, leading to a renewed emphasis on the importance of general mental ability. This development has in turn stimulated considerable research effort in the noncognitive domain, including biodata. There is renewed interest in personality testing and personality constructs, particularly employee reliability (or dependability) and conscientiousness. A relatively favorable APA report has raised the status of integrity testing in personnel selection in the eyes of many, and may stimulate considerable research. Application of meta-analysis has had an impact. In these noncognitive domains, the validity evidence—and the generalizability of this evidence—is already fairly impressive. More progress can be expected in the future.

Considerable progress has been made in understanding job-performance ratings. Much evidence now exists that single-rater reliabilities above .50 are rarely to be expected, that halo should perhaps not be viewed as error, and that complex rating-scale technologies do not improve job performance ratings. Also, there is increasing evidence that validities of many predictors do not decline with increasing time intervals, although research on this question will (and should) continue. Progress has been made in elucidating the constructs underlying job performance, in large part because of the contributions of Project A. Finally, there is increasing interest in developing explanatory theories of job performance, stimulated in part by the fact that meta-analysis has provided stable and precise estimates of the relationships among many variables. Efforts to develop such theories are an indication that the field is maturing.

From a broader perspective, the present period is one of both dramatic progress and clear dangers for personnel selection. Validity generalization and utility research has established the wide applicability and economic importance of personnel selection. Yet research has not, and cannot, resolve the conflict between the competing American values of individual merit, economic efficiency, and international competitiveness, on the one hand, and economic equality and opportunity for minorities, on the other.

The struggle to resolve this conflict may soon come to a head in the political and governmental domains. The Supreme Court's Wards Cove decision has opened the way to improved selection and major increases in economic gains from selection. Yet some perceive it as detrimental to minority advancement. The Civil Rights Bill of 1991, if passed into law, would make widespread use of optimally valid selection methods difficult if not impossible. Which road will we take? The US Employment Service's nationwide validity generalization–based testing program has collided with the same dilemma. The government's options were to continue the program with the subgroup test score adjustments and face mounting criticisms of reverse discrimination, or to drop the score adjustments and face attacks on grounds of "adverse impact." The desire to avoid either of these unpleasant and politically dangerous outcomes led to the proposal of the two year suspension. But the public reaction (in written comments) was so negative (96% of the 1600 responses were negative) that it has been necessary to suspend the suspension itself! Will it be politically and legally possible to employ valid selection procedures, with or without subgroup adjustments, in our litigious and multicultural society? The stakes are enormous—not merely for the field of personnel psychology, but for the economy and the nation as a whole. The jury is still out. But Congress may soon deliver its verdict, in the form of a new Civil Rights Bill.

Literature Cited

Ackerman, P. L. 1989. Within-task intercorrelations of skill performance: implications for predicting individual differences? (A comment on Henry & Hulin, 1987). *J. Appl. Psychol.* 74:360–64

Ackerman, P. L. 1987. Individual differences in skill learning: an integration of psychometric and information processing perspectives. *Psychol. Bull.* 102:3–27

Ackerman, P. L., Humphreys, L. G. 1990. Individual differences theory in industrial and organizational psychology. See Dunnette & Hough 1990, pp. 223–82

Alexander, R. A. 1988. Group homogeneity, range restriction, and range enhancement effect on correlations. *Personnel Psychol.* 41:773–7

Alexander, R. A., Carson, K. P., Alliger, G. M., Cranshaw, S. F. 1989. Empirical distributions of range restricted SD$_x$ in validity studies. *J. Appl. Psychol.* 74:253–58

Alexander, R. A., Hanges, P. J., Alliger, G. M. 1989. The sample-based estimation of parameters under range restriction. Paper presented at the 4th Annu. Conf. Soc. Indust. Org. Psychol., Boston

Alexander, R. A., Scozzaro, M. J., Borodkin, L. J. 1989. Statistical and empirical examination of the chi-square test for homogeneity of correlations in meta-analysis. *Psychol. Bull.* 106:329–31

Alexander, R. A., Carson, K. P., Alliger, G. M., Carr, L. 1987. Correcting doubly truncated correlations: an improved approximation for correcting the bivariate normal correlation when truncation has occurred on both variables. *Educ. Psychol. Meas.* 47: 309–15

Anastasi, A. 1989. Ability testing in the 1980's and beyond: some major trends. *Public Personnel Manage. J.* 18:471–84

Anderson, W. W., Stewart, O. J. 1989. Testing, job-specific literacy of industrial workers: cooperation between education and industry. Paper presented at the meeting of the Am. Educ. Re. Assoc., San Francisco

Armstrong, T. R., Chalupsky, A. B., McLaughlin, D. H., Dalldorf, M. R. 1988. *Armed Services Vocational Aptitude Battery: Validation for Civilian Occupations.* Brook Air Force Base, TX: Air Force Human Resources Laboratory

Arthur, W. Jr., Barrett, G. V., Doverspike, D. 1990. Validation of information-processing-based test battery for the prediction of handling accidents among petroleum-product transport drivers. *J. Appl. Psychol.* 75:621–28

Arvey, R. D., Salas, E., Gialluca, K. A. 1989. Using task inventories to forecast skills and abilities. Paper presented at Annu. Meet. Soc. Indust. Org. Psychol., Boston

Arvey, R. D., Strickland, W., Drauden, G., Martin, C. 1990. Motivational components of test taking. *Personnel Psychol.* 43:695–716

Ash, P. 1991. A history of honesty testing. In *Pre-employment Honesty Testing: Current Research and Future Directions,* ed. J. W. Jones, pp. 3–20. Westport, CT: Greenwood Publishing Group. In press

Ash, R. A., Johnson, J. L., Levine, E. L., McDaniel, M. A. 1989. Job applicant training and work experience evaluation in personnel selection. *Res. Personnel Hum. Resourc. Manage.* 7:183–226

Ash, P., Slora, K., Britton, C. 1990. Police agency officer selection practices. *J. Police Sci. Admin.* 17:258–69

Association of Personnel Test Publishers. 1990. *Model Guidelines for Pre-employment Integrity Testing Programs.* Washington DC: Assoc. Personnel Test Publ.

Austin, J. T., Hanisch, K. A. 1990. Occupational attainment as a function of abilities and interests: a longitudinal analysis using project TALENT data. *J. Appl. Psychol.* 75:77–86

Austin, J. F., Humphreys, L. G., Hulin, C. L. 1989. Another view of dynamic criteria: a critical reanalysis of Barrett, Caldwell, Alexander. *Personnel Psychol.* 42:583–96

Avolio, B. J., Waldman, D. A. 1990. An examination of age and cognitive test performance across job complexity and occupational types. *J. Appl. Psychol.* 75:43–50

Baker, L. 1989. Metacognition comprehension monitoring, and the adult reader. *Educ. Psychol. Rev.* 1:3–38

Barrett, G. V., Alexander, R. A. 1989. Rejoinder to Austin, Humphreys, Hulin: critical reanalysis of Barrett, Caldwell, Alexander. *Personnel Psychol.* 42:597–612

Barrett, G. V., Caldwell, M. S., Alexander, R. A. 1985. The concept of dynamic criteria: a critical reanalysis. *Pers. Psychol.* 38:41–56

Barrick, M. R., Mount, M. K. 1991. The big five personality dimensions and job performance: a meta analysis. *Personnel Psychol.* 41:1–26

Barrick, M. R., Barrett, G. V., Doverspike, D., Robison, S. J., Grubs, L. L. 1990. Central tendency and its impact on three SD_y procedures: a case study. *J. Occup. Psychol.* 63:265–8

Becker, B. E. 1989. The influence of labor markets on human resources utility estimates. *Personnel Psychol.* 42:531–46

Ben-Shakhar, G. 1989. Non-conventional methods in personnel selection. In *Assessment in Selection in Organizations,* ed. P. Herriot. New York: John Wiley & Sons Ltd

Binning, J. F., Barrett, G. V. 1989. Validity of personnel decisions: a conceptual analysis of the inferential and evidential bases. *J. Appl. Psychol.* 74:478–94

Blits, J. H., Gottfredson, L. S. 1990. Employment testing and job performance. *Public Interest* 98:18–25

Blits, J. H., Gottfredson, L. S. 1990. Equality or lasting inequality? *Soc. Sci. Modern Society* 27:4–11

Bosshardt, M. J., DuBois, D. A., Paullin, C., Carter, G. W. 1989. The Investigative Interview: A Review of Practice and Related Research. Inst. Rep. 160. Minneapolis: Pers. Decisions Res. Inst. 146 pp.

Brannick, M. T., Michaels, C. E., Baker, D. P. 1989. Construct validity of in-basket scores. *J. Appl. Psychol.* 74:957–63

Brown, S. H., Stout, J. D., Dalessio, A. 1988. Stability of validity indices through test score ranges. *J. Appl. Psychol.* 73:736–42

Burke, M. J., Doran, L. I. 1989. A note on the economic utility of generalized validity coefficients in personnel selection. *J. Appl. Psychol.* 76:171–75

Burke, M. J., Normand, J., Doran, L. I. 1989. Estimating unrestricted population parameters from restricted sample data in employment testing. *Appl. Psychol. Meas.* 3:161–66

Callender, J. C., Osburn, H. G. 1988. Unbiased estimation of sampling variance of correlations. *J. Appl. Psychol.* 73:312–15

Campbell, C. H., Ford, P., Rumsey, M. G., Pulakos, E. D., Borman, W. C., et al. 1990. Development of multiple job performance measures in a representative sample of jobs. *Personnel Psychol.* 43:277–300

Campbell, J. 1990. An overview of the army selection and classification project (Project A). *Personnel Psychol.* 43:231–39

Campbell, J. P. 1990. Modeling the performance prediction problem in industrial and organizational psychology. See Dunnette & Hough 1990, pp. 687–732

Campbell, J. P., Campbell, R. J. 1988. *Productivity in Organizations: New Perspectives from Industrial and Organization-*

al Psychology. San Francisco: Jossey-Bass

Campbell, J. P., McHenry, J. J., Wise, L. L. 1990. Modeling job performance in a population of jobs. *Personnel Psychol.* 43:313–33

Campion, M. A., Pursell, E. D., Brown, B. K. 1988. Structured interviewing: raising the psychometric properties of the employment interview. *Personnel Psychol.* 41:25–42

Campion, M. A. 1989. Ability requirement implications of job design: an interdisciplinary perspective. *Personnel Psychol.* 42:1–24

Carey, N. B. 1990. An assessment of surrogates for hands-on tests: selection standards and training needs. Cent. Naval Anal. Res. Memo. 90–47

Carretta, T. R. 1989. USAF pilot selection and classification systems. *Aviat. Space Envir.* 60:46–49

Carrier, M. R., Dalessio, A. T., Brown, S. H. 1990. Correspondence between estimates of content and criterion-related validity values. *Personnel Psychol.* 43:85–100

Cascio, W. F., Morris, J. K. 1990. A critical reanalysis of Hunter, Schmidt, and Coggins' 1988 "Problems and pitfalls in using capital budgeting and financial accounting techniques in assessing utility of personnel programs." *J. Appl. Psychol.* 75:410–17

Colberg, M. 1985. Logic-based measurement of verbal reasoning: a key to increased validity and economy. *Personnel Psychol.* 38:347–59

Colberg, M., Nestor, M. A. 1987. The use of illogical biases in psychometrics. Paper presented at the Eighth Int. Congr. Logic, Methodol., Philos. Sci., Moscow

Cook, M. 1988. *Personnel Selection and Productivity.* Chichester, England: Wiley

Coward, W. M., Sackett, P. R. 1990. Linearity of ability-performance relationships: a re-confirmation. *J. Appl. Psychol.* 75:297–300

Crawley, B., Pinder, R., Herriott, P. 1990. Assessment center dimensions, personality, and aptitudes. *J. Occup. Psychol.* 63:211–16

Cronbach, L. J. 1970. *Essentials of Psychological Testing.* New York: Harper & Row. 3rd. ed.

Cronshaw, S. F. 1988. Future directions for industrial psychology in Canada. *Can. Psychol.* 29:30–41

Cronshaw, S. F., Alexander, R. A. 1991. Why capital budgeting techniques are suited for assessing the utility of personnel programs: a reply to Hunter, Schmidt, Coggin. *J. Appl. Psychol.* 76:454–57

Cunningham, J. W., Scott, B. M. 1988. The dimensionality of uses and OAI worker-oriented job variables. Presented at the 96th Annu. Convent. Am. Psychol. Assoc., Atlanta

Dachler, H. P. 1989. Selection and the organizational context. In *Handbook of Assessment in Organizations,* ed. P. Herriot, pp. 45–69. New York: Wiley & Sons

Day, D. V., Silverman, S. B. 1989. Personality and job performance: evidence of incremental validity. *Personnel Psychol.* 42:25–36

Deadrick, D. L., Madigan, R. M. 1990. Dynamic criteria revisited: a longitudinal study of performance stability and predictive validity. *Personnel Psychol.* 43:717–44

Digman, J. M. 1990. Personality Structure: Emergence of the five factor model. *Annu. Rev. Psychol.* 41:417–40

Dipboye, R. L., Gaugler, B. B., Hayes, T. L., Parker, D. S. 1990. Individual differences in the incremental validity of interviewers' judgments. Poster presented at Annu. Meet. Soc. Indust. Org. Psychol., Miami, Fla.

Dobson, P., Williams, A. 1989. The validation of the selection of male British Army officers. *J. Occup. Psychol.* 62:313–25

Dreher, G. F., Ash, R. A., Hancock, P. 1988. The role of the traditional research design in underestimating the validity of the employment interview. *Personnel Psychol.* 41:315–24

Dunnette, M. D. 1989. Validation of selection tests for electrical power plant operators. *Advances in Industrial and Organizational Psychology,* ed. B. J. Fallon, H. B. Pfister, J. Brebner, pp. 377–87. New York: Elsevier/North-Holland

Dunnette, M. D., Hough, L. M. 1990. *Handbook of Industrial & Organizational Psychology.* Palo Alto: Consulting Psychologists Press. Vol. 1, 2nd ed.

Eaves, L. J., Eysenck, H. J., Martin, N. E. 1989. *Genes, Culture, and Personality.* New York: Academic

Edwards, J. E., Frederick, J. T., Burke, M. J. 1988. Efficacy of modified CREPID SD_ys on the basis of archival organizational data. *J. Appl. Psychol.* 7:529–35

Feltham, R. 1988. Assessment center decision making: judgmental vs. mechanical. *J. Occup. Psychol.* 61:237–41

Feltham, R. 1988. Validity of a police assessment center: a 1–19-year follow-up. *J. Occup. Psychol.* 61:129–44

Fiedler, F. E. 1989. The effective utilization of intellectual abilities and job-relevant knowledge in group performance: cognitive resource theory and an agenda for the future. *Appl. Psychol.: Int. Rev.* 38:289–304

Fraser, S. L., Kroeck, K. G. 1989. The impact of drug screening on selection decisions. *J. Bus. Psychol.* 3:403–11

Gael, S., ed. 1988. *The Job Analysis Handbook for Business, Industry and Government.* New York: Wiley

Gandy, J. A., Outerbridge, A. N., Sharf, J. C., Dye, D. A. 1989. *Development and*

Initial Validation of the Individual Achievement Records (IAR). Washington DC: US Office of Personnel Management

Gardner, D. G., Discenza, R. 1988. Sex effects in evaluating applicant qualifications: a re-examination. Sex Roles 18:297–308

Gatewood, R. D., Field, H. S. 1990. Human Resource Selection. Orlando: Dryden Press

Gaugler, B. B., Rosenthal, D. B., Thorton, G. C., Bentson, C. 1987. Meta-analysis of assessment center validity. J. Appl. Psychol. 72:493–511

Gaugler, B. B., Thornton, G. C. 1989. Number of assessment center dimensions as a determinant of assessor accuracy. J. Appl. Psychol. 74:611–18

Geyer, P. D., Hice, J., Hawk, J., Boese, R., Bannon, Y. 1989. Reliabilities of ratings available from the Dictionary of Occupational Titles. Personnel Psychol. 42:547–60

Ghorpade, J. V. 1988. Job Analysis: A Handbook for the Human Resource Director. Englewood Cliffs, NJ: Prentice-Hall

Gibson, F. W., Fiedler, F. E., Daniels, K. M. 1990. Determinants of effective utilization of leader abilities: stress, babble and the utilization of leader intellectual abilities. Tech. Rep. 90–1. Univ. Washington, Seattle

Giffin, M. E. 1989. Personnel research on testing, selection, and performance appraisal. Public Personnel Manage. J. 18:127–37

Glaser, R. 1989. Learning theory and the study of instruction. Annu. Rev. Psychol. 40:631–66

Goldberg, L. R. 1990. An alternative "description of personality": the big five factor structure. J. Pers. Soc. Psychol. 59:1216–29

Goldberg, L. R., Grenier, J. R., Guion, R. M., Sechrest, L. B., Wing, H. 1991. Questionnaires Used in the Prediction of Trustworthiness in Pre-employment Selection Decisions: An A. P. A. Task Force Report. Washington DC: Am. Psychol. Assoc. 31 pp.

Gomez-Mejia, L. R. 1988. Evaluating employee performance: Does the appraisal instrument make a difference? J. Org. Behav. Manage. 9:155–72

Gottfredson, L. S., Sharf, J. C. 1988. Fairness in employment testing. J. Vocat. Behav. 33 (Spec. Issue)

Graves, L. M., Powell, G. N. 1988. An investigation of sex discrimination in recruiters' evaluations. J. Appl. Psychol. 73:20–29

Griggs v. Duke Power Co. 401 U.S. 424 (1971)

Hammer, E. G., Kleiman, L. A. 1988. Getting to know you. Personnel Admin. 34:86–92

Hanges, P. J., Schneider, B., Niles, K. 1990. Stability of performance: an interactionist perspective. J. Appl. Psychol. 75:658–67

Hansen, C. P. 1989. A causal model of the relationship among accidents, biodata, personality, and cognitive factors. J. Appl. Psychol. 74:81–90

Harris, M. M. 1989. Reconsidering the employment interview: a review of recent literature and suggestions for future research. Personnel Psychol. 42:691–726

Hartigan, J. A., Wigdor, A. K., eds. 1989. Fairness in Employment Testing: Validity Generalization, Minority Issues, and the General Aptitude Test Battery. Washington DC: Natl. Acad. Press

Hattrup, K., Schmitt, N. 1990. Prediction of trades apprentices' performance on job sample criteria. Personnel Psychol. 43:453–66

Hedges, L. V. 1989. An unbiased correction for sampling error in validity generalization studies. J. Appl. Psychol. 74:469–77

Hembree, R. 1988. Correlates, causes, effects, and treatment of test anxiety. Rev. Educ. Res.. 58:44–77

Henry, R. A., Hulin, C. L. 1987. Stability of skilled performance across time: some generalizations and limitations on utilities. J. Appl. Psychol. 72:457–62

Henry, R. A., Hulin, C. L. 1989. Changing validities: ability-performance relations and utilities. J. Appl. Psychol. 74:365–67

Hogan, J., Hogan, R. 1989. How to measure employee reliability. J. Appl. Psychol. 74:273–79

Hough, L. M. 1988. Development of personality measures to supplement selection decisions. Presented at the 24th Annu. Int. Congr. Psychol. Convent., Sydney, Australia

Hough, L. M., Eaton, N. K., Dunnette, M. D., Kamp, J. D., McCloy, R. A. 1990. Criterion-related validities of personality constructs and the effect of response distortion on those validities. J. Appl. Psychol. Monogr. 75:581–95

Hughes, G. L., Prien, E. P. 1989. Evaluation of task and job skill linkage judgements used to develop test specifications. Personnel Psychol. 42:283–92

Hulin, C. L., Henry, R. A., Noon, S. L. 1990. Adding a dimension: time as a factor in the generalizability of predictive relationships. Psychol. Bull. 107:328–40

Hunter, J. E. 1983a. A causal analysis of cognitive ability, job knowledge, job performance, and supervisor ratings. In Performance Measurement and Theory, ed. F. Landy, S. Zedeck, J. Cleveland, pp. 257–66. Hillsdale, NJ: Earlbaum

Hunter, J. E. 1983b. The Dimensionality of the General Aptitude Test Battery (GATB) and the Dominance of General Factors over Specific Factors in the Prediction of Job Performance for the U. S. Employment Service. USES Test Res. Rep. No. 44. Washington DC: U. S. Dept. Labor

Hunter, J. E. 1986. Cognitive ability, cognitive aptitudes, job knowledge, and job performance. *J. Vocat. Behav.* 29:340–62

Hunter, J. E., Hunter, R. F. 1984. Validity and utility of alternate predictors of job performance. *Psychol. Bull.* 96:72–98

Hunter, J. E., Schmidt, F. L. 1976. A critical analysis of the statistical and ethical implications of various definitions of "test bias." *Psychol. Bull.* 83:1053–71

Hunter, J. E., Schmidt F. L. 1990a. *Methods of Meta-analysis: Correcting Error and Bias in Research Findings.* Newbury Park, CA: Sage Publications

Hunter, J. E., Schmidt F. L. 1990b. Dichotomization of continuous variables: the implications for meta-analysis. *J. Appl. Psychol.* 75:334–49

Hunter, J. E., Schmidt, F. L. 1991. Credibility intervals in meta-analysis. Unpublished manuscript

Hunter, J. E., Schmidt, F. L., Coggin, T. D. 1988. Problems and pitfalls in using capital budgeting and financial accounting techniques in assessing the utility of personnel programs. *J. Appl. Psychol.*. 73:522–28

Hunter, J. E., Schmidt, F. L., Judiesch, M. K. 1990. Individual differences in output as a function of job complexity. *J. Appl. Psychol.* 75:28–46

Hurd, S. N. 1990. Genetic testing: your genes and your job. *Employ. Responsib. Rights J.* 3:239–52

Jeanneret, P. R. 1988. Position requirements for space station personnel and linkages to portable microcomputer performance assessment. Tech. Rep. Jeanneret & Assoc., Houston, TX

Jensen, A. R. 1986. G: artifact or reality? *J. Vocat. Behav.* 29:301–31

Johnson, C. D., Zeidner, J., Scholarios, D. 1990. *Improving the Classification Efficiency of the Armed Services Vocational Aptitude Battery through the Use of Alternative Test Selection Indices.* Alexandria, VA: Inst. Defense Anal.

Jones, J. W., Joy, D. 1989. Empirical investigation of job applicants reactions to taking a pre-employment honesty test. Paper presented at the 97th Annu. Conf. Am. Psychol. Assoc., New Orleans

Jones, J. W., Ash, P., Soto, C. 1990a. Employment privacy rights and pre-employment honesty tests. *Employ. Relat. Law J.* 15:561–75

Jones, J. W., Arnold, D., Harris, W. G. 1990b. Introduction to the model guidelines for pre-employment integrity testing. *J. Bus. Psychol.* 4:525–32

Jones, G. E. 1988. *Investigation of the efficacy of general ability versus specific ability as predictors of occupational success.* Masters Thesis, St. Mary's University

Judiesch, M. K., Schmidt, F. L., Mount, M. K. 1991. Estimates of the dollar value of

employee output in utility analyses: An empirical test of two theories. *J. Appl. Psychol.* In press

Kemery, E. R., Mossholder, K. W., Dunlap, W. P. 1989. Meta-analysis and moderator variables: a cautionary note on transportability. *J. Appl. Psychol.* 74:168–70

Kinicki, A. J., Lockwood, C. A., Hom, P. W., Griffeth, R. W. 1990. Interviewer predictions of applicant qualifications and interviewer validity: aggregate and individual analyses. *J. Appl. Psychol.* 75:477–86

Kleiman, L. S., Biderman, M. 1989. Job analysis for managerial selection: a guidelines-based approach. *J. Bus. Psychol.* 3:353–59

Kleiman, L. S., Faley, R. H. 1990. A comparative analysis of the empirical validity of past and present-oriented biographical items. *J. Bus. Psychol.* 4:431–37

Klimoski, R. J., Refaeli, A. 1983. Inferring personal qualities through handwriting analysis. *J. Occup. Psychol.* 56:191–202

Klitgaard, R. 1986. *Elitism and Meritocracy in Developing Countries (Selection Policies for Higher Education).* Baltimore, MD: Johns Hopkins Univ. Press

Kraiger, K., Ford, J. K. 1990. The relation of job knowledge, job performance, and supervisory ratings as a function of ratee race. *Hum. Perform.* 3:269–79

Landy, F. J., ed. 1991. *Handbook of Test Validity.* Monterey, CA: Brooks-Cole Publishing Company

Lautenschlager, G. J. 1990. Sources of imprecision in formula cross-validated multiple correlations. *J. Appl. Psychol.* 75:460–62

Lawshe, C. H. 1987. Adverse impact: Is it a viable concept? *Prof. Psychol. Res. Pract.* 18:492–97

Lawshe, C. H. 1974. A quantitative approach to content validity. *Personnel Psychol.* 28: 563–75

Lee, R., Foley, P. P. 1986. Is the validity of a test constant throughout the test score range? *J. Appl. Psychol.* 71:641–44

Levy, R. 1979. Handwriting and hiring. *Dun's Rev.* March:72–79

Lowry, P. E. 1988. The assessment center: pooling scores or arithmetic decision rule? *Public Personnel Manage. J.* 17:63–71

Macan, T. H., Dipboye, R. L. 1990. The relationship of interviewers' preinterview impressions to selection and recruitment outcomes. *Personnel Psychol.* 43:745–68

Manhardt, P. J. 1989. Base rates and test of deception: Has I/O psychology shot itself in the foot? *Indust.-Org. Psychol.* 26:48–50

Martin, S. L. 1989. Honesty testing: estimating and reducing the false positive rate. *J. Bus. Psychol.* 3:255–67

Martin, C. L., Nagao, D. H. 1989. Some effects of computerized interviewing on job applicant responses. *J. Appl. Psychol.* 75: 72–80

Martin, S. L., Terris, W. 1990. The four-cell classification table in personnel selection heuristic device gone awry. *Indust.-Org. Psychol.* 27(3):49–55

Martin, S. L., Terris, W. 1991. Predicting infrequent behavior: classifying the impact on false positive rates. *J. Appl. Psychol.* 76:484–87

Mathieu, J. E., Tannenbaum, S. I. 1989. A process-tracing approach toward understanding supervisors' SD$_y$ estimates: results from five job classes. *J. Occup. Psychol.* 62:249–56

Maurer, S. D., Fay, C. 1988. Effect of situational interviews, conventional structured interviews, and training on interview rating agreement: an experimental analysis. *Personnel Psychol.* 41:329–44

McCormick, E. J., Mecham, R. C., Jeanneret, P. R. 1989. *Technical Manual for the Position Analysis Questionnaire.* West Lafayette, IN: Purdue Res. Found.

McDaniel, M. A. 1988. Does pre-employment drug use predict on-the-job suitability? *Personnel Psychol.* 41:717–29

McDaniel, M. A. 1989. Biographical constructs for predicting employee suitability. *J. Appl. Psychol.* 74:464–70

McDaniel, M. A., Schmidt, F. L., Hunter, J. E. 1988. A meta-analysis of the validity of methods for rating training and experience in personnel selection. *Personnel Psychol.* 41:283–314

McDaniel, M. A., Whetzel, D. L., Schmidt, F. L., Hunter, J. E., Russell, J. 1990. The validity of employment interviews: A review and meta-analysis. Unpublished manuscript

McEvoy, G. M., Beatty, R. W. 1989. Assessment centers and subordinate appraisals of managers: a seven-year examination of predictive validity. *Personnel Psychol.* 42:37–52

McHenry, J. J., Hough, L. M., Toquam, J. L., Hanson, M. L., Ashworth, S. 1990. Project A validity results: the relationship between predictor and criterion domains. *Personnel Psychol.* 43:335–54

McIntyre, R. M. 1990. Spurious estimation of validity coefficients in composite samples: some methodological considerations. *J. Appl. Psychol.* 75:91–94

Millsap, R. E. 1988. Tolerance intervals: alternatives to credibility intervals in validity generalization research. *Appl. Psychol. Meas.* 12:27–32

Millsap, R. E. 1989. Sampling variance in the correlation coefficient under range restriction: a Monte Carlo Study. *J. Appl. Psychol.* 74:450–61

Molcan, J. R., Orban, J. A. 1989. Selecting and developing entry-level managers with the Management Readiness Profile. *J. Bus. Psychol.* 4:221–35

Motowidlo, S. J., Carter, G. W., Dunnette, M. D. 1989. A situational inventory for entry-level management positions. Presented at the 4th Annu. Conf. Soc. Indust. Org. Psychol., Boston

Motowidlo, S. J., Dunnette, M. D., Carter, G. W. 1990. An alternative selection procedure: the low-fidelity simulation. *J. Appl. Psychol.* 75:640–47

Murphy, K. R. 1987. Detecting infrequent deception. *J. Appl. Psychol.* 72:611–14

Murphy, K. R. 1989. Is the relationship between cognitive ability and job performance stable over time? *Hum. Perform.* 2:183–200

Murphy, K. R., Balzer, B. Y. 1989. Rater errors and rating accuracy. *J. Appl. Psychol.* 74:619–24

Murphy, K. R., Thornton, G. C., Reynolds, D. H. 1990. College students' attitudes toward employee drug testing programs. *Personnel Psychol.* 43:615–31

Murphy, S. E., Blyth, D., Fiedler, F. E. 1990. Cognitive resource theory and the utilization of the leader's and group members' technical competence. Tech. Rep. 90–2, Univ. Washington, Seattle

Nathan, B. R., Alexander, R. A. 1988. A comparison of criteria for test validation: a meta-analytic investigation. *Personnel Psychol.* 41:517–35

Nathan, B. R., Tippins, N. 1990. The consequences of halo "error" in performance ratings: a field study of the moderating effect of halo on test validation results. *J. Appl. Psychol.* 75:290–96

Neter, E., Ben-Shakhar, G. 1989. Predictive validity of graphological inferences: a meta-analytic approach. *Pers. Indiv. Diff.* 10:737–45

Nevo, B., Jager, R. S., eds. 1987. *Psychological Testing: The Examinee Perspective,* Vol. 25. Frankfurt: Dtsch. Inst. Int. Pedagog. Forsch. Stud. Pedagog. Psychol.

Normand, J., Salyards, S. D., Mahoney J. J. 1990. An evaluation of pre-employment drug testing. *J. Appl. Psychol.* 75:629–39

Office of the Assistant Secretary of Defense, Force Management and Personnel. 1990. Report to the House Committee on Appropriations. Joint-Service efforts to link enlistment standards to job performance. Washington DC: Off. Assist. Sec. Defense. 33 pp.

Office of Technology Assessment. 1990. *The Use of Integrity Tests for Pre-employment Screening,* OTA-SET-442. Washington DC: USGPO

O'Bannon, M. R., Goldinger, L. A., Appleby, G. S. 1989. *Honesty and Integrity Testing: A Practical Guide.* Atlanta, GA: Applied Information Resources

Olian, J. D., Schwab, D. P., Haberfeld, Y. 1988. The impact of applicant gender compared to qualifications on hiring recommendations (a meta-analysis of experiment-

668   SCHMIDT ET AL

al studies). *Org. Behav. Hum. Decis. Process.* 41:180–95

Ones, D. S., Viswesvaran, C., Schmidt, F. L. 1991. Moderators of the validity of integrity tests. Presented at Annu. Meet. Soc. Indust. Org. Psychol., St. Louis

Orr, J. M., Sackett, P. R., Mercer, M. 1989. The role of prescribed and nonprescribed behaviors in estimating the dollar value of performance. *J. Appl. Psychol.* 74:34–40

Osburn, H. G., Callender, G. C. 1990. Bias in validity generalization variance estimates: a reply to Hoben Thomas. *J. Appl. Psychol.* 75:328–33

Peterson, N. S., Novick, M. R. 1976. An evaluation of some models for culture-fair selection. *J. Educ. Meas.* 13:3–39

Phillips, A. P., Dipboye, R. L. 1989. Correlational tests of predictions from a process model of the interview, *J. Appl. Psychol.* 74:41–52

Potter, E. E. 1989. Supreme Court's Wards Cove Packing decision redefines the adverse impact theory under Title VII. *Indust.-Org. Psychol.* 27(1):25–33

Prediger, D. J. 1989. Ability differences across occupations: more than g. *J. Vocat. Behav.* 34:1–27

Pulakos, E. D., White, L. A., Oppler, S. H., Borman, W. C. 1989. Examination of race and sex effects on performance ratings. *J. Appl. Psychol.* 74:770–80

Pynes, J., Bernardin, H. J., Benton, A. L., McEvoy, G. M. 1988. Should assessment center dimension ratings be mechanically-derived? *J. Bus. Psychol.* 2:217–27

Pynes, J., Bernardin, H. J. 1989. Predictive validity of an entry-level police officer assessment center. *J. Appl. Psychol.* 74:831–33

Rafilson, F. M., Frost, A. G. 1989. Overt integrity tests versus personality-based measures of delinquency: an empirical comparison. *J. Bus. Psychol.* 3:269–78

Raju, N. S., Pappas, S., Williams, C. P. 1989. An empirical Monte Carlo test of the accuracy of the correlation, covariance, and regression slope models for assessing validity generalization. *J. Appl. Psychol.* 74:901–11

Raju, N. S., Burke, M. J., Normand, J. 1991. A new meta-analytic approach. *J. Appl. Psychol.* 76:432–46

Raju, N. S., Burke, M. J., Normand, J. 1990. A new approach for utility analysis. *J. Appl. Psychol.* 75:3–12

Ree, M. J., Earles, J. A. 1990a. *Differential Validity of a Differential Aptitude Test.* Brooks Air Force Base, TX: Air Force Human Resources Laboratory

Ree, M. J., Earles, J. A. 1990b. *Relationships of General Ability, Specific Ability, and Job Category for Predicting Training Performance.* Brooks Air Force Base, TX: Air Force Human Resources Laboratory

Ree, M. J., Earles, J. A. 1990c. *Estimating the General Cognitive Component of the Armed Services Vocational Aptitude Battery (ASVAB): Three Faces of G.* Brooks Air Force Base, TX: Air Force Human Resources Laboratory

Robertson, I. T., Downs, S. 1989. Work-sample tests of trainability: a meta-analysis. *J. Appl. Psychol.* 74:402–10

Roth, P. L. 1992. Research trends in judgment and their implications for the Schmidt-Hunter global estimation procedure. *Org. Behav. Hum. Decis. Process.* In press

Rothstein, H. R. 1990. Interrater reliability of job performance ratings: growth to asymptote level with increasing opportunity to observe. *J. Appl. Psychol.* 75:322–27

Rothstein, H. R., Schmidt, F. L., Erwin, F. W., Owens, W. A., Sparks, C. P. 1990. Biographical data in employment selection: Can validities be made generalizable? *J. Appl. Psychol.* 75:175–84

Russell, C. J. 1990. Selecting top corporate leaders: an example of biographical information. *J. Manage.* 16:73–86

Russell, C. J., Mettson, J., Devlin, S. E., Atwater, D. 1990. Predictive validity of biodata items generated from retrospective life experience essays. *J. Appl. Psychol.* 75:569–80

Ryan, A. M., Sackett, P. R. 1987. Pre-employment honesty testing: fakability, reactions of test takers, and company image. *J. Bus. Psychol.* 1:248–56

Rynes, S., Gerhart, B. 1990. Interviewer assessments of applicant "fit": an exploratory investigation. *Personnel Psychol.* 43:13–34

Sackett, P. R., Burris, L. R., Callahan, C. 1989. Integrity testing for personnel selection: an update. *Personnel Psychol.* 42:491–525

Sackett, P. R., Dreher, G. F. 1982. Constructs and assessment center dimensions: some troubling empirical findings. *J. Appl. Psychol.* 67:401–10

Sackett, P. R., Harris, M. M. 1984. Honesty testing for personnel selection: a review and critique. *Personnel Psychol.* 37:221–45

Sackett, P. R., Harris, M. M. 1988. A further examination of the constructs underlying assessment center ratings. *J. Bus. Psychol.* 3:214–29

Sackett, P. R., Larson, J. R. 1990. Research strategies and tactics in industrial and organizational psychology. See Dunnette & Hough 1990, pp. 419–90

Sadacca, R., Campbell, J. P., DiFazio, A. S., Schultz, S. R., White, L. A. 1990. Scaling performance utility to enhance selection/classification decisions. *Personnel Psychol.* 32:367–78

Schippmann, J. S., Prien, E. P., Katz, J. A. 1990. Reliability and validity of in-basket performance measures. *Personnel Psychol.* 43:837–59

Schippmann, J. S., Prien, E. P. 1989. An assessment of the contributions of general mental ability and personality characteristics to management success. *J. Bus. Psychol.* 3:423–37

Schmidt, F. L. 1988. The problem of group difference in ability test scores in employment selection. *J. Vocat. Behav.* 33:272–92 (Special Issue: "Fairness in Employment Testing")

Schmidt, F. L. 1988. Validity generalization and the future of criterion related validity. In *Test Validity*, ed. H. Wainer and H. I. Braun, pp. 173–90. Hillsdale, NJ: Erlbaum

Schmidt, F. L., Rothstein, H. R. 1991. Application of validity generalization methods of meta-analysis to biographical data scales used in employment selection. In *Advances in Biodata Research*, ed. M. D. Mumford and G. S. Stokes. Palo Alto: Consulting Psychologists Press

Schmidt, F. L., Hunter, J. E. 1989. Interrater reliability coefficients cannot be computed when only one stimulus is rated. *J. Appl. Psychol.* 74:368–70

Schmidt, F. L., Hunter J. E., Larson, M. 1988a. General cognitive ability versus general and specific aptitudes in the prediction of training performance: some preliminary findings. Rep. for Navy Personnel Res. Dev. Cent., Contract Number 0053

Schmidt, F. L., Hunter, J. E., McKenzie, R., Muldrow, T. 1979. The impact of valid selection procedures on workforce productivity. *J. Appl. Psychol.* 64:609–26

Schmidt, F. L., Hunter, J. E., Outerbridge, A. N. 1986. The impact of job experience and ability on job knowledge, work sample performance, and supervisory ratings of job performance. *J. Appl. Psychol.* 71:432–39

Schmidt, F. L., Hunter, J. E., Outerbridge, A. N., Goff, S. 1988b. Joint relation of experience and ability with job performance: test of three hypotheses. *J. Appl. Psychol.* 73: 46–57

Schmidt, F. L., Hunter, J. E., Pearlman, K., Hirsh, H. R. 1985. Forty questions about validity generalization and meta-analysis. *Personnel Psychol.* 38:697–798

Schmidt, F. L., Kaplan, L. B. 1971. Composite vs. multiple criteria: a review and resolution of the controversy. *Personnel Psychol.* 24:419–34

Schmitt, N., Cohen, S. A. 1989. Internal analyses of task ratings by job incumbents. *J. Appl. Psychol.* 74:96–104

Schmitt, N., Klimoski, R. J. 1991. *Research Methods in Human Resource Management*. Cincinnati, OH: Southwestern Books

Schmitt, N., Schneider, J. R., Cohen, S. A. 1990. Factors affecting validity of a regionally administered assessment center. *Personnel Psychol.* 43:1–12

Shechtman, Z., Sansbury, D. 1989. Validation of a group assessment procedure for the selection of teacher-education candidates. *Educ. Psychol. Meas.* 49:653–61

Shore, T. H., Thornton, G. C., Shore, L. 1990. Construct validity of two categories of assessment center dimension ratings. *Personnel Psychol.* 43:101–14

Smith, J. 1989. Some British Data concerning the standard deviation of performance. *J. Occup. Psychol.* 62:184–90

Smith, M., Robertson, I. T. 1989. *Advances in Selection and Assessment*. London: St. Edmundsbury Press

Sowell, T. 1989. Affirmative action: a worldwide disaster. *Commentary* Dec.:21–41

Sparrow, J. 1989. The utility of PAQ in relating job behaviors to traits. *J. Occup. Psychol.* 62:151–62

Spector, P. E., Levine, E. L. 1987. Meta-analysis for integrating study outcomes: a Monte Carlo Study of its susceptibility to Type I and Type II Errors. *J. Appl. Psychol.* 72:3–9

Spencer, J. M. 1989. When preferential hiring becomes reverse discrimination. *Employ. Relat.* 14:513–29

Sperl, T. C., Ree, M. J., Steuck, K. W. 1990. *Air Force Officer Qualifying Test (AFOQT) and Armed Services Vocational Aptitude Battery (ASVAB): Analysis of Common Measurement Attributes*. Brooks Air Force Base, TX: Air Force Human Resources Laboratory

Squires, P., Ross, R. G. 1990. Literacy requirements for customer service jobs. Paper presented at the Annu. Convent. Am. Psychol. Assoc., Boston

Steffy, B. De, Ledvinka, J. 1989. The long-range impact of definitions of "fair" employee selection on black employment and employee productivity. *Org. Behav. Hum. Decis. Process.* 449?–324

Stone, D. L., Kotch, D. A. 1989. Individuals' attitudes toward organizational drug testing policies and practices. *J. Appl. Psychol.* 74: 518–21

Stone, E. F., Stone, D. L., Glueutal, H. G. 1990. Influence of cognitive ability on responses questionnaire measures: measurement precision and missing response problems. *J. Appl. Psychol.* 75:418–27

Tenopyr, M. L. 1990. Fairness in employment testing. *Soc. Sci. Modern Society* 27:17–20

Tenopyr, M. L. 1990. Practical implications of the Americans with Disabilities Act. Paper presented at Soc. Indust. Org. Psychol. Annu. Conf., Miami

Thomas, H. 1988. What is the interpretation of the validity generalization estimate $S^2_p = S^2_r - S^2_e$? *J. Appl. Psychol.* 73:679–82

Thomas H. 1990. A likelihood-based model for validity generalization. *J. Appl. Psychol.* 75:13–20

Thomas H. 1989. *Distributions of Correlation Coefficients* New York: Springer-Verlag

Thorndike, R. L. 1986. The role of general ability in prediction. *J. Vocat. Behav.* 29:332–39

Tullar, W. L. 1989. Relational control in the employment interview. *J. Appl. Psychol.* 74:971–77

Turban, D. B., Sanders, P. A., Francis, D. J., Osburn, H. G. 1989. Constructive equivalence as an approach to replacing validated cognitive ability selection tests. *J. Appl. Psychol.* 74:62–71

US Department of Labor. 1990. Employment and training administration: dictionary of occupational titles, issue paper and initiative notice. *Fed. Reg.* Aug. 10 (Part VI)

Vance, R. J., Coovert, M. D., MacCallum, R. C., Hedge, J. W. 1989. Construct models of task performance. *J. Appl. Psychol.* 74:447–55

Vandenberg, R. J., Scarpello, V. 1990. The matching model: an examination of the processes underlying realistic job previews. *J. Appl. Psychol.* 75:60–67

Waldman, D. A., Avolio, B. J. 1989. Homogeneity of test validity. *J. Appl. Psychol.* 76:371–76

Wanous, J. P. 1989. Installing a realistic job preview: ten tough choices. *Personnel Psychol.* 42:117–34

Wanous, J. P. 1980. *Organizational Entry: Recruitment, Selection, Socialization of Newcomers.* Reading, MA: Addison-Wesley

Wanous, J. P., Sullivan, S. E., Malinek, J. 1989. The role of judgment calls in meta-analyses. *J. Appl. Psychol.* 74:259–64

Wards Cove Packing Co. v. Atonio 109 S. Ct. 3115 (1989)

Warner, R. L., Steele, B. S. 1989. Affirmative action in times of fiscal stress and changing value priorities: a case of women in policing. *Public Personnel Manage. J.* 18:291–309

Watson v. Fort Worth Bank & Trust 108 S Ct. 2177 (1988)

Weekley, J. A., Gier, J. A. 1989. Ceilings in the reliability and validity of performance ratings: the case of expert raters. *Acad. Manage. J.* 32:213–22

Weisner, W. H., Cronshaw, S. F. 1988. A meta-analytic investigation of the impact of interview format and degree of structure on the validity of the employment interview. *J. Occup. Psychol.* 61:275–90

Weiss, M., Lotan, I., Kedar, H., Ben-

Shakhar, G. 1988. Selecting candidates for a medical school: an evaluation of a selection model based on cognitive and personality predictors. *Med. Educ.* 22:492–97

Welsh, J. R., Kucinkas, S. K., Curran, L. T. 1990. *Armed Services Vocational Battery (ASVAB): Integrative Review of Validity Studies.* Brooks Air Force Base, TX: Air Force Human Resources Laboratory

Welsh, J. R., Watson, T. W., Ree, M. J. 1990. *Armed Services Vocational Aptitude Battery (ASVAB): Predicting Military Criteria from General and Specific Abilities.* Brooks Air Force Base, TX: Air Force Human Resources Laboratory

Werner, J. M., Jones, J. W., Steffy, B. D. 1989. The relationship between intelligence, honesty, and theft admissions. *Educ. Psychol. Meas.* 49:921–27

Whetzel, D. L., McDaniel, M. A. 1988. Reliability of validity generalization databases. *Psychol. Rep.* 63:131–234

Whitener, E. M. 1990. Confusion of confidence intervals and credibility intervals in meta-analysis. *J. Appl. Psychol.* 75:315–21

Wigdor, A. K. 1990. Fairness in employment testing. *Issues Sci. Technol.* Spring, pp. 54–58

Windolf, P., Wood, S. 1988. *Recruiting and Selection in the Labor Market: A Comparative Study of Britain and West Germany.* Brookfield, VT: Gower Publishing

Wise, L. L., McHenry, J., Campbell, J. P. 1990. Identifying optimal predictor composites and testing for generalizability across jobs and performance factors. *Personnel Psychol.* 43:355–66

Wright, P. M., Lichtenfels, P. A., Pursell, E. D. 1989. The structured interview: additional studies and a meta-analysis. *J. Occup. Psychol.* 62:191–99

Young, W. Y., Houston, J. S., Harris, J. H., Hoffman, R. G., Wise, L. L. 1990. Large-scale predictor validation in Project A: data collection procedures in data base preparation. *Personnel Psychol.* 43:301–11

Zeidner, M. 1988. Cultural fairness in aptitude testing revisited: across-cultural parallel. *Prof. Psychol. Res. Pract.* 19:257–62

Zeidner, J., Johnson, C. D. 1989a. *The Utility of Selection for Military and Civilian Jobs.* Rep. for Off. Under Secretary of Defense for Acquisition (Research and Advanced Technology). Alexandria, VA: Inst. Defense Anal.

Zeidner, J., Johnson, C. D. 1989b. *Economic Benefits of Predicting Job Performance.* Rep. for Off. Under Secretary of Defense for Acquisition (Research and Advanced Technology). Alexandria, VA: Inst. Defense Anal. on of Newcomers Reading, MA: Addison-Wesley

Annu. Rev. Psychol. 1992. 43:671–710

COMPARATIVE COGNITION:
Representations and Processes in
Learning and Memory

Herbert L. Roitblat

Department of Psychology, University of Hawaii, Honolulu, Hawaii 96822

Lorenzo von Fersen

Allgemeine Psychologie, Universität Konstanz, D-7750 Konstanz, Germany

KEY WORDS: animal cognition, neural network models, mental representation, concept
learning

CONTENTS

0066-4308/92/0201-0671$02.00

INTRODUCTION

For much of scientific history, animals were seen as passive mechanistic entities with few, if any, mental processes. Animals were viewed as mere passive stimulus-response devices, controlled by characteristics of their immediate environment and their history in it. To the extent that they formed and used representations of the events and environment around them they did so by passively recording traces of the neural activity recorded by their senses. In contrast to this passive view, a more active perspective on animal representation has been emerging in recent years. This view sees animals as active information processors that seek information in their environment, encode it, and use it for their benefit in flexible and intelligent ways (Gallistel 1989; Roitblat 1982, 1987a).

Comparative cognition is the study of the minds of organisms and the ways those minds produce adaptive behaviors. It is an approach to understanding behavior that emphasizes what an animal knows and how it uses that information. Comparative cognition is a part of the larger fields of comparative psychology, cognitive psychology, and cognitive science, and a relative of the fields of physiological psychology and behavioral and computational neuroscience. Recent developments in these fields are both supported by and contribute to a renewed interest in the cognitive processes of animals. They support comparative cognition by providing tools and theories for understanding animal behavior. They are in turn supported by the evidence that investigations of comparative cognition provide about the operation of basic cognitive processes.

Natural and Artificial Neural Network Research and Comparative Cognition

Among the factors that broadened the appeal of comparative cognition were some recent developments in artificial neural network theories (See Wasserman 1989 for a summary of these theories). Neural networks and related connectionist systems have historical roots in traditional accounts of behavior (e.g. Hebb 1949). Few investigators were interested in these systems for a number of years, however, in part because such networks were difficult to program (Minsky & Pappert 1969). Interest began to be revived with the publication of a two-volume set by Rumelhart & McClelland (Rumelhart & McClelland 1986; McClelland & Rumelhart 1986) that reminded cognitive scientists of the potential utility of such theories and described in a more or less accessible way algorithms that addressed the problem of organizing these systems.

Neural networks provide an interesting system for the development of animal cognition theories because they are based on a brain metaphor that could be related to the actual functioning of animal brains, they do not involve any particular symbolic or linguistic inputs, they show how a system that starts in a naive unorganized state can come to organize itself on the basis of experience, and they provide means by which to represent plausibly the processes that animals may undergo during conditioning. Animals provide a useful comparative basis for testing the development of artificial neural network systems. Like these systems, they start in an uninstructed naive state (but unlike most neural network systems, their structure is not amorphous; evolution and their preexperimental experience have equipped animals with some preexisting structure). Animals do not require any explicit verbal instruction; and animal learning situations provide well-structured, relatively simple problems (compared, for example, to learning to produce the past-tense verb transformation) with already known solutions. They also provide known patterns of performance during acquisition based on partial solutions and provide the opportunity for physiological investigations that examine the biological neural system directly. The behavior of whole organisms, of network models, and of the underlying neural substrate can be examined in a unified way that relates behavior to computational algorithms and to its physiological implementation (cf Marr 1982).

An artificial neural network is a parallel computational system metaphorically based on the kind of processing apparently performed by the brain (McClelland & Rumelhart 1986; McClelland et al 1986; Smolensky 1988). Unlike standard computer systems that consist of a single central processor operating serially, the brain consists of many simple processing units or neurons that are organized into a highly interconnected network. Each neuron receives information from many (even thousands) of other neurons and transmits information, in turn, to many other neurons. The output of each neuron depends on the pattern of inputs it receives.

Artificial neural networks are similarly structured as interconnected networks of relatively simple processing units, although still on a relatively tiny scale when compared to biological brains. A network consists of many simple processing units, each of which receives inputs from other units or from the environment and produces an output value according to some usually non-linear transfer function. When organized into networks, these collections of simple processing elements are capable of substantial and complex processing. Artificial neural networks have been applied in a number of domains, such as pattern recognition, to solve problems that have otherwise been resistant to computational solutions. Their success recommends the fruitfulness of the approach. They have contributed understanding to artificial intelligence, pattern recognition, neuroscience, and cognition (e.g. Zornetzer et al 1990).

One of the most interesting properties of these systems is that they self-organize on the basis of the experience or examples they receive. For example, one kind of neural network architecture is trained to produce the desired outputs whenever certain inputs are presented to it. This training is accomplished by repeatedly presenting pairs of inputs and outputs, such as echo spectra (Gorman & Sejnowski 1988; Roitblat et al 1989), and corresponding labels for the object that returned that echo. Rumelhart et al (1986) developed a back-error propagation algorithm that adjusts the connection strengths between the artificial neurons in response to the difference between the obtained output of the network and the desired output (i.e. the label). After several presentations of these pairs, the network produces successively more accurate reproductions of the desired output patterns in response to the specific inputs. Such networks have also been shown to generalize to related input patterns.

The algorithm described by Rumelhart and his associates resembles the linear operator learning model described by Bush & Mosteller (1951), as well as the model described by Rescorla & Wagner (1972). The resemblance led to a renewed interest in such learning mechanisms and in the literature describing their application. Furthermore, the general success of neural network models with varying architectures led to renewed interest in other theories of animal learning, and to investigations of such putatively "simple" phenomena as classical conditioning (e.g. Grossberg & Levine 1987) in order to illustrate the effectiveness of these networks as self-adapting systems that mimic real but simple biological information processing. Recent evidence, however, suggests that even these simple phenomena have a considerable degree of complexity.

LEARNING

Learning is one of the traditional areas in comparative cognition research that has received renewed interest from a representational perspective (Roitblat 1987a). We limit our comments to three areas: learning in invertebrates, contextual conditioning and occasion setting, and neural-network models of learning and conditioning.

Learning in Invertebrates

Learning in invertebrates is especially interesting because of the tremendous differences between invertebrate and vertebrate nervous systems and because of the relative accessibility of invertebrate brains. Current wisdom (e.g. Hawkins & Kandel 1984) is that the structure of invertebrate nervous systems is grossly different from that of vertebrates, but the functionalities of both kinds of nervous system at the level of individual neurons and of the organism are similar. Bitterman and his colleagues, for example, investigate appetitive learning capabilities of honeybees. They have found substantial similarity between the learning abilities of honeybees and vertebrates, and no differences. Every phenomenon of vertebrate learning that has been investigated has been found in identical form in bees (Bitterman 1988; Bitterman & Couvillon 1991; Couvillon & Bitterman 1991). These results are also interesting because of the claims that have been made for species-specific learning capacities (e.g. Gould 1986; Menzel 1990).

One example suffices to illustrate the specializations attributed to honeybees. Gould (1988) and Menzel (1990) have argued that the specialized learning of honeybees is shown by what they learn and when they learn it. Gould (1988) has claimed that honeybees learn about landmarks near the food source only on departure from the food source (suggesting excitatory backward conditioning, a phenomenon rarely observed among vertebrates; but see Ayers et al 1987; Hearst 1989). In contrast to this claim Couvillon et al (1991) found that bees learn about the color and shape of nearby landmarks on both arrival and departure. Individual honeybees in this experiment were allowed to forage at a wooden table on which a small target of beige Plexiglas was presented. This target was baited with a drop of sucrose solution. The landmark was a small wooden block placed next to the target. The block was either blue or orange and oriented either horizontally or vertically. For one group, the landmark was present both on arrival and departure; for another, it was present only on arrival, and was removed while the bee foraged. For the third group the landmark was placed near the target only after the bee had arrived and had started feeding. The bee's preference for the target was assessed during a 10-min unrewarded test following six training trials. Two identical targets (the beige plastic feeder) were placed on the table. One target was accompanied by the landmark used during training, the other by a similar landmark differing either in color (color comparison) or in orientation (shape comparison). Learning was measured as a preference for the target near the landmark that had been present during training.

Preference for the familiar landmark was strongest when it was available during the bees' arrival on the feeding target. All bees showed significant learning about the landmark color, whether they were trained with the color present only on arrival, only on departure, or on both arrival and departure. In fact, discrimination between colors was identical for both groups, indicating that the bees learned about color on arrival, contrary to Gould's (1988) prediction. Preference for the training color was also above chance for the group that saw the landmark only on departure, suggesting that the bees learned about color both on arrival and on departure. Similarly, bees showed significant preference for the shape of the landmark, whether the shape was presented on arrival or on departure (but, curiously, not when the landmark was present on both arrival and departure). This experiment demonstrates that bees learn about nearby landmarks on both arrival at and departure from a food source. They learn most readily about the landmarks that precede the food, in preference to learning about landmarks that only follow food (i.e. those that are present only on departure).

The experiments with bees suggest that all animals share a "library" of essentially identical learning mechanisms. Macphail (1987) has extended this notion to argue that there are essentially no differences in intelligence among various nonhuman species. Although the learning abilities of many species share many common aspects, these have generally involved relatively few phenomena. In fact, Macphail's claim rests on a peculiar definition of intelligence, which is related to the animals' performance on tests of general problem solving in arbitrary environments. He specifically excludes potential species adaptations (such as song learning in song birds versus other bird species). This approach seems arbitrarily to define out of existence the question of whether there are species differences in intelligence (see Roitblat 1987b). As the work with bees makes clear, psychologists should not be too quick to decide that some species' performance is due to species-unique or specialized mechanisms. At the same time, the only way to determine whether there are differences among species is to explore their performance in a careful way in both the kinds of situations for which they are presumably specialized and in a battery of relatively standardized tasks.

All species may be expected to share a common complement of basic learning and problem-solving mechanisms as a result of shared evolutionary history or as a result of adaptive response to the causal structure of nature.

For example, classical conditioning may be the result of the animal's sensitivity to causation and prediction in which the cause of an important event occurs and is generally detected before the event that it causes. All animals may show similar patterns of classical conditioning either because they all contain neurons with essentially the same functional characteristics (e.g. McCulloch & Pitts 1943) or because causation takes essentially the same form, whatever the signal or whatever the event being caused (or both).

Neural Networks and Learning Theory

Interest in artificial neural networks and related mechanisms has grown explosively over the last five years. [For example, a recent bibliography of the artificial neural network literature lists 4661 entries up to 1989 (Wasserman & Oetzel 1990).] Part of that effort has involved modeling what many consider to be more elementary cognitive processing.

Interest in neural network models of conditioning has led to increased understanding of the mechanisms and processes underlying the psychological phenomenon and to increased understanding of neural systems and their construction (e.g. Barto & Sutton 1982; Card & Moore 1990; Donegan et al

1989; Gluck & Thompson 1987). Models based on artificial neural network systems have been effective in providing accounts of basic conditioning and of such phenomena as blocking (Grossberg & Levine 1987; Grossberg & Schmajuk 1987; Klopf 1988) and negative-pattern learning (Kehoe 1988, 1989). In the latter problem, an animal is trained with two conditional stimuli (CSs), each of which, when presented separately, is followed by an unconditional stimulus (US). When the two CSs are presented together, however, they are not followed by the US (A+B+/AB-). Animals learn to discriminate compound presentations from individual stimulus presentations. They continue responding to the individual stimuli but do not respond to the same stimuli when presented in compound. This problem is revealing, because correct performance conflicts with a class of associative models that says that response level is a linear function of input activation levels.

For example, according to a simple model, the animal learns to associate the CS with the US by correlating the occurrence of the two events. The strength of the connection between the CS and the US depends on the magnitude of the correlation, and the activation of the response depends on the input value as modulated by the connection between the CS and the US. Finally, either the strength of the response or its probability is presumed to be a simple monotonic function of the activation level of the output. By this model, the stronger the input, the stronger or more likely is the response. If the animal responds to the individual stimuli, then clearly it has learned an association between those CSs and the US that allows activation of the response. Therefore, when the two CSs are combined, the animal should respond with even more vigor to the compound than to the individual stimuli because the total input strength must be higher than that obtained with either stimulus alone. Despite the predictions of such a linear-response model, animals do learn the negative-pattern relation and withhold responding to the compound while responding to each of its elements. In fact, no monotonic function of the two CSs can acquire the negative-patterning relation. Therefore, this performance rules out the class of models that says that responding is simply a learned monotonic function of input intensities. Solution of the negative-patterning problem, and related problems, requires some additional element that represents the combination of the two inputs. Some models employ a sensory unit that responds only to the joint occurrence of the two CSs, but the large number of stimuli that can effectively be trained as CSs implies a combinatorially explosive number of these joint-occurrence units, one for each pair of potential CSs (Kehoe & Gormezano 1980).

In connectionist terms, the class of monotonic-response associators corresponds to a single-layer network in which each input leads directly to an output. Such single-layer networks have been shown inadequate to learn problems, like the negative-patterning problem, that are not linearly separable

(Minsky & Pappert 1969). The concept of linear separability is similar to the concept of monotonic response just described but includes a threshold that can separate one class of inputs from other classes of inputs. A single-layer network cannot solve problems, such as the logical exclusive-or function (XOR: 01+, 10+, 00-, 11-) that cannot be solved by a linear function.

The addition of joint-occurrence input units makes the negative patterning problem into a linearly separable one (i.e. a problem in which some value of activity can be used to determine the class of the inputs, such as whether or not a response is appropriate) but in a somewhat ad hoc manner. In contrast, many current connectionist models include not only inputs and outputs but also a layer of elements that intervenes between the inputs and the outputs (called hidden units, because they are neither inputs nor outputs and so are "hidden" from the environment). Networks with hidden layers are capable of solving complex problems, such as XOR and the negative-patterning problem. The hidden layer constitutes an internal representation of the relevant aspects of the input patterns (e.g. Elman & Zipser 1987). Hence, application of this kind of model both solves knotty problems in animal learning and suggests a structure for the kinds of representations animals form during learning. The units in the hidden layer form internal representations of the relations among events.

Networks and their learning rules show how simple algorithms, mechanisms, and methods can solve sophisticated computational problems without positing a conscious agent or homunculus. They also suggest the possibility of a unified account of human and nonhuman cognition at a subsymbolic level (Gluck & Bower 1988; Smolensky 1988).

Contextual Conditioning and Occasion Setting

Another phenomenon that demonstrates that even basic conditioning phenomena are not as simple as traditional analysis would indicate is "occasion setting" (e.g. Colwill & Rescorla 1990). Standard conditioning theory (e.g. Hull 1943) describes instrumental conditioning as the result of a learned association between the stimulus and the instrumental response (see also Roitblat 1987a for a description of the Standard Associative Model). The reinforcer serves as a catalyst to strengthen this connection but is not explicitly represented. Two-process theories (e.g. Rescorla & Solomon 1967; Trapold & Overmier 1972) add an explicit representation for the reinforcer by positing that two associations are learned during instrumental conditioning, one between the stimulus and the outcome, and a second between the response and the outcome. Occasion-setting theories (Colwill & Rescorla 1986, 1989; Mackintosh & Dickinson 1979) suggest that the stimulus becomes associated with and modulates the response-outcome relation by specifying the occasion on which the response produces the outcome. On this view, the occasion-setting stimulus acts as a modulator or shunt (Grossberg & Schmajuk 1987) that controls the activity of the response-outcome association and its ability to produce behavior.

The standard traditional account of instrumental conditioning is inadequate because it fails to include information about the outcome of an instrumental behavior (see Roitblat 1987a for a discussion of this issue). The two-process account and the occasion-setting account include information about the outcome in different ways. The two-process account argues that behavior is controlled by the interaction between two separate associations, that between the contextual stimulus and the outcome and that between the response and the outcome. The occasion-setting account, on the other hand, proposes a hierarchical relation in which the contextual stimulus "dominates" the response-outcome relation.

Several studies have provided evidence against the dual-process account by demonstrating an effect of the stimulus on responding under conditions that do not support the formation of stimulus-outcome associations. The crucial factor that determines the degree of classical conditioning is the correlation between the CS and the US (Rescorla 1966). Presenting the reinforcer equally often in the presence of a stimulus and in its absence (all other things being equal) prevents the development of a conditional response (Durlach 1983; Gamzu & Williams 1973; Rescorla 1968). Therefore, if it can be shown that presentation of a stimulus trained in this way affects responding, one can conclude that the animal has learned something about the stimulus that is different from an association between the stimulus and the outcome. The data support such a conclusion (e.g. Holland 1983, 1989a,b). For example, in a classical conditioning situation, the topography of a rat's response to an occasion-setting stimulus that preceded the target CS was different from the response the animal made to the target or to the same stimulus when presented simultaneously with the target CS (Ross & Holland 1981). Additionally, extending the interval between the putative occasion-setting stimulus and the target CS enhanced occasion setting but hindered the growth of simple associations (e.g. the occasion-setting stimulus when tested alone did not elicit a conditional response).

Additional data from instrumental conditioning also support the special properties acquired by occasion-setting stimuli. In one experiment (Colwill & Rescorla 1990), rats were trained to perform a nose-poke response (i.e. to insert their noses in a small opening) for one reward (e.g. food pellets) in the presence of a noise, and for another reward (e.g. sucrose solution) in the presence of a light (factors were properly counterbalanced). Nose-poking was ineffective in producing the reward when the stimuli were not present, but in the absence of stimuli the rewards were delivered with the same frequency at which they had been delivered in the presence of the stimuli. Under these conditions, the two stimuli, tone and light, signaled when responding would lead to specific outcomes but did not signal when the reinforcer would be delivered (reinforcers were equally likely in the presence and in the absence of the stimuli). Subjects were then trained to perform two new responses in the absence of the noise and light. Finally, during an extinction test, the rats were allowed to perform either response, and their rate of responding was measured in the presence of the two original stimuli and in their absence. Each stimulus was consistent with one of the new response-outcome pairings. For example, during the first stage of the experiment the noise had signaled when nose-poking would be followed by food pellets and the light had signaled when nose-poking would be followed by sucrose. During the second stage of the experiment, bar-pressing was followed by food pellets and chain-pulling was followed by sucrose. During stage 3, in the extinction test, the noise was presented, and its effect on chain-pulling and bar-pressing was measured. Presentation of the noise increased the rats' rate of bar-pressing, relative to the rate in the presence of the light and relative to the rate in the absence of either stimulus. In general, presentation of the stimulus that had previously signaled the effectiveness of a specific response in producing a specific outcome increased the rate of another response previously paired with that outcome. Thus a stimulus that had been trained under conditions that prevent the formation of stimulus-outcome associations transfers its control to a new response trained with the same outcome.

Converging evidence for the modulating effect of these stimuli was obtained in a subsequent experiment (Colwill & Rescorla 1990, Experiment 2) by devaluing one of the reinforcers. Rats were trained in the presence of one stimulus (e.g. noise) that one response (e.g. bar-pressing) produced food pellets, and another response (e.g. chain-pulling) produced another outcome (e.g. sucrose). The response outcome was reversed in the presence of the other stimulus (e.g. bar-pressing produced sucrose and chain-pulling pro-duced food pellets). During the second stage of the experiment, the value of one of these reinforcers was reduced by pairing it with illness. This procedure had previously been shown to reduce a response that had produced that outcome (e.g. Dickinson et al 1983; Holland & Straub 1979). In this experi-ment, however, both responses were equally paired with this devalued rein-forcer but were signaled by the occasion-setting stimulus. Therefore, if the stimuli had become modulators of the response-outcome relation, then one response should be depressed in the presence of one stimulus, and the other response should be depressed in the presence of the other stimulus. Such a relationship was indeed found. In the presence of each stimulus, the rats selectively suppressed the response that had produced the now devalued outcome, relative to the other response. In a manner consistent with the hierarchical, occasion-setting view, this experiment clearly demonstrates that the stimuli came to modulate selectively the animals' expectations about the outcome of their behavior. Subsequent experiments have extended this modulation effect to higher-order relations (Arnold et al 1991).

REPRESENTATIONS IN WORKING MEMORY

Outcome Expectancies

Outcome expectancies can also play an important role in other tasks. For example, pigeons' performance on delayed matching-to-sample tasks is enhanced when correct choices of each comparison stimulus are followed by an outcome unique to that stimulus (Brodigan & Peterson 1976; Peterson 1984; Urcuioli 1990a,b, 1991; Urcuioli & Zentall 1990; Williams et al 1990). In a delayed matching-to-sample task, a sample stimulus is presented for a short time (typically a color or a pattern projected onto a pecking key for a few seconds). Then, after a delay (one to a few seconds) two or more alternatives are presented, one of which is designated the correct choice for that sample. In identity matching, the correct comparison is identical to the sample, but in so-called symbolic matching, the comparison stimulus can be only arbitrarily paired with sample. Acquisition of the task (Peterson 1984; Urcuioli 1991; Williams et al 1990), performance of the task, and retention of sample information over delays (Urcuioli & Zentall 1990) are facilitated by this differential outcome procedure. This facilitation suggests that the pigeons code the comparison stimulus and its outcome prospectively. Presumably, the uniqueness of the outcome makes the comparison stimuli more distinct and hence more memorable.

The use of the so-called symbolic matching procedure makes clear that the effect of differential outcomes is produced by a prospective rather than a retrospective (Honig & Thompson 1982; Roitblat 1980) facilitation. Pigeons were trained in a fully counterbalanced matching task in which multiple samples signaled the same correct choice (Urcuioli 1990b). Samples were solid blue or yellow, or black and white horizontal, or vertical lines. The comparison stimuli were red and green. The differential outcomes were produced by reinforcing some correct choices 100% of the time and reinforcing other correct choices only 20% of the time. Red was always the correct choice following either vertical or blue samples, and green was the correct choice following either horizontal or yellow samples. One group, the correlated group, was trained with correct choices of the red stimulus always followed by 100% reinforcement and correct choices of the green stimulus followed by reinforcement on only 20% of the trials. Pigeons in the uncorrelated group received 100% reinforcement following the vertical and the yellow samples and received 20% reinforcement following the horizontal and blue samples. Hence, for all birds each sample was uniquely associated with a specific outcome. Only birds in the correlated group, however, received a consistent pairing between the correct comparison stimulus and an outcome. Birds in the uncorrelated condition were rewarded on 100% of the trials on which they chose red following a vertical sample or on which they chose green following a yellow sample. They were rewarded on 20% of the trials on which they chose green following a horizontal sample or chose red following a blue sample. Birds in the correlated condition were rewarded on 100% of the trials on which they correctly chose red, regardless of the sample, and were rewarded on 20% of the trials on which they correctly chose green. In a manner consistent with the hypothesis that the pigeons prospectively code the outcome as part of their representation of the correct choice on a trial, the birds in the correlated condition acquired the task more quickly and showed better retention over 0–4 sec delays than the birds in the uncorrelated condition. These results cannot be explained on the basis of the reliability of the relation between the samples and the outcomes but must be explained on the basis of the reliability of the relation between correct choices and the outcomes when these are unconfounded. Hence, these data, like the data on occasion-setting, demonstrate that animals include information about the outcome of their responses as part of their representation of events. They further demonstrate that memories, even for nominally simple events such as yellow or blue samples, contain substantial internal structure, including hierarchical relations (also see Roitblat et al 1991; Terrace 1991) and response outcomes.

Other Working Memory Processes

DECISION PROCESSES IN MEMORY USAGE   The previous section suggested that pigeons encode information about a matching-to-sample trial in terms of the choice they will make at the end of the trial (Roitblat 1980) and its outcome (Brodigan & Peterson 1976). In addition to encoding information about the sample and/or the choice on each trial, the animal must also be able to use that information. Little information is available about the decision strategies animals employ when selecting the correct match, in part because obtaining such data is difficult. For example, all of the comparison stimuli are visible simultaneously in the typical matching task, and so data are not readily available concerning how the animal compares the stimuli. Wright & Sands (1981) addressed this problem by testing pigeons on a hue matching task in which the stimuli were presented behind small windows. The stimuli were thus invisible except when the pigeon stood directly in front of the window. The position of the bird's head was thereby an indicator of where the bird was looking. Using this technique, the investigators could determine the sequence in which two comparison stimuli were examined and the relation between these examinations and the bird's decision. Based on these observations,

Wright & Sands developed a model of pigeon decision making in the matching task that combines a random walk process with a signal-detection-based analysis of stimulus identification.

Wright & Sands (1981) assumed that the pigeon randomly selects one of the comparison stimuli to observe. This choice must be random because the location of the correct match varies randomly from trial to trial and the bird cannot know the identity of a stimulus until it is observed. The psychophysical effect of the observed stimulus is compared with a criterion representation of the choice stored in memory, and the bird decides whether to accept it as a match or to reject it. Because of psychophysical variability, the observed stimulus may not be accepted on a particular look even if it nominally does match the correct choice. If the bird rejects this observation as an adequate match, then it moves to observe the other stimulus and repeats this decision process, again either accepting or rejecting the stimulus and switching following a rejection. In a later, simpler version of this experiment, Wright (1990) found that the pigeons would switch as often as 8–10 times before making a final decision and a response.

Roitblat et al (1990) extended this kind of analysis to examine the decision strategies of an echolocating dolphin. Echolocation provides an excellent means of collecting fine-grained information about the information used by an animal in a delayed matching task. The echolocating dolphin obtains information about the identity of the stimuli by actively interrogating them in the form of generated echolocation clicks. Each click is generated in the dolphin's melon or forehead and transmitted through the water in a narrow directional beam. The dolphin directs a train of these clicks at an object and listens to the returning echo. The clicks can be individually recorded. Because of their directional selectivity, it is possible to know where the dolphin is directing the signal and hence which stimulus it is examining. It is also possible to record the echoes returning from the examined objects and perform simulated psychophysical experiments on these recorded echoes (Moore et al, in press).

Roitblat et al (1990) modeled the dolphin's decision processes as a sequential sampling problem. Although Wright & Sands had to treat each of the pigeon's observations as a single look, Roitblat et al were able to treat each click as an independent observation. The dolphin tended to emit a train of clicks at each target, ended either by a switch to scan another target or by a decision (indicated by a touch of a marker in front of the matching stimulus). Following sequential sampling theory, Roitblat et al assumed that: 1. Each click has some cost to the animal. 2. Each click provides a sample of evidence about the target that returned the echo. 3. Information from successive looks is combined to identify the stimulus. 4. The animal attempts to minimize the number of looks subject to meeting a confidence criterion for identifying the stimulus. 5. As a result, confidence in identifying the stimulus grows monotonically with increasing numbers of clicks but at the expense of making those clicks. 6. As a result of averaging multiple samples, the marginal contribution of each additional echo to the animal's confidence in identifying the target diminishes with the number of echoes already directed at that target (Dye & Hafter 1984).

According to the Roitblat et al (1990) model, the dolphin selects a target according to preexisting biases and scans the target in that location until one of four conditions is met. Scans terminate when (*a*) the probability that the target is the correct match exceeds an acceptance criterion, (*b*) the probability goes below a rejection criterion, (*c*) a maximum number of clicks has been emitted, or (*d*) the change in the posterior probability from successive clicks (the marginal rate of information returned from an echo) decreases below another criterion. On terminating a scan the dolphin uses the information obtained in that scan to adjust the estimated probabilities that the matching stimulus is located in each position, and as a result of this revised estimate, either selects another target for scanning or indicates a choice. Simulations based on this model gave a reasonable account of the dolphin's performance. The decision-making data and the models for those data suggest that both encoding and use of matching-to-sample information rely on sophisticated computational processes.

PROACTIVE INTERFERENCE   Other evidence for active coding comes from list-learning experiments. Several studies have demonstrated the existence of a serial position effect in animals that is similar to the pattern of results seen with human subjects. Early studies demonstrated only a recency effect (e.g. Thompson & Herman 1977; Gaffan 1977), but later studies have found both a primacy and a recency effect (Bolhuis & van Kampen 1988; DiMattia & Kesner 1984; Wright et al 1985). That is, retention of the middle items in a list is poorer than retention of the items at either the start or the end of the list.

The serial position effect in humans has been attributed either to a combination of representations in short-term and long-term memory or to a combination of proactive and retroactive interference. According to the short/long-term memory account (e.g. Glanzer & Cunitz 1966), items at the start of a list are encoded into long-term memory and so are remembered well. Items at the end of the list are in short-term or sensory memory, so they are also remembered well; but items in the middle of the list are not yet encoded into long-term memory and have faded substantially from short-term memory, and so are remembered poorly. Other data argue against such an interpretation, however, by showing that memory for an item is affected not just by its position in the list but also by its categorical relation to other items in the list. The von Restorff effect, for example, (von Restorff 1933; Wallace 1965) occurs when an item in the middle of a list is somehow made distinctive. In one experiment (Detterman & Ellis 1972) human subjects were asked to recall serially presented lists of common objects represented by line drawings. For some of the lists the middle item was replaced by a photograph of male and female nudes. Recall of the nudes was nearly perfect, even though the photograph occurred in a serial position that was otherwise recalled with less than 40% accuracy. The von Restorff effect indicates that serial position per se is not the determinant of the serial position effect; rather, the serial position effect is more likely produced by differential allocation of effort (e.g. rehearsal) to the various items or differential amounts of interference. Items at the start of a list are more distinctive (Radtke et al 1982) and are rehearsed more than items later in the list (Rundus & Atkinson 1970). Items at the end of a list may also be more distinctive. Furthermore, items in the middle of the list receive more proactive interference than items at the start and more retroactive interference than items at the end of the list (Melton 1963).

The existence of a serial position effect in animal performance suggests the presence of similar processes in animal memory. Several studies have found both a primacy and a recency effect in animals. An effect analogous to the von Restorff effect has also been described (Reed et al 1991). Rats were trained in a Y maze to perform a running oddity task. Each trial consisted of five forced-choice entries into distinctively decorated goal boxes followed by a free choice between two goal boxes, one of which had been entered earlier in the trial and the other which had not. The rat was rewarded for selecting the novel goal box. A total of 50 distinctive goal boxes were used in the experiment. Choice accuracy (i.e. avoidance of the familiar design) was generally highest for the goal boxes visited either first or last in the sequence, and poorest for the middle goal box. Hence, this experiment demonstrated a marked serial position effect. In a second experiment, the middle stimulus on half the trials was marked by changing the illumination level while the rat was in the goal box (for half the animals the illumination level increased and for half it decreased). This treatment significantly increased the rats' ability to remember the middle goal box as shown by an increase in the accuracy with which the rat avoided it.

The occurrence of a von Restorff–like effect in this experiment demonstrates that, as in human memory, the serial position effect is not simply a product of the item's location in the list. Additional processes can affect the item's memorability. A change in illumination made the item more memorable, presumably by making it more salient. Two questions remain, however. First, what was the mechanism by which this salience was increased, and second, how did this increase in salience improve memorability? One possible explanation that addresses both of these questions is that the change in illumination affected the memory of the goal box by making the outcome of entering the box different from the outcomes of entering the other goal boxes in the trial (Fedorchak & Bolles 1986). All of the forced-choice entries in the trial were accompanied by the delivery of a food pellet. Entry into the distinctive goal box was accompanied by a food pellet and an illumination change. As the research described above suggests, differential outcomes make events more distinct, and so more memorable.

A similar release from proactive interference effect was found in a monkey's memory for lists of pictures (Jitsumori et al 1989). A monkey was trained to perform a serial probe recognition (SPR) task analogous to human list-learning experiments (e.g. Wickens 1970) and similar to that used by Reed et al (1991). Each session consisted of 20 warm-up trials using travel slides, followed by 80 experimental trials. The same category, either slides of flowers or primate faces, was presented for 40 trials in a row, followed by 40 trials testing the other category. Each trial presented 4 slides from the same category, followed by a probe slide also from the same category. The monkey was required to indicate, by moving a lever, whether or not the probe slide had been presented in the previous list of four. Choice accuracy on this task declined significantly over the course of the 40 trials with the same category, but rebounded at the start of the second category to match the accuracy found at the start of the session. As in studies of humans (Bennett & Bennett 1974; Wickens 1970, 1973; Wickens et al 1981) a change in the category of item to be remembered caused release from proactive interference. The buildup and release from proactive interference in this experiment imply that the monkey categorically coded the stimuli. Although other factors may differ between the slides representing the two categories, a control experiment in which the color of the stimuli was changed halfway through a category block of trials failed to produce a similar effect. Short of additional data with other sets of stimuli, the observed buildup and release from proactive interference are most likely due to repetitive experience with the same category or group of items. Hence, this procedure provides a converging measure for the assessment of category membership in animals (see below).

VISUO-SPATIAL REPRESENTATION

Imagery

Imagery is a controversial topic in many areas of cognitive science. At different times in the history of the field, images have been taken as the most elementary and parsimonious form of representation and at other times as less parsimonious than other representational codes (see Finke 1985; Kosslyn 1983; Premack 1983). The importance of this oscillation is in determining what kind of data are necessary to address the question of imagery in animals. If images are more parsimonious than other forms of representation, then one must provide evidence justifying the existence of these other forms. On the other hand, if images are less parsimonious, then one must provide compelling evidence justifying the hypothesis of imagery.

It is widely accepted among students of human cognition that humans employ some sort of propositional representation when performing at least some tasks (e.g. Paivio 1986). Therefore, by reason of parsimony, some investigators claim that all human representations are propositional (e.g. Pylyshyn 1984). A propositional representation is one that expresses symbolically a relationship between a predicate and its arguments. A proposition is the smallest unit of representation that has a truth value (i.e. that can be either true, "grass is green" or false, "grass is purple"). Propositions are naturally expressed in a language, in which each word stands either for a predicate (e.g. "green") or one of its arguments (e.g. "grass"). Some investigators have even proposed that such propositions are not only common in human thought, but are absolutely essential. Although propositions need not be expressed in any external human language, they must be expressed in some internal "mentalese" that has the power and structure of human language (Fodor 1987). As a result, many investigators are reluctant to attribute such language-like representations to animals. Therefore, it is not entirely clear what approach to take to claims of imagery in animals (see Boakes 1984). Premack (1983), for example, has taken the position that images are relatively simple forms of representation. He proposed that all animals use concrete or "imaginal" representations to solve problems, but other sorts of proposition-like representations are restricted to language trained animals. Animals demonstrate the use of nonimaginal codes when they solve problems that require the animal to judge the relations between relations (e.g. that a whole apple is to a cut apple as a full glass is to a half-full glass). According to an opposing view, animals may not use propositional representations like those presumably used by humans, but the use of images implies a mentalism that stretches the bounds of parsimony (e.g. Skinner 1984).

Part of the difficulty concerning imagery is its definition. Representations of visuo-spatial information must clearly include information about the visual and spatial properties of objects, but the question revolves around the way those representations are coded and stored. The ability of animals to live in a spatially distributed environment (Gallistel 1989) clearly indicates that they have perceptual and representational mechanisms to obtain, store, and process information about the environment (even if only to recognize landmarks in it), but it is not clear how they represent that information. Use of images has something to do with preserving information in a form similar to that in which it was obtained during perception. The use of images allows transformations of the representations that are isomorphic with transformations performed on the represented objects. One system is an analog representation of another when continuous changes in the represented item produce continuous changes in the representation. Analog representations preserve "betweenness." Two items that are different by a certain amount may have another item between them. This item will be represented by a code that is intermediate between the representations of the first two. A traditional clock is an analog for the passage of time because continuous changes in the time of day correspond to continuous changes in the position of the hands. A time between noon and six is represented by a hand position between 12 and 6. A digital clock is not an analog representation, because intermediate times correspond to symbolically intermediate representations, but the representation itself does not preserve the similarity structure. For example, the digital representation of 9:59 shares many features with the digital representation of 9:58 (two of the digits are the same), but it shares few features with the digital representation of 10:00 (none of the digits is the same). Hence two pairs of times that are equally different from one another do not correspond to two representations that are equally different from one another.

Studies of human imagery find that people can perform transformations on representions of objects that correspond to transformations that could be performed on real objects. Mental rotation experiments, for example, show that people rotate putatively imaged representations at about 50–60°/sec (Shepard & Metzler 1971). By certain hypotheses, however, these apparent rotations could correspond to transformations performed on symbolic pro-positional representations (Pylyshyn 1981). For example, subjects could pre-dict the orientation of an item that they are to rotate mentally, transform the description to match that orientation, and then wait an appropriate amount of time to respond based on their tacit knowledge of the task. The strongest evidence that the representations are analogs of the visual stimuli they represent is seen in an experiment that prevents the subject from knowing what the final transformation will be.

Metzler (1973) estimated the subject's rate of mental rotation. She asked subjects to start mentally rotating a figure from various initial orientations. After some amount of time she then presented a target figure at different orientations, and the subject was asked to decide as quickly as possible whether or not the target matched the original stimulus. If the subject were able to rotate the image continuously, then the latency to respond to the target stimulus should depend on the angular disparity between the target and the image at that point in time. For example, if the subject were found to rotate mental images at a rate of 60°/sec, then the image would be expected to be mentally rotated to a position of 60° after 1 sec, 120° after 2 sec, 180° after 3 sec, and so on. The time to decide whether the target matches the initial stimulus is predicted to depend, therefore, on the amount of time allowed for rotation of the image and the angular disparity between the target and the putative image. Whatever the disparity between the orientation of the initial stimulus and the target, if the target is presented at an orientation that is predicted to correspond to that of the rotated image, then response latencies should be minimal.

On the other hand, if subjects do not rotate images, but instead transform descriptive propositional representations, then the amount of time allowed for rotation of the image should be irrelevant to the subject's response latency. Response latency should depend on the angular disparity between the initial stimulus and the target, because the subject cannot know what transformation to work on the description of the initial stimulus until the target is presented.

Metzler (1973) found that the latency to decide whether the initial and target stimuli matched or were mirror images depended an the disparity between the predicted orientation of the mentally rotated image and the target rather than on the disparity between the stimuli as presented. These data thus support strongly the hypothesis that subjects were actually rotating continuously an image of the initial stimulus rather than arbitrarily transforming its description.

Similar data are available from animal studies (e.g. Neiworth, in press; Neiworth & Rilling 1987; Rilling & Neiworth 1987; cf Hollard & Delius 1982). Pigeons were trained to discriminate a clock hand that revolved at a constant velocity from one that moved at an apparently nonconstant velocity. The clock hands were displayed on the screen of a computer monitor. Three types of simulated movement were investigated. In the perceptual condition, the clock hand moved from its starting position at 12:00 to a position of 135° (4:30) or 180° (6:00) at a constant velocity of 90°/sec. On imagery trials, the hand moved from its 0° vertical position to 90° (3:00) at which point it disappeared. After an appropriate amount of time (0.5 sec for the 135° position and 1 .0 sec for the 180° position) it then reappeared at a position of 135° (4:30) or 18° (6:00). On violation trials the hand also disappeared at 90° but then reappeared an inappropriate amount of time later in one of the two positions (1.0 sec for the 135° position and 0.5 sec for the 180° position). The discrimination of primary interest in this experiment is that between the imagery condition and the violation condition. In both cases, the simulated clock hand disappeared at the 3:00 position and then reappeared at either the 4:30 or the 6:00 position. Hence, the discrimination had to be based on the bird's estimate of the time that passed while the hand was invisible and the location at which it reappeared. One way to summarize this performance is to assume that the bird employed an image of the moving hand and estimated its position as a function of its velocity. Another alternative is that the birds learned a conditional discrimination involving time and position. Pigeons can discriminate with reasonable accuracy durations similar to those used in this experiment (pigeon temporal discrimination in the 0.5–1 sec range). Evidence favoring an image account over this conditional discrimination account depends on showing that the birds estimated the hand's position while it was invisible, not just its time and position of reappearance. Evidence for this possibility is found in the generalization test, in which the hand reappeared at a 158° position after 0.75 sec during imagery trials and appeared at the same position after 0.5 or 1.0 sec on violation trials. The pigeons transferred their discrimination and were able to discriminate constant velocity imagery trials from nonconstant velocity violation trials at the new position intermediate between the two previous positions. Furthermore, subsequent data (Neiworth, in press) showed that pigeons can also generalize their performance to displays that simulated movement at either twice or half the speed of the original training stimuli. These data provide strong support for the notion that pigeons employ images when solving this problem.

Cognitive Maps

Images may also be used by animals to construct representations of their environment. Homing pigeons, for example, can discriminate photographs of an area near their home coop from photographs of other areas and can generalize this discrimination to other photographs of the same vicinity (Wilkie et al 1989; also see Honig & Stewart 1988). Such representations may be organized into an image-like cognitive map. Gallistel (1989) has recently reviewed much of the research on spatial representations. The evidence seems clear that many animals maintain rich representations of their environment. This is especially evident among the food-caching birds. Food storage is found in 12 families of birds (Sherry 1985), but data are primarily available from two of these, the Corvidae and the Paridae. Clark's nutcracker (*Nucifraga columbiana*) is a corvid species that lives in high mountain coniferous forests of western North America. These birds harvest pine seeds during the late summer and hide them in thousands of discrete subterranean caches. Few, if any, signs of a cache are left on the surface, so the cache sites are difficult to detect visually. A single bird can cache up to 33,000 seeds in 6,600 separate cache locations (Vander Wall & Balda 1977) and must recover approximately 1,980 caches to survive the winter and breed successfully in the early spring (Kamil & Balda 1990). Apparently these birds recover their own caches by remembering where they were stored (Balda et al 1987).

Laboratory investigations support the claim that nutcrackers remember where they have stored food and use visual cues to identify those locations. For example, Kamil & Balda (1985) allowed nutcrackers to store pine seeds in a randomly preselected set of sand-filled locations in a room. After retention intervals of 10–15 days, the birds selectively searched holes in which seeds had been placed, despite the fact that these sites were selected by the experimenters and not by the birds. Various procedures were used to ensure that the birds were not somehow directly sensing the seeds. A comparison of three caching corvid species (scrub jays, *Apelocoma coerulescens*; pinyon jays, *Gymnorhinus cyanophalus*, and Clark's nutcrackers) revealed that after a 7-day retention interval, all three species recovered caches with greater than chance accuracy, but the accuracy of the nutcrackers and pinyon jays was higher than that of the scrub jays. Furthermore, the pinyon jays had a strong tendency to clump their caches. These behavioral differences correspond to differences in the species' dependence on recovered caches for survival. Clark's nutcrackers rely almost 100% on stored food, pinyon jays obtain 70–90% of their winter diet from stored food, and scrub jays obtain about 60% of their winter diet from stored food (Balda & Kamil 1989).

Food storing is also known to be used by 14 of the 47 species of parids. Several parid species have demonstrated good memory for cache locations over delays measured in hours or days. Marsh tits (*Parus palustris*) in the field recover whatever caches they will use within about 3 days of making those caches (Stevens & Krebs 1986). In the laboratory chickadees (*Parus atricapillus*) can remember caches over 28 days (Hitchcock & Sherry 1990), a delay comparable to that over which Clark's nutcracker has been tested in the laboratory.

As in the corvids (Balda & Kamil 1989), the parids' ability to remember cache sites in which food has been stored is correlated with the use of this strategy in the field (Krebs et al 1990). Coal tits (*Parus atur*), which store food, were more likely to return to sites in which they had seen food than were great tits (*Parus major*), which do not cache (cf Hilton & Krebs 1990).

These studies show that certain animals have evolved specializations for representing information related to food storage sites. Other mechanisms could be used for food storage and retrieval (e.g. hoarding), but many of these alternatives are not as secure (do not prevent loss of the cache as well) as distributed caching (Shettleworth 1990). Several observations support the idea of specialized capacities: Many of the food storing birds also have other specializations, such as a sublingual pouch in Clark's nutcracker, used for carrying seeds (Bock et al 1973), and increased hippocampal size relative to brain and body size in food storing birds compared to other species (Krebs 1990; Krebs et al 1989; Sherry et al 1989). The hippocampus has been implicated in spatial and other forms of memory in mammals (O'Keefe & Nadel 1978; Sherry & Vaccarino 1989). Hence, these animals seem specially adapted to form representations of their environment and food sites within it, and to maintain those representations over long periods.

ABSTRACT AND NATURAL CONCEPTS

Categorization is essential to all cognitive processes. In the absence of categorization, each object or event would be perceived as unique and no generalizations could be used to govern behavior. Our knowledge about the world and many of our reactions depend on concepts that we have formed from our experiences. Humans begin to integrate new information into knowledge categories in a rather sophisticated way by 10 months of age (Younger & Cohen 1985). Because the ability to form concepts is closely linked with language it was long assumed to be a uniquely human property, but in the last 20 years, work on complex discrimination learning in animals has changed that position.

Two different approaches have been used to investigate concepts. One of these concerns the use by animals of abstract concepts, such as same versus different, symmetric versus asymmetric, and novel versus familiar. The other concerns the use of natural concepts, such as classifying monkey versus human faces, or discriminating slides that have pictures of fish versus those that lack fish. Both lines of investigation are related, in that the rules formed to solve the problems are not stimulus specific. Animals apparently abstract the classification rules from the set of exemplars and extend these rules to novel examples. As Lea (1984) correctly remarks, it is still an open question whether the animal forms a concept or uses a concept it already had. In the case of pigeon studies, for example, the concept of "pigeon" or "human" was probably formed before the experiment started. There are only a few experiments that investigate the ontogeny of concepts. Animals appear capable of using sophisticated conceptual categories, whether these preexist or are induced from the set of exemplars.

Abstract Concepts

SIMILARITY   Conditional discriminations such as matching-to-sample and oddity are frequently used to investigate such abstract concepts as same/ different. In a matching task, the animal must choose the comparison stimulus that is the same as the sample. In an oddity task, the animal must choose the comparison stimulus that does not match the sample. Animals could learn to perform the task on the basis of individual responses to specific stimuli or specific stimulus combinations, especially when only a few combinations are presented. On the other hand, some animals seem able to use the more abstract similarity among the elements to solve the problem. Support for the use of an abstract matching concept is obtained when the animal not only performs accurately on the initial training task but also can transfer this performance to novel stimuli, about which specific rules could not have been learned. The use of a generalized matching concept and the use of stimulus-specific rules are not mutually exclusive. An animal could use both strategies simultaneously.

Testing for the use of a matching concept is a complex problem. An animal that learned a conditional discrimination wholly on the basis of stimulus-specific rules would be expected to show little transfer to novel stimuli, unless those stimuli resembled the training stimuli or there was a significant learning-to-learn effect or other effect of shared task demands between the training set and a set of novel stimuli (Wilson et al 1985a). Similarly, perfect transfer might be expected based on the use of a generalized matching concept, but many animals are neophobic and may fail to attend to or interact with some transfer stimuli (D'Amato et al 1985; Zentall et al 1984).

Pigeons seem biased toward using stimulus-specific rules in a conditional discrimination, though some evidence of a generalized matching concept has been found. To the extent that pigeons are using stimulus-specific rules, or are demonstrating transfer on the basis of task-related factors, they should transfer to a formally identical task to the same degree whether the transfer task employs the same matching relation or a different relation. Original training on a matching task should transfer equally to a subsequent matching or oddity task if the pigeon does not use a generalized matching concept. On the other hand, if the pigeon does use a generalized matching concept, then rule-congruent transfer (i.e. from matching to matching or from oddity to oddity) should result in more accurate performance than rule-incongruent transfer (i.e. from matching to oddity or from oddity to matching). This general pattern of results has been observed (Zentall et al 1984). Pigeons showed above-chance accuracy on rule-congruent transfer and below-chance performance on rule-incongruent transfer, although in both cases the differences were small. These data suggest that pigeons make at least some use of a generalized matching concept in addition to stimulus-specific rules.

Another study using this rule-congruent versus incongruent transfer paradigm also found some limited support for the use of a matching concept by pigeons (Wilson et al 1985a). Wilson et al observed an asymmetry in the degree of transfer depending on whether the transfer task employed matching or oddity. Transfer performance on the oddity task was the same, whether the birds had initially been trained on the matching or on the oddity task. Transfer performance on the matching task, however, was higher when the birds had initially been trained on the matching task than when they had been trained on the oddity task. In a second experiment, pretraining on a symbolic matching task (in which the samples and correct comparison stimuli are only arbitrarily related) produced the same level of performance on a subsequent matching task as did pretraining on a matching task. Wilson et al concluded from this result that there was no benefit of pretraining on the matching relation, and that, therefore, the birds did not use this relation in learning the task. The difference in the size of the effect of task congruence on oddity versus matching transfer tasks they attributed to "the initial preference for the odd stimulus that pigeons usually display when first given stimulus arrays of this kind" (Wilson et al 1985a:308). In short, they attribute this transfer to the existence of an abstract concept of same versus different, and a preference for the different stimulus. Hence, although the data reflect a bias, they also seem to compel an analysis based on an abstract same/different concept.

Transfer of matching (Pisacreta et al 1984) and oddity (Pisacreta et al 1985) were also reported for pigeons using a six-key matching/oddity procedure. The birds' task was to peck the sample key until the matching (in the matching task) or the nonmatching stimulus (in the oddity task) appeared on one of the comparison keys. Pecks to the above-mentioned keys produced reinforcement. Novel stimuli were introduced following acquisition. Above-chance performance with these new stimulus combinations in the first sessions and faster learning of the new task reveal matching and oddity concept formation. The degree to which pigeons seem to use a generalized matching concept depends on the number of stimuli in the training set. Lombardi et al (1984) trained pigeons on a matching task involving 20 visual patterns. After reaching asymptotic performance with these stimuli, the pigeons showed accurate performance with completely new stimuli. These novel stimuli were presented under extinction conditions to avoid associations between test-stimulus and reinforcement. The results of this study seem to support the use of a generalized matching concept, but they might also be explained on the basis of stimulus generalization. Choice accuracy on novel transfer stimuli that were completely different from those used during training was poorer than was performance on stimuli that were similar to those used during training.

Stronger support for a generalized matching concept that cannot be so easily dismissed was obtained when pigeons were trained with an even larger stimulus set (Wright et al 1988). One group of pigeons (trial-unique group), which was trained with 152 stimuli, did not show any decline in their performance when confronted with novel trial-unique test stimuli. Another group of pigeons trained with only two stimuli showed no evidence of transfer. The fact that these birds were tested with each stimulus only once also supports the conclusion that the pigeons were using a generalized matching concept, because they had no opportunity to learn stimulus-specific responses during the transfer test. Although these data support the use of a generalized matching concept by pigeons, this form of concept learning does not appear to be the pigeon's preferred strategy (Wright et al 1988). Rather, they seem to rely primarily on stimulus-specific rules unless the situation demands that they employ a more abstract concept.

Results suggest that other bird species are more likely to employ a generalized matching concept. Jackdaws (*Corvus monedula*), jays (*Garrulus glandarius*), and rooks (*C. frugilegus*) all showed positive transfer to novel stimuli when the transfer task employed the same rule as the training task (Wilson et al 1985b). In the first experiment, pigeons and jackdaws were trained either on an arbitrary symbolic matching conditional discrimination or on a matching problem. The pigeons in both groups performed equally well on the transfer matching problem. In contrast, the jackdaws trained on the arbitrary task performed worse than chance during the first few sessions of the transfer task, whereas the jackdaws trained on the matching task performed at chance during these same sessions. Eventually both groups showed improved performance, but the group trained initially on the arbitrary task did not improve above chance during the six transfer sessions. The jackdaws thus showed the same kind of negative transfer observed by Wilson et al in pigeons tested on a matching task. Like the pigeon data, the performance of the jackdaws on the transfer test is consistent with the use of a generalized same/different concept coupled to a bias to choose the odd stimulus.

In a second experiment with jays (Wilson et al 1985b) and pigeons, the birds were transferred either to congruent or incongruent matching or oddity tasks using line-orientation stimuli following training on three previous matching or oddity tasks using color stimuli. Clear evidence of concept-mediated transfer was provided by the jays, who performed about 65% correct in the first transfer session when transferred to congruent matching or oddity and about 42% correct when transferred to an incongruent task. Similar data were obtained from rooks performing a related transfer task. These data thus provide clear evidence for the use of an abstract same/different concept by jays and rooks and provide somewhat weaker evidence for the use of a matching concept by jackdaws.

In another study of a bird species (Pepperberg 1987), an African gray parrot, Alex, was able to respond appropriately to questions concerning the concept of same versus different. Alex was previously taught to use vocal English labels to discriminate more than 80 different objects and could respond to questions concerning categorical concepts of shape and color. For example, on some trials he was shown two objects that were of the same color but differed in shape, or two objects that were of the same shape but differed in color. When asked "What is same?" he responded "color same" to the first pair and "shape same" to the second pair. Because he responded accurately to novel pairs of items, his responses were not stimulus specific. This experiment shows that Alex comprehends the concept of same/different, but it provides no evidence concerning his ability to produce items that correspond to the relationship. This experiment did not require him, for example, to select one object, from among many, that was the same as a target object.

Unlike pigeons, rats showed no evidence of oddity transfer using either visual or olfactory stimuli (Thomas & Noble 1988). Two groups were trained using 10 visual objects and 5 odors. After acquisition, the rats performed at chance levels of accuracy on novel trial-unique oddity problems. Other mammalian species, however, show evidence of possessing a generalized matching concept. For example, California sea lions (*Zalophus californianus*)

696   ROITBLAT & VON FERSEN

seem to employ a hierarchy of learning patterns depending on the task demands. In the first two experiments (Hille 1988), two sea lions were trained in an oddity task with a small number of stimuli (5 for one experiment and 10 for the other). Although the animals learned to perform the task, there was no evidence that they had learned a generalized oddity concept. Furthermore, there was no evidence of savings over successive problems. In a third experiment, with a single sea lion, trial-unique stimuli were used, and the animal reached 90% correct performance in 120 trials, thus indicating the use of a generalized oddity concept. It seems that sea lions, like pigeons, tend to learn stimulus-specific rules rather than abstract concepts when dealing with a small number of stimuli. Another sea lion also provided evidence for the use of a generalized matching concept in a delayed matching-to-sample task (Pack et al 1991). Following acquisition with a two-stimulus set, the animal performed significantly above chance when new object combinations were shown.

Bottlenosed dolphins (*Tursiops truncatus*) have also demonstrated the use of a generalized matching concept with auditory (Herman & Gordon 1974) as well as visual stimuli (Herman et al 1989). In the visual study, the dolphin was trained to match three-dimensional objects. Following acquisition, the dolphin transferred to novel objects, choosing correctly 16 out of 18 objects the first time they were presented. The immediate transfer observed to new objects is the strongest evidence for a generalized visual matching.

Studies done with monkeys report comparable results. Like dolphins, monkeys were tested using both visual and auditory stimuli. For example, of 8 cebus monkeys (*Cebus apella*) trained with two-dimensional stimuli (D'Amato et al 1985), four showed transfer performance according to D'Amato et al's criterion (above 70% correct performance in test sessions 2–4), but the extent to which the monkeys discriminated the test stimuli on a conceptual basis is difficult to assess because learning during the test sessions cannot be ruled out. Performance during the first session may be too conservative a measure of the degree of transfer because monkeys are frequently neophobic and this neophobia may interfere with their initial performance. Nevertheless, the fact that two of the monkeys did show 75% accurate first-session transfer demonstrates that monkeys are capable of learning and using a same/different concept. Spontaneous transfer of the matching rule was also demonstrated by chimpanzees (Oden et al 1988). Four young chimpanzees (14 to 16 months old) spontaneously transferred the matching rule to new objects after being trained with only one pair of objects. In this case it is highly probable that the utilization of three-dimensional objects and the familiarity of the objects to the animals (the subjects were preexposed to the new objects in a free play situation) had a positive influence on performance.

Three other experiments done with monkeys show that they also perform well when dealing with auditory stimuli. Both cebus monkeys (D'Amato &

Colombo 1985) and Rhesus monkeys (*Macaca mulatta;* Shyan et al 1987; Wright et al 1990) showed that test performance was mediated by a generalized matching concept. D'Amato and colleagues used only two auditory stimuli during training. They found that 4 of their 8 monkeys learned the task and transferred to novel stimuli. Shyan et al and Wright et al used a training set of 38 sounds and found more convincing results. In a total of 92 transfer test trials, each with unique stimuli, both monkeys reached 78.8% correct responses (compared with 77.3% in training).

SYMMETRY   Another property of objects and (in particular) animals is bilateral symmetry. The fact that bilateral symmetry is a widespread phenomenon suggests that symmetry detection could be a useful competence (Braitenberg 1986), for example, for finding camouflaged prey (Curio 1976). Discrimination of symmetric from nonsymmetric objects is also important because there is no simple algorithm available by which such decisions can be made. An object is symmetrical when every point on one side of its axis of symmetry has a corresponding point with the same value and same relative position on the opposite side of the axis. These corresponding points can occur at any distance from one another, in any orientation, and can be distorted by perspective or by occlusion of intervening objects. Therefore, the ability to recognize symmetric from asymmetric objects indicates a powerful computational mechanism. In one study demonstrating discrimination on the basis of symmetry, pigeons were trained to discriminate 26 symmetric two-dimensional visual patterns from an equal number of asymmetric patterns (Delius & Nowak 1982). Following this training, the pigeons were able to apply this same discrimination to novel exemplars.

FAMILIARITY   In addition to learning to respond to objects on the basis of their similarity, animals can also respond on the basis of the overall familiarity of the objects (MacPhail & Reilly 1989). Pigeons were trained using a successive discrimination task in which responses to novel slides were rewarded and responses to familiar stimuli (seen once before) were not rewarded. The animals rapidly learned to categorize the stimuli on the basis of familiarity. In a final experiment, the pigeons responded to a set of new duplicates of previously presented slides as familiar.

In summary, at least some animals can abstract general rules from specific problems. The formation of these rules is not linked to language, though the use of more complex rules may be (Premack 1983; Roitblat 1987a).

Categories and Concepts

The data described above make it clear that animals can learn to respond to abstract relations (e.g. similarity, novelty) among stimuli. Animals also seem to employ categorical representations of classes of objects and treat members of the category in similar ways. The basis for this categorization may be as simple as perceptual similarity, or it may depend on such abstract relations as functional similarity (cf Lea 1984; D'Amato & Van Sant 1988). Categorization thus spans a class of mechanisms. Perceptual similarity, however, is not as simple as it might appear. For example, one investigator has suggested that pigeons discriminate photographs containing trees from photographs not containing trees because slides in the reinforced class simply look like trees. It is one thing to say that a photograph looks like it contains a tree and quite another to specify the algorithm by which trees can be recognized (Duda & Hart 1973; Biederman 1990; Yuille & Ullman 1990).

PERCEPTUAL CATEGORIES   In a standard test of concept discrimination (e.g. Herrnstein 1984, 1985), subjects were trained with a certain number of different slides. Half of the slides, defined as the positive set, contain a particular feature—for example, a tree—and responses in the presence of these slides is rewarded. The other half of the slides, defined as the negative set, contain other features but not trees. After the subjects learned to discriminate these slides, they were tested with hundreds of new slides. The results of the experiments show that novel slides depicting trees tend to receive more responses than the nontree slides. Using this training procedure, investigators have found that pigeons can classify new instances of natural categories such as humans, trees, fish, and water. This pattern of results is consistent with the use of a general concept for the class depicted in the positive slides (see also Bhatt et al 1988; Wasserman et al 1988).

Probably one of the first steps in the process of categorization is to group objects according to simple exterior outlines. For example, the ability to sort objects according to their form (angular vs round) has been shown by many animals. In one of these studies, Delius (1991), using three-dimensional stimuli, demonstrated that pigeons trained with a large number of angular and round objects transfer this categorization to novel objects and photographs. Following the experiments demonstrating that pigeons and monkeys can learn to recognize classes of natural objects (e.g. Herrnstein 1984, 1985; see also Bhatt et al 1988; Wasserman et al 1988), several studies have investigated animals' ability to discriminate classes representing primates. Pigeons showed evidence of learning a category based on the presence of humans (Edwards & Honig 1987). The positive and negative exemplars included the same background setting. A scene was photographed without any people, then the same scene was photographed with one or more people present somewhere in the scene. Unlike previous studies (Herrnstein et al 1976; Mallot & Siddall 1972) that investigated pigeons' abilities to discriminate slides with people from slides without people, the positive and negative slides in the latter study were identical except for the presence of people. Hence, this experiment provides stronger evidence that the pigeons were actually using people as the discriminative element.

In another experiment, Rhesus monkeys were trained to discriminate slides containing Rhesus monkeys from similar pictures showing Japanese macaques (Yoshikubo 1985). The extent to which these monkeys extended their discrimination on a conceptual basis to novel photographs is difficult to assess, however, because the data are pooled over three sessions and therefore learning was possible during the generalization test. Rhesus monkeys were also trained to discriminate more than 1000 scenes on the basis of whether or not they contained humans (Schrier & Brady 1987). This categorization then generalized to novel exemplars including some with distorted images. The use of such a large training set speeded learning and improved accuracy compared to an earlier study employing fewer slides in the training set (Schrier et al 1984). Other evidence for spontaneous categorization of new slides that differed in the presence or absence of humans came from a study done by D'Amato & Van Sant (1988). In contrast to the experiment of Schrier & Brady (1987), in which a large number of slides led to the formation of a generalized matching concept, one monkey (*Cebus apella*) in this study showed accurate transfer performance after only 20 exemplars (10 of each class). These data must also be interpreted with caution, however, because the monkeys may have discriminated examples in this study on the basis of some correlated feature (e.g. the color red was more frequent in the human slides than in the slides without humans; D'Amato & Van Sant 1988). This result makes clear that alternative explanations must be examined before concept formation is asserted.

All the prior experiments report categorization of visual patterns. A few studies also report results with auditory categorization, primarily with categorical perception of sounds. Experiments on categorical perception with nonhuman animals are particularly informative with respect to the uniqueness of human speech perception processes. Both monkeys and chinchillas can discriminate synthetic speech sounds, such as /da/ and /ta/, which differ only in voice onset time (VOT; Kuhl 1987). In the first experiment the chinchillas were trained to distinguish synthesized examples of /da/ from /ta/. Following training on these two syllables, generalization tests presented syllables with voice onset times intermediate between those in the two training examples. These were discriminated with a sharp boundary between categories. Hence, these results show that, like humans, chinchillas perceive these tests sounds discretely as either /da/ or /ta/ and not as intermediate sounds. Another interesting finding was that the perceptual boundary (point on the VOT scale where the animal changes its assignment from /da/ to /ta/) was the same for chinchillas and English speakers. Similar results were obtained when /ga/-/ka/ and /ba/-/pa/ syllables were used. This last finding suggests that the boundaries for human phonemic categories might coincide with animals' natural perceptual boundaries.

In another study, Japanese quail (*Coturnix coturnix*) were taught to discriminate natural syllables (Kluender et al 1987). First the birds learned to discriminate syllables that began with the consonant /d/ followed by one of four vowels (positive set) from other syllables that began with the consonants /b/ or /g/ followed by the same four vowels. After acquisition, the quail correctly categorized new syllables in which the same consonants preceded eight novel vowels. In contrast, it seems that great tits do not classify continuous variations in the phrase length of their own songs into discrete categories. Weary (1989) trained great tits with two reference songs that differed only in phrase length. The animals in this experiment did not discriminate sharply between the two song categories but assigned novel test songs to categories as a function of song length.

In contrast, Japanese macaques do seem to represent some of their calls categorically. Japanese macaques were trained to discriminate two groups of natural sounds: smooth late high "coos" and smooth early high "coos" (May et al 1988). Faster acquisition of subsequently introduced sounds and spontaneous transfer to new natural sounds (from other animals) and computer synthesized stimuli demonstrate that the animals developed a category for each type of sound. Similar results were obtained with vervet monkeys (*Cercopithecus aethiops*). These monkeys issue characteristic alarm calls in the vicinity of specific classes of predators such as snakes, eagles, or leopards and take specific actions when hearing those calls (Cheney & Seyfarth 1980). Acoustic analyses of these alarm calls show that examples of the same call, that is calls in response to the same class of predator, vary substantially between instances. Owren (1990a) trained vervet monkeys to discriminate two acoustically different alarm calls (snake and eagle) recorded from a single animal. After reaching criterion on these stimuli, the subjects had no difficulty in discriminating 48 novel versions of the same calls. Similar results were obtained using synthetic calls (Owren 1990b).

Mechanisms of Categorization

Although the studies described above lend strong support to the notion that animals employ categorical representations of some stimuli, they do not specify the nature of the underlying mechanism responsible for such categorization or for its acquisition (if such categories are, indeed, acquired). The mechanisms responsible for categorization processes are problematic, particularly because of the polymorphous nature of many of the categories investigated. These categories are not definable in terms of any single stimulus dimension, and no single perceptual feature is likely to be a necessary or sufficient condition for category membership (Herrnstein 1985). In the case of the category "tree" already mentioned, no single set of features could be found that was necessary or sufficient to account for the birds' behavior. Four different theories about object recognition have been proposed to explain stimulus categorization and generalization.

TEMPLATE MATCHING   This theory holds that the brain constructs templates for different figures. Identification of an object involves a matching process between a perceptual pattern and all of the stored templates. The object is recognized by selecting the template that most closely matches it. The main difficulty with this system is the large number of templates that would have to be stored if items are to be recognized in a wide variety of distances, orientations, and positions. Another obstacle is that generalization to new exemplars is difficult to explain using templates (see Yuille & Ullman 1990 for an alternative view concerning templates).

FEATURE ANALYSIS   According to the feature-analysis hypothesis objects are characterized by the set of perceptual features of which they are composed. For example, the letter "A" is recognized when (simplifying somewhat) a concave-downward acute angle, a horizontal bar, and a forward and a backward slanting line are detected. This approach seemed to be suggested by Hubel & Wiesel's (1977) demonstration that the brain contains cells that appear to be selective for certain line orientations and other characteristics of visual input. The essence of feature analysis is that several different features of each of the stimuli are measured and as a result of reinforcement a weighting factor is assigned to each feature. On this basis, response rates can be predicted from the sum of the weighted features. One model of this sort was investigated by Cerella (1986). Cerella compared pigeons' performance on categorical discrimination tasks to a perceptron (Rosenblatt 1962) that classifies patterns on the basis of local features but does not respond specifically to combinations of features. For example, by manipulating negative instances, Cerella was able to determine that pigeons discriminated the leaves of one oak species from others on the basis of a local feature, rounded lobes, not present in any of the other leaves. Neither his perceptron model nor the pigeons could discriminate oak leaves that differed from the positive species in overall shape but also included rounded lobes.

One difficulty with the feature-analysis approach to pattern recognition is that the necessary features that underlie some categories cannot be specified. Although animals are sometimes capable of detecting features that escape the attention of human experimenters, they also sometimes fail to take advantage of features that the experimenters considered obvious (Lea & Ryan 1990). Another experiment, however, did find evidence that the pigeons made use of specific features (von Fersen & Lea 1990). In this experiment the authors trained pigeons with a set of photographs of two buildings. Each slide was characterized by five bipolar features: building (pub or university), orientation (vertical or oblique), weather (sunny or cloudy), height (low or high), and distance (near or far). One value of each feature was designated positive, the other as negative. The subjects were reinforced for pecking at stimuli in which three or more of the five positive values appeared. Hence, assuming equal weighting, the birds could employ a linear threshold and accept any items as positive that had a score of 1.0 or above (three features at $+1.0$ and two features at -1.0). According to the linear feature model all the systematic variation in the response rates should be accounted for by the main effects of the five features. Four of the eight pigeons trained used spontaneously all five features to discriminate both categories. Within the positive class the stimuli with more positive-valued features controlled higher response rates, indicating that the birds did not employ a simple all-or-none criterion for category membership. Instead, the variations in response rate to different stimuli suggested that they employed a fuzzy set (Zadeh 1971) to represent the category. Finally, although the experimenters specified nominal categories along which the items varied, they could not specify the precise perceptual features that the pigeons presumably used in identifying such nominal features as the pub versus university.

PROTOTYPE MATCHING   According to prototype theory, recognition occurs by comparing perceived figures to prototypes for their various categories. A prototype is a central tendency, average, or typical example of the category (Posner & Keele 1970; Rosch & Mervis 1975).

RELAXATION   Relaxation is a relatively new theory of pattern recognition that incorporates feature analysis and prototype theories. It views a template as a special kind of prototype. Relaxation is the name for a family of mathematical processes that have long been used for solving constraint-satisfaction problems (e.g. Allen 1954). Waltz (1975) showed how such techniques could be applied to object recognition. Hopfield & Tank (1985) showed how a connectionist system could be used to implement a relaxation constraint-satisfaction system. According to the relaxation theory of pattern recognition the perception of an object provides evidence for one or more hypotheses. Each hypothesis corresponds to a possible interpretation or categorization for that object. Some of the features of the perceived object are more consistent with one hypothesis than with another. The system oscillates among the alternative hypotheses until it finds the one that best satisfies the constraints provided by the evidence and the mutual relations among the hypotheses (see also McClelland 1986).

    According to the relaxation model, object recognition is an interactive process. In a connectionist implementation of the model, each of the hypotheses and each object feature to which the system responds is represented by a formal neuron. Connections between these formal neurons represent the constraints and associations among the hypotheses and inputs. For example, in one experiment (Bhatt et al 1988), pigeons were trained to classify photographic slides as flowers, cats, cars, or chairs. Because flowers are often pastel, the presence of pastel colors in the slide would support the hypothesis that it pictures flowers, but the slide could also depict a cat or an object in one of the other categories positioned near a pastel object. The combination of green and a pastel color is more supportive of the flower hypothesis but still not compelling. To the extent that a feature co-occurs with some class, indicated to the animal by reinforcement during training, the connection weight between the feature and the hypothesis is strengthened. To the extent that a feature is negatively correlated with a hypothesis (e.g. certain shapes may only rarely occur in flower pictures), the connection weight between the feature and the hypothesis is weakened (made more negative). Activation of a set of features in the input leads to partial activation of the alternative hypotheses. The degree of activation of an input feature is a function of the strength or clarity of the feature in the input (e.g. a partially occluded circle will activate its respective input unit less strongly than an unoccluded one). The activation of each hypothesis is a function of the total contribution (both supportive and detractive) of the inputs. An active hypothesis will lend support to the inputs that support it, thereby strengthening their activation, which will contribute support to the hypothesis, and so on. The network will oscillate in this way until it finds the combination of input and hypothesis activations that minimizes the "stress" of the system—that is, until it finds the most consistent classification of the input pattern.

A relaxation system solves a number of problems inherent in other classification models. It includes both bottom-up (stimulus-feature driven) and top-down (hypothesis driven) processes. It includes features and representations of the central tendency of categories but allows for more flexibility in recognizing members of each category. It does not require a perfect match for recognition as a template model might but seeks to find the best match between category and exemplar.

CONCLUSIONS

In contrast to the historic view of animals as passive responders to environmental change, the experiments reviewed above show that animals are active processors of information about their environment. Recent advances in understanding both natural and artificial neural networks show how known neural mechanisms can be combined to produce sophisticated learning and representational processes. These advances have supported progress in comparative cognition by suggesting mechanisms animals might use during learning and memory, and by showing how those mechanisms might plausibly be physically implemented. The success of relatively simple computational systems implementing putatively cognitive functions supports the plausibility of similar mechanisms in animals. Neural network investigations also support comparative cognition research by raising application-oriented questions. One of the major interests in artificial neural network research is applying these systems to the solution of real-world problems such as robotic control (e.g. Beer 1990). Many investigators have taken the brain metaphor seriously and sought examples in animal behavior that can provide suggestions for the design of artificial neural network systems (Meyer & Wilson 1991). Understanding animals and their behavior can greatly facilitate the development of real-world applications.

Although these studies reveal that animals are not as simple as many had previously thought, they also demonstrate that the complexity of animal cognition is tractable. At least some aspects of animal cognition may be easier to understand than related phenomena in humans. Continued progress in understanding cognition and the brain mechanisms responsible for it requires a more complete understanding of animals and their cognitive capacities.

Finally, a growing body of evidence demonstrates good continuity among the processes of animals and humans. Space limitations have prevented us from discussing a substantial body of work concerning language-like processes in animals (see Roitblat et al 1992). Considerable progress has been made in recent years in the investigation of grammatical (Greenfield & Savage-Rumbaugh 1990, 1992) and symbolic processes (Savage-Rumbaugh 1986; Savage-Rumbaugh et al 1990) in chimpanzees (*Pan troglodytes*) and bonobos (*Pan paniscus*). These studies suggest that these animals are capable of extremely sophisticated representational systems similar to those seen in human language.

ACKNOWLEDGMENTS

L. von Fersen was supported during the preparation of this paper by Grant #FE 278/2-1 from the German Science Foundation, Deutsche Forschungs-Gemeinschaft. We thank Boris Goldowsky and Constance Manos for their careful reading of earlier drafts.

Literature Cited

Allen, D. N. 1954. *Relaxation Methods in Engineering and Science.* NY: McGraw Hill

Arnold, H. M., Grahame, N. J., Miller, R. R. 1991. Higher order occasion setting. *Anim. Learn. Behav.* 19:58–64

Ayers, J. J. B., Haddad, C., Albert, M. 1987. One trial excitatory backward conditioning as assessed by conditioned suppression of licking in rats: concurrent observations of lick suppression and defensive behaviors. *Anim. Learn. Behav.* 15:212–17

Balda, R. P., Kamil, A. C. 1989. A comparative study of cache recovery by three corvid species. *Anim. Behav.* 38:486–95

Balda, R. P., Bunch, K. G., Kamil, A. C., Sherry, D. F., Tomback, D. F. 1987. Cache site memory in birds. In *Foraging Behavior,* ed. A. C. Kamil, J. R. Krebs, H. R. Pulliam, pp. 645–66. NY: Plenum

Barto, A. G., Sutton, R. S. 1982. Simulation of anticipatory responses in classical conditioning by a neuron-like adaptive element. *Behav. Brain Res.* 4:221–35

Beer, R. 1990. *Intelligence as Adaptive Behavior*. NY: Academic

Bennett, R. W., Bennett, I. F. 1974. PI release as a function of the number of prerelease trials. *J. Verb. Learn. Verb. Behav.* 13:573–84

Bhatt, R. S., Wasserman, E. A., Reynolds, W. F., Knauss, K. S. 1988. Conceptual behavior in pigeons: categorization of both familiar and novel examples from four classes of natural and artificial stimuli. *J. Exp. Psychol.: Anim. Behav. Proc.* 14:219–34

Biederman, I. 1990. Higher level vision. In *Visual Cognition and Action: An Invitation to Cognitive Science*, ed. D. N. Osherson, S. M. Kosslyn, J. M. Hollerbach, pp. 41–72. Cambridge, MA: MIT Press

Bitterman, M. E. 1988. Vertebrate-invertebrate comparisons. In *Intelligence and Evolutionary Biology*, ed. H. J. Jerison, I. Jerison, pp. 251–75. NY: Springer-Verlag

Bitterman, M. E., Couvillon, P. A. 1991. Failures to find evidence of adaptive specialization in the learning of honeybees. In *The Behaviour and Physiology of Bees*, ed. L. J. Goodman R. C. Fischer. Wallingford, UK: CAB International. In press

Boakes, R. 1984. *From Darwin to behaviorism: Psychology and the Minds of Animals*. NY: Cambridge Univ. Press

Bock, W. J., Balda, R. P., Vander Wall, S. B. 1973. Morphology of the sublingual pouch and tongue musculature in Clark's nutcracker. *Auk* 90:491–519

Bolhuis, J. J., van Kampen, H. S. 1988. Serial position curves in spatial memory of rats: primacy and recency effects. *Q. J. Exp. Psychol.* 40B:135–49

Braitenberg, V. 1986. *Vehicles*. Cambridge: MIT Press

Brodigan D. L., Peterson, G. B. 1976. Two-choice conditional discrimination performance as a function of reward expectancy, prechoice delay, and domesticity. *Anim. Learn. Behav.* 4:121–24

Bush, R. R., Mosteller, F. 1951. A mathematical model for simple learning. *Psychol. Rev.* 58:313–23

Card, H. C., Moore, W. R. 1990. Silicon models of associative learning in *Aplysia. Neural Networks* 3:333–46

Cerella, J. 1986. Pigeons and perceptrons. *Pattern Recog.* 19:431–38

Cheney, D. L., Seyfarth, R. M. 1980. Vocal recognition in free-ranging vervet monkeys. *Anim. Behav.* 28:362–67

Colwill, R. M., Rescorla, R. A. 1986. Associative structures in instrumental learning. *Psychol. Learn. Motiv.* 20:55–104

Colwill, R. M., Rescorla, R. A. 1989. Associations with anticipated and obtained outcomes in instrumental learning. *Anim. Learn. Behav.* 17:291–303

Colwill, R. M., Rescorla, R. A. 1990. Evidence for the hierarchical structure of instrumental learning. *Anim. Learn. Behav.* 18:71–82

Couvillon, P. A., Bitterman, M. E. 1991. How honeybees make choices. In *The Behaviour and Physiology of Bees*, ed. L. J. Goodman, R. C. Fischer. Wallingford, UK: CAB International

Couvillon, P. A., Leiato, T. G., Bitterman, M. P. 1991. Learning in honeybees (*Apis mellifera*) on arrival at and departure from a feeding place. *J. Comp. Psychol.* 105:177–84

Curio, E. 1976. *The Ethology of Predation*. Berlin: Springer Verlag

D'Amato, M. R., Colombo, M. 1985. Auditory matching-to-sample in monkeys (*Cebus apella*). *Anim. Learn. Behav.* 13:375–82

D'Amato, M. R., Salmon, D. P., Colombo, M. 1985. Extent and limits of the matching concept in monkeys (*Cebus apella*). *J. Exp. Psychol.: Anim. Behav. Proc.* 11:31–51

D'Amato, M. R., Van Sant, P. 1988. The person concept in monkeys (*Cebus apella*). *J. Exp. Psychol.: Anim. Behav. Proc.* 14:43–55

Delius, J. D. 1991. Categorical discrimination of objects and pictures by pigeons. *Anim. Learn. Behav.* In press

Delius, J. D., Nowak, B. 1982. Visual symmetry recognition by pigeons. *Psychol. Res.* 44:199–212

Detterman, D. K., Ellis, N. R. 1972. Determinants of induced amnesia in short-term memory. *J. Exp. Psychol.* 95:308–16

Dickinson, A., Nicholas, D. J., Adams, C. D. 1983. The effect of instrumental training contingency on susceptibility to reinforcer devaluation. *Q. J. Exp. Psychol.* 35B:35–51

DiMattia, B. V., Kesner, R. P. 1984. Serial position curves in rats: automatic versus effortful information processing. *J. Exp. Psychol.: Anim. Behav. Proc.* 10:557–63

Donegan, N. H., Gluck, M. A., Thompson, R. F. 1989. Integrating behavioral and biological models of classical conditioning. *Psychol. Learn. Motiv.* 23:109–56

Duda, R. O., Hart, P. E. 1973. *Pattern Classification and Scene Analysis*. NY: Wiley

Durlach, P. J. 1983. The effect of signaling intertrial USs in autoshaping. *J. Exp. Psychol.: Anim. Behav. Proc.* 9:374–89

Dye, R. H. Jr., Hafter, E. R. 1984. The effects of intensity on the detection of interaural differences of time in high frequency trains of clicks. *J. Acoust. Soc. Am.* 75:1593–98

Edwards, C. A., Honig, W. K. 1987. Memorization and "feature selection" in the acquisition of natural concepts in pigeons. *Learn. Motiv.* 18:235–60

Elman, J. L., Zipser, D. 1987. Representation and structure in connectionist models. CRL Tech. Rep. 8903. Cent. Res. Lang., Univ. Calif., San Diego

Fedorchak, P. M., Bolles, R. C. 1986. Differential outcome effects using a biologically neutral outcome difference. *J. Exp. Psychol.: Anim. Behav. Proc.* 12:125–30

Finke, R. A. 1985. Theories relating mental imagery to perception. *Psychol. Bull.* 98:236–59

Fodor, J. A. 1987. *Psychosemantics.* Cambridge, MA: MIT Press

Gaffan, D. 1977. Recognition memory after short retention intervals in fornix-transected monkeys. *Q. J. Exp. Psychol.* 29:577–88

Gallistel, C. R. 1989. Animal cognition: the representation of space time and number. *Annu. Rev. Psychol.* 40:155–90

Gamzu, E. R., Williams, D. R. 1973. Associative factors underlying the pigeon's keypecking in autoshaping procedures. *J. Exp. Anal. Behav. 1* 9:225–32

Glanzer, M., Cunitz, A. R. 1966. Two storage mechanisms in free recall. *J. Verb. Learn. Verb. Behav.* 5:351–60

Gluck, M. A., Bower, G. H. 1988. From conditioning to category learning: an adaptive network model. *J. Exp. Psychol.: Gen.* 117:225–44

Gluck, M. A., Thompson, R. F. 1987. Modeling the neural substrates of associative learning and memory: a computational approach. *Psychol. Rev.* 94:176–91

Gorman, R. P., Sejnowski, T. J. 1988. Analysis of hidden units in a layered network trained to classify sonar targets. *Neural Networks* 1:75–89

Gould, J. L. 1986. The biology of learning. *Annu. Rev. Psychol.* 37:163–92

Gould, J. L. 1988. Timing of landmark learning by honey bees. *J. Insect Behav.* 1:373–78

Greenfield, P. M., Savage-Rumbaugh, E. S. 1990. Grammatical combination in *Pan paniscus.* Processes of learning and invention. In *"Language" and Intelligence in Monkeys and Apes: Comparative Developmental Perspectives,* ed. S. T. Parker K. R. Gibson. NY: Cambridge Univ. Press

Greenfield, P. M., Savage-Rumbaugh, E. S. 1992. Imitation, grammatical development, and the invention of protogrammar. In *Biobehavioral Foundations of Language Development,* ed. N. Krasnagor, D. M. Rumbaugh, M. Studdert-Kennedy, D. Scheifelbusch. Hillsdale, NJ: Erlbaum Associates

Grossberg, S., Levine, D. S. 1987. Neural dynamics of attentionally modulated Pavlovian conditioning: blocking, inter-stimulus

interval, and secondary reinforcement. *Appl. Optics* 26:5015–30

Grossberg, S., Schmajuk, N. A. 1987. Neural dynamics of attentionally modulated Pavlovian conditioning: conditioned reinforcement, inhibition, and opponent processing. *Psychobiology* 15:195–240

Hawkins, R. D., Kandel, E. R. 1984. Is there a cell biological alphabet for simple forms of learning? *Psychol. Rev.* 91:375–91

Hearst, E. 1989. Backward associations: differential learning about stimuli that follow the presence versus the absence of food in pigeons. *Anim. Learn. Behav.* 17:280–90

Hebb, D. O. 1949. *The Organization of Behavior.* NY: Wiley

Herman, L. M., Gordon, J. A. 1974. Auditory delayed matching in the bottlenose dolphin. *J. Exp. Anal. Behav.* 21:19–26

Herman, L. M., Hovancik, J. R., Gory, J. D., Bradshaw, G. L. 1989. Generalization of matching by a bottlenosed dolphin (*Tursiops truncatus*): evidence for invariance of cognitive performance with visual and auditory materials. *J. Exp. Psychol.: Anim. Behav. Proc.* 15:124–36

Herrnstein, R. J. 1984. Objects, categories, and discriminative stimuli. In *Animal Cognition,* ed. H. L. Roitblat, T. G. Bever, H. S. Terrace, pp. 233–62. Hillsdale, NJ: Erlbaum

Herrnstein, R. J. 1985. Riddles of natural categorization. *Philos. Trans. R. Soc. London Ser. B* 308:129–44

Herrnstein, R. J., Loveland, D. H., Cable, C. 1976. Natural concepts in pigeons. *J. Exp. Psychol.: Anim. Behav. Proc.* 2:285–302

Hille, P. 1988. Versuche zur Ungleicherkennung beim Kalifornischen Seeloewen (*Zalophus californianus*) unter besonderer Berücksichtigung der Begriffsbildung. Ms. thesis, Westfälische Wilhelms-Univ., Münster, Germany

Hilton, S. C., Krebs, J. R. 1990. Spatial memory of four species of *Parus:* performance in an open-field analogue of a radial maze. *Q. J. Exp. Psychol.* 42B:345–68

Hitchcock, C. L., Sherry, D. F. 1990. Long-term memory for cache sites in the black-capped chickadee. *Anim. Behav.* 40:701–12

Holland, P. C. 1983. Occasion setting in Pavlovian feature positive discriminations. In *Quantitative Analyses of Behavior: Discrimination Processes,* ed. M. L. Commons, R. J. Herrnstein, A. R. Wagner, 4:223–345. NY: Ballinger

Holland, P. C. 1989a. Acquisition and transfer of conditional discrimination performance. *J. Exp. Psychol.: Anim. Behav. Proc.* 15:154–65

Holland, P. C. 1989b. Feature extinction enhances transfer of occasion setting. *Anim. Learn. Behav.* 17:269–79

Holland, P. C., Straub, J. J. 1979. Differential effects of two ways of devaluing the unconditioned stimulus after Pavlovian appetitive conditioning. *J. Exp. Psychol.: Anim. Behav. Proc.* 5:65–68

Hollard, V. D., Delius, J. D. 1982. Rotational invariance in visual pattern recognition by pigeons and humans. *Science* 218:802–4

Honig, W. K., Stewart, K. E. 1988. Pigeons can discriminate locations presented in pictures. *J. Exp. Anal. Behav.* 50:541–51

Honig, W. K., Thompson, R. K. R. 1982. Retrospective and prospective processing in animal working memory. *Psychol. Learn. Motiv.* 16:239–83

Hopfield, J. J., Tank, D. 1985. "Neural" computation of decisions in optimization problems. *Biol. Cybernet.* 52:141–52

Hubel, D. H., Wiesel, T. N. 1977. Functional architecture of macaque monkey visual cortex. *Proc. R. Soc. London Ser. B* 198:1–59

Hull, C. L. 1943. *Principles of Behavior.* NY: Appleton-Century-Crofts

Jitsumori, M., Wright, A. A., Shyan, M. R. 1989. Buildup and release from proactive interference in a rhesus monkey. *J. Exp. Psychol.: Anim. Behav. Proc.* 15:329–37

Kamil, A. C., Balda, R. P. 1985. Cache recovery and spatial memory in Clark's nutcrackers (*Nucifraga columbiana*). *J. Exp. Psychol.: Anim. Behav. Proc.* 11:95-111

Kamil, A. C., Balda, R. P. 1990. Spatial memory in seed-caching corvids. *Psychol. Learn. Motiv.* 26:1–25

Kehoe, E. J. 1988. A layered network model of associative learning: learning to learn and configuration. *Psychol. Rev.* 95:411–53

Kehoe, E. J. 1989. Connectionist models of conditioning: a tutorial. *J. Exp. Anal. Behav.* 52:427–40

Kehoe, E. J., Gormezano, I. 1980. Configuration and combination laws in conditioning with compound stimuli. *Psychol. Bull.* 87:351–78

Klopf, A. H. 1988. A neuronal model of classical conditioning. *Psychobiology* 16:85–125

Kluender, K. R., Diehl, R. L., Killeen, P. R. 1987. Japanese quail can learn phonetic categories. *Science* 237:1195–97

Kosslyn, S. M. 1983. *Ghosts in the Mind's Machine.* NY: Norton

Krebs, J. R. 1990. Food storing birds: adaptive specialization in brain and behaviour. *Philos. Trans. R. Soc. London Ser. B.* 329:55–62

Krebs, J. R., Healy, S. D., Shettleworth, S. J. 1990. Spatial memory of paridae: comparison of a storing and a non-storing species, the coal tit, *Parus ater,* and the great tit, *P. major. Anim. Behav.* 39:1127–37

Krebs, J. R., Sherry, D. F., Healy, S. D., Perry, V. H., Vaccarino, A. L. 1989. Hippocampal specialization of food-storing birds. *Proc. Natl. Acad. Sci. USA* 86:1388–92

Kuhl, P. K. 1987. The special-mechanisms debate in speech research: categorization tests on animals and infants. In *Categorical perception,* ed. S. Harnad, pp. 355–86. Cambridge: Cambridge Univ. Press

Lea, S. E. G. 1984. In what sense do pigeons learn concepts? See Herrnstein 1984, pp. 263–77

Lea, S. E. G., Ryan, D. 1990. Unnatural concepts and the theory of concept discrimination in birds. In *Models of Behavior: Behavioral Approaches to Pattern Recognition and Concept Formation,* ed. M. L. Commons, R. J. Herrnstein, S. Kosslyn, D. Mumford, pp. 165–85. Hillsdale, NJ: Erlbaum

Lombardi, C., Fachinelli, C., Delius, J. D. 1984. Oddity of visual patterns conceptualized by pigeons. *Anim. Learn. Behav.* 12:2–6

Mackintosh, N. J., Dickinson, A. 1979. Instrumental (Type II) conditioning. In *Mechanisms of Learning and Motivation,* ed. A. Dickinson, R. A. Boakes. Hillsdale, NJ: Lawrence Erlbaum Associates

MacPhail, E. M. 1987. The comparative psychology of intelligence. *Behav. Brain Sci.* 10:645–95

MacPhail, E. M., Reilly, S. 1989. Rapid acquisition of a novelty versus familiarity concept by pigeons (*Columba livia*). *J. Exp. Psychol.: Anim. Behav. Proc.* 15:242–52

Mallot, R., Siddall, J. W. 1972. Acquisition of the people concept in pigeons. *Psychol. Rep.* 31:3–13

Marr, D. 1982. *Vision.* NY: Freeman

May, B., Moody, D. B., Stebbins, W. C. 1988. The significant features of Japanese macaque coo sounds: a psychological study. *Anim. Behav.* 36:1432–44

McClelland, J. L. 1986. The programmable blackboard model of reading. See McClelland & Rumelhart, pp. 122–69

McClelland, J. L., Rumelhart, D. E. 1986. *Parallel Distributed Processing: Explorations in the Microstructure of Cognition.* Vol. 2. *Psychological and Biological Models.* Cambridge, MA: MIT Press

McClelland, J. L., Rumelhart, D. E., Hinton, G. E. 1986. The appeal of parallel distributed processing. See Rumelhart McClelland, 1986, pp. 3–44

McCulloch, W. W., Pitts, W. 1943. A logical calculus of the ideas imminent in nervous activity. *Bull. Math. Biophys.* 5:115–33

Melton, A. W. 1963. Implications of short-term memory for a general theory of memory. *J. Verb. Learn. Verb. Behav.* 2:1–21

Menzel, R. 1990. Learning, memory, and "cognition" in honeybees. In *Neurobiology of Comparative Cognition,* ed. R. P. Kesner, D. S. Olton, pp. 237–92. Hillsdale, NJ: Erlbaum

Metzler, J. 1973. *Cognitive analogs of the rotation of three-dimensional objects*. PhD thesis, Stanford Univ.

Meyer, J. A., Wilson, S. W. 1991. *From Animals to Animats*. Cambridge, MA: MIT Press

Minsky, M., Pappert, S. 1969. *Perceptrons*. Cambridge, MA: MIT Press

Moore, P. W. B., Roitblat, H. L., Penner, R. H., Nachtigall, P. E. 1991. Recognizing successive dolphin echoes with an integrator gateway network. *Neural Networks*. In press

Neiworth, J. J. 1992. Cognitive aspects of movement estimation: a test of imagery in animals. In *Cognitive Aspects of Stimulus Control*, ed. W. K. Honig, G. Fetterman. Hillsdale. NJ: Lawrence Erlbaum Associates. In press

Neiworth, J. J., Rilling, M. E. 1987. A method for studying imagery in animals. *J. Exp. Psychol.: Anim. Behav. Proc.* 13:203–14

O'Keefe, J., Nadel, L. 1978. *The Hippocampus as a Cognitive Map*. Oxford: Clarendon Press

Oden, D. L., Thompson, R. K. R., Premack, D. 1988. Spontaneous transfer of matching by infant chimpanzees. *J. Exp. Psychol.: Anim. Behav. Proc.* 14:140–45

Owren, M. J. 1990a. Acoustic classification of alarm calls by vervet monkeys (*Cercopithecus aethiops*) and humans (*Homo sapiens*). I. Natural calls. *J. Comp. Psychol.* 104:20–28

Owren, M. J. 1990b. Acoustic classification of alarm calls by vervet monkeys (*Cercopithecus aethiops*) and humans (*Homo sapiens*). II. Synthetic calls. *J. Comp. Psychol.* 104:29–40

Pack, A. A., Herman, L. M., Roitblat, H. L. 1991. Generalization of visual matching and delayed matching by a California sea lion (*Zalophus Californianus*). *Anim. Learn. Behav.* 19:37–48

Paivio, A. 1986. *Mental Representations: A Dual Coding Approach*. NY: Oxford Univ. Press

Pepperberg, I. 1987. Acquisition of the same/different concept by an African Grey parrot (*Psittacus erithacus*): learning with respect to categories of color, shape, and material. *Anim. Learn. Behav.* 15:423–32

Peterson, G. B. 1984. How expectancies guide behavior. In *Animal Cognition,* ed. H. L. Roitblat, T. G. Bever, H. S. Terrace, pp. 135–47. Hillsdale, NJ: Erlbaum

Pisacreta, R., Lefave, P., Lesneski, T., Potter, C. 1985. Transfer of oddity learning in the pigeon. *Anim. Learn. Behav.* 13:403–14

Pisacreta, R., Redwood, E., Witt, K. 1984.

Transfer of matching-to-figure samples in the pigeon. *J. Exp. Anal. Behav.* 42:223–37

Posner, M. I., Keele, S. 1970. Retention of abstract ideas. *J. Exp. Psychol.* 83:304–8

Premack, D. 1983. The codes of man and beasts. *Behav. Brain Sci.* 6:125–67

Premack, D. 1983. Animal cognition. *Annu. Rev. Psychol.* 34:351–62

Pylyshyn, Z. W. 1981. The imagery debate: analogue media versus tacit knowledge. *Psychol. Rev.* 88:16–45

Pylyshyn, Z. W. 1984. *Computation and Cognition.* Cambridge, MA: MIT Press

Radtke, R. C., Grove, E. K., Talasi, U. 1982. PI in short-term and delayed recall. *J. Exp. Psychol.: Learn. Mem. Cogn.* 8:117–25

Reed, P., Chih-Ta, T., Aggleton, J. P., Rawlins, J. N. 1991. Primacy, recency, and the Von Restorff effect in rats' nonspatial recognition memory. *J. Exp. Psychol.: Anim. Behav. Proc.* 17:36–44

Rescorla, R. A. 1966. Predictability and number of pairings in Pavlovian fear conditioning. *Psychonom. Sci.* 4:383–84

Rescorla, R. A. 1968. Probability of shock in the presence and absence of CS in fear conditioning. *J. Comp. Physiol. Psychol.* 66:1–5

Rescorla, R. A., Solomon, R. L. 1967. Two process learning theory: relationship between Pavlovian and instrumental learning. *Psychol. Rev.* 88:151–82

Rescorla, R. A., Wagner, A. R. 1972. A theory of Pavlovian conditioning: variations in the effectiveness of reinforcement and nonreinforcement. In *Classical Conditioning II: Current Research and Theory,* ed. A. H. Black, W. F. Prokasy. pp. 64–99. NY: Appleton-Century-Crofts

Rilling, M. E., Neiworth, J. J. 1987. Theoretical and methodological considerations for the study of imagery in animals. *Learn. Motiv.* 18:57–79

Roitblat, H. L. 1980. Codes and coding processes in pigeon short-term memory. *Anim. Learn. Behav.* 8:341–51

Roitblat, H. L. 1982. The meaning of representation in animal memory. *Behav. Brain Sci.* 5:353–406

Roitblat, H. L. 1987a. *Introduction to Comparative Cognition.* NY: Freeman

Roitblat, H. L. 1987b. Metacomparative psychology. *Behav. Brain Sci.* 10:677–78

Roitblat, H. L., Bever, T. G., Harley, H. E., Helweg, D. A. 1991. Online choice and the representation of serially structured stimuli. *J. Exp. Psychol.: Anim. Behav. Proc.* 17:55–67

Roitblat, H. L., Herman, L. M., Nachtigall, P. E., eds. 1992. *Language and Communication: Comparative Perspectives.* Hillsdale, NJ: Lawrence Erlbaum Associates. In press

Roitblat, H. L., Moore, P. W. B., Nachtigall, P. E., Penner, R. H., Au, W. W. 1989. Dolphin echolocation: identification of returning echoes. In *Proceedings of the International Joint Conference on Neural Networks—89*, R. Hecht-Nielsen, Program Chair, pp. 295–300. Washington, DC: Inst. Electr. Electron. Eng.

Roitblat, H. L., Penner, R. H., Nachtigall, P. E. 1990. Matching-to-sample by an echolocating dolphin (*Tursiops truncatus*). *J. Exp. Psychol.: Anim. Behav. Proc.* 16:85–95

Rosch, E. H., Mervis, C. B. 1975. Family resemblances: studies in the internal structure of categories. *Cogn. Psychol.* 7:573–605

Rosenblatt, F. 1962. *Principles of Neurodynamics.* NY: Spartan Books

Ross, R. T., Holland, P. C. 1981. Conditioning of simultaneous and serial featurepositive discriminations. *Anim. Learn. Behav.* 9:293–303

Rumelhart, D. E., McClelland, J. L. 1986. *Parallel Distributed Processing: Explorations in the Microstructure of Cognition.* Vol. 1. *Foundations.* Cambridge, MA: MIT Press

Rumelhart, D. E., Hinton, G. E., Williams, R. J. 1986. Learning internal representations by error propagation. See McClelland & Rumelhart 1986, pp. 318–62

Rundus, D., Atkinson, R. C. 1970. Rehearsal processes in free recall: a procedure for direct observation. *J. Verb. Learn. Verb. Behav.* 9:99–105

Savage-Rumbaugh, E. S. 1986. *Ape Language: From Conditioned Response to Symbols.* NY: Columbia Univ. Press

Savage-Rumbaugh, E. S., Rumbaugh, D. M., Smith, S. T., Lawson, J. 1980. Reference: the linguistic essential. *Science* 210:922–25

Savage-Rumbaugh, S., Sevcik, R. A., Brakke, K. E., Rumbaugh, D. M., Greenfield, P. M. 1990. Symbols. Their communicative use, comprehension, and combination by bonobos (*Pan paniscus*). In *Advances in Infancy Research*, ed. C. Rovee-Collier, L. P. Lipsitt, 6:221–71. Norwood, NJ: Ablex

Schrier, A. M., Angarella, R., Povar, M. L. 1984. Studies of concept formation by stumptailed monkeys: concept humans, monkeys, and letter A. *J. Exp. Psychol.: Anim. Behav. Proc.* 4:564–84

Schrier, A. M., Brady, P. M. 1987. Categorization of natural stimuli by monkeys (*Macaca mulatta*): effects of stimulus set size and modification of exemplars. *J. Exp. Psychol.: Anim. Behav. Proc.* 13:136–43

Shepard, R. N., Metzler, J. 1971. Mental rotation of three-dimensional objects. *Science* 171:701–3

Sherry, D. F. 1985. Food storage by birds and mammals. *Adv. Stud. Behav.* 15:153–88

Sherry, D. F., Vaccarino, A. L. 1989. Hippocampal aspiration disrupts cache recovery in black-capped chickadees. *Behav. Neurosci.* 103:308–17

Sherry, D. F., Vaccarino, A. L., Buckenham, K., Herz, R. 1989. The hippocampal complex of food-storing birds. *Brain Behav. Evol.* 34:308–17

Shettleworth, S. J. 1990. Spatial memory in food-storing birds. *Philos. Trans. R. Soc. London Ser. B.* 329:45–53

Shrier, A. M., Brady, P. M. 1987. Categorization of natural stimuli by monkeys (*Macaca mulatto*): effects of stimulus set size and modification of exemplars. *J. Exp. Psychol.: Anim. Behav. Proc.* 13:136–43

Shyan, M. R., Wright, A., Cook, R., Jitsumori, M. 1987. Acquisition of the auditory same/different task in a rhesus monkey. *Bull. Psychonom. Soc.* 25:1–4

Skinner, B. F. 1984. The canonical papers of B. F. Skinner. *Behav. Brain Sci.* 7:473–764

Smolensky, P. 1988. On the proper treatment of connectionism. *Behav. Brain Sci.* 11:1–74

Stevens, T. A., Krebs, J. R. 1986. Retrieval of stored seeds by marsh tits *Parus palustris* in the field. *Ibis* 128:513–25

Terrace, H. S. 1991. Chunking during serial learning by a pigeon: I. Basic evidence. *J. Exp. Psychol.: Anim. Behav. Proc.* 17:81–93

Thomas, R. K., Noble, L. M. 1988. Visual and olfactory oddity learning in rats: What evidence is necessary to show conceptual behavior? *Anim. Learn. Behav.* 16:157–63

Thompson, R. K. R., Herman, L. M. 1977. Memory for lists of sounds by bottlenosed dolphins: convergence of memory processes with humans? *Science* 195:501–3

Trapold, M. A., Overmier, J. B. 1972. The second learning process in instrumental learning. See Rescorla & Wagner 1972, pp. 427–52

Urcuioli, P. J. 1990a. Some relationships between outcome expectancies and sample stimuli in pigeons' delayed matching. *Anim. Learn. Behav.* 18:302–14

Urcuioli, P. J. 1990b. Differential outcomes and many-to-one matching: effects of correlation with correct choice. *Anim. Learn. Behav.* 18:410–22

Urcuioli, P. J. 1991. Retardation and facilitation of matching acquisition by differential outcomes. *Anim. Learn. Behav.* 19:29–36

Urcuioli, P. J., Zentall, T. R. 1990. On the role of trial outcomes in delayed discrimination. *Anim. Learn. Behav.* 18:141–50

Vander Wall, S. B., Balda, R. P. 1977. Codaptation of the Clark's nutcracker and

710   ROITBLAT & VON FERSEN

the pinyon pine for efficient seed harvest
and dispersal. *Ecol. Monogr.* 47:89–111
von Fersen, L., Lea, S. E. G. 1990. Category
discrimination by pigeons using five
polymorphous features. *J. Exp. Anal. Behav.* 54:69–84
von Restorff, H. 1933. Über die Wirkung von
Bereichsbildungen im Spurenfeld [The
effect of organization in perceptual fields].
Psychol. Forsch. 18:299–342
Wallace, W. P. 1965. Review of the historical, empirical, and theoretical status of the
von Restorff phenomenon. *Psychol. Bull.*
63:410–25
Waltz, D. 1975. Understanding line drawings
of scenes with shadows. In *The Psychology
of Computer Vision,* ed. P. H. Winston, pp.
19–91. NY: McGraw Hill
Wasserman, E. A., Kiedinger, R. E., Bhatt,
R. S. 1988. Conceptual behavior in pigeons: categories, subcategories, and
pseudocategories. *J. Exp. Psychol.: Anim.
Behav. Proc.* 14:235–46
Wasserman, P. D. 1989. *Neural Computing:
Theory and Practice.* NY: Van Nostrand
Reinhold
Wasserman, P. D., Oetzel, R. M. 1990. *Neural Source: The Bibliographic Guide to
Artificial Neural Networks.* NY: Van Nostrand Reinhold
Weary, D. M. 1989. Categorical perception of
bird song: How do great tits (*Parus major*)
perceive temporal variation in their song? *J.
Comp. Psychol.* 103:320–25
Wickens, D. D. 1970. Encoding categories of
words: an empirical approach to meaning.
Psychol. Rev. 77:1–15
Wickens, D. D. 1973. Some characteristics of
word encoding. *Mem. Cogn.* 1:485–90
Wickens, D. D., Moody, M. J., Dow, R.
1981. The nature and timing of the retrieval
process and of interference effects. *J. Exp.
Psych: Gen.* 110:1–20
Wilkie, D. M., Willson, R. J., Kardal, S.
1989. Pigeons discriminate pictures of a
geographic location. *Anim. Learn. Behav.*
17:163–71
Williams, D. A., Butler, M. M., Overmier, J.
S. 1990. Expectancies of reinforcer location
and quality as cues for conditional discrimination in pigeons. *J. Exp. Psychol.:
Anim. Behav. Proc.* 16:3–13
Wilson, B., Mackintosh, N. J., Boakes, R. A.

1985a. Matching and oddity learning in the
pigeon: transfer effects and the absence of
relational learning. *Q. J. Exp. Psychol.*
37B:295–311
Wilson, B., Mackintosh, N. J., Boakes, R. A.
1985b. Transfer of relational rules in matching and oddity learning by pigeons and corvids. *Q. J. Exp. Psychol.* 37B:313–32
Wright, A. A. 1990. Markov choice processes
in simultaneous matching-to-sample at different levels of discriminability. *Anim.
Learn. Behav.* 18:277–86
Wright, A. A., Cook, R. G., Rivera, J. J.,
Sands, S. F., Delius, J. D. 1988a. Concept
learning by pigeons: matching-to-sample
with trial-unique video picture stimuli.
Anim. Learn. Behav. 16:436–44
Wright, A. A., Sands, S. F. 1981. A model of
detection and decision processes during
matching to sample by pigeons: performance with 88 different wavelengths in delayed and simultaneous matching tasks. *J.
Exp. Psychol.: Anim. Behav. Proc.* 7:191–
216
Wright, A. A., Shyan, M. R., Jitsumori, M.
1990. Auditory same/different concept
learning by monkeys. *Anim. Learn. Behav.*
18:287–94
Wright, A. A., Santiago, H. C., Sands, S. F.,
Kendrick, D. F., Cook, R. G. 1985. Memory processing of serial lists by pigeons,
monkeys, and people. *Science* 229:287–89
Yoshikubo, S. 1985. Species discrimination
and concept formation by rhesus monkeys
(*Macaca mulatta*). *Primates* 26:285–99
Younger, B. A., Cohen, L. B. 1985. How
infants form categories. *Psychol. Learn.
Motiv.* 19:211–47
Yuille, A. L. Ullman, S. 1990. Computational
theories of low-level vision. In *Visual
Cognition and Action: An Invitation to
Cognitive Science,* ed. D. N. Osherson, S.
M. Kosslyn, J. M. Hollerbach, pp. 5–39.
Cambridge, MA: MIT Press
Zadeh, L. 1971. Quantitative fuzzy semantics.
Info. Sci. 3:159–76
Zentall, T. R., Hogan, D. E., Edwards, C. A.
1984. Cognitive factors in conditional learning by pigeons. See Herrnstein 1984, pp.
389–408
Zornetzer, S. F., Davis, J. L., Lau, C. 1990.
*An Introduction to Neural and Electronic
Networks.* NY: Academic

Annu. Rev. Psychol. 1992. 43:711–42

ATTENTION

R. A. Kinchla

Department of Psychology, Princeton University, Princeton, New Jersey 08544-1010

KEY WORDS: visual search, priming, set-size effects, directing attention

CONTENTS

This is a selective review of attentional research, primarily that involving the detection or identification of visual targets. Such work is central to the study of attention and currently among the most active areas of attentional research. By restricting the review to this narrower focus it is possible to describe the studies in more detail, raise some critical questions about their interpretation, and point out their relation to earlier research. While the studies reviewed are primarily behavioral, a brief description of some important neurological work is also presented.

WHAT IS ATTENTION?

Although the term attention is often used as if its meaning were self-evident it has remained a remarkably elusive concept. There are overt forms of attending or orienting that can be studied directly, such as the way we shift our gaze to bring one object or another into view. There are also covert forms of attending, whereby we choose to listen to one voice or another among the babble of simultaneous voices at a party, or attend to different parts of a visual image without moving our eyes. The studies reviewed here are primarily concerned with overt forms of attending. I argue that the fundamental empirical bases for the concept of covert attention are the processing tradeoffs one often seems to make when simultaneously presented with multiple "sources" of information. By tradeoff I mean that better processing of one source seems to require poorer processing of another. The covert adjustments one makes to adopt a particular tradeoff I will term an *allocation of attention*. For example, the multiple sources of information might be the simultaneous voices at a party, or the individual letters in a tachistoscopically viewed letter matrix. Attempting to process ("attend to") a particular voice, letter, or row of letters, defines a particular allocation of attention.

It should be emphasized that the processing of simultaneously presented sources of information does not always reflect a need for processing tradeoffs. It sometimes seems possible to process sources simultaneously as well as they can be processed singly. In such cases the simultaneous processing is said to require less than one's "attentional capacity," or the processing of at least one source is said to "occur in parallel," "automatically," "pre-attentively," or "without needing attention."

In any case, the manner in which people process simultaneously presented sources of information, "shared allocation of attention," the degree to which they can process one source and ignore another, "focal allocation of attention," and the manner in which they shift from one allocation of attention to another, "attention switching," are all central to the study of attention.

PROCESSING TRADEOFFS AND SET-SIZE EFFECTS

In discussing experiments involving multiple sources of information it will be useful to denote n such sources by $S_1, S_2, \ldots, S_n$. In the simplest paradigm there may be only two sources, S_1 and S_2; $n = 2$—for example, two simultaneous voices or two positions in a visual display. In such cases it is possible to characterize a subject's processing options by what has been variously referred to as an *attention operating characteristic*, AOC (Kinchla 1969; Sperling & Melchner 1978), a *performance operating characteristic*, POC (Norman & Bobrow 1975) or, in a slightly different form, a *cost-benefit analysis*

(Posner & Boies 1971). The AOC form of representation is illustrated in Figure 1a, which shows three ways (I, II, III) in which a subject's ability to process each of two sources might be related. In some studies "processing" is assessed in terms of accuracy; in others, in terms of speed (the faster a subject can respond to information from a source, the better the processing). The open points in Figure 1a indicate the quality of processing when a subject is directed to "attend to S_1 only" (ordinate) or "to S_2 only" (abcissa), so called "focal attention" instructions. The solid points indicate how well each source is processed when the subject is instructed to "attend to both S_1 and S_2"—"divided" or "shared attention" instructions. Note that Curve I indicates that S_1 and S_2 can not be processed simultaneously as well as either can be processed alone, while Curve II indicates a similar but less severe cost of "sharing attention." Usually a subject can also be induced to perform at intermediate points if instructed to "pay attention to both sources, but more to one than the other." Curves I and II, then, are examples of the processing tradeoffs, AOC functions, which underlie the concept of attention. A subject can operate at any point along the function by adopting a particular allocation of attention, but improved processing of one source inevitably means poorer processing of the other.

In contrast, note Curve III in Figure 1a. Here there is no evidence of a processing tradeoff: The subject can process S_1 and S_2 at the same time (solid point) as well as either source alone (open points). As will be shown, such an absence of a processing tradeoff, plus the often involuntary nature of such processing, underlies the concept of "automatic" or "pre-attentional" processing.

A currently popular method of studying attentional processes uses visual search tasks in which subjects are asked to decide rapidly whether or not an n-element visual array contains a particular "target" element. In some cases response times increase with n, a so-called *set-size effect*, which is often interpreted as implying a serial (one-after-another) processing of the n elements—i.e. a successive "attending" to each element. In other cases response times are independent of n, which is often taken to imply parallel (simultaneous) processing. The relationship of such arguments to those based on AOC functions is illustrated in Figure 1b, which replots the same three sets of hypothetical data (I, II, and III) shown in Figure 1a. In Figure 1b the two "sources," S_1 and S_2, correspond to the elements in a two-element array that must be "searched" for the presence of a target, perhaps a left element and a right one. Here the data labeled I and II are said to indicate a "set-size effect": Subjects take longer to evaluate both elements for the presence of a target than when told to evaluate only one of the elements (e.g. "the left one only"). In contrast the data labeled III in Figure 1b indicate no set-size effect: A two element array can be "searched" for a target as rapidly as a single-element array. Thus processing tradeoffs and set-size effects are essentially similar.

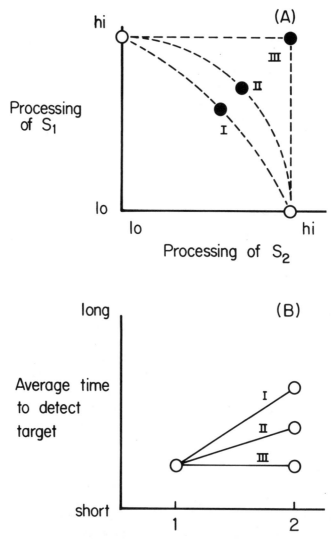

Figure 1   Three illustrative performances (I, II, III) represented in the form of (*a*) an attention operating characteristic and (*b*) reaction time as a function of set-size. Only performances I and II indicate an attentional or set-size effect. Performance III is often characterized as indicating "pre-attentive," "parallel," or "non-attentional" processing.

Their presence suggests an attentional process and their absence a "pre-attentional," "non-attentional," or "automatic" one. A major advantage of the representation shown in Figure 1b is that it can be used when *n* is greater than 2. However note that in Figure 1b response times are averaged across sources so the time to detect targets in specific sources (e.g. positions) is suppressed.

Before going on to consider research on visual search, it seems useful to show how a cost-benefit analysis (Posner & Boies 1971; Juola et al 1991) is simply another way of representing the processing tradeoffs revealed by AOC functions. Such an analysis is illustrated in Figure 2, which presents hypothetical data from a divided attention task, first in the form of an AOC function (Figure 2a) and then as a cost-benefit analysis (Figure 2b). These data are typical of those obtained in divided attention tasks where a subject monitors two sources of information (S_1 and S_2) for the occurrence of a target or signal (e.g. a brightness increment at one of two locations on a visual display), and where reaction time is the primary dependent variable. The three performances (data points) defining the AOC function in Figure 2a are the sort that can be obtained by varying the relative frequency of signals from each source. Specifically, suppose signals occurred at S_1 with probability P_1 or at S_2 with probability P_2, with $P_1 = 1 - P_2$. The three data points in Figure 2a are representative of those that might be obtained when P_1 equalled .8, .5, or .2. It is as if the subject processes S_1 more rapidly if signals are more likely at that source ($P_1 = .8$), processes S_1 and S_2 about equally well if they are equally likely to contain a signal ($P_1 = .5$), and processes S_2 faster if it is more likely to contain a signal ($P_1 = .2$). Naturally, error rates would have to be evaluated to insure these changes in mean reaction time reflected more than a "speed-accuracy tradeoff" (RT and error rates would have to be positively correlated).

Figure 2b shows how the same data might be represented as a cost-benefit analysis (how quickly the subject can respond following the occurrence of a signal). Here the value P_1 (.8, .5, or .2) is normally indicated by a cue prior to each test trial. The cue is said to be "valid" if a signal occurs at S_1 when $P_1 = .8$, or at S_2, when $P_1 = .2$, or "invalid" if the signal occurs at the less likely source. The cue is considered to be "neutral" when $P_1 = .5$. Figure 2a shows the average reaction time to signals given valid (V), invalid (I), and neutral (N) cues. Using the mean reaction time to signals with neutral cues as a reference point, one can define, the "gain" (reduced RT) when the cue is valid and the "cost" (increased RT) when the cue is invalid. If cues indicating which source is more likely to yield a signal produce *no cost or gain,* there is *no evidence of any attentional process* (just as with the data labeled III in Figure 1a and 1b).

It is argued here that the AOC/POC form of analysis is preferable to cost-benefit analysis on the following grounds. There is no reason to assume the neutral cue ($P_1 = .5$) actually produces an equal "allocation of attention," whereas the AOC representation allows one to assess this. The three data values in Figure 2b are the result of *averaging* responses to targets in S_1 and S_2 for valid, neutral, and invalid cues, whereas all six measures of the dependent variable are represented by the coordinates of the three data points in Figure 2a. And finally, the subject in a cost-benefit analysis is never given

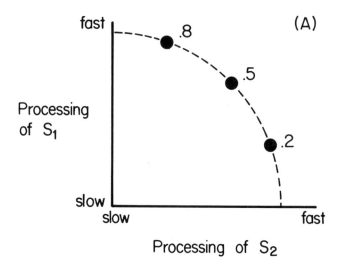

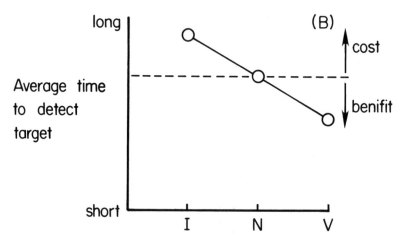

Figure 2 (*a*) An AOC function based on performance when targets occurred in S₁ with
probability .8, .5, or .2 as indicated on the graph. (*b*) The same data shown as a "cost-benefit
analysis" when cues were valid (V), invalid (I), or neutral (N). See the text for further discussion.

the opportunity to "attend" exclusively to either source as they did for the
AOC functions in Figure 1 (open points). In the cost-benefit analysis it is
often assumed that subjects always "attend" to the source that has the .8
probability of containing the signal. Yet much research on statistical "guessing games" (see Neimark & Estes 1967) suggest that subjects would actually
"match": attend primarily to the more likely source 80% of the time and to the

less likely 20%. This of course raises the question of whether subjects can actually "share attention" or must "switch" in an all-or-none fashion. In either case, directly comparing performances in focal and divided attention tasks seems necessary in order to assess the true "cost" of dividing attention. Finally "costs" and "benefits" are often compared directly as if they were linearly related to some underlying cognitive variable. Yet it seems clear that under extreme speed pressure it may be much harder for a subject to reduce reaction time than to increase it; e.g. 100 msec of "gain" should not be equated with 100 msec of "loss."

VISUAL SEARCH

Figure 3 shows some search data reported by Steinman (1987). Subjects had to search n-element arrays for a target element. Each "element" was formed by three parallel lines and could vary along the two dimensions illustrated in Figure 3a: separation, equally separated or not, and orientation, lines vertical or slightly tilted. Search times for various targets are shown in Figure 3b. If the target was defined by a value on one dimension (e.g. "tilted"), the median time to detect a target appeared to be independent of the set-size. However, if the target was defined by a conjunction of values on both dimensions (e.g. "tilted and equally separated"), and some of the nontargets included each of these values alone, there was a strong set-size effect.

The general pattern of results illustrated in Figure 3 has been reported by many investigators using a wide variety of stimuli—i.e. a set-size effect for targets defined by the conjunction of values on two dimensions, and none for targets defined by a value on one dimension. A highly influential explanation of these results has been advanced by Treisman and her associates (Treisman 1977, 1982, 1988, and Treisman & Sato 1990). Her *feature-integration theory* depicts the conjoining of features as a process that "requires attention." Thus searching an n-element array for a conjunction target requires a successive shifting of attention from one element to the next. This accounts (among other things) for the linear set-size effects often found with such targets: Equal increments in set size produce equal increments in response time. Furthermore, the slope of the search function for "detect" responses is often half that for nondetect responses, as if the search process was serial and self-terminating (so that, on average, only half the array elements need be searched to detect a target). In contrast, searching for a target defined by a value on only one dimension seems to involve a parallel ("pre-attentive") process, since there is no set-size effect (the search function is flat).

The idea that one perceives complex objects by "conjoining" separately processed sensory dimensions stems partially from the discovery of specialized neural "channels" (modules or subsystems) that appear to process specif-

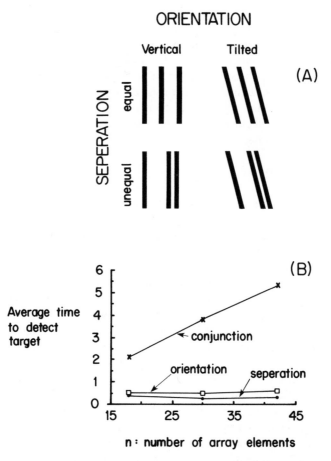

Figure 3 (*a*) The four types of stimuli defined by combinations of values on two dimensions. Each array contained *n* such stimuli. (*b*) Search times for targets defined by a value on one stimulus dimension (orientation or separation), or by a conjunction of values on both (e.g. tilted and equally separated). Data from Steinman (1987)

ic aspects of a visual stimulus, such as color, form, and motion (see Graham 1985; Livingston & Hubel 1987). Search for a target value on a single dimension might involve the output of only one such channel, while search for a conjunction target would involve the conjoining of outputs from two independent channels. This notion is also consistent with a finding by Gra-browecky & Treisman (see Treisman 1988:212–14) that the probability of detecting a conjunction can be predicted from the product of detecting the individual values.

Another aspect of Treisman's theory is her explanation of *conjunction errors,* the illusionary perception of improperly conjoined stimulus values—

e.g. "seeing" a red candle in a green holder as a green candle in a red holder. Such errors of visual perception have been demonstrated with a wide variety of stimuli and are most likely to arise with objects outside the region you are told to attend to, or when you are asked to "spread your attention over the entire visual field." It is as if accurate conjunctions require focal attention (Julesz 1986; Treisman & Gormican 1988; and Treisman & Paterson 1984).

Treisman's is not the only interpretation of set-size effects in visual search. It is true that a linear set-size effect can be interpreted as a serial process in which the evaluation of each additional element takes the same amount of time; but this does not rule out a parallel-processing interpretation—e.g. one in which each additional item is processed at the same time but at a lower rate, as if a limited resource were being divided among more elements. Classic papers on the difficult problem of distinguishing parallel and serial processes are those by Townsend (1971, 1976, 1990).

Another problem with interpreting set-size effects as implying a serial shifting of attention can be illustrated as follows: Suppose a subject viewed n briefly exposed letters, presented in slow succession at the rate of one letter per second, and then reported whether at least one of the letters had been a target letter F. Note that subjects can allocate all of their attention to viewing each letter, since the letters occur sequentially rather the simultaneously. Yet it has been shown that so long as each letter is presented briefly enough, the accuracy of the subjects' decisions diminishes as n increases—that is, there is a set-size effect on accuracy (Eriksen & Spencer 1969). A similar effect is obtained if a subject listens to n successively presented bursts of white noise and then reports whether at least one of them was accompanied by a weak tone signal (Kinchla 1969).

An explanation of these effects in terms of the "noise" or "confusability" contributed by each array element can be made in terms of the following integration model (this is a slightly simplified version of a model presented in Kinchla 1969, 1974):

1. Let each element S in an n-element array evoke a "subjective impression" X_i ($i = 1, 2, \ldots n$).
2. Let each X_i be a Gaussian random variable with variance σ^2, and an expected value of one if S_i is a target, or of zero if S_i is a nontarget.
3. Let the subject report a target if an "integrated impression" equal to $\Sigma\, X_i$ exceeds some response criterion C.

It can easily be shown these assumptions imply that a subject's ability to discriminate between arrays containing one target and those containing none can be characterized by the following "d-prime" measure (see Green & Swets 1966):

$$d' = 1/(n\ \sigma^2)^{1/2}$$

Note that discriminability, d', diminishes as the square-root of n increases, a set-size effect. This is due to the "noise" (σ^2) or "confusability" contributed by each display element, which tends to obscure the single target's contribution to the integrated impression, ΣX_i.

The point to be made here is that a simultaneous presentation of the n-elements in an array could produce the same set-size effect, even if there were no need to attend serially to each of the n-elements. This is why Kinchla (1969) and Shaw (1982) argued that *an "attentional" explanation is required only if the set-size effect on accuracy with simultaneous presentation exceeds that obtained with sequential presentation.* In fact Eriksen & Spencer (1969) found no difference in a subject's accuracy with (virtually) simultaneous or slow sequential presentation. Thus those data do not suggest any "attentional" problem in processing simultaneously presented arrays, only the same confusability problem encountered with sequentially presented arrays. Further evidence for this view is presented by Shiffrin & Gardner 1972.

It should be noted that the preceding model also predicts a *redundant targets effect* when more than one target appears in an array. Specifically, if an n-element array contains t targets $(t = 1, 2, \ldots n)$, a subject's ability to discriminate it from arrays containing no targets is given by:

$$d' = t/(n\ \sigma^2)^{1/2} \qquad\qquad 2.$$

Again, the improvement in discriminability with redundant targets is explained solely in terms the increased expected value of the integrated impression (ΣX_i), not to an increased likelihood of "attending" to a target.

These issues have also been dealt with in terms of reaction time in studies by Shaw (1978, 1982, 1984), van der Heijden et al (1984), and Ulrich & Giray (1986). Two general types of model have been studied—*race models* and *integration models*. The simple model we have just considered is a type of integration model, where information about each element is combined or integrated prior to any decision. In contrast, race models represent each element as being independently processed, with a positive search response made as soon as any element is identified as a target. To a large extent the effects of set size and redundant targets can be accounted for in terms of either type of model (see Bundesen 1990; Miller 1986; Shaw 1982). However, in some studies certain properties of the latency distribution have been inconsistent with the fully independent race model (see Miller 1982).

Such findings lead Mordkoff & Yantis (1992) to propose an "Interactive Race Model" that is somewhere between a fully independent race model and a conventional integration model. While elements are fully processed in separate channels, with an affirmative response made as soon as any channel detects a target, the channels are not completely independent. For example, if one channel identifies an element as a nontarget it can influence the process-ing in another channel. This is particularly important if the elements in an array are correlated, as they are in most visual search tasks. This can be illustrated by a search task involving two-element arrays. Suppose half the arrays contained one target, and the other half no targets, so that prior to a trial, each element in a randomly selected array had a one fourth probability of being a target. Note that as soon as one of the four elements was processed to a point where it was clearly a nontarget, the remaining element would then have a one third probability of being a target. Thus identifying one element as a nontarget contains information about the other element. It is primarily this correlational information that Mordkoff & Yantis propose the channels share, rather than a complete integration of impressions. They also assume that identification can activate common memory representations to produce in-teractions. This sort of model provides yet another way of interpreting set-size and redundant-target effects.

In addition to the preceding general considerations several other types of evidence raise questions about Treisman's original feature-integration theory in which set-size effects are interpreted as the product of serial shifts in attention.

There is evidence that certain multidimensional targets may have "emer-gent" or "higher-level" properties that also produce flat search functions ("allow one to search for them in parallel"). For example, Enns (1990) employed drawings of many three-dimensional cubes oriented in one direc-tion and asked subjects to search for a target cube oriented in a different direction (see Figure 4). The subjects yielded flat search functions and reported the target seemed to "pop out" of the display, easily discriminable from the differently oriented cubes. Similar results have been obtained with other relatively complex targets defined by the direction of lighting (Enns & Rensick 1990) or gradients of shading (Ramachandran 1988). Treisman & Paterson (1984) also obtained flat search functions when they had subjects search for a triangle among clusters of component lines and angles that were not joined. They concluded that the emergent Gestalt property of "closure" allowed the triangle to be searched for in parallel. However Treisman & Gormican (1988) were unable to produce flat search functions when they formed potentially emergent forms such as intersections and junctions formed by two straight lines.

Several investigators have found virtually flat search functions for a variety of conjunction targets so long as the values on each stimulus dimension were highly discriminable (McLeod et al 1988; Nakayama & Silverman 1986ab; Steinman 1987; Wolfe et al 1989). Phenomena of this sort led some in-vestigators to contrast feature and conjunction searches in terms of the discriminability of targets and distractors. It was pointed out that targets are

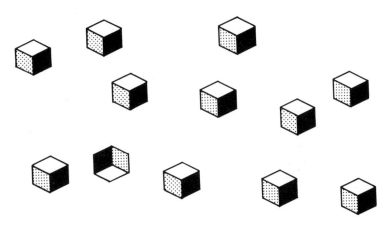

Figure 4   Enns (1990) obtained flat search functions for complex forms when targets were defined by their apparent three-dimensional orientation. They seemed to "pop out".

generally less discriminable when embedded in heterogeneous sets of distractors than they are in homogeneous sets (Duncan & Humphreys 1989; Humphreys & Riddoch 1989; Quinlan & Humphreys 1987). For example, the three rows of symbols in Figure 5 represent three arrays, each containing a target letter A flanked by two distractors. The top two arrays (rows) have homogeneous distractors (only one type), while the bottom array has heterogeneous distractors (more than one type). Note that the target in the top two arrays is distinguished from the distractors by a single "feature": the right diagonal component of the A in the top array, and the horizontal component in the middle array. However, neither "feature" alone is sufficient in the bottom array; only when both "features" are present (a "conjunction") can a viewer be sure the symbol is the target letter A. Thus increased heterogeneity among distractors may require more extensive processing to distinguish targets, since it may involve a search for conjunctions of features. Differences among distractors have also been termed "internal noise," while differences between distractors and the target have been termed "target salience." Thus serial search is necessary when internal noise is high and salience low (Wolfe and Cave 1990).

These findings have suggested alternatives to Treisman's original feature-integration theory. For example, Wolfe et al (1989), Cave & Wolfe (1990), and Wolfe et al (1990) proposed *guided-search* models similar to one proposed earlier by Hoffman (1978, 1979). These models depict a subject as guiding a conjunction search by (at least partially) limiting search to those elements that had one of the conjoined features. For example, a serial search for a red triangle among red circles, green circles, and green triangles, might

Figure 5   The three rows correspond to three arrays containing the target letter A flanked by distractors. In the top and middle array (row) the distractors are homogeneous, in the bottom row heterogeneous.

only evaluate red elements or triangular elements, thereby not wasting time on green circles. High discriminability of the values on each dimension should enhance the subject's ability to process selectively only values common to the target (see Duncan & Humphreys 1989; Humphreys & Riddoch 1989). Treisman & Sato (1990) have proposed a similar elaboration of Treisman's original feature-integration theory except that they emphasize a selective search based on an "inhibition" of irrelevant features rather than the "facilitation" of relevant ones suggested by Wolfe et al (1989, 1990). Nevertheless, the ideas are essentially the same: Search is limited to elements having at least one of the conjoined values.

Another complexity in evaluating feature-integration theory is that most visual-search studies employed large sets of elements (*n* greater than 10). However, Houch & Hoffman (1986) and Pashler (1987) studied visual search using arrays containing fewer than 8 elements. They found parallel set-size functions for positive and negative responses rather than the 2:1 ratio expected in a serial exhaustive search. Pashler felt his results suggested at least a partial parallel search of four or five elements at a time followed by a serial identification stage. Models of this sort have been developed by Pashler (1987) and Duncan & Humphreys (1989) and have proven successful in accounting for several aspects of search data.

Finally, extensive practice alters set-size effects. The data shown earlier in Figure 3 were obtained by Steinman (1987) after his subjects had practiced for only about 200 trials. The same subjects were then given extensive additional practice for about 10,000 trials. Gradually the set-size effect for conjunction targets disappeared and the search function became flat. It was as if with sufficient practice the search for a conjunction target became a parallel search process—i.e. as if the conjunction were eventually processed "pre-attentively," "without attention," or "automatically."

The circumstances under which extensive practice leads to perceptual automaticity have been systematically investigated by a number of psychologists (e.g. LaBerge 1975; Shiffrin & Schneider 1977; Schneider et al 1984; and Logan 1988). For example, Shiffrin & Schneider found that visual search for a target letter among distractors changes character with extensive practice, so long as the letter is always a target ("constant mapping"), rather than sometimes a target and sometimes a distractor ("varied mapping"). Not only does such extensive practice lead to a performance without any evidence of processing tradeoffs, but also the processing seems to occur almost involuntarily—that is, you perceive it whether you wish to or not. For example, as a highly practiced reader of English you are unable to look at the word "DOG" without rapidly activating or retrieving both phonetic and semantic knowledge consistently associated with the word (which would not be true if you had only learned to read Arabic).

DIRECTING COVERT VISUAL ATTENTION

While one has considerable flexibility in allocating or directing covert attention, there are limits. First of all there are limits to how precisely one can focus attention on specific sources to the total exclusion of others. Second, it takes time to shift from one allocation to another (switch attention). This section of the paper considers several representative lines of research bearing on these issues.

Focusing Visual Attention

Early in the study of attention it became clear that one could not always focus attention on one source to the exclusion of others. For example, while trying to listen exclusively to one of two voices in dichotic listening tasks, subjects often reported hearing highly familiar words such as their own names spoken by the "ignored" voice (Moray 1959). It was as if the processing of such highly familiar and normally relevant words was so automatic that they were processed involuntary, without attention.

Such failures of focal attention led some investigators to argue that selective (attentional) mechanisms operate much later in the perceptual process than simple "sensory filters" (e.g. Deutsch & Deutsch 1963; Treisman 1969). The idea is that selection operates on representations (e.g. semantic) activated relatively late in the perceptual process. The primary evidence for this late selection view are Stroop-like interference effects where one seems unable to ignore certain stimuli. For example, failures of focal attention have been demonstrated in visual letter-detection tasks where subjects sometimes seem unable to ignore letters adjacent to a target letter (Eriksen & Eriksen 1974; Eriksen & Schultz 1979). These adjacent "flanking" letters can reduce the time to respond to the target if they are associated with the same response, or lengthen response times if they are associated with a different response. Murphy & Eriksen (1987) found such interference occurred only if the flanking letters were within about a 1° visual angle of the target letter, so long as the subject knew exactly where the target would occur. If, on the other hand, the subject was uncertain about target location, interference from flankers up to 2–3° from the target could occur. This led Eriksen to liken attention to the field of a "zoom-lens": To monitor a wide area the lens widens its field, leading to flanker effects; but when a target can occur in only one place, the lens zooms in on that location, largely eliminating flanker effects. Recently Yantis & Johnston (1990) developed procedures that seem optimally to cue subjects concerning target position and virtually eliminate flanker effects. LaBerge et al (1991) developed another procedure for eliminating flanker effects. They presented a digit at the target location just before the target and flankers were presented. Subjects were to respond to the target only if the preceding digit was a seven. As recognition of the digit was made more difficult (by shortening its duration from 250 to 50 ms) flanker effects gradually disappeared (as if the increased difficulty of processing the digit prevented processing of the flankers). The preceding results are consistent with the recent proposals of Lavie & Tsal (unpublished), who argue that early selection (effective focal attention) occurs only if the processing load is sufficiently high to preclude the incidental processing of irrelevant stimuli. Furthermore, the relevant stimuli must be clearly discriminable from irrelevant stimuli. They present a series of experiments in which perceptual load and discriminability influenced the success of focal attention as their theory would predict.

Thus under certain conditions it seems attention can be allocated to a small region, with little processing of some stimulus events outside that region. It also seems clear that one can allocate attention over a wider area, perhaps the whole visual field (Eriksen 1990). If visual attention is like a spotlight (Posner 1980), that spotlight has a variable diameter (see Eriksen & St. James 1986, 1989; Eriksen & Yeh 1985; LaBerge & Brown 1986, 1989). Other aspects of the spotlight metaphor must also be clarified. For example, it has been argued that sensitivity to stimuli seems to fall off slowly at the edge of the area attended to—a gradient of attention (Eriksen & St. James 1986; Downing & Pinker 1985). Also, while the previously cited studies indicate one can eliminate flanker effects under certain circumstances, other sorts of peripheral stimuli, such as motion or a brief flash, seem to command attention auto-matically (Miller 1989; Kröse & Julesz 1990; Müller & Rabbit 1989; Tipper et al 1990).

Switching Attention

The most widely used method for inducing a shift in visual attention is to pre-cue a subject concerning the likely location of a subsequent target. If the time between cue and target is sufficiently short, subjects don't have time to move their eyes, and any enhancement of processing at the target location can be attributed to a covert shift in attention induced by the cue (assuming that any general alerting or warning effect of the cue is assessed by occasionally presenting a positionally neutral version of the cue as a control condition; see Remington & Pierce 1984). After over 20 years of research on the effect of pre-cuing, Eriksen (1990) concluded that an enhancement of processing at the cued location (a reduction in response time, or an increase in accuracy) begins within 50 msec of a cue and continues to grow until it reaches asymptote about 200 msec after the cue—i.e. there doesn't appear to be an abrupt, all-or-none switching but instead a gradual buildup of "attention" at the cued location, which reaches a peak after about 200 msec. In terms of the spotlight metaphor, it is as if the spotlight went off at one point and then gradually came on again at the target location. This can be contrasted with a con-tinuously illuminated spotlight that illuminates intervening points while mov-ing in analog fashion from one point in the visual field to another. Data that seemed to support the analog view had been presented much earlier by Shulman et al (1979) and Tsal (1983). However, rather telling critiques of the earlier interpretations of those data have recently been presented by Yantis (1988) and Eriksen (1990). Furthermore, a study by Eriksen & Webb (1989) failed to show a relation between time to shift attention and distance between elements to be attended.

The idea that it takes time to switch or shift one's allocation of attention goes back at least to the beginning of experimental psychology and the so called "complication clock experiment" in which subjects tried to report where a moving clock hand was positioned when a bell sounded. Subjects tended to report the hand as further along than it really was. This phenomenon was attributed to the time it took to "switch attention" from "listening for the bell" to "seeing the clock." Sperling & Reeves (1980) employed a more sophisticated but conceptionally similar approach to measuring attention switching. Their subjects fixated on a stream of successively superimposed digits while attending to an adjacent stream of letters. When a subject detected a target letter C in the letter stream she was to switch her attention im-mediately to the fixated digit stream and report the first digit she saw. Subjects typically reported a digit that occurred 300–400 msec after the target, independently of the rate at which the digits were presented. Note that this

"attention reaction time" ostensibly includes the time to recognize the target letter, as well as the time to switch attention, and the two are hard to separate.
More recently, Weichselgartner & Sperling (1987) employed a variant of this task. Subjects fixated on a digit stream until they saw a square appear around a digit. They were then to report the digit within the square, as well as the subsequent three digits. Based on both subjects' subjective statements and the bimodal nature of the digits reported, the authors identified two processes: an automatic process consisting of a rapid, effortless, "first glimpse" of the digit within the square; and a controlled process producing a slower, effortful, "second glimpse" of digits occurring more than 200 or 300 msec after the square.

The idea that both automatic and controlled processes mediate shifts in attention is suggested by other research as well. As noted earlier, visually pre-cuing a subject to direct attention to particular parts of a visual array produces substantial shifts of attention within as little as 50 msec of cue onset (see Eriksen 1990). However, some cues seem to induce shifts of attention more rapidly than others, the most effective being cues at or near locations to which attention is to be directed. Cues such as a centrally located number indicating that attention should be shifted to a specific peripheral region induce much slower shifts (see Yantis & Jonides 1990).

This and other evidence has led a number of investigators to postulate two types of attention shifts. For example, Mackeben & Nakayama (1987; see also Nakayama & Mackeben 1989) argued that there are both sustained and transient components of visual attention. The sustained component is maintained through effortful control and is shifted more slowly than the transient component, which is automatically evoked by the cue. Müller & Rabbitt (1989) told subjects to allocate visual attention on the basis of a centrally located arrow and to ignore briefly brightened squares that occasionally came on prior to the test stimulus. In spite of these instructions subjects revealed an increased sensitivity to targets presented within a brightened square. The experimenters concluded that attention allocation based on the fixated arrow was a controlled process while that evoked by the peripheral squares was essentially an automatic capture of attention. Kröse & Julesz (1990) similarly concluded that visual cues presented in the same position as a subsequent target produce a fast, automatic, "bottom-up" control of attention that can be distinguished from a slower, voluntary, "top-down" mode of control.

DISTINGUISHING ALLOCATION AND DECISION-MAKING

Faster responding to targets at pre-cued locations doesn't necessarily imply enhanced information processing. Faster responding may reflect more liberal decision-making. Shaw (1984) in fact concluded that pre-cuing effects in luminance detection reflected only changes in decision criteria (see also Sperling & Dosher 1986). However, Shaw did find evidence of an "attentional" (quality of processing) effect in letter identification. One problem with this distinction should be noted. If luminance increments are more likely to occur at pre-cued locations, the cue carries information concerning the appropriate response ("increment"/"no increment"). In contrast, the cue in a letter identification task need not carry the same sort of information. For example, suppose a subject were asked to decide whether a briefly presented letter was an F or a K. A pre-cue could indicate the most likely location for the letter to occur without indicating anything about which letter is more likely. Thus the difference between luminance detection and letter identification may be confounded with the difference in correlation between location and response. Furthermore, even if a cue doesn't indicate which response is more likely, it can indicate which areas of an array should be given more weight when the decision process involves a weighted integration of impressions (Kinchla 1980).

In the last few years several studies have been designed to separately assess the effects of pre-cues on "decision-making" and "quality of processing" (Downing 1988; Müller & Findlay 1987; and Müller & Humphreys 1991). Each used an approach based on Signal Detection Theory (Green & Swets 1966) whereby shifts in decision-making are indicated by estimates of β, the decision criterion, and shifts in the quality of processing by d', the sensitivity measure.

Downing (1988) had subjects maintain central fixation while monitoring a circular array of 12 small squares in which targets could occur. Each trial began with either an arrow cue indicating a specific square or a circle cue indicating all 12 squares. A stimulus pattern was then presented consisting of targets shown at from 0–4 of the square locations. Four locations were then successively indicated by a probe stimulus. During each probe the subject used a four-valued rating scale to indicate how confident he was that a target had just occurred in the probed location. If a location was pre-cued with an arrow, a target occurred in it with probability .8, and the position was always probed. Otherwise all the probed locations were selected quasi-randomly on each trial, and a target occurred in each with probability .5. The nature of these targets depended on the task. In a luminance-detection task the target was a luminance increment and nontargets no change in luminance. In three discrimination tasks targets were either a luminance increment, a vertical line, or two perpendicular lines, while the nontargets were, respectively, a luminance decrement, a horizontal line, or two parallel lines. Downing found enhanced processing (larger d' estimates) at the arrow-cued location in all four tasks, with progressively poorer processing at other probed locations as their distance from the cued location increased. Subjects were also more liberal in reporting targets (lower d') at the cued location. While it is not clear how powerful her tests were, Downing found no evidence of an order of report effect, nor any dependence among the four responses on each trial.

While Downing's study is impressive, it does involve a rather complex paradigm in which subjects must retain information about the sensory events evoked at many locations until the end of the probe sequence. One could argue that subjects might immediately code the sensory event at an arrow-cued location into one of the rating responses, since that location was always probed, then code the information in the other locations less carefully into a less precise code. A similar proposal was made by Duncan & Humphreys (1989), except they suggest that it is simply the order of encoding from a rapidly decaying iconic store that determines the information lost from each location. In any case, if sensory information were differentially lost during these initial encodings, rather than during the probe sequence, Downing's test for order of report would not reveal it. Such an encoding enhancement of d' at the pre-cued location would not reflect a difference in the initial quality of information, but simply a differential encoding of sensory information be-cause of the need to retain it during the long probe sequence. (Downing acknowledges this possibility but asserts it would simply be another aspect of attention.) Finally, since there were so many (12) locations to monitor, subjects might mistakenly attribute a strong sensory impression of a target to the wrong location, thereby inflating estimates of false-alarm rates.

In an attempt to avoid some of these issues Hawkins et al (1990) conducted a similar study using a simplified detection paradigm. Their subjects moni-tored four locations for the occurrence of a target (a luminance increment). Each trial began with a pre-cue indicating one of the four locations, or all four. (This pre-cue occurred either near fixation or near the cued locations.) Following the pre-cue a target occurred at one of the four locations or at none of them. This was followed by a half-second mask and finally a single probe indicating that the subject should rate his confidence that a target had been presented in the probed location. If a single location was pre-cued it was probed with probability .76, otherwise one of the other locations was equally likely (.8) to be probed. If all four locations had been pre-cued, each was equally likely (.25) to be the one probed. In all cases, a target was presented in the probed location with probability .5. As in the Downing study, the results were seen as indicating an enhanced quality of processing (d') at the cued location (for both central and peripheral cuing).

While this study involved a simpler paradigm than Downing's, it too required subjects to retain sensory information from four locations until a probe is presented (after the half-second mask). Thus here again subjects might more carefully or quickly encode the sensory information evoked at the single pre-cued location, since it was most likely to be probed. There are also significant correlations among pre-cued, probed, and target locations. For example, when only one location was pre-cued it had a .76 × .05, or .34 probability of containing a target on that trial, and each of the other three locations a probability of $(1 - .76) × .33 × .5$, or .04. However as soon as a location was probed it had a .5 probability of having contained a target. These complex correlations among events at the four locations are a form of redundancy that the subject might use in determining a response.

Recently Juola et al (1991) conducted a series of experiments designed to evaluate variants of the "attentional spotlight" idea. Their subjects viewed briefly presented (150 msec) arrays of 12 letters arranged such that four letters fell within each of three concentric rings—an inner ring, a middle ring, and an outer ring (none of the letters was at a more than 3-degree visual angle from a central fixation point). On each test trial 11 of the 12 letters were distractor Xs while the other target letter was either an L or an R. The subjects' task was to identify this target letter. Of principle interest was the effect of pre-cuing the subject concerning which ring was most likely to contain the target with the cue valid on 80% of the trials. The results indicated subjects were both faster and more accurate in identifying targets in the cued ring.

Juola and his colleagues used these data to evaluate three models: one considering attention as analogous to a variable-diameter spotlight (the "zoom lens" model); one in which attention was likened to a narrowly focused spotlight that serially scanned the letters; and one in which attention could be allocated to any one of the three rings. They concluded that this later model provided the best account of the data; e.g. attention could be allocated in an O-shaped pattern to include only the outer, or the middle, ring.

The problem with this conclusion is that Joula et al only consider models in which the "quality" of information processing differed in the cued and non-cued regions. They failed to consider models in which the cue effects were mediated solely by decision processes. For example, suppose the quality of processing was the same in cued and noncued regions but *the subject simply give more weight or credence to the information extracted from the cued region*. On a particular trial, he might be fairly sure he saw an L in the outer ring, and also feel he saw a K in the middle ring. He might resolve these conflicting impressions by giving more weight to his impression of the outer ring if it had been cued on that trial. Since the cues were valid on 80% of the trials, this *weighted integration of information* could account for the faster and more accurate responses to targets in cued regions and there wouldn't be a simple speed-accuracy trade-off. Note that this interpretation could be tested experimentally by presenting cues after the letter array but before the re- sponse. A similar pattern of results would support the view that the cues influenced decision-making rather than the initial processing of visual in- formation. Unfortunately this was not done in the Juola et al study, so their data are inconclusive. A more extensive and formal development of the weighted-integration idea applied to the detection of target letters in multi-letter displays is presented in Kinchla (1977).

EXPECTANCY AND PRIMING AS ATTENTIONAL PROCESSES

Much of the work we have considered to this point has involved cuing a subject about where a stimulus is most likely to occur. Enhanced processing at that location and poorer processing at other locations have been interpreted as being due to a spatial allocation of attention. Similar processing tradeoffs can be produced by cuing a subject about the type of stimulus most likely to occur, rather than about where it will occur. This procedure often leads to enhanced processing of the anticipated stimulus and poorer processing of less likely stimuli. Such a processing tradeoff is often interpreted in terms of the subject's "preparation" or "set." This view goes back at least to William James, who wrote:

> The effort to attend . . . consists in nothing more nor less than the effort to form as clear an IDEA as is possible of what is there portrayed. The idea is to come to the help of the sensation and make it more distinct (James 1904:239).

Pre-cuing the "idea" of the stimulus facilitated its subsequent recognition, a process James referred to as "preperception."

More specific theories of how one prepares to process specific stimuli have been developed to account for data from choice–reaction time studies. For example, Falmange & Theios (1969) developed a model in which subjects processed a test stimulus by sequentially comparing it to a "stack" of stimuli held in memory. Cuing a subject to anticipate a particular stimulus caused it to be placed near the top of the stack. This sort of preparation produced faster responses to likely stimuli and slower ones to unlikely stimuli. There are also many other ways of explaining the effects of a priori stimulus probabilities in choice–reaction time tasks, including shifts in decision criteria and muscle preparation for a particular response (see Luce 1986 for a review of such theories). However, there do seem to be tasks in which the subject actually prepares to process a particular type of stimulus. For example, Figure 6 presents four stimulus patterns composed of Xs and Os, which are susceptible to alternative figure-ground organization. The top two patterns define the large letters L and H if the Os are seen as "figure" against a "ground" of Xs, while seeing the same large letters requires the opposite organization in the lower two patterns. Leading a subject to anticipate one type of organization speeds recognition of large letters defined in that fashion and slows recognition when the less likely organization is required. The fact that this tradeoff in

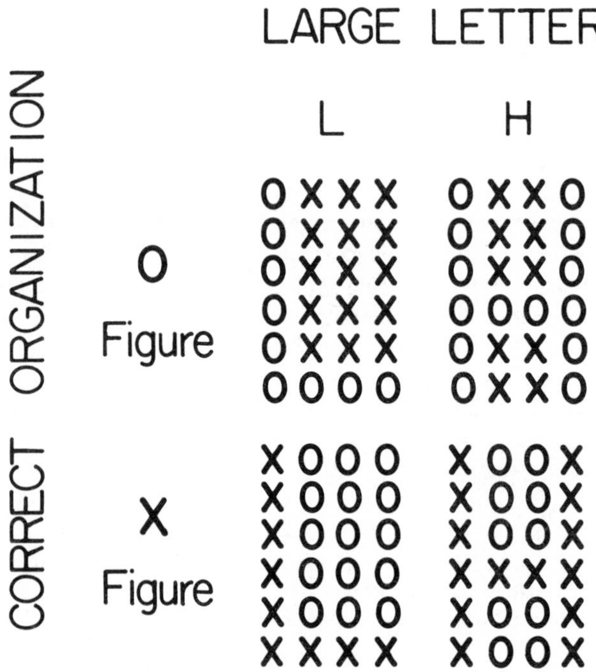

LARGE LETTER

ORGANIZATION

CORRECT

		L	H
	O Figure	O X X X O X X X O X X X O X X X O X X X O O O O	O X X O O X X O O X X O O O O O O X X O O X X O
	X Figure	X O O O X O O O X O O O X O O O X O O O X X X X	X O O X X O O X X O O X X X X X X O O X X O O X

Figure 6   Four stimulus patterns employed by Kinchla (1974) susceptible to alternate figure-ground organization: Xs as figure and Os as ground (top two patterns), or vice versa (bottom two). If subjects are prepared to make the correct organization they identify the large letter about one half second faster than if they are prepared to make the wrong organisation.

reaction time is linear is consistent with a mixture of fast responses when the subject's initial organization is correct and slow responses when it isn't (Kinchla 1974).

Certain ideas about "filters" that enhance processing of relevant stimuli and inhibit processing of irrelevant ones can be interpreted as preparation for specific types of stimuli (rather than a spatial allocation of attention). It is also possible to view such effects as an allocation of attention to specific channels or sensory modalities. For example, Shulman & Wilson (1987) had subjects view large letters made up of smaller ones. Their detection of high-frequency gratings was enhanced while the subjects tried to identify the smaller letters, and their detection of low-frequency gratings was enhanced while they tried to identify the larger one. It was as if they could alternatively "filter" or enhance high or low spatial frequency channels, much as one might attend to high- or low-frequency components of a sound (see Green & Swets 1966).

Viewing the matter in the broadest way one could argue that the recent priming or activation of any sort of knowledge makes it more accessible and therefore more influential in processing new stimuli. This knowledge becomes James's "preperceptive idea," which enhances the processing of related stimuli. In recent years a number of studies have shown how a prior stimulus ("prime") can enhance the processing of subsequent stimuli—for example, speeding such processes as lexical decision-making or completing fragments of words and pictures (see Richardson-Klavehn & Bjork 1988 for a review of such work). Thus either explicitly cuing a subject to expect a particular type of stimulus or implicitly priming related knowledge may lead to enhanced processing of the expected or primed class of stimuli; the processing of unexpected or unprimed classes is slower. In fact there is even evidence of a sort of negative priming. Tipper & Driver (1988) presented subjects with a series of overlapping red and green forms, with instructions to identify forms of one color while ignoring those of the other color. They found that if a specific form was the to-be-ignored color on one trial and the to-be-identified color on the next trial, the identification response was slowed. It was as if the form's appearance in the to-be-ignored color had produced a sort of negative priming, an inhibition of the form's identification on the next trial. It would thus seem that preparation based on expectancy or priming is another form of attending; it involves processing tradeoffs that enhance the processing of some stimuli while reducing that of others.

NEUROLOGICAL STUDIES OF ATTENTION

While an extensive review of neurological studies of attention is beyond the scope of this paper it seems useful to mention some of the more promising lines of research.

Basically there are four major pathways for visual information. Two of these, the geniculostriate and tectopulvinar pathways, carry visual information from the eye to visual areas in the occipital lobe of the cortex. From these areas information is carried to other visual areas in the parietal lobe via a dorsal or occipitoparietal pathway, and to the temporal lobe via a ventral or occipitotemporal pathway. Visual areas in the temporal lobe seem to be primarily engaged in processing spatial location and movement, and those in the temporal lobe with pattern recognition and color. (These functional differences can to some degree be traced all the way back to the retina in terms of the types of retinal ganglion cells, magnocells, and parvocells, feeding into the higher systems.) The dorsal and ventral cortical "pathways" are actually composed of many different visual areas with many reciprocal interconnections. The organization of these areas seems to be hierarchical, as evidenced by the progressive latency of evoked neuronal responses and the progressively larger receptive fields (for reviews of these neural systems see DeYoe & Van Essen 1988; Desimone & Ungerleider 1989; and Maunsell & Newsome 1987).

Following the seminal work of Wurtz & Albano (1980) many studies have focused on what might be termed the cognitive aspects of stimulus-evoked activity in the visual system; they have shown that such neural activity depends on more than the physical properties of the evoking stimulus. For example, light-evoked (event-related) potentials in visual cortex are larger if the subject is pre-cued to expect a stimulus at the location where it occurred, rather than some other location (Hillyard & Hansen 1986).

Cognitive aspects of receptive fields have also been identified. Moran & Desimone (1985) trained monkeys to respond to one or the other of two visual stimuli within the receptive field of a cell in visual area V4. The currently relevant stimulus was indicated by a cue. If this currently relevant stimulus had not previously been effective in evoking a response while the other stimulus had, the response occurred as before. However, if the relevant stimulus had not previously evoked a response while the other stimulus had, the cell's response was highly attenuated (even though the previously effective but nonrelevant stimulus was present in the cell's original receptive field). It was as if the cell's receptive field had contracted to include only the relevant stimulus. This relevance effect occurred only when both stimuli fell within the cell's original receptive field. If one of the stimuli fell outside the field, relevance had no effect on the cell's response. While these effects were not found in V1 or V2 cells, similar results were obtained with cells in the monkey's inferior temporal cortex, although the receptive fields of these cells were so large that both stimuli were always within the field. Moran & Desimone interpreted their results as reflecting an "attentional" process beginning in V4 that contracted a receptive field around the "attended to" (relevant) stimulus whenever two or more stimuli fell within the cell's original field (with a finer spatial tuning of this process in V4 cells than in inferior temporal cells).

Just as the sizes of receptive fields have been shown to contract about critical stimuli, tuning curves for both color- and orientation-sensitive cells in V4 have been shown to contract or sharpen when an animal's task requires a finer discrimination of those dimensions. It is as if the animal is "attending more closely" to that dimension (Spitzer et al 1988; Spitzer & Richmond 1990).

While the contraction of receptive fields and the sharpening of tuning curves would seem to serve a selective or "attentional" function, where does the control of such processes reside? A number of investigators have concluded that the pulvinar nucleus of the thalamus serves such a function (e.g. Crick 1984; LaBerge & Buchsbaum 1990; and Posner & Petersen 1990). It seems a likely candidate because it has reciprocal connections with areas throughout the occipitotemporal system (Ungerleider et al 1983), and patients with pulvinar lesions exhibit deficits in directing visual attention (Rafal & Posner 1987). The pulvinar nucleus also exhibits increased blood flow in PET scans when subjects are asked to ignore a particular stimulus, as if it were engaged in filtering out that stimulus. (LaBerge & Buchsbaum 1990).

Desimone et al (1991) examined the role of the pulvinar nucleus by first training a monkey to respond on the basis of one visual stimulus while ignoring a second stimulus in the opposite visual field. They then chemically disabled the monkey's lateral pulvinar nucleus and found the monkey had great difficulty in ignoring a distractor in the affected (contralateral) field when the target was located in the other (normal) field. However, only when there was a competing stimulus present did deactivation of the pulvinar nucleus produce performance deficits. Thus Desimone et al concluded that the deactivated nucleus interfered with the same sort of attentional gating they had observed in inferior temporal cells whenever two stimuli were presented simultaneously.

Other cortical areas involved in oculomotor control have, not surprisingly, been implicated in the control of covert spatial attention (attending without eye movements). These include, in addition to the pulvinar nucleus, the posterior parietal cortex and the superior colliculus. (See Goldberg & Colby 1989 for a review of this work.) Some of the evidence implicating these areas is clinical. Posner & Petersen (1990) assert that while patients with damage to any of these show deficits in shifting visual attention there are subtle differences among these deficits. Damage to the posterior parietal lobe reduces the patient's ability to disengage from an existing focus of attention so as to shift that focus to a position opposite to the side of the lesion. In contrast, lesions to the superior colliculus show shifts whether or not attention was initially focused. Thalamic (pulvinar) lesions seem to reduce the patient's ability to maintain focused attention. It is as if "The parietal lobe first disengages attention from its present focus, then the midbrain area acts to move the index of attention to the area of the target, and the pulvinar is involved with reading out data from the indexed locations" (Posner & Petersen 1990:28).

Other areas in the associative cortex undoubtedly serve selective or attentional functions that are slowly being revealed by PET studies of blood flow during various cognitive tasks (see LaBerge & Buchsbaum 1990; Posner & Petersen 1990; Petersen et al 1988)—for example, the type of cognitive task discussed earlier, in which a word can prime or activate semantic knowledge that then facilitates or enhances the subsequent processing of semantically related words.

DISCUSSION

Discoveries in neuroscience are at last identifying neural systems that underlie attentional processes studied at the behavioral level. In a much earlier review of work on attention I argued that "Attention should not be thought of as a single entity. It seems more useful to assume that a variety of cognitive mechanisms mediate selectivity in information processing" (Kinchla 1980:214). More recently, in his excellent review of work on attention in the *Annual Review of Neuroscience,* Posner concluded that research "suggests to us a possible hierarchy of attention systems,. . .. [It] involves the operation of a separate set of neural areas whose interaction with domain specific systems (e.g. visual word form or semantic association) is the proper subject for empirical investigation" (Posner & Petersen 1990:34, 39).

Neural centers in the tectum and hypothalamus seem to modulate specific components of incoming sensory information, providing the sort of filtering of irrelevant information and enhancement of relevant information that theories based or purely behavioral evidence have long suggested. These effects are apparent in the cognitive aspects of cortical receptive fields described earlier (e.g. Desimone et al 1991; Spitzer & Richmond 1990). Other attentional centers involved in higher-order modes of selection such as semantic priming are being identified through altered patterns of cerebral blood flow during various cognitive tasks (e.g. LaBerge & Buchsbaum 1990; Posner & Petersen 1990).

This review has dealt primarily with behavioral research, especially that on visual search, and the directing of visual attention. A number of general comments may be made about each.

Visual Search

Some search studies attempt to limit the role of overt eye movements by using tachistoscopic presentation or instructing subjects to hold their eyes still (e.g. Enns & Rensink 1992); other studies place no constraints on eye movements (e.g. Treisman & Sato 1990). Most of the data supporting Treisman's feature-integration theory or its alternatives were collected with no constraints on eye movements. Since these studies often involved response times as long as 1 or 2 sec, subjects had ample time to make several eye movements. Little research has been done on the role of such eye movements. This is surprising because questions about the "serial" versus "parallel" nature of the search process are ubiquitous in the literature. If, for example, perceiving the details or colors defining a target required direct fixation (foveal processing), the search process would necessarily be serial as the subject shifted fixation from one array element to the next. Even if the situation were less extreme so that target processing were simply enhanced on the fovea, the interplay of overt and covert shifts of attention should be complex. It seems particularly relevant to assess the degree to which foveation facilitates the processing of targets, or to use smaller stimulus arrays that can be presented so briefly that eye movements can't occur.

In most of the search literature reaction time is the most frequently used independent variable. Subjects are normally requested to "respond as rapidly as possible while avoiding errors" (Cavanagh et al 1990). A problem with this strategy is that it leads subjects to perform at a point on the speed/accuracy–tradeoff function where small shifts in error rates (e.g. 1%–2%) may be associated with large shifts in mean reaction time (see Luce 1986). Such small shifts in error rates are unlikely to be statistically significant given the typical amount of data collected in these studies. Thus experimenters often conclude that shifts in mean reaction times are not due to speed/accuracy tradeoffs if the independent variable has no significant effect on error. This is clearly inappropriate since one doesn't prove the null-hypothesis; nonsignificance simply means there is insufficient evidence to reject it. It would seem useful actually to trace out some of the speed/accuracy functions for search paradigms of this sort (see Luce 1986).

Other questions regarding visual search were raised earlier in the paper: Are small arrays ($n < 8$) searched in the same way as larger ones (see Pashler 1987)? Can extensive practice gradually flatten search functions (see Steinman 1987)?

Directing Attention

The balance of evidence at this point seems to support the idea that subjects can rapidly switch attention on the basis of a pre-cue so as to enhance the processing of stimuli at the cued location. Analyses of data from several studies using the signal detection measures d' and β has supported this view: The cues apparently influenced both d' and β. Nevertheless, the studies involve complex paradigms in which subjects are required to maintain considerable sensory information until a response is called for or probed. Thus critics can question whether the sensory information initially available at the cued location was actually enhanced, or whether it was preferentially encoded into a form better suited for retention until the probe.

It should also be noted that the apparently separate assessment of "sensitivity" by d' and of "response criterion" by β may be misleading. For example, it is conventional to treat β as constant during a long series of detection trials. Suppose it were actually a Gaussian random variable. Then the conventional measure of β would be an estimate of its expected value, and its variance would influence d'. In other words, variability in a subject's decision criterion (a parameter of the decision process) would be represented in d', the sensitivity measure (see Green & Swets 1966). If pre-cuing a location could evoke a more stable (less variable) decision criterion for that location it would have the same effect on d' as reducing sensory "noise." Thus interpretation of

738 KINCHLA

pre-cue effects as influencing "sensory" versus "decision-making" processes requires caution.

Evidence is also accumulating that there are at least two forms of attention: cuing: a rapid, to some degree involuntary, automatic, switching; and a slower, more controlled form of switching. Cues such as sudden light onsets or motion near the cued location seem most likely to induce the automatic form of attention switching.

Another type of attention switching would seem to be involved in the "preparation" one sometimes seems to make to enhance the processing of a particular type of stimulus. For example, suppose you were asked to process rapidly the type of patterns shown in Figure 6. Before the pattern was presented you might alternatively be prepared to organize the Xs as "figure" and the Os as "ground," or vice versa. Data I have collected (R. Kinchla, unpublished observations) indicates that something like this occurs, and that it takes about one half a second to switch from one form of preparation to the other.

"Priming" a subject so as to "activate" certain knowledge in memory (make it more accessible or salient) seems to enhance the subject's ability to process related stimuli (compared to other, nonprimed stimuli). Thus priming seems to be a way of allocating attention. If one could assess the time required to "deactivate" or "unprime" knowledge and prime or activate other knowledge it would represent the time required to switch to another form of attention. In fact, it may be a special case of the rather lengthy and difficult process whereby one switches from performing one type of complex cognitive task (calculating on your income tax) to another (writing a poem). There is clearly a considerable startup period during which knowledge required to work on each task is progressively "primed" or "activated." This is why it is much more efficient to work on one task for a long time, or to completion, than it is to switch back and forth between two tasks.

In conclusion, then, it appears there are many mechanisms that mediate selectivity in human cognition, ranging from systems that alter the early flow of sensory input to higher-order associative processes that prime or activate knowledge and thereby enhance subsequent processing.

Literature Cited

Bundesen, C. 1990. A theory of visual attention. *Psychol. Rev.* 97:523–47

Cavanagh, P., Arguin, M., Treisman, A. 1990. Effect of surface medium on visual search for orientation and size features. *J. Exp. Psychol.: Hum. Percept. Perform.* 3:479–91

Cave, K. R., Wolfe, J. M. 1990. Modeling the role of parallel processing in visual search. *Cogn. Psychol.* 22:225–71

Crick, F. 1984. The function of the thalamic reticular complex: the searchlight hypothesis. *Proc. Natl. Acad. Sci. USA* 81:4586–90

Desimone, R., Ungerleider, L. G. 1989. Neural mechanisms of visual processing in monkeys. In *Handbook of Neuropsychology*, ed. F. Boller, J. Grafman, 2:267–99. Amsterdam: Elsevier

Desimone, R., Wessinger, M., Thomas, L., Schneider, W. 1991. Attentional control of visual perception: cortical and subcortical mechanisms. *Cold Spring Harbor Symp. Quant. Biol.* 55:963–71

Deutsch, J. A., Deutsch, D. 1963. Attention: some theoretical considerations. *Psychol. Rev.* 70:80–90

DeYoe, E. A., Van Essen, D. C. 1988. Concurrent processing streams in monkey visual cortex. *Trends Neurosci.* 11:219–26

Downing, C. G. 1988. Expectancy and visual spatial attention: effects on perceptual quality. *J. Exp. Psychol.: Hum. Percept. Perform.* 14:188–202

Downing, C. G., Pinker, S. 1985. The spatial structure of visual attention. In *Mechanisms of Attention: Attention and Performance* ed. M. I. Posner, O. S. Marin, 11:171–87. Hillsdale, NJ: Erlbaum

Duncan, J., Humphreys, G. W. 1989. Visual search and stimulus similarity. *Psychol. Rev.* 96:433–58

Enns, J. T. 1990. Three-dimensional features that pop out in visual search. In *Visual Search,* ed. D. Brogan. London: Taylor Francis

Enns, J. T., Rensink, R. A. 1992. Sensitivity to three-dimensional orientation in visual search. *Psychol. Sci.* 5:323–26

Enns, J. T., Rensink, R. A. 1990. Influence of scene-based properties on visual search. *Science* 247:721–23

Eriksen, C. W. 1990. Attentional search of the visual field. See Enns 1990. pp. 221–40

Eriksen, B. A., Eriksen, C. W. 1974. Effects of noise letters upon the identification of a target letter in a nonsearch task. *Percept. Psychophys.* 1:143–49

Eriksen, C. W., Schultz, D. W. 1979. Information processing in visual search: a continuous flow conception and experimental results. *Percept. Psychophys.* 25:249–63

Eriksen, C. W., Spencer, T. 1969. Rate of information processing in visual perception: some results and methodological considerations. *J. Exp. Psychol. Monogr.* 79(2)

Eriksen, C. W., St. James, J. D. 1986. Visual attention within and around the field of focal attention: a zoom lens model. *Percept. Psychophys.* 40:225–40

Eriksen, C. W., Webb, J. 1989. Shifting of attentional focus within and about a visual display. *Percept. Psychophys.* 42:60–68

Eriksen, C. W., Yeh, Y. Y. 1985. Allocation of attention in the visual field. *J. Exp. Psychol.: Hum. Percept. Perform.* 11:583–97

Falmagne, J. C., Theios, J. 1969. On attention and memory in reaction time experiments. *Acta Psychol.* 30:316–23

Goldberg, M. E., Colby, C. L. 1989. The neurophysiology of spatial vision. In *Handbook of Neuropsychology,* ed. F. Boller, J. Grafman, 2:267–99. Amsterdam: Elsevier

Graham, N. 1985. Detection and identification of near-threshold visual patterns. *Opt. Soc. Am.* 2:1468–82

Green, D. M., Swets, J. A. 1966. *Signal Detection Theory and Psychophysics.* NY: Wiley

Hawkins, H. L., Hillyard, S. A., Luck, S. J., Mouloua, M., Downing, C. G., Woodward, D. P. 1990. Visual attention modulates signal detection. *J. Exp. Psychol.: Hum. Percept. Perform.* 16:802–11

Hillyard, S. A., Hansen, J. C. 1986. Attention: electrophysiological approaches. *Psychophysiol.: Syst., Process., Appl.* 11:227–43

Hoffman, J. E. 1978. Search through a sequentially presented visual display. *Percept. Psychophys.* 23:1–11

Hoffman, J. E. 1979. A two-stage model of visual search. *Percept. Psychophys.* 25: 319–27

Houck, M. R., Hoffman, J. E. 1986. Conjunction of color and form without attention: evidence from an orientation-contingent color aftereffect. *J. Exp. Psychol.: Hum. Percept. Perform.* 12:186–99

Humphreys, G. W., Riddoch, M. 1989. Grouping processes in visual search: effects with single- and combined-feature targets. *J. Exp. Psychol.: Gen.* 118(3):258–79

James, W. 1904. *Psychology.* NY: Henry Holt & Co.

Juola, J. F., Bouwhuis, D. G., Cooper, E. E., Warner, C. B. 1991. Control of attention around the fovea. *J. Exp. Psychol.: Hum. Percept. Perform.* 17(1):125–41

Julesz, B. 1986. Texton gradients: the texton theory revisited. *Biol. Cybernet.* 54:464–69

Kinchla, R. A. 1969. An attention operating characteristic in vision. Tech. Rept., No. 29, Dept. Psychol., McMaster Univ., Hamilton, Ontario

Kinchla, R. A. 1974. Detecting target elements in multi-element arrays: a confusability model. *Percept. Psychophys.* 15:149–58

Kinchla, R. A. 1977. The role of structural redundancy in the perception of visual targets. *Percept. Psychophys.* 22(1):19–30

Kinchla, R. A. 1980. The measurement of attention. In *Attention and Performance,* ed. R. S. Nikerson, Vol. 8. Hillsdale, NJ: Erlbaum

Kinchla, R. A., Solis-Macias, V., Hoffman, J. 1983. Attending to different levels of structure in a visual image. *Percept. Psychophys.* 33:1–10

Kröse, B. J. A., Julesz, B. 1990. Automatic or voluntary allocation of attention in a visual search task. See Enns 1990, pp. 321–30

LaBerge, D. 1975. Acquisition of automatic processing in perceptual and associative learning. In *Attention and Performance,* ed. P. M. A. Rabbitt, S. Dornic, Vol. 5. London: Academic

740   KINCHLA

LaBerge, D., Brown, V. 1986. Variations in size of the visual field in which targets are presented: an attentional range effect. *Percept. Psychophys.* 8:188–200

LaBerge, D., Brown, V. 1989. Theory of attentional operations in shape identification. *Psychol. Rev.* 96:101–24

LaBerge, D., Brown, V., Carter, M., Bash, D., Hartley, A. 1991. Reducing the effects of adjacent distractors by narrowing attention. *J. Exp. Psychol.: Hum. Percept. Perform.* 17:90–95

LaBerge, D., Buchsbaum, M. S. 1990. Positron emission tomographic measurements of pulvinar activity during an attention task. *J. Neurosci.* 10:613–19

Livingstone, M. S., Hubel, D. H. 1987. Psychological evidence for separate channels for the perception of form, color, movement and depth. *J. Neurosci.* 7:3416–68

Logan, G. D. 1988. Toward an instance theory of automatization. *Psychol. Rev.* 95:492–527

Luce, R. D. 1986. *Reaction Times.* NY: Oxford Univ. Press

Mackeben, M., Nakayama, K. 1987. Sustained and transient aspects of extra-foveal visual attention. Presented at Assoc. Res. Vis. Ophthalmol., May

Maunsell, J. H. R., Newsome, W. T. 1987. Visual processing in monkey extrastriate cortex. *Annu. Rev. Neurosci.* 10:363–401

McLeod, P., Driver, J., Crisp, J. 1988. Visual search for a conjunction of movement and form is parallel. *Nature* 332:154–55

Miller, J. 1982. Divided attention: evidence for coactivation with redundant signals. *Cogn. Psychol.* 14:247–79

Miller, J. 1986. Timecourse of coactivation in bimodal divided attention. *Percept. Psychophys.* 40:331–43

Miller, J. 1989. The control of attention by abrupt visual onsets and offsets. *Percept. Psychophys.* 45:567–71

Moran, J., Desimone, R. 1985. Selective attention gates visual processing in the extrastriate cortex. *Science* 229:782–84

Moray, N. 1959. Attention in dichotic listening: affective cues and the influence of instructions. *Q. J. Exp. Psychol.* 11:56–60

Mordkoff, J. T., Yantis, S. 1992. An interactive race model of divided attention. *J. Exp. Psychol.: Hum. Percept. Perform.* In press

Müller, H. J., Findlay, J. M. 1987. Sensitivity and criterion effects in the spatial cuing of visual attention. *Percept. Psychophys.* 42:383–99

Müller, H. J., Humphreys, G. W. 1991. Luminance-increment detection: capacity limited or no? *J. Exp. Psychol.: Hum. Percept. Perform.* 17–1:107–24

Müller, H. J., Rabbitt, P. M. 1989. Reflexive and voluntary orienting of visual attention: time course of activation and resistance to interruption. *J. Exp. Psychol.: Hum. Percept. Perform.* 15:315–30

Murphy, T. D., Eriksen, C. W. 1987. Temporal changes in the distribution of attention in the visual field in response to precues. *Percept. Psychophys.* 42:576–86

Nakayama, K., Mackeben, M. 1989. Sustained and transient components of focal visual attention. *Vis. Res.* 29:1631–47

Nakayama, K., Silverman, G. H. 1986a. Serial and parallel processing of visual feature conjunctions. *Nature* 320:264–65

Nakayama, K., Silverman, G. H. 1986b. Serial and parallel encoding of visual feature conjunctions. *Invest. Ophthalmol. Visual Sci.* 27(Suppl. 182):128–31)

Neimark, E. D., Estes, W.K. *1967. Stimulus Sampling Theory.* San Francisco: Holden-Day

Norman, D. A., Bobrow, D. G. 1975. On data-limited and resource-limited processes. *Cogn. Psychol.* 7:44–64

Pashler, H. 1987. Detecting conjunctions of color and form: reassessing the serial search hypothesis. *Percept. Psychophys.* 41:191–201

Peterson, S. E., Fox, P. T., Miezin, F. M., Raichle, M. E. 1988. Modulation of cortical visual responses by direction of spatial attention measured by PET. *Assoc. Res. Vis. Ophthalmol. Abstr.*, p. 22

Posner, M. I. 1980. Orienting of attention. *Q. J. Exp. Psychol.* 32:3–25

Posner, M. I., Boies, S. J. 1971. Components of attention. *Psychol. Rev.* 78:391–408

Posner, M. I., Petersen, S. E. 1990. The attention system of the human brain. *Annu. Rev. Neurosci.* 13:25–42

Quinlan, P. T., Humphreys, G. W. 1987. Visual search for targets defined by combinations of color, shape and size: an examination of the task constraints on feature and conjunction searches. *Percept. Psychophys.* 41:455–72

Rafal, R. D., Posner, M. I. 1987. Deficits in human visual spatial attention following thalamic lesions. *Proc. Natl. Acad. Sci. USA* 84:7349–53

Ramachandran, V. 1988. Perceiving shape from shading. *Sci. Am.* 259:76–83

Remington, R., Pierce, L. 1984. Moving attention: evidence for time-invariant shifts of visual selective attention. *Percept. Psychophys.* 35:393–99

Richardson-Klavehn, A., Bjork, R. A. 1988. Measures of memory *Annu. Rev. Psychol.* 39:475–543

Schneider, W., Dumas, S. T., Shiffrin, R. M. 1984. Automatic and control processing and attention. In *Varieties of Attention,* ed. R.

Parasuraman, D. R. Davies, pp. 1–27. NY: Academic

Shaw, M. L. 1978. A capacity allocation model for reaction time. *J. Exp. Psychol.: Hum. Percept. Perform.* 4:586–98

Shaw, M. L. 1982. Attending to multiple sources of information: I. The integration of information in decision making. *Cogn. Psychol.* 14:353–409

Shaw, M. L. 1984. Division of attention among spatial location: a fundamental difference between detection of letters and detection of luminance increments. In *Attention and Performance,* ed. H. Bouma, D. G. Bouwhuis, Vol. 10. Hillsdale, NJ: Erlbaum

Shiffrin, R. M. 1988. Attention. In *Stevens' Handbook of Experimental Psychology,* ed. R. C. Atkinson, R. J. Herrnstein, G. Lindzey, and R. D. Luce. New York: Wiley and Sons. 2nd ed.

Shiffrin, R. M., Gardner, G. T. 1972. Visual processing capacity and attentional control. *J. Exp. Psychol.* 93:72–83

Shiffrin, R. M., Schneider, W. 1977. Controlled and automatic human information processing. II. Perceptual learning, automatic attending, and a general theory. *Psychol. Rev.* 84:127–90

Shulman, G. L., Remington, R., McLean, J. P. 1979. Moving attention through visual space. *J. Exp. Psychol.: Hum. Percept. Perform.* 5:522–26

Shulman, G. L., Wilson, J. 1987. Spatial frequency and selective attention to local and global structure. *Perception* 16:89–101

Sperling, G., Dosher, B. A. 1986. Strategy and optimization in human information processing. In *Handbook of Perception and Performance,* ed. K. Boff, L. Kaufman, J. Thomas, 1:2.1–2.65. NY: Wiley

Sperling, G., Melchner, M. J. 1978. The attention operating characteristic: examples from visual search. *Science* 202:315–18

Sperling, G., Reeves, A. 1980. Measuring the reaction time of a shift of visual attention. *Attention Perform.* 8:347–60

Spitzer, H., Desimone, R., Moran, J. 1988. Increased attention enhances both behavioral and neuronal performance. *Science* 240:338–40

Spitzer, H., Richmond, B. J. 1990. Task difficulty: ignoring, attending to, and discriminating a visual stimulus yield progressively more activity in inferior temporal neurons. *Exp. Brain Res.* 38:120–31

Steinman, S. B. 1987. Serial and parallel search in pattern vision. *Perception* 16:389–98

Tipper, S., Brehaut, J., Driver, J. 1990. Selection of moving and static objects for the control of spatially directed action. *J.*

Exp. Psychol.: Hum. Percept. Perform. 16:492–504

Tipper, S. P., Driver, J. 1988. Negative priming between pictures and words in a selective attention task: evidence for semantic processing of ignore stimuli. *Mem. Cogn.* 16:64–70

Townsend, J. T. 1971. A note on the identification of parallel and serial processes. *Percept. Psychophys.* 10:161–63

Townsend, J. T. 1976. Serial and within-stage independent parallel model equivalence on the minimum completion time. *J. Math. Psychol.* 14:219–39

Townsend, J. T. 1990. Serial vs. parallel processing: Sometimes they look like Tweedledum and Tweedledee but they can (and should) be distinguished. *Psychol. Sci.* 1:46–54

Treisman, A. 1969. Strategies and models of selective attention. *Psychol. Rev.* 76:282–99

Treisman, A. 1977. Focused attention in the perception and retrieval of multidimensional stimuli. *Percept. Psychophys.* 22:1–11

Treisman, A. 1982. Perceptual grouping and attention in visual search for features and for objects. *J. Exp. Psychol.: Hum. Percept. Perform.* 8:194–214

Treisman, A. 1988. Features and objects: the Fourteenth Bartlett Memorial Lecture. *Q. J. Exp. Psychol.* 40A:201–37

Treisman, A., Gormican, S. 1988. Feature analysis in early vision: evidence from search asymmetries. *Psychol. Rev.* 95:15–48

Treisman, A., Paterson, R. 1984. Emergent features, attention and object perception. *J. Exp. Psychol.: Hum. Percept. Perform.* 10:12–31

Treisman, A., Sato, S. 1990. Conjunction search revisited. *J. Exp. Psychol.: Hum. Percept. Perform.* 16:459–78

Tsal, Y. 1983. Movements of attention across the visual field. *J. Exp. Psychol.: Hum. Percept. Perform.* 9:523–30

Ulrich, R., Giray, M. 1986. Separate-activation models with variable base times: testability and checking of cross-channel dependency. *Percept. Psychophys.* 39:248–54

Ungerleider, L. G., Gattass, R., Sousa, A. P. A., Mishkin, P. 1983. Projections of area V2 in the macaque. *Soc. Neurosci. Abstr.* 9, p. 152

van der Heijden, A. H. C., Schreuder, R., Maris, L., Neerincx, M. 1984. Some evidence for correlated separate activations in a simple letter-detection task. *Percept. Psychophys.* 36:577–85

Weichselgartner, E., Sperling, G. 1987. Dynamics of automatic and controlled visual attention. *Science* 238:778–80

Wolfe, J. M., Cave, K. R., Franzel, S. L.

1989. Guided search: an alternative to the modified feature integration model for visual search. *J. Exp. Psychol.: Hum. Percept. Perform.* 15:419–33

Wolfe, J. M., Cave, K. R. 1990. Deploying visual: the guided search model. In *AI and the Eye*, ed. A. Blake, T. Troscianko. New York: Wiley and Sons

Wolfe, J. M., Yu, K. P., Stewart, M. I., Shorter, A. D., Stacia, R., Cave, K. R. 1990. Limitations on the parallel guidance of visual search: color × color and orientation × orientation conjunctions. *J. Exp. Psychol: Hum. Percept. Perform.* 16: 869–92

Wurtz, R. H., Albano, J. E. 1980. Visualmotor function of the primate superior colliculus. *Annu. Rev. Neurosci.* 3:189–226

Yantis, S. 1988. On analog movements of visual attention. *Percept. Psychophys.* 43: 203–6

Yantis, S., Johnston, J. C., 1990. On the locus of visual selection: evidence from focused attention tasks. *J. Exp. Psychol.: Hum. Percept. Perform.* 16:135–49

Yantis, S., Jonides, J. 1990. Abrupt visual onsets and selective attention: voluntary versus automatic allocation. *J. Exp. Psychol.: Hum. Percept. Perform.* 16:121–34

AUTHOR INDEX

746   AUTHOR INDEX

Claes, R., 514, 515
Clancey, W. J., 607
Clark, D. A., 249
Clark, D. M., 244, 248, 249
Clark, H. H., 155
Clark, K. E., 428
Clark, L. A., 181, 187, 236, 237, 261, 327, 479
Clark, M. B., 428
Clark, M. S., 66
Clark, N. B., 453
Clark, R. C., 405, 406
Clark, S. E., 36, 208, 215, 216, 219, 226-28
Clark, W. C., 269
Clarke, J. C., 256
Clayton, P. J., 320
Clerebaut, N., 513
Cleveland, J. N., 407, 408
Cliff, N., 26, 175, 180
Clipp, E. C., 490
Cloninger, C. R., 327
Clore, G. L., 57, 59, 60, 65
Clough, E. E., 363
Clum, G. A., 257
Cluydts, R., 513
Cobb, J., 252
Codol, J. P., 512
Cody, M. J., 134, 143
Coetsier, P., 514, 515
Coffey, H. S., 485
Coggin, T. D., 652
Cohen, A. S., 248, 249, 251
Cohen, B. L., 97
Cohen, D., 392, 570
Cohen, D. J., 385, 417, 419
Cohen, E. G., 613
Cohen, J., 609
Cohen, L. B., 344, 692
Cohen, N. J., 213
Cohen, P. A., 608
Cohen, S., 73, 295
Cohen, S. A., 635, 655
Cohen, S. P., 561, 570
Cohn, J. F., 73
Colberg, M., 632
Colby, C. L., 735
Cole, A. J., 178
Cole, C. A., 115
Cole, D. A., 423, 424
Cole, M., 588, 606
Coleman, L. M., 156
Coley, J. D., 357
Colle, L. M., 457
Collier, T. J., 447
Collins, A., 57, 59, 60, 588, 605-7
Collins, L. M., 175
Collins, R. L., 143
Collman, P., 362, 363
Colombo, M., 693, 696
Coltrane, S., 290, 292
Colvin, C. R., 494, 495

Colwill, R. M., 678-80
Combs, B., 289
Condelli, L., 290
Conger, R., 71
Conley, M., 543, 546
Conlon, D. E., 562, 565, 567, 568
Conn, S. R., 478
Connell, J. P., 56, 62, 63
Connelly, S., 608
Conner, H. S., 447
Content, A., 511
Converse, S. A., 431, 432
Conway, M. A., 67, 76
Cook, D. A., 291
Cook, M., 246, 652
Cook, R. G., 451, 684, 694, 697
Cook, S. W., 293
Cook, T. D., 423
Cook, W. D., 187
Cooke, N. J., 402, 404, 405
Cooke, N. M., 174, 183, 402
Cooley, C. H., 135
Cooley, T. F., 284
Cooney, J. B., 597
Cooper, E. E., 715, 730
Cooper, M. C., 181, 188
Cooper, N. A., 257
Coopersmith, R., 381-84, 386-88
Coovert, M. D., 660
Coppi, R., 171, 180, 187
Corbett, D., 455
Cordell, L. H., 156
Corkin, S., 458
Cornell, D. P., 139
Corno, L., 590, 601, 602
Cornwell, C. A., 381
Corpet, F., 182
Correa, A., 386
Corter, C. M., 61, 63
Corter, J. E., 39, 178
Corveleyn, J., 514
Costa, P. T., 69
Costa, P. T. Jr., 474, 475, 477, 479, 480, 489
Costanzo, M., 284, 285, 290
Costanzo, M. A., 291, 293
Costermans, J., 510
Cottam, G. L., 237
Cottrill, K. L., 454
Couch, S. R., 294, 295
Coulombe, D., 449
Coupey, E., 101, 113
Couvillon, P. A., 675
Coward, W. M., 630, 647, 652
Cox, A. D., 106
Cox, D. R., 175
Coxon, A. P. M., 176, 189
Coyette, F., 513
Coyne, J. C., 73

Craik, K. H., 10, 11, 479, 488, 496, 497
Crandall, C. S., 105
Cranny, C. J., 400
Cranshaw, S. F.
Craske, M. G., 246, 248, 249, 253-55
Crawley, B., 636
Crawley, E., 184
Crews, R., 281
Creyer, E. H., 113, 115
Crick, F., 734
Crisp, J., 721
Critchley, F., 174, 176, 181, 186
Critchlow, D. E., 187
Crits-Christoph, P., 76
Crocker, J., 160, 547, 557
Croeders, M. E., 452
Crombez, G., 514
Cronbach, L. J., 416, 494, 585, 591, 611, 614, 634
Cronshaw, S. F., 641, 652, 660
Crosby, L. A., 280, 287
Cross, D., 344
Cross, D. R., 404, 417, 584
Croul, C. E., 454
Crow, T. J., 311, 312, 332
Crowell, J. A., 62
Cruikshank, J., 561
Crum, R., 97
Crutcher, M. D., 461
Crutcher, R. J., 424
Crutchfield, R. S., 5
Cruz, C. J., 452
Cubiciotti D. D. III, 381
Cucumel, G., 180
Cudeck, R., 599
Cudeck, R. A., 175
Cullington, A., 251, 252
Cullver, C., 69
Cummings, E. M., 62, 74
Cummings, R. G., 121
Cunha, D. A., 539
Cunitz, A. R., 684
Cunningham, J. P., 30
Cunningham, J. W., 655
Curbow, B., 290
Curio, E., 697
Curley, S. P., 110
Curran, L. T., 631, 646
Curtis, G. C., 253, 254
Cuthbert, B. N., 57
Cutler, B. L., 147
Czaja, S. J., 557, 570
Czekanowski, J., 175

D

Dachler, H. P., 660
Dahl, H., 76
Dahlström, A., 455
Dahlström, A. C., 455

K

Kadlec, H., 43, 44
Kagel, J., 534
Kahan, J. P., 544
Kahle, L. R., 282, 284, 294
Kahlehzan, B. M., 485
Kahleifeh, B., 594
Kahn, B. E., 110
Kahneman, D., 90, 94, 95, 97, 99, 100, 103, 104, 108, 109, 113, 120-22, 289, 414, 554, 555, 568
Kail, R., 339
Kaiser, M. K., 347, 348
Kakihara, C., 160
Kakkar, P., 97
Kalish, C. W., 368
Kalish, H. I., 459
Kalisky, Z., 446
Kallgren, C. A., 284
Kam, R., 452
Kameda, M., 162, 163
Kamensky, V., 173
Kamil, A. C., 690, 691
Kamlet, M. S., 97
Kamp, J. D., 638, 639
Kandel, E. R., 674
Kanerva, P., 210, 221
Kanfer, F. H., 406
Kanfer, R., 405, 414, 432, 599
Kaniel, S., 593
Kannappan, S., 30
Kantola, S. J., 290
Kaplan, C. A., 115
Kaplan, J. N., 381
Kaplan, K., 62, 72
Kaplan, L. B., 657
Kaplan, R. E., 429, 430
Kaplan, S., 284
Kapp, B. S., 447
Karambayya, R., 561
Kardal, S., 690
Kargbo, D., 363
Kargon, R., 596
Karmiloff-Smith, A., 338
Karnas, G., 514
Karren, R. K., 422, 432
Kasamatsu, T., 383
Kasperson, R. E., 270
Kaspi, S. P., 75, 241
Kasvikis, Y., 260
Kates, R. W., 269, 272
Katon, W., 261
Katz, J. A., 636
Katz, L., 185
Katz, R., 328
Katz, T., 569
Katzev, R. D., 274, 282, 291, 294
Kauer, J. S., 386
Kaufman, C. M., 139
Kaufmann, C. A., 304

Kavanagh, L., 63
Kawai, Y., 452
Kaye, H., 379, 381
Kaye, K., 6
Kayser, E., 538
Kazak, A. E., 5
Keane, T. M., 257, 258
Keashly, L., 562
Keating, M., 557, 570
Kedar, H., 645
Keeble, S., 344
Keefe, J. W., 599
Keele, S., 702
Keenan, P. A., 541, 556, 557, 560, 569
Keeney, R. L., 119, 121, 290
Kegley, C. W. Jr., 563
Kehoe, E. J., 677
Keiffer, M., 537, 546
Keil, F. C., 351, 357, 359, 362, 363, 368
Keinan, G., 114
Keith, J. G., 284
Kelleher, D., 429
Keller, K. L., 98
Keller, L. R., 89, 119
Kellerman, H., 60
Kelley, A. E., 455, 459
KELLEY, H. H., 1-23; 4, 11, 537, 538, 543, 544, 546, 547, 549, 551, 559, 567
Kelly, A. E., 604
Kelly, G. A., 496
Kelly, J. B., 563
Kelly, P. J., 363
Kelman, H. C., 561, 570
Keltner, J., 562
Kemery, E. R., 629
Kemper, T. D., 56
Kempton, W., 278, 284, 290, 293
Kendall, P. C., 236
Kendell, R. E., 313
Kendler, K. S., 310, 313, 327
Kendrick, D. F., 684
Kennedy, C. R., 256, 257
Kennedy, D. A., 385
Kenny, J. T., 382
Kenrick, D. T., 474
Keren, G., 109
Kerpel, L., 569
Kerr, C., 562
Kerr, N. L., 547
Kesner, I., 545
Kesner, R. P., 447, 448, 684
Kessler, S., 562
Kestenbaum, N. R., 347
Kestenbaum, R., 62
Kettenring, J. R., 181
Keys, B., 407, 408, 427
Keys, C., 545, 562, 566
Kidd, K. D., 183
Kiecolt-Glaser, J. K., 320

Kiedinger, R. E., 698
Kiesler, D. J., 481, 484, 486
Kihlstrom, J., 134, 239
Kihlstrom, J. F., 497
Killam, K. F., 455
Killeen, P. R., 700
Kilpatric, D. W., 30
Kilpatrick, J., 587
Kilts, C. D., 452
Kim, E., 241
Kim, J., 181
Kim, K. H., 174, 320
Kim, M.-H., 387
Kim, S. H., 558, 561
Kimmel, M., 545, 549, 552, 558, 571
Kimmel, M. J., 534
Kimuar, F., 383
KINCHLA, R. A., 711-42; 712, 719, 720, 728, 731, 732, 736
King, R. A., 451
Kinicki, A. J., 642
Kintsch, W., 594
Kinzie, M. B., 406
Kirby, M., 327
Kirkendo, S. E., 151
Kirkpatrick, D. L., 425
Kirkpatrick, S., 179
Kirson, D., 19, 61, 76
Kirstein, C. L., 384
Kister, M. C., 365
Kistner, J., 71
Kitamura, S., 588
Kite, W. R., 550
Klaber, M., 584
Klar, Y., 557, 561
Klastorin, T. D., 179, 184
Klauer, K. C., 183, 515
Klauer, K. J., 593
Klayman, J., 89, 98, 113
Kleber, H., 320
Kleiman, L. S., 637, 654
Klein, D. G., 247
Klein, D. N., 311
Klein, N. M., 114
Klein, R. W., 179
Kleinknecht, R. A., 253
Kleinmuntz, B., 120
Kleinmuntz, D. N., 88, 119
Klimes, I., 251, 252
Klimes-Dougan, B., 71
Klimoski, R. J., 418, 419, 432, 545, 643, 660
Kling, A., 458
Klinnert, M. D., 63
Klitgaard, R., 648, 652
Klopf, A. H., 677
Klosko, J. S., 248, 249, 251
Kluender, K. R., 700
Klüver, H., 458
Knapp, W. M., 562, 564
Knauer, M. J., 157

.

MacLeod, C., 66, 75, 241, 242
MacPhail, E. M., 676, 697
Macpherson, D. K., 290
MacQueen, J. B., 179, 181
Macrides, F., 384
Madden, N. A., 608
Maddox, W. T., 45, 47
Madigan, R. M., 645, 659
Magat, W. A., 118
Magenau, J., 545, 549, 552, 558, 571
Maggiolo, W. A., 562
Magjuka, R. J., 414, 418, 419, 422, 432
Magliozzi, T., 536, 544, 555
Mahajan, V., 180
Mahjoub, A., 515
Mahoney J. J., 644
Maier, S. F., 240
Maier, V., 390, 391, 393
Main, M., 62, 71, 72
Mainardi, D., 381
Major, B., 160
Major, R., 449-51
Malatesta, C. Z., 69
Malinek, J., 628
Mallot, R., 698
Malone, M. P., 553
Malone, T. W., 599
Mandel, I. D., 173
Mandinach, E. B., 615
Mandl, H., 584, 602
Mandler, G., 58, 72
Mandler, J., 345, 370
Mandler, J. M., 369, 596
Mangelsdorf, S., 62, 490
Manhardt, P. J., 640
Manis, M., 103
Mann, M. F., 415
Manning, C., 89
Manning, D. J., 160
Mano, H., 117
Manstead, A., 56
Manstead, A. R. S., 136, 152, 153, 155
Mantel, N., 185
Manz, C., 406
Manzo, L. C., 287
Marayama, G., 612
March, J. G., 89, 99
Marchione, K., 248
Marcoen, A., 511, 512
Marcotorchino, F., 186, 187
Marcus, S. A., 98
Margraf, J., 241
Margules, C. R., 180
Marhoefer-Dvorak, S., 257
Maris, L., 720
Markessini, J., 358
Marks, I. M., 259, 260
Markus, H., 139, 145
Marlatt, G. A., 258
Marley, A. A. J., 31

Marques, J., 512
Marquis, M. A., 115
Marr, D., 673
Marriot, C., 351
Marriott, F. H. C., 178
Marsan, M., 381
Marshall, J. F., 383-85, 457
Marshall, S. P., 596
Marshello, A., 542, 548, 570
Marsick, V., 430
Martin, C., 634
Martin, C. L., 642
Martin, J. J., 186
Martin, N. E., 638
Martin, N. G., 327
Martin, S. L., 640, 641
Martinak, R., 604
Martinez, J. L., 451, 452
Martin-Iverson, M. T., 456
Martinko, M. J., 136
Martlew, M. C., 355
Marton, F., 596-98
Martres, M. P., 385
Marvinney, D., 490
Marx, R. D., 415, 422, 426, 432
Maschmeyer, C. J., 178
Maser, J. D., 235, 327
Masi, W., 392
Massaro, D. W., 35
Massey, C. M., 359
Masters, R. D., 67
Masur, E. F., 355
Mathaney, A. P. Jr., 489
Mathews, A., 66, 241, 242, 252
Mathews, A. M., 66, 75, 247, 252
Mathews, J. T., 269
Mathieu, J. E., 414, 415, 418, 419, 425, 426, 431, 653
Matias, R., 73
Matsuomoto, D., 57
Mattick, R., 239, 259, 260
Mattick, R. P., 255, 256
Mattingly, B. A., 246
Matula, D. W., 174, 180
Maunsell, J. H. R., 734
Maurer, D., 392
Maurer, S. D., 641
Maury, R., 88, 560
Mavissakalian, M., 247
Maxwell, S. E., 424
May, B., 382, 700
May, J., 66, 242
Mayer, R. E., 587, 595, 598
Mayer, S. J., 411, 412
Mayfield, D. L., 402
Mayr, E., 363
Mazurski, E. J., 457
McAdam, D., 286
McAdams, D. P., 474, 487, 489

McAndrew, W., 547
McArthur, D., 603
McCabe, B. J., 393
McCabe, V., 588
McCall, M. W. Jr., 407, 429
McCallum, G. A., 431
McCarthy, J. D., 286
McCarty, R., 452
McCauley, C. D., 428, 429
McClelland, G., 121
McClelland, J. L., 213, 220, 672, 673, 702
McClelland, L., 293
McClintock, C. G., 539
McCloskey, M., 213, 347, 348, 596
McCloy, R. A., 638, 639
McCombs, B. L., 601
McCord, M. R., 119
McCormick, D. J., 175
McCormick, E. J., 654
McCormick, M., 368
McCormick, W. T. Jr., 186
McCrae, R. R., 69, 474-77, 479, 489
McCulloch, W. W., 676
McDaniel, M. A., 628, 638, 641, 642, 644
McDaniels, T., 121
McDonald, J. E., 183
McDonald, R. J., 459
McDonald, R. P., 171, 180, 187
McDonough, L., 369
McEvoy, G. M., 635, 637
McGaugh, J., 383, 384
McGaugh, J. L., 446-48, 450-52
McGehee, W., 401
McGillicuddy, N. B., 536, 537, 544, 548, 549, 552, 560, 563, 564, 566-68
McGillis, D., 561
McGlashan, T. H., 313
McGrath, J. E., 571
McGue, M., 305
McGuffin, P., 305, 306, 309, 310, 312, 328, 332
McGuire, W. J., 14
McHenry, J. J., 632, 639, 657-59
McHugo, G. J., 67
McIntyre, R. M., 647
McKeachie, W. J., 404, 417, 584, 585, 596
McKeithen, K. B., 184
McKenna, D. D., 428
McKenzie, C. R. M., 115
McKenzie, R., 652, 653
McKeough, A., 596
McKersie, R., 534, 536, 545, 569
McKibbin, L., 427

Shields, M. D., 98
Shields, S. A., 78
SHIFFRIN, R. M., 205-34; 36,
206-8, 215, 216, 218, 219,
223, 224, 226-28, 230,
720, 724
Shiina, K., 184
Shin, H. J., 35, 36
Shine, K. P., 274, 275
Shinkman, P. G., 448
Shipley, M. T., 383
Shizgal, P., 456
Shocker, A. D., 102
Shoda, Y., 495
Shohan-Solomon, V., 485
Shore, L., 636
Shore, T. H., 636
Shorter, A. D., 722, 723
Shotter, J., 21
Shuell, T. J., 589
Shulman, G. L., 726, 732
Shulman, L. S., 587, 606
Shultz, T. R., 347, 349, 354,
361
Shute, V. J., 405, 586, 587,
606, 610, 611
Shvartser, L. V., 175
Shweder, R. A., 18, 19, 338
Shyan, M. R., 686, 697
Sia, A. P., 284
Sibson, R., 174, 175, 178, 181,
186
Siddall, J. W., 698
Siegal, M., 352, 362, 365
Siegel, J., 451
Siegel, S., 96, 544
Siegler, R. S., 337, 360, 369,
588, 598
Signorella, M. L., 362
Sikes-Nova, V. E., 486
Silber, S., 352
Sillars, A. L., 549, 559
Silver, C. S., 270
Silverman, G. H., 721
Silverman, S. B., 639
Silvern, L., 337
Silverstein, J. W., 210, 217
Sim, J. P., 486
Simmons, R., 587
Simon, H. A., 88, 92, 96, 113,
115, 116, 340, 450, 560,
584, 586
Simons, P. R. J., 601
Simons, R. L., 71
Simonson, I., 88, 102
Sims, H., 406
Singer, J., 58
Singer, W., 383
Singh, P. J., 381
Singley, M. K., 588
Sipusic, M., 607, 611
Sistrunk, F., 534, 562, 568
Sivek, D. J., 284

Sjöberg, L., 40, 272
Skaalvik, E. M., 601
Skaggs, L. P., 613
Skelton, J. A., 147
Skinner, B. F., 443, 687
Skitka, L., 154
Skon, L., 612
Skwarecki, E., 605
Slavin, R. E., 608, 612
Sleeman, D., 604
Sleeman, D. H., 603
Slim, R. M., 569
Sloboda, J. A., 587
Sloman, S., 213
Sloore, H., 512
Slora, K., 633
Slovic, P., 89-91, 93, 94, 97,
98, 101, 102, 109, 117,
119, 280, 289
Sluckin, W., 392
Smaltz, V. E., 431
Smedslund, J., 4, 19, 20
Smiley, P., 64
Smith, C. A., 60, 65, 346
Smith, D. A. F., 596
Smith, D. L., 537, 544, 546,
547
Smith, D. R., 182, 588
Smith, E. E., 108, 230, 593
Smith, J. E. K., 31, 170, 363,
452, 455, 651
Smith, L. B., 359
Smith, M. A., 74, 660
Smith, N. D., 415
Smith, P. B., 62
Smith, S. H., 160
Smith, S. M., 173
Smith, T. C., 546
Smith, V. K., 118
Smith, W. P., 534, 537, 546,
562, 568
Smolensky, P., 673, 678
Smotherman, W. P., 382
Smouse, P. E., 185
Sneath, P. H. A., 172, 175
Snell, J., 99
Sniezek, J. A., 115
Snijders, T. A. B., 177
Snow, D. A., 294
SNOW, R. E., 583-626; 416,
417, 588-90, 592, 593,
596, 600, 602, 611, 614,
615
Snyder, C. R., 139, 155, 158,
159, 161, 162
Snyder, C. W. Jr., 171, 180,
187
Snyder, K., 320, 321
Snyder, M., 9, 136, 146, 151,
491
Snyder, S. H., 314
Soderstrom, E. J., 290, 291
Sodian, B., 353

Soetens, E., 510, 513
Soffie, M., 511, 513
Sokal, R. R., 172, 173, 180,
182, 183, 185
Sokol, L., 249
Solomon, D., 545, 547
Solomon, E. P., 73
Solomon, J., 62
Solomon, R. C., 57, 58
Solomon, R. L., 678
Solomon, S., 138, 139
Soloway, E., 607
Solyom, C., 246
Somerville, S. C., 587
Sommers, A. A., 311, 312, 316
Somoza, M. P., 150
Sonnemans, J., 59
Sonnenfeld, J. A., 401
Sonsalla, P. K., 452
Sorce, J. F., 63
Sorcher, M., 411
Sorrentino, R. M., 561, 601
Soto, C., 640
Sousa, A. P. A., 735
Sowell, T., 649
Spaeth, H., 172, 179, 180
Span, P., 584
Sparks, C. P., 637
Sparrow, J. A., 402, 654
Spear, N. E., 387
Spears, R., 280, 286
Spector, P. E., 628
Speer, J., 421
Spelke, E. S., 344, 345, 358,
369
Spencer, J. M., 649
Spencer, T., 719, 720
Sperl, T. C., 634
Sperling, G., 712, 726-28
Spetner, N. B., 354
Spiegler, B. J., 459
Spiehler, V. R., 451
Spielberger, C. D., 73
Spindel, M. S., 65
Spindler, J., 457
Spiro, A., 242
Spitzer, H., 734, 736
Spitzer, R. L., 480
Spoehr, K. T., 405
Spoont, M. R., 316, 326
Sprangers, M., 424
Spring, B., 308
Springer, K., 363
Spyraki, C., 451, 452
Squires, P., 651
Sredl, K., 284
Srinivasan, V., 121, 178
Sriram, N., 174
Srivasta, S., 428
Sroufe, L. A., 63, 71, 490
Srull, T. K., 103, 144
Stacia, R., 722, 723
Staddon, J. E. R., 29

SUBJECT INDEX

A

Ability grouping
teaching and learning and,
614
Ability testing
in personnel selection, 631-35
Abstract conceptualization, 692-
97
Achievement motivation
learning and, 600
ACTE model, 206, 216
Action control
learning and, 601
Action-identification theory, 150
Action learning
in management development,
430
Action tendencies
in anxiety and depression,
237, 245
Activism
environmental protection and,
294
Activity-withdrawal
in affective disorders, 330
in schizophrenia, 310-11
ACT model, 219
ACT* model, 206-7, 215-16,
218, 220, 223
Act Report, 479
ACT theory, 207
Adaptations
global environmental change
and, 288-89
Adaptive instruction, 602-14
ADCLUS model, 178
Additive trees
in combinatorial data analysis,
183-84
Additive utility strategy, 113
Adjustment
negotiation and, 555
Adjustment heuristic
decision behavior and, 103
Affect
negative
in anxiety and depression,
236-37
behavioral inhibition system
and, 325-26
in diathesis-stress, 327-28
positive
behavioral activation system
and, 237, 325-26
in diathesis-stress, 328-29
negotiation and, 559

Affective aptitudes, 599-601
Affective disorders
activity-withdrawal in, 330
bipolar
dopamine and, 316-17
neurobehavioral theory of,
304
continuity in, 70-71
polygenic influences in, 306
schizophrenia and, 313-14
Affective distress
in anxiety and depression,
236-37
Affect regulation
self-esteem maintenance and,
139
Affirmative action plans, 648
Agendas, 134-35
Aggression
childhood antecedents of,
490
children exposed to anger
and, 74
impression management and,
136
Agoraphobia
etiology of
uncontrollability in, 240
panic disorder with
threatening interpretations
of ambiguous scenarios
in, 242
treatment of, 247-50
Agreeableness
interpersonal behavior and,
481
job performance and, 638
Air Force Officer Qualifying
Test, 634
Akinesia syndrome, 316
Alcohol dependence
posttraumatic stress disorder
and, 258
All-or-none activation model,
206
Alprazolam
for panic disorder, 249
Alternative generation
behavioral decision research
and, 89
Altruism
anthropocentric
environmental concern and,
280
negotiation and, 539
Altruistic behavior
norm-activation model of, 280

Altruistic behavior theory
human-environment relations
and, 272
Ambiguity
risky choice and, 109-11
Americans with Disabilities Act
(1990), 650
Amnesia
retrograde, 446
Amphetamine
olfactory preference learning
and, 383, 385
posttraining administration of
memory enhancement due
to, 450-51
psychosis due to, 319
Amygdala
conditioned emotional re-
sponse and, 458-60
local electrical stimulation of
memory loss due to, 447
Amygdalectomy
neophobia and, 459
Analysis of covariance
designs for training evaluation
and, 423-24
Analysis of variance
designs for training evaluation
and, 424
Analysis of variance model
of attribution, 4
Analytic reasoning ability
fluid, 592-93
Anchoring
negotiation and, 555
Anchoring heuristic
decision behavior and, 103
Anesthetization
memory loss due to, 446-
47
Anger
children exposed to, 74
in psychopathology, 70
Anger management
posttraumatic stress disorder
and, 257
Anhedonia, 310
Animals
cognition in, 674-76
Animate/inanimate distinction
children's understanding of,
358-59
infants' understanding of,
359-60
Animism, 358
Anoxia
memory loss due to, 446

784   SUBJECT INDEX

Self-construction
  impression regulation and,
    139-40
Self-criticism
  consequences of, 163
Self-discrepancy theory, 140
Self-efficacy
  learning and, 601
  trainee
    training outcomes and,
      415
Self-efficacy theory, 20
  cognitive-mediational con-
    structs in, 244
Self-esteem
  impression management and,
    152
  maintenance and enhancement
    of
    impression regulation and,
      138-39
Self-evaluation maintenance
  theory, 157
Self-glorification
  impression regulation and,
    138-40
Self-handicapping
  impression management and,
    136, 161
Self-identification, 138
  audiences and, 157
  believability of, 144-45
  beneficiality of, 143-44
  desirable, 142-52
Self-identification theory, 142
Self-monitoring
  impression management and,
    151-52
Self-monitoring scale, 152
Self-presentation, 136-38
  acquisitive, 147
  automatic vs. controlled, 147-
    49
  control of, 149-50
  deception and, 150-51
  ingratiation and, 143
  protective, 147
  self-beliefs and, 145-46
Self-regulation
  learning and, 601
  self-consciousness and, 157-
    58
  in symbolic interactionism,
    135
Self-verification theory, 140-41
Semantic similarity
  scientific psychology and, 18-
    19
Sensitivity analysis
  contingent judgments and,
    119
Sentence parsing

reading comprehension and,
    594-95
Septo-hippocampal system
  behavioral inhibition system
    and, 325
  fight-or-flight response and,
    238
Seriation, 171-72
Set-size effects
  in attention, 712-17
Set theory
  clustering algorithms and,
    174
Short-term memory
  caudate-putamen lesions and,
    461
  conditioning mediation by,
    244
Signal detection theory, 43
Similarity
  in abstract conceptualization,
    692-97
  universal laws of, 27-30
Similarity choice model, 27
  identification performance
    and, 31-32
Similarity judgments
  general recognition theory
    and, 46
Similarity scaling, 25-50
SIMNET, 410-11
Simple phobia
  selective interference effect
    in, 241
  treatment of, 253-54
Simulation
  as training method, 407-
    8
Simulator networking
  large-scale, 410-11
Skill acquisition
  stages of, 404
Social anxiety
  impression management and,
    136, 152
  self-consciousness and, 149
Social behavior
  dramaturgical analysis of,
    135
  See also Interpersonal pro-
    cesses
Social-competency perspective,
    479
Social desirability
  impression management and,
    152
Social dilemma theory
  human-environment relations
    and, 272
Social facilitation
  impression management and,
    136

Social interaction
  functions and effects of emo-
    tions in, 67-68
  self-concept and, 145
Social learning theory, 401
  behavioral role modeling and,
    412
  self-efficacy in, 415
Social loafing
  public scrutiny and, 154-
    55
Social maladjustment
  industrial accidents and, 639
Social phobia
  selective interference effect
    in, 241
  treatment of, 255-57
Social psychology
  in Belgium, 512
  cluster analysis in, 182
  quantitative impact of, 5
Social reality
  selective explanations of, 158-
    63
Social referencing, 63-64
  in infants, 355-56
Sociometry
  cluster analysis in, 182
Species extinction
  human activities responsible
    for, 276
Speech recognition
  equipment simulators and,
    410
Speech simulation
  equipment simulators and,
    410
Startle response
  amygdala lesions and, 459
Status quo bias
  decision behavior and, 97
Stimulus sampling theory,
    209
Strategy compatibility
  procedural variance and, 95
Stress
  in diathesis-stress, 327-29
  dimensions of
    conceptualization of, 324-
      29
  emotional effects of, 72-73
Stress inoculation training
  posttraumatic stress disorder
    and, 257-58
Striatum
  conditioned motivation and,
    460-61
Structural Analysis of Social
  Behavior, 486-87
Struggle
  opposing preferences and,
    532-33

CUMULATIVE INDEXES

CONTRIBUTING AUTHORS, VOLUMES 35–43

W

Wallach, H., 38:1–27
Walton, E., 38:339–67
Weary, G., 35:427–59
Weigold, M. F., 43:133–68
Weinstein, C. S., 42:493–525
Wellman, H. M., 43:337–75
Westheimer, G., 35:201–26
Wexley, K. N., 35:519–51
Whalen, R. E., 35:257–76
White, N. M., 43:443–71

Wickens, C. D., 36:307–48
Widiger, T. A., 42:109–33
Wiggins, J. S., 43:473–504
Wilcox, R. R., 38:29–60
Willerman, L., 39:101–34
Wimer, C. C., 36:171–218
Wimer, R. E., 36:171–218
Winkel, G., 41:441–77
Wise, R. A., 40:191–225
Wolfe, B., 37:321–49
Woody, C. D., 37:433–93
Wortman, C. B., 36:531–72
Wurf, E., 38:299–337

Y

Young, F. W., 35:55–81
Yukl, G., 43:399–441

Z

Zajonc, R. B., 40:249–80
Zedeck, S., 35:461–518
Zigler, E., 42:29–50
Zinbarg, R. E., 43:235–67

CHAPTER TITLES, VOLUMES 35–44

ANNUAL REVIEWS INC.

a nonprofit scientific publisher
4139 El Camino Way
P. O. Box 10139
Palo Alto, CA 94303-0897 · USA

Annual Reviews Inc. publications may be ordered directly from our office; through booksellers and subscription agents, worldwide; and through participating professional societies.
Prices are subject to change without notice.   ARI Federal I.D. #94-1156476

- **Individuals:** Prepayment required on new accounts by check or money order (in U.S. dollars, check drawn on U.S. bank) or charge to MasterCard, VISA, or American Express.
- **Institutional Buyers:** Please include purchase order.
- **Students:** $10.00 discount from retail price, per volume. Prepayment required. Proof of student status must be provided. (Photocopy of Student I.D. is acceptable.) Student must be a degree candidate at an accredited institution. Order direct from Annual Reviews. Orders received through bookstores and institutions requesting student rates will be returned.
- **Professional Society Members:** Societies who have a contractual arrangement with Annual Reviews offer our books at reduced rates to members. Contact your society for information.
- **California orders** must add applicable sales tax.
- **CANADIAN ORDERS:** We must now collect 7% General Sales Tax on orders shipped to Canada. Canadian orders will not be accepted unless this tax has been added. Tax Registration # R 121 449-029. **Note:** Effective 1-1-92 Canadian prices increase from USA level to "other countries" level. See below.
- **Telephone orders,** paid by credit card, welcomed. Call Toll Free **1-800-523-8635** (except in California). California customers use 1-415-493-4400 (not toll free). M-F, 8:00 am - 4:00 pm, Pacific Time. Students ordering by telephone must supply (by FAX or mail) proof of student status if proof from current academic year is not on file at Annual Reviews. Purchase orders from universities require written confirmation before shipment.
- **FAX: 415-855-9815   Telex: 910-290-0275**
- **Postage paid by Annual Reviews** (4th class bookrate). UPS domestic ground service (except to AK and HI) available at $2.00 extra per book. UPS air service or Airmail also available at cost. UPS requires street address. P.O. Box, APO, FPO, not acceptable.
- **Regular Orders:** Please list below the volumes you wish to order by volume number.
- **Standing Orders:** New volume in the series will be sent to you automatically each year upon publication. Cancellation may be made at any time. Please indicate volume number to begin standing order.
- **Prepublication Orders:** Volumes not yet published will be shipped in month and year indicated.
- **We do not ship on approval.**

ANNUAL REVIEWS SERIES *Volumes not listed are no longer in print*		Prices, postpaid, per volume		Regular Order Please send Volume(s):	Standing Order Begin with Volume:
		Until 12-31-91 USA & Canada / elsewhere	After 1-1-92 USA / other countries (incl. Canada)		
Annual Review of ANTHROPOLOGY					
Vols. 1-16	(1972-1987)	$33.00/$38.00			
Vols. 17-18	(1988-1989)	$37.00/$42.00	$41.00/$46.00		
Vols. 19-20	(1990-1991)	$41.00/$46.00			
Vol. 21	(avail. Oct. 1992)	$44.00/$49.00	$44.00/$49.00	Vol(s)._____	Vol._____
Annual Review of ASTRONOMY AND ASTROPHYSICS					
Vols. 1, 5-14, 16-20	(1963, 1967-1976) (1978-1982)	$33.00/$38.00			
Vols. 21-27	(1983-1989)	$49.00/$54.00	$53.00/$58.00		
Vols. 28-29	(1990-1991)	$53.00/$58.00			
Vol. 30	(avail. Sept. 1992)	$57.00/$62.00	$57.00/$62.00	Vol(s)._____	Vol._____
Annual Review of BIOCHEMISTRY					
Vols. 30-34, 36-56	(1961-1965, 1967-1987)	$35.00/$40.00			
Vols. 57-58	(1988-1989)	$37.00/$42.00	$41.00/$47.00		
Vols. 59-60	(1990-1991)	$41.00/$47.00			
Vol. 61	(avail. July 1992)	$46.00/$52.00	$46.00/$52.00	Vol(s)._____	Vol._____

ANNUAL REVIEWS SERIES

Volumes not listed are no longer in print

			Prices, postpaid, per volume			
			Until 12-31-91 USA & Canada / elsewhere	After 1-1-92 USA / other countries (incl. Canada)	Regular Order Please send Volume(s):	Standing Order Begin with Volume:

Annual Review of BIOPHYSICS AND BIOMOLECULAR STRUCTURE

Vols.	1-11	(1972-1982)	$33.00/$38.00			
Vols.	12-18	(1983-1989)	$51.00/$56.00 } $55.00/$60.00			
Vols.	19-20	(1990-1991)	$55.00/$60.00			
Vol.	21	(avail. June 1992)	$59.00/$64.00	$59.00/$64.00	Vol(s)._____	Vol.____

Annual Review of CELL BIOLOGY

Vols.	1-3	(1985-1987)	$33.00/$38.00			
Vols.	4-5	(1988-1989)	$37.00/$42.00 } $41.00/$46.00			
Vols.	6-7	(1990-1991)	$41.00/$46.00			
Vol.	8	(avail. Nov. 1992)	$46.00/$51.00	$46.00/$51.00	Vol(s)._____	Vol.____

Annual Review of COMPUTER SCIENCE

Vols.	1-2	(1986-1987)	$41.00/$46.00	$41.00/$46.00		
Vols.	3-4	(1988, 1989-1990)	$47.00/$52.00	$47.00/$52.00	Vol(s)._____	Vol.____

Series suspended until further notice. Volumes 1-4 are still available at the special promotional price of $100.00 USA /$115.00 other countries, when all 4 volumes are purchased at one time. Orders at the special price must be prepaid.

Annual Review of EARTH AND PLANETARY SCIENCES

Vols.	1-10	(1973-1982)	$33.00/$38.00			
Vols.	11-17	(1983-1989)	$51.00/$56.00 } $55.00/$60.00			
Vols.	18-19	(1990-1991)	$55.00/$60.00			
Vol.	20	(avail. May 1992)	$59.00/$64.00	$59.00/$64.00	Vol(s)._____	Vol.____

Annual Review of ECOLOGY AND SYSTEMATICS

Vols.	2-18	(1971-1987)	$33.00/$38.00			
Vols.	19-20	(1988-1989)	$36.00/$41.00 } $40.00/$45.00			
Vols.	21-22	(1990-1991)	$40.00/$45.00			
Vol.	23	(avail. Nov. 1992)	$44.00/$49.00	$44.00/$49.00	Vol(s)._____	Vol.____

Annual Review of ENERGY AND THE ENVIRONMENT

Vols.	1-7	(1976-1982)	$33.00/$38.00			
Vols.	8-14	(1983-1989)	$60.00/$65.00 } $64.00/$69.00			
Vols.	15-16	(1990-1991)	$64.00/$69.00			
Vol.	17	(avail. Oct. 1992)	$68.00/$73.00	$68.00/$73.00	Vol(s)._____	Vol.____

Annual Review of ENTOMOLOGY

Vols.	10-16, 18	(1965-1971, 1973)				
	20-32	(1975-1987)	$33.00/$38.00			
Vols.	33-34	(1988-1989)	$36.00/$41.00 } $40.00/$45.00			
Vols.	35-36	(1990-1991)	$40.00/$45.00			
Vol.	37	(avail. Jan. 1992)	$44.00/$49.00	$44.00/$49.00	Vol(s)._____	Vol.____

Annual Review of FLUID MECHANICS

Vols.	2-4, 7	(1970-1972, 1975)				
	9-19	(1977-1987)	$34.00/$39.00			
Vols.	20-21	(1988-1989)	$36.00/$41.00 } $40.00/$45.00			
Vols.	22-23	(1990-1991)	$40.00/$45.00			
Vol.	24	(avail. Jan. 1992)	$44.00/$49.00	$44.00/$49.00	Vol(s)._____	Vol.____

Annual Review of GENETICS

Vols.	1-12, 14-21	(1967-1978, 1980-1987)	$33.00/$38.00			
Vols.	22-23	(1988-1989)	$36.00/$41.00 } $40.00/$45.00			
Vols.	24-25	(1990-1991)	$40.00/$45.00			
Vol.	26	(avail. Dec. 1992)	$44.00/$49.00	$44.00/$49.00	Vol(s)._____	Vol.____

Annual Review of IMMUNOLOGY

Vols.	1-5	(1983-1987)	$33.00/$38.00			
Vols.	6-7	(1988-1989)	$36.00/$41.00 } $41.00/$46.00			
Vol.	8	(1990)	$40.00/$45.00			
Vol.	9	(1991)	$41.00/$46.00	$41.00/$46.00		
Vol.	10	(avail. April 1992)	$45.00/$50.00	$45.00/$50.00	Vol(s)._____	Vol.____